Advanced Torts

Carolina Academic Press
Context and Practice Series
Michael Hunter Schwartz
Series Editor

Administrative Law
Richard Henry Seamon

Advanced Torts
Alex B. Long and Meredith J. Duncan

An Intersex Athlete's Constitutional Challenge, Hastings v. USATF, IAAF, and IOC
Olivia M. Farrar

Civil Procedure for All States
Benjamin V. Madison, III

Constitutional Law
David Schwartz and Lori Ringhand

Contracts
Michael Hunter Schwartz and Denise Riebe

Current Issues in Constitutional Litigation
Sarah E. Ricks, with contributions by Evelyn M. Tenenbaum

Employment Discrimination
Second Edition
Susan Grover, Sandra F. Sperino, and Jarod S. Gonzalez

Evidence
Pavel Wonsowicz

International Business Transactions
Amy Deen Westbrook

International Women's Rights, Equality, and Justice
Christine M. Venter

The Lawyer's Practice
Kris Franklin

Professional Responsibility
Barbara Glesner Fines

Sales
Edith R. Warkentine

Torts
Paula J. Manning

Workers' Compensation Law
Michael C. Duff

Advanced Torts

A Context and Practice Casebook

Alex B. Long
University of Tennessee College of Law

Meredith J. Duncan
University of Houston Law Center

Carolina Academic Press
Durham, North Carolina

ISBN 978-1-61163-099-2
LCCN 2013958181

Carolina Academic Press
700 Kent Street
Durham, North Carolina 27701
Telephone (919) 489-7486
Fax (919) 493-5668
www.cap-press.com

Printed in the United States of America

Contents

Part 2 · Legal Malpractice and Breach of Fiduciary Duty

Table of Cases

Series Editor's Preface

Welcome to a new type of casebook. Designed by leading experts in law school teaching and learning, Context and Practice casebooks assist law professors and their students to work together to learn, minimize stress, and prepare for the rigors and joys of practicing law. Student learning and preparation for law practice are the guiding ethics of these books.

Why would we depart from the tried and true? Why have we abandoned the legal education model by which we were trained? Because legal education can and must improve.

In Spring 2007, the Carnegie Foundation published *Educating Lawyers: Preparation for the Practice of Law* and the Clinical Legal Education Association published *Best Practices for Legal Education*. Both works reflect in-depth efforts to assess the effectiveness of modern legal education, and both conclude that legal education, as presently practiced, falls quite short of what it can and should be. Both works criticize law professors' rigid adherence to a single teaching technique, the inadequacies of law school assessment mechanisms, and the dearth of law school instruction aimed at teaching law practice skills and inculcating professional values. Finally, the authors of both books express concern that legal education may be harming law students. Recent studies show that law students, in comparison to all other graduate students, have the highest levels of depression, anxiety and substance abuse.

The problems with traditional law school instruction begin with the textbooks law teachers use. Law professors cannot implement *Educating Lawyers* and *Best Practices* using texts designed for the traditional model of legal education. Moreover, even though our understanding of how people learn has grown exponentially in the past 100 years, no law school text to date even purports to have been designed with educational research in mind.

The Context and Practice Series is an effort to offer a genuine alternative. Grounded in learning theory and instructional design and written with *Educating Lawyers* and *Best Practices* in mind, Context and Practice casebooks make it easy for law professors to change.

I welcome reactions, criticisms, and suggestions; my e-mail address is mhschwartz@ualr.edu. Knowing the author(s) of these books, I know they, too, would appreciate your input; we share a common commitment to student learning. In fact, students, if your professor cares enough about your learning to have adopted this book, I bet s/he would welcome your input, too!

Michael Hunter Schwartz, Series Designer and Editor
Dean and Professor of Law
UALR William H. Bowen School of Law

Preface

As professors who write and teach in the fields of Torts and Professional Responsibility, we feel *Advanced Torts: A Context and Practice Casebook* fills several needs.

First, as the first part of its title implies, the book can be used as casebook for an Advanced Torts class at those law schools that do not require two semesters of Torts. The cases included cover nearly every subject covered in an upper-level Torts elective, and the book includes most of the cases (*New York Times v. Sullivan, Ultramares Corp. v. Touche,* etc.) one would expect to find in an Advanced Torts casebook. However, our book also includes material on subjects such as bad faith claims and consumer protection statutes that contain a wealth of interesting material, but that often go uncovered in the typical Torts class. Thus, the book can be used by any Torts professor and any student interested in learning about the array of theories of civil liability beyond negligence and the intentional torts covered in a first-year Torts class.

In addition to being an Advanced Torts casebook, the book is designed specifically to expose aspiring lawyers to the theories of civil liability that may impact them in their professional lives. It is no secret to those who study legal ethics that the threat of legal malpractice and related claims may pose a greater deterrent to attorney misconduct than the threat of professional discipline. While law students will inevitably take some type of course on professional responsibility while in law school, few have the opportunity to take a course that addresses in any detail the general and specific theories of civil liability they themselves might one day face as professionals.

Therefore, we conceive of this book as a means of bridging this gap. The book can certainly be used as part of a standard Advanced Torts class, but many of the cases included involve lawyers as plaintiffs and (more often) defendants. Students are therefore able to see the potential pitfalls they may face in practice as well as some of the special legal rules that apply when a lawyer is a party to the ensuing lawsuit. Thus, the subject matter of *Advanced Torts: A Context and Practice Casebook* should resonate with students.

In addition, the book can be used as part of a course devoted to legal malpractice and related torts. Again, as professors who teach and write in the areas of Torts and Professional Responsibility, we tend to think that, historically, too few law schools have offered such courses. For those like-minded individuals, this book may serve as a resource. The first part of the book is devoted to the special rules regarding legal malpractice. The material that follows—while more general in nature—devotes significant time to legal theories that may have special relevance for lawyers in their professional lives. For example, in addition to exploring the torts of malicious prosecution and abuse of process, the chapter on misuse of the legal process also addresses spoliation of evidence and anti-SLAPP suits. While covering more general topics, we have attempted to identify at least some of the special rules and issues that have developed with regard to lawyers engaged in the practice of law.

Regardless of how an instructor decides to use this book, part of our goal in writing it was to help law students develop a sense of professionalism. Throughout this book, readers will read about defendant-lawyers who have engaged in egregious behavior, behavior that is entirely consistent with the lawyer's ethical responsibilities, and behavior that falls somewhere in between these extremes. We hope that this focus on lawyers acting in their professional capacities will force students and their instructors to think more deeply about what it means to practice law in a professional manner. To aid in that goal, nearly every chapter contains a reference to the relevant rules of professional conduct so that students can see how a lawyer's ethical responsibilities square with the lawyer's legal responsibilities.

Finally, throughout the process of writing the book, we have endeavored to keep the goals of the Context and Practice Series (CAP) in mind. A set of focus questions precedes all of the major cases in the book in order to better focus students' attention to the important issues. We have incorporated problems—some detailed, some relatively short—to allow students to extract the relevant legal principles from the material they have read and apply those principles in a more practical way. Finally, all of the cases were selected not just with the goal of helping students understand the material, but with the goal of helping them understand how the material applies to them as future lawyers.

Alex B. Long
Meredith J. Duncan

Part 1

Advanced Torts for Lawyers

Chapter 1

Introduction

A. Advanced Torts: The Lawyer's Perspective

The Enron scandal of 2001 brought renewed attention to the role that lawyers play in advising clients. Through "creative" accounting, Enron, a Houston-based energy corporation, was able to conceal billions of dollars of debt from investors while reporting inflated earnings. When its practices came to light, the company collapsed, criminal charges were brought against company executives, and shareholders brought suit against various financial institutions accused of helping to further the fraud. Civil litigation against the company ultimately settled for $7.2 billion in 2008. Juan A. Lozano, *Enron Investors to Share $7.2 Billion Settlement*, Wash. Post, Sep. 10, 2008.

But accounting firms and Enron executives were not the only parties accused of wrongdoing. The Houston law firm of Vinson & Elkins was also sued as part of the "MegaClaims" litigation involving Enron. As part of Enron's bankruptcy proceedings, a court-appointed examiner into Enron's affairs identified possible claims of legal malpractice and aiding and abetting corporate fraud against Enron's in-house lawyers as well as the company's outside counsel, Vinson & Elkins. The examiner's report raised concerns that Vinson & Elkins "provided legal opinions that were used to support Enron's aggressive accounting techniques ... despite questions about whether they could be used to support beneficial accounting treatment." Richard Acello, *Enron Lawyers in the Hot Seat*, ABA Journal, June 1, 2004. According to the report, these opinion letters were crucial to Enron's ability to perpetrate its fraud. The firm was also accused of conducting an inadequate investigation into illegal accounting practices after warnings surfaced about the practices, and reassuring company officials that there was little cause for alarm. Jeanne Cummings et al., *Vinson & Elkins Discounted Warnings By Employee About Dubious Accounting*, Wall Street Journal, Jan. 16, 2002.

Vinson & Elkins eventually settled with Enron's estate for $30 million, while denying any wrongdoing. Part of $30 million included over $10 million in legal fees previously charged to Enron. Vinson & Elkins also agreed to waive an additional $4 million in legal fees it was never paid by the company. John C. Roper, *Vinson & Elkins Settles with Enron for $30 Million*, Houston Chronicle, June 2, 2006.

* * *

This book focuses primarily on tort theories of recovery that are not covered in significant detail in the standard first-semester Torts course, hence the inclusion of the phrase "Advanced Torts" in the title. But the book explores the topics with a particular emphasis on how these tort theories apply to lawyers engaged in the practice of law. To be sure, there are plenty of cases herein—maybe even a majority—that do not involve lawyers as either plaintiffs or defendants. Thus, students should come away from the course with a solid understanding of the legal issues and concepts lawyers in a sophisticated, general civil practice can be expected to encounter. But why the special focus on how the legal theories discussed apply to lawyers engaged in the practice of law?

There are several reasons. One is the reality that the threat of civil liability is (or should be) of greater concern to lawyers in their daily practice than professional discipline. Lawyers who violate the rules of professional conduct are, of course, subject to professional discipline. But the reality is that professional discipline is relatively uncommon. *See* Anita Bernstein, *Pitfalls Ahead: A Manifesto for the Training of Lawyers*, 94 CORNELL L. REV. 479, 487 (2009) (referring to "the relatively rare occasion that an errant lawyer receives some form of professional discipline"). Indeed, the *Restatement (Third) of the Law Governing Lawyers* notes that "the remedy of malpractice liability ... [is] practically of greater importance in most law practice than is the risk of disciplinary proceedings." Foreword to *Restatement (Third) of the Law Governing Lawyers*, at XXI (2000); *see also* Douglas R. Richmond, *For a Few Dollars More: The Perplexing Problem of Unethical Billing Practices by Lawyers*, 60 S.C. L. REV. 63, 79 (2008) ("[P]otential civil liability often deters lawyer misconduct more effectively than does the threat of professional discipline."). Thus, anyone who aspires to be a practicing lawyer should have a basic understanding of not just the professional rules of professional conduct, the violation of which may subject the lawyer to discipline, but the civil theories of recovery that a lawyer may confront should the lawyer's conduct cause harm.

Another reason is that the interplay between the disciplinary rules and the legal rules sometimes presents some interesting and intellectually challenging issues. Consider the Enron scandal. The Enron scandal attracted worldwide attention. For some time, Enron management was able to effectively hide the company's debt from investors, thereby increasing the value of Enron stock. When Enron's house of cards eventually collapsed, the public began trying to determine who was to blame. Not surprisingly, some eventually pointed a finger at the lawyers who were involved in Enron's dealings. To hide the company's debt, Enron had to use lawyers. Lawyers are, of course, ethically prohibited from assisting a client in conduct they know to be criminal or fraudulent. ABA MODEL RULES OF PROF'L CONDUCT R. 1.2(d). But this prohibition applies only when the lawyer knows the conduct in question is criminal or fraudulent. In the Enron matter, Vinson & Elkins was accused of adopting a policy of conscious avoidance when it came to learning of its clients' actions. This might have amounted to negligence on the part of the lawyers at Vinson & Elkins. But, if so, who would have a right to recover? Enron itself? Its shareholders? *See* Roger C. Crampton, *Enron and the Corporate Lawyer: A Primer on Legal and Ethical Issues*, 58 BUS. LAW. 143, 167–73 (2002).

Some lawyers go beyond consciously avoiding unpleasant facts about their clients. Some lawyers have been accused of actively assisting their clients in wrongful conduct to the detriment of third parties. When questioned about their conduct, some lawyers tend to cite a lawyer's ethical duty to diligently (or, as some lawyers insist on saying, zealously) represent their clients as justifying their behavior. MODEL RULES OF PROF'L CONDUCT R. 1.3. The question in some cases then becomes where to draw the line between diligent representation and assisting a client's crime or fraud.

The fact that a defendant in a tort case is a lawyer tends to complicate the legal analysis in many cases. The special obligations that a lawyer owes a client and the special set of rules of professional conduct to which a lawyer is subject may require a court to modify existing legal rules in order to balance the competing interests. As an example, one noted contracts scholar once observed that "the law of lawyers' contracts is different" from the general law of contracts. Joseph M. Perillo, *The Law of Lawyer's Contracts Is Different*, 67 FORDHAM L. REV. 443 (1998). The same might also be said of tort law as applied to lawyers.

According to some, it is different in a way that favors the interests of the legal profession. Professor Benjamin H. Barton has advanced what he calls "the lawyer-judge bias" hypothesis: "when given the chance, judges favor the interests of the legal profession over the public." BENJAMIN H. BARTON, THE LAWYER-JUDGE BIAS IN THE AMERICAN LEGAL SYSTEM 2 (2011). Barton provides numerous examples of this supposed bias, some of which are addressed in this book.

In other instances, the fact that a defendant is a lawyer would seem to make it easier for a plaintiff to recover. After all, lawyers are subject to their own rules of professional conduct, many of which directly relate to the legal theories covered in this book. Therefore, it seems logical that the fact that *a lawyer*—an officer of the court with a "special obligation to protect the integrity of the courts and foster their truth-telling function," *Amalfitano v. Rosenberg*, 903 N.E.2d 265, 269 (N.Y. 2009), from whom the law demands "the utmost good faith in the conduct and management of the business intrusted to them," *id.* (quoting *Looff v. Lawton*, 14 Hun. 588, 590 (2d Dept. 1878))—has violated a rule of professional conduct would tend to make it easier to establish the tortiousness of the conduct. This is another theme that is explored throughout the book.

In light of all of the above, consider the following cases involving tort claims every law student is familiar with—intentional infliction of emotional distress—that were brought against lawyers.

Focus Questions: *McDaniel v. Gile*

1. *Why is there a jury question as to whether the defendant's conduct was extreme and outrageous?*
2. *Would the plaintiff have avoided summary judgment if the defendant had been an auto mechanic hired to fix the plaintiff's car?*

McDaniel v. Gile

230 Cal.App.3d 363
(Cal. Ct. App. 1991)

[Defendant and cross-complainant Patricia Gile was represented in her marital dissolution action by plaintiff and cross-defendant attorney James H. McDaniel. McDaniel sued Gile for unpaid legal fees, and Gile cross-claimed for, *inter alia*, intentional infliction of emotional distress. The lower court entered in a summary disposition in favor of McDaniel on Gile's IIED claim.]

The facts are taken from defendant's answers to plaintiff's interrogatories, which were submitted by plaintiff in support of his motion for summary adjudication. In January of 1985, plaintiff met with defendant and "fill[ed] out a lengthy and intimate self-characterization document, seeking intimate details of [her] personal and sexual life." At their next meeting plaintiff "continually referred to [sic] back to the more intimate parts of [her] personal life, particularly remarking about the sexual problems [she] had in [her] marriage."

Several weeks later, when plaintiff and defendant were at the courthouse, plaintiff took defendant into a small room and when she attempted to leave he grabbed her and "pinned [her] against the wall and kissed [her] on the mouth." ...

On numerous occasions during the following weeks, plaintiff called defendant both at home and at her work place and made "sexually suggestive remarks." When defendant asked plaintiff if he always talked to his clients like that, he answered, "that he only did so with 'the sexy ones.'" Plaintiff would also call defendant at home in the late evening and ask her to come to his office.

After defendant refused to have sexual relations with plaintiff, plaintiff abandoned her and failed to "[r]epresent [her] interests, appear in court to represent [her] interests, negotiate a complete and fair property settlement..., properly advise [her] of [her] rights," return her phone calls, or take any action at all except after numerous requests. In January of 1986, defendant needed a restraining order because she was having a problem with her ex-husband involving the police. She called plaintiff at his office for days. When she finally spoke to him, he told her that "if [she] had played the game 'the right way' [she] would have the right phone number to reach him immediately. [She] understood this to mean that if [she] gave him sexual favors he would have been available for [her] as an attorney and not otherwise."

When defendant brought a friend to meetings to protect herself from plaintiff, he made sexually suggestive remarks about her and other women. One time he told defendant's friend that "when a woman client came to him, she was extremely vulnerable, so if she went to bed to get better service from him, 'so be it.'" Defendant had heard that plaintiff had done the same things to other women in her position and that his reputation for this was "well known around the Ontario courthouse."

Plaintiff advised defendant that she had no community property interest in her ex-husband's retirement of $18,000, and, as a consequence, she lost her one-half interest. Ultimately, she was forced to settle her case alone to her disadvantage.

Defendant has suffered emotionally from plaintiff's acts and failures to act. [At the conclusion of the dissolution proceedings, defendant owed plaintiff a sum for attorney's fees and costs which she did not pay.]

Discussion

Intentional Infliction of Emotional Distress

Defendant contends that there are triable issues of fact as to her cause of action for intentional infliction of emotional distress. She further contends that the trial court erred in granting summary adjudication of issues based on plaintiff's assertions that: (1) the cause of action was barred by Civil Code section 43.5; and (2) his conduct was not "outrageous" as a matter of law. We agree.

To recover for intentional infliction of emotional distress a plaintiff must show: "(1) outrageous conduct by the defendant, (2) intention to cause or reckless disregard of the probability of causing emotional distress, (3) severe emotional suffering and (4) actual and proximate causation of the emotional distress." (3) Outrageous conduct is that which exceeds "'... all bounds usually tolerated by a decent society, [and is] of a nature which is especially calculated to cause, and does cause, mental distress. Ordinarily mere insulting language, without more, does not constitute outrageous conduct.... Behavior may be considered outrageous if a defendant (1) abuses a relation or position which gives him power to damage the plaintiff's interest; (2) knows the plaintiff is susceptible to injuries through mental distress; or (3) acts intentionally or unreasonably with the recognition that the acts are likely to result in illness through mental distress.'"

Moreover, "'[t]he extreme and outrageous character of the conduct may arise from an abuse by the actor of a position, or a relation with the other, which gives him actual or apparent authority over the other, or power to affect his interests.... The extreme and outrageous character of the conduct may arise from the actor's knowledge that the other is peculiarly susceptible to emotional distress, by reason of some physical or mental condition or peculiarity. The conduct may become heartless, flagrant, and outrageous when the actor proceeds in the face of such knowledge, where it would not be so if he did not know.'"

Plaintiff does not contend that there are no triable issues of fact as to the intentional nature of the conduct, the existence of emotional distress, or causation. His sole contention is that his conduct, as set forth in defendant's responses to interrogatories, is insufficient as a matter of law to constitute outrageous conduct. This contention is without merit.

A fiduciary relationship exists between attorneys and clients. An attorney must act with the most conscientious fidelity. A breach of fiduciary duty by an attorney is actionable whether it involves financial claims or physical damage resulting from the violation.

Defendant had a special relationship with plaintiff in that she was a client and plaintiff was her attorney representing her in a dissolution of marriage proceeding. Plaintiff was in a position of actual or apparent power over defendant. Defendant was peculiarly susceptible to emotional distress because of her pending marital dissolution. Plaintiff was aware of defendant's circumstances. The withholding by a retained attorney of legal services when sexual favors are not granted by a client and engaging in sexual harassment of the client constitutes acts of outrageous conduct under these circumstances.

Nevertheless, plaintiff predicts "a floodgate of litigation" which will require courts to determine standards as to what statements can be made by an individual to a member of the opposite sex. Plaintiff's sweeping prediction belies the facts of this case and ignores his fiduciary relationship and coercive conduct toward a vulnerable woman. Indeed, the facts of this case are no different than those alleging sexual harassment in the workplace. Furthermore, our Supreme Court has held that fear of unfounded or fraudulent claims is not a valid reason for disallowing a tort action predicated upon a meritorious claim.

We conclude that the summary adjudication of defendant's claim for intentional infliction of emotional distress was improper.

Focus Questions: *Motheral v. Burkhart* and *Cunningham v. Jensen*

1. *Assuming the facts as alleged in* Motheral *were true, does the fact that the defendant Lesko was an attorney make her actions more extreme and outrageous or less extreme and outrageous? Assuming the facts as alleged were true, could a reasonable juror conclude the actions extreme and outrageous? In your opinion, were they extreme and outrageous?*
2. *Why was there not issue for the jury to decide on the issue of whether the defendant's actions in* Cunningham *were extreme and outrageous? Assuming there actually was a jury question on this issue, should the law firm's actions be considered to be absolutely privileged?*

Motheral v. Burkhart

583 A.2d 1180
(Pa. Super. 1990)

ROWLEY, Judge:

During the course of a bitter custody dispute between appellant G. Brinton Motheral and his wife, Gretchen Burkhart, from whom he is now divorced, appellant allegedly threatened his wife's mother, Ann Burkhart. The incident resulted in the filing of criminal charges against appellant, all of which were later dropped or nolle prossed. As a result of the filing of the criminal charges, which he contends were unfounded, appellant instituted the present civil action. In a multi-count complaint he asserted claims of malicious prosecution and intentional infliction of emotional distress against appellees Ann Burkhart and Deborah Lesko, who was Gretchen Burkhart's attorney in the divorce action, as well as claims of malicious prosecution and negligence against appellee Kratzenberg, Shields and Lesko, P.C., Lesko's law firm.

...

II. COUNTS III AND IV: APPELLEE LESKO

We turn next to the merits of appellant's appeal from the orders dismissing Counts III and IV of his complaint. In doing so, we are mindful of our scope of review as set forth in *Field v. Philadelphia Electric Company*:

> When preliminary objections in the nature of a demurrer are filed, we must accept as true all the well-pleaded material facts set forth in the complaint and all reasonable inferences deducible from those facts. Accepting these facts and inferences, we then determine whether the pleader has failed to state a claim for which relief may be granted, and we will affirm the grant of a demurrer only if there is certainty that no recovery is possible. All doubts are resolved in favor of the pleader.

Id. 388

... In his amended complaint, appellant makes broad allegations that Lesko provided information to Officer Blodgett, the police officer who filed the criminal complaint. Appellant claims that Lesko knew, or in the exercise of reasonable diligence should have known, that the information which she provided was false and that her actions were done "solely for her benefit and for the anticipated beneficial effect on the pending custody proceedings and not with any reasonable belief that any criminal conduct had actually occurred." Appellant specifically alleges that Lesko falsely informed Officer Blodgett that appellee Burkhart was to testify in the impending custody proceeding and that appellant had sexually molested his daughter.

Even accepting as true the allegation that Lesko made these statements to Officer Blodgett, we agree with the trial court that appellant has not pled sufficient facts to support a cause of action for malicious prosecution against Lesko. In order to prevail in an action for malicious prosecution ... the plaintiff must show, *inter alia*, that the defendant instituted the criminal proceedings against the plaintiff. Appellant was arrested for intimidation of a witness, simple assault, terroristic threats, and harassment. [He was not charged with sexual molestation of the children.] We conclude, therefore, that the trial court did not err in dismissing Count III of appellant's complaint.

In Count IV of his complaint appellant attempts to state a claim for intentional infliction of emotional distress based on the actions attributed to Lesko in Count III. Appellant cannot recover on such a claim ... unless the conduct complained of was "so outrageous in character, and so extreme in degree, as to go beyond all possible bounds of decency, and to be regarded as atrocious, and utterly intolerable in a civilized community." The conduct attributed to Lesko-making accusations to a police officer that she knew or reasonably should have known were false-was not of such a character. Accordingly, we affirm the trial court's dismissal of Count IV.

* * *

Cunningham v. Jensen

2004 WL 2034988
(Idaho Ct App. 2004)

I.
FACTS AND PROCEDURE

In 1998, the Cunninghams and Donald Jensen and Charolette Jensen entered into a contract for the purchase and sale of real property. Subsequently, the parties became involved in a dispute over the transaction in which the Cunninghams asserted that the Jensens made misrepresentations to entice them to purchase the property. In 2002, the Cunninghams filed a complaint against the Jensens and the Jensens' grandson, Arthur Hansen. In their complaint, the Cunninghams alleged, among other things, that the Jensens and Hansen wrongfully concealed property defects; misrepresented property boundaries, size, and conditions; and falsely promised to improve or repair irrigation equipment. In that lawsuit, the Jensens and Hansen retained the law firm of Brassey, Wetherell, Crawford, and McCurdy, LLP, (hereinafter BWC & M) to represent them.

The Cunninghams asserted that during the course of the litigation, the Jensens, Hansen, and BWC & M engaged in wrongful and abusive actions for the purpose of delaying, stalling, and subverting the Cunninghams' case. The Cunninghams requested that the district court impose sanctions and enter a default judgment. The district court imposed sanctions against the Jensens, Hansen, and BWC & M but denied the request to enter a default judgment. The Jensens and Hansen filed a motion to reconsider the sanctions and the district court issued a decision affirming the sanctions and the denial of a default judgment. Ultimately, the lawsuit alleging misrepresentation and fraud was settled and the case was dismissed.

Prior to settlement, the Cunninghams filed a complaint against the Jensens, Hansen, William McCurdy, J. Nick Crawford, and the law firm of BWC & M (respondents), alleging abuse of process, conspiracy to abuse process, and intentional infliction of emotional distress. More specifically, the Cunninghams alleged that the respondents intentionally delayed the filing of an answer, intentionally delayed the taking of discovery depositions, intentionally refused to appear for scheduled depositions, refused to comply with requests for production of documents, presented false and perjured testimony, presented false and perjured affidavits, refused to comply with the district court's order compelling discovery, filed motions and pleadings which were not intended to advance the litigation, and made unsworn statements to the district court which were false and/ or misleading. According to the complaint, the Cunninghams incurred injuries as a result of these alleged actions, including the loss of their anticipated trial date, the inability to use the real property for its intended purpose, the inability to cultivate crops, a delay in the construction of their home, the inability to divide and develop a section of the property, and the inability to develop and expand a horse boarding operation.

McCurdy, Crawford, and BWC & M filed a motion to dismiss pursuant to I.R.C.P. 12(b)(6)....

In the present case, the district court dismissed the Cunninghams' intentional infliction of emotional distress claim finding that the respondents' actions, as alleged in the complaint, were not extreme and outrageous. The district court further found that policy considerations dictate that the remedy available to litigants in the form of court sanctions is the appropriate remedy rather than a separate tort action. Moreover, the district court found that the respondents benefited from an absolute privilege in defamation for statements made during a judicial proceeding and that privilege extends to the claim of intentional infliction of emotional distress.

The Cunninghams assert that the respondents' actions were extreme and outrageous as demonstrated by sanctions imposed by the district court and the attorney fees awarded to the Cunninghams in the previous litigation. Additionally, the Cunninghams argue that the district court's ruling that the proper remedy for the respondents' actions should come from court sanctions rather than a separate tort action is error because court sanctions are not designed, nor appropriate, to fully compensate the victims of intentional infliction of emotional distress.

In determining whether the actions committed by the respondents rose to the level of extreme and outrageous conduct, the district court reviewed cases of similar conduct and concluded that many courts have addressed conduct similar to or more egregious than the allegations in the present case and those courts concluded that the conduct fails to rise to the level of extreme and outrageous. The district court cited two cases involving negotiations in bad faith, allegations of financial ruin to opposing litigants, threats of continued litigation, and the filing of multiple lawsuits which were frivolous and contained false allegations. *See* O'Neil v. Vasseur, 796 P.2d 134 (Idaho Ct.App.1990); Ulmer v. Frisard, 694 So.2d 1046 (La.Ct.App.1997).

Having reviewed these cases, we agree with the district court's analysis. Because we find no error in the district court's conclusion that the respondents' conduct did not rise to the level of extreme and outrageous conduct for purposes of the intentional infliction of emotional distress tort, we need not address the other grounds for dismissal cited by the district court.

* * *

B. Organization of the Book

Because many of the cases in this book involve plaintiffs seeking to hold an organization vicariously liable for the torts of an employee, the book begins with a chapter on vicarious liability. This is a subject that is usually addressed in a one-semester Torts class but not usually in any great detail.

In keeping with the focus on the threat of civil liability as it impacts lawyers, the book then addresses breach of fiduciary duty and legal malpractice claims in considerable detail.

This section devotes considerable time to the issues surrounding breach of fiduciary duty and professional negligence, two theories that any lawyer engaged in a sophisticated civil practice is likely to encounter at some point. However, in keeping with the unifying theme of this book that future lawyers should be particularly well versed when it comes to issues of professionalism and professional misconduct as it relates to their chosen profession, the section focuses almost exclusively on the fiduciary duties lawyers owe to clients and the related theory of legal malpractice.

After that, the book then transitions to a study of the broad range of tort theories lawyers may encounter in practice. The book devotes several chapters to the study of defamation, a theory with application to lawyers and nonlawyers alike. Next, the book turns to the various economic and dignitary torts. There are three chapters relating to theories involving misrepresentation and deceit, including a chapter covering consumer protection law and other alternatives to traditional misrepresentation claims. The next chapter focuses in considerable detail on the torts of interference with contractual relations and interference with prospective contractual relations, two torts that have bedeviled defendants and courts alike. Next, the book covers the various theories grouped under the broad heading of "invasion of privacy." This section ends with an in-depth coverage of misuse of the legal process, including the torts of malicious prosecution and abuse of process as well as a discussion of anti-SLAPP statutes.

Finally, the book concludes with something of a catch-all section that deals with liability for aiding and abetting another's tortious conduct, bad faith claims in the insurance context, and the employment-based claim of wrongful discharge in violation of public policy.

Chapter 2

Vicarious Liability

Exercise 2.1: Chapter Problem

Like many large law firms, Apple & Bosh has a practice of hiring contract attorneys for work on specific matters. These contract attorneys work on a temporary basis and typically devote their time to specific projects, for example doing document review in complex litigation. The firm pays these contract attorneys an hourly wage that (if extrapolated over the course of an entire year) is slightly less than the starting salary of a first-year associate of the firm. Contract attorneys do not receive most of the benefits that regular attorneys in the firm receive, such as health insurance. The firm bills the work of its contract attorneys out to clients at a substantially reduced rate. Thus, most of the firm's clients are generally pleased with the firm's practice of using contract attorneys. Contract attorneys are free to decline any work they do not wish to undertake. Most of the contract attorneys at Apple & Bosh work for only a few months at most.

Carl had a tough time finding a job after finishing law school, so he agreed to take a contract attorney job with Apple & Bosh. One assignment led to another and Carl wound up working at the firm for almost two years. Carl spent most of his time reviewing documents with a team of other contract attorneys who were all operating under the supervision of Dennis, a fifth-year associate. The members of the team were responsible for determining which documents were relevant to discovery requests and which were subject to the attorney-client privilege. Dennis was ultimately responsible within the firm for the team's work.

One week, the team was facing a deadline and worked long hours under extreme pressure. After the team finally finished the work at around 11 p.m. one night, Dennis offered to take his team out to a nearby bar for celebratory drinks. One drink became several and soon Carl, Dennis, and several other members were slightly intoxicated. Dennis remembered that he needed to pick up something from his office, so he and Carl stopped back by the office before heading home. While inside Dennis' office, Carl began complaining about what he perceived to be Dennis' lack of supervision of the team. The two men began to argue heatedly. Eventually, Carl became so enraged that he physically attacked Dennis, causing serious injuries.

As a result of this altercation, Carl's contract was terminated. Several months later, one of Apple & Bosh's clients was sanctioned by a judge for failing to adequately respond to discovery requests. Further investigation by the firm revealed that the failure was Carl's responsibility. The client has now sued the firm, seeking to hold it vicariously liable for Carl's alleged malpractice.

Dennis left the firm for other reasons a few months later and decided to sue Carl for battery. He also seeks to hold Apple & Bosh vicariously liable for Carl's actions.

Is Apple & Bosh likely to be held liable under either theory?

Throughout this book, you will encounter cases in which an injured party attempts to hold liable not only the individual who caused the injury, but the employer or other entity with which the individual is associated. As you probably learned in your basic Torts course, sometimes a defendant may be held vicariously liable for the torts of others. Vicarious liability is a form of strict liability. A defendant who is held vicariously liable is not being held liable for his or her own shortcomings. Instead, the defendant is held liable because someone else committed a wrong. This chapter explores the general rules regarding vicarious liability as well as some of the special issues raised when an individual attempts to hold a defendant vicariously liable for the torts of another.

A. Scope of Employment

1. Vicarious Liability Stemming from Negligent Conduct

Focus Questions: *Chorey, Taylor & Feil, P.C. v. Clark* and *O'Toole v. Carr*

1. *Why were the employees in these cases determined not to be acting within the scope of employment?*
2. *What is the difference between the scope of employment test found in the Restatement (Second) of Agency and the enterprise theory of liability?*

Chorey, Taylor & Feil, P.C. v. Clark

539 S.E.2d 139
(Ga. 2000)

BENHAM, Chief Justice.

In April 1996, appellee Dannice Clark was injured when her automobile was struck by a car driven by Wanda Chatham. [At the time, Chatham was an employee of a law firm named Chorey, Taylor & Feil, P.C. ("Chorey Taylor").*] The collision occurred while Ms. Chatham was on her way in her personal vehicle to deliver a check for telephone service for Vincent, Berg, Stalzer & Menendez, P.C. ("Vincent Berg"). Vincent Berg was a new law firm not yet open for business that had been established by some of [Chorey Taylor's] attorneys, and was the law firm for which Chatham had agreed to begin work in May 1996.... Appellee Clark filed a personal injury action against Chatham and, citing

* Editor's note: The history surrounding the firm's name is somewhat complicated. This aspect of the opinion has been edited for the sake of simplicity.

the doctrine of *respondeat superior,* included as defendants Chatham's employer at the time of filing suit (Vincent Berg) and Chorey Taylor. The trial court awarded summary judgment to both Vincent Berg and Chorey Taylor, and Clark appealed the entry of judgment in favor of Chorey Taylor. A divided Court of Appeals reversed the grant of summary judgment to Chorey Taylor after concluding that a factfinder should determine whether Chatham was acting within the scope of her employment at the time of the collision. The Court of Appeals opined that it could be inferred from the facts that Chatham's mission was not a purely personal pursuit entirely disconnected from her employment, and that it could be inferred that Chatham's attempt to deliver the check on behalf of Vincent Berg was not voluntary since her employment at [Chorey Taylor] and her future employment at Vincent Berg could have been adversely affected had she not delivered the check. We granted Chorey Taylor's petition for a writ of certiorari.

"The clearest case of vicarious liability [that is, liability for the tort of another] is that of a master for harm caused by acts of his servant." Harper, James & Gray, The Law of Torts, § 26.6, p. 23 (2nd ed. 1986). Under the principle of *respondeat superior,* "employers are generally jointly and severally liable along with the tortfeasor employee for the torts of employees committed within the scope of employment." Dobbs, The Law of Torts, § 333, p. 905 (2000). In Georgia, the common law principle is codified in OCGA § 51-2-2: "Every person shall be liable for torts committed by his ... servant by his command or in the prosecution and within the scope of his business, whether the same are committed by negligence or voluntarily."

When an employee causes an injury to another, the test to determine if the employer is liable is whether the employee was acting within the scope of the employee's employment and on the business of the employer at the time of the injury. The employer is not liable for the employee's tort if the tort was committed, "not by reason of the employment, but because of matters disconnected therewith...." Frazier v. Southern R. Co., 200 Ga. 590(2), 37 S.E.2d 774 (1946). Stated another way, if the employee was authorized to accomplish the purpose in pursuance of which the tort was committed, the employer is liable.

While the question of whether or not an employee was acting within the scope of employment at the time of the tort is generally one for the jury, summary judgment for the employer is appropriate where the evidence and all reasonable inferences drawn therefrom show that the employee was not engaged in furtherance of the employer's business, but was on a private enterprise of the employee's own. In the case at bar, Chatham was asked by a fellow employee to deliver a check issued by an entity other than Chatham's employer for initiation of phone service for an entity other than Chatham's employer. There is no evidence that Chatham's attempt to deliver the check was in furtherance of her employer's business. In fact, it appears that the opposite is true inasmuch as the delivery of the check would aid some of Chatham's fellow employees in their effort to open a business in competition with Chatham's employer. The fact that some of her fellow employees might benefit from her delivery of the check is not evidence that Chatham was on the business of her employer when she attempted to deliver the check. Without evidence that Chatham's employer's business was to assist in the set up of new law firms, the fact that the fellow employee who asked the favor of Chatham later described herself as having acted in her capacity as an employee of Chatham's employer when she made the request is not evidence that Chatham was on the business of her employer when she collided with Ms. Clark.

However willing we are to commit to the jury the solution of every question of fact, yet in the very nature of things, when the determination of the issue rests not on direct proof, but on circumstances, there exists a point where the inferences to be drawn can not, as a matter of law, be sufficient to [defeat the grant of summary judgment].

Accordingly, we reverse the judgment of the Court of Appeals and order the reinstatement of the trial court's entry of summary judgment in favor of Chorey Taylor.

Judgment reversed.

* * *

O'Toole v. Carr

786 A.2d 121
(N.J. Super. A.D. 2001)

CONLEY, J.A.D.

This appeal is generated by an automobile accident caused by defendant Paul J. Carr while driving from his home to his municipal court judgeship employment. The accident victims sued not only Carr but the Murray and Carr law firm in which, at the time of the accident, Carr was a partner. The law firm's alleged liability was premised upon principles of agency and respondeat superior vicarious liability. On leave granted by the Supreme Court, the firm appeals a March 16, 2001, order granting plaintiffs' and Carr's motion for summary judgment. In granting the motion, the judge concluded as a matter of law that the law firm was vicariously liable for Carr's negligence.

Although recognizing that more modern approaches in other jurisdictions to *respondeat superior* liability might provide a basis for vicarious liability under the particular circumstances here, we are constrained to abide by what we believe to be the current law in New Jersey and reverse. Under our existing law, Carr's automobile negligence while driving to the location of his municipal court judgeship cannot be imputed to the private law practice of Murray and Carr.

Most of the particular circumstances are not in dispute. On January 8, 1998, the O'Tooles' vehicle was struck by Carr's vehicle on Route 9 in the Township of Eagleswood. At the time of the accident, Carr was driving to the Tuckerton Municipal Court, where he presided as a part-time municipal judge. His car was leased. Lease payments, in addition to gas, tolls and other car expenses, were paid from Carr's corporate account. Income in this corporate account was derived from law firm disbursements after partnership overhead expenses were paid. No income, however, from Carr's judgeships, or Murray's (who also was a part-time municipal judge) judgeships, went into the partnership business account or their separate corporate accounts. Carr's vehicle was not leased in either the partnership or corporate name, but rather was leased by Carr in his personal capacity. The vehicle was insured by First Trenton Indemnity with bodily injury limits of $100,000 for each person and $300,000 for each accident. In contrast, the law firm had a million dollar automobile policy with CNA. The judge noted that plaintiffs had no underinsured motorists' coverage, thus enabling them to recover from either policy.

There are a few disputed facts. Carr had a portable cellular phone at the time of the accident which he had with him in the vehicle. Sometime before the accident, he claims to have made several law firm-related calls, one to his secretary to check his diary for the day and one or two to law firm clients. It was his deposition testimony that were it not for the accident, these clients would have been billed for the phone calls. Some question is raised as to the existence of the calls as phone bills purporting to be those of Carr's cell phone do not reflect the calls. The authenticity and accuracy of these records is disputed. Were there some basis for concluding that the accident occurred while Carr was engaged in one of the firm-related phone calls he claims to have made, the dispute of fact as to their existence might be critical. Carr, however, admitted in deposition testimony that he had finished the phone calls and was not on the cell phone at the time of the accident. There is no basis for concluding, therefore, that at the time of the accident, Carr was directly engaged in law firm business.

Nonetheless, the motion judge imposed vicarious liability upon the firm concluding that:

> [A]ny attorney who is also a municipal court judge even though the direct contributions may not be going back into the firm, there is a sufficient nexus and a sufficient benefit to that firm from that activity which inures to the benefit of all partners in that firm.... That is a sufficient connection so as to make [the law firm's] excess policy available for this accident.
>
> ....
>
> That [Carr] was in fact on sufficient law firm business at the time of the event so as to be, "legally designated as an agent." To the extent that we need that designat[ion] to implicate the policy.

The judge acknowledged that he was "expanding the definition of agency to cover this activity."

The focus here is upon the "going and coming" or commuting anomalies that have been engrafted upon *respondeat superior* liability principles. *See generally* Christopher Vaeth, Annotation, *Employer's Liability for Negligence of Employee in Driving His or Her Own Automobile,* 27 A.L.R. 5th 174 (1995); Rhett B. Franklin, *Pouring New Wine Into an Old Bottle: A Recommendation for Determining Liability of an Employer Under Respondeat Superior,* 39 S.D. L. Rev. 570 (1994). A number of different tests have been employed by jurisdictions throughout the country to determine whether *respondeat superior* principles apply to commuting accidents so as to make the employer liable for the commuting employee's negligence. *Ibid.* By far, the most liberal is that utilized in California. Employing what has been referred to as an enterprise theory of liability,[3] California has concluded that "if the employee's trip to or from work 'involves an incidental benefit to the employer, not common to commute trips made by ordinary members of the work force,' the 'going and coming' rule will not apply." Henderson v. Adia Servs. Inc., 182 Cal.App.3d 1069, 227 Cal.Rptr. 745, 747–48 (1986) (quoting Hinman v. Westinghouse Elec. Co., 2 Cal.3d 956, 88 Cal.Rptr. 188, 471 P.2d 988 (1970)). "Categorization of an employee's action as within or outside the scope of employment thus begins with a question of foreseeability, i.e., whether the accident is part of the inevitable toll of a lawful enterprise." The enterprise theory inquires whether "in the context of the particular enterprise the employee's conduct was 'so unusual or startling that it would seem unfair to include the loss resulting from it among other costs of the employer's business.'" It is not some element of control by the employer that is seen as the basis for imposing vicarious liability "but [rather] because the employer's enterprise creates inevitable risks as a part of doing business."

---

3. The enterprise theory, has been described in the following fashion:[w]hat has emerged as the modern justification for vicarious liability is a rule of policy, a deliberate allocation of a risk. The losses caused by the torts of employees, which as a practical matter are sure to occur in the conduct of the employer's enterprise, are placed upon that enterprise itself, as a required cost of doing business. They are placed upon the employer because, having engaged in an enterprise, which will on the basis of all past experience involve harm to others through the torts of employees, and sought to profit by it, it is just that he, rather than the innocent injured plaintiff, should bear them; and because he is better able to absorb them, and to distribute them, through prices, rates or liability insurance, to the public, and so to shift them to society, to the community at large. W. Page Keeton, et al., Prosser and Keeton on the Law of Torts, 499, 500–01 (5th ed.1984) (footnotes omitted).

Applying this rationale here, it might be said that the law firm could have anticipated or foreseen that Carr would be engaged in commuting to the municipal court as both Murray and Carr were each part-time municipal judges. Indeed, the partnership was formed to provide a mechanism, primarily for accounting purposes, by which each could continue with their part-time municipal judgeships but also engage in their respective private practices. It was also understood that while commuting, each attorney might conduct some firm business with their cell phones. Carr's automobile negligence under these circumstances might not be "so unusual or startling that it would seem unfair to" impose liability upon the partnership as a risk of its enterprise.

We do not believe New Jersey's application of *respondeat superior* liability principles to "going and coming"/commuting circumstances has yet gone so far as the California approach. Fundamentally, the California enterprise liability eschews the scope of employment test set forth in the *Restatement (Second) of Agency* §§218, 228, 229 (1957). As described by one commentator: "Under [the enterprise liability theory], the reason for imposing vicarious liability on employers is because their businesses should bear the losses incidental to those enterprises. [On the other hand] [t]he [*Restatement's*] "scope of employment" test attempts to limit the reach of *respondeat superior.*" Rhett B. Franklin, *supra,* 39 S.D.L. Rev. at 593 (footnotes omitted). Thus far, New Jersey follows the principles of the *Restatement.*

Under the *Restatement* principles, an employer is vicariously liable for the torts of an employee if the employee was acting within the scope of his or her employment at the time the tort was committed. An employee is acting within the scope of employment if the action is "'of the kind [the employee] is employed to perform; it occurs substantially within the authorized time and space limits; [and] it is actuated, at least in part, by a purpose to serve the master.'"[4]

Generally, the *Restatement* scope of employment principles do not recognize ordinary travel commute as within the scope of employment. "[A]n employee driving his or her own vehicle to and from the employee's workplace is not within the scope of employment for the purpose of imposing vicarious liability upon the employer for the negligence of the employee-driver." Mannes v. Healey, *supra,* 306 N.J.Super. at 353–54, 703 A.2d 944. Some courts ascribe this rule to the theory that "employment is suspended from the time

---

4. The *Restatement* defines scope of employment in §228 and describes the type of conduct which falls within that scope in §229. §228 states:(a) it is of the kind he is employed to perform;(b) it occurs substantially within the authorized time and space limits;(c) it is actuated, at least in part, by a purpose to serve the master, and(d) if force is intentionally used by the servant against another, the use of force is not unexpectable by the master.(2) Conduct of a servant is not within the scope of employment if it is different in kind from that authorized, far beyond the authorized time or space limits, or too little actuated by a purpose to serve the master.

> §229 states: (1) [t]o be within the scope of the employment, conduct must be of the same general nature as that authorized, or incidental to the conduct authorized.
> (2) In determining whether or not the conduct, although not authorized, is nevertheless so similar to or incidental to the conduct authorized as to be within the scope of employment, the following matters of fact are to be considered:
> (a) whether or not the act is one commonly done by such servants; (b) the time, place and purpose of the act; (c) the previous relations between the master and the servant; (d) the extent to which the business of the master is apportioned between different servants; (e) whether or not the act is outside the enterprise of the master or, if within the enterprise, has not been entrusted to any servant; (f) whether or not the master has reason to expect that such an act will be done; (g) the similarity in quality of the act done to the act authorized; (h) whether or not the instrumentality by which the harm is done has been furnished by the master to the servant; (i) the extent of departure from the normal method of accomplishing an authorized result; and (j) whether or not the act is seriously criminal.

the employee leaves the work-place until he or she returns, or that in traveling to and from work, the employee is not rendering service to the employer."

We recognize a number of exceptions to the general rule that ordinary travel commute is not within the scope of employment. Where, at the time of the negligent conduct, the employee is serving an interest of the employer as well as his or her own private interest, a "dual purpose" is established and the employer is vicariously liable. Such liability will also be imposed when the employee can be considered to have been on a special errand or mission on behalf of the employer. Another exception exists where the employee is required to drive his or her vehicle to work so that the vehicle is available for work-related duties. Finally, where an employee is "on call" and becomes involved in an accident while, at the request of the employer, is traveling to a work site, respondeat superior liability will attach.

Several recent cases are illustrative. Pfender v. Torres, 336 N.J.Super. 379, 392–94, 765 A.2d 208 (App.Div.), *certif. denied,* 167 N.J. 637, 772 A.2d 938 (2001), is an example of the employer required vehicle availability. There, defendant was a salesman for a car dealership which had provided its salesmen with vehicles for business as well as personal use, albeit retaining ownership. During working hours, the assigned vehicles were used for customer "demonstrators" and to run work-related errands. The vehicles so provided displayed the dealership's identification and were considered to serve promotional and advertising benefits when used by the salesmen. At the time of the accident, defendant was driving to work and was not serving any particular purpose of the dealership. In, nonetheless, imposing vicarious liability upon the dealership, we said: "[The dealership's] liability under [the] well-recognized exception is clear since [defendant employee] was driving to work when the accident happened and he was required to use the car in the performance of his employment as a demonstrator to encourage sales and to run work-related errands." *Id.* at 394, 765 A.2d 208.

In *Carter v. Reynolds,* 345 N.J.Super. 67, 783 A.2d 724 (App.Div.2001), we concluded vicarious liability should be imputed to the employer for an auto accident that occurred when the employee was commuting home from work because the employee's employment responsibilities required her to have a vehicle at work for off-site client visits. We pointed out that at least a third of her work time was off-site. *Id.* at 74, 783 A.2d 724.

In contrast, we declined in *Mannes v. Healey, supra,* 306 N.J.Super. at 355, 703 A.2d 944, to impose vicarious liability under the special mission or special errand exception. There, defendant was driving her own vehicle from her home to her place of employment when she struck a pedestrian at 8:30 p.m. She had an undefined and flexible nature of employment which allowed her to go to the office after regular business hours. But we viewed this employment flexibility as an employee benefit, not a requirement of the job. Moreover, we noted that the varying hours and unrestricted access to the employer's office underscored the absence of control by the employer, often considered a necessary element of respondeat superior liability. *Id.* at 355, 703 A.2d 944. We also pointed out that defendant was using her own car and that the employer did not control the manner in which defendant operated her car, the route of travel or when she chose to commute to the office for business purposes. *Ibid.* All of these *Restatement* factors convinced us that the employee in *Mannes* was not acting within the scope of employment at the time of the accident and that none of the exceptions thereto applied.

We believe a similar result must be reached here under our existing *respondeat superior* law. To begin with, it would be violative of Canon 2 of the Code of Judicial Conduct[5] to

5. Canon 2 instructs, in part, that a "judge should not lend the prestige of office to advance the private interests of others...."

say that Carr was serving any purpose of the law firm while commuting to his municipal judgeship position and thus the dual purpose exception does not apply. And, certainly he was not on a law firm special errand or mission. Neither does the record support a finding that the firm's practice required him to have a vehicle for off-site firm business. Finally, he was not in an "on-call" capacity.

We can, therefore, find no authority in New Jersey for imposing vicarious liability upon the law firm for Carr's auto negligence under the particular circumstances as they are reflected by the present record. We add the following brief comments. As we have said, were this jurisdiction to have adopted the enterprise liability approach that exists in California, the result might be different....

We are an appellate court bound to follow the law as we believe it to be in this jurisdiction.

Until and unless our Supreme Court rejects the *Restatement (Second) of Agency,* §§ 218, 228, 229, as the appropriate governing principles for resolving *respondeat superior* liability issues in the "going and coming"/commuting context or concludes that enterprise liability is consistent with the *Restatement* principles, we cannot expand those principles to encompass such liability. We, thus, conclude that the motion judge erred in imposing vicarious liability upon the law firm for Carr's negligence.

Reversed.

* * *

1. Enterprise liability. The *O'Toole* court sees a sharp distinction between the *Restatement's* scope of employment test and the enterprise liability theory. Are they really so different? For example, would the factors included in the *Restatement's* test have any relevance in a jurisdiction that relied on the enterprise liability theory? Can you articulate why the defendants in *Pfender* and *Carter* cases might be held liable under an enterprise liability analysis?

2. The need for an anchor claim. In *National Union Fire Ins. Co. of Pittsburgh, PA v. Wuerth,* 913 N.E.2d 939 (Ohio 2009), the client retained a law firm to defend a lawsuit. The lawyer primarily responsible for the case allegedly committed malpractice. The client sued the lawyer and the firm for malpractice, and also sought to hold the firm vicariously liable for the lawyer's malpractice. The malpractice claim against the firm was dismissed because only individuals, not entities, can commit malpractice. The claim against the individual attorney was dismissed due to the failure to file the claim within the one-year statute of limitations. Finally, the court concluded that if there was no finding of liability against the individual attorney, there could be no vicarious liability against the firm. "Although a party injured by an agent may sue the principal, the agent, or both, a principal is vicariously liable only when an agent could be held directly liable." *Id.* at 944; *see also Owens v. McLeroy, Litzler, Rutherford, Bauer & Friday, P.C.,* 235 S.W.3d 388 (Tex. Ct. App. 2007) (concluding law firm could not be vicariously liable for alleged wrongdoing of attorney in whose favor a final take-nothing summary judgment had been granted).

3. Model Rule comparison. Rule 5.1(c) of the *ABA Model Rules of Professional Conduct* provides that a law firm partner or lawyer with direct supervisory authority is responsible for another lawyer's violation of an ethical rule if, *inter alia* the first lawyer knew of the misconduct but failed to take remedial action when the consequences of the misconduct could have been avoided or mitigated.

* * *

2. Vicarious Liability Stemming from Intentional Misconduct and Breach of Fiduciary Duty

Focus Question: *Lyon v. Carey*

How could a jury find that this employee was acting within the scope of his employment at the time of the injury?

Lyon v. Carey

533 F.2d 649
(D.C. Cir. 1976)

McMILLAN, District Judge:

Corene Antoinette Lyon, plaintiff, recovered a $33,000.00 verdict in the United States District Court for the District of Columbia before Judge Barrington T. Parker and a jury, against the corporate defendants, George's Radio and Television Company, Inc., and Pep Line Trucking Company, Inc. The suit, for damages, arose out of an assault, including rape, committed with a knife and other weapons upon the plaintiff on May 9, 1972, by Michael Carey, a nineteen-year-old deliveryman for Pep Line Trucking Company, Inc. Three months after the trial, Judge Parker set aside the verdict and rendered judgment for both defendants notwithstanding the verdict. Plaintiff appealed.

Plaintiff was twenty-five years old, an employee of the D. C. Metropolitan Police Department. She is a twin sister of Irene Yvette Lyon, whose home was in an apartment at 5218 Fifth Street, S. E., in the District of Columbia. Irene Yvette Lyon had bought a mattress and springs for her bed from the defendant George's Radio and Television Company, Inc. The merchandise was to be delivered on May 9, 1972. Irene Lyon had to be at work and the plaintiff, Corene Lyon, had agreed to wait in her sister's apartment to receive the delivery.

A C.O.D. balance of $13.24 was due on the merchandise, and Irene Lyon had left a check for $13.24 to cover that balance. Plaintiff had been requested by her sister to "wait until the mattress and the springs came and to check and make sure they were okay."

Plaintiff, fully clothed, answered the door. Her description of what happened is sufficiently brief and unqualified that it will bear repeating in full. She testified, without objection, as follows:

> A. I went to the door, and I looked in the peephole, and I asked who was there. The young man told me he was a delivery man from George's. He showed me a receipt, and it said, 'George's.'
>
> He said he couldn't take a COD, so I let him in, and I told him to bring the mattress upstairs and he said, 'No,' that he wasn't going to lug them upstairs, and he wanted the COD first, and I told him I wanted to see the mattress and boxsprings to make sure they were okay, and he said no, he wasn't going to lug them upstairs. So this went back and forwards and so he was getting angry, and I told him to wait right here while I go get the COD.
>
> I went to the bedroom to get the check, and I picked it up, and I turned around and he was right there.

Q. Keep on.

A. And then I was giving him the check and then he told me that his boss told him not to accept no check, that he wanted cash money, and that if I didn't give him cash money, he was going to take it on my ass, and he told me that he was no delivery man, he was a rapist and then

THE COURT: Talk a little louder, young lady. Just a second. The ladies over in the jury box are raising their hands indicating that they are unable to hear you.

Q. Now you say there came a time when he said he could not take any check?

A. His boss only told him to accept cash.

Q. All right. Now turn your head toward the ladies and gentlemen of the jury, and relate what happened after that.

A. And then he told me that his boss wanted him only to accept cash, that he could not take any checks, and then he said that if I don't give him cash money, he was going to take it out of my ass, and then he threw me on the bed.

Q. Talk louder, young lady.

A. And then he threw me on the bed, and he had a knife to my throat.

Q. Then what happened?

A. And then he raped me.

Plaintiff's pre-trial deposition was a part of the record on appeal, and it shows that Carey raped plaintiff at knife point; that then he chased her all over the apartment with a knife and scissors and cut plaintiff in numerous places on her face and body, beat and otherwise attacked her. All of the physical injury other than the rape occurred after rather than before the rape had been accomplished.

Carey was tried for rape, pleaded guilty, and was sentenced to an active term in prison. Although he was named as a defendant, no one bothered to procure service of process upon him. Because Carey is not even a party, no question is presented on this appeal as to his liability.

Carey was an employee of the defendant Pep Line Trucking Company, Inc. Pep Line had an independent contract arrangement to make deliveries for George's Radio and Television Company, Inc. Carey was not an employee of George's. Carey was on the Lyon apartment premises for the purpose of delivering the mattress and springs which plaintiff's sister had bought from George's. Carey had the delivery receipt, and obtained entrance into the apartment upon the basis that he was making the delivery for George's. Plaintiff did not release the door chain until Carey displayed the George's delivery receipt.

As to the defendant Pep Line Trucking Company, Inc., the evidence will not support a finding that Pep Line knew or should have known that Carey had any proclivity or history more pronounced than that of any other nineteen-year-old boy for assaults, sexual or otherwise which would make Pep Line liable because of knowledge of a dangerous propensity.

The principal question, therefore, is whether the evidence discloses any other basis upon which a jury could reasonably find Pep Line, the employer of Carey, liable for the assault.

Michael Carey was in the employment of the defendant Pep Line as a deliveryman. He was authorized to make the delivery of the mattress and springs plaintiff's sister had bought. He gained access to the apartment only upon a showing of the delivery receipt for the merchandise. His employment contemplated that he visit and enter that particular apartment. Though the apartment was not owned by nor in the control of his employer, it was nevertheless a place he was expected by his employer to enter.

After Carey entered, under the credentials of his employment and the delivery receipt, a dispute arose naturally and immediately between him and the plaintiff about two items of great significance in connection with his job. These items were the request of the plaintiff, the customer's agent, to inspect the mattress and springs before payment (which would require their being brought upstairs before the payment was made), and Carey's insistence on getting cash rather than a check.

The dispute arose out of the very transaction which had brought Carey to the premises, and, according to the plaintiff's evidence, out of the employer's instructions to get cash only before delivery.

On the face of things, Pep Line Trucking Company, Inc. is liable, under two previous decisions of the Court of Appeals for the District of Columbia Circuit. *Tarman v. Southard,* 92 U.S. App. D.C. 297, 205 F.2d 705 (1953) held a taxi owner liable for damages (including a broken leg) sustained by a customer who had been run over by the taxi in pursuit of a dispute between the driver and the customer about a fare. *Dilli v. Johnson,* 71 U.S. App. D.C. 139, 107 F.2d 669 (1939), held a restaurant owner liable to a restaurant patron who was beaten with a stick by one Propst, a restaurant employee, after a disagreement over the service. The theory of *Dilli,* 71 U.S. App. D.C. 139, 107 F.2d at 670, was that:

> It is well established that an employer may be held responsible in tort for assaults committed by an employee while he is acting within the scope of his employment, even though he may act wantonly and contrary to his employer's instructions. Axman v. Washington Gaslight Co., 38 App.D.C. 150; Davis v. Merrill, 133 Va. 69, 112 S.E. 628; *see* New York Central & H. R. R. Co. v. United States, 212 U.S. 481, 493, 29 S.Ct. 304, 53 L.Ed. 613.
>
> ... having placed Propst in charge and committed the management of the business to his care, defendants may not escape liability either on the ground of Propst's infirmity of temperament or because, under the influence of passion aroused by plaintiff's threat to report the circumstances, he went beyond the ordinary line of duty and inflicted the injury shown in this case. Davis v. Merrill, 133 Va. 69, 112 S.E. 628.

In 1 Thompson, Negligence, § 554, it is pointed out that, unless the above principle is maintained:

> It will always be more safe and profitable for a man to conduct his business vicariously than in his own person. He would escape liability for the consequences of many acts connected with his business, springing from the imperfections of human nature, because done by another, for which he would be responsible if done by himself. Meanwhile, the public, obliged to deal or come in contact with his agent, for injuries done by them must be left wholly without redress. He might delegate to persons pecuniarily irresponsible the care of large factories, of extensive mines, of ships at sea, or of railroad trains on land, and these persons, by the use of the extensive power thus committed to them, might inflict wanton and malicious injuries on third persons, without other restraint than that which springs from the imperfect execution of the criminal laws. A doctrine so fruitful of mischief could not long stand unshaken in an enlightened jurisprudence.

Grimes v. Saul, 60 App.D.C. 47, 47 F.2d 409 (1931), does not require a different result. In that case the defendant Saul Company, an owner of real estate, was held not liable for an attempted rape committed one afternoon in the building by a janitor on a tenant. A demurrer to the complaint was sustained because there was no allegation that the assault arose out of any business being transacted or any duty being performed for the employer, or that the janitor in committing the assault had any motive whatever connected with the business of the employer, the only intent alleged being simply the assault with the personal intent to commit rape. The case was decided upon the basis that

> The act of a servant done to effect some independent purpose of his own and not with reference to the service in which he is employed, or while he is acting as his own master for the time being, is not within the scope of his employment so as to render the master liable therefor. In these circumstances the servant alone is liable for the injury inflicted.
>
> ... The general idea is that the employee at the time of doing the wrongful act, in order to fix liability on the employer, must have been acting in behalf of the latter and not on his own account.

The principal physical (as opposed to psychic) damage to the plaintiff is a number of disfiguring knife wounds on her head, face, arms, breasts and body. If the instrumentalities of assault had not included rape, the case would provoke no particular curiosity nor interest because it comes within all the classic requirements for recovery against the master. The verdict is not attacked as excessive, and could not be excessive in light of the physical injuries inflicted.

It may be suggested that *Dilli v. Johnson* [is] distinguishable because ... the plaintiff was a business visitor on the defendant's "premises."

... [T]he premises of a deliveryman may fairly include the places where he goes to make deliveries, Davis v. J. & B. Motor Lines, 193 Tenn. 233, 245 S.W.2d 769 (1951) (A contractor's premises include the highway, when his business is hauling freight.); *see* Babine v. Cane Const. Corp., 153 Me. 339, 138 A.2d 625 (1958) (When a contractor takes his employees onto the premises of another, to perform the contract, such premises become the contractor's premises.); Ganassi v. Pittsburgh Coal Co., 162 Pa.Super. 289, 57 A.2d 717 (1948) (A public way may be the premises of an employer.).

Home delivery customers are usually in their homes, sometimes alone; and deliveries of merchandise may expose householders to one-on-one confrontations with deliverymen. It would be a strange rule indeed which, while allowing recovery for assaults committed in "the store," would deny a master's liability for an assault committed on a lone woman in her own home, by a deliveryman required by his job to enter the home.

If, as in *Grimes v. Saul, supra,* the assault was not motivated or triggered off by anything in the employment activity but was the result of only propinquity and lust, there should be no liability.

However, if the assault, sexual or otherwise, was triggered off or motivated or occasioned by a dispute over the conduct then and there of the employer's business, then the employer should be liable.

It is, then, a question of fact for the trier of fact, rather than a question of law for the court, whether the assault stemmed from purely and solely personal sources or arose out of the conduct of the employer's business; and the trial judge so instructed the jury.

It follows that, under existing decisions of the District of Columbia Circuit, plaintiff has made out a case for the jury against Pep Line Trucking, Inc. unless the sexual character of one phase of the assault bars her from recovery for damages from all phases of the assault.

... It is a jury's job to decide how much of plaintiff's story to believe, and how much if any of the damages were caused by actions, including sexual assault, which stemmed from job-related sources rather than from purely personal origins.

The judgment is affirmed as to the defendant George's and reversed as to the defendant Pep Line Trucking Company, Inc.

Focus Questions: *Goodman v. Holmes & McLaurin Attorneys at Law* and *Federal Savings & Loan Ins. Corp. v. McGinnis, Juban, Bevan, Mullins*

1. *Can these two decisions be reconciled?*
2. *What should be the relevance of the fact that an employee violates a rule of professional conduct? What should be the relevance of the fact that an employer instructed an employee not to perform the act that forms the basis of the vicarious liability claim?*

Goodman v. Holmes & McLaurin Attorneys at Law

665 S.E.2d 526

(N.C. App. 2008)

On 31 July 1992, David M. Goodman (plaintiff) was injured in an automobile collision. Plaintiff hired the law firm of Holmes & McLaurin (H & M Partnership) to represent him with respect to his personal injury and property damage claims. Edward McLaurin, Jr. (McLaurin) had primary responsibility for plaintiff's representation and filed a complaint on 28 July 1995. On 21 October 1997, McLaurin filed a voluntary dismissal without prejudice, without the knowledge or consent of plaintiff. When McLaurin failed to re-file plaintiff's lawsuit within one year, plaintiff's claims against the original tortfeasors were barred by the three year statute of limitations pursuant to N.C. Gen.Stat. §§ 1A-1, Rule 41(a) and 1-52(5).

Following the filing of the voluntary dismissal, McLaurin took affirmative steps to conceal his action, or lack of action, from plaintiff. He advised plaintiff that the insurer of the tortfeasors in the 1992 accident was St. David's Trust, located in Barcelona, Spain. In fact, no such entity ever existed. McLaurin advised plaintiff that he was negotiating a settlement with St. David's Trust, and in June 2000, faxed a purported "settlement offer" to plaintiff. This offer was rejected by plaintiff. Subsequently, two further offers, supposedly made by St. David's Trust, were submitted to plaintiff. Plaintiff eventually "accepted" a settlement in the amount of $200,000. McLaurin forwarded to plaintiff a "Trust Memorandum" allegedly from St. David's Trust, dated 29 September 2000, showing that the settlement would be paid in two installments of $100,000 on 31 December 2001 and 31 December 2002. The settlement was to be funded by St. David's Trust or the Landau Foundation. Between January and July of 2001, there were three transfers of funds from the H & M Partnership's Trust Account to plaintiff's bank account, totaling $25,000. McLaurin represented to plaintiff that these funds represented "interim payments" by St. David's Trust to assist plaintiff with his medical bills.

From 2001 through 2003, McLaurin continued to assure plaintiff that he was still "dealing with" St. David's Trust to obtain the monies provided for in the "Trust Memorandum." In January 2004, McLaurin sent plaintiff a copy of a purported complaint against the original tortfeasors and St. David's Trust. The complaint sought damages from St. David's Trust for breach of the settlement agreement and for unfair and deceptive trade practices. McLaurin asked plaintiff to execute a verification of the complaint. Plaintiff was told by McLaurin that the complaint had been filed. When plaintiff pressed McLaurin for confirmation on the status of this matter, McLaurin sent plaintiff a copy of an e-mail supposedly from a lawyer in Spain.

On 11 December 2001, plaintiff was injured in a second automobile accident. He hired the H & M partnership to represent him with respect to his personal injury claim. In November 2005, plaintiff learned for the first time of McLaurin's 1997 dismissal of plaintiff's claims and his subsequent failure to re-file the action within one year. Plaintiff also learned that McLaurin had not filed suit against St. David's Trust.

On 9 May 2006 Plaintiff filed a complaint against defendants, seeking to recover damages based upon the negligent and fraudulent conduct of McLaurin, which plaintiff alleged was imputed to the other defendants by virtue of their relationship with McLaurin. The complaint asserted five causes of action [including fraud arising out of the alleged cover-up of McLaurin's actions concerning the 1992 accident. This is the issue on appeal.]

III. Partnership Law

... The Holmes defendants acknowledge that McLaurin's representation of plaintiff for his claims associated with the 1992 accident was with the authority of the partnership. They contend, however, that the fraudulent concealment of McLaurin's negligence "took him outside the scope of any arguable agency of the firm" and "went so far beyond a lawyer's legitimate role as to place it outside the ordinary scope of business of a law partnership."

A partnership is liable for loss or injury caused by any wrongful act or omission of any partner acting in the ordinary course of business of the partnership or with the actual or apparent authority of his copartners. "The rules governing partnership tort liability are fully applicable to law partnerships." Jackson v. Jackson, 20 N.C.App. 406, 407, 201 S.E.2d 722, 723 (1974). "The general rule in this jurisdiction is that a partner or officer cannot bind the partnership or corporation beyond the normal scope of his authority." Thus the question at issue is whether a lawyer who engages in fraudulent concealment of his professional negligence is acting in the ordinary course of his law firm's business.

In *Jackson,* a law partnership was sued on the grounds that one of the partners instituted a malicious prosecution. In determining whether the attorney's conduct was within the scope of the partnership, this Court noted that the Rules of Professional Conduct prohibit an attorney from instituting an action on behalf of his client that he knows would merely serve to harass or maliciously injure another. Based on these rules, we concluded that malicious prosecution was not within the ordinary course of business of a law partnership.

The Rules of Professional Conduct of the North Carolina State Bar require:

Rule 1.4: Communication

(a) A lawyer shall:

(1) promptly inform the client of any decision or circumstance with respect to which the client's informed consent..., is required by these Rules;

...

(3) keep the client reasonably informed about the status of the matter

(4) promptly comply with reasonable requests for information

...

(b) A lawyer shall explain a matter to the extent reasonably necessary to permit the client to make informed decisions regarding the representation.

As previously discussed, the statute of repose barred plaintiff's claims for professional negligence and malpractice. Thus, the only remaining claim for which the Holmes defendants could be liable was McLaurin's fraudulent concealment of his professional negligence. As in *Jackson,* the representation of a plaintiff in a personal injury action is clearly within the normal range of activities for a typical law partnership. However, fraud associated with such representation, including the failure to keep a client informed about the status of his or her case and the active concealment of the true state of affairs, in violation of the standards of the legal profession, is not in the ordinary course of the partnership business. There is nothing in plaintiff's complaint to suggest that the Holmes defendants authorized, participated in, or even knew about McLaurin's fraudulent conduct.

The trial court did not err in dismissing plaintiff's claims against the Holmes defendants.

* * *

Federal Savings & Loan Ins. Corp. v. McGinnis, Juban, Bevan, Mullins

808 F. Supp. 1263
(E.D. La. 1992)

FELDMAN, District Judge.

Before the Court are several motions. Defendant moves for summary judgment: (1) dismissing some of the FDIC's malpractice claims because the alleged negligence acts were not done in the course of a duty owed to the failed institution, (2) dismissing the FDIC's conflict of interest claims, (3) dismissing all the FDIC's claims because the FDIC is estopped from advancing them, and (4) ordering that the McGinnis, Juban firm is not vicariously liable for some of the alleged acts of malpractice committed by one of its partners.

Plaintiff has responded to defendants' motions with its own motions for summary judgment: (1) dismissing the estoppel defenses and (2) ordering that the McGinnis, Juban firm is vicariously liable for all its partner's alleged wrongdoing. Plaintiff has also filed motions for summary judgment (1) dismissing the defenses based on the comparative fault of the failed institution's former officers and directors, and (2) dismissing the defenses alleging that the FDIC was contributorily negligent and that it failed to mitigated its damages.

BACKGROUND

In this case, still another federal court is left to pick up the pieces after a bank failure. In late Spring 1986, Sun Belt Federal Bank, F.S.B., a Louisiana savings and loan institution, was declared insolvent and the Federal Savings and Loan Insurance Company was appointed receiver of the failed institution. The FDIC has sued the defendants, alleging that George Bevan, a Baton Rouge lawyer, committed malpractice in the course of representing Sun Belt as the closing attorney on a loan that ended up in default.

In late February 1985, Sun Belt extended an $898,000 loan to Mande Cove, Inc. In preparing the deal, Sun Belt hired, as is apparently customary, Mr. Bevan to serve as the closing attorney on the loan. George Bevan was a partner in the firm of McGinnis, Juban,

Bevan, Mullins & Patterson, P.C. At the very least, the closing attorney's duties included (1) performing a title search on any real estate advanced as collateral and preparing a certificate of title examination, (2) preparing the necessary loan and mortgage documents, and (3) closing the transaction (including any act of sale involved). The FDIC, however, contends that the responsibilities of such a professional extend further and require the closing attorney to advise the institution concerning all relevant legal matters affecting the transaction, and to otherwise protect the bank's interests in the deal.

Ultimately, Mande Cove defaulted on the Sun Belt loan. The FDIC contends that had Bevan not committed certain acts of malpractice while acting as the closing attorney for Sun Belt, the bank would have learned that the transaction was ill-advised and either would have not made the loan, or would have restructured the deal to make it less risky.

Specifically, the FDIC maintains that Bevan breached his duties as the closing attorney in three ways. First, the FDIC says that Bevan performed a negligent title search on the property that was used for collateral. The FDIC maintains that Sun Belt required at least a second mortgage on the property. According to the FDIC, Bevan certified to Sun Belt that the subject property was only encumbered by a $175,000 first mortgage. Thus, Bevan apparently told Sun Belt, the bank could get the required second mortgage. The FDIC says that Sun Belt relied on Bevan's assurance and extended credit to Mande Cove. However, the FDIC contends that the property was in fact subject to a $1 million mortgage in addition to the $175,000 encumbrance Bevan had disclosed.

The FDIC says that if Sun Belt had known of the existing second mortgage, it either would have somehow restructured the deal to obtain a better position, or it would have refused to lend Mande Cove the money. Instead, Sun Belt made the loan, and when Mande Cove defaulted, it recovered only $25,000 of its lien on the property.

The FDIC also asserts that Bevan either intentionally or negligently failed to reveal crucial facts he knew concerning Mande Cove's circumstances that would have affected Sun Belt's willingness to go through with the loan. The FDIC claims that Bevan knew that Mande Cove had been formed just before it sought the loan, and was composed solely of three people who had previously borrowed substantial amounts of money from the bank. The FDIC adds that Bevan knew that the Mande Cove principals were hoping to borrow this money so that they could use it to pay past due interest on their prior loans from Sun Belt. Moreover, the FDIC contends that Bevan knew, or should have known, that because of the substantial amounts of money the Mande Cove people had previously borrowed, the February 1986 loan would violate the federal one-borrower regulations. The FDIC says that Bevan violated his fiduciary duties to Sun Belt as its closing attorney, and if he had revealed what he knew to the uninvolved officers and directors of the institution, the bank would have refused the loan.

Finally, the FDIC concludes that Bevan violated his fiduciary responsibilities to Sun Belt by not informing the uninvolved officers and directors that he was representing the Mande Cove principals at the same time that he was acting as Sun Belt's closing attorney in the February 1986 transaction. The FDIC claims that Bevan should have revealed that he had represented the Mande Cove principals in the previous dealings. If the uninterested officers and directors had known of this alleged conflict of interest, the FDIC contends, they would have had the chance to block the loan.

This is not the only civil suit arising out of Sun Belt's failure that the banking authorities brought. In 1986, FSLIC sued some of the officers and directors of Sun Belt, alleging that their negligent, intentional and even criminal conduct in loan approval led to the failed institution's demise. At issue in the prior litigation, called FSLIC v. Wendell P. Shelton, et al., was officer and director misconduct with respect to numerous loan transactions, including the Mande Cove deal. Earlier this year, the FDIC and the officer-director defendants settled the case for $60 million. The Sun Belt disgrace has become permanent lore in the annals of the epidemic of failed financial institutions in this country.

LAW AND APPLICATION

[In Parts I and II of the opinion the court denied the defendant's motion for summary judgement because "fact issues remain as to (1) whether there was a potential conflict; (2) whether Bevan informed Sun Belt's uninvolved directors of any conflict that may have existed; (3) what the uninvolved directors may have known from sources other than Bevan; (4) if Bevan did fail to notify the uninvolved directors of any potential conflict, whether he was negligent; and (5) if there was negligence in this regard, whether that negligence caused Sun Belt any injury."]

III. Vicarious Liability

The McGinnis, Juban defendants[6] contend that, even if Bevan is liable to the FDIC for malpractice, they cannot be held vicariously responsible for the wrongful acts about which the FDIC complains because (1) there is no partnership liability for a member's fraudulent or intentional torts or breach of fiduciary duty; and (2) Bevan was not acting within the course and scope of the McGinnis, Juban partnership business. The FDIC responds that, at the very least, factual issues remain for trial on vicarious liability. But the FDIC goes further, and moves for summary judgment that, as a matter of law, the McGinnis, Juban defendants are vicariously liable for all the wrongdoing alleged against Bevan (provided, of course, that the FDIC proves Bevan's fault). The Court agrees with the FDIC, although the decision is not a pleasant one to make.

A.

In Louisiana, as elsewhere, a partnership and its individual members are vicariously liable for torts committed by any partner in the course and scope of the partnership business. Vicarious liability, obviously, is liability without fault. That is, the partnership and partners are responsible even though they neither participated in, nor knew of, the other partner's wrongdoing.

However, the McGinnis, Juban defendants contend that there can be no partnership liability for a member's intentional or fraudulent misconduct, or for a member's breach of a fiduciary duty. Therefore, these defendants say, whatever may be true as to their liability for Bevan's negligence,[8] they cannot be held responsible for any of Bevan's other alleged misconduct, even if arguably done in the course and scope of the partnership business.

Louisiana law has not so restricted partner liability. The Louisiana Supreme Court held almost seventy-five years ago that "[p]artners are liable in civil actions upon the principle of agency for the fraudulent or malicious conduct of one of their number done without the knowledge of the others for the benefit of the partnership and within the

6. These defendants include the McGinnis, Juban law firm and the firm's malpractice liability insurance carrier, New England Insurance Company.

8. The McGinnis, Juban defendants admit that they are vicariously liable for any negligence of Bevan "within the scope of the normal business of the firm: performing the title examination, preparing the loan and mortgage documents, and passing the act of sale."

scope of its business" (internal quotation omitted). Guarantee Trust & Safe Deposit Co. v. E.C. Drew Investment Co., 107 La. 251, 31 So. 736, 738 (1908). Vicarious liability, therefore, depends on whether the act was done in the course and scope of the partnership business for the benefit of the partnership, and not, as harsh is it may seem, on the wrongdoer's state of mind.

Case literature in Louisiana defining "the course and scope of the partnership business" is sparse. However, partnership liability is grounded in agency principles because "each partner acts both as principal and agent of the other as to acts done within the apparent scope of the business and purpose of the partnership and for its benefit." *McCaskill, supra.* Thus, the Court looks to Louisiana agency law, which, like partnership law, holds the principal (the master) vicariously liable for even the intentional torts of his the agent (the servant) provided the servant was acting within the course and scope of his employment. *See* LeBrane v. Lewis, 292 So.2d 216, 217 (La.1974) (supervisor's stabbing of recently discharged employee is within the course and scope of employment); Home Life Ins. Co. v. Equitable Equipment Co., 680 F.2d 1056, 1058–59 (5 Cir.1982) (interpreting Louisiana law). In *LeBrane,* the Louisiana Supreme Court wrote that an intentional tort is committed within the scope of employment if:

> the tortious conduct ... was so closely connected in time, place, and causation as to be regarded as a risk of harm fairly attributable to the employer's business, as compared with conduct motivated by purely personal considerations entirely extraneous to the employer's interests.

B.

These guiding principles and the undisputed facts compel the conclusion that all the allegations against Bevan implicate conduct that, if proven, will have necessarily been done in the course of the McGinnis, Juban partnership business.

Defendants admit that Bevan was a partner in the firm, that Bevan was considered by firm members to have special expertise in real estate matters, that Sun Belt retained Bevan to close the Mande Cove deal, and that the firm received $3,750 in legal fees in connection with the loan closing. And so, defendants cannot seriously contest that loan closings were "done by [McGinnis, Juban] lawyers with such frequency or appropriateness as to [have] become a phase of the practice." Rouse v. Pollard, 130 N.J.Eq. 204, 21 A.2d 801 (Ct. Err. & App.1941).

In Count I-A of the FDIC's amended complaint, the FDIC maintains that Bevan knew of facts surrounding this loan that should have indicated to him that the Mande Cove transaction would violate federal regulations, and that he failed, either intentionally or negligently, to tell the disinterested Sun Belt directors of these circumstances. The FDIC says that this was a violation of Bevan's fiduciary duty to the bank as its closing attorney. Defendants hotly contest that Bevan's responsibilities as closing attorney required him to disclose to Sun Belt the circumstances that may have made the loan unwise.

The only way the FDIC can win on its claim is to prove that Bevan breached a duty imposed in Louisiana on closing attorneys generally, and that Bevan and Sun Belt had not contractually narrowed that duty. The FDIC will not recover on Count I-A unless it can prove that Bevan's representation of Sun Belt included the fiduciary duty to reveal the allegedly detrimental circumstances of the loan. McGinnis, Juban concede, as they must, that Bevan was acting within the scope of the partnership business when he represented Sun Belt in connection with the Mande Cove transaction. Thus, Bevan's breach, if any, of a duty that the Sun Belt representation imposed would clearly "be regarded as a risk of harm fairly attributable to [McGinnis, Juban's] business." *LeBrane, supra.* McGinnis, Juban's only argument is that the representation did not impose a duty to disclose the facts Bevan allegedly knew. However, that goes to whether Bevan committed malpractice, and not to whether McGinnis, Juban are vicariously responsible if it is determined that Bevan is liable.

In Count I-B, the FDIC alleges that Bevan breached his fiduciary responsibilities to Sun Belt by (1) failing to disclose that he was representing the Mande Cove's principals in the Mande Cove transaction while simultaneously acting as Sun Belt's closing attorney; and (2) failing to disclose that he had represented the Mande Cove principals in their earlier dealings with Sun Belt. The FDIC maintains that if disinterested Sun Belt directors and officers had known of this alleged conflict of interest, they would have refused to extend the Mande Cove loan.

Again, in disputing vicarious liability, McGinnis, Juban mistakenly argue the merits of Bevan's responsibility. They contend that at least one, if not all, of the Sun Belt officers knew of Bevan's dual representation. If the FDIC is to recover on this Count, it will have to prove that Bevan had a duty as Sun Belt's closing attorney (a role McGinnis, Juban admit Bevan assumed as part of the partnership business) to disclose the alleged conflict of interest. Whether negligent or intentional, a lawyer's breach of a duty to a firm client imposed by the representation is within the course of the partnership's business.

Thus, the Court grants partial summary judgment that any liability the FDIC eventually proves against George Bevan under Counts I, I-A, or I-B of the complaint is attributable to the McGinnis, Juban defendants under general principles of partnership liability.

Exercise 2.2

The accountant for a law firm converts client funds for her own use. One of the affected clients seeks to recover from the firm on theories of vicarious liability and negligent supervision of the accountant. *See generally* ABA Model Rule of Professional Conduct Rule 5.3 (requiring proper supervision of non-lawyer employees of a firm). The negligent supervision claim is dismissed because the firm exercised reasonable care in supervising the accountant. Is vicarious nonetheless liability appropriate under the *McGinnis* approach?

B. Independent Contractors and Nondelegable Duties

Respondeat superior is not appropriate where the wrongdoer is merely an independent contractor, rather than an employee of the party sought to be held vicariously liable. Thus, it may be imperative to first determine whether the wrongdoer is an employee or an independent contractor. Even where it is determined that the wrongdoer is an independent contractor, there are limited circumstances in which an employer may nonetheless be held liable for harm caused by the contractor.

In *Pusey v. Bator*, 762 N.E.2d 968 (Ohio 2002), the Ohio Supreme Court described the notion of a nondelegable duty as follows:

> [A]n employer is generally not liable for the negligent acts of an independent contractor. There are, however, exceptions to this general rule, several of which stem from the nondelegable duty doctrine. Nondelegable duties arise in various situations that generally fall into two categories: (1) affirmative duties that are imposed on the employer by statute, contract, franchise, charter, or common law and (2) duties imposed on the employer that arise out of the work itself because its performance creates dangers to others, i.e., inherently dangerous work. If the work to be performed fits into one of these two categories, the employer may delegate the work to an independent contractor, but he cannot delegate the duty. In other words, the employer is not insulated from liability if the independent contractor's negligence results in a breach of the duty.

Pusey involved a business owner who hired an independent contractor, a security company, to supply armed security to deter theft and vandalism. This type of work, the court concluded, was inherently dangerous. Thus, the court concluded that if the security company performed its duties negligently and someone was injured as a result, the business owner was vicariously liable under the nondelegable duty doctrine.

The type of work need not involve an abnormally dangerous activity for a nondelegable duty to arise. For example, the *Restatement (Third) of Torts* explains that a nondelegable duty arises where the work involves a "peculiar risk." An activity involves a peculiar risk when "if reasonable care is not exercised, the resulting risk differs from the types of risk usual in the community." Restatement (Third) of Torts § 59. For example, transporting flammable chemicals might not be an abnormally dangerous activity, but it does impose risks that are different in kind than other activities on the highway. *Id.* cmt. c. According to one author, "[t]he most often cited formulation is that a duty will be deemed nondelegable when the responsibility is so important to the community that the employer should not be permitted to transfer it to another." 5 HARPER, JAMES AND GRAY, TORTS § 26.11, at 73 (2d ed.) (quoted in Kleeman v. Rheingold, 614 N.E.2d 712, 716 (N.Y. 1993)).

Focus Questions: *Kersten v. Van Grack, Axelson & Williamowsky, P.C.*

1. *What distinguishes an employee (or agent) from an independent contractor?*
2. *Should service of process be treated as involving a nondelegable duty?*

Kersten v. Van Grack, Axelson & Williamowsky, P.C.

608 A.2d 1270
(Md. App. 1992)

HARRELL, Judge.

This appeal from a summary judgment proceeding in the Circuit Court for Montgomery County raises the issue of whether a law firm may be held vicariously liable for the alleged bad acts of a private process server. The circuit court (Cave, J.) ruled that appellee, Van Grack, Axelson & Williamowsky, P.C., neither possessed nor exercised that degree of control over the private process server which would give rise to vicarious liability. We find no error and affirm.

Facts

The events leading up to this appeal are undisputed and may be summarized briefly. Appellee was retained by Charlene Baden in connection with an action brought against her by Private Mortgage Investors Trade Association (PMITA). On behalf of Baden, appellee filed a third-party complaint against appellants, Carol and Peggy Kersten and Lucille and Jeffrey Schneyer. Appellee engaged Richard Alan James to serve process on appellants. James submitted purported affidavits of service to appellee and to the circuit court stating that he had personally served appellants on 30 and 31 May 1987. The affidavits were false; James never personally served appellants.

Not having received notice of Baden's complaint, appellants failed to respond to it. Upon the written request of appellee, therefore, the circuit court entered an order of default against Carol Kersten and the Schneyers pursuant to Md. Rule 2-613. The circuit court notified Carol Kersten and the Schneyers that an order of default had been entered against them and that they could move to vacate the order within 30 days after its entry. Thereafter, they successfully moved to vacate the order. Judgment was ultimately entered in favor of appellants in the PMITA action.

On 5 May 1988, appellants filed the instant action against appellee, James, and Baden.[3] In their complaint, appellants alleged that, as a result of discovering they were potentially subject to a substantial default judgment, they suffered severe emotional distress. Appellants also sought to recover financial losses sustained in defending against the entry of the default order. Their complaint contained two counts, one of which charged appellee with vicarious liability for James' actions. Appellee moved for summary judgment on 29 March 1991. After hearing arguments on 29 August 1991, the circuit court granted appellee's motion for summary judgment.

Although there were a number of issues raised before the circuit court at the summary judgment hearing, the sole issue on appeal is whether liability may be imputed to appellee for the alleged bad acts of James. Appellants contend that an employer-employee relationship existed between appellee and James, such that liability may be imputed to appellee under the doctrine of *respondeat superior.* Alternatively, appellants contend that appellee may be held vicariously liable under one of the exceptions to the general rule that an employer of an independent contractor is not liable for the conduct of the contractor. We reject both contentions.

I.

Under the doctrine of *respondeat superior,* an employer is vicariously liable for the tortious conduct of an employee when the employee is acting within the scope of the employer-employee relationship. Brady v. Ralph Parsons Co., 308 Md. 486, 511, 520 A.2d 717 (1987). Converse to this doctrine is the general rule that an employer of an independent contractor is not vicariously liable for the conduct of the contractor. *Id.* at 512, 520 A.2d 717; Rowley v. Mayor of Baltimore, 305 Md. 456, 461, 505 A.2d 494 (1986). An independent contractor is "one who contracts to perform a certain work for another according to his own means and methods, free from control of his employer in all details connected with

3. Fittingly, James vanished before appellants filed this action and was never personally served.

the performance of the work except as to its product or result." Gale v. Greater Washington Softball Umpires Ass'n, 19 Md.App. 481, 487, 311 A.2d 817 (1973).

> Various reasons have been advanced for it [the rule that an employer is not liable for conduct of an independent contractor], but the one most commonly accepted is that, since the employer has no right of control over the manner in which the work is to be done, it is to be regarded as the contractor's own enterprise, and he, rather than the employer, is the proper party to be charged with the responsibility for preventing the risk, and administering and distributing it.

Rowley, 305 Md. at 462, 505 A.2d 494, quoting 5 Prosser and Keeton on the Law of Torts, §71 at 509 (1984).

As one might expect based upon the above rationale, the distinction between an employee and an independent contractor hinges on the right of control and supervision.

> [T]he cases list a number of subsidiary factors that may be considered, but stress the right of control and supervision retained by the employer. To put it in terms of an employer-employee relationship, the decisive test in determining whether the relation of master and servant exists is whether the employer has *the right to control and direct the servant in the performance of his work and in the manner in which the work is to be done* (emphasis in original) (citations omitted).

Gale, 19 Md.App. at 487, 311 A.2d 817.

Other factors considered by courts in determining the existence of an employer-employee relationship include (1) the selection and engagement of the servant, (2) the payment of wages, (3) the power of dismissal, and (4) whether the work is a part of the regular business of the employer. Keitz v. National Paving and Contracting Co., 214 Md. 479, 491, 134 A.2d 296, 136 A.2d, 229 (1957). These factors are relevant to the extent that the right of overall control is implicit in each. L.M.T. Steel Products, Inc. v. Pierson, 47 Md.App. 633, 636, 425 A.2d 242 (1981). However, "these are but *indicia* of the employment relationship-factors or criteria to look at." *Id.* at 635, 425 A.2d 242 (emphasis in original). The only test with "any special conclusive significance" is the power or right of control and supervision.

> To have an employment relationship, the 'employer' must have some ability, should he care to exercise it, to tell the 'employee' what to do and how and when to do it. If there is not this minimal power of control—if the worker's agreement is to perform the work 'according to his own means and methods free from control of his employer in all details connected with the performance of the work except as to its product or result'—the worker is deemed to be an independent contractor and not an employee/servant.

L.M.T. Steel Products, 47 Md.App. at 636, 425 A.2d 242, quoting *Gale,* 19 Md.App. at 481, 311 A.2d 817.

The undisputed facts adduced by the parties regarding the terms and manner of James' employment with appellee are as follows: In May 1987, James had been serving process papers for appellee for approximately eighteen months. James was the sole process server engaged by appellee for collections matters. He served process for matters other than collections as well. James did not have a written contract with appellee. He was under no obligation to accept assignments from appellee. It was assumed, however, that he would be available to serve process for appellee. James received a flat, agreed upon fee for each assignment which he successfully completed. He was generally paid out of appellee's collections trust account. No ordinary payroll deductions were made on his checks. James maintained his own offices and made his services available to the general public. He also provided his own forms for affidavits of service and his own notary public to notarize the affidavits.

Once a week at irregular intervals, James met with someone from appellee's office to report on assignments he had successfully completed and to receive new assignments. He generally met with Katrina March, a paralegal in appellee's office who was in charge of appellee's collections. Occasionally, he also met with the attorney in charge of the matter for which he was serving process. When James met with March, she would review a copy of his affidavits of service to verify that they had been completed and signed by him. In addition, she would attempt to verify that James had served the proper person and that he had filed the affidavits in court, usually by asking James these questions directly. March would also give James the names of persons to be served and addresses or locations where they might be found.

Based upon these facts, we find that the circuit court was correct in determining that the undisputed facts, and the reasonable inferences possible therefrom, did not demonstrate the degree of control required to establish an employer-employee relationship. James set his own hours of work and established his own work sequence. There is nothing in the record to suggest that James was subject to any instructions from appellee regarding the order in which process was to be served. Although he reported to appellee once a week at irregular intervals, the reports were only for the purpose of verifying that James had successfully completed particular assignments and giving him information necessary to carry out new assignments. The only instructions James received were whom to serve and where they might be found. Thus, there is no basis in the record for the conclusion that appellee ever dictated, or had a right to dictate, when, where or how James served process. While appellee directed James as to the product or result of his work, James was free from appellee's control as to the details and means by which that result was accomplished. In addition, appellee did not have the right to discharge James. If James failed to pick up papers to serve or to complete service, appellee's recourse was simply not to refer more business to him. In sum, the only conclusion that may be drawn from the record is that James was an independent contractor in his relationship with appellee.

...

II.

We turn to appellants' contention that vicarious liability may be imposed upon appellee under [the nondelegable duty exception] to the general rule that an employer is not liable for the tortious conduct of an independent contractor....

> The statement commonly made in ... cases [imposing a nondelegable duty upon an employer] is that the employer is under a duty which he is not free to delegate to the contractor. Such a 'nondelegable duty' requires the person upon whom it is imposed to answer for it that care is exercised by anyone, even though he be an independent contractor, to whom the performance of the duty is entrusted.

Rowley v. Mayor of Baltimore, 305 Md. 456, 463, 505 A.2d 494 (1986), quoting Restatement (Second) of Torts §§416–429 (introductory note). Employers are liable under this exception irrespective of whether they themselves have been at fault. Whether vicarious liability should be imposed upon an employer by application of this exception is a matter of policy.

Appellants assert that imposition of a nondelegable duty in the instant case is necessary to protect innocent members of the public from the actions of private process servers. Appellants rely primarily upon the Maryland Rules of Professional Conduct, which they offer as an expression of a public policy that service of process should be a nondelegable duty of attorneys. The Maryland Rules of Professional Conduct, however, are not a reflection of public policy, nor do they provide a basis upon which to impose liability.

> Violation of a Rule should not give rise to a cause of action nor should it create any presumption that a legal duty has been breached. The Rules are designed to provide guidance to lawyers and to provide a structure for regulating conduct through disciplinary agencies. They are not designed to be a basis for civil liability.... [N]othing in the Rules should be deemed to augment any substantive legal duty of lawyers or the extra-disciplinary consequences of violating such a duty.

In re Criminal Investigation No. 13, 82 Md.App. 609, 612–13, 573 A.2d 51 (1990) (citations omitted).

Aside from the Maryland Rules of Professional Conduct, appellants offer *Rowley*, 305 Md. At 456, 505 A.2d 494, in support of their position. We find *Rowley* to be distinguishable from the instant case. In that decision, the Court of Appeals held that the City of Baltimore had a nondelegable duty to maintain the premises of the Baltimore City Convention Center in a reasonably safe condition, but that the duty did not extend to an employee of an independent contractor with respect to defects arising from the failure of the independent contractor to accomplish repairs it had undertaken to perform. The foundation on which the Court based the City's nondelegable duty in *Rowley* was the liability of a landowner for injuries received on the land. A like foundation does not exist here.

We also observe that Md.Rule 2-123 provides for service of process "by a sheriff or, except as otherwise provided in this Rule, by a competent private person, 18 years of age or older, including an attorney of record, but not by a party to the action." The argument advanced by appellants supports the absurd notion that a law firm may be vicariously liable for the acts of a sheriff as well as a private process server. We cannot accept this notion. Under the circumstances, we are not persuaded that imposition of a nondelegable duty on appellee is warranted.

* * *

1. Service of process as a nondelegable duty. Under similar facts, the New York Court of Appeals disagreed with *Kersten* and concluded that a lawyer has a duty to the lawyer's client to exercise care in the service of process and that this duty is nondelegable. *Kleeman v. Rheingold*, 614 N.E.2d 712 (N.Y. 1993). "Manifestly, when an individual retains an attorney to commence an action, timely and accurate service of process is an integral part of the task that the attorney undertakes." *Id.* at 716. Thus, vicarious liability was appropriate. Unlike *Kersten*, the New York Court of Appeals relied on the ethical rules governing attorneys to reinforce its conclusion that a nondelegable duty existed in the case.

2. A client's vicarious liability. *Horwitz v. Holabird & Root*, 816 N.E.2d 272 (Ill. 2004), presented a twist on the typical lawyer vicarious liability case. In *Horwitz*, a company sought to hold a client vicariously liable for the torts of the client's lawyers. After concluding that lawyers are generally considered independent contractors for purposes of their representation of clients, the Illinois Supreme Court addressed whether a lawyer's misconduct could be imputed to a client:

> That someone is an independent contractor does not bar the attachment of vicarious liability for her actions if she is also an agent. *See* Petrovich v. Share Health Plan of Illinois, Inc., 188 Ill.2d 17, 31, 241 Ill. Dec. 627, 719 N.E.2d 756 (1999) ("[a]s a general rule, no vicarious liability exists for the actions of independent contractors. Vicarious liability may nevertheless be imposed for the actions of independent contractors where an agency relationship is established"). A person may be both an independent contractor and an agent with the authority both to control the details of the work and also "the power to act for and to bind the principal in business negotiations within the scope of [the] agency." ... As a general rule, attorneys fit squarely within this category. Nonetheless, when attorneys act pursuant to the exercise of independent professional judgment, they possess such considerable autonomy over the details and manner of performing their work that they are presumptively independent contractors for purposes of imposing vicarious liability. Accordingly, where a plaintiff seeks to hold a client vicariously liable for the attorney's allegedly intentional tortious conduct, a plaintiff must prove facts demonstrating either that the client specifically directed, controlled, or authorized the attorney's precise method of performing the work or that the client subsequently ratified acts performed in the exercise of the attorney's independent judgment. If there is no evidence that the client directed, controlled, authorized, or ratified the attorney's allegedly tortious conduct, no vicarious liability can attach.

3. Competence as a nondelegable duty. A local county does not have a public defender's office, so it relies on local lawyers to represent indigent criminal defendants on a contract basis. Lawyer Kristi was appointed to represent Rafael, an indigent defendant. Kristi is generally competent, but her representation of Rafael was so deficient that it rose to the level of ineffective assistance of counsel. As a result of Kristi's malpractice, Rafael spent five years in prison before eventually being released on the grounds of ineffective assistance of counsel. He then sued Kristi for negligence and sought to hold the county liable for Kristi's negligence. Can the county be held vicariously liable for Kristi's actions? *See State v. Hicks,* 198 P.3d 1200 (Ariz. 2009).

* * *

C. Other Forms of Vicarious Liability

A partner in a partnership is not an employee. However, as a practical matter, the test for imposing vicarious liability on a partnership for the acts of a partner essentially mirrors the scope of employment test. As the *Goodman* court stated, "A partnership is liable for loss or injury caused by any wrongful act or omission of any partner acting in the ordinary course of business of the partnership." Indeed, the *O'Toole* court applied the *Restatement's* "scope of employment" test in assessing whether the firm could be vicariously liable for the acts of the firm's partner.

Even if a partner's wrongful act or omission is not within the ordinary course of business of the partnership, *Goodman* notes another way the partnership can be held vicariously liable: if the wrongdoing partner acted with the actual or apparent authority of his copartners. *Goodman* briefly explored this issue. The following problem explores it in more detail. The case after that examines the possibility of vicarious liability stemming from a joint venture.

1. Partners and Apparent Authority

The rules regarding nondelegable duties notwithstanding, before vicarious liability can attach, the purported agent must have authority to act on behalf of the principal. Authority may be actual or apparent. An agent may have actual authority, *i.e.*, authority that the principal intended to confer upon the agent. In contrast, apparent authority is "that semblance of authority which a principal, through his own acts or inadvertences, causes or allows third persons to believe his agent possesses." Gordon v. Tobias, 817 A.2d 683, 689 (Conn. 2003). "First, it must appear from the principal's conduct that the principal held the agent out as possessing sufficient authority to embrace the act in question, or knowingly permitted [the agent] to act as having such authority ... Second, the party dealing with the agent must have, acting in good faith, reasonably believed, under all the circumstances, that the agent had the necessary authority to bind the principal to the agent's action." *Id.*

Exercise 2.3

Attorney Liddy was previously a partner in the firm of Chatham, Liddy & Scott. Liddy withdrew from the firm, and the partnership was dissolved and renamed Chatham & Scott. Liddy opened up a solo practice in the same building. Six months after withdrawing from the original firm, Liddy agreed to represent White in a civil matter. White ended up suing Liddy for legal malpractice, but also sought to hold the firm of Chatham & Scott vicariously liable on an apparent authority theory. White testified in a deposition that Liddy introduced himself as a partner in the firm of Chatham & Scott, although White acknowledges that he never received any letters from the firm and that his fee agreement never referenced the firm. White also testified that when he met with Liddy at Liddy's office, there was a business sign on the lawn that read "Chatham, Liddy & Scott, Attorneys at Law." (Chatham & Scott acknowledge that the sign remained on the property for nearly a year after Liddy left the firm.) Moreover, White testified that when discussing his case, Liddy informed White that he would "run the case by Chatham, my litigation guy who handles a lot of these kinds of cases." Based on all of this, White says he believed Liddy was acting as an agent of Chatham & Scott. Did Liddy have apparent authority to act on behalf of Chatham & Scott?

---

2. Co-Counsel and Joint Ventures

Focus Questions: *Armor v. Lantz*

1. *What qualifies as a joint venture?*
2. *Why did the arrangement at issue in Armor not qualify?*

Armor v. Lantz

535 S.E.2d 737
(W.Va. 2000)

McGRAW, Justice:

[Attorneys Smith and Sipe represented Armor in a personal injury action filed in West Virginia against Michelin Tire Corp. Neither attorney was licensed in West Virginia, so they contracted with Lantz for Lantz to serve as local counsel. Sipe prepared a complaint.] After reviewing the complaint, Lantz authorized Sipe to sign his name as local counsel. Lantz later testified that he viewed his role as local counsel at this stage to be limited to reviewing the complaint as to form, that is, in Lantz's words, "Does this complaint state a cause of action and have all the particulars in it that are necessary and required in the Southern District of West Virginia...."

After the action was filed in the District Court, Michelin moved for summary judgment on the ground that the action was time barred under W. Va. Code § 55-2-12(b) (1959), which imposes a two-year limitation period for bringing personal injury claims. The District Court granted Michelin's motion on April 23, 1996 ...

[Armor sued Smith, Sipe, and Lantz for legal malpractice. Armor also alleged that Lantz was vicariously liable for the negligence of Smith and Sipe.]

In asserting that Lantz is vicariously liable for the actions of co-counsel Sipe and Smith, based upon his association with them as local counsel, Appellants are essentially arguing that a joint venture was formed among these lawyers for purposes of prosecuting their case. We therefore turn to basic principles of joint-venture and partnership law to resolve this question.

A joint venture "is an association of two or more persons to carry out a single business enterprise for profit, for which purpose they combine their property, money, effects, skill, and knowledge. It arises out of a contractual relationship between the parties. The contract may be oral or written, express or implied." Syl. pt. 2, Price v. Halstead, 177 W.Va. 592, 355 S.E.2d 380 (1987). While this Court has frequently likened a joint venture to a partnership, we have nevertheless distinguished the two: "[A] partnership relates to a general business ... while [a] joint adventure relates to a single business transaction."

Because of the basic similarities between these two forms of business association, joint ventures and partnerships are governed generally by the same basic legal principles. Thus, since all partners are jointly liable for all debts and obligations of a partnership, members of a joint venture are likewise jointly and severally liable for all obligations pertaining to the venture, and the actions of the joint venture bind the individual co-venturers.

Our primary concern here, of course, is whether Lantz's assent to acting as local counsel was sufficient to constitute an express or implied agreement to form a joint venture. This

Court has never formulated any broad analytical test by which to determine the existence of a joint venture. In *Pownall v. Cearfoss,* 129 W.Va. 487, 40 S.E.2d 886 (1946), however, the Court did note the existence of certain "distinguishing elements or features" essential to the creation of a joint venture:

> As between the parties, a contract, written or verbal, is essential to create the relation of joint adventurers.... To constitute a joint adventure the parties must combine their property, money, efforts, skill, or knowledge, in some common undertaking of a special or particular nature, but the contributions of the respective parties need not be equal or of the same character. There must, however, be some contribution by each party of something promotive of the enterprise.... An agreement, express or implied, for the sharing of profits is generally considered essential to the creation of a joint adventure, and it has been held that, at common law, in order to constitute a joint adventure, there must be an agreement to share in both the profits and the losses. It has also been held, however, that the sharing of losses is not essential, or at least that there need not be a specific agreement to share the losses, and that, if the nature of the undertaking is such that no losses, other than those of time and labor in carrying out the enterprise, are likely to occur, an agreement to divide the profits may suffice to make it a joint adventure, even in the absence of a provision to share the losses.

Our most recent cases have concentrated primarily upon the presence or absence of an agreement to share in the profits and losses of an enterprise.

In the context of determining whether lawyers have formed a joint venture for purposes of vicarious liability, other courts have likewise concentrated upon whether there is an agreement to share in the potential profits and losses of the representation. In *Duggins v. Guardianship of Washington,* 632 So.2d 420 (Miss.1993), the guardianship of a minor child brought suit for an accounting against two lawyers who had represented the child in a medical malpractice action. One of the lawyers had misappropriated a portion of the funds obtained from settlement. The Mississippi Supreme Court held that the second lawyer, who had not engaged in any improper conduct, was nevertheless vicariously responsible, stating that "the intent to share both the responsibility and profits from th[e] representation clearly demonstrate the presence of a joint venture." 632 So.2d at 428. This holding was predicated in large part upon the fact that the two lawyers had agreed to split equally the fees generated by the case. *Id.* at 426. *See also* Fitzgibbon v. Carey, 70 Or.App. 127, 688 P.2d 1367 (1984) (finding joint venture between law firms based upon, inter alia, agreement to divide fees equally); Floro v. Lawton, 187 Cal.App.2d 657, 10 Cal.Rptr. 98 (1960) (joint venture found based upon agreement between lawyers to share fees on equal basis).

The Virginia Supreme Court in *Ortiz v. Barrett,* 222 Va. 118, 278 S.E.2d 833 (1981), applied similar reasoning to reject a claim of vicarious liability. In *Ortiz,* lead counsel Edward Barrett, who was not licensed to practice law in Virginia, filed a personal injury suit in Virginia on behalf of his clients, signing the name of Ronald Barrett, an unrelated Virginia lawyer. Ronald had not authorized Edward to sign the pleading, and when Ronald later became aware that suit had been filed under his signature, he agreed to serve as "co-counsel without active participation" for a fixed fee. In holding that Edward's subsequent mishandling of the case did not impose liability on Ronald, the Virginia court reasoned that Edward and Ronald were not joint venturers, based upon the fact that "Ronald was employed by Edward to perform limited services for a fixed fee regardless of results."

One noted commentator has echoed the *Ortiz* court's reluctance to find vicariously liable [sic] based solely upon the lawyers [sic] status as local counsel:

> A rule commonly encountered is that a lawyer from another jurisdiction must associate with local counsel when temporarily appearing in litigation in a state.... In most such situations the designated local lawyer plays a largely passive role. Courts should therefore be reluctant to visit the local lawyer with vicarious liability. But if the relationship is one of more nearly equal responsibility, authority, and profit sharing, it may fit the legal description of a joint venture, permitting an injured party to hold both foreign and local lawyer to joint and several liability.

Charles W. Wolfram, Modern Legal Ethics § 5.6.6, at 238 (1986) (footnotes omitted).

In the present case, it is undisputed that there were no discussions between Lantz and Sipe concerning how Lantz would be paid. Indeed, Sipe testified that in another case in which both he and Lantz were involved, Lantz had received a flat $1,000 fee for acting as local counsel. By contrast, Sipe and Smith had agreed in this case to share the expenses and fees equally. While Lantz did testify at deposition that he expected to be compensated for his services, this falls far short of demonstrating the requisite agreement to share in the profits and losses of the joint representation.

Other courts delineating the contours of joint ventures have also emphasized the necessity of joint venturers having equal control over the common commercial pursuit. "An essential element of a partnership or joint venture is the right of joint participation in the management and control of the business.... Absent such right, the mere fact that one party is to receive benefits in consideration of services rendered or for capital contribution does not, as a matter of law, make him a partner or joint venturer." Bank of California v. Connolly, 36 Cal.App.3d 350, 364, 111 Cal.Rptr. 468, 478 (1973) (citations omitted). As one Illinois court observed, "[p]ossibly the most important criterion of a joint venture is joint control and management of the property used in accomplishing its aims." Barton v. Evanston Hosp., 159 Ill.App.3d 970, 974, 111 Ill.Dec. 819, 513 N.E.2d 65, 67 (1987) (citation omitted). Importantly, "[t]he control required for imputing negligence under a joint enterprise theory is not actual physical control, but the legal right to control the conduct of the other with respect to the prosecution of the common purpose." Slaughter v. Slaughter, 93 N.C.App. 717, 721, 379 S.E.2d 98, 101 (1989) (citation omitted).

Our review of the record fails to uncover any evidence showing that Lantz agreed to undertake active management and control of Appellants' lawsuit in federal court. Although raised only obliquely, Appellants suggest that the District Court's requirement regarding the association of local counsel implies an agreement regarding joint control over the lawsuit. We are not persuaded by this argument. Rule 2.02 [of the District Court's local rules] does require that a visiting attorney "associate" with a permanent member of the District Court's bar, and that such local counsel sign all pleadings; however, the rule also permits local counsel to "be excused from further attendance during the proceedings" by consent of court. The rule is ambiguous as to the precise responsibilities of local counsel, and, while it certainly calls upon local counsel to perform a supervisory role with respect to visiting counsel, it does not necessarily require that local counsel take equal charge of preparing and prosecuting a case. Consequently, we conclude that Appellants have failed to raise a triable issue of fact as to whether a joint venture existed in this case.

[The court also concluded that Lantz had not assumed a duty to ascertain whether the personal injury complaint was time-barred and therefore was not subject to liability for malpractice.]

* * *

1. The role of local counsel. If a lawyer in Lantz's situation has no legal duty to the client to determine whether a complaint is time-barred and if that lawyer cannot be held vicariously liable for the other lawyers' failure to determine this fact, what purpose, exactly, does the requirement that local counsel (like Lantz) sign a pleading serve?

2. Fee splitting and vicarious liability. Rule 1.5(e) of the ABA Model Rules of Professional Conduct permits lawyers who are not in the same firm to split fees in limited circumstances. The division of fees must either be in proportion to the services performed by each lawyer (which necessarily assumes that each lawyer has rendered *some* service) or where each lawyer assumes joint responsibility for the representation. "Joint responsibility" in this instance includes vicarious liability. *Id.* cmt. 7; New York County Lawyers Assn. Ethics Opinion 715 (1996).

* * *

D. Limited Liability Partnerships and Insurance Coverage

If a company is held vicariously liable for the torts of an employee, the individual members and partners might also theoretically be held vicariously liable. Partly as an attempt to limit liability, every state has some type of limited liability company (LLC) or limited liability partnership (LLP) statute that protects individual partners and members from liability. The nation's first LLP statute was drafted with the specific intent of protecting law firms from malpractice and related forms of liability. RONALD E. SMITH & JEFFREY M. SMITH, LEGAL MALPRACTICE (2011) §5:6, at 485; Susan Saab Fortney, *Law as Profession: Examining the Role of Accountability*, 40 FORDHAM URB. L.J. 177, 181–84 (2012) (discussing the rise of such statutes).

Under many LLP statutes, individual partners remain liable for their own wrongdoing and the partnership itself may be vicariously liable for such wrongdoing, but the individual partners may not be held vicariously liable for another partner's wrongdoing. This is true regardless of whether the claim sounds in tort or contract. Some statutes explicitly provide that this type of "full-shield" protection applies to claims of intentional misconduct as well as mere negligence. RONALD E. SMITH & JEFFREY M. SMITH, LEGAL MALPRACTICE (2011) §5:6, at 493.

Lawyers and law firms may also attempt to limit liability through professional liability insurance. Although Oregon is the only state to require lawyers to carry legal malpractice insurance, malpractice insurance plays an important role in the practice of law in the United States. Most policies are claims-made policies, meaning that an attorney is covered for all claims made against the attorney and reported to the insurer while the policy is in effect. The attorney's failure to comply with the insurer's notice requirements may preclude coverage. If a policy lists a partnership as the insured, all of the partners are covered under the policy. Most policies are not limited to coverage for malpractice or negligence or confined to particular legal theories. Instead, they typically extend coverage for acts, errors, or omissions occurring while an attorney was providing services to a client of the insured.

Because many professional liability policies are not worded specifically in terms of negligence or malpractice, their coverage could, in theory, be quite broad. However, most policies contain a number of exclusions that limit their reach. The following case explores one common policy exclusion.

Focus Questions: *Mendel v. Home Ins. Co.*

1. *Why does the relevant coverage exclusion apply? To what other kinds of claims would a similar exclusion apply?*
2. *What was the gist of the innocent party clause?*

Mendel v. Home Ins. Co.

806 F. Supp. 1206
(E.D. Pa. 1992)

BARTLE, District Judge.

Plaintiffs M. Mark Mendel, Esquire ("Mendel"), Daniel E. Murray, Esquire ("Murray"), and M. Mark Mendel, Ltd. ("Mendel Ltd.") (collectively "the insureds"), have instituted this diversity action against their professional liability insurance carrier, The Home Insurance Company ("Home"). The insureds seek to compel Home to pay on their behalf a judgment of $1,690,670 which was jointly and severally entered against them as a result of an adverse jury verdict in this Court on December 9, 1991, in the case of Silver v. Mendel, et al., Civil Action No. 86-7104 ("Silver"). Home has counterclaimed for a declaratory judgment, seeking a declaration that it has no obligation to its insureds under the policy. Before the Court are cross-motions for summary judgment.

The backdrop for this action arises out of a highly charged business dispute between Marc Silver ("Silver"), a principal in the Marshall-Silver Construction Company ("Marshall-Silver") and its subcontractor Barton and Company ("Barton"). During 1984 insureds Mendel and Murray, in addition to practicing law, were officers of Barton. The Barton-Silver dispute escalated to the point where, in mid-1984, Mendel apparently made certain threats, including a threat to destroy Silver's business. Thereafter, in December, 1984, the law firm of Mendel Ltd., representing Barton and two other creditors, filed in this District, under Murray's signature, a petition for involuntary bankruptcy against Marshall-Silver. Several months later, the Bankruptcy Court dismissed the petition because the additional creditors failed to post the required bond.

In December, 1986 Silver and Marshall-Silver filed separate actions in this Court against the insureds arising out of the allegedly wrongful bankruptcy filing. Substantial activity in both cases, including various motions and appeals to the Court of Appeals of this Circuit, followed. As of June 14, 1990, upon the resolution of the pretrial appeals, the Marshall-Silver suit had been dismissed. In the Silver case, however, three claims remained against the insureds: (1) intentional interference with contractual relations; (2) intentional interference with prospective contractual relations; and (3) intentional infliction of emotional distress. Only after the completion of the pretrial appellate process did Home attempt to reserve its right to cover the insureds based on the intentional nature of the acts alleged.

[Eventually, a jury returned a verdict in favor of Silver and against the insureds for $1,690,670 on the interference claims. Judgment was entered on the verdict.]

The insureds argue that they are entitled to summary judgment on all claims on one or more of the following grounds: (1) the exclusion clause of the Home policy does not exclude coverage for the intentional economic torts which gave rise to the Silver judgment; (2) Mendel Ltd. is an "innocent party" and is protected by a waiver clause in the policy which exempts innocent parties from the exclusion clause upon which Home relies; (3) Home is estopped from denying coverage because, even if it is assumed that the company's reservation of rights letter was sent as early as September of 1990, the nearly four year delay in giving notice prejudiced the insureds as a matter of law; and (4) there is no evidence whatsoever that Home ever notified its insured Murray of any reservation of rights before November, 1991, on the eve of the Silver trial.

The Exclusion Clause

The exclusion clause of the Home professional liability policy issued to the insureds, provides in Section I(a) that:

> I. This policy does not apply:
>
> (a) to any judgment or final adjudication based upon or arising out of any dishonest, deliberately fraudulent, criminal, maliciously or *deliberately wrongful acts* or omissions committed by the insured. However, notwithstanding the foregoing, the Company will provide a defense for any such claim without any liability on the part of the Company to pay such sums as the insured shall become legally obligated to pay as damages (emphasis added).

The parties agree that the question of the applicability of this exclusion clause to the judgment returned in the Silver case is a question of law as to which extrinsic evidence need not be considered.

Home has invoked the clause, and has refused to indemnify the insureds as to the Silver judgment on the ground that the intentional torts which resulted in that judgment were "deliberately wrongful acts" included in the exclusion clause. The insureds, however, argue (1) that their intentional economic torts were not "deliberately wrongful acts" under the exclusionary clause; (2) that the term "deliberately wrongful acts," which was not defined in the policy, is unclear and ambiguous; and (3) that such ambiguity requires that the exclusionary clause be construed in favor of the insureds.

Under Pennsylvania law, which both parties agree is applicable, policy ambiguities must be resolved in favor of the insured. An ambiguity exists "if words may *reasonably admit* of different meanings." Mellon Bank N.A. v. Aetna Business Credit, Inc., 619 F.2d 1001, 1011 (3d Cir.1980) (emphasis added). Policy language must not be tortured, however, to create an ambiguity where none exists and policy provisions should be read to avoid ambiguities if possible.

No basis exists for concluding that the subject exclusion clause is ambiguous....

An intentional and unprivileged interference must be established to prove an intentional interference with contractual relations, or with prospective contractual relations. The terms "deliberate" and "intentional" are synonymous. *See* Home Ins. Co. v. Bullard, *supra*; Warren v. Lemay, *supra*.[6] Thus, in *United States Fidelity & Guaranty Co. v. Fireman's Fund*

6. *See also Webster's New Universal Unabridged Dictionary* which defines "deliberate," in pertinent part, as:

> 1. carefully thought out or formed; premeditated; done on purpose.

and gives "intentional" as a synonym. It defines "intentional" as:

> 1. having to do with intention or purpose. [Rare.]
>
> 2. intended; designed; done with design or purpose; as the act was intentional, not accidental.

and gives "deliberate" as a synonym.

Ins. Co., 896 F.2d 200 (6th Cir.1990), the Court agreed with the District Court's "determination that the only reasonable construction of the exclusionary clause, which similarly prohibited coverage for 'dishonest, fraudulent, criminal or malicious acts,' is that Fireman's Fund contracted to provide coverage for negligent—not intentional—acts ..." *See also* Employers Reinsurance Corp. v. Martin, Gordon & Jones, Inc., 767 F.Supp. 1355, 1359–1361 (S.D.Miss.1991).

There can be no question that the Home policy excludes coverage for the individual insureds Mendel and Murray since the jury found that they were each liable to Silver for intentional interference with contractual and prospective contractual relations.

The "Innocent Party" Clause

The issue remains, however, whether the exclusion extends to the law firm of Mendel Ltd., a corporation. Mendel Ltd. claims entitlement to coverage based on an "innocent party" policy provision which provides that insureds "who did not personally participate" in the acts giving rise to an exclusion are not subject to that exclusion. It further argues that Pennsylvania law does not allow innocent insureds to be deprived of coverage because of the intentional acts of their co-insureds.

It is, of course, axiomatic that a corporation is a creature of fiction that can only act through its officers, directors and other agents. A corporation is, however, bound by its agent's acts so long as those acts are "performed within the agent's implied or apparent authority, unless the agent acted for his own benefit without the corporation's ratification of his action." Lokay v. Lehigh Valley Cooperative Farmers, Inc., 492 A.2d 405, 409 (1985).

In this case, the acts at issue are those of one or more corporate officers or directors of Mendel Ltd. Mendel and Murray, officers or directors of Mendel Ltd., here spoke and acted for the corporation. Murray signed the bankruptcy filing which the Silver jury found amounted to an intentional interference with contractual relations and with prospective contractual relations. Further, the record establishes that Murray was not only a 12% shareholder in the corporation, but also the "administrative partner" and Secretary-Treasurer of the corporation, and its only corporate officer besides the President. Equally significant, was a statement made by Mendel, the corporation's President and controlling shareholder, when he completed the corporation's 1986 policy renewal application statement for the Home professional liability policy. In discussing the corporation's representation of Barton, in connection with the Marshall-Silver bankruptcy filing, Mendel declared that "*This law firm is acting on behalf of* its client and *itself*" (emphasis added).

Thus, the insureds do not and could not argue that the bankruptcy filing either exceeded Murray's implied or actual corporate authority or was not ratified by the corporation. Accordingly, "... the unauthorized and unpredictable act of [a corporate] agent ..." is not at issue here.

In this case, as in *FDIC v. Mmahat*, 907 F.2d 546 (5th Cir.1990), there was a jury finding against the corporation itself. In that case coverage was denied to a law firm despite an "innocent party" clause, because there was a finding that the law firm, as well as the individual lawyer, had breached a duty.

Here, Mendel Ltd. was not an innocent party. As the jury in Silver found, it "personally participated" in the intentional acts against Silver as a result of the acts of its officers or directors. Consequently, Mendel Ltd. is subject to the exclusion clause in Home's policy.

Reservation of Rights

The insureds, as a ground for summary judgment, argue that Home is estopped from relying on the "deliberately wrongful acts" policy exclusion because of its failure to reserve its rights under this provision until November 21, 1991, on the eve of the Silver trial when Mendel and Murray claim that they first saw the letter. Alternatively, the insureds claim that Home is still estopped even if they received such a letter in September, 1990, almost 4 years after the Silver case was initiated and some 14 months before the trial commenced. Home, in its cross-motion for summary judgment, argues that it reserved its rights in a timely manner.

The first question which must be resolved is whether there exist genuine issues of material fact with respect to Home's contention that it mailed a reservation of rights letter on September 4, 1990, and that the insureds received it on September 7, 1990, more than 14 months before the commencement of the Silver trial.

[The court concluded that there was sufficient evidence that the letter had been mailed and received by Mendel Ltd. as described.]

The Issue of Prejudice

Although the exclusionary clause of the policy is applicable to all of the insureds, the remaining question is whether Home is estopped from relying on the exclusion because it delayed until September 4, 1990, nearly four years after the filing of the Silver action, to issue its reservation of rights letter in that action.

At the time of the issuance of the reservation of rights letter, virtually all discovery remained to be completed because that process had been held in abeyance pending disposition of the various motions and appeals. Moreover, as previously noted, the trial did not begin until more than 14 months after the letter's issuance.

Home therefore argues that no basis exists for finding that the insureds were prejudiced by the issuance of the reservation of rights letter in September, 1990. Insureds, on the other hand, contend that the delay of nearly four years creates an irrebuttable presumption of prejudice, entitling them to a judgment against Home as a matter of law.

[The court concluded that the evidence as to prejudice was conflicting and that summary judgment for either party on this issue was inappropriate.]

* * *

1. Innocent insureds. If one partner in a firm engages in dishonest conduct that triggers a policy exclusion similar to that at issue in *Mendel*, other members of the firm may also be unable to claim coverage under the policy unless there is also an "innocent insured" or "innocent party" clause. Some innocent insured clauses provide limited protection to other firm members who were not involved in and did not have knowledge of the underlying dishonest conduct. Sunrise Props., Inc. v. Bacon, Wilson, Ratner, Cohen, Salvage, Fialky & Fitzgerald, P.C., 679 N.E.2d 540 (Mass. 1997).

2. Other exclusions. Other common exclusions include bodily injury or property damage, damage resulting from the lawyer's business pursuits (including where the lawyer is engaged in business with a client), and damages stemming from a lawyer acting in a fiduciary capacity outside the normal role of a lawyer. Ronald E. Smith & Jeffrey M. Smith, Legal Malpractice (2013) §§ 38:24–29. In addition, public policy may prevent an insurer from providing coverage for punitive damages awards. *Id.* § 38-23.

Part 2

Legal Malpractice and Breach of Fiduciary Duty

Chapter 3

Breach of Fiduciary Duty

Exercise 3.1: Chapter Problem

Nick, a new client, contacts a partner in the firm at which you currently work as an associate about a potential claim against his former counsel, Attorney Alpha. Nick explains to Partner that Attorney Alpha recently represented Nick in a breach of contract action brought against Company. Attorney Alpha collected $1000 in fees up front from Nick to evaluate whether Nick had a viable cause of action against Company and to cover additional preliminary costs associated with filing a claim. After looking into Nick's claim further, Attorney Alpha informed Nick that Nick would likely never be able to recover from Company due to a variety of evidentiary and other obstacles in the way of a successful claim. Surprisingly, Nick subsequently learned that at some point during the discovery process, Company and Attorney Alpha had discussed Company's willingness to settle Nick's claim for an amount well above any amount that Attorney Alpha had hoped to recover. Unfortunately, Attorney Alpha had never discussed the settlement with Nick. Even after Attorney Alpha received a check in settlement of Nick's claim, Attorney Alpha never contacted Nick. Attorney Alpha also failed to deposit the check promptly, and the check became misplaced on his desk in a large pile of papers.

Several months later, when Nick learned that Company had issued a settlement check, Nick contacted Attorney Alpha about it. Attorney Alpha was able to locate the check, but when he attempted to deposit it, the bank informed him that Company had since filed bankruptcy and the check therefore was no longer any good. Attorney Alpha told Nick that although he is sorry, he would not be able to recover anything on Nick's behalf. Partner has already had another lawyer at the firm research whether Nick might be able to sue his Attorney Alpha for his negligence. Partner now wants you to research whether Nick might have a viable breach of fiduciary duty action against Attorney Alpha and, if so, what potential damages would be recoverable. In preparing to conduct the requested research for Partner, make a list of questions that you will need to answer in conducting your research.

A. Breach of Fiduciary Duty to a Client

A fiduciary relationship is created when one party—the beneficiary—instills certain confidence in another—the fiduciary—who is then to act loyally and in good faith with regard to the beneficiary's interests. The attorney-client relationship is just one example of many different types of fiduciary relationships. In the attorney-client relationship, the attorney is the agent (the fiduciary) who is entrusted to act on behalf of her client (the beneficiary or principal). Typically, a fiduciary is entrusted with important responsibilities, and it is the transfer of power from principal to fiduciary that gives rise to the need for laws protecting the interests of the principal. This, a fiduciary is obligated by law to exercise the most abundant good faith in the interest of the beneficiary. This good faith requirement necessitates that the fiduciary place the principal's needs before that of her own. It is sometimes stated that the fiduciary must exercise the utmost loyalty to the interests of the entrustor—*uberrima fides*, the most abundant good faith. In the attorney-client context, this fiduciary relationship is founded on principles of trust, loyalty, and confidentiality. *See, e.g., Costa v. Allen,* 274 S.W.3d 461, 462 (Mo. 2008) ("Although the attorney-client relation is fiduciary, and breach of a fiduciary obligation is constructive fraud, not all lawyer obligations are fiduciary duties, nor counsel's every failure a constructive fraud. An attorney's fiduciary duties equate specifically to client loyalty and confidentiality.")

When a fiduciary overreaches or abuses the power with which she has been entrusted, the principal may sue for such violations. One such action—the tort action for breach of fiduciary duty—is available to a principal against the fiduciary when the fiduciary has abused the position of trust. This cause of action for breach of fiduciary duty arises by operation of law rather than, for example, as a result of the agreement between the parties, which would be contractual in nature. Distinct from a negligence action (which is also a tort action), a breach of fiduciary duty action is equitable in nature and, in the attorney-client context, may arise when the attorney has violated her trust position. Consider the following cases.

Focus Questions: *Klemme v. Best*

1. *What elements are required for proof of breach of fiduciary duty?*
2. *What was the alleged violation of trust in* Klemme?
3. *Did the plaintiff prevail in his breach of fiduciary duty action against attorney Best? Why or why not?*

Klemme v. Best

941 S.W.2d 493
(Mo. 1997)

BENTON, Judge.

Byron Klemme sued attorney Robert B. Best, Jr., and his law firm Watson & Marshall, L.C., alleging breach of fiduciary duty and constructive fraud. The circuit court dismissed the petition due to failure to state a claim upon which relief can be granted and the bar of the statute of limitations. Following opinion by the Court of Appeals, this Court granted transfer. Affirmed.

I.

[In the underlying litigation, attorney Best represented police officer Klemme who was a defendant in a 42 U.S.C. § 1983 claim in which the claimants alleged that officer Klemme along with others intentionally killed their 19-year-old daughter in violation of her civil rights.] Best represented all defendants until February 1987, when Klemme retained separate counsel. On February 19, 1987, the federal court dismissed Klemme with prejudice because the facts did not support a claim against him.

On February 19, 1988, Klemme filed a malicious prosecution action in state court against the Linzies and their attorneys. On September 19, 1994, Klemme filed a fourth amended petition joining Best and Watson & Marshall for the first time.

On April 25, 1995, the circuit court dismissed Best and Watson & Marshall [for failure to state a claim. The court also found that the claims against defendants Best and Watson & Marshall L.C. were barred by the applicable statute of limitations. This action ensued.]

II.

....

... Before the filing of the federal complaint, Klemme's attorney Best discussed with opposing counsel the identity of each officer involved in the shooting. Opposing counsel presented Best a draft copy naming "Officer Klemme" as a defendant. Although Best knew Klemme did not participate in the shooting, he did not so inform opposing counsel, allegedly to advance the interest of the city of Columbia and its self-insured association that had retained Best. Best did, however, inform opposing counsel that another officer named in the draft complaint did not participate, and opposing counsel eliminated him as a defendant in the filed complaint....

Klemme asserts that[, in so doing] Best violated the fiduciary duties of fidelity, loyalty, devotion, and good faith. Summarizing these allegations, Klemme characterizes his claims as "constructive fraud and breach of fiduciary duty."

A.

[A]n attorney [owes a client] the basic fiduciary obligations of undivided loyalty and confidentiality.

A breach of a fiduciary obligation is constructive fraud. Constructive fraud is a long-recognized cause of action. Missouri courts typically label these claims as breach of fiduciary duty. Whether characterized as breach of fiduciary duty or constructive fraud, the elements of such a claim are: (1) an attorney-client relationship; (2) breach of a fiduciary obligation by the attorney; (3) proximate causation; (4) damages to the client; (5) no other recognized tort encompasses the facts alleged.

The second and fifth elements distinguish [a breach of fiduciary duty] claim from a legal malpractice action. The rationale for the second element is clear: "[A] breach of the standard of care is negligence, and a breach of a fiduciary obligation is constructive fraud." The fifth element flows from *Donahue* [*v. Shughart, Thomson & Kilroy, P.C.*, 900 S.W.2d 624 (Mo. 1995)]. Because the alleged breach of fiduciary duty in *Donahue* was "dependent on" the existence of attorney negligence, this Court held that the alleged breach was "no more than an action for attorney malpractice." *Donahue*, 900 S.W.2d at 629–30. If the alleged breach can be characterized as both a breach of the standard of care (legal malpractice based on negligence) and a breach of a fiduciary obligation (constructive fraud), then the sole claim is legal malpractice. *See Donahue,* 900 S.W.2d at 630. *Donahue* does not, however, preclude an action for breach of fiduciary duty or constructive fraud where the alleged breach is independent of any legal malpractice.

B.

Best consistently denies that Missouri recognizes breach of fiduciary duty or constructive fraud as a claim against one's attorney. Best relies on the following court of appeals' statement: "An attorney's breach of duty to a client during the course of representation of the client is legal malpractice, *not* breach of fiduciary duty as a separate tort. However, a breach of trust which arises out of the relationship, but occurs outside the time frame of the representation of plaintiff, could be a breach of fiduciary duty." *Williams v. Preman,* 911 S.W.2d 288, 301 (Mo.App.1995) (emphasis added). As support, the court of appeals cited this Court's decision in *Donahue*[*supra*].

This interpretation of *Donahue* is incorrect. Clients may sue their attorneys for torts other than legal malpractice. As indicated, an attorney may breach a fiduciary duty to a client at any time during their relationship. *Williams v. Preman* is overruled insofar as it holds otherwise.

...

C.

Klemme has alleged facts that constitute the tort of breach of fiduciary duty or constructive fraud against his attorney: Best and Klemme had an attorney-client relationship; Best breached his fiduciary obligation by placing the interests of other clients before Klemme's; this breach proximately caused Klemme damages; no other recognized tort encompasses Klemme's claim. The circuit court erred in finding that Klemme's petition failed to state a claim.

III.

The trial court did not err, however, in dismissing Klemme's petition against Best and Watson & Marshall....

....

... Klemme waited over seven years to sue Best and Watson & Marshall. By then, the five-year statute of limitations in § 516.120(4) had run against Best and Watson & Marshall.

IV.

The judgment of the circuit court is affirmed.

* * *

1. Can an attorney be sued for breach of fiduciary duty in Missouri? If yes, why was plaintiff Klemme's breach of fiduciary duty action denied against Attorney Best?

2. According to the *Klemme* court, are the torts of negligence and breach of fiduciary duty mutually exclusive torts (*i.e.,* may both causes of action be brought arising from the same facts)?

Focus Questions: *Burrow v. Arce*

1. *How does the* Burrow *court define a breach of fiduciary duty action?*
2. *According to the court, what is the appropriate remedy for breach of fiduciary duty?*
3. *What is the central purpose for providing a remedy for breach of fiduciary duty?*

Burrow v. Arce

997 S.W.2d 229

(Tex. 1999)

Justice HECHT delivered the opinion of the Court.

The principal question in this case is whether an attorney who breaches his fiduciary duty to his client may be required to forfeit all or part of his fee, irrespective of whether the breach caused the client actual damages. Like the court of appeals, we answer in the affirmative and conclude that the amount of the fee to be forfeited is a question for the court, not a jury. We reverse....

I.

Explosions at a Phillips 66 chemical plant in 1989 killed twenty-three workers and injured hundreds of others, spawning a number of wrongful death and personal injury lawsuits. One suit on behalf of some 126 plaintiffs was filed by five attorneys ... and their law firm. The case settled for something close to $190 million, out of which the attorneys received a contingent fee of more than $60 million.

Forty-nine of these plaintiffs then filed this suit against their attorneys in the Phillips accident case alleging professional misconduct and demanding forfeiture of all fees the attorneys received. More specifically, plaintiffs alleged that the attorneys, in violation of rules governing their professional conduct, solicited business through a lay intermediary,[2] failed to fully investigate and assess individual claims,[3] failed to communicate offers received and demands made,[4] entered into an aggregate settlement with Phillips of all plaintiffs' claims without plaintiffs' authority or approval,[5] agreed to limit their law practice by not representing others involved in the same incident,[6] and intimidated and coerced their clients into accepting the settlement.[7] Plaintiffs asserted causes of action for breach of fiduciary duty [and other causes of action]. The attorneys have denied any misconduct and plaintiffs' claim for fee forfeiture.

The parties paint strikingly different pictures of the events leading to this suit:

> The plaintiffs contend: In the Phillips accident suit, the defendant attorneys signed up plaintiffs *en masse* to contingent fee contracts, often contacting plaintiffs

2. *See* Tex. Disciplinary R. Prof'l Conduct 7.03(b), *reprinted in* Tex. Gov't Code Ann., tit. 2, subtit. G app. A (1998) (Tex. State Bar R. art. X, §9).
3. *See id.* Rules 1.01, 2.01.
4. *See id.* Rule 1.03.
5. *See id.* Rule 1.08(f).
6. *See id.* Rule 5.06(b).
7. *See id.* Rules 1.02, 2.01.

> through a union steward. In many instances the contingent fee percentage in the contract was left blank and 33–1/3% was later inserted despite oral promises that a fee of only 25% would be charged.... No plaintiff was allowed to meet with an attorney for more than about twenty minutes, and any plaintiff who expressed reservations about the settlement was threatened by the attorney with being afforded no recovery at all.
>
> The defendant attorneys contend: No aggregate settlement or any other alleged wrongdoing occurred, but regardless of whether it did or not, all their clients in the Phillips accident suit received a fair settlement for their injuries, but some were disgruntled by rumors of settlements paid co-workers represented by different attorneys in other suits. After the litigation was concluded, a Kansas lawyer invited the attorneys' former clients to a meeting, where he offered to represent them in a suit against the attorneys for a fee per claim of $2,000 and one-third of any recovery. Enticed by the prospect of further recovery with minimal risk, plaintiffs agreed to join this suit, the purpose of which is merely to extort more money from their former attorneys.

[T]he [district] court granted summary judgment for the defendant attorneys on the grounds that the settlement of plaintiffs' claims in the Phillips accident suit was fair and reasonable, plaintiffs had therefore suffered no actual damages as a result of any misconduct by the attorneys, and absent actual damages plaintiffs were not entitled to a forfeiture of any of the attorneys' fees....

....

All but one of the plaintiffs ... appealed....

....

[T]he court of appeals reversed the summary judgment and remanded the case for a determination of whether the defendants breached their fiduciary duty to their former clients, and if so, what amount, if any, of their fee should be forfeited to plaintiffs....

....

III

[We consider the following] issues: (a) are actual damages a prerequisite to fee forfeiture? (b) is fee forfeiture automatic and entire for all misconduct? [and] (c) if not, is the amount of fee forfeiture a question of fact for a jury or one of law for the court? ... We address each issue in turn.

A

...

[S]ection 49 of the proposed *Restatement (Third) of The Law Governing Lawyers* [provides that] lawyers ... stand in a relation of trust and agency toward their clients. Section 49 states in part: "A lawyer engaging in clear and serious violation of duty to a client may be required to forfeit some or all of the lawyer's compensation for the matter."

... Th[is] rule is founded both on principle and pragmatics. In principle, a person who agrees to perform compensable services in a relationship of trust and violates that relationship breaches the agreement, express or implied, on which the right to compensation is based. The person is not entitled to be paid when he has not provided the loyalty bargained for and promised....

Along the same lines, comment *b* to section 49 ... explains: "The remedy of fee forfeiture presupposes that a lawyer's clear and serious violation of a duty to a client destroys or severely impairs the client-lawyer relationship and thereby the justification of the lawyer's claim to compensation." Pragmatically, the possibility of forfeiture of compensation discourages an agent from taking personal advantage of his position of trust in every situation no matter the circumstances, whether the principal may be injured or not. The remedy of forfeiture removes any incentive for an agent to stray from his duty of loyalty based on the possibility that the principal will be unharmed or may have difficulty proving the existence or amount of damages....

To limit forfeiture of compensation to instances in which the principal sustains actual damages would conflict with both justifications for the rule. It is the agent's disloyalty, not any resulting harm, that violates the fiduciary relationship and thus impairs the basis for compensation. An agent's compensation is not only for specific results but also for loyalty. Removing the disincentive of forfeiture except when harm results would prompt an agent to attempt to calculate whether particular conduct, though disloyal to the principal, might nevertheless be harmless to the principal and profitable to the agent. The main purpose of forfeiture is not to compensate an injured principal, even though it may have that effect. Rather, the central purpose of the equitable remedy of forfeiture is to protect relationships of trust by discouraging agents' disloyalty.

...

Texas courts of appeals, as well as courts in other jurisdictions[36] and respected commentators,[37] have also held that forfeiture is appropriate without regard to whether the breach of fiduciary duty resulted in damages.

....

We therefore conclude that a client need not prove actual damages in order to obtain forfeiture of an attorney's fee for the attorney's breach of fiduciary duty to the client.

36. *See, e.g., Hendry v. Pelland,* 73 F.3d 397, 402 (D.C.Cir.1996) ("[C]lients suing their attorney for breach of the fiduciary duty of loyalty and seeking disgorgement of legal fees as their sole remedy need prove only that their attorney breached that duty, not that the breach caused them injury."); *In re Estate of Corriea,* 719 A.2d 1234, 1241 (D.C.1998) (holding that the plaintiff's inability to quantify the damages suffered did "not disqualify the profits ordered disgorged as 'just compensation for the wrong' ") (quoting *Sheldon v. Metro-Goldwyn Pictures Corp.,* 309 U.S. 390, 399, 60 S.Ct. 681, 84 L.Ed. 825 (1940)); *Eriks v. Denver,* 118 Wash.2d 451, 824 P.2d 1207, 1213 (1992) (en banc) (rejecting the argument that a finding of damages and causation is required to order fee forfeiture); *Rice v. Perl,* 320 N.W.2d 407, 411 (Minn.1982) (holding that the client need not prove actual harm to obtain fee forfeiture); *Searcy, Denney, Scarola, Barnhart & Shipley, P.A. v. Scheller,* 629 So.2d 947, 952 (Fla.Dist.Ct.App.1993) (holding that "fee forfeiture should be considered only when an ordinary remedy like offsetting damages is plainly inadequate"); *see also Frank v. Bloom,* 634 F.2d 1245, 1258 (10th Cir.1980) (recognizing that "when the attorney is representing clients with actual existing conflicts of interest ... the attorney's compensation may be withheld even where no damages are shown").

37. *See, e.g.,* Restatement (Third) of the Law Governing Lawyers § 49 cmt. d (Proposed Final Draft No. 1, 1996) ("But forfeiture is justified for a flagrant violation even though no harm can be proved."); Thomas D. Morgan, *Sanctions and Remedies for Attorney Misconduct,* 19 S. Ill. U.L.J., 351 (1995) ("[T]he fee forfeiture sanction is available even where a client has suffered no loss as a result of an attorney's alleged misconduct."); 1 Geoffrey C. Hazard, Jr. & W. William Hodes, The Law of Lawyering § 1.5:108 (2d ed. Supp.1998) ("Generally speaking, where the claim rests on the disloyalty of the lawyer, and the remedy sought is forfeiture or disgorgement of fees already paid, rather than compensatory damages for poor service, the breach of the duty of loyalty *is* the harm, and the client is not required to prove causation or specific injury.").

B

The Clients argue that an attorney who commits a serious breach of fiduciary duty to a client must automatically forfeit all compensation to the client. [However, t]o require an agent to forfeit all compensation for every breach of fiduciary duty, or even every serious breach, would deprive the remedy of its equitable nature and would disserve its purpose of protecting relationships of trust....

The proposed *Restatement (Third) of The Law Governing Lawyers* rejects a rigid approach to attorney fee forfeiture. Section 49 states:

> A lawyer engaging in clear and serious violation of duty to a client may be required to forfeit some or all of the lawyer's compensation for the matter. In determining whether and to what extent forfeiture is appropriate, relevant considerations include the gravity and timing of the violation, its wilfulness, its effect on the value of the lawyer's work for the client, any other threatened or actual harm to the client, and the adequacy of other remedies.[39]

The remedy is restricted to "clear and serious" violations of duty. Comment *d* to section 49 explains: "A violation is clear if a reasonable lawyer, knowing the relevant facts and law reasonably accessible to the lawyer, would have known that the conduct was wrongful." The factors for assessing the seriousness of a violation, and hence "whether and to what extent forfeiture is appropriate", are set out in the rule. Elaborating on the rule, the comments to section 49 make it clear that forfeiture of fees for clear and serious misconduct is not automatic and may be partial or complete, depending on the circumstances presented....omment *e* observes: "Ordinarily, forfeiture extends to all fees for the matter for which the lawyer was retained...." But comment *e* adds: "Sometimes forfeiture for the entire matter is inappropriate, for example when a lawyer performed valuable services before the misconduct began, and the misconduct was not so grave as to require forfeiture of the fee for all services." And comment *b* expands on the necessity for exercising discretion in applying the remedy:

> Forfeiture of fees, however, is not justified in each instance in which a lawyer violates a legal duty, nor is total forfeiture always appropriate. Some violations are inadvertent or do not significantly harm the client. Some can be adequately dealt with by the remedies described in Comment *a* or by a partial forfeiture (see Comment *e*). Denying the lawyer all compensation would sometimes be an excessive sanction, giving a windfall to a client. The remedy of this Section should hence be applied with discretion.

The *Restatement*'s approach, as a whole, is consistent with Texas law concerning constructive trusts, and we agree with the forfeiture rule stated in section 49 as explained in the comments we have quoted. This rule, or something similar, also appears to have been adopted in most other jurisdictions that have considered the issue.[45]

---

39. Restatement (Third) of the Law Governing Lawyers § 49 (Proposed Final Draft No. 1, 1996).

45. *See, e.g., International Materials Corp. v. Sun Corp.,* 824 S.W.2d 890, 895 (Mo.1992) (en banc) (holding that complete forfeiture is not warranted unless there is a clear and serious violation of the lawyer's duty destroying the client-lawyer relationship, thereby removing the justification for the lawyer's compensation, and that recovery could be in quantum meruit for benefits conferred); *Kidney Ass'n of Oregon, Inc. v. Ferguson,* 315 Or. 135, 843 P.2d 442, 447 (1992) (favoring consideration of factors in determining whether attorney's fee should be reduced or denied when attorney breaches duty of loyalty); *In re Marriage of Pagano,* 154 Ill.2d 174, 180 Ill.Dec. 729, 607 N.E.2d 1242, 1249–1250 (1992) ("[W]hen one breaches a fiduciary duty to a principal the appropriate remedy is within the equitable discretion of the court. While the breach may be so egregious as to require the forfeiture of compensation by the fiduciary as a matter of public policy, such will not always be the case.")

. . . .

To the factors listed in section 49 we add another that must be given great weight in applying the remedy of fee forfeiture: the public interest in maintaining the integrity of attorney-client relationships.oncern for the integrity of attorney-client relationships is at the heart of the fee forfeiture remedy. The Attorneys' argument that relief for attorney misconduct should be limited to compensating the client for any injury suffered ignores the main purpose of the remedy.

. . .

Accordingly, we conclude that whether an attorney must forfeit any or all of his fee for a breach of fiduciary duty to his client must be determined by applying the rule as

---

(citations omitted); *Gilchrist v. Perl,* 387 N.W.2d 412, 417 (Minn.1986) (holding that the amount of fee forfeiture should be determined by consideration of the relevant factors set out in the state's punitive damage statute); *Crawford v. Logan,* 656 S.W.2d 360, 365 (Tenn.1983) (holding that any misconduct of an attorney does not automatically result in fee forfeiture but rather "[e]ach case ... must be viewed in the light of the particular facts and circumstances of the case"); *Cal Pak Delivery, Inc. v. United Parcel Serv., Inc.,* 52 Cal.App.4th 1, 60 Cal.Rptr.2d 207, 216 (1997) (recognizing California courts allowed partial fee recovery by the attorney "for services rendered before the ethical breach ... or ... on an unjust enrichment theory where the client's recovery was a direct result of the attorney's services"); *Fairfax Sav., F.S.B. v. Weinberg & Green,* 112 Md.App. 587, 685 A.2d 1189, 1209 (1996) (holding that law firm was not obligated to disgorge entire fee because firm rendered valuable legal services to clients, and because other remedies of actual and punitive damages and sanctions would be adequate); *Lindseth v. Burkhart,* 871 S.W.2d 693, 695 (Tenn.Ct.App.1993) (holding that fee forfeiture for a breach of fiduciary duty is not automatic but depends on the facts and circumstances of each case); *Searcy, Denney, Scarola, Barnhart & Shipley, P.A. v. Scheller,* 629 So.2d 947, 953 (Fla.Dist.Ct.App.1993) (rejecting a mechanical application of fee forfeiture and approving the multi-factor approach to fee forfeiture as stated in the *Restatement (Third) of The Law Governing Lawyers*); *Seeman v. Gumbiner (In re Life Ins. Trust Agr. of Julius F. Seeman),* 841 P.2d 403, 405 (Colo.Ct.App.1992) ("[A] conflict of interest is only one of many factors to be considered in determining the award of fees; it does not mandate a denial of all compensation."); *Lurz v. Panek,* 172 Ill.App.3d 915, 123 Ill.Dec. 200, 527 N.E.2d 663, 671 (1988) ("[W]e do not believe defendant should have to forfeit the entire fee.... Rather, we agree with the trial court that the jury was capable of apportioning the contingent fee."); *Mar Oil, S.A. v. Morrissey,* 982 F.2d 830, 840 (2d Cir.1993) (stating that "[u]nder New York law, attorneys may be entitled to recover for their services, even if they have breached their fiduciary obligations"); *Sweeney v. Athens Reg'l Med. Ctr.,* 917 F.2d 1560, 1573–1574 (11th Cir.1990) (holding that under Georgia law, if an attorney has engaged in unethical conduct, "the court may thus have a duty to require forfeiture of some portion of the fees"); *Iannotti v. Manufacturers Hanover Trust Co. (In re New York, New Haven & Hartford R.R. Co.),* 567 F.2d 166, 180–181 (2d Cir.1977) (holding that the court properly tailored the amount of fee forfeiture based on the nature of the breach of fiduciary duty found, as well as evidence that the attorney had, prior to the breach, performed valuable services for the estate); *see also Brandon v. Hedland, Fleischer, Friedman & Cooke (In re Estate of Brandon),* 902 P.2d 1299, 1317 (Alaska 1995) (noting that existing Alaska law appeared to require full fee forfeiture, but directing the trial court on remand to make alternative findings under the multi-factor approach in *Kidney Ass'n* "to reduce chances of a second remand following further appeal"); *Hendry v. Pelland,* 73 F.3d 397, 403 (D.C.Cir.1996) (leaving open the extent of forfeiture to which the plaintiffs might be entitled if they succeed in proving that the attorney breached his duty of loyalty); *Musico v. Champion Credit Corp.,* 764 F.2d 102, 112–113 (2d Cir.1985) (describing trend in New York law away from automatic full fee forfeiture); *Littell v. Morton,* 369 F.Supp. 411, 425 (D.Md.1974) (characterizing strict fee forfeiture as "inequitable" unless a deliberate scheme to defraud the client exists). *But see, e.g., Pessoni v. Rabkin,* 220 A.D.2d 732, 633 N.Y.S.2d 338, 338 (N.Y.App.Div.1995) (holding that an attorney who violates the disciplinary rules is not entitled to fees for any services rendered); *In re Estate of McCool,* 131 N.H. 340, 553 A.2d 761, 769 (1988) (holding that "an attorney who violates our rules of professional conduct by engaging in clear conflicts of interest, of whose existence he either knew or should have known, may receive neither executor's nor legal fees for services he renders an estate").

stated in section 49 of the proposed *Restatement (Third) of The Law Governing Lawyers* and the factors we have identified to the individual circumstances of each case.

C

....

Forfeiture of an agent's compensation, we have already explained, is an equitable remedy similar to a constructive trust. As a general rule, a jury "does not determine the expediency, necessity, or propriety of equitable relief." ... However, when contested fact issues must be resolved before equitable relief can be determined, a party is entitled to have that resolution made by a jury.

....

Thus, when forfeiture of an attorney's fee is claimed, a trial court must determine from the parties whether factual disputes exist that must be decided by a jury before the court can determine whether a clear and serious violation of duty has occurred, whether forfeiture is appropriate, and if so, whether all or only part of the attorney's fee should be forfeited.... Once any necessary factual disputes have been resolved, the court must determine, based on the factors we have set out, whether the attorney's conduct was a clear and serious breach of duty to his client and whether any of the attorney's compensation should be forfeited, and if so, what amount. Most importantly, in making these determinations the court must consider whether forfeiture is necessary to satisfy the public's interest in protecting the attorney-client relationship ...

....

For the reasons explained, we modify the court of appeals' judgment to reverse the district court's judgment ... and we remand the case to the district court for further proceedings.

* * *

1. Violation of Disciplinary Rules as Proof of Breach of Fiduciary Obligations. Like Texas, most jurisdictions have in place rules of professional conduct that govern lawyers' ethical obligations and responsibilities. Most jurisdictions' ethical rules are based on some variation of the Model Rules of Professional Conduct, and courts widely regard violations of the professional ethics rules as constituting a violation of a lawyer's fiduciary obligations. For example, in *Burrow,* the court discusses a number of alleged violations of the Texas Rules of Disciplinary Conduct, conduct that would also amount to violations of the Model Rules of Professional Conduct as well. *See, e.g.,* Model Rules of Prof'l Conduct R. 7.3(b) (solicitation of conduct through a lay intermediary), 2.1 (failing to investigate and assess individual claims fully), 1.3 (failing to communicate offers received and demands made), 1.8 (entering into an aggregate settlement without plaintiff's authority or approval), 5.6 (agreeing to limit law practice) 2.1 (intimidating and coercing clients into accepting settlement); *see also* Charles E. Rounds, Jr., *Lawyer Codes Are Just About Licensure, the Lawyer's Relationship with the State: Recalling the Common Law Agency, Contract, Tort, Trust, and Property Principles That Regulate the Lawyer-Client Fiduciary Relationship,* 60 Baylor L. Rev. 771, 785–86 (2008) (explaining that compensation contract between lawyer and client is incident to the agency relationship, not the other way around).

2. In *Kirsch v. Duryea,* 146 Cal. Rptr. 218 (Cal. 1978), the court referred to the California Rules of Professional Conduct, which provided:

> (A) member of the State Bar shall not withdraw from employment until he has taken reasonable steps to avoid foreseeable prejudice to the rights of his client,

> including giving due notice to his client, allowing time for employment of other counsel, delivering to client all papers and property to which the client is entitled, and complying with applicable laws and rules. (See A.B.A. CODE OF PROF. RESPONSIBILITY, DR 2-110(A)(2).)

The *Kirsch* court explained that "[w]hile this rule was not in effect at the time of the actions at issue, the rule states a long-accepted standard of professional conduct":

> A valid purpose is served by the requirement that the withdrawing attorney delay seeking court approval to permit his client to secure other representation. When the attorney seeks to withdraw without consent of client, there is an obvious inference his withdrawal is not for the client's purpose but for the attorney's purpose, usually a lack of confidence in the merits of the case. The inference is obvious to the parties in the case and will ordinarily gravely jeopardize any chance of settlement. On the other hand, consensual withdrawal or substitution of another attorney as opposing counsel are well-aware may be due to numerous reasons even personal casting no reflection on the client's case. Accordingly, an attorney should not seek a nonconsensual withdrawal immediately upon determination that the case lacks merit, but should delay to give his client an opportunity to obtain other counsel or to file a consensual withdrawal.

Kirsch v. Duryea, 146 Cal. Rptr. 218 (Cal. 1978). Can you articulate how not providing one's client an opportunity to obtain other counsel or file a consensual withdrawal might form the basis for a breach of fiduciary duty action?

3. Breach of Fiduciary Duty and Damages. Note that the *Burrow* court expressly provides that "a client need not prove actual damages in order to obtain forfeiture of an attorney's fee for the attorney's breach of fiduciary duty to the client." In other words, unlike a negligence action, which requires actual damages as part of the plaintiff's *prima facie* case, *see* Chapter 6, *infra* (discussing damages required for legal malpractice action), actual damages are not required for a plaintiff to establish a breach of fiduciary duty action.

4. In accord with *Burrow v. Arce* is *Eriks v. Denver*, 824 P.2d 1207 (Wash. 1992), in which the court explained that disgorgement of fees is an appropriate remedy for some breaches of fiduciary duty: "Disgorgement of fees is a reasonable way to discipline specific breaches of professional responsibility, and to deter future misconduct of a similar type."

Exercise 3.2

Associate has recently left his position at Big Firm to work at a smaller firm specializing in plaintiff class action litigation. While employed at Big Firm, Associate helped to defend Car Company against various claims of products liability that were allegedly caused by defective braking systems in various Car Company's automobiles. In representing Car Company, Associate worked under the supervision of several attorneys and engaged in various tasks, including drafting motions and briefs, conducting discovery, and communicating frequently with Car Company representatives as well as opposing counsel. More specifically, as part of Big Firm's representation of Car Company, Associate identified various potential experts to testify regarding plaintiffs' alleged damage claims, worked on opposition briefs to plaintiffs' class action certification motions, and participated in discussions with Car Company regarding class action defense issues and settlement strategies. He billed in excess of 500 hours to Car Company matters.

After receiving a substantially higher salary offer to work at ABC Firm, Associate gave notice at Big Firm and took a position at ABC Firm. At the time that he moved to ABC Firm, ABC Firm had no clients who were suing Car Company. However, after working there for two years, ABC Firm has been presented with the opportunity to represent clients in a class action against Car Company for injuries allegedly sustained by defectively designed seatbelt restraint systems.

As a member of ABC Firm's ethics compliance board, you have been asked by Managing Partner at ABC Firm whether ABC Firm taking on such a representation will potentially open the firm up to liability, especially considering Associate's former employment at Big Firm. It is Managing Partner's opinion, however, that the Rules of Professional Conduct—especially 1.9*—are not implicated because Associate defended Car Company on different matters (breaking systems) than what would be the subject of ABC Firm's new representation (seat belts and restraint system issues). Prepare a memorandum advising Managing Partner about whether ABC Firm could be subject to liability if it took on this new class representation against Car Company.

---

* Model Rule 1.9 provides:

Rule 1.9 Duties To Former Clients

(a) A lawyer who has formerly represented a client in a matter shall not thereafter represent another person in the same or a substantially related matter in which that person's interests are materially adverse to the interests of the former client unless the former client gives informed consent, confirmed in writing.

(b) A lawyer shall not knowingly represent a person in the same or a substantially related matter in which a firm with which the lawyer formerly was associated had previously represented a client

(1) whose interests are materially adverse to that person; and

(2) about whom the lawyer had acquired information protected by Rules 1.6 and 1.9(c) that is material to the matter;

unless the former client gives informed consent, confirmed in writing.

(c) A lawyer who has formerly represented a client in a matter or whose present or former firm has formerly represented a client in a matter shall not thereafter:

(1) use information relating to the representation to the disadvantage of the former client except as these Rules would permit or require with respect to a client, or when the information has become generally known; or

(2) reveal information relating to the representation except as these Rules would permit or require with respect to a client.

Lawyers owe a multitude of fiduciary obligations to their clients, including (but not limited to) duties of loyalty, confidentiality, and to avoid conflicts of interests, all of which are explored in the materials that follow.

1. Duty of Loyalty

Focus Questions: *Stanley v. Richmond*

1. *How is the scope of an attorney's breach of fiduciary duty established?*
2. *Describe the fiduciary obligation(s) allegedly violated in the* Stanley *case.*
3. *Is expert testimony required to establish breach of fiduciary duty?*
4. *Are emotional injuries recoverable in a breach of fiduciary duty action?*

Stanley v. Richmond

35 Cal. App. 4th 1070
(1995)

PHELAN, J.

Linda E. Stanley (appellant) timely appeals from a judgment of nonsuit entered as to her claims for breach of fiduciary duty [and other actions]. These claims against respondents Diana Richmond (Richmond or respondent) and her law firm, Richmond & Chamberlin (collectively, hereinafter, respondents), arose out of a dissolution [of marriage] proceeding in which Richmond represented appellant, and C. Rick Chamberlin (Chamberlin), an attorney with whom Richmond was in the process of forming a new law firm, represented appellant's husband, Dr. John Stanley (Dr. Stanley). At the close of appellant's evidence in a jury trial, the court granted respondents' motion for nonsuit..., ruling that ... that appellant failed to present evidence that, but for Richmond's alleged breach(es) of fiduciary duty, appellant would have obtained a better result in the dissolution proceedings.

We conclude that appellant established a prima facie case of breach of fiduciary duty [and other actions]. Accordingly, we reverse the judgment of the trial court and remand for a new trial.

I. Factual and Procedural Background

....

Appellant and Dr. Stanley were married in 1958 and separated on January 6, 1986....

Appellant is a litigation attorney specializing in bankruptcy matters. She was a partner in the law firm of Dinkelspiel & Dinkelspiel until June 1986, when she left to start a new firm, Taylor & Stanley. On February 1, 1989, Taylor & Stanley was acquired by Nossaman, Gunther, Knox & Elliot (the Nossaman firm)....

In June 1987, appellant retained Richmond to represent her in the marital dissolution proceedings. At the time, Richmond's law offices were located ... in space she subleased from the Nossaman firm....

Dr. Stanley retained Chamberlin as his attorney for the dissolution proceedings in or about February 1988. Chamberlin was at the time a partner with Stotter, Chamberlin & Coats....

A. *June 1988 Trial re Division of Marital Property.*

A three-day trial on the marital property issues was held in June 1988. Two of the issues at trial were the division of the family residence in Belvedere, which was valued at $825,000, and disposition of Dr. Stanley's University of California (UC), Veterans' Administration (VA), and "TIAA/CREF" retirement accounts. The retirement accounts were worth over $600,000....

At the end of the trial, the court ... ordered the [family] home sold, but provided that either party could bid on the [remaining] property. The court further ordered ... that Dr. Stanley's retirement plans should be divided equally in kind. On June 21, 1988, the parties were directed to draft a proposed final judgment for the court's approval. Over the following eight months, the parties continued to dispute many specifics of the property division, and exchanged six drafts of the form of judgment before finally settling the matter.[1]

B. *Posttrial Efforts to Finalize the Marital Property Division.*

After the trial of the property issues was concluded, appellant began to complain that Richmond had become ineffectual in efforts to wind up the dissolution. For example, on December 9, 1988, appellant wrote to Richmond and expressed concern about Richmond's apparent unwillingness to challenge Chamberlin on key issues. Unknown to appellant, Richmond had met with Chamberlin in July or August of 1988 and invited him to join her in the practice of law. Richmond wanted Chamberlin to relocate with her when she moved her offices later in the year. At that time, Chamberlin declined the invitation....

....

[O]n or about January 25, Chamberlin called Richmond to inquire if she was still interested in having him join her in the practice of law. Richmond told Chamberlin that she was, indeed, still interested, and agreed to check if there was additional space in the building where she had leased offices to relocate her law practice.

Also on January 25, Richmond called appellant to tell her that she and opposing counsel Chamberlin were "seriously discussing taking offices together within the next 60 days." Richmond confirmed their conversation in a letter dated January 26. Stanley testified about her reaction to Richmond's news: "My first impression was to laugh in disbelief. I was just amazed that here I was in a situation where the opposing counsel and my attorney were going to go [in]to practice or going to share offices together. But I said, well, that's all the more reason to get this judgment finished, which has languished all this time." Stanley further testified that she understood "taking offices together" to mean that Richmond and Chamberlin would be renting space in the same building ... but not that they would be starting a new law firm together. Apparently, Richmond's and Chamberlin's plan was to open the new law firm within 60 days of January 25, *i.e.*, by March 26, when Richmond's sublease with the Nossaman firm expired.[2] ... In her confirming letter of January 26,

1. At least two of these drafts were exchanged after Richmond's alleged conflict of interest arose.

2. In fact, Richmond and Chamberlin probably began practicing fewer than 60 days after giving appellant notice of their plan. On or about March 22, 1989, appellant received some papers in an envelope bearing a mailing label with the firm name "Richmond & Chamberlin" printed on it.

Richmond also noted that her plan to go into practice with Chamberlin was "yet another reason to conclude [appellant's] dissolution as soon as we possibly can."

Contrary to Richmond's representations to her client on January 25 and 26 that she and Chamberlin were merely "discussing taking offices together," a jury could infer from their conduct that, by that time, they had already agreed to go into practice together and were actively organizing their new law firm, Richmond & Chamberlin. Richmond admitted that within 48 hours of her telephone call to appellant on January 25, she and Chamberlin met with a realtor to acquire additional office space for their new law firm. While continuing to represent opposing parties in ongoing litigation, Richmond and Chamberlin also selected associates (from among the attorneys employed by their separate law firms), stationery, forms of retainer, announcements, computers, and a telephone system for Richmond & Chamberlin. A bank account was also established in the firm name.... By February 1, Richmond and Chamberlin had made arrangements for the additional office space Chamberlin needed. Attorney fees due Chamberlin from [his representation of Dr. Stanley in the divorce proceeding] would be used to finance his move into Richmond's law offices.

....

[Attorney Richmond appeared to be working with opposing counsel to make appellant agree to the sale of property with terms unfavorable to her client.]

On Tuesday, February 7, appellant wrote to Chamberlin and threatened to seek to disqualify him because of a conflict of interest, saying, "Business partners should not be representing parties on the opposite sides of the lawsuit." On the same day, appellant [wrote to Richmond] and complained that she had been unavailable and ineffective in representing appellant's interests. Appellant also specifically charged that she was being "adversely affect[ed]" by Richmond's conflict of interest "now that you and Rick will be practicing in the same offices starting on March 1."

[O]n Wednesday, February 8, she served a substitution of attorneys by which she would have been replaced as counsel of record by appellant proceeding in *propria persona*.... Appellant refused to sign the substitution form because she did not believe she could competently represent herself or obtain new counsel on such short notice....

....

[W]ithout doing any research on the law governing federal pensions, Richmond advised appellant to waive her interest in the VA pension.

On February 16, the parties appeared in Marin County Superior Court.... Richmond met with appellant in the corridor of the Marin County Superior Court and induced her to enter into a settlement which was read into the record. Appellant objected that she did not understand the agreement she was being asked to make. In response, Richmond told her client, "Don't be a baby, this is the way you will get your house." Appellant explained that she went ahead with the settlement "at the request of Diana Richmond," as follows: "I was—I had—I had a lawyer who was—basically abandoned me, and I was looking at losing my house, and she said that's the only way I could get the house, so I walked in and agreed."

Under the terms of the settlement entered on the record on February 16, appellant ceded her entire interest in Dr. Stanley's VA pension to him, received the entire cash settlement from the buyout of her partnership interest in Dinkelspiel & Dinkelspiel without any allowance for the tax consequences to her, and approved a division of the community property which miscalculated the amount of rent due the community from ... Dr. Stanley's use of the family home during the pendency of the dissolution.

....

On March 15, John McCall substituted into the case to represent appellant. McCall felt that his hands were tied with respect to obtaining relief from the February 16 settlement.... Appellant paid McCall fees totaling $2,290.60 to "mitigate the damages caused by Richmond's conflict of interest."

In August 1989, appellant learned that, although she was an otherwise eligible unremarried ex-spouse of a civil service employee, she was not allowed to enroll in the Federal Employees' Health Benefits (FEHB) Program because she had ceded her entire interest in Dr. Stanley's VA pension. Had she retained a minimum $1 interest in the VA pension, she would have been eligible for lifetime health insurance from the FEHB at very low cost, as well as a possible survivor's annuity.

....

C. *Expert Testimony re Breach of Fiduciary Duty and Malpractice.*

Professor Richard Zitrin, an expert in legal ethics, testified that Richmond had a conflict of interest [at least] as of January 25, as follows: "She had decided just at a time when a lot of things were happening on the case, ... that she and Mr. Chamberlin were going to join forces in some way and open a law office, and that created a conflict of interest between her desire to open a law office with Mr. Chamberlin, who is opposing counsel, and her obligation to represent [appellant] in the domestic relations matter." [Professor Zitrin testified further that the conflict of interest was not adequately cured with the informed consent of the appellant, and therefore Richmond had a duty pursuant to the California Rules of Professional Conduct to withdraw from the representation. At the trial, Richmond also testified as an expert in family law.]

....

II. Discussion

The issue presented in this appeal is whether appellant presented substantial evidence—including any required expert testimony—to support a prima facie claim of breach of fiduciary duty [and her additional claims].

A. *Professor Zitrin's Expert Testimony Was Sufficient to Establish Both the Duty and Breach Elements of a Cause of Action for Breach of Fiduciary Duty.*

[A] breach of fiduciary duty is a species of tort distinct from a cause of action for professional negligence. The elements of a cause of action for breach of fiduciary duty are: (1) existence of a fiduciary duty; (2) breach of the fiduciary duty; and (3) damage proximately caused by the breach.

The scope of an attorney's fiduciary duty may be determined as a matter of law based on the Rules of Professional Conduct which, "together with statutes and general principles relating to other fiduciary relationships, all help define the duty component of the fiduciary duty which an attorney owes to his [or her] client." (*Mirabito v. Liccardo* (1992) 4 Cal.App.4th 41, 45) Whether an attorney has breached a fiduciary duty to his or her client is generally a question of fact. Expert testimony is not required, but is admissible to establish the duty and breach elements of a cause of action for breach of fiduciary duty where the attorney conduct is a matter beyond common knowledge.

Professor Zitrin's testimony about the Rules of Professional Conduct and the common law of attorney fiduciary duty, and his opinions that Richmond violated her duties under each, were plainly sufficient to establish the first two elements of a cause of action for breach of fiduciary duty. Indeed, when taken together with Richmond's own expert testimony and her denials, Zitrin's testimony was more than sufficient to raise questions of fact whether Richmond had an actual conflict of interest by virtue of her agreement to go into practice with Chamberlin, whether she obtained an informed consent to her continued employment as appellant's counsel of record after that conflict arose, whether her representation of appellant was compromised by her relationship with Chamberlin, and whether she breached her fiduciary duties with respect to withdrawal from the action.

... Professor Zitrin provided two theories under which appellant could establish that Richmond's loyalty to appellant was impaired by her agreement to go into practice with Chamberlin before the dissolution action was wrapped up. First, by entering into and commencing performance under an agreement to form a new law firm with her opposing counsel, Richmond arguably moved into an attorney-client relationship with Dr. Stanley that "flowed through" her prospective law partner, Chamberlin. Notwithstanding the fact that she and Chamberlin were not yet sharing office space, a jury could reasonably find that, by assuming such a position without obtaining written consent from appellant, Richmond (and Chamberlin) violated both the literal proscription on simultaneous representation of conflicting interests (rule 5-102(A) & (B)), and the common law fiduciary duties she owed to appellant.

....

What was at stake when Richmond agreed to form a new law firm with her opposing counsel, while they continued simultaneously to represent adverse parties in a highly contentious dissolution action, was her *duty of loyalty* to appellant. Our Supreme Court recently reaffirmed the long-standing definition of an attorney's duty of loyalty to his or her client, as follows: "'One of the principal obligations which bind[s] an attorney is that of fidelity, the maintaining inviolate the confidence reposed in him by those who employ him, and at every peril to himself to preserve the secrets of his client. [Citations.] This obligation is a very high and stringent one. It is also an attorney's duty to protect his client in every possible way, and it is a violation of that duty to assume a position adverse or antagonistic to his client without the latter's free and intelligent consent given after full knowledge of all the facts and circumstances. [Citation.] *By virtue of this rule an attorney is precluded from assuming any relation which would prevent him from devoting his entire energies to his client's interests.* Nor does it matter that the intention and motives of the attorney are honest. The rule is designed not alone to prevent the dishonest practitioner from fraudulent conduct, but as well to preclude the honest practitioner from putting himself in a position where he may be required to choose between conflicting duties, or be led to attempt to reconcile conflicting interests, rather than to enforce to their full extent the rights of the interest which he should alone represent.'" (*Flatt v. Superior Court, supra*, 9 Cal.4th at p. 289, quoting *Anderson v. Eaton* (1930) 211 Cal. 113, 116 [293 P. 788], italics in *Flatt*).

Because a reasonable trier of fact could find that Richmond and Chamberlin agreed on or about January 25 to go into practice together, and were well underway with the logistics of establishing their new law firm, Richmond would have been subject to immediate and "'automatic'" disqualification under the rule applicable to cases of dual representation. (*Flatt v. Superior Court, supra*, 9 Cal.4th at pp. 284–285.) "The reason for such a rule is evident, even (or perhaps especially) to the nonattorney. A client who learns that his or her lawyer is also representing a litigation adversary ... cannot long be expected to sustain the level of confidence and trust in counsel that is one of the foundations of the professional relationship. All legal technicalities aside, few if any clients would be willing to suffer the prospect of their attorney continuing to represent them under such circumstances." (*Id.*

at p. 285.) At a minimum, Richmond was required to make full and timely disclosure of the extent of her relationship with Chamberlin and to obtain appellant's intelligent, informed consent to the dual representation. This, of course, she did not do. [A]ppellant testified that she would have fired Richmond on January 26 and hired substitute counsel if she had known the extent of Richmond's involvement with Chamberlin on January 25. Instead, Richmond concealed from her client the fact that she had made a commitment to join forces with opposing counsel. On this view of the evidence, Richmond surely violated her duty of loyalty to appellant.

Perhaps more importantly, the evidence is sufficient to show that Richmond's personal interests in having Chamberlin join her in the practice of law as "ostensible partners," before appellant's case could be wrapped up, actually conflicted with her duty to obtain for her client a reasonable settlement of the outstanding property division issues in the dissolution action. Both appellant and Professor Zitrin testified about several instances of Richmond placing herself in a position where she was required to choose between conflicting duties to her client and her new law partner (or her own self-interest), and arguably resolved those conflicts adversely to her client.... Based on this evidence, a reasonable trier of fact could find that Richmond undermined her client's position before the court and weakened her position in the settlement negotiations.

....

C. *There Are Questions of Fact Whether Respondent's Breach of Fiduciary Duty ... Caused Appellant's Claimed Damages.*

The only remaining question is whether there was sufficient evidence, either disputed or undisputed, that the alleged breach of fiduciary duty ... [was a] legal cause[] of damage to appellant. It is plaintiff's burden to establish "'a reasonable basis for the conclusion that it was more likely than not that the conduct of the defendant was a substantial factor in the result.'" We conclude that appellant's evidence is sufficient to raise questions of fact under this standard of causation.

[T]here is substantial evidence that, because of Richmond's plan to go into practice with Chamberlin before the expiration of appellant's right of first refusal, Richmond placed undue pressure on her client to settle the property division issues more quickly than necessary and on less favorable terms than appellant could have obtained without the time constraints....

....

Of course, as Richmond correctly notes, a violation of the Rules of Professional Conduct does not, in and of itself, render an attorney liable for damages. However, the evidence in this case is capable of showing that appellant's interests in an equal division of the marital property were prejudiced by Richmond's conduct in violation of her fiduciary duties....

Finally, we note that appellant appears to claim a right to recover damages for emotional distress suffered as a result of Richmond's conflict of interest. Richmond impliedly concedes that such damages are recoverable if directly caused by the attorney's conduct in breach of her fiduciary duties. If credited by the jury, appellant's testimony about the extreme pressure she was under and her state of mind during the last few weeks of Richmond's representation including feelings of abandonment and betrayal by her attorney, anxiety over her possible loss of her family home, and undue pressure to obtain financing on a timetable established for the benefit of her attorney and opposing counsel as well as her loss of lifetime health benefits, may well be sufficient to support an award of damages for emotional distress from the alleged breaches of fiduciary duty.

III. Conclusion

... We ... hold that the trial court erred by ruling that [appellant] did not make a prima facie showing of each element ... for [a] breach of fiduciary duty [action].... For all the foregoing reasons, the judgment of the trial court is reversed and the cause remanded for a new trial....

* * *

1. Expert testimony. As discussed in the principal case, in a breach of fiduciary duty action, expert testimony is not necessarily required in order for the plaintiff to prevail. *See, e.g., Crist v. Loyacono*, 65 So. 3d 837, 842 (Miss. 2011) (explaining that expert testimony is not necessarily required for prevailing in a breach of fiduciary duty action); *Lane v. Oustalet*, 873 So. 2d 92, 99 (Miss. 2004) ("[W]hen the claim is for breach of the standard of conduct [*i.e.* breach of fiduciary duty], we conclude that lack of expert testimony should not preclude the issue from being heard by a jury.").

2. Fiduciary Obligations and Attorneys-in-fact. An attorney-in-fact is one who has been designated to serve as another's legal agent or to transact business on behalf of another, even if not a lawyer. Attorneys-in-fact owe fiduciary obligations to their principals, the violation of which may result in liability for breach of fiduciary duty. *See, e.g., Schock v. Nash*, 732 A.2d 217 (Del. 1999), in which Ms. Dever executed a durable power of attorney naming Irma Schock as attorney-in-fact. When Schock breached her fiduciary duty of loyalty by making gratuitous transfers to herself, the court explained:

> The creation of a power of attorney imposes the fiduciary duty of loyalty on the attorney-in-fact.... [¶] The common law fiduciary relationship created by a durable power of attorney is like the relationship created by a trust. The fiduciary duty principles of trust law must, therefore, be applied to the relationship between a principal and her attorney-in-fact. An attorney-in-fact, under the duty of loyalty, always has the obligation to act in the best interest of the principal unless the principal voluntarily consents to the attorney-in-fact engaging in an interested transaction after full disclosure. At common law, transactions which violated the fiduciary duty of loyalty were void.... If the transaction is challenged, the burden of persuasion to justify upholding the transaction is on the fiduciary. Thus, Irma Schock ... had the burden to establish that Anna Dever consented to the gratuitous transfers to Irma and her family after full disclosure of all the facts....

* * *

2. Duty of Confidentiality

A lawyer's duty of confidentiality is broad and long-lasting. Simply put, an attorney has an obligation to keep confidential all information relating to the representation of a client whatever its source. *See, e.g.*, MODEL RULES OF PROF'L CONDUCT R. 1.6 (Duty of Confidentiality). This duty of confidentiality applies to all information, whether received from the client or another source and whether received before, during, or after the representation. The duty to maintain confidences remains in effect forever, even after the representation has terminated, unless the client gives permission for confidences to be shared or unless one of the recognized exceptions to the duty of confidentiality is implicated. *See* MODEL RULES OF PROFESSIONAL CONDUCT R. 1.6(b) (setting forth exceptions to confidentiality). The improper disclosure of confidences may give rise to a breach of fiduciary duty claim. Consider the following materials.

Focus Questions: *Sealed Party v. Sealed Party*

1. *For how long does an attorney's fiduciary duty of confidentiality last?*
2. *Does an attorney owe a* former *client a fiduciary obligation of confidentiality?*
3. *Is breach of fiduciary duty a tort action or does other law govern?*
4. *What is the breadth of an attorney's obligation of confidentiality?*

Sealed Party v. Sealed Party

2006 WL 1207732
(S.D. Tex. 2006)

AMENDED OPINION [REDACTED]

ATLAS, J.

The only remaining claim pending before the Court in this case is a breach of fiduciary duty cross-claim asserted by Cross-Plaintiff ("the Client") against Cross-Defendants, the "Attorney" and his law firm (collectively, "the Attorney"). The merits of this cross-claim were tried to the Court without a jury.... The Client contends the Attorney breached his fiduciary duty to the Client by issuing a June 2004 press release, which was published on the Internet, among other places. The Client seeks disgorgement of the attorney's fee the Attorney received from the Client in a lawsuit (the "State Suit") filed by the Attorney on behalf of the Client against Plaintiff Company ("Company")....

Having heard and observed the witnesses, and having reviewed all matters of record in this case, the Court makes the following findings of fact and conclusions of law.

I. *FINDINGS OF FACT*

The Client, an insurance broker, initially contacted a Louisiana law firm (the "Louisiana Firm") to handle a dispute with the Company. That firm referred the Client to the Attorney, a Texas lawyer, who was one of two equity partners at his law firm (the "Original Firm"). The Attorney analyzed the facts and issues presented by the Client and agreed to handle the case through the Original Firm. The Attorney enlisted the help of an associate at that Firm (the "Associate"). The Attorney engaged in pre-suit negotiations with the Company's high level representatives and/or attorneys.

Negotiations were futile and, on April 26, 2002, the Attorney and Associate filed the State Suit on behalf of the Client against the Company and several other entities and individuals in Texas state court. The Attorney was listed on the pleadings as lead counsel. Both he and the Associate were listed as the attorneys of record. At the Attorney's request, the Associate handled virtually all the day-to-day work on the matter.

... The Associate performed the vast majority of the work on the case and became the Client's primary contact person at the Original Firm.

... The parties and counsel finally agreed to mediate on January 9, 2004, a date the Attorney was not available.

Meanwhile, in December 2003, the two principals in the Original Firm decided to dissolve their partnership. The Associate asked the Client to choose which firm he wanted as his counsel in the State Suit, either the Attorney's new firm ("Attorney's New Firm") or his former partner's new firm (the "Partner's Firm"), where the Associate was to work. The Client told the Associate he wanted the Partner's Firm as his counsel and accordingly the file was transferred. On January 1, 2004, the Original Firm formally dissolved. That day, the Attorney began practicing under a new firm name, Attorney's New Firm, and the Partner's Firm opened for business. The Associate maintained physical possession and control over the State Suit's file. The Associate became the Client's primary attorney. The Attorney's New Firm and the Partner's Firm shared office space until some time in February 2004.

Although still listed as the formal attorney of record on the State Suit's pleadings, the Attorney did no substantive work on the State Suit during the latter part of 2003 or thereafter.

On January 9, 2004, the Associate filed a pleading entitled "Notice of Counsel's Change of Law Firm." This notice directed that the Partner's Firm receive all further pleadings and correspondence in the State Suit. From this time onward, the Associate and the Louisiana lawyer were the only attorneys listed as counsel on the court filings.

Also on January 9, 2004, the parties and counsel participated in mediation. The Associate and the Louisiana lawyer appeared and represented the Client. The Attorney did not attend, did not participate in any way, and gave no substantive advice about resolving the litigation.[6] The parties reached a settlement and late in the evening finalized and signed a formal agreement titled "Confidential Settlement and Mutual Release Agreement" ("Settlement Agreement"). The Associate and the Louisiana lawyer signed the Settlement Agreement as attorneys for the Client. The Associate signed as an attorney with the Partner's Firm. Neither the Attorney nor the Attorney's New Firm was a signatory. Upon the parties' stipulation of dismissal, the State Suit was dismissed with prejudice.

The Settlement Agreement included a confidentiality provision ("Confidentiality Provision"), which provided [that information related to the settlement not be disclosed]....

On or about March 1, 2004, the Attorney received $66,153.41 out of the settlement proceeds, the Partner received $66,153.41, and the Louisiana Firm received $176,409.10.

The Associate left the Attorney a brief voicemail message late in the day on January 9, 2004, stating that the State Suit had been settled and that the Company had insisted upon stringent confidentiality terms....

[I]t is clear that before, during and after the settlement, the Attorney knew that the Company was highly sensitive about the existence of the State Suit and the claims alleged. The Company made it clear to him personally during the pre-suit and early post-filing negotiations that he conducted with the Company's officers and attorneys that the Company wanted any settlement they might reach to be confidential.

Sometime near the end of May 2004, the Attorney began drafting a press release to announce the settlement of the State Suit ("Press Release").... On June 3, 2004, PR Newswire published the Press Release, which appeared on the Internet and other news sources. The Press Release stated:

---

6. The Attorney's only involvement occurred the night before the January 9 mediation, when the Client saw him in the hallway of the joint offices of the two new law firms. The Client and the Attorney briefly discussed the mediator's style, and the Attorney gave a general recommendation on how to handle the mediator at the outset of the mediation process. There was no discussion about the substance of the State Suit.

> [The Client].... alleged that a secret [Company] plan to reduce or underpay sales commissions and damage marketing partners such as [the Client] was concealed by pervasive problems with [the Company's] information systems.
>
> [The Client] had sued [the Company] ... in Texas state district court for fraud, tortious interference and breach of contract, and sought seven-figure damages. (The defendants denied the allegations.)
>
> According to [the Attorney], the lead lawyer for [the Client], the terms of the settlement are confidential. [The Attorney] said, "[the Client] valued [his] long relationship with [the Company] and regretted having to pursue legal action, but [the Client is] satisfied with the resolution of the matter."
>
> [The Client's] interests were represented by [the Attorney] of [Attorney's New Firm] in Houston and New York, and [the Louisiana lawyer with the Louisiana Firm], in New Orleans.
>
> ....

... The Attorney ... never sought permission to make the particular statements he included in the Press Release. He did not seek approval from the Client, the Associate, or anyone else involved in the State Suit to issue any press release at all.

... The sentiments the Attorney attributed to the Client were based on the Attorney's personal opinion of the Client's views over almost two years. The Attorney, however, made no effort to ascertain the Client's actual thoughts about the settlement when the Client agreed to it in January or at the time of the Press Release in June. The Court nonetheless is persuaded that the Attorney's characterizations of the Client's opinions in June 2004 were essentially correct.

On June 9, 2004, upon learning of the Press Release, the Company filed suit against the various Defendants in this federal case claiming breach of contract and other causes of action associated with alleged violations of the Confidentiality Provision and duties arising from the parties' relationships.

In March and April 2005, the Company dismissed its claims against all Defendants except the Attorney. Most pertinent to the cross-claim, on April 1, 2005, the Company and the Client agreed in a settlement agreement in the federal action:

> [The Company] represents that it would not have brought suit against [the Client] ... but for the fact that [the Attorney] named [the Client] in the Press Release and quoted [the Client] in the Press Release.
>
> ....

II. *CONCLUSIONS OF LAW*

Justice Benjamin Cardozo, at the time Chief Judge of the New York State Court of Appeals, defined the duty the common law imposes upon fiduciaries in *Meinhard v. Salmon,* 249 N.Y. 458, 464, 164 N.E. 545 (1928): "A trustee is held to something stricter than the morals of the market place. Not honesty alone, but the punctilio of an honor the most sensitive, is then the standard of behavior."

A. *Jurisdiction and Burden of Proof*

....

The elements of a breach of fiduciary duty claim are: (1) a fiduciary relationship between the plaintiff and defendant; (2) the defendant's breach of its fiduciary duty owed to the plaintiff; and (3) injury to the plaintiff or benefit to the defendant resulting from the defendant's fiduciary duty breach.[23] *Kelly v. Gaines,* 181 S.W.3d 394, 414 (Tex.App.—Waco 2005, pet filed); *Punts v. Wilson,* 137 S.W.3d 889, 891 (Tex.App.—Texarkana 2004, no pet.) (citing *Burrow v. Arce,* 997 S.W.2d 229, 238–39 (Tex. 1999). For reasons explained hereafter, the Court concludes that at the time the Attorney issued the Press Release, the Attorney still owed a fiduciary duty to the Client, despite the fact that at that time the attorney-client relationship had terminated. The Court also concludes that the Attorney breached that duty. Nevertheless, the Attorney is entitled to judgment on the Client's fiduciary duty claim because the Client has not proven that, as a result of the breach, he was injured or that the Attorney benefitted in legally cognizable ways.

B. *Existence of a Fiduciary Relationship*

To prevail on a breach of fiduciary duty claim, the Client must first establish that he was in a fiduciary relationship with the Attorney. Under Texas law, "[t]here are two types of fiduciary relationships—a formal fiduciary relationship that arises as a matter of law, such as principal/agent or partners, and an informal fiduciary relationship arising from a confidential relationship 'where one person trusts in and relies upon another, whether the relation is moral social, domestic or merely personal.'" *Hoggett v. Brown,* 971 S.W.2d 472, 487 (Tex.App.—Houston [14th Dist.] 1997, pet. denied) (quoting *Crim Truck & Tractor Co. v. Navistar Int'l Transp. Corp.,* 823 S.W.2d 591, 593–94 (Tex.1992)). The existence of a fiduciary relationship is a question of fact. Once the relationship is created through formal or informal means, the "fiduciary duty requires the fiduciary to place the interest of the other party before his or her own." *Hogget,* 971 S.W.2d at 487.

Formal fiduciary duties arise as a matter of law in certain relationships, including attorney-client ... relationships. ...

"The relationship existing between attorney and client is characterized as 'highly fiduciary,' and requires proof of 'perfect fairness' on the part of the attorney." *See Jackson Law Office, P .C. v. Chappell,* 37 S.W.3d 15, 22 (Tex.App.—Tyler 2000, pet. denied) (quoting *Archer v. Griffith,* 390 S.W.2d 735, 739 (Tex.1964)). Specifically, the relationship between attorney and client has been described as one of *uberrima fides,* which means, "most abundant good faith," requiring absolute and perfect candor, openness and honesty, and the absence of any concealment or deception..

In the absence of an agreement to the contrary, or special circumstances, an attorney-client relationship generally terminates upon the completion of the purpose of the employment. ...

It is undisputed that by June 2004, when the Attorney issued the Press Release, he was no longer the Client's attorney [and] that the Client was the Attorney's *former* client.... The Court turns to the issue of whether the Attorney had any continuing fiduciary duties to his former client after the attorney-client relationship ended.

C. *Scope of Fiduciary Duties Owed by Attorneys to Former Clients*

... The specific question here is whether there is a "fiduciary duty" under Texas law that an attorney not reveal a former client's confidential information when the revelation

23. Certain Texas courts require a plaintiff on a fiduciary duty claim to prove: (1) the existence of a fiduciary duty, (2) breach of the duty, (3) causation, and (4) damages. *E.g., Greene's Pressure Treating & Rentals, Inc. v. Fulbright and Jaworski, L.L.P.,* 178 S.W.3d 40, 43 (Tex.App.—Houston [1st Dist.] 2005, no pet.).

is without the client's permission. The Court concludes [that] an attorney has a fiduciary obligation to not reveal to third parties confidential information received from a client, or obtained by reason of the representation of that client, and that obligation survives termination of the attorney-client relationship in the absence of permission from the former client to make the disclosure.

[G]enerally a fiduciary's duty to preserve confidential information survives the termination of the fiduciary relationship. Courts interpreting tort law from other jurisdictions similarly suggest that a fiduciary's duty to preserve confidential information survives cessation of the fiduciary relationship.[24]

....

... Texas and Federal courts regularly have referred to the Texas Rules [of Professional Conduct] to help define standards of attorney conduct in tort cases. Thus, although the Texas Rules are not dispositive, they may be considered evidence and significantly inform the analysis of the scope of fiduciary duties between attorneys and their clients, as well as between attorneys and their former clients.

...

There is no question that at the time he issued the Press Release, under the Texas Rules, the Attorney owed a duty to his former client not to "reveal" "confidential information" to others unless authorized expressly or implicitly by former client to do so. *See generally Perez,* 822 S.W.2d at 265–66; *see also* TEX. R. 1.05(b), (c). The parties do not dispute that "reveal" means "to make known" or "disclose" to another person.

....

[U]nder Texas Rule 1.05(b), ... the Attorney had a continuing duty to not knowingly reveal confidential information relating to the Client or obtained from the Client or other sources without the client's permission. The Court holds that this duty was a continuing fiduciary duty that survived the Client's termination of the attorney-client relationship.

24. *See NCH Corp. v. Broyles,* 749 F.2d 247, 254–55 (5th Cir.1985) (affirming district court's finding that, under Louisiana law, defendant was under fiduciary duty not to use former employer's confidential information for defendant's benefit); *Wilson P. Abraham Const. Corp. v. Armco Steel Corp.,* 559 F.2d 250, 253 (5th Cir.1977) (holding that when information is exchanged between co-defendants and their attorneys in a criminal case, an attorney who is the recipient of such information breaches his fiduciary duty under Louisiana law if he later, in his representation of another client, is able to use this information to the detriment of one of the co-defendants); *ABKCO Music, Inc. v. Harrisongs Music, Ltd.,* 722 F.2d 988, 994–95 (2d Cir.1983) (finding songwriter's former manager breached his fiduciary duty to plaintiff by revealing confidential information after the fiduciary relationship ended); *Boettcher DTC Building Joint Venture v. Falcon Ventures,* 762 P.2d 788, 790 (Colo.App.1988) ("Upon termination of the agency, an agent owes a continuing duty not to use or disclose confidential information obtained during the course of the agency. However, the remaining fiduciary obligations which arose during the agency, including the duty of loyalty, no longer exist."); *David Welch Co. v. Erskine & Tulley,* 250 Cal.Rptr. 339, 342 (Cal.Ct.App.1988) (holding that attorney's "duty to protect confidential information continues after the formal [attorney-client] relationship ends" in affirming breach of fiduciary duty judgment in favor of law firm's former client); *see also Bank Saderat Iran v. Telegen Corp.,* 1997 WL 685247, at *7 (N.D.Cal. Oct. 16, 1997), *aff'd in part, rev'd in part on other grounds,* 30 Fed. Appx. 741 (9th Cir. Feb. 6, 2006) ("Following termination of representation, an attorney owes a continuing obligation to his former clients.... [C]ourts have recognized a breach of fiduciary duty where an attorney gains an unfair advantage over a former client by using confidential information obtained during the relationship.") (internal citations omitted)).

D. *Application to the Press Release of Texas Rule 1.05 and the Related Fiduciary Duty of Confidentiality*

The Attorney asserts that issuance of the Press Release violated no duties to the Client because the Release revealed only information that either was not "confidential" at all or was at the time of the Press Release in publicly available court records, and thus was "generally known." ...

1. Attorney's Right to Reveal "Confidential Information" and "Unprivileged Client Information"

a. *Legal Analysis*

....

... "[A]n attorney's duty of confidentiality is broader than just client communications, and extends to all confidential information, whether privileged or unprivileged, and whether learned directly from the client or from another source." *Perillo v. Johnson*, 205 F.3d 775, 799, (5th Cir.2000) (applying Texas law); *see also* STEPHEN GILLERS & ROY D. SIMON, REGULATION OF LAWYERS, STATUTES AND STANDARDS 86–87 (2002).

Texas courts have stated that "virtually any information relating to a case should be considered confidential [under Rule 1.05]." *Phoenix Founders, Inc. v. Marshall*, 887 S.W.2d 831, 834 (Tex.1994).

....

... Nothing in Texas Rule 1.05(a) or elsewhere in the Texas Rules suggests that client information loses its status as "confidential" vis à vis the former attorney merely because the information has been disclosed in court pleadings.

....

These rules apply equally to the attorney's conduct during and after the representation. *See* TEX. R. 1.05(b)(1) (rule is applicable to former clients). Furthermore, the rules apply equally to information learned before, during, and after the representation. The exceptions to the blanket rule of confidentiality permitting an attorney to "reveal" client information are balanced to enable an attorney to perform services for the client by communicating client information to opponents and others formally in court pleadings and correspondence, and informally either to further the goals of the representation or to protect the attorney in defense of claims against him.

....

The Court concludes ... that an attorney generally owes a former client a continuing duty to not reveal to third parties confidential client information without the client's express or implicit permission.

b. *Discussion*

... The Attorney's Press Release contained the following information: (i) identification of the Attorney and the fact that he had filed the State Suit in Texas court against the Company on behalf of the Client; (ii) the claims asserted against the Company with factual allegations in support; (iii) the fact that the parties settled the State Suit; and (iv) the Attorney's impressions of the Client's views about his prior relationship with the Company, the filing of the State Suit, and the State Suit settlement.... The Attorney knew about the Client's allegations, claims, and related matters solely because of his representation of the Client.... [A]ll information in the Press Release was acquired "during the course of or by reason of [the Attorney's] representation" of the Client, and thus was confidential information. *See* TEX. R. 1.05(a). For reasons described above, the mere fact that some of the disclosed information already had been included in court pleadings does not remove that information from the realm of "confidential information" ... or alter an attorney's fiduciary duty of confidentiality to a former client under the circumstances of this case.

The Court also concludes that, through the Press Release, the Attorney "revealed" confidential information in contravention of Texas Rule 1.05(b)(1). The Attorney had no authority to disclose the information in the Press Release. Even if third parties might have found the information on their own, the Attorney had a continuing fiduciary duty not to be the conduit or source of others learning about that information.

....

Therefore, the Attorney's disclosure in the Press Release of the settlement and private Client opinions violated the Attorney's continuing fiduciary duty of confidentiality owed to the Client under Texas law.

....

3. The Attorney's Conduct Was "Knowing"

The Attorney made the disclosures in the Press Release intentionally and deliberately, not by accident. Accordingly, he acted "knowingly." Moreover, the Attorney purposefully disclosed information that he knew "relat[ed] to a client ... [and which information he] acquired ... during the course of or by reason of the representation of the client." *See* TEX. R. 1.05(a). The Attorney thus knowingly revealed information that was "confidential information" under the Texas Rules and applicable law. *See id.*

....

E. *Appropriate Remedies*

1. Compensatory Damages

An award of actual damages for breach of fiduciary duty requires a showing of injury and causation.

The Client has not proven by a preponderance of the evidence that he suffered any actual monetary damages as a result of the Attorney's breach of fiduciary duty. The Client testified that he paid $4,000 to $5,000 in attorneys' fees in defending against the Company's claims. However, the Court credits the billing records the Client submitted from the attorney who defended him against the Company's claims. These records establish that two companies, the Client's insurer and a corporation the Client controls but does not wholly-own, together expended a total of $45,637 defending the Client against the Company's claims. There is no probative evidence the Client personally has paid any of the fees or costs incurred defending against the Company's claims....

....

Another avenue the Client might have utilized to prove the "damages" element of his claim was to demonstrate that the Attorney "benefitted" from his breach of the duty of confidentiality.... The Client, however, neither pleaded nor offered proof of any value or benefit received by the Attorney from the Press Release. No damages are warranted.

2. Forfeiture

Under Texas law, where a court finds a "clear and serious" breach of fiduciary duty, a party is not required to prove injury or causation where the remedy sought is partial or total forfeiture. *Burrow v. Arce*, 997 S.W.2d 229, 240–41 (Tex.1999). The party need not prove actual damages in order to obtain a fee forfeiture for the breach of a fiduciary duty owed to him because "[i]t is the agent's disloyalty, not any resulting harm, that violates the fiduciary relationship and thus impairs the basis for compensation." *Burrow*, 997 S.W.2d at 238. Forfeiture is an equitable remedy. *Id.* at 234.

"A violation is clear if a reasonable lawyer, knowing the relevant facts and law reasonably accessible to the lawyer, would have known that the conduct was wrongful." *Burrow*, 997 S.W.2d at 241. The Court concludes that the Attorney's violation of the continuing fiduciary duty of confidentiality (founded in part on Texas Rule 1.05(b)(1)) as a result of the Press Release disclosure of confidential client information was clear in some respects and not in others. As explained above, *see supra* Part II.D, the Court's conclusions about the scope of the continuing fiduciary duty of confidentiality are based in no small measure on the language of Texas Rule 1.05. There is a dearth of Texas judicial authority, however, about whether disclosure by an attorney of matters concerning a former client is a revelation of confidential information when the matters are included in court pleadings the attorney filed on behalf of that client.... Therefore, to the extent the information in the Press Release was a matter of public record in the State Suit, the Attorney's fiduciary duty violation is not "clear" under *Burrow*.

...

... It is permissible and equitable to award a forfeiture only if the violation was both "clear" and "serious." *See Burrow*, 997 S.W.2d at 240–41. The Attorney's breach of fiduciary duty was serious insofar as he disclosed in the Press Release the existence of the State Suit, the names of the parties, and the inflammatory allegations by the Client.

....

"[T]he remedy of forfeiture must fit the circumstances presented." *Id.* at 241. On balance, the Court cannot conclude that any component of the Attorney's violation of his fiduciary duty of continued confidentiality was both clear and serious. Some of the disclosures constitute ... clear but not serious violations of fiduciary duty, and some amounted to serious but not clear violations. In the exercise of the Court's broad discretion, *see id.* at 243, the Court concludes that the public interest in maintaining the integrity of attorney-client relationships is served by the conclusions herein that the Attorney breached a fiduciary duty to the Client, but not ordering a forfeiture.

Accordingly, although the Attorney had a fiduciary duty to the Client as his former client, and the Attorney breached that duty, the Client is not entitled to judgment on his breach of fiduciary duty claim. The Client has not shown that the Attorney's breach either resulted in injury to the Client or benefit to the Attorney, *see Kelly*, 181 S.W.3d at 414; *Punts*, 137 S.W.3d at 891, and has not shown entitlement to a forfeiture. The client thus has failed to prove the last element of his breach of fiduciary claim, and the Attorney is entitled to judgment in his favor.

....

Law Students and the Duty of Confidentiality. Lawyers are not the only persons that may owe fiduciary obligations to clients. Law students should remain aware that information obtained during summer employment or employment during law school may form the basis for breach of fiduciary duty actions. *See, e.g., La. Crisis Assistance Ctr. v. Marzano-Lesnevich*, 827 F. Supp. 2d 668 (E.D. La. 2011) (breach of fiduciary duty action brought against law clerk who disclosed confidential information acquired while working as an unpaid summer clerk while in law school); *see also* MODEL RULES OF PROF'L CONDUCT

R. 1.10 cmt. [4] (explaining that law students have a duty to avoid communication of confidential information to others).

3. Duty to Avoid Conflicts of Interest

Focus Questions: *So v. Suchanek*

1. *How does the* So *court define a conflict of interest?*
2. *When can a conflict of interest support a breach of fiduciary duty action?*
3. *What is the court's ruling regarding the appropriate measure of damages?*

So v. Suchanek

670 F.3d 1304
(D.C. Cir. 2012)

RANDOLPH, Senior Circuit Judge:

This case is here on appeal and cross-appeal from the judgment of the district court ordering attorney Leonard Suchanek to pay his former client Kevin So $455,933.52, an amount representing a portion of the legal fees Suchanek collected from So, plus interest.

So is a citizen of the People's Republic of China ... and the general manager of his family's cosmetics company. He does not speak, read, or write English. So met Lucy Yan Lu in 2004 through a business partner. Convinced of Lu's expertise, So granted her written authorization to serve as his agent in investment matters. In April 2005 Lu signed an agreement between So and Land Base, LLC, a California entity operated by Boris Lopatin. The agreement called for Land Base to make investments on So's behalf, and periodically to disburse to him fifty percent of any profits. Pursuant to the agreement, So transferred $30 million to a HSBC Bank account in London, England. An "Irrevocable Bank Instruction" appended to the agreement called for the funds to be administered by 5th Avenue Partners Ltd., a Land Base affiliate controlled by Michael Brown.

The investment initially appeared to be a success. So received nearly $3 million in profits between May and August of 2005. These "profits" turned out to be fictitious. As HSBC later discovered, Brown had been running a Ponzi scheme. So first learned this in early 2006. By that time, his $30 million investment had disappeared and HSBC had brought suit in London against Brown, Lu, So, and others seeking to absolve itself of any responsibility for the loss. HSBC alleged that the bank instruction was fraudulent; that Brown had used it to mislead So into thinking his deposit was secure; and that Land Base's agreement with So was "designed to lend an appearance of legitimacy to arrangements made for the purpose of money laundering or some other unlawful purpose."

Early in the litigation, Lopatin—who ran Land Base—referred Lu to Leonard Suchanek, a former administrative law judge with an office in Washington, D.C. Lu met with Suchanek in July 2006 and hired him to assist in recovering So's funds. She explained to So, through an intermediary, that Suchanek was a "very powerful U.S. judge" who was willing to help them "without any service fee." Lopatin provided a resume listing Suchanek's title as "Chief Judge Emeritus" of the "U.S. Federal Special

Contract Court" ... [a position from which he had] resigned in 1992 and entered private practice.)

Suchanek began representing Lu and So in July 2006 despite the fact that he was already representing Land Base in connection with the HSBC suit. While Suchanek was simultaneously representing Lu, So, and Land Base, he prepared a twelve-page legal opinion on Land Base's behalf. The opinion concluded that Land Base's agreements with So and other investors did not facilitate an "illegal scheme," and that any claim to the contrary was "frivolous." Suchanek terminated his representation of Land Base on August 24, 2006. He then sent an engagement letter to Lu and So on September 10, 2006, confirming that the representation had begun in July and that its scope included "obtaining compensation and damages due as the result of any wrong-doing against you that has been committed by any person, firm, [or] company." So paid Suchanek $99,000 shortly after receiving the letter.

Suchanek coordinated what he described as a "complex worldwide litigation" campaign on So's behalf. In this role, Suchanek served primarily as an administrator. He hired counsel to represent So in London, Hong Kong, New York, and several other jurisdictions, and managed So's communication with these firms, but did not appear in court on So's behalf. Suchanek also oversaw the campaign's finances, including payment of the various law firms and processing of sums recovered by them in the HSBC litigation—all through a trust account he maintained for So. In August 2007, Suchanek instructed So to wire $2.1 million to this account for litigation expenses.[1] So expressed reservations about the cost, describing it as "so much higher than my budget," but complied after Suchanek assured him a "minimum recovery" of $160 million.

So began to lose trust in Lu, his agent, just a few months into the joint representation. In December 2006, he informed Suchanek that Lu had attempted to fire Kendall Freeman, the law firm representing them in London, without his consent. And in February 2007, So complained that Lu had lied to Suchanek about So's willingness to pay for her share of the legal fees. These developments led So to contemplate cancelling Lu's authority to act as his agent. Suchanek encouraged So to "keep the status with [Lu] the same" despite her actions. He attempted to hold the relationship together by maintaining—or at least purporting to maintain—separate, confidential correspondence with Lu and So. The effort fell apart, however, when So notified Suchanek that Lu had falsified a witness statement bearing his name in August 2007 (the statement was prepared for use in the HSBC litigation). Suchanek responded by urging So to cut off Lu's authority, but continued to represent Lu and So jointly until January 31, 2008, when Suchanek terminated his representation of So.

At the conclusion of the representation, Suchanek held back $400,000 of the funds remaining in So's trust account for his "invoice." So objected, demanding that Suchanek remit the withheld funds to him and provide a full accounting. When Suchanek refused, So filed suit ... [for] breach of fiduciary duty [and other actions].

The district court conducted a bench trial and eventually winnowed the case down to a single claim for breach of fiduciary duty. On that claim, the court held that Suchanek had violated the District of Columbia Rules of Professional Conduct governing conflicts of interest—and thus breached his fiduciary duty to So—during two distinct periods. The first involved Suchanek's simultaneous representation of So and Land Base in July and August of 2006. The second arose from Suchanek's continued representation of Lu

1. Suchanek represented—as it turns out, falsely—that none of these funds would be used to pay for his services. Suchanek never sent So an invoice at any point in the representation.

and So after August 21, 2007, when So reported that Lu had falsified his witness statement. To remedy these breaches, the court ordered Suchanek to disgorge $400,000 plus interest, for a total of $455,933.52. The court reasoned that this amount was roughly equal to the sum Suchanek collected "during the two conflicted periods."

Suchanek seeks to have the judgment reversed. So's cross appeal seeks disgorgement of the rest of the approximately $1 million Suchanek covertly paid himself over the course of the representation....

I

Suchanek denies that he breached his fiduciary duty to So. Under District of Columbia law, a violation of the Rules of Professional Conduct "can constitute a breach of the attorney's common law fiduciary duty to the client." *Griva v. Davison,* 637 A.2d 830, 846–47 (D.C.1994). Although not every ethics violation rises to the level of a breach of fiduciary duty, a breach occurs "when an attorney represents clients with conflicting interests," *Hendry v. Pelland,* 73 F.3d 397, 401 (D.C. Cir.1996).

Rule 1.7 provides the general rule governing conflicts. D.C. Rules of Prof'l Conduct R. 1.7. It states, in relevant part, that a lawyer may not represent a client when the representation "will be or is likely to be adversely affected by representation of another client." *Id.* R. 1.7(b)(2). This prohibition is conditional, and ceases to apply when two criteria are satisfied. *See id.* R. 1.7(c). First, each of the affected clients must provide informed consent "after full disclosure of the existence and nature of the possible conflict and the possible adverse consequences of [the joint] representation." *Id.* R. 1.7(c)(1). Second, the lawyer must "reasonably believe[ ]" that he "will be able to provide competent and diligent representation to each affected client." *Id.* R. 1.7(c)(2). "The underlying premise" of these restrictions "is that disclosure and informed consent are required [whenever] ... there is any reason to doubt the lawyer's ability to provide wholehearted and zealous representation...." *Id.* R. 1.7 cmt. 7. Thus, "if an objective observer would have any reasonable doubt on that issue, the client has a right to disclosure of all relevant considerations and the opportunity to be the judge of its own interests." *Id.*

The district court correctly held that Suchanek violated Rule 1.7 by simultaneously representing So and Land Base in July and August of 2006. During that period, Suchanek never advised So that he might have claims against Land Base. Yet So's agreement with Land Base was a but-for cause of So's loss, and the Land Base agreement made certain warranties against any loss to the $30 million So initially deposited in the HSBC account. As the district court found, "Suchanek could not have advised So to pursue his warranty claims against Land Base ... without violating his obligations to Land Base."

Suchanek also prepared the Land Base opinion while he was representing Land Base and So. The opinion, which was filed as an attachment to Lopatin's witness statement in the HSBC litigation, undercut any claims So might have had against Land Base by concluding that the Land Base agreements did not facilitate an unlawful scheme. *See* D.C. Rules of Prof'l Conduct R. 1.7 cmt. 13 (stating that a conflict exists when "there is a significant risk that a lawyer's action on behalf of one client ... will adversely affect the lawyer's effectiveness in representing another"). Under these circumstances, Suchanek's representation of Land Base clearly compromised his representation of So. And, because Suchanek could not have "reasonably believe[d]" that he was capable of "provid[ing] competent and diligent representation to each affected client," he breached his fiduciary duty to So.

The district court's analysis of the second conflict period, between August 2007 and January 2008, is also sound. Before August 2007, So regularly informed Suchanek that Lu was undermining him, often by acting outside the scope of her authorization. Then, on

August 21, 2007, So notified Suchanek that Lu had falsified a witness statement bearing his name. These developments would have caused an objective observer to doubt whether Suchanek could continue to "wholeheartedly and zealously" represent both So and Lu. Suchanek recognized the gravity of Lu's transgression, describing it as "very serious," and even recommended that So immediately terminate Lu's authority to act on his behalf. He also told So that a court order issued in the HSBC litigation was "based upon misrepresentations by [Lu]." Yet he continued the joint representation, without making any effort to secure So's informed consent, in clear contravention of his ethical and fiduciary duties.

....

II

On cross-appeal, So contends that the district court erred in ordering disgorgement of only some of the fees Suchanek collected. Total disgorgement is required, So maintains, because Suchanek's conflicts of interest were not limited to the two periods identified by the district court.... The sources of these conflicts included Suchanek's personal interests, those of his assistant, Mira Meltzer, and Suchanek's representation of several other parties involved in the HSBC litigation.

Disgorgement is an equitable remedy entrusted to the sound discretion of the district court. *See United States v. Nacchio,* 573 F.3d 1062, 1080 (10th Cir.2009). Here, the district court misapplied Rule 1.7—and thus abused its discretion—when it held that Suchanek had a conflict of interest only during the two periods described above.

... Suchanek claims that he did not initially perceive a conflict between Lu and So, but we are not concerned with his subjective impressions. Under Rule 1.7, the question is whether there was "any reason to doubt [Suchanek's] ability to provide wholehearted and zealous representation" to both Lu and So. D.C. RULES OF PROF'L CONDUCT R. 1.7 cmt. 7. This depends on whether an objective observer—with Suchanek's prior knowledge of Lopatin, Land Base, and the particulars of the fraudulent scheme—would have had a "reasonable doubt" of his ability to represent jointly a victim of the scheme and the person who got him involved in it in the first place. The answer, we think, is clearly yes.

....

We ... therefore remand the case to the district court for further review of the record and issuance of a supplemental remedy, greater than the amount already ordered. On remand, the district court should consider the conflict between Lu and So, as well as the variety of other serious conflicts of interest alleged in So's brief. The remedy it fashions should account for the full extent of the conflicts found; the need to deter attorney misconduct; the "fundamental principle of equity ... that fiduciaries should not profit from their disloyalty"; and the decreased value of the services provided to So resulting from Suchanek's rampant misconduct. *Hendry,* 73 F.3d at 402; *see also* RESTATEMENT (THIRD) OF THE LAW GOVERNING LAWYERS § 37 cmt. e (2000) ("Ordinarily, forfeiture extends to all fees for the matter for which the lawyer was retained....").

* * *

Although most courts recognize a breach of fiduciary duty action as arising in tort law, not all courts do. For example, in *Doe v. Roe,* 289 Ill. App. 3d 116 (1997), plaintiff sued defendant attorney and his law firm for breach of fiduciary duty and other actions, claiming that the defendant attorney coerced her into a sexual relationship with him while representing her in a divorce proceeding:

... The plaintiff was involved in an emotionally trying divorce that included ongoing concerns over the custody of her child. In Spring of 1983, she was introduced to the defendant, who assured her that he could represent her more effectively than the attorney she had engaged. The defendant also promised to help secure a rapid settlement of her case. Based upon these statements, the plaintiff engaged the defendant, and in July of 1983, paid him a retainer of $7,500. The defendant did not furnish the plaintiff with a written fee agreement, but orally stated that any additional legal fees would be borne by her husband, who was believed to possess substantial assets. The plaintiff alleged that she lacked significant financial resources and would not have employed or continued to employ the defendant had she known that she would be required to pay additional attorney fees.

... During one of the plaintiff's initial visits to the defendant's office, the defendant began making unwanted sexual advances towards her.... she submitted to the defendant's sexual demands out of fear that he would discontinue or compromise his representation of her if she did not comply and because she could not afford to pay the retainer for another attorney. Thereafter, the defendant made repeated sexual demands on the plaintiff. According to the plaintiff, she continued to engage in sexual relations with the defendant because she had become very dependent upon him for legal as well as emotional support.

....

In June 1985, while the parties were in court awaiting a hearing, the defendant presented the plaintiff with a proposed settlement agreement, and instructed her to sign the document without apprising her of its terms. The plaintiff contended that she did so, unaware that it included provisions enabling the defendant to procure a $2,500 judgment against her for his fees and granting the defendant a lien on her home as security. On July 30, 1985, the defendant obtained the judgment against the plaintiff.

....

When the plaintiff subsequently began having difficulty enforcing the terms of her dissolution judgment, the defendant agreed to represent her on the "same terms" as in the past.... the plaintiff interpreted this statement as a demand for her continuance of sexual relations. The plaintiff terminated her employment of the defendant in early 1989, and commenced the instant action.

The court denied her causes of action against the attorney and his firm.

Doe v. Roe, 289 Ill. App. 3d 116, 121–22 (1997). The court explained that "the mere fact that an attorney may have violated professional ethics does not, of itself give rise to a cause of action for damages." It further clarified that in Illinois, a "breach of fiduciary duty is not a tort, [but] rather it is governed by the substantive law of contracts." Can you see why the theory of recovery—be it in tort or in contract—might matter to the parties involved? Briefly make a chart illustrating how the theory of recovery might impact a plaintiff's or a defendant's case.

* * *

B. Breach of Fiduciary Duties Owed to Partners, Associates, and the Firm

So far, we have been focusing on lawyers' fiduciary obligations owed to their clients. However, in the practice of law, lawyers may owe fiduciary obligations to persons other than their clients. For example, in working at a law firm, a lawyer may owe fiduciary obligations to partners or associates working at the firm or even to the firm itself. Consider the following case.

Focus Questions: *Starr v. Fordham*

1. *Do partners at law firms owe fiduciary obligations to other partners at the firm? To the firm itself?*
2. *How does the* Starr *court characterize such fiduciary obligations, if any?*

Starr v. Fordham

648 N.E.2d 1261
(Mass. 1995)

NOLAN, Justice.

The plaintiff, Ian M. Starr, was a partner in the Boston law firm Fordham & Starrett (firm). After the plaintiff withdrew from the firm, he commenced this action to recover amounts to which he claimed that he was entitled under the partnership agreement. The plaintiff also sought damages for breach of fiduciary duty and [other claims]. The defendants, his former partners at the firm, counterclaimed that the plaintiff had violated his fiduciary duties to his partners and breached the terms of the partnership agreement.

After a jury-waived trial, a Superior Court judge concluded that Fordham, P.C., and Starrett, P.C. (founding partners), had violated their fiduciary duties to the plaintiff ... when they determined the plaintiff's share of the firm's profits for 1986. The judge awarded the plaintiff damages of $75,538.48.... The judge also found that Fordham, in his individual capacity, had misrepresented to the plaintiff the basis on which the founding partners would allocate the firm's profits among the partners.... Finally, the judge entered judgment for the plaintiff on the defendants' counterclaims.

The plaintiff appeals from the judge's entry of judgment against him on his claim ... The founding partners and Attorneys Fordham and Starrett, in their individual capacities, cross appeal from the judge's finding that they violated their fiduciary duties ... We affirm.

... In 1984, the plaintiff was a partner in the Boston law firm Foley, Hoag & Eliot (Foley Hoag). The plaintiff specialized in corporate and business law. Although the plaintiff had become a partner at Foley Hoag in 1982, he was actively seeking to leave the firm in early 1984. During this time, the founding partners were also partners at Foley Hoag. Both men enjoyed outstanding professional reputations among their colleagues. Nevertheless, they agreed that they would withdraw from Foley Hoag in early 1985 in order to establish a new law firm with another established Boston attorney, Frank W. Kilburn.

Fordham invited the plaintiff to join the new law firm Kilburn, Fordham & Starrett in January, 1985. At first, the plaintiff was somewhat hesitant to accept the offer because he was not known as a "rainmaker" (i.e., an attorney responsible for significant client origination) at Foley Hoag. Fordham, however, assured the plaintiff that business origination would not be a significant factor for allocating the profits among the partners. Relying on this representation, the plaintiff withdrew from Foley Hoag on March 1, 1985. [The founding partners] withdrew from Foley Hoag on March 4, 1985.

Prior to executing the partnership agreement, the plaintiff informed Fordham that certain provisions in the agreement disturbed him.... Fordham summarily dismissed the plaintiff's concerns, telling him, in effect, to "take it or leave it." On March 5, 1985, the founding partners, Kilburn, and LeClair each executed the partnership agreement for Kilburn, Fordham & Starrett. The plaintiff also signed the agreement without objection and without making any revisions. The defendant Barry A. Guryan joined the new firm on March 11, 1985.

... Subsequently, the firm assumed the name Fordham & Starrett. In September, 1985, the partners met to consider entering into a ten-year lease for office space.... [T]he partners agreed to enter into the lease.

The founding partners had divided the firm's profits equally among the partners in 1985. Each of the five partners received $11,602. In 1986, the firm's financial fortunes improved significantly. On December 31, 1986, the firm's profits were $1,605,128. In addition, the firm had $1,844,366.59 in accounts receivable and work in progress.

The plaintiff withdrew from the firm on December 31, 1986.... The founding partners determined the plaintiff's share of the firm's profits for 1986 to be 6.3% of the total profits. In allocating the firm's profits among the partners, the founding partners did not consider any of the firm's accounts receivable or work in process. In addition, the founding partners refused to assign any of the firm's accounts receivable or work in process to the plaintiff when he withdrew from the firm. The founding partners claimed that the express provisions of Paragraph 3 of the partnership agreement barred the plaintiff from recovering any share of his accounts receivable or work in process because the firm's liabilities exceeded its gross accounts receivable and work in process.

... [A] judge's finding is not to be set aside "unless clearly erroneous, and due regard shall be given to the opportunity of the trial court to judge of the credibility of the witnesses." We apply this standard both to findings of subsidiary facts and to ultimate findings.

....

Partners owe each other a fiduciary duty of the highest degree of good faith and fair dealing. When a partner has engaged in self-dealing, that partner has the burden to prove the fairness of his actions and to prove that his actions did not result in harm to the partnership. In the present case, it is clear that the judge concluded that the founding partners had engaged in self-dealing. The judge found that the founding partners' determination of the plaintiff's share of the profits "positioned them on both sides of the transaction" because the percentage of the profits which they had assigned to the plaintiff had a direct impact on their own share of the profits. We cannot say that this conclusion was clearly erroneous. The founding partners were responsible for dividing the partnership's profits and assigning to each partner his respective share of the profits. Thus, the founding partners had some self-interest in designating each partner's respective share of the profits because the percentage of profits which they were assigning to the other partners had a direct effect on their own percentage of the profits. As a result, we conclude that there was no error in the judge's imposing on the founding partners the burden of proving that their distribution of the firm's profits to the plaintiff was fair and reasonable.

....

... The founding partners argue that the judge's conclusion that they had violated both their fiduciary duties ... when they allocated only 6.3% of the firm's profits for 1986 to the plaintiff was clearly erroneous. We disagree.

[A]n unfair determination of a partner's respective share of a partnership's earnings is a breach ... of one's fiduciary duty.... A court has the power to determine whether a partner's share of the profits is fair and equitable as a matter of law. In the present case, the judge "vigorously scrutinized" the founding partners' determination of the plaintiff's share of the profits. The judge then made extensive findings concerning the fairness of the plaintiff's share of the profit distribution. The judge found that the plaintiff had produced billable hour and billable dollar amounts that constituted 16.4% and 15%, respectively, of the total billable hour and billable dollar amounts for all of the partners as a group. The judge noted, however, that the founding partners distributed only 6.3% of the firm's 1986 profits to the plaintiff. Meanwhile, the other partners received substantially greater shares of the profits.[4] The judge concluded, therefore, that the founding partners had decided to exclude billable hour and billable dollar totals as a factor in determining compensation. The judge determined that this decision to exclude billable hour figures was unfair to the plaintiff and indicated that the founding partners had selected performance criteria in order to justify the lowest possible payment to the plaintiff. The judge also noted that Fordham had fabricated a list of negative factors that the founding partners had used in determining the plaintiff's share of the firm's profits. As a result, the judge concluded that the founding partners had violated their respective fiduciary duties to the plaintiff....[6] The judge also concluded that the plaintiff was entitled to 11% of the firm's profits for 1986 and awarded the plaintiff damages.

Having examined the record, all 127 exhibits, and the judge's own findings of fact and rulings of law, we conclude that the judge's ultimate finding of liability was not clearly erroneous.... We cannot conclude that the judge committed a mistake in finding that the founding partners had violated ... their fiduciary duties....

....

Judgment affirmed.

* * *

---

4. The plaintiff received $101,025.60. Meanwhile, the defendants Guryan and LeClair each received 18.75% ($301,025.60) of the firm's total profits. As a result, each of the managing partners kept for himself a 28.1% share of the profits, or $451,025.60 each. The judge did note, however, that the founding partners were not unfair in allocating to the plaintiff 7.2% of the firm's expenses in 1986.

6. The judge noted that Fordham and Starrett were the sole shareholders of Fordham, P.C., and Starrett, P.C., respectively. As the sole shareholders of a corporate general partner, the judge concluded that Fordham and Starrett were personally liable for the breaches of fiduciary duty by the founding partners.

C. Breach of Fiduciary Duties to "Non-Clients"

In addition to obligations owed to clients and members of their firms, lawyers may also find themselves in the position of owing fiduciary duties to others outside of the official (or even intended) attorney-client relationship. Lawyers practicing law believing that they can be single-mindedly devoted only to their clients do so at their peril. Consider the following case.

Focus Questions: *Fassihi v. Sommers, Schwartz, Silver, Schwartz & Tyler, P.C.*

1. *How does the court define the relationship between the plaintiff and the defendant's attorneys in* Fassihi?
2. *May a "non-client" impose liability for breach of fiduciary duty against an attorney? If so, what is the basis for liability and when may liability be imposed?*

Fassihi v. Sommers, Schwartz, Silver, Schwartz & Tyler, P.C.

309 N.W.2d 645
(Mich. Ct. App. 1981)

Per Curiam.

... In his complaint, plaintiff asserted that he was a 50% shareholder, officer, and director of Livonia Physicians X-Ray, P.C., a professional medical corporation. The various allegations included breach of the attorney-client relationship, breach of fiduciary, legal, and ethical duties, fraud, and legal malpractice. Defendant filed a motion for summary judgment on the basis that ... no attorney-client relationship existed with plaintiff....

Following the trial court's order denying defendant's motion for summary judgment, plaintiff deposed attorney Donald Epstein. However, during the deposition Epstein repeatedly refused to answer questions, claiming an attorney-client privilege. Plaintiff moved for an order compelling discovery, but the trial court denied the motion.... This order also extended to both parties the opportunity to take an interlocutory appeal from the denial of their respective motion.

This Court granted leave to take the interlocutory appeals....

The following factual recitation comes from plaintiff's complaint and the statement of facts appearing in his brief. [W]e are obligated to consider the facts in the light most favorable to the nonmoving party when passing on a motion for summary judgment....

In the summer of 1973, plaintiff, a radiologist practicing medicine in Ohio, was asked by Dr. Rudolfo Lopez to come to Michigan and join him in the practice of radiology at St. Mary's Hospital in Livonia. In August, 1973, the doctors formed a professional corporation known as Livonia Physicians X-Ray. Each doctor owned 50% of the stock, was an employee of the corporation, and received an identical salary. Plaintiff contends that the by-laws adopted by the two shareholders made each of them a member of the Board of Directors and that the two of them constituted the entirety of the board. Dr. Lopez was president of the corporation, and Dr. Fassihi was the secretary-treasurer.

Shortly after the corporation was organized, plaintiff sought and obtained medical staff privileges at St. Mary's. For a period of approximately 18 months, the doctors practiced together at the hospital in the radiology department.

Some time on or before June 4, 1975, Dr. Lopez decided that he no longer desired to be associated with plaintiff. Consequently, Lopez requested that the attorney for the professional corporation, the defendant, ascertain how plaintiff could be ousted from Livonia Physicians X-Ray.

On or about June 6, 1975, defendant's agent, Donald Epstein, Esquire, personally delivered to plaintiff a letter dated June 4, 1975, purporting to terminate his interest in the professional corporation. The letter stated that this termination followed a meeting of the board of directors.[2] Plaintiff denies that any such meeting ever occurred. On June 9, 1975, plaintiff went to St. Mary's to perform his duties as a staff radiologist. At this time officials at the hospital told him that, due to his "termination" from the professional corporation, he was no longer eligible to practice at St. Mary's.

Dr. Lopez had an agreement with St. Mary's Hospital prior to plaintiff's association with Livonia Physicians X-Ray giving him personal and sole responsibility for staffing the radiology department. This agreement necessitated membership in Livonia Physicians X-Ray, P.C.

Defendant was responsible for drafting all the agreements pertaining to membership in the professional corporation. Defendant, and specifically Donald Epstein, had knowledge of the arrangements between Dr. Lopez and the hospital but never disclosed these facts to plaintiff. Plaintiff finally states that defendant has represented both Lopez individually and the professional corporation without disclosing to him this dual representation.

This case presents us with the difficult question of what duties, if any, an attorney representing a closely held corporation has to a 50% owner of the entity, individually. This is a problem of first impression in Michigan.

We start our analysis by examining whether an attorney-client relationship exists between plaintiff and defendant....

A corporation exists as an entity apart from its shareholders, even where the corporation has but one shareholder. While no Michigan case has addressed whether a corporation's attorney has an attorney-client relationship with the entity's shareholders, the general proposition of corporate identity apart from its shareholders leads us to conclude, in accordance with decisions from other jurisdictions, that the attorney's client is the corporation and not the shareholders.

Although we conclude that no attorney-client relationship exists between plaintiff and defendant, this does not necessarily mean that defendant had no fiduciary duty to plaintiff. The existence of an attorney-client relationship merely establishes a per se rule that the lawyer owes fiduciary duties to the client.

---

2. Whether or not the by-laws of the professional corporation made Drs. Fassihi and Lopez the sole directors of the organization, Donald Epstein in a deposition contended that a Joseph Carolan was a third director. Mr. Carolan was apparently the business manager of Livonia Physicians X-Ray. We assume that at least defendant considers him a proper director. Otherwise, it would have been impossible for Lopez to effect his scheme of terminating Fassihi's association with the professional corporation as Fassihi would have undoubtedly opposed the plan. In any case, a corporate arrangement whereby one 50% shareholder can oust the other 50% shareholder whether individually or with the assistance of a third director seems highly unusual and comes to us on a stipulated hypothetical for purposes of this appeal.

A fiduciary relationship arises when one reposes faith, confidence, and trust in another's judgment and advice. Where a confidence has been betrayed by the party in the position of influence, this betrayal is actionable, and the origin of the confidence is immaterial. Furthermore, whether there exists a confidential relationship apart from a well defined fiduciary category is a question of fact. Based upon the pleadings, we cannot say that plaintiff's claim is clearly unenforceable as a matter of law.

Plaintiff asserts that he reposed in defendant his trust and confidence and believed that, as a 50% shareholder in Livonia Physicians X-Ray, defendant would treat him with the same degree of loyalty and impartiality extended to the other shareholder, Dr. Lopez. In his complaint plaintiff states that he was betrayed in this respect. Specifically, plaintiff asserts that he was not advised of defendant's dual representation of the corporate entity and Dr. Lopez personally. Plaintiff also alleges that he was never informed of the contract between Lopez and St. Mary's which gave Lopez sole responsibility in the staffing of the radiology department and, more importantly, that defendant actively participated with Lopez in terminating plaintiff's association with the corporation and using the Lopez-St. Mary's contract to his detriment.

... Instances in which the corporation attorneys stand in a fiduciary relationship to individual shareholders are obviously more likely to arise where the number of shareholders is small. In such cases it is not really a matter of the courts piercing the corporate entity. Instead, the corporate attorneys, because of their close interaction with a shareholder or shareholders, simply stand in confidential relationships in respect to both the corporation and individual shareholders.[6]

....

... While defendant should have, and likely did, consider the effect that its relationship with Lopez might have on the representation of the corporation and incidentally plaintiff, as a 50% shareholder, officer, and director, it was not prohibited from representing both if its employees' independent professional judgment on behalf of either would not likely be adversely affected by representation of the other. Code of Professional Responsibility and Canons DR 5-105(C).[8]

Plaintiff's complaint does state a cause of action ... [W]e affirm the trial court's order denying summary judgment....

....

Affirmed in part, reversed in part and remanded for proceedings consistent with this opinion....

---

6. Although factually different, Prescott v. Coppage, 266 Md. 562, 296 A.2d 150 (1972), is illuminating in its discussion of an attorney's obligations to third parties apart from a specific attorney-client relationship. In Prescott, the Maryland court found that the attorney owed a duty to a preferred creditor on a third-party beneficiary theory. The question in any given case is whether, irrespective of an actual attorney-client relationship, plaintiff has pled sufficient allegations tending to show some legal duty on the part of the attorney to him personally.

8. To the extent the complaint alleges that defendants conspired with Dr. Lopez after plaintiff became a 50% shareholder of the corporation to use the Lopez-St. Mary's agreement to deprive him of the business opportunity he thought he had obtained, a cause of action is stated for breach of a fiduciary duty. It is not the failure to divulge the existence of the Lopez-St. Mary's Hospital contract in the first instance which is the basis of the action, however. The cause of action arises because of defendant's fiduciary duty to plaintiff and breach of this duty by covertly colluding with Dr. Lopez to deprive plaintiff of the business opportunity.

Focus Questions: *Chem-Age Indus., Inc. v. Glover*

1. *According to the* Chem-Age Industries *court, might an attorney owe a fiduciary obligation to one who is not a client? If so, under what circumstances?*
2. *Under what conditions may an attorney be held liable for aiding and abetting another's breach of fiduciary duty?*

Chem-Age Indus., Inc. v. Glover

652 N.W.2d 756
(S.D. 2002)

KONENKAMP, Justice.

We are confronted with the question whether a lawyer who incorporates a business on behalf of an individual client owes any duty of care to the corporation thus created and to its director-investors who have no contractual relationship with the lawyer.... [T]he client misappropriated the investors' funds and gave some money and property to the lawyer. The investors and the corporation sued the lawyer, his client, and others to recover all the funds and property, alleging ... breach of fiduciary duty [and other actions]. The circuit court granted summary judgment to the lawyer on all issues, ruling, among other things, that no privity of contract existed between anyone other than the lawyer and his individual client. We conclude that there are material questions of fact on whether the lawyer ... knowingly assisted his client in breaching a fiduciary duty to the director-investors and the corporation. We affirm in part, reverse in part, and remand for trial.

A.
Background

In the past twenty years, attorney Alan F. Glover of Brookings, South Dakota, has represented Byron Dahl, a Watertown entrepreneur, in various transactions and lawsuits around the country. In March 1997, Dahl interested two Watertown businesspersons, Roger O. Pederson and Garry Shepard, in investing in a start-up firm, under the name Chem-Age Industries. Dahl would contribute equipment and expertise; Pederson, and, to a lesser extent, Shepard, would contribute capital. According to attorney Glover's deposition, Dahl had told him "that [Dahl] had basically started up a business in Watertown with the assistance of some people who had chosen to invest their money with him in this business." That is, Chem-Age as a brand new business did not preexist the agreement made by Dahl, Pederson, and Shepard.

Sometime during their business engagement (the exact timing is disputed), Pederson obtained a report from a private investigator warning him that Dahl was a "crook." According to Pederson, the report indicated that Dahl had done this all over the country....

Pederson executed two "Stock Agreements" and a "Subscription Agreement and Letter of Investment," and despite this report continued to invest thousands of dollars in Dahl's enterprise. According to the terms of the stock agreements as prepared by Dahl, Pederson was to receive 48 shares of common stock in exchange for his investments. Pederson had originally given Dahl $25,000, but both Pederson and Shepard wanted the business to be incorporated before they invested more money. They pressed Dahl to get an attorney involved to set up the corporation. At some point between March and October

1997, Pederson, Shepard, and Dahl decided that Chem-Age Industries would be incorporated under the name "Chem-Age Industries, Inc." Pederson and Shepard agreed to serve as incorporators and directors of the corporation; Dahl agreed to serve as chief executive officer. With this understanding, Dahl engaged Glover to draw up articles of incorporation.

Glover prepared the articles and faxed them, either to Dahl alone or to both Pederson and Shepard: the parties disagree on this point. In either case, Dahl secured the signatures of Pederson and Shepard. The articles were dated October 30, 1997. When Dahl delivered the signed articles to him, Glover notarized Pederson's and Shepard's signatures, despite the fact that they had not signed the document in his presence. On the same day, Glover signed a Consent of Registered Agent, agreeing to act as registered agent for "Chem-Age Industries, Inc." Soon thereafter, at Dahl's request, Glover filed the articles with the South Dakota Secretary of State. On November 6, 1997, the Secretary of State issued a Certificate of Incorporation. Glover then sent a letter to the company, attaching an application to obtain a federal tax identification number for the corporation.

....

In March 1998, Glover received a desk as a "gift" from Dahl. It was charged on the Chem-Age corporate credit card for $1,113. In August 1998, Sioux Valley Cooperative commenced a lawsuit against Chem-Age, Inc.; Glover was engaged as the attorney for the defendant in that case, serving and filing an answer and counterclaim on behalf of Chem-Age, Inc.

By early fall of 1998, Pederson and Shepard became suspicious that they were being swindled: Dahl had accumulated large balances on the company's credit cards for what appeared to be personal items. They engaged attorney John L. Foley of Watertown for legal advice. According to Foley's affidavit, a meeting was held in his office in October 1998. Present were plaintiffs Pederson and Shepard as well as defendants Glover and Dahl. At that meeting, Glover stated that he was representing "the corporation, Chem-Age Industries, Inc.," and that Dahl owned that entity....

On July 1, 1999, the Secretary of State sent to Glover, as agent of Chem-Age Industries, Inc., a Notice of Pending Administrative Dissolution. Glover was thereby notified that Chem-Age Industries, Inc., was delinquent in filing its annual report ... and that the corporation would be administratively dissolved if the report was not filed before September 13, 1999. After receiving this notice, Glover had separate conversations with Dahl and attorney Foley. Glover decided not to file the annual report, thus allowing an administrative dissolution. (Asserting attorney-client privilege, Glover did not reveal the substance of his conversation with Dahl, though his deposition testimony reveals that he made the decision not to file the report directly after his conversation with Dahl.) Glover did not notify directors Pederson and Shepard of his decision. The Secretary issued a Certificate of Administrative Dissolution on September 19, 1999.

A year later, in apparent preparation for suit, new counsel obtained a legal reinstatement of the corporation with the Secretary of State. Thereafter, ... plaintiffs Chem-Age Industries, Inc., Pederson, and Shepard sued Dahl, Glover, and certain others who were later released by stipulation. Dahl was scheduled to give a deposition on May 3, 2001, but he failed to appear.... Glover moved for summary judgment on all claims against him. Plaintiffs, in turn, moved for summary judgment on two questions: whether Glover owed them a duty, and whether he had breached a fiduciary duty to them. The trial court denied plaintiffs' motion and granted summary judgment to Glover on all plaintiffs' claims.

Plaintiffs now appeal [several issues including whether attorney Glover breached a fiduciary duty owed to plaintiffs or whether attorney Glover may be liable for aiding and abetting a breach of fiduciary duty].

....

E.
Breach of Fiduciary Duty

1. Direct Breach of Fiduciary Duty to Nonclients

[T]here remains a question of material fact whether an attorney-client relationship existed between Glover and Chem-Age Industries, Inc. If such a relationship did exist, then Glover owed a fiduciary duty to the corporation. If, in turn, Glover had such a fiduciary duty, then there remains a question of material fact whether Glover breached that duty. A fiduciary duty to the corporation, in that circumstance, would arise from the attorney-client relationship.

We earlier found that no attorney-client relationship existed between Glover and the two investor-directors, Pederson and Shepard. We now turn to the question whether Glover may have owed a fiduciary duty to them or to the corporation, even in the absence of an attorney-client relationship. The existence and scope of a fiduciary duty are questions of law. Whether a breach of a fiduciary duty occurred, however, is a question of fact.

To ascertain a fiduciary duty, we must find three things: (1) plaintiffs reposed "faith, confidence and trust" in Glover, (2) plaintiffs were in a position of "inequality, dependence, weakness, or lack of knowledge" and, (3) Glover exercised "dominion, control or influence" over plaintiffs' affairs. *Garrett v. BankWest Inc.*, 459 N.W.2d 833, 838 (S.D.1990) (citing *Union State Bank v. Woell*, 434 N.W.2d 712, 721 (N.D.1989)). "Fiduciary relationships juxtapose trust and dependence on one side with dominance and influence on the other." *High Plains Genetics Research, Inc.*, 535 N.W.2d at 842. To recover for breach of fiduciary duty, a plaintiff must prove: (1) that the defendant was acting as plaintiff's fiduciary; (2) that the defendant breached a fiduciary duty to plaintiff; (3) that plaintiff incurred damages; and (4) that the defendant's breach of the fiduciary duty was a cause of plaintiff's damages.

We have always recognized the lawyer-client relationship as highly fiduciary. In South Dakota, however, we have not extended a cause of action for breach of fiduciary duty to instances involving lawyers and nonclients, but other jurisdictions have opened the door to this claim. In those cases, when attorneys breach a fiduciary duty to nonclients, liability typically arises when a trust or guardianship beneficiary sues the trust or guardianship attorney for failing to prevent the misappropriation and mismanagement of the estate.[9]

---

9. The Restatement (Third) of the Law Governing Lawyers § 51 defines a lawyer's duties to a nonclient, when the lawyer's client is a fiduciary:

> For purposes of liability under § 48, a lawyer owes a duty to use care within the meaning of § 52 in *each* of the following circumstances:
> (4) to a nonclient when and to the extent that:
> (a) the lawyer's client is a trustee, guardian, executor, or fiduciary acting primarily to perform similar functions for the nonclient;
> (b) the lawyer knows that appropriate action by the lawyer is necessary with respect to a matter within the scope of the representation to prevent or rectify the breach of fiduciary duty owed by the client to the nonclient, where (i) the breach is a crime or fraud or (ii) the lawyer has assisted or is assisting the breach;
> (c) the nonclient is not reasonably able to protect its rights; and
> (d) such a duty would not significantly impair the performance of the lawyer's obligations to the client.

RESTATEMENT (THIRD) OF THE LAW GOVERNING LAWYERS § 51(4) (1998).

But liability also occurs in the corporate sphere. *Collins v. Telcoa Intern. Corp.*, 283 A.D.2d 128, 726 N.Y.S.2d 679 (2nd Dept. 2001) (allegations by minority shareholder that corporation's attorney had duty to act responsibly to protect shareholder's interests adequately stated cause of action for attorney's breach of fiduciary duty); *Fassihi v. Sommers, Schwartz, Silver, Schwartz & Tyler*, 107 Mich.App. 509, 309 N.W.2d 645, 648 (1981) (question of fact existed whether confidential relationship existed between the two shareholders of a closely-held corporation and the corporation's attorney, even if no attorney-client relationship existed between them). *But see Angel, Cohen & Rogovin v. Oberon Inv., N.V.*, 512 So.2d 192 (Fla.1987).

Plaintiffs Pederson and Shepard have submitted no evidence to show how they were in a confidential relationship with Glover, where they depended on him specifically to protect their investment interests, and where Glover exercised dominance and influence over their business affairs. On the contrary, they never consulted with Glover during the time he is alleged to have breached a fiduciary duty to them. Aside from simple avowals that they believed Glover was watching out for their interests, their claim that Glover was entrusted with explicit responsibility for their investments is "factually unsupported." *Celotex*, 477 U.S. 317, 323–324. Likewise for the corporation: outside the existence of an attorney-client relationship, we detect no facts justifying a fiduciary duty owed to the company. We conclude that there was no direct fiduciary relationship between Glover and plaintiffs.

2. Aiding and Abetting Breach of Fiduciary Duty

Although he may not have directly breached a fiduciary duty, if Glover assisted Dahl in a breach of Dahl's fiduciary duty, Glover may still be subject to liability. Plaintiffs' complaint alleges that both Dahl and Glover breached their fiduciary duties. The Restatement provides:

> For harm resulting to a third person from the tortious conduct of another, one is subject to liability if he knows that the other's conduct constitutes a breach of duty and gives substantial assistance or encouragement to the other so to conduct himself.

Restatement (Second) of Torts § 876(b) (1977). *See also* SDCL 15-8-11 (defining joint tortfeasor). Several courts recognize a cause of action for aiding and abetting the breach of fiduciary duty. *See, e.g., Blow v. Shaughnessy*, 88 N.C.App. 484, 364 S.E.2d 444 (N.C.App.1988); *Holmes v. Young*, 885 P.2d 305, 308 (Colo.App.1994) (claim against attorney for aiding and abetting the breach of fiduciary duty in the partnership context). When they participate in their clients' tortious acts, lawyers are not exempt from liability under this theory.

Legal authorities ... are unanimous in expressing the proposition that one who knowingly aids another in the breach of a fiduciary duty is liable to the one harmed thereby. That principle readily extends to lawyers....

In *Granewich* [*v. Harding*, 329 Or. 47, 985 P.2d 788, 793–94 (1999)] the defendant attorneys provided substantial assistance to the controlling shareholders to squeeze out the minority shareholder in breach of the fiduciary duties the majority shareholders owed to the minority shareholder. Unlike the fraud allegations against Glover, which require proof of misrepresentations, liability for aiding and abetting breach of a fiduciary duty requires only the giving of substantial assistance and encouragement. *See* Restatement (Second) of Torts § 876 cmt. b (1979) (one who gives advice or encouragement to a tortfeasor is also a tortfeasor).

Dahl, as the operating officer of the corporation, owed a fiduciary duty to the company and to its investors. Like controlling shareholders, officers and directors possessing discretion in the management of a company have a fiduciary duty "to use their ability to control the corporation in a fair, just, and equitable manner...." *Jones v. H.F. Ahmanson & Co.,* 1 Cal.3d 93, 81 Cal.Rptr. 592, 460 P.2d 464, 471 (1969). For summary judgment purposes, the evidence that Dahl breached his fiduciary duties to the corporation and the investor-directors remains wholly uncontradicted. He used corporate funds for personal expenditures; he failed to deliver promised stock issues; he sold corporate assets and kept the proceeds. Now the question is whether his lawyer may be subject to liability for assisting Dahl in his breach of fiduciary duties.

Holding attorneys liable for aiding and abetting the breach of a fiduciary duty in rendering professional services poses both a hazard and a quandary for the legal profession. On the one hand, overbroad liability might diminish the quality of legal services, since it would impose "self protective reservations" in the attorney-client relationship. *Goodman v. Kennedy,* 18 Cal.3d 335, 134 Cal.Rptr. 375, 556 P.2d 737, 743 (1976). Attorneys acting in a professional capacity should be free to render advice without fear of personal liability to third persons if the advice later goes awry. On the other hand, the privilege of rendering professional services not being absolute, lawyers should not be free to substantially assist their clients in committing tortious acts. To protect lawyers from meritless claims, many courts strictly interpret the common law elements of aiding and abetting the breach of a fiduciary duty.

The substantial assistance requirement carries with it a condition that the lawyer must actively participate in the breach of a fiduciary duty. *See Spinner v. Nutt,* 417 Mass. 549, 631 N.E.2d 542, 546 (1994) (allegation that trustees acted under legal advice of defendants, without more, is insufficient to give rise to claim that attorney is responsible to third persons for fraudulent acts of clients); *Schatz v. Rosenberg,* 943 F.2d 485, 487 (4thCir.1991) (attorney's liability for aiding and abetting a breach of duty under federal securities law). Merely acting as a scrivener for a client is insufficient. A plaintiff must show that the attorney defendant rendered "substantial assistance" to the breach of duty, not merely to the person committing the breach. *Id. See also Witzman,* 601 N.W.2d at 188 ("substantial assistance" means more than providing routine professional services). In *Granewich,* the lawyers facilitated the squeeze-out, not just by providing legal advice and drafting documents, but by sending letters containing misrepresentations and helping to amend by-laws eliminating voting requirements that protected the minority shareholder's interest.

Another condition to finding liability for assisting in the breach of a fiduciary duty is the requirement that the assistance be "knowing." RESTATEMENT (SECOND) OF TORTS § 874 cmt. c (1979). Knowing participation in a fiduciary's breach of duty requires both knowledge of the fiduciary's status as a fiduciary and knowledge that the fiduciary's conduct contravenes a fiduciary duty. Although in some instances actual knowledge may be required, constructive knowledge will often suffice. Constructive knowledge is adequate when the aider and abettor has maintained a long-term or in-depth relationship with the fiduciary.

In accordance with these principles, we hold that to establish a cause of action for aiding or assisting in the breach of a fiduciary duty, a plaintiff must prove that (1) the fiduciary breached an obligation to plaintiff; (2) defendant substantially assisted the fiduciary in the achievement of the breach; (3) defendant knew that the fiduciary's conduct constituted a breach of duty; and (4) damages were sustained as a result of the breach. *See Holmes v. Young,* 885 P.2d 305, 309 (Colo.Ct.App.1994) (attorney's substantial assistance is the gravamen of aiding and abetting breach of fiduciary duty (citation omitted)); *Witzman,* 601 N.W.2d at 187–188 (accountant liability) (citing RESTATEMENT (SECOND) OF TORTS § 876(b) (1977)).

Glover recounts that shortly after incorporation, Dahl told him that the two investors, Pederson and Shepard, had decided not to proceed and that the business would be solely controlled by Dahl as a proprietorship. Because no shares were issued, Glover took the position that the company had no official existence. But we think that what Glover actually knew and what he should have known are questions of credibility. After all, Glover notarized Pederson's and Shepard's signatures on corporate documents without having them in his presence. If he did not know his client was in the midst of a swindle, he certainly knew Dahl had several questionable investment schemes in the past, leaving unhappy investors in his wake. Thus his decision to notarize these signatures may or may not have been an altogether innocuous act. Perhaps if Glover had met with Pederson and Shepard at that time, instead of simply notarizing their signatures unseen, and heard their expectations, he could have disabused them of any misunderstanding or encouraged them to seek independent legal advice. Pederson and Shepard allege that this was part of a pattern in which Glover allowed Dahl to use his legal services as a means to allow Dahl to misappropriate investor funds. The creation of a corporation with the assistance of an attorney gave a patina of authenticity to Dahl's otherwise rogue activities. Moreover, Glover listed himself as registered agent for the company. Pederson and Shepard claim that they began investing more heavily once they learned the company had been incorporated and an attorney was onboard. They say that they felt reassured upon incorporation that the business would proceed with all the formalities required of corporations.

Four months after the business was incorporated, Glover received a "gift" of office furniture from Dahl, bought with the company credit card. Glover claimed he did not know how the furniture was paid for. Accepting such a "gift" from a client like Dahl, who Glover knew had longstanding financial problems, raises a question of constructive knowledge and exposes the problem of improper, personal financial gain in assisting Dahl.

We think it also significant that Glover assisted Dahl in selling assets that were obtained with investor funds in the corporation. In a meeting with the investors and their lawyer, Glover was present when Dahl assured the investors that upon the sale, they would be receiving their money back. The next month, with Glover's help, the company's assets were sold to a Wisconsin business. Dahl and Glover had taken the position that Chem-Age Industries, Inc., was not a corporation but a proprietorship owned solely by Dahl. Yet Glover helped to arrange the sale of Chem-Age assets through another entity: "Byron Dahl d/b/a BMD Associates, a South Dakota sole proprietorship." Glover later testified that he did not know the relationship between BMD and Chem-Age.

Although Glover may not have taken any active role in defrauding the investor-directors and may not have owed any direct fiduciary duty to them, Dahl did owe such a duty, and a material question of fact exists on whether Glover substantially assisted Dahl in breaching that duty. It may be that Glover, as much as Pederson and Shepard, was duped by Dahl's conniving business dealings, but that is for a jury to decide.

....

* * *

1. Aiding and Abetting Breach of Fiduciary Duty. As discussed in *Chem-Age Industries, supra*, lawyers must be careful not to assist a client in breaching the client's fiduciary responsibilities. In *Spinner v. Nutt*, 631 N.E.2d 542 (Mass. 1994), plaintiffs were beneficiaries of a testamentary trust having two trustees. Over ninety percent of the trust's value was comprised of stock in Salem News Publishing Company. The trustees received written offers for all the stock of the company for $42,000,000, but they could not agree to make the purchase. Subsequently, Salem News Publishing Company's value was substantially reduced, and the plaintiffs brought suit against the trustees' attorneys under several theories of recovery, including aiding and abetting a client's breach of fiduciary duty. The court affirmed dismissal of the plaintiffs' claims after noting that "the plaintiff[s] must show that the defendant[s] knew of the breach and actively participated in it such that [they] could not reasonably be held to have acted in good faith." *Id.* at 546. "An allegation that the trustees acted under the legal advice of the defendant [attorneys], without more, is insufficient to give rise to a claim that an attorney is responsible to third persons for the fraudulent acts of his clients." *Id; see also Alleco Inc. v. Harry & Jeanette Weinberg Found. Inc.*, 665 A.2d 1038 (Md. 1995) (claim for aiding and abetting client's breach of fiduciary obligation precluded by failure to establish client's breach of fiduciary obligation).

2. For a thoughtful exploration of the increase of lawsuits against lawyers for aiding and abetting clients' breaches of fiduciary obligations, *see* Katerina P. Lewinbuk, *Let's Sue All the Lawyers: The Rise of Claims Against Lawyers for Aiding and Abetting a Client's Breach of Fiduciary Duty*, 40 Ariz. St. L.J. 135, 136 (2008) (exploring the "tremendous expansion of claims accusing attorneys of aiding and abetting their clients' breach of fiduciary duty"). Liability for aiding and abetting another's wrongful act is explored in greater detail in Chapter 17.

* * *

D. Remedies

The previous cases have discussed remedies available when a lawyer breaches his fiduciary obligations owed to his client, most often focusing on the appropriateness of disgorgement of the lawyer's fees. However, other remedies for breach of fiduciary duty may be more appropriate, depending on the circumstances, a subject that is explored in the next opinion.

Focus Questions: *Maritrans GP Inc. v. Pepper, Hamilton & Scheetz*

1. *Describe the factual basis of the attorney's alleged breach of fiduciary duty.*
2. *What remedy for breach of fiduciary duty are the plaintiffs seeking in* Maritrans?

Maritrans GP Inc. v. Pepper, Hamilton & Scheetz

602 A.2d 1277
(Pa. 1992)

PAPADAKOS, Justice.

This case involves the question of whether the conduct of Appellee-attorneys is actionable independent of any violation of the Code of Professional Responsibility. While we agree that violations of the Code do not *per se* give rise to legal actions that may be brought by clients or other private parties, we, nevertheless, conclude that the record supports a finding that Appellees' conduct here constituted a breach of common law fiduciary duty owed to Appellant-clients and that, contrary to Appellees' argument that they cannot be prevented from representing a former client's competitors, the injunction issued by the trial court against Appellees should have been sustained by the Superior Court. As a result, we reverse the decision of the Superior Court, as more fully explained below.

Appellants, plaintiffs in the trial court and appellees in the Superior Court, are Maritrans GP Inc., Maritrans Partners L.P. and Maritrans Operating Partners L.P. (hereinafter, collectively, "Maritrans"). Appellees, defendants in the trial court and appellants in the Superior Court, are the Philadelphia law firm of Pepper, Hamilton & Scheetz (hereinafter "Pepper"), and one of Pepper's partners, J. Anthony Messina, Jr. (hereinafter "Messina"). In February, 1988, Maritrans brought an action for preliminary and permanent injunctive relief, as well as for compensatory and punitive damages, against Pepper and Messina, its former attorneys of more than ten years. Maritrans' action arises out of Pepper and Messina's representation of Maritrans' competitors, entities whose interests were found to be adverse to the interests of Maritrans, in matters substantially related to matters in which they had represented Maritrans.

On May 1, 1989, the Court of Common Pleas of Philadelphia County entered an order preliminarily enjoining Pepper and Messina from continuing to act as labor counsel for seven of Maritrans' New York-based competitors, with the exception of one discrete piece of litigation then scheduled to commence on May 8, 1989. The trial court ruled that preliminary injunctive relief was necessary given the existence of a substantial relationship (*i.e.,* a conflict of interest in derogation of Pepper and Messina's fiduciary duties to Maritrans) between Pepper and Messina's current representation of the New York companies, whose interests were adverse to the interests of Maritrans, and their former longstanding representation of Maritrans. Pepper and Messina then moved in the trial court for a stay pending appeal, and certain of the New York competitors moved for leave to intervene in the action. Both motions were denied.

Pepper and Messina then appealed the trial court's preliminary injunction order ... reversing the preliminary injunction order. Maritrans' subsequent applications for a stay or an order restoring the preliminary injunction pending appeal were denied first by [a panel] of the Superior Court ... and then by Chief Justice Nix, Jr., acting as a single justice, and not on behalf of the Court, pursuant to Rule 123 of the Pennsylvania Rules of Appellate Procedure. The matter is now on full appeal to this Court. For the reasons explained below, we reverse.

The facts taken in a light most favorable to Maritrans, the winner at the trial court level, are as follows:

Maritrans is a Philadelphia-based public company in the business of transporting petroleum products along the East and Gulf coasts of the United States by tug and barge. Maritrans competes in the marine transportation business with other tug and/or barge companies, including a number of companies based in New York. Pepper is an old and established Philadelphia law firm. Pepper and Messina represented Maritrans or its predecessor companies in the broadest range of labor relations matters for well over a decade. In addition, Pepper represented Maritrans in a complex public offering of securities, a private offering of $115 million in debt, a conveyance of all assets, and a negotiation and implementation of a working capital line of credit. Over the course of the representation, Pepper was paid approximately $1 million for its labor representation of

Maritrans and, in the last year of the representation, approximately $1 million for its corporate and securities representation of Maritrans.

During the course of their labor representation of Maritrans, Pepper and Messina became "intimately familiar with Maritrans' operations" and "gained detailed financial and business information, including Maritrans' financial goals and projections, labor cost/savings, crew costs and operating costs." This information was discussed with Pepper's labor attorneys, and particularly with Messina, for the purpose of developing Maritrans' labor goals and strategies. In addition, during the course of preparing Maritrans' public offering, Pepper was furnished with substantial confidential commercial information in Maritrans' possession—financial and otherwise—including projected labor costs, projected debt coverage and projected revenues through the year 1994, and projected rates through the year 1990. Pepper and Messina, during the course of their decade-long representation of Maritrans, came to know the complete inner-workings of the company along with Maritrans' long-term objectives, and competitive strategies in a number of areas including the area of labor costs, a particularly sensitive area in terms of effective competition. In furtherance of its ultimate goal of obtaining more business than does its competition, including the New York-based companies, Maritrans analyzed each of its competitors with Pepper and Messina. These analyses included an evaluation of each competitor's strengths and weaknesses, and of how Maritrans deals with its competitors.

Armed with this information, Pepper and Messina subsequently undertook to represent several of Maritrans' New York-based competitors. Indeed, Pepper and Messina undertook to represent the New York companies in their labor negotiations, albeit with a different union, during which the New York companies sought wage and benefit reductions in order to compete more effectively with, *i.e.*, to win business away from, Maritrans.

In September, 1987, Maritrans learned from sources outside of Pepper that Pepper and Messina were representing four of its New York-based competitors in their labor relations matters. Maritrans objected to these representations, and voiced those objections to many Pepper attorneys, including Mr. Messina. Pepper and Messina took the position that this was a "business conflict," not a "legal conflict," and that they had no fiduciary or ethical duty to Maritrans that would prohibit these representations.

To prevent Pepper and Messina from taking on the representation of any other competitors, especially its largest competitor, Bouchard Transportation Company, Maritrans agreed to an arrangement proposed by Pepper whereby Pepper would continue as Maritrans' counsel but would not represent any more than the four New York companies it was then already representing. In addition, Messina—the Pepper attorney with the most knowledge about Maritrans—was to act not as counsel for Maritrans but, rather, as counsel for the New York companies, while two other Pepper labor attorneys would act as counsel for Maritrans; the attorneys on one side of this "Chinese Wall" would not discuss their respective representations with the attorneys on the other side. Maritrans represented that it agreed to this arrangement because it believed that this was the only way to keep Pepper and Messina from representing yet more of its competitors, especially Bouchard.

Unbeknownst to Maritrans, however, Messina then "parked" Bouchard and another of the competitors, Eklof, with Mr. Vincent Pentima, a labor attorney then at another law firm, at the same time that Messina was negotiating with Pentima for Pentima's admission into the partnership at Pepper. Moreover, notwithstanding Pepper's specific agreement not to represent these other companies, Messina for all intents and purposes was representing Bouchard and Eklof, as he was conducting joint negotiating sessions for those companies and his other four New York clients. On November 5, 1987, Maritrans executives discussed with Pepper attorneys, *inter alia,* Maritrans' plans and strategies of an aggressive nature in the event of a strike against the New York companies. Less than one month later, on December 2, 1987, Pepper terminated its representation of Maritrans in all matters. Later that month, on December 23, 1987, Pepper undertook the representation of the New York companies. Then, on January 4, 1988, Mr. Pentima joined Pepper as a partner and brought with him, as clients, Bouchard and Eklof. In February, 1988, Maritrans filed a complaint in the trial court against Pepper and Messina.

....

[T]he trial court determined that preliminary injunctive relief was both justified and appropriate.

... Concluding that Maritrans was entitled to be able to proceed in its business with confidence that its plans and strategies would not be disclosed or used by Appellees, even inadvertently, the trial court ruled that preliminary injunctive relief was warranted given the existence of material adversity between Maritrans and the New York competitors, of a substantial relationship between the representations, and the fact that Maritrans had carried its burden in proving the necessity for a preliminary injunction.

The Superior Court reversed stating that the trial court erred by issuing a preliminary injunction based upon Pepper's alleged violation of the [Pennsylvania] Rules of Professional Conduct without making any independent finding that Pepper's conduct was actionable. The Superior Court found that the trial court's use of Pennsylvania Rules of Professional Conduct 1.7 and 1.9 as points of reference for its breach of fiduciary duty analysis improperly augmented the substantive law of our Commonwealth. The Superior Court did not analyze whether the common law principles of fiduciary duty, embodied in those rules, nonetheless apply to this case. The Superior Court then held that an attorney's conflict of interest in representing a subsequent client whose interests are materially adverse to a prior client in a substantially related matter is not "actionable" in Pennsylvania. [W]e reverse.

The public's trust in the legal profession undoubtedly would be undermined if this Court does not correct the Superior Court's failure to recognize the common law foundation for the principle that an attorney's representation of a subsequent client whose interests are materially adverse to a former client in a matter substantially related to matters in which he represented the former client constitutes an impermissible conflict of interest actionable at law. The Superior Court's decision is diametrically opposed to law established by the courts of this Commonwealth and throughout the United States which have imposed civil liability on attorneys for breaches of their fiduciary duties by engaging in conflicts of interest, notwithstanding the existence of professional rules under which the attorneys also could be disciplined.

I.
Actionability and Independent Fiduciary Duty at Common Law of Avoiding Conflicts of Interest—Injunctive Relief

A preliminary injunction is a harsh remedy for which "essential prerequisites" must be proven. *See, e.g., Public Utility Commission v. Process Gas Consumers Group,* 502 Pa. 545, 467 A.2d 805 (1983). These are:

1) The Petitioner makes a strong showing that he is likely to prevail on the merits.

2) The Petitioner has shown that without the requested relief, he will suffer irreparable injury.

> 3) The issuance of a stay will not substantially harm other interested parties in the proceedings.
>
> 4) The issuance of a stay will not adversely affect the public interest.

502 Pa. at 552–553, 467 A.2d 805.

In *John G. Bryant, Inc. v. Sling Testing & Repair, Inc.*, 471 Pa. 1, 6–7, 369 A.2d 1164, 1166–67 (1977), we declared it "essential" that the "activity sought to be restrained is actionable."

Activity is actionable if it constitutes breach of a duty imposed by statute or by common law. Our common law imposes on attorneys the status of fiduciaries *vis a vis* their clients; that is, attorneys are bound, at law, to perform their fiduciary duties properly. Failure to so perform gives rise to a cause of action....

At common law, an attorney owes a fiduciary duty to his client; such duty demands undivided loyalty and prohibits the attorney from engaging in conflicts of interest, and breach of such duty is actionable. The Superior Court here emasculated these common law principles, in effect turning the ethical or disciplinary rules governing lawyers into a grant of civil immunity for conduct which has been condemned from time immemorial. As stated by the United States Supreme Court in 1850:

> There are few of the business relations of life involving a higher trust and confidence than those of attorney and client or, generally speaking, one more honorably and faithfully discharged; few more anxiously guarded by the law, or governed by sterner principles of morality and justice; and it is the duty of the court to administer them in a corresponding spirit, and to be watchful and industrious, to see that confidence thus reposed shall not be used to the detriment or prejudice of the rights of the party bestowing it.

Stockton v. Ford, 52 U.S. (11 How.) [232,] 247 [(1850)]. By ignoring the common law principles of fiduciary duty, the Superior Court elevated attorneys above the law and granted to them greater rights and protection than are enjoyed by any other fiduciaries in this Commonwealth. No rule so preferring attorneys can be permitted to stand.[3] Adherence to those fiduciary duties ensures that clients will feel secure that everything they discuss with counsel will be kept in confidence. Pepper and Messina, as attorneys, had a duty to administer properly their responsibilities to respect the confidences of Maritrans.

Our courts clearly have the power to enjoin an attorney from breaching his duty to a client:

> While the breach by a lawyer of his duty to keep the confidences of his client and to avoid representing conflicting interests may be the subject of appropriate disciplinary action, a court is not bound to await such development before acting to restrain improper conduct where it is disclosed in a case pending in that court.

Slater v. Rimar, Inc., supra, 462 Pa. at 148–49, 338 A.2d at 589 (footnote omitted). The power to enjoin the threatened violation of an attorney's fiduciary duty not to engage in conflicting representations dates at least to the early 1900's ....

---

3. The *Tri-Growth* court explained the concept of a fiduciary relationship as follows: "A fiduciary or confidential relationship can arise when confidence is reposed by persons in the integrity of others, and if the latter voluntarily accept or assume to accept the confidence, they cannot act so as to take advantage of the others' interests without their knowledge or consent. The attorney/client relationship is a fiduciary one, binding the attorney to the most conscientious fidelity." 216 Cal. App. 3d at 1150, 265 Cal.Rptr. at 334–35 (citations omitted).

... Moreover, "[a] court may restrain conduct which it feels may develop into a breach of ethics; it 'is not bound to sit back and wait for a probability to ripen into a certainty.'" *United States v. RMI Co.*, 467 F.Supp. 915, 923 (W.D.Pa.1979) (citation omitted)....

Accordingly, the trial court's preliminary injunction was a proper mechanism to abate an unlawful and actionable breach of fiduciary duties to Maritrans where the facts support such a conclusion.

II.
An Attorney's Common Law Duty is Independent of the Ethics Rules

Contrary to the arguments raised by Pepper and Messina, we conclude that the Superior Court badly confused the relationship between duties under the rules of ethics and legal rules that create actionable liability apart from the rules of ethics....

....

Long before the Code of Professional Responsibility was adopted, and before the Rules of Professional Conduct were adopted, the common law recognized that a lawyer could not undertake a representation adverse to a former client in a matter "substantially related" to that in which the lawyer previously had served the client....

....

The legal obligation of a lawyer to refrain from misuse of a client's confidences goes even further back, predating the ABA Canons of Professional Ethics promulgated in 1908....

The Superior Court seems to have the idea that because conduct is not a tort simply because it is a disciplinary violation, then conduct ceases to be a tort when it is at the same time a disciplinary violation. This is an inversion of logic and legal policy and misunderstands the history of the disciplinary rules.... As regards misuse of a former client's confidences, the disciplinary rules derive from the lawyer's common law duties, not the other way around.

III.
Scope of Duties at Common Law

We next must discuss the scope or the contours of remedy for an attorney's breach of duty to his or her client at common law....

Courts throughout the country have ordered the disgorgement of fees paid or the forfeiture of fees owed to attorneys who have breached their fiduciary duties to their clients by engaging in impermissible conflicts of interests.

....

IV.
Equity

Injunctive relief will lie where there is no adequate remedy at law. The purpose of a preliminary injunction is to preserve the status quo as it exists *or previously existed before the acts complained of*, thereby preventing irreparable injury or gross injustice. A preliminary injunction should issue only where there is urgent necessity to avoid injury which cannot be compensated for by damages....

Pepper and Messina argue that a preliminary injunction was an abuse of discretion where it restrains them from representing a former client's competitors, in order to supply the former client with a "sense of security" that they will not reveal confidences to those competitors where there has been no revelation or threat of revelations up to that point. We disagree. Whether a fiduciary can later represent competitors or whether a law firm can later represent competitors of its former client is a matter that must be decided from case to case and depends on a number of factors. One factor is the extent to which the fiduciary was involved in its former client's affairs. The greater the involvement, the greater the danger that confidences (where such exist) will be revealed. Here, Pepper and Messina's involvement was extensive as was their knowledge of sensitive information provided to them by Maritrans. We do *not* wish to establish a blanket rule that a law firm may not later represent the economic competitor of a former client in matters in which the former client is not also a party to a law suit. But situations may well exist where the danger of revelation of the confidences of a former client is so great that injunctive relief is warranted. This is one of those situations. There is a substantial relationship here between Pepper and Messina's former representation of Maritrans and their current representation of Maritrans' competitors such that the injunctive relief granted here was justified.... As fiduciaries, Pepper and Messina can be fully enjoined from representing Maritrans' competitors as that would create too great a danger that Maritrans' confidential relationship with Pepper and Messina would be breached.

... On these facts, it was perfectly reasonable [for the trial court] to conclude that Maritrans' competitive position could be irreparably injured if Pepper and Messina continued to represent their competitors and that Maritrans' remedy at law, that is their right to later seek damages, would be difficult if not impossible to sustain because of difficult problems of proof, particularly problems related to piercing what would later become a confidential relationship between their competitors and those competitors' attorneys (Pepper and Messina).... [E]quitable principles establish that injunctive relief here was just and proper. Damages might later be obtained for breach of fiduciary duties and a confidential relationship, but that remedy would be inadequate to correct the harm that could be prevented by injunctive relief, at least until the court could examine the case in greater detail.

....

The order of the Superior Court is reversed and the order of the Court of Common Pleas granting a preliminary injunction is reinstated. The matter is remanded to the trial court for further proceedings consistent with this opinion.

NIX, Chief Justice, dissenting.

In the instant matter the majority has concluded that appellee, Pepper, Hamilton & Scheetz ("Pepper"), was properly enjoined from representing Maritrans' competitors because of the significant risk of the disclosure of confidential information. The majority finds the creation of the relationship which harbors this risk to be a breach of Pepper's fiduciary duty to Maritrans. I believe that in reaching this result, the majority overlooks the significant body of case law that has developed in this area, as well as a key factor that renders its conclusion unreasonable.

The Chinese wall defense is set forth in the Model Rules of Professional Conduct, Rule 1.11.[2] The procedure established is one whereby a single attorney or group of attorneys who has represented a particular client is isolated from another attorney or attorneys

---

2. In Pennsylvania, the same procedure is found at Rule 1.10(a) and (b) of the Rules of Professional Conduct. That Rule provides as follows:

(a) While lawyers are associated in a firm, none of them shall knowingly represent a client

within the same firm who represent a client whose interests are substantially related but materially adverse to those of the initial client. The goal of such a procedure is to minimize the potential for the transmission of confidential information between attorneys representing clients with competing interest.

The Chinese wall defense is asserted in the following manner. First, in attempting to have an attorney disqualified, the former client must show that matters embraced within a pending lawsuit, in which his former attorney appears on behalf of an adversary, are substantially related to matters wherein the attorney had previously represented the former client. Once this burden, called the "substantial relationship test," is met, and the complainant has shown that the former representation exposed the attorney to confidences or secrets arguably pertinent in the present dispute, a rebuttable presumption arises that those confidences were shared.

To overcome this presumption, the Chinese wall defense is asserted, and the attorney and firm must demonstrate sufficient facts and circumstances of their particular case to establish the probable effectiveness of the wall....

[However,] *Maritrans was informed of this peculiar arrangement and consented to it.* It is well-settled in the field of legal ethics *that a client's consent,* upon full disclosure of a conflict of interest, *is sufficient to permit the attorney to continue the otherwise objectionable representation.* Thus, while Maritrans' concerns may have been legitimate, their initial acquiescence must be construed as a forbearance of any objections based upon the *potential* for breach of confidentiality. Having consented to the arrangement, they are now bound by their consent until such time as an actual breach of confidentiality occurs. [N]o actual disclosure of confidential information has occurred.[4] Maritrans' prior consent amounts to a waiver of their right to an objection based upon the fear of disclosure.

Accordingly, I dissent.

....

* * *

As the preceding cases indicate, various remedies are potentially available when a plaintiff can establish that a lawyer has breached his fiduciary obligations owed to the plaintiff. As breach of fiduciary duty as a tort is equitable in nature, the remedy most often awarded involves disgorgement of fees, whether the full amount of the fee or a portion thereof. However, in addition, courts have also recognized the need for imposing

---

when any one of them practicing alone would be prohibited from doing so by Rules 1.7, 1.8(c), 1.9 or 2.2.

(b) When a lawyer becomes associated with a firm, the firm may not knowingly represent a person in the same or substantially related matter in which that lawyer, or a firm with which the lawyer was associated, had previously represented a client whose interests are materially adverse to that person and about whom the lawyer had acquired information protected by Rules 1.6 and 1.9(b) that is material to the matter unless:

(1) the disqualified lawyer is screened from any participation in the matter and is apportioned no part of the fee therefrom; and

(2) written notice is promptly given to the appropriate client to enable it to ascertain compliance with the provisions of this rule.

4. Although Maritrans repeatedly insists that it has no way of knowing whether confidences have actually been disclosed because attorney-client privilege makes that fact difficult, if not impossible, to ascertain, it does not deny conceding the absence of disclosure at the prior proceeding before this Court. Moreover, the majority in the instant appeal concedes that the concern is not that actual disclosure has occurred, but that the circumstances create significant potential for such disclosure.

damages to compensate for actual injuries caused by the attorney's breach of fiduciary duty as well as ordering injunctive relief when appropriate.

* * *

E. Defenses to Claims of Breach of Fiduciary Duty

As with other torts, traditional defenses such as immunities and statutes of limitations are available as defenses to actions for breach of fiduciary duty. However, as a breach of fiduciary duty action is not a negligence action, defenses unique to negligence are typically not available in breach of fiduciary duty actions. As one court explained, "With respect to the claim of breach of a fiduciary duty, it has been held that the defense of contributory negligence is not available to what is an action in equity." *Jackson State Bank v. King,* 844 P.2d 1093, 1097 (Wyo. 1993) (citing *Federal Savings & Loan Insurance Corporation v. Huff,* 237 Kan. 873, 704 P.2d 372 (1985); *see also* Chapter 7, *infra,* exploring defenses to legal malpractice actions.

* * *

For a thoughtful exposition and further exploration of breach of fiduciary duty claims against lawyers, *see* Charles W. Wolfram, *A Cautionary Tale: Fiduciary Breach as Legal Malpractice,* 34 Hofstra L. Rev. 689 (2006).

Chapter 4

Professional Malpractice: Duty and Breach

Exercise 4.1: Chapter Problem

Client hired Attorney Adams to pursue a sexual harassment claim against Employer for inappropriate conduct she was exposed to at her former workplace. Attorney Adams agreed to represent Client in the sexual harassment claim against Employer, but failed to advise Client that in order to file a successful sexual harassment claim, she was first required to file her claim with the Equal Employment Opportunity Commission ("EEOC"), the federal law enforcement agency charged with enforcing laws against workplace discrimination, within 300 days of the alleged incidents. Instead, without filing with the EEOC, Attorney Adams filed a complaint against Employer on Client's behalf, alleging the sexual discrimination. Employer immediately moved for summary judgment based on Client's failure to file with the EEOC. Attorney Adams did not respond to Employer's summary judgment motion, which the trial judge granted. However, even when asked directly by Client, Attorney Adams did not disclose to Client that her case had been dismissed. Instead, Client was led to believe that her case was still pending and that the litigation was scheduled to resume in full swing in a few months. After a year had passed and she still had not heard anything on her claim, Client finally learned of the dismissal of her claim. If she had learned of the dismissal of the sexual harassment claim earlier, she would have been able to pursue a negligence action against Employer, but since so much time had now passed, the statute of limitations on any negligence action had also run. As one can imagine, Client is emotionally distraught over not being able to hold her Employer liable for the conduct she endured while working at that job.

Client has contacted your firm to determine the prudence of filing a legal malpractice action against Attorney Adams for his mishandling of her sexual harrassment claim. You have been asked by your supervising attorney to put together a memo with questions that Client is likely to need to have answered regarding the viability of a legal malpractice claim and the answers to those questions. Please draft a memo to your supervising attorney, enumerating the legally relevant questions and their corresponding answers. Be sure to conclude whether, in your professional opinion, Client has a viable legal malpractice action against her former attorney, Attorney Adams.

A. Generally

In the preceding chapter, we explored the tort of breach of fiduciary duty, a tort separate and distinct from a legal malpractice action, which is a negligence action brought against an attorney acting in his professional capacity as an attorney. *See, e.g., Beverly Hills Concepts, Inc. v. Schatz & Schatz, Ribicoff & Kotkin*, 717 A.2d 724 (Conn. 1998) (defendant attorney may be liable for professional negligence, but professional negligence does not automatically give rise to a breach of fiduciary duty claim). You will likely recall from an introductory torts course, which most first year law students are required to take, that all negligence actions—including those against professionals such as attorneys—require the plaintiff to prove four elements to establish the *prima facie* case:

(1) a duty of care owed to the plaintiff (sometimes referred to as the standard of care or standard of conduct);

(2) breach of that duty of care;

(3) causation (comprised of both causation in fact and proximate or legal cause); and

(4) actual damage or loss.

In the next several chapters, we will explore each of these elements of a negligence action brought against an attorney, beginning with the elements of duty and breach.

Focus Questions: *Togstad v. Vesely, Otto, Miller & Keefe*

1. *What are the elements of a legal malpractice action?*
2. *How does the court characterize the relationship between the plaintiffs and the defendant firm?*
3. *Does the duty in a lawyer-client relationship arise by operation of contract law or negligence law? What if anything distinguishes the two bodies of law?*

Togstad v. Vesely, Otto, Miller & Keefe

291 N.W.2d 686
(Minn. 1980)

PER CURIAM.

This is an appeal by the defendants from a judgment of the Hennepin County District Court involving an action for legal malpractice. The jury found that the defendant attorney Jerre Miller was negligent and that, as a direct result of such negligence, plaintiff John Togstad sustained damages in the amount of $610,500 and his wife, plaintiff Joan Togstad, in the amount of $39,000. Defendants (Miller and his law firm) appeal to this court from the denial of their motion for judgment notwithstanding the verdict or, alternatively, for a new trial. We affirm.

In August 1971, John Togstad began to experience severe headaches and on August 16, 1971, was admitted to Methodist Hospital where tests disclosed that the headaches were caused by a large aneurism on the left internal carotid artery. The attending physician,

Dr. Paul Blake, a neurological surgeon, treated the problem by applying a ... clamp ... in Togstad's neck to allow the gradual closure of the artery over a period of days.

... The greatest risk associated with this procedure is that the patient may become paralyzed if the brain does not receive an adequate flow of blood. In the event the supply of blood becomes so low as to endanger the health of the patient, the adjustable clamp can be opened to establish the proper blood circulation.

In the early morning hours of August 29, 1971, a nurse observed that Togstad was unable to speak or move. At the time, the clamp was one-half (50%) closed. Upon discovering Togstad's condition, the nurse called a resident physician, who did not adjust the clamp. Dr. Blake was also immediately informed of Togstad's condition and arrived about an hour later, at which time he opened the clamp. Togstad is now severely paralyzed in his right arm and leg, and is unable to speak.

Plaintiffs' expert, Dr. Ward Woods, testified that Togstad's paralysis and loss of speech was due to a lack of blood supply to his brain. Dr. Woods stated that the inadequate blood flow resulted from the clamp being 50% closed and that the negligence of Dr. Blake and the hospital precluded the clamp's being opened in time to avoid permanent brain damage....

....

About 14 months after her husband's hospitalization began, plaintiff Joan Togstad met with attorney Jerre Miller regarding her husband's condition. Neither she nor her husband was personally acquainted with Miller or his law firm prior to that time. John Togstad's former work supervisor, Ted Bucholz, made the appointment and accompanied Mrs. Togstad to Miller's office. Bucholz was present when Mrs. Togstad and Miller discussed the case.[3]

Mrs. Togstad had become suspicious of the circumstances surrounding her husband's tragic condition due to the conduct and statements of the hospital nurses shortly after the paralysis occurred. One nurse told Mrs. Togstad that she had checked Mr. Togstad at 2 a.m. and he was fine; that when she returned at 3 a.m., by mistake, to give him someone else's medication, he was unable to move or speak; and that if she hadn't accidentally entered the room no one would have discovered his condition until morning. Mrs. Togstad also noticed that the other nurses were upset and crying, and that Mr. Togstad's condition was a topic of conversation.

Mrs. Togstad testified that she told Miller "everything that happened at the hospital," including the nurses' statements and conduct which had raised a question in her mind. She stated that she "believed" she had told Miller "about the procedure and what was undertaken, what was done, and what happened." She brought no records with her. Miller took notes and asked questions during the meeting, which lasted 45 minutes to an hour. At its conclusion, according to Mrs. Togstad, Miller said that "he did not think we had a legal case, however, he was going to discuss this with his partner." She understood that if Miller changed his mind after talking to his partner, he would call her. Mrs. Togstad "gave it" a few days and, since she did not hear from Miller, decided "that they had come to the conclusion that there wasn't a case." No fee arrangements were discussed, no medical authorizations were requested, nor was Mrs. Togstad billed for the interview.

Mrs. Togstad denied that Miller had told her his firm did not have expertise in the medical malpractice field, urged her to see another attorney, or related to her that the statute of limitations for medical malpractice actions was two years. She did not consult

3. Bucholz, who knew Miller through a local luncheon club, died prior to the trial of the instant action.

another attorney until one year after she talked to Miller. Mrs. Togstad indicated that she did not confer with another attorney earlier because of her reliance on Miller's "legal advice" that they "did not have a case."

On cross-examination, Mrs. Togstad was asked whether she went to Miller's office "to see if he would take the case of [her] husband * * *." She replied, "Well, I guess it was to go for legal advice, what to do, where shall we go from here? That is what we went for." Again in response to defense counsel's questions, Mrs. Togstad testified as follows:

> Q And it was clear to you, was it not, that what was taking place was a preliminary discussion between a prospective client and lawyer as to whether or not they wanted to enter into an attorney-client relationship?
>
> A I am not sure how to answer that. It was for legal advice as to what to do.
>
> Q And Mr. Miller was discussing with you your problem and indicating whether he, as a lawyer, wished to take the case, isn't that true?
>
> A Yes.

On re-direct examination, Mrs. Togstad acknowledged that when she left Miller's office she understood that she had been given a "qualified, quality legal opinion that (she and her husband) did not have a malpractice case."

Miller's testimony was different in some respects from that of Mrs. Togstad. Like Mrs. Togstad, Miller testified that Mr. Bucholz arranged and was present at the meeting, which lasted about 45 minutes. According to Miller, Mrs. Togstad described the hospital incident, including the conduct of the nurses. He asked her questions, to which she responded. Miller testified that "[t]he only thing I told her [Mrs. Togstad] after we had pretty much finished the conversation was that there was nothing related in her factual circumstances that told me that she had a case that our firm would be interested in undertaking."

Miller also claimed he related to Mrs. Togstad "that because of the grievous nature of the injuries sustained by her husband, that this was only my opinion and she was encouraged to ask another attorney if she wished for another opinion" and "she ought to do so promptly." He testified that he informed Mrs. Togstad that his firm "was not engaged as experts" in the area of medical malpractice, and that they associated with the Charles Hvass firm in cases of that nature. Miller stated that at the end of the conference he told Mrs. Togstad that he would consult with Charles Hvass and if Hvass's opinion differed from his, Miller would so inform her. Miller recollected that he called Hvass a "couple days" later and discussed the case with him. It was Miller's impression that Hvass thought there was no liability for malpractice in the case. Consequently, Miller did not communicate with Mrs. Togstad further.

On cross-examination, Miller testified as follows:

> Q Now, so there is no misunderstanding, and I am reading from your deposition, you understood that she was consulting with you as a lawyer, isn't that correct?
>
> A That's correct.
>
> Q That she was seeking legal advice from a professional attorney licensed to practice in this state and in this community?
>
> ...
>
> THE WITNESS: ... Certainly, she was seeking my opinion as an attorney in the sense of whether or not there was a case that the firm would be interested in undertaking.

Kenneth Green, a Minneapolis attorney, was called as an expert by plaintiffs. He stated that in rendering legal advice regarding a claim of medical malpractice, the "minimum" an attorney should do would be to request medical authorizations from the client, review the hospital records, and consult with an expert in the field. John McNulty, a Minneapolis attorney, and Charles Hvass testified as experts on behalf of the defendants. McNulty stated that when an attorney is consulted as to whether he will take a case, the lawyer's only responsibility in refusing it is to so inform the party. He testified, however, that when a lawyer is asked his legal opinion on the merits of a medical malpractice claim, community standards require that the attorney check hospital records and consult with an expert before rendering his opinion.

Hvass stated that he had no recollection of Miller's calling him in October 1972 relative to the Togstad matter. He testified that:

> A * * * when a person comes in to me about a medical malpractice action, based upon what the individual has told me, I have to make a decision as to whether or not there probably is or probably is not, based upon that information, medical malpractice. And if, in my judgment, based upon what the client has told me, there is not medical malpractice, I will so inform the client.

Hvass stated, however, that he would never render a "categorical" opinion. In addition, Hvass acknowledged that if he were consulted for a "legal opinion" regarding medical malpractice and 14 months had expired since the incident in question, "ordinary care and diligence" would require him to inform the party of the two-year statute of limitations applicable to that type of action.

This case was submitted to the jury.... The jury found that Dr. Blake and the hospital were negligent and that Dr. Blake's negligence (but not the hospital's) was a direct cause of the injuries sustained by John Togstad; that there was an attorney-client contractual relationship between Mrs. Togstad and Miller; that Miller was negligent in rendering advice regarding the possible claims of Mr. and Mrs. Togstad; that, but for Miller's negligence, plaintiffs would have been successful in the prosecution of a legal action against Dr. Blake; and that neither Mr. nor Mrs. Togstad was negligent in pursuing their claims against Dr. Blake. The jury awarded damages to Mr. Togstad of $610,500 and to Mrs. Togstad of $39,000.

On appeal, defendants raise the following issues:

> (1) Did the trial court err in denying defendants' motion for judgment notwithstanding the jury verdict?
>
> (2) Does the evidence reasonably support the jury's award of damages to Mrs. Togstad in the amount of $39,000?

....

1. In a legal malpractice action of the type involved here, four elements must be shown: (1) that an attorney-client relationship existed; (2) that defendant acted negligently or in breach of contract; (3) that such acts were the proximate cause of the plaintiffs' damages; (4) that but for defendant's conduct the plaintiffs would have been successful in the prosecution of their medical malpractice claim.

This court first dealt with the element of lawyer-client relationship in the decision of *Ryan v. Long*, 35 Minn. 394, 29 N.W. 51 (1886). The *Ryan* case involved a claim of legal malpractice and on appeal it was argued that no attorney-client relation existed. This court, without stating whether its conclusion was based on contract principles or a tort theory, disagreed:

> [I]t sufficiently appears that plaintiff, for himself, called upon defendant, as an attorney at law, for "legal advice," and that defendant assumed to give him a professional opinion in reference to the matter as to which plaintiff consulted him. Upon this state of facts the defendant must be taken to have acted as plaintiff's legal adviser, at plaintiff's request, and so as to establish between them the relation of attorney and client.

Id. (citation omitted). More recent opinions of this court, although not involving a detailed discussion, have analyzed the attorney-client consideration in contractual terms....

We believe it is unnecessary to decide whether a tort or contract theory is preferable for resolving the attorney-client relationship question raised by this appeal. The tort and contract analyses are very similar in a case such as the instant one,[4] and we conclude that under either theory the evidence shows that a lawyer-client relationship is present here. The thrust of Mrs. Togstad's testimony is that she went to Miller for legal advice, was told there wasn't a case, and relied upon this advice in failing to pursue the claim for medical malpractice. In addition, according to Mrs. Togstad, Miller did not qualify his legal opinion by urging her to seek advice from another attorney, nor did Miller inform her that he lacked expertise in the medical malpractice area. Assuming this testimony is true, as this court must do, we believe a jury could properly find that Mrs. Togstad sought and received legal advice from Miller under circumstances which made it reasonably foreseeable to Miller that Mrs. Togstad would be injured if the advice were negligently given. Thus, under either a tort or contract analysis, there is sufficient evidence in the record to support the existence of an attorney-client relationship.

Defendants argue that even if an attorney-client relationship was established the evidence fails to show that Miller acted negligently in assessing the merits of the Togstads' case. They appear to contend that, at most, Miller was guilty of an error in judgment which does not give rise to legal malpractice. However, this case does not involve a mere error of judgment. The gist of plaintiffs' claim is that Miller failed to perform the minimal research that an ordinarily prudent attorney would do before rendering legal advice in a case of this nature. The record, through the testimony of Kenneth Green and John McNulty, contains sufficient evidence to support plaintiffs' position.

In a related contention, defendants assert that a new trial should be awarded on the ground that the trial court erred by refusing to instruct the jury that Miller's failure to inform Mrs. Togstad of the two-year statute of limitations for medical malpractice could not constitute negligence. The argument continues that since it is unclear from the record on what theory or theories of negligence the jury based its decision, a new trial must be granted.

The defect in defendants' reasoning is that there is adequate evidence supporting the claim that Miller was also negligent in failing to advise Mrs. Togstad of the two-year

---

4. Under a negligence approach it must essentially be shown that defendant rendered legal advice (not necessarily at someone's request) under circumstances which made it reasonably foreseeable to the attorney that if such advice was rendered negligently, the individual receiving the advice might be injured thereby. *See, e.g., Palsgraf v. Long Island R. Co.*, 248 N.Y. 339, 162 N.E. 99, 59 A.L.R. 1253 (1928). Or, stated another way, under a tort theory, "[a]n attorney-client relationship is created whenever an individual seeks and receives legal advice from an attorney in circumstances in which a reasonable person would rely on such advice." 63 Minn.L.Rev. 751, 759 (1979). A contract analysis requires the rendering of legal advice pursuant to another's request and the reliance factor, in this case, where the advice was not paid for, need be shown in the form of promissory estoppel. See, 7 C.J.S., *Attorney and Client*, §65; *Restatement (Second) of Contracts*, §90.

medical malpractice limitations period and thus the trial court acted properly in refusing to instruct the jury in the manner urged by defendants. One of defendants' expert witnesses, Charles Hvass, testified:

> Q Now, Mr. Hvass, where you are consulted for a legal opinion and advice concerning malpractice and 14 months have elapsed [since the incident in question], wouldn't—and you hold yourself out as competent to give a legal opinion and advice to these people concerning their rights—wouldn't ordinary care and diligence require that you inform them that there is a two-year statute of limitations within which they have to act or lose their rights?
>
> A Yes. I believe I would have advised someone of the two-year period of limitation, yes.

Consequently, based on the testimony of Mrs. Togstad, *i.e.*, that she requested and received legal advice from Miller concerning the malpractice claim, and the above testimony of Hvass, we must reject the defendants' contention, as it was reasonable for a jury to determine that Miller acted negligently in failing to inform Mrs. Togstad of the applicable limitations period.

....

There is also sufficient evidence in the record establishing that, but for Miller's negligence, plaintiffs would have been successful in prosecuting their medical malpractice claim. Dr. Woods, in no uncertain terms, concluded that Mr. Togstad's injuries were caused by the medical malpractice of Dr. Blake. Defendants' expert testimony to the contrary was obviously not believed by the jury. Thus, the jury reasonably found that had plaintiff's medical malpractice action been properly brought, plaintiffs would have recovered.

Based on the foregoing, we hold that the jury's findings are adequately supported by the record. Accordingly we uphold the trial court's denial of defendants' motion for judgment notwithstanding the jury verdict.

....

Affirmed.

* * *

1. Professional negligence and malpractice. "To prevail in a legal malpractice claim, a plaintiff must prove: (1) the existence of an attorney-client relationship giving rise to a duty; (2) the attorney, either by an act or a failure to act, breached that duty; (3) the attorney's breach of duty proximately caused injury to the client; and (4) the client sustained actual damage." *Chem-Age Indus., Inc. v. Glover,* 652 N.W.2d 756, 767 (S.D. 2002).

2. A legal malpractice action is not materially different from the ordinary negligence action. It is just a negligence action brought against a lawyer. It is simply a variety of negligence in which a special relationship—the attorney-client relationship—gives rise to a particular duty that goes beyond the ordinary duty to avoid a foreseeable risk of harm. As such, in order to prevail in a legal malpractice action, a plaintiff must allege and prove "(1) a *duty* that runs from the defendant to the plaintiff; (2) a *breach* of that duty; (3) a resulting *harm* to the plaintiff measurable in damages; and (4) *causation, i.e.,* a causal link between the breach of duty and the harm." *Stevens v. Bispham,* 316. Or. 221, 227–28, 851 P.2d 556 (1993) (emphasis in original); *see also Harding v. Bell,* 265 Or. 202, 204 (1973) ("An action for negligence by an attorney is not fundamentally different from other more typical actions for negligence.").

3. Definition of an attorney-client relationship. An attorney-client relationship may be formed as a result of an agreement between an attorney and the client. However, the formation of an attorney-client relationship is not solely dependent upon an agreement or contract between the parties, but rather may be created when one consults an attorney reasonably believing that they are doing so for the purpose of seeking legal advice. As one court explained: "[T]he duty upon the attorney to exercise reasonable care, skill, and diligence on behalf of the client arises out of the relationship of the parties, irrespective of a contract, and the attorney's breach of that duty, *i.e.*, the appropriate standard of care, constitutes negligence." *Lyle, Siegel, Croshaw & Beale, P.C. v. Tidewater Capital Corp.*, 249 Va. 426 (1995).

4. Duty and Breach as "Negligence." Legal malpractice actions are a subset of the larger tort category of negligence actions. However, some courts (confusingly) refer to the first two elements of a negligence action, *i.e.*, (1) the defendant's duty owed to the plaintiff and (2) the defendant's breach of that duty, as constituting "negligence." Do not allow this shorthand for breach of the standard of care to confuse you: using the term "negligence" in this manner means that the plaintiff has proven just the first two elements of the legal malpractice action and is still required to prove the remaining elements, namely (3) causation (comprised of both causation in fact and proximate cause) and (4) an actual loss. *See, e.g., State v. Therrien*, 830 A.2d 28, 36 (Vt. 2003) ("[T]he rules that apply to all legal malpractice actions founded on negligence apply here: defendant can recover if she can demonstrate that attorney Howe was negligent and that such negligence [breach of the standard of care] was the proximate cause of her injury.").

B. Standard of Care in Professional Malpractice — Duty

Focus Questions: *Kirsch v. Duryea*

1. *Define a lawyer's duty in negligence owed to a client. Upon what is a lawyer's duty of care based?*
2. *Upon what element did the plaintiff's negligence claim in* Kirsch *fail?*
3. *According to the* Kirsch *court, when is expert testimony to establish the duty of care in a legal malpractice action necessary?*

Kirsch v. Duryea

146 Cal.Rptr. 218
(Cal. 1978)

CLARK, Justice.

Defendant, an attorney, appeals from a legal malpractice judgment following jury verdict. We conclude the evidence is insufficient to support the judgment.

Evidence at trial revealed that in February 1963 plaintiff fell injuring his left shoulder while employed. A preoperative diagnosis revealed "probable tear, musculotendinitus cuff, left shoulder." The tear was repaired surgically and the arm placed in an airplane splint. An airplane splint is designed to hold the patient's arm in the air perpendicular to the axis of the body with the forearm bent forward at the elbow in a 45 degree angle. The splint must be carefully applied and padded to prevent pressure on the elbow area against the ulnar nerve, commonly called the crazy bone.

The splint was removed five days after plaintiff's release from the hospital.

On 29 February 1964, plaintiff was examined by Dr. Hickey who found plaintiff had pain and numbness in parts of his left shoulder, forearm and some numbness in the shoulder area near the surgical scar. The anterior portion of the deltoid muscle was atrophic and the lateral extension of the left arm was about 60 percent less than normal. Dr. Hickey diagnosed the problem as ulnar nerve damage, believing it was due to an improper airplane splint. He operated on plaintiff to relieve pressure on the ulnar nerve and to prevent paralysis of the hand. Before the operation plaintiff had no feeling in his lower arm, elbow and fingers, but following the operation some feeling was restored. Numbness continued in the forearm and in areas that Dr. Hickey believed were not caused by ulnar nerve damage.

In November 1964 Dr. Hickey sent plaintiff to a neurologist who, on the basis of his examination and tests performed, concluded that the surface of the ulnar nerve was intact and that the plaintiff's injury was due to neurosis of the brachial plexus. In December 1964 Dr. Hickey wrote a report to the workers' compensation carrier stating he agreed with the neurologist's report. However, he raised a third possible cause, pointing out that X-ray reports showed cervical spine changes and stating: "This sort of picture makes one think of degenerative disc disease with nerve root and spinal cord compression and this may be his reason for the pain and his disability now rather than a true ulnar nerve peripheral lesion." Dr. Hickey recommended a cervical myelogram. The myelogram indicated plaintiff's injury was not due to spine changes.

A few days before the statute of limitation would bar any medical malpractice action, plaintiff was referred by his workers' compensation attorney to defendant who was experienced in medical malpractice litigation. The latter filed a complaint on 23 March 1965. Shortly after suit was filed, plaintiff moved to New Mexico, and subsequent communication between them was by telephone or mail.

Defendant reviewed the workers' compensation file including its medical records, conversed with physicians, and did medical and legal research, but did not depose any of the doctors. At some point prior to 21 July 1969, he concluded trial was not justified because of insufficient evidence of malpractice.

Of the several doctors whose reports were examined, only Dr. Hickey indicated that the injury might be due to cause involving medical malpractice ulnar nerve damage from an improper airplane splint and his December 1964 report, as indicated above, stated that continuing disability was due to other causes, including the possibility of a spinal disorder, warranting a myelogram. Plaintiff failed to inform defendant that a myelogram had been performed and defendant was unaware of it.

On 21 July 1969 defendant informed plaintiff by mail of his conclusion the case could not be established and that he would proceed no further. He enclosed a substitution of attorneys form, substituting plaintiff in propria persona and asked that the form be signed and returned within 15 days. Defendant pointed out that until another attorney was retained plaintiff must act as his own attorney. Offering full cooperation with any attorney plaintiff designated, defendant repeatedly stressed the need to bring the case to trial within five years, specifying in capital letters, "THIS CASE MUST BE BROUGHT TO TRIAL AND TRIAL MUST BE COMMENCED BEFORE MARCH 23, 1970."

Not hearing from plaintiff, defendant sent a second letter on 5 September 1969, stating that if the substitution form was not signed and returned within 10 days, defendant would move for withdrawal from the case. No date for the motion was given in the letter. Defendant then filed his motion to withdraw on 25 November and hearing was set for 9 January. Plaintiff was not served with notice of motion. The matter was continued by the court to 27 January 1970 and notice was mailed by defendant to plaintiff. The motion was granted without opposition or appearance by plaintiff. Plaintiff testified he did not receive notice and was unaware of the motion and hearing.

After receipt of the July letter, plaintiff consulted various attorneys. One of them, a San Francisco attorney, examined the file and agreed with defendant's assessment of the case, sending defendant a copy of his letter declining employment. A New Mexico attorney referred plaintiff to a Texas attorney who, according to plaintiff, made arrangements with two California attorneys to represent him. However, plaintiff never replied to the two letters from defendant, and defendant did not hear from the two California attorneys until April 1970, after the March trial deadline.

The medical malpractice case was dismissed on 12 May 1970 for failure to comply with the five-year trial requirement of Code of Civil Procedure section 583.

At the instant legal malpractice trial, John Lewis, a Sacramento attorney, testified a lawyer owes a continuous duty to represent a client and to do nothing which would prejudice the case irrespective of its lack of merit. He recognized lawyers frequently withdraw from cases and sometimes another will proceed to obtain a significant recovery. However, he concluded that it is improper for an attorney to withdraw when only two months remain to bring the matter to trial. He further testified it would have been proper for defendant, after concluding the case lacked merit, to withdraw the prior summer, allowing the client nine months to find another attorney.

The jury found defendant attorney negligent, assessed damages of $237,100, found plaintiff 2.5 percent negligent, and reduced the award to $231,175.50.

GENERAL RULE

"The general rule with respect to the liability of an attorney for failure to properly perform his duties to his client is that the attorney, by accepting employment to give legal advice or to render other legal services, impliedly agrees to use such skill, prudence, and diligence as lawyers of ordinary skill and capacity commonly possess and exercise in the performance of the tasks which they undertake.... The attorney is not liable for every mistake he may make in his practice; he is not, in the absence of an express agreement, an insurer of the soundness of his opinions or of the validity of an instrument that he is engaged to draft; and he is not liable for being in error as to a question of law on which reasonable doubt may be entertained by well-informed lawyers.... These principles are equally applicable whether the plaintiff's claim is based on tort or breach of contract." (*Lucas v. Hamm* (1961) 56 Cal.2d 583, 591, 15 Cal.Rptr. 821, 825, 364 P.2d 685, 689; *Smith v. Lewis* (1975) 13 Cal.3d 349, 358, 118 Cal.Rptr. 621, 530 P.2d 589).

CONFLICTING OBLIGATIONS

Frequently an attorney is confronted with legitimate but competing considerations, and we have recently recognized a latitude granted the attorney engaged in litigation in choosing between alternative tactical strategies.

In addition to competing strategies, an attorney is often confronted with clashing obligations imposed by our system of justice. An attorney has an obligation not only to protect his client's interests but also to respect the legitimate interests of fellow members of the bar, the judiciary, and the administration of justice.

In absence of a specific rule of conduct governing the situation before him, determination of the attorney's duty of care when conflicting interests arise is made by balancing those interests, keeping in mind that it would be unfair to require the attorney to pay damages merely upon a showing of a mistake in choice. To hold the attorney responsible in damages whenever in retrospect it appears he mistakenly sacrificed his client's interests in favor of his public obligations would place an impossible burden on the practice of law. Moreover, awarding damages against the attorney would violate sound public policy, because an attorney frequently faced with the question whether vigorous advocacy in favor of a client must be curtailed in light of public obligation would tilt in favor of the client at the expense of our system of justice.

When apparent conflict exists between the attorney's duty to his client on the one hand and his public obligation on the other, it is not sufficient to show that some or many prudent attorneys would not have made the mistake. The attorney's choice to honor the public obligation must be shown to have been so manifestly erroneous that no prudent attorney would have done so.

Here, defendant was confronted with a choice between his duty to advance his client's cause by continuing to prosecute the action and his duty to fair administration of justice to refuse to maintain actions believed to lack merit.

An attorney's duty is to maintain only such actions as appear to him legal or just. "When an attorney loses faith in his cause he should either retire from the case or dismiss the action." (*Larimer v. Smith* (1933) 130 Cal.App. 98, 101, 19 P.2d 825, 827.)

....

... Viewing the evidence in the light most favorable to plaintiff, the evidence available to defendant at the time he determined the action lacked legal merit reflected that several doctors believed plaintiff's ailment resulted from something other than negligence. There was no direct evidence that the airplane splint was faulty. The one doctor who first believed that the injury was due to a defective splint, in a subsequent letter of December 1964, questioned his own initial opinion.... Based on the materials available to defendant, the possibility of recovery was remote; certainly the determination that the action was not meritorious cannot be characterized as manifestly erroneous.

WITHDRAWAL

Plaintiff further contends the judgment may be upheld upon the theory that defendant improperly delayed in securing court discharge.

....

Plaintiff's expert testified that the attorney who concludes his client's case lacks merit should quickly proceed to obtain a nonconsensual discharge. This is contrary both to our rules of professional conduct and the American Bar Association's disciplinary rule.

Defendant gave due notice by letter in July and in September of his intended withdrawal. He offered all materials pertaining to the case, and advised plaintiff of the need for quick action. He sent the file to one of the attorneys consulted by defendant.

Defendant did all he could to avoid the inference of lack of merit by delaying his non-consensual withdrawal. His delay in seeking the formal order does not reflect absence of due care but rather compliance with the rules.

INVESTIGATION

The third basis urged in support of the finding of attorney negligence is that defendant should have investigated further. But no expert testimony was elicited warranting a determination of negligent investigation. Although in some cases expert testimony is not required to establish standard of care (see *Wright v. Williams* (1975) 47 Cal.App.3d 802, 810, 121 Cal.Rptr. 194), this is not one of them. The extent to which an attorney, in the exercise of due care, will advance funds to hire investigators, depose witnesses, or perform tests on a client is not a matter of common knowledge.

The judgment is reversed.

* * *

1. Statutes of Limitation. Note that in *Kirsch*, the underlying medical malpractice litigation was dismissed for failure to comply with the five-year trial requirement. Although most statutes of limitation limit the time by which a plaintiff's lawsuit must be *filed*, note that the statute at issue in *Kirsch* dictated the time by which the *trial* of the plaintiff's lawsuit must take place. The medical malpractice case was dismissed for failure to comply with the statute requiring the date by which the trial must take place.

2. Comparative Fault/Comparative Negligence. In *Kirsch*, the jury found in favor of the plaintiff but found the plaintiff partially responsible for his damages. Due to the plaintiff's comparative fault of 2.5%, the jury's award of $237,100 was reduced by 2.5%, and the plaintiff was awarded instead $231,175.50. For more discussion and explanation of comparative fault as a defense to a legal malpractice action, *see* Chapter 7, *infra.*

3. Should a lawyer's duty to his client include the duty to inform of his own malpractice? *See* Benjamin P. Cooper, *The Lawyer's Duty to Inform His Client of His Own Malpractice,* 61 Baylor L. Rev. 174 (2009).

4. Criminal Malpractice. Legal malpractice actions where the underlying litigations involved lawyers representing defendants in criminal matters are often referred to as criminal malpractice actions. As an illustration, consider the next case.

Focus Questions: *Simko v. Blake*

1. *What is the standard of care in a criminal malpractice action* (i.e., *a legal malpractice action brought against a criminal defense attorney)?*
2. *Does the standard of care in a criminal malpractice action differ from the standard of care when the underlying matter is a civil action?*
3. *What are the elements of a criminal malpractice action?*
4. *What is the dissent's primary disagreement with the majority of the court in* Simko?
5. *Are you more persuaded by the majority or the dissent? Defend your position.*

Simko v. Blake

448 Mich. 648
(1995)

MALLETT, Justice.

This case presents the question whether an attorney's duty to his client extends beyond what is legally adequate to win a client's case. We hold that attorneys must only act as would an attorney of ordinary learning, judgment, or skill under the same or similar circumstances.

Defendant Blake raised a complete defense, did what was legally sufficient to fully vindicate his client's interest, and acted as would an attorney of ordinary learning, judgment, or skill under the same or similar circumstances. His alleged acts and omissions were trial tactics based on good faith and reasonable professional judgment. Further, no amount of factual development could reveal a case of malpractice. Thus, we affirm the decision of the Court of Appeals in favor of the defendant.

I

Plaintiffs Arthur Louis Simko, Margaret Simko, and Tara Marie Simko filed suit against defendant Marvin Blake, an attorney, alleging that the defendant committed professional malpractice in failing to adequately represent Arthur Simko in a prosecution of possessing over 650 grams of cocaine ... and possession of a firearm in the commission or attempt to commit a felony.... Although the defendant was convicted and the conviction eventually was reversed by the Court of Appeals, Mr. Simko spent more than two years in prison.

In the underlying criminal case, on the night of March 6, 1987, a state police officer observed a speeding car traveling with its lights flashing in an apparent effort to attract the officer's attention. The car exited the highway and stopped to wait for the police car. The driver of the vehicle alighted from his car and told the police that the passenger, Arthur Simko, needed medical attention.

Plaintiff appeared flushed, was perspiring, and his breathing was labored. The officer summoned an ambulance. While waiting for the ambulance to arrive, the officer discovered what appeared to be drug paraphernalia on the floor of the car. A further search of the car revealed a cup containing cocaine residue, a bullet in plaintiff's pocket, a pistol in the glove compartment, a pistol in the trunk, several rounds of ammunition, and 988 grams of a substance containing cocaine.

Arthur Simko was represented by Marvin Blake. At the close of the prosecution's case, and again at the close of defendant's case, Mr. Blake moved for a directed verdict on the ground that the evidence was insufficient to convict plaintiff. The trial judge denied both motions. Mr. Simko was ultimately found guilty by the jury and sentenced to mandatory sentences of life without parole plus two years.

Arthur Simko then retained another attorney and appealed his conviction. The Court of Appeals reversed; however, by that time, he had already served two years of his prison sentence.

At the time plaintiff filed his appeal, he also filed a legal malpractice action against defendant. Arthur Simko alleged that the defendant failed to properly investigate his case and failed to properly prepare to defend him. Specifically, Mr. Simko alleged that Mr. Blake did not produce any witnesses in his defense besides Mr. Simko himself, failed to produce plaintiff's personal physician who had been treating him for a pinched nerve and who prescribed medication that would have offered an explanation of his medical condition at the time of arrest, and failed to provide Mr. Simko with the name and location of the hotel where Mr. Simko had spent the day before he was arrested that may have protected him from impeachment.

The malpractice action was dismissed by the trial court when it granted defendant's motion for summary disposition....

....

The Court of Appeals affirmed, stating that

> [b]y challenging the sufficiency of the evidence against Simko, Blake raised a complete and ultimately successful defense to both charges.... Blake was not Simko's insurer against all possible misfortune.... His duty was to raise an adequate defense to the criminal charges, not to protect Simko from judge and jury. [201 Mich.App. 191, 195, 506 N.W.2d 258 (1993).]

We affirm the decision of the Court of Appeals and hold that Marvin Blake fulfilled his duty to Arthur Simko.

II

We hold that defendant's motion for summary disposition was properly granted by the trial court because the plaintiffs failed to state a claim upon which relief can be granted.

Plaintiffs' complaint and pleadings failed to state a breach of duty.

... A motion of summary disposition is tested on the pleadings alone, and all factual allegations contained in the complaint must be accepted as true.

III

In order to state an action for legal malpractice, the plaintiff has the burden of adequately alleging the following elements:

(1) the existence of an attorney-client relationship;

(2) negligence in the legal representation of the plaintiff;

(3) that the negligence was a proximate cause of an injury; and

(4) the fact and extent of the injury alleged.

...

The first element the plaintiff must prove is "duty." "Duty" is any obligation the defendant has to the plaintiff to avoid negligent conduct. In negligence actions, the existence of duty is a question of law for the court.

In legal malpractice actions, a duty exists, as a matter of law, if there is an attorney-client relationship.... In the instant case, the parties admitted that an attorney-client relationship existed between Mr. Simko and Mr. Blake. Thus, the issue is not whether a duty existed, but rather the extent of that duty once invoked.

It is well established that "[a]n attorney is obligated to use reasonable skill, care, discretion and judgment in representing a client." *Lipton v. Boesky*, 110 Mich.App. 589, 594, 313 N.W.2d 163 (1981),.... Further, ... all attorneys have a duty to behave as would an attorney "of ordinary learning, judgment or skill ... under the same or similar circumstances...."

An attorney has the duty to fashion such a strategy so that it is consistent with prevailing Michigan law. However, an attorney does not have a duty to insure or guarantee the most favorable outcome possible. An attorney is never bound to exercise extraordinary diligence, or act beyond the knowledge, skill, and ability ordinarily possessed by members of the legal profession....

....

To require attorneys, or other professionals, to act over and beyond average skill, learning, and ability, would be an unreasonable burden on the profession and the legal system. As the Court of Appeals stated:

> There is no motion that can be filed, no amount of research in preparation, no level of skill, nor degree of perfection that could anticipate every error or completely shield a client from the occasional aberrant ruling of a fallible judge or an intransigent jury. To impose a duty on attorneys to do more than that which is legally adequate to fully vindicate a client's rights would require our legal system, already overburdened, to digest unnecessarily inordinate quantities of additional motions and evidence that, in most cases, will prove to be superfluous. And, *because no amount of work can guarantee a favorable result, attorneys would never know when the work they do is sufficiently more than adequate to be enough to protect not only their clients from error, but themselves from liability* [201 Mich.App. at 194, 506 N.W.2d 258 (emphasis added)].

In *Denzer v. Rouse,* 48 Wis.2d 528, 534, 180 N.W.2d 521 (1970), the court noted that an attorney cannot possibly be required to predict infallibly how a court will rule. "A lawyer would need a crystal ball, along with his library, to be able to guarantee that no judge, anytime, anywhere, would disagree with his judgment or evaluation of a situation." Similarly, this Court refuses to impose any greater duty on attorneys than to act as would an attorney of ordinary learning, judgment, or skill under the same or similar circumstances.

Lastly, mere errors in judgment by a lawyer are generally not grounds for a malpractice action where the attorney acts in good faith and exercises reasonable care, skill, and diligence. Where an attorney acts in good faith and in honest belief that his acts and omissions are well founded in law and are in the best interest of his client, he is not answerable for mere errors in judgment.... :

> [T]here can be no liability for acts and omissions by an attorney in the conduct of litigation which are based on an honest exercise of professional judgment. This is a sound rule. Otherwise every losing litigant would be able to sue his attorney if he could find another attorney who was willing to second guess the decisions of the first attorney with the advantage of hindsight.... To hold that an attorney may not be held liable for the choice of trial tactics and the conduct of a case based on professional judgment is not to say, however, that an attorney may not be held liable for any of his actions in relation to a trial. He is still bound to exercise a reasonable degree of skill and care in all his professional undertakings. [*Woodruff v. Tomlin,* 616 F.2d 924, 930 (C.A.6 1980) (citations omitted).]

IV

We find that the defendant acted as would an attorney of ordinary learning, judgment, or skill under the same or similar circumstances, and his alleged acts and omissions were a matter of trial tactics based on reasonable professional judgment.

....

We find, as a matter of law, that the plaintiffs' allegations could not support a breach of duty because they are based on mere errors of professional judgment and not breaches of reasonable care.... Plaintiffs alleged that defendant should have called other witnesses besides Mr. Simko, including Mr. Simko's physician, Dr. Michael Karbal, and Mr. Simko's wife, Margaret Simko. In addition, [the plaintiff alleges that] Mr. Blake failed to ascertain the name and location of the hotel where Mr. Simko had allegedly spent the day before he was arrested.

First, it is a tactical decision whether to call particular witnesses, as long as the attorney acts with full knowledge of the law and in good faith. [A] charge of malpractice on the basis of an attorney's decision to not cross-examine an expert witness did not constitute malpractice. Similarly, in *Frank v. Bloom,* 634 F.2d 1245, 1256–1257 (C.A. 10 1980), the court stated that it will afford latitude to the attorney when making tactical strategies:

> [I]t is the duty of the attorney who is a professional to determine trial strategy. If the client had the last word on this, the client could be his or her own lawyer.

Here, plaintiffs are alleging that defendant was negligent in not calling Dr. Karbal and Mrs. Simko. This, however, is a tactical decision that this Court may not question. Perhaps defendant made an error of judgment in deciding not to call particular witnesses, and perhaps another attorney would have made a different decision; however, tactical decisions do not constitute grounds for a legal malpractice action. Plaintiffs' claim that certain witnesses should have been called is nothing but an assertion that another lawyer might have conducted the trial differently, a matter of professional opinion that does not allege violation of the duty to perform as a reasonably competent criminal defense lawyer.

Second, the failure to ascertain the name and location of the hotel where a client was located at a particular time does not constitute negligence. There is no duty to infallibly protect a client from impeachment. This would be an impossible standard for defense counsel to meet and would violate and extend beyond the well-established reasonable care standard.

V

We conclude that there was no legal basis for holding that Mr. Blake's actions constituted negligence, or otherwise constitute malpractice. When an attorney fashions a trial strategy consistent with the governing principles of law and reasonable professional judgment, the attorney's conduct is legally adequate. Accordingly, we affirm the decision of the Court of Appeals and hold that the defendant fulfilled his duty to his client.

MICHAEL F. CAVANAGH, BOYLE and RILEY, JJ., concur.

LEVIN, Justice (dissenting).

This is an action for legal malpractice. Plaintiff Arthur Louis Simko was convicted of possessing over 650 grams of cocaine and sentenced to the mandatory term of life in prison. Defendant Marvin Blake represented Simko at the trial. His motion for a directed verdict was denied.

The Court of Appeals reversed Simko's conviction finding that there was insufficient evidence that Simko possessed the cocaine found in the vehicle in which he was a passenger. The Court thus implicitly ruled that Blake's motion in Simko's behalf for a directed verdict should have been granted.

Although Simko's conviction was reversed without a new trial, he was imprisoned under a life sentence for more than two years. Simko, his wife, Margaret A. Simko, and his daughter, Tara Marie Simko, commenced this action against Blake alleging errors of omission and commission and failure to observe the standard of care required of a lawyer.

....

[The trial court granted summary judgment in favor of defendant attorney Blake.] The Court of Appeals acknowledged that "[p]roximate cause in attorney malpractice is a question for the trier of fact," and "*accept[ed] that a trier of fact could find that it was because Blake did not present additional evidence that Simko spent two years in prison unnecessarily.*" The Court nevertheless affirmed, one judge dissenting, on the basis that Blake had discharged his "duty" to Simko when he "identified correctly the legal inadequacy" of the people's case and thus had no duty to "be prepared to present additional evidence in support of alternative theories just in case the trial court erroneously should deny the motions."

The majority, adopting essentially the same analysis, affirms. I would reverse the Court of Appeals and reinstate the complaint because, although stated in terms of "duty," the majority in this Court

. . .

- in effect redefines the standard of care to require of a lawyer less than ordinary learning, judgment, diligence, and skill in the representation of a client;
- in effect invades the province of the trier of fact by finding that "the" only cause/ proximate cause of Simko's injury was the trial judge's error in denying the motion for directed verdict rather than allowing the trier of fact to determine whether "a" cause was error by Blake;
- indulges in further fact finding in stating that Blake's "alleged acts and omissions were trial tactics based on good faith and reasonable professional judgment."

A physician who operated successfully on a patient, whose malady could have been cured with a pill that a physician of ordinary learning, judgment, diligence or skill would have administered, would be subject to liability for the unnecessary inconvenience, pain, and suffering, even if endured for only a few weeks, and not two years. So, too, should a lawyer be subject to liability if the trier of fact finds that a lawyer of ordinary learning, judgment, diligence, and skill would have advanced alternative theories that would have avoided Simko enduring over two years' imprisonment.

The Supreme Court of North Dakota ruled in a legal malpractice action, *Klem v. Greenwood,* 450 N.W.2d 738, 744 (N.D.1990), that "merely because this court reversed Klem's conviction does not mean that any alleged malpractice caused no damage." The court said that in holding that the trial court had erred and that Greenwood, Klem's lawyer, had preserved the issue for appellate review, the court "did not hold, as a matter of law, that Greenwood had met the degree of skill, care, *diligence,* and knowledge commonly possessed and exercised by a reasonable, careful, and prudent attorney" (emphasis added).[7]

The majority states:

> [A]ttorneys must only act as would an attorney of ordinary learning, judgment, or skill under the same or similar circumstances.

A

I agree that a lawyer need "only act" as would a lawyer of ordinary learning, judgment, diligence, or skill under the same or similar circumstances. But he must *so act.* If the majority were to allow this case to come to trial, the evidence were to show, and a trier of fact were to find, that a lawyer of ordinary learning, judgment, diligence, or skill, under the same or similar circumstances, would have avoided errors that Blake allegedly committed, then Blake is, or should be, subject to liability for damage found to have resulted from conviction of an offense subjecting Simko to a sentence of life in prison and actual incarceration for over two years.

---

7. The court observed that Klem had alleged "acts of malpractice, including, but not limited to, the failure to adequately cross-examine a complaining witness."

In holding as a matter of law that Blake is not subject to liability because it was ultimately determined that he interposed a legally adequate defense even though, had he avoided error, Simko would not have been convicted and served over two years in prison, the majority requires less of Blake than the conduct of a lawyer of "ordinary learning, judgment, or skill under the same or similar circumstances."

B

The majority also states that "mere errors in judgment by a lawyer are *generally* not grounds for a malpractice action where the attorney acts in good faith and exercises reasonable care, skill, and diligence" (emphasis added). It is implicit in the formulation adopted by the majority, requiring a lawyer to act as would a lawyer of "ordinary learning, *judgment*, or skill," that errors of judgment may constitute negligence. Whether an error of judgment, or a "mere" error of judgment, constitutes negligence depends on whether a lawyer of ordinary learning, judgment, diligence, or skill would have avoided the error or "mere" error of judgment. That "generally" is a question of fact for the trier of fact to decide.

....

III

Blake's motion for summary disposition was filed on the basis that the Simkos "failed to state a claim on which relief can be granted." In finding facts on this second appellate review, the majority ignores that only the pleadings may be considered by the circuit court and the appellate courts in ruling on such a motion.

The majority finds, as a matter of fact or law, that the "alleged acts and omissions were trial tactics based on good faith and reasonable professional judgment." ... In response to the motion for summary disposition, the Simkos filed an affidavit of a lawyer stating that in his opinion Blake had erred. Blake did not file an affidavit in support of the motion for summary disposition, probably because no such support is required or permitted. Nevertheless the majority finds, as a matter of fact or law, that Blake acted in good faith and exercised reasonable professional judgment.

The majority finds, as a matter of fact or law, that certain witnesses were not called because Blake "did not feel that they would be beneficial to the defense's case."

Because Blake did not file an affidavit in support of his motion for summary disposition, ... there is no record support for fact finding by the majority.

... The silent record no more justifies a finding that Blake had a reason for not calling the witnesses, than it would a finding that he simply neglected or overlooked calling them. A silent record supports no finding of fact at all.

IV

The majority states, quoting with approval the opinion of the Court of Appeals:

> "To impose a duty on attorneys to do more than that which is legally adequate to fully vindicate a client's rights would require our legal system, already overburdened, to digest unnecessarily inordinate quantities of additional motions and evidence that, in most cases, will prove to be superfluous."

....

The Simkos ... complain ... about [Blake's] asserted lack of diligence in preparing for trial, and in failing to call witnesses during trial.

Lowering the standard of care for lawyers will not reduce the burden of over-lawyering by lawyers who fail to recognize their professional responsibility....

....

BRICKLEY, C.J., concurs.

* * *

Criminal Malpractice Actions and the Requirement of Post-Conviction Relief. In a section of the *Simko* dissent not included above, Judge Levin explains:

> In *Gebhardt v. O'Rourke,* 444 Mich. 535, 554, 510 N.W.2d 900 (1994), this Court said that "successful postconviction relief is not a prerequisite to the maintenance of a claim for legal malpractice arising out of negligent representation in a criminal matter." The Court, thus, implicitly said that a legal malpractice action may be maintained against a lawyer who represented a plaintiff in a criminal matter without establishing that he rendered "ineffective assistance."[20]
>
> Simko is at least entitled to maintain this damage action for legal malpractice if he can establish that Blake failed to render effective assistance within the meaning of the "ineffective assistance" standard.[21] The majority should at least remand to the circuit court for determination of the effective assistance issue.[22]
>
> We would reverse the Court of Appeals and remand for determination under the standard of care heretofore applicable in actions asserting legal malpractice in the conduct of criminal as well as civil cases.

What is your opinion regarding whether a plaintiff in a criminal malpractice action should be required to prove that he was denied the effective assistance of counsel in violation of the 6th Amendment of the U.S. Constitution prior to bringing a criminal malpractice action? Defend your position. For further exploration of this interesting issue, *see* Chapter 5, *infra* (examining special issues in proving causation in criminal malpractice actions).

* * *

---

20. See *People v. Pickens,* 446 Mich. 298, 521 N.W.2d 797 (1994).

21. Simko sought reversal in the Court of Appeals not only on the basis of insufficiency of the evidence but also on the basis that he was denied the effective assistance of counsel. Because the Court of Appeals reversed his conviction on the basis that there was insufficient evidence, it did not reach the question whether he was denied the effective assistance of counsel. Simko thus did not obtain a ruling from the Court of Appeals on his claim that he was denied the effective assistance of counsel.

22. In *Gebhardt, supra* at 548, n. 13, 510 N.W.2d 900, this Court said:

> We do not accept the "no relief-no harm" rule because it is a legal fiction with serious analytical flaws.[13]
>
> > [13] Rather than being a legal definition of harm, the rule is a legal fiction that divorces the law from reality. "[P]ersons convicted of a crime will be astonished to learn that, even if their lawyers' negligence resulted in their being wrongly convicted and imprisoned, they were not harmed when they were wrongly convicted and imprisoned but, rather, that they are harmed only if and when they are exonerated."

The Court also said at 552, 510 N.W.2d 900:

> ... In this case, a cause of action for malpractice could well exist regardless of the outcome of post-judgment proceedings in the underlying case.

1. The Role of the Expert in Establishing Duty and Breach

The *Kirsch* opinion, *supra,* touched on the issue of the need for expert testimony in establishing duty in a legal malpractice action by briefly explaining: "Although in some cases expert testimony is not required to establish standard of care, this is not one of them. The extent to which an attorney, in the exercise of due care, will advance funds to hire investigators, depose witnesses, or perform tests on a client is not a matter of common knowledge." This issue of when expert testimony is required to establish the standard of care in a legal malpractice action is more thoroughly explored in the following case.

Focus Questions: *Rizzo v. Haines*

1. *When is expert testimony necessary to establish the standard of care in a legal malpractice action?*
2. *What is the appropriate measure of damages in a legal malpractice action?*

Rizzo v. Haines

555 A.2d 58
(Pa. 1989)

STOUT, Justice.

Barton A. Haines, Esquire, appeals from the order of the Superior Court ... affirming in part, and reversing and remanding in part, the judgment order of the Court of Common Pleas of Philadelphia County that held that he negligently, and in bad faith, conducted settlement negotiations for his client Frank L. Rizzo, that he had fraudulently induced his client to transfer $50,000 to him, and that he improperly accounted for costs and expenses. The trial court entered a judgment against him in the amount of $530,000 in compensatory damages and $150,000 in punitive damages.... We affirm.

On September 20, 1968, Rizzo, while stopped in a vehicle at an intersection, was rear-ended by a City of Philadelphia police vehicle. At the time, Rizzo was an off-duty police officer for the City of Philadelphia. Rizzo's soft-tissue neck, back, and arm injuries, sustained in the accident, eventually worsened, and he came under the supervision of Henry T. Wycis, M.D. After three surgical procedures..., he became permanently partially paralyzed. Once a handsome and vital police officer, he became a comparatively helpless and pitiful invalid.

Rizzo originally retained Anthony J. Caiazzo, Esquire, to institute a suit against the City of Philadelphia [hereinafter "*City*" case]. Later he retained the law firm of Richter, Syken, Ross & Levant, which assigned the case to Haines, an associate with the firm. The relationship between Haines and the Richter firm deteriorated, and Haines left the firm. He copied the Rizzo file and took it and the client, who by this time had become a personal friend, with him. Frank and Lena Rizzo, under Haines' counsel, instituted a medical malpractice action against Dr. Wycis and the hospital where the surgeries were performed [hereinafter "*Wycis*" case]. The instant action arises from Haines' representation of Rizzo in these two lawsuits.

Haines did not pursue consolidation of the two cases. Rather, after a failed attempt on the part of the City to join Dr. Wycis' estate, the *City* case was listed for a jury trial before the Honorable Merna B. Marshall. The jury returned a verdict in favor of Mr. Rizzo for $450,000. Reassuring the Rizzos that the *Wycis* case was still viable, Haines recommended that Rizzo take the money. Neither party filed post-trial motions.

....

Throughout the course of the *City* case, Haines repeatedly led the Rizzos to believe that the *Wycis* case had a recovery value of between $800,000 and $1 million. The record reveals, however, that there was insufficient evidence of Dr. Wycis' malpractice to justify this figure. Furthermore, the doctor's professional liability insurance coverage was only $100,000. In addition, there was insufficient evidence that the hospital was negligent either in extending staff privileges to Dr. Wycis or in caring for Rizzo. On January 23, 1978, the *Wycis* case was dismissed on a summary judgment motion ... on the basis that, *inter alia,* the recovery in the *City* suit had fully compensated Rizzo for his injuries.

The Rizzos instituted the instant malpractice action against Haines alleging, *inter alia,* professional negligence in settling the *City* case, breach of fiduciary duties with respect to the $50,000 transfer, and improper accounting of costs and expenses. The case was tried without a jury.... On January 18, 1984, the judge found for the Rizzos. He awarded $300,000 compensatory damage for negligent settlement.... Lastly, the court awarded $150,000 in punitive damages.... Judge Kremer denied the post-trial motions.... The Superior Court affirmed....

In reviewing the factual determinations of the trial court sitting as finder of fact, we must attribute to them the same force and effect as a jury's verdict. Accordingly, we view the evidence and all reasonable inferences therefrom in the light most favorable to the Rizzos, as verdict winners. We will only upset the findings if there is insufficient evidence, or if the trial court committed an error of law....

....

... Haines argues that the trial court improperly imposed liability based on his exercise of judgment on matters of strategy and tactics, and that the trial court improperly imposed on him a duty to elicit his adversary's undisclosed settlement authority. The court also erred, according to Haines, by holding that expert testimony was not needed to detail the appropriate standard of care, and by holding that the damages were not speculative. In addition, Haines asserts that the trial court ... erred by imposing punitive damages....

In *Schenkel v. Monheit,* 266 Pa.Super. 396, 405 A.2d 493 (1979), the Superior Court held that an allegedly aggrieved client must establish three elements in order to recover for legal malpractice. They are:

"1. The employment of the attorney or other basis for duty;

2. The failure of the attorney to exercise ordinary skill and knowledge; and

3. That such negligence was the proximate cause of damage to the plaintiff."

We believe that the necessity for an attorney's use of ordinary skill and knowledge extends to the conduct of settlement negotiations. As this Court stated in *Rothman v. Fillette,* 503 Pa. 259, 469 A.2d 543 (1983), in addition to the fact that settlement is the faster way to get money into the hands of the victims of tortious conduct,

> "[v]oluntary settlement of civil controversies is in high judicial favor. Judges and lawyers alike strive assiduously to promote amicable adjustments of matters in dispute, as for the most wholesome of reasons they certainly should. When the

> effort is successful, the parties avoid the expense and delay incidental to litigation of the issues; the court is spared the burdens of a trial and the preparation and proceedings that must forerun it."

Id. at 267, 469 A.2d at 546 (footnote omitted) (quoting *Autera v. Robinson,* 419 F.2d 1197, 1199 (D.C.Cir.1969)). We recognize that a disappointed client may be inclined to subject his or her attorney to the standard that only hindsight may provide, and as a general policy there should be judicial reluctance to relitigate suits in the guise of legal malpractice. Nevertheless, as stated in *Gans v. Mundy,* 762 F.2d 338 (3d Cir.1985):

> "[A]n attorney's considered decision *involving at a minimum the requisite exercise of 'ordinary skill and capacity,'* and which is an 'informed judgment,' does not constitute malpractice." *Id.* at 341 (emphasis added). Therefore, an attorney may not shield himself from liability in failing to exercise the requisite degree of professional skill in settling the case by asserting that he was merely following a certain strategy or exercising professional judgment. Rather, the importance of settlement to the client and society mandates that an attorney utilize ordinary skill and knowledge.

Consistent with ordinary skill and knowledge, it was incumbent upon Haines, as a matter of law, to communicate all settlement offers to his client.[9] This rule derives from the settled principle that an attorney must have express authority from the client to settle the case. Since the client's choice to accept or reject a settlement offer must be an informed one, we further believe that Haines was also under a duty to investigate the offers that were proposed by the City. Thus, contrary to Haines' assertion, the duty imposed by the trial court was not simply that he elicit his opponent's maximum settlement authority in the form of an offer. Rather, it was a duty to take reasonable steps to investigate the inquiries or offers that the City extended.

....

... Haines clearly breached this duty to investigate settlement offers by failing to respond to Moran's comment at trial that he could get more than $550,000. Despite the comment, he took no steps to ascertain how much "more" the City was willing to pay. He also breached the duty to communicate this settlement offer to his client. Since the other elements of attorney malpractice have been met, we hold that breach of these duties is sufficient to support a malpractice action.

Concerning the necessity for expert testimony to establish the standard of care, ... this Court [has previously] noted the general rule that expert testimony is essential where it would help the finder of fact understand an issue that is beyond the knowledge of the average person. Clearly, where the issues are not beyond such knowledge, the appropriate standard of care can be established without expert testimony. Where the issue is simple, and the lack of skill obvious, the ordinary experience and comprehension of lay persons can establish the standard of care.

Instantly, the Rizzos presented the expert testimony of M. Mark Mendel, Esquire.... [W]e agree with the trial court that breach of the duty to investigate, and to inform one's

9. Similarly, the Rules of Professional Conduct provide:

> (a) A lawyer shall abide by a client's decisions concerning the objectives of representation ... and shall consult with the client as to the means by which they are to be pursued. *A lawyer shall abide by a client's decision whether to accept an offer of settlement of a matter.*

Rules of Professional Conduct 1.2(a) (1988) (emphasis added).

client of, settlement offers does not require expert testimony. *See Joos, supra,* 94 Mich.App. at 423, 288 N.W.2d at 445 ("It is well within the ordinary knowledge and experience of a layman jury to recognize that ... the failure of an attorney to disclose [settlement offers] is a breach of the professional standard of care."). *See also Wright v. Williams,* 47 Cal.App.3d. 802, 810, 121 Cal.Rptr. 194, 200 (1975) ("In some circumstances, the failure of attorney performance may be so clear that the trier of fact may find professional negligence unaided by the testimony of experts."). Instantly, there was sufficient nonexpert testimony to support the finding that Haines breached the standard of care by failing to investigate and inform his client of the City's settlement offer.

....

[I]n order for one to prevail on a claim of legal malpractice, one must establish that the party against whom the initial claim was asserted, in this case the City, would have reached agreement upon a settlement in an ascertainable amount.... Sheldon Albert testified that Mr. Moran had the authority to settle the case for $300,000 plus a lifetime pension, and Mr. Moran testified that, at trial, he had the authority to settle the case for $750,000.... Instantly, firm settlement offers *were* communicated to Haines, and the attorney making the offers had the authority to settle. In addition, Haines was authorized to settle at about $750,000. Thus, we are unpersuaded by Haines' assertion that the damages were uncertain. The trial court awarded $300,000 in compensatory damages based on the difference between Rizzo's actual recovery and what he would have recovered except for Haines' negligence. We believe that this calculation was proper.

....

[T]he Superior Court was correct in holding that Haines must pay interest at the market rate on the $50,000 that he fraudulently induced his client to transfer to him. Courts in this Commonwealth should not permit a person guilty of fraudulently withholding the funds of another to profit therefrom. Accordingly, where funds are wrongfully and intentionally procured or withheld from one who seeks their restoration, the court should calculate interest on these monies at the market rate.

....

The Order of the Superior Court is affirmed.

FLAHERTY, Justice, concurring.

I join the majority but express my concern about creating precedent which imposes liability on an attorney for a settlement strategy and for not "second guessing" a jury or being unaware of the actual limits of authority of an opposing attorney during settlement negotiations of a civil law suit; certainly a dangerous step and one which should be approached with the utmost caution. I do not believe, however, this case sets such a precedent.

ZAPPALA, J., joins this concurring opinion.

* * *

More on Expert Testimony in Legal Malpractice. In addition to suing her former divorce attorney for breach of fiduciary duty, the plaintiff in *Stanley v. Richmond,* 35 Cal. App. 4th 1070 (1995), excerpted in Chapter 3, *supra,* sued her former divorce attorney alleging professional malpractice. On appeal, the plaintiff alleged that the trial court erred in ruling that she did not present sufficient expert testimony about the applicable standard of care and the breach of that standard by Attorney Richmond:

> ... Where a malpractice action is brought against an attorney holding [herself] out as a legal specialist and the claim against the attorney relates to [her] expertise, then only a person knowledgeable in the specialty can define the applicable duty of care and render an opinion on whether it was met. However, '[w]here the failure of attorney performance is so clear that a trier of fact may find professional negligence unassisted by expert testimony, then expert testimony is not required.' In other words, if the attorney's negligence is readily apparent from the facts of the case, then the testimony of an expert may not be necessary. (*Goebel v. Lauderdale* (1989) 214 Cal.App.3d 1502, 1508 [263 Cal.Rptr. 275] [expert testimony from bankruptcy specialist not necessary to establish professional negligence claim against bankruptcy attorney who failed to perform even the most perfunctory legal research and, thus, advised his general contractor client to handle financial affairs in a manner that violated Penal Code section 484b].)
>
> ....
>
> [R]espondent's advice with respect to [her client's husband's] VA pension "demonstrates a total failure to perform even the most perfunctory research" on the *legal* issues presented by [the representation]. The testimony of a family law expert was not necessary to establish whether respondent was negligent by failing to perform a simple research task, and by responding to a client's request for advice about the "pluses and minuses" of a decision without the benefit of valuable, and readily available, information. This was *not* an unsettled question of law....
>
> An attorney who has conducted a "thorough, contemporaneous research effort," demonstrated "detailed knowledge of legal developments and debate in the field," and made a decision which represented a "reasoned exercise of an informed judgment grounded upon a professional evaluation of applicable legal principles," may be entitled to judgment as a matter of law.... [Attorney] Richmond ... completely failed to research standard legal materials containing information that was important to her client's [representation]. We hold that it was a question of fact within the ken of a lay jury to decide whether respondent's failure to conduct a few minutes—or even a few hours—of legal research, and her failure to discover information that could have been "easily discovered through standard research techniques," was a violation of the applicable standard of care....

Stanley v. Richmond, 35 Cal. App. 4th 1070 (1995).

2. The Role of Professional Standards (Including Disciplinary Rules) in Establishing Duty and Breach

In presenting evidence regarding the applicable standard of care—particularly expert testimony regarding the standard of care—a common question regarding the role of the applicable professional or ethical standards may arise, an issue addressed in the following case.

Focus Questions: *Hizey v. Carpenter*

1. *May ethics rules desgined to govern the conduct of lawyers be used to establish the standard of care in a legal malpractice action?*
2. *What policy considerations are of concern in determining whether legal ethics or disciplinary rules may be used to establish the standard of care in a legal malpractice action?*
3. *Should the legal "specialist" be held to a differing standard of care in a legal malpractice action?*

Hizey v. Carpenter

119 Wash.2d 251
(1992)

DOLLIVER, Justice.

In an action for legal malpractice, plaintiffs attempted to apprise the jury of the Code of Professional Responsibility (CPR) and the Rules of Professional Conduct (RPC) through expert testimony and jury instructions. The trial court excluded reference to the CPR and the RPC, through either an expert's mention of them or their use as jury instructions. The jury returned a verdict in favor of the defendants.

Plaintiffs appealed the trial court's ruling disallowing reference to the CPR and RPC, and the Court of Appeals certified the issue to this court for resolution. We accepted certification and transferred the case to this court for disposition.... We now affirm the trial court, holding an expert witness may neither explicitly refer to the CPR or RPC nor may their existence be revealed to the jury via instructions.

Gordon and Jessie Hizey, Baryldean Jo Carlson, Guy and Doris Fenimore, and Jeri Pickering sought legal advice from Timothy Carpenter regarding the sale of an 11.5 acre parcel of commercially zoned property in Mount Vernon, Washington. Plaintiffs had purchased the property in 1968 for $80,000 and, prior to the transaction at issue, had sold two portions of the property to unrelated purchasers and were trying to sell the remainder.

In 1978, plaintiffs borrowed a $249,000 development loan from Mount Baker Bank and made interest-only payments on the loan. By 1983, plaintiffs were behind in interest payments and delinquent in tax payments. Additionally, there were liens against the property as a result of lawsuits against the Fenimores. Mount Baker Bank, which was considering foreclosure, would not make a new loan to plaintiffs alone.

In late 1982 or early 1983, plaintiffs were approached by the Four Star Group—of which James and May Finnegan were members—which wished to purchase the subject property for $950,000. Plaintiffs intended to give the purchasers a $270,000 "credit" against the price for paying off the underlying obligation to Mount Baker Bank. Plaintiffs signed a purchase and sale agreement with the buyers on June 18, 1983. Shortly thereafter, they met with Mount Baker Bank's Lynn Carpenter (wife of the defendant attorney herein), to discuss ways to restructure their loan based on the purchase and sale agreement. The bank would not agree to a straight sale without a substantial cash payment. In addition, the bank considered all members of the Four Star Group less than credit worthy except for the Finnegans, who planned to incorporate as Finnco. Given Mr. Finnegan's financial strength, the bank was willing to consider another loan provided all the original parties remained obligated under it. At this juncture, plaintiffs believed their negotiations with the buyers should be put in writing; they needed a document drafted to replace the original, unacceptable purchase and sale agreement, and they contacted Mr. Carpenter.

Plaintiffs brought the rejected purchase and sale agreement to their meeting with Mr. Carpenter, asking him to prepare a joint venture agreement (JVA) using the terms they gave him. They were anxious to have the documents prepared quickly so the loan would be extended and foreclosure avoided. Mr. Carpenter felt the plaintiffs and Finnegans' group were in "total agreement" on what they wanted, as there was no negotiating or disagreement. He prepared a JVA which did not personally obligate the Finnegans, but obligated their corporation, Finnco; Mr. Carpenter testified he did not inform plaintiffs who was obligated.

As a result of the JVA, a $425,000 loan was approved, which was used to pay off the $249,000 existing loan, back taxes, and liens. Mr. Finnegan then worked on obtaining construction financing to build a hotel. As a prerequisite to obtaining construction financing, it was necessary to have title in the Finnegans' name. To achieve this, plaintiffs asked Mr. Carpenter to draft an agreement converting the JVA to a limited partnership. The limited partnership necessarily converted plaintiffs from creditors to investors or, as Mr. Carpenter admitted, from a debt to an equity situation.

In early 1986, although they had begun building the hotel, the Finnegans/Finnco were nearing bankruptcy. Around July 1986, Mr. Carpenter drafted a proposed furniture, fixtures, and equipment agreement (FF & E) in the hopes of saving the hotel project. The FF & E would have further subordinated plaintiffs' interest in the property, and Mr. Carpenter therefore advised them, for the first time, to seek independent counsel.

The Finnegans ultimately went bankrupt. Plaintiffs filed a claim, but the Finnegans' bankruptcy attorney took the position plaintiffs were owed nothing, since they were investors, not creditors. Plaintiffs eventually settled for $300,000, were awarded $150,000, and netted around $99,000.

Plaintiffs sued Mr. Carpenter in 1987, claiming they were unaware he "represented" both them and the Finnegans/Finnco in drafting documents. At trial, defendants moved to exclude the testimony of Professor David Boerner—one of plaintiffs' expert witnesses—on grounds he was not an expert in real estate law, but would testify to the ethical obligations of an attorney. Such testimony was inadmissible, they argued, because the CPR and RPC do not create standards of civil liability. The trial court ruled Professor Boerner could not "ground" his testimony on the CPR and RPC, *i.e.,* he could not refer to specific rules or testify as to the existence of a codified body of ethics rules for attorneys. In addition, he could not testify the CPR or RPC set the standard of care in an action for legal malpractice. Professor Boerner was, however, allowed to testify that an attorney has ethical duties and to explain what those duties were in this case. As well as expounding on many other ethical aspects of the client-lawyer relationship, Professor Boerner defined a conflict of interest and explained an attorney's obligations when a conflict arises. He claimed there was a conflict of interest in this case and concluded Mr. Carpenter failed to fulfill his obligations in the conflict setting.

The jury returned a verdict in favor of defendant Carpenter, finding he had not been negligent. Plaintiffs moved for judgment notwithstanding the verdict (judgment n.o.v.) or, in the alternative, new trial. Both were denied. This appeal followed.

In addition to the issue certified to this court, plaintiffs claim the trial court erred in refusing to instruct the jury on the standard of care required of a "real estate specialist".... We address the issues seriatim.

(1) In a legal malpractice action, may the jury be informed of the Code of Professional Responsibility or the Rules of Professional Conduct either directly through jury instructions or by the testimony of experts who refer to the CPR or RPC?

During the period in which Mr. Carpenter was representing plaintiffs, his actions were governed by the CPR and the RPC. The CPR applied until September 1, 1985, when it was superseded by the RPC. Plaintiffs contend the jury should have been informed of the existence of the CPR and RPC, as well as informed of the relevant provisions of each, either through the expert testimony of Professor David Boerner, or through jury instructions. Plaintiffs' argument, essentially, is that the CPR and RPC conclusively establish ethical standards of care for attorneys, and those ethical standards should also be relevant to the legal standard of care in a malpractice action. A violation of the CPR or RPC, they argue, is evidence of a breach of the attorney's duty and their expert should have been able to refer to specific provisions of the CPR and RPC in testifying as to the standard of care and its breach. Plaintiffs also argue the jury should have been instructed on the relevant portions of the CPR and RPC. The provisions of which plaintiff wanted the jury made aware were CPR DR 4-101(B) (preserving confidences and secrets of a client), CPR DR 5-105 (refusing to accept or continue employment if interests of another client may impair independent professional judgment of lawyer); CPR DR 7-101 (zealous representation); RPC 1.1 (competence); RPC 1.2 (scope of representation); RPC 1.4 (communication); RPC 1.6 (confidentiality); RPC 1.7 (conflicts of interest); and RPC 2.1 (advisor).

Neither the CPR nor the RPC purport to set the standard for civil liability. Quite to the contrary, the preliminary statement to the RPC states:

> The rules make no attempt to prescribe either disciplinary procedures or penalties for violation of a rule, nor do they undertake to define standards for civil liability of lawyers for professional conduct.

The CPR contained a similar disclaimer:

> The code makes no attempt to prescribe either disciplinary procedures or penalties for violation of a Disciplinary Rule, nor does it undertake to define standards for civil liability of lawyers for professional conduct.

Preliminary Statement, CPR.

Based on such language, most courts that have addressed the issue hold violations of the CPR or RPC do not give rise to an independent cause of action against the attorney.

The result of such holdings, with which we concur, has been that breach of an ethics rule provides only a public, *e.g.*, disciplinary, remedy and not a private remedy. Because the CPR and RPC explicitly, and in what we deem to be clear and unambiguous language, disclaim any intent to create civil liability standards, we refuse to hold their violation creates a cause of action for malpractice.

Plaintiffs argue even if a violation of the CPR or RPC does not *create* a cause of action, such violation nonetheless provides evidence of malpractice. We are aware several commentators adhere to plaintiffs' view. In addition, we note several courts have adopted plaintiffs' position, but with little or no supporting rationale. Some courts simply assumed, with no analysis as to *why*, the CPR and RPC constitute evidence of the legal standard of care required of attorneys. One court found it "anomalous" to hold professional standards of ethics not relevant in a tort action, while another simply found it "unfair". Still others attempted some analysis of the issue, and ultimately equated the CPR and RPC with statutes—an analogy which we explore below.

We disagree with plaintiffs'—and the aforementioned courts' and commentators'—position that violation of the CPR or RPC may be used as evidence of malpractice. Again, we find the disclaimer language in both the CPR and RPC to be clear and unambiguous. In addition, there are significant policy reasons for barring the use of a violation of the CPR or RPC as evidence of attorney malpractice.

The CPR and RPC are ill-suited for use in the malpractice arena.

To establish a claim for legal malpractice, a plaintiff must prove the following elements: (1) The existence of an attorney-client relationship which gives rise to a duty of care on the part of the attorney to the client; (2) an act or omission by the attorney in breach of the duty of care; (3) damage to the client; and (4) proximate causation between the attorney's breach of the duty and the damage incurred.

To comply with the duty of care, an attorney must exercise the degree of care, skill, diligence, and knowledge commonly possessed and exercised by a reasonable, careful, and prudent lawyer in the practice of law in this jurisdiction. In Washington, the standard of care for lawyers is a statewide, rather than a local or community standard.

Plaintiffs would have the fact finder in a legal malpractice action rely, at least in part, on an alleged ethical violation to find a breach of the legal standard of care. In furtherance of their argument, plaintiffs analogize the CPR and RPC to statutes or administrative regulations, the violation of which produces evidence of negligence or, in some jurisdictions, negligence per se. This analogy is flawed. The CPR and RPC are not statutes or administrative regulations. This court, not the Legislature, adopted the Code of Professional Responsibility and the Rules of Professional Conduct by court order, pursuant to its power to regulate the practice of law within the state.

Furthermore, because they were never intended as a basis for civil liability, the CPR and RPC contain standards and phrases which, when relied upon to establish a breach of the legal standard of care, provide only vague guidelines ... Indeed, the Rules of Professional Conduct purport only to "state the minimum level of conduct below which no lawyer can fall without being subject to disciplinary action." Preliminary Statement, RPC. Malpractice liability, on the other hand, is premised on the conduct of the "reasonable" lawyer. One court has succinctly stated the problem created when an alleged code violation is used as evidence of a breach of the standard of care:

> [I]n a civil action charging malpractice, the standard of care is the *particular duty* owed the client under the circumstances of the representation, which may or may not be the standard contemplated by the Code.

(Italics ours.) *Lazy Seven Coal Sales, Inc. v. Stone & Hinds, P.C.*, 813 S.W.2d 400, 405 (Tenn.1991).

We are not persuaded that either standard should be abandoned in favor of the other. On the contrary, both should continue to operate in their relative, *separate* spheres. As two noted commentators in the area of legal malpractice explain:

> There are several significant differences between a civil malpractice action and a disciplinary proceeding. First, a lawyer may be disciplined even if the misconduct does not cause any damage. The rationale is the need for protection of the public and the integrity of the profession. Second, although the severity of the breach may affect the nature of the discipline, the prophylactic purpose of the ethical rules may result in a sanction even if the conduct would not otherwise constitute a civil wrong. Third, even if the injured party initiates a disciplinary complaint, that individual is not a party to the proceeding. *These differences often mean that*

> *a rule promulgated for discipline is inappropriate as a principle of law or standard for defining proper civil conduct* (italics ours; footnotes omitted).

1 Mallen & Smith § 1.9, at 33.

Use of the CPR and RPC in the malpractice arena would contravene their purpose.

As Mallen and Smith point out, ethics rules protect both the public *and* the integrity of the profession. They do so by establishing and regulating a balance among the court, attorneys, and clients.... Adoption of plaintiffs' position would upset that balance.

In evaluating the usefulness of the model rules as a standard of civil liability, two Montana commentators recognized their state supreme court adopted the rules to aid the legal system:

> The Model Rules exist to ensure the integrity of the legal system as a whole by forcefully reminding attorneys that their first loyalty is to the court. Taking the Model Rules out of this context removes the motivating force behind them. A legal malpractice suit neglects the party most involved in and affected by the professional standards of the Model Rules—the legal system itself. In a legal malpractice suit, however, the court reverts to its accustomed role as arbiter. The suit focuses on the relationship between the attorney *and* the client. Using the Model Rules in this context renders two harms. First, their use would emphasize only one aspect of the Model Rules—the attorney/client—to the exclusion of the Model Rules' impact on the legal system. Second, their use would encourage attorneys to elevate those Model Rules which relate to the attorney-client relationship. Attorneys would thereby distance themselves from the court system and consider more important their relationship with clients than their relationship with the legal system.

Faure & Strong at 375.

We concur with these observations.

Underlying our decision not to extend the CPR and RPC into the malpractice arena is the conviction that plaintiffs already have available adequate and recognized common law theories under which to bring malpractice actions....

....

To avoid confusion in practice, we point out experts on an attorney's duty of care may still properly base their opinion, as Professor Boerner did in this case, on an attorney's failure to conform to an ethics rule. In so testifying, however, the expert must address the breach of the *legal* duty of care, and not simply the supposed breach of the ethics rules. Such testimony may not be presented in such a way that the jury could conclude it was the ethical violations that were actionable, rather than the breach of the legal duty of care. In practice, this can be achieved by allowing the expert to use language from the CPR or RPC, but prohibiting explicit reference to them. The expert must testify generally as to ethical requirements, concluding the attorney's violations of the ethical rules constituted a deviation from the legal standard of care. Without this evidentiary link, the plaintiff risks dismissal of the malpractice case for failure properly to establish the breach of the duty of care....

Jury instructions, moreover, may not refer to the CPR or RPC. An expert's mention of them or their use as the basis of jury instructions could mislead the jury into believing the CPR and RPC conclusively establish the standard of care—precisely the result we wish to avoid. A balance must be maintained between legally enforceable standards of care—*i.e.*, an existing common law sufficient to support civil grievances—and the professional autonomy and the enforcement of ethical standards by the professional rules. We believe an appropriate balance will continue to be maintained in this jurisdiction by the position we adopt in this case.

We therefore hold in a legal malpractice action that the jury may not be informed of the CPR or RPC, either directly through jury instructions or through the testimony of an expert who refers to the CPR or RPC.

....

[The court's discussion regarding the appropriate standard of care for legal specialists is excerpted in Section D, *infra.*]

... We affirm the trial court in all respects.

* * *

C. The Locality Rule

As discussed in the previous cases, the standard of care in a negligence action arises by operation of tort law, and in the legal professional context a lawyer owes a duty of care to act as the reasonable prudent professional under the same or similar circumstances. Questions sometimes arise regarding how inclusive those "circumstances" should be. Consider the following materials, which consider whether a legal professional's circumstances should take into account the location of the legal services rendered.

Focus Questions: *Chapman v. Bearfield*

1. *What is the locality rule?*
2. *What are the justifications in favor of and in opposition to adopting the locality rule?*
3. *What rule does the* Chapman *court adopt for Tennessee?*

Chapman v. Bearfield

207 S.W.3d 736
(Tenn. 2006)

CORNELIA A. CLARK, J.

We accepted this appeal to clarify whether experts testifying in legal malpractice cases must be familiar with a single, statewide professional standard of care or a standard of care for a particular locality within the state. Because we hold that a single, statewide professional standard of care exists for attorneys practicing in Tennessee, expert witnesses testifying in legal malpractice cases must be familiar with the statewide professional standard. The judgment of the Court of Appeals is affirmed. We remand the case to the trial court for further proceedings consistent with this opinion.

BACKGROUND

Cathy L. Chapman and other members of the Chapman family ("the Chapmans") retained Johnson City attorney Rick J. Bearfield ("Bearfield") in 2001 to represent them in a medical malpractice action resulting from a Chapman family member's death. The Chapmans became dissatisfied with Bearfield's representation and obtained new counsel. After reviewing the case, the Chapmans' new counsel advised them to file a legal malpractice suit against Bearfield. On July 8, 2004, in the Washington County Circuit Court, the Chapmans filed pro se the legal malpractice action against Bearfield that has generated this appeal.

Bearfield answered the Chapmans' complaint and denied numerous factual allegations. Bearfield subsequently moved for summary judgment. In support of his motion, Bearfield filed a Statement of Material Facts ... and his own affidavit. In the affidavit, Bearfield opined that neither he nor any attorney under his direction had committed malpractice, citing as his authority the professional standard of care applicable to attorneys "in the upper East Tennessee area."

The Chapmans responded to Bearfield's motion, submitting their own Statement of Material Facts and the affidavit of Richard L. Duncan, a Knoxville medical malpractice attorney. Duncan asserted that he was "familiar with the standard of care for attorneys in medical malpractice cases in Tennessee" and opined that Bearfield's prosecution of the Chapmans' medical malpractice claim fell below the standard of what "a reasonable attorney under similar circumstances" would have done.

....

... Bearfield attacked the sufficiency of Duncan's affidavit because Duncan did not demonstrate a familiarity with the professional standard of care required of attorneys in upper east Tennessee....

....

... [T]he trial court granted summary judgment to Bearfield because ... the Duncan affidavit did not meet what the judge termed "the locality rule": the affidavit did not demonstrate Duncan's familiarity with the professional standard of care required of attorneys in that part of east Tennessee....

The Chapmans appealed. The Court of Appeals vacated the grant of summary judgment. First, the intermediate appellate court could find no basis for a "locality rule" that governs the conduct of an attorney practicing law in Tennessee. Second, the court found the Duncan affidavit technically deficient but reasoned that the Chapmans should have received extra time to correct the mistake.

We accepted this appeal to clarify whether experts testifying in legal malpractice cases must be familiar with a single statewide professional standard of care or a standard of care for a particular locality within the state. We hold that a single, statewide professional standard of care exists for attorneys practicing in Tennessee and that expert witnesses testifying in legal malpractice cases must be familiar with the statewide professional standard of care.

DISCUSSION

....

A Statewide Professional Standard of Care for Tennessee Attorneys

In *Spalding v. Davis,* 674 S.W.2d 710 (Tenn.1984), the Court noted that "[t]he settled general rule in most if not all [United States] jurisdictions is that an attorney ... may be held liable to his client for damages resulting from his failure to exercise [the] ordinary care, skill, and diligence ... which is commonly possessed and exercised by attorneys in practice in the *jurisdiction.*" *Id.* at 714 (emphasis added)....

Since 1984, various panels of the Court of Appeals have been inconsistent in defining the "jurisdiction" referenced in *Spalding.* On the one hand, two reported opinions of the Court of Appeals have linked the legal malpractice standard of care with the medical malpractice standard, which is governed by a statutory locality rule. *See Underwood v. Waterslides of Mid-Am., Inc.,* 823 S.W.2d 171, 183 (Tenn.Ct.App.1991) (finding that a professional's familiarity with "the local standard of care is the exception rather than the rule," with the principal exceptions being law and medicine); *Cleckner v. Dale,* 719 S.W.2d 535, 539 (Tenn.Ct.App.1986) ("a lawyer's standard of care does not differ markedly from that of physicians or other professionals") (internal quotation marks and citations omitted). On the other hand, one intermediate appellate court panel understood "jurisdiction" to mean "Tennessee." *See Wood v. Parker,* 901 S.W.2d 374, 379 (Tenn.Ct.App.1995) ("[w]e find nothing ... to show that defendant ... deviated from the accepted standard of care for attorneys in *Tennessee*") (emphasis added). In this case, the Court of Appeals, in its opinion below, also adopted a statewide professional standard of care.

We agree with the instant decision of the Court of Appeals. A "jurisdiction" is "[a] geographic area within which political or judicial authority may be exercised." *Black's Law Dictionary* 855 (7th ed.1999); *see also Webster's Third New International Dictionary* 1227 (1993) (defining jurisdiction as "the limits or territory within which any particular power may be exercised"). This Court allows an attorney with a Tennessee law license to practice anywhere in the state.... An attorney practicing in Tennessee, then, must exercise the ordinary care, skill, and diligence commonly possessed and practiced by attorneys *throughout the state.* Indeed, while there may be local *rules of practice* within the various judicial districts of our State, there are no local *standards of care.* There is only one standard of care for attorneys practicing in Tennessee: a statewide standard. By extension, an expert who opines in a legal malpractice case about an attorney's adherence to our professional standard of care must be familiar with the statewide professional standard of care.

Bearfield argues that the medical malpractice locality rule should be extended to legal malpractice actions. However, the locality rule for medical malpractice is a creature of statute. *See* Tenn.Code Ann. § 29-26-115(a)(1) (Supp.2005) (standard of care relates to "the community in which the defendant practices or in a similar community"). Neither this Court nor the legislature has created a similar standard for the legal profession, and we decline to create one here.

We also believe the adoption of a statewide professional standard of care for attorneys who practice law in Tennessee is good policy. Three concerns motivate our conclusion. First, if a local professional standard of care prevailed, plaintiffs might have difficulty proving their legal malpractice cases because local attorneys might not be willing to speak against their colleagues.... Second, local variations in the standard of care could create an inefficient and inequitable morass of professional standards of care, reducing the likelihood that some attorneys would face malpractice claims while increasing the likelihood for others.... Finally, the emergence of the internet as a primary tool for legal research undercuts historical transportation and communications arguments favoring local variations in the standard of care. We join those states which have accepted these and other rationales for maintaining a statewide standard of professional care for their attorneys. *See, e.g., Brett v. Berkowitz,* 706 A.2d 509, 517 (Del.Super.Ct.1998); *Kellos v. Sawilowsky,* 254 Ga. 4, 325 S.E.2d 757, 758 (1985); *Fenaille v. Coudert,* 44 N.J.L. 286, 289 (N.J.1882); *Little v.*

Matthewson, 114 N.C.App. 562, 442 S.E.2d 567, 570 (1994), *aff'd* 340 N.C. 102, 455 S.E.2d 160 (1995); *Feil v. Wishek,* 193 N.W.2d 218, 225 (N.D.1971); *Smith v. Haynsworth, Marion, McKay & Geurard,* 322 S.C. 433, 472 S.E.2d 612, 614 (1954); *Russo v. Griffin,* 147 Vt. 20, 510 A.2d 436, 438 (1986); *Cook, Flanagan & Berst v. Clausing,* 73 Wash.2d 393, 438 P.2d 865, 866 (1975); *Moore v. Lubnau,* 855 P.2d 1245, 1250 (Wyo.1993).

Because there is a statewide professional standard of care for attorneys practicing in Tennessee, the Court of Appeals correctly overturned the trial court's award of summary judgment to Bearfield. The Chapmans' expert affiant did not need to assert knowledge of any practice standards peculiar to the "upper East Tennessee area." To the contrary, he correctly asserted his knowledge of the professional standard of care for attorneys practicing in Tennessee....

....

CONCLUSION

A single, statewide professional standard of care exists for attorneys practicing law in Tennessee. Therefore, experts testifying in legal malpractice cases in Tennessee must be familiar with the professional standard of care for the entire state. We affirm the judgment of the Court of Appeals and remand this case to the trial court for further proceedings consistent with this opinion....

* * *

1. In accord with *Chapman* is *Hizey v. Carpenter,* 119 Wash.2d 251 (1992) ("In Washington, the standard of care for lawyers is a statewide, rather than a local or community standard."). *See* Section B.2, *supra.*

2. In *Russo v. Griffin,* 510 A.2d 436 (Vt. 1986), a case referenced in *Chapman,* Justice Hayes, concurring in part and dissenting in part, explained:

> I agree with the majority that the correct standard to which an attorney should be held in the performance of professional services is *not* the standard of his or her locality. If there are only two lawyers in a small town, and both are incompetent, they cannot set a standard of inferiority for a third who comes to town.
>
> I disagree with the Court's holding that the applicable standard of care should be a *state* standard. Doctors in Vermont are required to adhere to standards based upon the medical profession generally. Lawyers should be subject to a similar standard of care based on their profession.
>
> The scope of an attorney's obligation to his or her client should not vary with geography. The law schools of today are truly national in legal training. Vermont and almost all other states give a multistate bar examination. Much of our continuing legal education is national in scope. Why then must candidates for admission to the Vermont bar clear a multistate hurdle, and be required to meet only a state standard for performance once admitted?
>
> I would require that the standard of care for Vermont lawyers be based upon the legal profession generally, and I would reject a state or local standard.
>
> We are members of a profession that has not won a full measure of public confidence. To adopt a state standard is to say that what may be considered attorney negligence in New Hampshire may not violate the standard of adequacy of legal services in Vermont. Such a caliper to measure attorney conduct will lower public esteem for the Vermont legal profession and will arouse suspicions

> in lay circles that we have selected a cemetery in the Green Mountains in which quietly to bury the faults of our legal brothers and sisters.

Do you agree or disagree with Justice Hayes? Explain your position.

D. Specialists

Focus Questions: *Hizey v. Carpenter*

1. *According to the* Hizey *court, are legal specialists held to a different standard of care?*
2. *If so, define the standard of care in a legal malpractice action brought against a lawyer specializing in a particular area of law.*

Hizey v. Carpenter

119 Wash.2d 251
(1992)

DOLLIVER, Justice.

[The facts of this case and the court's discussion of whether the legal ethics rules may be used to establish the standard of care in a negligence action are set forth in section B.2, *supra.*]

....

(2) Did the trial court err in refusing to instruct the jury on the standard of care required of a "real estate specialist"?

Plaintiffs' proposed jury instruction 14, which the trial court declined to give, provided:

> A lawyer who holds himself out as a specialist in real estate related legal matters has a duty to exercise the degree of skill, care and learning reasonably expected of a reasonably prudent lawyer in the State of Washington acting in the same or similar circumstances at the time in question. Failure to exercise such skill, care and learning is negligence.

Clerk's Papers, at 165.

The trial court's instruction ... addressed the standard of care as follows:

> A lawyer has a duty to exercise the degree of skill, care and learning expected of a reasonably prudent lawyer in the State of Washington acting in the same or similar circumstances at the time such services are provided. Failure to exercise such skill, care and learning is negligence.

Clerk's Papers, at 189.

Each party to a lawsuit is entitled to have its theories presented to the jury if such theories are supported by the evidence. *Gammon v. Clark Equip. Co.,* 104 Wash.2d 613, 616, 707 P.2d 685 (1985). Plaintiffs contend the refusal of the trial court to allow proposed jury instruction 14 deprived them of that right. They argue Mr. Carpenter's conduct should have been evaluated under a higher standard of care because he held himself out as a specialist in real estate law....

The courts of this state have frequently held the general "reasonably prudent lawyer" standard applies in legal malpractice cases. In a legal malpractice case involving the mishandling of a federal maritime personal injury action, we stated:

> Generally, one who holds himself out as specializing and as possessing greater than ordinary knowledge and skill in a particular field, will be held to the standard of performance of those who hold themselves out as specialists in that area.

Walker v. Bangs, 92 Wash.2d 854, 860, 601 P.2d 1279 (1979) (citing Restatement (Second) of Torts § 299A, comment *d* (1965)).

....

There is support for the notion that the standard of care should be different for those who hold themselves out as specialists in a particular area of law. In Washington, however, there is no "real estate specialist" standard of care. Moreover, the [Code of Professional Responsibility] and the [Rules of Professional Conduct] prohibit a lawyer from holding himself out as a specialist in certain fields, with few exceptions not applicable in this case. The trial court informed the jury the applicable standard was that of an attorney in the same or similar circumstances. Plaintiffs were not precluded from arguing one of those circumstances was Mr. Carpenter's assertion that he handled real estate matters almost exclusively.

... Based on the lack of authority in Washington for a "specialist" instruction in legal malpractice cases, it was not an abuse of discretion for the trial court to refuse plaintiffs' proposed jury instruction 14.

....

... We affirm the trial court in all respects.

* * *

E. Special Issues: Duties to "Non-Clients" in Legal Malpractice

Lawyers can subject themselves to criticism and liability by practicing law while being single-mindedly devoted to the interests of their clients. Lawyers may unwittingly open themselves up to liability in tort for practicing as if they owe no duty of care to others outside of the official attorney-client relationship. This notion of single-minded devotedness to the client was further perpetuated with the privity requirement in legal malpractice actions. However, the privity requirement has been eliminated in most jurisdictions as a bar to recovery for legal malpractice, and courts now widely recognize a lawyer's potential duty to those outside of the attorney-client relationship to those with whom the lawyer is not in privity. As the court explained in *Chem-Age Indus., Inc. v. Glover*, 652 N.W.2d 756, 770–71 (S.D. 2002):

> Perhaps cognizant that legal malpractice is one of the last citadels of the privity doctrine, the Restatement (Third) of the Law Governing Lawyers sanctions limited instances where a lawyer owes a duty of care to nonclients. *See* Restatement (Third) of the Law Governing Lawyers § 51 (1998). Of course, the Restatement's pronouncements are not binding on this Court; nevertheless, we have found its reasoning persuasive in many instances. Subsections (2) and (3) of § 51 provide in pertinent part:
>
>> For purposes of liability under § 48, a lawyer owes a duty to use care within the meaning of § 52 in *each* of the following circumstances:
>>
>> (2) to a nonclient when and to the extent that:
>>
>>> (a) the lawyer or (with the lawyer's acquiescence) the lawyer's client invites the nonclient to rely on the lawyer's opinion or provision of other legal services, and the nonclient so relies; and
>>>
>>> (b) the nonclient is not, under applicable tort law, too remote from the lawyer to be entitled to protection;
>>
>> (3) to a nonclient when and to the extent that:
>>
>>> (a) the lawyer knows that a client intends as one of the primary objectives of the representation that the lawyer's services benefit the nonclient;
>>>
>>> (b) such a duty would not significantly impair the lawyer's performance of obligations to the client; and
>>>
>>> (c) the absence of such a duty would make enforcement of those obligations to the client unlikely; ...
>
> ... The comment from § 51 further explains this requirement:
>
>> A nonclient's claim under Subsection (3) is recognized *only* when doing so will both implement the client's intent and serve to fulfill the lawyer's obligations to the client without impairing performance of those obligations in the circumstances of the representation. A duty to a third person hence exists *only* when the client intends to benefit the third person as one of the primary objectives of the representation.
>
> Restatement (Third) of the Law Governing Lawyers § 51 cmt. f (1998). Under this limited exception, to establish a duty owed by the attorney to the nonclient, the nonclient
>
>> must allege and prove that the intent of the client to benefit the nonclient was a direct purpose of the transaction or relationship. In this regard, the test for third party recovery is whether the intent to benefit actually existed, not whether there could have been an intent to benefit the third party.
>
> *Flaherty*, 492 A.2d at 625. Thus, an incidental benefit to a nonclient is not sufficient. *Id.* at 625 n. 6.

Chem-Age Indus., Inc. v. Glover, 652 N.W.2d 756, 770–71 (S.D. 2002); *see also* Symposium, *The Lawyer's Duties and Liabilities to Third Parties*, 37 S. Tex. L. Rev. 957–1313 (1996). *But see* C. Chase Senk, Note, *Another Missed Opportunity in* Shoemaker v. Gindlesberger: *Strict Privity Lives on in Ohio Legal Malpractice Cases*, 43 Akron L. Rev. 291 (2010); Tracy M. Mason, Note, *Privity, Duty, and Loss: In* Swanson v. Ptak, *268 Neb. 265, 682 N.W.2d 225 (2004), the Nebraska Supreme Court Again Endorses Privity in Legal Malpractice Actions*, 84 Neb. L. Rev. 369 (2005).

Focus Questions: *Greycas, Inc. v. Proud*

1. *What duty of care is generally owed to a non-client or someone outside of the attorney-client relationship?*
2. *What is the basis of Chief Judge Bauer's concurrence? Why does he write separately?*
3. *According to the majority opinion, what is the distinction between professional malpractice and negligent misrepresentation?*

Greycas, Inc. v. Proud

826 F.2d 1560
(7th Cir. 1987)

POSNER, Circuit Judge.

Theodore S. Proud, Jr., a member of the Illinois bar who practices law in a suburb of Chicago, appeals from a judgment against him for $833,760, entered after a bench trial. The tale of malpractice and misrepresentation that led to the judgment begins with Proud's brother-in-law, Wayne Crawford, like Proud a lawyer but one who devoted most of his attention to a large farm that he owned in downstate Illinois. The farm fell on hard times and by 1981 Crawford was in dire financial straits. He had pledged most of his farm machinery to lenders, yet now desperately needed more money. He approached Greycas, Inc., the plaintiff in this case, a large financial company headquartered in Arizona, seeking a large loan that he offered to secure with the farm machinery. He did not tell Greycas about his financial difficulties or that he had pledged the machinery to other lenders, but he did make clear that he needed the loan in a hurry. Greycas obtained several appraisals of Crawford's farm machinery but did not investigate Crawford's financial position or discover that he had pledged the collateral to other lenders, who had perfected their liens in the collateral. Greycas agreed to lend Crawford $1,367,966.50, which was less than the appraised value of the machinery.

The loan was subject, however, to an important condition, which is at the heart of this case: Crawford was required to submit a letter to Greycas, from counsel whom he would retain, assuring Greycas that there were no prior liens on the machinery that was to secure the loan. Crawford asked Proud to prepare the letter, and he did so, and mailed it to Greycas, and within 20 days of the first contact between Crawford and Greycas the loan closed and the money was disbursed. A year later Crawford defaulted on the loan; shortly afterward he committed suicide. Greycas then learned that most of the farm machinery that Crawford had pledged to it had previously been pledged to other lenders. 

The machinery was sold at auction. The Illinois state court that determined the creditors' priorities in the proceeds of the sale held that Greycas did not have a first priority on most of the machinery that secured its loan; as a result Greycas has been able to recover only a small part of the loan. The judgment it obtained in the present suit is the district judge's estimate of the value that it would have realized on its collateral had there been no prior liens, as Proud represented in his letter.

That letter is the centerpiece of the litigation. Typed on the stationery of Proud's firm and addressed to Greycas, it identifies Proud as Crawford's lawyer and states that, "in such capacity, I have been asked to render my opinion in connection with" the proposed loan to Crawford. It also states that "this opinion is being delivered in accordance with the requirements of the Loan Agreement" and that I have conducted a U.C.C., tax, and judgment search with respect to the Company [i.e., Crawford's farm] as of March 19, 1981, and ... are free and clear of all liens or encumbrances....

The reference to the lender's security interest is to Greycas's interest; Crawford, pursuant to the loan agreement, had filed a notice of that interest with the recorder....

Proud never conducted a search for prior liens on the machinery.... His brother-in-law ... and told him there were no liens other than the one that Crawford had just filed for Greycas. Proud made no effort to verify Crawford's statement. The theory of the complaint is that Proud was negligent in representing that there were no prior liens, merely on his brother-in-law's say-so. No doubt Proud *was* negligent in failing to conduct a search, but we are not clear why the *misrepresentation* is alleged to be negligent rather than deliberate and hence fraudulent, in which event Greycas's alleged contributory negligence would not be an issue (as it is, we shall see), since there is no defense of contributory or comparative negligence to a deliberate tort, such as fraud. Proud did not merely say, "There are no liens"; he said, "I have conducted a U.C.C., tax, and judgment search"; and not only is this statement, too, a false one, but its falsehood cannot have been inadvertent, for Proud knew he had not conducted such a search. The concealment of his relationship with Crawford might also support a charge of fraud. But Greycas decided, for whatever reason, to argue negligent misrepresentation rather than fraud. It may have feared that Proud's insurance policy for professional malpractice excluded deliberate wrongdoing from its coverage, or may not have wanted to bear the higher burden of proving fraud, or may have feared that an accusation of fraud would make it harder to settle the case—for most cases, of course, are settled, though this one has not been. In any event, Proud does not argue that either he is liable for fraud or he is liable for nothing.

He also does not, and could not, deny or justify the misrepresentation; but he argues that it is not actionable under the tort law of Illinois, because he had no duty of care to Greycas. (This is a diversity case and the parties agree that Illinois tort law governs the substantive issues.) He argues that Greycas had an adversarial relationship with Proud's client, Crawford, and that a lawyer has no duty of straight dealing to an adversary, at least none enforceable by a tort suit. In so arguing, Proud is characterizing Greycas's suit as one for professional malpractice rather than negligent misrepresentation, yet elsewhere in his briefs he insists that the suit was solely for negligent misrepresentation—while Greycas insists that its suit charges both torts. Legal malpractice based on a false representation, and negligent misrepresentation by a lawyer, are such similar legal concepts, however, that we have great difficulty both in holding them apart in our minds and in understanding why the parties are quarreling over the exact characterization; no one suggests, for example, that the statute of limitations might have run on one but not the other tort. So we shall discuss both.

Proud is undoubtedly correct in arguing that a lawyer has no general duty of care toward his adversary's client; it would be a considerable and, as it seems to us, an undesirable novelty to hold that every bit of sharp dealing by a lawyer gives rise to prima facie tort liability to the opposing party in the lawsuit or negotiation. The tort of malpractice normally refers to a lawyer's careless or otherwise wrongful conduct toward his own client. Proud argues that Crawford rather than Greycas was his client, and although this is not so clear as Proud supposes—another characterization of the transaction is that Crawford undertook to obtain a lawyer for Greycas in the loan transaction—we shall assume for purposes of discussion that Greycas was not Proud's client.

Therefore if malpractice just meant carelessness or other misconduct toward one's own client, Proud would not be liable for malpractice to Greycas. But in *Pelham v. Griesheimer,* 92 Ill.2d 13, 64 Ill.Dec. 544, 440 N.E.2d 96 (1982), the Supreme Court of Illinois discarded the old common law requirement of privity of contract for professional malpractice; so now it is possible for someone who is not the lawyer's (or other professional's) client to sue him for malpractice. The court in *Pelham* was worried, though, about the possibility of a lawyer's being held liable "to an unlimited and unknown number of potential plaintiffs," so it added that "for a nonclient to succeed in a negligence action against an attorney, he must prove that the primary purpose and intent of the attorney-client relationship itself was to benefit or influence the third party." That, however, describes this case exactly. Crawford hired Proud not only for the primary purpose, but for the sole purpose, of influencing Greycas to make Crawford a loan....

All this assumes that *Pelham* governs this case, but arguably it does not, for Greycas, as we noted, may have decided to bring this as a suit for negligent misrepresentation rather than professional malpractice. We know of no obstacle to such an election; nothing is more common in American jurisprudence than overlapping torts.

The claim of negligent misrepresentation might seem utterly straightforward. It might seem that by addressing a letter to Greycas intended (as Proud's counsel admitted at argument) to induce reliance on the statements in it, Proud made himself prima facie liable for any material misrepresentations, careless or deliberate, in the letter, whether or not Proud was Crawford's lawyer or for that matter anyone's lawyer. Knowing that Greycas was relying on him to determine whether the collateral for the loan was encumbered and to advise Greycas of the results of his determination, Proud negligently misrepresented the situation, to Greycas's detriment. But merely labeling a suit as one for negligent misrepresentation rather than professional malpractice will not make the problem of indefinite and perhaps excessive liability, which induced the court in *Pelham* to place limitations on the duty of care, go away....

....

Later Illinois cases ... influenced by section 552 of the Second Restatement of Torts (1977), state the limitation on liability for negligent misrepresentation in more compact terms.... These are cases in the intermediate appellate court, but, as we have no reason to think the Supreme Court of Illinois would reject them, we are bound to follow them. They hold that "one who in the course of his business or profession supplies information for the guidance of others in their business transactions" is liable for negligent misrepresentations that induce detrimental reliance. *Penrod v. Merrill Lynch, Pierce, Fenner & Smith,* 68 Ill.App.3d 75, 81–82, 24 Ill.Dec. 464, 469, 385 N.E.2d 376, 381 (1979) ... Whether there is a practical as distinct from a merely semantic difference between this formulation of the duty limitation and that of *Pelham* may be doubted but cannot change the outcome of this case. Proud, in the practice of his profession, supplied information (or rather misinformation) to Greycas that was intended to guide Greycas in commercial dealings with Crawford. Proud therefore had a duty to use due care to see that the information was correct. He used no care.

....

There is no serious doubt about the existence of a causal relationship between the misrepresentation and the loan. Greycas would not have made the loan without Proud's letter. Nor would it have made the loan had Proud advised it that the collateral was so heavily encumbered that the loan was as if unsecured, for then Greycas would have known that the probability of repayment was slight. Merely to charge a higher interest rate would not have been an attractive alternative to security; it would have made default virtually inevitable by saddling Crawford with a huge fixed debt. To understand the astronomical interest rate that is required to make an unsecured loan a paying proposition to the lender when the risk of default is high, notice that even if the riskless interest rate is only 3 percent, the rate of inflation zero, the cost of administering the loan zero, and the lender risk-neutral, he still must charge an annual interest rate of 106 percent if he thinks there is only a 50 percent chance that he will get his principal back.

Proud argues, however, that his damages should be reduced in recognition of Greycas's own contributory negligence, which, though no longer a complete defense in Illinois, is a partial defense, renamed "comparative negligence." *Alvis v. Ribar,* 85 Ill.2d 1, 52 Ill.Dec. 23, 421 N.E.2d 886 (1981) ... It is as much a defense to negligent misrepresentation as to any other tort of negligence. On the issue of comparative negligence the district court said only that "defendant may have proved negligence upon the part of plaintiff but that negligence, if any, had no causal relationship to the malpractice of the defendant or the damages to the plaintiff." This comment is not easy to fathom. If Greycas was careless in deciding whether to make the loan, this implies that a reasonable investigation by Greycas would have shown that the collateral for the loan was already heavily encumbered; knowing this, Greycas would not have made the loan and therefore would not have suffered any damages.

But we think it too clear to require a remand for further proceedings that Proud failed to prove a want of due care by Greycas. Due care is the care that is optimal given that the other party is exercising due care. It is not the higher level of care that would be optimal if potential tort victims were required to assume that the rest of the world was negligent. A pedestrian is not required to exercise a level of care (e.g., wearing a helmet or a shin guard) that would be optimal if there were no sanctions against reckless driving. Otherwise drivers would be encouraged to drive recklessly, and knowing this pedestrians would be encouraged to wear helmets and shin guards. The result would be a shift from a superior method of accident avoidance (not driving recklessly) to an inferior one (pedestrian armor).

So we must ask whether Greycas would have been careless not to conduct its own UCC search had Proud done what he had said he did—conduct his own UCC search. The answer is no. The law normally does not require duplicative precautions unless one is likely to fail or the consequences of failure (slight though the likelihood may be) would be catastrophic. One UCC search is enough to disclose prior liens, and Greycas acted reasonably in relying on Proud to conduct it. Although Greycas had much warning that Crawford was in financial trouble and that the loan might not be repaid, that was a reason for charging a hefty interest rate and insisting that the loan be secured; it was not a reason for duplicating Proud's work. It is not hard to conduct a UCC lien search; it just requires checking the records in the recorder's office for the county where the debtor lives.... So the only reason to backstop Proud was if Greycas should have assumed he was careless or dishonest; and we have just said that the duty of care does not require such an assumption. Had Proud disclosed that he was Crawford's brother-in-law this might have been a warning signal that Greycas could ignore only at its peril. To go forward in the face of a known danger is to assume the risk. But Proud did not disclose his relationship to Crawford.

The last issue concerns the amount of damages awarded Greycas. In estimating what Proud's negligence had cost Greycas, the judge relied heavily on the state court's finding that Greycas's lien was subordinate to other liens. Proud complains that it was wrong to give collateral estoppel effect to a finding in a case to which he was not a party. But we do not understand the district judge to have been using the judgment to prevent further inquiry into the question of Greycas's damages. The state court's judgment determining the priority of the liens was merely some evidence of the degree to which Proud's misconduct had injured Greycas; for the injury depended on the size of the perfected liens that were prior to its lien. No one tried to prevent Proud from proving, if he could, that the judgment in the state court was erroneous and that Greycas's lien had actually enjoyed the priority that Proud had represented it to have. Proud offered no such evidence. His attack on the state court judgment must fail.

....

It may seem that the judge was, if anything, unduly generous to Proud, in giving Greycas only the value of the collateral on the date of default, rather than the unpaid principal of the loan. But for Proud's misrepresentations, Greycas would not have made the loan, so its damages are not just the collateral but the entire uncollectable portion of the loan together with the interest that the money would have earned in an alternative use.... We therefore conclude that the realizable value of Greycas's collateral on the date of Crawford's default was a real loss.

A final point. The record of this case reveals serious misconduct by an Illinois attorney. We are therefore sending a copy of this opinion to the Attorney Registration and Disciplinary Commission of the Supreme Court of Illinois for such disciplinary action as may be deemed appropriate in the circumstances.

AFFIRMED.

BAUER, Chief Judge, concurring.

I am in agreement with the majority opinion. I believe that Proud would be liable without reference to legal malpractice or negligent misrepresentation. The evidence in this case indicates that he is guilty of fraud or intentional misrepresentation. He was lying when he represented that he had made U.C.C., tax and judgment searches on his brother-in-law's farm. He intended the misrepresentation to induce Greycas to make a loan to his brother-in-law; Greycas justifiably relied upon the misrepresentation in making the loan and was injured as a result. Under these facts, Proud's misrepresentation was indefensible.

Focus Questions: *Lucas v. Hamm*

1. *According to* Lucas v. Hamm, *might an attorney owe a duty of care to one outside of the attorney-client relationship? If so, how does the court define the contours of that duty?*
2. *What did precedent in this jurisdiction provide regarding whether an attorney owes a duty of care to one outside of the attorney-client relationship?*
3. *Did the defendant attorney in* Lucas v. Hamm *owe a duty of care to the plaintiffs (non-client beneficiaries)? Were the plaintiffs permitted to recover in negligence from the attorney? Why or why not?*

Lucas v. Hamm

364 P.2d 685
(Cal. 1961)

GIBSON, Chief Justice.

Plaintiffs, who are some of the beneficiaries under the will of Eugene H. Emmick, deceased, brought this action for damages against defendant L. S. Hamm, an attorney at law who had been engaged by the testator to prepare the will. They have appealed from a judgment of dismissal....

The allegations of the first and second causes of action are summarized as follows: Defendant agreed with the testator, for a consideration, to prepare a will and codicils thereto for him by which plaintiffs were to be designated as beneficiaries of a trust provided for by paragraph Eighth of the will and were to receive 15% of the residue as specified in that paragraph. Defendant, in violation of instructions and in breach of his contract, negligently prepared testamentary instruments containing phraseology that was invalid by ... relating to restraints on alienation and the rule against perpetuities.[1]

Paragraph Eighth of these instruments 'transmitted' the residual estate in trust and provided that the 'trust shall cease and terminate at 12 o'clock noon on a day five years after the date upon which the order distributing the trust property to the trustee is made by the Court having jurisdiction over the probation of this will.' After the death of the testator the instruments were admitted to probate. Subsequently defendant, as draftsman of the instruments and as counsel of record for the executors, advised plaintiffs in writing that the residual trust provision was invalid and that plaintiffs would be deprived of the entire amount to which they would have been entitled if the provision had been valid unless they made a settlement with the blood relatives of the testator under which plaintiffs would receive a lesser amount than that provided for them by the testator. As the direct and proximate result of the negligence of defendant and his breach of contract in preparing the testamentary instruments and the written advice referred to above, plaintiffs were compelled to enter into a settlement under which they received a share of the estate amounting to $75,000 less than the sum which they would have received pursuant to testamentary instruments drafted in accordance with the directions of the testator.

....

It was held in Buckley v. Gray, 110 Cal. 339, 42 P. 900, 31 L.R.A. 862, that an attorney who made a mistake in drafting a will was not liable for negligence or breach of contract to a person named in the will who was deprived of benefits as a result of the error. The court stated that an attorney is liable to his client alone with respect to actions based on negligence in the conduct of his professional duties, and it was reasoned that there could be no recovery for mere negligence where there was no privity by contract or otherwise between the defendant and the person injured.... For the reasons hereinafter stated the case is overruled.

The reasoning underlying the denial of tort liability in the Buckley case, i.e., the stringent privity test, was rejected in Biakanja v. Irving, 49 Cal.2d 647, 648–650, 320 P.2d 16, 65

1. Former section 715.1 of the Civil Code, as it read at the times involved here, provided: 'The absolute power of alienation cannot be suspended, by any limitation or condition whatever, for a period longer than 21 years after some life in being at the creation of the interest and any period of gestation involved in the situation to which the limitation applies. The lives selected to govern the time of suspension must not be so numerous or so situated that evidence of their deaths is likely to be unreasonably difficult to obtain.'
Section 715.2 reads as follows: 'No interest in real or personal property shall be good unless it must vest, if at all, not later than 21 years after some life in being at the creation of the interest and any period of gestation involved in the situation to which the limitation applies. The lives selected to govern the time of vesting must not be so numerous or so situated that evidence of their deaths is likely to be unreasonably difficult to obtain. It is intended by the enactment of this section to make effective in this State the American common-law rule against perpetuities.'
....

A.L.R.2d 1358, where we held that a notary public who, although not authorized to practice law, prepared a will but negligently failed to direct proper attestation was liable in tort to an intended beneficiary who was damaged because of the invalidity of the instrument. It was pointed out that since 1895, when Buckley was decided, the rule that in the absence of privity there was no liability for negligence committed in the performance of a contract had been greatly liberalized. In restating the rule it was said that the determination whether in a specific case the defendant will be held liable to a third person not in privity is a matter of policy and involves the balancing of various factors, among which are the extent to which the transaction was intended to affect the plaintiff, the foreseeability of harm to him, the degree of certainty that the plaintiff suffered injury, the closeness of the connection between the defendant's conduct and the injury, and the policy of preventing future harm. The same general principle must be applied in determining whether a beneficiary is entitled to bring an action for negligence in the drafting of a will when the instrument is drafted by an attorney rather than by a person not authorized to practice law.

[O]ne of the main purposes which the transaction between defendant and the testator intended to accomplish was to provide for the transfer of property to plaintiffs; the damage to plaintiffs in the event of invalidity of the bequest was clearly foreseeable; it became certain, upon the death of the testator without change of the will, that plaintiffs would have received the intended benefits but for the asserted negligence of defendant; and if persons such as plaintiffs are not permitted to recover for the loss resulting from negligence of the draftsman, no one would be able to do so, and the policy of prevent future harm would be impaired.

Since defendant was authorized to practice the profession of an attorney, we must consider ... whether the recognition of liability to beneficiaries of wills negligently drawn by attorneys would impose an undue burden on the profession. Although in some situations liability could be large and unpredictable in amount, this is also true of an attorney's liability to his client. We are of the view that the extension of his liability to beneficiaries injured by a negligently drawn will does not place an undue burden on the profession, particularly when we take into consideration that a contrary conclusion would cause the innocent beneficiary to bear the loss....

It follows that the lack of privity between plaintiffs and defendant does not preclude plaintiffs from maintaining an action in tort against defendant.

....

The general rule with respect to the liability of an attorney for failure to properly perform his duties to his client is that the attorney, by accepting employment to give legal advice or to render other legal services, impliedly agrees to use such skill, prudence, and diligence as lawyers of ordinary skill and capacity commonly possess and exercise in the performance of the tasks which they undertake. The attorney is not liable for every mistake he may make in his practice; he is not, in the absence of an express agreement, an insurer of the soundness of his opinions or of the validity of an instrument that he is engaged to draft; and he is not liable for being in error as to a question of law on which reasonable doubt may be entertained by well-informed lawyers....

The complaint, as we have seen, alleges that defendant drafted the will in such a manner that the trust was invalid because it violated the rules relating to perpetuities and restraints on alienation. These closely akin subjects have long perplexed the courts and the bar.... Of the California law on perpetuities and restraints it has been said that few, if any, areas of the law have been fraught with more confusion or concealed more traps for the unwary draftsman....

In view of the state of the law relating to perpetuities and restraints on alienation and the nature of the error, if any, assertedly made by defendant in preparing the instrument, it would not be proper to hold that defendant failed to use such skill, prudence, and diligence as lawyers of ordinary skill and capacity commonly exercise. The provision of the will quoted in the complaint, namely, that the trust was to terminate five years after the order of the probate court distributing the property to the trustee, could cause the trust to be invalid only because of the remote possibility that the order of distribution would be delayed for a period longer than a life in being at the creation of the interest plus 16 years (the 21-year statutory period less the five years specified in the will). Although it has been held that a possibility of this type could result in invalidity of a bequest, the possible occurrence of such a delay was so remote and unlikely that an attorney of ordinary skill acting under the same circumstances might well have 'fallen into the net which the Rule spreads for the unwary' and failed to recognize the danger. We need not decide whether the trust provision of the will was actually invalid or whether, as defendant asserts, the complaint fails to allege facts necessary to enable such a determination, because we have concluded that in any event an error of the type relied on by plaintiffs does not show negligence ... on the part of defendant. It is apparent that plaintiffs have not stated and cannot state causes of action with respect to the first two counts, and the trial court did not abuse its discretion in denying leave to amend as to these counts.

....

The judgment is affirmed.

* * *

Exercise 4.2: Review Problem

Your firm is considering hiring an expert witness in the matter described in Problem 4.1. Through your practice, you have come to think highly of Douglas McDonnell, a labor and employment lawyer from the western side of your state, and think he might make a good expert witness. McDonnell has handled dozens of employment discrimination cases for plaintiffs in state and federal court and has been certified as an employment discrimination specialist by the state bar. McDonnell has told you that he is willing to testify that Attorney Adams failed to live up to the standard of care required under the circumstances. He says he will testify that Adams was incompetent under Rule 1.1 of the jurisdiction's Rules of Professional Conduct insofar as he failed to exhibit the thoroughness and preparation reasonably necessary for the representation. Moreover, McDonnell is also prepared to testify that Adams violated Rule 1.4 insofar as he failed to keep Client "reasonably informed about the status of [Client's] matter."

Research the relevant law in your jurisdiction concerning the admissibility of expert testimony in legal malpractice actions and prepare a brief (1,500 words or less) memorandum identifying the relevant legal issues regarding McDonnell's possible testimony and their likely resolution.

Chapter 5

Professional Malpractice: Causation

A. Generally

The third element of a plaintiff's *prima facie* case of legal malpractice in negligence is the causation component, arguably the most complex and difficult element to prove. Recall that the typical legal malpractice action is a negligence action. As such, the *prima facie* case requires proof of breach of a duty of care that caused in fact and proximately caused damages to the plaintiff. In the previous chapter, we focused on the duty and breach components of a legal malpractice action. This chapter is devoted to the causation element.

Causation is comprised of two components—(1) causation in fact (which is sometimes referred to as actual causation) and (2) proximate causation (which is sometimes referred to as legal causation). To prove causation in legal malpractice, proof of both causation in fact and proximate causation is required. The following materials explore each of these concepts in turn.

Exercise 5.1: Chapter Problem

Attorney Alpha represented Clint in a slip and fall case against Mom 'N Pop Grocers ("MNP") after Clint slipped on a banana peel and fell while shopping in MNP's one day. The fall fractured Clint's leg and caused severe and permanent head injuries. Clint hired Attorney Alpha immediately following his accident, requesting that Attorney Alpha immediately file suit against MNP. Unfortunately, Attorney Alpha negligently failed to do so prior to the expiration of the applicable statute of limitation. As a result, Clint was unable to recover from MNP as his case was barred. (Since Clint's accident, MNP has gone out of business, having to declare bankruptcy for reasons not related to Clint's claim against it.) Clint has incurred substantial medical bills as a result of his fall, and he has now hired your firm to file a legal malpractice action against Attorney Alpha. Your boss at your firm wants you to draft the body of the complaint on behalf of Clint. In the jurisdiction where the malpractice action will be filed, litigants are required to plead with particularity each element of the asserted cause of action as well as supporting facts as they are reasonably believed to be established. Please draft the body of the complaint in the matter of Clint v. Attorney Alpha. Be sure to include in your pleading every required element to plead a malpractice action successfully.

Focus Questions: *Smith v. Lewis*

1. *In imposing liability against the defendant lawyer, upon what element(s) of the plaintiff's legal malpractice action did the majority of the court focus in* Smith v. Lewis *(duty, breach, causation, or harm)?*
2. *What element of the plaintiff's claim was the focus of the dissenting justice's opinion?*
3. *According to the dissent, what must a plaintiff prove to establish a legal malpractice claim and in what way was the plaintiff's claim deficient?*
4. *What must a plaintiff prove to establish causation in a legal malpractice action?*

Smith v. Lewis

530 P.2d 589
(Cal. 1975)

MOSK, Justice.

Defendant Jerome R. Lewis, an attorney, appeals from a judgment entered upon a jury verdict for plaintiff Rosemary E. Smith in an action for legal malpractice. The action arises as a result of legal services rendered by defendant to plaintiff in a prior divorce proceeding. The gist of plaintiff's complaint is that defendant negligently failed in the divorce action to assert her community interest in the retirement benefits of her husband.

Defendant principally contends, *inter alia*, that the law with regard to the characterization of retirement benefits was so unclear at the time he represented plaintiff as to insulate him from liability for failing to assert a claim therefor on behalf of his client. We conclude defendant's appeal is without merit, and therefore affirm the judgment.

In 1943 plaintiff married General Clarence D. Smith. Between 1945 and his retirement in 1966 General Smith was employed by the California National Guard. As plaintiff testified, she informed defendant her husband 'was paid by the state ... it was a job just like anyone else goes to.' For the first 16 years of that period the husband belonged to the State Employees' Retirement System, a contributory plan. Between 1961 and the date of his retirement he belonged to the California National Guard retirement program, a non-contributory plan. In addition, by attending National Guard reserve drills he qualified for separate retirement benefits from the federal government, also through a noncontributory plan. The state and federal retirement programs each provide lifetime monthly benefits which terminate upon the death of the retiree. The programs make no allowance for the retiree's widow.

On January 1, 1967, the State of California began to pay General Smith gross retirement benefits of $796.26 per month. Payments under the federal program, however, will not begin until 1983, *i.e.*, 17 years after his actual retirement, when General Smith reaches the age of 60. All benefits which General Smith is entitled to receive were earned during the time he was married to plaintiff.

On February 17, 1967, plaintiff retained defendant to represent her in a divorce action against General Smith. According to plaintiff's testimony, defendant advised her that her husband's retirement benefits were not community property. Three days later defendant filed plaintiff's complaint for divorce. General Smith's retirement benefits were not pleaded as items of community property, and therefore were not considered in the litigation or apportioned by the trial court. The divorce was uncontested and the interlocutory decree divided the minimal described community property and awarded Mrs. Smith $400 per month in alimony and child support. The final decree was entered on February 27, 1968.

On July 17, 1968, pursuant to a request by plaintiff, defendant filed on her behalf a motion to amend the decree, alleging under oath that because of his mistake, inadvertence, and excusable neglect ... the retirement benefits of General Smith had been omitted from the list of community assets owned by the parties, and that such benefits were in fact community property. The motion was denied on the ground of untimeliness. Plaintiff consulted other counsel, and shortly thereafter filed this malpractice action against defendant.

Defendant admits in his testimony that he assumed General Smith's retirement benefits were separate property when he assessed plaintiff's community property rights. It is his position that as a matter of law an attorney is not liable for mistaken advice when well informed lawyers in the community entertain reasonable doubt as to the proper resolution of the particular legal question involved. Because, he asserts, the law defining the character of retirement benefits was uncertain at the time of his legal services to plaintiff, defendant contends the trial court committed error in refusing to grant his motions for nonsuit and judgment notwithstanding the verdict and in submitting the issue of negligence to the jury under appropriate instructions.

The law is now settled in California that 'retirement benefits which flow from the employment relationship, to the extent they have vested, are community property subject to equal division between the spouses in the event the marriage is dissolved.' Because such benefits are part of the consideration earned by the employee, they are accorded community treatment regardless of whether they derive from a state, federal, or private source, or from a contributory or non-contributory plan. In light of these principles, it becomes apparent that General Smith's retirement pay must properly be characterized as community property.

We cannot, however, evaluate the quality of defendant's professional services on the basis of the law as it appears today. In determining whether defendant exhibited the requisite degree of competence in his handling of plaintiff's divorce action, the crucial inquiry is whether his advice was so legally deficient when it was given that he may be found to have failed to use 'such skill, prudence, and diligence as lawyers of ordinary skill and capacity commonly possess and exercise in the performance of the tasks which they undertake.' (Lucas v. Hamm (1961) 56 Cal.2d 583, 591, 15 Cal.Rptr. 821, 825, 364 P.2d 685, 689.) We must, therefore examine the indicia of the law which were readily available to defendant at the time he performed the legal services in question.

The major authoritative reference works which attorneys routinely consult for a brief and reliable exposition of the law relevant to a specific problem uniformly indicated in 1967 that vested retirement benefits earned during marriage were generally subject to community treatment.[5] ... A typical statement appeared in The California Family Lawyer, a work with which defendant admitted general familiarity: 'Of increasing importance is the fact that pension or retirement benefits are community property, even though they are not paid or payable until after termination of the marriage by death or divorce.' (1 Cal.Family Lawyer, supra, at p. 111.)

5. In evaluating the competence of an attorney's services, we may justifiably consider his failure to consult familiar encyclopedias of the law.

Although it is true this court had not foreclosed all conflicts on some aspects of the issue at that time, the community character of retirement benefits had been reported in a number of appellate opinions often cited in the literature and readily accessible to defendant. ...

We are aware, moreover, of no significant authority existing in 1967 which proposed a result contrary to that suggested by the cases and the literature, or which purported to rebut the general statutory presumption, as it applies to retirement benefits, that all property acquired by either spouse during marriage belongs to the community....

On the other hand, substantial uncertainty may have existed in 1967 with regard to the community character of General Smith's Federal pension. The above-discussed treatises reveal a debate which lingered among members of the legal community at that time concerning the point at which retirement benefits actually vest.... Because the federal payments were contingent upon General Smith's survival to age 60, 17 years subsequent to the divorce, it could have been argued with some force that plaintiff and General Smith shared a mere expectancy interest in the future benefits. Alternatively, a reasonable contention could have been advanced in 1967 that federal retirement benefits were the personal entitlement of the employee spouse and were not subject to community division upon divorce in the absence of express congressional approval....

Of course, the fact that in 1967 a reasonable argument could have been offered to support the characterization of General Smith's federal benefits as separate property does not indicate the trial court erred in submitting the issue of defendant's malpractice to the jury. The State benefits, the large majority of the payments at issue, were unquestionably community property according to all available authority and should have been claimed as such. As for the Federal benefits, the record documents defendant's failure to conduct any reasonable research into their proper characterization under community property law.[7] Instead, he dogmatically asserted his theory, which he was unable to support with authority and later recanted, that all noncontributory military retirement benefits, whether state or federal, were immune from community treatment upon divorce. The jury could well have found defendant's refusal to educate himself to the applicable principles of law constituted negligence which prevented him from exercising informed discretion with regard to his client's rights.

As the jury was correctly instructed, an attorney does not ordinarily guarantee the soundness of his opinions and, accordingly, is not liable for every mistake he may make in his practice. He is expected, however, to possess knowledge of those plain and elementary principles of law which are commonly known by well informed attorneys, and to discover

---

7. At trial defendant testified that prior to the division of property in the divorce action, he had assumed the retirement benefits were not subject to community treatment, despite the fact General Smith had already begun to receive payments from the state; that he did not at that time undertake any research on the point nor did he discuss the matter with plaintiff; that subsequent to the divorce plaintiff asked defendant to research the question whereupon defendant discovered the *French* case which contained dictum in support of plaintiff's position; that the *French* decision caused him to change his opinion and conclude 'that the Supreme Court, when it was confronted with this (the language in *French*) may hold that it (vested military retirement pay) is community property.' On the basis of *French* defendant filed his unsuccessful motion to amend the final decree of divorce to allow plaintiff an interest in the retirement benefits. Defendant admitted at trial, 'I would have been very willing to assert it (a community interest) on her behalf had I known of the dictum in the *French* case at the time.'

those additional rules of law which, although not commonly known, may readily be found by standard research techniques. (Lucas v. Hamm (1961) 56 Cal.2d 583, 591, 15 Cal.Rptr. 821, 364 P.2d 685;.... If the law on a particular subject is doubtful or debatable, an attorney will not be held responsible for failing to anticipate the manner in which the uncertainty will be resolved. But even with respect to an unsettled area of the law, we believe an attorney assumes an obligation to his client to undertake reasonable research in an effort to ascertain relevant legal principles and to make an informed decision as to a course of conduct based upon an intelligent assessment of the problem. In the instant case, ample evidence was introduced to support a jury finding that defendant failed to perform such adequate research into the question of the community character of retirement benefits and thus was unable to exercise the informed judgment to which his client was entitled....

We recognize, of course, that an attorney engaging in litigation may have occasion to choose among various alternative strategies available to his client, one of which may be to refrain from pressing a debatable point because potential benefit may not equal detriment in terms of expenditure at time and resources or because of calculated tactics to the advantage of his client. But, as the Ninth Circuit put it somewhat brutally in Pineda v. Craven (9th Cir. 1970) 424 F.2d 369, 372: 'There is nothing strategic or tactical about ignorance....' In the case before us it is difficult to conceive of tactical advantage which could have been served by neglecting to advance a claim so clearly in plaintiff's best interest, nor does defendant suggest any. The decision to forego litigation on the issue of plaintiff's community property right to a share of General Smith's retirement benefits was apparently the product of a culpable misconception of the relevant principles of law, and the jury could have so found.

Furthermore, no lawyer would suggest the property characterization of General Smith's retirement benefits to be so esoteric an issue that defendant could not reasonably have been expected to be aware of it or its probable resolution.... Certainly one of the central issues in any divorce proceeding is the extent and division of the community property. In this case the question reached monumental proportions, since General Smith's retirement benefits constituted the only significant asset available to the community.[8] In undertaking professional representation of plaintiff, defendant assumed the duty to familiarize himself with the law defining the character of retirement benefits; instead, he rendered erroneous advice contrary to the best interests of his client without the guidance through research of readily available authority.

Regardless of his failure to undertake adequate research, defendant through personal experience in the domestic relations field had been exposed to community property aspects of pensions. Representing the wife of a reserve officer in the National Guard in 1965, defendant alleged as one of the items of community property 'the retirement benefits from the Armed Forces and/or the California National Guard.' On behalf of the husband in a 1967 divorce action, defendant filed an answer admitting retirement benefits were community property, merely contesting the amount thereof. In 1965 a wife whom he was representing was so insistent on asserting a community interest in a pension, over defendant's contrary views, that she communicated with the state retirement system

8. It is undisputed that the only assets the parties had to show as community property after 24 years of marriage, aside from General Smith's retirement benefits, were an equity of $1,800 in a house, some furniture, shares of stock worth $2,800, and two automobiles on which money was owing.

and brought to defendant correspondence from the state agency describing her interest in pension benefits. And representing an army colonel, defendant filed a cross-complaint for divorce specifically setting up as an item of community property 'retirement benefits in the name of the defendant with the United States Government.' It is difficult to understand why defendant deemed the community property claim to pensions of three of the foregoing clients to deserve presentation to the trial court, but not the similar claim of this plaintiff.

In any event, as indicated above, had defendant conducted minimal research into either hornbook or case law, he would have discovered with modest effort that General Smith's state retirement benefits were likely to be treated as community property and that his federal benefits at least arguably belonged to the community as well. Therefore, we hold that the trial court correctly denied the motions for non-suit and judgment notwithstanding the verdict and properly submitted the question of defendant's negligence to the jury under the instructions given.... For the same reasons, the trial court correctly refused to instruct the jury at defendant's request that 'he is not liable for being in error as to a question of law on which reasonable doubt may be entertained by well informed lawyers.' Even as to doubtful matters, an attorney is expected to perform sufficient research to enable him to make an informed and intelligent judgment on behalf of his client.[9]

....

The judgment is affirmed.

CLARK, Justice (dissenting).

I dissent.

The evidence is insufficient to prove plaintiff lost $100,000 from her lawyer's negligence in 1967. There is no direct evidence a well-informed lawyer would have obtained an award of the husband's pensions in the wife's divorce, nor does the record provide such inference. Rather, the state of the law and the circumstances of the parties reveal lawyer Lewis reached a reasonable result for his client in 1967.

To establish liability for negligence, a plaintiff must show defendant's negligence contributed to injury so that 'but for' the negligence the injury would not have been sustained. If the injury would have occurred anyway—whether or not the defendant was negligent—the negligence was not a cause in fact ... It is not enough merely to show that the probabilities were evenly divided. The evidence must be such that it could be found the balance of probabilities was in plaintiff's favor....

---

9. The principal thrust of the dissent is its conclusion ... that 'even assuming that defendant was negligent in failing to research the pension questions, the record does not furnish a balance of probabilities that his negligence—rather than the uncertain status of the law and the availability of uncontested alimony—caused plaintiff to lose a $100,000 pension award.' Whether defendant's negligence was a cause in fact of plaintiff's damage—an element of proximate cause—is a factual question for the jury to resolve.... Here the jury was correctly instructed that plaintiff had the burden of proving, inter alia, that defendant's negligence was a proximate cause of the damage suffered, and proximate cause was defined as 'a cause which, natural and continuous sequence, produces the damage, and *without which the damage would not have occurred.*' (Italics added.) Under the strict standards governing appellate review of dispute questions of fact..., we see no reason on the present record to disturb the jury's implied finding of proximate cause.

This fundamental principle is reflected in legal malpractice cases. Prior to today's majority opinion, a lawyer was 'not liable for being in error as to a question of law on which reasonable doubt may be entertained by well-informed lawyers. (Citations.)' (Lucas v. Hamm (1961) 56 Cal.2d 583, 591, 15 Cal.Rptr. 821, 825, 364 P.2d 685, 689.) ...

....

When we consider the law existing in 1967 and the circumstances of the parties, it cannot be concluded on the record before us that it was probable another lawyer would have obtained pension rights for plaintiff in addition to the award obtained for her by defendant.

As the majority opinion points out, when defendant was employed to procure the divorce in 1967, the law was clear that, other than military retirement payments, pension *payments* constituted community property.... However, no reported California case prior to 1967 stated that a court was empowered to award an employee's future pension benefits to his spouse in a divorce action. To the contrary, there were strong indications from statutory and case authorities that such an award could not be obtained. Further, in every reported case where a spouse sought award of the employee's pension, that spouse lost.

....

Because of the relationship between community properly and alimony awards, it was to be anticipated that had defendant succeeded through litigation in establishing a right to assignment of the pensions, the alimony award would have been greatly reduced or eliminated altogether and the award of the remaining community property possibly altered. Although an award of part of the pension would no doubt have been more valuable than an alimony award of equal amount, the benefit pales in significance when viewed in light of the uncertainty of the law and the large expense required to establish the right to assignment....

....

Given the uncertain status of the law, the circumstances of the parties, and the close relationship between property division and alimony payment, an ethical, diligent and careful lawyer would have avoided litigation over pension rights and instead would have sought a compensating alimony award for any inequity.... So far as appears, defendant secured such compensating award.

Accordingly, even assuming that defendant was negligent in failing to research the pension questions, the record does not furnish a balance of probabilities that his negligence—rather than the uncertain status of the law and the availability of uncontested alimony—caused plaintiff to lose a $100,000 pension award.

....

I would reverse the judgment.

* * *

1. Based on your understanding of negligence law, which opinion was most persuasive to you in *Smith v. Lewis*? Why?

2. Explain the significance of the dissent's explanation that there was not proof of a "balance of probabilities" that the defendant's negligence lead to plaintiff's loss of the pension award.

B. Causation in Fact: The "Case-within-a-Case" Issue in Legal Malpractice

Focus Questions: *Vahila v. Hall*

1. *According to the court in* Vahila, *must a legal malpractice plaintiff prove that he would have been successful in the underlying matter giving rise to the malpractice action? Why or why not?*
2. *What must a legal malpractice plaintiff prove to establish causation?*

Vahila v. Hall

674 N.E.2d 1164
(Ohio 1997)

Syllabus by the Court

To establish a cause of action for legal malpractice based on negligent representation, a plaintiff must show (1) that the attorney owed a duty or obligation to the plaintiff, (2) that there was a breach of that duty or obligation and that the attorney failed to conform to the standard required by law, and (3) that there is a causal connection between the conduct complained of and the resulting damage or loss.

On July 1, 1993, appellants, Terry R. Vahila, James G. Vahila, and Vahila Insurance Agency, filed a legal malpractice action against Charles D. Hall III, Ralph F. Dublikar, and the law firm of Baker, Meekison & Dublikar, appellees. Appellants' malpractice action arose in connection with appellees' representations of appellants in several civil matters, appellees' representations of Terry Vahila with respect to certain criminal charges that had been brought against her, and appellees' representation of Terry during an investigation of her by the Ohio Department of Insurance. In their complaint, appellants claimed that they had sustained damages as the direct and proximate result of appellees' negligent representations in the various civil, criminal, and administrative matters. Appellants further set forth claims against appellees for "extreme" emotional distress. Additionally, James Vahila sought recovery against appellees for loss of consortium.

Appellees answered appellants' complaint and denied any negligence in their prior representations of appellants. Appellees also filed a counterclaim to recover attorney fees allegedly owed by appellants. Thereafter, the matter proceeded to discovery.

On April 15, 1994, appellees filed a motion for summary judgment. In their motion, appellees asserted, among other things, that there was "[a] complete absence of any evidence of damages proximately caused by the alleged acts and/or omissions of the defendants[.]" With respect to this assertion, appellees claimed essentially that they were entitled to summary judgment because appellants were required to, but could not, prove that they would have been successful in the underlying civil, criminal, and administrative matters in which the alleged malpractice had occurred....

Appellants responded to the motion for summary judgment. In support of their response, appellants submitted the affidavits of James and Terry Vahila and the affidavits of two expert witnesses, Bennett J. Wasserman and Eric A. Mertz. James and Terry Vahila indicated in their affidavits that they had sustained damages as the direct and proximate result of appellees' negligence. James stated that as a result of appellees' negligence they (appellants) had suffered damages of $100,000 and that they had lost profits "of at least" $200,000. Wasserman and Mertz indicated in their affidavits that they had reviewed the events surrounding the malpractice action, that appellees had breached various duties owed to appellants in connection with these matters, and that such negligent acts and/or omissions had been the direct and proximate cause of appellants' damages.

On May 26, 1994, the trial court granted appellees' motion for summary judgment. The trial court held that "there are no material issues of fact in controversy as to proximate cause and Plaintiffs have failed to establish the essential element of damages proximately caused by the Defendants' alleged negligence on all of their claims. Further, this Court finds that Plaintiffs have not demonstrated that, absent the alleged negligent conduct, Plaintiffs would have been successful at trial. As such, this case is not an appropriate one for a legal malpractice claim."

On June 23, 1994, appellants filed a motion with the trial court, requesting that the court reconsider its May 26, 1994 decision. In support of their motion, appellants attached supplemental affidavits of Wasserman and Mertz. Thereafter, on June 24, 1994, appellants filed a notice of appeal with the trial court regarding the court's May 26, 1994 decision.

On appeal, the Court of Appeals for Stark County affirmed the judgment of the trial court. The court of appeals ... held that appellees were entitled to summary judgment on appellants' claims because appellants, in response to appellees' motion for summary judgment, failed to prove that they sustained damages proximately caused by the alleged negligence of appellees. The court of appeals determined that "[t]o establish a genuine issue of material fact regarding proximate cause, the Vahilas were required to present evidence which, if believed, would have proved that the outcome of one or more of the matters in which defendants represented them would have been more favorable to them but for defendants' alleged breaches of duty." Specifically, the court of appeals concluded that "[i]n their response to defendants' motion for summary judgment, the Vahilas did not point to 'specific facts showing that there [was] a genuine issue for trial' regarding whether any of the matters in which defendants represented them would have resulted in a more favorable outcome to them but for defendants' alleged breaches of duty. They pointed to no evidence that any judgment entered against them in the civil matters would have been for a lesser amount, or that those civil matters would have been settled on a more favorable basis, but for defendants' mishandling of them; they pointed to no evidence that any cross-claim or counterclaim that defendants allegedly failed to assert would have been successful; they pointed to no evidence that the criminal prosecutions against Ms. Vahila would have been resolved more favorably to her but for defendants' alleged mishandling; and they pointed to no evidence that the investigation of Ms. Vahila by the Ohio Department of Insurance would have been resolved more favorably to her but for the alleged mishandling of that investigation by defendants."

The cause is now before this court pursuant to the allowance of a discretionary appeal.

DOUGLAS, Justice.

The primary issue in this case is whether the trial court and court of appeals properly concluded that appellees were entitled to summary judgment on the claims set forth in appellants' legal malpractice complaint. For the reasons that follow, we find that summary judgment should not have been granted in favor of appellees. Accordingly, we reverse the judgment of the court of appeals and remand this cause to the trial court for further proceedings.

Initially, we note that the trial court and court of appeals determined that appellees were entitled to summary judgment because appellants failed to establish that they sustained any damages proximately caused by the alleged negligent acts and/or omissions of appellees. The trial court's determination was based in part on the fact that appellants had failed to establish that, but for the negligence of their attorneys, appellants would have been successful in the underlying actions and proceedings in which the alleged malpractice had occurred. It appears that the court of appeals agreed with the findings of the trial court in this regard. However, we disagree with the conclusions reached by the trial court and court of appeals.

In *Krahn v. Kinney* (1989), 43 Ohio St.3d 103, 106, 538 N.E.2d 1058, 1061, we held that "a plaintiff need not allege a reversal of his or her conviction in order to state a cause of action for legal malpractice arising from representation in a criminal proceeding. To plead a cause of action for attorney malpractice arising from criminal representation, a plaintiff must allege (1) an attorney-client relationship giving rise to a duty, (2) a breach of that duty, and (3) damages proximately caused by the breach."[1]

....

We ... reject any finding that the element of causation in the context of a legal malpractice action can be replaced or supplemented with a rule of thumb requiring that a plaintiff, in order to establish damage or loss, prove in every instance that he or she would have been successful in the underlying matter(s) giving rise to the complaint. This should be true regardless of the type of representation involved. In fact, one legal authority has severely criticized imposing such a burden on victims of legal malpractice:

> "A standard of proof that requires a plaintiff to prove to a virtual certainty that, but for the defendant's negligence, the plaintiff would have prevailed in the underlying action, in effect immunizes most negligent attorneys from liability. No matter how outrageous and morally reprehensible the attorney's behavior may have been, if minimal doubt exists as to the outcome in the original action, the plaintiff may not recover in the malpractice action. Except in those rare instances where the initial action was a 'sure thing,' the certainty requirement protects attorneys from liability for their negligence.
>
> "A strict 'but for' test also ignores settlement opportunities lost due to the attorney's negligence. The test focuses on whether the client would have won in the original action. A high standard of proof of causation encourages courts' tendencies to exclude evidence about settlement as too remote and speculative. The standard therefore excludes consideration of the most common form of client recovery.
>
> "In addition, stringent standards of proving 'but for' require the plaintiff to conduct a 'trial within a trial' to show the validity of his underlying claim. A full, theoretically complete reconstruction of the original trial would require evidence about such matters as the size of jury verdicts in the original jurisdiction. For example, an experienced attorney could testify that juries in that jurisdiction typically award verdicts of x dollars in similar cases. But such evidence is too

---

1. We also noted in *Krahn v. Kinney* (1989), 43 Ohio St.3d 103, 105, 538 N.E.2d 1058, 1060–1061, that the elements required to state a cause of action for malpractice arising out of legal representation in criminal matters also apply to a cause of action for legal malpractice relating to civil matters.

> remote and speculative; the new factfinder must try the merits of both the malpractice suit and the underlying claim to make an independent determination of the damage award. The cost and complexity of such a proceeding may well discourage the few plaintiffs otherwise willing to pursue the slim chance of success.
>
> "Other problems await those who do proceed with the 'trial within a trial.' For example, the attorney in the original action may have negligently failed to pursue the discovery that would have insured success. If the results of that same discovery are now necessary to prove the merit of the underlying claim—and the passage of time has precluded obtaining that information—the attorney by his own negligence will have protected himself from liability. In such a case, the more negligent the attorney, the more difficult is the plaintiff's task of proving causation" (footnotes omitted). Note, The Standard of Proof of Causation in Legal Malpractice Cases (1978), 63 Cornell L.Rev. 666, 670–671 ("Note").

The inequity of requiring appellants to prove that they would have been successful in the underlying matters giving rise to their malpractice action is duly apparent from the facts of this case. Appellants' malpractice suit is premised on multiple negligent acts and/or omissions that had allegedly been committed by their attorneys. The majority of the allegations stem from the failure of appellees to properly disclose all matters and/or legal consequences surrounding the various plea bargains entered into by Terry Vahila and the settlement arrangements agreed to by appellants with respect to the several civil matters. According to appellants, the pleas and settlements were obtained under duress and/or coercion and were not entered into voluntarily. Moreover, appellants have also asserted that appellees failed to adequately protect their interests in many of the underlying matters and negligently failed to secure viable defenses on their (appellants') behalf. Thus, given the facts of this case, appellants have arguably sustained damage or loss regardless of the fact that they may be unable to prove that they would have been successful in the underlying matter(s) in question.

Accordingly, we hold that to establish a cause of action for legal malpractice based on negligent representation, a plaintiff must show (1) that the attorney owed a duty or obligation to the plaintiff, (2) that there was a breach of that duty or obligation and that the attorney failed to conform to the standard required by law, and (3) that there is a causal connection between the conduct complained of and the resulting damage or loss. We are aware that the requirement of causation often dictates that the merits of the malpractice action depend upon the merits of the underlying case. Naturally, a plaintiff in a legal malpractice action may be required, depending on the situation, to provide some evidence of the merits of the underlying claim. However, we cannot endorse a blanket proposition that requires a plaintiff to prove, in every instance, that he or she would have been successful in the underlying matter. Such a requirement would be unjust, making any recovery virtually impossible for those who truly have a meritorious legal malpractice claim.

....

In conclusion, we find that appellees were not entitled to have summary judgment granted in their favor on any of the claims set forth in appellants' complaint. Appellants were not required to establish that they would have been successful in the underlying civil, criminal, and administrative matters giving rise to the malpractice action.... Construing the evidence most favorably toward appellants, reasonable minds could differ as to the proximate cause(s) of the various alleged negligent representations and the alleged damages or losses flowing therefrom.

Accordingly, we reverse the judgment of the court of appeals and remand this cause to the trial court for further proceedings consistent with this opinion.

Judgment reversed and cause remanded.

* * *

1. *Vahila v. Hall* represents the minority position on establishing causation in a legal malpractice action. The *Vahila* court rules that legal malpractice plaintiffs are not required to establish that they would have been successful in the underlying representation. As indicated by the following cases, courts in most jurisdictions require legal malpractice plaintiffs to prove success in the underlying representation.

2. In Chapter 3, we explored the tort of breach of fiduciary duty, which is a tort action, but which is a tort separate and distinct from a negligence action. Although like a negligence action, a breach of fiduciary duty claim requires a showing of causation (*i.e,* that the defendant's breach of fiduciary duty is causally linked to the plaintiff's alleged injuries or damages), unlike the causation element in negligence a breach of fiduciary duty action does not require proof of success for the "case within the case." As explained in *Crist v. Loyacono,* 65 So. 3d 837 (Miss. 2011):

> It is true—and well established—that a plaintiff in a *negligence-based* malpractice action must establish proximate cause by the so-called "trial-within-a-trial" test. That is to say, the client "must show that, but for [his] attorney's negligence, he would have been successful in the prosecution or defense of the underlying action." But we have never required a legal-malpractice plaintiff alleging breach of fiduciary duty to establish that, but for the breach, the plaintiff would have won the underlying case. Rather, the proof of proximate cause in such cases is "to be tailored to the injury the client claims and the remedy he elects." This means that expert testimony is not always necessary.
>
> The law recognizes a clear distinction between allegations of legal malpractice based on negligence ... and those based on breach of fiduciary duty.... When a legal-malpractice claim is based on an allegation of breach of fiduciary duty, the plaintiff must establish (1) the existence of an attorney-client relationship; (2) the acts constituting a violation of the attorney's fiduciary duty; (3) that the breach proximately caused the injury; and (4) the fact and extent of the injury.
>
> This dichotomy is consistent with the differing characters of these two theories. Because attorneys are afforded a degree of professional autonomy, proof of success in the underlying case is an appropriate test for proximate cause in a negligence-based action because it ensures that attorneys are only held professionally liable where their failures to adhere to the standard of care actually impacted the plaintiff's interests in the case. But an attorney's breach of his fiduciary duties to his client may cause injury to the client entirely separate from the merits of the underlying case.

Crist v. Loyacono, 65 So. 3d 837, 842–43 (Miss. 2011).

* * *

1. Litigation Malpractice

Focus Questions: *Garcia v. Kozlov, Seaton, Romanini & Brooks, P.C.*

1. *What is required to prove causation in a legal malpractice action?*
2. *According to the* Garcia *court, what element in a legal malpractice action does proof of the "suit within a suit" clarify?*
3. *In New Jersey, is proof of the "suit within a suit" required to prevail in a legal malpractice action?*

Garcia v. Kozlov, Seaton, Romanini & Brooks, P.C.

845 A.2d 602
(N.J. 2004)

Justice LONG delivered the opinion of the Court.

The issue before us arises out of a legal malpractice case. Plaintiff sued her former lawyers for failing to join an arguably integral party in a personal injury lawsuit. In the subsequent legal malpractice action, plaintiff claimed that she was forced to settle the personal injury case with the named defendants for less than full value as a result of the absence of the negligently omitted party. Because defendant raised the settlement first as a bar and then as a defense in the malpractice case, plaintiff sought to present her case, in part, through expert testimony. The trial court acceded to that request in reliance on *Lieberman v. Employers Insurance of Wausau*, 84 N.J. 325, 419 *A.*2d 417 (1980), wherein we signaled that the traditional "suit within a suit" format is not the only way to proceed in a legal malpractice action. Plaintiff obtained a verdict and defendant appealed.

The Appellate Division reversed, advocating strict adherence to the "suit within a suit" format in the absence of the precise factors considered in *Lieberman*. The Appellate Division misreads that case. In *Lieberman*, we specifically recognized that a legal malpractice case may proceed in any number of ways depending on the issues. Included among those options are a "suit within a suit," any "reasonable modification thereof," and a suit based on "expert testimony." *Lieberman, supra*, 84 N.J. at 343–44, 419 *A.*2d 417. The ruling in *Lieberman* did not establish a hierarchy among those approaches nor did it suggest that there is a presumption in favor of the "suit within a suit" scheme. We hold today that the proper approach in each case will depend upon the facts, the legal theories, the impediments to one or more modes of trial, and, where two or more approaches are legitimate, to plaintiff's preference. Courts are not to become involved in determining how a legal malpractice case is tried unless the parties disagree, in which case the final determination of the court is a discretionary judgment that is entitled to deference.

I

Plaintiff, Karen Garcia, was injured in a multi-vehicle automobile accident ... in East Windsor, New Jersey on a rainy night in April 1992. The accident began with a collision between vehicles driven by Carol Ertel and Emily Forman. That accident cut power to the Forman car leaving it disabled and unlit in the roadway. Immediately following the crash, Ertel temporarily left the scene without taking steps to warn oncoming traffic about the Forman vehicle. Within minutes, another vehicle driven by Karen Marut struck the Forman vehicle. A chain-reaction crash followed in which a vehicle driven by Charlotte Ignall struck plaintiff's vehicle, which struck Marut's vehicle.

On November 1, 1993, the law firm of Kozlov, Seaton, Romanini & Brooks, filed a complaint prepared by its associate, Elizabeth Sylvester, Esq., on behalf of plaintiff against Forman, Marut, and Ignall for negligence. The complaint inexplicably omitted Ertel. The law firm then discovered a conflict of interest with an insurance company implicated in the case and referred the matter to Michael Gentlesk, Esq., who was then retained by plaintiff. Gentlesk moved to amend the complaint to include a claim against Ertel. After the court granted the motion, Ertel successfully moved for summary judgment based on the applicable statute of limitations. Plaintiff later settled her claims against the other drivers for $87,000. Thereafter, she filed a complaint for malpractice against the Kozlov firm and Sylvester (collectively, defendant) alleging that defendant's negligence in failing to name Ertel caused her to settle her case for less than its true value.

The trial of plaintiff's legal malpractice claim began on July 31, 2000. After jury selection, the trial court was presented with motions *in limine* from both parties....

The court granted plaintiff's motion and denied that of defendant[, stating in part that] "of course, the settlement of the prior case doesn't bar her from proceeding in this case.["]

....

[P]laintiff testified to her conversations with Gentlesk ... and her reasons for settling the claim. She testified that Gentlesk told her the value of her case was between $200,000–$250,000 and that she should take the settlement offered, basically because the absence of Ertel was a problem to full recovery. According to plaintiff, Gentlesk told her Ertel was at fault for the accident and that she should settle with the remaining defendants and sue the law firm.

She also testified that another partner at defendant's firm, Frank DiGiacomo, told her to take the settlement because "some money is better than no money at all." Plaintiff stated that she would not have taken the settlement in full satisfaction of all of her claims if it were not for the reservation of the right to bring the malpractice action.

Gentlesk testified that he estimated the "full value" of plaintiff's claim to be at or around $200,000, although he acknowledged that he could have said $250,000 to her.[5] When the defendants in the underlying suits made settlement offers totaling $87,000 ($65,000 from Ignall, $10,000 from Marut, $12,000 from Forman), Gentlesk recalled that in each instance "[m]y recommendation was that it was a settlement that she should consider accepting." His advice reflected the absence of Ertel as a defendant because of the "leverage" it afforded the defendants at trial. Gentlesk testified that "[t]he defendants that remained in the case indicated to me that their defense would be that Ertel caused the first accident," and consequently, bore primary responsibility for plaintiff's injuries. He further acknowledged that due to the fact that the police report recounted the statement of an eyewitness who claimed to have seen plaintiff hit Marut prior to being hit by Ignall, the potential of plaintiff's own comparative negligence relative to the named defendants influenced his thinking. In other words, absent Ertel, all other parties were, to Gentlesk, similarly situated. When asked whether he would have recommended a settlement of $87,000 if Ertel had been a defendant in the case, Gentlesk responded, "[p]robably not."

5. By the time of trial, Gentlesk was employed at defendant's firm and plaintiff's lawyer was permitted to inquire into the effect of that employment on his recollections. DiGiacomo denied ever having recommended settlement.

Plaintiff also presented the testimony of a malpractice expert, Douglas Calhoun, Esq., who weighed in on two aspects of her claim. First, Calhoun expressed his opinion that defendant deviated from the standard of care when it failed to sue Ertel within the statute of limitations. Second, he testified regarding the effect of defendant's negligence on the underlying suit. Calhoun described the mechanism of New Jersey's comparative negligence statute and how, in combination with the omission of Ertel from the underlying action, it hampered plaintiff's ability to recover full compensation for her injuries.[6] It was his view that, absent Ertel, plaintiff could not fairly argue that she was less negligent than the other defendants. Calhoun also explained how the omission of Ertel handicapped plaintiff by affording the accident defendants an "empty chair" defense.

....

Defendant also produced expert testimony. Timothy Barnes, Esq., expressed the opinion that the defendant's failure to include Ertel in the suit was not malpractice because plaintiff's deposition testimony showed that she had come to a full stop prior to colliding with the Marut vehicle. According to Barnes, that placed primary responsibility for the accident on Ignall, who hit plaintiff. Therefore, because Ertel's negligence was not a proximate cause of plaintiff's injuries, Barnes opined it would not have been ethical to name Ertel as a defendant. Thus, Barnes concluded that the $87,000 plaintiff received was a reasonable settlement of her case with the only liable defendants, given her own negligence for failing to activate her hazard lights or pull off to the right.

....

At the close of the presentation of evidence, the trial court decided the issue of negligence in favor of plaintiff as a matter of law. The court found

> that after examining the record and the testimony of Mr. Barnes that he did not articulate a reason for finding no negligence. In fact, [ ] part of his reason was contrary to accepted New Jersey law, that is that the [ ] initial car, the Ertel car could [not] be a contributing cause to the happening of the accident and for that reason among others I found that his opinion in that regard was basically a net opinion and his testimony concerning ethical considerations was just really to muddle the record. There was nothing in the record to suggest that any one would have had any ethical breach by bringing suit against the Ertel vehicle.

In addition, the court ruled that plaintiff acted reasonably in settling the underlying case against the party defendants. Those rulings are not challenged here.

After complete instructions regarding the considerations relevant to assessing responsibility for the accident and to valuing plaintiff's injuries, the trial court put two questions to the jury for consideration. The first was whether defendant was a proximate cause of plaintiff's loss. The second asked for "the reasonable settlement value" of plaintiff's claim in November of 1996. The jury responded affirmatively to the first question and

---

6. At the time of the trial, *N.J.S.A.* 2A:15-5.3 stated that only a defendant determined to be 60% or more responsible for damages would be liable for the total amount of the award. A defendant found to be more than 20% but less than 60% liable would be responsible for the total amount of any economic loss but only that percentage of the noneconomic loss directly attributable to his negligence. A defendant found to be 20% or less responsible for the damages would be liable only for the percentage of the award directly attributable to his negligence.

During his testimony, Calhoun estimated the liability of Ertel at "a minimum of fifty if not sixty percent." That estimate, along with Gentlesk's testimony regarding the potential full value of plaintiff's underlying claims, and the litigation risks generated by the omission of Ertel, led Calhoun to assert that plaintiff acted reasonably in settling her case for $87,000.

set the reasonable settlement value of plaintiff's claim at $225,000. Based on those findings, the court molded the verdict and awarded plaintiff $92,460 in actual damages plus prejudgment interest.[7]

Defendant appealed, arguing, among other things, that the traditional "suit within a suit" method of trying a legal malpractice case was violated. The Appellate Division reversed, addressing only that issue. The court "[was] satisfied that in a complex matter such as this, there was no sound basis to depart from the 'suit within a suit' format," which it apparently viewed as presumptive. Accordingly, it held that the trial court erroneously exercised its discretion when it granted plaintiff's application to try the case in hybrid fashion.

In ruling, the Appellate Division accepted as a given that defendant was negligent when it failed to name Ertel in the underlying suit and that the "suit within a suit" format was not necessary in order to prove that legal malpractice took place. Further, the Appellate Division acknowledged that *Lieberman* left the decision regarding the mode of trial of a legal malpractice claim within the "sound discretion of the trial court." Despite those findings, the panel concluded that the trial court abused that discretion. Because of the conflicting factual versions of the accident and because Ertel's liability was pivotal, the panel viewed the "suit within a suit" model as the proper tool to resolve the case. In reaching that conclusion, the court concluded that there were no factors, within the meaning of *Lieberman,* compelling divergence from the "suit within a suit" scheme.

Having determined to reverse, the Appellate Division turned its attention to the question of whether to remand for a new trial. The court ruled: "Plaintiff adopted a certain litigation strategy. That it proved incorrect does not entitle her to a new trial with a different strategy." Accordingly, the court concluded that the doctrine of invited error compelled a reversal without a remand. We granted plaintiff's petition for certification, 176 N.J. 280, 822 *A.*2d 609 (2003), and now reverse.

II

Plaintiff attacks the Appellate Division decision on two fronts. She argues that under *Lieberman,* the trial court was within its discretion in admitting expert testimony on damages inflicted by defendant's malpractice, and that in any event, the decision of the Appellate Division reflects a misapplication of the doctrine of invited error and produced an unjust result.

Defendant counters, on the merits, that the Appellate Division correctly ruled that departure from the "suit within a suit" format was not warranted under *Lieberman* and reasserts the invited error doctrine as a ground to justify the denial of a retrial.

III

Legal malpractice is a variation on the tort of negligence. Thus, a plaintiff must prove a deviation from the standard, proximate causation, and damages. There is no question in this case regarding the threshold issue of whether defendant committed professional negligence. Indeed, that issue, on which the trial court directed a verdict, is not contested on this appeal. What is at issue here is whether defendant's failure to sue Ertel proximately caused plaintiff to be damaged and if so, in what amount.

---

7. The verdict for $225,000 was reduced by the $87,000 already received and the $45,540 in counsel fees arising out of the first case.

Where, as here, the claim of malpractice alleges a failure to meet a time-bar, "a client must establish 'the recovery which the client would have obtained if malpractice had not occurred.'" *Frazier v. New Jersey Mfrs. Ins. Co.,* 142 N.J. 590, 601, 667 A.2d 670 (1995) (quoting *Osborne v. O'Reilly,* 267 N.J.Super. 329, 331, 631 A.2d 577 (Law Div.1993)); *see also Gautam v. De Luca,* 215 N.J.Super. 388, 397, 521 A.2d 1343 ("[T]he measure of damages is ordinarily the amount that the client would have received but for his attorney's negligence."), *certif. denied,* 109 N.J. 39, 532 A.2d 1107 (1987).

The most common way to prove the harm inflicted by such malpractice is to proceed by way of a "suit within a suit" in which a plaintiff presents the evidence that would have been submitted at a trial had no malpractice occurred. The "suit within a suit" approach aims to clarify what would have taken place but for the attorney's malpractice. At such a trial, "plaintiff has the burden of proving by a preponderance of the evidence that (1) he would have recovered a judgment in the action against the main defendant, (2) the amount of that judgment, and (3) the degree of collectibility of such judgment." *Hoppe v. Ranzini,* 158 N.J.Super. 158, 165, 385 A.2d 913 (App.Div.1978).

The "suit within a suit" format is regularly employed in most jurisdictions, including New Jersey. R. Mallen & V. Levit, *Legal Malpractice,* § 33.8, vol. 5, at 69 (5th ed. 2000); *Lieberman, supra,* 84 N.J. at 342, 419 A.2d 417. Yet, it has been subjected to criticism.

First, the rule wholly ignores the possibility of settlement. The simple fact is that many, if not most, legal claims are not tried to conclusion, but rather are amicably adjusted. Second, it is often difficult for the parties to present an accurate evidential reflection or semblance of the original action. Finally, the passage of time itself can be a significant factor militating against the "suit within a suit" approach.

Further, in some situations, a "suit within a suit" cannot accurately reconstruct the underlying action. Often, parties must cope with the disadvantage of not having the same access to evidence or of having evidence grow stale with the passage of time. Evidentiary concerns loom large for underlying suits that never reach trial.

The "suit within a suit" format has also drawn fire for being unfair to plaintiffs who must litigate the underlying claim against the lawyer who originally prepared it. Courts and commentators alike acknowledge the various ways in which the "suit within a suit" method can distort the underlying action. Such shortcomings have created the need for alternative approaches and a measure of willingness to accept such alternatives when the situation demands.

....

[Quoting *Lieberman,* the court also observed that "the passage of time itself can be a significant factor militating against the 'suit within a suit' approach. ... For example, [important] witnesses ... may no longer be available or their testimony and other evidence, if generally available, may not be susceptible of recapture in the same form or with the same effect as in the original action."]

In terms of procedure, [in *Lieberman*]we stated, "it should be within the discretion of the trial judge as to the manner in which the plaintiff may proceed to prove his claim for damages and that the appropriate procedure should, if not otherwise agreed upon between the parties, be settled through pretrial proceedings." By way of example, but not of limitation, we detailed some possible approaches, including:

> [T]he "suit within a suit" approach or any reasonable modification thereof. Another option, which may be apposite in this case in light of the duality of de-

> fendants, the factor of role reversal, and the passage of time, is to proceed through the use of expert testimony as to what as a matter of reasonable probability would have transpired at the original trial. *Cf. Shields v. Campbell*, 277 *Or.* 71, 559 *P.*2d 1275, 1279 (1977) (in action for attorney malpractice, plaintiff introduces expert who testifies as to the effect malpractice had upon outcome of suit). Such experts would testify, in light of their experience and expertise, concerning the outcome of the DeSarno claim if the case had been brought to trial as anticipated by McDonough and had been defended in the manner McDonough had initially planned. *Cf. Rempfer v. Deerfield Packing Corp.*, 4 N.J. 135, 141–142, 72 A.2d 204 (1950) (where jury does not have sufficient knowledge with which to decide an issue, expert testimony is appropriate).

What is important about *Lieberman* is the flexibility it accorded to lawyers and judges to limn an appropriate procedure in each case based on the facts and on the claims, without favoring one approach over another....

IV

We turn now to the facts of this case. In our view, the trial court was empowered fully to allow this case to proceed as it did. As in nearly all malpractice cases, plaintiff needed to produce an expert regarding deviation from the appropriate standard.... Ordinarily, a "suit within a suit" would follow.

What complicated matters was defendant's position that plaintiff willingly and reasonably accepted $87,000 as the full value of the case. That leg of the case required Gentlesk to testify, as a fact witness, why in the absence of Ertel, he recommended that plaintiff settle with the remaining defendants for $87,000, although he considered the case to be worth much more. Plaintiff likewise had to explain why she agreed to do so. An expert was proffered to show how Ertel's absence negatively affected plaintiff's litigation and settlement posture in 1996 and why the settlement with the named defendants was a reasonable strategy under the then-existing circumstances. Again, Calhoun provided that evidence. It is important to note, however, that Calhoun's testimony was not presented as a substitute for the jury's evaluation of the case, but only to explain the reason for the settlement.

In addition, ... plaintiff presented a full "suit within a suit" by adducing all of the circumstances surrounding the accident, along with factual and expert testimony regarding the damages she sustained. That evidence provided the jury with an independent basis to determine the effect of Ertel's absence from the case and to value plaintiff's losses.

[I]n this case, a full "suit within a suit," providing evidence to support the jury verdict, was produced. The expert testimony was not offered as a substitute for that evidence, but as an adjunct to address a different issue—the effect of the earlier settlement.

Hence, the Appellate Division erred ... in failing to recognize that a "suit within a suit," providing the jury with a basis for its determination, in fact took place.... Therefore, ... we reverse the judgment of the Appellate Division to the contrary.

Because the Appellate Division based its opinion on the single issue to which we have adverted, it did not reach the remaining questions raised by defendant.... Because ... issues remain outstanding, we remand the case to the Appellate Division for disposition....

V

The judgment of the Appellate Division is reversed. The case is remanded for further proceedings consistent with this opinion.

* * *

1. As discussed in the principal case, the suit-within-a-suit or case-within-a-case format is required to prove causation in the majority of jurisdictions. Consider the *Vahila* case, *supra*, where the court refused to hold that proof of success in the underlying matter was necessary to establishing causation. With which position do you agree most?

2. Although typically employed in situations where the underlying litigation never proceeded to trial, the trial-within-a-trial doctrine may also be applied even when the underlying litigation has actually taken place. *See, e.g.*, *Suder v. Whiteford, Taylor & Preston, LLP*, 992 A.2d 413 (Md. 2010):

> The trial-within-a-trial doctrine is unique to legal malpractice cases. The doctrine provides a mechanism we do not see elsewhere for a tribunal to resolve a proximate cause query. When the doctrine is applicable, the litigants reconstruct the underlying action, absent the supposed breach of duty. The tribunal must not only determine how the parties would have proceeded had there been no breach, but must also assume the role of the earlier adjudicator in order to ascertain the probable outcome of the action. Simply put, the court must try a case within a case.
>
> We have previously recognized the trial-within-a-trial doctrine when the legal malpractice claimant was denied a trial due to the attorney's alleged malpractice. In this appeal, we are asked to determine whether the doctrine may apply when the underlying trial or other proceeding has already been litigated. We hold that it can....
>
> ....
>
> The trial-within-a-trial doctrine exposes "what the result 'should have been' or what the result 'would have been'" had the lawyer's negligence not occurred. Ronald E. Mallen & Jeffrey M. Smith, *Legal Malpractice* § 35:12 (2010).
>
> Suder argues that the trial-within-a-trial doctrine cannot be utilized here, where the underlying case has been litigated ... As support, she cites several cases in which courts have applied the doctrine to investigate allegations that the attorney's malpractice prevented a trial from ever taking place. These cases, however, do not say that the doctrine is limited to "no-trial" situations....
>
> Indeed, in other cases, outside of Maryland, the doctrine has been applied after the completion of a trial in the underlying case. *See McIntire v. Lee*, 149 N.H. 160, 816 A.2d 993 (2003) (malpractice established after jury determined that evidence that was not introduced in the underlying trial was relevant and should have been introduced); *Prince v. Garruto, Galex & Cantor, Esqs.*, 346 N.J.Super. 180, 787 A.2d 245 (App.Div. 2001) (ordering a trial on the merits to determine when omission of a witness in previous trial constituted malpractice); *see also Meyer v. Maus*, 626 N.W.2d 281, 287 (N.D.2001) ("The case-within-a-case doctrine requires that, but for the attorney's alleged negligence, litigation

would have ended with a more favorable result for the client."); *Aubin v. Barton*, 123 Wash.App. 592, 98 P.3d 126, 134 (2004) ("[T]he trial court hearing the malpractice claim retries, or tries for the first time, the client's cause of action that the client contends was lost or compromised by the attorney's negligence, and the trier of fact decides whether the client would have fared better but for the alleged mishandling.").

....

Ultimately, the triggering mechanism for the trial-within-a-trial doctrine is a dispute over proximate cause, not whether the client lost the chance of a trial....

Suder v. Whiteford, Taylor & Preston, LLP, 992 A.2d 413 (Md. 2010).

2. Transactional Malpractice

Focus Questions: *Viner v. Sweet*

1. *What was the issue in* Viner?
2. *How does the court distinguish between the concepts of causation in fact and proximate or legal cause?*
3. *What are the reasons upon which the defendant attorneys base their position that the causation in fact determination should be different in the transactional malpractice context? Was the court persuaded? Are you persuaded?*

Viner v. Sweet

135 Cal. Rptr. 2d 629
(Cal. 2003)

KENNARD, J.

In a client's action against an attorney for legal malpractice, the client must prove, among other things, that the attorney's negligent acts or omissions caused the client to suffer some financial harm or loss. When the alleged malpractice occurred in the performance of transactional work (giving advice or preparing documents for a business transaction), must the client prove this causation element according to the "but for" test, meaning that the harm or loss would not have occurred without the attorney's malpractice? The answer is yes.[1]

---

1. Causation analysis in tort law generally proceeds in two stages: determining cause in fact and considering various policy factors that may preclude imposition of liability. This case concerns only the element of cause in fact.

I.

In 1984, plaintiffs Michael Viner and his wife, Deborah Raffin Viner, founded Dove Audio, Inc. (Dove). The company produced audio versions of books read by the authors or by celebrities, and it did television and movie projects.

In 1994, Dove went public by issuing stock at $10 a share. In 1995, the Viners and Dove entered into long-term employment contracts guaranteeing the Viners, among other things, a certain level of salaries, and containing indemnification provisions favorable to the Viners. The Viners received a large share of Dove's common stock and all of its preferred cumulative dividend series "A" stock.

Thereafter, Michael Viner discussed with longtime friend David Povich, a partner in defendant law firm Williams & Connolly in Washington, D.C., the possibility of selling the Viners' interest in Dove. In the fall of 1996, Norton Herrick proposed buying the Viners' entire interest in Dove. Attorney Povich assigned the matter to his partner, defendant Charles A. Sweet, a corporate transactional attorney.... During the negotiations with Herrick, Sweet learned that under the Viners' employment agreements with Dove, the latter owed the Viners a substantial amount of unpaid dividends on their preferred stock. Sweet also learned that the Viners wanted to preserve their right to engage in the television and movie businesses.

When the negotiations with Herrick were unsuccessful, Ronald Lightstone of Media Equities International (MEI) approached the Viners. Thereafter, in March 1997, the Viners and MEI entered into an agreement under which MEI was to invest $4 million, and the Viners $2 million, to buy Dove stock. By May 1997, disputes arose, and the parties to the agreement each threatened litigation. That same month, Ronald Lightstone of MEI and Michael Viner, without defendant attorney Sweet's involvement, agreed that MEI would buy the Viners' stock in Dove and the Viners would terminate their employment with Dove.

Defendant attorney Sweet and Lightstone of MEI negotiated the final agreement, which the parties signed on June 10, 1997. The deal consisted of a securities purchase agreement and an employment termination agreement. Under the former, MEI agreed to buy a significant portion of the Viners' stock for more than $3 million. Under the latter agreement, the Viners' employment with Dove was terminated, mutual general releases were given, and Dove was to pay the Viners a total of $1.5 million over five years in monthly payments, with Dove's series "E" preferred stock to be held in escrow for distribution to the Viners if Dove defaulted on the monthly payments to them.

The employment termination agreement contained a noncompetition provision stating that the Viners would not " 'compete' in any way, directly or indirectly, in the audio book business for a period of four years" in any state in which Dove was doing business. The agreement also had a nonsolicitation provision that the Viners would not "directly or indirectly contract with, hire, solicit, encourage the departure of or in any manner engage or seek to employ any author or, for purposes of audio books, reader, currently under contract or included in the Company's book or audio catalogues for a period of four years."

In addition, the employment termination agreement provided that Deborah Raffin Viner would receive "Producer Credit" on audiobook work initiated during her employment with Dove; that Dove would not amend documents to terminate or reduce its obligation to indemnify the Viners; and that disputes would be submitted to arbitration, whose costs were to be split equally between the parties, with attorney fees to the party seeking to enforce the arbitration in court.

Defendant attorney Sweet led the Viners to believe that the employment termination agreement gave them three years of monthly payments by Dove, retained the indemnity protection they had with Dove, and provided credit for work done before their departure from Dove. The Viners also thought that they could use their celebrity contacts for any work that did not compete with Dove's audiobook business and involvement in film and television productions, and that if Dove defaulted on the agreed-upon monthly payments to them, the noncompetition clauses would be voided. The contracts did not so provide.

Later, several arbitration proceedings took place to resolve disputes between the Viners and MEI, including a claim by the Viners that the noncompetition provision of the employment termination agreement violated Business and Professions Code section 16600's restrictions on noncompetition agreements. The arbitrator rejected the claim, and the superior court confirmed the arbitrator's decision.

On June 3, 1998, the Viners brought a malpractice action against Attorney Sweet and the law firm of Williams & Connolly. Presented at trial were these seven claims: (1) Sweet told the Viners that the nonsolicitation clause of the employment termination agreement prohibiting plaintiffs from using their contacts to obtain work in television and movie projects applied only to the book and audiobook parts of Dove's business, but Dove, because the clause was ambiguous, asserted that the clause also encompassed Dove's television and movie projects; (2) Sweet negligently agreed to the noncompetition provision, which violated Business and Professions Code section 16600's restrictions on such provisions; (3) the Viners had asked for an attorney fees provision, but the employment termination agreement disallowed attorney fees in any disputes, permitting them only in enforcing an arbitration award; (4) ambiguous language in the Producer Credit provision caused Dove not to give Deborah Raffin Viner credit as a producer; (5) the Viners lost rights to dividends on Dove's series "A" preferred stock; (6) the employment termination agreement did not contain an indemnity provision providing the same level of protection as the Viners' agreement with Dove; and (7) the series "E" stock afforded inadequate security to the Viners if Dove defaulted on the monthly payments due them under the employment termination agreement.

After deliberating five days, the jury found defendants liable on all seven claims of malpractice, awarding the Viners $13,291,532 in damages. Defendants moved for judgment notwithstanding the verdict or in the alternative for a new trial, arguing that the trial court erred in not instructing the jury that the Viners needed to prove they would have received a better deal "but for" defendant attorney Sweet's negligence. The trial court denied both motions.

The Court of Appeal reduced the damage award to $8,085,732, but otherwise affirmed the judgment. The court first noted that it was undisputed that the Viners did not attempt to prove that without defendants' alleged negligence MEI would have given them a better deal on the contract terms here in issue. The court determined that the case presented a pure question of law: whether plaintiffs in a transactional legal malpractice action must show that the harm would not have occurred *but for* the alleged negligence. It held that the "but for" test of causation did not apply to transactional malpractice.

The Court of Appeal distinguished transactional malpractice from litigation malpractice, in which the plaintiff is required to prove the harm would not have occurred without the alleged negligence, and it offered three reasons for treating the two forms of malpractice differently. First, the court asserted that in litigation a gain for one side is always a loss for the other, whereas in transactional work a gain for one side could also be a gain for the other side. Second, the court observed that litigation malpractice involves past historical facts while transactional malpractice involves what parties would have been willing to accept for the future. Third, the court stated that "business transactions generally involve a much larger universe of variables than litigation matters." According to the Court of Appeal, in "contract negotiations the number of possible terms and outcomes is virtually unlimited," and therefore the "jury would have to evaluate a nearly infinite array of 'what-ifs,' to say nothing of 'if that, then whats,' in order to determine whether the plaintiff would have ended up with a better outcome 'but for' the malpractice."

We granted defendants' petition for review, and thereafter limited the issues to whether the plaintiff in a transactional legal malpractice action must prove that a more favorable result would have been obtained *but for* the alleged negligence.[2]

II

Defendants contend that in a transactional malpractice action, the plaintiff must show that *but for* the alleged malpractice, a more favorable result would have been obtained. Thus, defendants argue, the Viners had to show that without defendants' negligence (1) they would have had a more advantageous agreement (the "better deal" scenario), or (2) they would not have entered into the transaction with MEI and therefore would have been better off (the "no deal" scenario).

The Viners respond that in *Mitchell v. Gonzales* (1991) 54 Cal.3d 1041 [1 Cal.Rptr.2d 913, 819 P.2d 872], this court repudiated the "but for" test of causation in tort cases alleging negligence. Not so.

In *Mitchell*, the parents of a boy who died while on a picnic with neighbors sued the neighbors for wrongful death. The child, who could not swim, was riding a paddleboard in a lake when the paddleboard capsized and he drowned. Addressing causation, a majority of this court held that, for use in jury instructions, the term "proximate cause" was "conceptually and grammatically deficient" because it could mislead jurors into focusing on the cause that as to time and space was nearest to the injury.

In so holding, *Mitchell* did not abandon or repudiate the requirement that the plaintiff must prove that, *but for* the alleged negligence, the harm would not have happened. On the contrary, *Mitchell* stated that jury instructions on causation in negligence cases should use the "substantial factor" test articulated in the Restatement Second of Torts (Restatement), and *Mitchell* recognized that "the 'substantial factor' test *subsumes* the 'but for' test." ...

The text of Restatement section 432 demonstrates how the "substantial factor" test subsumes the traditional "but for" test of causation. Subsection (1) of section 432 provides: "Except as stated in Subsection (2), the actor's negligent conduct is *not a substantial factor* in bringing about harm to another *if the harm would have been sustained even if the actor had not been negligent*." (Italics added.) Subsection (2) states that if "two forces are actively operating ... and each of itself is sufficient to bring about harm to another, the actor's negligence may be found to be a substantial factor in bringing it about."

Thus, in Restatement section 432, subsection (1) adopts the "but for" test of causation, while subsection (2) provides for an exception to that test. The situation that the exception

2. The trial court refused defendants' requested instruction on "but for" causation. The court did instruct the jury that a cause of an injury "is something that is a substantial factor in bringing about" the harm. Because the Court of Appeal addressed this case as presenting the "pure question of law" of whether the legal requirement of showing "but for" causation applies at all to transactional malpractice cases, and because we limited our review to that issue, we have not framed our discussion in terms of instructional error.

addresses has long been recognized, but it has been given various labels, including "concurrent independent causes," "combined force criteria," and "multiple sufficient causes".

This case does not involve concurrent independent causes, which are multiple forces operating at the same time and independently, each of which would have been sufficient by itself to bring about the harm. Here, the Viners argued that their losses were caused by defendants' negligence, the actions of MEI exploiting that negligence, the underlying economic situation, and "other factors." ... Because these forces operated in combination, with none being sufficient in the absence of the others to bring about the harm, they are not concurrent *independent* causes.[3] ... Accordingly, the exception stated in subsection (2) of Restatement section 432 does not apply, and this case is governed by the "but for" test stated in subsection (1) of Restatement section 432.[4]

The Court of Appeal here held that a plaintiff suing an attorney for transactional malpractice need not show that the harm would not have occurred in the absence of the attorney's negligence. We disagree. We see nothing distinctive about transactional malpractice that would justify a relaxation of, or departure from, the well-established requirement in negligence cases that the plaintiff establish causation by showing either (1) *but for* the negligence, the harm would not have occurred, or (2) the negligence was a concurrent independent cause of the harm.

> "When a business transaction goes awry, a natural target of the disappointed principals is the attorneys who arranged or advised the deal. Clients predictably attempt to shift some part of the loss and disappointment of a deal that goes sour onto the shoulders of persons who were responsible for the underlying legal work. Before the loss can be shifted, however, the client has an initial hurdle to clear. *It must be shown that the loss suffered was in fact caused by the alleged attorney malpractice.* It is far too easy to make the legal advisor a scapegoat for a variety of business misjudgments unless the courts pay close attention to the cause in fact element, and deny recovery where the unfavorable outcome was likely to occur anyway, the client already knew the problems with the deal, or where the client's own misconduct or misjudgment caused the problems. It is the failure of the client to establish the causal link that explains decisions where the loss is termed remote or speculative. Courts are properly cautious about making attorneys guarantors of their clients' faulty business judgment." (Bauman, *Damages for Legal Malpractice: An Appraisal of the Crumbling Dike and Threatening Flood* (1988) 61 Temp. L.Rev. 1127, 1154–1155, fns. omitted, italics added (hereafter Bauman, *Damages for Legal Malpractice*).)

In a litigation malpractice action, the plaintiff must establish that *but for* the alleged negligence of the defendant attorney, the plaintiff would have obtained a more favorable judgment or settlement in the action in which the malpractice allegedly occurred. The purpose of this requirement, which has been in use for more than 120 years, is to safeguard against speculative and conjectural claims. It serves the essential purpose of ensuring

---

3. "Concurrent independent causes" should not be confused with "concurrent causes." The former refers to multiple forces operating at the same time and independently, each of which would have been sufficient by itself to bring about the harm. The latter refers simply to multiple forces operating at the same time.

4. The requirement that the plaintiff prove causation should not be confused with the method or means of doing so. Phrases such as "trial within a trial," "case within a case," "no deal" scenario, and "better deal" scenario describe methods of proving causation, not the causation requirement itself or the test for determining whether causation has been established.

that damages awarded for the attorney's malpractice actually have been caused by the malpractice.

The Court of Appeal here attempted to distinguish litigation malpractice from transactional malpractice in order to justify a relaxation of the "but for" test of causation in transactional malpractice cases. One of the distinguishing features, according to the court, was that in litigation a gain for one side necessarily entails a corresponding loss for the other, whereas in transactional representation a gain for one side does not necessarily result in a loss for the other. We question both the accuracy and the relevance of this generalization. In litigation, as in transactional work, a gain for one side does not necessarily result in a loss for the other side. Litigation may involve multiple claims and issues arising from complaints and cross-complaints, and parties in such litigation may prevail on some issues and not others, so that in the end there is no clear winner or loser and no exact correlation between one side's gains and the other side's losses. In addition, an attorney's representation of a client often combines litigation and transactional work, as when the attorney effects a settlement of pending litigation. The "but for" test of causation applies to a claim of legal malpractice in the settlement of litigation, even though the settlement is itself a form of business transaction.

Nor do we agree with the Court of Appeal that litigation is inherently or necessarily less complex than transactional work. Some litigation, such as many lawsuits involving car accidents, is relatively uncomplicated, but so too is much transactional work, such as the negotiation of a simple lease or a purchase and sale agreement. But some litigation, such as a beneficiary's action against a trustee challenging the trustee's management of trust property over a period of decades, is as complex as most transactional work.

It is true, as the Court of Appeal pointed out, that litigation generally involves an examination of past events whereas transactional work involves anticipating and guiding the course of future events. But this distinction makes little difference for purposes of selecting an appropriate test of causation. Determining causation always requires evaluation of hypothetical situations concerning what might have happened, but did not. In both litigation and transactional malpractice cases, the crucial causation inquiry is *what would have happened* if the defendant attorney had not been negligent. This is so because the very idea of causation necessarily involves comparing historical events to a hypothetical alternative.

The Viners also contend that the "but for" test of causation should not apply to transactional malpractice cases because it is too difficult to obtain the evidence needed to satisfy this standard of proof. In particular, they argue that proving causation under the "but for" test would require them to obtain the testimony of the other parties to the transaction, who have since become their adversaries, to the effect that they would have given the Viners more favorable terms had the Viners' attorneys not performed negligently. Not so. In transactional malpractice cases, as in other cases, the plaintiff may use circumstantial evidence to satisfy his or her burden. An express concession by the other parties to the negotiation that they would have accepted other or additional terms is not necessary. And the plaintiff need not prove causation with absolute certainty. Rather, the plaintiff need only "'introduce evidence which affords a reasonable basis for the conclusion that it is more likely than not that the conduct of the defendant was a cause in fact of the result.'" In any event, difficulties of proof cannot justify imposing liability for injuries that the attorney could not have prevented by performing according to the required standard of care.

....

For the reasons given above, we conclude that, just as in litigation malpractice actions, a plaintiff in a transactional malpractice action must show that *but for* the alleged malpractice, it is more likely than not that the plaintiff would have obtained a more favorable result.

Disposition

The judgment of the Court of Appeal is reversed, and the matter is remanded to the Court of Appeal for proceedings consistent with the views expressed here.

* * *

1. In accord is *Watson v. Meltzer*, 270 P.3d 289, 293–94 (Or. Ct. App. 2011), in which the court explained:

> Under Oregon negligence law, the element of "causation" ordinarily refers to "causation-in-fact" or "but-for" causation. That is to say, in order to prevail in a negligence action, a plaintiff must establish that *but for* the negligence of the defendant, the plaintiff would not have suffered the harm that is the subject of the claim. *See Joshi v. Providence Health System*, 198 Or.App. 535, 538–39, 108 P.3d 1195 (2005), *aff'd*, 342 Or. 152, 149 P.3d 1164 (2006) ("'Cause-in-fact' also has a well-defined legal meaning: it generally requires evidence of a reasonable probability that, *but for the defendant's negligence, the plaintiff would not have been harmed*" (emphasis added).).
>
> In the legal malpractice context, that means that, to prevail, a plaintiff must show, "'not only that the attorney was negligent, but also that the result would have been different except for the negligence.'" *Harding*, 265 Or. at 205, 508 P.2d 216 (quoting John H. Wade, *The Attorney's Liability for Negligence in Professional Negligence* 231–32 (Thomas G. Roady & William R. Anderson eds. 1960)); *see also Jeffries v. Mills*, 165 Or.App. 103, 122, 995 P.2d 1180 (2000) ("To show causation in a legal malpractice action, a plaintiff must demonstrate that she would have obtained a more favorable result" but for the negligence of the defendant).
>
> In the more specific context of legal malpractice that occurred during the course of litigation, the general requirement that a plaintiff demonstrate that he or she would have obtained a more favorable result but for the negligence of the defendant has been referred to as a requirement of proving a "case within a case." *See, e.g., Drollinger v. Mallon*, 350 Or. 652, 668, 260 P.3d 482 (2011) (referring to "the 'case within a case' methodology that is typically used to prove legal malpractice in a litigation context"). It may well be that the shorthand expression of "case within a case" makes sense only in the litigation context, where it may be said that the malpractice occurred in an actual "case." But the underlying requirement—that a plaintiff demonstrate that, but for the malpractice of the defendant, he or she would have obtained a more favorable result—is not a special rule that applies only in litigation malpractice cases. It is simply the application of the but-for causation requirement that applies in ordinary negligence cases.
>
> ....
>
> Aside from that, plaintiffs' argument further assumes that there is a meaningful *a priori* distinction between malpractice that occurs during the course of transactions, as opposed to litigation. The distinction is not obvious to us. It is not clear, for example, whether malpractice committed during the course of settling a lawsuit in the middle of trial would be appropriately classified as malpractice of a "litigation" or "transactional" variety.
>
> Plaintiffs insist that transactional legal malpractice is qualitatively different because requiring proof of what would have been the outcome of a negotiation but for a

defendant's negligence necessitates proof of something that never happened. The same, however, may be said of any litigation legal malpractice case. The very nature of the requirement of causation requires a comparison of what actually happened with what, hypothetically, would have happened but for the defendant's conduct.

2. *Conklin v. Hannoch Weisman,* 678 A.2d 1060 (N.J. 1996) is a transactional legal malpractice action in which the plaintiffs sought recovery against their lawyer who represented them in the sale of real estate but who allegedly failed to inform them of some of the risks of the deal as well as the risk of the buyer's insolvency. In explaining causation in fact (and the preferable use of the substantial factor test) in transactional legal malpractice actions, the court stated:

> Generally, our concepts of causation for failure to act are expressed in terms of whether the negligent conduct may be considered a substantial factor contributing to the loss. *See Brown v. United States Stove Co.,* 98 N.J. 155, 171, 484 A.2d 1234 (1984) ("With respect to concurrent proximate causation, a tortfeasor will be held answerable if its 'negligent conduct was a substantial factor in bringing about the injuries,' even where there are 'other intervening causes which were foreseeable or were normal incidents of the risk created.'") (quoting *Rappaport v. Nichols,* 31 N.J. 188, 202, 156 A.2d 1 (1959)). Although the law of negligence recognizes that there may be any number of concurrent causes of an injury, "[n]evertheless, these acts need not, of themselves, be capable of producing the injury; it is enough if they are a 'substantial factor' in bringing it about." *Scott v. Salem County Memorial Hosp.,* 116 N.J.Super. 29, 33–34, 280 A.2d 843 (App.Div.1971).
>
> The substantial factor test accounts for the fact that there can be any number of intervening causes between the initial wrongful act and the final injurious consequence and does not require an unsevered connecting link between the negligent conduct and the ultimate harm. The test is thus suited for legal malpractice cases in which inadequate or inaccurate legal advice is alleged to be a concurrent cause of harm. To relate the concepts to the facts, a court might instruct the jury to consider whether a reasonably competent transactional lawyer would have advised the clients of the economic risks that they took and whether the lack of the benefit of that advice was a substantial factor in causing them harm....
>
> ....
>
> The Appellate Division was thus concerned that it would be unfair to require the Conklins to prove that the specific events leading to their losses (the bankruptcy of and default by [the buyer]) were foreseeable at the time of sale. *See id.* at 454, 658 A.2d 322. The court remarked that "[t]here is a distinction between whether defendant's conduct caused the foreclosure and bankruptcies, and whether it caused plaintiffs' losses resulting from those events." However, "[i]f conduct creates an unreasonable risk of foreseeable harm, it matters not that the precise injury which occurred was not foreseen. If it is within the realm of foreseeability that some harm might result, negligence may be found." Thus, although it may not have been foreseeable that the [buyer] would become insolvent, the consequences of insolvency were always plainly foreseeable.

Conklin v. Hannoch Weisman, 678 A.2d 1060, 1070–72 (N.J. 1996).

3. For an interesting exposition on transactional legal malpractice and the issue of proving causation in fact, *see* George S. Mahaffey, Jr., *Cause-In-Fact and the Plaintiff's*

Burden of Proof with Regard to Causation and Damages in Transactional Legal Malpractice Matters: The Necessity of Demonstrating the Better Deal, 37 SUFFOLK U. L. REV. 393 (2004).

3. Reverse Bifurcation

As explained in the preceding sections, without proof of causation in fact, the plaintiff's legal malpractice action will fail. Recognizing that proof of causation in fact may be difficult for various reasons, some courts opt to reverse bifurcate legal malpractice actions. A trial is bifurcated when it is divided into two stages pursuant to the applicable rules of civil procedure. In the legal malpractice context, bifurcating the trial may involve determining the causation in fact component of the negligence action prior to proceeding with the additional elements of the plaintiff's legal malpractice action (duty, breach, and actual injury). It is termed "reverse bifurcation" because it permits the jury to determine causation and accompanying damages prior to determining whether the defendant attorney breached a duty of care owed to the plaintiff. Courts opting to conduct a legal malpractice trial in reverse bifurcation format justify its use as a means of preventing jury confusion of the issues. *See, e.g., Kearns v. Horsley*, 552 S.E.2d 1, 7 (N.C. Ct. App. 2001) (explaining that trying the cases together would be confusing to the jury and prejudicial to the defendant). *See generally* FED. R. CIV. P. 42(b) (permitting trial court "in furtherance of convenience or to avoid prejudice" to order separate trial of any claim or separate issue); Dwayne J. Hermes, Jeffrey W. Kemp & Paul B. Moore, *Leveling the Legal Malpractice Playing Field: Reverse Bifurcation of Trials*, 36 ST. MARY'S L.J. 879 (2005).

* * *

C. Loss of Chance

Focus Questions: *Daugert v. Pappas*

1. *What is "loss of chance" in legal malpractice?*
2. *Is a plaintiff entitled to bring a legal malpractice action based upon his previous counsel's failure to timely appeal his case?*
3. *How did the court's previous decision in* Herskovits *inform the court's decision in* Daugert?

Daugert v. Pappas

704 P.2d 600
(Wash. 1985)

PEARSON, Justice.

This case involves a legal malpractice claim against an attorney for failure to file timely a petition for review with this court of a Court of Appeals decision. The issues presented concern the proper standard for determining proximate cause in a legal malpractice action. The trial court concluded that proximate cause was a question for the jury and instructed the jury to decide whether the attorney's negligence was a substantial factor in causing the client's loss and whether the client lost a chance to recover. We hold this was error and reverse.

The underlying suit upon which this malpractice action is based arose out of a contract dispute between Black Mountain Development Company (developer) and Black Mountain Ranch (ranch). The ranch purchased a recreation complex built by the developer. Over a period of years a number of disputes arose about alleged deficiencies in the complex and its facilities and who should make the repairs. In an attempt to resolve these disputes, the parties signed an agreement purported to be a full and complete settlement of all disputes, past, present and future, between the ranch and the developer. Pursuant to this agreement the parties agreed to abide by the findings of an independent appraiser, the Anvil Corporation. Anvil completed the study called for in the agreement and concluded the problems were caused by a design defect. The developer disagreed with the findings and refused to correct the deficiencies. The ranch filed suit against the developer alleging breach of the settlement agreement.

Following trial the court concluded, contrary to Anvil's findings, that the deficiencies resulted from the ranch's negligent failure to maintain properly and adequately the facility so as to prevent deterioration. Thus, judgment was entered in favor of the developer. The ranch appealed and the Court of Appeals reversed based on a finding that without a showing of fraud, mistake, or arbitrariness, the settlement agreement was binding and enforceable.

Immediately following the Court of Appeals decision, the developer instructed its attorney, John Pappas, to petition the Supreme Court for review. The petition was filed a day late and Pappas failed to follow the proper procedure for requesting an extension of time. Having lost any right to a further appeal, judgment was entered against the developer. Thereafter, the developer, through its trustee, Larry Daugert, brought suit against Pappas and his law firm for malpractice. The issues of duty and breach of duty were resolved on summary judgment. The only issue disputed at trial was whether Pappas' negligence was the proximate cause of the judgment being entered against the developer. At trial both parties presented expert testimony on the likelihood of review and reversal of the Court of Appeals decision by the Supreme Court. In addition the trial judge, believing that proximate cause was a jury question, instructed the jury that:

The Plaintiffs have the burden of proving the following:

1. That Defendants' malpractice proximately caused the loss of chance for Plaintiffs to avoid damage;

2. The percentage chance, if any, that the Supreme Court would have accepted review and reversed the decision of the Court of Appeals;

3. Whether the percentage chance, if any, for Plaintiffs to avoid damage that was lost by Defendants' malpractice was a substantial factor in bringing about damage to Plaintiffs.

This instruction apparently was based on this court's opinion in *Herskovits v. Group Health Coop. of Puget Sound,* 99 Wash.2d 609, 664 P.2d 474 (1983). Upon returning its verdict, the jury found there was a 20 percent chance the Supreme Court would have granted review and reversed. Hence, judgment was entered against Pappas.[1] Pappas then sought review in the Court of Appeals. The case was transferred to this court.

---

1. The judgment equaled $71,341.84, representing 20 percent of the total amount of damages incurred in the underlying action against the ranch, plus $5,000 awarded to Pappas as a fee for handling

The first question presented by this case is whether it is proper, in a legal malpractice action involving an attorney's failure to perfect an appeal, for the jury to decide the issue of proximate cause. Washington law recognizes two elements to proximate cause: cause in fact and legal causation. The instant case concerns only cause in fact; therefore, any use herein of the term proximate cause concerns only the question of cause in fact. Furthermore, any reference to questions of law bears no relation to the concept of legal causation.

In most instances the question of cause in fact is for the jury.... The principles of proof and causation in a legal malpractice action usually do not differ from an ordinary negligence case. For instance, when an attorney makes an error during a trial, the causation issue in the subsequent malpractice action is relatively straightforward. The trial court hearing the malpractice claim merely retries, or tries for the first time, the client's cause of action which the client asserts was lost or compromised by the attorney's negligence, and the trier of fact decides whether the client would have fared better but for such mishandling. In such a case it is appropriate to allow the trier of fact to decide proximate cause. In effect the second trier of fact will be asked to decide what a reasonable jury or fact finder would have done but for the attorney's negligence. Thus, it is obvious that in most legal malpractice actions the jury should decide the issue of cause in fact.

In cases involving an attorney's alleged failure to perfect an appeal, however, the burden of proving causation takes on a different light. The cause in fact inquiry becomes whether the frustrated client would have been successful if the attorney had timely filed the appeal. Specifically, the client must show that an appellate court would have (1) granted review, and (2) rendered a judgment more favorable to the client. Not surprisingly, numerous other courts confronted with making this causation determination have not delegated it to the jury. Rather, they have consistently recognized that these latter two determinations are within the exclusive province of the court, not the jury, to decide.

The rationale for these decisions is clear. The overall inquiry is whether the client would have been successful if the attorney had timely filed the appeal. The determination of this issue would normally be within the sole province of the jury. Underlying the broad inquiry, however, are questions bearing legal analysis. The determination of whether review would have been granted and whether the client would have received a more favorable judgment depends on an analysis of the law and the rules of appellate procedure. Clearly, a judge is in a much better position to make these determinations. Thus, as two commentators have indicated:

> This decision must be made by the trial judge as an issue of law, based upon review of the transcript and record of the underlying action, the argument of counsel, and subject to the same rules of review as should have been applied by the appellate courts.

R. Mallen & V. Levit, *Legal Malpractice* §583, at 738 (2d ed. 1981).

We believe the rule articulated above constitutes the proper procedure for determining cause in fact in a legal malpractice action involving an attorney's failure to file an appeal in a timely manner. Although some courts have expressed concern over the idea of a trial judge attempting to predict the outcome of an appellate case, *see Better Homes, Inc. v. Rodgers*, 195 F.Supp. 93, 95 (N.D.W.Va.1961), the needs of both the client and the legal profession dictate adoption of the rule. On balance, the rule protects a client who is

---

the appeal. It should be noted that Pappas does not dispute the finding that he should return the $5,000 given to him for handling the appeal.

without fault from bearing the loss of an unappealed claim and prevents the jury from speculating over what an appellate court might have done by requiring the trial judge to make the determination by reviewing the record and applying the rules of appellate procedure. Hence, we hold that the determination of what decision would have followed if the attorney had timely filed the petition for review is a question of law for the judge, irrespective of whether the facts are undisputed. Therefore, in the instant case the trial court erred in instructing the jury on proximate cause.

Notwithstanding our finding that it was procedural error for the jury rather than the judge to decide cause in fact, the question remains: What is the appropriate test for determining cause in fact for failure to file timely a petition for review in a legal malpractice action? The trial court determined that the proper test was whether the client lost a chance to reverse the judgment and whether the attorney's negligence was a substantial factor in causing the client's loss. Appellant argues that the proper test is whether but for the attorney negligence the judgment would have been entered.

Traditionally, cause in fact has referred to the "but for" consequences of an act—the physical connection between an act and an injury. The "but for" test requires a plaintiff to establish that the act complained of probably caused the subsequent disability. Plaintiff's case must be based on more than just speculation and conjecture.

Courts have consistently applied the "but for" test in legal malpractice cases. A majority of courts have therefore concluded that when an attorney is negligent in filing an appeal, the client bears the burden of proving that the underlying case would have been successful but for the negligence of the attorney.

Application of the "but for" test to legal malpractice claims has not, however, gone uncontested. Furthermore, this court recently reevaluated the "but for" test in reference to a medical malpractice claim. *Herskovits v. Group Health Coop. of Puget Sound,* 99 Wash.2d 609, 664 P.2d 474 (1983).

Herskovits involved a wrongful death claim against a doctor for the death of a cancer patient. Expert testimony given at trial indicated the doctor's failure to diagnose the disease at an earlier date reduced decedent's chances of survival from 39 percent to 25 percent. Under the traditional "but for" test, the plaintiff could not prove the doctor probably caused decedent's death since decedent more likely than not would have died anyway. Recognizing the harsh consequences of applying the "but for" test in the traditional manner, a majority of this court allowed the question to go to a jury. Two justices held that plaintiff need not show decedent would have had a 51 percent chance of survival if the hospital had not been negligent; rather, plaintiff need only show defendant's negligence was a substantial factor contributing to decedent's death. In a concurring opinion four other justices concluded the disability involved was not death but rather the loss of a chance to survive and, under traditional causation analysis, defendant probably caused this disability.

Despite the *Herskovits* opinion and the questioning by commentators of the use of the "but for" test in legal malpractice claims, we believe it inappropriate at this time to change the test. The primary thrust of *Herskovits* was that a doctor's misdiagnosis of cancer either deprives a decedent of a chance of surviving a potentially fatal condition or reduces that chance. A reduction in one's opportunity to recover (loss of chance) is a very real injury which requires compensation. On the other hand, where the issue is whether the Supreme Court would have accepted review and rendered a decision more favorable to the client, there is no lost chance. The client in a legal malpractice case can eventually have the case reviewed. For example, in the instant case the client's underlying claim was not reviewed by the court initially because of the attorney's negligence. However, in the subsequent malpractice action the trial judge should have decided whether the Supreme Court would have accepted review and held in favor of the client. If the trial judge found review would have been denied, the client could have sought review in the Court of Appeals and ultimately in the Supreme Court. Hence, the client would eventually regain the opportunity to have the claim reviewed by the Supreme Court. On the other hand, in the medical context, when a patient dies all chances of survival are lost. Furthermore, unlike the medical malpractice claim wherein a doctor's misdiagnosis of cancer causes a separate and distinguishable harm, *i.e.*, diminished chance of survival, in a legal malpractice case there is no separate harm. Rather, the attorney will be liable for all the client's damages if review would have been granted and a more favorable decision rendered, and none if review would have been denied. Thus, clearly the loss of chance analysis articulated in *Herskovits* is inapplicable in a legal malpractice case.

....

In summary, we hold the client must prove that, but for the attorney's negligence, the plaintiff would probably have prevailed upon appeal in a legal malpractice action wherein the negligence occurs at the appellate level. Such a determination is for the trial judge, based upon a review of the transcript and record of the underlying action and subject to the same rules of review as would be applied by the appellate courts.

We turn now to the case at hand which has already been through the appellate process once. The client who may be without fault may or may not have suffered from the negligence of his attorney. Hence, rather than merely remanding the case for a determination of causation by the trial judge, we believe it appropriate in the interest of judicial economy and fairness to the client to permit the client to file a petition for review in this court pertaining to review of the original action. This court will then decide whether review would have been accepted and whether the client would have received a more favorable decision. Our determination will not, however, change the outcome of the underlying claim. Rather, it will decide the causation issue in the malpractice action. [Because] client's attorney did not argue the "but for" theory at trial [due to] confusion prompted by the *Herskovits* decision, [w]e reverse the trial court and invite the client to submit his petition for review within 30 days of the filing of this opinion.

* * *

1. In the *Daugert* opinion, the court discusses at length an opinion that many first year law students are introduced to in their introductory torts class, *Herskovits v. Grp. Health Coop. of Puget Sound*, 99 Wash. 2d 609, 664 P.2d 474 (1983). Were you persuaded by the court's reasoning that the rule from *Herskovits* should not be extended to the legal malpractice context?

2. Consider *Rivers v. Moore, Myers & Garland, LLC*, 236 P.3d 284, 293–94 (Wyo. 2010), in which the plaintiff complained that his attorney's negligence cost him the opportunity to build a larger building than the one he was permitted to build due to restrictions on a lot he had purchased with his attorney's help. The plaintiff sought to persuade the court that the recognition of loss of a chance in the medical malpractice context should be extended to the legal malpractice content as well. Ruling against allowing proof of loss of a chance in the legal malpractice context, the court explained:

> The loss-of-chance doctrine typically arises when a plaintiff seeks to recover damages against a medical provider who has reduced the plaintiff's chances of survival. To prevail on a loss-of-chance claim, the plaintiff must show: 1) that the patient has been deprived of the chance for successful treatment; and 2) that

the decreased chance for successful treatment more likely than not resulted from the provider's negligence.

To date, we have permitted recovery of damages under the loss-of-chance doctrine in only medical malpractice cases. This case does not present the proper circumstance to address the doctrine's application to legal malpractice cases.

....

We do not with this decision declare that there can never be a circumstance under which the loss-of-chance doctrine may apply to a legal malpractice claim. This case does, however, fit squarely within the parameters of the type of case in which the doctrine should have no application.

Observing that the jury in a legal malpractice action has the opportunity to decide, in retrospect, the probable outcome of the "case within the case" also helps capture why the analogy to suits against physicians ultimately breaks down. The critical prerequisite to employment of loss of a chance in the medical context is the existence of reliable statistical information, gleaned from rigorous studies that are typically generated outside the context of litigation, as to the survival rates of patients who are classified by reference to various objective characteristics. This is the sort of information that tells us that a Hispanic woman who is forty years old, and presents a certain medical profile, has a thirty percent chance of surviving a cancer of a given type if it is diagnosed and treated in a certain way. The presence of this sort of reliable statistical information, which is capable of being introduced to the jury at trial by a competent expert witness, helps explain the concern behind, and perhaps the propriety of, the adoption of loss of a chance in the medical setting. For certain kinds of patients, we know with some confidence that three out of ten would survive without malpractice. Yet we also know that, absent a change in the rules on proof of causation, none of those who suffer malpractice and would have survived in its absence will ever recover.

There is simply no comparable ground motivating the adoption of loss of a chance in legal malpractice. Because we are dealing with outcomes determined almost entirely by human interactions, rather than events dominated by biological processes, there is now, and may always be, a dearth of controlled studies and meaningful statistical information that might permit a qualified expert justifiably to assign a percentage chance of success to a given type of legal claim. Likewise, there is no well-defined body of expertise that purports to set standards for the drawing of sound inferences about the chances of prevailing on a given kind of legal claim. In short, the jury in a legal malpractice claim is not being presented with sound statistical information as to whether, absent malpractice, this sort of client, in this sort of circumstance, has a three in ten chance of prevailing. Rather, the jury is necessarily required to consider the "case within the case" as a one-off event. Thus, even granting that attorneys, like doctors, owe it to their clients to take reasonable steps to provide them with the best odds of prevailing, loss of a chance seems out of place in the realm of legal malpractice.

Do you agree or disagree with the *Rivers* court? *See also* John C.P. Goldberg, *What Clients Are Owed: Cautionary Observations on Lawyers and Loss of a Chance*, 52 Emory L.J. 1201, 1212–13 (2003).

* * *

D. Proximate Cause

We now turn to the issue of proximate causation (sometimes referred to as "legal causation"). As some of the previous cases indicated and unfortunately illustrated, the terms causation in fact and proximate causation are sometimes confused for each other. It is important to remember that these are two distinct legal doctrines with particular meanings. Causation in fact requires a showing of but for causation (but for the defendant's breach of the duty of care, the plaintiff more likely than not (*i.e.,* probably) would not have suffered the injury about which she complains). Causation in fact is different than proximate cause; the proximate or legal causation inquiry is whether there is some reason (or multiple reasons) justifying not holding the defendant liable in negligence despite proof that his breach of the standard of care in fact caused the plaintiff's complained of injury. Proximate or legal cause determinations are most often simply policy examinations. Consider the next cases.

Focus Questions: *Cleveland v. Rotman*

1. *What was the issue in* Cleveland*?*
2. *Was the defendant attorney's conduct a cause in fact of the decedent's death?*
3. *How does the court define proximate (or legal) causation?*
4. *Was the defendant attorney's conduct a proximate cause of the decedent's death?*

Cleveland v. Rotman

297 F.3d 569

(7th Cir. 2002)

COFFEY, MANION, and EVANS, Circuit Judges.

TERENCE T. EVANS, Circuit Judge.

Rose Cleveland is executrix of the estate of her late husband, Robert Cleveland, who committed suicide in 1998. Cleveland alleges that events surrounding 15 years of tax collection proceedings caused her husband severe depression and led to his suicide. She filed a four-count suit on the estate's behalf against the Internal Revenue Service, an IRS officer, and her husband's tax attorney, Michael Rotman. We address only the claims against Rotman, which are for legal malpractice.... Cleveland's estate appeals from the district court's dismissal for failure to state a claim for which relief can be granted under Federal Rule of Civil Procedure 12(b)(6).

... We will affirm the dismissal if it appears beyond doubt that the plaintiff cannot prove any set of facts entitling it to relief.

In the late 1960's, Robert Cleveland, who was an attorney, became involved in a dispute with the IRS over a tax issue. The tax proceedings stretched over 15 years, involving multiple trials and appeals. Cleveland's estate alleges that the IRS engaged in a campaign of unauthorized activities that stripped Cleveland of all assets and income. Unable to pay his legal bills and the interest and penalties that the IRS assessed (which totaled $250,000), Cleveland went into debt. Starting in 1991, the IRS confiscated Cleveland's social security income. The estate also alleges that the IRS levied on money that Cleveland obtained in a settlement for one of his law clients, causing the client to wait for years to receive his settlement money. The estate alleges that this is "one example of how ... the IRS caused Mr. Cleveland to get disbarred from practicing law in Illinois." The tax dispute caused Cleveland to suffer severe depression. As a result, Cleveland's therapist informed the IRS in writing that Cleveland was suicidal.

In 1996 Cleveland retained Rotman for advice in resolving the tax dispute. At the time, Cleveland's therapist informed Rotman of Cleveland's poor financial status, his severe depression, and his suicidal tendencies. Rotman advised Cleveland that he needed to file tax returns for a 10-year period, but Cleveland claimed that he was unable to calculate his income and expenses for this period because his financial records had been lost during office moves and discarded by others during divorce proceedings (involving a different wife, not Rose). As a result, it is alleged that Rotman told Cleveland to estimate his income and expenses for the relevant years.

Apparently, Cleveland's estimates did not agree with IRS figures, and although the IRS had previously declared Cleveland's account uncollectible, it decided to audit him again. It notified Cleveland of the impending audit in February 1997. Because she was concerned over Cleveland's suicidal depression, Cleveland's therapist intervened and succeeded in postponing the audit until January 1998. On January 26, 1998, shortly before the audit was scheduled to take place, Cleveland shot himself in the head at home in his wife's presence. He was 74 years old.

Cleveland's estate alleges that Rotman committed malpractice, which triggered the IRS's proposed 1998 audit, which in turn triggered Cleveland's suicide. The estate argues that the district court erred in ruling that, as a matter of law, a plaintiff's allegations were insufficient under Rule 12(b)(6).

[T]he elements of a legal malpractice claim are (1) an attorney-client relationship establishing a duty on the attorney's part, (2) breach of that duty, (3) proximate cause establishing that but for the breach the plaintiff would not have been injured, and (4) resulting damages.

It is well-established under Illinois law that a plaintiff may not recover for a decedent's suicide following a tortious act because suicide is an independent intervening event that the tortfeasor cannot be expected to foresee. The district court ... therefore dismissed the estate's claims arising from Cleveland's suicide.

We agree with the district court that Cleveland's suicide was an independent intervening event that broke the chain of causation from Rotman's alleged malpractice to Cleveland's death. Cleveland was an adult, and the estate has not alleged that he was mentally unstable. *See Kleen,* 321 Ill.App.3d at 643, 255 Ill.Dec. 246, 749 N.E.2d 26; *Jarvis,* 517 F.Supp. at 1175 (recognizing exception to suicide rule where, as proximate result of a head injury caused by tortfeasor's negligence, victim becomes "insane and bereft of reason" and commits suicide as a result). Therefore, we assume that Cleveland was a competent adult who clearly understood what he was doing and intentionally took his own life. Moreover, Cleveland's estate fails to establish that Rotman breached a duty to Cleveland, or that Rotman's alleged negligence proximately caused Cleveland's suicide.

Essentially, Cleveland's estate seeks to impose on Rotman a duty to foresee and avoid a client's suicide. Although an Illinois court imposed such a duty on a psychiatrist who knew of his patient's history of suicidal depression and yet failed to protect the patient from self-harm, the estate here points to no case law extending such a duty to the attorney-client context. Because of the differences between the psychiatrist-patient relationship and the attorney-client relationship, we see no justification for extending such a duty to attorneys. Psychiatrists are health care professionals trained to care for their patients' mental and emotional health. By contrast, attorneys are medical laypeople who cannot be reasonably expected to anticipate the mental health consequences of their legal advice.

Whether Rotman had a duty to prevent Cleveland's suicide depends on the suicide's foreseeability, its likelihood, the magnitude of the burden of guarding against it, and the potential consequences of placing that burden on Rotman. As we just noted, because Rotman was not a medical professional, he could not have reasonably been expected to foresee that his allegedly erroneous advice would drive Cleveland to suicide. Cleveland's estate urges, however, that Rotman should have foreseen that bad tax advice could drive Cleveland to suicide because he knew that Cleveland was suffering from severe depression triggered by his tax woes. Nonetheless, based on his lack of psychological training, Rotman cannot have reasonably been expected to foresee Cleveland's suicide.

Additionally, suicide is generally not a likely result of bad tax advice, especially when that advice concerns the relatively routine matter of filing tax returns. By the time Cleveland retained Rotman, the tax dispute had been going on for 15 years, and Cleveland was already suffering from severe depression. In the context of the entire series of events arising from Cleveland's IRS dispute, Rotman's allegedly erroneous advice was not more likely than any of the other events to cause Cleveland's suicide.

Moreover, the magnitude of placing the burden on an attorney to foresee and prevent a client's suicide is very great. Attorneys cannot reasonably be expected to screen potential clients for suicidal tendencies. Imposing such a burden would expose attorneys to an unreasonable risk of liability, which would ultimately deprive visibly depressed people of competent legal advice. Therefore, Cleveland's estate fails to establish that Rotman had a duty to foresee and avoid Cleveland's suicide.

Even assuming that Rotman had such a duty, the estate fails to show that Rotman's allegedly erroneous advice proximately caused Cleveland's suicide. A proximate cause is one that produces an injury through a natural and continuous sequence of events unbroken by any effective intervening cause. Proximate cause is composed of two elements: legal cause and cause in fact. Legal cause exists where the injury was of a type that a reasonable person would foresee as a likely result of his or her conduct.

As we've noted, it was not reasonably foreseeable that Cleveland's suicide was a likely result of Rotman's advice. Additionally, the timing of events weakens the proximate cause argument. Rotman advised Cleveland to file estimated tax returns in 1996. The IRS notified Cleveland of its intended audit in February 1997. Cleveland did not commit suicide until almost a year later, in January 1998. Even assuming that Rotman's allegedly erroneous advice precipitated the audit, Cleveland was aware of the impending audit for almost a year before taking his life. Given the significant time lapse between the alleged triggering event and Cleveland's suicide, as well as Cleveland's history of depression, which had its origins in events that preceded his relationship with Rotman—including the loss of his legal practice, his disbarment, the confiscation of his assets and income, and his mounting debt—Cleveland's suicide did not follow Rotman's advice through a natural and continuous sequence of events unbroken by any effective intervening cause. Therefore, Rotman's allegedly erroneous advice did not proximately cause Cleveland's suicide. Thus, the district court correctly held that the estate cannot recover for Cleveland's suicide.

....

AFFIRMED.

Focus Questions: *Andrews v. Saylor*

1. *Is proximate causation in a legal malpractice action typically an issue of fact or a question of law?*
2. *May there be more than one proximate or legal cause of an injury?*
3. *What policy considerations were important to the* Andrews *court in determining the appropriateness of potentially extending legal malpractice liability to successor counsel?*

Andrews v. Saylor

80 P.3d 482
(N.M. Ct. App. 2003)

ALARID, Judge.

This case presents us with a question of first impression concerning proximate cause in legal malpractice cases: does the judge or the jury decide whether an attorney's failure to appeal was a proximate cause of injury to the client? We hold that questions of proximate cause in legal malpractice cases are to be treated as questions of fact for the factfinder—in this case, the jury. We also consider the question of whether malpractice by successor attorneys hired to respond to the original attorney's malpractice is a foreseeable consequence of the original attorney's malpractice. We hold that it is.

...

BACKGROUND

Plaintiff-Appellant, Deborah Andrews, and her husband, Stephen Andrews, were divorced in 1986, after approximately twelve years of marriage. During the marriage, Stephen worked for the Bernalillo County Fire Department (BCFD) and made contributions towards a pension pursuant to the Public Employees Retirement Act (PERA). Plaintiff was aware that Stephen made contributions to a PERA account.

A final decree granting the divorce was signed by District Judge Robert L. Thompson and was filed on May 29, 1986. The final decree contained the following provision dividing the parties' property:

> [P]etitioner shall have as her sole and separate property the "Golden Body Gym" business, the 1976 MG, and all other property presently in her possession; and, Respondent shall have as his sole and separate property the house at 2936 Dakota, N.E., the 1981 Honda, the 1973 Ford, and all other property presently in his possession.

The final decree was prepared by Plaintiff's attorney, Defendant-Appellant, Susan J. Scarborough, who was employed by Defendants-Appellants, Albuquerque Law Clinic, and Bruce W. Barrett & Associates. Stephen was not represented by an attorney. There is no provision in the final decree expressly declaring the parties' respective interests in the PERA benefits.

In early 1996, Plaintiff encountered a friend who some years previously had also divorced an employee of the BCFD. By this time, both Stephen and the friend's former husband had retired from the BCFD, and were receiving PERA retirement benefits. Plaintiff's friend mentioned that she had been awarded, and was receiving, a share of the PERA benefits earned during her husband's employment with the BCFD.

The friend's remarks led Plaintiff to hire an attorney to investigate Plaintiff's entitlement to a portion of the PERA benefits earned by Stephen during their marriage. In April 1996, this second attorney, Claudia Work, filed a "Petition to Divide Undivided Marital Property." The petition alleged that, by operation of community property law, Plaintiff was entitled to a 24% interest in Stephen's PERA retirement account. The petition requested that the district court divide Stephen's retirement account pursuant to the community property laws of the State of New Mexico. The petition to divide was docketed separately from the original divorce case and was assigned to District Judge William Lang. Judge Lang conducted an evidentiary hearing at which both Plaintiff and Stephen testified....

At the end of the hearing, Judge Lang ruled that the parties had intended to accomplish a complete division of all community property and that the 1986 final decree clearly and unambiguously divided all of the parties' community property, including the PERA account:

> [T]here is an argument advanced by the petitioner, that somehow the state had possession of the account, and that I agree with [counsel for Stephen,] is a red herring indeed[.] [I]t is the money of the contributor or in this instance Mr. Andrews, subject to the community interest at least during their marriage. The real issue is the language entered in the final decree and does it contemplate a final division of all of the property and debts of the parties, and in my estimation and in this court[']s estimation having viewed a number of these, this final decree did that. The petitioner was represented by coun[sel].... Ms. Scarborough was a licensed attorney at the time[.] [H]er failure to investigate, should in no way prejudice the rights of the parties, either of them, with respect to what is contained in the language of the decree. The language being clear and unambiguous that all community property was divided, that each takes the specifically enumerated items plus all other items in their personal property or property in your possession ... [T]here was a failure to investigate apparently by petitioner's agent and that in no way induces or brings up any issue of fraud, there was no evidence that there was any attempt to hide anything, in fact it is clear and was stated by both parties that the petitioner knew of the existence of the retirement all during the course of the marriage[.] [E]ssentially, this is [r]es [j]udicata[.] [T]he issue of the retirement was negotiated and was resolved by the terms of the final decree. As is indicated by the clear and unambiguous language contained in the final decree, if there is a remedy in this matter, that the petitioner may have, it does not lie versus the respondent[,] but perhaps it lies elsewhere. I do not reach the issue of laches for the forgoing reasons; as there is legal defense and on the basis of what was presented in court today I will decree that the retirement benefits of the respondent were previously divided to the satisfaction of the parties as eviden[ced] by the clear and [un]ambiguous language of the final decree.

After the hearing, but prior to entry of an order, Plaintiff hired attorney Thomas Nance Jones to take over the case from Work. Jones advised Plaintiff that he did not believe there was a good chance of successfully appealing Judge Lang's ruling and that the cost of an appeal would be substantial. Plaintiff also consulted attorney William Gilstrap about pursuing a malpractice claim against Defendants. Gilstrap consulted with Jones regarding the viability of an appeal. The case was reassigned to District Judge Mark Macaron who entered an order denying Plaintiff's motion to divide the PERA benefits on April 15, 1998.

Plaintiff did not appeal from the April 15, 1998 order. Instead, Plaintiff filed the present malpractice action on May 26, 1998. The malpractice action was assigned to Judge Robert L. Thompson, the same judge who had signed the 1986 final decree.

Defendants moved for summary judgment on the ground that Plaintiff's failure to appeal from Judge Lang's ruling was the proximate cause of the loss of Plaintiff's share of PERA benefits. According to Defendants, Judge Lang erred by ruling that Stephen's interest in his PERA account constituted property presently in his possession.... Defendants argued that Stephen's PERA benefits were in the possession of the Retirement Board, which held them as a statutory trustee. Defendants argued that Plaintiff should have appealed the April 15, 1998 order.

Plaintiff responded that (1) Judge Lang did not err in finding that Plaintiff and Stephen intended to include the PERA account in property presently in Stephen's possession; and (2) even if Judge Lang erred, his conduct was not an independent intervening cause. Plaintiff attached to her response portions of the deposition of her expert witness, attorney Barbara Shapiro. In her deposition testimony, Shapiro discussed the likelihood of successfully appealing from the April 15, 1998, order denying the motion to divide. In Shapiro's view, Plaintiff had a "good chance ... of losing the appeal."

In their reply, Defendants asserted that they were not claiming that the alleged negligence of Plaintiff's successor attorneys was an "intervening cause"; rather, it was Defendants' position that Plaintiff had not established causation "in the first place."

Judge Thompson granted Defendants' motion for summary judgment. At the conclusion of the hearing on the motion, he explained his reasoning:

> Let me just say three or four things that I think cap it. The language [of the final decree] itself, I think, is clear and unambiguous. And I don't think the PERA is included, okay? I think had there been a timely appeal, the plaintiff would not have suffered injury.
>
> There's an undivided community asset protected by law, and I don't think she had any damages at the time of the decree because they were protected by law. And had the—and I hate to disagree with my fellow judge, because I may get reversed, but I think had he ruled according to the law, that my interpretation is there would have been no damages.

Plaintiff filed a timely notice of appeal.

DISCUSSION

1. Who Determines Proximate Cause in a Legal Malpractice Case?

"With few exceptions, proximate cause is a question of fact to be determined by the factfinder." *Lerma v. State Highway Dep't*, 117 N.M. 782, 784–85, 877 P.2d 1085, 1087–88 (1994). Defendants argue that Plaintiff's failure to appeal from the April 15, 1998, order was the proximate cause of Plaintiff's loss of her community share of retirement benefits from PERA because, according to Defendants, in a hypothetical past in which Plaintiff pursued an appeal, Plaintiff necessarily would have prevailed. Defendants argue that it would be improper to allow a jury to reconstruct this hypothetical past because, in doing so, the jury must decide the appeal, a task that in an actual appeal is the function of judges. Thus, Defendants ask us to create a legal-malpractice exception to the general rule that proximate cause is a question of fact to be determined by the factfinder.

In a legal malpractice action involving a failure to appeal, proximate cause ultimately reduces to a prediction as to what the outcome of a hypothetical appeal would have been. Significantly, under the preponderance-of-the-evidence standard applicable to legal malpractice actions, complete certainty as to the outcome of the hypothetical appeal is not required: the party bearing the burden of proof need only persuade the jury that the likelihood of a favorable outcome in the hypothetical appeal was greater than even. Unlike an actual appellate decision, the jury's answer to the question of who more likely than not should have prevailed had an appeal been taken does not change the result in the earlier lawsuit and does not establish binding legal precedent in future lawsuits.

We see no need for treating legal malpractice any differently than other types of professional malpractice. Although a district judge, as a lawyer, will have a general knowledge of the law and likely will have expertise in some areas, no lawyer is presumed to know all the law, much less to be an expert in every area of the law. We are confident that a jury, aided by the testimony of experts versed in the relevant area of the law, is capable of making a prediction as to the outcome of a hypothetical appeal with the degree of certainty required by a preponderance-of-the-evidence standard of proof. We are concerned that our adoption of a special rule that insulates malpracticing lawyers from jury scrutiny of their conduct would give the public the impression that we are simply lawyers protecting other lawyers. *Millhouse v. Wiesenthal*, 775 S.W.2d 626, 629 (Tex.1989) (Mauzy, J., dissenting) (observing that "to say that the court is entitled to rule upon the question of causation as a matter of law in an appellate legal malpractice case gives the appearance that the bench is in the position of protecting the bar"; arguing that "[t]he privilege of being an attorney should not carry with it immunity from the jury system"). We therefore hold that in a legal malpractice action, the issue of proximate cause is a question of fact for the jury, and this is so even when proximate cause depends upon whether or not an appeal would have been successful.

... Contrary to Defendants' position, New Mexico case law recognizes that in legal malpractice cases expert testimony is admissible to establish that an attorney breached the standard of care and that the breach resulted in damage to the client.

In the present case, the district court decided the issue of proximate cause by ruling as a matter of law that an appeal inevitably would have succeeded. In doing so, the district court usurped the jury's function as factfinder.

....

... We therefore reverse the grant of summary judgment in Defendants' favor.

3. The District Court Committed Substantive Error in Treating the Alleged Malpractice of Successor Counsel as "the" Proximate Cause

In addition to its error in deciding the question of proximate cause as a question of law, the district court committed substantive error by ruling that malpractice by Plaintiff's successor attorneys would constitute "the" proximate cause of Plaintiff's loss and would necessarily prevent Scarborough's initial malpractice from being a proximate cause of the loss of Plaintiff's community share of PERA benefits.

As noted above, Plaintiff alleges that Scarborough negligently failed to protect Plaintiff's community interest in Stephen's PERA benefits by failing to include in the final decree express language awarding Plaintiff her community share. If the jury finds that Scarborough was negligent, then, in determining whether Scarborough's negligence was a cause of the loss of Plaintiff's community share of PERA benefits, the jury will decide what would have happened if Scarborough had included in the 1986 final decree a provision awarding Plaintiff her community interest in the PERA benefits. We believe it is open to proof that had Scarborough included a provision expressly awarding Plaintiff her community share of Stephen's PERA benefits, there would have been no need to bring a ... motion to divide the PERA benefits, the hearing before Judge Lang would not have occurred, and the question of appealing the April 15, 1998, order would not have arisen. Thus, a jury could find that Scarborough's negligence was a cause in fact of the loss of Plaintiff's share of benefits—*i.e.*, a factor "without which the [loss of PERA benefits] would not have occurred." UJI 13-305 NMRA 2003.

Proximate cause superimposes considerations of foreseeability on causation in fact. *See Torres v. El Paso Elec. Co.*, 1999-NMSC-029, ¶ 14, 127 N.M. 729, 987 P.2d 386 (noting the necessity of limiting "potentially limitless liability arising from mere cause in fact"). New Mexico follows the rule that " '[a]ny harm which is in itself foreseeable, as to which the actor has created or increased the recognizable risk, is always "proximate," no matter how it is brought about.' " *Id.*, ¶ 23 (quoting Restatement (Second) of Torts § 442B cmt. b (1965)). Our Supreme Court has held that medical malpractice is a foreseeable consequence of negligent operation of a motor vehicle resulting in an injury to the plaintiff that requires medical treatment. If medical malpractice is a foreseeable consequence of negligent operation of a motor vehicle in a manner that results in physical injury to another, then, *a fortiori*, the alleged legal malpractice of Plaintiff's successor attorneys was a foreseeable consequence of Scarborough's negligence in preparing the decree. *See Collins v. Perrine*, 108 N.M. 714, 718, 778 P.2d 912, 916 (Ct.App.1989) (observing that "where the negligent conduct of an actor creates or increases the risk of a particular harm and is a substantial factor in causing that harm, the fact that the harm is brought about through the intervention of another force does not relieve the actor of liability").

Under New Mexico law, there may be more than one proximate cause of an injury. Thus, a finding that the failure of Plaintiff and her successor attorneys to appeal from the April 15, 1998 order was a proximate cause of Plaintiff's loss does not foreclose a finding that Scarborough's negligence also was a proximate cause.

....

CONCLUSION

The summary judgment in Defendants' favor is reversed and this matter is remanded to the district court for further proceedings consistent with this opinion.

IT IS SO ORDERED.

* * *

1. Causation in Fact and Proximate Causation. It is very important to understand the distinctions between causation in fact and proximate (or legal) causation. The causation element in a negligence action requires proof of both causation in fact and proximate causation. Causation in fact is the connecting link between the defendant's breach of the standard of care (sometimes also confusingly referred to as negligence) and the plaintiff's complained-of actual damages. Without a determination of causation in fact, the plaintiff's *prima facie* case fails. Proximate (or legal) causation is a policy determination—a determination that even though the defendant's breach of the standard of care has resulted in the plaintiff's damages, there is some other reason that the defendant should not be subject to liability.

2. Expert Testimony to Establish Proximate Causation. In *Carbone v. Tierney*, 151 N.H. 521 (2004), plaintiff sued his former attorney for legal malpractice when his attorney failed to properly plead subject matter jurisdiction (due to her lack of knowledge of the Federal Rules of Civil Procedure) and also failed to contest the dismissal of her client's cause of action in state court (due to, the trial court said, "an obvious breach of an equally obvious professional norm") in a tort litigation. In addressing the defendant-attorney's argument that the plaintiff's claim against the attorney should fail for failure to provide expert testimony on the issue of proximate causation, the court explained:

> It is well established that expert testimony is required where the subject presented is so distinctly related to some science, profession or occupation as to be beyond the ken of the average layperson. On the other hand, expert testimony is not required where the subject presented is within the realm of common knowledge and everyday experience. These general principles are applicable to legal malpractice actions.
>
> To establish legal malpractice, a plaintiff must prove: (1) that an attorney-client relationship existed, which placed a duty upon the attorney to exercise reasonable professional care, skill and knowledge in providing legal services to that client; (2) a breach of that duty; and (3) resultant harm legally caused by that breach.
>
> We have previously held that, absent exceptional circumstances, expert testimony is necessary to inform the jury regarding the skill and care ordinarily exercised by lawyers and to prove a breach thereof. We have also assumed, without deciding, that expert testimony is required to prove proximate cause. Today, we resolve this issue, and conclude that, in most instances, expert testimony is required to prove causation in a legal malpractice action.
>
> In legal malpractice cases, "[e]xpert testimony may be essential for the plaintiff to establish causation. The trier of fact must be able to determine what ... result should have occurred if the lawyer had not been negligent." 5 R. Mallen & J. Smith, *Legal Malpractice* § 33.16, at 116 (5th ed. 2000). "[U]nless the causal link is obvious or can be established by other evidence, expert testimony may be essential to prove what the lawyer should have done." *Id.* We thus hold that expert testimony on proximate cause is required "in cases where determination of that issue is not one that lay people would ordinarily be competent to make." *Delp v. Douglas*, 948 S.W.2d 483, 495 (Tex.App.1997), *rev'd in part and vacated in part on other grounds*, 987 S.W.2d 879 (Tex.1999).
>
> In the present case, the trial court characterized [Attorney] Tierney's lack of knowledge about the Federal Rules of Civil Procedure and her failure to contest the dismissal of Carbone's case in the Essex County Superior Court as "obvious breach[es] of ... equally obvious professional norm[s]." ... The trial court thus ruled that [former client] Carbone was not required to offer expert testimony and granted summary judgment in his favor on the legal malpractice claim.
>
> Even assuming that no expert testimony was required to establish the appropriate standard of care and Tierney's breach of that standard, Carbone was nonetheless required to provide expert testimony to establish that Tierney's breach was the legal cause of his injuries. As set forth above, the trier of fact must be able to determine what result would have occurred if the attorney had not been negligent. An analysis of what Tierney should have done and whether her

negligence was the legal cause of Carbone's injuries is so distinctly related to the practice of law as to be beyond the ken of the average layperson.

We disagree that this is one of those exceptional cases where Tierney's breach of the standard of care was so obviously the legal cause of Carbone's injuries that expert testimony was not required. The trial court was correct in characterizing Tierney's conduct as egregious. She demonstrated a fundamental lack of knowledge about the Federal Rules of Civil Procedure and about the remedies available when a case is dismissed in both federal and state court. Nonetheless, it is unclear which egregious conduct, if any, was the legal cause of Carbone's injuries. Accordingly, expert testimony was required to explain whether, if the underlying case had not been dismissed in federal or state court, Carbone would have prevailed in the cause of action against his son. Expert testimony was also required to explain whether Tierney's failure to represent Carbone's interests in Lisa's bankruptcy proceeding actually resulted in harm to Carbone. The facts of this case are thus sufficiently complicated to require expert testimony with respect to causation.

Carbone v. Tierney, 151 N.H. 521 (2004).

3. In a legal malpractice action in which the plaintiffs (who were selling real estate) complained that the defendant attorney did not adequately explain the risks of subordination of claims and the risk of the buyer's potential insolvency, the court explained the distinction between causation in fact and proximate (or legal) causation in this manner:

Although it sounds simple, "'causation' is an inscrutably vague notion, susceptible to endless philosophical argument, as well as practical manipulation." Glen O. Robinson, *Multiple Causation in Tort Law: Reflections on the DES Cases*, 68 VA. L. REV. 713, 713 (1982). Dean Prosser observed almost fifty years ago that "'Proximate cause remains a tangle and a jungle, a palace of mirrors and a maze ... [it] covers a multitude of sins ... [and] is a complex term of highly uncertain meaning under which other rules, doctrines and reasons lie buried.'"[5]

The first and most basic concept "buried" within proximate cause is that of causation in fact. Cause in fact is sometimes referred to as "but for" causation. In the routine tort case, "the law requires proof that the result complained of probably would not have occurred 'but for' the negligent conduct of the defendant." The simplest understanding of cause in fact in attorney malpractice cases arises from the case-within-a-case concept. For example, if a lawyer misses a statute of limitations and a complaint is dismissed for that reason, a plaintiff must still establish that had the action been timely filed it would have resulted in a favorable recovery....

Those cases present the easier aspects of causation. More complex are cases in which the attorney's negligent conduct combines with other causes that lead to the client's injury.... The negligent attorney ... often does not "create" the risk of intervening harm (the attorney does not make the borrower more likely to become insolvent), but rather fails to take the steps that competent counsel should take to protect a client from the risks that ultimately produce the injury.

---

5. We have been candid in New Jersey to view this doctrine not so much as an expression of the mechanics of causation, but as an expression of line-drawing by courts and juries, an instrument of "overall fairness and sound public policy." *Brown v. United States Stove Co.*, 98 N.J. 155, 173, 484 A.2d 1234 (1984). Juries, like courts, should understand the doctrine to be based on "'logic, common sense, justice, policy and precedent.'" *Caputzal v. The Lindsay Co.*, 48 N.J. 69, 78, 222 A.2d 513 (1966) (quoting *Powers v. Standard Oil Co.*, 98 N.J.L. 730, 734, 119 A. 273 (Sup.Ct.), *aff'd*, 98 N.J.L. 893, 121 A. 926 (E. & A.1923)).

....

... Traditionally, proximate cause has been defined "as being any cause which in the natural and continuous sequence, unbroken by an efficient intervening cause, produces the result complained of and without which the result would not have occurred." Similarly, the jury charge [in this case] stated that, to be a proximate cause of plaintiffs' losses, defendants' negligence had to be "an efficient cause of the plaintiffs' losses, *a cause which necessarily set the other causes in motion* and was a substantial factor in bringing about the plaintiffs' losses" (emphasis added). The problem with this language is that defendants' failure to inform plaintiffs about the risks of subordination did not in any sense "set in motion" the chain of events that led to the bankruptcy of Longview Estates, the other primary cause of plaintiffs' losses.

Language concerning the "cause that sets the other causes in motion" relates to the concept of cause in fact, not to the value driven aspects of proximate cause....

Conklin v. Hannoch Weisman, 678 A.2d 1060, 1070–72 (N.J. 1996).

* * *

E. Special Issues in Proving Causation

1. Proof of Collectibility

Exercise 5.2

Dr. Zeta is a resident of State A and a practicing periodontist. On September 3, 1989, Dr. Zeta was injured in a two-car automobile accident during his vacation in State B. The traffic collision report for the accident stated that a vehicle being driven by Evan Trapp crossed a highway on-ramp into the path of Dr. Zeta's automobile after striking a curb and a cyclone fence. The traffic collision report also indicated that Trapp was driving while intoxicated and that his vehicle was being operated at the time of the accident at a high rate of speed. After the accident, Dr. Zeta returned to the Philadelphia area in order to begin treatment for his injuries. As a result of this automobile accident, Dr. Zeta avers that he suffers from a degenerative and arthritic back condition, which makes it difficult for him to work full-time as a periodontist. On September 9, 1989, Dr. Zeta retained Attorney Corbman to pursue his claim against Trapp for the personal injuries he sustained in the accident. Attorney Corbman is licensed to practice law in State A. Attorney Corbman proceeded to obtain Dr. Zeta's medical reports. After reviewing the medical reports, Attorney Corbman made a claim on Dr. Zeta's behalf against Trapp's insurance carrier, State B Automobile Association ("SBAA"). During settlement negotiations with SBAA, Attorney Corbman learned that Trapp's insurance policy had a limit of $25,000. On September 17, 1990, more than one year after the accident, Attorney Corbman discovered that the State B statute of limitations for injuries such as those suffered by Dr. Zeta was only one year as opposed to the two-year statute of limitations in State A. SBAA ultimately informed Attorney Corbman that it would not make a settlement offer to Dr. Zeta because the one-year statute of limitations had passed without Attorney Corbman instituting a formal legal action. As soon as Attorney Corbman learned this information, he met with Dr. Zeta and informed him that his claim had been terminated because no suit was filed and settlement had not been reached within the one-year statute of limitations period. Upon hearing this news, Dr. Zeta becomes upset and threatens to sue Attorney Corbman for malpractice. Your firm has been contacted by Dr. Zeta to file the legal malpractice action against Dr. Zeta's former counsel, Attorney Corbman. Please draft the body of a complaint alleging legal malpractice against Attorney Corbman, being sure to plead each element of the negligence action with particularity.

Focus Questions: *Paterek v. Petersen & Ibold*

1. *Explain how proof of collectibility relates to the causation in fact determination.*
2. *What are the majority and minority positions regarding proof of collectibility? Which position does the* Paterek *court adopt?*
3. *According to* Paterek, *is proof of collectibility part of the plaintiff's* prima facie *case or an affirmative defense to be pleaded and proven by the defendant?*
4. *How does the ruling in* Paterek *differ from the ruling in* Kituskie? *With which position do you agree most? Why?*

Paterek v. Petersen & Ibold

890 N.E.2d 316
(Ohio 2008)

PFEIFER, J.

We hold today that in an attorney-malpractice case, proof of the collectibility of the judgment lost due to the malpractice is an element of the plaintiff's claim against the negligent attorney.

Factual and Procedural Background

This is an attorney-malpractice case involving the mishandling of a personal-injury claim. On May 28, 1997, Kristopher Richardson negligently injured Edward Paterek in an automobile accident. Richardson had no personal assets or earning capacity with which to compensate Paterek for his injuries, but did carry $100,000 of auto liability coverage.

After the accident, Paterek and his wife, appellee Irene Paterek, retained an attorney, Jonathon Evans, of the law firm of Peterson & Ibold, appellants, to represent them in a personal-injury action against Richardson. On May 11, 1998, Evans filed a lawsuit against Richardson, but subsequently dismissed it on October 6, 2000, without prejudice. He then failed to refile the claim within one year of the dismissal, and the suit was dismissed for want of prosecution. Both Evans and Peterson & Ibold admitted liability for the damages proximately caused by Evans's breach of the standard of care.

On October 2, 2002, the Patereks filed this legal-malpractice suit....

On September 17, 2003, appellants filed a motion for partial summary judgment. They argued that since the maximum recovery available to Irene from the tortfeasor was $100,000, the court should cap any damages against the appellants at that amount.

The trial court overruled appellants' motion on October 21, 2003, holding that the collectibility of a judgment against the underlying tortfeasor was not an element Irene would have to prove at trial:

> "Although Plaintiffs will have to prove the 'case within the case', such proof does not have to go so far as to demonstrate that the tortfeasor in the underlying case was not judgment proof or, conversely stated, that the tortfeasor had assets from which a judgment could be collected."

....

... The legal-malpractice claim against the firm and Evans proceeded to trial on December 13, 2004. The parties jointly submitted stipulations to the court. The appellants stipulated that Richardson was at fault in the underlying accident and that Edward Paterek was not comparatively negligent. The appellants also admitted that Evans missed a filing deadline, causing the Pautereks to lose their cause of action. The parties stipulated that Richardson carried a $100,000 automobile liability insurance policy that would have been available to satisfy a judgment against him. The parties further stipulated that Richardson had no other assets:

> "Kristopher Richardson did not at the time of the accident, nor does he presently, have any personal assets or earning capacity sufficient to satisfy any judgment against him in excess of the $100,000 automobile liability coverage."

The parties also stipulated that the Patereks held a valid UIM policy:

> "[T]he Plaintiffs had underinsured motorist coverage with Beacon One [sic] in the amount of $250,000 at the time of the accident in question ($150,000 of which may be available to the plaintiffs to cover damages, if necessary, after set-off of the $100,000 available from the tortfeasor's policy)."

Finally, the parties stipulated that "these stipulations will be entered into the record by the Court but the jury will only be told that a filing deadline was missed by Mr. Evans (and the firm) and that there is no issue of liability regarding the underlying accident. The jury will be asked to just return a verdict regarding the value of the Plaintiff's damages."

The court thus advised the jury at the outset of the proceedings that they needed to consider only the amount of damages suffered by the Patereks.

At the close of the plaintiff's case, the defense moved the court to limit the damages in the case to the amount of Richardson's insurance policy. Consistently with its summary-judgment ruling, the trial court again rejected the argument that damages should be capped at $100,000.

On December 15, 2004, the jury returned a verdict of $382,000 for Irene Paterek. In response to interrogatories, the jury stated that it had awarded the decedent's estate $282,000 for his medical bills, pain and suffering, and inability to perform usual activities, and $100,000 for loss of consortium to Irene.

On December 30, 2004, appellants filed a motion for judgment notwithstanding the verdict.... In its February 16, 2005 decision, the trial court granted that motion, holding that the Patereks' recovery was restricted to the $100,000 liability policy limits maintained by the original tortfeasor, Richardson.

The court based its decision on two factors. First, the court found that the jury's award was based only upon the injuries suffered by the Patereks in the automobile accident; the jury did not find any separate injuries related to the firm's breach:

> "Although the instructions given to the jury permitted them to consider awarding damages beyond the amounts of Plaintiff's underlying personal injury and loss of consortium claims, the interrogatories establish that the jury chose not to do so. The jury limited its award to those sums it determined arose from Mr. Paterek's personal injury and Mrs. Paterek's loss of consortium" (footnote omitted).

Second, the court found that the Patereks had failed to submit any proof that Richardson would have been able to pay anything beyond the amount of his insurance:

> "It can be argued that the value of the opportunity to collect in this case was limited to the policy limits of $100,000. It is also conceivable that an expert witness could be found who would opine that statistically the value of a $382,000 judgment against a person of Mr. Richardson's age and financial status is of a particular worth. If that is so, no such expert testified in this trial."

The court concluded:

> "The determination that Plaintiff suffered damages in the amount of $382,000 as a result of Kristopher Richardson's negligence does not mean that Plaintiff suffered damages in that same amount as a result of the negligence of Jonathon Evans and Petersen & Ibold. It is possible that Plaintiff could be entitled to damages from Defendants in addition to those resulting from the injuries caused by Mr. Richardson upon proper proof that additional damages existed. In the same vein, although Mr. Richardson caused injuries that were assigned a monetary value of $382,000, the damages actually caused by the negligence of these Defendants must be limited to the amount that Plaintiff could be reasonably certain of receiving had Defendant not been negligent."

....

Irene appealed the trial court's decision, and on August 14, 2006, the Eleventh District Court of Appeals reversed the lower court's judgment and remanded for an order reinstating the jury verdict. The appellate court held that the trial court had erred in making collectibility from Richardson an element of Irene's case:

> "Under Civ.R. 50(B) the trial court had no duty to examine the collectability of Richardson. * * * We accept that the jury limited its verdict of $382,000 to the personal injuries suffered by the Patereks, and did not enhance the award with any other damages that may have related to the malpractice committed by Evans and Petersen & Ibold, but this fact by itself did not enable the trial court to step in and reduce the jury verdict due to considerations of collectability of the verdict. Its duty was to examine whether the verdict was supported by 'substantial evidence,' not whether the verdict was collectible."

The cause is before this court upon the acceptance of a discretionary appeal.

Law and Analysis

In *Vahila v. Hall* (1997), 77 Ohio St.3d 421, 674 N.E.2d 1164, this court set forth the elements of a claim for legal malpractice:

...

> "To establish a cause of action for legal malpractice based on negligent representation, a plaintiff must show (1) that the attorney owed a duty or obligation

> to the plaintiff, (2) that there was a breach of that duty or obligation and that the attorney failed to conform to the standard required by law, and (3) that there is a causal connection between the conduct complained of and the resulting damage or loss."

The only dispute in this case concerns the measure of the damages that resulted from the appellants' negligence. When an attorney commits malpractice in a civil case, the lion's share of the damages derives from the value of the lost claim....

The dispute concerns whether the collectibility of any judgment that might have resulted from the lost claim is relevant to calculating the malpractice damages. This court has not specifically addressed this question, but the answer can be found within our holding in *Vahila* that there must be a causal connection between the conduct complained of and the resulting loss.

The jury in this case arrived at a figure for damages that was not necessarily reflective of the value of the Patereks' claim against their lawyers; the jury's damage award reflects what the Patereks suffered through the negligence of Richardson. But the appellant attorneys in this case are not responsible for Richardson's negligent conduct; they are responsible for their own. This case is not about what Irene Paterek suffered on account of Richardson's bad driving, but what she suffered on account of the appellants' bad lawyering. The proper inquiry, then, is this: Had the appellants not been negligent, how much could Irene have received from a settlement or a judgment?

A judgment amount that is shown to be collectible provides a realistic picture of what a malpractice claimant actually lost. To find collectibility of the lost judgment irrelevant would "go beyond the usual purpose of tort law to compensate for loss sustained and would give the client a windfall opportunity to fare better as a result of the lawyer's negligence than he would have fared if the lawyer had exercised reasonable care." David A. Barry, *Legal Malpractice in Massachusetts: Recent Developments* (1993), 78 Mass. L. Rev. 74, 81–82. The finest attorneys in the world cannot coax blood from a stone.

"The prevailing rule is that the client's recovery is limited to the amount that would have been collectible." 4 Ronald E. Mallen and Jeffrey M. Smith, Legal Malpractice (2008), Section 31:17. Indeed, among other jurisdictions, the only dispute regarding collectibility concerns which party must prove it. The majority of jurisdictions have held that the burden of proving collectibility of the lost judgment lies with the plaintiff; in those jurisdictions, the plaintiff must prove the realistic value of a judgment against the underlying defendant as an element of his or her case.

A minority of jurisdictions consider lack of collectibility to be an affirmative defense to be pleaded and proven by the defendant attorneys. The court in *Kituskie,* [714 A.2d 1027 (Pa. 1998)] explains the minority view:

> "These courts have recognized that the plaintiff must prove a case within a case. These minority of courts, however, do not believe that it logically follows from the case within a case burden of proof that the plaintiff must also prove that the damages in the underlying case would have been collectible. Instead, these courts believe that the burden of proof in a legal malpractice action only requires the plaintiff to prove a loss of judgment on a valid claim. To require the plaintiff to also prove collectibility of damages would result in placing an unfair burden on the plaintiff where the plaintiff's legal malpractice action is often brought years after the initial accident causing his injuries solely because the defendant/lawyer failed to act in a timely and competent manner. Thus, the minority of courts

> believe that it is more logical and fair to treat collectibility as an affirmative defense which the defendant/attorney must plead and prove in order to avoid or mitigate the consequences of that attorney's negligent acts. Moreover, this minority has criticized the majority position because it ignores the possibility of settlement between the plaintiff and the underlying tortfeasor and also overlooks that the passage of time itself can be a militating factor either for or against collectibility of the underlying case." *Kituskie,* 552 Pa. at 284–285, 714 A.2d 1027.

In *Smith v. Haden* (D.D.C.1994), 868 F.Supp. 1, 2, the court opined:

> "In a normal civil lawsuit, * * * a plaintiff must prove each required element to make out a case against the defendant in order to obtain a judgment. It is not necessary to demonstrate that plaintiff will successfully be able to execute on the judgment or that the judgment is collectible. Normally, enforcement of the judgment remains for another day. In a legal malpractice action alleging that an attorney failed to timely file suit, a plaintiff is required only to prove the loss of a judgment on a valid claim."

We disagree with the minority view. We hold that collectibility is logically and inextricably linked to the legal-malpractice plaintiff's damages, for which the plaintiff bears the burden of proof. In proving what was lost, the plaintiff must show what would have been gained. The *Smith* court is correct that in other types of civil cases, the plaintiff is not required to prove collectibility. The malpractice plaintiff need not prove the collectibility of the attorney she is suing, but she must prove that the attorney she is suing has indeed injured her through neglecting to properly handle a lawsuit that would have generated recompense. And her injury is measured by what she actually would have collected.

...

Moreover, we disagree with the *Kituskie* court that the majority position ignores the possibility of settlement between the plaintiff and the underlying tortfeasor and overlooks the mitigating nature of the passage of time. To the contrary, courts need not—and should not—overlook the possibility of settlement or the passage of time in determining damages suffered by a malpractice plaintiff. However, those factors should be a part of the plaintiff's case.

...

Given our requirement that plaintiffs in legal-malpractice cases must prove a causal connection between the attorney's malpractice and their damages, we adopt the majority view that collectibility is an element of the plaintiff's case that must be proved by the plaintiff.

Thus, it was up to the Irene Paterek to prove what she lost because of the appellants' negligence. She stipulated that she would have received nothing toward a judgment from the tortfeasor himself. The stipulation stated that Richardson did not have sufficient assets to satisfy any judgment beyond his $100,000 automobile liability coverage.

The stipulation does not speak to the future ability of Richardson to pay off a judgment. Richardson was 17 years old at the time of the accident. The trial court opined that Irene Paterek might have found an expert to testify as to the value of a judgment against a person of Richardson's age and financial status. But she offered no such evidence. Thus, the record does not show that she could have collected more than $100,000 from sources related to Richardson.

....

Accordingly, we reverse the judgment of the court of appeals, remand the cause to the trial court, and instruct the trial court to enter judgment in favor of the appellees....

Judgment reversed and cause remanded.

[The concurring opinion is omitted.]

* * *

1. The *Paterek* case refers to *Kituskie v. Corbman,* 714 A.2d 1027 (Pa. 1998), a case in which the Pennsylvania Supreme Court for the first time was presented with the issue regarding "whether collectibility should be part of a legal malpractice action and, if so, which party bears the burden of proof as to that issue." In adopting the minority position on the issue of proof of collectability, the court reasoned:

> [C]ollectibility of damages in the underlying action should ... be part of the analysis in a legal malpractice action. We [conclude] so because we recognize that a legal malpractice action is distinctly different from any other type of lawsuit brought in the Commonwealth. A legal malpractice action is different because ... a plaintiff must prove a case within a case since he must initially establish by a preponderance of the evidence that he would have recovered a judgment in the underlying action.... It is only after the plaintiff proves he would have recovered a judgment in the underlying action that the plaintiff can then proceed with proof that the attorney he engaged to prosecute or defend the underlying action was negligent in the handling of the underlying action and that negligence was the proximate cause of the plaintiff's loss since it prevented the plaintiff from being properly compensated for his loss. However, ... the plaintiff in a legal action should only be compensated for his actual losses. Actual losses in a legal malpractice action are measured by the judgment the plaintiff lost in the underlying action and the attorney who negligently handled the underlying action is the party held responsible for the lost judgment. However,... "it would be inequitable for the plaintiff to be able to obtain a judgment against the attorney which is greater than the judgment that the plaintiff could have collected from the third party; the plaintiff would be receiving a windfall at the attorney's expense." Thus, we now hold that collectibility of damages in the underlying case is a matter which should be considered in legal malpractice actions.
>
> [W]e now must decide who bears the burden of proof. While other jurisdictions considering the issue of collectibility of damages have unanimously concluded that collectibility is a part of a legal malpractice action, they have been split on which party in the legal malpractice action bears the burden of proof. A majority of courts in other jurisdictions have placed the burden of proving collectibility on the plaintiff because it is viewed as being closely related to the issue of proximate cause, a burden which clearly the plaintiff bears as part of his *prima facie* case. In doing so, these courts place the burden on the plaintiff because a plaintiff can prove that the attorney's malfeasance was the proximate cause of his loss only if he demonstrates that he would have succeeded on the underlying action and that he would have succeeded in collecting on the resulting judgment.
>
> A minority of courts in other jurisdictions, however, have rejected the majority's line of reasoning and placed the burden of proving non-collectibility on the defendant/attorney. These courts have recognized that the plaintiff must prove a case within a case. These minority of courts, however, do not believe that it logically follows from the case within a case burden of proof that the

> plaintiff must also prove that the damages in the underlying case would have been collectible. Instead, these courts believe that the burden of proof in a legal malpractice action only requires the plaintiff to prove a loss of judgment on a valid claim. To require the plaintiff to also prove collectibility of damages would result in placing an unfair burden on the plaintiff where the plaintiff's legal malpractice action is often brought years after the initial accident causing his injuries solely because the defendant/lawyer failed to act in a timely and competent manner. Thus, the minority of courts believe that it is more logical and fair to treat collectibility as an affirmative defense which the defendant/attorney must plead and prove in order to avoid or mitigate the consequences of that attorney's negligent acts. Moreover, this minority has criticized the majority position because it ignores the possibility of settlement between the plaintiff and the underlying tortfeasor and also overlooks that the passage of time itself can be a militating factor either for or against collectibility of the underlying case.
>
> After considering both positions, this Court finds the reasoning of the minority position to be more persuasive. Thus, we adopt the minority position and hold that a defendant/lawyer in a legal malpractice action should plead and prove the affirmative defense that the underlying case was not collectible by a preponderance of the evidence.

Which position do you find to be more persuasive? Why?

2. *Carbone v. Tierney*, 151 N.H. 521 (2004), is in accord with the *Kituskie* court in adopting the minority position that the defendant attorney in a legal malpractice action has the burden of proving collectibility of the underlying action as an affirmative defense:

> "[A] growing minority of jurisdictions holds uncollectibility to be an affirmative defense that must be pleaded and proved by the negligent attorney." These jurisdictions have advanced a number of reasons for rejecting the majority rule.
>
> First, these jurisdictions reject the proposition that the plaintiff should bear the burden of proving collectibility because collectibility is closely related to proximate causation, which is an element of the plaintiff's *prima facie* case. Rather, these jurisdictions contend that although the plaintiff has the burden of proving that he or she would have been successful in the underlying claim, "it does not logically follow that [the plaintiff] must also prove that if [the plaintiff] had obtained a judgment it would have been collectible."
>
> Second, these jurisdictions maintain: "To require the plaintiff to ... prove collectibility of damages would result in placing an unfair burden on the plaintiff." This is particularly true "when a legal malpractice suit is ... brought years after the underlying events and when the delay by the plaintiff in bringing such a suit is because of the defendant-lawyer's failure to act in a timely manner in the first place."
>
> We find the reasoning advanced by the minority of jurisdictions that have considered this issue to be persuasive. Accordingly, we hold that, in a legal malpractice action, noncollectibility of the underlying judgment is an affirmative defense that must be proved by the defendant.

Carbone v. Tierney, 151 N.H. 521, 532–33 (2004). Before adopting the minority position, the *Carbone* court explained:

> A majority of courts that have considered this issue view collectibility as being closely related to proximate cause, a burden which the plaintiff bears as part of his or her prima facie case. *See, e.g., Whiteaker v. State,* 382 N.W.2d 112, 115 (Iowa 1986); *Jernigan v. Giard,* 398 Mass. 721, 500 N.E.2d 806, 807 (1986); *Rorrer v. Cooke,* 313 N.C. 338, 329 S.E.2d 355, 369 (1985); *Haberer v. Rice,* 511 N.W.2d 279, 285 (S.D.1994); *DiPalma v. Seldman,* 27 Cal.App.4th 1499, 33 Cal.Rptr.2d 219, 223 (1994); *Fernandes v. Barrs,* 641 So.2d 1371, 1376 (Fla.Dist.Ct.App.1994); *Lavigne v. Chase, Haskell, Hayes & Kalamon,* 112 Wash.App. 677, 50 P.3d 306, 310–11 (2002). Consequently, these courts have concluded that the plaintiff must demonstrate that if the defendant had performed adequately, "the plaintiff would have succeeded on the merits in the underlying case *and* would have succeeded in collecting on the resulting judgment, because only then would [the] plaintiff have proven that the lawyer's malfeasance was the proximate cause of [the] plaintiff's loss." *Smith v. Haden,* 868 F.Supp. 1, 2 (D.D.C.1994).
>
> As the Washington Court of Appeals noted, this approach avoids "awarding the aggrieved more than he or she would have recovered had the attorney not been negligent." *Lavigne,* 50 P.3d at 310.

Carbone v. Tierney, 151 N.H. 521, 531–32 (2004). In considering the policy issues at stake, which is the better position? Explain your answer.

* * *

2. Criminal Malpractice, Actual Innocence, and Post-Conviction Relief

---

Focus Questions: *Wiley v. County of San Diego*

1. *What is a criminal malpractice action?*
2. *What policy issues are at stake in determining whether a plaintiff in a criminal malpractice action should be permitted to recover from his former defense attorney?*
3. *Do you agree that allowing a criminal defendant to recover civil damages is of questionable public policy?*

Wiley v. County of San Diego

966 P.2d 983
(Cal. 1998)

BROWN, Justice.

When a former criminal defendant sues for legal malpractice, is actual innocence a necessary element of the cause of action? For reasons of policy and pragmatism, we conclude the answer is yes.

FACTUAL AND PROCEDURAL BACKGROUND

... In September 1990, plaintiff Kelvin Eugene Wiley (Wiley) was arrested and charged with burglary and various assaultive crimes against Toni DiGiovanni, a former girlfriend with whom he had a stormy relationship. At arraignment, he denied the charges and Deputy Public Defender John Jimenez was appointed to represent him. Wiley claimed he had been at his apartment at the time of the alleged crimes, and Jimenez arranged for an investigator to contact witnesses and prepare a report. The investigator had only limited success in finding anyone to establish an alibi. In the meantime, Wiley took a polygraph test, which Jimenez was informed he "had not passed."

At trial, DiGiovanni, the only percipient witness, testified that after Wiley entered her condominium in a rage, he hit her repeatedly with a wrench, threatened to kill her, and strangled her with a belt until she lost consciousness. Her 11-year-old son, Eric, testified that he found his mother lying on the floor and that Wiley had physically abused her on prior occasions. He also stated he saw Wiley's truck drive into the cul-de-sac where they lived the morning of the alleged attack. Taking the stand in his own behalf, Wiley denied attacking DiGiovanni and said she had been following and harassing him because he wanted to break off their relationship. According to his landlord, Wiley's truck was parked outside his duplex early on the morning of the alleged assault, and he did not see Wiley enter or leave his residence. Numerous character witnesses also attacked DiGiovanni's credibility.

A jury convicted Wiley of battery causing serious bodily injury, but could not reach verdicts on the remaining counts, which the prosecutor dismissed. Wiley was sentenced to four years in state prison. While his appeal was pending, he filed a petition for writ of habeas corpus challenging Jimenez's representation as ineffective due to his inadequate investigation of the defense. In support of the petition, he submitted declarations from several of DiGiovanni's neighbors, none of whom had been contacted by the defense investigator. In sum, they stated they had seen DiGiovanni driving away from her residence early on the morning in question and later saw a man other than Wiley banging on her door and shouting, "Let me in." They noticed no signs of injury in the days following the incident. The trial court denied the petition, finding Wiley had failed to establish the investigation, preparation, or trial strategy had been inadequate.

A year later, Wiley filed a second habeas corpus petition. In addition to the previous declarations, he submitted evidence DiGiovanni's son had recanted his statement that Wiley's truck was at the condominium the morning of the alleged attack. The court granted the petition, finding that the son had lied at trial and that his testimony was crucial to the conviction. As a second basis for granting relief, the court determined Jimenez's inadequate investigation had deprived Wiley of exculpatory witnesses. The prosecutor later dismissed the case.

Wiley then filed the present legal malpractice action against Jimenez and the County of San Diego (defendants). Prior to trial, the court determined Wiley's innocence was not an issue and refused to require proof on the matter or submit the question to the jury. The jury found in favor of Wiley and awarded him $162,500. On appeal, defendants challenged, *inter alia*, the trial court's ruling on the issue of actual innocence. In support of their argument, they cited *Tibor v. Superior Court* (1997) 52 Cal.App.4th 1359, 61 Cal.Rptr.2d 326, in which the appellate court "concluded that, as a matter of sound public policy, a former criminal defendant, in order to establish proximate cause [in a legal malpractice action], must prove, by a preponderance of the evidence, not only that his former attorney was negligent in his representation, but that he (the plaintiff) was innocent of the criminal charges filed against him." (Id. at p. 1373, 61 Cal.Rptr.2d 326.)

The Court of Appeal reversed the judgment because the trial court erroneously admitted the transcript of the second habeas corpus hearing and erroneously excluded certain evidence on which Jimenez based his trial strategy: the polygraph examination, a psychological evaluation of Wiley, and a prior domestic violence incident. Defendants' arguments on the question of actual innocence were rejected, however. The court acknowledged the "visceral appeal" of imposing such a requirement, but declined to do so for several reasons. First, "it is 'difficult to defend logically a rule that requires proof of innocence as a condition of recovery, especially if a clear act of negligence of defense counsel was obviously the cause of the defendant's conviction of a crime' (Glenn [v. Aiken (1991)] 409 Mass. 699, 569 N.E.2d [783,] 787, fn. omitted)." Second, creating a separate standard for clients represented in a criminal setting is "fundamentally incompatible" with the constitutional guaranty of effective assistance of counsel. Third, no empirical evidence supported the rationale, advanced by some courts, that the threat of malpractice claims would discourage representation of criminal defendants, particularly those who are indigent. Finally, an actual innocence requirement would create "rather artificial distinctions" between criminal defense attorneys and civil attorneys.

We granted review to resolve the conflict in the Courts of Appeal and settle an important issue of state law.

DISCUSSION

In their seminal commentary, Justice Otto Kaus and Ronald Mallen remarked on the "dearth of criminal malpractice litigation," noting only a handful of reported cases nationwide as of 1974. (Kaus & Mallen, The Misguiding Hand of Counsel—Reflections on "Criminal Malpractice" (1974) 21 UCLA L.Rev. 1191, 1193 (Kaus & Mallen).)[1] Today by contrast, they would find a plethora of decisions, generated by the ever-rising tide of professional negligence actions generally. Nevertheless, this court has yet to address any aspect of criminal malpractice, including the relevance of the plaintiff's actual innocence.

In civil malpractice cases, the elements of a cause of action for professional negligence are: "(1) the duty of the attorney to use such skill, prudence and diligence as members of the profession commonly possess; (2) a breach of that duty; (3) a proximate causal connection between the breach and the resulting injury; and (4) actual loss or damage. [Citations.]" In criminal malpractice cases, the clear majority of courts that have considered the question also require proof of actual innocence as an additional element.[2]

---

1. As the authors explain, "[t]he term 'criminal malpractice' implies no criminality on the part of the attorney. We use it elliptically to mean 'legal malpractice in the course of defending a client accused of crime.' Its counterpart is, of course, civil malpractice." (Kaus & Mallen, supra, 21 UCLA L.Rev. at p. 1191, fn. 2.) For purposes of our discussion, we adopt the same terminology.

2. Many of these decisions further require that "the person's conviction has been reversed, ... on appeal or through post-conviction relief, or the person otherwise has been exonerated." (Stevens v. Bispham (1993) 316 Or. 221, 230, 851 P.2d 556, 561; *see also, e.g.,* Morgano v. Smith (1994) 110 Nev. 1025, 1029, 879 P.2d 735, 737; Peeler v. Hughes & Luce (Tex.1995) 909 S.W.2d 494, 497.) In Weiner v. Mitchell, Silberberg & Knupp (1980) 114 Cal.App.3d 39, 170 Cal.Rptr. 533, the Court of Appeal impliedly imposed such a requirement. In that case, the plaintiff remained convicted on charges of federal securities violations when he brought his malpractice action. (*Id.* at p. 48, 170 Cal.Rptr. 533.) The trial court sustained a demurrer, which the appellate court affirmed in part because the doctrine of collateral estoppel precluded relitigation of his guilt "and we must, therefore, accept as the proximate cause of his indictment, and of all the damages which occurred to him by reason of it, his guilt and his guilt alone." (*Ibid.*) Under our holding today, the decision in Weiner would be correct independent of any consideration of postconviction relief. Whether such relief is a prerequisite to maintaining a criminal malpractice action has significant implications, *e.g.,* for determining statute of limitations and collateral estoppel issues. Since Wiley's conviction was overturned on habeas corpus and the

Common to all these decisions are considerations of public policy: "'[P]ermitting a convicted criminal to pursue a legal malpractice claim without requiring proof of innocence would allow the criminal to profit by his own fraud, or to take advantage of his own wrong, or to found [a] claim upon his iniquity, or to acquire property by his own crime. As such, it is against public policy for the suit to continue in that it "would indeed shock the public conscience, engender disrespect for courts and generally discredit the administration of justice."' [Citations.]" "'[C]ourts will not assist the participant in an illegal act who seeks to profit from the act's commission.'"

Additionally, "allowing civil recovery for convicts impermissibly shifts responsibility for the crime away from the convict. This opportunity to shift much, if not all, of the punishment assessed against convicts for their criminal acts to their former attorneys, drastically diminishes the consequences of the convicts' criminal conduct and seriously undermines our system of criminal justice. [Citation.]" "[I]f plaintiffs engaged in the criminal conduct they are accused of, then they alone should bear full responsibility for the consequences of their acts, including imprisonment. Any subsequent negligent conduct by a plaintiff's attorney is superseded by the greater culpability of the plaintiff's criminal conduct. [Citation.]" Accordingly, "[t]hese cases treat a defendant attorney's negligence as not the cause of the former client's injury as a matter of law, unless the plaintiff former client proves that he did not commit the crime."

Notwithstanding these policy considerations, actual innocence is not a universal requirement. Those courts declining to require such proof generally do not discuss the public policy implications but simply consider criminal malpractice as indistinguishable from civil malpractice. For example, in Krahn v. Kinney, supra, 43 Ohio St.3d 103, 538 N.E.2d 1058, defense counsel failed to convey a plea bargain offer and his client ultimately pled guilty to a more serious charge than offered. The reviewing court allowed the client's subsequent criminal malpractice action to proceed without proof of innocence, analogizing to what it considered comparable negligence in a civil context. "The situation is like that in a civil action where the attorney fails to disclose a settlement offer. Such failure [exposes] the attorney to a claim of legal malpractice. [Citations.]"

We find these latter decisions unpersuasive. To begin, the public policy reasons articulated in favor of requiring proof of actual innocence are compelling. Our legal system is premised in part on the maxim, "No one can take advantage of his own wrong." (Civ.Code, § 3517; see Prob.Code, § 250 et seq. [prohibiting financial gain by one who feloniously and intentionally kills]; Whitfield v. Flaherty (1964) 228 Cal.App.2d 753, 758, 39 Cal.Rptr. 857; cf. Civ.Code, § 3333.3 [no tort recovery if plaintiff's injury caused by own commission of felony].) Regardless of the attorney's negligence, a guilty defendant's conviction and sentence are the direct consequence of his own perfidy. The fact that nonnegligent counsel "could have done better" may warrant postconviction relief, but it does not translate into civil damages, which are intended to make the plaintiff whole. While a conviction predicated on incompetence may be erroneous, it is not unjust....

Only an innocent person wrongly convicted due to inadequate representation has suffered a compensable injury because in that situation the nexus between the malpractice and palpable harm is sufficient to warrant a civil action, however inadequate, to redress the loss. In sum, "the notion of paying damages to a plaintiff who actually committed the criminal offense solely because a lawyer negligently failed to secure an acquittal is of questionable public policy and is contrary to the intuitive response that damages should

---

charge was ultimately dismissed, we have no occasion on these facts to address this distinct question.

only be awarded to a person who is truly free from any criminal involvement." We therefore decline to permit such an action where the plaintiff cannot establish actual innocence.

The public policy rationale is strongest when the malpractice plaintiff claims that some species of trial-related error resulted in a conviction. In other circumstances, where guilt is conceded or undeniable, it admittedly gives rise to a certain tension if counsel's negligence nonetheless caused a less favorable outcome. Kaus and Mallen anticipated this conflict: "Paradoxically, perhaps, the temptation to urge the relevance of actual guilt is strongest in situations in which the malpractice may be the least excusable, such as the lawyer's failure to raise a defense available to the client which would have prevented the prosecution from even going to trial. Thus, if the lawyer failed to make a motion to suppress a balloon of heroin which had been stomach-pumped from the client after he swallowed it when threatened by an illegal arrest, the client should be entitled to a directed verdict on the issues of malpractice and causation; yet if actual guilt is relevant, he should be nonsuited. The paradox arises, of course, from the fact that the malpractice is liable to be most obvious where it consists of a failure to raise what, for want of a better word, we may call a 'technical' defense—one which would result in a favorable disposition of the criminal proceedings without the issue of the client's guilt ever being submitted to a jury. In many cases the 'technical' defense will be the only one the client has: if not asserted, a conviction is a foregone conclusion." (Kaus & Mallen, supra, 21 UCLA L.Rev. at p. 1205; see also Silvers v. Brodeur, supra, 682 N.E.2d at p. 818 ["[C]riminal defendants who are harmed by their attorneys' negligence in ways other than conviction, such as by the imposition of lengthier sentences, will be completely without relief."].)

Even courts adopting an actual innocence prerequisite have noted this quandary. "[A] requirement that a plaintiff, the former criminal defendant, must prove his innocence of the crime with which he was charged may relieve the defendant attorney, his former counsel, of liability for harm that the plaintiff suffered only because of his defense counsel's negligence. For example, if a defendant attorney failed to assert a clearly valid defense of the statute of limitations, a client who did commit the crime, but should not have been convicted of it, sustained a real loss, but he may not recover against the attorney defendant.... [¶] ... [¶] It may be difficult to defend logically a rule that requires proof of innocence as a condition of recovery, especially if a clear act of negligence of defense counsel was obviously the cause of the defendant's conviction of a crime" (Glenn v. Aiken, supra, 569 N.E.2d at p. 787, fn. omitted).

This theoretical dilemma is predicated in part on too literal a translation of the civil malpractice model, which operates on strict "but for" principles of causation. In a civil malpractice action, the focus is solely on the defendant attorney's alleged error or omission; the plaintiff's conduct is irrelevant. In the criminal malpractice context by contrast, a defendant's own criminal act remains the ultimate source of his predicament irrespective of counsel's subsequent negligence. Any harm suffered is not "only because of" attorney error but principally due to the client's antecedent criminality. Thus, it is not at all difficult to defend a different rule because criminal prosecution takes place in a significantly different procedural context, "and as a result the elements to sustain such a cause of action must likewise differ." (Bailey v. Tucker, supra, 621 A.2d at p. 114)

In larger part, the expressed concern fails to account for the nature and function of the constitutional substructure of our criminal justice system. For example, "it is clear that our society has willingly chosen to bear a substantial burden [by requiring proof beyond a reasonable doubt] in order to protect the innocent...." "The standard provides concrete substance for the presumption of innocence—that bedrock 'axiomatic and elementary' principle whose 'enforcement lies at the foundation of the administration of our criminal law.' [Citation.]" (In re Winship (1970) 397 U.S. 358, 363, 90 S.Ct. 1068, 25 L.Ed.2d 368.) Indeed, "[c]ompliance with the standard of proof beyond a reasonable doubt is the defining, central feature in criminal adjudication, unique to the criminal law. [Citation.] Its effect is at once both symbolic and practical, as a statement of values about respect and confidence in the criminal law, [citation], and an apportionment of risk in favor of the accused [citation]." (Foucha v. Louisiana (1992) 504 U.S. 71, 93, 112 S.Ct. 1780, 118 L.Ed.2d 437 (dis. opn. of Kennedy, J.).) Simply put, it is "bottomed on a fundamental value determination of our society that it is far worse to convict an innocent man than to let a guilty man go free." (In re Winship, supra, 397 U.S. at p. 372, 90 S.Ct. 1068 (conc. opn. of Harlan, J.).

....

These and other constitutional protections are to safeguard against conviction of the wrongly accused and to vindicate fundamental values. They are not intended to confer any direct benefit outside the context of the criminal justice system. Thus, defense counsel's negligent failure to utilize them to secure an acquittal or dismissal for a guilty defendant does not give rise to civil liability. Rather, the criminal justice system itself provides adequate redress for any error or omission and resolves the apparent paradox noted in case and commentary. All criminal defendants have a Sixth Amendment right to effective assistance of counsel, that is, counsel acting reasonably "'within the range of competence demanded of attorneys in criminal cases.' [Citation.]" (Strickland v. Washington (1984) 466 U.S. 668, 687, 104 S.Ct. 2052, 80 L.Ed.2d 674.) Not only does the Constitution guarantee this right, any lapse can be rectified through an array of postconviction remedies, including appeal and habeas corpus. Such relief is afforded even to those clearly guilty as long as they demonstrate incompetence and resulting prejudice, *i.e.*, negligence and damages, under the same standard of professional care applicable in civil malpractice actions.

....

In contrast to the postconviction relief available to a criminal defendant, a civil matter lost through an attorney's negligence is lost forever. The litigant has no recourse other than a malpractice claim. The superficial comparison between civil and criminal malpractice is also faulty in other crucial respects. Tort damages are in most cases fungible in the sense that the plaintiff seeks in a malpractice action exactly what was lost through counsel's negligence: money. "Damages" in criminal malpractice are difficult to quantify under any circumstances. Calculating them when, for example, counsel's incompetence causes a longer sentence would be all the more perplexing.

...

Moreover, "[t]he underpinnings of common law tort liability, compensation and deterrence, do not support a rule that allows recovery to one who is guilty of the underlying criminal charge. A person who is guilty need not be compensated for what happened to him as a result of his former attorney's negligence. There is no reason to compensate such a person, rewarding him indirectly for his crime." (Glenn v. Aiken, supra, 569 N.E.2d at p. 788.)

Reinforcing this conclusion are the pragmatic difficulties that would arise from simply overlaying criminal malpractice actions with the civil malpractice template. In civil actions, carrying the burden on causation is relatively straightforward and comprehensible for the jury, even if it necessitates a "trial within a trial." The factual issues in the underlying action are resolved according to the same burden of proof, and the same evidentiary rules apply. Thus, it is reasonably possible for the malpractice jury to assess whether and to what extent counsel's professional lapse compromised a meritorious claim or defense.

By contrast, "the prospect of retrying a criminal prosecution [is] 'something one would not contemplate with equanimity....'" The procedure outlined in Shaw v. State, Dept. of Admin., supra, 861 P.2d at page 573, suggests this estimation is not exaggerated: "[T]he standard of proof will be a complex one, in essence, a standard within a standard. [Plaintiff] must prove by a preponderance of the evidence that, but for the negligence of his attorney, the jury could not have found him guilty beyond a reasonable doubt." Moreover, while the plaintiff would be limited to evidence admissible in the criminal trial, the defendant attorney could introduce additional evidence, including "any and all confidential communications, as well as otherwise suppressible evidence of factual guilt." (Bailey v. Tucker, supra, 621 A.2d at p. 115, fn. 12;). The mental gymnastics required to reach an intelligent verdict would be difficult to comprehend much less execute. ...

We would also anticipate attorneys might practice "defensive" law more frequently to insulate their trial court decisions. "[I]n our already overburdened system it behooves no one to encourage the additional expenditure [of] resources merely to build a record against a potential malpractice claim." (Bailey v. Tucker, supra, 621 A.2d at p. 114.)

For the foregoing reasons, we hold that in a criminal malpractice action actual innocence is a necessary element of the plaintiff's cause of action. Therefore, on retrial Wiley will have to prove by a preponderance of the evidence that he did not commit battery with serious bodily injury.

DISPOSITION

We affirm the judgment of the Court of Appeal and remand to that court with directions to remand the cause to the superior court for further proceedings not inconsistent with this opinion.

GEORGE, C.J., and KENNARD, J., BAXTER, J., and CHIN, J., concur.

Concurring Opinion of WERDEGAR, J.

I agree with the majority that plaintiff's guilt or innocence of the 1990 battery is relevant to his malpractice claim and that the case must therefore be remanded for further proceedings. Accordingly, I concur in the judgment. I do not, however, agree with the majority's decision to add a new element to the tort of malpractice, nor do I agree with the method by which the majority reaches that decision.

....

One problem with announcing a new, policy-based rule is that unintended consequences invariably follow. So it is here. Our court has in recent cases made it abundantly clear that we will strictly follow the statute that governs the accrual and limitation of claims for attorney malpractice. Under this statute, an action against an attorney for a wrongful act or omission must ordinarily be commenced within one year after the plaintiff discovers, or should have discovered, the facts constituting the wrongful act or omission. In view of the time required to decide appeals and petitions for habeas corpus in criminal cases, the statute of limitations in most cases likely will run long before the convicted person has a chance to have the conviction set aside and, thus, remove the bar (collateral estoppel) to establishing his or her actual innocence. The majority alludes to this problem, but offers no solution.... Indeed, I see no ready solution, considering that we have soundly condemned all nonstatutory tolling rules ... How, without [reversing previous decisions] might we hold that a cause of action for criminal malpractice does not accrue until the underlying conviction is set aside?

Another problem with rules of law that spring to life full-grown from the mind of policy, rather than by evolving through the ordinary process of the common law, is that they tend not to be well articulated. That is the case here. What, precisely, is "actual innocence"? The majority does not tell us. If a criminal defendant, for example, is convicted of two different crimes, must he or she prove innocence of both, even if the alleged legal malpractice affected only one of the convictions? Must a convicted malpractice plaintiff prove innocence of all related offenses that might have been charged, or only of those that were charged or necessarily included in those that were? Should the plaintiff's ability to recover for malpractice depend on the fortuities of prosecutorial charging discretion? The answer to these questions is far from obvious.

The common law of torts, as articulated by successive generations of judges, typically has enough depth and subtlety to do justice in unusual cases. To turn our backs on this collective wisdom by adopting a rule apparently designed to cut off whole categories of litigation seems ill advised. It is not beyond imagination that a particular defendant's offense might be so insignificant, and the attorney's malpractice so egregious, that reasonable jurors instructed on the relevant principles of tort law might well conclude the latter was in fact a proximate cause of some of the ensuing consequences. The majority's new rule seems to foreclose such possibilities.

In conclusion, although I share the majority's intuition that a guilty person ordinarily should not be able to recover damages based on a defense attorney's malpractice, I do not agree that it is either necessary or desirable to remake the law to conform to our own views of good policy. Rather, we would do better to ask whether any legitimate policy concerns already find expression in existing principles of tort law and, if so, to leave the law alone.

Dissenting Opinion by MOSK, J.

As the majority acknowledge, the usual elements of a legal malpractice cause of action are: "(1) the duty of the attorney to use such skill, prudence and diligence as members of the profession commonly possess; (2) a breach of that duty; (3) a proximate causal connection between the breach and the resulting injury; and (4) actual loss or damage." The majority add the element of "actual innocence" in criminal malpractice cases. In effect, the majority hold that a defense attorney owes no duty cognizable in tort to act competently toward a client he or she knows to be guilty of a crime of which the client is charged. I decline to join the majority for reasons stated in the Court of Appeal opinion, set forth below.

> "First, as recognized by the court in [Glenn v. Aiken (1991) 409 Mass. 699, 569 N.E.2d 783, 787, fn. omitted], it is 'difficult to defend logically a rule that requires proof of innocence as a condition of recovery, especially if a clear act of negligence of defense counsel was obviously the cause of the defendant's conviction of a crime.' [Citation.] For example, where the attorney fails to seek to suppress evidence seized in clear violation of his client's constitutional rights, a bright line rule would preclude the guilty client from recovering damages for the malpractice. Similarly, the rule would preclude recovery where the client was incarcerated after his attorney failed to communicate the prosecutor's offer to dismiss charges against him in exchange for testimony against another of that attorney's clients. (Cf. Krahn v. Kinney [(1989) 43 Ohio St.3d 103] 538 N.E.2d 1058.) In such instances, requiring proof of innocence would have the effect of 'just about destroy[ing] criminal malpractice as an actionable tort in the very type of situation where the lawyer's incompetence is most flagrant and its consequences most easily

demonstrable.' (Kaus & Mallen, The Misguiding Hand of Counsel-Reflections on "Criminal Malpractice," [(1974)] 21 UCLA L.Rev. 1191, 1205.)

"Second, the rule is clearly intended to create a separate standard for clients represented in a criminal setting. However, it is precisely in this setting that the state and federal Constitutions guarantee effective assistance of counsel. (Cal. Const., art. I, § 15; U.S. Const., 6th Amend.; People v. Ledesma [(1987) 43 Cal.3d 171,] 215, 233 Cal.Rptr. 404, 729 P.2d 839; Strickland v. Washington [(1984)] 466 U.S. [668,] 684–685, 104 S.Ct. 2052, 80 L.Ed.2d 674.) A rule relieving criminal defense counsel from liability for harm resulting from his clear negligence is fundamentally incompatible with this constitutionally guaranteed right.

"While the court in Glenn believed that the possibility the client is innocent will act as a sufficient deterrent to negligent conduct by defense counsel in criminal cases, we are not aware of any evidence to support this proposition. Even if such a deterrent effect could be established, it is difficult to accept that the client who has suffered loss of personal liberty as a result of his counsel's negligence must make a more onerous showing to recover for those losses than his civil counterpart, whose losses are purely monetary.

"Third, while [ ] the public has an interest in encouraging representation of criminal defendants, [ ] this [is not] a valid policy reason to support the imposition of an 'actual innocence' requirement in the absence of any empirical evidence suggesting that the threat of malpractice claims, as defined by the traditional elements, has deterred public defenders or retained counsel from representing criminal defendants.

"Finally, the rule creates rather artificial distinctions between public defenders and retained criminal defense attorneys, on one hand, and civil attorneys on the other. [ ]

"For these reasons, we [should not] alter the traditional elements of a malpractice cause of action for claims arising out of criminal proceedings."

[I]t has been the rule in the state [since 1980] that a criminal defendant must obtain postconviction relief before pursuing a malpractice action. It is also noteworthy that proving ineffective assistance of counsel in order to obtain such relief, and for purposes of proving criminal malpractice liability, is very difficult. When considering a trial counsel's performance in an ineffective assistance claim, we "indulge a strong presumption that counsel's conduct falls within the wide range of reasonable professional assistance." (Strickland v. Washington (1984) 466 U.S. 668, 689, 104 S.Ct. 2052.) This stringent rule will screen out frivolous malpractice claims. There is no need for the actual innocence requirement to further limit these claims.

....

For all of the foregoing, I would affirm the judgment of the Court of Appeal.

* * *

1. Do you agree with the majority that allowing a criminal defendant to recover civil damages is of questionable public policy?

2. In *Rantz v. Kaufman,* 109 P.3d 132 (Colo. 2005), Rantz was convicted of sexually assaulting two boys and sentenced to sixty-six years in prison. The defendants (collectively "Kaufman") represented him at trial. Rantz filed a motion for post-conviction relief and a motion for new trial. He alleged ineffective assistance of counsel based on Kaufman's refusal to call a particular witness. The witness, a runaway minor, had contacted Kaufman while still on the run. Kaufman did not report the contact to the authorities and lied to the court about the contact. Rantz contended that Kaufman opted not to call the witness for personal reasons and claimed that he would have testified on his own behalf had he known the witness would not be called. The post-conviction court denied Rantz's motions. Rantz appealed the denial and filed a malpractice action against Kaufman. Kaufman moved to dismiss on the grounds that Rantz failed to obtain post-conviction relief and therefore could not state a claim. In resolving the case, the Colorado Supreme Court began by discussing majority law on the issues of post-conviction relief and actual innocence as applied to the element of causation in legal malpractice cases, explaining that many jurisdictions require post-conviction relief, some require an affirmative showing of innocence, and some require neither. The court cited an Oregon case in which the Oregon Supreme Court determined that, pursuant to public policy, all convictions are valid until reversed. Thus, the harm caused by legal malpractice in criminal actions occurs not upon conviction, but on reversal of conviction. The Oregon Supreme Court therefore concluded that causation requires a showing of post-conviction relief.

The court then cited its decision in *Morrison v. Goff*, 91 P.3d 1050 (Colo. 2004), which held that malpractice actions are not tolled by the pursuit of post-conviction relief. Defendants must file their malpractice actions and, if necessary, can request a stay until the post-conviction relief is either granted or denied. The court explained:

> The idea that a former client must obtain postconviction relief before bringing a malpractice suit against his or her criminal defense attorney appears to have had its genesis in a 1974 law review article. Otto M. Kaus & Ronald E. Mallen, *The Misguiding Hand of Counsel—Reflections on "Criminal Malpractice"*, 21 U.C.L.A.L.Rev. 1191 (1974). Since then, many jurisdictions that have considered the question have adopted some form of postconviction relief as a prerequisite to maintaining the malpractice action. The requirement is sometimes referred to as the "exoneration rule." *See, e.g., Canaan*, 72 P.3d at 914.
>
> Several other jurisdictions have directly or impliedly declined to make prior postconviction relief a requirement for suit, although some insist on an affirmative demonstration of innocence of the underlying crime from the former client. Most jurisdictions cite various public policy reasons to justify their decision either to adopt or reject the exoneration rule.
>
> Those jurisdictions that adopt the exoneration rule often also assert that, absent postconviction relief, the former client cannot, as a matter of law, establish either the causation or damages element necessary to sustain a malpractice claim. In *Stevens*, [851 P.2d 556 (Or. 1993)], the Oregon Supreme Court reasoned that "what constitutes legally cognizable harm is a policy choice." 851 P.2d at 560. Reviewing the overall "legislative scheme" for procedural criminal law in Oregon, the court determined that it was the policy of the state "to treat any person who has been convicted of any criminal offense as validly convicted unless and until the person's conviction has been reversed." *Id.* at 561. Because persons convicted of crimes are already afforded many protections and opportunities for relief from negligence of counsel, the court concluded that it would be "inappropriate to treat victims of alleged negligence by defense counsel as having been 'harmed,'" unless they had been exonerated. *Id.* at 562.
>
> Jurisdictions and commentators disagreeing that prior exoneration should be a precondition to suit, dismiss this argument as a legal fiction. *See, e.g., Gebhardt*, 510 N.W.2d at 906 n. 13; *Duncan*, 936 P.2d at 867–68; *Stevens* at 566 (Unis, J.,

concurring); *cf. Coscia,* 108 Cal.Rptr.2d 471, 25 P.3d at 680 (declining "to adopt the legal fiction that an innocent person convicted of a crime suffered no actual injury until he or she was exonerated through postconviction relief," but adopting exoneration rule). The legal malpractice plaintiff in *Stevens* pleaded guilty on the advice of his attorney and was exonerated when another person confessed to the crimes. Under the *Stevens* majority's theory of damages, had the actual perpetrator not come forward, the plaintiff would not have been harmed by the wrongful conviction. Reacting to the absurd result created by the majority's "no relief/no harm" rule, the specially concurring justice noted that persons

> convicted of a crime will be astonished to learn that, even if their lawyers' negligence resulted in their being wrongly convicted and imprisoned, they were not harmed when they were wrongly convicted and imprisoned, but, rather, that they are harmed only if and when they are exonerated.

Stevens, 851 P.2d at 566 (Unis, J., concurring). The Michigan Supreme Court also rejected the related notion that damages were not final until exoneration, stating that "harm is established not by the finality of the damages, but by the occurrence of an identifiable and appreciable loss." *Gebhardt,* 510 N.W.2d at 904.

Putting any analytical flaws aside, our decision in *Morrison* necessarily rejected the *Stevens* majority's construction of harm in malpractice suits between former clients and their criminal defense attorneys. In *Morrison,* we decided that the statute of limitations for a criminal defendant's malpractice action is not tolled while he or she pursues direct appeal or postconviction relief. The General Assembly in Colorado has adopted the discovery rule for determining when a cause of action accrues for statute of limitations purposes. Applying the discovery rule to legal malpractice actions, we concluded that the claim accrues when a plaintiff learns "facts that would put a reasonable person on notice of the general nature of *damage* and that the *damage* was caused by the wrongful conduct of an attorney."

Under the "two-track" approach adopted in *Morrison,* "the criminal defendant must file a malpractice claim within the specified period after the defendant learns or should have learned of the injury and its cause." *Id.* at 1055. The criminal defendant may then seek a stay in the malpractice suit, which the trial court has the discretion to grant or deny, until all appellate and postconviction matters concerning the criminal case are resolved. *Id.* Implicit in this approach and Colorado's definition of accrual for legal malpractice claims is the notion that the criminal defendant can suffer damages prior to exoneration. If a criminal defendant were unable to suffer damages before exoneration, then the claim could not accrue before postconviction proceedings are concluded. However, *Morrison* clearly holds to the contrary. As a result, we reject the notion that a former client cannot establish the damage element necessary to sustain a malpractice action against his or her criminal defense attorney unless he or she first obtains postconviction relief.

We also reject the concept that, as a matter of law, a criminal defendant cannot establish the causation element of a malpractice claim unless he or she has been exonerated through postconviction relief. In order to demonstrate causation in a legal malpractice case, the client must prove the "case within a case," meaning he or she must show that "the claim underlying the malpractice action should have been successful if the attorney had acted in accordance with his or her duties." *Bebo Construction Co. v. Mattox & O'Brien, P.C.,* 990 P.2d 78, 83

(Colo.1999). It may be that in some or even the majority of legal malpractice suits against criminal defense attorneys, their former clients will not be able to prove that the outcome of the criminal case would have been successful unless they prevail in some manner in appellate or postconviction proceedings. Causation should be evaluated on the facts of a particular case, and we discern no reason for erecting a permanent barrier to malpractice claims with a blanket rule. *See Krahn,* 538 N.E.2d at 1062 ("We reject the suggestion that a proximate cause analysis can be eliminated and replaced by a rule of thumb based on whether the malpractice plaintiff has succeeded in overturning the underlying criminal conviction.").

Having determined that the existing elements of a malpractice claim do not dictate that a criminal defendant must obtain postconviction relief before he or she can maintain suit, we now consider whether other reasons compel adoption of such a requirement. We are not persuaded by the policy arguments advanced by jurisdictions that impose an exoneration requirement. Several of the justifications offered for the exoneration rule, such as promoting judicial economy, providing a convenient date for triggering the statute of limitations, and protecting criminal defendants, are satisfied or rendered moot by the "two-track" approach adopted in *Morrison.*

Affording the trial court the discretion to stay the civil suit while the criminal proceedings are completed serves the interests of judicial economy in the same manner that the exoneration rule does. ... The requirement that the criminal defendant prove the "case within the case" is also a heavy burden that will screen out frivolous claims. Furthermore, the judicial economy consideration cuts both ways. The exoneration rule forces the criminal defendant to file two suits, because he or she cannot go forward on a malpractice suit without attacking the criminal conviction. Without a prior exoneration requirement, the criminal defendant may decide to file the civil suit only, thereby conserving judicial resources.

Similarly, the rights of criminal defendants are adequately protected by the *Morrison* "two-track" approach. Imposing a further requirement of obtaining prior postconviction relief is therefore unnecessary. With the civil suit stayed, the criminal defendant is able to pursue postconviction relief free from distraction or the fear that the former attorney will reveal information damaging to the criminal proceedings. Finally, the statute of limitations issue was squarely presented and addressed in *Morrison* and a bright line rule was rejected.

Many jurisdictions that have adopted the exoneration rule also point to the policy of ensuring that criminals do not profit from their criminal conduct as justification. This argument bears similarity to the idea that a criminal defendant cannot demonstrate harm or causation unless and until formal exoneration has been achieved. Like those proposed barriers to maintaining a malpractice suit, preventing an individual from profiting from criminal conduct is better addressed at the individual case level. Before recovering damages, a criminal defendant will have to demonstrate that the negligence of his or her attorney caused legally cognizable harm. A criminal defendant who prevails in a malpractice action is receiving compensation for an injury suffered, in the form of time spent in prison or the burden of a criminal record, not a windfall.

Policy reasons do, however, persuade us that obtaining prior postconviction relief should not be an element of legal malpractice claims against criminal

> defense attorneys. We see no reason why criminal defense lawyers should be afforded greater protection against liability for negligence than other professionals. Jurisdictions adopting the exoneration rule sometimes justify the disparate treatment of malpractice claims brought against civil and criminal attorneys, or against criminal attorneys and other licensed professionals, by arguing that criminal malpractice claims are unique due to the postconviction remedies available to criminal defendants. Postconviction remedies exist to protect the constitutional rights of criminal defendants, not to protect negligent defense attorneys. Accordingly, the availability of such remedies should not serve as an additional shield for attorneys who practice a particular form of law. Physicians who practice a particular type of medicine may be able to persuasively argue that their practice is unique, but they would still be subject to the same set of malpractice elements as other physicians.
>
> Even without considering policy, our decision in *Morrison* strongly suggests that prevailing in postconviction proceedings is not a prerequisite to maintaining a malpractice suit in Colorado. In *Morrison* we held that:
>
>> *In the event* that a *particular* criminal defendant must obtain appellate relief to avoid dismissal of a pending malpractice action, or if proceeding with a malpractice action would jeopardize the criminal defendant's rights, the trial court *may* stay the malpractice action pending resolution of the criminal case.
>
> *Id.* at 1058 (emphasis added).... We recognized that certain cases may present factual situations necessitating a final determination of postconviction relief, but that not all would. Because of this recognition, we chose flexibility over a bright line rule.
>
> Today, we make the same choice and hold that former clients are not required to obtain postconviction relief before bringing a malpractice action against their criminal defense attorneys. While some criminal defendants may not be able to establish causation without obtaining such relief, we find that this element of the claim should be addressed individually rather than through adoption of the exoneration rule.

Rantz v. Kaufman, 109 P.3d 132, 137–38 (Colo. 2005).

3. In *Ang v. Martin,* 114 P.3d 637 (Wash. 2005), the Angs owned a company that provided the Washington State Department of Labor and Industries with independent medical examinations of injured workers. Dr. Ang became a person of interest in a government investigation of social security fraud, and a warrant was executed on his office. The task force seized copies of two sets of signed tax returns that reported conflicting amounts of income, and the Angs were indicted on 18 criminal counts, including fraud and conspiracy. The Angs retained the defendants (collectively "Martin") and engaged in a series of plea discussions. They accepted an unfavorable plea deal based on Martin's recommendation and assertion that Mrs. Ang could face sexual assault in prison. The Angs then retained Hester (not a defendant), who concluded that the government had not met its burden of proof and that the plea deal provided the Angs with no material benefit. The Angs withdrew the plea and proceeded to a bench trial; they were acquitted on all 18 counts.

The Angs and their company filed a malpractice action against Martin. The trial court instructed the jury that the Angs must prove by a preponderance of the evidence that they were innocent of the charged crimes. The jury found that the Angs had not adequately proven innocence. The court of appeals affirmed.

In the criminal malpractice context, Washington state has added two elements to its proximate causation analysis: (1) post-conviction relief, and (2) proof of innocence. The court first noted that the Angs had met the first requirement by demonstrating that the Angs had withdrawn their pleas and had been acquitted of all charges. *Ang*, 114 P.3d at 641. The court then made a distinction between legal innocence and actual innocence, holding that plaintiffs in a criminal malpractice case must prove the latter, not the former. In other words, criminal malpractice plaintiffs must show that deficient representation, not their illegal acts, was the proximate cause of their harm: "Unless criminal malpractice plaintiffs can prove by a preponderance of the evidence their actual innocence of the charges [not just that the court found them not guilty, which would constitute mere legal innocence], their own bad acts, not the alleged negligence of defense counsel, should be regarded as the cause in fact of their harm." *Id.* The court declined to put the burden of showing actual guilt on the defendant, noting that if the plaintiff is actually innocent, he is in the best position to prove it. Do you agree with this position?

There were three dissenting opinions to the *Ang* majority opinion. One of the dissenting justices wrote:

> I ... write separately to express my indignation that this court, based upon the policy of protecting lawyers, would carve out a special protection for criminal defense attorneys whose acts of professional negligence are harmful to their clients. Under this logic, it is not enough for the injured client to prove actual harm from the attorney's failure to meet professional standards; the injured client must also prove that her hands were always clean....
>
> But this logic ignores the fact that professionals owe a duty to the sick as well as the healthy; to the scrupulously honest business woman as well as the one looking for the angle; to the guilty as well as the innocent. Those of us caught in the grip of the law are always entitled to competent legal representation whether or not we are totally innocent. The heart of the criminal defense lawyer's job is often not to prove absolute innocence; the irreducible core of the job is to make the state prove its case and make the best case for the defendant possible. Often the sole issue is the level of culpability and the sanction to be imposed upon the client. The government may seek multiple counts where a single count is appropriate, seek charges of a higher degree than the evidence supports, or seek a sentence disproportionate to the offense. The negligence of her lawyer may cost her client her fortune, her liberty, or her life. The "actual innocence" requirement is impractical and harmful in the area of criminal malpractice law; it creates an almost impossible burden and provides almost absolute immunity to criminal defense lawyers.
>
> The most troubling aspect of the actual innocence requirement announced by the majority lies with its origin. It is based upon a policy to protect *lawyers* from lawsuits. Tort actions are maintained for a variety of reasons, including the deterrence of wrongful conduct. As a matter of basic policy, accountability, compensation, and deterrence of wrongful conduct should trump protecting lawyers from lawsuits. *See generally* Meredith J. Duncan, *Criminal Malpractice: A Lawyer's Holiday*, 37 GA. L. REV. 1251 (2003) (advocating greater use of malpractice to police quality of criminal defense).
>
> Second, while it may be true that a majority of courts that have reached the issue require the plaintiff to establish actual innocence, the numbers do not appear to be great. Only Missouri, New York, Massachusetts, Alaska, Pennsylvania, California, New Hampshire, Nebraska, Illinois, Florida, and Wisconsin require

> either proof of actual innocence or that the conviction was set aside on postconviction relief. This is hardly a national consensus.
>
> This court should protect the public from lawyers' misdeeds, not the other way around. A plaintiff who is not categorically innocent seeking compensation under ordinary principles of tort law faces no light burden. Such a guilty plaintiff must prove a duty, a breach of that duty, injuries proximately caused by the breach, and the amount of his damages. I see no reason to provide additional protections for lawyers.

Ang, 114 P.3d at 645–46 (Chambers, J. concurring in dissent).

4. As the previous materials seek to demonstrate, jurisdictions vary on whether, in the criminal malpractice context, proof of innocence is required, whether post-conviction relief is required, or both. *See, e.g., Rodriguez v. Nielsen,* 609 N.W.2d 368, 374–75 (Neb. 2000) (adopting requirement of actual innocence of the underlying crime, but declining to adopt a requirement of post-conviction relief). Which combination of post-conviction relief or innocence do you conclude is the most prudent?

5. What is the injury sought to be remedied in a criminal malpractice action? Consider an excerpt from *Vahila v. Hall,* 674 N.E.2d 1164 (Ohio 1997):

> In *Krahn,* Lynn B. Krahn managed a bar owned by High Spirits, Inc. ("High Spirits"). Krahn hired Winfield E. Kinney III to defend her with respect to three misdemeanor gambling charges that had been brought against her. High Spirits retained Kinney to represent it in connection with a citation issued by the Ohio Department of Liquor Control. However, following pretrial negotiations between Kinney and the prosecutor, Kinney failed to convey to Krahn that the prosecutor had offered to dismiss the charges in exchange for Krahn's testimony against her gambling-device supplier. On the day of trial, Krahn followed Kinney's recommendation to withdraw her plea of not guilty and enter a plea of guilty to one of the charges. Further, Kinney failed to appear at a hearing before the Ohio Liquor Control Commission to defend the citation that had been issued against High Spirits. As a result of Kinney's conduct, Krahn and High Spirits sued Kinney and the law firm for malpractice. The trial court granted summary judgment in favor of Kinney and the firm. The court of appeals reversed the judgment of the trial court.
>
> Kinney and the law firm appealed to this court, arguing, among other things, that relief should not be granted in these types of cases unless the plaintiff first obtains a reversal of his or her underlying conviction on grounds of ineffective assistance of counsel. We rejected this argument and stated that:
>
> > "The inequity of requiring a plaintiff to obtain a reversal of his or her conviction before bringing a malpractice action is apparent from the facts in the present case. Krahn's claim is based in part on Kinney's alleged failure to communicate the prosecutor's offer. Consequently, Krahn was forced into the situation of having to plead to a more serious charge or risk a still greater conviction and sentence. Krahn may have made a valid plea on the day of trial, but she would have been better served had she accepted the earlier bargain. As aptly stated by the court of appeals, *the injury in such a situation 'is not a bungled opportunity for vindication, but a lost opportunity to minimize her criminal record.'*
> >
> > "The situation is like that in a civil action where the attorney fails to disclose a settlement offer. Such failure may expose the attorney to a claim

> of legal malpractice. *Lysick v. Walcom* (1968), 258 Cal.App.2d 136, 65 Cal.Rptr. 406. See, also, *Smiley v. Manchester Ins. & Indemn. Co.* (1978), 71 Ill.2d 306 [16 Ill.Dec. 487], 375 N.E.2d 118, where the attorney failed to effect a settlement on a client's behalf" (emphasis added and footnote omitted). *Krahn*, 43 Ohio St.3d at 105–106, 538 N.E.2d at 1061.

We also found in favor of High Spirits and further observed that:

> "We also find that High Spirits has stated a cause of action. High Spirits incurred extra attorney fees in rectifying Kinney's failure to appear at the original commission hearing. *The injury is not the penalty ultimately imposed by the commission, but the expenses involved in rectifying Kinney's failure. High Spirits states a cause of action regardless of whether the ultimate penalty imposed by the commission is reversed.*
>
> "Having enunciated the elements of a claim sounding in malpractice and arising from criminal representation, we note that in most cases the failure to secure a reversal of the underlying criminal conviction may bear upon and even destroy the plaintiff's ability to establish the element of proximate cause. In other words, we do not relieve a malpractice plaintiff from the obligation to show that the injury was caused by the defendant's negligence. But the analysis should be made in accordance with the tort law relating to proximate cause. The analysis should focus on the facts of the particular case. *We reject the suggestion that a proximate cause analysis can be eliminated and replaced by a rule of thumb based on whether the malpractice plaintiff has succeeded in overturning the underlying criminal conviction*" (emphasis added and footnote omitted). *Id.*, 43 Ohio St.3d at 106, 538 N.E.2d at 1061–1062.

Do you agree or disagree? Explain the rationalization for your answer.

Chapter 6

Professional Malpractice: Damages

The final element of the plaintiff's *prima facie* case in a legal malpractice action requires proof of actual loss or damages. Nominal damages are not recoverable in a negligence action. One of the difficulties in determining this final element in the legal malpractice context is resolving what losses may account for a plaintiff's actual damages, the subject of this chapter. As one court explained, "An essential element to this cause of action [for legal malpractice] is proof of actual loss rather than a breach of a professional duty causing only nominal damages, speculative harm or the threat of future harm. Damages are considered remote or speculative only if there is uncertainty concerning the identification of the existence of damages rather than the ability to precisely calculate the amount or value of damages. In essence, a legal malpractice action ... requires the plaintiff to prove that he had a viable cause of action against the party he wished to sue in the underlying case and that the attorney he hired was negligent in prosecuting or defending that underlying case...." *Kituskie v. Corbman,* 714 A.2d 1027, 1030 (Pa. 1998).

Typically, plaintiffs in negligence actions are permitted to recover compensatory damages—the purpose being to restore the plaintiff to her pre-tort condition as much as it is possible to do so—and punitive damages, where appropriate.

> **Compensatory damages** typically are comprised of both economic losses and non-economic losses. Economic losses—sometimes referred to as pecuniary losses—seek to compensate for injuries associated with the plaintiff's lost earnings, loss or impairment of future earning capacity, and past and future medical expenses. Non-economic or general damages seek to compensate the plaintiff for injuries not easily translated into dollar figures, such as for physical pain and suffering, mental pain, and emotional distress.
>
> **Punitive damages** are a sum of money above and beyond compensatory damages that are designed for the distinct purpose of punishing a defendant for engaging in particularly egregious conduct. An award of punitive damages is in addition to compensatory damages, and, as such, is sometimes considered a windfall to plaintiffs receiving the award. Punitive damage awards are also often constrained by constitutional considerations.

In the context of legal malpractice actions, keep in mind that there are two different damage considerations—(1) the damages to which the plaintiff would have been entitled in the underlying litigation, which is the subject of the legal malpractice action; and (2) the damages that the plaintiff is seeking to recover in the legal malpractice action, namely the damages caused by the lawyer's breach of the standard of care in handling the underlying suit.

e 6.1: Chapter Problem

..t hired Attorney to represent her in a personal injury suit against a uriver who struck her while she was on duty as a crossing guard. The driver had bodily injury insurance of $10,000, and Client had uninsured and underinsured motorist insurance of $100,000 apiece through Insur Co. Her policy required the insured to obtain Insur Co.'s consent before pursuing a claim against an alleged tortfeasor. Attorney, not realizing that the policy covered *under*insured as well as *un*insured drivers, proceeded with a claim against the driver's $10,000 insurance policy. Attorney was successful and deducted its fees and expenses from the recovery. Client later pursued her own underinsured motorist coverage, but was told by Insur Co. that the unconsented claim against the driver's policy effectively voided the underinsured policy. Client then brought suit against Attorney for malpractice.

Attorney asserted several defenses in his answer, one of which was a request to reduce any damage award by the contingency fee and expenses his firm would have received in the underlying personal injury action. Client has filed a motion with the trial court to strike Attorney's defense of reducing the damage award by the contingency fee and expenses. You are clerking for the judge to whose court this case has been assigned. Advise the judge on how the judge should rule on Client's motion and the reasons supporting your recommendation.

A. Compensatory Damages

1. Pecuniary Harm

Focus Questions: *Carbone v. Tierney*

1. *How are damages calculated for a legal malpractice action?*
2. *According to the* Carbone *court, are the defendant attorney's fees that would have been paid according to the agreement between the attorney and his client in the underlying litigation taken into consideration in calculating the plaintiff's actual loss? Why or why not?*
3. *Did the court apply the doctrine of* quantum meruit *in calculating the plaintiff's actual loss? Why or why not?*
4. *According to the court, is prejudgment interest included in a legal malpractice plaintiff's calculation of actual damages? Was the plaintiff in* Carbone *entitled to recovery for prejudgment interest? Why or why not?*

Carbone v. Tierney

151 N.H. 521
(2004)

DUGGAN, J.

The defendant, Nancy S. Tierney, appeals a jury verdict in Superior Court ... finding her liable for legal malpractice in her representation of the plaintiff, Alfred Carbone. We affirm in part, reverse in part and remand.

Tierney's representation of Carbone arose out of a dispute between Carbone and his son, Daniel. In 1994, Carbone purchased a home in Londonderry. Because he is an inventor, he converted a two-car garage on the property into a laboratory, which he used to conduct research and test his inventions. Carbone used two additional buildings on the property for a woodworking shop and for the storage of chemicals.

Daniel lived in Danvers, Massachusetts with his wife, Lisa, and their two children. Daniel visited Carbone on numerous occasions and encouraged him to sell his home and move into their home in Danvers.

After approximately two years of discussions, Carbone entered into an agreement with his son. Carbone agreed to sell his home and give Daniel the proceeds from the sale. Daniel, in turn, would sell his Danvers home, combine the proceeds from the two sales and purchase a bigger home, large enough to accommodate Daniel's family, as well as Carbone and his laboratory. Carbone and his son further agreed that "if this thing didn't work out," Daniel would return Carbone's money.

To effectuate this plan, on September 9, 1996, Carbone transferred the deed to his home to Daniel's wife, Lisa. Later that month, Lisa sold Carbone's home to a third party and collected $69,812.41 at the closing.

Because Daniel and Lisa's home had not yet been sold, Carbone moved into their basement. He stored two or three pieces of laboratory equipment in their garage and put the rest of the equipment in storage.

Carbone found his new living situation to be "nerve-racking [*sic*]." As a result, in late October or early November 1996, he told Daniel that he wanted to leave and asked for his money back. Daniel told his father that he could not return the money because he had used it to pay other bills. Because Carbone received only $550 per month in social security benefits and had no other resources, he remained in Daniel and Lisa's basement.

On November 27, 1996, Daniel and Lisa purchased a new home in Danvers. The new home included an apartment for Carbone. It also had a small shed in the yard but, according to Carbone, the shed was not large enough to accommodate his laboratory. Consequently, Carbone purchased a box trailer, placed it on a friend's property and set up his laboratory in the trailer.

After the purchase of the new home, Carbone's relationship with Daniel and Lisa went "[f]rom bad to worse." Carbone had no space for his laboratory and was disturbed by the noisy surroundings. He subsequently moved out of Daniel and Lisa's home.

Approximately one month later, Carbone's friend told him that he had to move the trailer containing the laboratory off the friend's property. Carbone stored some pieces of equipment with other friends and sold, or otherwise disposed of, the rest of the equipment. Eventually, all of the equipment was either sold or destroyed.

In 1998, Carbone hired Tierney to represent him in an action against Daniel and Lisa. Tierney agreed to represent Carbone on a contingency fee basis.

On August 8, 1998, Tierney filed a complaint on Carbone's behalf in the United States District Court for the District of New Hampshire. The complaint alleged diversity of citizenship as the basis for the court's jurisdiction and that the "amount in controversy exceed[ed] $10,000.00 exclusive of interest and costs."

On September 24, 1998, Daniel and Lisa moved to dismiss the complaint. The next day, Tierney sent Carbone a letter informing him that a motion to dismiss had been filed. The letter stated that the motion to dismiss "alleg[ed] no copy of the Complaint was attached with the Summons." Tierney's letter did not mention that the motion to dismiss was also based on the failure to state an adequate amount in controversy. On October 22, 1998, the court dismissed Carbone's complaint for failure to establish subject matter jurisdiction because the complaint failed to allege that Carbone's damages exceeded $75,000—a requirement for federal jurisdiction in a diversity of citizenship action.

On October 27, 1998, Tierney moved to amend the complaint and for late entry. She also filed three objections to the September 24, 1998 motion to dismiss. Two days later, the motions were returned to Tierney with the following notation: "Motion denied. Case has been dismissed."

On October 30, 1998, Tierney sent Carbone a second letter which stated:

> At the present time, we are in the process of re-serving the complaint. This is being done for the purpose of increasing the requested damage amount to include your laboratory facilities and the like. Needless to say, the other side has filed Motions to Dismiss and we have countered with Objections to said Motions.

On December 2, 1998, Tierney filed a second complaint in the United States District Court for the District of New Hampshire. This time, the complaint alleged that the amount in controversy exceeded $75,000 exclusive of interest and costs. On April 7, 1999, the district court issued an order which, in pertinent part, stated:

> Plaintiff had a full and fair opportunity to litigate the jurisdictional issue in the former action. He chose not to appeal the district court's adverse ruling in that action. He cannot avoid the effect of that ruling simply by filing a new action. Accordingly, the case is dismissed without prejudice to plaintiff's right to reinstate his claim in a state court of competent jurisdiction.

Two days later, Tierney sent Carbone a third letter. She informed her client that she had "received notice from the United States District Court for the District of New Hampshire ... indicating they believe the law suit should be brought in the United States District Court for the District of Massachusetts even though there is diversity of citizenship." Tierney told Carbone that she presumed the court believed that Carbone "would have an easier time collecting from [his] son if the Order issued from a Massachusetts based court."

In April 1999, Tierney filed a complaint in the United States District Court for the District of Massachusetts. The complaint alleged diversity of citizenship as the basis for the court's jurisdiction and that the amount in controversy exceeded $75,000 exclusive of interest and costs. On February 9, 2000, the court dismissed the complaint because Tierney had "failed to establish federal jurisdiction" in the United States District Court for the District of New Hampshire.

On June 9, 1999, while the district court complaint was still pending, Tierney filed a complaint in the Massachusetts Superior Court in Essex County. On March 14, 2000, the superior court sent Tierney a form entitled "Notice of Status Review of the Docket." The form stated: "If this report is not completed and returned to the Clerk's Office within [t]wenty days a dismissal will enter and the docket closed out." Tierney completed the form and, on March 16, 2000, she sent it to the superior court by Federal Express. Nonetheless, in April 2000, the superior court dismissed the complaint. It was later discovered that the court had misplaced the form. Tierney, however, did not inquire of the court as to why the case had been dismissed.

Instead, on May 4, 2000, Tierney wrote to the plaintiff. In pertinent part, she wrote:

> Your matter was ... brought before the Superior Court. On April 28, 2000, an Order of Dismissal was published and sent to this office. At this time, the case could be appealed to the Supreme Judicial Court. However, I believe the effort would be futile as every court which could have heard the matter has quashed all attempts for the case to be heard. We believe, to appeal this, or any of these decisions, would be fruitless and would be a financial hardship to you.

While Carbone's action against Daniel and Lisa was still pending, Lisa filed for bankruptcy. Carbone contacted Tierney and asked her to represent his interests in the bankruptcy by opposing the homestead exemption that Lisa was seeking and the discharge of the debt that was owed to him. A paralegal for Tierney subsequently sent Carbone a letter outlining the steps that Tierney planned to take to represent his interests in Lisa's bankruptcy proceeding. Tierney, however, did not appear at the first meeting of creditors and did not oppose the homestead exemption. Lisa was discharged in bankruptcy on August 18, 1999.

In September 2000, Carbone filed the instant action claiming that Tierney committed legal malpractice when she represented him in his action against Daniel and Lisa. He moved for summary judgment on the legal malpractice claim, as well as his claim for damages. The trial court ruled that Carbone was entitled to summary judgment on the legal malpractice claim but denied summary judgment with respect to damages.

A jury trial was held in January 2003. The jury returned a verdict in Carbone's favor, awarding $69,812.41 in damages for the loss of his residence and laboratory. It also awarded $105,000 to Carbone for the loss of his laboratory equipment. The trial court subsequently ordered interest to be added to the judgment.... This appeal followed.

....

On appeal, Tierney argues that the trial court erred when it: (1) entered summary judgment in favor of Carbone on liability; (2) ruled that Carbone's claims were not barred by his failure to mitigate his damages; (3) sustained the jury's award of $105,000 in damages for Carbone's lost laboratory equipment; (4) ruled that Tierney had the burden of proving collectibility; and (5) failed to reduce the damage award to reflect the contingency fee that Carbone agreed to pay Tierney. In addition, Carbone cross-appeals, arguing that the trial court erred when it calculated the amount of interest due on the judgment. We address each argument in turn.

Tierney first argues that expert testimony is required to prove proximate causation in a legal malpractice action. Because Carbone failed to provide any expert testimony in the present case, Tierney contends that the trial court erred when it granted Carbone's motion for summary judgment on liability. We agree.

[The court's discussion requiring expert testimony to establish proximate cause is omitted. *See* Chapter 5.D, *supra*, and Notes exploring Expert Testimony to Establish Proximate Causation for an excerpt from this court's opinion.]

Tierney next contends that the trial court erred when it denied her motion for judgment notwithstanding the verdict and ruled that Carbone's claims were not barred by his failure to mitigate his damages. We disagree.

....

In April 2000, the Essex County Superior Court notified Tierney that Carbone's complaint had been dismissed. At that time, Tierney did not inquire of the court as to the basis for the dismissal. Carbone brought the instant action against Tierney in September 2000. In the fall of 2001, Tierney learned that the court had dismissed the case because it had misplaced the "Notice of Status Review of the Docket" form that she had returned. Tierney's attorney subsequently informed Carbone of the court's error.

... Tierney contends that ... Carbone could have moved the Essex County Superior Court to correct its error and reopen his action. Because Carbone failed to do so, Tierney argues that he is precluded from bringing the instant action.

We hold that the trial court did not err when it denied Tierney's motion for judgment notwithstanding the verdict. As set forth above, Tierney bears the burden of proving that Carbone failed to mitigate his damages. She has not satisfied her burden. Tierney failed to present any evidence at trial to establish that moving the Essex County Superior Court to correct its error would have lessened Carbone's resultant loss. Viewing the evidence in the light most favorable to Carbone, we conclude that the trial court did not commit an unsustainable exercise of discretion when it denied Tierney's motion for judgment notwithstanding the verdict.

Tierney next argues that the trial court erred when it sustained the jury's award of $105,000 in damages for Carbone's lost laboratory equipment. Specifically, Tierney argues that the trial court erred in sustaining the jury's award because "[a] review of the evidence offered to support the valuation of lost laboratory equipment demonstrates that [Carbone's] testimony cannot properly establish an appropriate foundation for such an award." As set forth above, we will not overturn the trial court's decision to deny a motion for judgment notwithstanding the verdict absent an unsustainable exercise of discretion.

"In tort, one to whom another has tortiously caused harm is entitled to compensatory damages for the harm if, but only if, he establishes by proof the extent of the harm and the amount of money representing adequate compensation with as much certainty as the nature of the tort and the circumstances permit." New Hampshire does not require that damages be calculated with mathematical certainty, and the method used to compute damages need not be more than an approximation.

In the instant case, Carbone testified about the value of his lost laboratory equipment. On direct examination, he explained that in order to calculate his loss, he created a handwritten list of his laboratory equipment from memory. He then used old catalogues to estimate the purchase price of new equipment. In a few instances, he obtained the purchase price of used laboratory equipment and included that information on the list. On cross-examination, Carbone admitted that he had no information about the price he actually paid for his equipment. On appeal, Tierney argues that because there is "nothing scientifically valid" about Carbone's calculations, the evidence presented at trial was insufficient to establish an appropriate foundation for the jury's damage award.

We hold that the trial court did not err in upholding the jury's damage award for Carbone's lost laboratory equipment. Carbone is not, as Tierney suggests, required to use a scientifically valid method to calculate his damages. Instead, Carbone must establish the extent of his loss with as much certainty as the circumstances permit. By creating an inventory of his lost items and estimating the cost of those items, the jury could find that Carbone satisfied his burden. Tierney had the opportunity to cross-examine Carbone about the method he used to calculate his loss. Moreover, the jury was free to accept or reject Carbone's calculations. We thus conclude that the trial court did not commit an unsustainable exercise of discretion when it upheld the jury's award of damages.

Tierney next argues that the trial court erred when it ruled that she had the burden of proving that the judgment in the underlying action would not have been collectible. We disagree.

[The court's ruling that the issue of collectibility is relevant to a legal malpractice action, but is in this jurisdiction an affirmative defense with the burden of proof on the defendant has been omitted. *See* Chapter 5.E.1, *supra,* exploring collectibility and Chapter 7, *infra,* exploring the issue of defenses to legal malpractice actions.] ...

....

... For the reasons set forth above, we agree with the trial court's determination and conclude that the trial court did not err when it ruled that Tierney had the burden of proving that the judgment against Carbone's son, Daniel, would not have been collectible.

Tierney next argues that the trial court erred when it denied her motion to reduce the jury verdict "to reflect the amount that [Carbone] would have paid [her] in accordance with the contingency fee agreement." Although we reject the theory that the trial court employed in reaching its conclusion, we agree with its result.

Because the issue of whether a verdict should be reduced to reflect a contingency fee is a question of law, we review the trial court's ruling de novo.

To begin, we recognize that whether a plaintiff's legal malpractice recovery should be reduced by the amount of attorney's fees the plaintiff would have paid for the defendant's competent performance is "still [an] unsettled issue." 3 Mallen & Smith, *supra* § 20.18, at 161. Indeed, it is a question of first impression for this court.

[T]he well-established principle that in a legal malpractice action [is that] a plaintiff is entitled to recover damages for his actual loss, which is "measured by the judgment the plaintiff lost in the underlying action." *Kituskie,* 714 A.2d at 1030. This principle is the foundation of our analysis.

Some jurisdictions that have addressed this issue have held that the verdict should be reduced by the amount of the contingency fee because only then would the verdict reflect what the plaintiff would have recovered had the defendant performed competently in the underlying action. *See, e.g., Moores v. Greenberg,* 834 F.2d 1105, 1113 (1st Cir.1987) (applying Maine law); *McGlone v. Lacey,* 288 F.Supp. 662, 665 (D.S.D.1968) (applying South Dakota law).

We disagree that reducing the verdict by the amount of the contingency fee puts the plaintiff in the same position that he or she would have been in if the defendant had performed competently in the underlying action. If we were to hold that the verdict must be reduced by the amount of the contingency fee, at the conclusion of the malpractice action, the verdict would be reduced by the amount of the contingency fee, *and* the plaintiff would have to pay his or her new attorney for the services that the new attorney provided in the prosecution of the malpractice action. We think this is an inequitable result.

On the other hand, if the defendant is barred from reducing the verdict to reflect the contingency fee, the plaintiff is in the same position he would have been in if the defendant had performed competently in the underlying action. The plaintiff will still be required to compensate his or her new attorney for the services the attorney provided in pursuit of the malpractice action. The plaintiff, however, will not be penalized for having to employ two attorneys to get the result the plaintiff should have obtained in the original action. Accordingly, we hold that, in a legal malpractice action, the verdict should not be reduced to reflect the amount of a contingency fee agreement. Our holding is consistent with a number of other jurisdictions that have addressed this issue. *Accord Winter v. Brown,* 365 A.2d 381, 386 (D.C.1976); *Togstad v. Vesely, Otto, Miller & Keefe,* 291 N.W.2d 686, 696 (Minn.1980); *Saffer v. Willoughby,* 143 N.J. 256, 670 A.2d 527, 534 (1996); *Campagnola v. Mulholland, Minion & Roe,* 76 N.Y.2d 38, 556 N.Y.S.2d 239, 555 N.E.2d 611, 613–14 (1990); *Kane, Kane & Kritzer, Inc. v. Altagen,* 107 Cal.App.3d 36, 165 Cal.Rptr. 534, 538 (1980); *McCafferty v. Musat,* 817 P.2d 1039, 1045 (Colo.Ct.App.1990).

We additionally recognize that, in what appears to be a recent trend, several jurisdictions have applied the doctrine of *quantum meruit* to determine whether a verdict should be reduced to reflect a negligent attorney's fee. Under this approach, the damage award is reduced by the amount the negligent attorney would have been compensated for services that were actually rendered. If we were to adopt this approach, the jury would be required to decide whether the first lawyer provided services that ultimately benefited the plaintiff. If the jury found that the lawyer did provide services that benefited the plaintiff, the jury would then be required to assign a value to those services and reduce the damage award accordingly. We think, as a practical matter, that it would be difficult for a jury to assign a value to the services provided by the first lawyer, particularly where there is considerable disagreement about whether those services benefited the client in any meaningful way. Consequently, we decline to adopt the quantum meruit approach.

In the present case, Carbone hired Tierney to represent him in an action against his son. Carbone agreed to pay Tierney one-third of the amount he recovered in the underlying action. When Carbone later brought suit against Tierney alleging legal malpractice, Tierney argued that the jury verdict should be reduced by one-third to reflect the contingency fee agreement. The trial court rejected Tierney's argument and stated that she "did not provide any services for Mr. Carbone for which she is entitled to a deduction in the malpractice award on a theory of *quantum meruit*." As a result, the court denied Tierney's motion to reduce the verdict to reflect the contingency fee.

As we explained above, we reject the application of a *quantum meruit* approach to determine whether the verdict should be reduced by the amount of the contingency fee. Instead, we hold that Tierney is not entitled to have the verdict reduced. Although the trial court employed a different theory than the one that we adopt today, it reached the correct result. We thus conclude that the court did not err in denying Tierney's motion to reduce the jury verdict.

Finally, Carbone argues that the trial court erred in calculating the prejudgment interest that was due on the jury verdict. More specifically, Carbone urges us to adopt a rule under which a plaintiff's damages in a legal malpractice action include interest the plaintiff would have recovered on the judgment in the underlying action. Although we agree that the damages in a legal malpractice action may include interest in the underlying case, we conclude that Carbone did not properly raise his claim for interest as damages.

In the present case, the jury returned a verdict in Carbone's favor, awarding $69,812.41 in damages for the loss of his residence and laboratory, as well as $105,000 for the loss of his laboratory equipment. The jury was not asked to calculate the amount of interest Carbone would have recovered on the judgment in the underlying action. Nor was any evidence introduced that would have assisted the jury in making this determination. Instead, after the jury returned its verdict, Carbone filed a motion requesting that the trial judge calculate the interest on the judgment in the underlying action and add that interest to the damage award. The trial judge denied the motion, ruling that Carbone "did not plead or prove interest as an element of damages."

In this case, the amount of interest Carbone was entitled to as damages depended upon several unresolved factual issues, including when and where Carbone would have obtained a judgment. Accordingly, the jury was required to determine these factual issues. Because Carbone did not present any evidence relating to interest, the trial court was correct to deny his motion.

....

Affirmed in part; reversed in part; and remanded.

* * *

1. Proper Measure of Damages in a Legal Malpractice Action

> Few cases have considered what constitutes the proper measure of damages in a legal malpractice action. The general rule is that a plaintiff is entitled only to be made whole: *i.e.*, when the attorney's negligence lies in his failure to press a meritorious claim, the measure of damages is the value of the claim lost. (Lally v. Kuster (1918) supra 177 Cal. 783, 791, 171 P. 961.) Or, as stated by Justice Peters in *Pete v. Henderson* (1954) 124 Cal.App.2d 487, 489, 269 P.2d 78, 79, an attorney's 'liability, as in other negligence cases, is for all damages directly and proximately caused by his negligence.'

Smith v. Lewis, 530 P.2d 589 (Cal. 1975).

2. Proof of collectibility. Note that the court in *Carbone* adopted a minority position regarding proof of collectibility. *See* Chapter 5.E.1, *supra* (exploring the majority and minority positions on the burden of proof on the issue of collectibility in a legal malpractice action).

Focus Questions: *Ferguson v. Lieff, Cabraser, Heimann & Bernstein, LLP*

1. *In tort law, what is the purpose of a punitive damages award?*
2. *Are punitive damages, which would potentially have been awarded in the underlying lawsuit, properly included in a legal malpractice plaintiff's calculation of compensatory damages? Upon what policy considerations does the* Ferguson *majority place base its decision?*
3. *According to the majority in* Ferguson, *may an attorney who has been found liable for legal malpractice be subject to punitive damages?*
4. *What is the basis of Justice Kennard's disagreement with the majority opinion? With which opinion do you agree most? Why?*

Ferguson v. Lieff, Cabraser, Heimann & Bernstein, LLP

30 Cal. 4th 1037
(2003)

BROWN, J.

In a mass tort action, class counsel stipulated to the certification of a mandatory, non-opt-out class with respect to punitive damages. To settle the action, class counsel agreed to dismiss the punitive damages class claims with prejudice. Despite objections from some class members, the trial court dismissed the punitive damages claims and approved the settlement. Two of these objectors now contend class counsel committed legal malpractice and seek to recover the punitive damages they would have recovered but for counsel's negligence. We now consider whether plaintiffs in a legal malpractice action may recover as compensatory damages the punitive damages they allegedly lost due to the negligence of their attorneys in the underlying litigation (lost punitive damages). We conclude they may not.

Facts

A. *The Underlying Class Action*

In 1994, a processing tower at a refinery in Rodeo, California, released hydrogen sulfide and a toxic chemical called Catacarb into the atmosphere. The release of these substances affected thousands of residents living near the refinery.

Soon thereafter, respondent Lieff, Cabraser, Heimann & Bernstein, LLP (Lieff Cabraser), filed a class action lawsuit against Union Oil Company of California (Unocal), the owner of the refinery. The complaint sought, among other things, punitive damages. Other law firms also filed individual and class action lawsuits against Unocal—including Casper, Meadows & Schwartz (Casper Meadows), which had entered into contingent fee contracts with and filed suit on behalf of appellants Brent Ferguson and Florencia Prieto (collectively appellants) and other individuals.

Pursuant to a pretrial order, the trial court consolidated these actions against Unocal and designated them as complex litigation. The court gave primary responsibility for managing the consolidated actions to a steering committee of plaintiffs' counsel—which included Lieff Cabraser and Casper Meadows. The court designated Lieff Cabraser as co-lead class counsel and Casper Meadows as co-lead direct action counsel.

Lieff Cabraser then filed a first amended model complaint identifying four potential classes: (1) personal injury, (2) property damage, (3) medical monitoring, and (4) punitive damages (Unocal Class Action). Several months later, Lieff Cabraser, its co-lead class counsel, and Unocal entered into a stipulation and order approved by the trial court. Under the stipulation and order, the class action plaintiffs agreed to withdraw the allegations of the personal injury and property damage classes. The parties also stipulated to the "certification of a mandatory, non-opt-out" punitive damages class and agreed to schedule the issue of certification of the medical monitoring class for briefing and decision. Finally, the stipulation and order gave individuals with claims for personal injury or property damage 60 days to file their claims and gave plaintiffs the right to seek certification of the personal injury and property damage classes if Unocal moved to decertify or substantially modify the punitive damages class.

Following extensive discovery, Lieff Cabraser engaged in settlement negotiations with Unocal under the aegis of Retired Judge Daniel H. Weinstein, the court-appointed settlement master. After "extensive negotiations and discussion," the parties tentatively agreed to an $80 million global settlement of the consolidated class and individual actions. The settlement required the dismissal of the punitive damages class claims with prejudice.

The parties then stipulated to an order referring all issues concerning the good faith and scope of the settlement and the allocation of settlement proceeds to Judge Weinstein. Pursuant to this order, Judge Weinstein reported that the settlement negotiations "were conducted at arm's length by highly qualified counsel who were thoroughly knowledgeable about the evidence and the law." He further concluded that the $80 million settlement was "a fair, reasonable, and just settlement for all of the settling parties." Observing that the settlement "could not have been achieved without Class Counsel's agreement to dismiss with prejudice the punitive damages allegations of the non-opt-out punitive damages class" and finding "the handful of objections to the proposed dismissal ... to be unpersuasive," Judge Weinstein recommended "that the Court grant Class Counsel's motion to dismiss the punitive damages class claims with prejudice."

After providing notice of the proposed dismissal of the punitive damages class claims, Lieff Cabraser filed the motion to dismiss. The motion included authorizations from the various attorneys representing the individual plaintiffs-including Casper Meadows-to dismiss their clients' claims in exchange for participation in the $80 million global settlement.

Over 12,000 individual members of the punitive damages class received notice of the motion; eight, including appellants, filed objections. Appellants focused on the purported inadequacy and unfairness of the settlement and asked the court to allocate the $80 million settlement solely to the punitive damages claims. Ferguson himself attended the hearing on the motion and personally voiced his objections to the court. Appellants proceeded *in propria persona* because Casper Meadows refused to represent them in opposing the motion and settlement and because they could not find another attorney to assist them.

At the hearing, the trial court approved the settlement and dismissed the punitive damages class claims with prejudice. In doing so, the court stated: "I'm ... satisfied that those concerns that you [the objectors] have [have] been fully considered by the class counsel that are proposing this settlement. And I'm satisfied that this appears to be a fair and reasonable settlement for all parties involved.... [¶] My understanding of the settlement ... [is] that the $80 million settlement does encompass all punitive damages claims that have been filed, and I'm hearing from everyone that I have a great deal of confidence in that this is a settlement that should be approved and that the dismissal of the punitive claims would be appropriate."

In its written order dismissing the punitive damages class claims, the court concluded "that the public's interest in punishing Unocal for its conduct" at its Rodeo "refinery, and in deterring Unocal from future such conduct has been achieved." The court also issued an order finding that the settlement "is fair, reasonable and made in good faith ...."

Appellants did not appeal the dismissal of the punitive damages claims. Instead, represented by Casper Meadows, they participated in the claims process created by the settlement. Ferguson received an award of $125,000 and Prieto received an award of $100,000 from the $80 million settlement. Neither Ferguson nor Prieto appealed or otherwise challenged these awards.

B. *The Legal Malpractice Action*

A few weeks after receiving the settlement awards, appellants filed the instant action against, among others, Lieff Cabraser and the individual attorneys at Lieff Cabraser involved in the settlement of the Unocal Class Action—respondents William Bernstein, Donald C. Arbitblit, and Jonathan D. Selbin (collectively respondents). After initial demurrer rulings by the trial court, appellants filed a third amended complaint.

The complaint stated 11 causes of action, including: ... negligence [and] ... legal malpractice.... The gist of the complaint was that the settlement and related notices were inadequate and that respondents breached their fiduciary duty and committed malpractice by certifying the non-opt-out punitive damages class, negotiating and recommending the settlement, and refusing to support appellants' objections to the settlement. As compensatory damages, appellants alleged they lost a potential award of punitive damages against Unocal and received an award of compensatory damages far below the amount they would have received but for respondents' tortious conduct.

... The court ... granted summary judgment for respondents on appellants'... claims [and] the court entered judgment in favor of respondents.

The Court of Appeal affirmed.... The court then upheld the summary judgment because ... "as a matter of law, lost punitive damages are not recoverable as compensatory damages for legal malpractice." ...

We granted review solely to determine whether lost punitive damages are recoverable in a legal malpractice action and conclude they are not.

Discussion

[A]ppellants contend they merely "seek[] the value of the recovery [they] lost through [respondents'] negligence"—*i.e.*, the punitive damages they should have recovered from Unocal. Because these lost punitive damages "are compensatory, not punitive," in the context of a legal malpractice, they contend they may recover these damages even though respondents did not act oppressively, fraudulently, or maliciously (see Civ. Code, § 3294, subd. (a)). Respondents counter that appellants may not recover lost punitive damages as compensatory damages for attorney negligence.... According to respondents, allowing recovery of lost punitive damages contravenes the purpose of punitive damages awards and cannot be justified "as a matter of policy." We agree with respondents, and find that legal malpractice plaintiffs may not recover lost punitive damages as compensatory damages.

"Detriment is a loss or harm suffered in person or property." "For the breach of an obligation not arising from contract, the measure of damages ... is the amount which will compensate for all the detriment *proximately caused* thereby, whether it could have been anticipated or not." Thus, "an attorney's 'liability, as in other negligence cases, is for all damages directly and proximately caused by his negligence.'" (*Smith v. Lewis* (1975) 13 Cal.3d 349, 362 ...).

"Proximate cause involves *two* elements." "One is *cause in fact*. An act is a cause in fact if it is a necessary antecedent of an event." "Whether defendant's negligence was a cause in fact of plaintiff's damage ... is a factual question for the jury to resolve."

By contrast, the second element focuses on public policy considerations. Because the purported causes of an event may be traced back to the dawn of humanity, the law has imposed additional "limitations on liability other than simple causality." "These additional limitations are related not only to the degree of connection between the conduct and the injury, but also with public policy." Thus, "proximate cause 'is ordinarily concerned, not with the fact of causation, but with the various considerations of policy that limit an actor's responsibility for the consequences of his conduct.'"

....

[W]e conclude that public policy considerations strongly militate against allowing a plaintiff to recover lost punitive damages as compensatory damages in a legal malpractice action. First, allowing recovery of lost punitive damages would defeat the very purpose behind such damages.... "Punitive damages by definition are not intended to compensate the injured party, but rather to punish the tortfeasor whose wrongful action was intentional or malicious, and to deter him and others from similar extreme conduct." "The essential question therefore in every case must be whether the amount of [punitive] damages awarded substantially serves the societal interest."

... Making a negligent attorney liable for lost punitive damages would not serve a societal interest, because the attorney did not commit and had no control over the intentional misconduct justifying the punitive damages award. Imposing liability for lost punitive damages on negligent attorneys would therefore neither punish the culpable tortfeasor (see *Newport*, *supra*, 453 U.S. at p. 267 [101 S.Ct. at p. 2760] ["Under ordinary principles of retribution, it is the wrongdoer himself who is made to suffer for his unlawful conduct"]), nor deter that tortfeasor and others from committing similar wrongful acts in the future (see *Cappetta v. Lippman* (S.D.N.Y. 1996) 913 F.Supp. 302, 306). Indeed, allowing appellants to recover lost punitive damages would not effectuate the public purpose behind such damages in this case because, as the trial court in the Unocal Class Action found, "the public's interest in punishing Unocal ... and in deterring Unocal from future such conduct has been achieved" by the $80 million settlement. (See *ante*, at p. 1043.)

Allowing recovery of lost punitive damages as compensatory damages in legal malpractice actions would also violate public policy, because the amount of the award bears no relation to the gravity of the attorney's misconduct or his or her wealth. A plaintiff seeking to recover lost punitive damages from his negligent attorney is "deliberately seeking an award disproportionate (or at least unrelated) to the [attorney's] ability to pay. That result ... is contrary to the public purpose of punitive damages." (*Adams v. Murakami*, *supra*, 54 Cal.3d at p. 122.)

Contrary to appellants' assertion, awarding lost punitive damages would not indirectly further the deterrent purpose of punitive damages by encouraging attorneys "to exercise reasonable care in investigating or defending punitive damages claims." (*Jacobsen v. Oliver* (D.D.C. 2002) 201 F.Supp.2d 93, 102.) " ""The policy considerations in a state where, as in [California], punitive damages are awarded for punishment and deterrence, would seem to require that the damages rest *ultimately* as well as *nominally* on the party actually responsible for the wrong."" " (*Peterson v. Superior Court* (1982) 31 Cal.3d 147, 157, fn. 4 [181 Cal.Rptr. 784, 642 P.2d 1305], italics added.) By ultimately and nominally imposing damages on an attorney, purporting to punish and deter a wrongdoer who was not responsible for the wrong, an award of lost punitive damages necessarily frustrates the purpose of such damages.

Even assuming an award of lost punitive damages may have some indirect deterrent effect, it still conflicts with the public purpose behind punitive damages.... [A]n award of lost punitive damages can only further the goal of deterrence if it deters "without being excessive." Because an award of lost punitive damages bears no relation to the gravity of the attorney's misconduct or his or her wealth, it cannot further the deterrent purpose behind such damages. Indeed, where, as here, the intentional wrongdoer is a wealthy corporation whose alleged misconduct was especially reprehensible, any award of lost punitive damages is likely to be "disproportionate to the [attorney's] ability to pay" and may financially destroy the attorney. Such a result would undoubtedly contravene the purpose of punitive damages, which "is to deter, not destroy."

Second, permitting recovery of lost punitive damages would violate the public policy against speculative damages.... "[D]amages may not be based upon sheer speculation or surmise, and the mere possibility or even probability that damage will result from wrongful conduct does not render it actionable." "Damage to be subject to a proper award must be such as follows the act complained of as a legal certainty...."

... Because an award of punitive damages constitutes a moral determination, lost punitive damages are too speculative to support a cause of action for attorney negligence.... In determining compensatory damages in a legal malpractice action, "'the jury's task is to determine what a reasonable judge or fact finder would have done'" in the underlying action absent attorney negligence. The standard is "an *objective* one." Lost punitive damages, however, are not amenable to an objective determination.

"'Unlike the measure of actual damages suffered, which presents a question of historical or predictive fact, [citation], the level of punitive damages is not really a "fact" "tried" by the jury.'" Instead, a jury's "imposition of punitive damages is an expression of its moral condemnation." Indeed, a plaintiff is not "'*entitled*, as of right'" to an award of punitive damages, even if the jury finds the defendant "guilty of oppression, fraud, or malice" Thus, to award lost punitive damages, the trier of fact must determine what *moral* judgment would have been made by a reasonable jury.

Because moral judgments are inherently subjective, a jury cannot objectively determine whether punitive damages should have been awarded or the proper amount of those damages with any legal certainty. Lost punitive damages are therefore too speculative to support a cause of action for legal malpractice.

Third, the complex standard of proof applicable to claims for lost punitive damages militates against the recovery of such damages. Because the standards of proof governing compensatory and punitive damages are different (compare Evid. Code, § 115 ["Except as otherwise provided by law, the burden of proof requires proof by a preponderance of the evidence"] with Civ. Code, § 3294, subd. (a) [plaintiff may recover punitive damages only "where it is proven by *clear and convincing evidence* that the defendant has been guilty of oppression, fraud, or malice" (italics added)]), the standard of proof for lost punitive damages will be, in essence, a standard within a standard. To recover lost punitive damages, a plaintiff must prove *by a preponderance of the evidence* that but for attorney negligence the jury would have found *clear and convincing evidence* of oppression, fraud or malice. In light of this complex standard, "[t]he mental gymnastics required to reach an intelligent verdict would be difficult to comprehend much less execute." This pragmatic difficulty provides additional support for barring recovery of lost punitive damages in a legal malpractice action.

Fourth, allowing recovery of lost punitive damages in this case would hinder the ability of trial courts to manage and resolve mass tort actions by discouraging the use of mandatory, non-opt-out punitive damages classes. "[C]ourts have encouraged the use of mandatory class actions to handle punitive damages claims in mass tort cases. Mandatory class actions avoid the unfairness that results when a few plaintiffs—those who win the race to the courthouse—bankrupt a defendant early in the litigation process. They also avoid the possible unfairness of punishing a defendant over and over again for the same tortious conduct." Making class counsel liable for lost punitive damages would, however, discourage counsel from using these mandatory classes because counsel would otherwise face the specter of multiple legal malpractice lawsuits from disgruntled class members.

Indeed, allowing lost punitive damages may adversely impact the overall ability of courts to manage their caseloads by making settlement more difficult in cases involving punitive damages claims. Because dissatisfied clients may seek such damages based solely on an allegation of negligent undervaluation of the punitive damages claims, the settlement of such claims exposes plaintiffs' attorneys to potentially devastating liability. Faced with this risk, plaintiffs' attorneys will likely be more hesitant to settle and more intransigent in their settlement demands.

Finally, allowing recovery of lost punitive damages as compensatory damages in a legal malpractice action may exact a significant social cost. Exposing attorneys to such liability would likely increase the cost of malpractice insurance, cause insurers to exclude coverage for these damages, or further discourage insurers from providing professional liability insurance in California. The resulting financial burden on attorneys would probably make it more difficult for consumers to obtain legal services or obtain recovery for legal malpractice. At a minimum, the specter of lost punitive damages would encourage the practice of "'defensive' law." "'[I]n our already overburdened system it behooves no one to encourage the additional expenditure [of] resources merely to build a record against a potential malpractice claim.'" Even though respondents and amici curiae provide no concrete evidence that this parade of horribles will occur, "we deem it unwise to inflict the risk" "[a]bsent a compelling reason" to do so.

And appellants offer no compelling reason to take this risk. The general rule that "the measure of damages [in a legal malpractice action] is the value of the claim lost" does not preclude us from barring recovery of lost punitive damages for public policy reasons. A plaintiff in a legal malpractice action "is entitled only to be made whole." But "[i]t should be presumed a plaintiff has been made whole for his injuries by compensatory damages...." Thus, "[b]y definition [punitive damages] are not intended to make the plaintiff whole by compensating for a loss suffered." "An award of punitive damages, though perhaps justified for societal reasons of deterrence, is a boon for the plaintiff. 'Such damages constitute a windfall....'" Although the plaintiff is "'entitled [as] of right to compensatory damages,'" he or she is "'never entitled to'" punitive damages. Because legal malpractice plaintiffs are made whole for their injuries by an award of lost compensatory damages, allowing these plaintiffs to recover lost punitive damages would give them an undeserved windfall. This is especially true where, as here, the plaintiffs have been fully compensated for their injuries.

The fear that insulating negligent attorneys from liability for lost punitive damages will foster misconduct is also overblown. Given the potential size of punitive damage awards and the typical contingent fee arrangements, attorneys already have a strong incentive to properly pursue these claims without subjecting them to liability for lost punitive damages. Moreover, in most cases, potential liability for lost compensatory damages—which are often substantial—provides an adequate deterrent to attorney misconduct. Finally, the specter of disciplinary action, increases in malpractice premiums, and losses in future business gives attorneys more than enough incentive to handle their cases properly. In any event, we believe the overwhelming public policy considerations militating against recovery of lost punitive damages significantly outweigh any countervailing risk of encouraging attorney negligence.

Neither *Granquist v. Sandberg* (1990) 219 Cal.App.3d 181 [268 Cal.Rptr. 109] nor *Norton v. Superior Court* (1994) 24 Cal.App.4th 1750 [30 Cal.Rptr.2d 217] (*Norton*) dictates a contrary result. In *Granquist*, the Court of Appeal held that the personal representative of a deceased tort victim may recover pain, suffering, or disfigurement damages in a legal malpractice action. [T]he [*Granquist*] court found no reason to deviate from the general rule that the measure of damages in a legal malpractice action is the value of the claim lost. By contrast, strong public policy considerations militate against allowing recovery of lost punitive damages. *Norton* is also inapposite. In *Norton*, the Court of Appeal held that the collateral source rule applied in legal malpractice actions as a matter of "practicality." According to the court, "the defendant attorney stands in the shoes of the underlying tortfeasor insofar as the collateral source rule is concerned." The court carefully limited its holding to the collateral source rule and did not address the question of proximate causation. Indeed, the court apparently found that no public policy barred the application of the collateral source rule. That is not true here. Finally, the court concluded that "[t]he result ... in this case merely allows the plaintiffs in a legal malpractice action to be made whole." By contrast, an award of lost punitive damages gives appellants a windfall that they were not entitled to in the underlying action.

Finally, we decline to follow the out-of-state cases cited by appellants. Most of these cases provide little or no analysis and permit recovery of lost punitive damages solely based on the general rule that the measure of damages in a legal malpractice action is the value of the lost claim. These cases largely ignore public policy—including the public purpose of punitive damages.... Accordingly, we ... hold that a plaintiff in a legal malpractice action may not recover lost punitive damages as compensatory damages.[3] ...

...

We affirm the judgment of the Court of Appeal.

George, C. J., Baxter, J., and Chin, J., concurred.

KENNARD, J., Concurring and Dissenting.

I agree with the majority that these two plaintiffs in a legal malpractice action may not recover as compensatory damages the punitive damages they allegedly lost when, as part of a settlement in the underlying class action, the attorneys for the class stipulated to a dismissal of the punitive damages sought by the class. But, unlike the majority, I would leave for another day the determination whether today's holding applies to cases outside the class action context, when considerations different from those involved here may lead to a different conclusion.

I.

Plaintiffs are two of over 12,000 individuals who, after exposure to a toxic chemical emanating from a leak at a refinery, joined a class action against the refinery's owner. Plaintiffs were among eight objectors to the $80 million settlement, which included a stipulation for dismissal of the punitive damage claims. The trial court approved the settlement, finding that "the public's interest in punishing ... and deterring" the defendant had been achieved, and that the settlement was made in good faith (Code Civ. Proc., § 877.6).

Under the terms of the settlement, plaintiffs were free to seek a jury trial on their compensatory damage claims, but they did not do so. After receiving their arbitration awards, plaintiffs collaterally attacked the settlement through this malpractice action against class counsel, asking for punitive damages lost to them, when as part of the settlement, counsel stipulated to a dismissal of the punitive damage claims of the non-opt-out class.

I agree with the majority that this case presents important issues of public policy. In my view, however, the crucial policy issues spring from both the nature and resolution

3. Of course, plaintiffs may recover punitive damages in a legal malpractice action if the attorneys, *themselves*, are guilty of "oppression, fraud, or malice", but the measure of punitive damages would depend on the gravity of the attorneys' misconduct and their wealth.

of the underlying class action lawsuit. This court long ago acknowledged that public policy encourages the use of class actions. Settlement of class actions is encouraged precisely because they "consume substantial judicial resources and present unusually large risks for the litigants." (*In re General Motors Corp. Pick-Up Truck Fuel Tank Products Liability Litigation* (3d Cir. 1995) 55 F.3d 768, 805.)

If we permitted all dissident members of a class to pursue a malpractice action against class counsel for punitive damages relinquished by settlement, attorneys would have little incentive to bring class actions and even less incentive to settle them. Counsel acting pro bono would be especially unlikely to undertake class representation. (See *Thomas v. Albright* (D.D.C. 1999) 77 F.Supp.2d 114, 123 ["In a world fraught with numerous injustices that can only be vindicated through the vehicle of a class action, attorneys should not be dissuaded from bringing meritorious actions by the threat of a state court malpractice law suit."].) And, as this case illustrates, permitting such a collateral attack undermines the very authority of the judiciary. Here, two of 12,000 class members sought to recoup from class counsel potential punitive damages based on a claim that had been bargained away in exchange for a global settlement of $80 million, even though the trial court expressly found the settlement to have been made in good faith and to have vindicated the public interest in "punishing ... and deterring" the defendant's conduct.

To permit plaintiffs to now collaterally attack what they perceive to be an insufficiently lucrative settlement in the underlying class action violates an overriding public policy favoring settlement of class actions. On this point, I agree with the majority. Unlike the majority, however, I would stress the narrowness of the holding, leaving for another day whether the same considerations would apply outside the class action context. I outline my concerns below.

II.

The vast majority of legal malpractice claims do not arise from class actions or from class action settlements, as in this case. Probably the most frequent type of attorney malpractice occurs when counsel fails to timely file a complaint or preserve a claim, leaving the client with no recourse except a malpractice action against counsel. The measure of damages for legal malpractice is the value of the claim lost (*Smith v. Lewis* (1975) 13 Cal.3d 349, 361 [118 Cal.Rptr. 621, 530 P.2d 589, 78 A.L.R.3d 231]) or all detriment proximately caused by the malpractice (Civ. Code, § 3333). But often an injured client suffers only a small economic loss or incurs substantial noneconomic harm not easily valued in dollars and cents. When the client's injury is caused by especially egregious conduct, the value of the client's claim may lie almost entirely in a large punitive damage recovery. (See *BMW of North America, Inc. v. Gore* (1996) 517 U.S. 559, 582 [116 S.Ct. 1589, 1602, 134 L.Ed.2d 809] [in such cases low compensatory damages will support higher ratio of punitive damages].) By denying recovery for lost punitive damages in *every* legal malpractice action, instead of limiting today's holding to the confines of a class action settlement, the majority effectively denies such injured clients anything but a nominal recovery of compensatory damages, insulating the attorneys while failing to fully compensate the clients for the loss caused by the malpractice.

The majority condemns a claim of lost punitive damages as too speculative. Yet, whether a jury trying the underlying claim would have awarded punitive damages, and how much it would have awarded but for the claim's forfeiture, are no more speculative than whether the client would have prevailed had the claim gone to trial and how much in compensatory damages the jury would have awarded. Lost punitive damages, like any other item of compensatory damage in a malpractice action, must be proven to a degree of reasonable certainty.

In a malpractice action, punitive damages lost because of attorney error are not true punitive damages but are merely *a measure* of some of the injury resulting from the attorney's malpractice. Thus, lost punitive damages are a form of compensatory damages. In tort law, a goal of awarding compensatory damages is to deter harmful conduct by making the wrongdoer compensate the person harmed. As Justice Puglia explained in *Merenda v. Superior Court* (1992) 3 Cal.App.4th 1 [4 Cal.Rptr.2d 87], a legal malpractice plaintiff "should be entitled to recover ... as compensatory damages the amount of punitive damages [the plaintiff] proves she would have obtained ... in the underlying action. This amount is a portion of the difference between the amount of the actual recovery ... and the amount which would have been recovered but for" the attorney's negligence. *(Id.* at p. 12.)

When the majority here suggests that an award of lost punitive damages inappropriately punishes a merely negligent attorney, it conflates lost punitive damages as one measure of compensatory damage with punitive damages assessed against a particularly culpable party. If the attorney has not performed competently, the attorney is liable for the client's injury, including punitive damages lost to the client because of the attorney's deficient performance. Only if an attorney commits malpractice and does so oppressively, fraudulently, or maliciously is the attorney liable for punitive damages. Conceivably, an attorney could be liable for both types of damages, but analytically only the latter would be punitive damages.

Not only are lost punitive damages subject to proof at trial of the malpractice claim, but the amount of an award for lost punitive damages is ultimately constrained by due process. As the United States Supreme Court held recently, "few awards [of punitive damages] exceeding a single-digit ratio between punitive and compensatory damages ... will satisfy due process." (*State Farm Mutual Automobile Ins. Co. v. Campbell* (2003) 538 U.S. 408, ___ [123 S.Ct. 1513, 1524, 155 L.Ed.2d 585].) The high court went on to note that "[w]hen compensatory damages are substantial, then a lesser ratio, perhaps only equal to compensatory damages can reach the outermost limit of the due process guarantee." (*Ibid.*)

The majority here observes that permitting recovery of lost punitive damages in legal malpractice actions may "exact a significant social cost" by driving insurers offering professional liability coverage out of the California market. That is an issue to be addressed to the Legislature, not to this court. Moreover, the majority's observation assumes that until now, both in this state and in the majority of other jurisdictions that have addressed the question, legal malpractice actions have not permitted recovery of lost punitive damages as an item of compensatory damage. Not so. So far, only one state excludes recovery of lost punitive damages. Thus, the general rule is this: "Attorneys can be liable for exemplary or punitive damages lost or imposed because of their negligence" (3 Mallen & Smith, Legal Malpractice (5th ed. 2000) Damages, § 20.7, p. 136, fn. omitted). The majority does not explain why a malpractice insurance crisis will result from leaving in place a rule that has prevailed until now in many jurisdictions, including California.

In sum, I am not persuaded that the public policy rationales the majority advances support the broad rule it announces.

III.

....

In a client's action against an attorney for lost punitive damages, ... only one of the parties—the attorney—is blameworthy. The client is a victim twice over—a victim first of the third party's intentional tort and second of the attorney's malpractice. Such an action ... does not involve a more culpable party's attempt to shift to a less culpable party a liability resulting from its own intentional wrongdoing; instead, it involves a nonculpable party's attempt to obtain full compensation from a culpable party for the complete financial loss caused by the culpable party's negligence. No public policy forbids such compensation.

For the reasons given above, I join in affirming the judgment of the Court of Appeal, but I do not join in either the majority's reasoning or the broad application of the rule it announces.

* * *

1. Compare the principal case to *Haberer v. Rice*, 511 N.W.2d 279 (S.D. 1994), a legal malpractice decision in which the plaintiff Haberer sued his former attorney for the attorney's negligent representation of Haberer on a matter against a bank. In the underlying suit, the Bank's tortious conduct against Haberer merited a punitive damage award, but due to the defendant attorney's negligence, Haberer was unable to prevail in the suit against the Bank, thereby also losing out on the punitive damages that would have been awarded. The Supreme Court of South Dakota ruled that because absent the attorney's negligence Haberer would have been able to obtain punitive damages against the bank in the underlying litigation, that punitive damage award was properly included in the calculation of compensatory damages in the legal malpractice action. The *Haberer* court concluded that lost punitive damages are recoverable as a component of compensatory damages in legal malpractice actions. *Id.* at 288. It explained that proof of damages in a legal malpractice action "necessarily involves analysis of the value of that underlying cause of action," and if the attorney's negligence results in a judgment that would not have otherwise been rendered, "the proper measure of damages is the entirety of the prior judgment regardless of the theory upon which the prior judgment was entered or the nature of the damages assessed thereunder." *Id.* at 287–88.

2. For an interesting exploration of the issue of recovering punitive damages as part of compensatory damages in legal malpractice, *see* Charles Marshall Thatcher, *Recovery of "Lost Punitive Damages" as "Compensatory Damages" in Legal Malpractice Actions: Transference of Liability or Transformation of Character?*, 49 S.D. L. Rev. 1 (2003).

* * *

2. Emotional Distress Damages

The recovery of emotional distress damages for negligence has been somewhat controversial. In typical negligence actions, most modern courts allow for the recovery of emotional distress damages as part of compensatory damages as long as there are other substantiated personal or property injuries proven. Recovery for mere emotional distress, in the absence of physical injury to the plaintiff, is highly scrutinized and disfavored. The following materials explore whether emotional distress injuries should be recoverable in legal malpractice.

Focus Questions: *Long-Russell v. Hampe*

1. *Are emotional distress damages typically recoverable in negligence actions?*
2. *Are emotional distress damages recoverable in a legal malpractice action based on an attorney's mere negligence?*

Long-Russell v. Hampe

39 P.3d 1015
(Wyo. 2002)

HILL, Justice.

In this matter we are asked to answer questions certified to this Court.... Appellant, Sharon Long-Russell (Long-Russell), seeks an opinion of this Court which would resolve the question of whether damages for emotional suffering may be awarded in the context of a legal malpractice case wherein mere negligence on the part of the attorney is the basis for the claim of emotional damages. Appellee, Robert A. Hampe (Hampe), Attorney-at-Law, asks that those questions be answered in the negative.

1

We will answer the certified questions in the negative. Such emotional damages may be an element of a claim for damages, in the context of a legal malpractice action, under certain limited circumstances, but not the circumstance of mere negligence.

THE CERTIFIED QUESTIONS

The issues certified to this Court, by the district court, are:

1. Are damages for emotional suffering available in a legal malpractice case which alleges that an attorney negligently failed to properly assert property claims in a divorce, or negligently gave bad advice resulting in a client's eviction from her place of residence?

2. Are damages for emotional suffering available in a legal malpractice case which alleges that an attorney negligently gave incorrect legal advice about a child visitation order?

FACTUAL BACKGROUND

... The certified questions assume a factual circumstance wherein an attorney is alleged to have been negligent in the performance of his services for a client.

Long-Russell was divorced from her second husband, Gary Long (Long), in September, 1982. The property settlement agreed to in that divorce made no mention of the parties owning a home. Hampe played no role in that divorce. At the time of that divorce, Long-Russell and Long were apparently renting a home from Long's parents and completing repairs on that home with a view to ultimately buying it from Long's parents. Some time after that divorce was final, Long obtained title to the home from his parents. The most significant complicating factor in this case is that Long-Russell continued to live in that house, apparently without paying rent, until Long had her evicted in 1995. Hampe did not represent Long-Russell in the eviction action either. However, Long-Russell did hire Hampe in 1995 to try to undo the eviction. At the time Hampe began representing Long-

Russell, she was still residing in the home but was forcibly evicted pursuant to court order shortly after retaining Hampe as her lawyer.

At the time of her divorce from Long, Long-Russell was pregnant with Richard Russell's (Russell) child. Long-Russell then married Russell, and the two of them (and eventually their two children) continued living in Long's house, with the Russell family living in the upstairs portion of the house and Long living in the basement. In January, 1995, Long-Russell was divorced from Russell. The decree of divorce in that case made no reference to Long-Russell or Russell owning any interest in Long's home. During this divorce and even after the divorce was final, custody of the children born of Long-Russell's marriage to Russell was in dispute. Hampe did not represent Long-Russell during this divorce or in the child custody proceedings which resulted in her temporary loss of the custody of the children. However, Long-Russell did hire Hampe to attempt to undo the loss of the custody of her children. Eventually, Russell was given permanent custody of the children and Long-Russell was accorded liberal visitation. The record extant suggests that all parties continue to reside in Cheyenne.

The essence of Long-Russell's malpractice claim against Hampe is that he accepted her payment of attorney's fees in the approximate amount of $9,500.00 and did no meaningful work for her, gave her bad advice which complicated her legal problems, pursued hopeless claims and failed to pursue hopeful ones, and made promises of success in the legal arena that were irresponsible and, of course, they did not come to pass. In addition to the loss of the $9,500.00 in attorney's fees, Long-Russell sought damages for loss of her alleged interest in Long's home, emotional damages for the emotional upheaval that attended her eviction from Long's home, and the loss of the custody of her children. It is the claim of emotional damages that is our sole concern in this matter.

DISCUSSION

....

[T]he decision of the Minnesota Supreme Court in the case *Lickteig v. Alderson, Ondov, Leonard & Sween, P.A.*, 556 N.W.2d 557 (Minn.1996), comports well with our previous decisions with respect to many aspects of the matter before us, and we will adopt its decision in that case, to govern in similar cases in Wyoming. Lickteig was injured in an automobile accident, and the attorneys who represented her admitted their negligence in their representation of her. The issue of damages was submitted to binding arbitration, and a claim for emotional damages in the amount of $45,000.00 was awarded. *Lickteig*, 556 N.W.2d at 559. The decision of the Minnesota Supreme Court is as follows:

> We first consider the issue of emotional distress damages. We have not been anxious to expand the availability of damages for emotional distress. *K.A.C. v. Benson*, 527 N.W.2d 553, 559 (Minn.1995); *Hubbard v. United Press Int'l, Inc.*, 330 N.W.2d 428, 437–38 (Minn.1983). This reluctance has arisen from the concern that claims of mental anguish may be speculative and so likely to lead to fictitious allegations that there is a potential for abuse of the judicial process. *Hubbard*, 330 N.W.2d at 438. Thus, we have been careful to limit the availability of such damages to "those plaintiffs who prove that emotional injury occurred under circumstances tending to guarantee its genuineness." *Id.* at 437.
>
> In tort cases, emotional distress may be an element of damages in only three circumstances. First, a plaintiff who suffers a physical injury as a result of another's negligence may recover for the accompanying mental anguish. *Langeland v. Farmers State Bank of Trimont*, 319 N.W.2d 26, 31 (Minn.1982). Second, a plaintiff

may recover for negligent infliction of emotional distress when physical symptoms arise after and because of emotional distress, if the plaintiff was actually exposed to physical harm as a result of the negligence of another (the "zone-of-danger" rule). *K.A.C.*, 527 N.W.2d at 559; *Langeland*, 319 N.W.2d at 31; *Stadler v. Cross*, 295 N.W.2d 552, 554 (Minn.1980). Finally, a plaintiff may recover emotional distress damages when there has been a "direct invasion of the plaintiff's rights such as that constituting slander, libel, malicious prosecution, seduction, or other like willful, wanton, or malicious conduct." *State Farm Mut. Auto. Ins. Co. v. Village of Isle*, 265 Minn. 360, 368, 122 N.W.2d 36, 41 (1963). *See also, M.H. v. Caritas Family Services*, 488 N.W.2d 282, 290 (Minn.1992); *Hubbard*, 330 N.W.2d at 437–38; *Langeland*, 319 N.W.2d at 31–32.

We have also recognized the independent tort of intentional infliction of emotional distress. *Hubbard*, 330 N.W.2d at 438. This independent tort differs from the "willful conduct" category above in that it can stand alone as a separate action, whereas in the "willful conduct" category, emotional distress is only an element of the damages arising from an intentional tort that constitutes a direct violation of the plaintiff's rights, such as defamation.

The respondent in this case did not suffer any physical injury; neither was she in any "zone of danger," nor is she alleging intentional infliction of emotional distress. Damages for emotional distress could be justified only had the appellants violated her rights by willful, wanton or malicious conduct. We note at the outset that respondent's complaint contained no allegations of willfulness or malice; it alleged only negligent representation and breach of contract....

Appellants argue that, in the absence of any allegation of willful conduct, evidence of willful conduct, or finding of willful conduct by the arbitrator, emotional distress damages were wrongfully awarded in this legal malpractice action.

Despite the absence of an allegation or finding of willful conduct, respondent contends that willfulness was shown and found here ... and that in this case, it can be inferred from the arbitrator's finding that she suffered "compensable" emotional distress, that the arbitrator made the requisite finding of willfulness. Further, she points to allegations presented to the arbitrator in her arbitration brief which, she asserts, support a finding of willful conduct on the part of the appellants.

Our analysis is complicated by the hybrid nature of claims for legal malpractice. To state a claim for legal malpractice, one must show that the "defendant acted negligently *or* in breach of contract." *Togstad v. Vesely, Otto, Miller & Keefe*, 291 N.W.2d 686, 692 (Minn.1980) (emphasis added); *Admiral Merchants Motor Freight, Inc. v. O'Connor & Hannan*, 494 N.W.2d 261, 265 (Minn.1992). We have recognized that the two theories will frequently be interchangeable in legal malpractice cases. *Togstad*, 291 N.W.2d at 693.

However, the availability of emotional distress damages in contract actions has been even more restricted than for actions in tort. In general, extra-contractual damages, including those for emotional distress, are not recoverable for breach of contract except in those rare cases where the breach is accompanied by an independent tort. *Olson v. Rugloski*, 277 N.W.2d 385, 388 (Minn.1979); *Haagenson v. National Farmers Union Property and Cas. Co.*, 277 N.W.2d 648, 652 (Minn.1979); *Beaulieu v. Great Northern Ry. Co.*, 103 Minn. 47, 53, 114 N.W. 353, 355 (1907). The accompanying independent tort must be willful. *Olson*,

> 277 N.W.2d at 388. That is, it must support the extra-contractual damages in its own right as a tort. *See Barr/Nelson, Inc. v. Tonto's, Inc.,* 336 N.W.2d 46, 52–53 (Minn.1983). Thus, even a malicious or bad-faith motive in breaching a contract does not convert a contract action into a tort action sufficient to support an award of emotional distress damages, *Haagenson,* 277 N.W.2d at 652, or other extra-contractual damages, such as punitive damages, *Moore v. John E. Blomquist, Inc.,* 256 N.W.2d 518, 518 (Minn.1977); *Wild v. Rarig,* 302 Minn. 419, 440–42, 234 N.W.2d 775, 789–90 (1975), *cert. denied,* 424 U.S. 902, 96 S.Ct. 1093, 47 L.Ed.2d 307 (1976).
>
> Here, the breach of contract and tort claims are not independent: they are interchangeable. Appellants admitted negligence in the loss of respondent's claim against the other driver. From that, the trial court concluded, "An admission to negligence is also an admission to breach of the attorney-client relationship." Moreover, this will be the case in almost all legal malpractice cases. If we were to affirm the award of damages for emotional distress in this case, we would be sanctioning a similar award whenever a lawyer breached his or her contract with a client by negligently performing the promised legal services. This we are not willing to do.
>
> Nor does the conduct giving rise to the purported breach of contract support an award of emotional distress damages *on its own.* The court of appeals seems to imply that a breach of the attorney-client contract is inherently willful. *See Lickteig,* 556 N.W.2d at 560. It is simply not the case that professional malpractice and willful indifference to another's rights are always one and the same. *See Admiral Merchants,* 494 N.W.2d at 267–68. Moreover, a willful breach of contract, in and of itself, is not enough to justify an award of extra-contractual damages. *Haagenson,* 277 N.W.2d at 652; *Barr/Nelson,* 336 N.W.2d at 52–53; *Wild,* 302 Minn. at 440–42, 234 N.W.2d at 789–90. While cases may arise where an attorney acts so egregiously that emotional distress damages may be appropriate, the creation of a per se rule for such damages in every legal malpractice case is not warranted, based on the longstanding limitation of such damages to those instances where there has been a willful violation of another's rights.
>
> We therefore hold that, as in other negligence actions, emotional distress damages are available in limited circumstances. There must be a direct violation of the plaintiff's rights by willful, wanton or malicious conduct; mere negligence is not sufficient. Here, in the absence of an allegation or proof on these essential elements, the award of emotional distress damages was improper.

Lickteig, 556 N.W.2d at 560–62 (footnotes omitted). Thus, based solely on an allegation of negligence, a litigant is not entitled to present an emotional damages claim to a jury.

The standard we have adopted above is fully consistent with the RESTATEMENT (THIRD) OF THE LAW, THE LAW GOVERNING LAWYERS, §§48, 50, 52 and 53 (*also see* comment g. to §53) (2000).

....

This matter is remanded to the district court for further proceedings consistent with this opinion.

* * *

1. In *Douglas v. Delp,* 987 S.W.2d 879 (Tex. 1999), the plaintiff filed a malpractice action against her attorney who had represented her when a business deal between her and her business partner went awry. As part of her legal malpractice claim, she sought to recover damages for her alleged decline in net worth, lost earning capacity, lost credit reputation, and mental anguish. In addressing her claim for mental injuries, the Texas Supreme Court explained:

> This Court has not yet addressed whether mental anguish damages are recoverable for legal malpractice.... Reasoning that mental anguish is not generally a foreseeable consequence of an attorney's negligence, and that recovery of economic loss usually suffices to make a plaintiff whole, other courts have concluded that a plaintiff may not recover mental anguish damages when those damages are a consequence of economic loss. *See generally Boros v. Baxley,* 621 So.2d 240, 244 (Ala.1993); *Reed v. Mitchell & Timbanard, P.C.,* 183 Ariz. 313, 903 P.2d 621, 626–27 (App.1995); *Merenda v. Superior Court,* 3 Cal.App.4th 1, 4 Cal.Rptr.2d 87, 92 (1992); *Gavend v. Malman,* 946 P.2d 558, 563 (Colo.Ct.App.1997); *Segall v. Berkson,* 139 Ill.App.3d 325, 93 Ill.Dec. 927, 487 N.E.2d 752, 756 (1985); *Richards v. Cousins,* 550 So.2d 1273, 1278 (La.Ct.App.1989); *Lickteig v. Alderson, Ondov, Leonard & Sween, P.A.,* 556 N.W.2d 557, 562 (Minn.1996); *Selsnick v. Horton,* 96 Nev. 944, 620 P.2d 1256, 1257 (1980); *Gautam v. DeLuca,* 215 N.J.Super. 388, 521 A.2d 1343, 1348–49 (App.Div.1987); *Sanders v. Rosen,* 159 Misc.2d 563, 605 N.Y.S.2d 805, 810 (N.Y.Sup.Ct.1993); *Hilt v. Bernstein,* 75 Or.App. 502, 707 P.2d 88, 95–96 (1985); *Wehringer v. Powers & Hall, P.C.,* 874 F.Supp. 425, 429–30 (D.Mass.1995) (applying Massachusetts law); *see also* 2 Ronald E. Mallen & Jeffrey M. Smith, LEGAL MALPRACTICE § 19.11, at 612 (4th ed. 1996) ("The prevailing rule is that damages for emotional injuries are not recoverable if they are a *consequence* of other damages caused by the attorney's negligence."). *But see Beis v. Bowers,* 649 So.2d 1094, 1096 (La.Ct.App.1995) (permitting recovery of mental anguish damages for legal malpractice); *Salley v. Childs,* 541 A.2d 1297, 1300 (Me.1988) (same); *Gore v. Rains & Block,* 189 Mich.App. 729, 473 N.W.2d 813, 818–19 (1991) (same).
>
> Some courts have allowed mental anguish claims to proceed when the client's direct injury is not exclusively economic, but is more personal in nature, for example, loss of child custody or loss of liberty.[1] These courts recognize that economic recovery alone would not make the plaintiff whole because of the very personal nature of the injury. *See Wagenmann v. Adams,* 829 F.2d 196, 221 (1st Cir.1987) (applying Massachusetts law) (confinement in mental hospital); *Snyder v. Baumecker,* 708 F.Supp. 1451, 1464 (D.N.J.1989) (applying New Jersey law) (incarceration); *Holliday v. Jones,* 215 Cal.App.3d 102, 264 Cal.Rptr. 448, 458 (1990) (criminal conviction later reversed); *Bowman v. Doherty,* 235 Kan. 870, 686 P.2d 112, 118 (1984) (arrest); *Kohn v. Schiappa,* 281 N.J.Super. 235, 656 A.2d 1322, 1324–25 (Law Div.1995) (adoption).
>
> Some of the same courts following the general rule that mental anguish is not a compensable element of damages in legal malpractice cases would permit such damages when an attorney has acted with heightened culpability. *See, e.g., Boros,*

1. We note that under Texas law, plaintiffs convicted of a crime may maintain legal malpractice claims in connection with that conviction "only if they have been exonerated on direct appeal, through post-conviction relief, or otherwise." *Peeler v. Hughes & Luce,* 909 S.W.2d 494, 497–98 (Tex.1995). We express no opinion on what kinds of damages a plaintiff able to make that required showing may recover.

621 So.2d at 244–45; *Bowman*, 686 P.2d at 118; *Lickteig*, 556 N.W.2d at 562; *Selsnick*, 620 P.2d at 1257; *Gautam*, 521 A.2d at 1348; *Timms*, 713 F.Supp. at 954. The court of appeals in this case ... focused, however, not on any heightened culpability on the part of [the law firm], but on the severity of the anguish [the plaintiff] suffered. We have discovered no other court explicitly adopting such a test that focuses not on the attorney's conduct but on the client's condition.

In *City of Tyler v. Likes*, 962 S.W.2d 489 (Tex.1997), our most recent comprehensive discussion of mental anguish damages, we reaffirmed the importance of awarding sufficient damages to make the plaintiff whole. In so doing, we disallowed mental anguish damages to a plaintiff whose property was negligently harmed. We concluded that damages measured by the economic loss would be "an adequate and appropriate remedy for negligent harm to real or personal property." We reasoned that, "[w]hile few persons suffering serious bodily injury would feel made whole by the mere recovery of medical expenses and lost wages, many whose property has been damaged or destroyed will be entirely satisfied by recovery of its value." Although *Likes* did not involve an attorney-client relationship, we think the principles announced in *Likes* support our conclusion that when the injuries caused by an attorney's negligence are economic, the plaintiff can be fully recompensed by the recovery of any economic loss. Restoration of the pecuniary interest suffices to return a plaintiff to her prior circumstances.

... In *Likes* we did point out that recovery of mental anguish damages has been permitted as the foreseeable result of breach of duties arising from "certain special relationships," including that of physician-patient. *Likes*, 962 S.W.2d at 496. In particular we noted that mental anguish is a foreseeable result of most doctors' negligence, "perhaps because most physicians' negligence also causes bodily injury." The foreseeable result of an attorney's negligence, on the other hand, typically extends only to economic loss. Therefore, consistent with the policy goals set forth in *Likes* and by the majority of courts that have thus far addressed this issue, and in keeping with the well-established principle that a plaintiff should receive an amount of damages sufficient to make her whole, we hold that when a plaintiff's mental anguish is a consequence of economic losses caused by an attorney's negligence, the plaintiff may not recover damages for that mental anguish. As [plaintiff's] claim for mental anguish damages is a consequence of her economic loss, she may not maintain that claim in this case. We express no opinion on what standard may be appropriate when additional or other kinds of loss are claimed or when heightened culpability is alleged.

Douglas v. Delp, 987 S.W.2d 879, 884–85 (Tex. 1999).

2. The *Douglas* court expressly reserves opinion regarding whether criminal malpractice clients should be permitted to recover for emotional injuries. (Reread footnote 1 excerpted from the *Douglas* opinion, *supra*). What is your opinion on this issue? Should mental anguish damages be recoverable for a lawyer's negligence in a criminal malpractice action? *See, e.g.*, Chapter 5.E.2 (exploring the challenges associated with bringing criminal malpractice actions).

3. Other decisions are in accord with the principal case. For example, the court explained in *Paterek v. Petersen & Ibold*, 890 N.E.2d 316 (Ohio 2008),

"'[t]he vast majority of appellate decisions that have considered the issue have held that an attorney is not liable for emotional distress damages where the attorney's conduct has been merely negligent.' Joseph J. Kelleher, An Attorney's Liability for the Negligent Infliction of Emotional Distress (1990), 58 FORDHAM L. REV. 1309, 1319. This court has recognized that a plaintiff in a legal-malpractice case may seek other types of consequential damages, such as additional attorney fees incurred to correct the mistakes of the malpracticing attorney, *Krahn v. Kinney* (1989), 43 Ohio St.3d 103, 106, 538 N.E.2d 1058.... Thus, the focus of this [legal malpractice] case is the value of the lost cause of action." *Paterek*, 890 N.E.2d at 320.

B. Punitive Damages

Focus Questions: *Metcalfe v. Waters*

1. *When may a legal malpractice plaintiff recover punitive damages as an award separate and distinct from compensatory damages?*
2. *What is the purpose of imposition of a punitive damage award?*

Metcalfe v. Waters

970 S.W.2d 448
(Tenn. 1998)

ANDERSON, Chief Justice.

We granted this appeal to determine whether the Court of Appeals erred in reversing the jury's verdict awarding punitive damages in this legal malpractice action. The appeals court held that punitive damages were improper because the defendant's malpractice did not constitute intentional, fraudulent, malicious or reckless conduct and because the defendant's efforts to conceal his actions were not contemporaneous with his malpractice. The court affirmed the jury's verdict as to liability, but reversed the jury's verdict as to compensatory damages because it was excessive.

After our review of the record and applicable authority, we hold that as to punitive damages, the evidence supported a finding that the defendant engaged in intentional, fraudulent, malicious, or reckless conduct and that there is no requirement that a defendant's attempts to lie about or conceal his conduct must be contemporaneous with the underlying malpractice. The judgment of the Court of Appeals is therefore reversed in part and the jury's verdict as to punitive damages is reinstated. The case is remanded to the trial court for a new trial solely on the issue of compensatory damages for the reasons expressed by the Court of Appeals.

BACKGROUND

In September of 1986, the plaintiff, Billie Metcalfe, was a passenger in a car that was involved in a head-on collision with another automobile. Metcalfe, who was age 16 at the time, suffered a broken leg, a concussion, facial cuts, and had to have a pin surgically placed in her hip. She spent thirteen days in the hospital.

The plaintiff and her parents, Julia and Johnny Metcalfe, later hired the defendant, Larry Waters, to represent them in connection with the accident. In September of 1987,

Waters filed a complaint against the driver of the vehicle Billie Metcalfe had been riding in, the driver's parents, and several other defendants. The complaint was non-suited by Waters on March 15, 1990, because Waters was not prepared on the day of trial. The complaint was re-filed on March 6, 1991; however, Waters did not pay the filing fee, nor did he properly issue summons.

The complaint was dismissed by the trial court against some of the defendants in December of 1992, due to the expiration of the statute of limitations. It was dismissed as to the remaining defendants on May 14, 1993, when Waters failed to appear for the trial. Waters lied to the plaintiffs about the status of the case for several months, telling them that it was still pending even though he knew it had been dismissed. When he finally informed the Metcalfes that the case had been dismissed, he did not state the reason for the dismissal but nevertheless told them it was not worth appealing.

The Metcalfes initiated a legal malpractice suit against Waters. In his amended answer to the complaint and in his testimony, Waters admitted that he failed to apprise the plaintiffs of the status of their case, failed to adequately prepare for trial, failed to refile the suit properly after taking a non-suit, failed to file summons properly, failed to appear the second time the case was set for trial, and failed to file a notice of appeal on behalf of the plaintiffs. Waters conceded that his failure to inform the plaintiffs that the case had been dismissed was an intentional, fraudulent, malicious, or reckless effort to conceal his mistakes. He nonetheless denied that punitive damages were warranted.

At trial, the trial court directed a verdict for the plaintiffs on liability. The jury, having been instructed on the law, returned a verdict that included $100,000 in punitive damages against Waters. In approving the verdict, the trial court found that "the conduct of the defendant Waters in not keeping the plaintiffs informed about the status of their case and of lying to the plaintiffs about the dismissal is the gravamen of the punitive damage award." The trial court also stressed that Waters "did not take any action to set aside the dismissal of the case or to protect his clients' interests after the case was dismissed."

In reversing the trial court, the Court of Appeals found that Waters' malpractice amounted to negligent conduct and not intentional, fraudulent, malicious or reckless conduct. Although the intermediate court also found that the defendant's effort to conceal his malpractice was "egregious," it could not serve as the basis for punitive damages:

> [A]n award of punitive damages must be made on the basis of the same conduct that warrants an award of compensatory damages. In the case before us, compensatory damages were awarded for the negligent conduct of Waters in allowing the dismissal of the underlying case. Subsequent to this negligent conduct, Waters committed the egregious act of lying to the Metcalfes about the dismissal of the case. Certainly, his conduct after the dismissal of the case cannot be condoned, but at the same time it is conduct that was not included in the negligent act or acts that resulted in the award of compensatory damages.

We granted the plaintiffs' application for permission to appeal.

ANALYSIS

This Court historically has recognized that "in an action of trespass the jury [is] not restrained, in their assessment of damages, to the amount of the mere pecuniary loss sustained by the plaintiff, *but may award damages in respect of the malicious conduct of the defendant, and the degree of insult with which the trespass had been attended.*" *Wilkins v. Gilmore,* 21 Tenn. 140 (1840) (emphasis added). The purpose of such damages is not to compensate the plaintiff but to punish the wrongdoer for conduct that is egregious and to deter others from engaging in similar conduct. *Huckeby v. Spangler,* 563 S.W.2d 555, 558 (Tenn.1978).

In *Hodges v. S.C. Toof & Co.,* 833 S.W.2d 896 (Tenn.1992), we traced the history of our case law and determined that punitive damages are only available where a defendant has acted either intentionally, fraudulently, maliciously or recklessly. We explained:

> A person acts intentionally when it is the person's conscious objective or desire to engage in the conduct or cause the result. A person acts fraudulently when (1) the person intentionally misrepresents an existing, material fact or produces a false impression, in order to mislead another or to obtain an undue advantage, and (2) another is injured because of reasonable reliance upon that representation. A person acts maliciously when the person is motivated by ill will, hatred, or personal spite. A person acts recklessly when the person is aware of, but consciously disregards, a substantial and unjustifiable risk of such a nature that its disregard constitutes a gross deviation from the standard of care that an ordinary person would exercise under all the circumstances.

Id. at 901 (citations omitted).

To achieve the twin purposes of punishment and deterrence, the defendant's conduct must be established by "clear and convincing" evidence. In determining *liability* for punitive damages, evidence of the defendant's financial condition is inadmissible. *Id.* In determining the *amount* of punitive damages, the following factors may be considered in a separate, bifurcated proceeding: the defendant's financial condition and net worth; the nature and reprehensibility of the defendant's conduct; the impact of the defendant's conduct on the plaintiff; the relationship of the defendant to the plaintiff; the defendant's awareness of the harm and motivation in causing the harm; the duration of the defendant's misconduct and *whether the defendant attempted to conceal the conduct;* the expense the plaintiff has incurred in recovering any losses; whether the defendant profited from the conduct, and if so, whether damages in excess of the profit are necessary to deter future conduct; whether the defendant has been subjected to previous punitive damage awards based upon the same wrongful act; and whether the defendant made any effort to take remedial action or to offer a fair and prompt settlement for the actual harm caused. *Id.* at 901–902 (emphasis added).

In the present case, the Court of Appeals reversed the jury's award of punitive damages, finding that Waters' malpractice amounted to negligence and not intentional, fraudulent, malicious, or reckless conduct. The court further stated that Waters' conduct in concealing and lying about his malpractice, although "egregious," was not contemporaneous with the underlying malpractice and was therefore, under *Hodges,* relevant only to the amount of, but not the liability for, punitive damages. We disagree with both conclusions.

A majority of jurisdictions have recognized that punitive damages may be proper in a legal malpractice case. Annotation, *Allowance of Punitive Damages Against Attorney For Malpractice,* 13 A.L.R.4th 95 (1982 & Supp.1997); *see also Elliott v. Videan,* 164 Ariz. 113, 791 P.2d 639, 644 (1989) ("punitive damages have historically been awarded against attorneys for legal malpractice"). As in any case involving punitive damages, however, the plaintiff must prove that the defendant engaged in the requisite culpable conduct. The Alabama Supreme Court has said, for instance, that "some showing of fraudulent, malicious, willful, wanton, or reckless behavior or inaction must be made to support a claim for punitive damages in a legal malpractice case." *Boros v. Baxley,* 621 So.2d 240,

245 (Ala.1993). Other courts have used similar terms in describing the culpable conduct for an award of punitive damages in a legal malpractice case.[2]

We join these jurisdictions in recognizing that punitive damages may be awarded in a legal malpractice claim, provided the culpable conduct established in *Hodges, supra,* i.e., intentional, fraudulent, malicious, or reckless, is proven by clear and convincing evidence. In this regard, we disagree with the intermediate court's conclusion that Waters' conduct was merely negligent. In addition to failing to prosecute the Metcalfes' claim, Waters' failed to keep them informed about the status of their lawsuit, failed to prepare when the case was set for trial, failed to re-file the case properly after taking a nonsuit, failed to pay the filing fee, failed to issue summons properly, failed to appear when the case was set a second time for trial, failed to file a notice of appeal, and failed to take any actions in an effort to preserve the Metcalfes' right of appeal. Given Waters' repeated transgressions and callous disregard for the rights of his clients, there was overwhelming evidence from which the jury could find, at a minimum, reckless conduct, that is, conduct constituting a gross deviation from the applicable standard of care. *See, e.g., Patrick v. Ronald Williams P.A.,* 102 N.C.App. 355, 402 S.E.2d 452, 460 (1991) ("repeated course of conduct which constituted a callous or intentional indifference to the plaintiff's rights" stated a claim for punitive damages).

We also disagree with the conclusion that punitive damages were improper because Waters' malpractice was not contemporaneous with his efforts to lie about and conceal his wrongdoing. Although the Court of Appeals correctly observed that the concealment of wrongdoing is listed among the factors in *Hodges* that may be considered in determining the *amount* of punitive damages, nothing in *Hodges* precludes the factor from being considered with regard to a defendant's *liability* for punitive damages. Indeed, other factors listed among those for consideration with respect to the amount of punitive damages are also necessarily considered with respect to the threshold liability issue; for instance, the "nature and reprehensibility of the defendant's wrongdoing." *Hodges,* 833 S.W.2d at 901. A close reading of *Hodges,* in fact, indicates that only evidence of a defendant's net worth or financial condition is deemed inadmissible in determining a defendant's liability for punitive damages. *Id.* at 901–902.

Finally, we believe that limiting consideration of a defendant's efforts to conceal his or her wrongdoing is inconsistent with the purpose of punitive damages: to punish egregious acts and deter others from committing the same or similar acts. As other courts have recognized, an attorney's concealment of wrongdoing and/or misrepresentations affecting the client's case relate directly to the punitive damages issue. *See, e.g., Houston v. Surrett,* 222 Ga.App. 207, 474 S.E.2d 39, 41 (1996) ("an attorney's concealment and misrepresentation of matters affecting his client's case will give rise to a claim for punitive damages."); *Asphalt Engineers, Inc. v. Galusha,* 160 Ariz. 134, 770 P.2d 1180 (1989) ("the

---

2. *See, e.g., Hyatt Regency v. Winston & Strawn,* 184 Ariz. 120, 907 P.2d 506, 518 (1995) ("aggravated or outrageous conduct"); *Orsini v. Larry Moyer Trucking, Inc.,* 310 Ark. 179, 833 S.W.2d 366, 368 (1992) (wanton conduct; conscious indifference; malice); *Miller v. Byrne,* 916 P.2d 566, 580 (Colo.Ct.App.1995) ("willful and wanton"); *Ray-Mar Beauty College, Inc. v. Ellis Rubin Law Offices,* 475 So.2d 718, 719 (Fla.Dist.Ct.App.1985) ("gross malpractice"); *Houston v. Surrett,* 222 Ga.App. 207, 474 S.E.2d 39, 41 (1996) ("willful misconduct, malice, fraud, wantonness, oppression"); *Fitzgerald v. Walker,* 121 Idaho 589, 826 P.2d 1301, 1305 (1992) ("extreme deviation from reasonable standards of conduct"); *Belford v. McHale, Cook & Welch,* 648 N.E.2d 1241, 1245 (Ind.Ct.App.1995) ("malice, fraud, gross negligence, or oppressiveness"); *McAlister v. Slosberg,* 658 A.2d 658 (Me.1995) (malice); *Gautam v. DeLuca,* 215 N.J.Super. 388, 521 A.2d 1343, 1347 (1987) (wanton, reckless or malice; conscious wrongdoing); *but see Cripe v. Leiter,* 291 Ill.App.3d 155, 225 Ill.Dec. 348, 683 N.E.2d 516 (1997) (discussing statute which precluded punitive damages for attorney malpractice).

record also supports an inference that [the attorney] attempted to cover up his misconduct."). In sum, the harm resulting from the original wrongdoing, as in the present case, may be exacerbated by intentional, fraudulent, malicious, or reckless efforts that prevent the plaintiff from taking immediate corrective action.

CONCLUSION

We have concluded that the Court of Appeals erred in reversing the jury's verdict awarding punitive damages. There was clear and convincing evidence of intentional, fraudulent, malicious, or reckless conduct on the part of Waters, and there is no requirement that attempts to conceal be contemporaneous with the original wrongdoing.

The judgment of the Court of Appeals is therefore reversed in part and the jury's verdict as to punitive damages is reinstated. The case is remanded to the trial court for a new trial solely on the issue of compensatory damages....

* * *

1. In *Rizzo v. Haines* (in a section of the court's opinion edited out of the excerpt of the case appearing in Chapter 4, *supra*) on the issue of punitive damages, the court explained:

> [Attorney] Haines ... argues that the trial court erred by imposing $150,000 in punitive damages. This Court ... permits punitive damages for conduct that is "outrageous because of the defendant's evil motives or his reckless indifference to the rights of others." Restatement (Second) of Torts § 908(2) (1977). A court may award punitive damages only if the conduct was malicious, wanton, reckless, willful, or oppressive.... The proper focus is on "the act itself together with all the circumstances including the motive of the wrongdoer and the relations between the parties...." In addition, the actor's state of mind is relevant. The act or omission must be intentional, reckless, or malicious.
>
> Based on this standard, we believe that the trial court acted properly in awarding the [legal malpractice plaintiffs] Rizzos $150,000 in punitive damages. [Attorney] Haines used his confidential position to persuade his injured client ... that he should transfer to him the $50,000 that Judge Marshall had awarded him due to Haines' misconduct. Haines secured this transfer after intentionally withholding Judge Marshall's findings of misconduct, in order to evade her ruling. He also secured this transfer by telling his client that he needed the money to pursue a claim against the doctor and the hospital. That claim, however, proved meritless.... [Attorney's conduct was] more than sufficient to justify the punitive damage award.

Rizzo v. Haines, 555 A.2d 58 (Pa. 1989).

2. In Section A, *supra*, the court in *Ferguson v. Lieff, Cabraser, Heimann & Bernstein* considered whether punitive damages were recoverable as a component of a legal malpractice plaintiff's *compensatory* damage award. The court in *Metcalfe v. Waters* and the materials following it above consider the issue of recovering of punitive damages as an award separate and distinct from compensatory damages. Do you understand the distinction between the two? Explain your understanding.

Chapter 7

Professional Malpractice: Defenses

Exercise 7.1: Chapter Problem

Husband, Wife, and Business Partner each held 500 shares of stock in Company. Ten years ago, Attorney was retained to prepare and review a new Company shareholder agreement because Wife had decided to give up her stock in Company. Husband's belief was that as a result of the new shareholder agreement, Company's by-laws gave Husband the right to acquire all of Wife's shares and with those shares, Husband would have a controlling two-thirds interest in Company. Because Husband did not follow his stock ownership reports carefully, Husband was unaware that the shareholder agreement actually caused 2.5 of Wife's shares to be transferred to Business Partner instead.

Husband's belief was that by Attorney reviewing and preparing the shareholder agreement, Attorney was representing Husband's and the company's interests, which he believed to be in alignment. After Wife gave up her stock in Company, Husband operated the company for nearly 10 years under the revised shareholder agreement, generating profit. However, eventually a dispute within Company arose, and Business Partner informed Husband that the changes to the shareholder agreement 10 years earlier had in fact provided Business Partner with 2.5 shares from Wife, thereby preventing Husband from exercising full control of Company. Business Partner then sued Husband for control of Company, basing his lawsuit on the fact that Business Partner had veto power over Husband's decisions about Company because of the 2.5 share transfer of Wife's shares. Husband was placed in the untenable position of having to settle that litigation brought by Business Partner, which resulted in a significant legal and reputational injury to Husband.

Husband wishes to sue Attorney for legal malpractice, as he has recently learned that Attorney had a prior attorney-client relationship with Business Partner previous to being retained to work on the shareholder agreement, a fact that was not disclosed to Husband at the time of the representation. Husband also believes that Attorney was negligent toward Husband in not fully explaining the significance of Wife's sale of stock pursuant to the new shareholder agreement that Attorney had reviewed and drafted.

This jurisdiction has adopted a pure comparative fault scheme for negligence actions, and the statute of limitation governing negligence actions is two years.

Husband is now consulting you, a practicing attorney, seeking your professional advice regarding the viability of a legal malpractice action against Attorney. Please prepare talking points for your upcoming office meeting with Husband.

Because a legal malpractice action is a type of negligence claim, a legal malpractice defendant may avail himself of the typical defenses available to negligence actions. You may recall from your introductory torts course that traditional defenses to negligence actions include assertions based on the plaintiff's conduct, such as contributory negligence, comparative negligence (sometimes termed comparative fault), and assumption of the risk. Remember that most jurisdictions today have eliminated the traditional contributory negligence defense to negligence actions, which operated as a complete bar to a plaintiff's recovery if the plaintiff's conduct contributed at all to his complained of injuries. In the many jurisdictions that have eliminated contributory negligence as a defense, comparative negligence or comparative fault schemes have replaced that defense. Although they vary from jurisdiction to jurisdiction, comparative fault schemes may reduce a plaintiff's recovery or may eliminate his recovery all together, depending on the facts of the case and the particular scheme in place. The materials that follow provide an overview of some of the schemes in place and how they may be at play in the legal malpractice context, beginning with a jurisdiction (Virginia) which still recognizes contributory negligence as a defense to negligence.

A. Plaintiff's Conduct

Focus Question: *Lyle, Siegel, Croshaw & Beale, P.C. v. Tidewater Capital Corp.*

Is a legal malpractice plaintiff's contributory negligence a bar to recovery in Virginia?

Lyle, Siegel, Croshaw & Beale, P.C. v. Tidewater Capital Corp.

249 Va. 426
(1995)

STEPHENSON, Justice.

In this appeal, we determine whether the trial court erred in (1) ruling, as a matter of law, that the plaintiff was not guilty of contributory negligence; (2) striking the defendant's evidence and entering summary judgment in favor of the plaintiff; (3) striking the defendant's expert testimony; (4) refusing to strike the plaintiff's evidence; and (5) making certain discovery and other evidentiary rulings.

I

Tidewater Capital Corporation (Tidewater) sued the law firm of Lyle, Siegel, Croshaw & Beale, P.C. and its successor in interest, Croshaw, Siegel, Beale, Hauser & Lewis, P.C.

(the Firm), for malpractice. At a jury trial, at the conclusion of the Firm's evidence, the trial court struck the Firm's evidence, entered summary judgment in favor of Tidewater, and fixed damages at $2.4 million. The Firm appeals.

II

Tidewater is a real estate investment company of which Lawrence R. Siegel was president, a director, and 50% shareholder. Siegel also was a partner in the Firm.

Galaxy-Wide Products, Inc. (Galaxy) is in the business of purchasing consumer contracts from companies engaged in door-to-door sales of products (primarily encyclopedias). After purchasing the contracts, Galaxy delivers the products and collects the installment payments.

In late 1988 and early 1989, Galaxy was seeking a loan to fund its purchase of contracts. During that time, Joseph B. Ketaner, Galaxy's chief executive officer, asked Siegel for assistance in locating a lender. Unable to find any other lenders, Siegel approached his fellow Tidewater directors and obtained authority to enter into loan negotiations with Galaxy.

In April 1989, Siegel drafted a proposed "term sheet" outlining the basic provisions of the loan. Tidewater's board of directors approved these terms, and Ketaner, for Galaxy, agreed to them. Thereafter, between May 1, 1989, and August 23, 1989, Tidewater disbursed to Galaxy a total of $2.5 million, consisting of 16 separate draws. The loan was secured by all of Galaxy's assets; however, the principal collateral consisted of Galaxy's consumer contracts.

Siegel instructed Laurie L. Dawson, a first-year associate attorney in the Firm, to draft the requisite loan documents and to ensure that Tidewater perfected a security interest in all of Galaxy's assets. Siegel requested two of his law partners, David N. Reda and Wayne G. Souza, to assist him in supervising Dawson's work. Reda and Dawson testified, however, that Siegel was in charge of the loan transaction and was responsible for reviewing all loan documents and for approving any substantive changes to them. Indeed, Siegel was both the "lead attorney" and the authorized representative of Tidewater in the transaction.

Prior to May 1, 1989, Siegel had reviewed copies of some of Galaxy's contracts that were "supposedly representative" of Tidewater's collateral. From this review, Siegel had concluded that the contracts were "accounts receivable." Thus, based on Siegel's conclusion and his instructions to other lawyers in the Firm, the lawyers, *i.e.*, Dawson, Reda, and Souza, all understood that Tidewater held a security interest in Galaxy's accounts receivable.

Thereupon, Dawson took the necessary steps to perfect Tidewater's security interest in all of Galaxy's assets, including accounts receivable. She drafted the May 1, 1989 security agreement that accompanied the initial loan documents. Siegel reviewed and signed the security agreement as "President of Tidewater Capital Corporation." Dawson then filed the necessary financing statements with the State Corporation Commission and with the Circuit Court of the City of Virginia Beach. Code § 8.9-401. The Firm, however, never required Tidewater to take possession of any of the collateral.

On May 12, 1989, Siegel sent a memorandum to Stephen B. Sandler, a fellow Tidewater director, recommending that Galaxy sell $500,000 of its contracts to "Household Finance Corp. and/or Beneficial Finance Corp." at "approximately 88–90¢ per dollar." This, Siegel estimated, would generate about $440,000 for Galaxy's benefit.

Shortly thereafter, Siegel reviewed and signed in his capacity as Tidewater's president a security agreement dated May 17, 1989. Unlike the May 1, 1989 security agreement, the May 17 agreement allowed Galaxy to sell the loan collateral "in the normal course of business" and gave Tidewater a security interest in all "proceeds" from the sales of "accounts receivable." Siegel testified that he did not know how or why this change was made in the May 17 security agreement. Dawson and Reda also did not know how the change was made, and Souza also offered no explanation therefor. Dawson testified, however, that she would not have added the language "except upon the direction of [Siegel]," and Reda testified that Siegel always reviewed all documents and made changes in documents "all the time, even right up to closing."

A third security agreement was executed on July 27, 1989. It also allowed Galaxy to sell the collateral "in the normal course of business."

On July 21, 1989, Galaxy began selling its contracts to Beneficial Finance Corporation (Beneficial). In late August, David S. Rudiger, a member of the Firm, told Siegel that Tidewater needed to obtain physical possession of the contracts in case their characterization as accounts was incorrect and Galaxy tried to sell them or filed for bankruptcy. Tidewater, however, took no action at that time.

On September 1, 1989, after all the funds had been disbursed, Tidewater and the Firm learned that Galaxy had sold some of its contracts to Beneficial, free of Tidewater's lien. On September 27, 1989, Tidewater declared Galaxy in default on the loan, and the Firm recommended that Tidewater file a detinue action to obtain possession of the collateral. Tidewater did obtain possession, but was required to post a $10 million bond. Faced with having $10 million of its cash tied up and possibly with a determination in Galaxy's threatened bankruptcy proceeding that it was unsecured, Tidewater settled with Galaxy in December 1989. By this time, Galaxy had sold collateral for approximately $1.1 million.

Tidewater then looked to the Firm to indemnify it against any losses it would incur. When it became apparent that the Firm was not willing to do so, Tidewater instituted the present action.

On March 13, 1989, Siegel, as Tidewater's lawyer, began recording his time in negotiating and structuring the business transaction between Tidewater and Galaxy. The fees charged by the Firm in connection with the transaction totalled $123,000. The Firm had been Tidewater's exclusive legal counsel from the time Tidewater was incorporated through the business transaction that is the subject of this litigation.

III

The Firm contends that Tidewater's malpractice action is barred by its contributory negligence. The Firm asserts that, when Siegel engaged in loan negotiations, reviewed the loan collateral, and signed various documents as Tidewater's president, Siegel "acquired critical knowledge about Galaxy and the loan transaction during the scope of [his] agency with Tidewater" and that Siegel's actions are imputed to Tidewater. The Firm further asserts that Siegel, in his capacity as president and director of Tidewater, formulated the proposed loan structure and negotiated the terms of the loan "in an effort to forge a favorable business transaction acceptable to his corporation."

The trial court, in rejecting the Firm's contributory negligence defense, ruled that Siegel's actions and knowledge were not imputed to Tidewater. The court reasoned that "all of [Siegel's] actions in drafting legal papers, construing legal papers, giving legal advice, was as Siegel the lawyer, and not as Siegel the lender."

A

Initially, we must decide whether the defense of contributory negligence is available in a legal malpractice action, an issue we previously have not addressed. We have recognized, however, that, in certain circumstances, contributory negligence may be a defense in a medical malpractice action. *See Eiss v. Lillis,* 233 Va. 545, 552–53, 357 S.E.2d 539, 543–44 (1987); *Lawrence v. Wirth,* 226 Va. 408, 412–13, 309 S.E.2d 315, 317–18 (1983).

In contending that contributory negligence is not available as a defense in a legal malpractice action, Tidewater relies mainly upon *Oleyar v. Kerr,* 217 Va. 88, 225 S.E.2d 398 (1976). In that case, we held that the statute of limitations applicable to contracts governed legal malpractice actions. *Id.* at 90, 225 S.E.2d at 400. We did not, however, consider whether contributory negligence was available as a defense.

Clearly, as *Oleyar* teaches, the attorney-client relationship is formed by a contract. Nonetheless, the duty upon the attorney to exercise reasonable care, skill, and diligence on behalf of the client arises out of the relationship of the parties, irrespective of a contract, and the attorney's breach of that duty, *i.e.,* the appropriate standard of care, constitutes negligence.

With respect to contributory negligence, we discern no logical reason for treating differently legal malpractice and medical malpractice actions. Both are negligence claims, and actions against attorneys for negligence are governed by the same principles applicable to other negligence actions. *See Allied Productions v. Duesterdick,* 217 Va. 763, 765, 232 S.E.2d 774, 775 (1977). Therefore, we hold that contributory negligence is available as a defense in a legal malpractice action.

B

Next, we consider whether Siegel's knowledge and actions may be imputed to Tidewater. It is undisputed that Siegel acted in a dual role. He was a partner in the Firm, and he was president, a director, and 50% shareholder of Tidewater. Clearly, a jury issue was presented whether Siegel acted solely in his capacity as lawyer and whether his knowledge and actions may be imputed to Tidewater. Thus, the trial court erred in ruling otherwise.

We think, therefore, that, considering all the evidence and reasonable inferences deducible therefrom, a jury issue was presented whether Tidewater's claim is barred by contributory negligence.

....

Affirmed in part, reversed in part, and remanded.

* * *

1. Comparative Fault and Legal Malpractice. In *Andrews v. Saylor,* 80 P.3d 482 (N.M. Ct. App. 2003), the plaintiff argued for an exception to the doctrine of pure comparative fault in that jurisdiction in the context of legal malpractice. In a *pure comparative fault* jurisdiction, a plaintiff's negligence is not a complete bar to recovery, but rather just operates to reduce the amount of the plaintiff's recovery by the amount of fault attributable to the plaintiff. The court explained:

> Plaintiff argues that the question of whether an attorney sued for legal malpractice may base the defense of comparative fault on the alleged malpractice of successor attorneys presents a question of "general public interest." Rule 12-216(B)(1) NMRA 2003. We agree, and therefore address this question.
>
> "More is involved in pure comparative negligence than the removal of contributory negligence as a bar to recovery." *Bartlett v. N.M. Welding Supply, Inc.,* 98 N.M. 152, 155, 646 P.2d 579, 582 (Ct.App.1982). Our system of pure comparative negligence is based on fairness to both plaintiffs *and defendants. Id.* We must apply several liability/comparative fault principles unless their application

would be inconsistent with public policy. *Reichert v. Atler,* 117 N.M. 623, 625, 875 P.2d 379, 381 (1994).

[W]e think that it is possible to protect the rights of plaintiff-former clients without depriving defendant-attorneys of the defense of comparative fault. *See Parler & Wobber v. Miles & Stockbridge, P.C.,* 359 Md. 671, 756 A.2d 526 (2000) (allowing original counsel to assert a contribution claim against allegedly negligent successor counsel; rejecting the argument that by suing former counsel for malpractice, the client puts the negligence of successor counsel at issue, thereby impliedly waiving the attorney-client privilege as to communications between the client and successor counsel). We therefore reject Plaintiff's request that we recognize a legal malpractice exception to the doctrine of comparative fault.

2. Statutes of Limitation. A statute of limitation is a defined period of time during which a plaintiff's claim must be filed or it is forever barred. As a statute of limitation may bar a plaintiff from recovering from a defendant, it is a defense to a legal malpractice action. Note that in *Lyle, Siegel,* the court mentioned that it had previously held that a legal malpractice action was governed by the statute of limitation dictating the time by which a contract action must be filed, which is typically a longer period of time than the limitations period is for a negligence action. However, the court concluded in *Lyle, Siegel* that contributory negligence (a defense to a negligence action, not a contract action) was available. Can these two declarations be reconciled?

Focus Questions: *Behrens v. Wedmore*

1. *What is contributory negligence? What is assumption of the risk? How are these two doctrines related?*
2. *What conduct was the defendant attorney asserting constituted contributory negligence in* Behrens?
3. *What conduct was the defendant attorney asserting amounted to assumption of the risk in* Behrens?
4. *According to the court, are either or both contributory negligence or assumption of the risk defenses to a legal malpractice action?*

Behrens v. Wedmore

698 N.W.2d 555
(S.D. 2005)

ZINTER, Justice.

Jon and Don Behrens (jointly referred to as Behrens) owned and operated a funeral home in Rapid City. Without the assistance of legal counsel, they negotiated an agreement to sell their business to Loewen International, Inc. After signing the agreement, Behrens engaged Melvin Wedmore, their long-time attorney, to close the transaction with Loewen. Some time after the transaction was closed, Loewen filed for bankruptcy protection and Behrens were unable to recover the full purchase price they had negotiated. Not satisfied with the outcome of the bankruptcy, Behrens filed this malpractice action against Wedmore. They contended that Wedmore should have better collateralized the transaction, should have advised them of the risks of an installment sale in bankruptcy, and that he charged an unreasonable attorney fee. A jury found for Wedmore on all issues. We affirm.

Facts and Procedural History

Behrens Mortuary was founded in 1879 by Behrens' great-grandfather. It was the second largest funeral home in South Dakota at the time of its sale to Loewen International, Inc. in 1997. Jon and Don began working in this family business in 1970 and 1983, respectively. They enhanced the business in many ways. Despite the success of the business, Behrens believed that they would have to sell it at some time because the next generation of their family was not interested in operating the business.

Robert Eastgate, a regional manager for Loewen, contacted Jon in the mid 1990's about buying the business. Jon told Eastgate that they were not interested in selling. Service Corp. International (SCI), Loewen's competitor, also contacted Behrens about buying the business. Behrens again indicated that they were not interested in selling.

Loewen continued to pursue the purchase by making a $2 million offer. The terms of this offer included a $1 million cash down payment, with the balance financed by Behrens on a ten-year, interest-free note. After Behrens rejected the offer, Loewen made another offer, this time in the amount of $4.1 million. Behrens responded with a counteroffer. The terms of the counteroffer included a $2.55 million cash down payment and an additional $2 million to be financed by Behrens on an interest-free note payable in ten equal payments.

Loewen was eager to acquire Behrens Mortuary because it was fighting a takeover bid from SCI and wanted a presence in the Rapid City market. Consequently, Loewen wrote a letter to Behrens containing the following alternate offers:

1. $4,100,000, which included the entire business, as well as the mortuary property and the retort (crematory) property; or
2. $3,400,000, (with $2,400,000 cash at closing) with a lease of the retort property.

Because the funeral home (mortuary property) was owned by Jon's and Don's fathers, these offers indicated that the mortuary property was included in the purchase price. The offer further indicated that Jon and Don were to determine how to allocate the total purchase price to that part of the business.

On March 25, 1997, Behrens responded with a counteroffer informing Loewen that its proposal to purchase the complete package was acceptable with the following changes in price and financing:

1. $2,550,000 cash at closing [$500,000 of this to be allocated to the purchase of the building from Behrens' fathers];
2. 10 equal annual payments of $200,000 commencing on the first anniversary of the Closing Date. (Unsecured promissory note to be defined.)

On April 16, 1997, Behrens and Loewen met and executed a writing that incorporated the terms of Behrens' March 25, 1997 counteroffer. Although the document included a provision noting that it was an offer open for acceptance until 5:00 p.m. on April 17, 1997, Behrens signed it the same day, April 16, 1997. By its terms, the writing provided that Behrens agreed to sell the entire business (including the mortuary property owned by their fathers and the crematory owned by Don and Jon) for $4.55 million. $2.55 million was to be paid on closing, and the $2 million balance was to be financed by Behrens on a no-interest, unsecured promissory note. The agreement further provided that closing would occur within ninety days. Loewen also had the right to execute a more detailed purchase agreement that included ancillary documents necessary to transfer all of the business assets.

A central issue in this litigation involved the legal characterization of this written agreement. Behrens contended that it was only a non-binding letter of intent. Therefore, Behrens argued that Wedmore was required to use his legal expertise to change the terms and better collateralize the sale in the event of a bankruptcy. On the other hand, Wedmore contended that it was a binding contract, and that the financing terms, including the $2 million unsecured note, could not have been renegotiated without losing the entire sale. For ease of reference, we refer to this writing as the "Initial Agreement."

Two days after signing the Initial Agreement, Behrens first consulted Wedmore about legal representation. According to Jon, they took the Initial Agreement to Wedmore and told him: that they were going to sell Behrens Mortuary; that there would be more information forthcoming; that "if you want to make any changes or anything you want to do to [the Initial] agreement, contact [Loewens][sic]"; and, that the "deal" was scheduled to close by June 30, 1997. However, according to Wedmore, he was only to close the transaction based on the Initial Agreement. Therefore, Wedmore contended that he was to review the closing documents and update the corporate records. Wedmore specifically contended that he was not hired to renegotiate the Initial Agreement or to change its terms, including the provision that called for the unsecured promissory note.

Negotiations to close the transaction continued over two months. Changes were made even after the July 15, 1997 stated expiration date of the Initial Agreement. During these negotiations, Wedmore contends that he unsuccessfully asked for additional security (including a guarantee, stock pledge, security interest, and letter of credit). He was successful in obtaining a $500,000 contract for deed for the mortuary. Wedmore also drafted a mortgage and promissory note that included interest. Together, these secured transactions reduced the $2 million unsecured indebtedness called for in the Initial Agreement by approximately $1 million. Wedmore also included bankruptcy-default and cross-default provisions in the contract for deed, promissory note, and mortgage. These provisions were intended to tie the assets together in order to prevent Loewen from defaulting on one, but not all of the assets sold. There was not, however, any cross-collateralization of the contract for deed and the promissory note.

The transaction finally closed on July 24, 1997. Sometime after closing, Loewen filed for bankruptcy. The evidence reflects that, as a result of Wedmore's involvement, Behrens were better protected in the bankruptcy than they would have been had they only held the $2 million unsecured note described in the Initial Agreement. However, they were oversecured on the contract for deed and unsecured on the promissory note. Furthermore, the cross-default provisions (purportedly triggered by bankruptcy) and the foreclosure provisions were not fully enforceable in bankruptcy. Consequently, Behrens were unable to get their business back. Furthermore, because the indebtedness was not cross-collateralized, they were unable to use excess equity in the mortuary building (subject to the contract for deed) to secure the promissory note.

Behrens alleged that as a result of these problems, they incurred a $462,890 loss in the bankruptcy. They were also required to spend $14,579 in bankruptcy attorney fees. Behrens claimed that if Wedmore had better collateralized the promissory note, they would have been paid in full or they would have gotten their business back. Although Wedmore's efforts resulted in Behrens being better positioned than most other creditors in the Loewen bankruptcy, Behrens contended that Wedmore committed malpractice. Behrens specifically alleged that Wedmore was negligent in negotiating and preparing the transactional documents and in failing to warn them of the potential risks of an installment sale in bankruptcy.

On the other hand, Wedmore's experts testified that Wedmore could not have better collateralized the transaction because the Initial Agreement was legally enforceable and it finalized the terms of the sale, which included the $2 million unsecured note. Under Wedmore's theory, his ability to negotiate for additional security was limited because the Initial Agreement was binding and further security demands risked a loss of the entire sale. He further contended that he did make additional efforts to obtain more security, but those efforts were rejected by Loewen. Wedmore finally contended that Behrens ultimately received approximately $4,088,286 after bankruptcy, which was substantially more than they could have received under the Initial Agreement that they had negotiated on their own.

....

On appeal, Behrens raise the following issues:

...

2. Whether the trial court improperly instructed the jury on contributory negligence and assumption of the risk;

...

Analysis and Decision

....

2. Whether the trial court improperly instructed the jury on contributory negligence and assumption of the risk.

Wedmore argued that Behrens were contributorily negligent and assumed the risk by entering into the Initial Agreement without obtaining legal advice. Wedmore introduced expert testimony that the terms of the Initial Agreement were binding and prevented him from negotiating terms that would better collateralize the note. Therefore, over Behrens' objection, the trial court instructed the jury that contributory negligence and assumption of the risk were defenses to Behrens' malpractice claim.[8]

....

8. Instruction 39:

Plaintiffs cannot recover damages if they were contributorily negligent and their contributory negligence was a proximate cause of their damage except as provided in the next instruction.

Instruction 40:

If you find Plaintiffs were contributorily negligent, they may still recover damages for their damage if you find that their contributory negligence was slight compared with the negligence of MELVIN WEDMORE.

If you find Plaintiffs' contributory negligence was more than slight compared with the negligence of MELVIN WEDMORE, they cannot recover.

"Slight" means whether Plaintiffs' negligence was small in comparison with the negligence of MELVIN WEDMORE.

If you find Plaintiffs' contributory negligence was slight and that they are still entitled to

a. Contributory Negligence

Behrens assert that the contributory negligence instructions were improper because their negligence, if any, in negotiating the Initial Agreement was made before Wedmore was hired. Behrens argue that "if a professional accepts a duty to serve a client, the professional is [thereafter] liable for negligence in the performance of that duty regardless of how or why the client got involved in the matter in which the professional was retained." We generally agree.

As the Utah Supreme Court noted:

> [A] preexisting condition that a professional is called upon to resolve cannot be the cause, either proximate or direct, of the professional's failure to exercise an appropriate standard of care in fulfilling his duties. To decide otherwise would allow professionals to avoid responsibility for the very duties they undertake to perform. A doctor, for example, might be able to avoid liability for negligently treating an injured person because the patient negligently had run a traffic light and was injured. Such a result would be clearly unsound.

Steiner Corp. v. Johnson & Higgins of California, 996 P.2d 531, 533 (Utah 2000) (internal citation omitted). Thus, if a professional accepts a duty to serve a client, the professional is generally liable for negligence in the performance of that duty regardless of how or why the client became involved in the matter for which the professional was retained.

This, of course, is not to say that a professional is responsible for *the pre-existing condition* that was the proximate cause of the client's injury. The professional is not. *Staab v. Cameron,* 351 N.W.2d 463, 466 (S.D.1984) (stating that attorney is not responsible for a client's loss when client entered into a valid contract *before* seeking attorney representation). Thus, there is no liability where there was nothing that the attorney could have done to remedy the harm that was already and inexorably in place before the attorney agreed to represent the client. *Id.* In those circumstances, "the overwhelming majority [of courts] have recognized that a client's recovery for legal malpractice can be either entirely foreclosed, or proportionally diminished, as the result of his or her own negligence." *Gorski v. Smith,* 812 A.2d 683, 698 (Pa.Super.Ct.2002). *See also* Susan L. Thomas, J.D., Annotation, *Legal Malpractice: Negligence or Fault of Client as Defense,* 10 A.L.R.5th 828 (1993–2004) (noting in a legal malpractice claim the "usual defenses are applicable, including the defense that the client contributed to or was solely responsible for his or her own harm"); *Shaw v. State of Alaska, Dep't. of Admin.,* 861 P.2d 566 (Alaska 1993) (recognizing contributory negligence and assumption of the risk as traditional defenses to legal malpractice claim);

> recover, then the damages must be reduced in proportion to the amount of []their contributory negligence.

Instruction 41:

> DON BEHRENS & JON BEHRENS cannot recover damages if they assumed the risk by voluntarily placing themselves at risk or voluntarily continuing at risk when they knew the risk. MELVIN WEDMORE must show that DON BEHRENS & JON BEHRENS not only knew the specific risk and appreciated its character, but also that they voluntarily assumed the risk. MELVIN WEDMORE must also show that DON BEHRENS & JON BEHRENS had sufficient time, knowledge and experience to make an intelligent choice.

Instruction 42:

> There is a distinction between the defenses of assumption of risk and contributory negligence. Contributory negligence must be a proximate cause of the damage. Assumption of risk, however, bars recovery of damages although it did not cause the damage but merely exposed the person to damage. The same conduct may be both contributory negligence and assumption of the risk.

Western Fiberglass, Inc. v. Kirton, McConkie and Bushnell, 789 P.2d 34, 36 (Utah Ct.App.1990) (affirming judgment that plaintiff was equally negligent in action against a law firm because plaintiff failed to keep the law firm fully informed and failed to be represented by counsel at closing of a transaction).

Moreover, in this case, the trial court modified the general contributory negligence instructions to ensure that, to the extent the Initial Agreement was not the proximate cause of Behrens' loss, the jury would not apply Behrens' contributory negligence to Wedmore's post-Initial Agreement representation. The trial court did so by specifically instructing the jury that:

Instruction 44a:

> A client who retains an attorney to perform legal services has a justifiable expectation that the attorney will exhibit reasonable care in the performance of those services. The client is under no duty to guard against the failure of the attorney to exercise the reasonable standard of professional care in the performance of the legal services for which the attorney was retained. A client cannot be found contributorily negligent for failing to anticipate or guard against his attorney's negligence in the performance of legal services within the scope of the attorney's representation of the client.

Thus, the jury was specifically instructed that Behrens could expect to receive reasonable care, that they were "under no duty to guard against" any negligence of Wedmore for the services for which he was retained, and that Behrens could not be contributorily negligent by failing to anticipate or guard against Wedmore's negligence that was within the scope of his post-Initial Agreement representation.

We finally observe that the modified contributory negligence instructions were supported by the evidence. A number of Wedmore's expert witnesses testified that because of the terms of the Initial Agreement, an attorney exercising due care could not have obtained a more favorable result in the bankruptcy. Wedmore's experts first opined that if a client came in and stated that they had made a "deal" for the sale of their business, had signed an agreement, and it looked like the Initial Agreement in this case, the standard of care was that an attorney would conduct himself as if they had made a binding agreement. Another expert opined that "having no evidence that the clients were telling me to get out of this agreement," he would treat the agreement as a starting point, i.e., what the client wanted, and he would try to get it closed. Another expert indicated that Behrens had negotiated their best deal before they came to see Wedmore, and as such, the next step for a transaction lawyer was to get the deal closed.

With respect to getting additional collateral or security in anticipation of bankruptcy, Wedmore introduced expert testimony that an attorney's duty to get more security was dependent upon when that attorney came into the transaction. In this case, there was evidence that because the Initial Agreement indicated that the storage facility and the mortuary were to be delivered free and clear of any liens or encumbrances, Wedmore went "out on a limb" to even ask for additional security for his clients. Another expert indicated that because Behrens did not come to Wedmore early on to ask how to negotiate this sale, there were "a lot of things they didn't do that precluded [Wedmore] from having the opportunity to look at a lot of things." Finally, with respect to the proximate cause of Behrens' loss, one expert, who has practiced bankruptcy law since 1978, opined that Behrens were actually paid more in the bankruptcy than the value of their collateral, and therefore, even if there had been a stacking of mortgages, Behrens' recovery in bankruptcy would not have changed.

Thus, there was evidence that Behrens' conduct in negotiating the Initial Agreement without professional assistance was the sole proximate cause of their loss. Considering this expert testimony, the jury could have found that the Initial Agreement was binding, that it proximately caused Behrens' damages, and that nothing Wedmore did in his subsequent representation contributed to Behrens' loss. Under these circumstances, the trial court did not err in giving its contributory negligence instructions.

b. Assumption of the Risk

In order to assume the risk of one's own loss, a person must know that the danger exists, appreciate the character of the danger, and "voluntarily accept such risk by having a sufficient amount of time, knowledge, and experience to make an intelligent choice." Behrens contend that they could not have assumed the risk because they knew nothing about bankruptcy.

This contention requires us to consider whether Behrens could have been charged with knowledge of the risk by negotiating the Initial Agreement without the assistance of counsel. On that issue, we observe that Wedmore's expert testimony indicated that experienced business people should know that when one makes a loan there is a risk of nonpayment. Here, by the terms of the Initial Agreement, Behrens clearly agreed to assume the risk of a $2 million unsecured loan. Even after the security Wedmore obtained, Behrens remained saddled with an approximate $1.5 million note secured by a mortgage on property worth only $425,000. Consequently, according to one expert, Behrens "had to know that they weren't fully protected because they've got ... a note secured by an asset worth" substantially less than the value of the note. Considering all of the evidence, Behrens must be charged with the knowledge that by negotiating a $2 million *unsecured* loan, they incurred a risk of not being repaid in full.

We, therefore, agree that there was sufficient evidence to charge these businessmen with having voluntarily assumed the risk of agreeing to a $2 million unsecured note. Because there was sufficient evidence for Behrens to be charged with knowledge of the risk of making an unsecured loan, the trial court did not err in giving an assumption of the risk instruction.

....

Affirmed.

* * *

1. Plaintiff's Failure to Mitigate Damages. In *Carbone v. Tierney*, 151 N.H. 521 (2004), the court explained that in a legal malpractice action, a plaintiff's failure to mitigate damages is a partial defense, to be established by the defendant in order to reduce the damage award against him or her: "It is settled law that a party seeking damages occasioned by the fault of another must take all reasonable steps to lessen the resultant loss. The defendant bears the burden of proving that the plaintiff failed to mitigate damages."

2. Plaintiff's Intentional Conduct as a Bar to Recovery for Legal Malpractice. What about a plaintiff's *intentional* conduct? What policy considerations are at stake in courts' recognition of (or refusal to recognize) defenses to legal malpractice actions based on the plaintiffs' conduct? Consider *State v. Therrien*, 830 A.2d 28 (Vt. 2003), in which the court explained:

> Although an attorney whose negligence was not the sole proximate cause of the injury may be shielded from liability by the doctrine of *in pari delicto*, see *McKinley v. Weidner*, 73 Or.App. 396, 698 P.2d 983, 985–86 (1985) (applying in pari delicto doctrine to legal malpractice claim); *Gen. Car & Truck Leasing Sys., Inc. v. Lane & Waterman*, 557 N.W.2d 274, 279, 283 (Iowa 1996) (same), a client's own intentional wrongful conduct does not automatically shield the attorney from all

> liability. See *Heyman*, 1999 OK CIV APP 132, at ¶7, 994 P.2d 92 (Stubblefield, J., concurring) ("[A] plaintiff's fraud alone would [not], as a matter of law, relieve a defendant of potential liability for professional negligence, unless, without factual dispute, the fraud was the sole cause of a plaintiff's damages."); 3 R. Mallen & J. Smith, Legal Malpractice §21.4, at 191 (5th ed. 2000) ("When [the client's] motives involve intentional misconduct by the client, which was *a* cause of the loss, a complete defense *may* be available to the attorney.") (emphasis added). The *in pari delicto* doctrine serves as a bar against a defendant's liability only where "the plaintiff has been guilty of illegal or fraudulent conduct ... [and] was equally or more culpable than the defendant or acted with the same or greater knowledge as to the illegality or wrongfulness of the transaction." *Lane & Waterman,* 557 N.W.2d at 279 (internal citations omitted). Thus, the issue of an attorney's liability cannot be resolved without examining the actions of both the attorney and the client.

State v. Therrien, 830 A.2d 28, 36 (Vt. 2003).

Focus Questions: *Jackson State Bank v. King*

1. *Is a legal malpractice action a negligence action in Wyoming?*
2. *Does the comparative fault statute in Wyoming provide a defense to legal malpractice actions in this jurisdiction?*
3. *Why does the concurring justice write separately?*
4. *What is the basis of the dissenting justice's disagreement with the majority of the court?*
5. *Which of the various opinions do you find to be most doctrinally sound? Be able to defend your position.*

Jackson State Bank v. King

844 P.2d 1093
(Wyo. 1993)

THOMAS, Justice.

The questions in this case are certified to this court by the United States Court of Appeals for the Tenth Circuit....

The questions certified by the federal court are:

> A. Does Wyoming's comparative negligence statute, Wyo. Stat. §1-1-109(a) (1977), bar plaintiff's recovery in a legal malpractice action based on claims for breach of contract and breach of fiduciary duty when the jury apportions fault in the following manner: plaintiff, thirty-five percent; defendant, thirty-five percent; and a third party, thirty percent?
>
> B. If the comparative negligence statute does not bar recovery on these claims, does it or some other principle of Wyoming law require that plaintiff's recovery be reduced by his percentage of fault?

We answer both of the certified questions in the negative.

On February 26, 1973, Rosemary Miles died, and her husband, Maurice Miles (Miles), and her son from a previous marriage, William Hutson, and his family (Hutsons) survived her. Her will divided her estate into two parts. One part, equivalent to the maximum marital deduction, was left directly to Miles. The other portion was left in a testamentary trust for the benefit of the Hutsons. Her will also provided that Miles should be appointed as the executor of her estate. Floyd R. King (King) was retained by Miles to represent him in accomplishing his duties as executor of the estate.

In April of 1979, the probate court entered an order approving the accounting and a decree of distribution in Rosemary Miles' estate, and the estate was closed in October, 1979. In July of 1986, the Hutsons brought an action against Miles in the federal district court asserting breach of his fiduciary duties as executor of the estate. Miles then filed a third-party complaint against King, alleging legal malpractice in connection with King's representation of Miles as the executor of the Rosemary Miles estate and asserting claims based on theories of negligence, breach of contract, and breach of a fiduciary duty.

Miles entered into an agreement with the Hutsons, settling their claim against him, and pursued his malpractice action against King. The legal malpractice action was tried before a jury and, on June 30, 1989, following a five-day trial, the jury returned a verdict finding that Miles had suffered damages in the amount of $46,500 as the result of King's actions. In its verdict, the jury apportioned fault, defined as "negligence causing damage," for Miles' damages, as follows: Miles 35%; King 35%; and the Jackson State Bank, not a party to the action, 30%. The jury found that King, in his attorney-client relationship with Miles, had been negligent, had breached the fiduciary duty owed by an attorney to a client, and had breached his contract with Miles.

On August 17, 1989, the United States District Court for the District of Wyoming ruled that the assessment of comparative fault by the jury applied to all three of Miles' claims, and it denied recovery. Miles then took an appeal to the United States Court of Appeals for the Tenth Circuit asserting that there was error in this ruling by the United States District Court, and that is the thrust of the questions certified to this court. We disagree with the ruling of the United States District Court.

At the time this case arose, the comparative negligence statute in effect in Wyoming provided:

> Contributory negligence shall not bar a recovery in an action by any person or his legal representative to recover damages for negligence resulting in death or in injury to person or property, if the contributory negligence was not as great as the negligence of the person against whom recovery is sought. Any damages allowed shall be diminished in proportion to the amount of negligence attributed to the person recovering.

Wyo. Stat. § 1-1-109(a) (1977).

...

....

In *Phillips*[*v. Duro-Last Roofing, Inc.,* 806 P.2d 834, 837 (Wyo.1991)], we refused to extend our comparative negligence statute, beyond its intended and express application to negligence.... *Phillips,* of course, did not encompass an issue of legal malpractice but, nevertheless, we perceive the case as controlling. Both Miles and King agreed in the briefs they submitted to this court that *Phillips* is controlling, but they disagreed as to the result it directed.

King urges *Phillips* as controlling on the premise that even though, concededly, § 1-1-109 applies only to those cases involving negligence, Miles' claim in the trial court was founded in negligence, no matter how it might be characterized. This was the view adopted by the United States District Court, and King argues that decision manifested the correct application of § 1-1-109 to the case involved. Miles, on the other hand, distinguishes between a cause of action based on contract theories and a cause of action based on tort theories. Miles agrees *Phillips* stood for the proposition that § 1-1-109 reached only to those causes of action arising out of negligence. Miles argues, therefore, that the statute has no application to a legal malpractice action, which is a contractual claim based on the implied warranty that the work performed by an attorney for his client will be performed in a skillful and professional manner.

We agree with Miles that the cause of action in a legal malpractice claim is contractual in nature and that § 1-1-109 is not applicable based upon its clear and unambiguous language. We reach that result, however, upon a different analysis from that urged by Miles.

The relationship of attorney and client is contractual in nature. The contract may be an express contract, or it may be implied from the actions of the parties, such as, the furnishing of advice and assistance or even the awareness of the attorney of reliance on the relationship. The attorney-client relationship can be created by a retainer or an offer to retain or the payment of a fee. Even though legal malpractice may be attributable to negligence on the part of the attorney, still the right to recompense is based upon the breach of the contract with the client. It follows that, because this relationship is contractual in nature and is to be treated according to the law of contracts, there is no justification to invoke the comparative negligence statute.

In *Cline v. Sawyer,* 600 P.2d 725 (Wyo.1979), *appeal after remand,* 618 P.2d 144 (Wyo.1980), this court held the trial court was obligated to make special findings of fact in determining the amount of damages and the percentage of negligence attributable to each party under § 1-1-109(b).[1] ...

....

[T]he Wyoming Comparative Negligence Statute, as drafted by the legislature and interpreted by this court, is limited to those actions based on negligence only. Clearly, it should not be extended to actions based on contract. We, therefore, hold that § 1-1-109(a) does not bar recovery by a plaintiff in a legal malpractice action, which necessarily is based on claims for breach of contract and breach of fiduciary duty.

....

With respect to the claim of breach of a fiduciary duty, it has been held that the defense of contributory negligence is not available to what is an action in equity. *Federal Savings & Loan Insurance Corporation v. Huff,* 237 Kan. 873, 704 P.2d 372 (1985)....

We are in accord with Miles' position that the plain and unambiguous language of § 1-1-109(a) demonstrates that the statute applies only to those causes of action arising out

---

1. Wyo. Stat. § 1-1-109(b) (1977) provided, in pertinent part:

(b) The court may, and when requested by any party shall:

(i) If a jury trial, direct the jury to find separate special verdicts;

(ii) If a trial before the court without jury, make special findings of fact, determining the amount of damages and the percentage of negligence attributable to each party. The court shall then reduce the amount of such damages in proportion to the amount of negligence attributed to the person recovering;

(iii) Inform the jury of the consequences of its determination of the percentage of negligence.

of negligence. It does not extend to those that are based upon a theory of contract or a theory of breach of fiduciary duty. It follows that the statute does not serve as a bar to those claims by Miles, nor can it be invoked to reduce his recovery by any percentage of fault. We are not cognizant of, nor has anyone called to our attention, any other principle of Wyoming law that would require Miles to reduce his recovery by his percentage of fault as to his claims on contract theories.

In summary, we hold that Wyoming's comparative negligence statute, Wyo.Stat. § 1-1-109(a) (1977), does not bar plaintiff's recovery in a legal malpractice action based on claims for breach of contract and breach of fiduciary duty, even though the jury has apportioned fault in the following manner: plaintiff, 35%; defendant, 35%; and a third party, 30%. We further hold that neither the comparative negligence statute nor any other principle of Wyoming law requires that the plaintiff's recovery be reduced by his percentage of fault.

URBIGKIT, Justice, concurring in the result.

I concur in the result of this decision, but have a concern that the opinion is directed beyond the certified question and may be clearly wrong in the context of the extended discussion.

The question presented, by certification from the Tenth Circuit Court of Appeals, was clearly limited to a legal malpractice claim based on a contractual theory of liability. I find no justification to extend our discussion into questions of legal malpractice that might be based on negligent theories of actionable wrong.

Even worse, in my opinion, is the further mistake in opinion evaluation that legal malpractice proceedings *must* be contractual in nature. A review of the law demonstrates that either or both contract and tort theories have interchangeably been used by the client to pursue attempted recovery for the claimed wrong from his attorney. Even though I consider this portion of the decision pure dictum, I still find the possibility of confusion to be created for trial judges and the practicing bar.

The concept is stated in the standard authority, 2 Ronald E. Mallen & Jeffrey M. Smith, *Legal Malpractice*, § 27.4 (3rd ed. 1989), and similarly found in Irving J. Sloan, *Professional Malpractice* at 65 (1992), that "[c]ourts disagree on the underlying theory of the attorney malpractice action." ... 1 Mallen & Smith, *supra*, § 8.10 (footnote omitted) describe in their final conclusion:

> The most common form of a legal malpractice action is for negligence. The cause of action for legal malpractice involves the same basic elements as any ordinary negligence action: duty, negligent breach of duty, proximate cause and damage. Yet, one court, emphasizing the contractual nature of the attorney-client relationship, stated that a legal malpractice action is not an action in tort. That, however, is not the rule.

A valuable text, Duke Nordlinger Stern & Jo Ann Felix-Retzke, *A Practical Guide to Preventing Legal Malpractice*, § 1.01 (1983) (emphasis in original), delineates the definitional confusion:

> Defining *legal malpractice* can be an exercise in frustration. The many courts that have addressed the question are prone to add their personalized verbiage to what has become many definitions. Some sound in tort while others are framed in terms of express or implied contract. Still others tend to combine both theories, and some courts have said that neither approach is correct. Yet, by whatever definition, legal malpractice is increasing in frequency of occurrences and severity of loss payments.

> The more practical approach is to analyze attorney malpractice not in terms of theoretical definitions, but rather by the multitude of claims that have been made against members of the legal profession. The substantial majority of claims are never tried, and of those that are, even fewer are appealed. The body of case law pales by comparison to the body of *claim law.* Even the significant percentage of claims which result in no indemnity payments still can result in substantial sums being paid for defense. The cost in terms of damage to an attorney's reputation can be still greater.

2 Mallen & Smith, *supra,* at § 27.4 (footnotes omitted), recognizes the significance of the selection of a legal theory which motivates my concern about the text of this majority decision:

> On occasion, the legal theories available to a plaintiff may involve choice of law issues. The issue may concern the principle governing the underlying action or the legal malpractice action itself. For a federal court, choice of law principles are those of the forum in which it sits.
>
> In most jurisdictions, the plaintiff in a legal malpractice action may have a choice between proceeding upon the theory of negligence, breach of contract, or a statutory remedy. Although the plaintiff may have facts available which constitute an express promise, the contract action can sometimes be based upon the implied promise to exercise ordinary skill and knowledge. The implied promise usually has the same legal and practical result as a tort claim.
>
> In some instances, however, a contract theory may not only be preferable, but also the only viable course of action. Thus, if either the attorney or client is deceased, survival of the cause of action can depend upon the theory of liability asserted. A statute of limitations applicable to tort actions usually expires well before a statute applying to an action founded upon a contract. A suit predicated upon a contract or statute may be preferable because it may not be subject to the contributory negligence defense. Interest may be recoverable for a breach of contract but not for negligence. Punitive damages, however, are not usually recoverable for breach of a contract.

Consequently, I concur in the majority decision, but would leave for another day, when the issue is directly presented, whether either or both contract or negligence confine or describe a legal malpractice proceeding.

CARDINE, Justice, dissenting.

Each case of this kind presents a new and different problem that adds confusion to what ought to be simple. This case creates an injustice by requiring a party to pay 100 percent of a loss of which he caused only 35 percent. I would hold that when negligence is asserted and, as in this case, is an element of a claim, the case sounds in negligence, and negligence law and principles apply. Should the injured party sue only upon the contract, negligence principles would not apply. This would leave intact a pure contract action and result in a more reasonable approach to justice between the parties.

B. Release

Focus Questions: *Rich v. Ellingson*

1. *What is the defendant's defense to the legal malpractice action?*
2. *What is a release?*

Rich v. Ellingson

174 P.3d 491
(Mont. 2007)

Justice PATRICIA O. COTTER delivered the Opinion of the Court.

Kiersten Rich (Rich) appeals the grant of summary judgment in favor of Jeffrey Ellingson (Ellingson) and the Attorney's Liability Protection Society (ALPS). Rich was involved in two separate motor vehicle accidents, one occurring in 1993 and the other in 1994. She hired Ellingson to represent her in securing uninsured motorists' (UM) and underinsured motorists' (UIM) coverage from her insurer State Farm for the respective accidents, and to assert Unfair Trade Practice (UTPA or bad faith) claims for the handling of both claims. Due to Ellingson's failure to timely serve a summons upon State Farm after filing the UIM claim, Rich's UIM claim was dismissed in both state and federal court. As a result, she filed the first of two legal malpractice claims against Ellingson and ALPS, Ellingson's malpractice insurer. Rich settled with ALPS and signed a Limited General Release (Release) releasing ALPS and Ellingson from any and all future malpractice claims that may arise as a result of Ellingson's representation of Rich against her insurer.

Later, Rich's UTPA claims against her insurer were dismissed because the statute of limitations had run. Rich in turn filed a second legal malpractice claim against Ellingson. In response, Ellingson and ALPS argued that the unambiguous terms of the Release barred future, unknown claims, arising from Ellingson's representation of Rich against her insurer. The parties stipulated that there were no material issues of fact. The District Court found the Release dispositive, clearly barring the second malpractice claim asserted by Rich, and entered summary judgment. We affirm.

ISSUE

Does the Release signed upon settlement of one malpractice claim (for failure to timely issue a summons) bar a subsequent malpractice claim discovered two years later arising out of the same legal representation?

FACTUAL AND PROCEDURAL BACKGROUND

Rich was involved in two motor vehicle accidents within a period of one year, the first on November 28, 1993, and the second on October 21, 1994. At the time of these accidents, Rich had medical payments (Med Pay), (UIM) and (UM) coverage through State Farm Mutual Automobile Insurance Company (State Farm). She made a claim for Med Pay and UIM benefits as a result of the 1993 accident and a claim for Med Pay and UM benefits as a result of the 1994 accident. On April 10, 1995, Rich sought legal representation from Ellingson in connection with her claims against State Farm.

On November 22, 1996, Rich, through Ellingson, filed a complaint against State Farm in the Eleventh Judicial District, Flathead County, seeking UIM coverage in relation to the November 28, 1993 accident. That same day a summons was issued to State Farm, but it was never served.

On January 2, 2001, Rich filed an action against State Farm in the United States District Court of Montana, Missoula Division, for breach of contract for failure to pay Med Pay and UIM benefits, and for damages for State Farm's alleged violations of the UTPA with respect to its handling of the 1993 accident. She also sought damages for breach of contract for failure to pay Med Pay and UM coverage for the 1994 accident, and sought damages for State Farm's alleged violations of UTPA in handling the claims arising out of that accident as well.

On June 11, 2001, due to the lack of timely service of summons, Rich filed a notice of voluntary dismissal without prejudice in the state court UIM action pursuant to Mont. R. Civ. P. 41(a)(1).

On June 13, 2001, State Farm filed a motion for partial summary judgment in the federal action seeking dismissal of the UIM claim arising out of the 1993 accident because Rich had failed to comply with Mont. R. Civ. P. 41(e), in the state court action, and thus the federal action for the same relief was automatically barred. The federal court granted partial summary judgment on the UIM claim relative to the 1993 accident.

On June 18, 2001, State Farm then filed an amended answer to Rich's complaint in federal court, alleging affirmative defenses of statute of limitations and res judicata with respect to the remaining claims.

After her federal UIM claims against State Farm were dismissed, Rich filed a claim against Ellingson for legal malpractice, seeking benefits from his malpractice insurance carrier, ALPS. On November 18, 2003, Rich settled her malpractice claim against Ellingson in exchange for payment of $175,000. Rich signed the Settlement Agreement and entered into the Release, which contained the following language:

> Description of Casualty: Alleged legal malpractice of any kind arising out of or related to the representation of Kiersten Rich by Jeffrey D. Ellingson.
>
> ....
>
> 1. *Release*
>
> The undersigned Releasor acknowledges receipt of the above sum of money and in consideration for payment of such sum, fully and forever releases and discharges Releasee, Releasee's heirs, personal representatives, successors, assigns, agents, partners, employees and attorneys from any and all actions, claims causes of action, demands, or expenses for damages or injuries, whether asserted or unasserted, known or unknown, foreseen or unforeseen, arising out of or related to the described casualty.
>
> 2. *Future Damages*
>
> Inasmuch as the injuries, damages, and losses resulting from the events described herein may not be fully known and may be more numerous or more serious than it is now understood or expected, the Releasor agrees, as a further consideration of this agreement, that this Release applies to any and all injuries, damages and losses resulting from the casualty described herein, even though now unanticipated, unexpected and unknown, as well as any and all injuries, damages and losses which have already developed and which are now known or anticipated.
>
> ....

6. *Reservation of Claims*

While this release fully and finally releases Releasee of any and all claims of any kind whatsoever which Releasor does or could have against him, Releasor specifically reserves any and all claims she may have against State Farm Insurance Companies, including her bad faith claim.

7. *Disclaimer*

Releasor has carefully read the foregoing, discussed its legal effect with Releasor's attorney, understands the contents thereof, and signs the same of Releasor's own free will and accord.

On October 7, 2005, a U.S. Magistrate Judge dismissed Rich's remaining federal court claims, concluding that res judicata barred Rich's claims for Med Pay benefits and the statute of limitations barred her UTPA claims. Following dismissal of her remaining breach of contract claims and her bad faith claims, Rich filed this action against Ellingson and ALPS, alleging that Ellingson was guilty of legal malpractice. Rich argued that the Release applied only to the malpractice "alleged" prior to the execution of the Release, thus limiting its application to the UIM complaint and not the bad faith complaints. Ellingson and ALPS raised the Release, signed on November 19, 2003, as a bar to suit. They further asserted that certain negotiated provisions demonstrate that the Release was not a standard boilerplate form. In their reply brief, they argued that even if the Release arguably covered only known claims, Rich had had notice of the statute of limitations affirmative defense in the UTPA actions *prior to* her execution of the Release; thus, that claim was barred under either theory. On May 30, 2006, the parties submitted to the District Court a statement of stipulated facts upon which the court relied in making its determination.

On October 3, 2006, the District Court granted the Defendants' motion for summary judgment, holding that the Release was dispositive in that it clearly barred Rich from bringing future claims against Ellingson arising from his representation of Rich in her actions against her insurer. The court further pointed out that the plaintiff offered no evidence of fraud, duress or mutual mistake, nor did she offer admissible extrinsic or parol evidence to contradict the clear terms of the Release; therefore, the court had no basis on which to find that the parties' intent differed from the express terms of the Release. Rich timely appeals.

....

DISCUSSION

Rich argues that a plain reading of the Release limits the effect of the Release to "alleged" malpractice claims that arose prior to the settlement. Relying on § 28-3-301, MCA, she maintains it was the parties' intent *at the time of contracting* that the Release would bar future malpractice claims only insofar as they might apply to the 1993 contract claims. She asserts that (1) the specific mention in the Release of the 1993 complaint overrides the general boilerplate provisions; (2) any ambiguity that exists should be construed against the drafter, ALPS, who provided the form; and (3) the lack of consideration for the bad faith claims demonstrates that there was an intent to bar only the malpractice claims arising from the 1993 contract claim and, therefore, her claims for malpractice against Ellingson relative to her Med Pay and bad faith claims should remain viable.

ALPS argues that the terms of the Release unambiguously bar future claims such as this one because this claim arises out of Ellingson's legal representation of Rich. ALPS asserts that Rich's reliance on principles of contract interpretation is misplaced, and that her argument about consideration is irrelevant.

As we have stated many times, where the language of an agreement is clear and unambiguous, and as a result, susceptible to only one interpretation, the court's duty is to apply the language as written. *Doble v. Bernhard,* 1998 MT 124, ¶ 19, 289 Mont. 80, ¶ 19, 959 P.2d 488, ¶ 19. Both parties refer to this rule of contract interpretation, but reach opposite conclusions. This does not, however, make the Release ambiguous. "Whether or not an ambiguity exists is a question of law for the court to decide [citation omitted]. Only where an ambiguity exists may the court turn to extrinsic evidence of contemporaneous or prior oral agreements to determine the intent of the parties [citations omitted]." *Doble,* ¶ 19.

"An ambiguity exists when the contract taken as a whole in its wording or phraseology is reasonably subject to two different interpretations." *Wray v. State Compensation Ins. Fund,* 266 Mont. 219, 223, 879 P.2d 725, 727 (1994) (quoting *Morning Star Enterprises v. R.H. Grover,* 247 Mont. 105, 111, 805 P.2d 553, 557 (1991)). If the terms of the contract are clear, however, the court must determine the intent of the parties from the wording of the contract alone. We also must consider the document as a whole, giving effect to each part in interpreting it, rather than attaching a meaning to a single word not supported by the rest of the document. Section 28-3-202, MCA.

Here, the Release clearly and unambiguously bars future claims arising from Ellingson's representation of Rich in her multiple actions against State Farm. Although Rich contends that the use of the term "[a]lleged" in the "Description of Casualty" provision limits the application of the Release to only claims made prior to the settlement agreement, we find this argument unpersuasive.

The two plain, everyday meanings of "alleged," are (1) asserted to be true or to exist; and (2) questionably true or of a specified kind. *Webster's Third New International Dictionary, Unabridged* 55 (Philip Babcock Gove, ed., Merriam-Webster, Inc. 2002). Thus, the reference to "alleged legal malpractice" would be understood to mean malpractice asserted but not confirmed to exist, or malpractice that is questionably true. Implying a more temporal meaning would be attaching a greater meaning than the writing expresses. We decline to interpret the term in such a way as would create discordance with the other provisions in the Release.

From beginning to end, the Release consistently demonstrates the intent of the parties to resolve all disputes arising from Ellingson's representation of Rich, known or unknown, anticipated or unanticipated, regardless of the particular complaint alleged. The sole reservation in the document was for Rich's claims against State Farm for bad faith; no reservations were made as to present or future claims against Ellingson. Rich's present allegation of her past intent, without more, cannot change the unambiguous intent of the Release, as indicated through its express terms. The District Court correctly concluded that the terms of the agreement and Release were clear and unambiguous and that Rich was bound by those terms.

We likewise reject Rich's assertion that the consideration paid in exchange for the Release was inadequate to encompass all of her possible claims against Ellingson. The Release clearly provided that the amount paid was consideration for "alleged malpractice of any kind." A written instrument is presumptive evidence of sufficient consideration and the burden of attacking the sufficiency of such consideration is on the party seeking to invalidate the instrument. Section 28-2-804, MCA; *Archer v. LaMarch Creek Ranch,* 174 Mont. 429, 435, 571 P.2d 379, 382 (1977). According to a treatise on automobile insurance releases,

> [i]t has been held that the amount paid for the release is not material or open for question provided it has been accepted in full satisfaction and discharge of the claim.

> *McCloskey v. Porter,* 161 Mont. 307, 312, 506 P.2d 845, 848 (1973) quoting Blashfield, *Automobile Law and Practice,* vol. 6, § 257.52 (3rd Ed.). Here, Rich provides us with excerpts of the ALPS "Claim Action Summary," which she contends establish that the intent was to cover only the 1993 contract claims. The contents of this internal insurance company document, however, dated weeks before the date the Release was signed, are insufficient to overcome the presumption of sufficient consideration.

A party's "latent discontent" with a release, without more, is an insufficient basis upon which to premise an alteration of an express agreement. *Hanson v. Oljar,* 231 Mont. 272, 277, 752 P.2d 187, 190 (1988). This is especially so when the document is unambiguous. *Doble,* ¶ 19.

CONCLUSION

For the foregoing reasons, we conclude that the District Court did not err in entering summary judgment in favor of Ellingson and ALPS. Therefore, we affirm.

* * *

Part 3

Defamation

Good name in man and woman, dear my lord,
Is the immediate jewel of their souls.
Who steals my purse steals trash;
'Tis something, nothing;
'Twas mine, 'tis his, and has been slave to thousands;
But he that filches from me my good name
Robs me of that which not enriches him,
And makes me poor indeed.

William Shakespeare, *Othello*, Act III, Scene 3

The defamation tort is difficult to deal with. It seems simple enough on its face: an individual who publishes a false and defamatory statement concerning another is subject to liability. In reality, things are not that simple. Historically, the tort presented practitioners with a variety of challenges stemming from a host of highly specialized rules. Beginning in the 1960s, the Supreme Court began addressing constitutional issues raised by the application of common law defamation rules. The result was a further muddying of the waters of the law regarding defamation. Today, there may be questions in each case as to the level of fault required on the part of the defendant in order for liability to exist; what damages, if any, must result from the defamatory publication; which of the many, many recognized privileges may apply to the publication in question; and even more basic questions, such as whether the publication is, in fact, false to begin with. Indeed, the tort has so many intertwining standards and recognized privileges that it is difficult to even state with precision the elements of a prima facie case.

These complexities pose special challenges for lawyers. Obviously, if it is difficult to define the elements of a prima facie case, it may be difficult for a lawyer to advise a client in an effective manner. Clients who seek to recover for damage to their reputation must be made to understand the numerous obstacles to recovery as well as the reality that by claiming damage to one's good name, a client is, in fact, raising the issue of whether the client had a good name to begin with.

The defamation tort may pose other challenges for lawyers, both in terms of representing clients and being a party. A lawyer must diligently (some would say "zealously") represent the interests of their clients. In doing so, lawyers may sometimes say things that damage the reputation of others, thereby making themselves potential targets for lawsuits. In other instances, a lawyer's representation of a client may result in the lawyer attracting substantial public attention. With public attention often comes public criticism. Thus, there may be instances in which a lawyer becomes a defamation plaintiff as a result of comment related to his or her professional activities.

The following chapters attempt to make sense of the defamation tort generally while highlighting some of the special concerns lawyers may face in their practice. Chapter 8 deals with the prima facie case. Chapter 9 covers the special constitutional rules that have developed over the past half century regarding defamation. Finally, Chapter 10 addresses the various common law and statutory privileges that may shield a defendant from liability.

Chapter 8

Defamation: The Prima Facie Case at Common Law

Exercise 8.1: Chapter Problem

Samantha Brill is the legal affairs correspondent for the *Blackacre Times*. In addition to being a reporter of local trials, Brill also writes a column for the Sunday edition of the paper. In her column, which appears as part of the paper's "Local Community" section, Brill comments on local politics and other newsworthy issues. Brill often includes biting humor in her opinion pieces. Recently, Brill wrote a piece entitled "A Fairytale in Blackacre." The column focused on a local high-profile civil lawsuit alleging police brutality and the decision of the plaintiff's lawyers to add lawyer Billy Bales to the team. Bales is a nationally famous lawyer who first gained notoriety as one of the lawyers representing Terri Sirico, a teenage girl who was accused of murdering a classmate. As part of Sirico's defense team, Bales had argued to the jury that two police investigators had framed Sirico. Brill began her column in the following manner: "There is an old joke that goes, 'how can you tell if a lawyer is lying?' Answer: his lips are moving. Well, Billy Bales does a lot of talking." The column then went on to criticize the decision of the lawyers in the local police brutality case to hire Bales.

> Bales made a name for himself by telling a fairytale to New York jurors in the Sirico lawsuit and somehow persuading them to swallow his story. As a result, the good names of a couple of good cops were ruined and Bales walked away with a truckload in attorney's fees. His past record demonstrates that Bales is willing to say whatever it takes to win a case. Now Bales is bringing his peculiar brand of legal snake oil to Blackacre.

The column went on to question why the lawyers representing the plaintiff in the local matter chose to hire Bales. "When you lie down with dogs," Brill wrote, "you are likely to get fleas."

Bales and the local lawyers have decided to sue Brill and the *Blackacre Times* on a libel theory. Putting aside any issues of privilege or constitutional law, can they make out a prima facie case of libel against either defendant?

The term "defamation" covers both slander and libel. Slander is typically thought of as the spoken form of defamation, whereas libel is defamation in more tangible or written form. Historically, the distinction between slander and libel was significant for purposes of a defamation claim, and in some jurisdictions the difference may still matter in terms of the plaintiff's burden of proof. If the defamatory statement was libelous, the plaintiff's burden was likely to be less substantial than if the defamatory statement was slanderous. Until well into the 20th century, a defamation plaintiff's burden could be quite light, regardless of whether the defamatory statement amounted to slander or libel. For instance, while a defamation plaintiff might be required to allege that a defamatory statement was false, proof of falsity was not part of the plaintiff's prima facie case at common law. The fact that the statement was true was an absolute defense to a defamation claim and, therefore, often at issue. But the burden was on the defendant to establish the truthful nature of the statement. A plaintiff was often not even required to establish that the defendant was somehow at fault in making the defamatory statement; defamation was, in effect, a strict liability tort.

Eventually, the Supreme Court dramatically altered the plaintiff's prima facie case through a series of decisions involving the application of the First Amendment to common-law defamation claims. These decisions, which dealt largely with the plaintiff's burden of establishing fault on the part of the defendant, will be explored in Chapter 9. Even with the Supreme Court's "clarification" of the law, jurisdictions still vary wildly in their enunciation of the rules governing defamation. As one of the leading treatises on the subject puts it, "[t]here is simply no way succinctly to state the elements of a modern cause of action for defamation." RODNEY A. SMOLLA, 2 LAW OF DEFAMATION § 1:34 (2d ed.). With that disclaimer in mind, this chapter examines the elements of a defamation claim as they existed at common law.

A. Publication

The most basic requirement of a defamation claim is the publication requirement. Liability for defamation requires publication of a defamatory statement. In order for there to be publication, the defendant must communicate to at least one person other than the person defamed. Doe v. Am. Online, Inc., 783 So.2d 1010, 1016 (Fla. 2001). Regardless of whether the defamatory communication takes the form of libel or slander, the recipient must actually understand the communication. Thus, the publication element is not satisfied if the defendant says something defamatory about the plaintiff to an individual who does not speak the same language. The publication element is satisfied by either an intentional publication (where the defendant acts for the purpose of communicating with the third person or knows that such communication is substantially certain to occur) or a negligent publication (for example, where the defendant leaves a defamatory letter lying around in plain sight and the letter is read by another). Restatement (Second) of Torts § 577 cmt. k. A person who repeats a defamatory statement originally made by another is treated as having published the statement; a talebearer may cause as much damage to the reputation of another as the original talemaker. Harris v. Minvielle, 19 So. 925 (La. 1896).

Despite the relatively straightforward nature of the publication element, there are several recurring issues or wrinkles that may sometimes require more consideration. For example, under the "single publication rule," each defamatory statement is generally treated as a separate publication. An exception exists in the case of publication of a newspaper edition or book, in which case there has been only one publication per edition. Restatement (Second) of Torts § 577A.

Exercise 8.2

Based on the above information and keeping in mind the basic purposes of the defamation tort, decide whether there has there been a publication for purposes of a defamation claim in each of the following instances:

(1) One day, Alice walked around town telling a defamatory story about Bob to twenty different people. That same day, *The Whiteacre Post*, a daily newspaper, published a defamatory story about Bob. The edition containing the defamatory statement was delivered to 100,000 subscribers. Has Alice made one publication or twenty? Has *The Whiteacre Post* made one publication or 100,000? *See* Restatement (Second) of Torts § 577A.

(2) *The Blackacre Times*, a daily newspaper, republishes a defamatory news story that was originally published in *The Whiteacre Post*. Timmy, a newspaper delivery boy, delivers multiple editions of *The Blackacre Times* to subscribers. The victim of the defamatory news story now wishes to sue *The Whiteacre Post*, *The Blackacre Times*, and Timmy. Has each defendant made a publication for purposes of a defamation claim? *See* Restatement (Second) of Torts §§ 578, 581.

(3) Employer fires Employee and gives as the reason the Employer's conclusion that Employee sexually harassed a coworker. However, Employer is mistaken. Employee did not harass anyone. When Employee applies for a new job, he is asked why he is no longer employed. After trying to avoid the question, Employee is finally forced to admit that he was fired after Employer concluded that he had sexually harassed a coworker. As a result, Employee does not get the job. Employee now wishes to sue Employer for defamation. Did Employer publish the statement about Employee to the prospective employer, even though Employee was the one who told the prospective employer about the sexual harassment charge? *See* Cweklinsky v. Mobil Chemical Co., 837 A.2d 759, 765 (Conn. 2004); Lewis v. Equitable Life Assurance Society of the United States, 389 N.W.2d 876, 886–88 (Minn. 1986); Martika D. Cooper, *Between A Rock and Hard Case: Time for a New Doctrine of Compelled Self-Publication*, 72 Notre Dame L. Rev. 373 (1997).

(4) Partner Cooley conducts the annual evaluation for associates of Law Firm. In discussing Associate Finn's performance with other partners in the firm, Cooley makes several defamatory statements about Finn's sense of professional ethics. As a result of the negative evaluations, Finn is fired. Finn sues Cooley under a defamation theory. Cooley responds that there was no publication to a third party in this instance because he was acting within the scope of employment when he spoke to the other partners and, therefore, the communication was, in effect, the partnership speaking to itself. Putting aside for now the question of whether Cooley should have some sort of privilege to make such statements, was there a publication? *See* Bals v. Verduzco, 600 N.E.2d 1353 (Ind. 1992).

Defamation in the Digital Age. Defamation law developed in an age when gossipy neighbors were the primary vehicles for the spread of defamatory statements. Eventually, the development of the printing press, radio, and television made it possible to publish defamatory statements more easily. However, in terms of their ability to serve as a vehicle for the publication of defamatory statements, these vehicles pale in comparison to the Internet.

The growth of the Internet has made it possible for one to publish a defamatory statement to millions instantly. So-called "Twitter Defamation" has attracted widespread news coverage. For example, in 2011 musician/actress Courtney Love agreed to a $430,000 settlement of a defamation claim brought by a fashion designer whom Love had allegedly defamed in a series of 140-character tweets. Jennifer Preston, *Courtney Love Settles Twitter Defamation Case*, N.Y. TIMES, March 4, 2011, *available at* http://artsbeat.blogs.nytimes.com/2011/03/04/courtney-love-settles-twitter-defamation-case/.

By and large, the basic rules for liability for defamation (and for the element of publication in particular) transfer relatively easily to the digital world. However, new technology does present some interesting challenges. Consider the following hypothetical: Law Student posts a defamatory comment about Classmate in the comment section of a popular legal blog. Classmate notifies the operator of the blog about the existence and the defamatory nature of the comment, but the operator declines to remove the comment, citing his policy of "uninhibited expression of ideas." The operator of the blog has, however, taken down offensive material in the past on occasion. Classmate now wishes to sue the operator of the blog under a defamation theory. Can Classmate recover from the blog operator?

At first glance, the answer would seem to be "yes." The general rule is that a property owner who unreasonably fails to remove defamatory material is as liable as the person who posted the material. However, the Communications Decency Act (CDA) provides immunity in these kinds of situations. Section 230(c) of the CDA provides that "[n]o provider or user of an interactive computer service shall be treated as the publisher or speaker of any information provided by another information content provider." *Id.* § 230(c). *See, e.g.*, Zeran v. America Online, Inc., 129 F.3d 327 (4th Cir. 1997). This provision has been held to shield online service providers from liability for defamation and related torts where the law historically has provided for such liability. Classmate could, however, still recover from Law Student. Why would Congress want to shield online service providers from liability in these kinds of cases, even when service providers are aware that they are providing a forum for people who are making false and defamatory statements about others?

* * *

B. Defamatory Statements

1. Generally

Focus Questions: Marcone v. Penthouse International Magazine

1. *What does it mean to say that a statement is "defamatory"?*
2. *In order to establish that a statement was defamatory, must a plaintiff establish that the allegedly defamatory statement actually damaged the plaintiff's reputation?*

Marcone v. Penthouse International Magazine for Men

754 F.2d 1072
(3d Cir. 1985)

ADAMS, Circuit Judge.I.

Marcone is an attorney residing in Delaware County, a suburb of Philadelphia. During the mid-1970's he gained notoriety in part through his representation of the Pagans, a motorcycle gang headquartered in Marcus Hook, Pennsylvania, and a rival gang, the Warlocks. Marcone was also linked to these motorcycle gangs on a non-professional basis. In this regard, law enforcement agents stated that Marcone frequented "the Castle," a 40-room mansion in Delaware County which served as the Pagans' headquarters. Among other things, the Castle was connected with the disappearance and death of five young women in 1976. An article in the Philadelphia Inquirer dated March 18, 1976, reported that Marcone once stated that he "occasionally went on weekend trips" with one of the motorcycle gangs.

In February of 1976, a grand jury in Detroit, Michigan, handed down an indictment charging Marcone and 24 other co-defendants with conspiring "to knowingly, intentionally and unlawfully possess with intent to distribute, and to distribute marijuana" in violation of 21 U.S.C. §§ 841(a)(1), 846 (1982). In particular, the indictment charged that "[d]uring May, 1974, FRANK MARCONE gave $25,000 in United States currency to FREDERICK R. FREY in Philadelphia, Pennsylvania for the purpose of purchasing multi-hundred pound quantities of marijuana in California." Law enforcement agents stated that Marcone and the three other co-defendants from the Philadelphia area had frequent meetings at the Castle.

On May 19, 1976, the government withdrew the charges against Marcone without prejudice to his being reindicted in Philadelphia. An assistant United States Attorney in Detroit explained that the charges were dropped because of "legal technicalities" in tying Marcone to the larger conspiracy which involved defendants from San Diego to Montreal. For reasons not explained in the record, Marcone was not subsequently reindicted in Philadelphia.

Penthouse published an article in its November 1978 issue entitled "The Stoning of America." Written by Edward Rasen, the article concerned the emergence of marijuana trade as a multibillion dollar industry. The subtitle stated that "marijuana is now big agribusiness—a $12 billion a year corporate growth crop." The article proceeded to report, in part, about "criminal attorneys and attorney criminals" involved in drug transactions ...

Example[]: ... "Frank Marcone, an attorney from the Philadelphia area, contributed down payments of up to $25,000 on grass transactions. Charges against him were dismissed because he cooperated with further investigations."

Marcone brought suit against *Penthouse* charging that the article libeled him since it declared that he was guilty of an offense for which he was only indicted, and since it stated that charges were dropped against him because he cooperated with the authorities. Plaintiff alleges that these two statements are untrue and that they have caused him harm and subjected him to ridicule.

A.

First, defendant contends that plaintiff has not met the burden of proving the article's defamatory character. This is so, *Penthouse* maintains, because the questioned remarks are incapable of defamatory meaning. Whether a statement is capable of defamatory meaning is a question the judge, as distinguished from the jury, must determine, and the district court ruled that the article was capable of a defamatory meaning.

According to Pennsylvania law, a statement is defamatory if it "tends so to harm the reputation of another as to lower him in the estimation of the community or to deter third persons from associating or dealing with him." The threshold determination of whether a statement is capable of defamatory meaning depends "on the general tendency of the words to have such an effect"; no demonstration of any actual harm to reputation is necessary.

Penthouse attempts to demonstrate that each individual phrase in the article, in isolation, cannot be understood as libelous. Thus, for example, it asserts that "cooperated with further investigations" cannot be defamatory. The proper test, however, requires that the allegedly libelous communication be read as a whole, in context.

As the district court observed, "The Stoning of America" refers to "attorney criminals" and lists as one of the examples:

> Frank Marcone, an attorney from the Philadelphia area, contributed down payments of up to $25,000 on grass transactions. Charges against him were dismissed because he cooperated with further investigations.

This statement suggests that Marcone has committed a crime. Statements imputing the commission of an indictable offense are capable of defamatory meaning as a matter of law. Thus *Penthouse*'s argument that the article could not possibly have defamed Marcone is not valid.

* * *

1. **Defamatory statements.** Pennsylvania's definition of a "defamatory" publication is the same used by § 559 of the *Restatement (Second) of Torts*. Some decisions and statutes emphasize the idea that a statement is defamatory where it tends to subject the plaintiff to scorn, ridicule, contempt or the like. CA. CIV. CODE § 45 (defining libel as a publication that exposes a person to hatred, contempt, ridicule, or obloquy, or which causes him to be shunned or avoided); Independent Newspapers, Inc. v. Brodie, 966 A.2d 432, 441 (Md. 2009) ("[a] 'defamatory statement,' is one which tends to expose a person to public scorn, hatred, contempt or ridicule, thereby discouraging others in the community from having a good opinion of, or associating with, that person.") (internal quotations omitted).

2. **Reasonable construction vs. Innocent construction.** In considering whether a statement is defamatory, nearly every jurisdiction follows the rule of reasonable construction: "The meaning of a communication is that which the recipient correctly, or mistakenly but reasonably, understands that it was intended to express." Restatement (Second) Torts § 563 (1977). If the communication is capable of either a defamatory or innocent meaning, "the plaintiff has the burden of proving that it was reasonably understood in the sense that would make it defamatory." Restatement (Second) Torts § 613 cmt. c (1977).

3. **Defamatory/not defamatory.** Consider whether the following statements are defamatory:

> (a) Alice tells Bob that Carol's employment was terminated. Denny v. Mertz, 318 N.W.2d 141, 154 (Wis. 1982).
>
> (b) Manager tells his employees that their co-worker, Don [age 53], "is an old man." Howard v. Daiichiya-Love's Bakery, Inc., 714 F. Supp. 1108 (D. Hawaii).
>
> (c) "Elise's conduct violated several standards of professional ethics." Lewis v. Elliot, 628 F. Supp. 512, 516 (D.D.C. 1986).

(d) A newspaper reports that Fred, a prisoner, agreed to testify against alleged criminals. As a result of the report, fellow inmates shun Fred as an informer. Burrascano v. Levi, 452 F. Supp. 1066, 1072 (D. Md. 1978).

(e) Defendant wrote a newspaper story in which he said that two individuals were "eager for news about a junkie they both knew who was doing time in prison." The two individuals have now sued. Romaine v. Kallinger, 537 A.2d 284 (N.J. 1988).

(f) Alice tells Bob that Carol was born out of wedlock. Carol's mother now wishes to sue for defamation.

(g) Alice tells Bob that "Charles has lived with another man for 15 years."

Focus Questions: *James v. Gannett Co.*

1. *What approach does the court take with respect to analyzing the allegedly defamatory character of the two statements in question?*
2. *Why does the court conclude that the statements are not susceptible to a defamatory construction?*

James v. Gannett Co.

40 N.Y.2d 415
(N.Y. 1976)

On July 9, 1972, an article entitled "Samantha's Belly Business" appeared in the Sunday supplement, Upstate, of the *Rochester Democrat & Chronicle*, a newspaper published by the Gannett Co., Inc. The story, prepared by one of the newspaper's reporters based upon an interview with the plaintiff, described the plaintiff as the "undisputed queen of the exotic stages of Upstate New York, Rochester's belly dancer in residence." Without delving into unnecessary detail, it suffices to note that the four-page story discussed the plaintiff's background, set forth her views on life in general, her approach to her business, and described two of her dancing routines. Accompanying photographs depicted the plaintiff in her dressing room, on the stage, and arriving for work. Quotations from the interview with plaintiff are sprinkled liberally throughout the article.

[The trial court granted the defendant's summary judgment motion. The appellate court reversed. This appeal followed.]

The plaintiff finds fault with two sentences in the article, denying that she made statements attributed to her. Specifically, she objects to the statement that "she admits to selling her time to lonely old men with money, for as much as $400 an evening in one case, 'just to sit with him and be nice to him.'" In a later paragraph, the plaintiff is quoted as saying: "'Most men can talk to me. They can't talk to their wives because they're blocked by society. Do you understand what I'm saying? They're looking for something they've lost at home. This is my business. Men is my business.'" Of this paragraph, the plaintiff objects only to the phrase, "Men is my business." The plaintiff does not deny making any of the other quotations attributed to her in the article.

In her complaint, the plaintiff alleged that, by the two sentences cited, "the defendant meant, and intended to mean, and was understood by the readers of said newspaper as meaning that the plaintiff was acting as a prostitute who was offering her body and her time for sale at a price, was committing the crime of prostitution, was committing adultery, was sleeping and having intercourse with various and sundry male persons for a profit; that plaintiff was a person of low and despicable moral character." The plaintiff claimed that the allegedly false publication discredited her reputation in the community, resulting in damages of $500,000.

We agree with the dissenting Justices at the Appellate Division that the published article, when read in context, was not defamatory. It is old law that written charges imputing unchaste conduct to a woman are libelous per se ... However, whether the words complained of would constitute a libel..., it is for the court to decide whether the words are susceptible of the meaning ascribed to them. The court must decide whether there is a reasonable basis for drawing the defamatory conclusion. If the contested statements are reasonably susceptible of a defamatory connotation, then "it becomes the jury's function to say whether that was the sense in which the words were likely to be understood by the ordinary and average reader." In analyzing the words in order to ascertain whether a question of fact exists for resolution upon trial, the court will not pick out and isolate particular phrases but will consider the publication as a whole. The publication will be tested by its effect upon the average reader. The language will be given a fair reading and the court will not strain to place a particular interpretation on the published words. "The construction which it behooves a court of justice to put on a publication which is alleged to be libelous is to be derived as well from the expressions used as from the whole scope and apparent object of the writer."

In applying these traditional standards to this case, we find there is absolutely no basis from which the ordinary reader could draw an inference of prostitution from the paragraph containing the statement: "Men is my business." The thrust of the paragraph, read as a whole with the entire article, was that the plaintiff believed that men attended her shows in order to obtain a form of entertainment not available in their homes. It cannot be said, as a matter of law, that, so construed, these remarks may impute unchastity or prostitution to the plaintiff. Indeed, it is to be expected that the talents of a female belly dancer would generally hold a greater attraction for men than for women and, since the plaintiff's audience is predominately male, it is but a truism to suggest that men are her business. From the entire article, it is clear that her "business" consists of displaying her dancing ability and does not involve acts of illegality or promiscuity.

The second alleged libel, that plaintiff sold her time to lonely old men, is a bit more difficult. However, we again conclude that this sentence is not susceptible to a defamatory construction. Although, on its face, this portion of the article states that the plaintiff sold her time to men on occasion, the statement itself negates the possibility that the plaintiff was thereby committing an act of prostitution since her role was to do no more than "sit with him and be nice to him." Whether a publication alleging that a woman sold her time to men charges an act of prostitution depends necessarily upon what services were to be performed in exchange for the money tendered to the woman. For it is plain that many women sell legitimate, professional services, involving an expenditure of personal time, to male customers. Doctors, lawyers, designers, and nurses are but a few examples. Here, the publication does no more than allege that the plaintiff accepted money in return for providing a few hours of companionship to lonely men. There is nothing in the sentence complained of to support an inference that the sale of anything more was involved. Any lingering doubt is resolved by a review of the entire article which establishes that plaintiff is a professional belly dancer who markets her own nightclub act "as an all-but-lost art as much as erotic entertainment." We conclude that the article, read as a whole, is incapable, as a matter of law, of bearing the libelous meaning that plaintiff would ascribe to it. We reject plaintiff's attempt to pick at two sentences from a feature article and impute to them a libelous connotation that the whole article, let alone the specific sentences, will not bear.

* * *

2. Special Considerations: Defamation Per Se and Defamation Per Quod

The tort of defamation exists primarily to protect an individual's interest in his or her reputation. Historically, the distinction between libel and slander was significant in terms of an individual's ability to recover for damage to reputation. Today, the distinction has less significance, but continues to play a role in some jurisdictions with respect to a plaintiff's burden to plead and prove damages. There are three types of damages that are potentially relevant in a defamation action: (1) "special harm" or "special damages" *i.e.*, pecuniary damage, resulting from the defamatory statement; (2) general damages, *i.e.*, damage to reputation as well as emotional distress resulting from the defamatory statement; and (3) presumed damages, which are, as the name implies, damages that may be awarded without proof of any injury. Which type of damage a defamation plaintiff must plead and prove depends on the jurisdiction and perhaps whether the publication is classified as libel or slander. Some jurisdictions have done away with the distinction between libel and slander and struck a middle ground that requires a defamation plaintiff to plead and prove general damages. Sullivan v. Baptist Memorial Hospital, 995 S.W.2d 569, 571 (Tenn.1999). In a jurisdiction that retains the distinction between libel and slander, a plaintiff, as a general matter, is less likely to be required to establish special harm in the case of libel than slander. Rodney A. Smolla, 2 Law of Defamation § 1:15 (2d ed.).

a. Libel Per Se and Libel Per Quod

In the case of libel, a plaintiff did not have to establish special harm at common law. Economic damage could be presumed because of the "greater permanency, dissemination, and credence attached to printed as opposed to spoken words." Marcone v. Penthouse International Magazine for Men, 754 F.2d 1072, 1080 (3d Cir. 1985) (quotations omitted). This rule was quite beneficial for many plaintiffs given the difficulty of establishing that a defamatory statement resulted in economic loss somehow. This rule still exists in some jurisdictions.

Some jurisdictions developed (and continue to rely upon) a distinction between publications that were "libel per se" and "libel per quod." Written statements that were defamatory on their face ("Alice is a murderer") were classified as libel per se. Libel per se was actionable without proof of special harm. Statements that "required proof of facts and circumstances imparting a defamatory meaning" were termed libel per quod. *Id.* (quotations omitted). A statement that is libelous per quod may be neutral on its face ("Alice slept with Bob"), but is capable of a defamatory meaning once extrinsic evidence is introduced (Alice is actually married to Carl).

Where the distinction between libel per se and libel per quod still exists, it is relevant as to the plaintiff's burden in terms of establishing damages. If extrinsic evidence is required to establish the defamatory meaning of a statement (libel per quod), a plaintiff must introduce evidence of special harm. If, however, the libel is defamatory on its face (libel per se), a plaintiff is excused from this burden and, in some jurisdictions, damages may be presumed.

* * *

b. Slander Per Se and Slander Per Quod

At common law, slander typically required proof of special damage before a plaintiff could recover. Like libel, slander is also sometimes divided into per se and per quod categories. It would have been helpful if courts had simply used those terms in the same way they used them in the case of libel. Unfortunately, they didn't.

If a statement qualifies as "slander per se," the plaintiff is relieved of the burden of proving special harm caused by the slander. There are four recognized categories of statements that amount to slander per se. These are statements that impute to another

(a) a criminal offense,

(b) a loathsome disease,

(c) a matter incompatible with his business, trade, profession, or office, or

(d) serious sexual misconduct.

Restatement (Second) of Torts § 570.

With regard to the first category, the criminal offense in question must be relatively serious in the sense that it could result in imprisonment or that it involve "moral turpitude." Sexually-transmitted and other kinds of serious, communicable diseases may be considered "loathsome." Historically, the "serious sexual misconduct" category has been applied to allegations of unchastity directed at women rather than men.

The slanderous per se statement most directly applicable to lawyers is a statement imputing behavior incompatible with one's profession. To be slanderous per se, the statements must be "peculiarly harmful to one engaged in his trade or profession." Statements suggesting lack of skill in connection with the practice of the trade or profession typically fall into this category. However, the *Restatement* explains that, ordinarily, a statement imputing a single mistake or act of misconduct is only actionable "if the act fairly implies an habitual course of similar conduct, or the want of the qualities or skill that the public is reasonably entitled to expect of persons engaged in such a calling." Restatement (Second) of Torts § 573 cmt. d.

Slander per quod is actually fairly easy to describe. It is slander that is not slander per se. Thus, spoken defamation that does not fit within one of the four categories identified above is slander per quod, and a plaintiff must establish special harm.

Exercise 8.3

Assume that in *Marcone*, Pennsylvania still followed the traditional distinctions between the various forms of libel and slander. What kind of damages, if any, would Marcone need to plead and prove?

Exercise 8.4

Lawyer Smith tells Lawyer Jones that in an estate case, Lawyer Thompson charged a fee amounting to 80% of the value of the estate. In a jurisdiction that still retains the historical distinctions between the various forms of libel and slander, would the statement amount to libel per se, libel per quod, slander per se, slander per quod, or none of the above?

C. Of and Concerning the Plaintiff

Focus Questions: *Ratner v. Young* and *Handelman v. Hustler Magazine, Inc.*

1. *Why are the plaintiffs in* Ratner *suing the newspaper publisher?*
2. *In both* Ratner *and* Handelman, *the defendants do not specifically name the plaintiffs, yet the courts reach different conclusions on the questions of whether a juror could find the statements referenced the plaintiffs. Can the decisions be reconciled? Can they be explained by the types of lawyers involved and the nature of the alleged defamatory conduct?*

Ratner v. Young

465 F. Supp. 386
(D.C. Virgin Islands 1979)

[Plaintiff, Leroy A. Mercer, was appointed as defense counsel in a high-profile murder case. Famed lawyer William A. Kunstler and lawyer Margaret Ratner "promptly moved in, uninvited, and each one of them took over the defense of one of the defendants, without pay." According to the court, the "tactics of Kunstler and Ratner were scorched earth all the way," including "aiding and abetting" the criminal defendants in shouting obscenities at the trial judge, Judge Young.]

Shortly after the return of the verdicts of guilty and the sentencing of all five defendants, THE ST. CROIX AVIS published an article containing a letter which had been received during the trial by the presiding judge, Warren H. Young, from a state court judge in Baltimore, Maryland, complimenting him on the manner in which he had conducted the proceedings in the murder case. William M. Kunstler, Mrs. Margaret Ratner, Leroy A. Mercer and Mario De Chabert, four defense counsel in the murder case, then brought this suit against Jerome Dwyer, Managing Editor of THE ST. CROIX AVIS, and Brodhurst Printery, Inc., the publisher of the paper, and Judge Young, alleging that the letter was libelous and that they were entitled to $4,000,000.00 damages from such defendants by reason of the publication of it. The author of the letter has not been sued.

The Alleged Defamatory Statements Were Not Directed at Plaintiff, Leroy A. Mercer

The Court is of the opinion that summary judgment should be rendered against the plaintiff, Leroy A. Mercer, because the record shows without dispute that the alleged defamatory statements were not directed at him.

The letter to defendant, Judge Young, quoted in full in the article in THE ST. CROIX AVIS, was written by a state Criminal Court judge in Baltimore. It congratulated Judge Young on the manner in which he handled the Fountain Valley murder trial. The Maryland judge said he was in position to understand the situation that faced Judge Young because he had recently been in a trial where several Black Panthers had murdered a white police officer. He said that Kunstler had attempted to interject himself into the trial at the last minute. The following statement in the closing portion of the letter leaves no question about the fact that it was specifically directed at the conduct of Kunstler and Ratner, and not at local counsel, Leroy A. Mercer:

> It is for this reason that I have a great deal of sympathy for your present position. According to the newspaper clippings which were sent me, Mr. Kunstler and Mrs. Ratner are following the same tactics which the Black Panther organization attempted to do in the case tried by me.

At the time the alleged defamatory statements were published, there were no provisions in the Virgin Islands Code regarding civil liability for defamation. 1 V.I.C. §4 states that the rules of common law, as expressed in the restatements of law approved by the American Law Institute, and to the extent not so expressed, as generally understood and applied in the United States, shall be the rules of decision in the courts of the Virgin Islands in cases to which they apply, in the absence of laws to the contrary. *Restatement-Torts* §564 is applicable here. It reads:

> §564. Applicability of Defamatory Communication to Plaintiff
>
> "A defamatory communication is made concerning the person to whom its recipient correctly, or mistakenly but reasonably, understands that it was intended to refer."

In ... *Rosenblatt v. Baer*, 383 U.S. 75, 81 (1966), the Supreme Court, in discussing this question said:

> "... There must be evidence showing the attack was read as specifically directed at the plaintiff."

Mercer was only one of the local lawyers in the case. The record shows that Kunstler and Ratner had complete, active charge of the defense of the case. Mercer was not active enough for the author of the letter to know that he even existed. There is nothing before the Court in this summary judgment hearing that would indicate that "the attack was read as specifically directed at the plaintiff" (Mercer), or that a reader of the newspaper would understand it was intended to refer to anyone other than Kunstler and Ratner.

This is one of the grounds upon which a summary judgment will be entered against the plaintiff Mercer.

* * *

Handelman v. Hustler Magazine, Inc.

469 F. Supp. 1048
(S.D.N.Y. 1978)

SAND, District Judge.

Jurisdiction in this libel action is based upon diversity of citizenship. Plaintiff [Handelman] alleges that he was libeled by a *Hustler* feature article about William Loeb, publisher of the Manchester Union Leader and the New Hampshire Sunday News, which, among other matters, described the extensive litigation which raged over the estate of William Loeb's mother. The defendants in this case are Hustler Magazine, Inc., Larry C. Flynt, its publisher, and Kevin Cash, who allegedly wrote the article under the fictitious name, "Ben Steffens".

In his complaint, plaintiff states that he is the attorney who represented the executor of the Loeb estate. He alleges that he was libeled by one sentence in the *Hustler* article which reads: "Loeb, according to the book,[1] fought the will for about six years, letting high-priced New York lawyers eat up over $800,000 before withdrawing his complaint, leaving his daughter to pay taxes on the rest."[2] Defendants move for summary judgment on the grounds that (1) the statement is not actionable because it does not refer to plaintiff; ... For the reasons herein stated, summary judgment is denied.

Under New York law, the plaintiff must show that a libelous statement was published "of and concerning him." As the Second Circuit has stated, the question is whether:

> "the libel designates the plaintiff in such a way as to let those who knew him understand that he was the person meant. It is not necessary that all the world should understand the libel; it is sufficient if those who knew the plaintiff can make out that he is the person meant." Fetler v. Houghton Mifflin Co., 364 F.2d 650 (2d Cir. 1966).

Moreover, it is for the jury to decide whether a written defamatory statement applies to plaintiff. At trial, a plaintiff is entitled to prove this fact by the use of extrinsic evidence.

Defendants argue that this sentence does not refer to plaintiff. Under this interpretation:

> "(i)t is clear that ... the object of the sentence is Mr. Loeb, not the attorneys for the estate. The clear import of the sentence is that Loeb's destructive purposes created such litigation and other legal proceedings as to cause a good deal of legal work in opposition to him. No conclusion adverse to the attorneys' involvement in these proceedings can fairly be drawn from that statement." Defendant's Memo, p. 12.

Plaintiff, on the other hand, argues that in referring to the lawyers involved with the estate, the sentence clearly depicts the attorney of record for the estate.

Clearly, the primary target of the article is Mr. Loeb. One may also read the sentence in question as being highly critical of the lawyers retained by Mr. Loeb to pursue allegedly frivolous claims, later abandoned, against the estate. The question is, however, whether a jury could find that the term "lawyers" refers not only to Mr. Loeb's attorneys but to Mr. Handelman as well. Under this interpretation, Mr. Handelman, as a member of the group, would still be entitled to recover. When a defamatory matter refers to a small group of persons, an individual member may recover if (1) the group or class is so small that the matter can reasonably be understood to refer to the member, or (2) the circumstances of publication reasonably give rise to the conclusion that there is a particular reference to the member. *Restatement (Second) of Torts*, section 564A, Comment b, Illustration 3 (1977); *see* Neiman-Marcus v. Lait, 13 F.R.D. 311 (S.D.N.Y.1952).

Although we realize that the burden on plaintiff to show that a statement is "of and concerning him" is not a light one, we cannot conclude that these words are incapable of supporting a jury's finding that the allegedly libelous statements refer to plaintiff.

* * *

1. Vicarious defamation? According to §§ 561–562 of the *Restatement (Second) of Torts*, a for-profit corporation or partnership may have an action for defamation to the same

---

1. The article quotes extensively from a book on Loeb entitled "Who the Hell is William Loeb" written by Cash and published shortly before the end of 1975....

2. At oral argument of this motion and in his memorandum, plaintiff disclaimed any objection to the words "high priced New York lawyers". Indeed, he would take umbrage at any suggestion that he was not a "high priced New York lawyer".

extent as an individual if the defamatory matter about the entity "tends to prejudice it in the conduct of its business or to deter others from dealing with it." Assume that the defendant makes a defamatory statement about a lawyer, who happens to be a partner in a law firm. Does the firm have a cause of action? Have the other individual partners in the firm also been defamed?

2. Defamation of a group. *Handelman* references the rule regarding defamation of a group. If a defendant defames a law firm, have the individual lawyers in the firm also been defamed? According to the *Restatement*, a defamatory statement about a partnership "usually carries imputations defamatory of one or more of the individual partners." *Restatement (Second) of Torts* § 562 cmt. b. But is that right? Under the rule cited in *Handelman*, lawyers Smith & Jones would probably have a claim if the defendant defamed the two-person law firm of Smith & Jones. But do the 200 hundred partners of the Able & Baker law firm each have separate causes of action if an individual defames the firm as an entity? ("The Able & Baker firm is corrupt.") *See Restatement (Second) of Torts* § 564A.

3. Fictional characters. According to the *Restatement*, a statement is of and concerning the plaintiff if the "recipient correctly, or mistakenly but reasonably, understands that it was intended to refer" to the plaintiff. *Restatement (Second) of Torts* § 564. One recurring issue is whether an individual has been defamed through the creation of a supposedly fictional character that is based on or closely resembles the individual. If a reasonable listener or reader would understand that the fictional character is intended to portray the actual individual, liability may attach. What if the author of the fictional work did not intend to portray the plaintiff but a reasonable reader would conclude that the fictional character is meant to portray the plaintiff?

* * *

D. Damages

Damages recoverable for defamation include damage to one's reputation, as well as emotional distress and any resulting economic or physical harm. In *Marcone*, for example, Marcone testified that he was "frustrated, distraught, upset, and distressed about the article and its effect on his family and friends." He also stated that he feared "retribution against his family by clients who imagined themselves the victims of his alleged cooperation" with the government. *Id.* The Third Circuit held that this evidence was sufficient to permit recovery.

Recall from the earlier discussion regarding the distinction between libel and slander that, historically, unless the defamatory statement constituted libel or slander per se, a plaintiff had to establish special harm (i.e., pecuniary damage). In *Marcone*, for example, the court concluded that since the defamatory statement amounted to libel per se, the plaintiff was not required under Pennsylvania law to establish actual economic loss. Where a plaintiff established that the defamation consisted of libel or slander per se, some courts permitted a jury to award presumed damages, *i.e.*, recovery without any evidence of any kind of injury. This rather extraordinary form of compensatory damages was known as presumed damages. The ability of plaintiffs to recover presumed damages has been limited by the Supreme Court decisions in the next chapter. Indeed, some jurisdictions have abolished the doctrine altogether. Yet, others still cling to the doctrine, despite complaints about its arbitrary nature. Julie C. Sipe, "*Old Stinking, Old Nasty, Old Itchy Old Toad*": *Defamation Law, Warts and All (A Call for Reform)*, 41 IND. L. REV. 137 (2008).

Focus Questions: *Marcone v. Penthouse International Magazine*

1. *Which modern or recent historical figures would you consider to be libel-proof?*
2. *Even if Marcone was not libel-proof, what is the relevance of the prior negative publicity concerning Marcone?*

Marcone v. Penthouse International Magazine for Men

754 F.2d 1072
(3d Cir. 1985)

ADAMS, Circuit Judge.I.

[The facts in this case appear in Part B1 *supra*. The Third Circuit concluded that the statements concerning Marcone could be construed as being defamatory.]

Defendants next contend that even if its article was capable of being defamatory, Marcone's reputation in the community was so tarnished before the publication that no further harm could have occurred. Penthouse's assertion is that Marcone was, in effect, libel proof before the publication of the allegedly libelous statement. *See* Cardillo v. Doubleday & Co., 518 F.2d 638, 639–40 (2d Cir.1975); Sharon v. Time, Inc., 575 F.Supp. 1162, 1168–72 (S.D.N.Y.1983); Wynberg v. National Enquirer, Inc., 564 F.Supp. 924, 927–28 (C.D.Cal.1982).

In *Wynberg*, for example, the court held that a plaintiff, who had a brief but highly publicized romance with Elizabeth Taylor was libel proof. Wynberg had been convicted of criminal conduct on five separate occasions, including a conviction for contributing to the delinquency of minors. The court concluded that

> When, for example, an individual engages in conspicuously anti-social or even criminal behavior, which is widely reported to the public, his reputation diminishes proportionately. Depending upon the nature of the conduct, the number of offenses, and the degree and range of publicity received, there comes a time when the individual's reputation for specific conduct, or his general reputation for honesty and fair dealing is sufficiently low in the public's estimation that he can recover only nominal damages for subsequent defamatory statements.

To bolster its claim that Marcone is entitled only to nominal damages, *Penthouse* cites a string of items of negative publicity regarding Marcone, from 1976 onward. For example, his indictment in connection with drug trafficking in 1976 was widely publicized in the Philadelphia-area media. Moreover, a number of newspaper articles linked Marcone to the Castle, a gathering place for motorcycle gangs and a haven for a variety of illegal activities. In addition, in 1978 Marcone was tried for failing to file Federal Income tax returns for 1971 and 1972. Marcone was tried for criminal income tax evasion in 1978, and although the case ended in a hung jury, it was widely reported by the local media. Marcone was also fined at least twice for contempt of court for his failure to appear at scheduled hearings. The second of these contempt convictions occurred in 1979, however, after the Penthouse article was published. Finally, in 1978 Marcone was fined for punching a police officer who had stopped Marcone's car for a traffic violation.

While such evidence suggests that Marcone's reputation was sullied before the article was published, we cannot say as a matter of law that Marcone was libel proof. *See* Buckley v. Littell, 539 F.2d 882, 889 (2d Cir.1976) (libel proof doctrine is narrow), *cert. denied*,

429 U.S. 1062, 97 S.Ct. 785, 50 L.Ed.2d 777 (1977). Evidence of a tarnished reputation is admissible and should be considered as a factor to mitigate the level of compensatory damages. In the present case, the jury was informed of the evidence regarding Marcone's reputation, and its verdict for compensatory damages may well reflect the diminished status of Marcone in November of 1978.

* * *

Libel-proof plaintiffs. The *Wynberg* court referenced in *Marcone* explained the concept of a libel-proof plaintiff in the following manner: "Depending upon the nature of the conduct, the number of offenses, and the degree and range of publicity received, there comes a time when the individual's reputation for specific conduct, or his general reputation for honesty and fair dealing is sufficiently low in the public's estimation that he can recover only nominal damages for subsequent defamatory statements." Wynberg v. National Enquirer, Inc., 564 F. Supp. 924, 928 (C.D. Cal. 1982). As such, the libel-proof plaintiff's reputation "may be kicked and trod upon with impunity." Rodney A. Smolla, 2 Law of Defamation § 9:61 (2d ed.).

* * *

E. The Role of Truth

At common law, a plaintiff did not have to establish that the defendant's defamatory statement was false in order to make out a prima facie case of defamation. Instead, the fact that the defamatory statement was true was an absolute defense. Where the role of truth or falsity of a defamatory statement fits within the scheme of a defamation claim is examined in greater detail in the following chapter. However, regardless of whether it is the plaintiff's burden to establish that a statement is false or the defendant's burden to establish that the statement is true, if it is established that the statement was not false, there can be no liability.

What it means to say that a statement is "true" (or at least "not false"), however, is a complicated question. The line between a statement of fact and one of opinion can be blurry at best. Some statements may be mostly true but a little bit false. Sometimes the headline or teaser of a story may be misleading but the gist of the article as a whole is true. The following section explores the concept of truth in the context of defamation claims.

Focus Question: *Rouch v. Enquirer & News of Battle Creek*

What is the substantial truth doctrine?

Rouch v. Enquirer & News of Battle Creek

487 N.W.2d 205
(Mich. 1992)

This case began on December 21, 1979, with the arrest of David Rouch as a suspect in the rape of his former wife's baby-sitter. Rouch was arrested without a warrant, held by the police, booked on the charge of first-degree criminal sexual conduct, as authorized by the prosecutor, and released on $10,000 personal recognizance bond after an informal hearing before a magistrate. It is undisputed that Rouch was never formally arraigned on a warrant and that the police eventually pursued another suspect. The facts surrounding Rouch's arrest were set forth in an article published by the *Battle Creek News & Enquirer*. Mr. Rouch conceded that the article in question and its references to his arrest, booking, and release on bond were accurate. Plaintiff complained, however, about three supposedly material errors. First, plaintiff contended that the article falsely asserted that Rouch was "charged" with sexual assault. Second, the plaintiff complained that the article falsely stated that he was identified by his children when, in reality, he was identified by his former wife's children, his former stepchildren. Third, plaintiff complained that the article was inaccurate in that it asserted that the charge against Rouch was authorized by the Calhoun County Prosecutor's office.

The common law has never required defendants to prove that a publication is literally and absolutely accurate in every minute detail. For example, the *Restatement of Torts* provides that "[s]light inaccuracies of expression are immaterial provided that the defamatory charge is true in substance." Michigan courts have traditionally followed this approach. At early common law, Michigan courts predicated a claim for libel on the question whether the article was substantially true. In *McAllister v. Detroit Free Press*, 85 Mich. 453, 460–461, 48 N.W. 612 (1891), this Court explained that liability could not be imposed for a slight inaccuracy:

> It is sufficient for the defendant to justify so much of the defamatory matter as constitutes the sting of the charge, and it is unnecessary to repeat and justify every word of the alleged defamatory matter, so long as the substance of the libelous charge be justified.... [A] slight inaccuracy in one of its details will not prevent the defendant's succeeding, providing the inaccuracy in no way alters the complexion of the affair, and would have no different effect on the reader than that which the literal truth would produce....

Thus, the test looked to the sting of the article to determine its effect on the reader; if the literal truth produced the same effect, minor differences were deemed immaterial.

The substantial truth doctrine is frequently invoked to solve two recurring problems: minor inaccuracies and technically incorrect or flawed use of legal terminology. This case raises both questions. The Court of Appeals held that "whether the article is read for its gist or simply for the information presented as fact, plaintiff has met his burden of proving falsity." In reaching this result, the Court of Appeals focused on the assertions that the article indicated that plaintiff was "charged" with the crime of first-degree criminal sexual conduct, sexual assault, that "charges" had been authorized by the prosecutor when no formal arraignment had occurred, and that the article suggested that "his children" identified him as the person who committed the crime when the identification was made by his former wife's children. We disagree.

In order to properly evaluate the falsity of the article, we have reproduced the language from the article as published in the newspaper followed by a version that contains language which corrects the inaccuracies complained of by the plaintiff.

This is the text of the report and headline published by the Enquirer *& News of Battle Creek*:

Police arrest suspect in baby-sitter assault

> A 43-year-old man has been arrested and charged with the sexual assault of a 17-year-old woman who was babysitting with *his children* at his *ex-wife's house* on North Finlay Avenue in Bedford Township.

> The subject has been identified by Bedford Township Police as David J. Rouch of 631 Golden Avenue. He is free on a $10,000 personal recognizance interim bond pending his arraignment in District 10 Court next week. Rouch *is charged with* first-degree criminal sexual conduct.
>
> Police said Rouch allegedly entered the house about 4 a.m. Friday and attacked the young woman. He is said to have used a knife to cut the victim's clothes off, police said.
>
> The victim later called a relative, who took her to Community Hospital and then called police. The suspect was *identified by his children*, according to police.
>
> Rouch was arrested at his home by Emmett Township Police, who were informed where he lived by Bedford Township investigators.
>
> The *charge* against Rouch *was authorized Friday by the Calhoun County Prosecutor's Office.*

The following version substitutes language that the plaintiff asserts should have been used in the article:

> **Police arrest suspect in baby-sitter assault**
>
> A 43-year-old man has been *arrested and accused* of sexual assaulting a 17-year-old woman who was babysitting his ex-wife's children at her house on North Finlay Avenue in Bedford Township.
>
> The suspect has been identified by Bedford Township Police as David J. Rouch of 631 Golden Avenue. He is free on a $10,000 personal recognizance interim bond pending his arraignment in District 10 Court next week. Rouch *is accused of* committing first-degree criminal sexual conduct.
>
> Police said that Rouch allegedly entered the house about 4 a.m. Friday and attacked the young woman. He is said to have used a knife to cut the victim's clothes off, police said.
>
> The victim later called a relative, who took her to Community Hospital and then called police. The suspect was identified by *his ex-wife's children*, according to police.
>
> Rouch was arrested at his home by Emmett Township Police, who were informed where he lived by Bedford Township investigators.
>
> The Calhoun County Prosecutor's Office *authorized the incarceration* of Rouch on *allegations of criminal sexual conduct* in the first degree.

We cannot agree that the gist or sting of the article is changed by these minor differences.

The primary criticism that plaintiff raises is with the use of the word "charges," absent formal arraignment. The Court of Appeals ... relied upon a textual analysis of the plain meaning of the word "charge," questioning the defendant's suggestion that "charge" is synonymous with "accuse." Conceding that Webster's New World Dictionary of the American Language, Second College Edition (1984), includes "accuse" as one of the possible meanings of "charge," the Court pointed out the additional listed term "indictment." It also referred to The Random House College Dictionary, Revised Edition (1984), which defined "charge" as "to accuse formally or explicitly" and as "an accusation." On the basis of these authorities, the Court reasoned that "charge" carries a more serious connotation than "accuse" and that the article's use of the term "in a much more specific and legal sense" was false.

Technical inaccuracies in legal terminology employed by nonlawyers such as those at issue here fall within this category. Numerous courts have rejected claims of falsity when based on a misuse of formal legal terminology.[26] ...

... [P]laintiff asserts that "charge" should be limited to circumstances in which a formal arraignment has been held.... [T]he word at issue in this case encompasses the formal legal sense as well as a broader lay sense.... [W]e conclude that use of "charge" absent formal arraignment cannot be deemed materially false.

The word "charge" is an umbrella term covering all stages of the charging process. It is used by the law in contradistinction to a conviction. Even if plaintiff's argument that "charge" connotes a more serious formal involvement of judicial process than "accuse" were correct as a matter of law, we think it apparent that the word may be used in a popular sense as a synonym for accuse. While one meaning of "charge" is simply "accuse," carrying with it no intimation of governmental involvement, here, if the word "charge" is measured by the gist of what happened, there was not only a charge or accusation by an individual, but a booking by the police, an authorization by the prosecution to lodge the suspect on the charge, and an involvement by the magistrate recognizing these actions. Thus, even if "charge" connotes the existence of governmental involvement, that was present here.

At best, one might conclude that the use of "charge" in its technical formal sense was inaccurate. We cannot accept this as a basis for liability. To do so would totally eviscerate the "breathing space" that the constitution requires in order to protect important First Amendment rights. When writing about criminal justice or legal matters, newspapers would be forced to recapitulate technical legal terminology employed by courts or law enforcement personnel even where popular words might be clearer for the lay reader. Attempting to reframe legal documents and events with legal significance into popular or lay terminology would be fraught with peril, and newspapers would do so at their risk. As one court remarked, there is "no authority for plaintiff's contention that a newspaper article reporting a judicial proceeding must indicate every possible interpretation of every word used in a complaint or other legal document." We agree. Having conducted an independent review of the record to determine whether use of the word "charge" rendered the article materially false, we conclude that it did not.

Plaintiff's additional complaint falls within the second category of cases arising under the substantial truth doctrine, those that involve minor inaccuracies. Plaintiff protests the article's suggestion that he was identified by his children, rather than the children of his former wife. The Court of Appeals concluded that this constituted material falsity because it seemed to eliminate the possibility that there was a mistaken identification. We cannot accept this reasoning.

---

26. *See, e.g.*, Vachet v. Central Newspapers, Inc., 816 F.2d 313, 316 (CA 7, 1987) (the gist of the article concerned the plaintiff's association with a suspected rapist because he was arrested for harboring a fugitive, but the "particulars of the arrest—whether it was pursuant to an arrest warrant or authorized by a state statute—are inoffensive details of secondary importance"); Simonson v. United Press Int'l. Inc., 654 F.2d 478 (CA 7, 1981) (use of the technical term "ruled" for remarks made by the judge during a sentencing hearing and of "rape" where the defendant had pleaded no contest to a charge of second-degree sexual assault was not enough to establish falsity); Lambert v. Providence Journal Co., 508 F.2d 656 (CA 1, 1975), *cert. den.* 423 U.S. 828, 96 S.Ct. 45, 46 L.Ed.2d 45 (1975) (the use of the term "murder" where the defendant denied guilt did not constitute an actionable innuendo regarding his guilt despite the article's failure to use more neutral term like "homicide" or "shooting death"); Piracci v. Hearst Corp., 263 F. Supp. 511 (D. Md., 1966), *aff'd* 371 F.2d 1016 (CA 4, 1967) (per curiam) (a newspaper report that the plaintiff was arrested for "possession of marijuana" was substantially accurate despite the fact that the actual charge was "delinquency due to the act of possessing marijuana").

Like courts in other jurisdictions, Michigan courts have found substantial truth despite minor inaccuracies in the details of an article. *McCracken v. Evening News Ass'n*, 3 Mich.App. 32, 141 N.W.2d 694 (1966), epitomizes the reasoning that undergirds such a finding. The defendant newspaper reported that the plaintiff was charged with "$100,000 fraud" when, in fact, he had altered construction invoices in an amount between $37,000 and $39,000. The Court of Appeals rejected the plaintiff's claim that the article was substantially untrue, noting that this constituted "an inaccuracy that does not alter the complexion of the affair and would have no different effect on the reader than that which the literal truth would produce."

The essence of plaintiff's argument is that the statement in the article that his children had identified him would eliminate in the reader's mind the possibility of a mistake. We think the gist or sting of the article was that plaintiff was arrested on the basis of the identification of persons who knew him. While we might agree that a reader acquainted with the facts might have more reason to suspect the motives of the identifiers, this is an argument regarding the weight of the identification, not its truth or falsity.

In sum, neither of the asserted errors, taken individually or as a group, alters the gist or sting of the article. The sting of the article was that the plaintiff had been identified by persons to whom he was well known and was charged with CSC I. That is true. The question whether a formal warrant had been issued or an arraignment held, like the question whether it was his children or former stepchildren who identified him, did not affect the article's substantial truth. Thus, the Court of Appeals erred in affirming the trial court judgment on this issue.

* * *

1. Substantial truth. Which of the following statements are false (or substantially untrue) under the *Rouch* approach?

(a) A newspaper article stating that plaintiff had been charged in a lawsuit with "outright theft" (the word "theft" being a term used in the criminal context) when, in fact, the complaint alleged civil conversion. Handelsman v. San Francisco Chronicle, 11 Cal. App. 3d 381, 387, 90 Cal. Rptr. 188 (1970).

(b) A newspaper article stating, in the context of a story about public employees' use of tax-payer funded vehicles, that the plaintiff had used a state car to drive seventy-two miles to work when, in fact, the distance was only fifty-five miles. Stevens v. Independent Newspapers, Inc., 15 Media L.Rep. 1097, 1988 WL 25377 (Del. Super. Ct., 1988).

(c) A newspaper article stating that plaintiff, a candidate for office, had spent 24 hours in jail for firing a gun after a motorist accidentally leaned on her horn, when, in fact, plaintiff had spent 24 hours in jail for displaying a weapon after a motorist accidentally leaned on her horn. Read v. Phoenix Newspapers, Inc., 819 P.2d 939 (Ariz. 1991).

(d) A newspaper article stating that a police officer kidnapped a boy at a gunpoint after the boy got into a fight with another boy, when, in fact, the police officer did not point a gun and made no threat to the boy, who got into the police car with the officer. Akins v. Altus Newspapers, Inc., 609 P.2d 1263 (Okla. 1977).

2. Related issues. There are several other issues that are closely connected to the issue of truth and falsity. For example, to what extent may an opinion be actionable in defamation? To what extent is highly colorful and exaggerated language actionable? When, if ever, are satire and parody actionable? Given the overlap these issues have with constitutional law, they are discussed in the following chapter.

Chapter 9

Defamation: Constitutional Constraints

Exercise 9.1: Chapter Problem

Johnny "Jumpy" Garvin is a famous professional football player. He is famous not just for his athletic abilities, but for his seemingly pathological need to draw attention to himself. Whenever he scores a touchdown, Garvin does some new kind of dance or acts out some type of skit to celebrate; he has his own reality television show; and he is constantly engaged in some type of public spat with a sports writer or other athlete who has written something negative about him.

Garvin was entering the last year of his contract with the Boise Bruisers when he decided he was not being paid enough. He therefore decided not to report to training camp until his contractual demands were met. He spoke repeatedly to the press about his demands and his unhappiness with the general manager and owner of the Bruisers. Behind the scenes, his agent (and girlfriend), Teri Hayes, was negotiating with the general manager of the Bruisers in an attempt to secure a better deal. After leaving the Bruisers' complex one day, a reporter for the local newspaper asked Hayes to comment on Garvin's contract situation. Hayes replied, "I'm just trying to make sure that Jumpy gets paid what he's worth. I have a feeling that the fans recognize that Jumpy is underpaid and will put the blame for the holdout where it belongs: on Bruisers management."

Eventually, Garvin received a new contract, but the Bruisers general manager, Art Coy, was furious with Hayes' negotiating tactics. During an interview with the same reporter, Coy responded to a question about Garvin's new contract by saying, "There were times when I was ready to trade Garvin, just so I didn't have to deal with his crazy agent anymore. She's so dishonest, I can't stand it." Coy's comments were broadcast nationally. After controversy concerning the statements erupted, a rival sports agent, Tommy Paxton, told a reporter that Hayes was "a sleazy, incompetent idiot." Paxton has never met Hayes nor had any dealings with her, but he figured that more bad publicity affecting Hayes might help him land a few of her clients.

Hayes has now sued Coy and Paxton for defamation. What level of fault will Hayes need to establish on the part of Coy and Paxton? Will she able to satisfy her burden?

Defamation law took a dramatic turn in the 1960s. Prior to that time, the rules regarding libel and slander developed blissfully separate from constitutional law. Eventually, however, there was the realization that holding a defendant liable for defamation—a speech-related tort—had First Amendment implications. As a result, the Supreme Court changed the landscape of defamation law in some important ways. One of the most important changes occurred with respect to the concept of fault. Recall that as the defamation tort originally developed, liability was strict. A defendant might have various affirmative defenses at his or her disposal, but the fact that the defendant had no reason to know that a statement was false or defamatory was not, by itself, a bar to liability. In a series of important decisions, the Court changed all of that.

The following chapter examines the constitutional constraints that have developed regarding the tort of defamation.

A. The *New York Times v. Sullivan* Standard: Public Officials, Public Figures, and Actual Malice

---

Focus Questions: *New York Times Co. v. Sullivan*

1. *What does the court mean by "actual malice"?*
2. *When does this standard apply?*
3. *Why does the Court adopt this standard?*

New York Times Co. v. Sullivan

376 U.S. 254
(1964)

Mr. Justice BRENNAN delivered the opinion of the Court.

We are required in this case to determine for the first time the extent to which the constitutional protections for speech and press limit a State's power to award damages in a libel action brought by a public official against critics of his official conduct.

Respondent L. B. Sullivan is one of the three elected Commissioners of the City of Montgomery, Alabama. He testified that he was 'Commissioner of Public Affairs and the duties are supervision of the Police Department, Fire Department, Department of Cemetery and Department of Scales.' He brought this civil libel action against the four individual petitioners, who are Negroes and Alabama clergymen, and against petitioner the New York Times Company, a New York corporation which publishes the New York Times, a daily newspaper. A jury in the Circuit Court of Montgomery County awarded him damages of $500,000, the full amount claimed, against all the petitioners, and the Supreme Court of Alabama affirmed.

Respondent's complaint alleged that he had been libeled by statements in a full-page advertisement that was carried in the New York Times on March 29, 1960. Entitled 'Heed Their Rising Voices,' the advertisement began by stating that 'As the whole world knows by now, thousands of Southern Negro students are engaged in widespread non-violent demonstrations in positive affirmation of the right to live in human dignity as guaranteed by the U.S. Constitution and the Bill of Rights.' It went on to charge that 'in their efforts to uphold these guarantees, they are being met by an unprecedented wave of terror by those who would deny and negate that document which the whole world looks upon as setting the pattern for modern freedom.... Succeeding paragraphs purported to illustrate the 'wave of terror' by describing certain alleged events. The text concluded with an appeal for funds for three purposes: support of the student movement, 'the struggle for the right-to-vote,' and the legal defense of Dr. Martin Luther King, Jr., leader of the movement, against a perjury indictment then pending in Montgomery.

... The advertisement was signed at the bottom of the page by the 'Committee to Defend Martin Luther King and the Struggle for Freedom in the South,' and the officers of the Committee were listed.

Of the 10 paragraphs of text in the advertisement, the third and a portion of the sixth were the basis of respondent's claim of libel. They read as follows:

Third paragraph:

> In Montgomery, Alabama, after students sang 'My Country, 'Tis of Thee' on the State Capitol steps, their leaders were expelled from school, and truckloads of police armed with shotguns and tear-gas ringed the Alabama State College Campus. When the entire student body protested to state authorities by refusing to re-register, their dining hall was padlocked in an attempt to starve them into submission.

Sixth paragraph:

> Again and again the Southern violators have answered Dr. King's peaceful protests with intimidation and violence. They have bombed his home almost killing his wife and child. They have assaulted his person. They have arrested him seven times—for 'speeding,' 'loitering' and similar 'offenses.' And now they have charged him with 'perjury'—a felony under which they could imprison him for ten years....

Although neither of these statements mentions respondent by name, he contended that the word 'police' in the third paragraph referred to him as the Montgomery Commissioner who supervised the Police Department, so that he was being accused of 'ringing' the campus with police. He further claimed that the paragraph would be read as imputing to the police, and hence to him, the padlocking of the dining hall in order to starve the students into submission. As to the sixth paragraph, he contended that since arrests are ordinarily made by the police, the statement 'They have arrested (Dr. King) seven times' would be read as referring to him; he further contended that the 'They' who did the arresting would be equated with the 'They' who committed the other described acts and with the 'Southern violators.' Thus, he argued, the paragraph would be read as accusing the Montgomery police, and hence him, of answering Dr. King's protests with 'intimidation and violence,' bombing his home, assaulting his person, and charging him with perjury. Respondent and six other Montgomery residents testified that they read some or all of the statements as referring to him in his capacity as Commissioner.

It is uncontroverted that some of the statements contained in the two paragraphs were not accurate descriptions of events which occurred in Montgomery. [For example, "[t]he campus dining hall was not padlocked on any occasion, and the only students who may have been barred from eating there were the few who had neither signed a preregistration application nor requested temporary meal tickets. Although the police were deployed near the campus in large numbers on three occasions, they did not at any time 'ring' the campus, and they were not called to the campus in connection with the demonstration on the State Capitol steps, as the third paragraph implied."]

Respondent made no effort to prove that he suffered actual pecuniary loss as a result of the alleged libel.[3] One of his witnesses, a former employer, testified that if he had believed the statements, he doubted whether he 'would want to be associated with anybody who would be a party to such things that are stated in that ad,' and that he would not re-employ respondent if he believed 'that he allowed the Police Department to do the things that the paper say he did.' But neither this witness nor any of the others testified that he had actually believed the statements in their supposed reference to respondent.

The cost of the advertisement was approximately $4800, and it was published by *the Times* upon an order from a New York advertising agency acting for the signatory Committee.... The manager of the Advertising Acceptability Department testified that he had approved the advertisement for publication because he knew nothing to cause him to believe that anything in it was false, and because it bore the endorsement of 'a number of people who are well known and whose reputation' he 'had no reason to question.' Neither he nor anyone else at *the Times* made an effort to confirm the accuracy of the advertisement, either by checking it against recent Times news stories relating to some of the described events or by any other means.

In affirming the judgment, the Supreme Court of Alabama sustained the trial judge's rulings and instructions in all respects. It held that '(w)here the words published tend to injure a person libeled by them in his reputation, profession, trade or business, or charge him with an indictable offense, or tends to bring the individual into public contempt,' they are 'libelous per se'; that 'the matter complained of is, under the above doctrine, libelous per se, if it was published of and concerning the plaintiff'; and that it was actionable without 'proof of pecuniary injury..., such injury being implied.' It approved the trial court's ruling that the jury could find the statements to have been made 'of and concerning' respondent, stating: 'We think it common knowledge that the average person knows that municipal agents, such as police and firemen, and others, are under the control and direction of the city governing body, and more particularly under the direction and control of a single commissioner. In measuring the performance or deficiencies of such groups, praise or criticism is usually attached to the official in complete control of the body.' In sustaining the trial court's determination that the verdict was not excessive, the court said that malice could be inferred from *the Times'* 'irresponsibility' in printing the advertisement while '*the Times* in its own files had articles already published which would have demonstrated the falsity of the allegations in the advertisement'; from the Times' failure to retract for respondent while retracting for the Governor, whereas the falsity of some of the allegations was then known to *the Times* and 'the matter contained in the advertisement was equally false as to both parties'; and from the testimony of *the Times'* Secretary that, apart from the statement that the dining hall was padlocked, he thought the two paragraphs were 'substantially correct.' The court reaffirmed a statement in an earlier opinion that 'There is no legal measure of damages in cases of this character.' It rejected petitioners' constitutional contentions with the brief statements that 'The First Amendment of the U.S. Constitution does not protect libelous publications' and 'The Fourteenth Amendment is directed against State action and not private action.'

---

3. Approximately 394 copies of the edition of the Times containing the advertisement were circulated in Alabama. Of these, about 35 copies were distributed in Montgomery County. The total circulation of the Times for that day was approximately 650,000 copies.

I.

We may dispose at the outset of two grounds asserted to insulate the judgment of the Alabama courts from constitutional scrutiny. The first is the proposition relied on by the State Supreme Court—that 'The Fourteenth Amendment is directed against State action and not private action.' That proposition has no application to this case. Although this is a civil lawsuit between private parties, the Alabama courts have applied a state rule of law which petitioners claim to impose invalid restrictions on their constitutional freedoms of speech and press. It matters not that that law has been applied in a civil action and that it is common law only, though supplemented by statute. The test is not the form in which state power has been applied but, whatever the form, whether such power has in fact been exercised. *See* Ex parte Virginia, 100 U.S. 339, 346–347, 25 L. Ed. 676; American Federation of Labor v. Swing, 312 U.S. 321, 61 S. Ct. 568, 85 L. Ed. 855.

The second contention is that the constitutional guarantees of freedom of speech and of the press are inapplicable here, at least so far as *the Times* is concerned, because the allegedly libelous statements were published as part of a paid, 'commercial' advertisement....

[The Court held that the advertisement was not a commercial advertisement in the traditional sense in that it "communicated information, expressed opinion, recited grievances, protested claimed abuses, and sought financial support on behalf of a movement whose existence and objectives are matters of the highest public interest and concern." Accordingly, the Court held "that if the allegedly libelous statements would otherwise be constitutionally protected from the present judgment, they do not forfeit that protection because they were published in the form of a paid advertisement."]

II.

Under Alabama law as applied in this case, a publication is 'libelous per se' if the words 'tend to injure a person ... in his reputation' or to 'bring (him) into public contempt'; the trial court stated that the standard was met if the words are such as to 'injure him in his public office, or impute misconduct to him in his office, or want of official integrity, or want of fidelity to a public trust.... Once 'libel per se' has been established, the defendant has no defense as to stated facts unless he can persuade the jury that they were true in all their particulars. His privilege of 'fair comment' for expressions of opinion depends on the truth of the facts upon which the comment is based. Unless he can discharge the burden of proving truth, general damages are presumed, and may be awarded without proof of pecuniary injury. A showing of actual malice is apparently a prerequisite to recovery of punitive damages, and the defendant may in any event forestall a punitive award by a retraction meeting the statutory requirements. Good motives and belief in truth do not negate an inference of malice, but are relevant only in mitigation of punitive damages if the jury chooses to accord them weight.

The question before us is whether this rule of liability, as applied to an action brought by a public official against critics of his official conduct, abridges the freedom of speech and of the press that is guaranteed by the First and Fourteenth Amendments.

Respondent relies heavily, as did the Alabama courts, on statements of this Court to the effect that the Constitution does not protect libelous publications. Those statements do not foreclose our inquiry here. None of the cases sustained the use of libel laws to impose sanctions upon expression critical of the official conduct of public officials.... Like insurrection, contempt, advocacy of unlawful acts, breach of the peace obscenity, solicitation of legal business, and the various other formulae for the repression of expression that have been challenged in this Court, libel can claim no talismanic immunity from constitutional limitations. It must be measured by standards that satisfy the First Amendment.

The general proposition that freedom of expression upon public questions is secured by the First Amendment has long been settled by our decisions. The constitutional safeguard, we have said, 'was fashioned to assure unfettered interchange of ideas for the bringing about of political and social changes desired by the people.' Roth v. United States, 354 U.S. 476, 484, 77 S. Ct. 1304, 1308, 1 L. Ed.2d 1498. 'The maintenance of the opportunity for free political discussion to the end that government may be responsive to the will of the people and that changes may be obtained by lawful means, an opportunity essential to the security of the Republic, is a fundamental principle of our constitutional system.' Stromberg v. California, 283 U.S. 359, 369, 51 S. Ct. 532, 536, 75 L. Ed. 1117. '(I)t is a prized American privilege to speak one's mind, although not always with perfect good taste, on all public institutions,' Bridges v. California, 314 U.S. 252, 270, 62 S. Ct. 190, 197, 86 L. Ed. 192, and this opportunity is to be afforded for 'vigorous advocacy' no less than 'abstract discussion.' N.A.A.C.P. v. Button, 371 U.S. 415, 429, 83 S. Ct. 328, 9 L. Ed.2d 405. The First Amendment, said Judge Learned Hand, 'presupposes that right conclusions are more likely to be gathered out of a multitude of tongues, than through any kind of authoritative selection. To many this is, and always will be, folly; but we have staked upon it our all.' United States v. Associated Press, 52 F. Supp. 362, 372 (D.C. S.D.N.Y.1943). Mr. Justice Brandeis, in his concurring opinion in Whitney v. California, 274 U.S. 357, 375–376, 47 S. Ct. 641, 648, 71 L. Ed. 1095, gave the principle its classic formulation:

> Those who won our independence believed ... that public discussion is a political duty; and that this should be a fundamental principle of the American government. They recognized the risks to which all human institutions are subject. But they knew that order cannot be secured merely through fear of punishment for its infraction; that it is hazardous to discourage thought, hope and imagination; that fear breeds repression; that repression breeds hate; that hate menaces stable government; that the path of safety lies in the opportunity to discuss freely supposed grievances and proposed remedies; and that the fitting remedy for evil counsels is good ones. Believing in the power of reason as applied through public discussion, they eschewed silence coerced by law—the argument of force in its worst form. Recognizing the occasional tyrannies of governing majorities, they amended the Constitution so that free speech and assembly should be guaranteed.

Thus we consider this case against the background of a profound national commitment to the principle that debate on public issues should be uninhibited, robust, and wide-open, and that it may well include vehement, caustic, and sometimes unpleasantly sharp attacks on government and public officials. The present advertisement, as an expression of grievance and protest on one of the major public issues of our time, would seem clearly to qualify for the constitutional protection. The question is whether it forfeits that protection by the falsity of some of its factual statements and by its alleged defamation of respondent.

Authoritative interpretations of the First Amendment guarantees have consistently refused to recognize an exception for any test of truth—whether administered by judges, juries, or administrative officials—and especially one that puts the burden of proving truth on the speaker. The constitutional protection does not turn upon 'the truth, popularity, or social utility of the ideas and beliefs which are offered.' N.A.A.C.P. v. Button, 371 U.S. 415, 445, 83 S. Ct. 328, 344, 9 L. Ed.2d 405. As Madison said, 'Some degree of abuse is inseparable from the proper use of every thing; and in no instance is this more true than in that of the press.' 4 Elliot's Debates on the Federal Constitution (1876), p. 571. In Cantwell v. Connecticut, 310 U.S. 296, 310, 60 S. Ct. 900, 906, 84 L. Ed. 1213, the Court declared:

> In the realm of religious faith, and in that of political belief, sharp differences arise. In both fields the tenets of one man may seem the rankest error to his neighbor. To persuade others to his own point of view, the pleader, as we know, at times, resorts to exaggeration, to vilification of men who have been, or are, prominent in church or state, and even to false statement. But the people of this nation have ordained in the light of history, that, in spite of the probability of excesses and abuses, these liberties are, in the long view, essential to enlightened opinion and right conduct on the part of the citizens of a democracy.

That erroneous statement is inevitable in free debate, and that it must be protected if the freedoms of expression are to have the 'breathing space' that they 'need ... to survive,' N.A.A.C.P. v. Button, 371 U.S. 415, 433, 83 S. Ct. 328, 338, 9 L.Ed.2d 405, was also recognized by the Court of Appeals for the District of Columbia Circuit in Sweeney v. Patterson, 76 U.S. App. D.C. 23, 24, 128 F.2d 457, 458 (1942), cert. denied, 317 U.S. 678, 63 S. Ct. 160, 87 L. Ed. 544. Judge Edgerton spoke for a unanimous court which affirmed the dismissal of a Congressman's libel suit based upon a newspaper article charging him with anti-Semitism in opposing a judicial appointment. He said:

> Cases which impose liability for erroneous reports of the political conduct of officials reflect the obsolete doctrine that the governed must not criticize their governors.... The interest of the public here outweighs the interest of appellant or any other individual. The protection of the public requires not merely discussion, but information. Political conduct and views which some respectable people approve, and others condemn, are constantly imputed to Congressmen. Errors of fact, particularly in regard to a man's mental states and processes, are inevitable.... Whatever is added to the field of libel is taken from the field of free debate.

What a State may not constitutionally bring about by means of a criminal statute is likewise beyond the reach of its civil law of libel. The fear of damage awards under a rule such as that invoked by the Alabama courts here may be markedly more inhibiting than the fear of prosecution under a criminal statute. Alabama, for example, has a criminal libel law which subjects to prosecution 'any person who speaks, writes, or prints of and concerning another any accusation falsely and maliciously importing the commission by such person of a felony, or any other indictable offense involving moral turpitude,' and which allows as punishment upon conviction a fine not exceeding $500 and a prison sentence of six months. Alabama Code, Tit. 14, s 350.... The judgment awarded in this case—without the need for any proof of actual pecuniary loss—was one thousand times greater than the maximum fine provided by the Alabama criminal statute, and one hundred times greater than that provided by the Sedition Act. And since there is no double-jeopardy limitation applicable to civil lawsuits, this is not the only judgment that may be awarded against petitioners for the same publication. Whether or not a newspaper can survive a succession of such judgments, the pall of fear and timidity imposed upon those who would give voice to public criticism is an atmosphere in which the First Amendment freedoms cannot survive.

The state rule of law is not saved by its allowance of the defense of truth....

A rule compelling the critic of official conduct to guarantee the truth of all his factual assertions—and to do so on pain of libel judgments virtually unlimited in amount—leads to a comparable 'self-censorship.' Allowance of the defense of truth, with the burden of proving it on the defendant, does not mean that only false speech will be deterred.

Even courts accepting this defense as an adequate safeguard have recognized the difficulties of adducing legal proofs that the alleged libel was true in all its factual particulars. Under such a rule, would-be critics of official conduct may be deterred from voicing their criticism, even though it is believed to be true and even though it is in fact true, because of doubt whether it can be proved in court or fear of the expense of having to do so. They tend to make only statements which 'steer far wider of the unlawful zone.' Speiser v. Randall, *supra*, 357 U.S., at 526, 78 S. Ct. at 1342, 2 L. Ed.2d 1460. The rule thus dampens the vigor and limits the variety of public debate. It is inconsistent with the First and Fourteenth Amendments.

The constitutional guarantees require, we think, a federal rule that prohibits a public official from recovering damages for a defamatory falsehood relating to his official conduct unless he proves that the statement was made with 'actual malice'—that is, with knowledge that it was false or with reckless disregard of whether it was false or not.

...

III.

We hold today that the Constitution delimits a State's power to award damages for libel in actions brought by public officials against critics of their official conduct. Since this is such an action, the rule requiring proof of actual malice is applicable. While Alabama law apparently requires proof of actual malice for an award of punitive damages, here general damages are concerned malice is 'presumed.' Such a presumption is inconsistent with the federal rule.... Since the trial judge did not instruct the jury to differentiate between general and punitive damages, it may be that the verdict was wholly an award of one or the other. But it is impossible to know, in view of the general verdict returned. Because of this uncertainty, the judgment must be reversed and the case remanded.

Since respondent may seek a new trial, we deem that considerations of effective judicial administration require us to review the evidence in the present record to determine whether it could constitutionally support a judgment for respondent. This Court's duty is not limited to the elaboration of constitutional principles; we must also in proper cases review the evidence to make certain that those principles have been constitutionally applied. This is such a case, particularly since the question is one of alleged trespass across 'the line between speech unconditionally guaranteed and speech which may legitimately be regulated.' Speiser v. Randall, 357 U.S. 513, 525, 78 S. Ct. 1332, 1342, 2 L. Ed.2d 1460....

Applying these standards, we consider that the proof presented to show actual malice lacks the convincing clarity which the constitutional standard demands, and hence that it would not constitutionally sustain the judgment for respondent under the proper rule of law. The case of the individual petitioners requires little discussion. Even assuming that they could constitutionally be found to have authorized the use of their names on the advertisement, there was no evidence whatever that they were aware of any erroneous statements or were in any way reckless in that regard. The judgment against them is thus without constitutional support.

As to *the Times*, we similarly conclude that the facts do not support a finding of actual malice. The statement by *the Times*' Secretary that, apart from the padlocking allegation, he thought the advertisement was 'substantially correct,' affords no constitutional warrant for the Alabama Supreme Court's conclusion that it was a 'cavalier ignoring of the falsity of the advertisement (from which), the jury could not have but been impressed with the bad faith of *The Times*, and its maliciousness inferable therefrom.' The statement does not indicate malice at the time of the publication; even if the advertisement was not 'substantially correct'—although respondent's own proofs tend to show that it was—that opinion was at least a reasonable one, and there was no evidence to impeach the witness' good faith in holding it....

Finally, there is evidence that *the Times* published the advertisement without checking its accuracy against the news stories in *the Times*' own files. The mere presence of the stories in the files does not, of course, establish that *the Times* 'knew' the advertisement was false, since the state of mind required for actual malice would have to be brought home to the persons in *the Times*' organization having responsibility for the publication of the advertisement. With respect to the failure of those persons to make the check, the record shows that they relied upon their knowledge of the good reputation of many of those whose names were listed as sponsors of the advertisement, and upon the letter from A. Philip Randolph, known to them as a responsible individual, certifying that the use of the names was authorized. There was testimony that the persons handling the advertisement saw nothing in it that would render it unacceptable under *the Times*' policy of rejecting advertisements containing 'attacks of a personal character'; their failure to reject it on this ground was not unreasonable. We think the evidence against *the Times* supports at most a finding of negligence in failing to discover the misstatements, and is constitutionally insufficient to show the recklessness that is required for a finding of actual malice.

We also think the evidence was constitutionally defective in another respect: it was incapable of supporting the jury's finding that the allegedly libelous statements were made 'of and concerning' respondent.

[The proposition that criticism of a government body is attached to the official in control of the body] has disquieting implications for criticism of governmental conduct. For good reason, 'no court of last resort in this country has ever held, or even suggested, that prosecutions for libel on government have any place in the American system of jurisprudence.' The present proposition would sidestep this obstacle by transmuting criticism of government, however impersonal it may seem on its face, into personal criticism, and hence potential libel, of the officials of whom the government is composed.... We hold that such a proposition may not constitutionally be utilized to establish that an otherwise impersonal attack on governmental operations was a libel of an official responsible for those operations. Since it was relied on exclusively here, and there was no other evidence to connect the statements with respondent, the evidence was constitutionally insufficient to support a finding that the statements referred to respondent.

The judgment of the Supreme Court of Alabama is reversed and the case is remanded to that court for further proceedings not inconsistent with this opinion.

Reversed and remanded.

* * *

1. Extension to public figures. The *New York Times* case involved a public official as the plaintiff. Part D of this chapter will examine what it takes to qualify as a "public figure" for purposes of a defamation claim. In *Curtis Publishing Co. v. Butts*, 388 U.S. 130 (1967), the Court extended the *New York Times* standard to cases involving *public figures* as plaintiffs. That case involved an article alleging that Butts, the athletic director for the University of Georgia, conspired to fix a football game with the University of Alabama. Although Butts was the athletic director for a public university, "he was employed by the Georgia Athletic Association, a private corporation, rather than by the State itself." *Id.* at 135. Therefore, he could not be a public official. However, "Butts had previously served as head football coach of the University and was a well-known and respected figure in coaching ranks." *Id.* at 136. He continued to command "a substantial amount of independent public interest" at the time of the publication of the article. *Id.* at 154. Thus, the Court concluded he was a public figure. For reasons similar to those articulated in *New York Times Co. v. Sullivan*, the Court concluded that the actual malice standard applied to Butts' libel action. A later section in this chapter will explore the contours of public figure status in the defamation context.

2. The meaning of "actual malice." The Supreme Court's use of the term "actual malice" was rather unfortunate since malice in the traditional sense of the word is not actually required. Nor is the Court's "reckless disregard" language particularly illuminating. It took subsequent cases to develop the meaning of the term:

> In *St. Amant* [v. Thompson, 390 U.S. 727 (1968)] Deputy Sheriff Thompson sued St. Amant, a candidate for public office, for defamation. Based on a source whose reputation he did not know and without any independent investigation, St. Amant incorrectly asserted that Thompson had taken bribes. The Supreme Court held that on those facts actual malice was lacking because "[t]here must be sufficient evidence to permit the conclusion that the defendant in fact entertained serious doubts as to the truth of his publication." *St. Amant*, 390 U.S. at 731.

Marcone v. Penthouse International Magazine for Men, 754 F.2d 1072, 1089 (3d Cir. 1985). Future cases in this section will explore the actual malice in greater detail.

3. Actual malice in the disciplinary context. Rule 8.2(a) of the ABA's Model Rules of Professional Conduct borrows the actual malice language from *New York Times* and prohibits a lawyer from making a statement that "that the lawyer knows to be false or with reckless disregard as to its truth or falsity concerning the qualifications or integrity of a judge." The majority of courts have adopted an objective formulation of this standard for use in the disciplinary process. *See, e.g.,* In re Cobb, 838 N.E.2d 1197 (Mass. 2005); Florida Bar v. Ray, 797 So. 2d 556 (Fla. 2001).

* * *

B. Private Figures and Matters of Public Concern

Focus Questions: *Gertz v. Robert Welch, Inc.*

1. *Why does the Court conclude that the* New York Times v. Sullivan *standard is not constitutionally required in* Gertz*-type cases? What standard does apply?*
2. *What is the Court's holding with respect to presumed and punitive damages?*

Gertz v. Robert Welch, Inc.

418 U.S. 323

(1974)

Mr. Justice POWELL delivered the opinion of the Court.

This Court has struggled for nearly a decade to define the proper accommodation between the law of defamation and the freedoms of speech and press protected by the

First Amendment. With this decision we return to that effort. We granted certiorari to reconsider the extent of a publisher's constitutional privilege against liability for defamation of a private citizen.

I

In 1968 a Chicago policeman named Nuccio shot and killed a youth named Nelson. The state authorities prosecuted Nuccio for the homicide and ultimately obtained a conviction for murder in the second degree. The Nelson family retained petitioner Elmer Gertz, a reputable attorney, to represent them in civil litigation against Nuccio.

Respondent publishes *American Opinion*, a monthly outlet for the views of the John Birch Society. Early in the 1960's the magazine began to warn of a nationwide conspiracy to discredit local law enforcement agencies and create in their stead a national police force capable of supporting a Communist dictatorship. As part of the continuing effort to alert the public to this assumed danger, the managing editor of American Opinion commissioned an article on the murder trial of Officer Nuccio. For this purpose he engaged a regular contributor to the magazine. In March 1969 respondent published the resulting article under the title 'FRAME-UP: Richard Nuccio And The War On Police.' The article purports to demonstrate that the testimony against Nuccio at his criminal trial was false and that his prosecution was part of the Communist campaign against the police.

In his capacity as counsel for the Nelson family in the civil litigation, petitioner attended the coroner's inquest into the boy's death and initiated actions for damages, but he neither discussed Officer Nuccio with the press nor played any part in the criminal proceeding. Notwithstanding petitioner's remote connection with the prosecution of Nuccio, respondent's magazine portrayed him as an architect of the 'frame-up.' According to the article, the police file on petitioner took 'a big, Irish cop to lift.' The article stated that petitioner had been an official of the 'Marxist League for Industrial Democracy, originally known as the Intercollegiate Socialist Society, which has advocated the violent seizure of our government.' It labeled Gertz a 'Leninist' and a 'Communist-fronter.' It also stated that Gertz had been an officer of the National Lawyers Guild, described as a Communist organization that 'probably did more than any other outfit to plan the Communist attack on the Chicago police during the 1968 Democratic Convention.'

These statements contained serious inaccuracies. The implication that petitioner had a criminal record was false. Petitioner had been a member and officer of the National Lawyers Guild some 15 years earlier, but there was no evidence that he or that organization had taken any part in planning the 1968 demonstrations in Chicago. There was also no basis for the charge that petitioner was a 'Leninist' or a 'Communist-fronter.' And he had never been a member of the 'Marxist League for Industrial Democracy' or the 'Intercollegiate Socialist Society.'

The managing editor of American Opinion made no effort to verify or substantiate the charges against petitioner. Instead, he appended an editorial introduction stating that the author had 'conducted extensive research into the Richard Nuccio Case.' And he included in the article a photograph of petitioner and wrote the caption that appeared under it: 'Elmer Gertz of Red Guild harasses Nuccio.' Respondent placed the issue of American Opinion containing the article on sale at newsstands throughout the country and distributed reprints of the article on the streets of Chicago.

Petitioner filed a diversity action for libel in the United States District Court for the Northern District of Illinois. He claimed that the falsehoods published by respondent injured his reputation as a lawyer and a citizen.

II

The principal issue in this case is whether a newspaper or broadcaster that publishes defamatory falsehoods about an individual who is neither a public official nor a public figure may claim a constitutional privilege against liability for the injury inflicted by those statements.

III

We begin with the common ground. Under the First Amendment there is no such thing as a false idea. However pernicious an opinion may seem, we depend for its correction not on the conscience of judges and juries but on the competition of other ideas. But there is no constitutional value in false statements of fact. Neither the intentional lie nor the careless error materially advances society's interest in 'uninhibited, robust, and wide-open' debate on public issues. New York Times Co. v. Sullivan, 376 U.S., at 270, 84 S. Ct., at 721. They belong to that category of utterances which 'are no essential part of any exposition of ideas, and are of such slight social value as a step to truth that any benefit that may be derived from them is clearly outweighed by the social interest in order and morality.' Chaplinsky v. New Hampshire, 315 U.S. 568, 572, 62 S. Ct. 766, 769, 86 L. Ed. 1031 (1942).

The legitimate state interest underlying the law of libel is the compensation of individuals for the harm inflicted on them by defamatory falsehood. We would not lightly require the State to abandon this purpose....

Some tension necessarily exists between the need for a vigorous and uninhibited press and the legitimate interest in redressing wrongful injury.... In our continuing effort to define the proper accommodation between these competing concerns, we have been especially anxious to assure to the freedoms of speech and press that 'breathing space' essential to their fruitful exercise. To that end this Court has extended a measure of strategic protection to defamatory falsehood.

The *New York Times* standard defines the level of constitutional protection appropriate to the context of defamation of a public person. Those who, by reason of the notoriety of their achievements or the vigor and success with which they seek the public's attention, are properly classed as public figures and those who hold governmental office may recover for injury to reputation only on clear and convincing proof that the defamatory falsehood was made with knowledge of its falsity or with reckless disregard for the truth. This standard administers an extremely powerful antidote to the inducement to media self-censorship of the common-law rule of strict liability for libel and slander. And it exacts a correspondingly high price from the victims of defamatory falsehood. Plainly many deserving plaintiffs, including some intentionally subjected to injury, will be unable to surmount the barrier of the *New York Times* test. Despite this substantial abridgment of the state law right to compensation for wrongful hurt to one's reputation, the Court has concluded that the protection of the *New York Times* privilege should be available to publishers and broadcasters of defamatory falsehood concerning public officials and public figures. We think that these decisions are correct, but we do not find their holdings justified solely by reference to the interest of the press and broadcast media in immunity from liability. Rather, we believe that the *New York Times* rule states an accommodation between this concern and the limited state interest present in the context of libel actions brought by public persons. For the reasons stated below, we conclude that the state interest in compensating injury to the reputation of private individuals requires that a different rule should obtain with respect to them.

... [W]e have no difficulty in distinguishing among defamation plaintiffs. The first remedy of any victim of defamation is self-help-using available opportunities to contradict the lie or correct the error and thereby to minimize its adverse impact on reputation. Public officials and public figures usually enjoy significantly greater access to the channels of effective communication and hence have a more realistic opportunity to counteract false statements then private individuals normally enjoy. Private individuals are therefore more vulnerable to injury, and the state interest in protecting them is correspondingly greater.

More important than the likelihood that private individuals will lack effective opportunities for rebuttal, there is a compelling normative consideration underlying the distinction between public and private defamation plaintiffs. An individual who decides to seek governmental office must accept certain necessary consequences of that involvement in public affairs. He runs the risk of closer public scrutiny than might otherwise be the case. And society's interest in the officers of government is not strictly limited to the formal discharge of official duties. As the Court pointed out in *Garrison v. Louisiana*, 379 U.S., at 77, 85 S. Ct., at 217, the public's interest extends to 'anything which might touch on an official's fitness for office.... Few personal attributes are more germane to fitness for office than dishonesty, malfeasance, or improper motivation, even though these characteristics may also affect the official's private character.'

Those classed as public figures stand in a similar position. Hypothetically, it may be possible for someone to become a public figure through no purposeful action of his own, but the instances of truly involuntary public figures must be exceedingly rare. For the most part those who attain this status have assumed roles of especial prominence in the affairs of society. Some occupy positions of such persuasive power and influence that they are deemed public figures for all purposes. More commonly, those classed as public figures have thrust themselves to the forefront of particular public controversies in order to influence the resolution of the issues involved. In either event, they invite attention and comment.

Even if the foregoing generalities do not obtain in every instance, the communications media are entitled to act on the assumption that public officials and public figures have voluntarily exposed themselves to increased risk of injury from defamatory falsehood concerning them. No such assumption is justified with respect to a private individual. He has not accepted public office or assumed an 'influential role in ordering society.' He has relinquished no part of his interest in the protection of his own good name, and consequently he has a more compelling call on the courts for redress of injury inflicted by defamatory falsehood. Thus, private individuals are not only more vulnerable to injury than public officials and public figures; they are also more deserving of recovery.

For these reasons we conclude that the States should retain substantial latitude in their efforts to enforce a legal remedy for defamatory falsehood injurious to the reputation of a private individual.

We hold that, so long as they do not impose liability without fault, the States may define for themselves the appropriate standard of liability for a publisher or broadcaster of defamatory falsehood injurious to a private individual. This approach provides a more equitable boundary between the competing concerns involved here. It recognizes the strength of the legitimate state interest in compensating private individuals for wrongful injury to reputation, yet shields the press and broadcast media from the rigors of strict liability for defamation....

IV

Our accommodation of the competing values at stake in defamation suits by private individuals allows the States to impose liability on the publisher or broadcaster of defamatory falsehood on a less demanding showing than that required by *New York Times*. This conclusion is not based on a belief that the considerations which prompted the adoption of the *New York Times* privilege for defamation of public officials and its extension to public figures are wholly inapplicable to the context of private individuals. Rather, we endorse this approach in recognition of the strong and legitimate state interest in compensating private individuals for injury to reputation. But this countervailing state interest extends no further than compensation for actual injury. For the reasons stated below, we hold that the States may not permit recovery of presumed or punitive damages, at least when liability is not based on a showing of knowledge of falsity or reckless disregard for the truth.

The common law of defamation is an oddity of tort law, for it allows recovery of purportedly compensatory damages without evidence of actual loss. Under the traditional rules pertaining to actions for libel, the existence of injury is presumed from the fact of publication. Juries may award substantial sums as compensation for supposed damage to reputation without any proof that such harm actually occurred. The largely uncontrolled discretion of juries to award damages where there is no loss unnecessarily compounds the potential of any system of liability for defamatory falsehood to inhibit the vigorous exercise of First Amendment freedoms. Additionally, the doctrine of presumed damages invites juries to punish unpopular opinion rather than to compensate individuals for injury sustained by the publication of a false fact. More to the point, the States have no substantial interest in securing for plaintiffs such as this petitioner gratuitous awards of money damages far in excess of any actual injury.

We would not, of course, invalidate state law simply because we doubt its wisdom, but here we are attempting to reconcile state law with a competing interest grounded in the constitutional command of the First Amendment. It is therefore appropriate to require that state remedies for defamatory falsehood reach no farther than is necessary to protect the legitimate interest involved. It is necessary to restrict defamation plaintiffs who do not prove knowledge of falsity or reckless disregard for the truth to compensation for actual injury. We need not define 'actual injury,' as trial courts have wide experience in framing appropriate jury instructions in tort actions. Suffice it to say that actual injury is not limited to out-of-pocket loss. Indeed, the more customary types of actual harm inflicted by defamatory falsehood include impairment of reputation and standing in the community, personal humiliation, and mental anguish and suffering. Of course, juries must be limited by appropriate instructions, and all awards must be supported by competent evidence concerning the injury, although there need be no evidence which assigns an actual dollar value to the injury.

We also find no justification for allowing awards of punitive damages against publishers and broadcasters held liable under state-defined standards of liability for defamation. In most jurisdictions jury discretion over the amounts awarded is limited only by the gentle rule that they not be excessive. Consequently, juries assess punitive damages in wholly unpredictable amounts bearing no necessary relation to the actual harm caused. And they remain free to use their discretion selectively to punish expressions of unpopular views. Like the doctrine of presumed damages, jury discretion to award punitive damages unnecessarily exacerbates the danger of media self-censorship, but, unlike the former rule, punitive damages are wholly irrelevant to the state interest that justifies a negligence standard for private defamation actions. They are not compensation for injury. Instead, they are private fines levied by civil juries to punish reprehensible conduct and to deter its future occurrence. In short, the private defamation plaintiff who establishes liability under a less demanding standard than that stated by *New York Times* may recover only such damages as are sufficient to compensate him for actual injury.

V

Because the jury was allowed to impose liability without fault and was permitted to presume damages without proof of injury, a new trial is necessary. We reverse and remand for further proceedings in accord with this opinion.

* * *

1. Uncertainty following *Gertz*. *Gertz* involved defamatory statements that obviously involved matters of public concern. But there was some question as to whether the *Gertz* approach was limited to cases involving private-figure plaintiffs who had been defamed with reference to a matter of public concern, or whether it applied regardless of whether the statement implicated matters of public concern. *See Dun & Bradstreet, Inc. v. Greenmoss Builders, Inc.*, 472 U.S. 749, 785 (1985) (Brennan, J., dissenting). There was also some question—given the Court's repeated references in *Gertz* to publishers and broadcasters—whether *Gertz* was limited to cases involving media defendants. Both of these issues were resolved to some extent in *Dun & Bradstreet, Inc. v. Greenmoss Builders, Inc.*, which is covered in the next section.

2. The appropriate standard of liability. Following *Gertz*, state courts have struck the balance identified in *Gertz* in different ways. Some states have chosen to require a showing of actual malice in *Gertz*-type cases. *See* Bandido's, Inc. v. Journal Gazette Co., 575 N.E.2d 324, 326 (Ind. 1991). However, most states simply require the lesser standard of negligence. Rodney A. Smolla, 1 Law of Defamation § 3:30 (2d ed.).

* * *

C. Private Figures and Matters of Private Concern

Focus Questions: *Dun & Bradstreet, Inc. v. Greenmoss Builders, Inc.*

1. *How does the Court's holding in* Dun & Bradstreet *differ from its holding in* Gertz?
2. *What distinguishes a matter of public concern from a matter of private concern?*

Dun & Bradstreet, Inc. v. Greenmoss Builders, Inc.

472 U.S. 749
(1985)

Justice POWELL announced the judgment of the Court and delivered an opinion, in which Justice REHNQUIST and Justice O'CONNOR joined.

In *Gertz v. Robert Welch, Inc.*, 418 U.S. 323 (1974), we held that the First Amendment restricted the damages that a private individual could obtain from a publisher for a libel that involved a matter of public concern. More specifically, we held that in these circumstances the First Amendment prohibited awards of presumed and punitive damages for false and defamatory statements unless the plaintiff shows "actual malice," that is, knowledge of falsity or reckless disregard for the truth. The question presented in this case is whether this rule of *Gertz* applies when the false and defamatory statements do not involve matters of public concern.

I

Petitioner Dun & Bradstreet, a credit reporting agency, provides subscribers with financial and related information about businesses. All the information is confidential; under the terms of the subscription agreement the subscribers may not reveal it to anyone else. On July 26, 1976, petitioner sent a report to five subscribers indicating that respondent, a construction contractor, had filed a voluntary petition for bankruptcy. This report was false and grossly misrepresented respondent's assets and liabilities. That same day, while discussing the possibility of future financing with its bank, respondent's president was told that the bank had received the defamatory report. He immediately called petitioner's regional office, explained the error, and asked for a correction. In addition, he requested the names of the firms that had received the false report in order to assure them that the company was solvent. Petitioner promised to look into the matter but refused to divulge the names of those who had received the report.

After determining that its report was indeed false, petitioner issued a corrective notice on or about August 3, 1976, to the five subscribers who had received the initial report. The notice stated that one of respondent's former employees, not respondent itself, had filed for bankruptcy and that respondent "continued in business as usual." Respondent told petitioner that it was dissatisfied with the notice, and it again asked for a list of subscribers who had seen the initial report. Again petitioner refused to divulge their names.

Respondent then brought this defamation action in Vermont state court. It alleged that the false report had injured its reputation and sought both compensatory and punitive damages. The trial established that the error in petitioner's report had been caused when one of its employees, a 17-year-old high school student paid to review Vermont bankruptcy pleadings, had inadvertently attributed to respondent a bankruptcy petition filed by one of respondent's former employees. Although petitioner's representative testified that it was routine practice to check the accuracy of such reports with the businesses themselves, it did not try to verify the information about respondent before reporting it.

After trial, the jury returned a verdict in favor of respondent and awarded $50,000 in compensatory or presumed damages and $300,000 in punitive damages. Petitioner moved for a new trial. It argued that in *Gertz v. Robert Welch, Inc.*, *supra,* this Court had ruled broadly that "the States may not permit recovery of presumed or punitive damages, at least when liability is not based on a showing of knowledge of falsity or reckless disregard for the truth," and it argued that the judge's instructions in this case permitted the jury to award such damages on a lesser showing. The trial court indicated some doubt as to whether *Gertz* applied to "non-media cases," but granted a new trial "[b]ecause of ... dissatisfaction with its charge and ... conviction that the interests of justice require[d]" it. App. 26.

The Vermont Supreme Court reversed.... It held that the balance between a private plaintiff's right to recover presumed and punitive damages without a showing of special fault and the First Amendment rights of "nonmedia" speakers "must be struck in favor of the private plaintiff defamed by a nonmedia defendant." Accordingly, the court held "that as a matter of federal constitutional law, the media protections outlined in *Gertz* are inapplicable to nonmedia defamation actions."

Recognizing disagreement among the lower courts about when the protections of *Gertz* apply, we granted certiorari. We now affirm, although for reasons different from those relied upon by the Vermont Supreme Court.

IV

We have never considered whether the *Gertz* balance obtains when the defamatory statements involve no issue of public concern. To make this determination, we must employ the approach approved in *Gertz* and balance the State's interest in compensating private individuals for injury to their reputation against the First Amendment interest in protecting this type of expression. This state interest is identical to the one weighed in *Gertz*. There we found that it was "strong and legitimate." A State should not lightly be required to abandon it ...

The First Amendment interest, on the other hand, is less important than the one weighed in *Gertz*. We have long recognized that not all speech is of equal First Amendment importance. It is speech on " 'matters of public concern' " that is "at the heart of the First Amendment's protection." First National Bank of Boston v. Bellotti, 435 U.S. 765, 776, 98 S. Ct. 1407, 1415, 55 L.Ed.2d 707 (1978), citing Thornhill v. Alabama, 310 U.S. 88, 101, 60 S. Ct. 736, 743, 84 L.Ed. 1093 (1940). As we stated in Connick v. Myers, 461 U.S. 138, 145, 103 S. Ct. 1684, 1689, 75 L.Ed.2d 708 (1983), this "special concern [for speech on public issues] is no mystery":

> The First Amendment 'was fashioned to assure unfettered interchange of ideas for the bringing about of political and social changes desired by the people.' Roth v. United States, 354 U.S. 476, 484 [77 S. Ct. 1304, 1308, 1 L.Ed.2d 1498] (1957); New York Times Co. v. Sullivan, 376 U.S. 254, 269 [84 S. Ct. 710, 720, 11 L.Ed.2d 686] (1964). '[S]peech concerning public affairs is more than self-expression; it is the essence of self-government.' Garrison v. Louisiana, 379 U.S. 64, 74–75, [85 S. Ct. 209, 215–216, 13 L.Ed.2d 125] (1964). Accordingly, the Court has frequently reaffirmed that speech on public issues occupies the '"highest rung of the hierarchy of First Amendment values,'" and is entitled to special protection. NAACP v. Claiborne Hardware Co., 458 U.S. 886, 913, [102 S. Ct. 3409, 3425, 73 L.Ed.2d 1215] (1982); Carey v. Brown, 447 U.S. 455, 467 [100 S. Ct. 2286, 2293, 65 L.Ed.2d 263] (1980).

In contrast, speech on matters of purely private concern is of less First Amendment concern. As a number of state courts, including the court below, have recognized, the role of the Constitution in regulating state libel law is far more limited when the concerns that activated *New York Times* and *Gertz* are absent. In such a case,

> [t]here is no threat to the free and robust debate of public issues; there is no potential interference with a meaningful dialogue of ideas concerning self-government; and there is no threat of liability causing a reaction of self-censorship by the press. The facts of the present case are wholly without the First Amendment concerns with which the Supreme Court of the United States has been struggling. Harley-Davidson Motorsports, Inc. v. Markley, 279 Or. 361, 366, 568 P.2d 1359, 1363 (1977).

While such speech is not totally unprotected by the First Amendment, its protections are less stringent.... In light of the reduced constitutional value of speech involving no matters of public concern, we hold that the state interest adequately supports awards of presumed and punitive damages—even absent a showing of "actual malice."

V

The only remaining issue is whether petitioner's credit report involved a matter of public concern. In a related context, we have held that "[w]hether ... speech addresses a matter of public concern must be determined by [the expression's] content, form, and context ... as revealed by the whole record." Connick v. Myers, *supra*, 461 U.S., at 147–

148. These factors indicate that petitioner's credit report concerns no public issue. It was speech solely in the individual interest of the speaker and its specific business audience. *Cf.* Central Hudson Gas & Elec. Corp. v. Public Service Comm'n of New York, 447 U.S. 557, 561 (1980). This particular interest warrants no special protection when—as in this case—the speech is wholly false and clearly damaging to the victim's business reputation. Moreover, since the credit report was made available to only five subscribers, who, under the terms of the subscription agreement, could not disseminate it further, it cannot be said that the report involves any "strong interest in the free flow of commercial information." *Id.* at 764. There is simply no credible argument that this type of credit reporting requires special protection to ensure that "debate on public issues [will] be uninhibited, robust, and wide-open." New York Times Co. v. Sullivan, 376 U.S., at 270.

In addition, the speech here, like advertising, is hardy and unlikely to be deterred by incidental state regulation. It is solely motivated by the desire for profit, which, we have noted, is a force less likely to be deterred than others. Arguably, the reporting here was also more objectively verifiable than speech deserving of greater protection. In any case, the market provides a powerful incentive to a credit reporting agency to be accurate, since false credit reporting is of no use to creditors. Thus, any incremental "chilling" effect of libel suits would be of decreased significance.

VI

We conclude that permitting recovery of presumed and punitive damages in defamation cases absent a showing of "actual malice" does not violate the First Amendment when the defamatory statements do not involve matters of public concern. Accordingly, we affirm the judgment of the Vermont Supreme Court.

* * *

Exercise 9.2

The National Organization for College Women is an organization that is dedicated to improving the academic performance and experience of college-aged women. Over the years, the organization has compiled a list of attorneys in different states who have represented college-aged women in sexual harassment and discrimination cases, along with evaluations appearing by each lawyer's name from clients. The organization posts this list on its website, where it is intended to be used a resource for women in need of legal representation. The description appearing alongside the name of one attorney, Earl Flatt, says that Flatt "was totally disorganized, didn't seem to know what he was doing, and made me do all of the work." Flatt now wishes to sue the organization for defamation based on these statements. Assume that Flatt is a private figure. Based on the preceding opinions, what is the plaintiff's burden of proof on the questions of fault and damages?

D. Actual Malice and the Classification of Plaintiffs as Public Officials, Public Figures, or Private Figures

Gertz held that the *New York Times* actual malice standard did not apply to the plaintiff in that case, a lawyer, because he was not a public official or a public figure. It was fairly easy to conclude that *Gertz* was not a public official.

> Several years prior to the present incident, petitioner had served briefly on housing committees appointed by the mayor of Chicago, but at the time of publication he had never held any remunerative governmental position. Respondent admits this but argues that petitioner's appearance at the coroner's inquest rendered him a 'de facto public official.' Our cases recognized no such concept. Respondent's suggestion would sweep all lawyers under the *New York Times* rule as officers of the court and distort the plain meaning of the 'public official' category beyond all recognition. We decline to follow it.

Gertz v. Robert Welch, Inc., 418 U.S. 323, 351 (1974). In other cases, it is not quite so easy to distinguish between public officials, public figures, and private figures, yet how a court classifies an individual may, as a practical matter, be outcome determinative since the resulting classification may determine whether a plaintiff needs to establish that the defendant acted with actual malice. The following section explores these distinctions. In addition, it explores the concept of actual malice in greater detail.

1. Public Officials

Focus Question: *Tague v. Citizens for Law and Order, Inc.*

1. *Judges, district attorneys, and police chiefs have all been held to be public officials for purposes of* New York Times *analysis. Some firefighters and public school teachers have been held to not be public officials for defamation purposes. Based on the test used in Tague, are you able to articulate why?*
2. *Does the test the court applies for determining the public official status of a plaintiff provide sufficient guidance for judges and litigants?*

Tague v. Citizens for Law & Order, Inc.

142 Cal.Rptr. 689
(Cal. Super. 1977)

PHILLIPS, Judge.

I. INTRODUCTION

This appeal from a judgment in favor of an assistant public defender against a citizens' group and the editor of its newsletter for defamatory statements printed in the newsletter.

The principal issue before us on appeal is whether an assistant public defender is a public official within the meaning of *New York Times v. Sullivan* (1964), 376 U.S. 254, and is, therefore, required to prove actual malice to recover damages for defamatory falsehoods by the press. The trial judge, upon appellants' motion for partial summary judgment, ruled that an assistant public defender is not a public official....

II. FACTS

Respondent Peter Tague brought this libel action against Citizens for Law and Order (CLO) and Earl Huntting, appellants ... On September 6, 1974, the Oakland Tribune published a short article on the sentencing hearing of a person represented by respondent in his capacity as assistant public defender. The article stated that the trial court had discounted respondent's representation that his client had previously done well on parole. Solely on the basis of this article, appellant Huntting wrote a letter to respondent's superior, Public Defender James Hooley, and published an article in the CLO News stating that respondent had "misrepresented facts to the trial court." Upon respondent's demand for retraction, appellants published an article in the CLO News stating that respondent had not misrepresented facts in open court; the article falsely implied, however, that respondent had lied to the judge in chambers.

Appellants moved for summary judgment on the ground that respondent was a public official within the meaning of *New York Times* and that respondent was unable to show that the statement was made with actual malice, as required to overcome the resulting constitutional privilege. The court apparently found that respondent was not a public official and denied the motion. The jury returned a verdict for respondent, against CLO and Huntting, making a special finding of malice by a preponderance of the evidence. Appellants moved for a new trial and judgment notwithstanding the verdict, in part on the ground that the trial court improperly determined that respondent was not a public official. The motions were denied. This appeal followed.

III. DISCUSSION

A. Interests Involved

We note at the outset the fundamental interests involved in this case: the right of the press to criticize freely, without malice, those responsible for government affairs; the right of an assistant public defender to privacy and reputation and his interest in representing unpopular clients free from coercion and veiled threats by the press; the interest of the public in crime prevention and careful scrutiny of the operations of the criminal justice system; and the right of indigents to effective legal defense in criminal actions.

The gravity of these interests and the absence of case authority on the precise question of the public status of an assistant public defender compels us to reach a decision that both falls within prevailing legal boundaries and best accommodates the values embodied in these interests.

B. Assistant Public Defender as Public Official

Is Assistant Public Defender Tague a public official within the meaning of *New York Times* and therefore required to overcome this privilege by proving that CLO published the libelous statements with actual malice?

In *Rosenblatt v. Baer* (1966) 383 U.S. 75, 86 S. Ct. 669, 15 L.Ed.2d 597, the Supreme Court articulated the threshold test for determining whether a government employee is a public official:

> The public official designation applies at the very least to those among the hierarchy of government employees who have or appear to the public to have substantial responsibility for or control over the conduct of governmental affairs.

To determine whether a government employee, such as an assistant public defender, has or appears to have substantial responsibility for the conduct of governmental affairs, and is therefore to be deemed a public official, a court may properly look to the nature of his "functions, duties, and relationship with the public." (*See* People v. Tautfest, 274 Cal.App.2d 630, 79 Cal.Rptr. 478 (1969). Where that employee's duties or position in government has "such apparent importance the public has an independent interest in the qualifications and performance of the person who holds it," [*Rosenblatt*, 383 U.S. at 86] the public's interest in debate about public issues and those responsible for the resolution of those issues is best served by holding that employee to be a public official within the meaning of *New York Times*.

In *Tunnel v. Edwardsville Intelligencer, supra*, the Illinois Court of Appeals held that the plaintiff city attorney was a public official for the purpose of the underlying libel action.... In finding that the city attorney has or appears to the public to have substantial control over the conduct of government affairs, the court focused on the broad duties of the city attorney as defined in Illinois court decisions and in Attorney General opinions (legal adviser to city officers and the city council regarding their duties and powers; representative of the city on all legal matters; law officer of the city). The court also noted the public's interest in the subject about which the attorney was criticized (promotion of illegal acts) and the availability of opportunity for rebuttal (the public meetings of the city council were available to the attorney as a forum from which to expose the falsity of the defamatory statements).

Duties of Assistant Public Defender

In our case, as in *Tunnel*, the respondent was entrusted with specific duties and performed specific functions of considerable public importance. As an attorney in the office of the public defender, Tague was charged by state law with "representing those persons assigned to him as clients by the Public Defender of Alameda County," thereby serving to discharge the government's constitutionally prescribed duty to provide legal representation to indigent criminal defendants. (*See* Gideon v. Wainwright, 372 U.S. 335.)

As an attorney who attained the rank of Public Defender II, Tague was responsible for felony cases including discretionary control over pretrial matters (investigation, trial preparation, plea bargaining), trials and sentencing. It is apparent to us that Tague's performance of these governmental duties, for the direct benefit of those for whom the government is legally responsible, is precisely the "conduct of government affairs" deserving of public scrutiny that the court envisioned in *Rosenblatt*.

Subject of Public Concern

Moreover, the subject of crimes and criminals, the core of the public defender's practice, plunges deeply into the heart of public concern. The sword is double-edged. On the one hand, there is a strong societal interest in protecting the democratic rights of all people, including those who are indigent and in need of criminal defense. On the other hand, the increasing incidence of crime arouses public concern for safety and well-being. The public's dual interest in preventing crime and preserving democratic rights has given rise in recent years to careful scrutiny of the criminal justice system in America. Judges, district attorneys, and public defenders, as integral components of that system, are appropriate targets for scrutiny as to their qualifications and performances.

CLO, it appears, was organized to effect such scrutiny. Its newsletter, CLO News, is the means by which it apprises members of matters relating to law enforcement in Alameda

County. Its criticism of respondent Tague, however false, was addressed to his performance as a government employee involved in a matter of considerable public concern. Public defenders are paid by the taxpayers and entrusted with the duty of implementing public policy concerning crime and criminal justice. If they are allowed to perpetrate fraud on the court, in breach of that duty, dangerous individuals may be released at considerable risk to public safety. Both public and press, therefore, have an interest in robust criticism of even the appearance of unethical conduct on the part of public defenders. As assistant public defender, Tague's duties evoked public scrutiny; his reported actions warranted privileged comment about his qualifications and performance.

Finally, as a matter of constitutional policy in libel actions, we believe that any doubt as to the public status of a government employee should be resolved in favor of the First and Fourteenth Amendments' guarantees of freedom of the press and the public's interest in open criticism of government operations. (*See* Rosenblatt v. Baer, *supra*, 383 U.S. 75, 86 S. Ct. 669.)

Accordingly, we find that assistant public defender Tague has substantial responsibility for the conduct of government affairs and that his governmental duties involve a subject of such public importance as to justify public scrutiny and uninhibited comment about his performance of those duties. We therefore hold, in accordance with *Rosenblatt*, that an assistant public defender is a public official within the meaning of *New York Times* and its progeny, and must prove actual malice to recover damages in this libel action.[9]

To hold otherwise would hamper the press in its quest to speak freely and the public in its effort to scrutinize the workings of the criminal justice system. The threat of libel action by an assistant public defender or someone in a similar position of public trust would chill the unprotected press in its effort to scrutinize government conduct in criminal justice. The effect of our holding is to mitigate the impact of that potential threat by reducing, though not eliminating, the probability of recovery by such persons. In addition, by affording the press room to err in good faith in its criticism, the public is benefitted by the increased flow of information on crime and law enforcement and the greater assurance of ethical conduct by government employees. At the same time, the individual is afforded a reasonable measure of protection of reputation. He or she may demand retraction or, if no retraction is printed, recover punitive, special, and general damages where he or she proves that the defamatory statement was printed with knowledge that it was false or with reckless disregard as to its accuracy. The press, therefore, is prevented from using this decision as a legal veil for grossly irresponsible or vindictive behavior.

AVAKIAN, Judge, concurring.

I concur in the foregoing decision. In relation to footnote 9, … I would observe that I see no material distinction between an assistant public defender and a private attorney (whether court-appointed at public expense or privately compensated) performing the functions of respondent in this case. All of the public interest factors which militate in favor of restricting defamation actions to cases of actual malice apply equally to any attorney representing a litigant, regardless of the source of his compensation or the genesis of his assignment.

* * *

9. We do not hold that an attorney is a public official solely by reason of his membership in a state bar and his status as officer of the court. (*See* Gertz v. Robert Welch (1974), 418 U.S. 323, 94 S. Ct. 2997, 41 L.Ed.2d 789; Harkaway v. Boston Herald Traveler (1st Cir. 1969) 418 F.2d 56; Hotchner v. Castillo-Puche (S.D.N.Y.1975) 404 F. Supp. 1041.)

The public official status of government lawyers. A different California court concluded in *James v. San Jose Mercury News, Inc.*, 20 Cal.Rptr.2d 890, 896 (Cal. App. 6 Dist. 1993), that a deputy public defender was not a public official for purposes of *New York Times* analysis.

> We respectfully disagree with *Tague*. From a practical perspective a deputy public defender in the discharge of his or her duties differs from a private criminal defense attorney only in the happenstance of his or her employment. Such control as he or she may exercise over the management of a particular case must invariably be controlled in turn by considerations of the best interests of the individual client, tempered only by professional constraints applicable to all attorneys and not by any generalized public interest beyond the concern that indigent defendants should be competently and professionally represented. It would be a gross overstatement to say that a deputy public defender has, or would appear to the public to have, "substantial responsibility for or control over the conduct of governmental affairs" (citation omitted).

However, the court did conclude that that the deputy public defender's "performance, and administration of the criminal laws in general and laws relating to child molestation in particular, were matters of legitimate public interest and concern."

* * *

2. All-Purpose Public Figures and Limited-Purpose Public Figures

In *Gertz*, the Court concluded that designation as a public figure may rest on two possible bases:

> In some instances an individual may achieve such pervasive fame or notoriety that he becomes a public figure for all purposes and in all contexts. More commonly, an individual voluntarily injects himself or is drawn into a particular public controversy and thereby becomes a public figure for a limited range of issues. In either case such persons assume special prominence in the resolution of public questions.
>
> Petitioner has long been active in community and professional affairs. He has served as an officer of local civic groups and of various professional organizations, and he has published several books and articles on legal subjects. Although petitioner was consequently well known in some circles, he had achieved no general fame or notoriety in the community. None of the prospective jurors called at the trial had ever heard of petitioner prior to this litigation, and respondent offered no proof that this response was atypical of the local population. We would not lightly assume that a citizen's participation in community and professional affairs rendered him a public figure for all purposes. Absent clear evidence of general fame or notoriety in the community, and pervasive involvement in the affairs of society, an individual should not be deemed a public personality for all aspects of his life. It is preferable to reduce the public-figure question to a more meaningful context by looking to the nature and extent of an individual's participation in the particular controversy giving rise to the defamation.
>
> In this context it is plain that petitioner was not a public figure. He played a minimal role at the coroner's inquest, and his participation related solely to his

> representation of a private client. He took no part in the criminal prosecution of Officer Nuccio. Moreover, he never discussed either the criminal or civil litigation with the press and was never quoted as having done so. He plainly did not thrust himself into the vortex of this public issue, nor did he engage the public's attention in an attempt to influence its outcome. We are persuaded that the trial court did not err in refusing to characterize petitioner as a public figure for the purpose of this litigation.

Gertz v. Robert Welch, Inc., 418 U.S. 323, 351–52 (1974).

The following section examines the distinctions between all-purpose (or general-purpose) public figures, limited-purpose public figures, and private figures.

Focus Question: *Wolston v. Reader's Digest Ass'n, Inc.*

1. *What is the difference between a limited-purpose public figure and an all-purpose or general-purpose public figure?*
2. *How does one become a limited-purpose public figure?*

Wolston v. Reader's Digest Ass'n, Inc.

443 U.S. 157
(1979)

Mr. Justice REHNQUIST delivered the opinion of the Court.

In 1974, respondent Reader's Digest Association, Inc., published a book entitled KGB, the Secret Work of Soviet Agents (KGB), written by respondent John Barron. The book describes the Soviet Union's espionage organization and chronicles its activities since World War II. In a passage referring to disclosures by "royal commissions in Canada and Australia, and official investigations in Great Britain and the United States," the book contains the following statements relating to petitioner Ilya Wolston:

> Among Soviet agents identified in the United States were Elizabeth T. Bentley, Edward Joseph Fitzgerald, William Ludwig Ullmann, William Walter Remington, Franklin Victor Reno, Judith Coplon, Harry Gold, David Greenglass, Julius and Ethel Rosenberg, Morton Sobell, William Perl, Alfred Dean Slack, Jack Soble, Ilya Wolston, Alfred and Martha Stern.

In addition, the index to KGB lists petitioner as follows: "Wolston, Ilya, Soviet agent in U.S."

Petitioner sued the author and publishers of KGB in the United States District Court for the District of Columbia, claiming that the passages in KGB stating that he had been indicted for espionage and had been a Soviet agent were false and defamatory. The District Court granted respondents' motion for summary judgment. The court held that petitioner was a "public figure" and that the First Amendment therefore precluded recovery unless petitioner proved that respondents had published a defamatory falsehood with "'actual malice'—that is, with knowledge that it was false or with reckless disregard of whether it was false or not," New York Times Co. v. Sullivan, 376 U.S. 254, 280, 84 S. Ct. 710, 726, 11 L.Ed.2d 686 (1964). 429 F. Supp., at 172, 176. While the District Court agreed that the above-quoted portions of KGB appeared to state falsely that petitioner had been indicted for espionage, it ruled, on the basis of affidavits and deposition testimony, that the evidence raised no genuine issue with respect to the existence of "actual malice" on the part of respondents.

During 1957 and 1958, a special federal grand jury sitting in New York City conducted a major investigation into the activities of Soviet intelligence agents in the United States. As a result of this investigation, petitioner's aunt and uncle, Myra and Jack Soble, were arrested in January 1957 on charges of spying. The Sobles later pleaded guilty to espionage charges, and in the ensuing months, the grand jury's investigation focused on other participants in a suspected Soviet espionage ring, resulting in further arrests, convictions, and guilty pleas. On the same day the Sobles were arrested, petitioner was interviewed by agents of the Federal Bureau of Investigation at his home in the District of Columbia. Petitioner was interviewed several more times during the following months in both Washington and in New York City and traveled to New York on various occasions pursuant to grand jury subpoenas.

On July 1, 1958, however, petitioner failed to respond to a grand jury subpoena directing him to appear on that date. Petitioner previously had attempted to persuade law enforcement authorities not to require him to travel to New York for interrogation because of his state of mental depression. App. 91 (affidavit of petitioner, June 15, 1976). On July 14, a Federal District Judge issued an order to show cause why petitioner should not be held in criminal contempt of court. These events immediately attracted the interest of the news media, and on July 15 and 16, at least seven news stories focusing on petitioner's failure to respond to the grand jury subpoena appeared in New York and Washington newspapers.

Petitioner appeared in court on the return date of the show-cause order and offered to testify before the grand jury, but the offer was refused. A hearing then commenced on the contempt charges. Petitioner's wife, who then was pregnant, was called to testify as to petitioner's mental condition at the time of the return date of the subpoena, but after she became hysterical on the witness stand, petitioner agreed to plead guilty to the contempt charge. He received a 1-year suspended sentence and was placed on probation for three years, conditioned on his cooperation with the grand jury in any further inquiries regarding Soviet espionage. Newspapers also reported the details of the contempt proceedings and petitioner's guilty plea and sentencing. In all, during the 6-week period between petitioner's failure to appear before the grand jury and his sentencing, 15 stories in newspapers in Washington and New York mentioned or discussed these events. This flurry of publicity subsided following petitioner's sentencing, however, and, thereafter, he succeeded for the most part in returning to the private life he had led prior to issuance of the grand jury subpoena. At no time was petitioner indicted for espionage.

In *New York Times Co. v. Sullivan*, 376 U.S., at 279–280, 84 S. Ct., at 275–276, the Court held that the First and Fourteenth Amendments prohibit a public official from recovering damages for a defamatory falsehood relating to his official conduct absent proof that the statement was made with "actual malice," as that term is defined in that opinion. Three years later, the Court extended the New York Times standard to "public figures." Curtis Publishing Co. v. Butts, 388 U.S. 130, 162, 87 S. Ct. 1975, 1995, 18 L.Ed.2d 1094 (1967) (Warren, C.J., concurring in result). But in *Gertz v. Robert Welch, Inc.*, 418 U.S. 323, 344–347, 94 S. Ct. 2997, 3009–3010, 41 L.Ed.2d 789 (1974), we declined to expand the protection afforded by that standard to defamation actions brought by private individuals. We explained in *Gertz* that the rationale for extending the *New York Times* rule to public figures was two-fold. First, we recognized that public figures are less vulnerable to injury from defamatory statements because of their ability to resort to effective "self-help." They usually enjoy significantly greater access than private individuals to channels of effective communication, which enable them through discussion to counter criticism and expose the falsehood and fallacies of defamatory statements. Second, and more importantly, was a normative consideration that public figures are less deserving of protection than private persons because public figures, like public officials, have "voluntarily exposed themselves to increased risk of injury from defamatory falsehood concerning them." We identified two ways in which a person may become a public figure for purposes of the First Amendment:

> For the most part those who attain this status have assumed roles of especial prominence in the affairs of society. Some occupy positions of such persuasive power and influence that they are deemed public figures for all purposes. More commonly, those classed as public figures have thrust themselves to the forefront of particular public controversies in order to influence the resolution of the issues involved. 418 U.S., at 345, 94 S. Ct., at 3009.

Neither respondents nor the lower courts relied on any claim that petitioner occupied a position of such "persuasive power and influence" that he could be deemed one of that small group of individuals who are public figures for all purposes. Petitioner led a thoroughly private existence prior to the grand jury inquiry and returned to a position of relative obscurity after his sentencing. He achieved no general fame or notoriety and assumed no role of special prominence in the affairs of society as a result of his contempt citation or because of his involvement in the investigation of Soviet espionage in 1958.

Instead, respondents argue, and the lower courts held, that petitioner falls within the second category of public figures—those who have "thrust themselves to the forefront of particular public controversies in order to influence the resolution of the issues involved"—and that, therefore, petitioner is a public figure for the limited purpose of comment on his connection with, or involvement in, Soviet espionage in the 1940's and 1950's. Both lower courts found petitioner's failure to appear before the grand jury and citation for contempt determinative of the public-figure issue. The District Court concluded that by failing to appear before the grand jury and subjecting himself to a citation for contempt, petitioner "became involved in a controversy of a decidedly public nature in a way that invited attention and comment, and thereby created in the public an interest in knowing about his connection with espionage...." Similarly, the Court of Appeals stated that by refusing to comply with the subpoena, petitioner "stepped center front into the spotlight focused on the investigation of Soviet espionage. In short, by his voluntary action he invited attention and comment in connection with the public questions involved in the investigation of espionage."

We do not agree with respondents and the lower courts that petitioner can be classed as such a limited-purpose public figure. First, the undisputed facts do not justify the conclusion of the District Court and Court of Appeals that petitioner "voluntarily thrust" or "injected" himself into the forefront of the public controversy surrounding the investigation of Soviet espionage in the United States. It would be more accurate to say that petitioner was dragged unwillingly into the controversy. The Government pursued him in its investigation. Petitioner did fail to respond to a grand jury subpoena, and this failure, as well as his subsequent citation for contempt, did attract media attention. But the mere fact that petitioner voluntarily chose not to appear before the grand jury, knowing that his action might be attended by publicity, is not decisive on the question of public-figure status. In *Gertz*, we held that an attorney was not a public figure even though he voluntarily associated himself with a case that was certain to receive extensive media exposure. We emphasized that a court must focus on the "nature and extent of an individual's participation in the particular controversy giving rise to the defamation." In

Gertz, the attorney took no part in the criminal prosecution, never discussed the litigation with the press, and limited his participation in the civil litigation solely to his representation of a private client. Similarly, petitioner never discussed this matter with the press and limited his involvement to that necessary to defend himself against the contempt charge. It is clear that petitioner played only a minor role in whatever public controversy there may have been concerning the investigation of Soviet espionage. We decline to hold that his mere citation for contempt rendered him a public figure for purposes of comment on the investigation of Soviet espionage.

Petitioner's failure to appear before the grand jury and citation for contempt no doubt were "newsworthy," but the simple fact that these events attracted media attention also is not conclusive of the public-figure issue. A private individual is not automatically transformed into a public figure just by becoming involved in or associated with a matter that attracts public attention.... A libel defendant must show more than mere newsworthiness to justify application of the demanding burden of *New York Times*.

Nor do we think that petitioner engaged the attention of the public in an attempt to influence the resolution of the issues involved. Petitioner assumed no "special prominence in the resolution of public questions." *See* Gertz v. Robert Welch, Inc., 418 U.S., at 351, 94 S. Ct., at 3012. His failure to respond to the grand jury's subpoena was in no way calculated to draw attention to himself in order to invite public comment or influence the public with respect to any issue. He did not in any way seek to arouse public sentiment in his favor and against the investigation. Thus, this is not a case where a defendant invites a citation for contempt in order to use the contempt citation as a fulcrum to create public discussion about the methods being used in connection with an investigation or prosecution. To the contrary, petitioner's failure to appear before the grand jury appears simply to have been the result of his poor health. He then promptly communicated his desire to testify and, when the offer was rejected, passively accepted his punishment. There is no evidence that petitioner's failure to appear was intended to have, or did in fact have, any effect on any issue of public concern. In short, we find no basis whatsoever for concluding that petitioner relinquished, to any degree, his interest in the protection of his own name.

This reasoning leads us to reject the further contention of respondents that any person who engages in criminal conduct automatically becomes a public figure for purposes of comment on a limited range of issues relating to his conviction. Brief for Respondents 24; Tr. of Oral Arg. 15, 17. We declined to accept a similar argument in *Time, Inc. v. Firestone, supra*, 424 U.S., at 457, 96 S. Ct., at 966–67, where we said:

> [W]hile participants in some litigation may be legitimate 'public figures,' either generally or for the limited purpose of that litigation, the majority will more likely resemble respondent, drawn into a public forum largely against their will in order to attempt to obtain the only redress available to them or to defend themselves against actions brought by the State or by others. There appears little reason why these individuals should substantially forfeit that degree of protection which the law of defamation would otherwise afford them simply by virtue of their being drawn into a courtroom.... As to inaccurate and defamatory reports of facts, matters deserving no First Amendment protection..., we think *Gertz* provides an adequate safeguard for the constitutionally protected interests of the press and affords it a tolerable margin for error by requiring some type of fault.

We think that these observations remain sound, and that they control the disposition of this case. To hold otherwise would create an "open season" for all who sought to defame persons convicted of a crime.

Accordingly, the judgment of the Court of Appeals is

Reversed.

Mr. Justice BLACKMUN, with whom Mr. Justice MARSHALL joins, concurring in the result.

I agree that petitioner is not a "public figure" for purposes of this case. The Court reaches this conclusion by reasoning that a prospective public figure must enter a controversy "in an attempt to influence the resolution of the issues involved," and that petitioner failed to act in that manner purposefully here. The Court seems to hold, in other words, that a person becomes a limited-issue public figure only if he literally or figuratively "mounts a rostrum" to advocate a particular view.

I see no need to adopt so restrictive a definition of "public figure" on the facts before us. Assuming, arguendo, that petitioner gained public-figure status when he became involved in the espionage controversy in 1958, he clearly had lost that distinction by the time respondents published KGB in 1974. Because I believe that the lapse of the intervening 16 years renders consideration of this petitioner's original public-figure status unnecessary, I concur only in the result.

Focus Questions: *Ratner v. Young*

1. *Why is Kunstler deemed to be an all-purpose public figure? Why is Ratner a limited-purpose public figure?*
2. *Do you see any practical concerns with classifying lawyers (or other professionals) who participate in high-profile cases as public figures?*

Ratner v. Young

465 F. Supp. 386
(D.C. Virgin Islands 1979)

[Plaintiff, Leroy A. Mercer, was appointed as defense counsel in a high-profile murder case. Famed lawyer William A. Kunstler and lawyer Margaret Ratner "promptly moved in, uninvited, and each one of them took over the defense of one of the defendants, without pay." According to the court, "[the] tactics of Kunstler and Ratner were scorched earth all the way," including "aiding and abetting" the criminal defendants in shouting obscenities at the trial judge, Judge Young. Kunstler and Ratner sued a state court judge who sent a letter to the trial judge in the murder case. The letter contained allegedly defamatory statements about Kunstler and Ratner. See Chapter 8 for the contents of the letter. Kunstler and Ratner also sued the publisher of the newspaper that reprinted the letter.]

Kunstler was a public figure generally, and Ratner was one at least for the Fountain Valley murder case.

The affidavits and exhibits before the Court in support of the motions for summary judgment, together with admissions by counsel for the plaintiffs in the course of his argument on the motions, show that Kunstler was one of the leading lawyers in the country devoting his time to the defense of members of minority groups charged with crime. He styled himself "an itinerant lawyer." He defended many of the leaders in the revolt of the

1960's and early 1970's seeking to get rid of the "establishment." He was almost always on the unpopular side of controversial cases. His cases and trial tactics were widely publicized. Mr. Padilla, the attorney who represented the plaintiffs in the hearing on the motions, made the following admissions during his oral argument: "... Kunstler is a controversial figure, I'll admit. He glories in controversy. That's his life style ..."

When the Court asked him what was the extent of his admission whether he was a controversial figure on a local scale or a national scale, he stated: "I would have to say Mr. Kunstler is a controversial figure on a national scale."

Ratner is not shown to be the public figure that Kunstler has been, but the matters that the Court can consider on this hearing show that she was a public figure for the limited purpose of the Fountain Valley murder trial. One of the exhibits before the Court is the transcript of her testimony on the hearing of her motion requesting admission Pro Hac Vice for the defense of the charges in the Fountain Valley trial. She testified that Kunstler came to her office and invited her to go with him to St. Croix to offer their legal services free of charge to the defendants in the Fountain Valley trial; that they went to see the defendants without invitation; that their offer of their legal services without pay was accepted. She took a leading part in the trial, even to the point of joining the defendants when they were disrespectfully shouting at the Court.

It has been previously pointed out that Kunstler stated several times that the trial of the Fountain Valley murder case was a political trial. With its racial overtones and devastating effect on the economy of the Islands, it was unquestionably a public controversy of deep concern to all of the people in the Islands, and to those who owned property there but lived elsewhere. The oral admissions made during the argument of plaintiffs' counsel on the motions would be enough to support the statement just made.

Kunstler and Ratner voluntarily thrust themselves into the vortex of the case that had far-reaching and serious effect on many people not connected with it.

Under the circumstances, the *New York Times* rule is applicable to this case, and Kunstler and Ratner have failed to meet its requirements. This is one of the grounds for summary judgment against them.

* * *

1. A note on William Kunstler. The following is from Kunstler's obituary in the *New York Times*:

> Mr. Kunstler made not just a career but also a life out of representing people and movements that were disliked, even despised. His clients' unpopularity seemed to inspire Mr. Kunstler, who was recognized by admirers and detractors alike as a lawyer who embraced pariahs. He seemed to seek out the most loathed of people and causes.

http://www.nytimes.com/1995/09/05/obituaries/william-kunstler-76-dies-lawyer-for-social-outcasts.html. In response to the charge that he was a showoff or a publicity-seeker, Kunstler said this: "I enjoy the spotlight, as most humans do, but it's not my whole *raison d'etre*. My purpose is to keep the state from becoming all-domineering, all powerful." *Id.*

2. Professional identity and pretrial publicity. Lawyers are routinely advised of the dangers that pretrial publicity poses to the administration of justice. ABA Model Rule 3.6(a) prohibits a lawyer from making a public statement that is substantially likely to materially prejudice a proceeding. Yet, lawyers often make public statements before and during legal proceedings, some of which impugn the character of some of the participants. Why do they do this? When is it appropriate for a lawyer to "use the media" to help a client?

3. Public figures within a community. A person may be an all-purpose public figure within a particular community or geographic area despite not having attained pervasive fame or notoriety on a national level. *See* Steere v. Cupp. 602 P.2d 1267 (Kan. 1979).

Focus Question: *Bandelin v. Pietsch*

1. *Is Bandelin the type of public figure the Supreme Court seemed to have had in mind in* Gertz *and* Wolston?
2. *Why is the evidence insufficient to establish actual malice on the part of the defendant?*

Bandelin v. Pietsch

563 P.2d 395
(Idaho 1977)

DONALDSON, Justice.

This case is an action for libel.... Plaintiff-appellant Glenn Bandelin appeals from a grant of summary judgment. Glenn E. Bandelin is a North Idaho attorney and is also a former office holder in the state legislature. On December 19, 1968, the probate court of Bonner County appointed him guardian of the person and estate of one Muriel I. Talbot who had been found incompetent on the same date. She died on January 2, 1970. Bandelin did not initiate proceedings for a final accounting until March 25, 1971. At that time, the district court concluded that Bandelin's management of the estate had been negligent in the extreme and ordered the prosecuting attorney of Bonner County to initiate contempt proceedings against him.

Over a period of several months, the *Sandpoint News-Bulletin* reported the ensuing legal proceedings. Accounts of the proceedings occurred in eleven consecutive editions of the *Sandpoint News-Bulletin.* There were seventeen publications in total. These accounts gave rise to Bandelin's allegations of libel and invasion of privacy. He claims that the accounts contained misstatements of fact and that they were deliberately repetitious.

From the record it appears that misstatements appeared in the August 19 and August 26 editions of the *Sandpoint News-Bulletin.* The August 19 edition referred to two Sandpoint attorneys 'judged in contempt of a district court decision and order concerning their handling of the guardianship and estate of the late Mrs. Muriel Talbot.' At a later point in the article they were cited by name. In the August 26 edition the same misstatement is made twice. Although plaintiff was later judged in contempt by the district court (a conviction that was overturned by the Idaho Supreme Court on procedural grounds), at the time the above accounts were written his case had not come to trial and hence he had not as yet been adjudged in contempt. The *Sandpoint News-Bulletin* did accurately report future developments in the case—Bandelin's conviction, the appeal that followed and the Supreme Court's reversal of the lower court's decision, but it never made a retraction of the earlier misstatements.

Bandelin brought a libel action ... against the *Sandpoint News-Bulletin*, as well as its editor, L. E. Pietsch, and the reporter responsible for the allegedly defamatory publications, Morgan Monroe. After extensive discovery, the Sandpoint News-Bulletin moved for summary judgment. The district court, after examining the record as well as supplementary briefs and affidavits, granted the Sandpoint News-Bulletin's motion. This appeal followed.

[The issues on appeal were Bandelin's public figure status and whether there was sufficient evidence of actual malice.]

The United States Supreme Court in *Gertz* said that the designation of a public figure may rest on two alternative bases:

> In some instances an individual may achieve such persuasive fame or notoriety that he becomes a public figure for all purposes and in all contexts. More commonly, an individual voluntarily injects himself or is drawn into a particular public controversy and thereby becomes a public figure for a limited range of issues. 418 U.S. at 351, 94 S. Ct. at 3013.

A review of the record reveals that Bandelin was prominent in the local politics of Bonner County, had been a representative in the state legislature, was a leading attorney, and was well-known throughout the county. Counsel for Bandelin argues, however, that in recent years Bandelin's public role has subsided—that he has reverted to the 'simple small-town lawyer he was before he gained notoriety.' We concede that a public figure can revert back to the 'lawful and unexciting life lead by the great bulk of the community.' Prosser, Law of Torts, s 107 (1st ed. 1941). But it is far more common that a public figure will retain residual elements of his former status even when he returns to private life.

However, we do not affirm the district court's decision exclusively on the prominence that Bandelin enjoyed in the local community. We are sensitive to the consequences of being a public figure and we do not assume that a citizen's participation in community and professional affairs automatically renders him a public figure....

In the present case, Bandelin as the guardian of the estate of Muriel I. Talbot was the center of the controversy that gave rise to the *Sandpoint News-Bulletin*'s publications. The *Sandpoint News-Bulletin* initiated its coverage of the Talbot case when it became aware of the trial judge's criticism of Bandelin's handling of the Talbot guardianship. Under such circumstances, Bandelin cannot maintain that he is not a public figure and was just an attorney handling the probate affairs of a client. He was rather that court appointed guardian, a pivotal figure in the controversy regarding the accounting of the estate that gave rise to the defamation and invasion of privacy actions.

The fact that after a period of active involvement in the political and social affairs of Bonner County, Bandelin desired the personal anonymity of a private citizen, does not make him a private figure for first amendment purposes. Public figure status does not hinge upon an individual's preference in the matter. In most cases, a public figure will have become such by the active pursuit of the limelight; but the *Times* privilege is not precluded because an individual does not voluntarily pursue public acclaim. The privilege is based upon a value judgment that debate on public issues should be uninhibited. That judgment is applicable to both the individual who becomes embroiled in a public controversy through no effort of his own and the individual who actively generates controversy—both abdicate their anonymity.

Since the *Sandpoint News-Bulletin*'s coverage of Bandelin's role in the Talbot case was constitutionally privileged, in order to recover on his libel [action], Bandelin had to show that the publications were made with malice. We come then to the major issue which Bandelin raises on appeal—whether there were disputed issues of fact as to the existence of malice which should have been submitted to a jury.

[W]e agree with the district court that summary judgment should have been granted. Even viewing the evidence most favorably to Bandelin and giving him the benefit of all proper inferences, there is no evidence that shows with convincing clarity that the *Sandpoint News-Bulletin* acted with malice. The only errors appearing in the report were two statements that Bandelin had been judged in contempt when his case had not yet come to trial. The Supreme Court of the United States found that a reporter's failure to differentiate between allegations in a complaint and proven fact is not sufficient to sustain a jury finding of actual malice. Time, Inc. v. Pape, 401 U.S. 279, 91 S. Ct. 633, 28 L.Ed.2d 45 (1971). Like Morgan Monroe, the reporter in this case, the reporter in *Pape* professed some familiarity with legal concepts. The Supreme Court based its conclusion on the fact that the alleged libel in *Pape* arose from a misinterpretation of an ambiguous document. The district court's order directing the prosecuting attorney of Bonner County to initiate contempt proceedings against Bandelin was equally ambiguous. Malice cannot be predicated exclusively on misstatements having their genesis in an ambiguous document.

Bandelin also relies on the tone of the articles to sustain his claim that summary judgment was improvidently granted. The articles were evocative. Phrases such as the 'puzzling Talbot case,' 'rapid-fire developments,' 'shaken Bonner County legal community' blemish the articles. We do not applaud the *Sandpoint News-Bulletin*'s journalism. It was unjustifiably sensational. However, the tone of the articles, even when considered with the other evidence presented in the case, does not establish malice with convincing clarity. Malice is defined for first amendment purposes as knowledge of falsity or reckless disregard of truth. Its essence is a knowing state of mind on the part of the publisher. Although it is conceivable that the character and content of a publication could be so patently defamatory that a jury could infer a knowing state of mind on this basis alone, no case has so held....

Bandelin contends that the repetition of the news stories together with their misstatements and tone raise sufficient evidence of malice to justify submitting the question to a jury. The record establishes beyond factual dispute that the Talbot case was a continuing story—each of the articles was justified by a new development in the case. Morgan Monroe testified that standard journalism procedure is to summarize preceding developments in a continuing story, the assumption being that readers have not read the prior stories. Monroe's testimony is not challenged by any evidence to the contrary. We also take notice of the fact that the *Sandpoint News Bulletin* is a weekly paper. When a paper is not published daily, it may be more important to repeat what transpired previously so that readers will understand the least developments in a story.

Bandelin has not introduced any other evidence of malice. What he has introduced even if accepted by a jury would not establish malice under the less demanding preponderance of evidence standard. It falls far short of establishing malice with convincing clarity.

Focus Question: *Marcone v. Penthouse International Magazine*

1. *Is Marcone the type of public figure the Supreme Court seemed to have had in mind in* Gertz *and* Wolston*?*
2. *Why is the evidence insufficient to establish actual malice on the part of the defendant?*

Marcone v. Penthouse International Magazine for Men

754 F.2d 1072
(3d Cir. 1985)

Penthouse published an article in its November 1978 issue entitled "The Stoning of America." Written by Edward Rasen, the article concerned the emergence of marijuana trade as a multibillion dollar industry. The subtitle stated that "marijuana is now big agribusiness—a $12 billion a year corporate growth crop." The article proceeded to report, in part, about "criminal attorneys and attorney criminals" involved in drug transactions ...

Examples: ... Frank Marcone, an attorney from the Philadelphia area, contributed down payments of up to $25,000 on grass transactions. Charges against him were dismissed because he cooperated with further investigations.

Marcone brought suit against Penthouse charging that the article libeled him since it declared that he was guilty of an offense for which he was only indicted, and since it stated that charges were dropped against him because he cooperated with the authorities. Plaintiff alleges that these two statements are untrue and that they have caused him harm and subjected him to ridicule.

III.

Penthouse ... argues that because Marcone was a public figure the district court erred in applying a negligence rather than an actual malice standard to prove liability for actual damages....

A.

In considering a defamation case after *Gertz*, a court is required to ascertain in the first instance whether the plaintiff is a public figure.[4] Public officials and public figures must prove actual malice. Regarding private figures, however, the Court held that states could define the appropriate standard for liability, "so long as they do not impose liability without fault." *Gertz*, 418 U.S. at 347, 94 S. Ct. at 3010.

The Supreme Court has not provided a detailed chart of the contours of the public and private figure categories. In an attempt to avoid "unpredictable results and uncertain expectations," the Court elected to paint with a broad brush rather than to adopt a case by case approach. Without a precise diagram for guidance, courts and commentators have had considerable difficulty in determining the proper scope of the public figure doctrine. One district court opined that the task of demarcating between public and private figures "is much like trying to nail a jelly fish to the wall." Rosanova v. Playboy Enterprises, Inc., 411 F. Supp. 440, 443 (S.D.Ga.1976), *aff'd*, 580 F.2d 859 (5th Cir.1978).

...

B.

Penthouse does not contend and we cannot hold that Marcone developed such pervasive notoriety in the community that he should be deemed a public figure for all purposes. Rather, the defendant maintains that the trial judge erred in not classifying Marcone as a public figure in the limited circumstance of his connection with illicit drug activities....

4. The classification of a plaintiff as a public or private figure is a question of law to be determined initially by the trial court and then carefully scrutinized by an appellate court.

Since it is clear that the alleged libel involves a public controversy, it is necessary to examine the nature and extent of Marcone's participation in it. In general, to be a limited purpose public figure, the plaintiff must voluntarily thrust himself into the vortex of the dispute. From the voluntary act is derived the notion of assumption of the risk and the consequent fairness in labeling the person a public figure. In the typical limited purpose public figure case, the plaintiff actively participates in the public issue in a manner intended to obtain attention. For example, a meat producer that aggressively advertised its product in the media becomes a limited purpose public figure for comment on the quality of its product. *See* Steaks Unlimited, Inc. v. Deaner, 623 F.2d 264, 273–74 (3d Cir.1980). Similarly, an agent who holds news conferences to attract media attention for himself and his client is a public figure in that context. Woy v. Turner, 573 F. Supp. 35 (N.D.Ga.1983).

In other defamation cases, the plaintiff's action may itself invite comment and attention, and even though he does not directly try or even want to attract the public's attention, he is deemed to have assumed the risk of such attention.

Somewhat related, courts have classified some people as limited purpose public figures because of their status, position or associations. For example, sports figures are generally considered public figures because of their position as athletes or coaches. *See, e.g.*, Chuy v. Philadelphia Eagles Football Club, 595 F.2d 1265 (3d Cir.1979) (en banc); Barry v. Time, Inc., 584 F. Supp. 1110, 1113 (N.D.Cal.1984). If a position itself is so prominent that its occupant unavoidably enters the limelight, then a person who voluntarily assumes such a position may be presumed to have accepted public figure status. The district court in *Chuy* stated

> Where a person has, however, chosen to engage in a profession which draws him regularly into regional and national view and leads to "fame and notoriety in the community," even if he has no ideological thesis to promulgate, he invites general public discussion.... If society chooses to direct massive public attention to a particular sphere of activity, those who enter that sphere inviting such attention must overcome the Times standard.... This is especially so in this case where the subject matter pertained to Donald Chuy's ability to continue playing professional football, a matter in which the sports loving public had a not insignificant interest.

Chuy v. Philadelphia Eagles Football Club, 431 F.Supp. 254, 267 (E.D.Pa.1977), *aff'd*, 595 F.2d 1265 (3d Cir.1979) (en banc).

In addition to sports figures, others have been classified as limited purpose public figures by virtue of their associations or positions. For example, the Fifth Circuit deemed Louis Rosanova, a reputed underworld personality, a public figure in the context of his connection to organized crime. Rosanova v. Playboy Enterprises, Inc., 411 F.Supp. 440 (S.D.Ga.1976), aff'd, 580 F.2d 859 (5th Cir.1978). Although never convicted of a crime, Rosanova had been the subject of governmental investigations and criminal prosecutions. Moreover, his alleged underworld ties had been the subject of considerable media attention. Asserting that he never sought such a status, Rosanova vigorously argued he was not a public figure. However, because some of his contacts with underworld figures were not denied, the court held that Rosanova voluntarily engaged in a course of activity that was bound to invite attention and comment. The Fifth Circuit went on to say

> In our view of the law resulting from the inevitable collision between First Amendment freedoms and the right of privacy, the status of public figure *vel non* does not depend upon the desires of an individual. The purpose served by limited protection to the publisher of comment upon a public figure would

> often be frustrated if the subject of the publication could choose whether or not he would be a public figure. Comment upon people and activities of legitimate public concern often illuminates that which yearns for shadow. It is no answer to the assertion that one is a public figure to say, truthfully, that one doesn't choose to be. It is sufficient, as the district court found, that "Mr. Rosanova voluntarily engaged in a course that was bound to invite attention and comment."

580 F.2d at 861.[9]

C.

With regard to the nature and extent of Marcone's participation in drug activities, Penthouse points to three factors which it asserts establish Marcone as a limited purpose public figure: (1) Marcone's indictment in the drug trafficking conspiracy and the attendant publicity; (2) his representation of motorcycle gang members; and (3) his non-representational ties to the Pagans and Warlocks.

... Marcone, along with 24 other co-defendants was indicted in Detroit for allegedly participating in a nationwide drug trafficking ring which at that time reportedly was the largest drug smuggling case in United States history. Marcone's indictment was widely reported by the Philadelphia area media. The headline story in *The Evening Bulletin* on February 11, 1976, the day after the indictment was handed down, was entitled "Media Lawyer Accused of Role in Drug Ring." ... *The Evening Bulletin* article quoted Marcone as expressing his surprise and professing his innocence with respect to his indictment.

Penthouse points to Marcone's indictment and the accompanying publicity to establish him as a limited purpose public figure. In *Wolston*, the Supreme Court rejected the contention that "any person who engages in criminal conduct automatically becomes a public figure for purposes of comment on a limited range of issues relating to his conviction." 443 U.S. at 168, 99 S. Ct. at 2708; *cf. Firestone*, 424 U.S. at 457, 96 S. Ct. at 966 (status as participant in litigation does not automatically render one a public figure). Although the criminal activity, by itself, may not create public figure status, such activity may, nevertheless, be one element in a mix of factors leading to that classification. *See Rosanova*, 580 F.2d at 861; Orr v. Argus-Press Co., 586 F.2d 1108, 1116 (6th Cir.1978), cert. denied, 440 U.S. 960, 99 S. Ct. 1502, 59 L.Ed.2d 773 (1979). Moreover, the crime involved in *Wolston* was particularly passive—a contempt citation for failure to appear at a grand jury hearing because of ill health. In the present case, however, Marcone was indicted for

9. Some courts and commentators have questioned whether *Gertz* also created a third class of public figures: the involuntary public figure. *See, e.g., Waldbaum*, 627 F.2d at 1295 n. 18; *Steaks Unlimited*, 632 F.2d at 272–73; Note, *The Involuntary Public Figure Class of Gertz v. Robert Welch: Dead or Merely Dormant?*, 14 U.Mich.J.L. Ref. 71 (1980). In general, rather than creating a separate class of public figures, we view such a description as merely one way an individual may come to be considered a general or limited purpose public figure. Thus, to the extent a person attains public figure status by position, status, or notorious act he might be considered an involuntary public figure. The one group of individuals that might truly be considered involuntary public figures are relatives of famous people. *See* Meeropol v. Nizer, 381 F. Supp. 29 (S.D.N.Y.1974) (children of Julius and Ethyl Rosenberg are public figures), *aff'd in relevant part*, 560 F.2d 1061 (2d Cir.1977), *cert. denied*, 434 U.S. 1013, 98 S. Ct. 727, 54 L.Ed.2d 756 (1978); *see also* Carson v. Allied News Co., 529 F.2d 206, 210 (7th Cir.1976) (wife of famous entertainer a public figure); Note, *An Analysis of the Distinction Between Public Figures and Private Defamation Plaintiffs Applied to Relatives of Public Persons*, 49 S.Cal.L.Rev. 1131 (1976). In *Gertz*, the Supreme Court cautioned that "the instances of truly involuntary public figures must be exceedingly rare." 418 U.S. at 345, 94 S. Ct. at 3009.

participating, not in a passive manner, in a drug conspiracy. This factor may be considered in our analysis of Marcone's status.

Marcone's indictment was widely reprinted in the local media. Moreover, the drug ring with its prominent local connection became the subject of intense attention by the Philadelphia media. In this regard, federal law enforcement agents were quoted as saying that the four Philadelphia-area co-indictees frequently met at the Castle, a large mansion in Delaware County which served as the headquarters for the Pagans motorcycle gang. Numerous news stories focused on the Castle and a list of illegal activities connected with it, including drugs, stolen goods, and the disappearance and suspected murder of five young women. Subject to even closer scrutiny were the occupants of the Castle, the Pagans, and a rival gang, the Warlocks. Federal sources linked the Pagans and their illegal drug activities to the two billion dollar drug-smuggling ring brought to light by the Detroit indictment.

Plaintiff was closely linked to the Castle and the Pagans in a number of ways. Marcone had a significant criminal practice and frequently represented the Pagans and Warlocks in legal matters. Representation of such notorious groups does invite attention, and, in fact, this legal relationship was widely reported in the Philadelphia-area media. Nevertheless this evidence is not determinative in our analysis. Legal representation of a client, by itself, does not establish an individual as a public figure. To hold otherwise would place an undue burden on attorneys who represent famous or notorious clients. *See Gertz*, 418 U.S. at 352, 94 S. Ct. at 3013; Steere v. Cupp, 226 Kan. 566, 571, 602 P.2d 1267, 1273–74 (1979).

Of course, if an attorney does more than merely represent the client in a strictly legal context—such as holding news conferences or otherwise affirmatively making a public issue of the case—then those activities may be counted in the public figure calculus. *See, e.g.*, Ratner v. Young, 465 F. Supp. 386, 399–400 (D.V.I.1979) (defense attorneys in widely publicized trial deemed public figures because of their out of court activities). Nothing in the record of the present case indicates that Marcone was engaged in bringing attention to his clients or himself in regard to their legal relationship. Thus we may give only limited significance to Marcone's representational activities in the public figure analysis.

More important for the limited public figure determination are Marcone's non-representational contacts with the Pagans. As noted, Marcone reportedly met at the Pagans' headquarters with Frey, Heron and Mealy. In addition, one newspaper article reported that Marcone admitted to going on occasional weekend trips with motorcycle gang members. For purposes of public figure analysis we must look to Marcone's actions in addition to his intentions. There is no evidence that his conduct was intended to attract attention; but this does not end our inquiry. As the Fifth Circuit noted in *Rosanova*, it may be sufficient that Marcone engaged in a course of conduct that was bound to attract attention and comment.

In this regard, Marcone's non-representational connections to the Castle and the Pagans are sufficient to tip the balance in the calculation. Both the Pagans and their headquarters were linked to the two billion dollar drug ring, i.e., the public controversy surrounding the alleged libel. We find that Marcone's voluntary connection with motorcycle gangs—including his meetings at the Castle with Frey and his occasional weekend trips with them—in conjunction with the intense media attention he engendered is sufficient to render Marcone a public figure for the limited purpose of his connection with illicit drug trafficking.

This is a close case, and if each element of the equation is taken separately it may be argued that no one aspect may be sufficient to create public figure status. Nevertheless, when all the relevant factors are considered in context and as a whole, we believe that Marcone has crossed the line from private to limited purpose public figure.

... We recognize that there are counterveiling dangers from a media that has untrammeled freedom to publish inaccurate and damaging statements with impunity. Moreover, when a sensational story by one news organization is picked up by many, the snowballing of media attention may transform an unknown individual into a virtual celebrity almost overnight. The possibility therefore exists that by relying on this snowballing of attention a media defendant might be able to bootstrap itself into first amendment protection. Such a sequence of events might concededly defeat public figure status in an appropriate case, but plaintiff's situation is not such a case.

Given the public nature of the activities at issue here, the widespread media attention and the significant contact to the Pagans of a non-representational type, we hold that Marcone has crossed the threshold and become a limited purpose public figure. Accordingly, the district court erred in not classifying Marcone as a limited purpose public figure.[11]

IV.

Since Marcone is a limited purpose public figure, he must establish libel under the *New York Times* actual malice standard. Because the district court ruled that Marcone was a private figure, it permitted the jury to award compensatory damages upon a demonstration that *Penthouse* merely was negligent in publishing the article. [The court concluded that the trial court's instructions to the jury were erroneous.]

VI.

Penthouse's article [was inaccurate in that] it states as a fact that Marcone purchased $25,000 worth of marijuana when Marcone was only indicted but never convicted of such conduct....

The original draft of the article, submitted by free-lance author Edward Rasen, apparently made the assertion that Marcone had purchased marijuana. Penthouse points to three sources to demonstrate that this factual error was made without actual malice. First, the magazine relied on the experience and reputation of Rasen. Mr. Goode, Penthouse's editorial director in 1978, had known Rasen as an investigative reporter and writer since the early 1970's. In 1971, when Goode was at Earth Magazine, he hired Rasen to provide information about Vietnam and found Rasen's material to be reliable. In 1978 Rasen approached Penthouse regarding a series of articles on drugs. Goode appointed John Lombardi, an articles editor, to work with Rasen. Lombardi testified, by deposition, that Rasen had previously written for several west coast newspapers, including the Los Angeles Times, and worked in electronic journalism for west coast television stations. Lombardi, like Goode, found Rasen to be a very professional investigative journalist. Reliance on the professional reputation of an author may help to defeat an allegation of actual malice.

Failure to investigate, without more, does not demonstrate actual malice. In *St. Amant*, [the Court held that in order to find actual malice,] "[t]here must be sufficient evidence to permit the conclusion that the defendant in fact entertained serious doubts as to the truth of his publication." *St. Amant*, 390 U.S. at 731, 88 S. Ct. at 1325; *see also New York*

---

11. This decision is tied to the facts of this case. We emphasize that we do not hold that an attorney whose connection to notorious clients remains purely professional or any person charged with a crime automatically becomes a limited purpose public figure.

Times, 376 U.S. at 288, 84 S. Ct. at 730 (failure of newspaper's employees to verify the facts contained in an advertisement against new stories in its own files amounted at most to negligence, and was "constitutionally insufficient to show the recklessness that is required for a finding of actual malice.")

The Court noted that there are limitations on the actual malice element of First Amendment protection. A mere assertion by the publisher that he thought the statement published to be true does not automatically defeat actual malice. In some instances, bare professions of good faith may be unpersuasive, such as where the "publisher's allegations are so inherently improbable that only a reckless man would have put them in circulation. Likewise, recklessness may be found where there are obvious reasons to doubt the veracity of the informant or the accuracy of his reports." *St. Amant*, 390 U.S. at 732, 88 S. Ct. at 1326. But, the Court reiterated, mere failure to investigate does not establish bad faith.

Thus even if *Penthouse* had failed to investigate, its reasonable reliance on Rasen arguably would have been sufficient to defeat plaintiff's attempt to show actual malice. Here, however, Penthouse did attempt to verify the assertions in the article; its editors obtained a copy of the Detroit indictment that charged Marcone with the crime for which the article stated he committed. In addition, the magazine had an article from the *Philadelphia Inquirer*, dated March 18, 1976, which reported on Marcone's indictment. Consequently, in publishing the information about Marcone, Penthouse relied on the apparent reputation of Rasen, partially based on his prior relationship with *Penthouse* staffers, Rasen's notes, a copy of the Detroit indictment, and the article in the *Philadelphia Inquirer*. The statement was not so "inherently improbable" that defendant should have been put on notice as to its probable falsity. *See St. Amant*, 390 U.S. at 732, 88 S. Ct. at 1326. While the newspaper article and indictment do not prove the truth of the assertion, they are sufficiently related to the statement in question that we cannot say the whole story is a fabrication or a product of the author's imagination. *Penthouse* may have been negligent in not investigating further to determine the veracity of the statement and in failing to distinguish between an allegation and a proven fact. But the failure to use the word "alleged," under these circumstances, does not establish actual malice.

Thus based on our independent review of the record we conclude that the plaintiff failed to prove, either by clear and convincing evidence or even by a preponderance of the evidence, that the libelous statement was published with actual malice.

* * *

1. Representing the famous or the controversial. Other courts have expressed greater reluctance to classify a lawyer as a public figure by virtue of the fact that he lawyer represents a famous or controversial client. In *Spence v. Flynt*, 816 P.2d 771, 777 (Wyo. 1991), the Wyoming Supreme Court held that "a lawyer who is merely advocating for a famous or controversial client is not a public figure merely because he has taken on the cause as advocate."

2. Involuntary Public Figures. *Gertz* introduced the idea of an involuntary public figure: someone who becomes a public figure "through no purposeful action of his own" and is instead dragged into the spotlight. *Marcone* also mentions this idea. Some courts have been willing to recognize this as a category of public figures. According to the Fourth Circuit Court of Appeals, to be an involuntary public figure, one must (1) be a central figure in a significant public controversy and (2) have assumed the risk of publicity, even if one did not seek to publicize her views or influence discussion on an issue of public controversy. Wells v. Liddy, 186 F.3d 505, 540 (4th Cir. 1999). Would the attorney in *Bandelin* qualify as such a figure?

Exercise 9.3

You are scheduled to have a meeting with Lawrence Gatton, a local lawyer, about the possibility of representing Gatton in a defamation action. You have spoken briefly with Gatton on the phone, but know only a few details about his situation. Gatton is outraged about a recent story in the local newspaper that reported that Gatton was under investigation for insurance fraud in connection with his representation of the state teacher's union in an insurance matter. When you spoke briefly with Gatton, all you could really get from him was that the story was false, that Gatton was not under investigation, and that the person actually under investigation was another individual.

Prepare an outline of topics that you need to discuss with Gatton (along with a few tentative questions you might ask related to each topic) in order to determine which of the constitutional rules that have evolved from *New York Times v. Sullivan* is likely to apply to Gatton's case.

E. Actionable and Non-Actionable Statements

The Supreme Court's decision in *Gertz* contained the following dictum: "Under the First Amendment there is no such thing as a false idea. However pernicious an opinion may seem, we depend for its correction not on the conscience of judges and juries but on the competition of other ideas. But there is no constitutional value in false statements of fact." *Gertz*, 418 U.S. at 339–340. Based on this statement, some argued that only false statements of fact were actionable under a defamation theory; statements of opinion were constitutionally protected. The following decisions attempt to articulate standards for determining when statements may be actionable under a defamation theory.

Focus Question: *Milkovich v. Lorain Journal Co.*

1. *When, if ever, are statements of opinion actionable?*
2. *Why was the statement in* Milkovich *actionable?*

Milkovich v. Lorain Journal Co.

497 U.S. 1
(1990)

Chief Justice REHNQUIST delivered the opinion of the Court.

Respondent J. Theodore Diadiun authored an article in an Ohio newspaper implying that petitioner Michael Milkovich, a local high school wrestling coach, lied under oath in a judicial proceeding about an incident involving petitioner and his team which occurred at a wrestling match. Petitioner sued Diadiun and the newspaper for libel, and the Ohio Court of Appeals affirmed a lower court entry of summary judgment against petitioner. This judgment was based in part on the grounds that the article constituted an "opinion" protected from the reach of state defamation law by the First Amendment to the United States Constitution....

This lawsuit is before us for the third time in an odyssey of litigation spanning nearly 15 years. Petitioner Milkovich, now retired, was the wrestling coach at Maple Heights High School in Maple Heights, Ohio. In 1974, his team was involved in an altercation at a home wrestling match with a team from Mentor High School. Several people were injured. In response to the incident, the Ohio High School Athletic Association (OHSAA) held a hearing at which Milkovich and H. Don Scott, the Superintendent of Maple Heights Public Schools, testified. Following the hearing, OHSAA placed the Maple Heights team on probation for a year and declared the team ineligible for the 1975 state tournament. OHSAA also censured Milkovich for his actions during the altercation. Thereafter, several parents and wrestlers sued OHSAA in the Court of Common Pleas of Franklin County, Ohio, seeking a restraining order against OHSAA's ruling on the grounds that they had been denied due process in the OHSAA proceeding. Both Milkovich and Scott testified in that proceeding. The court overturned OHSAA's probation and ineligibility orders on due process grounds.

The day after the court rendered its decision, respondent Diadiun's column appeared in the News-Herald, a newspaper which circulates in Lake County, Ohio, and is owned by respondent Lorain Journal Co. The column bore the heading "Maple Beat the Law with the 'Big Lie,'" beneath which appeared Diadiun's photograph and the words "TD Says." The carryover page headline announced "... Diadiun says Maple told a lie." The column contained the following passages:

> "'... [A] lesson was learned (or relearned) yesterday by the student body of Maple Heights High School, and by anyone who attended the Maple-Mentor wrestling meet of last Feb. 8.
>
> "'A lesson which, sadly, in view of the events of the past year, is well they learned early.
>
> "'It is simply this: If you get in a jam, lie your way out.
>
> "'If you're successful enough, and powerful enough, and can sound sincere enough, you stand an excellent chance of making the lie stand up, regardless of what really happened.
>
> "'The teachers responsible were mainly head Maple wrestling coach, Mike Milkovich, and former superintendent of schools H. Donald Scott.
>
> ....
>
> "'Anyone who attended the meet, whether he be from Maple Heights, Mentor, or impartial observer, knows in his heart that Milkovich and Scott lied at the hearing after each having given his solemn oath to tell the truth.
>
> "'But they got away with it.
>
> "'Is that the kind of lesson we want our young people learning from their high school administrators and coaches?
>
> "'I think not.'"

Milkovich v. News-Herald, 46 Ohio App.3d 20, 21, 545 N.E.2d 1320, 1321–1322 (1989).

The common law generally did not place any ... restrictions on the type of statement that could be actionable. Indeed, defamatory communications were deemed actionable regardless of whether they were deemed to be statements of fact or opinion. As noted in the *1977 Restatement (Second) of Torts* § 566, Comment a:

> Under the law of defamation, an expression of opinion could be defamatory if the expression was sufficiently derogatory of another as to cause harm to his reputation, so as to lower him in the estimation of the community or to deter third persons from associating or dealing with him.... The expression of opinion was also actionable in a suit for defamation, despite the normal requirement that the communication be false as well as defamatory.... This position was maintained even though the truth or falsity of an opinion—as distinguished from a statement of fact—is not a matter that can be objectively determined and truth is a complete defense to a suit for defamation.

However, due to concerns that unduly burdensome defamation laws could stifle valuable public debate, the privilege of "fair comment" was incorporated into the common law as an affirmative defense to an action for defamation. "The principle of 'fair comment' afford[ed] legal immunity for the honest expression of opinion on matters of legitimate public interest when based upon a true or privileged statement of fact." 1 F. Harper & F. James, Law of Torts § 5.28, p. 456 (1956) (footnote omitted). As this statement implies, comment was generally privileged when it concerned a matter of public concern, was upon true or privileged facts, represented the actual opinion of the speaker, and was not made solely for the purpose of causing harm. *See Restatement of Torts, supra,* § 606. "According to the majority rule, the privilege of fair comment applied only to an expression of opinion and not to a false statement of fact, whether it was expressly stated or implied from an expression of opinion." *Restatement (Second) of Torts, supra,* § 566, Comment a. Thus under the common law, the privilege of "fair comment" was the device employed to strike the appropriate balance between the need for vigorous public discourse and the need to redress injury to citizens wrought by invidious or irresponsible speech.

... Respondents would have us recognize, in addition to the established safeguards discussed above, still another First-Amendment-based protection for defamatory statements which are categorized as "opinion" as opposed to "fact."

If a speaker says, "In my opinion John Jones is a liar," he implies a knowledge of facts which lead to the conclusion that Jones told an untruth. Even if the speaker states the facts upon which he bases his opinion, if those facts are either incorrect or incomplete, or if his assessment of them is erroneous, the statement may still imply a false assertion of fact. Simply couching such statements in terms of opinion does not dispel these implications; and the statement, "In my opinion Jones is a liar," can cause as much damage to reputation as the statement, "Jones is a liar." As Judge Friendly aptly stated: "[It] would be destructive of the law of libel if a writer could escape liability for accusations of [defamatory conduct] simply by using, explicitly or implicitly, the words 'I think.'" It is worthy of note that at common law, even the privilege of fair comment did not extend to "a false statement of fact, whether it was expressly stated or implied from an expression of opinion." Restatement (Second) of Torts, § 566, Comment a (1977).

[R]espondents do not really contend that a statement such as, "In my opinion John Jones is a liar," should be protected by a separate privilege for "opinion" under the First Amendment. But they do contend that in every defamation case the First Amendment mandates an inquiry into whether a statement is "opinion" or "fact," and that only the latter statements may be actionable.... But we think the "'breathing space'" which "'[f]reedoms of expression require in order to survive,'" *Hepps*, 475 U.S., at 772, 106

S.Ct., at 1561, is adequately secured by existing constitutional doctrine without the creation of an artificial dichotomy between "opinion" and fact.

Foremost, we think *Hepps* stands for the proposition that a statement on matters of public concern must be provable as false before there can be liability under state defamation law, at least in situations, like the present, where a media defendant is involved. Thus, unlike the statement, "In my opinion Mayor Jones is a liar," the statement, "In my opinion Mayor Jones shows his abysmal ignorance by accepting the teachings of Marx and Lenin," would not be actionable. *Hepps* ensures that a statement of opinion relating to matters of public concern which does not contain a provably false factual connotation will receive full constitutional protection.

Next, [another] line of cases provides protection for statements that cannot "reasonably [be] interpreted as stating actual facts" about an individual. *Falwell*, 485 U.S., at 50, 108 S.Ct., at 879. This provides assurance that public debate will not suffer for lack of "imaginative expression" or the "rhetorical hyperbole" which has traditionally added much to the discourse of our Nation. *See id.*, at 53–55, 108 S.Ct., at 880–882.

We are not persuaded that, in addition to these protections, an additional separate constitutional privilege for "opinion" is required to ensure the freedom of expression guaranteed by the First Amendment. The dispositive question in the present case then becomes whether a reasonable factfinder could conclude that the statements in the Diadiun column imply an assertion that petitioner Milkovich perjured himself in a judicial proceeding. We think this question must be answered in the affirmative. As the Ohio Supreme Court itself observed: "[T]he clear impact in some nine sentences and a caption is that [Milkovich] 'lied at the hearing after ... having given his solemn oath to tell the truth.'" *Scott*, 25 Ohio St.3d, at 251, 496 N.E.2d, at 707. This is not the sort of loose, figurative, or hyperbolic language which would negate the impression that the writer was seriously maintaining that petitioner committed the crime of perjury. Nor does the general tenor of the article negate this impression.

We also think the connotation that petitioner committed perjury is sufficiently factual to be susceptible of being proved true or false. A determination whether petitioner lied in this instance can be made on a core of objective evidence by comparing, *inter alia*, petitioner's testimony before the OHSAA board with his subsequent testimony before the trial court. As the Scott court noted regarding the plaintiff in that case: "[W]hether or not H. Don Scott did indeed perjure himself is certainly verifiable by a perjury action with evidence adduced from the transcripts and witnesses present at the hearing. Unlike a subjective assertion the averred defamatory language is an articulation of an objectively verifiable event." *Id.* at 252, 496 N.E.2d, at 707. So too with petitioner Milkovich.

The numerous decisions discussed above establishing First Amendment protection for defendants in defamation actions surely demonstrate the Court's recognition of the Amendment's vital guarantee of free and uninhibited discussion of public issues. But there is also another side to the equation; we have regularly acknowledged the "important social values which underlie the law of defamation," and recognized that "[s]ociety has a pervasive and strong interest in preventing and redressing attacks upon reputation." ...

We believe our decision in the present case holds the balance true. The judgment of the Ohio Court of Appeals is reversed, and the case is remanded for further proceedings not inconsistent with this opinion.

Reversed.

* * *

Opinions and Fair Comment. In *Milkovich*, the Court discussed the venerable fair comment privilege, a privilege still in existence in many jurisdictions. Chapter 10 will revisit the fair comment privilege within the context of a broader discussion of qualified privileges to defamation claims.

Focus Question: *Standing Committee on Discipline v. Yagman*

1. *Why would the defendant's statement that the judge was a "buffoon" not be actionable under a defamation theory?*
2. *Why was the statement about the judge being anti-Semitic not actionable?*

Standing Committee on Discipline v. Yagman

55 F.3d 1430
(9th Cir. 1995)

KOZINSKI, Circuit Judge.

Never far from the center of controversy, outspoken civil rights lawyer Stephen Yagman was suspended from practice before the United States District Court for the Central District of California for impugning the integrity of the court and interfering with the random selection of judges by making disparaging remarks about a judge of that court. We confront several new issues in reviewing this suspension order.

I

The convoluted history of this case begins in 1991 when Yagman filed a lawsuit pro se against several insurance companies. The case was assigned to Judge Manuel Real, then Chief Judge of the Central District. Yagman promptly sought to disqualify Judge Real on grounds of bias. The disqualification motion was randomly assigned to Judge William Keller, who denied it ... and sanctioned Yagman for pursuing the matter in an "improper and frivolous manner."

A few days after Judge Keller's sanctions order, Yagman was quoted as saying that Judge Keller "has a penchant for sanctioning Jewish lawyers: me, David Kenner and Hugh Manes. I find this to be evidence of anti-Semitism." Susan Seager, *Judge Sanctions Yagman, Refers Case to State Bar*, L.A. Daily J., June 6, 1991, at 1. The district court found that Yagman also told the *Daily Journal* reporter that Judge Keller was "drunk on the bench," although this accusation wasn't published in the article....

Around this time, Yagman received a request from Prentice Hall, publisher of the much-fretted-about *Almanac of the Federal Judiciary*,[1] for comments in connection with a profile of Judge Keller. Yagman's response was less than complimentary.[2]

---

1. The *Almanac* is a loose-leaf service consisting of profiles of federal judges. Each profile covers the judge's educational and professional background, noteworthy rulings, and anecdotal items of interest.

2. The portion of the letter relevant here reads as follows:

> It is outrageous that the Judge wants his profile redone because he thinks it to be inaccurately harsh in portraying him in a poor light. It is an understatement to characterize the Judge as "the worst judge in the central district." It would be fairer to say that he is ignorant, dishonest, ill-tempered, and a bully, and probably is one of the worst judges in the United States. If television cameras ever were permitted in his courtroom, the other federal judges

A few weeks later, Yagman placed an advertisement (on the stationary of his law firm) in the *L.A. Daily Journal*, asking lawyers who had been sanctioned by Judge Keller to contact Yagman's office.

Soon after these events, Yagman ran into Robert Steinberg, another attorney who practices in the Central District. According to Steinberg, Yagman told him that, by leveling public criticism at Judge Keller, Yagman hoped to get the judge to recuse himself in future cases. Believing that Yagman was committing misconduct, Steinberg described his conversation with Yagman in a letter to the Standing Committee on Discipline of the U.S. District Court for the Central District of California (the Standing Committee)....

A few weeks later, the Standing Committee received a letter from Judge Keller describing Yagman's anti-Semitism charge, his inflammatory statements to Prentice Hall and the newspaper advertisement placed by Yagman's law firm. Judge Keller stated that "Mr. Yagman's campaign of harassment and intimidation challenges the integrity of the judicial system. Moreover, there is clear evidence that Mr. Yagman's attacks upon me are motivated by his desire to create a basis for recusing me in any future proceeding." ... Judge Keller suggested that "[t]he Standing Committee on Discipline should take action to protect the Court from further abuse ..."

After investigating the charges in the two letters, the Standing Committee issued a Petition for Issuance of an Order to Show Cause why Yagman should not be suspended from practice or otherwise disciplined.... [T]he matter was then assigned to a panel of three Central District judges, which issued an Order to Show Cause and scheduled a hearing. Prior to the hearing, Yagman raised serious First Amendment objections to being disciplined for criticizing Judge Keller. Both sides requested an opportunity to brief the difficult free speech issues presented, but the district court never acted on these requests. The parties thus proceeded at the hearing without knowing the allocation of the burden of proof or the legal standard the court intended to apply.

...

III

Local Rule 2.5.2 ... enjoins attorneys from engaging in any conduct that "degrades or impugns the integrity of the Court." ...

A.

Attorneys who make statements impugning the integrity of a judge are ... entitled to ... First Amendment protections applicable in the defamation context. To begin with, attorneys may be sanctioned for impugning the integrity of a judge or the court only if their statements are false; truth is an absolute defense. Moreover, the disciplinary body bears the burden of proving falsity.

It follows that statements impugning the integrity of a judge may not be punished unless they are capable of being proved true or false; statements of opinion are protected by the First Amendment unless they "imply a false assertion of fact." *See* Milkovich v. Lorain Journal Co., 497 U.S. 1, 19 (1990). Even statements that at first blush appear to be factual are protected by the First Amendment if they cannot reasonably be interpreted

in the Country would be so embarrassed by this buffoon that they would run for cover. One might believe that some of the reason for this sub-standard human is the recent acrimonious divorce through which he recently went: but talking to attorneys who knew him years ago indicates that, if anything, he has mellowed. One other comment: his girlfriend..., like the Judge, is a right-wing fanatic.

as stating actual facts about their target. *See* Hustler Magazine, Inc. v. Falwell, 485 U.S. 46, 50, 108 S.Ct. 876, 879, 99 L.Ed.2d 41 (1988). Thus, statements of "rhetorical hyperbole" aren't sanctionable, nor are statements that use language in a "loose, figurative sense." *See* National Ass'n of Letter Carriers v. Austin, 418 U.S. 264, 284 (1974) (use of word "traitor" could not be construed as representation of fact); Greenbelt Coop. Publishing Ass'n v. Bresler, 398 U.S. 6, 14 (1970) (use of word "blackmail" could not have been interpreted as charging plaintiff with commission of criminal offense).

With these principles in mind, we examine the statements for which Yagman was disciplined.

We first consider Yagman's statement in the *Daily Journal* that Judge Keller "has a penchant for sanctioning Jewish lawyers: me, David Kenner and Hugh Manes. I find this to be evidence of anti-Semitism." Though the district court viewed this entirely as an assertion of fact, ... we conclude that the statement contains both an assertion of fact and an expression of opinion.

Yagman's claim that he, Kenner and Manes are all Jewish and were sanctioned by Judge Keller is clearly a factual assertion: The words have specific, well-defined meanings and describe objectively verifiable matters.... Thus, had the Standing Committee proved that Yagman, Kenner or Manes were not sanctioned by Judge Keller, or were not Jewish, this assertion might have formed the basis for discipline. The committee, however, didn't claim that Yagman's factual assertion was false, and the district court made no finding to that effect. We proceed, therefore, on the assumption that this portion of Yagman's statement is true.

The remaining portion of Yagman's *Daily Journal* statement is best characterized as opinion; it conveys Yagman's personal belief that Judge Keller is anti-Semitic. As such, it may be the basis for sanctions only if it could reasonably be understood as declaring or implying actual facts capable of being proved true or false....

In applying this principle, we are guided by section 566 of the *Restatement (Second) of Torts*, which distinguishes between two kinds of opinion statements: those based on assumed or expressly stated facts, and those based on implied, undisclosed facts....

A statement of opinion based on fully disclosed facts can be punished only if the stated facts are themselves false and demeaning. The rationale behind this rule is straightforward: When the facts underlying a statement of opinion are disclosed, readers will understand they are getting the author's interpretation of the facts presented; they are therefore unlikely to construe the statement as insinuating the existence of additional, undisclosed facts. Moreover, an opinion which is unfounded reveals its lack of merit when the opinion-holder discloses the factual basis for the idea; readers are free to accept or reject the author's opinion based on their own independent evaluation of the facts. A statement of opinion of this sort doesn't "imply a false assertion of fact," ... and is thus entitled to full constitutional protection.

Yagman's *Daily Journal* remark is protected by the First Amendment as an expression of opinion based on stated facts.... Yagman disclosed the basis for his view that Judge Keller is anti-Semitic and has a penchant for sanctioning Jewish lawyers: that he, Kenner and Manes are all Jewish and had been sanctioned by Judge Keller. The statement did not imply the existence of additional, undisclosed facts; it was carefully phrased in terms of an inference drawn from the facts specified rather than a bald accusation of bias against Jews.[3] Readers were "free to form another, perhaps contradictory opinion from the same facts," ... as no doubt they did.

3. Even if Yagman's statement were viewed as a bare allegation of anti-Semitism, it might well qualify for protection under the First Amendment as mere "name-calling." *Cf.* Stevens v. Tillman, 855

The district court also disciplined Yagman for alleging that Judge Keller was "dishonest." This remark appears in the letter Yagman sent to Prentice Hall in connection with the profile of Judge Keller in the *Almanac of the Federal Judiciary*. The court concluded that this allegation was sanctionable because it "plainly impl[ies] past improprieties." ... Had Yagman accused Judge Keller of taking bribes, we would agree with the district court. Statements that "could reasonably be understood as imputing specific criminal or other wrongful acts" are not entitled to constitutional protection merely because they are phrased in the form of an opinion ...

When considered in context, however, Yagman's statement cannot reasonably be interpreted as accusing Judge Keller of criminal misconduct. The term "dishonest" was one in a string of colorful adjectives Yagman used to convey the low esteem in which he held Judge Keller. The other terms he used—"ignorant," "ill-tempered," "buffoon," "sub-standard human," "right-wing fanatic," "a bully," "one of the worst judges in the United States"—all speak to competence and temperament rather than corruption; together they convey nothing more substantive than Yagman's contempt for Judge Keller. Viewed in context..., the word "dishonest" cannot reasonably be construed as suggesting that Judge Keller had committed specific illegal acts.... Yagman's remarks are thus statements of rhetorical hyperbole, incapable of being proved true or false. *Cf.* In re Erdmann, 301 N.E.2d 426, 427 (1973) (reversing sanction against attorney who criticized trial judges for not following the law, and appellate judges for being "the whores who became madams"); State Bar v. Semaan, 508 S.W.2d 429, 431–32 (Tex. Civ. App. 1974) (attorney's observation that judge was "a midget among giants" not sanctionable because it wasn't subject to being proved true or false).

Were we to find any substantive content in Yagman's use of the term "dishonest," we would, at most, construe it to mean "intellectually dishonest"—an accusation that Judge Keller's rulings were overly result-oriented. Intellectual dishonesty is a label lawyers frequently attach to decisions with which they disagree. An allegation that a judge is intellectually dishonest, however, cannot be proved true or false by reference to a "core of objective evidence." Because Yagman's allegation of "dishonesty" does not imply facts capable of objective verification, it is constitutionally immune from sanctions.

Finally, the district court found sanctionable Yagman's allegation that Judge Keller was "drunk on the bench." Yagman contends that, like many of the terms he used in his letter to Prentice Hall, this phrase should be viewed as mere "rhetorical hyperbole." The statement wasn't a part of the string of invective in the Prentice Hall letter, however; it was a remark Yagman allegedly made to a newspaper reporter. Yagman identifies nothing relating to the context in which this statement was made that tends to negate the literal meaning of the words he used. We therefore conclude that Yagman's "drunk on the bench" statement could reasonably be interpreted as suggesting that Judge Keller had actually, on at least one occasion, taken the bench while intoxicated. Unlike Yagman's remarks in his letter to Prentice Hall, this statement implies actual facts that are capable of objective verification. For this reason, the statement isn't protected under [prior cases].

For Yagman's "drunk on the bench" allegation to serve as the basis for sanctions, however, the Standing Committee had to prove that the statement was false.... This it failed to do ... Without proof of falsity, Yagman's "drunk on the bench" allegation, like

F.2d 394, 402 (7th Cir. 1988) (allegation that plaintiff was a "racist" held not actionable); Buckley v. Littell, 539 F.2d 882, 894 (2d Cir. 1976) (allegation that plaintiff was a "fascist" held not actionable); Ward v. Zelikovsky, 136 N.J. 516, 643 A.2d 972, 983 (1994) (allegation that plaintiffs "hate Jews" held not actionable).

the statements discussed above, cannot support the imposition of sanctions for impugning the integrity of the court....

Conclusion

We can't improve on the words of Justice Black in *Bridges*, 314 U.S. at 270–71:

> The assumption that respect for the judiciary can be won by shielding judges from published criticism wrongly appraises the character of American public opinion. For it is a prized American privilege to speak one's mind, although not always with perfect good taste, on all public institutions. And an enforced silence, however limited, solely in the name of preserving the dignity of the bench, would probably engender resentment, suspicion, and contempt much more than it would enhance respect.

REVERSED.

* * *

1. Falsity and the disciplinary process. *Yagman* is obviously not a tort case. Still, the *Yagman* court wrestled with the question of whether the standards articulated by the Supreme Court in cases dealing with the applicability of the First Amendment to state law defamation claims are applicable to the lawyer disciplinary process. The court explains that lawyers facing disciplinary charges based on the content of their speech are still entitled to the protections of the First Amendment.

2. Satire and parody. In *New Times, Inc. v. Isaacks*, 146 S.W.3d 144 (Tex. 2004), a local paper had published a parody inspired by the recent arrest of a thirteen-year old who had written a Halloween story that depicted the deaths of several individuals. The parody reported the arrest of a six-year old girl who had written a book report about "'cannibalism, fanaticism, and disorderly conduct' in Maurice Sendak's classic children's book, *Where the Wild Things Are*." The piece included several fictitious quotes from the local judge and prosecutor, such as "[a]ny implication of violence in a school situation, even if it was just contained in a first grader's book report, is reason enough for panic and overreaction." The judge and prosecutor were not amused and sued under a defamation theory. The Texas Supreme Court sided with the defendant, concluding that the proper test was whether the statements "could reasonably be interpreted as stating actual facts." *Id.* at 163. Will this test always be appropriate in the case of satire and parody? What about the case of a fake letter to the editor that speaks ill of another that appears on April Fool's Day? *See* S.F. Bay Guardian, Inc. v. Superior Court, 21 Cal. Rptr. 2d 464 (Cal. Ct. App. 1993); Joseph H. King, *Defamation Claims Based on Parody and Other Fanciful Communications Not Intended to be Understood as Fact*, 2008 Utah L. Rev. 875 (2008).

Chapter 10

Defamation: Privileges and Defenses

Exercise 10.1: Chapter Problem

Memorandum

To: Associate
From: Senior Partner
Re: Griffey Arbitration

As part of his agreement with his cell phone company, Cell Telephone and Technology (CT&T), George Griffey agreed to waive any right to bring a lawsuit in state or federal court and instead submit any legal claims he might have against CT&T to binding arbitration. Under the agreement, the arbitration is to be conducted in accordance with the rules of a national arbitration association. Under these rules, discovery is permitted, but the arbitrator retains the authority to limit the discovery process. The parties are required to exchange copies of all exhibits they intend to submit at the hearing at least five days before the arbitration hearing. Each side may introduce evidence, but formal, legal rules of evidence do not apply. The national arbitration association selects an arbitrator for the parties from a list of potential arbitrators. The arbitrator must render a written decision within 30 days of the completion of the arbitration, but the opinion is not published in any type of official reporter. All decisions of the arbitrator are final and not appealable, except on grounds of corruption, fraud, partiality, or misconduct on the part of the arbitrator.

Griffey's fraud claim against CT&T was submitted for arbitration. During the arbitration, several CT&T employees, acting as witnesses, made false and defamatory statements about Griffey's credit rating, as did the CT&T employee representing CT&T during the process. Eventually, the arbitrator ruled against Griffey's claim. In her written decision provided to the parties, the arbitrator repeated the defamatory statements made about Griffey's credit rating.

Coincidentally, a Supreme Court decision on the subject of consumer arbitration was released the same week as the arbitrator's decision. While writing a story about the Supreme Court decision, a local newspaper reporter contacted CT&T and obtained a copy of the arbitrator's decision. The reporter accurately quoted from the decision, including the parts about Griffey's credit rating. Griffey claims that as a result of the article, he was turned down for a job for which he was well-qualified. He has now sued CT&T, CT&T's employees who spoke at the hearing, the arbitrator, and the newspaper that published the story. We represent Griffey in that matter.

Assess whether any of the defendants can successfully assert the existence of a privilege that would defeat Griffey's claims. As you do so, note what other information we need to obtain in order to respond to any assertion of privilege.

A. Absolute Privileges

1. The Judicial Proceedings Privilege

The privilege described in this section will reappear throughout the book. Courts frequently extend the protection of the privilege to other tort theories involving judicial proceedings, such as interference with contractual relations. However, the basic privilege originally developed in the defamation context, and it is in this context that nearly every jurisdiction recognizes the existence of the privilege.

The judicial proceedings privilege dates back over 500 years to English common law. Paul T. Hayden, *Reconsidering the Litigator's Absolute Privilege to Defame*, 54 OHIO ST. L.J. 985, 985 (1993). This section uses the phrase "judicial proceedings privilege" to describe the privilege at issue, but different jurisdictions may use different terminology, such as the litigation privilege. In some jurisdictions, the privilege is named in reference to the party that can assert the existence of the privilege (e.g., the litigator's privilege or the witness' privilege). Regardless, the basic idea is the same in most jurisdictions: a publication made in the course of a judicial proceeding, by a privileged person, is absolutely privileged if there is a sufficient relation to the proceeding.

a. Made in the Course of Judicial Proceedings

In order for the privilege to attach, the defamatory statement must be made in a judicial proceeding. Obviously, a statement made during a civil or criminal trial—such as a lawyer's statement during closing argument—would qualify. Jackson v. Sloan, 931 S.W.2d 807 (Mo. Ct. App.1996) (closing argument). However, the privilege typically also "attaches to all aspects of the proceedings, including statements made in open court, pre-trial hearings, depositions, affidavits, and any of the pleadings or other papers in the case." James v. Brown, 637 S.W.2d 914, 916–17 (Tex.1982). Therefore, the more challenging issues involve statements made in other contexts, such as administrative or quasi-judicial proceedings, and statements made preliminary to a proceeding.

Focus Questions: *Miner v. Novotny*

1. *Why are statements made by participants in a judicial proceeding afforded an absolute, as opposed to conditional, privilege?*
2. *In what circumstances is the privilege extended to administrative or quasi-judicial proceedings?*

Miner v. Novotny

498 A.2d 269
(Md. 1985)

MURPHY, Chief Judge.

We granted certiorari in this case to decide whether a law enforcement officer against whom a brutality complaint has been filed may maintain a defamation action against the complainant based upon the contents of the complaint.

I.

On July 14, 1982, Joseph A. Novotny was arrested by John J. Miner, a deputy sheriff for Harford County, and charged with driving while intoxicated in violation of Maryland Code (1977, 1982 Cum.Supp.), § 21-902 of the Transportation Article. The arrest was apparently not a peaceful one. Although the record is not entirely clear, it appears that Novotny was also charged with assaulting Miner. Two days after his arrest, Novotny filed a "Complaint of Brutality" with the Harford County Sheriff's Office, alleging that he had been kicked, choked, and otherwise abusively treated by Miner during and after the arrest.

Upon receiving Novotny's complaint, the sheriff's office conducted an internal investigation and concluded that Miner was not guilty of any misconduct. Miner then brought suit against Novotny in the Circuit Court for Harford County, asserting ... [a claim for, *inter alia*,] defamation, based on the contents of the brutality complaint; Novotny's demurrer was sustained without leave to amend.... On appeal, Miner sought review only of the defamation count.

II.

For reasons of public policy, the law of defamation recognizes certain communications as privileged, and thereby affords those who publish such communications immunity from liability. The privilege, and the resultant immunity enjoyed by the publisher, may be either absolute or qualified. As we explained in *DiBlasio v. Kolodner*, 233 Md. 512, 197 A.2d 245 (1964), "[a]n absolute privilege is distinguished from a qualified privilege in that the former provides immunity regardless of the purpose or motive of the defendant, or the reasonableness of his conduct, while the latter is conditioned upon the absence of malice and is forfeited if it is abused." 233 Md. at 522, 197 A.2d 245. *See also* Adams v. Peck, 288 Md. 1, 3, 415 A.2d 292 (1980) ("absolute privilege protects the person publishing the defamatory statement from liability even if his purpose or motive was malicious, he knew that the statement was false, or his conduct was otherwise unreasonable"); Orrison v. Vance, 262 Md. 285, 292, 277 A.2d 573 (1971) (qualified privilege "must be exercised in a reasonable manner and for a proper purpose" or the speaker "will forfeit his immunity"); Note, *Developments in the Law-Defamation*, 69 HARV.L.REV. 875, 917 (1956).

B. Common Law Privilege for Testimony in Administrative Proceedings

In Maryland, a witness who testifies in the course of judicial proceedings is protected by an absolute privilege against liability for defamatory statements made during the testimony. *Adams, supra*, 288 Md. at 3, 415 A.2d 292; Korb v. Kowaleviocz, 285 Md. 699, 701–04, 402 A.2d 897 (1979)....

The absolute privilege for judicial testimony is based upon sound considerations of public policy. As our predecessors observed in *Hunckel v. Voneiff*, 69 Md. 179, 187, 14 A. 500 (1888), "it is of the greatest importance to the administration of justice that witnesses should go upon the stand with their minds absolutely free from apprehension that they may subject themselves to an action of slander for what they may say while giving their testimony." *See also Adams, supra*, 288 Md. at 5, 415 A.2d 292. The absolute nature of this privilege is intended "not merely to protect the witness from ultimate liability, but to protect him from the annoyance of suit itself." Gersh v. Ambrose, 291 Md. 188, 192, 434 A.2d 547 (1981).

The absolute privilege extends not only to oral testimony given in open court, but also to statements contained in documents which have been filed in a judicial proceeding. Statements contained in documents prepared for possible use in a pending judicial proceeding, but never actually filed in the proceeding, are similarly shielded by absolute immunity. *Adams, supra*, 288 Md. at 8–9, 415 A.2d 292. *See generally Annotation: Libel and Slander: Application of Privilege Attending Statements Made in Course of Judicial Proceedings to Pretrial Deposition and Discovery Procedures*, 23 A.L.R.3d 1172 (1969). Professors Prosser and Keeton have suggested that "an informal complaint to a prosecuting attorney or a magistrate is to be regarded as an initial step in a judicial proceeding, and so entitled to an absolute, rather than a qualified immunity." W. Prosser & W. Keeton, The Law of Torts, § 114, at 819–20 (5th ed. 1984) (citations omitted).

In *Gersh, supra*, we addressed for the first time the question of whether the absolute privilege afforded judicial testimony should extend as well to defamatory statements made in the course of administrative proceedings. The allegedly defamatory statements in that case were published by a witness testifying at a public hearing before the Baltimore City Community Relations Commission. In the ensuing defamation action, the defendant maintained that his testimony before the Commission was protected by an absolute privilege.

After reviewing the relevant case law from other jurisdictions, we concluded that

> "[t]he nature and scope of such proceedings are too varied to be circumscribed by specific criteria. Rather, [the question of] whether absolute witness immunity will be extended to any administrative proceeding will have to be decided on a case-by-case basis and will in large part turn on two factors: (1) the nature of the public function of the proceeding and (2) the adequacy of procedural safeguards which will minimize the occurrence of defamatory statements."

Applying these principles to the facts of that case, we observed that the Commission's hearing—which was essentially an "ordinary open public meeting"—lacked the procedural safeguards traditionally provided in judicial proceedings. Furthermore, we found that "[t]he public benefit to be derived from testimony at Commission hearings of this type is not sufficiently compelling to outweigh the possible damage to individual reputations to warrant absolute witness immunity." We therefore declined to extend absolute immunity to the defendant's testimony before the Commission.

III.

By filing his sworn brutality complaint with the Harford County Sheriff's Office, Novotny initiated an administrative disciplinary proceeding governed by Maryland Code (1957, 1982 Repl.Vol.), Art. 27, §§ 727–734D, generally known as the "Law-Enforcement Officers' Bill of Rights" (the "LEOBR"). The LEOBR was enacted by the General Assembly in 1974, and was designed to provide a law-enforcement officer covered by the statute with substantial procedural safeguards during any inquiry into his conduct which could lead to the imposition of a disciplinary sanction. As a deputy sheriff in Harford County, Miner clearly was covered by the LEOBR.

The administrative proceeding contemplated by the LEOBR was well summarized in *Jacocks*:

> The law ... looks to what is essentially a two-phase administrative process. The first phase involves an internal investigation to determine whether there is some substance to the complaint or suspicion. If it appears that there is, a recommendation for some disciplinary action is made. At that point, phase two begins—an adjudicatory hearing before a departmental hearing board to determine (1) whether the charge itself is valid, and (2) if so, what the punishment should be. If the board finds the officer innocent of the charge, that ends the proceeding. If it finds him guilty, it then makes a recommendation to the chief of police as to an appropriate punishment. The chief is bound by a determination of innocence, but not a proposed punishment in the event of a finding of guilt. As to that, his decision (rather than that of the Board) is final.

As we indicated in *Gersh*, the availability of absolute immunity to witnesses in administrative proceedings depends to a large extent upon "the adequacy of procedural safeguards which will minimize the occurrence of defamatory statements." The procedural safeguards provided by the LEOBR in this case are, we believe, entirely adequate in this regard.

Under the statute, no brutality complaint may be investigated by a law-enforcement agency unless the complaint is duly sworn to by the aggrieved person, a member of the aggrieved person's immediate family, a person with firsthand knowledge of the alleged incident, or the parent or guardian in the case of a minor child. § 728(b)(4). A person who knowingly makes a false complaint is subject to criminal liability. § 734C. Prior to any interrogation, the law-enforcement officer under investigation must be informed in writing of the nature of the investigation. § 728(b)(5). The officer under investigation must also be informed of the name, rank, and command of the officer in charge of the investigation, the interrogating officer, and all persons present during the interrogation. § 728(b)(3). At all times during the interrogation, the officer under investigation has the right to be represented by counsel. § 728(b)(10). A complete record of the interrogation must be kept, and must be made available to the officer upon request at the completion of the investigation, and at least ten days before any hearing. § 728(b)(8).

If at the conclusion of the investigatory phase of the proceeding disciplinary sanctions are recommended, the officer under investigation must be given notice of his right to a hearing. The notice must inform the officer of the issues involved, as well as of the time and place of the hearing. § 730(a). At least ten days before the hearing, the officer under investigation must also be notified of the names of all witnesses. § 728(b)(5).

The hearing phase of the proceeding is adversarial in nature. The hearing is ordinarily conducted before a board of at least three officers, none of whom had any role in the investigatory phase of the proceeding. §§ 730(b), 727(d). The law-enforcement agency and the officer under investigation each have the right to be represented by counsel, and each must be given an adequate opportunity to present its case. § 730(b).

Each party may request that the hearing board issue summonses compelling the attendance and testimony of witnesses, and the production of documents. § 730(h)(1). The hearing board's summons may be enforced, in the proper circumstances, by an order of the circuit court. Failure to obey the court order is punishable as a contempt of court. § 730(h)(2). Witnesses must testify under oath, and are subject to criminal penalties for knowingly giving false testimony. §§ 730(f), 734C. Each party has the right to cross-examine witnesses, and to submit rebuttal evidence. § 730(d).

Although the formal rules governing the admissibility of evidence in a judicial proceeding do not apply, "[t]he hearing board conducting the hearing shall give effect to the rules of privilege recognized by law, and shall exclude incompetent, irrelevant, immaterial, and unduly repetitious evidence." §730(c). An official record of the hearing must be maintained, and must include all evidence, both testimonial and real, introduced during the hearing. §730(a), (c).

If the officer is exonerated of all charges contained in the complaint, he may require the law-enforcement agency to expunge from its files any record of the complaint three years after the investigation is completed. §728(12)(ii). Furthermore, no adverse material may be inserted into the officer's file until the officer receives a copy of the adverse material and has an opportunity to review it, comment upon it in writing, and sign it. §728(12)(i).

IV.

Our society vests its law-enforcement officers with formidable power, the abuse of which is often extremely detrimental to the public interest. Citizen complaints of such abuses, and the administrative disciplinary procedure which has been developed to investigate these complaints, serve a public function of vital importance by providing a mechanism through which abuses may be reported to the proper authorities, and the abusers held accountable.

The viability of a democratic government requires that the channels of communication between citizens and their public officials remain open and unimpeded. Were complaints such as Novotny's not absolutely privileged, the possibility of incurring the costs and inconvenience associated with defending a defamation suit might well deter a citizen with a legitimate grievance from filing a complaint. We therefore conclude that the possible harm a false brutality complaint may cause to a law-enforcement officer's reputation, despite the procedural safeguards provided by the LEOBR, is outweighed by the public's interest in encouraging the filing and investigation of valid complaints. Most other courts that have considered this issue have reached the same conclusion. *See, e.g.,* Putter v. Anderson, 601 S.W.2d 73, 76–77 (Tex.Civ.App.1980) (citizen's complaints of police misconduct were absolutely privileged); Campo v. Rega, 79 A.D.2d 626, 433 N.Y.S.2d 630, 631 (N.Y.App.Div.1980), *motion for leave to appeal denied,* 52 N.Y.2d 705, 437 N.Y.S.2d 1028, 419 N.E.2d 876 (1981) (same); Larkin v. Noonan, 19 Wis. 93, 98 (1865) (citizen's complaint of sheriff's misconduct was absolutely privileged). *Cf.* Pena v. Municipal Court, 96 Cal.App.3d 77, 82–83, 157 Cal.Rptr. 584 (Cal.Ct.App.1979) (citizen's complaint of police misconduct was protected by absolute statutory privilege); Imig v. Ferrar, 70 Cal.App.3d 48, 55–56, 138 Cal.Rptr. 540 (Cal.Ct.App.1977) (same). *But see* Elder v. Holland, 208 Va. 15, 155 S.E.2d 369, 374–75 (1967) (witness's testimony at police disciplinary hearing was entitled to only a qualified privilege because procedural safeguards at hearing were inadequate).

We are not unmindful of the deeply disturbing and demoralizing effect a false accusation of brutality may have on a law-enforcement officer. As Judge Eldridge observed in his dissent in *Berkey,* "[n]o one likes to hear, or have his family and friends hear, such allegations." Id. at 341, 413 A.2d 170. It is regrettable that our holding here will, in some instances, "afford an immunity to the evil disposed and malignant slanderer." *Bartlett, supra,* 69 Md. at 226, 14 A. 518. We are satisfied, however, that the inhibition of citizens' criticism of those entrusted with their protection is a far worse evil. Accordingly, we hold that a citizen's brutality complaint filed against a law-enforcement officer is protected by the same absolute privilege as are statements made by witnesses in judicial proceedings, and that such complaints cannot, therefore, serve as the basis for a defamation suit.

* * *

1. Similar decisions. A number of other jurisdictions have reached the same conclusion as the *Miner* court under similar facts. Gray v. Rodriguez, 481 So.2d 1298, 1299–1300

(Fla.App.1986); Magnus v. Anpatiellos, 130 App.Div.2d 719, 720, 516 N.Y.S.2d 31 (1987); Campo v. Rega, 79 App.Div.2d 626, 433 N.Y.S.2d 630 (1980), *appeal denied*, 52 N.Y.2d 705, 419 N.E.2d 876, 437 N.Y.S.2d 1028 (1981); Putter v. Anderson, 601 S.W.2d 73, 76–77 (Tex.Civ.App.1980).

2. **Other types of proceedings.** Most courts have held that the privilege attaches to defamatory statements made in unemployment or workers' compensation hearings, *see, e.g.*, Dorn v. Peterson, 512 N.W.2d 902 (Minn. Ct. App. 1994) (unemployment); Tallman v. Hanssen, 427 N.W.2d 868 (Iowa 1988) (workers' compensation); *Libel and Slander: Privilege Applicable to Judicial Proceedings as Extending to Administrative Proceedings*, 45 A.L.R.2d 1296. In contrast, courts have split on the question of whether the privilege attaches to statements made as part of union/employer grievance process. Hasten v. Phillips Petroleum Co., 640 F.2d 274 (10th Cir. 1981) (absolute privilege applies); Wright v. Over-the-Road and City Transfer Drivers, Helpers, Dockmen and Warehousemen, 945 S.W.2d 481, 492 (Mo.App.1997) (qualified, not absolute privilege, applies).

Exercise 10.2

You are the trial court judge in a defamation case involving facts similar to *Miner*. As in *Miner*, the police internal investigation and disciplinary procedures are established by law. Most of the same procedural safeguards that applied in *Miner* apply in the present case. As the judge, which of the following safeguards (or which combination of safeguards), if lacking from the process, would lead you to conclude that an absolute privilege should not apply?

(a) The ability to compel the appearance of witnesses or the production of documents via an enforceable subpoena;

(b) a process to swear in witnesses;

(c) criminal penalties for the commission of perjury;

(d) the ability to cross-examine witnesses; and/or

(e) formal rules of evidence.

Exercise 10.3

In the District of Columbia, the Office of Bar Counsel investigates alleged violations of the ethical standards contained in the Rules of Professional Conduct for lawyers and prosecutes cases before the Board on Professional Responsibility and the D.C. Court of Appeals. Bar counsel has the authority to issue subpoenas to gather papers and documents and to compel the attendance of witnesses. A hearing committee hears each lawyer disciplinary case. According to the Board's website,

> Hearing Committees consider evidence and the testimony of witnesses, taken under oath. Committees are generally guided, but not bound, by provisions or rules of court practice, procedure, pleading and evidence. At the conclusion of the hearing, the parties file briefs, and the Committee drafts a report to the Board, with findings of fact and recommended conclusions of law.

http://www.dcbar.org/for_lawyers/ethics/discipline/board_on_professional_responsibility/bprmission.cfm. Disciplinary sanctions range from informal admonition to disbarment. The D.C. Court of Appeals retains the ultimate authority with respect to the discipline of lawyers, and lawyers found to have engaged in misconduct have the right to have the Board's findings and recommendations reviewed by the court.

Assuming the other requirements for application of the judicial proceedings privilege are satisfied, how would a D.C. court rule on the question of whether the absolute privilege should apply to statements contained in a complaint of attorney misconduct filed by a former client with the Board of Professional Responsibility? Should the privilege apply if the person filing the complaint is another lawyer and it can be established that the lawyer filing the complaint knew the charges of misconduct were false?

Focus Questions: *Messina v. Krakower*

1. *Based on* Messina, *are defamatory statements contained in a lawyer's advice to a client concerning a business transaction covered under the privilege?*
2. *Based on* Messina, *are defamatory statements made by a lawyer to a prospective witness in anticipation of litigation subject to the privilege? Statements contained in a draft complaint that is circulated to potential members of a class in a class action?*

Messina v. Krakower

439 F.3d 755
(D.C. Cir. 2006)

GARLAND, Circuit Judge.

Plaintiff Karyne Messina brought this diversity action charging attorney Daniel Krakower and his law firm, Shulman, Rogers, Gandal, Pordy & Ecker, P.A., with defamation. The district court concluded that the defendants were protected from liability for defamation by the judicial proceedings privilege and granted summary judgment in their favor. We affirm.

I

Karyne Messina and Susan Fontana were equal owners and co-presidents of a corporation called Totally Italian.com, Inc. By December 2002, the two had become embroiled in disputes regarding the management of the business. To assist her in resolving those conflicts, Fontana retained the services of Krakower and his law firm. Krakower drafted a letter to Messina, outlining Fontana's grievances and proposing a process that would allow one owner to buy out the other. The letter is the source of Messina's defamation claim against Krakower and the law firm.

In the letter, Krakower advised Messina that he understood "that disputes have arisen between you and [Fontana]," that he had "reviewed these circumstances with [Fontana]," and that he had "serious concerns about the propriety and legality" of Messina's actions. Krakower then enumerated a long list of concerns, including Messina's failure to share information with Fontana and to return Fontana's telephone calls, her lease of the corporation's headquarters and establishment of a corporate bank account without Fontana's consent, and her exertion of unilateral control over the corporation's internet accounts. "It seems abundantly clear to me," Krakower concluded, "that you cannot continue in business together," and he therefore proposed a detailed process "designed to result in one of you buying out the other at a fair price."

Krakower's proposal, he wrote, would "result[ ] in a win/win scenario, as compared to the inevitable lose/lose scenario that would result if you are unable to resolve this matter and [Fontana] was forced to commence legal proceedings and/or dissolution of the Corporation." J.A. 32. Krakower warned that if Messina were not "willing to deal with [Fontana] reasonably and fairly," Fontana would have to "consider taking appropriate legal action to protect her interest in the corporation." "If we do not hear from you (or your attorney if you are represented by one) by close of business on January 13, 2003," he said, "we will assume that you are not interested in resolving this matter amicably, and will proceed accordingly." Krakower closed by declaring that "[t]his letter is for settlement purposes only" and "is inadmissible in any legal proceeding."

On December 27, 2002, before sending the letter to Messina, Krakower emailed Fontana a draft for her review. He also sent a copy of the email to a businessman named Chaim Kalfon. Earlier that month, Fontana had sent Messina an email "to introduce" Kalfon and to authorize him "to negotiate an amicable settlement for our partnership." On December 31, 2002, Krakower sent the letter to Messina by Federal Express.

Messina never replied. Instead, she filed suit in the United States District Court for the District of Columbia, charging Krakower and his law firm with defamation. The complaint alleged that Krakower's letter constituted libel per se, because it imputed "unfitness to perform and/or the lack of integrity of performance of the duties of the job that [Messina] was designated to perform for the business enterprise." Compl. ¶5.

On January 31, 2003, Krakower and the law firm filed a motion to dismiss and/or for summary judgment. The defendants contended, *inter alia*, that they were absolutely protected by the judicial proceedings privilege. Messina opposed the motion and submitted an affidavit, pursuant to Federal Rule of Civil Procedure 56(f), requesting further discovery.

On May 8, 2003, the district court concluded that the defendants were protected from Messina's defamation claim by the judicial proceedings privilege and granted their motion for summary judgment.... This appeal followed.

III

The judicial proceedings privilege, upon which the district court grounded its grant of summary judgment, is well-settled in District of Columbia law. *See* Finkelstein, Thompson, & Loughran v. Hemispherx Biopharma, Inc., 774 A.2d 332 (D.C.2001); McBride v. Pizza Hut, Inc., 658 A.2d 205 (D.C.1995); Arneja v. Gildar, 541 A.2d 621 (D.C.1988); *see also* Brown v. Collins, 402 F.2d 209 (D.C.Cir.1968). The district has adopted the version of the privilege found in §586 of the *Restatement of Torts,* which states:

> An attorney at law is absolutely privileged to publish defamatory matter concerning another in communications preliminary to a proposed judicial proceeding, or in the institution of, or during the course and as a part of, a judicial proceeding in which he participates as counsel, if it has some relation to the proceeding.

Restatement (Second) Of Torts §586 (1977) (*Restatement*); *see Finkelstein*, 774 A.2d at 338; *McBride*, 658 A.2d at 207. Accordingly, for the privilege to apply, "two requirements must be satisfied: (1) the statement must have been made in the course of, or preliminary to a judicial proceeding; and (2) the statement must be related in some way to the underlying proceeding." Arneja, 541 A.2d at 623. If the privilege does apply, it "is absolute rather than qualified: it 'protects the attorney from liability in an action for defamation irrespective of his purpose in publishing the defamatory matter, his belief in its truth, or even his knowledge of its falsity.'" *Finkelstein*, 774 A.2d at 338 (quoting *Restatement* § 586 cmt. a). The privilege is "'based upon a public policy of securing to attorneys as officers of the court the utmost freedom in their efforts to secure justice for their clients.'" *Id.*

... First, [Messina] insists that the allegedly "defamatory communications ... merely involve a business dispute between two partners in a business that had hardly ripened into litigation." Appellant's Br. 12. But, "[d]espite its name, the judicial proceedings privilege does not protect only statements that are made in the institution of a lawsuit or in the course of litigation." *Finkelstein*, 774 A.2d at 341. Rather, the "privilege extends to some statements that are made prior to the commencement of litigation, for instance, 'in ... communications preliminary to the proceeding.'" *Id.* (quoting Restatement § 586 cmt. a). "An actual outbreak of hostilities is not required, so long as litigation is truly under serious consideration." *Finkelstein*, 774 A.2d at 343. In particular, the privilege applies to "written correspondence between parties' counsel concerning threatened lawsuit[s]," *id.* at 341 (*citing McBride*, 658 A.2d at 207–08); "statements relating to threat[s] of litigation," including statements "'analogous to [those] that are often contained in demand letters,'" *id.* (quoting Conservative Club of Washington v. Finkelstein, 738 F.Supp. 6, 14 (D.D.C.1990)); and statements made during "'settlement discussions,'" *id.* (quoting *Brown*, 402 F.2d at 213).

Krakower's letter plainly falls within these contours. The letter explained that it was "for settlement purposes," proposed a "win/win scenario," and warned of a "lose/lose scenario" if settlement failed and Fontana were "forced to commence legal proceedings and/or dissolution of the Corporation." It described possible causes of action available to Fontana, alleging that Messina's actions "constitute[d] a violation of [her] fiduciary duties" and were "in contravention [of] ... Delaware corporate law." Krakower then reiterated the threat of litigation twice more. He warned that if Messina were not "willing to deal with [Fontana] reasonably and fairly," Fontana would have to "consider taking appropriate legal action to protect her interest in the corporation." And he concluded with a more specific warning: "If we do not hear back from you ... by the close of business on January 13, 2003, we will assume that you are not interested in resolving this matter amicably, and will proceed accordingly." As the district court determined, it is plain on the face of the letter that it was "'preliminary to a judicial proceeding' in that it was sent for the very purpose of attempting settlement prior to litigation." *Messina v. Fontana*, 260 F.Supp.2d 173, 178 (D.D.C.2003) (quoting *Restatement* § 586).

* * *

b. By Privileged Parties

As *Miner, supra*, makes clear, the parties to a judicial proceeding may be entitled to claim the absolute privilege related to judicial proceedings. As articulated by one court, one traditional justification for the existence of the privilege is that it "is necessary to encourage citizens to peaceably resolve their differences in court through litigation (or the threat of litigation) by allowing them to speak to their adversaries freely without fear of facing liability for what they say, and without the prospect of having their good faith legal claims prompt the initiation of more claims." Paige Capital Management, LLC v. Lerner Master Fund, LLC, 22 A.3d 710 (Del. Ch. 2011). Accordingly, it is said that an absolute privilege is necessary "to facilitate the flow of communication between persons involved in judicial proceedings and, thus, to aid in the complete and full disclosure of facts necessary to a fair adjudication." Barker v. Huang, 610 A.2d 1341, 1345 (Del. 1992).

The testimony of a witness at a proceeding is also usually covered by the privilege. Restatement (Second) of Torts § 588. The testimony of witnesses is, of course, "of fundamental importance in the administration of justice," *id.* § 588 cmt. a, and witnesses sometime appear in a proceeding involuntarily. Thus, extending an absolute privilege is said to be essential so that witnesses do not fear the threat of a defamation action when they testify. Paul T. Hayden, *Reconsidering the Litigator's Absolute Privilege to Defame*, 54 OHIO ST. L.J. 985, 1054 (1993).

* * *

The litigator's privilege. As *Messina* makes clear, a lawyer representing a client in a proceeding may be entitled to claim the privilege. The so-called litigator's privilege has been in existence in most jurisdictions for many years. In addition, a lawyer's agent may also be able to claim the privilege if the other requirements are satisfied. *See* Leavitt v. Bickerton, 855 F. Supp. 284 (D. Mass. 1994) (attorney's private investigator). As *Messina* suggests, this privilege is often justified on the grounds that lawyers should not feel chilled in their ability to zealously advocate on behalf of their clients. Is an absolute (as opposed to qualified or conditional) privilege necessary to further this goal?

* * *

c. Having Some Relation to the Proceeding

Focus Questions: *Arneja v. Gildar*

1. *How are the defendant's statements in* Arneja *related to the proceeding?*
2. *Should it matter to the court's decision if it could be established that the parties were not engaged in settlement discussions at the time the statements were made?*
3. *Is it in the best interests of the legal profession for courts to extend the privilege in cases such as* Arneja?

Arneja v. Gildar

541 A.2d 621
(D.C. 1988)

GALLAGHER, Senior Judge:

Both appellant and appellee are attorneys licensed to practice law in the District of Columbia. They were representing opposing parties in a landlord-tenant dispute. Appellant represented the tenants, and appellee was counsel for the landlord. The proceeding involved an interpretation of the small landlord exemption of the Rental Housing Act of 1980. On behalf of the tenants, appellant filed a petition with the District of Columbia Rental Accommodations Office challenging an exemption from rent control granted to the landlord's property. The alleged slanderous statements were uttered while both parties and their clients were present in a hearing room at the Rental Accommodations Office, awaiting the imminent arrival of the hearing examiner to adjudicate the dispute.

Before the hearing examiner arrived, appellee concededly made the following unsolicited remarks to appellant:

> You're unnecessarily pursuing this case. You don't understand the law. Where did you go to law school; you should go back to law school before you practice law. You don't understand. You better learn your English, go to elementary school.[3]

Appellant asserts that these statements were *ad hominem* attacks on his ethnicity and educational background, which were said with malice to impugn his professional capacity as a lawyer. Appellant claims that, as a result, he suffered pecuniary losses as well as humiliation and embarrassment before his clients. Appellee, on the other hand, asserted that his statements were intended to lead to a settlement of the dispute, *viz.*, to induce appellant to cease the litigation by highlighting his supposed incredulous position.

After a hearing on appellee's motion for summary judgment, the trial court found the alleged defamatory statements to be sufficiently related to the underlying dispute—the interpretation of a statute—to fall within the protective scope of the absolute privilege, which affords attorneys absolute immunity from liability for statements made in the course of a judicial proceeding. The trial judge found "a very strong connection between the words alleged to have been said by [appellee] and the procedure that was involved in this landlord and tenant case." He further opined that "the English language is an issue" in disputes involving opposing interpretations of a statute. In addition, the trial judge considered that the physical location and temporal proximity of the parties—sitting in a hearing room awaiting the imminent arrival of the examiner—justified concluding the statements were made preliminary to a judicial proceeding.

In this jurisdiction, an attorney "is protected by an absolute privilege to publish false and defamatory matter of another" during the course of or preliminary to a judicial proceeding, provided the statements bear some relation to the proceeding. Mohler v. Houston, 356 A.2d 646, 647 (D.C.1976) (per curiam); *see* Restatement (Second) of Torts § 586 (1977).... For the absolute immunity of the privilege to apply, two requirements must be satisfied: (1) the statement must have been made in the course of or preliminary to a judicial proceeding; and (2) the statement must be related in some way to the underlying proceeding.

The scope of the absolute privilege has been extended to encompass quasi-judicial proceedings conducted by administrative agencies.... We therefore conclude that the proceeding conducted before the Rental Accommodations Office constituted a proceeding within the ambit of the judicial privilege.

... Given that the parties were involved in litigation, present in a hearing room, and awaiting commencement of the proceeding to adjudicate their dispute, we believe the trial court did not err in concluding the statements were made preliminary to a judicial proceeding.[5]

---

3. Appellant was born in India. He earned several academic degrees, including a Bachelor of Arts degree from Punjab University, a Master of Economics degree from Agra University, and a law degree from the University of New Delhi. Although his native language is Punjabi, appellant has spoken English since the fifth grade, and he received his formal legal training in English. Appellant emigrated to the United States in 1971. He earned a Master of Comparative Law (American Practice) degree from George Washington University. He became a member of the District of Columbia Bar in 1978. In reverence to the doctrines of his Sikh religion, appellant wears a turban while in public.

5. The parties' physical presence in the hearing room substantially affects our analysis of this issue. If these same remarks were uttered outside the courtroom, a different question might be presented on the issue of absolute privilege, depending upon the particular circumstances. *See, e.g.*, Petrus v. Smith, 91 A.D.2d 1190, 459 N.Y.S.2d 173 (1983) (absolute privilege may not extend to statements

The question of relevance is a question of law determined by the court. In assessing whether the statement bears some relation to the proceeding, "[t]he communication need not be relevant in the legal sense; the term is very liberally construed." Statements will be "absolutely privileged if they have enough appearance of connection with the case ... so that a reasonable man might think them relevant." Considering the statements in the context in which they were made, "[a]ll doubt should be resolved in favor of relevancy or pertinency...." Young v. Young, 57 App.D.C. 157, 159, 18 F.2d 807, 809 (1927). The trial court found a "strong connection" between the defamatory statements made in the hearing room and the underlying issue in the landlord-tenant dispute. The statements "you don't understand English" and "you don't understand the law," for example, were deemed by the trial court to be "related" to the disputed interpretation of the Rental Housing Act, i.e., the parties' understanding and legal interpretation of the statute was at the core of the dispute. Liberally considering the relation of the statements made in this context, we conclude that a reasonable person might construe the defamatory remarks to be sufficiently related to the merits of the proceeding to fall within the protective shield of the absolute privilege.

The issues of fact disputed by appellant, *viz.*, that (1) no settlement discussions transpired in the hearing room, and (2) the remarks were ethnic slurs, are not controlling in determining whether, as a matter of law, appellee is entitled to the immunity of absolute privilege. Furthermore, the motive of appellee in uttering these remarks is irrelevant under the doctrine of absolute privilege.

Although we must recognize the absolute privilege in this instance, we naturally do not wish to be understood as condoning remarks such as those concededly (for purposes of the motion) made by appellee. Attorneys do not possess a license to defame their adversaries in the course of a judicial proceeding. The immunity of the absolute privilege supports the public policy of allowing counsel to zealously represent a client's interests without fear of reprisal through defamation actions. A separate public policy concern, however, is the integrity and civility of legal proceedings, especially as perceived by the public. A potential alternative mechanism available to deal with outrageous conduct by an attorney in lieu of an action for damages in slander may be the policing function of the Bar Disciplinary Committee.

Affirmed.

PRYOR, Chief Judge, dissenting:

The majority opinion cogently states a view for affirming the trial court ruling. Critical to our decision is the determination whether the questioned statements were made in the course of a judicial proceeding or even a conference preliminary to a proceeding. Recognizing, as does the majority, that it is difficult to draw a boundary for this absolute privilege, I am unable to distinguish this case from a similar scenario which occurs in the hallway or just outside of the courthouse. I agree that the relevance of the statements are a question of law. However, I think in this case, in particular, it is a question of fact whether there was a conference or even a discussion between the lawyers or whether this was a circumstance where one attorney was simply unilaterally abusing the other. As liberally as the privilege is to be construed, I question if the latter conduct should be protected.

I would remand for resolution of the factual question which I have noted.

---

made outside the courthouse); Sussman v. Damian, 355 So.2d 809 (Fla.Dist.Ct.App.1977) (statements made on elevator held not absolutely privileged).

* * *

1. Witness testimony. As part of a Plaintiff's lawsuit against Defendant for consumer fraud, Defense Counsel conducts a deposition of Witness, a former employee of Defendant. During the deposition, Defense Counsel asks Witness why she is no longer employed with Defendant. Witness replies that she had to quit the job in order to return to school. "So," asked Defense Counsel, "your reason for leaving had nothing to do with any alleged fraud on the part of Defendant?" Witness replied, "that's right. It was because of school. I mean, I always thought Defendant was a jerk and everyone knows he's a coke addict, but that didn't really have anything to do with why I quit." Defendant has now sued Witness for defamation based on these statements. Witness claims the absolute privilege for a witness' testimony should apply. Should Witness' statement regarding Defendant's drug addiction be considered privileged?

2. Model Rule comparison. Rule 4.4(a) of the ABA Model Rules of Professional Conduct prohibits a lawyer, in representing a client, from using "means that have no substantial purpose other than to embarrass, delay, or burden a third person, or use methods of obtaining evidence that violate the legal rights of such a person."

Focus Question: *Green Acres Trust v. London*

1. *The publication in this case is directly "related to" the judicial proceeding in the sense that it involves the allegations in the proceeding. Why then does the court find that it is not "related to" the proceeding?*
2. *Under what circumstances, if any, should the privilege apply to statements made to reporters?*

Green Acres Trust v. London

688 P.2d 617
(Ariz. 1984)

HOLOHAN, Chief Justice.

Appellants Green Acres Trust and Green Acres Memorial Gardens, Inc. ("Green Acres") brought a defamation action against all of the appellees based on oral and written statements published by the appellees during a "press conference" preliminary to the initiation of a class action against Green Acres. The appellees May London, Arthur W. Yoder and Cecil M. Yoder are representative members of the class of plaintiffs in the action filed against Green Acres. Appellees Michael J. Valder, Harry E. Craig, David J. Rich and Douglas G. Martin ("lawyer defendants") are the lawyers for the plaintiffs in that action. The trial court entered summary judgment in favor of all of the appellees, and the Court of Appeals affirmed.

On Friday, March 5, 1976, the lawyer defendants met to review a draft of a class action complaint to be filed against Green Acres which challenged the particular sales technique employed by Green Acres to sell its "pre-paid funerals." Appellee May London, one of the elderly class action clients, also attended the meeting. Sometime during the meeting, Edythe Jensen, a reporter for the Phoenix Gazette newspaper, arrived at the law offices where the meeting was held. One of the lawyer defendants had invited Ms. Jensen to the offices to learn about the basis for the class action. Ms. Jensen received a copy of the drafted complaint and discussed the case with at least one of the lawyer defendants.

Based in part on information obtained from a draft of the complaint and conversations held with the lawyer defendants, Ms. Jensen wrote an article describing the grounds of the class action suit. She quoted the clients and lawyer defendants, and unfavorably characterized the manner in which Green Acres marketed their "pre-paid funerals." The Gazette published the article on the following Monday, March 8, 1976, the same day the lawyer defendants filed the class action complaint.

In due course, Green Acres sued the class action clients and lawyer defendants for defamation based on communications made by the lawyer defendants to Ms. Jensen. Green Acres did not, however, name Ms. Jensen nor her employer as party defendants. Green Acres' complaint alleged that the clients authorized, and the lawyer defendants published, the following statements by providing a copy of the drafted complaint and through conversations with Ms. Jensen:

1. That the State Attorney General's office had been investigating the Plaintiffs [Green Acres] for the purpose of filing criminal charges against them in the areas of security [sic] violations and fraud.

2. That the Plaintiffs [Green Acres] had "bilked" up to five thousand people.

3. That the Plaintiffs [Green Acres] had deliberately violated state laws.

4. The Plaintiffs [Green Acres] had "intentionally inflicted emotional distress on its victims."

The trial court entered summary judgment in favor of the defendants. The Court of Appeals affirmed, finding that both an absolute and a qualified privilege to defame protected the lawyer defendants and supported the entry of summary judgment. The court reasoned that the primary requirement for the absolute privilege was pertinence of the communication's content to the proposed or pending judicial proceeding. The court found such pertinence in the oral statements and the written statements contained in the drafted complaint. Finally, the court found a qualified privilege to defame "because the information affected an important interest of the newspaper reporter, i.e., investigating and reporting purported fraudulent business practices, and the comments were made in response to the reporter's request for information."

We consider two issues raised by the petition:

(1) Were the statements made by the attorney-defendants to the newspaper reporter protected from liability by a privilege?

(2) If so, was the privilege absolute or conditional?

ABSOLUTE PRIVILEGE

While we have not addressed the application of the absolute privilege to this kind of extra-judicial communication, other authorities have considered the "press conference" context and decided against the application of the privilege to communications made in that setting. Assay v. Hallmark Cards, Inc., 594 F.2d 692 (8th Cir.1979); Bradley v. Hartford Accident & Indemnity Co., supra; Kennedy v. Cannon, 229 Md. 92, 182 A.2d 54 (1962); Barto v. Felix, 250 Pa.Super. 262, 378 A.2d 927 (1977); Restatement (Second) of Torts § 586, Reporter's Note, Appendix p. 517 ("The absolute privilege does not extend to a press conference."); Prosser, *supra*, § 114, p. 781 ("It is clear, however, that statements given to the newspapers concerning the case are no part of a judicial proceeding, and are not absolutely privileged" (footnote omitted).); L. Eldredge, The Law of Defamation, § 73H, p. 355–356 (1978). These authorities generally conclude that since publication to the news media lacks a sufficient relationship to judicial proceedings, it should not be protected by an absolute privilege. See Asay v. Hallmark Cards, Inc., supra, 594 F.2d at 697.

The lawyer defendants maintain, and the Court of Appeals agreed, that *Johnston v. Cartwright*, 355 F.2d 32 (8th Cir.1966), established a reasonable rule which recognized an absolute privilege for attorney statements to newspaper reporters concerning litigation which was about to be pursued. The rule in the *Johnston* case has not survived in its own circuit. In *Asay v. Hallmark Cards, supra*, the 8th circuit took a different view on the applicability of the privilege defense to statements made to the news media concerning litigation. The *Asay* court concluded that the application of the absolute privilege defense was dependent upon an analysis of the occasion for the communication and the substance of the communication. Focusing on the occasion of the statements, the *Asay* court concluded that since "[p]ublication to the news media is not ordinarily sufficiently related to a judicial proceeding to constitute a privileged occasion," the absolute privilege should not immunize such publication to the media. The court found that this conclusion harmonized with the public policy underlying the privilege:

> The salutary policy of allowing freedom of communication in judicial proceedings does not warrant or countenance the dissemination and distribution of defamatory accusations outside of the judicial proceeding. No public purpose is served by allowing a person to unqualifiedly make libelous or defamatory statements about another, but rather such person should be called upon to prove the correctness of his allegations or respond in damages.

Id. at 698. We conclude that the *Asay* ruling represents the better position considering the competing interests to be protected. We believe that both content and manner of extra-judicial communications must bear "some relation to the proceeding." The requirements of *Asay* that the recipient of the extra-judicial communication have some relationship to the proposed or pending judicial proceeding for the occasion to be privileged is sound. Ordinarily the media will lack such a connection to a judicial proceeding.

In this case, the recipient of the communications, the newspaper reporter, had no relation to the proposed class action. The reporter played no role in the actual litigation other than that of a concerned observer. Since the reporter lacked a sufficient connection to the proposed proceedings, public policy would be ill served if we immunized the communications made to the reporter by the lawyer defendants. The press conference simply did not enhance the judicial function and no privileged occasion arose. Accordingly, the lawyer defendants were not absolutely privileged to publish the oral and written communications to the newspaper reporter.

Finally, the lawyer defendants argue that extending the protection of the absolute privilege in this case would be consistent with their ethical duty to effectively represent their clients. To the contrary, we consider their conduct to be inconsistent with our rules of ethics. Two ethical tenets directly counsel against the publicity courted by lawyer defendants. First, lawyers must avoid causing injury to their opponents.

> An attorney has a duty to represent his or her clients zealously. But an attorney has *as* compelling an obligation to avoid unnecessary harm to an adversary. The *Model Code of Professional Responsibility* expressly recognizes this dual obligation:
>
> > The duty of a lawyer to represent his client with zeal does not militate against his concurrent obligation to treat with consideration all persons involved in the legal process and to avoid the infliction of needless harm.

Schulman v. Anderson Russell Kill & Olick, P.C., 117 Misc.2d 162, 171, 458 N.Y.S.2d 448, 455 (Sup.Ct.1982), quoting Model Code of Professional Responsibility EC 7-10

(1979) (emphasis in original). In addition, a lawyer may not make or participate in making an extra-judicial statement which he expects will be disseminated by means of public communication which will likely interfere with the fairness of an adjudicative proceeding. DR 7-107(G), Rule 29(a), Rules of the Supreme Court, 17A A.R.S. These two principles, avoiding unnecessary harm and extra-judicial communications, do not affect a lawyer's ability to further his client's interest. Indeed, inflicting unnecessary harm and defaming the adversary during a press conference cannot be considered as legitimately advancing a client's interest. Therefore, by denying the absolute privilege in this case, we do not curtail zealous representation. We simply decide that "an attorney who wishes to litigate his case in the press will do so at his own risk." Bradley v. Hartford Accident & Indemnity Co., *supra*, 30 Cal.App.3d at 828, 106 Cal.Rptr. at 724.

... Although we recognize that the absolute privilege must protect some kinds of communications uttered preliminary to a judicial proceeding, we find no reason in the case at bar to extend an absolute privilege to the lawyer defendants for the communications made by them to the newspaper reporter. We hold that the lawyer defendants were not protected by an absolute privilege for the oral and written communications published by them to the newspaper reporter.

[The court also concluded that the statements were not protected by a qualified or conditional privilege.]

* * *

1. The British rule. Most jurisdictions follow the so-called American rule, which requires at least some relations between the defamatory statement and the judicial proceeding. However, a few jurisdictions still follow the British rule, "which afford[s] the absolute privilege to witnesses and parties without the necessity of demonstrating the relevance of the statement to the pending litigation." Keys v. Chrysler Credit Corp., 494 A.2d 200, 203 (Md. 1985). Would the result in *Green Acres Trust* change under this rule?

2. Model Rule comparison. The *Green Acres Trust* court referenced language from the older ABA *Model Code of Professional Responsibility*. A comment to Rule 1.3 of the ABA *Model Rules of Professional Conduct* similarly advise that a lawyer's duty to provide diligent representation does not require the use of offensive tactics. Model R. Prof'l Conduct R. 1.3 cmt. 1; *see also id.* R. 4.4 (providing that "[i]n representing a client, a lawyer shall not use means that have no substantial purpose other than to embarrass, delay, or burden a third person"). Model Rule 3.6 deals with trial publicity and similarly prohibits a lawyer from making extrajudicial statements that "that the lawyer knows or reasonably should know will be disseminated by means of public communication and will have a substantial likelihood of materially prejudicing an adjudicative proceeding in the matter."

* * *

2. The Privilege for Executive, Legislative, or Judicial Officers

Executive, legislative, and judicial officers may also be entitled to evoke an absolute privilege with respect to statements made in the performance of their official functions. The privilege would clearly apply to statements made, for example, by a legislator during debate on the floor of the legislature or by a judge during the course of a judicial proceeding. But the privilege is not necessarily limited to such statements. In the case of a judicial officer, for example, what matters is that the publication of the defamatory matter occurs in the performance of the judicial function. *See* Spoehr v. Mittelstadt, 150 N.W.2d 502 (Wis. 1967) (concluding that defamatory statement about party made by judge during pretrial conference was absolutely privileged). *See generally* Forrester v. White, 484 U.S. 219 (1981) (concluding that absolute immunity from § 1983 suit did not apply to claim stemming from the judge's firing of an employee). Should the privilege apply in the following circumstances?

(1) Judge, who sentenced a criminal defendant convicted of a felony, wrote a letter to the warden of the penitentiary housing the defendant. The letter contained false and defamatory statements about the acts committed by the criminal defendant. By statute, a sentencing judge is required to prepare and send to the warden an official statement of facts and circumstances surrounding the crime that bear on the question of whether the convict is capable of becoming a law-abiding citizen in the future. The criminal defendant has now sued the judge.

(2) While speaking at a local Rotary Club luncheon about why he opposed a piece of legislation, a state senator knowingly makes a false and defamatory statement about the bill's sponsor. *See generally* Hutchinson v. Proxmire, 443 U.S. 111 (1979).

(3) After a disagreement with Mayor, Plaintiff, the head of a local government agency, tendered his resignation. Mayor had accused Plaintiff of having conflicts of interest with respect to various city contracts and his hiring and firing of employees. Before Plaintiff's termination of employment could become official, the city council had to decide whether to accept the offer of resignation. Part of Mayor's duties involves acting as chair of the council. Mayor circulated a letter to the members of the council, detailing what he believed to be Plaintiff's conflicts of interest. Plaintiff has now sued Mayor for defamation based on the statements in the letters.

(4) The state attorney general filed a consumer fraud action against a number of individuals who had allegedly defrauded citizens of the state. After filing suit, the attorney general issued a press release detailing the allegations and informing the public of the nature of the suit. The defendants in the consumer fraud action sued, alleging that statements in the press release were defamatory.

* * *

In the case of legislators, the privilege has its roots in the Speech and Debate Clause of the U.S. Constitution, Article I, § 6, Clause 1, which has been held to provide a privilege for statements that are "an integral part of the deliberative and communicative processes by which Members participate in committee and House proceedings with respect to the consideration and passage or rejection of proposed legislation or with respect to other matters which the Constitution places within the jurisdiction of either House." Hutchinson v. Proxmire, 443 U.S. 111, 126 (1979) (quotations omitted). The privilege also applies to legislative aides and staff members who are engaged in a legislative function. Restatement (Second) of Torts § 590 cmt. c. Many state constitutions similarly provide for an absolute privilege for legislators. In some states, the privilege is extended to members of local legislative bodies, like city council. Restatement (Second) of Torts § 590 cmt. c.

A similar split exists with respect to state executive officers. In perhaps a majority of states, an absolute privilege protects only "superior officers" (individuals at the cabinet-level or above), leaving "lesser" officers with only a conditional privilege. *See id.* § 591; Stukuls v. State, 366 N.E.2d 829 (N.Y. 1977) (president of state college entitled to qualified privilege); Wardlow v. City of Miami, 372 So.2d 976, 978 (Fla. Ct. App. 1979) (deputy commander of city police department entitled to qualified privilege). The logic behind extending absolute immunity only to high offices is that "the higher the post, the broader the range of responsibilities, and the wider the scope of discretion." Barr v. Matteo, 360 U.S. 564, 573 (1959).

* * *

3. Consent

Exercise 10.4

Employer tells Employee he is being fired because he is a poor salesperson who has failed to generate sufficient revenue. Employee disputes this reason at the time of his firing. However, Employer insists that Employee has failed to generate enough money for the company and that this is why he is being fired. Employee applies for a new job. When he does, he signs a consent form, authorizing former employers to provide information about his past job performance to the company to which he is applying. In response to a reference request, Employer tells the prospective employer that Employee was fired for dishonesty in the form of padding his expense report. Employee had never padded his expense account. Employee is not hired. Employee then sues Employer on a defamation theory. Employer defends on the grounds that Employee consented to the release of the negative information. Is Employer's defense likely to succeed?

Focus Questions: *Smith v. Holley*

1. *Did the plaintiff have reason to know that the evaluation provided to the prospective employer may be defamatory?*
2. *Should it matter for purposes of the validity of the plaintiff's consent that the release did not name the defendant as a person authorized to disclose information about the plaintiff?*

Smith v. Holley

827 S.W.2d 433

(Tex. Ct. App.—San Antonio 1992)

PEEPLES, Justice.

Lonnie Smith appeals a judgment based on a jury finding that he defamed Jeannette Holley by allowing a prospective employer to review documents concerning her and by discussing her job performance. The jury awarded Holley $500,000 in actual damages, and a like amount in punitive damages based on a finding that Smith acted with malice.

In 1984 the Big Spring Police Department hired Holley as a probationary employee. After completing the police academy program, she began field training in the company of experienced officers. The first officer gave her favorable evaluations, but after that it was all downhill. Holley was assigned to ride with a second field training officer, who made her feel stupid for asking questions, gave no timely feedback, and asked that they not ride together again. She was assigned to a third training officer, but within a few days, on November 22, 1984, she was told that she would be terminated. Smith made this decision. Holley challenged the contents of the untimely evaluations made by the second training officer and appealed her dismissal, but she was unsuccessful and was terminated.

In December 1984, Holley and the city manager agreed that: (1) the police department would reinstate Holley, and she would tender her resignation effective retroactively to November 21, citing personal reasons; and (2) the City would purge from its personnel records all references to the involuntary termination, and would mark each page of her personnel file with a notice limiting the information available to anyone asking about Holley's employment record.[1]

In the spring of 1985, Holley applied for a job with the United States Marshals Service ("USMS") and executed a form authorizing persons contacted to give out information about job applicants. The relevant text of that authorization reads:

AUTHORIZATION FOR RELEASE OF INFORMATION

> I hereby authorize any Investigator or duly accredited representative of the United States Civil Service Commission bearing this release ... to obtain any information from schools, residential management agents, employers, criminal justice agencies, or individuals, relating to my activities. This information may include, but is not limited to, academic, residential, achievement, performance, attendance, personal history, disciplinary, arrest, and conviction records. I hereby direct you to release such information upon request of the bearer. I understand that the information released is for official use by the Commission and may be disclosed to such third parties as necessary in the fulfillment of official responsibilities.
>
> I hereby release any individual, including record custodians, from any and all liability for damages of whatever kind or nature which may at any time result to me on account of compliance, or any attempts to comply, with this authorization.

A USMS investigator contacted the Big Spring Police Department in the summer of the following year as part of the routine civil service background check. At that time, Smith was Big Spring's acting Chief of Police, with access to personnel files located in another building. After receiving a copy of Holley's authorization form, Smith told the

---

1. The notice was to read as follows:

> NOTICE
>
> TO BE PLACED IN THE TOP OF EACH CITY OF BIG SPRING FILE RELATING TO JEANNETTE (JANET) HOLLEY
>
> Anyone inquiring about the employment history of Jeannette (Janet) Holley with the City of Big Spring shall only be informed as follows:
>
> 1. Mrs. Holley began working for the Big Spring Police Department on June 1, 1984 as a police officer trainee.
>
> 2. Mrs. Holley resigned for personal reasons on November 21, 1984.
>
> 3. City policy prohibits any additional information about prior employees from being released.
>
> ABSOLUTELY NOTHING BUT THE ABOVE INFORMATION WILL BE RELEASED TO ANYONE BY ANYBODY.

The agreement also included this provision:

> In the event of any inquiry from any prospective employer ... only [these] three points ... will be read or given out. This information will be the *only* information given out regarding her termination as a police officer, either officially or unofficially by anyone connected with the City of Big Spring (emphasis in original).

USMS investigator about his dealings with Holley, and he had another officer talk to the investigator as well. Smith also shared documents with the investigator.

Several months later, USMS notified Holley that it would not hire her. Its rejection letter, based on information from Smith, said that she failed probation at Big Spring, was reinstated, and then resigned. The USMS investigation, said the letter, revealed that her failure of probation "was based on (1) pulling a weapon in a public place; (2) inconsistent facts or reports; and (3) failure to follow chain of command." The letter characterized these actions as "irresponsible behavior" and informed Holley that she would not be recommended for employment.

Holley sued Smith, the City of Big Spring, and three former officials (the former city manager, city attorney, and police chief). She alleged causes of action for defamation per se and breach of contract. Smith was found liable for defamation; the claims against all other defendants were resolved in their favor and are not involved in this appeal. Holley's defamation count concerns the three statements mentioned in the USMS letter. Her live pleading alleged, "Publication of those grounds to the U.S. Marshals Service for plaintiff's termination as a police officer in the City of Big Spring, Texas, constitutes defamation against your plaintiff."

Ordinarily a qualified privilege protects communications made in good faith on subject matter in which the author has a common interest with the other person, or with reference to which he has a duty to communicate to the other person. This qualified privilege protects a former employer's statements about a former employee to a prospective employer. We need not reach Smith's points dealing with qualified privilege because the "Authority for Release of Information" that Holley signed and gave to the USMS makes this a case of absolute privilege instead of qualified privilege.

In point one Smith argues that the authorization immunizes him from liability for any defamatory statements he made in response to it. Holley replies that (1) it would violate public policy to enforce a release of an intentional tort, such as defamation; (2) the authorization did not encompass the information given by Smith because her agreement with the city manager sheltered it; and (3) Smith was not released because the instrument did not specifically name him. We agree with Smith and hold that the authorization was a valid release or consent to defamation that bars Holley's defamation suit.

I.

Holley is incorrect in suggesting that one cannot consent to a defamation, and that an instrument that consents to intentional torts is per se against public policy. On the contrary, the efficacy of such consent is recognized and approved by the *Restatement of Torts*, learned treatises, Texas case law, and the law of other states. The scope and extent of a consent instrument will vary with each case, and we discuss the extent of Holley's consent in section two. But it is clear that one can consent to a defamation, and that consent creates an absolute bar to a defamation suit.

When a plaintiff has consented to a publication, the defendant is absolutely privileged to make it, even if it proves to be defamatory. "[T]he consent of another [the person defamed] to the publication of defamatory matter concerning him is a complete defense to his action for defamation." Restatement (2d) Of Torts § 583 (1977)....

Texas follows this general rule, and the courts have applied it when a defendant has given defamatory information in response to a plaintiff's general authorization or request for comments. "[I]f the publication of which the plaintiff complains was consented to, authorized, invited or procured by the plaintiff, he cannot recover for injuries sustained by reason of the publication." Lyle v. Waddle, 144 Tex. 90, 188 S.W.2d 770, 772 (1945) (plaintiff asked for or consented to defendant physician's writing of letter concerning her treatment)....

The consent privilege applies when the plaintiff has given references for a prospective employer to contact, and the former employer makes defamatory statements about her. "[T]he employee who has been discharged, but who consents to inquiries to previous employers for references in connection with an application for a new job, must be considered willing that presumably unfavorable views be published to the potential new employer." 2 F. Harper, F. James, & O. Gray, The Law Of Torts § 5.17, at 138–39 (2d ed. 1986). This principle has been applied in Texas. *See Duncantell*, 446 S.W.2d at 936. And in other jurisdictions a former employer has absolute immunity when he utters the alleged defamation in response to an inquiry from a prospective employer with the plaintiff's consent.

II.

We consider now the scope and extent of the consent signed by Holley. Consent does not necessarily give a former employer license to tell the world everything he knows about the plaintiff for an unlimited time, unless that is a reasonable interpretation of the consent. The extent of the consent does not exceed what is reasonable in light of the language or circumstances that created it:

> The extent of the privilege is determined by the terms of the consent. These again are to be determined by the language or acts by which it is manifested in the light of the surrounding circumstances. If the person to whom the consent is given reasonably interprets the language used or the acts done as a consent to the publication of the defamatory matter to any person, at any time, in any manner and for any purpose, the publication however made is privileged. On the other hand, a consent may be limited to a publication to a particular person or at a particular time or for a particular purpose.

Restatement (2d) Of Torts § 583, comment d. "As in other cases of consent, the privilege is limited by the scope of the assent apparently given, and consent to one form of publication does not confer a license to publish to other persons, or in a different manner." Prosser & Keeton On Torts § 114, at 823. "The scope of the immunity is determined by the terms of the consent. A consent to publish a statement to a particular person is not a license to publish it to the world." 2 F. Harper, F. James, & O. Gray, The Law Of Torts § 5.17, at 136.

Here Smith did not exceed the authorization. He responded promptly, he spoke only of Holley's job performance and her capabilities, and he gave the information to the investigator and no one else.

The authorization is worded broadly enough to reach all kinds of defamatory remarks, even those uttered by employees of the City of Big Spring. It does not authorize disclosures of true information only, or favorable information. It does not reserve the right to sue providers of information that Holley disagrees with. On the contrary, it is broad and all-encompassing in three different ways: it authorizes contact with a large and diverse group of people, it contemplates wide and probing inquiry into every aspect of Holley's background, and it then releases every kind of lawsuit imaginable.

The instrument first authorizes the marshals service to contact almost anyone and "to obtain any information from schools, residential management agents, employers, criminal justice agencies, or individuals, relating to my activities." Second, it authorizes the persons contacted to give a great variety of information, which "may include, but is not limited to, academic, residential, achievement, performance, attendance, personal history, disciplinary, arrest, and conviction records." It does not stop at *authorizing* the disclosure of information; it *directs* those who possess information about Holley to disclose it to the investigator, who is acting for the United States Civil Service Commission. Finally, it releases Holley's right to sue, using language as broad and inclusive as we can imagine. It says, "I hereby release *any individual*, including record custodians, from *any and all liability for damages of whatever kind or nature* which may *at any time* result to me on account of compliance, or any attempts to comply, with this authorization" (emphasis added).

The authorization simply does not permit the interpretation that the signer reserved the right to sue persons who honor it and give information fairly related to the matters covered. Nothing suggests that Holley authorized only the release of favorable replies. That construction would, of course, make authorizations to respond to background checks completely worthless. The release says, in effect, you may find out what other people say about me, and I will not litigate if the responses are unfavorable. Fairly viewed, it does not exclude from its reach defamatory remarks about Holley's job performance uttered to the investigator.

Consent does not immunize defamations that the plaintiff had no reason to anticipate. The *Restatement* makes this clear:

> It is not necessary that the [plaintiff] know that the matter to the publication of which he consents is defamatory in character. It is enough that he knows the exact language of the publication or that he has reason to know that it may be defamatory.... In such a case, by consent to its publication, he takes the risk that it may be defamatory.

Restatement (2d) Of Torts § 583, comment d. *See* Duncantell v. Universal Life Ins. Co., 446 S.W.2d 934, 937 (Tex.Civ.App.—Houston [14th Dist.] 1969, *writ ref'd n.r.e.*) ("plaintiff invited the publication ... when he should have known that [it] would adversely affect his opportunity for employment"); McDermott v. Hughley, 317 Md. 12, 561 A.2d 1038, 1045–46 (1989) (absolute privilege applies if plaintiff had reason to anticipate the defamation).

But this limitation on the privilege does not avail Holley because it is undisputed that she knew that Smith and others at the Big Spring Police Department held unfavorable opinions about her performance there....

The reach of the authorization is not affected by the city's agreement to keep secret the real reasons for Holley's departure from the police force. Smith was not a party to the city manager's agreement with Holley; and in any event, the jury found that no damages resulted from the city's breach of it, a finding that Holley does not appeal. The jury did find that Holley did not waive her right to insist on compliance with the agreement, but that finding has nothing to do with Smith because the agreement did not bind him in the first place. We note also that Holley did not merely authorize prior employers to let the USMS review documents in her file at the police department and other places; she authorized personal contact with individuals, and she authorized the release of information. Perhaps Holley thought the authorization did not consent to disclosure of unfavorable information about her employment at Big Spring. But unambiguous written instruments are interpreted according to their wording, not the unwritten subjective intentions of the parties. *See* Westwind Exploration, Inc. v. Home Sav. Ass'n, 696 S.W.2d 378, 382 (Tex.1985); City of Pinehurst v. Spooner Addition Water Co., 432 S.W.2d 515, 518–19 (Tex.1968). Those who respond to an authorization are entitled to interpret it objectively on its own terms, without trying to divine the signer's subjective understanding of it.

We hold that the authorization granted Smith the right to make the three statements he made to the USMS investigator.

... We sustain Smith's first point of error, reverse the judgment against him, and render judgment that Holley take nothing.

* * *

1. The meaning of consent. Section 892A of the *Restatement (Second) of Torts* contains the general consent rule that applies in other intentional tort cases. In order for consent to be effective, an individual must consent in advance to the particular conduct that occurs or substantially the same conduct. Therefore, a party's consent to permit a neighbor to "dump a few stones" on the party's land is not consent to the neighbor covering the party's land with large boulders. *Id.* § 892A cmt. c. Section 583 purports to be a special application of this general rule to the defamation context.

2. Invited or procured defamation. *Holley* mentions the concept of inviting or procuring a defamatory publication. Imagine that your employer tells you are fired. In the presence of several coworkers, you (bewildered) ask why you are being fired. Your employer tells you that it is because you have been stealing from the company. You have never stolen anything from the employer. Are you barred from recovering on a subsequent defamation claim on the basis that you invited or procured your employer's defamatory publication? Did you consent to this publication under § 583?

Exercise 10.5

Melvin was hired as an associate at the Baker & Lafayette Law Firm. Melvin was told when he was hired that his work performance would be subject to a yearly evaluation and that his advancement (and retention) in the firm would be influenced by these reviews. During his first year, Melvin had run-ins with one of the partners at the firm as well as a senior associate. When Melvin met with firm partners to discuss his annual evaluation, he learned that the two attorneys in question had told the reviewing partners that Melvin was frequently out of the office during work hours and that the quality of his work was so poor that several clients had requested that Melvin not be allowed to work on their matters. As a result of the poor evaluation, the firm fired Melvin. Melvin has now sued the two attorneys in question, alleging that their statements were simply false and were made out of personal dislike and malice. The two attorneys argue in response that by consenting to the performance evaluation, Melvin consented to any resulting defamatory publication. What should the result be?

B. Qualified Privileges

Absolute privileges are recognized when the societal interest implicated by the defendant's action is of utmost importance. Qualified or conditional privileges are recognized when the societal interest implicated "an intermediate degree of importance, so that the immunity conferred is not absolute, but is conditioned upon publication in a reasonable manner and for a proper purpose." Green Acres Trust v. London, 688 P.2d 617, 624 (Ariz.1984). The following section considers three widely-recognized qualified privileges, the first of which consists of three related, but distinct types.

1. The Common Interest Privilege

Focus Questions: *Zinda v. Louisiana Pacific Corp.*

1. *Under what circumstances may a conditional privilege be lost?*
2. *What other argument is there that the common interest privilege should not apply in this case?*

Zinda v. Louisiana Pacific Corp.

440 N.W.2d 548
(Wis. 1989)

BABLITCH, Justice.

Allan D. "Rick" Zinda (Zinda) brought ... a defamation ... action against his former employer, Louisiana Pacific Corporation (Louisiana Pacific), based on a statement concerning his discharge which was published in a company newsletter.

The essential facts are undisputed. Approximately two years prior to his employment with Louisiana Pacific, Zinda was injured as a result of falling through "waferboard" on the roof of a garage he was constructing at his home. Zinda sustained numerous injuries, including a broken rib, a broken bone in the back, and a broken heel.

In connection with his application for employment with Louisiana Pacific in 1983, Zinda completed a standard application form as well as a medical history form. In the "personal health history" portion of the medical form, Zinda provided the following answers:

Upper Back Trouble—No.

Middle Back Trouble—No.

Low Back Trouble—No.

Back Injury or Disability—No.

Fracture or Broken Bone—No.

Back X-ray—No.

In explaining a "yes" answer regarding previous hospitalizations and surgery, Zinda wrote: "[W]hen I was 15 years old for Hay Fever, Tonsil, Appendits [sic], and fall off roof." Later, during a pre-employment interview, Zinda clarified that he had previously fallen off a roof and broken some bones including his ribs and a heel, but that he had no present problems. Zinda signed both forms acknowledging that all answers were true and that any false statements or misrepresentations would result in immediate discharge, regardless of when such facts were discovered.

Approximately one year later, Zinda filed a products liability action against Louisiana Pacific, alleging that it negligently manufactured the "waferboard" involved in his fall off the roof. The complaint asserted that Zinda had suffered permanent disabilities as a result of the injuries, and sought substantial compensatory and punitive damages.

The complaint was served on the personnel manager of the Louisiana Pacific plant who compared the allegations against the answers Zinda gave on his application forms. Apparently concluding that Zinda had intentionally withheld adverse information concerning his physical condition, the personnel manager notified Zinda that his employment was suspended pending an investigation into possible fraud regarding his employment forms. Approximately three weeks later, Louisiana Pacific terminated Zinda's employment.

Subsequently, Louisiana Pacific published a notice regarding Zinda's termination on the seventh page of the plant newspaper, the "Waferboard Press," under the following heading:

COMINGS AND GOINGS

5/1/84	Death	Leland Thysen	
5/10/84	Voluntary Quit	Jeff Aiken	Back to Railroad
5/14/84	Hire	Paul Lueck	Electrician
5/25/84	Terminate	Al Christner	Falsification of Emp. forms
...			
5/29/84	Terminate	Larry Radzak	Theft
5/29/84	Terminate	Al Zinda	Falsification of Emp. forms
...			

Approximately 160 copies of the newsletter were distributed to employees by placement in the lunchroom. Employees were not restricted from taking the newsletter home, and employees regularly took the newsletters out of the workplace. Testimony indicates that a copy reached the local hospital, where Zinda's wife worked, and two of her co-workers read the reference to Zinda's termination.

Zinda amended his complaint to include allegations of defamation, invasion of privacy, and wrongful discharge. Louisiana Pacific answered, raising conditional privilege as a defense, asserting that it had no liability for good faith communications to employees concerning the reasons for the discharge of another employee.

... Regarding the defamation and invasion of privacy claims, the trial court refused without explanation to submit Louisiana Pacific's requested instruction on conditional privilege.

The jury returned a verdict awarding $50,000.00 for defamation....

Louisiana Pacific appealed, arguing that it was entitled to the instruction on conditional privilege....

I.

We turn first to the issue of liability for defamation. We conclude that the information published in the company newsletter was conditionally privileged as a communication of common interest concerning the employer-employee relationship. We further conclude that although the privilege may be lost if abused, a jury question was presented in this case as to whether the information was excessively published.

Privileged defamations may be either absolute or conditional. Absolute privileges give complete protection without any inquiry into the defendant's motives. This privilege has been extended to judicial officers, legislative proceedings, and to certain governmental executive officers.

The arguments in this case, however, are concerned only with conditional privilege. In the area of conditional privilege, we have endorsed the language of the *Restatement of Torts. See Converters Equipment*, 80 Wis.2d at 264, 258 N.W.2d 712. The *Restatement* recognizes the existence of a conditional privilege in a number of different situations. Among these are statements made on a subject matter in which the person making the statement and the person to whom it is made have a legitimate common interest.

Section 596 of the *Restatement 2d of Torts* defines the "common interest" privilege:

> An occasion makes a publication conditionally privileged if the circumstances lead any one of several persons having a common interest in a particular subject matter correctly or reasonably to believe that there is information that another sharing the common interest is entitled to know.

The common interest privilege is based on the policy that one is entitled to learn from his associates what is being done in a matter in which he or she has an interest in common. Thus, defamatory statements are privileged which are made in furtherance of common property, business, or professional interests. The *Restatement* extends such privilege to "partners, fellow officers of a corporation for profit, fellow shareholders, and fellow servants. . . ." *See id.*, Comment d. at 597.

The common interest privilege is particularly germane to the employer-employee relationship. We have applied a conditional privilege to various communications between employers and persons having a common interest in the employee's conduct. . . .

[I]n *Johnson v. Rudolph Wurlitzer Co.*, 197 Wis. 432, 440, 222 N.W. 451, 454 (1928), we held that a conditional privilege applied to defamatory statements by a store manager to other employees in the office about an alleged embezzlement involving a fellow employee. We stated that because of their employment, the employees had a common interest in discovering the source of the shortage that was being investigated.

We conclude that the common interest privilege attaches to the employer-employee relationship in this case. Employees have a legitimate interest in knowing the reasons a fellow employee was discharged. Conversely, an employer has an interest in maintaining morale and quieting rumors which may disrupt business. Here, Louisiana Pacific's personnel manager testified that at the time of Zinda's termination, the plant had been going through a rather extensive retooling and reprocessing. During that time, normal crews had been broken apart and there were prevailing rumors that Louisiana Pacific was laying off employees. The company believed for this reason that it would be the best policy to immediately suppress rumors by being completely honest concerning employees who were no longer with the company.

Moreover, we conclude that truthfulness and integrity in the employment application process is an important common interest. An employer who asks questions such as those involved here is entitled to receive an honest answer, and reasonable communication in a plant newsletter concerning terminations for misrepresentations discourages other employees from engaging in similar conduct. In addition, the employees have an interest in knowing how the rules are enforced, and the type of conduct that may result in their discharge from employment. Accordingly, Louisiana Pacific's communication to its employees concerning Zinda's discharge was entitled to a conditional privilege.

However, conditional privilege is not absolute and may be forfeited if the privilege is abused. The *Restatement 2d of Torts* lists five conditions which may constitute an abuse of the privilege, and the occurrence of any one causes the loss of the privilege. The privilege may be abused: (1) because of the defendant's knowledge or reckless disregard as to the falsity of the defamatory matter (*see* secs. 600–602); (2) because the defamatory matter is published for some purpose other than that for which the particular privilege is given (*see* sec. 603); (3) because the publication is made to some person not reasonably believed to be necessary for the accomplishment of the purpose of the particular privilege (*see* sec. 604); (4) because the publication includes defamatory matter not reasonably believed to be necessary to accomplish the purpose for which the occasion is privileged (*see* sec. 605); or (5) the publication includes unprivileged matter as well as privileged matter (*see* sec. 605A).

Zinda insists that any privilege which may have existed in this case was abused as a matter of law by excessive publication under condition (3). Essentially, Zinda argues that Louisiana Pacific made no attempt to restrict the publication to persons with a common interest in his termination. Zinda alludes to testimony elicited on cross-examination which purportedly indicates that the personnel manager had knowledge that employees routinely took the newsletters home. Furthermore, Zinda asserts that the content of the newsletter encouraged its removal from the plant.

We disagree that Louisiana Pacific abused its privilege as a matter of law. The question whether a conditional privilege has been abused is a factual question for the jury, unless the facts are such that only one conclusion can be reasonably drawn.

Contrary to Zinda's insistence, the evidence alluded to does not necessarily lead to the conclusion that Louisiana Pacific excessively published the statement concerning Zinda's discharge. Once it is determined by the court that the defamatory communication was made on an occasion of conditional privilege, the burden shifts to the plaintiff to affirmatively prove abuse. Here, despite allegations of widespread distribution throughout the community, Zinda's proof at trial was limited to the testimony of two unprivileged women who read the reference to Zinda's termination at the hospital where his wife worked.

An employer is entitled to use a method of publication that involves an incidental communication to persons not within the scope of the privilege. *See* Walters v. Sentinel Co., 168 Wis. 196, 203–04, 169 N.W. 564 (1918); Restatement 2d, Torts, sec. 604, Comment a. at 292. Often the only practical means of communicating defamatory information involves a probability or even a certainty that it will reach persons whose knowledge of it is of no value in accomplishing the purpose for which the privilege is given. In *Walters* this court stated that if "a newspaper, published primarily for a given constituency, such as county or state, church or lodge, have a small circulation outside such constituency, it is not deprived of its privilege in the discussion of matters of concern to its constituency because of such incidental outside circulation."

As previously discussed, Louisiana Pacific had an interest in informing each and every one of its employees about the subject of Zinda's discharge.[2] We cannot as a matter of law consider the communication in this case an unreasonable means to accomplish this purpose. Testimony indicates that the company attempted to correlate the number of copies printed to the number of employees in the plant. These copies were circulated only in the lunchroom, over the course of several days, so that every workshift would have an

2. To the extent that Zinda implies that the allegedly defamatory matter was indiscriminately taken home by the employees and communicated to various family members, we agree with courts of other jurisdictions which have held that defamatory communications made to family members are ordinarily subject to a conditional privilege. *See, e.g.*, Kroger Company v. Young, 210 Va. 564, 172 S.E.2d 720, 723 (1970).

opportunity to read the newsletter. Thus, despite the company's alleged knowledge that employees often took the newsletter home, a jury could conclude that the great bulk of its readers had a direct and legitimate interest in the information regarding Zinda's termination, and that the outside communication was reasonably believed to be necessary to communicate the privileged information. Accordingly, the privilege was not abused as a matter of law, and it was error to refuse the requested instruction.

* * *

1. The role of malice? What should be the result if the employer's primary motivation for publishing the defamatory statement had been to seek revenge on the employee, rather than to inform other employees about goings on in the company? *See* Restatement (Second) of Torts § 603 cmt. a.

2. Judge vs. Jury: Whether an occasion is privileged is a question of law for the court. "[W]hether the occasion for the privilege was abused is a question of fact for the jury." Green Acres Trust v. London, 688 P.2d 617, 624 (Ariz. 1984).

* * *

2. The Privilege to Publish in Defense of Oneself

A conditional privilege also exists for a publication made to protect one's own interest. In order for the privilege to apply, the defendant must at least reasonably believe that the publication of defamatory information will help protect an important interest of the defendant. Restatement (Second) of Torts § 594. The interest to be protected must be deemed sufficiently important in order for the privilege to apply. Examples include protecting one's right of inheritance or protecting one's property from theft. In addition, the person to whom the publication is made must reasonably be one who will be of service to the defendant in protecting her interest. Thus, telling the school principal that one is being bullied might be privileged, but telling one's next-door neighbor who has no connection to the school or the parties might not.

* * *

3. The Privilege to Publish in the Interest of Others

Focus Questions: *Kevorkian v. Glass*

1. *What is the relation between the statutory privilege at issue and the common law privilege to publish in the interest of others?*
2. *Was the court correct in its conclusion that there was insufficient evidence of malice to defeat the privilege?*

Kevorkian v. Glass

913 A.2d 1043
(R.I. 2007)

[The plaintiff, Kevorkian, was formerly employed by Pawtuxet Village. She "was suspended from work for three days for insubordination. Specifically, Glass, the director of nursing at the center, alleged that plaintiff had failed to dispense necessary medication to patients at Pawtuxet Village. Kevorkian disputed her employer's allegation, and, unwilling to continue to work under the shadow of such accusations, she resigned her position with Pawtuxet Village" and accepted employment elsewhere. Two years later, Kevorkian filled out an application with Mercury Medical, an employment placement service. Mercury Medical contacted Glass for an employment reference. Unbeknownst to Kevorkian, Glass responded that she would not rehire Kevorkian due to her "unacceptable work practice habits." Kevorkian began attending interviews with prospective employers set up by Mercury Medical, but received no offers. Upon learning of the contents of Glass' reference, Kevorkian sued Glass for defamation.]

[W]e agree with the motion justice that defendant's publication of the allegedly defamatory statement was clearly covered by a qualified privilege found in § 28-6.4-1(c).[3] Even before the statute was enacted, it was well settled in this jurisdiction that, "[t]he publisher of an allegedly defamatory statement may avoid liability if he or she is privileged to make the statement in question." In our opinion, the critical issues in this case are whether defendant enjoyed a qualified privilege under § 28-6.4-1(c) to make the allegedly defamatory statement and, if so, whether plaintiff pointed to anything tangible that would create a genuine issue regarding whether the privilege was abrogated by the conduct of the defendant.

In *Swanson v. Speidel Corp.*, 110 R.I. 335, 340, 293 A.2d 307, 310 (1972), a case factually similar to the matter now before us, we held that a former employer's communication to a prospective employer with regard to the work characteristics of a former employee was protected by a qualified privilege. *Id.* at 310. In that case, we said that:

> the public interest requires that the protection of the privilege be accorded to a communication by a former employer to a prospective employer with regard to a former employee's work characteristics where the publisher acts in good faith and has reason to believe that to speak out is necessary to protect " ... his own interests, or those of third persons, or certain interests of the public." *Swanson*, 110 R.I. at 340, 293 A.2d at 310 (quoting *Ponticelli*, 104 R.I. at 551, 247 A.2d at 305–06).

The qualified privilege can be overcome, however, when the plaintiff proves "that the person making the defamatory statements acted with ill will or malice." *Mills*, 837 A.2d at 720.

---

3. General Laws 1956 § 28-6.4-1(c) provides:
"An employer that, upon request by a prospective employer or a current or former employee, provides fair and unbiased information about a current or former employee's job performance is presumed to be acting in good faith and is immune from civil liability for the disclosure and the consequences of the disclosure. The presumption of good faith is rebuttable upon a showing by a preponderance of the evidence that the information disclosed was:
"(1) Knowingly false;
"(2) Deliberately misleading;
"(3) Disclosed for a malicious purpose; or
"(4) Violative of the current or former employee's civil rights under the employment discrimination laws in effect at the time of the disclosure."

When it enacted § 28-6.4-1(c), the General Assembly essentially codified the *Swanson* holding and created a statutory qualified privilege for former employers' communications to prospective employers concerning former employees.

Here, the motion justice found that defendant's statement that plaintiff had "unacceptable work practice habits" clearly was covered by the § 28-6.4-1(c) privilege. We agree. The defendant is a former supervisor of plaintiff who, at the request of both plaintiff and a placement agency (Mercury Medical), provided information about plaintiff's work performance while she was employed at Pawtuxet Village. Clearly, when she received an inquiry about Kevorkian from a prospective employer, Glass had a qualified privilege under § 28-6.4-1(c) to reveal her dissatisfaction with plaintiff's work during the time she worked at Pawtuxet Village. Thus, according to § 28-6.4-1(c), a presumption of good faith attached to defendant's publication and the burden of rebutting that presumption shifted to plaintiff.

At the summary judgment hearing, plaintiff argued that defendant's statement was made for a malicious purpose, thereby removing it from the scope of the privilege provided by § 28-6.4-1(c). However, we conclude that plaintiff did not meet the burden imposed on her by Rule 56 of directing the court to specific facts that raise a genuine issue about whether defendant made the publication for a malicious purpose. The plaintiff argues that the issue of whether a qualified privilege is abrogated by the malicious intentions of the publisher of a defamatory statement presents a question of fact to be resolved by the fact-finder at trial, and not by the judge on a motion for summary judgment. In our opinion, plaintiff misstates the summary judgment standard.

Although, it is true that, "[w]hether ill will or spite is the incentive for a publication is,..., a fact question and is ordinarily for the fact-finder to decide ... [,]" *Swanson*, 110 R.I. at 341, 293 A.2d at 311, to overcome a motion for summary judgment based on a qualified privilege, a plaintiff must point to some specific facts in the record that raise a genuine issue relative to the existence of such ill will....

On no less than three occasions, the motion justice asked plaintiff's counsel to point to some facts in the record demonstrating ill will on the part of defendant to rebut the presumption of § 28-6.4-1(c). The plaintiff failed to do so on each occasion.

Apparently, it was plaintiff's contention, as it is here on appeal, that if defendant considered plaintiff's work habits acceptable enough not to fire her, then a reasonable inference may be drawn that her negative reference must have been made with malice. It is our opinion, however, that plaintiff's contention constitutes nothing more than a conclusion devoid of factual foundation, and that such an inference would not be reasonable.

The plaintiff, as the party opposing summary judgment in this case, did not carry her burden, and, therefore, the motion justice appropriately pronounced her case "dead in the water."

* * *

1. Employer references. Some courts say that a former employer who provides a reference to a prospective employer shares a common interest in the employee and is therefore protected by the common interest privilege. *See, e.g.*, Hett v. Ploetz, 20 Wis.2d 55, 59–62, 121 N.W.2d 270 (1963). Alternatively, the former employer might be privileged to publish a defamatory statement about a former employee for the protection of the prospective employer's interests. *See, e.g.*, Delloma v. Consolidation Coal Co., 996 F.2d 168 (7th Cir. 1993).

Many employers are reluctant to provide an employment reference regarding a current or former employee for fear that if they say something negative, the employee may sue for defamation. As a result, many employers provide nothing more than a former employee's dates of employment and job titles when responding to a request for an employment reference. In an effort to ease the fears of employers, many states began enacting reference immunity statutes in the 1990s. These statutes typically provide employers with qualified immunity from suit stemming from a negative reference. In most cases, the reference statutes do little than codify the existing common law privileges. J. Hoult Verkerke, *Legal Regulation of Employment Reference Practices*, 65 U. Chi. L. Rev. 115, 132 (1998).

2. Other situations. The employer reference scenario is easily the most common situation in which the privilege to provide information for the protection of others applies. Other situations include where a credit reporting agency, upon request, provides false credit information about a plaintiff, *Krumholz v. TRW Inc.*, 360 A.2d 413 (N.J. Super. Ct. 1976), and a manufacturer's announcement to the public that it is discontinuing a product due to safety concerns about component parts provided by another company. *See* Flotech, Inc. v. E.I. du Pont de Nemours & Co., 814 F.2d 775 (1st Cir. 1987).

3. Communication to one who may act in the public interest. A conditional privilege may also apply where the defendant reasonably believes that it is necessary, in order to protect an important public interest, to provide defamatory information to a public officer or a private citizen who is authorized to take action if the defamatory matter is true. Restatement (Second) of Torts § 598. This would include the situation in which an individual reasonably believes a theft is taking place and notifies the police or a private security guard. *Id.* § 598 cmt. d.

4. Family members. Statements that a defendant reasonably believes are necessary to protect the well being of an immediate family member are also conditionally privileged. Restatement (Second) of Torts § 597.

5. Repeating rumors. As discussed in Chapter 8, a defendant who repeats a defamatory rumor and identifies the statement as being a rumor is still subject to liability. However, if the statement is otherwise subject to a qualified privilege, the privilege is not lost, *even if the defendant knows the rumor is untrue*, provided the defendant identifies the statement as a rumor and the publication is otherwise reasonable. Restatement (Second) of Torts § 602. An example might be where a parent informs a child of a rumor going around town about the child's fiancé, even though the parent does not believe the rumor. *See id.* § 602 cmt. b.

Exercise 10.6

You are an attorney licensed in Rhode Island who represents Rhode Island employers. One day, you get a call from the human resources person for one of your clients asking for your advice. A prospective employer has contacted your client and asked your client to provide it with any information it thinks is relevant about a job applicant who was formerly employed by your client. Although the prospective employer is not technically affiliated with your client, the two entities are in the same business and frequently refer business to each other and sometimes work together on various projects. The human resources person tells you that there were numerous rumors surrounding the former employee. The human resources person tells you that she received several complaints from co-workers about the former employee's sexual harassment of the co-workers, but an internal investigation proved inconclusive. After the former employee left, several employees told the human resources person that the employee had a drug problem and that they had personally witnessed him doing drugs in his car in the company parking lot during his lunch break. Otherwise, the employee's job performance was fine, and all of his annual personnel evaluations rate him as an average employee. The human resources person asks you what, if anything, she should tell the prospective employer about the employee. What is your advice?

C. Privileges Involving the Media

Imagine that one public figure files a lawsuit against another public figure. The first public figure is known for being eccentric, and the allegations in his lawsuit reflect this. Most people who read the allegations quickly conclude that the complaint is frivolous. Most news outlets would probably run a story on the filing of the lawsuit and repeat the allegations contained therein, even though they might entertain serious doubts as to the truth of the allegations. After all, the filing of a lawsuit by one celebrity against another is, by itself, a newsworthy event. However, the *New York Times v. Sullivan* actual malice standard might not shield the reporter or the newspaper who runs such a story from liability in this scenario since they probably have serious doubts about the truth of the allegations on the complaint. The following section deals with the various privileges that might apply in these kinds of situations and situations involving reporting and commentary more generally.

1. Fair Reporting Privilege

Focus Questions: *Express Pub. Co. v. Gonzalez*

1. *What are the likely rationales for the fair reporting privilege at issue in the case?*
2. *How does the fair reporting privilege relate to the idea that a defamatory publication must be false before it is actionable?*
3. *What is the relationship between the requirement that a report be "true" in order for the privilege to apply and the concept of "substantial truth" discussed in Chapter 8?*

Express Pub. Co. v. Gonzalez

326 S.W.2d 544

(Tex. Civ. App. 1959)

W. O. MURRAY, Chief Justice.

This suit was instituted in the District Court of Starr County by Enrique G. Gonzalez, seeking to recover damages for the publication of an article by the Express Publishing Company alleged to be libelous of him. The article was published in the San Antonio 'Sunday Express and News' on December 22, 1957, and reads as follows:

Sisters Win Oil Land Suit

> Ninety-nine-year-old twin sisters, perhaps the oldest twins in the United States, Saturday had won their suit for 13 acres of oil-rich land in Starr County.
>
> The sisters, Inez Garcia Ruiz, and Aniceta Garcia Barrera, had alleged that the land was fraudulently taken from them by a nephew, Benigno Barrera and Enrique G. Gonzalez, both of Starr County.
>
> The women said they signed a deed to the land when Barrera represented it as a document permitting him to erect a corral fence there. The sisters cannot read or write Spanish or English.
>
> Judge C. K. Quinn in 45th District Court last year returned the sisters the land, which had been in their family since a Spanish grant.
>
> Saturday it was announced the appeals court had ruled against Barrera and Gonzalez.
>
> The sisters' address was listed as 2605 Guadalupe Street, San Antonio.

Article 5432, Vernon's Ann.Civ.Stats., reads in part as follows:

> The publication of the following matters by any newspaper or periodical shall be deemed privileged and shall not be made the basis of any action for libel.
>
> 1. A fair, true and impartial account of the proceedings in a court of justice, unless the court prohibits the publication of same when in the judgment of the court the ends of justice demand that the same should not be published and the court so orders, or any other official proceedings authorized by law in the administration of the law.

The controverting affidavit of Gonzalez and his amended petition, which he had made a part of his controverting affidavit, show on their face that the alleged libelous article was published by appellant, Express Publishing Company, in an attempt to report the proceedings in a court of justice, or proceedings authorized by law in the administration of the law. The burden of proof was therefore upon appellee to both allege and prove by the preponderance of the evidence that the article complained of was either unfair, untrue or partial. Appellee undertook to establish that the statement that the twin sisters had alleged in their cause of action, that both he and Benigno Barrera had 'fraudulently taken from them' thirteen acres of oil-rich land in Starr County, was unfair, untrue and partial. In the original petition filed by the twin sisters this allegation is found. However, after appellee had filed a motion for summary judgment, the twin sisters asked leave of the court to take a nonsuit as to Gonzalez, which request was granted by the court and an order entered to that effect. Thereafter the twin sisters filed their first and second original amended petitions in which the name of appellee was not mentioned, and the case went to trial upon their second amended petition. It is apparent that after taking a nonsuit the twin sisters abandoned their original petition in which the allegation against appellee had been made.

The suit filed by the twin sisters in the District Court of Bexar County, was Cause No. F-95,430, styled *Inez Garcia Ruiz et al. v. Benigno Barrera et al.* The cause was heard on February 25, 1957, by District Judge C. K. Quinn and judgment rendered restoring the thirteen acres 'of oil-rich land' to the twin sisters. An appeal was taken from this judgment to the San Antonio Court of Civil Appeals, and transferred to the Fort Worth Court of Civil Appeals by the Supreme Court upon an equalization of dockets, and the case was decided by that Court on December 20, 1957. Barrera v. Ruiz, 308 S.W.2d 578. The appeal was by Benigno Barrera and Enrique G. Gonzalez was one of the sureties on his cost bond. The Fort Worth Court of Civil Appeals on December 20, 1957, rendered judgment affirming the judgment of the trial court and adjudging the court costs against Barrera, Gonzalez and the other surety on the cost bond.

The article alleged to be libelous is undoubtedly a report concerning official proceedings, authorized by law in the administration of the law, and if fair, true and impartial, it is privileged and cannot form the basis for a libel suit. Art. 5432, Vernon's Ann.Civ.Stats. The word true as used in the above article really means correct. Let us examine the statement and see if it is a fair, correct and impartial statement of what happened in Cause No. F-95,430, *styled Ruiz et al. v. Barrera et al.* The article must be read as it would be understood by an ordinary average reader of the paper. When this is done the article would seem to say that both Barrera and appellee were charged with fraud and that the land had been restored to the twin sisters by Judge C. K. Quinn, and further that the Fort Worth Court of Civil Appeals had held against both Barrera and appellee upon such charge of fraud. Unless the article was privileged under the statute, it would be libelous if untrue. The article was literally true, in that the twin sisters had charged Gonzalez with fraud in their original petition and the Fort Worth Court of Civil Appeals had found against Gonzalez as to court costs. The publication to be privileged must not only be literally true, but it must also be fair and impartial.

In their original petition, the twin sisters stated, in effect, that both Barrera and Gonzalez had defrauded them out of their oil-rich land. The petition was filed in August, 1955. As soon as Gonzalez was served with citation, on September 1, 1955, he filed a motion for summary judgment as to himself. This motion was set for hearing on September 19, 1955, and on that date the twin sisters came into court and asked leave to take a nonsuit as to Gonzalez, which was granted by the court and an order to that effect entered on the minutes. The sisters thereafter filed a first amended original petition, and on April 9, 1956, filed a second amended original petition, which was the pleading on which the case went to trial. In the amended petition the name of Gonzalez was not mentioned, and he was not thereafter charged with any fraud. It is unfair for appellant to go back to the original petition which had been abandoned and publish that Gonzalez had been charged with fraud, and not mention the fact that a nonsuit had been taken by the twin sisters as to Gonzalez and an order entered upon the minutes showing such nonsuit, and that the amended petition contained no reference whatever to Gonzalez, and we cannot say that such article was a fair report of the proceedings.... We are unable to say that the article was fair in not stating that the twin sisters had taken a nonsuit as to Gonzalez and had filed an amended pleading in which his name was not mentioned. The original petition was no part of the proceedings had in the trial court or in the appellate court.

Neither do we think it was fair for appellant, after being unfair in not mentioning the nonsuit, to say that the appellate court had held against Gonzalez, thereby indicating that he had been adjudged guilty of fraud, without going further and saying that the appellate court had only held against Gonzalez as to costs.

The article complained of by appellee, Gonzalez, was not a fair statement of the pleadings and proceedings had in Cause No. F-95,430, but, on the contrary, was an unfair statement, not protected by the provisions of Article 5432, Vernon's Ann.Civ.Stats., declaring a 'fair, true and impartial account of the proceedings in a court of justice' or 'official proceedings authorized by law in the administration of the law' to be privileged. Sutton v. A. H. Belo & Co., supra; Houston Chronicle Pub. Co. v. McDavid, Tex. Civ. App., 173 S.W. 467.

The judgment of the trial court overruling appellant's plea of privilege is affirmed.

* * *

1. Other public proceedings. The fair reporting privilege also often applies to reports of other public proceedings, including legislative proceedings, local board meetings, state agency proceedings, *etc.* What matters is that the proceeding be "official." The privilege has also been held to apply to the official communications of public officials. *See* Coleman v. Newark Morning Ledger Co., 149 A.2d 193 (N.J. 1959) (holding that newspaper article covering press conference of Sen. Joseph McCarthy privileged).

2. Public proceedings that are non-public. There is disagreement as to whether the privilege should apply to secret official proceedings. *See* Cianci v. New York Times Pub. Co., 639 F.2d 54, 67 (2d Cir. 1980) (stating that common law did not extend privilege to non-public judicial proceedings); Reeves v. American Broadcasting Companies, Inc., 719 F.2d 602, 607 (2d Cir. 1983) (noting that California law is broader and extends privilege to reports of secret proceedings).

3. Public records and documents. The privilege often also applies to official records or documents that are open to public inspection. Thus, a newspaper story that accurately recounts defamatory allegations in a police arrest report or some other type of law enforcement report should be subject to the privilege. Lavin v. New York News, Inc., 757 F.2d 1416 (3d Cir. 1985); Dinkel v. Lincoln Pub. (Ohio), Inc., 638 N.E.2d 611 (Ohio 1994). However, there is disagreement as to whether the privilege attaches to a report that accurately recounts the allegations contained in a complaint filed in court, but not yet acted upon the court. *See* Newell v. Field Enterprises, Inc., 415 N.E.2d 434, 443 (Ill. Ct. App. 1980) (describing split). What are the arguments for and against extending the privilege to such cases?

4. The effect of malice. Courts are split on the question of whether the existence of common law malice (in the sense of spite or ill will) or perhaps actual malice defeats the existence of the fair report privilege. Rodney A. Smolla, 2 Law of Defamation § 8:70.50 (2d ed.).

* * *

2. The Neutral Reporting Privilege

During a speech at a luncheon for a local private charitable organization, an official of the National Collegiate Athletic Association (NCAA), a private organization, made a statement accusing a nationally known college athletic coach of numerous violations of NCAA rules in the recruitment of players. The local newspaper in the town where the coach's college was located fairly and accurately reported the statements of the NCAA official. The story caused a huge outcry in town and generated wide discussion. No one in town (including the reporter who wrote the story) believed the accusations. The coach sued the newspaper for republishing the NCAA official's defamatory statements about him. The fair report privilege discussed above probably would not apply in this instance because the NCAA is not a government entity and the speech was given to a private entity; thus, there was no "official" proceeding. Should some type of qualified privilege nonetheless also apply?

In *Edwards v. National Audubon Society, Inc.*, 556 F.2d 113 (2d Cir. 1977), the Second Circuit Court of Appeals concluded that a qualified "neutral reporting" privilege should apply in such cases. According to the court, "when a responsible, prominent organization ... makes serious charges against a public figure, the First Amendment protects the accurate and disinterested reporting of those charges, regardless of the reporter's private views regarding their validity." Some courts have refused to recognize this privilege, arguing that the recognition of such a privilege is inconsistent with *New York Times v. Sullivan* and its progeny, which provide that liability exists when a defendant entertains serious doubts regarding the truth of the reported facts. *See* Dickey v. CBS, Inc., 583 F.2d 1221, 1225–1226 (3d Cir. 1978).

Courts that have recognized the existence of a neutral reporting privilege have sometimes differed in terms of defining the scope of the privilege. In which of the following situations, if any, should a court recognize the existence of a neutral reporting privilege?

(1) when the subject of the defamatory article is a public figure;

(2) when the source of the defamatory statement in the article is a public figure;

(3) when the source of the defamatory statement in the article is identified and is a responsible source; or

(4) when the defamatory statement in the article involves a matter of public concern, regardless of whether the subject or the source of the statement is a public figure.

* * *

3. Fair Comment

Vernon's Texas Statutes and Codes Annotated

§ 73.002

(a) The publication by a newspaper or other periodical of a matter covered by this section is privileged and is not a ground for a libel action. This privilege does not extend to the republication of a matter if it is proved that the matter was republished with actual malice after it had ceased to be of public concern.

(b) This section applies to:

...

(2) reasonable and fair comment on or criticism of an official act of a public official or other matter of public concern published for general information.

* * *

The common law has long recognized the fair comment privilege, and the privilege still exists in many jurisdictions. Under the rule, the publication of an honest opinion on a matter of public concern was conditionally privileged if it was based upon true statements of facts and was not rendered for the purpose of causing harm. Milkovich v. Lorain Journal Co., 497 U.S. 1, 13–14 (1990); Foley v. Press Pub. Co., 226 A.D. 535, 544 (N.Y.A.D. 1929). In some jurisdictions, a showing of actual malice may also defeat the privilege. Brasher v. Carr, 743 S.W.2d 674, 682 (Tex. Ct. App.-Hou. 1987); Dairy Stores, Inc. v. Sentinel Publ'g Co., 516 A.2d 220, 233 (N.J. 1986). Despite its pedigree, the fair comment privilege—like other areas of defamation law—has become a confusing area, due to state and Supreme Court developments. The *Restatement (Second) of Torts* did not include the fair report privilege in its restatement of existing qualified privileges. Instead, the *Restatement* included a similar rule, but one not limited to statements on matters of public concern, that provides that an opinion is not actionable unless "it implies the allegation of undisclosed defamatory facts as the basis for the opinion." Restatement (Second) of Torts § 566.

The *Restatement*'s omission of the fair comment privilege was premised on the assumption that the Supreme Court had concluded that statements of opinion were, as a matter of constitutional law, not actionable. Rodney A. Smolla, Law of Defamation § 6:7 (2d ed.) (citing Restatement (Second) of Torts § 566 cmt. c.). However, in *Milkovich* (discussed in Chapter 9), the Court disavowed any such bright-line rule and instead spoke at length about the ability of the fair comment privilege to protect commentary and criticism on matters of public concern. As a result, the fair comment privilege is still alive. However, when courts discuss the privilege, they often do so in somewhat confusing manner, combining (or ignoring) bits of constitutional and common law in their analysis of whether a defendant's comment on matters of public concern is privileged.

* * *

4. Retraction Statutes

Exercise 10.7

Gary posts a defamatory statement about Joan, a law school classmate, on a legal blog. Joan is angry and wants to sue Gary for defamation. She comes to you, her lawyer, for advice. What is your advice if Georgia law applies? Texas? California? What is the difference between the retraction statutes in these states?

Vernon's Texas Statutes and Codes Annotated

§ 73.003

(a) To determine the extent and source of actual damages and to mitigate exemplary damages, the defendant in a libel action may give evidence of the following matters if they have been specially pleaded:

(1) all material facts and circumstances surrounding the claim for damages and defenses to the claim;

(2) all facts and circumstances under which the libelous publication was made; and

(3) any public apology, correction, or retraction of the libelous matter made and published by the defendant.

(b) To mitigate exemplary damages, the defendant in a libel action may give evidence of the intention with which the libelous publication was made if the matter has been specially pleaded.

Code of Georgia

§ 51-5-11

(a) In any civil action for libel which charges the publication of an erroneous statement alleged to be libelous, it shall be relevant and competent evidence for either party to prove that the plaintiff requested retraction in writing at least seven days prior to the filing of the action or omitted to request retraction in this manner.

(b) In any such action, the defendant may allege and give proof of the following matters, as applicable:

(1)(A) That the matter alleged to have been published and to be libelous was published without malice;

(B) That the defendant, in a regular issue of the newspaper or other publication in question, within seven days after receiving written demand, or in the next regular issue of the newspaper or other publication following receipt of the demand if the next regular issue was not published within seven days after receiving the demand, corrected and retracted the allegedly libelous statement in as conspicuous and public a manner as that in which the alleged libelous statement was published; and

(C) That, if the plaintiff so requested, the retraction and correction were accompanied, in the same issue, by an editorial in which the allegedly libelous statement was specifically repudiated; or

(2) That no request for correction and retraction was made in writing by the plaintiff.

(c) Upon proof of the facts specified in paragraph (1) or (2) of subsection (b) of this Code section, the plaintiff shall not be entitled to any punitive damages and the defendant shall be liable only to pay actual damages. The defendant may plead the publication of the correction, retraction, or explanation, including the editorial, if demanded, in mitigation of damages.

California Civil Code

§ 48a

1. In any action for damages for the publication of a libel in a newspaper, or of a slander by radio broadcast, plaintiff shall recover no more than special damages [economic] unless a correction be demanded and be not published or broadcast, as hereinafter provided. Plaintiff shall serve upon the publisher, at the place of publication or broadcaster at the place of broadcast, a written notice specifying the statements claimed to be libelous and demanding that the same be corrected. Said notice and demand must be served within 20 days after knowledge of the publication or broadcast of the statements claimed to be libelous.

2. If a correction be demanded within said period and be not published or broadcast in substantially as conspicuous a manner in said newspaper or on said broadcasting station as were the statements claimed to be libelous, in a regular issue thereof published or broadcast within three weeks after such service, plaintiff, if he pleads and proves such notice, demand and failure to correct, and if his cause of action be maintained, may recover general [damage to reputation, emotional distress, etc.], special and exemplary damages; provided that no exemplary damages may be recovered unless the plaintiff shall prove that defendant made the publication or broadcast with actual malice and then only in the discretion of the court or jury, and actual malice shall not be inferred or presumed from the publication or broadcast.

* * *

Recall from Chapter 8 that the Communications Decency Act (CDA) provides immunity to online service providers. Section 230(c) of the CDA provides that "[n]o provider or user of an interactive computer service shall be treated as the publisher or speaker of any information provided by another information content provider." *Id.* § 230(c). *See, e.g.*, Zeran v. America Online, Inc., 129 F.3d 327 (4th Cir. 1997). This provision has been held to shield online service providers from liability for defamation and related torts where the law historically has provided for such liability. Thus, the blog owner in Exercise 10.7 might have immunity. But what about Gary?

Retraction statutes like those above exist in a majority of jurisdictions. The statutes vary considerably in terms of their structure. Nearly all were drafted before the advent of the Internet. Should these statutes apply to defamatory postings on the Internet? If so, should they apply to defamatory postings by private individuals? Why would a state enact such a statute in the first place?

* * *

Revisiting the Chapter Problem. Which of the defenses addressed in this chapter might have potential relevance in Griffey's case? How might some of the defenses in this chapter have less relevance in light of the Supreme Court's development of the constitutional rules covered in the previous chapter? Does defamation law really need to be this complicated?

Part 4

Economic and Dignitary Torts

Chapter 11

Fraudulent Misrepresentation

Exercise 11.1: Chapter Problem

Robin and Tom jointly represented Ben on a contingency fee basis in his personal injury action in state court in Indiana against Gas 'n Stuff Convenience Store. Ben had been referred to Robin by a mutual friend. At the time she agreed to represent Ben, Robin had just passed the bar and opened up her own law practice. Given her lack of experience, Robin decided to bring Tom in on the matter as co-counsel. Tom had several years of experience in personal injury matters. After several months of discovery, Gas 'n Stuff offered a "take-it-or-leave-it" offer of $10,000 to settle Ben's claims. Upon learning of the settlement offer, Tom emailed Robin and said they should advise Ben to take the $10,000 and run. Without consulting Tom, Robin advised Ben that Tom thought that Ben should settle the case, but that Robin disagreed. Robin told Ben that he had a great case and that if they went to trial, Ben would recover around $100,000. Ben told Robin that he wanted to roll the dice and go to trial. When Tom found out about what Robin had done, he got mad and withdrew. As you probably have already guessed, Robin took Ben's case to trial and recovered ... nothing. The jury found in favor of Gas 'n Stuff. Now, Ben and Tom are suing Robin.

Robin recently inquired about the willingness of our firm to defend her against these claims. Ben and Tom are both asserting, among other claims, fraudulent misrepresentation. Any legal malpractice claim that Ben might bring would be barred by the statute of limitations. What is the likelihood of success for Ben and Tom?

A. The Prima Facie Case

According to § 525 of the *Restatement (Second) of Torts*, a defendant "who fraudulently makes a misrepresentation of fact, opinion, intention or law for the purpose of inducing another to act or to refrain from action in reliance upon it, is subject to liability to the other in deceit for pecuniary loss caused to him by his justifiable reliance upon the misrepresentation." This sounds simple enough. In reality, many of the elements of a fraudulent misrepresentation (or "fraud" or "deceit") tend to blur together. For example, to be actionable, a misrepresentation must concern a material fact. Some courts speak of materiality as a separate element, whereas the *Restatement* subsumes the materiality concept within the concept of justifiable reliance. With that in mind, this section explores the core concepts associated with a claim of fraudulent misrepresentation.

1. Knowledge and Intent

Exercise 11.2

Alice, the owner of a financially distressed car dealership who is interested in unloading her unprofitable dealership, tells Bob that the state consumer protection agency will, in about a month from now, publicly announce that Alice's company had not engaged in any wrongdoing in connection with a highly publicized complaint of consumer fraud. Alice knows that Bob acts as an agent for several prominent business investors and that Bob has several meetings lined up that afternoon with some of his clients. (However, Alice has no idea which clients Bob is meeting with.) In fact, the consumer protection agency has not yet reached a decision in the matter. Alice does not know whether the agency has reached a decision or what that decision is; however, based on her conversations with the agency, she is optimistic that the agency will find in her favor. Bob relays Alice's statements to one of his clients, who promptly buys Alice's car dealership. When the consumer protection agency later finds against the car dealership, the buyer suffers pecuniary loss as a result. Assuming Alice made an otherwise actionable false statement, did she do so fraudulently? Did she do so with the requisite intent to support a fraudulent misrepresentation claim? Does it matter that she didn't make the statement to the client?

The hallmark of a fraudulent misrepresentation claim is that the representation was, in fact, fraudulently made. This is sometimes known as the scienter requirement. The defendant must know that the matter is not as he represents it to be. Some jurisdictions say the scienter requirement is satisfied if the defendant acts recklessly, i.e., with knowledge that he does not know. *See* Beeck v. Kapalis, 302 N.W.2d 90, 95 (Iowa 1981).

Closely related to this requirement is the requirement that the defendant act with the intent to deceive. A defendant is liable to the person or class of persons he intends to act or refrain from acting in reliance upon the misrepresentation. Restatement (Second) of Torts § 531. Note that the *Restatement* speaks of the defendant making the false statement for the *purpose* of inducing reliance on the part of the recipient. Some courts speak more generally of an intent to induce reliance, *Beeck*, 302 N.W.2d at 94. This could, in keeping with the definition of intent for purposes of other intentional torts, include the situation where the defendant does not necessarily desire to deceive the recipient but knows that recipient is substantially certain to be deceived.

* * *

2. Misrepresentation of Fact, Opinion, Intention, or Law

a. Misrepresentation of Fact

Schlaifer Nance & Co., Inc. v. Estate of Warhol

927 F. Supp. 650
(S.D.N.Y. 1996)

[Following the death of artist Andy Warhol, Warhol's estate and a licensing company (SNC) discussed a licensing program involving Warhol's photographs. Copyright and other issues eventually caused problems with the deal, and SNC sued on a fraud theory, alleging that "defendants fraudulently represented that the Estate controlled all the rights to all of Warhol's works, when defendants knew that many of Warhol's works had fallen into the public domain and that Warhol had also entered into agreements giving rights to others." SNC's claims were based on multiple alleged misrepresentations, two of which—made by Hayes—are discussed below.]

As a threshold matter, Hayes's two affirmative statements cannot support a fraud claim as a matter of law because they simply were not representations of fact. The statement "[n]o one is going to get away with using Andy Warhol for free" [made in response to SNC's expression of concern that people might produce "knock-offs" of Warhol's work] was a prediction or promise or statement of intent or puffery. *See, e.g.*, Cohen v. Koenig, 25 F.3d 1168, 1172 (2d Cir.1994) ("statements will not form the basis of a fraud claim when they are mere 'puffery' or are opinions as to future events"); Lathrop v. Rice & Adams Corp., 17 F.Supp. 622, 628 (W.D.N.Y.1936) (statement that party "intend[ed] to prosecute anyone who infringes upon his patent rights" is a statement of future intention and not a representation of fact); Zanani v. Savad, 217 A.D.2d 696, 630 N.Y.S.2d 89, 90 (2d Dep't 1995) ("In general, a representation of opinion or a prediction of something which is hoped or expected to occur in the future will not sustain an action for fraud."). Likewise, the statement "[i]t's a go" was not a representation of fact but simply a statement that the Estate was prepared to go forward with the transaction.

* * *

As *Schlaifer Nance & Company, Inc.* illustrates, it may sometimes be necessary to distinguish between, on the one hand, false statements of fact and, on the other, opinions, predictions as to future events, and statements of intention. Courts often say that statements falling into the latter category are generally not actionable or, alternatively, that a recipient is not justified in relying on such statements. Some of the special issues associated with opinions, predictions as to future events, and statements of intention (as well as statements of law) will be examined shortly. Assuming the other requirements of a deceit claim are satisfied, a false statement of fact is actionable.

Focus Questions: *Wright v. Pennamped*

1. *Should the court's reasoning regarding the issue of silence constituting a misrepresentation under the facts of this case be limited to cases involving attorneys?*
2. *What is the difference between a fraudulent misrepresentation claim and the "constructive fraud" theory the court identifies? In what other type of relationships might the constructive fraud theory be relevant?*

Wright v Pennamped

657 N.E.2d 1223
(Ind. App. 1995)

SHARPNACK, Chief Judge.

Donald H. Wright appeals the trial court's order of summary judgment in favor of the defendant-appellees, Bruce M. Pennamped and his law firm, Lowe Gray Steele & Hoffman ("the Appellees"). Wright is seeking damages arising from the Appellees' alleged deceptive and fraudulent conduct during a commercial loan transaction. Wright raises four issues for our review, which we consolidate and restate as whether the trial court erred in granting summary judgment. We affirm in part and reverse in part.

[Wright was a self-employed general contractor and real estate developer who was looking to refinance the apartment complex he owned, the Diplomat Apartments, in the amount of $500,000.00. On May 29, 1991, Ray Krebs, the vice president of mortgage banking at SCI Financial Corporation ("SCI"), submitted a proposal of financing to Wright. Wright accepted the proposal on June 3, 1991. The proposal contained a prepayment provision that Wright did not understand, but he anticipated that he would have his attorney, Richard L. Brown, explain any provisions he did not understand when Brown received the proposed loan documents prior to closing. After signing the proposal, Wright provided Brown's name, address, and telephone number to Krebs. Krebs then relayed this information to Pennamped. Pennamped, a partner in the law firm of Lowe Gray Steele & Hoffman, became involved in the loan transaction on July 2, 1991, when he had a luncheon meeting with Krebs. SCI retained Pennamped and the firm to represent its interests and to prepare the necessary loan documents. Pennamped drafted the loan documents on July 31, 1991, and forwarded copies marked "DRAFT DATED 7-31-91" to Krebs and Brown. The draft contained a prepayment provision.

On Friday, August 2, 1991, Brown reviewed the draft documents and discussed them with Wright. Brown and Wright discussed the prepayment provision as well as additional terms in the draft documents. Wright did not indicate to Brown that the prepayment provision in the draft note was any different than the one in the proposal for financing. Based on their discussion, both Wright and Brown accepted and approved the form and substance of the draft documents. In the meantime, Don Wilson, Senior Vice President of the funding bank, Kentland Bank, reviewed the draft and requested of Krebs that changes be made to the prepayment penalty provision. On August 5th, Pennamped and Wright's attorney, Brown, discussed the loan agreement. Pennamped never mentioned any changes to the document. Pennamped asked Brown if he had any problems with the proposed loan documents, and Brown responded that he did not. Brown informed Pennamped he had two cases set for the following morning and he would be unable to attend the closing set for 9:00 a.m the next day. Pennamped completed the changes to the loan documents that Wilson had requested on the afternoon of August 5, 1991. No one informed Brown or Wright about the changes, although Pennamped told Krebs that he should speak to Wright and explain the changes. Krebs said he would do so, but never did. Pennamped never made any further inquiry regarding the matter.

Because Brown was in court, Wright attended the closing alone. No one ever informed him about the changes to the agreement. Wright executed the documents. Wright learned of the new prepayment provision when he attempted to payoff the loan. Under the terms of the original agreement, Wright's prepayment penalty would have been $4,931.49. Under the terms as modified the prepayment penalty was $97,504.38.]

On July 18, 1993, Wright filed a complaint for damages against Kentland Bank, Krebs, SCI, Pennamped, and Lowe Gray Steele & Hoffman. Wright sought recovery from the defendants based on fraud [and] constructive fraud ...

... On March 4, 1994, the trial court issued its order granting the Appellees' motion for summary judgment. The trial court found that an essential element of each of Wright's non-contractual theories is the intent to deceive and that Wright failed to come forward with any evidence supporting an inference of fraud.... The trial held there was no just cause for delay and ordered the entry of final judgment in favor of the Appellees. Wright appeals this judgment.

II. Actual Fraud

The elements of actual fraud are: (1) the fraud feasor must have made at least one representation of past or existing fact; (2) which was false; (3) which the fraud feasor knew to be false or made with reckless disregard as to its truth or falsity; (4) upon which the plaintiff reasonably relied; (5) and which harmed the plaintiff. *Scott*, 571 N.E.2d at 319. An intent to deceive, or "scienter," is an element of actual fraud, whether classified as a knowing or reckless misrepresentation or as an additional element to a knowing or reckless misrepresentation.... Fraud may be proven by circumstantial evidence, provided there are facts from which the existence of all of the elements can be reasonably inferred....

Wright argues he has designated sufficient evidence to survive summary judgment on his actual fraud claim. Wright contends that we should reverse the granting of summary judgment because he has shown (1) that Pennamped made a representation of past or existing fact to Wright or Brown, (2) that Wright relied on representations by Pennamped, or (3) that Pennamped acted with actual knowledge of the falsity of any representations made or in reckless disregard of their falsity. We agree.

First, Wright claims Pennamped's failure to inform Brown of the changes in advance of the closing and Pennamped's presentation of the documents for Wright's signature, "while continuing to remain silent, constituted a representation by Pennamped that the documents so presented were in form and substance identical to the documents that had been submitted to Brown." ... Construing the facts in the light most favorable to Wright, we agree that Pennamped, by remaining silent and not informing Brown or Wright of the changes to the loan documents, impliedly represented that the final loan documents conformed to the draft loan documents which had been reviewed and approved by Brown. *See* Matter of Gerard (1994), Ind., 634 N.E.2d 51, 53 (implied in attorney's retention of excessive fee was the false representation that the services he provided roughly corresponded with the amount of compensation); *see also* Midwest Commerce Banking v. Elkhart City Centre (7th Cir.1993), 4 F.3d 521, 524 ("Omissions are actionable as implied representations when the circumstances are such that a failure to communicate a fact induces a belief in its opposite.").

The Appellees contend, however, that Pennamped's "silence" cannot be construed as a representation in the present case because Pennamped had no duty to speak. We disagree.

The Appellees are correct that silence will not support a claim for actionable fraud absent a duty to speak or to disclose facts.... In addition, the party alleging fraudulent concealment has the burden of demonstrating the existence of a duty to speak.... We conclude, however, that Wright has satisfied this requirement.

By undertaking the tasks of a drafting attorney, including the distribution of draft loan documents and the solicitation of review and approval of the documents, Pennamped assumed a duty to disclose any changes in the documents prior to execution to the other parties or their respective counsel. *See* Hughes v. Glaese (1994), 637 N.E.2d 822, 825 (duty to disclose material information arises where there is a fiduciary or confidential relationship between the parties). The existence of such as duty is supported by common sense and notions of fair dealing. Thus, Pennamped, as the drafting attorney, had a duty to inform Brown or, in his absence, Wright, of any changes occurring after Brown's review and approval of the loan documents. Were the rule otherwise, pre-closing review of loan documentation would become a futile act, and counsel would be required to scrutinize every term of each document at the moment of execution.

Wright's third contention is that Pennamped acted with actual knowledge of the falsity of any representations made or in reckless disregard of their falsity. Wright claims the trial court erred because the presence of fraudulent intent is a factual issue for the jury and the evidence supports a reasonable inference of intent to deceive when viewed in the light most favorable to Wright. We agree.

The determination of whether fraudulent intent is present is a question for the fact finder. "There is no precise formula for drawing the line as to when there are sufficient indicia to constitute a determination of fraud. The general rule is that when there is a concurrence of several 'badges of fraud'—'an inference of fraudulent intent *may* be warranted' (our emphasis). Arnold v. Dirrim (1979), Ind.App., 398 N.E.2d 442, 446. Because no one badge of fraud constitutes a per se showing of fraudulent intent the facts must be taken together to determine how many badges of fraud exist and if together they constitute a pattern of fraudulent intent. This determination is for the fact finder.

In the present case, the Appellees contend the trial court correctly determined the intent issue as a matter of law because the only reasonable inference to be drawn from the undisputed evidence is there was no fraudulent intent on the part of the Appellees. In issuing its ruling on the motion for summary judgment, the trial court held:

"Here, it is uncontroverted that attorney Pennamped, upon learning of his client's intention to make last minute changes in the loan documents, instructed his client to notify the Plaintiff immediately of such changes and stressed the importance of such notification. In the face of such uncontroverted evidence, it is incumbent upon the Plaintiff to come forward with some evidence supporting an inference of fraud. The Plaintiff has failed to do so."

Although we would agree that the evidence supports finding an absence of fraudulent intent, we do not agree that the evidence on this issue is uncontroverted. Viewing the evidence in the light most favorable to Wright, Pennamped first learned that changes would be made to the loan documents on Friday, August 2, 1991. Pennamped received the changes via facsimile during the morning hours of Monday, August 5, 1991, the day prior to closing. Although speaking with Brown by telephone on August 5th, and although aware that Brown would be unable to attend the closing, Pennamped did not tell Brown the documents had been or would be changed. Pennamped neither informed Wright that changes had been or would be made after Brown's review and approval nor made any attempt to confirm that Krebs had informed Wright of the changes.

Wright has designated evidence showing that Pennamped knew there were last minute changes made to the loan documents and that Pennamped failed to inform Wright and his counsel of these changes. This is evidence from which a jury might infer an intent to deceive on the part of Pennamped and the law firm. Although the designated evidence would also allow a jury to conclude that Pennamped and the law firm had no fraudulent intent, "[t]he mere improbability of recovery does not justify summary judgment and the procedure is not intended to be a summary trial." *Jones*, 547 N.E.2d at 891.

We conclude, therefore, that the trial court erred in granting summary judgment on Wright's claim for actual fraud.

III. Constructive Fraud

The elements of constructive fraud include:

1. a duty owing by the party to be charged to the complaining party due to their relationship,

2. violation of that duty by the making of deceptive material misrepresentations of past or existing facts or remaining silent when a duty to speak exists,

3. reliance thereon by the complaining party,

4. injury to the complaining party as a proximate result thereof, and

5. the gaining of an advantage by the party to be charged at the expense of the complaining party.

... Contrary to the trial court's ruling in the present case, intent to deceive is not an element of constructive fraud.... Instead, the law infers fraud from the relationship of the parties and the surrounding circumstances. The Appellees contend that the trial court nonetheless properly entered summary judgment in their favor on Wright's claim for constructive fraud because there is an absence of the type of relationship which may form a basis of a claim for constructive fraud. Furthermore, Appellees contend this relationship did not give rise to a legal duty to disclose....

As we have observed previously, however, "Defendants are mistaken in arguing that constructive fraud can only exist where there is a confidential or fiduciary relationship. In Indiana, the term constructive fraud encompasses several related theories. All of these theories are premised on the understanding that there are situations which might not amount to actual fraud, but which are so likely to result in injustice that the law will find a fraud despite the absence of fraudulent intent. Defendants are correct in asserting that a constructive fraud may be found where one party takes unconscionable advantage of his dominant position in a confidential or fiduciary relationship. This is not, however, the exclusive basis for the theory of constructive fraud. In Indiana constructive fraud also includes what other jurisdictions have termed 'legal fraud' or 'fraud in law.' This species of constructive fraud recognizes that certain conduct should be prohibited because it is inherently likely to create an injustice...." *Scott*, 571 N.E.2d at 323–24 (emphasis added). Thus, we find the Appellees' reliance upon *Hardy* and *Comfax* to be of no avail....

Considering the facts in the light most favorable to Wright and contrary to the Appellees' contentions on appeal, this case is amenable to the application of the doctrine of constructive fraud. The facts as alleged by Wright suggest a situation that is so likely to result in injustice that the law will find a fraud despite the absence of fraudulent intent. *See Scott*, 571 N.E.2d at 323–24. The material alteration of loan documents after the review and approval of those documents by opposing counsel and the presentation of the revised documents for execution with no indication that changes have been made is the sort of conduct which "should be prohibited because it is inherently likely to create an injustice...." *Id.* at 324.

In the alternative, Appellees contend this relationship did not give rise to a legal duty. Appellees claim that Pennamped did not owe Wright a duty to disclose the changes made to the loan documents. Furthermore, Appellees argue that even if Pennamped did have a duty, Pennamped satisfied this duty by delegating the performance to Krebs. We disagree.

A party to a contract has a duty to the other party to disclose changes. Peoples Trust & Savings Bank v. Humphrey, (1983), Ind.App., 451 N.E.2d 1104, 1112. The Appellees argue that although Pennamped altered the contract, he did not owe a duty to Wright because Pennamped was not a party to the contract.

Contrary to Appellees' contention, as discussed previously, we find that Pennamped had a duty to disclose. As the drafting attorney, Pennamped assumed a duty to inform Wright of any changes to the loan documents prior to their execution.... In opposing the motion for summary judgment, Wright submitted the affidavit of Richard L. Johnson, the senior partner in the law firm of Johnson Smith Densborn Wright & Heath. The significance of this affidavit was to establish the customs and practices of financing transactions. Johnson commenced the practice of law in 1972 and has concentrated his practice in the areas of banking law, real estate law, and commercial law. After setting forth his qualifications and extensive experience as lender's counsel and in drafting or preparing documents to be used in lending transactions, Johnson's affidavit states:

> "Based upon my experience as lender's counsel, I believe the following to be the customs and practices in the industry in relation to real estate and/or commercial financing transactions:
>
> (a) At any time changes or revisions are made to draft or proposed loan documents by the attorney charged with the responsibility of drafting such documents—no matter how trivial or seemingly insignificant such changes or revisions may be—it is expected and understood by all other attorneys involved in the transaction that the drafting attorney will take whatever steps are necessary and/or appropriate to fully disclose and identify all such document changes and revisions to other attorneys involved in the transaction.
>
> (b) Typically, when any changes or revisions are made to proposed or draft loan documents, the drafting attorney will circulate, in writing, a 'red-lined' copy or some other written materials which will highlight and/or more particularly identify and/or describe the changes and revisions that have been or are contemplated to be made.
>
> (c) At the very least, the drafting attorney is responsible to verbally disclose to all other attorneys involved in the transaction—prior to execution of final documents—any and all changes and revisions that the drafting attorney has made to previously-distributed draft documents.
>
> (d) Any changes or revisions to the substance or form of documents which have been previously circulated to the participating attorneys should be fully disclosed to such other attorneys.
>
> (e) The closing of the transaction should not occur until final revisions to the loan documents have been fully disclosed to and approved by all parties and their respective counsel."

Based on this relationship, Wright could expect that Pennamped would inform him of any changes in the loan documents. Therefore, Pennamped had a duty to disclose material information to Wright concerning the loan documents.

Furthermore, Appellees' argument is in contradiction with Rule 4.1(b) of the Rules of Professional Conduct which states, "[i]n the course of representing a client a lawyer shall not knowingly ... (b) fail to disclose that which is required by law to be revealed." Ind. Professional Conduct Rule 4.1(b). As previously stated, the drafting attorney assumes a duty to disclose any changes in the documents prior to execution to the other parties. *See id.*

Courts hold attorneys to a separate and more demanding standard than the attorneys' clients. *Fire Insurance Exchange*, 643 N.E.2d at 312. Pennamped may have assisted his client, Krebs, in the commission of constructive fraud by failing to disclose to Wright that Pennamped changed the loan documents. Since Pennamped knew the documents were altered, he had a duty to disclose.

Lastly, we address whether Pennamped delegated his duty to Krebs. Pennamped may have created an agency relationship where he was the principal and Krebs was his agent within this narrow scope of disclosing changes to Wright. Therefore, Pennamped may have discharged his duty by delegating it to Krebs. However, this raises a question of whether Pennamped actually instructed Krebs to inform Wright of the changes. The existence of an agency is a question of fact, therefore this issue should be decided by a trier of fact and not decided upon summary judgment. Bryan Mfg. Co. v. Harris (1984), Ind.App. 459 N.E.2d 1199, 1204.

We conclude, therefore, that the trial court erred in granting summary judgment on Wright's claim for constructive fraud.

To sum up, while we affirm the trial court's entry of summary judgment for the defendant on the theory of quasi-contract, we reverse summary judgment on the theories of actual and constructive fraud. The case is remanded to the trial court for further proceedings consistent with this opinion.

* * *

1. Special relationships imposing a duty to speak. Generally, the failure to disclose a fact does not amount to misrepresentation of fact absent some duty to speak. Bradford v. Vento, 48 S.W.3d 749, 755 (Tex. 2001). One situation in which such a duty may exist is where a confidential or fiduciary relationship exists between the parties. "In the absence of a formal fiduciary relationship, a confidential relationship may arise when the parties have dealt with each other in such a manner, for a long period of time, that one party is justified in expecting the other to act on its behalf." Greenberg Traurig of New York, P.C. v. Moody, 161 S.W.3d 56, 78 n.20 (Tex. Ct. App-Houston Div. 2004).

2. Customs of the trade imposing a duty to speak. Section § 551(e) of the *Restatement (Second) of Torts* explains that sometimes the "customs of the trade or other objective circumstances" may create a situation in which disclosure of a fact that is basic to the transaction is required.

3. Fiduciary's silence in the face of client fraud. If a client makes a false statement during a negotiation, does the failure of the client's attorney to later correct the false statement amount to an affirmative misrepresentation of the part of the attorney? *See* Schalifer Nance & Co. v. Estate of Warhol, 927 F. Supp. 650, 661 (S.D.N.Y. 1996) (dismissing fraud claims against attorney based on attorney's failure to volunteer information and failure to correct client's false statement because attorney owed no fiduciary duty to other side).

4. Active concealment. A defendant who conceals or otherwise intentionally prevents a party from learning information is subject to liability as if the defendant had affirmatively made a false statement of fact. Restatement (Second) of Torts § 550. Does *Pennamped* fall into this category of cases?

5. Model Rule comparison. Rule 4.1(a) of the ABA's *Model Rules of Professional Conduct* prohibits a lawyer from, in the course of representing a client, knowingly making a false statement of material fact or law to a third person. Note that there is no requirement that the third person justifiably rely on the false statement; all that is required before discipline is the making of the false statement.

* * *

b. Misrepresentation of Opinion

As a general rule, a misrepresentation of opinion is not actionable. This may just be a more direct way of saying that a party is generally not justified in relying on a statement of opinion. A party may be justified in relying on a false statement of fact. But generally, a party is not justified in basing his or her course of action on someone's opinion. Sometimes it may be difficult to distinguish between a statement of fact and a statement of opinion. But even where it is possible to do so, there may be times when a statement—although technically in the form of an opinion—should be treated as a statement of fact for purposes of a misrepresentation claim.

Focus Questions: *Presidio Enterprises, Inc. v. Warner Bros.*

1. *What qualifies as a statement of fact?*
2. *What qualifies as a statement of opinion?*
3. *What is the relationship between statements of opinion and the requirement in a misrepresentation case that a plaintiff establish that he or she justifiably relied on the defendant's statement?*
4. *What kinds of statements would qualify under the "special knowledge" exception the court identifies?*

Presidio Enterprises, Inc. v. Warner Bros. Distributing Corp.

784 F.2d 674
(5th Cir. 1986)

GOLDBERG, Circuit Judge:

The distinctly unsettling thought of angry "killer bees" terrorizing an unsuspecting Texas town lies at the heart of this case. Appellant Warner Bros. thought it could turn this idea into a "chilling, riveting, harrowing, cinematic experience," and spent $10 million trying to do so. Appellee Presidio Enterprises was apparently similarly affected, for it agreed to pay Warner $65,000 for the right to show the film, sight unseen, at two of its theatres in Austin, Texas. To make a long story short, the film was a flop. Stung by this turn of events, Presidio flew enraged into federal court, where it somehow managed to persuade a judge and jury that it had been tricked into purchasing a defective product and could collect damages under Texas consumer protection law. Through the vagaries of statutory provisions, Presidio was able to turn its damages of $56,000 into a judgment of more than $500,000. We reverse.

I. FACTUAL AND PROCEDURAL BACKGROUND

Plaintiffs-appellees Presidio Enterprises et al. ("Presidio") are experienced film exhibitors who own and successfully operate five movie theatres (with a total of 18 screens); their operations in Austin, Texas, date back to 1973. Defendant-appellant Warner Bros. Distributing Corporation ("Warner") is a major motion picture distributor; it licenses exhibitors to show films under copyright.

In late 1977 Warner was completing filming of a movie entitled *The Swarm*, which concerned an invasion of Texas by "killer bees" from South America. *The Swarm* was based on a best-selling novel by Arthur Herzog and was directed by Irwin Allen, who had an Oscar award to his credit and had recently produced two enormously successful "disaster" films, The Poseidon Adventure and The Towering Inferno. The cast of *The Swarm* included such well known stars as Michael Caine, Richard Chamberlain, Olivia de Havilland, Patty Duke Astin, Henry Fonda, Ben Johnson, Slim Pickens, Katharine Ross, and Richard Widmark. The production budget for *The Swarm* was about $10,000,000.

The Swarm was scheduled for release in July, 1978. As is the practice with such productions, Warner began advertising the film to potential exhibitors far in advance of the release date. In August, 1977, Warner sent Presidio and other exhibitors a brochure that read as follows:

> August 22, 1977
>
> Dear Mr. Exhibitor:
>
> "THE SWARM" IS COMING!
>
> Today, shooting started at Warner Bros. on your blockbuster for the summer of '78.
>
> "THE SWARM" IS COMING!
>
> From the man who brought you the stunning successes of "THE POSEIDON ADVENTURE" and "THE TOWERING INFERNO" now comes what we hope to be the greatest adventure-survival movie of all time.
>
> "THE SWARM" IS COMING!
>
> After more than two years of preparation, that master showman, Irwin Allen, combines terror, suspense and startling performances in an eleven million dollar spectacular intended for audiences of all ages.
>
> "THE SWARM" IS COMING!
>
> Starring Michael Caine, Katharine Ross, Richard Widmark, Olivia de Havilland, Ben Johnson, Lee Grant, Patty Duke Astin, Slim Pickens, Bradford Dillman, and Henry Fonda as Dr. Krim, this will be the most "want-to-see" movie of the year.
>
> "THE SWARM" IS COMING AND AVAILABLE July 14, 1978!
>
> Sincerely,
>
> /s/Terry Semel

Warner also ran similar advertisements in the trade press at this time. See Plaintiff's Exhibit 1.

In December, 1977, Warner sent Presidio and other exhibitors a second brochure, which read as follows:

> December 1, 1977
>
> Dear Exhibitor:
>
> "THE SWARM" IS COMING!
>
> Today, shooting was completed on your summer of '78 blockbuster.
>
> "THE SWARM" IS COMING!
>
> From Irwin Allen, the man who brought you astronomical grosses with "The Poseidon Adventure" and "The Towering Inferno" now comes one of the greatest adventure-survival movies of all time.
>
> "THE SWARM" IS COMING!
>
> And with it one of the greatest casts ever assembled for a motion picture; Michael Caine, Katharine Ross, Richard Widmark, Olivia de Havilland, Henry Fonda, Fred MacMurray, Richard Chamberlain, Jose Ferrer, Patty Duke Astin, Lee Grant, Bradford Dillman, Ben Johnson, and Slim Pickens.
>
> "THE SWARM" IS COMING!
>
> It is a chilling, riveting, harrowing, cinematic experience.
>
> *It promises to be Irwin Allen's biggest and best to date.*
>
> ...

On or about December 16, 1977, Warner sent a letter to Presidio and other exhibitors soliciting bids for *The Swarm*....

In effect, Presidio was being invited to bid for the exhibition rights to the film sight unseen. This practice, known as "blind bidding," is relatively common in the film industry. It apparently makes economic sense for both distributors and exhibitors to reserve theatres and films far in advance of the important Christmas and summer viewing seasons. Distributors want to be sure their films are solidly booked before they set in motion their expensive advertising campaigns (in this case, Warner spent over $4,000,000 advertising *The Swarm*), and exhibitors want to be sure they have promising films to show during periods of peak attendance. At any rate, *The Swarm* was blind bid, and Presidio knew that it was being invited to bid on a film that would not be complete or available for viewing until months later.

... Warner accepted Presidio's bids on January 30, 1978, and returned signed and completed copies of its standard form contracts to Presidio.

The Swarm opened as scheduled on July 14, 1978. It was not a big success. The film ran for only five weeks at one of Presidio's theatres, and four weeks at the other. Presidio calculated that, after subtracting the guarantees and operating expenses from box office revenues, it had sustained a loss of $56,056.69.

Instead of accepting this result as an unsuccessful business venture, Presidio brought suit against Warner in federal district court, alleging common law fraud and negligent misrepresentation. Presidio also charged that Warner had violated the Texas Deceptive Trade Practices-Consumer Protection Act ("DTPA") ... The district court entered judgment in Presidio's favor with an award of $521,483.23, which included trebled damages, attorney's fees, prejudgment interest, and costs. Warner appeals from this judgment, and Presidio has filed a cross-appeal limited to the district court's refusal to treble prejudgment interest.

II. EXPRESSIONS OF OPINION

The first obstacle in Presidio's path is the rule that expressions of opinion are not actionable.... [A]ctions for fraud or misrepresentation must be based on objective statements of fact, not expressions of personal opinion....

A statement of fact is one that (1) admits of being adjudged true or false in a way that (2) admits of empirical verification. The statements complained of by Presidio fail on both counts.

We turn first to the brochure of August 22, 1977. Here Warner announces that "'THE SWARM' IS COMING!" and that "Today, shooting started at Warner Bros." on the film, assertions that Presidio does not dispute. It is probably also indisputable that Warner "hope[d]" *The Swarm* would be "the greatest adventure-survival movie of all time." But then Mr. Semel goes on to term the film "your blockbuster for the summer of '78," and states that "this will be the most 'want-to-see' movie of the year." These assertions are disputable, but they are not statements of fact for two reasons: (1) they turn on vague, essentially indefinable terms; (2) they are predictions.

If we interpret Mr. Semel's phrase "your blockbuster for the summer of '78" as implying a statement of the form, "This film will be a blockbuster in the summer of '78," we encounter the problem of vagueness with the term "blockbuster." What does it mean? According to *Webster's New World Dictionary of the American Language* (College ed. 1966), a blockbuster is "a large bomb that is dropped from an airplane and can demolish an entire city block." *Id.* at 157. *Webster's Seventh New Collegiate Dictionary* (1965) elaborates that the term can be used of "something or someone notably effective or violent," *id.* at 91, and the *American Heritage Dictionary of the English Language* (1976) adds that it may refer to "Anything of devastating effect," *id.* at 142. We would be hard pressed to deny that *The Swarm* might qualify as a "blockbuster" under one or more of these definitions. Even Charles Chick, president of Presidio, seems unsure as to the meaning of the term; on direct examination he testified as follows: "By 'blockbuster,' I guess they mean it's going to do good box office business, be an important box office picture." A party complaining about the fraudulent and misleading use of language should, at the very least, know what he is complaining about. The term "blockbuster" is inherently vague; it can mean just about whatever Terry Semel wants it to, and that is probably why he used it.

Even if we interpret Mr. Semel's assertion in the way Presidio prefers, we still encounter the problem that it is a prediction, not a statement of fact. Assuming, arguendo, that Mr. Semel is saying something to the effect that "*The Swarm* will be far more profitable than your average summer of '78 film"—would that be a statement of fact? Does it admit of being adjudged true or false? Can it be empirically verified? We answer "no" on all counts.

A prediction, or statement about the future, is essentially an expression of opinion. When the weatherman says "It will rain tomorrow," he comes closest to making a verifiable statement of fact by correcting himself and rephrasing as follows: "I think (or: it is my opinion) that it will rain tomorrow." Another possible rephrasing is: "The readings on my instruments are now the way they usually are when rain is coming." (The first statement is a factual report on the weatherman's state of mind; the second is a factual report on the state of his instruments. Both can be empirically verified.) The weatherman does not know whether it will in fact rain tomorrow. No one does. Thus no one knows whether the statement is true or false; perhaps it would be better to say that it is neither true nor false. A statement about the future can be verified only in the future; but then, of course, it is no longer a statement about the future as such. When tomorrow finally comes, and it is indeed raining, one no longer says "It will rain tomorrow" but rather "It is now raining." That statement can be empirically verified as true or disconfirmed as false.

Complaining that a film turned out to be a flop six months after binding, "non-cancellable" bids on it were accepted is like suing the weatherman because rain spoiled a picnic when he predicted fair skies. When Terry Semel says "this will be the most 'want-to-see' movie of the year," he is, quite literally, speaking in the grand tradition of those who do not know what they are talking about, unless we understand him to be giving a report on the present state of his mind (e.g., "I think (or: it is my opinion) that this will be the most 'want-to-see' movie of the year"), or on the state of predictive information at his disposal (e.g., "I have reliable surveys on hand, and they indicate that folks will be swarming on to my movie next summer"). Under the first interpretation, the assertion is an explicit expression of personal opinion that is not actionable at law; the second interpretation goes far beyond any plausible reading of the brochure.

Our analysis of the December, 1977, brochure and bid letter is similar. The film is still a "blockbuster," but now it is also a "giant spectacular," "one of the greatest adventure-survival movies of all time," and a "chilling, riveting, harrowing, cinematic experience" that "promises to be Irwin Allen's biggest and best to date." We have difficulty discerning a single verifiable, factual claim in this excited welter of salesmen's hoopla. Presidio is perhaps on strongest ground in questioning whether *The Swarm* could possibly "promise" to be Irwin Allen's "biggest and best" in December, 1977, but even if Mr. Semel had made the stronger claim that "It is Irwin Allen's biggest and best to date," the law provides no guidance for the assessment of this claim. "Biggest" in what sense? ... "Best" for whom or for what purpose? If aesthetic evaluation were our task, we certainly could not simply assume that the "best" films were those that generated the highest box-office revenues; indeed, the converse relationship seems more likely. Fortunately, aesthetic evaluation is not our task, so we can note without discomfiture that the same film could find its way into a *New York Times* listing of the 10 Best Movies of the Year as well as a book on The Fifty Worst Movies of All Time.[15] Here, as elsewhere in the realm of opinion, one man's meat is another man's poison.

III. SPECIAL KNOWLEDGE, AND "PUFFERY"

Presidio's main argument on appeal seems to be that, even if the statements it complains of are expressions of opinion, a "special knowledge" exception to the opinion rule makes them actionable. Relying heavily on *Trenholm v. Ratcliff*, Presidio asserts that under Texas law

> statements that would otherwise be deemed mere opinions will be treated as facts, actionable as fraud, when the parties do not have equal information regarding the subject matter of the representations. Trenholm v. Ratcliff, 646 S.W.2d 927 (Tex.1983). The underlying rationale is that, lacking access to information in order to form an independent judgment, the purchaser has a right to expect the truth and to rely on the "opinions."

15. *See* Appellant's Brief at 26. The film was *Last Year at Marienbad*.

Appellees' Brief at 24–25 (footnote omitted). We have serious reservations about this argument because: (1) Warner's representations are salesmen's "puffery," which reasonable people do not take seriously; (2) Presidio's executives were experienced, professional film exhibitors who could not reasonably have relied on Warner's puffery; (3) the record amply supports Warner's contentions that its alleged "special knowledge," in the form of marketing surveys and sneak previews, was useful solely for purposes of improving the as yet incomplete film and planning advertising strategies for it; and, (4) in any event, the jury found, by special interrogatories, that Warner's failure to disclose whatever special knowledge it had was not a proximate or producing cause of Presidio's damages.

Presidio cites the *Restatement (Second) of Torts* §§ 539, 542 (1977),* in support of its "special knowledge" argument. But Presidio inadvertently neglects to call our attention to several highly relevant comments to the *Restatement* sections it cites. These comments indicate that the "special knowledge" exception is inapplicable where the opinion relied on is clearly salesmen's puffery. In explaining section 539, "Representation of Opinion Implying Justifying Facts," the *Restatement* comment elaborates:

> The habit of vendors to exaggerate the advantages of the bargain that they are offering to make is a well recognized fact. An intending purchaser may not be justified in relying upon his vendor's statement of the value, quality or other advantages of a thing that he is intending to sell as carrying with it any assurance that the thing is such as to justify a reasonable man in praising it so highly.

§ 539, Comment on Subsection (2). Similarly, the *Restatement* amplifies its discussion of "Opinion of Adverse Party" in section 542 with the following qualifying comment:

> [T]he purchaser of an ordinary commodity is not justified in relying upon the vendor's opinion of its quality or worth. For example, one who is purchasing a horse from a dealer is not justified in relying upon the dealer's opinion, although the latter has a greater experience in judging the effect of the factors which determine its value.
>
> e. *This is true particularly of loose general statements made by sellers in commending their wares, which are commonly known as "puffing," or "sales talk."* It is common knowledge and may always be assumed that any seller will express a favorable opinion concerning what he has to sell; and when he praises it in general terms, without specific content or reference to facts, buyers are expected to and do understand that they are not entitled to rely literally upon the words. "Such statements, like the claims of campaign managers before election, are rather

---

* [Editor's note. Section 539 provides

(1) A statement of opinion as to facts not disclosed and not otherwise known to the recipient may, if it is reasonable to do so, be interpreted by him as an implied statement

(a) that the facts known to the maker are not incompatible with his opinion; or

(b) that he knows facts sufficient to justify him in forming it.

(2) In determining whether a statement of opinion may reasonably be so interpreted, the recipient's belief as to whether the maker has an adverse interest is important.

Section 542 provides

The recipient of a fraudulent misrepresentation solely of the maker's opinion is not justified in relying upon it in a transaction with the maker, unless the fact to which the opinion relates is material, and the maker

(a) purports to have special knowledge of the matter that the recipient does not have, or

(b) stands in a fiduciary or other similar relation of trust and confidence to the recipient, or

(c) has successfully endeavored to secure the confidence of the recipient, or

(d) has some other special reason to expect that the recipient will rely on his opinion.

> designed to allay the suspicion which would attend their absence than to be understood as having any relation to objective truth." [Learned Hand, C.J., in *Vulcan Metals v. Simmons Mfg. Co.*, (2 Cir.1918) 248 Fed. 853, 856.]
>
> Thus no action lies against a dealer who describes the automobile he is selling as a "dandy," a "bearcat," a "good little car," and a "sweet job," or as "the pride of our line," or "the best in the American market."

§ 542, Comments d–e (emphasis added). The "special knowledge" exception applies typically to the opinions of specialized experts—such as jewelers, lawyers, physicians, scientists, and dealers in antiques—where their opinions are based on concrete, specific information and objective, verifiable facts. *See Restatement* § 542, comment f.

Presidio's claim that its experienced executives were hoodwinked by Warner's extravagant puffery has a distinctly hollow ring to it. The claim is facially implausible in light of the fact that Warner, all puffing aside, suggested only a relatively modest guarantee for the film; Presidio responded with what its own executives testified was only "a good medium-range bid." ...

Another Presidio executive testified that *The Swarm*'s promotional material did not even reach "the high water mark for puffery."[21] It was no doubt for reasons of this sort that Presidio did not rely solely on Warner's representations concerning *The Swarm* but instead got the opinion of a paid consultant in Hollywood, whose advice was: "Don't go out on it." And, in fact, Presidio did not "go out on it."

Our contemporary jurisprudence is in the process of eroding a number of common law asseverations, but *caveat emptor* has not yet been entirely replaced in our vocabulary by *caveat venditor*. The motion picture industry is entitled to the same license of hyperbole, exaggeration, bombasticism, and flamboyance that the makers of toothpaste and other commodities enjoy in advertising their products. The law recognizes that a vendor is allowed some latitude in claiming merits for his wares by way of an opinion rather than an absolute guarantee, so long as he hews to the line of rectitude in matters of fact. Opinions are not only the lifestyle of democracy, they are the brag in advertising that has made for the wide dissemination of products that otherwise would never have reached the households of our citizens. If we were to accept the thesis set forth by appellees, the advertising industry would have to be liquidated in short order.

[The court also concluded that the statements at issue were not actionable under the Texas Deceptive Trade Practices Act.]

V. CONCLUSION

The nub of Presidio's case is its charge of misrepresentation. Presidio must show that (1) Warner misrepresented its film; and (2) that Warner's misrepresentations were the cause of Presidio's injury. We conclude on the basis of the foregoing analysis that Warner's representations concerning its film *The Swarm* are not actionable as a matter of law.

* * *

1. Statements of opinion. The *Restatement* explains that a statement concerning an individual's judgment "as to quality, value, authenticity, or other matters of judgment" is an opinion. Similarly a statement that expresses the maker's belief, without certainty, as

---

21. Presidio was apparently so accustomed to dealing with film promoters' hyperbole that it even had a special stamp made up with which it could imprint the word "bullshit" on the more flagrantly offending documents....

to the existence of a fact ("I think the oven is five years old") is an opinion. *Restatement (Second) of Torts* § 538A.

2. Model Rule comparison. Comment 2 to Rule 4.1 of the ABA's Model Rules of Professional Conduct explains that "[u]nder generally accepted conventions in negotiation," some statements are not considered statements of fact for purposes of the disciplinary rule against the making of false statements. These include "[e]stimates of price or value placed on the subject of a transaction and a party's intentions as to an acceptable settlement of a claim." How does this compare to the *Restatement*'s definition?

* * *

c. Misrepresentation of Intention

Exercise 11.3

Alice enters into a contract with Bob to sell a painting. Alice had no intention of performing her end of the bargain when she entered into the agreement and entered into the contract primarily for the purpose of generating publicity for her artwork. When the time comes to sell the painting, Alice refuses to do so. Bob obviously might have a claim for breach of contract, but, based on the material so far in this chapter, does he also have a claim for fraudulent misrepresentation?

d. Misrepresentation of Law

Exercise 11.4

In the course of an argument over pension benefits, Employer tells Employee that there is a federal statute that requires that an employee consent to mandatory arbitration of any dispute over pension benefits in lieu of bringing a lawsuit. There is no such statute, but Employee relies on Employer's statement to her detriment. Based on the material so far in this chapter, is Employer's statement actionable?

3. Justifiable Reliance

The next element in a fraudulent misrepresentation claim is the justifiable reliance element. First, a plaintiff must actually rely on the false statement. In other words, the plaintiff must be deceived. This concept is sometimes referred to as "reliance in fact." In addition, the plaintiff's reliance must be justified. The *Restatement* says that for reliance to be justified, the false statement must be material. Ordinarily, a statement is "material" only where a reasonable person would attach importance to in making a decision. Restatement (Second) of Torts § 538. If, however, the defendant knows of a particular eccentricity on the part of the plaintiff that makes it likely that the plaintiff will attach importance to the statement, even though a reasonable person would not. *Id.*

In addition, the plaintiff's reliance must be "justified" in the sense that the plaintiff had a "right" to rely on the statement. The following case examines this issue.

Focus Questions: *Fire Insurance Exchange v. Bell*

1. *What effect does a plaintiff's failure to investigate a defendant's false statement of fact have on the question of justifiable reliance when the misrepresentation is fraudulent in nature?*
2. *For purposes of the justifiable reliance element, what is the significance of the fact that the defendant who fraudulently made the false statement of fact was in a position adverse to the plaintiff?*

Fire Insurance Exchange v. Bell

643 N.E.2d 310
(Ind. 1994)

DICKSON, Justice.

The principal issue in this case is whether, and to what extent, a party who is represented by counsel has the right to rely on a representation by opposing counsel during settlement negotiations. In this interlocutory appeal, the defendant-appellants, Fire Insurance Exchange, Illinois Farmers Insurance Company, and Farmers Group, Inc., d/b/a Farmers Underwriters Association (Farmers); the law firm of Ice Miller Donadio & Ryan (Ice Miller); and Phillip R. Scaletta (Scaletta), a partner in Ice Miller, are appealing the trial court's denial of their motions for summary judgment.

The factual allegations favoring the plaintiff as non-moving party are as follows. On May 28, 1985, sixteen-month-old Jason Bell was severely burned in a fire at the Indianapolis home of Joseph Moore (Moore), Jason's grandfather. Gasoline had leaked onto the floor of Moore's utility room and was ignited by a water heater. The fire department cited Moore for the careless storage of gasoline. The carrier for Moore's homeowner's policy was Farmer's, whose claims manager was Dennis Shank (Shank) and whose attorney was Scaletta. Jason's mother, Ruby Bell (Bell), retained attorney Robert Collins to represent Jason regarding his claims for injuries sustained in the fire. Collins communicated with Scaletta and Shank on many occasions in an effort to obtain information regarding the insurance policy limits. By October, 1985, Farmers informed Scaletta that Moore's policy limits were $300,000. In February, 1986, Scaletta told Collins that he did not know the policy limits, even though Farmers had already provided Scaletta with this information. Collins claimed that Scaletta and Shank told him on separate occasions that Moore had a $100,000 policy limit. Scaletta confirmed his misrepresentation to Collins in a letter he wrote to Shank on February 14, 1986. When Jason's condition stabilized, Shank and Scaletta each represented to Collins that Farmers would pay the $100,000 policy limit. As a result of these conversations, Collins advised Bell to settle. The agreement was approved by the probate court, and after settling with Farmers, Bell filed a products liability action against the manufacturer of Moore's water heater. Through negotiations with the water heater company, Collins learned that Moore's homeowner's policy limits were actually $300,000. Collins informed Bell that he had been deceived and advised her to seek independent counsel to assert claims against Farmers and Ice Miller. Bell filed a complaint against the appellants, alleging among other claims the fraudulent misrepresentation of the insurance policy limits.

Ice Miller and Scaletta each contend that they were entitled to summary judgment because of the absence of the right to rely, a component of the reliance element required to prove fraud. They contend that Bell's attorney had, as a matter of law, no right to rely on the alleged misrepresentations because he was a trained professional involved in adversarial settlement negotiation and had access to the relevant facts. With respect to the claims of Farmers, we agree with the analysis of the Court of Appeals ... and its conclusion that whether Collins had the right to rely upon the alleged misrepresentations by Farmers is a question of fact for the jury to decide....

With respect to the alleged misrepresentations of Scaletta and Ice Miller, ... we grant transfer to recognize a separate and more demanding standard. This Court has a particular constitutional responsibility with respect to the supervision of the practice of law. Ind. Const. art. VII, § 4. The reliability and trustworthiness of attorney representations constitute an important component of the efficient administration of justice. A lawyer's representations have long been accorded a particular expectation of honesty and trustworthiness.

Commitment to these values begins with the oath taken by every Indiana lawyer; it is formally embodied in rules of professional conduct, the violation of which may result in the imposition of severe sanctions; and it is repeatedly emphasized and reinforced by professional associations and organizations. The Indiana Oath of Attorneys includes the promise that a lawyer will employ "such means only as are consistent with truth." Ind.Admission and Discipline Rule 22. Indiana Professional Responsibility Rule 8.4 declares that it is professional misconduct for a lawyer to "engage in conduct involving dishonesty, fraud, deceit or misrepresentation." Numerous other sources of guidelines and standards for lawyer conduct emphasize this basic principle. The Preamble of the Standards for Professional Conduct within the Seventh Federal Judicial Circuit begins with the following statement:

> A lawyer's conduct should be characterized at all times by personal courtesy and professional integrity in the fullest sense of those terms. In fulfilling our duty to represent a client vigorously as lawyers, we will be mindful of our obligations to the administration of justice, which is a truth-seeking process designed to resolve human and societal problems in a rational, peaceful, and efficient manner.

143 F.R.D. 441, 448 (1992). The Seventh Circuit standards expressly include the following duty of lawyers to other counsel: "We will adhere to all express promises and to agreements with other counsel, whether oral or in writing...." *Id.* at 449. Similarly, the Tenets of Professional Courtesy adopted by the Indianapolis Bar Association declare, "A lawyer should never knowingly deceive another lawyer or the court," and "A lawyer should honor promises or commitments to other lawyers and to the court, and should always act pursuant to the maxim, 'My word is my bond.'" Tenets of Professional Courtesy, Indianapolis Bar Association (1989). The International Association of Defense Counsel likewise emphasizes that "[w]e will honor all promises or commitments, whether oral or in writing, and strive to build a reputation for dignity, honesty and integrity." *See, e.g.*, 60 Def.Coun.J. 190 (1993).

Ice Miller and Scaletta contend that the plaintiff's attorney "had no right to rely on the representations he claims because he had the means to ascertain relevant facts, was in an adverse position, was educated, sophisticated and not involved in any dominant-subordinate relationship." Brief of Appellants Ice Miller Donadio & Ryan and Scaletta in Support of Petition to Transfer at 18–19. They further argue "that the relationship was adverse, the negotiations were protracted and that both sides were at all times represented by counsel," *id.* at 19, and emphasize that policy limits information was available to Bell's attorney from a variety of sources, including the rules of discovery.

We decline to require attorneys to burden unnecessarily the courts and litigation process with discovery to verify the truthfulness of material representations made by opposing counsel. The reliability of lawyers' representations is an integral component of the fair and efficient administration of justice. The law should promote lawyers' care in making statements that are accurate and trustworthy and should foster the reliance upon such statements by others.

We therefore reject the assertion of Ice Miller and Scaletta that Bell's attorney was, as a matter of law, not entitled to rely upon their representations. However, rather than finding this to be an issue of fact for determination at trial, as did our Court of Appeals, we hold that Bell's attorney's right to rely upon any material misrepresentations that may have been made by opposing counsel is established as a matter of law. The resolution of the questions of what representations were actually made and the extent of reliance thereon are, along with any other remaining elements of plaintiff's case, issues of fact which must be determined at trial.

Transfer is granted. The opinion of the Court of Appeals is vacated in part and summarily affirmed in part. The trial court's denial of the motions for summary judgment filed by the defendant-appellants is affirmed. This cause is remanded for further proceedings consistent with this opinion.

* * *

1. **Adversarial relationships, statements of fact, and justified reliance.** The court in *Fire Insurance Exchange* focused heavily on the special role that lawyers play in the administration of justice. Would the result in the case have been different if the false statements of fact had come from a non-lawyer and were relied upon by a non-lawyer? *See* Restatement (Second) of Torts § 541A.

2. **Adversarial relationships, statements of opinion, and justified reliance.** The *Fire Insurance Exchange* case involved a misrepresentation of fact by an adversarial party. As discussed earlier, a plaintiff is generally not justified in relying on a statement of opinion or a prediction of future events. When, if ever, might an individual be justified in relying on a statement of opinion?

3. **Defining justified reliance.** In cases of fraudulent misrepresentation, the inquiry into whether a plaintiff's reliance was justified is a subjective one. As stated by one court, the question is "whether the complaining party, in view of *his own* information and intelligence, has a right to rely on the representations." Lockard v. Carson, 287 N.W.2d 871, 878 (Iowa 1980) (emphasis added). Assume that a defendant makes a misrepresentation of fact that no reasonable person would rely on, but the plaintiff, an extremely gullible individual with a low I.Q., is deceived by the misrepresentation. Was the plaintiff's reliance was justified?

Exercise 11.5

In *Schlaifer Nance & Co. v. Estate of Warhol*, discussed *supra*, Hughes, the executor of Warhol's estate, affirmatively told the plaintiffs that the estate controlled all of the rights to Warhol's works. This was untrue. When the plaintiffs sued, they alleged that they had justifiably relied on this misrepresentation of fact when entering into an agreement with the estate. Based on the following facts, did SNC justifiably rely on Hughes' statement? Would any of the facts, standing alone, have prevented SNC from justifiably relying on Hughes' statement?

– Hughes told SNC in December 1985 that "Warhol owns copyrights on most of his images";

– SNC reviewed a book prior to execution of the agreement that showed that some copyrights were held by third parties and suggested that many of Warhol's works did not have copyright notices on them;

– Because of the volume of works created by Warhol and the fact he was a commercial artist who sold his works in such a way as to exploit them, SNC's lawyers suspected, prior to execution of the Agreement, that Warhol might have transferred the copyright to some of his works;

– The Estate specifically asked, prior to execution of the Agreement, if it could provide the information on limitations on copyright ownership on a "best efforts basis" after execution of the Agreement upon request from SNC.

---

4. Reliance and securities fraud. Defrauded investors have sometimes brought securities fraud actions under Section 10(b) of the 1934 Securities and Exchange Act and SEC Rule 10b-5 against the attorneys for securities issuers based upon the attorneys' actions in preparing fraudulent documents that were relied upon by investors. The general rule that has emerged in these cases is that a secondary actor (such as a lawyer, accountant, or other individual not employed by the issuer) is not liable for fraud for the false statements contained in any filings unless the statements were attributable to the secondary actor. "Absent attribution," courts have reasoned, "plaintiffs cannot show that they relied upon" the secondary actor's own false statements. Stoneridge Inv. Partners, LLC v. Scientific-Atlanta, Inc., 552 U.S. 148, 148 (2008) Pacific Investment Management Co. v. Mayer Brown, LLP, 603 F.3d 144, 148 (2d Cir. 2010). At most, the secondary actor's actions amount to aiding and abetting, a topic covered in Chapter 17.

* * *

4. Causation and Damages

To be actionable, a misrepresentation must induce justifiable reliance on the part of the plaintiff. And this reliance must ultimately lead to pecuniary harm before recovery is permitted. In other words, there must be detrimental reliance on the misrepresentation. To be actionable, the misrepresentation must be a cause in fact (judged by either a "but-for" or "substantial factor" test) of the plaintiff's pecuniary loss, as well as a proximate cause of the loss. To constitute a proximate cause of the plaintiff's pecuniary loss, the loss must reasonably be expected to result from the plaintiff's reliance. Restatement (Second) of Torts § 548A.

One question looming throughout this chapter is why a plaintiff would choose to sue in tort in the case of a misrepresentation. Contract law already permits the victim of a fraudulent misrepresentation to avoid performance of a contract and to recover what he or she has paid. Restatement (Second) of Contracts § 376. Moreover, the victim is not necessarily required to establish that the misrepresentation was fraudulent in order to avoid performance. *Id.* § 164. Why then would a plaintiff choose the potentially more difficult tort route? The answer, not surprisingly, relates to damages.

In the case of a fraudulent misrepresentation, a plaintiff is entitled to receive

(a) the difference between the value of what he has received in the transaction and its purchase price or other value given for it; and

(b) pecuniary loss suffered otherwise as a consequence of the recipient's reliance upon the misrepresentation.

Id. § 549(1). Thus, the plaintiff is able to recover any out-of-pocket losses. If this type of recovery is inadequate, a plaintiff has the option of obtaining the benefit of the bargain with the defendant. *Id.* § 549(2). This measure of damages places the victim in the position he or she would have been in if the misrepresentation had been true.

The decisional law splits on the issue of whether a plaintiff alleging fraudulent misrepresentation is entitled to collect emotional distress damages. *See* Bates v. Allied Mut. Ins. Co., 467 N.W.2d 255, 260 (Iowa 1991) (no); Crowley v. Global Realty, Inc., 474 A.2d 1056, 1058 (N.H. 1984) (yes). The general rule, however, appears to be that emotional distress damages are not recoverable in the absence of some other tort. DAN B. DOBBS, DOBBS LAW OF REMEDIES DAMAGES § 9.2(4) (2d. ed. 1993). Punitive damages, however, are frequently awarded in the case of fraud. *Id.*

Exercise 11.6

Alice tells Bob that the vintage car she is selling contains all original parts. Bob buys the car for $12,000. The car does not contain all original parts, but is still worth $12,000. If the car had contained all original parts, it would have been worth $20,000. How much can Bob recover?

Exercise 11.7

Memo to Associate
Re: Ben v. Robin and Tom v. Robin (see Exercise 11.1)

Please prepare a memo that addresses the following issues:

(1) What factual research do we need to do in order defend Robin?

(2) Based on what we know so far, what is the likely outcome of Ben's fraudulent misrepresentation claim? Tom's fraudulent misrepresentation claim?

B. Defenses

1. The Litigation Privilege

As discussed in Chapter 10, an absolute privilege applies to defamatory statements made in the course of and pursuant to a judicial proceeding. Some courts have extended the privilege to claims of fraudulent misrepresentation. *See* Steiner v. Eikerling, 181 Cal. App.3d 639, 643 (Cal. Ct. App. 1986); Paul T. Hayden, *Reconsidering the Litigator's Absolute Privilege to Defame*, 54 OHIO ST. L.J. 985, 998 (1993). To the extent the misrepresentation occurs during the course of a judicial proceeding and the opposing party is not deceived by the misrepresentation, this result is largely consistent with the general rule that there is no civil claim for perjury. *See* Cooper v. Parker-Hughey, 894 P.2d 1096, 1100–01 (Okla. 1995) (stating the general rule). But the privilege can theoretically apply to misrepresentations occurring preliminary to a proposed judicial proceeding. Thus, the privilege potentially has a longer reach than the rule regarding perjury. Other courts have declined to extent the privilege to fraudulent conduct occurring during discovery or at trial. Robinson v. Volkswagnwerk AG, 940 F.2d 1369 (10th Cir. 1991); Thompson v. Paul, 657 F. Supp. 2d 1113, 1122–23 (D. Ariz. 2009).

Exercise 11.8

Robert and Donna were divorced ten years ago, and Robert was ordered to pay alimony. Two years ago, Donna filed a motion to modify the alimony payments. In motions to the court and in several proceedings attended by Robert's lawyers, Donna's lawyers represented that she was in grave economic circumstances. In so doing, Donna's lawyers concealed from the court and Robert's lawyers the fact that Donna had recently become the beneficiary of $500,000. Eventually, the truth came out, but not before Robert incurred substantial legal fees in defending against Donna's motion. Robert has now sued Donna's lawyers on a fraudulent misrepresentation theory. In response, Donna's lawyers have argued that they are immune from liability by virtue of the litigation privilege.

You are the trial judge in the case. There is no mandatory authority on point. Assuming Robert can establish the elements of a fraudulent misrepresentation claim, will you extend the privilege to Donna's lawyers?

---

2. The Economic Loss Rule

Although technically not a defense, the economic loss rule may potentially have some application in the case of a fraudulent misrepresentation claim. Stated generally, the economic loss rule, where recognized, precludes recovery in tort for merely economic losses. *See* Vincent R. Johnson, *The Boundary-Line Function of the Economic Loss Rule*, 66 Wash. & Lee L. Rev. 523, 525 (2009). The rule was originally developed in the products liability area in cases in which plaintiffs sought recovery in tort when a product was defective but did not produce any separate physical injury or damage to property other than the product itself. R. Joseph Barton, Note, *Drowning in a Sea of Contract: Application of the Economic Loss Rule to Fraud and Negligent Misrepresentation Cases*, 41 Wm. & Mary L. Rev. 1789, 1794–95 (2000). One of the more common rationales used to support the rule is that contract law already provides a remedy and thus permitting a plaintiff to choose a tort remedy would undermine contract law.

Some jurisdictions have applied the economic loss rule outside the products liability area to other kinds of tort claims. Fraudulent misrepresentation claims represent a common exception to the economic loss rule where the rule is recognized, at least where there is fraud in the inducement of the contract. However, a few courts have applied the rule to bar fraudulent misrepresentation claims resulting only in pecuniary harm. Barton, *supra*, at 1803. Critics have complained that contract law, which does not permit recovery for punitive damages, may fail to adequately deter fraud or even allow the victims of fraud to recover the costs of pursuing litigation. Jean Braucher, *Deception, Economic Loss and Mass-Market Customers: Consumer Protection Statutes as Persuasive Authority in the Common Law of Fraud*, 48 Ariz. L. Rev. 829, 845–46 (2006). The economic loss rule is discussed in greater detail in the next chapter.

Chapter 12

Negligent Misrepresentation

Exercise 12.1: Chapter Problem

The Smiths entered into a contract to purchase a house owned by the Kinneys. Foster & Bench Realty acted as the agent for the Kinneys. The purchase agreement signed by the parties contained the following clause:

> Seller agrees to furnish purchaser with a letter from a reliable termite company that the premises are free from termite damages and/or infestation at time of settlement.

Foster & Bench arranged for Perez Pest Control to conduct the termite inspection and gave Perez a copy of the purchase agreement containing the termite clause as a way of instructing Perez about the scope of the investigation. Perez conducted the inspection and found no evidence of current infestation, but did find evidence of prior infestation and damage.

When Perez conducts an investigation, it usually sends a report to the party requesting the inspection. The report contains three pages: (1) a cover page that briefly summarizes what the inspection covered and that contains a sentence stating that the document could not be used by or transferred to other persons without Perez's written consent; (2) a standardized page containing an itemized list of inspection details (infestation on the front of the house, infestation on the east side, etc.) along with a box for each entry that the inspector would check if applicable; and (3) a narrative summary of the inspection. For some reason, when Perez sent the inspection letter to Foster & Bench, it failed to attach the narrative summary. Instead, for the second page, it accidentally attached the itemized list of inspection details for a different inspection of a different house (the Stinson's house). For the third page, it attached the itemized list of the inspection of the Kinneys' house. The second page (the standardized page involving the Stinson inspection) contained an entry noting that there was evidence of prior termite infestation but that there was no damage and that the problem had been ameliorated. The page did not contain any checks or any other indication that there was current termite damage to the house. However, the third page (the standardized page involving the Kinney inspection) indicated that there was extensive termite damage in several parts of the house. When Foster & Bench received the three-page document, the realtor mistakenly assumed that the third page was just a duplicate of the second page and had been attached accidentally. Therefore, she threw it away without showing it to the Smiths.

Before the Smiths could review the inspection report, the deal with the Kinneys fell apart for other reasons. Fortunately, the Kinneys were able to enter into a new deal the next day to sell the house to the Marrs. The new purchase agreement contained the same language regarding the termite inspection, and since an inspection had already been performed, the parties agreed to rely on the previous inspection. Prior to closing, Mrs. Marr noticed what she believed to be termite tracks in an area of the house. The Foster & Bench agent who was showing the house (and who had seen the Perez inspection letter) said, "Not to worry. We've had the inspection done and everything checked out just fine. Your purchase agreement covers everything." The agent showed the Marrs the inspection report, and, believing there to be no current damage, the Marrs proceeded with the sale.

The Marrs have now sued Perez Pest Control and Foster & Bench on separate negligent misrepresentation claims in state court in Texas.

(1) You represent Perez Pest Control. Assess your client's potential liability.

(2) You represent Foster & Bench. Assess your client's potential liability.

If a plaintiff is unable to establish that the defendant made a misrepresentation in a fraudulent manner, a negligent misrepresentation might be another possibility. There are downsides to pursuing such a theory, however. Punitive damages are generally more difficult to recover when a defendant has merely acted in a negligent manner. Indeed, damages are generally of a more limited nature under a negligent misrepresentation theory than under a fraudulent misrepresentation theory. In addition, under a negligent misrepresentation theory the scope of liability is generally more narrow than it is under a fraudulent misrepresentation theory.

A. Determining the Scope of Liability

A physician negligently provides a faulty diagnosis of a patient's condition. The physician negligently tells the patient that she has Condition X and that it is safe for her to drive home, when in fact she has Condition Y and is a danger to herself and anyone else who happens to be on the road. The patient then leaves the physician's office and, as a result of her medical condition, crashes her car into Plaintiff, a pedestrian. Plaintiff suffers physical injuries. The physician has engaged in a form of negligent misrepresentation, and many courts would permit Plaintiff's negligence claim to reach a jury. *See, e.g.*, Freese v Lemmon, 210 N.W.2d 576 (Iowa 1973). After all, the physician negligently misrepresented a fact and Plaintiff's resulting physical injuries were foreseeable.

When a defendant's negligent misrepresentation of fact results only in pecuniary loss, however, courts tend to be far more circumspect in their willingness to permit recovery. In some instances, this reluctance is manifested in the application of the economic loss rule discussed at the end of the last chapter. Numerous courts have not applied the economic loss rule in misrepresentation cases or have held that negligent misrepresentation claims are an exception to the economic loss rule. A few, however, have applied the rule to claims of negligent misrepresentation. R. Joseph Barton, Note, *Drowning in a Sea of Contract: Application of the Economic Loss Rule to Fraud and Negligent Misrepresentation Cases*, 41 Wm. & Mary L. Rev. 1789, 1822 (2000).

Courts have almost uniformly held that a negligent misrepresentation claim will not lie where a party or the party's lawyer negligently makes a misrepresentation to the opposing party. Restatement (Third) of the Law Governing Lawyers § 51 cmt. c (2000). Where a party's lawyer is the defendant, courts have held as a matter of law that a lawyer owes no duty to the other side. Courts have reasoned that if a lawyer were to owe a duty of care to an adverse party, this might cause the lawyer to shirk the lawyer's duty to his or her own client, resulting in a conflict of interest and diminished loyalty. Garcia v. Rodey, Dickason, Sloan, Akin & Robb, 750 P.2d 118, 122 (N.M. 1988).

Tort law has also been reluctant to permit recover where a commercial transaction results in only economic harm to a third party. For many years, plaintiffs injured by defective products could not recover from the manufacturers of those products unless there was privity of contract with the manufacturer. Eventually, courts discarded the privity requirement in products liability cases resulting in personal injury, but the privity concept continued to loom large in cases in which the negligence of one party to an agreement resulted in pecuniary loss to a stranger to that agreement. In 1879, for example, the Supreme Court held that the absence of privity barred the claim of a bank that suffered pecuniary loss after loaning money to the lawyer's client based on the lawyer's faulty assertion that the client held clear title to a piece of property. National Savings Bank of District of Columbia v. Ward, 100 U.S. 195 (1879). While stating that the absence of privity would not bar a claim of *fraudulent* misrepresentation, "inasmuch as the defendant was never retained or employed by the plaintiffs, and never rendered any service at their request or in their, behalf, he cannot be held liable to them for any negligence or want of reasonable care, skill, or diligence in giving to a third party the certificates in question." *Id.* at 200.

The cases that follow in this section all involve fact patterns similar to that in *National Savings Bank*. Each involves a third party who relies to his or her detriment on information negligently supplied by a defendant. Note the various approaches courts have taken in attempting to deal with this recurring fact pattern.

1. The Privity Test

Focus Questions: *Ultramares Corp. v. Touche*

1. *What are the justifications for establishing a separate rule for negligent misrepresentation claims as opposed to other kinds of negligence claims?*
2. *Are the court's justifications persuasive?*

Ultramares Corp. v. Touche

174 N.E. 441
(N.Y. 1931)

CARDOZO, C. J.

The action is in tort for damages suffered through the misrepresentations of accountants, the first cause of action being for misrepresentations that were merely negligent, and the second for misrepresentations charged to have been fraudulent.

In January, 1924, the defendants, a firm of public accountants, were employed by Fred Stern & Co., Inc., to prepare and certify a balance sheet exhibiting the condition of its business as of December 31, 1923. They had been employed at the end of each of the three years preceding to render a like service. Fred Stern & Co., Inc., which was in substance Stern himself, was engaged in the importation and sale of rubber. To finance its operations, it required extensive credit and borrowed large sums of money from banks and other lenders. All this was known to the defendants. The defendants knew also that in the usual course of business the balance sheet when certified would be exhibited by the Stern Company to banks, creditors, stockholders, purchasers, or sellers, according to the needs of the occasion, as the basis of financial dealings. Accordingly, when the balance sheet was made up, the defendants supplied the Stern Company with thirty-two copies certified with serial numbers as counterpart originals. Nothing was said as to the persons to whom these counterparts would be shown or the extent or number of the transactions in which they would be used. In particular there was no mention of the plaintiff, a corporation doing business chiefly as a factor, which till then had never made advances to the Stern Company, though it had sold merchandise in small amounts. The range of the transactions in which a certificate of audit might be expected to play a part was as indefinite and wide as the possibilities of the business that was mirrored in the summary.

By February 26, 1924, the audit was finished and the balance sheet made up. It stated assets in the sum of $2,550,671.88 and liabilities other than capital and surplus in the sum of $1,479,956.62, thus showing a net worth of $1,070,715.26. Attached to the balance sheet was a certificate as follows:

> We have examined the accounts of Fred Stern & Co., Inc., for the year ending December 31, 1923, and hereby certify that the annexed balance sheet is in accordance therewith and with the information and explanations given us. We further certify that, subject to provision for federal taxes on income, the said statement, in our opinion, presents a true and correct view of the financial condition of Fred Stern & Co., Inc., as at December 31, 1923.

Capital and surplus were intact if the balance sheet was accurate. In reality both had been wiped out, and the corporation was insolvent. The books had been falsified by those in charge of the business so as to set forth accounts receivable and other assets which turned out to be fictitious. The plaintiff maintains that the certificate of audit was erroneous in both its branches. The first branch, the asserted correspondence between the accounts and the balance sheet, is one purporting to be made as of the knowledge of the auditors. The second branch, which certifies to a belief that the condition reflected in the balance sheet presents a true and correct picture of the resources of the business, is stated as a matter of opinion. In the view of the plaintiff, both branches of the certificate are either fraudulent or negligent. As to one class of assets, the item of accounts receivable, if not also as to others, there was no real correspondence, we are told, between balance sheet and books, or so the triers of the facts might find. If correspondence, however, be assumed, a closer examination of supporting invoices and records, or a fuller inquiry directed to the persons appearing on the books as creditors or debtors, would have exhibited the truth.

The plaintiff, a corporation engaged in business as a factor, was approached by Stern in March, 1924, with a request for loans of money to finance the sales of rubber. Up to that time the dealings between the two houses were on a cash basis and trifling in amount. As a condition of any loans the plaintiff insisted that it receive a balance sheet certified by public accountants, and in response to that demand it was given one of the certificates signed by the defendants and then in Stern's possession. On the faith of that certificate the plaintiff made a loan which was followed by many others. The course of business was for Stern to deliver to the plaintiff documents described as trust receipts which in effect were executory assignments of the moneys payable by purchasers for goods thereafter to be sold. When the purchase price was due, the plaintiff received the payment, reimbursing itself therefrom for its advances and commissions. Some of these transactions were effected without loss. Nearly a year later, in December, 1924, the house of cards collapsed. In that month, plaintiff made three loans to the Stern Company, one of $100,000, a second of $25,000, and a third of $40,000. For some of these loans no security was received. For some of the earlier loans the security was inadequate. On January 2, 1925, the Stern Company was declared a bankrupt.

This action, brought against the accountants in November, 1926, to recover the loss suffered by the plaintiff in reliance upon the audit, was in its inception one for negligence. On the trial there was added a second cause of action asserting fraud also. The trial judge dismissed the second cause of action without submitting it to the jury. As to the first cause of action, he reserved his decision on the defendants' motion to dismiss, and took the jury's verdict. They were told that the defendants might be held liable if with knowledge that the results of the audit would be communicated to creditors they did the work negligently, and that negligence was the omission to use reasonable and ordinary care. The verdict was in favor of the plaintiff for $187,576.32. On the coming in of the verdict, the judge granted the reserved motion. The Appellate Division (229 App. Div. 581, 243 N. Y. S. 179) affirmed the dismissal of the cause of action for fraud, but reversed the dismissal of the cause of action for negligence, and reinstated the verdict. The case is here on cross-appeals.

The two causes of action will be considered in succession, first the one for negligence and second that for fraud.

1. We think the evidence supports a finding that the audit was negligently made, though in so saying we put aside for the moment the question whether negligence, even if it existed, was a wrong to the plaintiff. [The court then explained how the audit was conducted.]

If the defendants owed a duty to the plaintiff to act with the same care that would have been due under a contract of employment, a jury was at liberty to find a verdict of negligence upon a showing of a scrutiny so imperfect and perfunctory. No doubt the extent to which inquiry must be pressed beyond appearances is a question of judgment, as to which opinions will often differ. No doubt the wisdom that is born after the event will engender suspicion and distrust when old acquaintance and good repute may have silenced doubt at the beginning. All this is to be weighed by a jury in applying its standard of behavior, the state of mind, and conduct of the reasonable man. Even so, the adverse verdict, when rendered, imports an alignment of the weights in their proper places in the balance and a reckoning thereafter. The reckoning was not wrong upon the evidence before us, if duty be assumed.

We are brought to the question of duty, its origin and measure.

The defendants owed to their employer a duty imposed by law to make their certificate without fraud, and a duty growing out of contract to make it with the care and caution proper to their calling. Fraud includes the pretense of knowledge when knowledge there is none. To creditors and investors to whom the employer exhibited the certificate, the defendants owed a like duty to make it without fraud, since there was notice in the circumstances of its making that the employer did not intend to keep it to himself. A different question develops when we ask whether they owed a duty to these to make it without negligence. If liability for negligence exists, a thoughtless slip or blunder, the failure to detect a theft or forgery beneath the cover of deceptive entries, may expose accountants to a liability in an indeterminate amount for an indeterminate time to an indeterminate class. The hazards of a business conducted on these terms are so extreme as to enkindle doubt whether a flaw may not exist in the implication of a duty that exposes to these consequences....

The assault upon the citadel of privity is proceeding in these days apace. How far the inroads shall extend is now a favorite subject of juridical discussion. In the field of the law of contract there has been a gradual widening of the doctrine of *Lawrence v. Fox*, 20 N. Y. 268, until today the beneficiary of a promise, clearly designated as such, is seldom left without a remedy. Seaver v. Ransom, 224 N. Y. 233, 238, 120 N. E. 639, 2 A. L. R. 1187. Even in that field, however, the remedy is narrower where the beneficiaries of the promise are indeterminate or general. Something more must then appear than an intention that the promise shall redound to the benefit of the public or to that of a class of indefinite extension. The promise must be such as to 'bespeak the assumption of a duty to make reparation directly to the individual members of the public if the benefit is lost.' Moch Co. v. Rensselaer Water Co., 247 N. Y. 160, 164, 159 N. E. 896, 897, 62 A. L. R. 1199; American Law Institute, *Restatement of the Law of Contracts*, § 145. In the field of the law of torts a manufacturer who is negligent in the manufacture of a chattel in circumstances pointing to an unreasonable risk of serious bodily harm to those using it thereafter may be liable for negligence though privity is lacking between manufacturer and user. MacPherson v. Buick Motor Co., 217 N. Y. 382, 111 N.E. 1050; American Law Institute, *Restatement of the Law of Torts*, § 262. A force or instrument of harm having been launched with potentialities of danger manifest to the eye of prudence, the one who launches it is under a duty to keep it within bounds. Moch Co. v. Rensselaer Water Co., *supra*, at page 168 of 247 N. Y., 159 N. E. 896, 898. Even so, the question is still open whether the potentialities of danger that will charge with liability are confined to harm to the person, or include injury to property. In either view, however, what is released or set in motion is a physical force. We are now asked to say that a like liability attaches to the circulation of a thought or a release of the explosive power resident in words.

[N]othing in our previous decisions commits us to a holding of liability for negligence in the circumstances of the case at hand, and that such liability, if recognized, will be an extension of the principle of those decisions to different conditions, even if more or less analogous. The question then is whether such an extension shall be made.

The extension, if made, will so expand the field of liability for negligent speech as to make it nearly, if not quite, coterminous with that of liability for fraud....

We have said that the duty to refrain from negligent representation would become coincident or nearly so with the duty to refrain from fraud if this action could be maintained. A representation, even though knowingly false, does not constitute ground for an action of deceit unless made with the intent to be communicated to the persons or class of persons who act upon it to their prejudice. Affirmance of this judgment would require us to hold that all or nearly all the persons so situated would suffer an impairment of an interest legally protected if the representation had been negligent. We speak of all 'or nearly all,' for cases can be imagined where a casual response, made in circumstances insufficient to indicate that care should be expected, would permit recovery for fraud if willfully deceitful. Cases of fraud between persons so circumstanced are, however, too infrequent and exceptional to make the radii greatly different if the fields of liability for negligence and deceit be figured as concentric circles. The like may be said of the possibility that the negligence of the injured party, contributing to the result, may avail to overcome the one remedy, though unavailing to defeat the other.

Liability for negligence if adjudged in this case will extend to many callings other than an auditor's. Lawyers who certify their opinion as to the validity of municipal or corporate bonds, with knowledge that the opinion will be brought to the notice of the public, will become liable to the investors, if they have overlooked a statute or a decision, to the same extent as if the controversy were one between client and adviser. Title companies insuring titles to a tract of land, with knowledge that at an approaching auction the fact that they have insured will be stated to the bidders, will become liable to purchasers who may wish the benefit of a policy without payment of a premium. These illustrations may seem to be extreme, but they go little, if any, farther than we are invited to go now. Negligence, moreover, will have one standard when viewed in relation to the employer, and another and at times a stricter standard when viewed in relation to the public. Explanations that might seem plausible, omissions that might be reasonable, if the duty is confined to the employer, conducting a business that presumably at least is not a fraud upon his creditors, might wear another aspect if an independent duty to be suspicious even of one's principal is owing to investors. 'Every one making a promise having the quality of a contract will be under a duty to the promisee by virtue of the promise, but under another duty, apart from contract, to an indefinite number of potential beneficiaries when performance has begun. The assumption of one relation will mean the involuntary assumption of a series of new relations, inescapably hooked together' Moch Co. v. Rensselaer Water Co., *supra,* at page 168 of 247 N. Y., 159 N. E. 896, 899. 'The law does not spread its protection so far' Robins Dry Dock & Repair Co. v. Flint, *supra,* at page 309 of 275 U. S., 48 S. Ct. 134, 135.

Our holding does not emancipate accountants from the consequences of fraud. It does not relieve them if their audit has been so negligent as to justify a finding that they had no genuine belief in its adequacy, for this again is fraud. It does no more than say that, if less than this is proved, if there has been neither reckless misstatement nor insincere profession of an opinion, but only honest blunder, the ensuing liability for negligence is one that is bounded by the contract, and is to be enforced between the parties by whom the contract has been made. We doubt whether the average business man receiving a certificate without paying for it, and receiving it merely as one among a multitude of possible investors, would look for anything more.

[The court concluded there was sufficient evidence to permit a jury to find in favor of the plaintiffs on the fraudulent misrepresentation claim.]

* * *

1. Subsequent developments in New York. *Ultramares* was an influential decision. A few courts continue to follow it. Citizen's Nat'l Bank of Wisner v. Kennedy and Coe, 441 N.W.2d 180 (Neb. 1989). The basic gist of *Ultramares* remains good law in New York, *Sykes v. RFD Third Ave. 1 Associates, LLC,* 938 N.E.2d 325, 326 (N.Y. 2010), although it has been expanded to include relationships that "sufficiently approach[] privity." Credit Alliance Corp. v. Arthur Anderson & Co., 483 N.E.2d 110 (N.Y. 1985). In the context of an accounting firm that provided inaccurate financial information, the New York Court of Appeals in *Credit Alliance Corp.* held that

> [b]efore accountants may be held liable in negligence to noncontractual parties who rely to their detriment on inaccurate financial reports, certain prerequisites must be satisfied: (1) the accountants must have been aware that the financial reports were to be used for a particular purpose or purposes; (2) in the furtherance of which a known party or parties was intended to rely; and (3) there must have been some conduct on the part of the accountants linking them to that party or parties, which evinces the accountants' understanding of that party or parties' reliance.

Id. at 118. A few other jurisdictions have adopted this newer "near privity" rule from New York. *See, e.g.,* Colonial Bank v. Ridley & Schweigert, 551 So.2d 390 (Ala. 1989).

2. Professional malpractice as an alternative theory? Why didn't the plaintiff simply bring a professional malpractice claim against the defendant-accountants?

* * *

2. The Section 552 Test

Focus Questions: *McCamish, Martin, Brown & Loeffler v. F.E. Appling Interests*

1. *How does the* McCamish *court respond to the policy concerns regarding the scope of liability for negligent misrepresentation raised in* Ultramares?
2. *How does the test the* McCamish *court ultimately adopts differ from New York's "near privity" rule?*
3. *Does the test the court adopts conflict with a lawyer's duty of diligent representation owed to a client?*

McCamish, Martin, Brown & Loeffler v. F.E. Appling Interests

991 S.W.2d 787
(Tex. 1999)

Justice HANKINSON delivered the opinion of the Court.

In this case, we determine whether McCamish, Martin, Brown & Loeffler, a law firm representing Victoria Savings Association (VSA), may be liable to F.E. Appling Interests, a general partnership, and Boca Chica Development Company, a joint venture partnership managed by Appling, both nonclients, for the tort of negligent misrepresentation, as defined by the *Restatement (Second) of Torts* § 552 (1977). At trial, McCamish, Martin moved for summary judgment on Appling's negligent misrepresentation claim on the sole ground that, absent privity, McCamish, Martin owed no duty to Appling. The trial court rendered a take-nothing summary judgment in favor of McCamish, Martin based on the lack of privity between the parties. The court of appeals reversed and remanded for a trial on the merits, holding that a negligent misrepresentation claim is not the equivalent of a legal malpractice claim and is not barred by the privity rule. We affirm the judgment of the court of appeals.

Appling, a general partnership comprising four family trusts, was the managing partner of Boca Chica, a joint venture formed to develop recreational property. According to Appling's affidavit, Boca Chica obtained a loan and line of credit from VSA in 1985 to finance a real estate project. Boca Chica accepted the loan based on VSA's oral representation that VSA would later expand the line of credit, provided that Boca Chica's lot sales justified completing the development. However, in 1987, VSA decided not to extend the additional credit, despite the continued viability of the project. In 1988, Boca Chica went bankrupt and brought a lender liability claim against VSA for $15 million in damages.

With trial set for March 13, 1989, Boca Chica feared that the Federal Savings & Loan Insurance Corporation would declare VSA insolvent and take it over before a judgment could be obtained. If VSA were placed in receivership, Boca Chica's claim, based on the breach of an oral promise, would be unenforceable against VSA. Boca Chica was, therefore, anxious to settle. Boca Chica and VSA entered into settlement negotiations in early March 1989. They reached an agreement, which called for Boca Chica to deed the development to VSA in exchange for forgiveness of the outstanding debt that Boca Chica owed to VSA. Once the parties agreed on these terms, Appling wanted to ensure that the settlement agreement would be enforceable against the FSLIC.

[In order to be enforceable, the agreement had to comply with a federal statute, 12 U.S.C. § 1823(e)(1).]

Appling distrusted VSA's representations that the agreement met the requirements of section 1823(e). Consequently, Appling agreed to sign the agreement only if VSA's lawyers would affirm that the agreement did, in fact, comply with the statute. The parties and their attorneys signed a settlement agreement, dated March 8 and 9, 1989, in which the requested representations were made:

> [B]oth Victoria and its counsel represent to Plaintiffs that (a) this agreement is in writing; (b) it is being executed by both Victoria and Plaintiffs contemporaneously with the acquisition of these assets by Victoria; (c) that the Agreement has been approved by the Board of Directors of Victoria Savings Association and that such approval is reflected in the minutes of said board (a copy of which shall be attached to this Agreement); and (d) that a copy of this Agreement shall be from the time of its execution continuously maintained as an official record of Victoria; all in accordance with 12 USC § 1823(e).

The settlement agreement also included a "full, mutual general release" by both parties as to "all claims and causes of action, known and unknown, asserted or which might have been asserted, in this litigation." The agreement did not contain any disclaimer of reliance on representations made by the other party.

[As it turned out, through a series of complicated events, the VSA Board had not approved the settlement agreement. This rendered the settlement agreement unenforceable under § 1823(e).]

On June 29, 1989, VSA was declared insolvent, and the FSLIC was appointed receiver. The FSLIC removed Appling's case against VSA to federal court. The federal court concluded that ... the settlement agreement was not binding on the FSLIC because it was not approved by the VSA Board as required by section 1823(e).

Appling then filed this suit, individually and on behalf of Boca Chica, against McCamish, Martin, alleging that McCamish, Martin negligently misrepresented that the VSA Board had approved the settlement agreement. McCamish, Martin moved for summary judgment on the negligent misrepresentation claim on the sole ground that the firm owed no duty to Appling. The trial court granted the motion. The trial court later rendered final judgment, ordering that Appling take nothing. Appling appealed. The court of appeals reversed and remanded on the theory that, even absent privity, an attorney may owe a duty to a third party to avoid negligent misrepresentation.

On petition for review, McCamish, Martin argues that Appling does not have a cause of action against McCamish, Martin for the tort of negligent misrepresentation, as defined by the *Restatement (Second) of Torts* § 552, because, under Texas law, an attorney owes no duty of care to a third party absent privity. In particular, McCamish, Martin contends that Texas law does not permit a nonclient to sue a lawyer for negligence arising out of the lawyer's representation of a client because the lawyer and nonclient are not in privity. According to McCamish, Martin, the Texas privity requirement reflects the importance of the attorney-client relationship and takes into account the nature and demands of the adversarial system.

Moreover, McCamish, Martin argues that under Texas law, the privity rule applies to all negligence-based causes of action, whether the nonclient's claims are characterized as legal malpractice or negligent misrepresentation. Because McCamish, Martin represented Appling's adversary in a litigation matter and was never in privity with Appling, the law firm claims that it cannot be held liable to Appling for negligent misrepresentation. Appling responds that the court of appeals correctly held that an attorney may be liable to a nonclient under the *Restatement (Second) of Torts* § 552. Specifically, Appling claims that both the *Restatement* and Texas law envision the application of section 552 to attorneys. Appling also argues that there is no strict privity requirement in a cause of action against an attorney under section 552. Thus, Appling urges this Court to recognize a distinction between cases of legal malpractice, which are subject to the privity rule, and cases of negligent misrepresentation, which are not.

Furthermore, according to Appling, applying section 552 to attorneys does not offend the policy justifications for the privity rule, such as exposure to conflicting duties and to unlimited liability. Appling points out that the rules of professional conduct require an attorney to make certain no conflict of interest exists and to obtain the client's consent before undertaking an evaluation for a nonclient. Additionally, Appling emphasizes that section 552 limits liability to a narrow class of persons. Finally, Appling asserts that allowing a negligent misrepresentation claim against an attorney will not only improve the legal profession's integrity and reputation, but will also promote desirable economic activity by protecting a commercial actor who justifiably relies on an evaluation provided by the attorney of another commercial actor.

Thus, the parties present this Court with one precise question: Whether the absence of an attorney-client relationship precludes a third party from suing an attorney for negligent misrepresentation under the *Restatement (Second) of Torts* § 552. We do not decide or address in any way the liability of McCamish, Martin in this case. Instead, we determine only whether Appling, a nonclient, may bring a negligent misrepresentation cause of action, as defined by section 552, against McCamish, Martin.

This Court has already adopted the tort of negligent misrepresentation as described by the *Restatement (Second) of Torts* § 552. *See* Federal Land Bank Ass'n of Tyler v. Sloane, 825 S.W.2d 439, 442 (Tex.1991). In *Sloane*, the Court endorsed section 552 to define the scope of a lender's duty to avoid negligent misrepresentations to prospective borrowers. Section 552(1) provides:

> One who, in the course of his business, profession or employment, or in any transaction in which he has a pecuniary interest, supplies false information for the guidance of others in their business transactions, is subject to liability for pecuniary loss caused to them by their justifiable reliance upon the information, if he fails to exercise reasonable care or competence in obtaining or communicating the information.

Courts applying Texas law have recognized a section 552 cause of action against other professionals as well. *See, e.g.*, Steiner v. Southmark Corp., 734 F.Supp. 269, 279–80 (N.D.Tex.1990) (auditor); Smith v. Sneed, 938 S.W.2d 181, 185 (Tex.App.—Austin 1997, no writ) (physician); Hagans v. Woodruff, 830 S.W.2d 732, 736 (Tex.App.—Houston 1992, no writ) (real-estate broker); Lutheran Bhd. v. Kidder Peabody & Co., 829 S.W.2d 300, 309 (Tex.App.—Texarkana 1992, writ granted w.r.m.) (securities placement agent); Blue Bell v. Peat, Marwick, Mitchell & Co., 715 S.W.2d 408, 411–12 (Tex.App.—Dallas 1986, writ ref'd n.r.e.) (accountant); Cook Consultants, Inc. v. Larson, 700 S.W.2d 231, 234 (Tex.App.—Dallas 1985, writ ref'd n.r.e.) (surveyor); Great

Am. Mortgage Investors v. Louisville Title Ins. Co., 597 S.W.2d 425, 429–30 (Tex.Civ.App.—Fort Worth 1980, writ ref'd n.r.e.) (title insurer); Shatterproof Glass Corp. v. James, 466 S.W.2d 873, 880 (Tex.Civ.App.—Fort Worth 1971, writ ref'd n.r.e.) (accountant).

We perceive no reason why section 552 should not apply to attorneys. First, nothing in the language of section 552 or in the reasoning of Sloane warrants such an exception. More importantly, allowing a nonclient to bring a negligent misrepresentation cause of action against an attorney does not undermine the general rule that persons who are not in privity with an attorney cannot sue the attorney for legal malpractice. Nor does applying section 552 to attorneys implicate the policy concerns behind our strict adherence to the privity rule in legal malpractice cases. Finally, the *Restatement (Third) of the Law Governing Lawyers* [§ 50], which sets forth certain circumstances in which an attorney may owe a duty of care to a nonclient, validates the application of section 552 to an attorney when the attorney invites a nonclient's reliance.

At common law, the rule of privity limits attorney liability to third parties. The general rule is that persons who are not in privity with the attorney cannot sue the attorney for legal malpractice. In practical terms, this privity requirement means that an attorney is not liable for malpractice to anyone other than her client.

As the court of appeals noted, a negligent misrepresentation claim is not equivalent to a legal malpractice claim. Under the tort of negligent misrepresentation, liability is not based on the breach of duty a professional owes his or her clients or others in privity, but on an independent duty to the nonclient based on the professional's manifest awareness of the nonclient's reliance on the misrepresentation and the professional's intention that the nonclient so rely. Therefore, an attorney can be subject to a negligent misrepresentation claim in a case in which she is not subject to a legal malpractice claim.

The theory of negligent misrepresentation permits plaintiffs who are not parties to a contract for professional services to recover from the contracting professionals. Likewise, section 552 imposes a duty to avoid negligent misrepresentation, irrespective of privity.

Several jurisdictions have held that an attorney can be liable to a nonclient for negligent misrepresentation, as defined in section 552, based on the issuance of opinion letters. *See, e.g., Greycas, Inc.*, 826 F.2d at 1564–65; ... Other jurisdictions have indicated a willingness to subject lawyers to a section 552 claim by a nonclient in connection with the preparation of different types of evaluations, given the proper circumstances. *See, e.g., Menuskin*, 145 F.3d at 762–63 (warranty deeds); ... Thus, section 552 has been cited favorably in a variety of lawyer liability contexts.

Moreover, applying section 552 to attorneys does not offend the policy justifications for the strict privity rule in legal malpractice cases. In *Barcelo v. Elliott*, 923 S.W.2d 575 (Tex.1996), this Court reaffirmed that an attorney does not owe a duty of care that could give rise to malpractice liability to will beneficiaries because the attorney does not represent the beneficiaries. The Court reasoned that, without a bright-line privity rule, clients would "lose control over the attorney-client relationship" and lawyers would be "subject to almost unlimited liability." *Id.* at 577. While these policy reasons for the privity rule are legitimate, they do not preclude a section 552 cause of action against an attorney by a nonclient.

First, the application of section 552 to attorneys does not cause a client to "lose control over the attorney-client relationship." McCamish, Martin argues that imposing a section 552 duty on an attorney to a nonclient damages an attorney's ability to zealously represent a client. More specifically, McCamish Martin cautions that this potential liability to third parties creates a conflict of duties and threatens the attorney-client privilege. In the negligent misrepresentation context, neither contention has merit.

A typical negligent misrepresentation case involves one party to a transaction receiving and relying on an evaluation, such as an opinion letter, prepared by another party's attorney. Under the Texas Disciplinary Rules of Professional Conduct, an attorney cannot give an evaluation to a third party unless she reasonably believes that making the evaluation is compatible with other aspects of the attorney-client relationship and the client consents after consultation. Tex. Disciplinary R. Prof'l Conduct 2.02. Once the lawyer is satisfied that no conflict of interest exists (between the client and the lawyer or the client and a third party), she should "advise the client of the implications of the evaluation, particularly the lawyer's responsibilities to third persons and the duty to disseminate the findings." Tex. Disciplinary R. Prof'l Conduct 2.02 cmt. 5. Thus, in the negligent misrepresentation context, rule 2.02 safeguards against a lawyer's exposure to conflicting duties and ensures that the client makes the ultimate decision of whether to provide an evaluation. Moreover, under rule 2.02, a lawyer should not allow a client to make this decision without advising the client about the potential impact such an evaluation may have on the scope of the attorney-client privilege.

Nor does section 552 threaten lawyers with "almost unlimited liability." In fact, section 552 adequately addresses this threat by narrowing the class of potential claimants and requiring that any claimant justifiably rely on the alleged negligent misrepresentation. Under section 552(2), liability is limited to loss suffered:

> (a) by the person or one of a limited group of persons for whose benefit and guidance [one] intends to supply the information or knows that the recipient intends to supply it; and (b) through reliance upon it in a transaction that [one] intends the information to influence or knows that the recipient so intends or in a substantially similar transaction.

This formulation limits liability to situations in which the attorney who provides the information is aware of the nonclient and intends that the nonclient rely on the information. In other words, a section 552 cause of action is available only when information is transferred by an attorney to a known party for a known purpose. A lawyer may also avoid or minimize the risk of liability to a nonclient by setting forth (1) limitations as to whom the representation is directed and who should rely on it, or (2) disclaimers as to the scope and accuracy of the factual investigation or assumptions forming the basis of the representation or the representation itself.

Neither section 552 nor *Sloane* limits the class of potential defendants under section 552 to nonlawyers. In addition, the theory of negligent misrepresentation and section 552 itself do not require privity or implicate the policy concerns behind the privity rule. Finally, the *Restatement (Third) of the Law Governing Lawyers* § [51(2)], which specifically addresses situations in which an attorney invites reliance by a nonclient, not only recognizes the tort of negligent misrepresentation, as defined by section 552, but also incorporates the limitations of section 552 into its duty analysis. We, therefore, conclude that there is no reason to exempt lawyers from the operation of section 552 or to impose a privity requirement on a negligent misrepresentation cause of action under section 552. In so holding, we disapprove of the language in ... Texas cases refusing to permit a nonclient to bring a section 552 claim against an attorney based on a lack of privity.

The trial court granted McCamish, Martin's motion for summary judgment on Appling's negligent misrepresentation claim on the sole ground that, absent privity, McCamish, Martin owed no duty to Appling. Because we hold that McCamish, Martin may owe a duty to Appling, irrespective of privity, we affirm the judgment of the court of appeals, remanding this cause to the trial court.

* * *

1. The influence of the *Restatement*. The § 552 test is now the most commonly-used test in these types of negligent misrepresentation cases.

2. Other applications of § 552. The primary focus of this chapter is on cases like *McCamish,* in which a defendant provides information about a client to a third party, who later becomes a plaintiff. This is perhaps the most common application of § 552, but it is not the only one. Some courts have held that § 552 applies where the defendant negligently misrepresents a fact directly to the plaintiff. Allen v. Steele, 252 P.2d 476 (Colo. 2011).

Some courts have applied § 552 outside of the traditional business context. In *Sain v. Cedar Rapids Community School Dist.,* 626 N.W.2d 115 (Iowa 2001), a high school guidance counselor provided incorrect information to a high school athlete about the academic course requirements necessary to be eligible for a college scholarship. As a result, the athlete was not eligible for the scholarship. The Iowa Supreme Court held that § 552 applied to the plaintiff's negligent misrepresentation claim and reversed the lower court's grant of summary judgment in favor of the school district.

3. The scope of § 552. During the discovery process in civil litigation, Defendant's attorney negligently misrepresented a fact that was material for purposes of the litigation. Plaintiff relied on the misrepresentation, causing the plaintiff to lose the opportunity to recover on a related theory of liability. Would § 552 permit recovery against the attorney?

4. Model Rule comparison. Like the Texas Disciplinary rule mentioned in *McCamish,* ABA Model Rule 2.3 contemplates a lawyer providing an evaluation of a matter affecting a client for the use of someone other than the client.

Exercise 12.2

You are an associate in a law firm in Texas. Your boss tells you that your firm has just agreed to represent an individual in a civil action against the individual's former lawyer. The facts of the case are almost identical to those in *McCamish.* Your boss instructs you to do some research to determine whether to file the claim as one of professional negligence (legal malpractice) or negligent misrepresentation. You read *McCamish* and § 51 of the *Restatement of the Law Governing Lawyers* (2000), which provides that while a lawyer generally does not owe a duty of care to nonclients, there are exceptions. One of those exceptions is where the lawyer's client (with the lawyer's acquiescence) invites the nonclient to rely on the lawyer's opinion or provision of other legal services, and the nonclient so relies. Based on your research and your reading of *McCamish,*

(1) Is there a difference between a legal malpractice claim and a negligent misrepresentation claim on these facts?

(2) If so, can you explain the difference to your boss?

(3) Can you think of any reason to prefer one claim over the other?

(4) What is your advice to your boss as to how to proceed in terms of filing a complaint?

Exercise 12.3

Lawyer is at a cocktail party where she meets Alice. Alice tells Lawyer that Alice was injured in a car accident some time ago and suffered personal injuries. However, Alice expresses some concern that she may have waited too long to sue the other driver. Lawyer responds, "That's okay, you've got three years in these kinds of cases before the statute of limitations runs." This is not true; the statute of limitations expires after two years. Relying on Lawyer's statement, Alice waits three weeks before contacting another lawyer about the possibility of bringing a lawsuit, but is (correctly) told by the other lawyer that the statute of limitations just ran one week ago and that Alice's claim is barred.

(1) Could Alice bring a legal malpractice claim against Lawyer?

(2) Putting aside any question as to whether Alice's reliance on Lawyer's statement was justified, can you make an argument, based on the language of § 552, that this section does not apply to any potential claim of negligent misrepresentation Alice might have?

3. Traditional Negligence/Foreseeability Principles

Focus Questions: *Citizens Bank v. Timm, Schmidt & Co.*

1. *Why wouldn't the § 552 approach provide a remedy for the plaintiff in this case?*
2. *Do the benefits of the* Citizens State Bank *approach outweigh its drawbacks?*
3. *Might the* Citizens State Bank *approach make sense for cases involving accountants but not other professionals? (Conversely, might it make sense for other professionals but not accountants?)*

Citizens State Bank v. Timm, Schmidt & Co., S.C.

335 N.W.2d 361
(Wis. 1983)

DAY, Justice.

The issue considered on review is: May an accountant be held liable for the negligent preparation of an audit report to a third party not in privity who relies on the report?

[Timm, Schmidt & Company (Timm) was an accounting firm that, for several years, prepared financial statements for Clintonville Fire Apparatus, Inc. (CFA), including opinion letters which stated the financial statements fairly presented the financial condition of CFA and that the statements were prepared in accordance with generally accepted accounting principles.]

In November, 1975, CFA obtained a $300,000 loan from Citizens. The loan was guaranteed by the Small Business Administration, a federal agency (hereinafter SBA). Citizens made the loan to CFA after reviewing the financial statements which Timm had prepared. Additional loans, apparently not SBA guaranteed, were made by Citizens to CFA in 1976. By the end of 1976, CFA had a total outstanding indebtedness to Citizens of approximately $380,000.

In early 1977, during the course of preparing CFA's financial statement for 1976, Timm employees discovered that the 1974 and 1975 financial statements contained a number of material errors totaling over $400,000 once all period adjustments were made.

Once these errors were corrected and Citizens, as a creditor of CFA, was informed by Timm of the errors, Citizens called all of its loans due. As a result, CFA went into receivership and was ultimately liquidated and dissolved. As of the date the complaint was filed, the amount outstanding on Citizens' loans to CFA was $152,214.44. [Citizens filed an action against Timm and its malpractice insurance company seeking to recover $152,214.44, the amount due on its loans to CFA.]

[Timm moved for summary judgment.] The affidavits submitted with the motion came from every member of the Timm firm who had worked on the CFA account. Each affidavit stated that the affiant had no knowledge, until after the fact, that CFA intended to or had obtained any loans from Citizens. The affidavit of Elmer Timm, president of the firm, also stated that he was never informed by any person that any audit report prepared by his firm for CFA would be used by any lender for the purpose of determining whether or not to make a loan to CFA.

... [T]he trial court granted Timm's motion for summary judgment. The court concluded that under the *Restatement of Torts (2d)* section 552, accountants may be held liable to third parties for their negligent acts. However, the judge also concluded that, based upon the affidavits before him, the *Restatement* did not extend Timm's liability to Citizens.

Citizens appealed. The court of appeals affirmed the trial court. It concluded that, even assuming that section 552 of the *Restatement* should be the law in this state, there was still no genuine issue of fact as to whether Citizens was within the class protected by its provisions. Therefore, the court of appeals concluded summary judgment was properly granted.

Accountants have long been held not liable for their negligence to relying third parties not in privity under an application of Judge Cardozo's decision in *Ultramares v. Touche,* 255 N.Y. 170, 174 N.E. 441 (1931). In *Ultramares,* Judge Cardozo absolved the defendant accountants from liability for overvaluing the assets of a company in an audit report to a plaintiff who had loaned money in reliance on a certified balance sheet in the report. Judge Cardozo expressed the concern that "if liability exists, a thoughtless slip or blunder ... may expose accountants to a liability in an indeterminate amount for an indeterminate time to an indeterminate class." 174 N.E. at 444.

In this state, although the liability of accountants to third parties not in privity has not been examined, the liability of an attorney to one not in privity was recently examined in *Auric v. Continental Casualty Co.,* 111 Wis.2d 507, 331 N.W.2d 325 (1983). This court concluded that an attorney may be held liable to a will beneficiary not in privity for the attorney's negligence in supervising the execution of a will. 111 Wis.2d at 514. Part of the rationale for this decision was that the imposition of liability would make attorneys more careful in the execution of their responsibilities to their clients.

That rationale is applicable here. Unless liability is imposed, third parties who rely upon the accuracy of the financial statements will not be protected. Unless an accountant can be held liable to a relying third party, this negligence will go undeterred.

There are additional policy reasons to allow the imposition of liability. If relying third parties, such as creditors, are not allowed to recover, the cost of credit to the general public will increase because creditors will either have to absorb the costs of bad loans made in reliance on faulty information or hire independent accountants to verify the information received. Accountants may spread the risk through the use of liability insurance.

We conclude that the absence of privity alone should not bar negligence actions by relying third parties against accountants.

Although the absence of privity does not bar this action, the question remains as to the extent of an accountant's liability to injured third parties. Courts which have examined this question have generally relied upon section 552 of the *Restatement* to restrict the class of third persons who could sue accountants for their negligent acts.

Under section 552, liability is not extended to all parties whom the accountant might reasonably foresee as using the information. Rather, as one commentator noted, "The *Restatement's* formulation of 'a limited group of persons' extends causes of action to a limited number of third parties who are expected to gain access to the financial statement information in an expected transaction." This limitation is stressed in comment h. to section 552 where it is noted that:

> It is not required that the person who is to become the plaintiff be identified or known to the defendant as an individual when the information is supplied. It is enough that the maker of the representation intends it to reach and influence either a particular person or persons, known to him, or a group or class of persons, distinct from the much larger class who might reasonably be expected sooner or later to have access to the information and foreseeably to take some action in reliance upon it.

The fundamental principle of Wisconsin negligence law is that a tortfeasor is fully liable for all foreseeable consequences of his act except as those consequences are limited by policy factors. The *Restatement's* statement of limiting liability to certain third parties is too restrictive a statement of policy factors for this Court to adopt.

We conclude that accountants' liability to third parties should be determined under the accepted principles of Wisconsin negligence law. According to these principles, a finding of non-liability will be made only if there is a strong public policy requiring such a finding. Liability will be imposed on these accountants for the foreseeable injuries resulting from their negligent acts unless, under the facts of this particular case, as a matter of policy to be decided by the court, recovery is denied on grounds of public policy. *See,* H. Rosenblum, Inc. v. Jack F. Adler, [461 A.2d 138, 153 (N.J. 1983)]. This Court has set out a number of public policy reasons for not imposing liability despite a finding of negligence causing injury:

> (1) The injury is too remote from the negligence; or (2) the injury is too wholly out of proportion to the culpability of the negligent tort-feasor; or (3) in retrospect it appears too highly extraordinary that the negligence should have brought about the harm; or (4) because allowance of recovery would place too unreasonable a burden on the negligent tort-feasor; or (5) because allowance of recovery would be too likely to open the way for fraudulent claims; or (6) allowance of recovery would enter a field that has no sensible or just stopping point [citations omitted].

The pleadings, affidavits and other information in the record before this court do not establish that Timm was entitled as a matter of law to summary judgment. Under the accepted principles of Wisconsin negligence law, Timm could be liable to Citizens if Timm's actions were the cause of Citizens' injuries and if the injuries were reasonably foreseeable unless public policy precluded recovery.

Timm's affidavits do not dispute that Citizen's reliance upon the financial statements led to the making of the loans and ultimately to the losses which were incurred. Each affidavit recites that Timm employees had no knowledge that the financial statements would actually be used by CFA to apply for a new bank loan or to increase existing loan indebtedness. However, the affidavit of Elmer Timm stated that "as a certified public accountant, I know that audited statements are used for many purposes and that it is common for them to be supplied to lenders and creditors, and other persons."

These affidavits and other information contained in the record do not dispose of the issue of whether it was foreseeable that a negligently prepared financial statement could cause harm to Citizens.

Therefore, Timm having failed to establish a prima facie case for summary judgment, we conclude the trial judge erred in granting the motion for summary judgment.

* * *

Application beyond accountants. The *Citizens State Bank* opinion references *H. Rosenblum, Inc. v. Adler,* a New Jersey decision that likewise adopted a foreseeability test. That decision was subsequently overturned by the New Jersey legislature, which adopted New York's "near privity" approach for negligent misrepresentation claims involving accountants. Interestingly, New Jersey still applies the foreseeability test to non-accountants. *E.g.*, Petrillo v. Bachenberg, 655 A.2d 1354, 1360 (N.J. 1995) (applying the foreseeability test to an attorney); Hopkins v. Fox & Lazo Realtors, 625 A.2d 1110 (N.J. 1993) (applying the foreseeability test to a real estate broker)." Robert K. Wise & Heather E. Poole, *Negligent Misrepresentation in Texas: The Misunderstood Tort,* 40 TEX. TECH L. REV. 845, 850 n.19 (2008). Mississippi likewise employs a foreseeability test and has applied it to non-accountants. Touche Ross & Co. v. Commercial Union Ins. Co., 514 So.2d 315 (Miss. 1987) (accountant); Century 21 Deep South Properties, Ltd. v. Corson, 612 So.2d 359, 373 (Miss. 1992) (attorney).

* * *

4. Justifiable Reliance

Regardless of which test a jurisdiction employs in these kinds of cases, in order to recover, a plaintiff must satisfy all of the requirements of the test. Thus, obviously, a defendant must actually be negligent before liability can attach. Likewise, a plaintiff must also actually rely on the information provided by the defendant. As with a fraudulent misrepresentation claim, that reliance must also be justified. The following cases explore the concept of justifiable reliance in the context of a negligent misrepresentation claim.

Focus Questions: *McCamish, Martin, Brown & Loeffler v. F.E. Appling Interests*

1. *What can the provider of information do to limit a party's justifiable reliance on the information provided?*
2. *Do the court's statements concerning justifiable reliance adequately limit the scope of liability under section 552?*

McCamish, Martin, Brown & Loeffler v. F.E. Appling Interests

991 S.W.2d 787
(Tex. 1999)

[In the portion of the opinion excerpted *supra,* the Texas Supreme Court held that section 552 applied to a law firm that provided information about a client to a third party.]

[S]ection 552 guards against exposure to unlimited liability by requiring that a claimant justifiably rely on a lawyer's representation of material fact. Thus, not every statement made by an attorney to a nonclient is actionable under section 552. For example, an attorney's statements communicating her client's negotiating position are not statements of material fact. *See, e.g.,* Tex. Disciplinary R. Prof'l Conduct 4.01 cmt. 1 (differentiating between representations of material fact and negotiating positions, specifically in the context of settlement claims).

In determining whether section 552's justifiable reliance element is met, one must consider the nature of the relationship between the attorney, client, and nonclient. Generally, courts have acknowledged that a third party's reliance on an attorney's representation is not justified when the representation takes place in an adversarial context. *See, e.g., Mehaffy,* 892 P.2d at 235, 237 (business transaction); L & H Airco, Inc. v. Rapistan Corp., 446 N.W.2d 372, 378–79 (Minn.1989) (arbitration proceeding); Garcia, 750 P.2d at 122–23 (N.M.1988) (litigation); Beeck v. Kapalis, 302 N.W.2d 90, 96–97 (Iowa 1981) (litigation); *see also* Mallen and Smith, § 7.10 (stating the same and noting that "[t]he adversary concept is not limited to litigation. The same policy considerations apply to business and commercial transactions."). This adversary concept reflects the notion that an attorney, hired by a client for the benefit and protection of the client's interests, must pursue those interests with undivided loyalty (within the confines of the Texas Disciplinary Rules of Professional Conduct), without the imposition of a conflicting duty to a nonclient whose interests are adverse to the client. Because not every situation is clearly defined as "adversarial" or "nonadversarial," the characterization of the inter-party relationship should be guided, at least in part, by "the extent to which the interests of the client and the third party are consistent with each other." *See* Feinman, 31 Tort & Ins. L.J. at 750.

In addition to these policy considerations, the *Restatement (Third) of the Law Governing Lawyers* [§ 50], entitled "Duty of Care to Certain Nonclients," also supports allowing a third party to bring a section 552 claim against a lawyer, irrespective of privity. Subsection [50(2)] covers situations in which an attorney invites reliance by a nonclient. Under this subsection, an attorney owes a duty of care to a nonclient:

> when and to the extent that: (a) a lawyer ... invites the non-client to rely on the lawyer's opinion or provision of other legal services, and the non-client so relies, and (b) the non-client is not, under applicable tort law, too remote from the lawyer to be entitled to protection.

In other words, a nonclient cannot rely on an attorney's statement, such as an opinion letter, unless the attorney invites that reliance.

Focus Questions: *Kastner v. Jenkens & Gilchrist, P.C.*

1. *How does the court's conception of the justifiable reliance concept in the negligent misrepresentation context compare to the general conception of justifiable reliance in the fraudulent misrepresentation context?*
2. *How does the "in the course of his business, profession or employment" language from § 552 relate to the concept of justifiable reliance?*

Kastner v. Jenkens & Gilchrist, P.C.

231 S.W.3d 571
(Tex.App.—Dallas 2007)

Opinion by Justice RICHTER.

I. BACKGROUND

A. Factual Background

Randy Box, a real estate broker, owned a company called Malebox Investment, Inc. In August 2000, Malebox contracted to purchase an apartment complex known as "the Lodges" for $6.9 million dollars. Box and a business associate, Fred Weinberg, planned to sell investment interests in the property. Box retained George Dunlap, an attorney employed by Jenkens & Gilchrist, to provide legal services in connection with the transaction. At Box's request, Dunlap formed Lodges Investors, L.P., a single-asset Texas limited partnership (the Partnership). The Partnership was formed as the purchasing entity to acquire the apartment complex. After Dunlap prepared the limited partnership agreement, Malebox assigned the agreement to purchase the apartment complex to the Partnership. Box and Weinberg then solicited participation in the venture through the sale of limited partnership interests in the Partnership.

The partnership agreement required the contributions of the limited partners to be made in cash. The Kastners subscribed to the Partnership as Class A limited partners with an initial capital contribution of $120,000. Some of the other class A limited partners who later became parties to this lawsuit include: Wenz & Associates, Box Interests, Loren Weinstein, and AJ Associates.

Dunlap prepared the partnership agreement in accordance with information provided by Box and Weinberg. On February 26, 2001, Dunlap mailed the partnership agreement to each of the limited partners. Exhibit A to the partnership agreement reflected the partnership percentages and capital contributions of the partners. In the accompanying cover letter, Dunlap explained that ... the final percentages in Exhibit A would be determined at the closing based upon the aggregate capital contributions of the partners. Some of the limited partners, including the Kastners, signed the partnership agreement and returned it to Dunlap. Others waited until the closing to sign.

... At the closing, the parties learned the Partnership did not have sufficient funds on deposit with the title company to complete the transaction. The amount of the short-fall was approximately $88,000. To facilitate the closing, the seller agreed to make a short-term loan to the Partnership. According to Dunlap, Weinberg suggested the short-term loan and assured everyone the necessary funds would be available to pay off the loan the next day. Dunlap informed those present that under the terms of the partnership agreement, a loan to the Partnership would require the unanimous consent of all the limited partners. According to Weinberg, the idea for the secondary financing originated with Dunlap. Regardless, there is no question that the limited partners present decided to proceed with the closing and the short-term loan. The loan was documented by a closing agreement prepared by the seller's attorney and signed by the general partner.

On March 8, 2001, based on information provided by Box and Weinberg, Dunlap provided each of the partners with a fully executed copy of the partnership agreement with Exhibit A attached. No one suggested to Dunlap that the partnership percentages were inaccurate.

At some point after the Partnership began operating the apartment complex it began to experience financial difficulties. On June 3, 2002, the Partnership filed for protection under Chapter 11 of the United States Bankruptcy Code, and the relationship between the general partner and the limited partners deteriorated. This lawsuit ultimately ensued.

III. DISCUSSION

A. Negligent Misrepresentation

In their first issue, the Kastners assert the trial court erred when it granted Dunlap's no evidence motion for summary judgment on their negligent misrepresentation claim. Negligent misrepresentation requires proof that: (1) the defendant in the course of his business or a transaction in which he had an interest; (2) supplied false information for the guidance of others; (3) without exercising reasonable care or competence in communicating the information; (4) the plaintiff justifiably relied on the information; (5) proximately causing the plaintiff's injury. In support of their claim, the Kastners contend Dunlap improperly identified the partners' contributions as cash contributions when they were not all made in cash, incorrectly quantified the general partner's interest, and created a document reflecting the incorrect amount of capital raised by the partnership. They further contend Dunlap represented he would adjust the partnership percentages at closing but failed to do so, and allowed the secondary financing to occur when he knew it violated the terms of the partnership agreement and the first mortgage. All of this conduct arises out of Dunlap's participation in the March 1, 2001 closing on the Partnership's purchase of the apartment complex. The Kastners acknowledge they had no attorney-client relationship with Dunlap, but insist that Dunlap's conduct falls within the narrow exception to attorney liability for negligent misrepresentation recognized by the Texas Supreme Court in *McCamish, Martin, Brown & Loeffler v. F.E. Appling Interests,* 991 S.W.2d 787, 791 (Tex. 1991). We disagree.

In *McCamish,* the court considered whether the absence of an attorney-client relationship precludes a third party from suing an attorney for negligent misrepresentation under section 552 of the *Restatement (Second) of Torts.* The court confirmed that negligent misrepresentation is distinct from malpractice. Negligent misrepresentation liability is not premised on a breach of duty a professional owes to his client or others in privity; instead, liability results from the "professional's manifest awareness of the non-client's reliance on the misrepresentation and the professional's intention that the non-client so rely." *Id.* at 792. Accordingly, the court concluded that the theory of negligent misrepresentation "permits plaintiffs who are not parties to a contract for professional services to recover from the contracting professionals." *Id.*

The duty imposed on an attorney to a non-client, however, is limited. The duty only arises when (1) the attorney is aware of the non-client and intends that the non-client rely on the representation; and (2) the non-client justifiably relies on the attorney's representation of a material fact. *Id.* at 794. For purposes of determining whether the nonclient justifiably relied on the representation, the reviewing court must consider the nature of the relationship between the attorney, client, and non-client. A non-client cannot rely on an attorney's representations unless the attorney invites that reliance. *Id.* at 795.

The reliance element is absent in this case. There is no evidence Dunlap invited or was aware of the Kastners' reliance. Prior to the closing, Dunlap prepared transactional documents for his clients based on the information and instructions his clients provided. After mailing the fully executed partnership agreement in March after the closing, Dunlap had no further involvement with the Partnership. The *McCamish* court observed that when attorneys have been held liable to non-clients for negligent misrepresentation in other jurisdictions, the situation typically involved the attorney's issuance of an opinion letter or some other type of evaluation. Here, the only communication Dunlap had with the Kastners consisted of a cover letter accompanying the partnership agreement. The cover letter contained no legal opinions or evaluations; it conveyed neutral information about the mechanics of the revisions he anticipated after the closing. The relationship of the parties is also significant. Dunlap represented the Partnership, the general partner, and Box. It is well-established that an attorney's representation of a partnership does not constitute representation of each of the individual partners. *See* Tex Disc R Prof Conduct 1.12(a) (lawyer retained by entity represents entity as distinct from its members). Therefore, Dunlap's representation of the Partnership and the Kastners' status as limited partners in and of itself is not sufficient to justify reliance. But the record shows nothing more than this representation. Under these circumstances, there was no reason for Dunlap to anticipate the non-client recipients might attach any extraordinary significance to his transmission of the partnership agreement or the accompanying correspondence.

The Kastners argue their reliance was justified because the correspondence they received was on the letterhead of "a large Dallas law firm." We are not persuaded such superficial indicia justifies reliance. Regardless of origin, the mere transmission of a partnership agreement from an attorney to a non-client cannot reasonably be construed as a legal opinion on the validity of the agreement or the propriety of investment in the partnership. We similarly reject the Kastners' attempt to characterize the contents of the partnership agreement as representations made by Dunlap. To do so would effectively require attorneys to adopt as their own the terms of—and representations made in—legal documents they prepare for their clients. Such an expansive interpretation far exceeds the scope of *McCamish* liability.

Exercise 12.4

Your firm has just agreed to provide a letter like that in issue in *McCamish* to a third party. Your firm is obviously concerned about the possibility of being sued if any of the information provided turns out to be inaccurate. What can you do to limit any reliance on the part of the third party?

B. Damages

Available damages are more limited in the case of negligent misrepresentation than in fraudulent misrepresentation cases. In fraud cases, the plaintiff is typically entitled to recover either out-of-pocket losses (the difference between the value of what he has received in the transaction and its purchase price or other value given for it) or benefit-of-the bargain damages (what is necessary to place the victim in the position he or she would have been in if the misrepresentation had been true). In negligent misrepresentation cases, a plaintiff is typically entitled to only out-of-pocket losses, as well as any losses suffered as a consequence of the plaintiff's reliance on the misrepresentation. Restatement (Second) of Torts § 552B(1)

* * *

C. Defenses: Comparative Negligence

Focus Question: *Greycas, Inc. v. Proud*

Is there a difference between comparative negligence and unjustified reliance in the case of a negligent misrepresentation claim?

Greycas, Inc. v. Proud

826 F.2d 1560
(7th Cir. 1987)

POSNER, Circuit Judge.

Theodore S. Proud, Jr., a member of the Illinois bar who practices law in a suburb of Chicago, appeals from a judgment against him for $833,760, entered after a bench trial. The tale of malpractice and misrepresentation that led to the judgment begins with Proud's brother-in-law, Wayne Crawford, like Proud a lawyer but one who devoted most of his attention to a large farm that he owned in downstate Illinois. The farm fell on hard times and by 1981 Crawford was in dire financial straits. He had pledged most of his farm machinery to lenders, yet now desperately needed more money. He approached Greycas, Inc., the plaintiff in this case, a large financial company headquartered in Arizona, seeking a large loan that he offered to secure with the farm machinery. He did not tell Greycas about his financial difficulties or that he had pledged the machinery to other lenders, but he did make clear that he needed the loan in a hurry. Greycas obtained several appraisals of Crawford's farm machinery but did not investigate Crawford's financial position or discover that he had pledged the collateral to other lenders, who had perfected their liens in the collateral. Greycas agreed to lend Crawford $1,367,966.50, which was less than the appraised value of the machinery.

The loan was subject, however, to an important condition, which is at the heart of this case: Crawford was required to submit a letter to Greycas, from counsel whom he would retain, assuring Greycas that there were no prior liens on the machinery that was to secure the loan. Crawford asked Proud to prepare the letter, and he did so, and mailed it to Greycas, and within 20 days of the first contact between Crawford and Greycas the loan closed and the money was disbursed. A year later Crawford defaulted on the loan; shortly afterward he committed suicide. Greycas then learned that most of the farm machinery that Crawford had pledged to it had previously been pledged to other lenders.

The machinery was sold at auction. The Illinois state court that determined the creditors' priorities in the proceeds of the sale held that Greycas did not have a first priority on most of the machinery that secured its loan; as a result Greycas has been able to recover only a small part of the loan. The judgment it obtained in the present suit is the district judge's estimate of the value that it would have realized on its collateral had there been no prior liens, as Proud represented in his letter.

That letter is the centerpiece of the litigation. Typed on the stationery of Proud's firm and addressed to Greycas, it identifies Proud as Crawford's lawyer and states that, "in such capacity, I have been asked to render my opinion in connection with" the proposed loan to Crawford. It also states that "this opinion is being delivered in accordance with the requirements of the Loan Agreement" and that

> I have conducted a U.C.C., tax, and judgment search with respect to the Company [i.e., Crawford's farm] as of March 19, 1981, and except as hereinafter noted all units listed on the attached Exhibit A ("Equipment") are free and clear of all liens or encumbrances other than Lender's perfected security interest therein which was recorded March 19, 1981 at the Office of the Recorder of Deeds of Fayette County, Illinois.

The reference to the lender's security interest is to Greycas's interest; Crawford, pursuant to the loan agreement, had filed a notice of that interest with the recorder. The excepted units to which the letter refers are four vehicles. Exhibit A is a long list of farm machinery—the collateral that Greycas thought it was getting to secure the loan, free of any other liens. Attached to the loan agreement itself, however, as Exhibit B, is another list of farm machinery constituting the collateral for the loan, and there are discrepancies between the two lists; more on this later.

Proud never conducted a search for prior liens on the machinery listed in Exhibit A. His brother-in-law gave him the list and told him there were no liens other than the one that Crawford had just filed for Greycas. Proud made no effort to verify Crawford's statement. The theory of the complaint is that Proud was negligent in representing that there were no prior liens, merely on his brother-in-law's say-so. No doubt Proud was negligent in failing to conduct a search, but we are not clear why the misrepresentation is alleged to be negligent rather than deliberate and hence fraudulent, in which event Greycas's alleged contributory negligence would not be an issue (as it is, we shall see), since there is no defense of contributory or comparative negligence to a deliberate tort, such as fraud. *See, e.g.*, Cenco Inc. v. Seidman & Seidman, 686 F.2d 449, 454 (7th Cir.1982) (Illinois law); *cf.* Teamsters Local 282 Pension Trust Fund v. Angelos, 762 F.2d 522, 528–29 (7th Cir.1985). Proud did not merely say, "There are no liens"; he said, "I have conducted a U.C.C., tax, and judgment search"; and not only is this statement, too, a false one, but its falsehood cannot have been inadvertent, for Proud knew he had not conducted such a search. The concealment of his relationship with Crawford might also support a charge of fraud. But Greycas decided, for whatever reason, to argue negligent misrepresentation rather than fraud. It may have feared that Proud's insurance policy for professional malpractice excluded deliberate wrongdoing from its coverage, or may not have wanted to bear the higher burden of proving fraud, or may have feared that an accusation of fraud would make it harder to settle the case—for most cases, of course, are settled, though this one has not been. In any event, Proud does not argue that either he is liable for fraud or he is liable for nothing.

[Applying the basic test from § 552 of the *Restatement,* the court concluded that Greycas had established liability on the negligent misrepresentation claim.]

Proud argues, however, that his damages should be reduced in recognition of Greycas's own contributory negligence, which, though no longer a complete defense in Illinois, is a partial defense, renamed "comparative negligence." It is as much a defense to negligent misrepresentation as to any other tort of negligence. On the issue of comparative negligence the district court said only that "defendant may have proved negligence upon the part of plaintiff but that negligence, if any, had no causal relationship to the malpractice of the defendant or the damages to the plaintiff." This comment is not easy to fathom. If Greycas was careless in deciding whether to make the loan, this implies that a reasonable investigation by Greycas would have shown that the collateral for the loan was already heavily encumbered; knowing this, Greycas would not have made the loan and therefore would not have suffered any damages.

But we think it too clear to require a remand for further proceedings that Proud failed to prove a want of due care by Greycas. Due care is the care that is optimal given that the other party is exercising due care. *See* McCarty v. Pheasant Run, Inc., 826 F.2d 1554, 1557 (7th Cir.1987); Davis v. Consolidated Rail Corp., 788 F.2d 1260, 1265 (7th Cir.1986) (both cases applying Illinois law). It is not the higher level of care that would be optimal if potential tort victims were required to assume that the rest of the world was negligent. A pedestrian is not required to exercise a level of care (e.g., wearing a helmet or a shin guard) that would be optimal if there were no sanctions against reckless driving. Otherwise drivers would be encouraged to drive recklessly, and knowing this pedestrians would be encouraged to wear helmets and shin guards. The result would be a shift from a superior method of accident avoidance (not driving recklessly) to an inferior one (pedestrian armor).

So we must ask whether Greycas would have been careless not to conduct its own UCC search had Proud done what he had said he did—conduct his own UCC search. The answer is no. The law normally does not require duplicative precautions unless one is likely to fail or the consequences of failure (slight though the likelihood may be) would be catastrophic. One UCC search is enough to disclose prior liens, and Greycas acted reasonably in relying on Proud to conduct it. Although Greycas had much warning that Crawford was in financial trouble and that the loan might not be repaid, that was a reason for charging a hefty interest rate and insisting that the loan be secured; it was not a reason for duplicating Proud's work. It is not hard to conduct a UCC lien search; it just requires checking the records in the recorder's office for the county where the debtor lives. *See* Ill.Rev.Stat. ch. 26, ¶ 9-401. So the only reason to backstop Proud was if Greycas should have assumed he was careless or dishonest; and we have just said that the duty of care does not require such an assumption. Had Proud disclosed that he was Crawford's brother-in-law this might have been a warning signal that Greycas could ignore only at its peril. To go forward in the face of a known danger is to assume the risk. *See, e.g.,* Davis v. Consolidated Rail Corp., supra, 788 F.2d at 1266–67 (Illinois law); Phillips v. Croy, 173 Ind.App. 401, 405, 363 N.E.2d 1283, 1285 (1977). But Proud did not disclose his relationship to Crawford.

A final point. The record of this case reveals serious misconduct by an Illinois attorney. We are therefore sending a copy of this opinion to the Attorney Registration and Disciplinary

Commission of the Supreme Court of Illinois for such disciplinary action as may be deemed appropriate in the circumstances.

Affirmed.

* * *

Application of the litigation privilege. The absolute litigation privilege developed in the defamation context has also been applied by some courts to negligent misrepresentation claims. Paul T. Hayden, *Reconsidering the Litigator's Absolute Privilege to Defame,* 54 Ohio St. L.J. 985, 985 (1993).

Chapter 13

Other Remedies for Deceptive Practices

Claims of negligent and fraudulent misrepresentation may be available to the victims of misrepresentations. But, as the previous chapters illustrated, there are a number of potential obstacles plaintiffs may face when proceeding under these theories. Even if a plaintiff can avoid pretrial dismissal on the issues of scienter, justifiable reliance, privity, or any of the other requirements that might trip up a fraudulent or negligent misrepresentation claim, the economic loss rule might mandate dismissal. *See* Force v. ITT Hartford Life & Annuity Ins. Co., 4 F. Supp. 2d 843 (D. Minn. 1998). In some instances, a business may have engaged in a deceptive practice or a pattern of deceptive practices, but the amount of damages may be so low as to discourage pursuit of a fraud claim. In short, a common law misrepresentation claim may provide insufficient protection for consumers. This chapter presents some possible alternative theories of recovery for the victims of misrepresentations.

A. Consumer Protection Statutes

Exercise 13.1

Defendant is a real estate developer who advertised the sale of lakefront lots. Plaintiff and Defendant signed a "Real Estate Reservation Agreement." The agreement contained the following language:

> 1. *Reservation of Residence Homes(s).* Purchaser hereby reserves the right to purchase the aforedescribed Residence Home(s) in Lot 10A at Hawk's Landing....
>
> 2. *Purchase Price.* The purchase price of the Residence Homes(s) hereby reserved by Purchaser shall be U.S. $1,200,000 (the "Purchase Price"). Seller assures Purchaser that the Purchase Price shall be that which is to be set forth in the Contract.
>
> 3. *Refundable Deposit.* Contemporaneously with Purchaser's execution of this Agreement, Purchaser agrees to deliver to Seller a check or payment by major credit card reasonably acceptable to Seller in the amount of U.S. $25,000 as a good faith deposit (hereinafter referred to as "Deposit") to be held by Seller in consideration for Seller's reservation of the aforedescribed Residence Home(s) in Purchaser's name.... In the event that the Purchaser elects for any reason not to purchase the aforedescribed Residence Home(s) prior to the time that a legally binding Contract is executed by Purchaser,

> then, pursuant to Section 4 below, the Deposit together with any interest that has accrued, shall promptly be refunded to Purchaser.
>
> 4. *No obligation.* Purchaser acknowledges that until both Purchaser and Seller have executed a Contract with respect to the aforedescribed Residence Home(s), Purchaser is under no obligation to purchase and Seller is under no obligation to sell such Residence Home(s). This agreement can be terminated by either party at any time, subject to a refund of Purchaser's Deposit in accordance with Section 5 below.

When the time came to execute the purchase agreement five months later, the defendant offered a contract for Lot 2C, not 10A. Lot 2C is significantly less desirable than Lot 10A. In addition, the contract contained a purchase price of $1,495,000, not $1,200,000. Plaintiff's lawyer originally planned to argue that the agreement constituted an option contract. However, he decided to abandon that theory because although options are generally irrevocable on the part of a seller, in this instance paragraph 4 allowed either party to terminate the agreement. Thus, the reservation agreement was not an option contract. Instead, Plaintiff is proceeding on the theory that Defendant's actions are in violation of the Florida Deceptive and Unfair Trade Practices Act (FDUTPA) (see *infra*). What is the likely result?

"Since the late 1960s, every state in the union has passed some form of legislation aimed at protecting consumers from sales abuses." DEE PRIDGEN & RICHARD A. ALDERMAN, CONSUMER PROTECTION AND THE LAW § 2:9 (2008–09 ed.). As a result, consumers are often no longer forced to rely on common law theories and may instead rely upon state unfair and deceptive acts or practices (or state UDAP) statutes.

The state statutes take a variety of forms. Most of the statutes, however, have their roots in Section 5 of the Federal Trade Commission (FTC) Act. 15 U.S.C. § 45. The Federal Trade Commission (FTC) is authorized to investigate alleged violations of the Act and to commence enforcement proceedings if it has reason to believe its provisions have been violated. Complaints are adjudicated before an administrative law judge. Some states modeled their consumer protection statutes after the FTC Act. (These are the so-called "little FTC Acts.") Other states use different approaches. But all provide expanded coverage for consumers who have been the victim of unfair or deceptive acts.

1. Prohibition of Unfair or Deceptive Acts

a. In General

Florida Statutes Annotated

§ 501.204

> (1) Unfair methods of competition, unconscionable acts or practices, and unfair or deceptive acts or practices in the conduct of any trade or commerce are hereby declared unlawful.
>
> (2) It is the intent of the Legislature that, in construing subsection (1), due consideration and great weight shall be given to the interpretations of the Federal Trade Commission and the federal courts relating to § 5(a)(1) of the Federal Trade Commission Act, 15 U.S.C. § 45(a)(1).

* * *

Tennessee Code, § 47-18-104

Unfair or deceptive acts prohibited.

(a) Unfair or deceptive acts or practices affecting the conduct of any trade or commerce constitute unlawful acts or practices and are Class B misdemeanors.

(b) The following unfair or deceptive acts or practices affecting the conduct of any trade or commerce are declared to be unlawful and in violation of this part:

(1) Falsely passing off goods or services as those of another;

(2) Causing likelihood of confusion or of misunderstanding as to the source, sponsorship, approval or certification of goods or services. This subdivision (b)(2) does not prohibit the private labeling of goods and services;

(3) Causing likelihood of confusion or misunderstanding as to affiliation, connection or association with, or certification by, another. This subdivision (b)(3) does not prohibit the private labeling of goods or services;

(4) Using deceptive representations or designations of geographic origin in connection with goods or services;

(5) Representing that goods or services have sponsorship, approval, characteristics, ingredients, uses, benefits or quantities that they do not have or that a person has a sponsorship approval, status, affiliation or connection that such person does not have;

(6) Representing that goods are original or new if they are deteriorated, altered to the point of decreasing the value, reconditioned, reclaimed, used or secondhand;

(7) Representing that goods or services are of a particular standard, quality or grade, or that goods are of a particular style or model, if they are of another;

(8) Disparaging the goods, services or business of another by false or misleading representations of fact;

(9) Advertising goods or services with intent not to sell them as advertised;

(10) Advertising goods or services with intent not to supply reasonably expectable public demand, unless the advertisement discloses a limitation of quantity;

(11) Making false or misleading statements of fact concerning the reasons for, existence of, or amounts of price reductions;

(12) Representing that a consumer transaction confers or involves rights, remedies or obligations that it does not have or involve or which are prohibited by law;

(13) Representing that a service, replacement or repair is needed when it is not;

(14) Causing confusion or misunderstanding with respect to the authority of a salesperson, representative or agent to negotiate the final terms of a consumer transaction;

(15) Failing to disclose that a charge for the servicing of any goods in whole or in part is based on a predetermined rate or charge, or guarantee or warranty, instead of the value of the services actually performed;

(16) Disconnecting, turning back, or resetting the odometer of any motor vehicle so as to reduce the number of miles indicated on the odometer gauge, except as provided for in § 39-14-132(b);

(17) Advertising of any sale by falsely representing that a person is going out of business;

(18) Using or employing a chain referral sales plan in connection with the sale or offer to sell of goods, merchandise, or anything of value, which uses the sales technique, plan, arrangement or agreement in which the buyer or prospective buyer is offered the opportunity to purchase goods or services and, in connection with the purchase, receives the seller's promise or representation that the buyer shall have the right to receive compensation or consideration in any form for furnishing to the seller the names of other prospective buyers if the receipt of compensation or consideration is contingent upon the occurrence of an event subsequent to the time the buyer purchases the merchandise or goods;

(19) Representing that a guarantee or warranty confers or involves rights or remedies which it does not have or involve; provided, that nothing in this subdivision (b)(19) shall be construed to alter the implied warranty of merchantability as defined in §47-2-314;

(20) Selling or offering to sell, either directly or associated with the sale of goods or services, a right of participation in a pyramid distributorship. As used in this subdivision (b)(20), a 'pyramid distributorship' means any sales plan or operation for the sale or distribution of goods, services or other property wherein a person for a consideration acquires the opportunity to receive a pecuniary benefit, which is not primarily contingent on the volume or quantity of goods, services or other property sold or delivered to consumers, and is based upon the inducement of additional persons, by such person or others, regardless of number, to participate in the same plan or operation;

(21) Using statements or illustrations in any advertisement which create a false impression of the grade, quality, quantity, make, value, age, size, color, usability or origin of the goods or services offered, or which may otherwise misrepresent the goods or services in such a manner that later, on disclosure of the true facts, there is a likelihood that the buyer may be switched from the advertised goods or services to other goods or services;

(22) Using any advertisement containing an offer to sell goods or services when the offer is not a bona fide effort to sell the advertised goods or services. An offer is not bona fide, even though the true facts are subsequently made known to the buyer, if the first contact or interview is secured by deception;

(23) Representing in any advertisement a false impression that the offer of goods has been occasioned by a financial or natural catastrophe when such is not true, or misrepresenting the former price, savings, quality or ownership of any goods sold; ... [Another 25 specific prohibited acts are omitted.]

* * *

Public interest requirement. The FTC's authority to pursue unfair and deceptive practice actions is limited to proceedings that "would be to the interest of the public." 15 U.S.C. §45(b). State agencies are under similar constraints in enforcing state statutes, and some states also require that individual consumers establish that a defendant's unfair or deceptive acts implicate the public interest. *See, e.g.*, Lightfoot v. MacDonald, 86 Wash.2d 331, 544 P.2d 88 (1976). In some states, this requirement appears in the statute itself. W. Va. Code §46A-6-101. Thus, a simple breach of contract action may not satisfy the public interest requirement, preventing plaintiffs from pursuing a statutory claim. *Lightfoot*, 544 P.2d at 91. Where, however, the defendant's conduct is repeated (or has the potential for repetition) and impacts (or may potentially impact) multiple consumers, the public interest requirement may be satisfied.

* * *

b. Unfair Acts

Exercise 13.2

Tom's Termite Control entered into contracts with several hundred Florida residents to provide extermination services. The contracts offered pest control and repair services with guarantees for the lifetime of the treated structure so long as the customer paid a specified annual renewal fee. Salespersons and sales brochures from Tom's led customers to believe that the annual fee could not be increased by Tom's during the life of the contract. The contract itself, however, was silent about Tom's ability to increase the fee. Two years ago, Tom's began charging an increased annual renewal fee to existing customers. Has Tom's committed an unfair act under § 501.204 of Florida's Deceptive and Unfair Trade Practices Act *supra*?

FTC Policy Statement on Unfairness

Appended to *International Harvester Co.*,
104 F.T.C. 949, 1070 (1984). *See* 15 U.S.C. § 45(n)

FEDERAL TRADE COMMISSION
WASHINGTON, D. C. 20580

December 17, 1980

The Honorable Wendell H. Ford
Chairman, Consumer Subcommittee
Committee on Commerce, Science, and Transportation
Room 130 Russell Office Building
Washington, D.C. 20510

The Honorable John C. Danforth
Ranking Minority Member, Consumer Subcommittee
Committee on Commerce, Science, and Transportation
Room 130 Russell Office Building
Washington, D.C. 20510

Dear Senators Ford and Danforth:

This is in response to your letter of June 13, 1980, concerning one aspect of this agency's jurisdiction over "unfair or deceptive acts or practices." ...

In response to your inquiry we have therefore undertaken a review of the decided cases and rules and have synthesized from them the most important principles of general applicability. Rather than merely reciting the law, we have attempted to provide the Committee with a concrete indication of the manner in which the Commission has enforced, and will continue to enforce, its unfairness mandate. In so doing we intend to address the concerns that have been raised about the meaning of consumer unfairness, and thereby attempt to provide a greater sense of certainty about what the Commission would regard as an unfair act or practice under Section 5.

Commission Statement of Policy on the Scope of the
Consumer Unfairness Jurisdiction

Section 5 of the FTC Act prohibits, in part, "unfair ... acts or practices in or affecting commerce." This is commonly referred to as the Commission's consumer unfairness jurisdiction. The Commission's jurisdiction over "unfair methods of competition" is not discussed in this letter. Although we cannot give an exhaustive treatment of the law of consumer unfairness in this short statement, some relatively concrete conclusions ran nonetheless be drawn.

The present understanding of the unfairness standard is the result of an evolutionary process. The statute was deliberately framed in general terms since Congress recognized the impossibility of drafting a complete list of unfair trade practices that would not quickly become outdated or leave loopholes for easy evasion. The task of identifying unfair trade practices was therefore assigned to the Commission, subject to judicial review, in the expectation that the underlying criteria would evolve and develop over time. As the Supreme Court observed as early as 1931, the ban on unfairness "belongs to that class of phrases which do not admit of precise definition, but the meaning and application of which must be arrived at by what this court elsewhere has called 'the gradual process of judicial inclusion and exclusion.'"

By 1964 enough cases had been decided to enable the Commission to identify three factors that it considered when applying the prohibition against consumer unfairness. These were: (1) whether the practice injures consumers; (2) whether it violates established public policy; (3) whether it is unethical or unscrupulous. These factors were later quoted with apparent approval by the Supreme Court in the 1972 case of *Sperry & Hutchinson* [405 U.S. 233, 244–45 n.5 (1972).] Since then the Commission has continued to refine the standard of unfairness in its cases and rules, and it has now reached a more detailed sense of both the definition and the limits of these criteria.

Consumer injury

Unjustified consumer injury is the primary focus of the FTC Act, and the most important of the three *S&H* criteria. By itself it can be sufficient to warrant a finding of unfairness. The Commission's ability to rely on an independent criterion of consumer injury is consistent with the intent of the statute, which was to "[make] the consumer who may be injured by an unfair trade practice of equal concern before the law with the merchant injured by the unfair methods of a dishonest competitor."

The independent nature of the consumer injury criterion does not mean that every consumer injury is legally "unfair," however. To justify a finding of unfairness the injury must satisfy three tests. It must be substantial; it must not be outweighed by any countervailing benefits to consumers or competition that the practice produces; and it must be an injury that consumers themselves could not reasonably have avoided.

Violation of public policy

The second *S&H* standard asks whether the conduct violates public policy as it has been established by statute, common law, industry practice, or otherwise. This criterion may be applied in two different ways. It may be used to test the validity and strength of the evidence of consumer injury, or, less often, it may be cited for a dispositive legislative or judicial determination that such injury is present.

Although public policy was listed by the *S&H* Court as a separate consideration, it is used most frequently by the Commission as a means of providing additional evidence on the degree of consumer injury caused by specific practices. To be sure, most Commission actions are brought to redress relatively clear-cut injuries, and those determinations are based, in large part, on objective economic analysis. As we have indicated before, the Commission believes that considerable attention should be devoted to the analysis of whether substantial net harm has occurred, not only because that is part of the unfairness test, but also because the focus on injury is the best way to ensure that the Commission acts responsibly and uses its resources wisely. Nonetheless, the Commission wishes to emphasize the importance of examining outside statutory policies and established judicial principles for assistance in helping the agency ascertain whether a particular form of conduct does in fact tend to harm consumers. Thus the agency has referred to First Amendment decisions upholding consumers' rights to receive information, for example, to confirm that restrictions on advertising tend unfairly to hinder the informed exercise of consumer choice.

Conversely, statutes or other sources of public policy may affirmatively allow for a practice that the Commission tentatively views as unfair. The existence of such policies will then give the agency reason to reconsider its assessment of whether the practice is actually injurious in its net effects. In other situations there may be no clearly established public policies, or the policies may even be in conflict. While that does not necessarily preclude the Commission from taking action if there is strong evidence of net consumer injury, it does underscore the desirability of carefully examining public policies in all instances. In any event, whenever objective evidence of consumer injury is difficult to obtain, the need to identify and assess all relevant public policies assumes increased importance.

...

To the extent that the Commission relies heavily on public policy to support a finding of unfairness, the policy should be clear and well-established. In other words, the policy should be declared or embodied in formal sources such as statutes, judicial decisions, or the Constitution as interpreted by the courts, rather than being ascertained from the general sense of the national values. The policy should likewise be one that is widely shared, and not the isolated decision of a single state or a single court. If these two tests are not met the policy cannot be considered as an "established" public policy for purposes of the *S&H* criterion. The Commission would then act only on the basis of convincing independent evidence that the practice was distorting the operation of the market and thereby causing unjustified consumer injury.

Unethical or unscrupulous conduct

Finally, the third *S&H* standard asks whether the conduct was immoral, unethical, oppressive, or unscrupulous. This test was presumably included in order to be sure of reaching all the purposes of the underlying statute, which forbids "unfair" acts or practices. It would therefore allow the Commission to reach conduct that violates generally recognized standards of business ethics. The test has proven, however, to be largely duplicative. Conduct that is truly unethical or unscrupulous will almost always injure consumers or violate public policy as well. The Commission has therefore never relied on the third element of *S&H* as an independent basis for a finding of unfairness, and it will act in the future only on the basis of the first two.

* * *

1. Other approaches. States take a variety of approaches when defining the concept of an unfair practice. For example, even after the FTC's 1980 policy statement, some courts continue to rely on the FTC's prior standard. PNR, Inc. v. Beacon Prop. Mgmt., Inc., 842 So. 2d 773, 777 (Fla. 2003); People ex rel Hartigan v. All American Alum. & Const. Co., Inc., 524 N.E.2d 1067, 1071 (Ill. Ct. App. 1988).

2. Unconscionable acts. Note that in addition to prohibiting unfair practices, Florida's statute also prohibits "unconscionable acts or practices." A significant number of states include this additional prohibition. The Uniform Sales Practices Act, on which some state statutes are based, contains a list of circumstances that might lead to a finding of unconscionability. Some of these circumstances (grossly excessive price, excessively one-sided terms, etc.) have their roots in the concept of unconscionability in contract law.

3. Acts covered. Common examples of unfair or unconscionable acts or practices include "(1) charging unconscionably high prices for consumer goods; (2) suing consumer debtors in distant forums; [and] (3) using duress or coercion to obtain an agreement from a consumer." DEE PRIDGEN & RICHARD A. ALDERMAN, CONSUMER PROTECTION AND THE LAW § 3:15, at 110 (2008–09 ed.).

* * *

c. Deceptive Acts

Exercise 13.3

Seller advertises a car as a 2008 model. However, Seller was aware when it purchased the car from another individual that the car was "clipped," meaning that the front of a 2008 model had been welded onto the back of a 2006 model. Thus, the rear wheels, trunk, and other parts of the car were from a 2006 model. Buyer purchases the vehicle without knowledge of this fact and only discovers the fact that the car had been clipped a year later. The fact that the car had been clipped did not affect its reliability, safety, or market value. Buyer brings suit under Florida's Consumer Protection Act. Has Seller engaged in a deceptive act or practice?

FTC Policy Statement on Deception

Appended to *Cliffdale Associates, Inc.*, 103 F.T.C. 110, 174 (1984)

FEDERAL TRADE COMMISSION
WASHINGTON, D.C. 20580

October 14, 1983

The Honorable John D. Dingell
Chairman
Committee on Energy and Commerce
U.S. House of Representatives
Washington, D.C. 20515

Dear Mr. Chairman:

This letter responds to the Committee's inquiry regarding the Commission's enforcement policy against deceptive acts or practices. We also hope this letter will provide guidance to the public.

Section 5 of the FTC Act declares unfair or deceptive acts or practices unlawful. Section 12 specifically prohibits false ads likely to induce the purchase of food, drugs, devices or cosmetics. Section 15 defines a false ad for purposes of Section 12 as one which is "misleading in a material respect." Numerous Commission and judicial decisions have defined and elaborated on the phrase "deceptive acts or practices" under both Sections 5 and 12. Nowhere, however, is there a single definitive statement of the Commission's view of its authority. The Commission believes that such a statement would be useful to the public, as well as the Committee in its continuing review of our jurisdiction.

We have therefore reviewed the decided cases to synthesize the most important principles of general applicability. We have attempted to provide a concrete indication of the manner in which the Commission will enforce its deception mandate. In so doing, we intend to address the concerns that have been raised about the meaning of deception, and thereby attempt to provide a greater sense of certainty as to how the concept will be applied.

I. SUMMARY

Certain elements undergird all deception cases. First, there must be a representation, omission or practice that is likely to mislead the consumer. Practices that have been found misleading or deceptive in specific cases include false oral or written representations, misleading price claims, sales of hazardous or systematically defective products or services without adequate disclosures, failure to disclose information regarding pyramid sales, use of bait and switch techniques, failure to perform promised services, and failure to meet warranty obligations.

Second, we examine the practice from the perspective of a consumer acting reasonably in the circumstances. If the representation or practice affects or is directed primarily to a particular group, the Commission examines reasonableness from the perspective of that group.

Third, the representation, omission, or practice must be a "material" one. The basic question is whether the act or practice is likely to affect the consumer's conduct or decision with regard to a product or service. If so, the practice is material, and consumer injury is likely, because consumers are likely to have chosen differently but for the deception. In many instances, materiality, and hence injury, can be presumed from the nature of the practice. In other instances, evidence of materiality may be necessary.

Thus, the Commission will find deception if there is a representation, omission or practice that is likely to mislead the consumer acting reasonably in the circumstances, to the consumer's detriment.

* * *

1. Scienter. Noticeably absent from the FTC's summary is any mention of the scienter requirement in common-law fraud actions. This is not an oversight. An intent to deceive is not required under the statutes; even innocent misrepresentations are actionable. Why should this be the case? As we will see, however, there may be a benefit in terms of recovery to establishing an intent to deceive on the part of the defendant.

2. Reliance. Also noticeably lacking in most state consumer protection statutes is any requirement that a consumer justifiably relied on the defendant's deceptive practice. Indeed, the FTC policy statement on deceptive practices defines a deceptive practice in terms of whether it is "likely to mislead the consumer...." As we will see, however, in order to recover under a consumer protection statute, a consumer will ultimately need to prove reliance in fact. Instead of the "likely to mislead" standard, some courts employ a "tendency or capacity to deceive" standard. Which would you prefer if you were the plaintiff's lawyer?

3. Acts covered. As the Tennessee statute, *supra*, illustrates, some jurisdictions include a laundry list of specific deceptive acts that are prohibited. Common examples of deceptive practices covered under statutes that take a more general approach include things like bait and switch advertising and deceptive pricing (e.g., claiming to sell a product at "factory invoice price"). Commonwealth v. Call River Motor Sales, Inc., 565 N.E.2d 1205 (Mass. 1991).

* * *

2. Coverage

Florida Statutes Annotated

§ 501.203

As used in this chapter, unless the context requires otherwise, the term:

(1) 'Consumer transaction' means a sale, lease, assignment, award by chance, or other disposition of an item of goods, a consumer service, or an intangible to an individual for purposes that are primarily personal, family, or household or that relate to a business opportunity that requires both his expenditure of money or property and his personal services on a continuing basis and in which he has not been previously engaged, or a solicitation by a supplier with respect to any of these dispositions.

(7) 'Consumer' means an individual; child, by and through its parent or legal guardian; firm; association; joint adventure; partnership; estate; trust; business trust; syndicate; fiduciary; corporation; or any other group or combination.

(8) 'Trade or commerce' means the advertising, soliciting, providing, offering, or distributing, whether by sale, rental, or otherwise, of any good or service, or any property, whether tangible or intangible, or any other article, commodity, or thing of value, wherever situated. 'Trade or commerce' shall include the conduct of any trade or commerce, however denominated, including any nonprofit or not-for-profit person or activity.

* * *

a. Transactions between Consumers and Merchants

The majority of jurisdictions, like Florida, limit the coverage of their statutes to consumers and consumer transactions. Thus, businesses typically cannot take advantage of the statutes. And, like Florida, most jurisdictions limit the coverage of their statutes to unfair or deceptive acts in the conduct of trade or commerce. One question that has arisen is whether the statutes are limited to unfair or deceptive acts by merchants or whether they cover transactions between consumers and nonmerchants (such as between the individual buyer and seller of a house).

Focus Questions: *Lantner v. Carson*

1. *What is the significance of section 11 of Massachusetts' statute in terms of deciding whether the statute applies to transactions between nonmerchants?*
2. *Assuming the same facts as in* Lantner, *should the result be the same in a jurisdiction whose statute does not contain language similar to that found in section 11?*

Lantner v. Carson

373 N.E.2d 973
(Mass. 1978)

HENNESSEY, Chief Justice.

In March, 1977, the plaintiffs commenced an action under G.L. c. 93A, inserted by St.1967, c. 813, § 1, commonly known as the Consumer Protection Act, against the defendants who as private individuals sold them their home. The complaint sought treble damages, attorneys' fees, and other relief in connection with the repair of several defects discovered by the plaintiffs after they took occupancy.

The defendants filed a motion to dismiss the complaint under Mass.R.Civ.P. 12(b)(6), 365 Mass. 754 (1974), which motion was allowed. Judgment was entered accordingly, and the case was dismissed. Thereafter, the plaintiffs appealed, asserting that the remedial provisions of G.L. c. 93A apply, even where the consumer transaction at issue is the isolated sale of a private home. We granted direct appellate review.

It is well established that in proscribing "unfair or deceptive acts or practices in the conduct of any trade or commerce" (G.L. c. 93A, § 2) the consumer protection statute reaches "(a) wide range of activities," including the "sale ... of any ... property, ... real, personal or mixed." G.L. c. 93A, § 1(b). We conclude, however, that as broadly and expansively as the statute applies to the regulation of business practices, G.L. c. 93A is not available where the transaction is strictly private in nature, and is in no way undertaken in the ordinary course of a trade or business. Accordingly, we affirm the dismissal of the plaintiffs' complaint.

For the purposes of our ruling on the motion to dismiss, we accept as true the factual allegations in the complaint. They are as follows. Under an agreement dated April 12, 1976, the plaintiffs agreed to buy and the defendants agreed to sell the premises at 48 Georgetown Road, Boxford, which property was the private residence of the defendants. The purchase and sale agreement, drawn by Wini McDuff as the broker,[2] provided in part that: "This agreement is made ... subject to the following: Water turned on, well functional, and water quality tests acceptable." Prior to this written agreement, the defendants had made other representations, namely that (1) the evident damage to second floor ceilings was a result of a defective roof which had since been repaired; and that (2) the second floor fireplace was stuffed with paper to avoid drafts, but was otherwise in complete working order.

The sale was consummated on or about May 19, 1976. The plaintiffs took occupancy on June 8, 1976. Almost immediately thereafter, difficulties developed. [It turned out

2. We observe that the real estate broker was not made a party to this case.

that, among other things, the roof that had supposedly been repaired had not, and that the fireplace that was supposedly stuffed with paper to prevent drafts had actually been reconstructed from newspaper "bricks."]

The plaintiffs repaired these defects. On January 17, and February 10, 1977, in compliance with G.L. c. 93A, s 9(3), the plaintiffs sent to the defendants a written demand for relief. Having received no tender of settlement from the defendants within thirty days of the demand, the plaintiffs commenced the instant action.

For the purpose of our subsequent analysis, it is useful at this time to review briefly the applicable sections of G.L. c. 93A. Through § 9(1), as amended through St.1971, c. 241, G.L. c. 93A provides a private right of action to "(a)ny person who purchases ... property ... primarily for personal, family or household purposes and thereby suffers any loss of money or property ... as a result of the use ... by another person of an unfair or deceptive act or practice declared unlawful by section two." Section 2 proscribes "unfair or deceptive acts or practices in the conduct of any trade or commerce," and § 1 states that "trade" and "commerce" shall include "the advertising, the offering for sale, ... (or) sale ... of any ... property ... real, personal, or mixed."

The plaintiffs argue that the terms of §§ 1 and 2 are broad enough to reach any type of commercial exchange, regardless of the nature of the transaction or the character of the parties involved. According to the plaintiffs, the Legislature made no distinction in the statute between the professional salesperson or business person, and the amateur, the individual who may sell a consumer item only on an isolated basis. Therefore, they argue, the remedial provisions of § 9 should be available to the consumer who purchases from an individual homeowner, regardless of the fact the transaction is not in pursuit of the seller's ordinary course of business. We do not agree with this expansive reading.

First, the statute does not specifically define the phrase "in the conduct of any trade or commerce." Nevertheless, we may infer its meaning from reading the statute as a whole. In so doing, we observe that, contrary to the plaintiffs' assertions, G.L. c. 93A creates a sharp distinction between a business person and an individual who participates in commercial transactions on a private, nonprofessional basis.

For example, where § 9 affords a private remedy to the individual consumer who suffers a loss as a result of the use of an unfair or deceptive act or practice, an entirely different section, § 11, extends the same remedy to "(a)ny person who engages in the conduct of any trade or commerce."[5] In Slaney v. Westwood Auto, Inc., 366 Mass. 688, 322 N.E.2d 768 (1975), we concluded that by these terms, s 11 extends the consumer protection remedies of G.L. c. 93A to the "businessman." Id. at 695–697, 322 N.E.2d 768. Indeed, this construction is a necessary one. Were we to interpret the phrase "in the conduct of any trade or commerce" as the plaintiffs suggest, to apply to any commercial transaction whatsoever, the "persons" covered by §§ 9 and 11 would be identical. Section 11 would thus be superfluous merely a repetition of § 9. We have stated that "(a)n intention to enact a barren and ineffective provision is not lightly to be imputed to the Legislature." Insurance Rating Bd. v. Commissioner of Ins., 356 Mass. 184, 189, 248 N.E.2d 500, 504 (1969). Therefore, we conclude that with respect to G.L. c. 93A, where the Legislature employed

5. Section 11, inserted by St.1972, c. 614, s 2, provides, in pertinent part: "Any person who engages in the conduct of any trade or commerce and who suffers any loss of money or property ... as a result of the use ... by another person who engages in any trade or commerce of an unfair ... or deceptive act or practice declared unlawful by section two ... may ... bring an action in the superior court...."

the terms "persons engaged in the conduct of any trade or commerce," it intended to refer specifically to individuals acting in a business context.

These considerations are helpful in determining the meaning of § 2, which employs the phrase "in the conduct of any trade or commerce." Following the rule of statutory construction which suggests that words used in one place within a statute be given the same meaning when found in other parts of the statute, we conclude that the terms of § 2 must be construed similarly to those in § 11. Thus, the proscription in § 2 of "unfair or deceptive acts or practices in the conduct of any trade or commerce" must be read to apply to those acts or practices which are perpetrated in a business context.

Finally, we note that our conclusions with respect to the scope of G.L. c. 93A are not inconsistent with the statute's broadly protective legislative purpose. In *Dodd v. Commercial Union Ins. Co.*, 365 N.E.2d 802 (Mass. 1977), we stated that the basic policy of G.L. c. 93A was "to regulate business activities with the view to providing ... a more equitable balance in the relationship of consumers to persons conducting business activities." An individual homeowner who decides to sell his residence stands in no better bargaining position than the individual consumer. Both parties have rights and liabilities established under common law principles of contract, tort, and property law. Thus, arming the "consumer" in this circumstance does not serve to equalize the positions of buyer and seller. Rather, it serves to give superior rights to only one of the parties, even though as nonprofessionals both stand on an equal footing.

Judgment affirmed.

* * *

1. Definition of "merchant" or "supplier." Some statutes explicitly limit coverage to transactions between consumers and "merchants" or "suppliers." In Kansas, for example, the term "supplier" means "a ... seller ... or other person who, *in the ordinary course of business*, solicits [or] engages in ... consumer transactions." K.S.A. § 50-624(i) (emphasis added). If a licensed real estate agent sells her own house and commits what would be a deceptive practice under the Act, does the Act apply to the transaction? *See* Heller v. Martin, 782 P.2d 1241 (Kan. Ct. App. 1989).

2. Transactions between consumers and nonmerchants. The majority of jurisdictions have concluded that transactions between individuals (i.e., two nonmerchants) are not covered by the statutes. Dee Pridgen & Richard A. Alderman, Consumer Protection and the Law § 4:16, at 213 (2008–09 ed.).

3. Treatment of real estate. Massachusetts's statute explicitly covers real estate transactions. Other statutes are silent on this issue. Thus, plaintiffs may be forced to argue that a deceptive act in the sale of real property is an act in the conduct of "trade or commerce" and hope that a court agrees. The question of which transactions are covered by consumer protection statutes is dealt with in the next section.

* * *

b. Covered Transactions

Focus Question: *Force v. ITT Hartford Life & Annuity Ins. Co.*

What is the basis for the court's holding?

Force v. ITT Hartford Life & Annuity Ins. Co.

4 F. Supp. 2d 843
(D. Minn. 1998)

The Plaintiffs base their claims on the allegedly false and misleading practices that ITT Hartford used to market life insurance policies under three separate "schemes." The three at issue are the "vanishing premium scheme," the "churning scheme," and the "retirement/ investment plan scheme." The gravamen of the Plaintiffs' claims is that ITT Hartford trained its sales agents to misrepresent to potential clients the true nature of the life insurance policies being offered, in an effort to boost the corporations' sales and profits.

In the 1980s, a change took place in the life insurance industry. Life insurance companies, including ITT Hartford, recognized that traditional life insurance was becoming obsolete in the face of other investment vehicles offering higher rates of return. Such companies faced increasing competition not only from mainstream investment funds, but also from insurers that would invest policyholders' premiums in high-risk investments like junk bonds. As a result, ITT Hartford, like other insurers, developed new types of life insurance, where the insurance company would invest the premiums more aggressively and policyholders could enjoy the returns of successful investments. The investment strategy behind this new type of policy was more volatile and complex than traditional life insurance policies.

[The plaintiffs brought a variety of common-law claims involving misrepresentation, most of which were dismissed due to the application of the economic loss rule. The court next considered whether to grant the defendant's motion to dismiss the plaintiffs' claims under Minnesota's Consumer Fraud Act.]

ITT Hartford argues that the Fraud Act does not apply because the Fraud Act has never been applied to an insurance contract. They argue that an insurance policy cannot be classified as "merchandise" and thereby come within the scope of the Fraud Act. The Plaintiffs cite to various other jurisdictions that have found insurance policies to be within the scope of similar statutes.

Minnesota's Consumer Fraud Act applies to any "objects, wares, goods, commodities, intangibles, real estate, loans, or services." Minn.Stat. § 325F.68 (1998). ITT Hartford argues that insurance does not come within the scope of this definition and, therefore, the Consumer Fraud Act is inapplicable to the instant case. In support of this argument, ITT Hartford relies on a Minnesota case which held that loan contracts were outside of the scope of the Act (prior to its amendment to specifically include "loans"), and a Vermont case which held that insurance was not a "good" or "service" within the scope of that state's consumer fraud statute. *See* Boubelik v. Liberty State Bank, 553 N.W.2d 393, 403 (Minn.1996); Wilder v. Aetna Life & Cas. Ins. Co., 140 Vt. 16, 433 A.2d 309, 310 (1981).

The court in *Boubelik* considered the issue of whether Minnesota's Consumer Fraud Act applied to bank loans. At the time, the Act defined "merchandise" as "any objects, wares, goods, commodities, intangibles, real estate, or services." Minn.Stat. § 325F.68, subd. 2.[18] The court held that bank loans were not covered by the Act, because the Legislature did not specifically include bank loans in the definition of "merchandise," and the loans did not fall within the meaning of either "intangibles" or "services." In reaching this conclusion, the court cited a federal case from Minnesota which held that loans of

18. After *Boubelik*, the Minnesota Legislature amended § 325F.68, subd. 2 to expressly include loans within the meaning of the term "merchandise."

money are not "sales," subject to the unfair trade practices provision of the Clayton Act, because "[o]ne does not 'sell' money in the usual business sense." United States v. Investors Diversified Services, Inc., 102 F.Supp. 645, 647 (D.Minn.1951). Relying on this reasoning, the *Boubelik* court held that to include loans in the scope of the Consumer Fraud Act would "extend the policy of consumer protection beyond the language of the statute" and would require the court to "invade the province of the legislature." *Boubelik*, 553 N.W.2d at 403.

While instructive, *Boubelik* does not control the instant case. Unlike money, one does sell insurance in the usual business sense. The Minnesota Supreme Court has held that, because "merchandise" is defined as including both "commodities" and "intangibles," the Act applies to the sale of investment contracts. Jenson v. Touche Ross & Co., 335 N.W.2d 720, 728 (Minn.1983). The Court finds *Jenson* to be more persuasive than *Boubelik* on this issue and, in accord with the majority of other jurisdictions that have considered this issue with regard to similarly worded statutes, holds that the Consumer Fraud Act does apply to the sale of insurance.

Because Minnesota's Consumer Fraud Act can be read to encompass the sale of insurance policies, the Court finds that ITT Hartford has not shown that the Plaintiffs have failed to state a claim upon which relief could be granted. Accordingly, the Court will deny ITT Hartford's Motion to Dismiss, with regard to the Plaintiffs' claim under the Consumer Fraud Act.

* * *

1. Majority approach. The majority of courts have agreed with the reasoning in *Force*.

2. Regulated industries. Similar issues regarding coverage have arisen regarding transactions in industries that are already specifically regulated. Thus, for example, some courts are split on the question of whether the extension of credit qualifies as a good or service under a consumer protection statute. *Compare* Boubelik v. Liberty State Bank, 553 N.W.2d 393 (Minn. 1996) *with* State ex rel. Stephan v. Brotherhood Bank & Trust Co., 649 P.2d 419 (Kan. 1982). The following section explores a similar issue.

* * *

c. Coverage of Professional Services

Focus Questions: *Short v. Demopolis*

1. *Does the court's holding provide sufficient guidance for future courts, litigants, and lawyers?*
2. *What is the basis for the distinction the court draws with respect to the acts that are and are not covered by the Consumer Protection Act?*

Short v. Demopolis

691 P.2d 163
(Wash. 1984)

DOLLIVER, Justice.

May lawyers be subject to liability under the Consumer Protection Act (CPA), RCW 19.86? Defendant Chris Demopolis appeals the Superior Court order which dismissed his counterclaims under CR 12(b)(6) for CPA violations against the plaintiffs' law firm of Short and Cressman.

In March 1980, Demopolis met with Douglas Hartwich, partner in plaintiffs' law firm, to discuss representation in two pending lawsuits. The first involved dissolution of a real estate partnership. The complaint alleged damages in excess of $200,000. After 2 days of trial, the action settled for $7,500. Attorney fees totaled $19,958.53. The second case involved a real estate forfeiture action. Defendant prevailed and was entitled to immediate possession of the premises, rental delinquencies, and damages.

A dispute ensued over the rendering of legal services. Defendant contends he hired Hartwich to handle personally his legal matters but that without his consent or knowledge Hartwich had a younger partner (Ferrell) and an associate (Mayotte) do the legal work. Plaintiffs maintain Hartwich personally introduced Ferrell and Mayotte to Demopolis, that he told Demopolis they would be handling the cases, and that Demopolis agreed to this arrangement.

The parties also contest the payment of attorney fees. Defendant asserts he rejected plaintiffs' first bill and made a final settlement of $14,000. The second bill for $29,122.80 is considered excessive by defendant as he holds numerous grievances with the quality of representation. Plaintiffs state they attempted to obtain payment from Demopolis but were unsuccessful. Subsequent to filing a notice of intent to withdraw in August 1980, but before the effective date, plaintiffs maintain they entered into an agreement with Demopolis.

In a letter dated September 3, 1980, Hartwich wrote Demopolis confirming (1) plaintiffs' acceptance of $14,000 as full payment for the partnership matter; (2) withdrawal of their notice to withdraw; (3) plaintiffs' intent to bill at their regular hourly rates for time expended on the second case; and (4) noting "You will be working on the [second] case directly with Don Ferrell and Jim Mayotte, as was the case in the partnership action." A handwritten statement, signed by Demopolis, to hold Short and Cressman harmless for the release of trust funds totaling $3,025.35 held by them for Demopolis' former attorney is on the first page of this letter. However, Demopolis' affidavit states he never received the original or a copy of the letter, he only agreed to hold plaintiffs harmless for the release of trust funds, and was not told he was waiving any legal rights to complain about the fees or the handling of the first case.

Plaintiffs sued Demopolis for breach of an express contract to pay for legal services. Demopolis denied liability and asserted affirmative defenses and counterclaims. He alleged 10 causes of action [including unfair and deceptive practices in violation of the Consumer Protection Act (CPA), RCW 19.86.]

Plaintiffs moved for summary judgment which was denied, except for defendant's claim for emotional distress damages which was dismissed. Subsequently, and before a second judge, plaintiffs made a CR 12(b)(6) motion to dismiss defendant's [CPA claim]. This latter motion was granted and the counterclaims were dismissed with prejudice. Three reasons were cited for dismissing defendant's counterclaims for CPA violations.

First, the practice of law did not constitute the conduct of any trade or commerce within the meaning of the CPA or Washington case law. Second, to regulate the legal profession through the CPA was an unconstitutional infringement on the power of the judiciary to regulate the practice of law. Third, other adequate remedies (breach of contract and malpractice) were available.

Defendant was granted direct discretionary review and assigns error to the dismissal of his CPA violation counterclaims pursuant to CR 12(b)(6) ("failure to state a claim upon which relief can be granted").

I

The first issue we consider is whether the practice of law falls within "trade or commerce" as that term is defined by RCW 19.86. RCW 19.86.020 provides:

> Unfair methods of competition and unfair or deceptive acts or practices in the conduct of any trade or commerce are hereby declared unlawful.

"'Trade' and 'commerce' shall include the sale of assets or services, and any commerce directly or indirectly affecting the people of the state of Washington." RCW 19.86.010(2).

The trial court, relying on *Lightfoot v. MacDonald*, 86 Wash.2d 331, 544 P.2d 88 (1976), interpreted the CPA as exempting the practice of law. In *Lightfoot*, a client allegedly suffered damages as a result of her attorney's nonfeasance. We disallowed her CPA claim because of her failure to show sufficient public impact.

> A breach of a private contract affecting no one but the parties to the contract, whether that breach be negligent or intentional, is not an act or practice affecting the public interest.

86 Wash.2d at 334, 544 P.2d 88. In dictum we "implicitly recognized the lack of precedent for the concept that the legal profession is involved in trade and commerce ..." Subsequent case law does not appear finally to have answered the question.

The CPA contains no language expressly including or excluding attorneys from its purview. The act, however, contains its own guide to statutory construction. RCW 19.86.920 provides:

> The legislature hereby declares that the purpose of this act is to complement the body of federal law governing restraints of trade, unfair competition and unfair, deceptive, and fraudulent acts or practices in order to protect the public and foster fair and honest competition. *It is the intent of the legislature that, in construing this act, the courts be guided by final decisions of the federal courts* ... interpreting the various federal statutes dealing with the same or similar matters and that in deciding whether conduct restrains or monopolizes trade or commerce ... To this end this act shall be liberally construed that its beneficial purposes may be served. (Italics ours.)

Some earlier cases from the United States Supreme Court seem by dictum to have recognized a "learned professions" exemption to the antitrust laws. This exemption was based on judicial interpretations of what constituted a trade—"[w]herever any occupation, employment, or business is carried on for the purpose of profit, or gain, or a livelihood, not in the liberal arts or in the learned professions ..." Atlantic Cleaners & Dyers, Inc. v. United States, 286 U.S. 427, 436, (1932). The question as to whether there could be restraint of "trade or commerce" when the activities restrained were the professional activities of members of a "learned profession" was not reached until Goldfarb v. Virginia State Bar, 421 U.S. 773, 95 S.Ct. 2004, 44 L.Ed.2d 572 (1975).

In *Goldfarb*, the United States Supreme Court held minimum fee schedules, published by a county bar association and enforced by the state bar, violated the Sherman Act, 15 U.S.C. § 1 (1976). The bar association argued immunity under the Sherman Act because the practice of law was a learned profession—not trade or commerce. The association maintained competition was inconsistent with the practice of a profession because enhancing profit was not the goal of professional activities; the goal was to provide community services. The Court said neither the nature of an occupation in and of itself nor the claim of public service controlled in determining whether section 1 included performance. The Court went on to state:

> The language of § 1 of the Sherman Act, of course, contains no exception.... And our cases have repeatedly established that there is a heavy presumption against implicit exemptions ... Indeed, our cases have specifically included the sale of services within § 1.... Whatever else it may be, ... the exchange of such a service for money is "commerce" in the most common usage of that word. It is no disparagement of the practice of law as a profession to acknowledge that it has this business aspect ... In the modern world it cannot be denied that the activities of lawyers play an important part in commercial intercourse, and that anticompetitive activities by lawyers may exert a restraint on commerce (footnote omitted).

421 U.S. at 787–88, 95 S.Ct. at 2013–14. (*Cf.*, however, footnote 17, where the *Goldfarb* Court acknowledged "[i]t would be unrealistic to view the practice of professions as interchangeable with other business activities ..." 421 U.S. at 788 n. 17, 95 S.Ct. at 2013 n. 17. *See* Bates v. State Bar of Ariz., 433 U.S. 350, 371–72, 97 S.Ct. 2691, 2702–03, 53 L.Ed.2d 810 (1977) ("the belief that lawyers are somehow 'above' trade has become an anachronism ...").

Federal courts generally have refused to adopt a blanket immunity for the "learned professions".

> The issue of whether a profession is a learned one is not seen by the Court as the appropriate approach for resolving the higher question of whether the Sherman Act is applicable to that profession. To engage in such an inquiry would chart the Court on a semantic adventure of questionable value. It would be a dangerous form of elitism, indeed, to dole out exemptions to our antitrust laws merely on the basis of the educational level needed to practice a given profession, or for that matter, the impact which the profession has on society's health and welfare. Clearly, the more appropriate and fairer course is to examine the nature and conduct involved in the profession on a case by case basis together with the context in which it is practiced.

United States v. National Soc'y of Professional Eng'rs, 389 F.Supp. 1193, 1198 (D.D.C.1974).

While federal courts have rejected professional immunity from the antitrust laws, state courts are split on this issue in construing their consumer protection laws. Defendant urges a literal interpretation of the express language of the CPA. He contends attorneys sell "assets" and "services". RCW 19.86.010(2). Hence, their conduct falls within the trade or commerce provision of RCW 19.86.020. Defendant states the purposes of the act, i.e., protection of the public from unfair or deceptive acts or practices, are served by its application to lawyers. RCW 19.86.920. He distinguishes *Lightfoot v. MacDonald*, 86 Wash.2d 331, 544 P.2d 88 (1976), as it never addressed whether an attorney's conduct was part of trade or commerce. Rather, *Lightfoot* is deemed the court's first attempt to articulate a theory which excluded from the Act purely private disputes.

Plaintiffs, however, assert that, as RCW 19.86 was adopted virtually verbatim from federal antitrust laws, the Legislature is presumed to have intended "trade or commerce" to be interpreted in accordance with then-existing construction of that term under federal law. Since before 1961, federal law did not consider the learned professions to be part of trade or commerce; ergo, the practice of law cannot constitute trade or commerce under the CPA. Plaintiffs distinguish *Goldfarb v. Virginia State Bar*, 421 U.S. 773, 95 S.Ct. 2004, 44 L.Ed.2d 572 (1975) as dealing with commercial aspects of the legal profession, and not with the practice of law itself.

Guided by the legislative prescription to follow federal law and to construe liberally the CPA, RCW 19.86.920, we hold that certain entrepreneurial aspects of the practice of law may fall within the "trade or commerce" definition of the CPA. The more recent federal cases stand for the principle that attorneys, as well as other professionals, are not exempt from antitrust laws. The CPA, on its face, shows a carefully drafted attempt to bring within its reaches every person who conducts unfair or deceptive acts or practices in any trade or commerce. There is no statutory exemption for lawyers. Moreover, to limit our interpretations to the inconclusive dictum of pre-1961 federal case law relative to the "learned profession" seems totally contrary to the legislative directive that the CPA be construed liberally.

Defendant's counterclaims do not principally attack the actual performance of Short and Cressman's legal advice and services. Nor is defendant urging that plaintiff attorneys be reprimanded, suspended, or disbarred. Rather, defendant's counterclaims primarily challenge the entrepreneurial aspects of legal practice—how the price of legal services is determined, billed, and collected and the way a law firm obtains, retains, and dismisses clients. These business aspects of the legal profession are legitimate concerns of the public which are properly subject to the CPA.

However, a few of defendant's claims as a matter of law are outside the purview of the CPA and were properly dismissed by the trial court. CR 12(b)(6). Defendant alleges plaintiffs' law firm neglected properly to gather essential facts and evaluate the dissolution of his real estate partnership such that settlement was untimely; to pursue claims against defendant's opponents causing him a loss of valuable rights; and failed in a timely manner to file a judgment in the second action. Defendant also claims that the judgment finally entered was defective in failing to hold one of defendant's opponents liable. These claims are not chiefly concerned with the entrepreneurial aspects of legal practice; rather, they concern the actual practice of law. Since these claims are directed to the competence of and strategy employed by plaintiffs' lawyers, they amount to allegations of negligence or malpractice and are exempt from the CPA.

In reaching this result, we are cognizant of the important public policy interests at stake. Current remedies available to the victims of professional malpractice or misconduct have shortcomings. Comment, *The Washington Consumer Protection Act vs. The Learned Professional*, 10 Gonz. L. Rev. 435, 436 (1975). Most actions are expensive and difficult to prove. "The injured client can take little comfort from the fact that the wrongdoer has been reprimanded or suspended or stripped of the right to practice his profession." 10 Gonz. L. Rev. at 437. In some actions, only the prospects of attorney fees and potential treble damages provide a complete remedy. The CPA should be "available as an efficient and effective method of filling the gaps left vacant by the existing common law ..." (footnote omitted), 10 Gonz. L. Rev. at 437, as well as the Code of Professional Responsibility.

II

Next, we consider whether the application of the CPA to attorneys would be an unconstitutional legislative invasion of the jurisdiction of the Supreme Court in its power to regulate the practice of law. [The court held it would it not.]

To conclude, lawyers may be subject to liability under the CPA. We hold entrepreneurial aspects of the practice of law, which are principally counterclaimed by defendant, fall within the sphere of "trade or commerce" under RCW 19.86.010(2) and 19.86.020. As to such claims, we reverse the trial court's dismissal of defendant's CPA counterclaims. Defendant's claims which purely allege negligence or legal malpractice are exempt from the CPA and were properly dismissed under CR 12(b)(6). While we hold the term "conduct of any trade or commerce" does not exclude all conduct of the profession of law, we do not decide in this case whether the CPA applies to every aspect of the practice of law in this state as to the performance of legal services. Whether Demopolis at trial can satisfy the Anhold public interest test or other requirements of the CPA is beyond our scope of review.

Finally, we hold application of the CPA to entrepreneurial aspects of the practice of law does not violate the separation of powers doctrine.

Focus Questions: *Cripe v. Leiter*

1. *As a matter of statutory interpretation, which decision do you find more persuasive:* Short *or* Cripe?
2. *Would the defendant's actions in* Cripe *be subject to a consumer protection statute under the reasoning of* Short?

Cripe v. Leiter

703 N.E.2d 100
(Ill. 1998)

Justice BILANDIC delivered the opinion of the court:

FACTS

The plaintiff's complaint alleges the following. August H. Schmitz, the husband of Roberta Schmitz, died on January 6, 1992, leaving two irrevocable trusts valued at approximately $583,000. Mrs. Schmitz was the sole beneficiary of the trusts and the First National Bank of Peoria was named as trustee. On February 12, 1992, Mrs. Schmitz discharged the attorney who had been their family attorney and who had drafted the trusts. Thereafter, attorney Thomas E. Leiter of The Leiter Group began representing Mrs. Schmitz in an attempt to transfer the trusts from First National Bank to South Side Trust and Savings Bank of Peoria (South Side Bank). On or about April 27, 1992, South Side Bank was appointed as successor trustee of the trusts. South Side Bank subsequently appointed attorney Leiter as the attorney for the trusts.

On March 12, 1992, the plaintiff, Mrs. Schmitz's daughter and present guardian, filed a petition for appointment of guardian for disabled person in Tazewell County probate court, alleging that Mrs. Schmitz lacked sufficient capacity to make responsible decisions about her own care and the management of her estate. Mrs. Schmitz retained Leiter to defend her in the Tazewell County guardianship proceeding. This guardianship petition was ultimately dismissed on Mrs. Schmitz's motion.

In December 1992, Mrs. Schmitz moved to Michigan and began living with the plaintiff. On March 22, 1993, the probate court of Midland County, Michigan, found Mrs. Schmitz to be legally incapacitated based upon the report of a physician that her condition was consistent with a progressive dementing illness such as Alzheimer's disease. A public guardian was appointed as Mrs. Schmitz's guardian and conservator. The plaintiff was subsequently appointed as successor guardian of Mrs. Schmitz by the Michigan probate court.

The plaintiff, in her capacity as Mrs. Schmitz's guardian, filed this action against Thomas Leiter and The Leiter Group in the circuit court of Peoria County on October 24, 1994. The complaint alleged that, between February 12, 1992, and June 1, 1994, South Side Bank paid $65,933.50 out of the Schmitz trusts to the defendants as fees for legal services. The complaint charged that the defendants' fees for legal services were "outrageously excessive and unreasonable and bear no relationship to the actual time spent by Attorney Leiter in allegedly representing Mrs. Schmitz as her personal attorney and as her trust attorney." As ultimately amended, the plaintiff's complaint charged the defendants with: (1) violation of the Consumer Fraud Act; (2) common law fraud; (3) breach of fiduciary duty; (4) legal malpractice; and (5) constructive fraud. Each of the counts was premised on the allegation that the defendants charged excessive and unreasonable legal fees. The complaint alleged that the defendants' overbilling caused the Schmitz trust accounts to be depleted in excess of $40,000 in order to pay the defendants' excessive legal fees.

Only counts I and VI, the Consumer Fraud Act counts, are at issue in this appeal. Count I alleged that attorney Leiter charged excessive and unreasonable fees that bore no relationship to the actual time spent by Leiter in representing Mrs. Schmitz, and listed numerous examples of allegedly excessive charges. Count I alleged that Leiter owed Mrs. Schmitz a fiduciary duty both as her personal attorney and as the attorney for the trusts. As a result of that duty, Leiter was required to charge Mrs. Schmitz "reasonable attorney's fees representing the actual time, effort, and skill required to serve as legal counsel for the Schmitz trust accounts." Count I charged that Leiter engaged in the deceptive business practice of mailing out monthly invoices which contained outrageously excessive charges for the legal services performed by Leiter and which represented charges for time not spent by Leiter in representing Mrs. Schmitz. In addition to compensatory damages, count I sought recovery of attorney fees and punitive damages. Count VI reiterated the allegations of count I against The Leiter Group, the law firm in which Leiter was a partner.

The defendants moved to dismiss the plaintiff's complaint. The circuit court granted the motion to dismiss the Consumer Fraud Act count against each defendant, pursuant to section 2-615 of the Code of Civil Procedure (735 ILCS 5/2-615 (West 1992)), on the ground that the Act does not apply to legal services or the billing of those services. The plaintiff's counts alleging fraud, constructive fraud, legal malpractice and breach of fiduciary duty against each defendant remain pending in the circuit court.

The plaintiff appealed the dismissal of the Consumer Fraud Act counts to the appellate court. The appellate court determined that the Consumer Fraud Act, although not applicable to the actual practice of law, is nonetheless applicable to the "commercial aspects" of a law practice, which include billing for legal services. The appellate court therefore reversed the dismissal of the plaintiff's Consumer Fraud Act counts. We allowed the defendants' petition for leave to appeal.

ANALYSIS

The defendants contend that the appellate court erred in reversing the dismissal of the plaintiff's Consumer Fraud Act claims. They assert that the Act does not apply to claims arising out of the provision of legal services and that billing is a part of the provision of legal services. The plaintiff argues, on the other hand, that only claims arising out of the "actual practice of law" are exempt from the Act. She asserts that the appellate court correctly held that billing for legal services falls within the "business" aspect of the legal profession and is therefore subject to application of the Act.

The Consumer Fraud Act is a regulatory and remedial statute intended to protect consumers, borrowers and business persons against fraud, unfair methods of competition, and other unfair and deceptive business practices. The Act is to be liberally construed to effectuate its purpose. Section 2 of the Act declares unlawful the following conduct:

> Unfair ... or deceptive acts or practices, including but not limited to the use or employment of any deception, fraud, false pretense, false promise, misrepresentation or the concealment, suppression or omission of any material fact, with intent that others rely upon the concealment, suppression or omission of such material fact ... in the conduct of any trade or commerce....

815 ILCS 505/2 (West 1992).

Section 10a(a) of the Act provides that "[a]ny person who suffers damage as a result of a violation of this Act committed by any other person may bring an action against such person." 815 ILCS 505/10a(a) (West 1992). The elements of a claim under the Act are: (1) a deceptive act or practice by the defendant; (2) the defendant's intent that the plaintiff rely on the deception; and (3) that the deception occurred in the course of conduct involving trade or commerce. The plaintiff need not establish any intent to deceive on the part of the defendant because even an innocent misrepresentation may be actionable under the Act. 658 N.E.2d 1325 (Ill. 1995). The Act allows for the imposition of punitive damages and for the award of attorney fees to the prevailing party. 815 ILCS 505/10a(a), (c) (West 1992).

This court has not previously addressed the applicability of the Act to the legal profession. Our appellate court has considered this question in several cases. In *Frahm v. Urkovich*, 447 N.E.2d 1007 (Ill. 1983), the plaintiffs brought a claim against their attorney under the Consumer Fraud Act claiming that the attorney's misrepresentations caused them to lose their entire investment in a real estate deal. The circuit court dismissed the consumer fraud count for failure to state a cause of action and the appellate court affirmed. The appellate court reasoned that:

> In essence, plaintiffs seek a broad interpretation of the Act which would impose statutory liability for misconduct amounting to professional malpractice. We do not believe, however, that even the most liberal statutory interpretation indicates the application of this consumer protection statute to the conduct of an attorney engaged in the actual practice of law and, accordingly, we find that plaintiffs do not fall within the class of 'consumers' which the statute was designed to protect."

The issue was also discussed in *Guess v. Brophy*, 517 N.E.2d 693 (Ill. 1987). That court agreed with *Frahm* that "the legislature did not intend to include the furnishing of legal services to clients within the [Consumer Fraud] Act." The *Guess* court reasoned that the legal profession is subject to "a policing more stringent than that to which purveyors of most commercial services are subject." The court ultimately concluded, however, that the defendants in that case were not entitled to the same immunity from the Act afforded the legal profession because they were not acting in the capacity of lawyers representing clients.

Courts in several other states have addressed the applicability of consumer protection statutes to the legal profession, with differing results. In *Rousseau v. Eshleman*, 519 A.2d

243 (N.H. 1986), the Supreme Court of New Hampshire held that the practice of law was exempt from New Hampshire's consumer protection statute, finding applicable an exemption for "trade or commerce otherwise permitted under laws as administered by any regulatory board." The court found that the supreme court's professional conduct committee qualified as a regulatory board within the meaning of that exemption. The *Rousseau* court concluded that, in view of the practical problems that might result, it was "reluctant" to interpret the statute as applying to the legal profession absent a "clearly expressed legislative intent." The New Jersey appellate court also concluded that attorneys' services were not covered by a consumer fraud statute in *Vort v. Hollander*, 607 A.2d 1339 (N.J. 1992). That court noted that the practice of law in the State of New Jersey is regulated, "in the first instance, if not exclusively," by the New Jersey Supreme Court. The court reasoned that, "[h]ad the Legislature intended to enter the area of attorney regulation it surely would have stated with specificity that attorneys were covered under the Consumer Fraud Act." Significantly, in a later case addressing an analogous issue, the New Jersey court relied on Illinois decisions, noting that the Illinois Consumer Fraud Act was "very similar" to New Jersey's. Hampton Hospital v. Bresan, 672 A.2d 725, 730 (1996) (addressing the application of the consumer fraud statute to hospital services).

Courts in other states have reached a contrary conclusion. In *Short v. Demopolis*, 691 P.2d 163 (Wash. 1984), the Washington Supreme Court held that the Washington consumer protection statute applied to "certain entrepreneurial aspects of the practice of law," including "how the price of legal services is determined, billed and collected." ... The *Short* court also held, however, that claims arising out of the "actual practice of law," as opposed to the entrepreneurial aspects of the profession, are exempt from the Act. The Supreme Court of Connecticut has also determined that lawyers are not entitled to a blanket exemption from consumer protection legislation. In *Heslin v. Connecticut Law Clinic*, 461 A.2d 938, 943 (Conn. 1983), the court held that the Connecticut Unfair Trade Practices Act's regulation of "trade or commerce" did not "totally exclude all conduct of the profession of law." The court also stated, however, that it need not decide in that case whether the Act permitted regulation of "every aspect of the practice of law."

Our Consumer Fraud Act, like those discussed in the preceding cases from other jurisdictions, contains no language expressly excluding or including the legal profession within its ambit. Despite the absence of such language, there appears to be little dispute among the decisions addressing this issue that consumer protection statutes do not apply to claims arising out of the "actual practice of law." The plaintiff in this case concedes that the Act does not apply to such claims. We are called upon here to decide whether an attorney's billing for legal services is included within that exemption. The plaintiff urges us to hold that billing is a part of the "business" aspect of the practice of law, entirely separate from the "actual practice of law." Therefore, the plaintiff argues, attorneys' billing practices should be regulated by the Act. The defendants argue, to the contrary, that billing is a part of the provision of legal services to which the Act was not intended to apply. We find no indication that the legislature intended the Consumer Fraud Act to apply to regulate attorneys' billing practices.

Historically, the regulation of attorney conduct in this state has been the prerogative of this court. In the exercise of this power, this court administers a comprehensive regulatory scheme governing attorney conduct. The Illinois Rules of Professional Conduct adopted by this court set forth numerous requirements to which attorneys in this state must adhere. Violation of these rules is grounds for discipline. This court has appointed an Attorney Registration and Disciplinary Commission (ARDC) to supervise the "registration of, and disciplinary proceedings affecting, members of the Illinois bar." This court has also created a procedural scheme under which the ARDC operates, providing detailed regulations involving inquiry, hearing and review boards. The purpose of this regulatory scheme is to protect the public and maintain the integrity of the legal profession.

This court's regulatory scheme extends to the area of attorneys' fees. Rule 1.5 of the Rules of Professional Conduct specifically addresses the subject, providing [that "a lawyer's fees shall be reasonable" and including numerous factors to consider in making this determination.].

Rule 1.5 also addresses the attorney's obligation to communicate to the client the basis or rate of the fee. Further, Rule 1.5 sets forth guidelines for contingent fee arrangements and the division of fees among attorneys.

An attorney who charges or collects an excessive fee in violation of this court's rules may be subjected to discipline. This court has also ordered an attorney to make restitution to a client who was charged excessive legal fees. The Rules of Professional Conduct further provide for discipline of an attorney who engages in conduct involving fraud, dishonesty, deceit or misrepresentation. In addition, this court has created a client protection program operating under the auspices of the ARDC to reimburse losses caused by the dishonest conduct of attorneys in the course of the attorney-client relationship.

Accordingly, the attorney-client relationship in this state, unlike the ordinary merchant-consumer relationship, is already subject to extensive regulation by this court. The legislature did not, in the language of the Consumer Fraud Act, specify that it intended the Act's provisions to apply to the conduct of attorneys in relation to their clients. Given this court's role in that arena, we find that, had the legislature intended the Act to apply in this manner, it would have stated that intention with specificity. Absent a clear indication by the legislature, we will not conclude that the legislature intended to regulate attorney-client relationships through the Consumer Fraud Act.

We note that, prior to the decision in this case, our appellate court had, since 1983, consistently held the Act to be inapplicable to claims arising out of the attorney-client relationship. The legislature is presumed to be aware of judicial decisions interpreting legislation. Kozak v. Retirement Board of the Firemen's Annuity & Benefit Fund, 447 N.E.2d 394 (Ill. 1983). The Consumer Fraud Act has been amended numerous times since the decisions in *Frahm* [and] *Guess* ... The legislature has not, however, included language in the Act to specify that it applies to the conduct of attorneys in relation to their clients. In amending a statute, "the legislature is presumed to know the construction the statute has been given and, by re-enactment, is assumed to have intended for the new statute to have the same effect." Sulser v. Country Mutual Insurance Co., 591 N.E.2d 427 (Ill. 1992). The legislature's failure to alter the Act in response to these appellate court holdings provides further support for our conclusion that the legislature did not intend the Act to apply to claims arising out of the attorney-client relationship.

The plaintiff nonetheless argues that an attorney's billing is simply a "business" aspect of the practice of law and is therefore within the intended scope of the Consumer Fraud Act. As discussed above, however, the comprehensive regulatory scheme administered by this court extends to attorney fees. Moreover, an attorney's billing for legal services cannot be separated from the attorney-client relationship. Unlike ordinary merchant-consumer relationships, the relationship between attorney and client is fiduciary in nature. Although an attorney's fees in a particular case will generally be governed by the contractual arrangement between the attorney and the client, the attorney's fiduciary position prohibits the attorney from charging an excessive fee. Fraudulent or excessive billing of a client violates the attorney's fiduciary duty to the client. Thus, an attorney's billing of a client is not simply a "business" aspect of the practice of law, but is tied to the attorney's fiduciary obligation to the client. Because of that fiduciary relationship, the attorney's fees are subject to scrutiny and regulation not applicable to the fees for most commercial services. The Consumer Fraud Act therefore was not intended to apply to an attorney's billing of a client for legal services.

Accordingly, we conclude that the legislature did not intend the Consumer Fraud Act to apply to regulate the conduct of attorneys in representing clients. We hold that, where allegations of misconduct arise from a defendant's conduct in his or her capacity as an attorney representing a client, the Consumer Fraud Act does not apply. An attorney's billing of a client for legal services is a part of the attorney's representation of the client and is therefore exempt from the Act. The circuit court properly dismissed the plaintiff's Consumer Fraud Act counts against the defendants in this case.

Justice HARRISON, dissenting:

The majority engages in a protracted discussion of the legislative intent behind the Consumer Fraud Act. It is axiomatic, however, that the best indication of the legislature's intent is the language it employed in drafting the law. Where the language of a statute is clear and unambiguous, the court should not resort to other tools of statutory interpretation. The court's only legitimate function is to enforce the law as written.

> Section 2 of the Consumer Fraud Act declares unlawful [u]nfair methods of competition and unfair or deceptive acts or practices, including but not limited to the use or employment of any deception, fraud, false pretense, false promise, misrepresentation or the concealment, suppression or omission of any material fact, with intent that others rely upon the concealment, suppression or omission of such material fact ... in the conduct of any trade or commerce ...

815 ILCS 505/2 (West 1992).

> The terms "trade" and "commerce" are defined by the law to mean the advertising, offering for sale, sale, or distribution of any services and any property, tangible or intangible, real, personal or mixed, and any other article, commodity, or thing of value wherever situated, and shall include any trade or commerce directly or indirectly affecting the people of this State.

815 ILCS 505/1(f) (West 1992).

> Pursuant to section 10a(a) of the Act, [a]ny person who suffers actual damage as a result of a violation of this Act committed by any other person may bring an action against such person.

815 ILCS 505/10a(a) (West 1992).

These provisions, which must be liberally construed to effect the Act's purposes (815 ILCS 505/11a (West 1992)), clearly and unambiguously embrace the sort of billing fraud claims advanced in counts I and IV of plaintiff's complaint. Accordingly, defendants cannot be removed from the Act's coverage without holding that the legislature did not mean what the plain language of the statute says. No rule of construction authorizes us to do that.

Had the General Assembly intended to exclude attorneys from the scope of the Act, it could easily have done so, just as it excluded real estate salesmen and brokers, newspaper and periodical publishers, and individuals associated with television and radio stations. 815 ILCS 505/10b (West 1992). Attorneys, however, are nowhere mentioned. It is a basic rule of statutory construction that the expression of certain exceptions in a statute should be construed as an exclusion of all others. State of Illinois v. Mikusch, 562 N.E.2d 168 (Ill. 1990). Courts are not at liberty to depart from the plain language of a statute by reading into it exceptions, limitations, or conditions that the legislature did not express. Kunkel v. Walton, 689 N.E.2d 1047 (1997). Accordingly, the absence of attorneys from the detailed exclusions enumerated in the statute is fatal to the majority's analysis.

Holding attorneys to the same standards of honesty and fair dealing that apply to other business people will inevitably affect the practice of law. In my view, the results can only be positive. Unlike my colleagues, I am not concerned about encroachment on this court's authority. While it is true that responsibility for regulating the legal profession and disciplining attorneys is vested in our court, the General Assembly has made specific provision in the Consumer Fraud Act to avoid separation of power problems. Section 10b(1) of the Act exempts from coverage "[a]ctions or transactions specifically authorized by laws administered by any regulatory body or officer acting under statutory authority of this State or the United States." 815 ILCS 505/10b(1) (West 1992). Accordingly, if an attorney's conduct were permissible under the rules we have enacted and the standards we have set, it would not be actionable under the Consumer Fraud Act.

The conduct alleged in this case, if proven, would not be permissible under the rules of our court. Although the attorneys involved might ultimately be subject to discipline, that is no reason to deny plaintiff her right to bring a statutory damage action against them. If what the attorneys did constituted a crime, we would surely not say that they are exempt from prosecution merely because they are subject to disbarment by us. The same principle applies here.

For the foregoing reasons, counts I and IV of plaintiff's complaint should not have been dismissed, and the judgment of the appellate court should be affirmed. I therefore dissent.

* * *

1. Other decisions. Most courts to address the issue have adopted either the *Short* or the *Cripe* standard when it comes to the practice of law.

2. Coverage of other professions. Some state consumer protection statutes expressly exclude certain professions, including, possibly, lawyers. Md. Code Ann. Com. Law § 13-104. Where the statutes are silent, some courts, as in *Short*, have held that the entrepreneurial aspects of a learned profession (such as medicine) are covered by their consumer protection statutes, but not the actual practice of the profession. Haynes v. Yale-New Haven Hosp., 699 A.2d 964, 972 (Conn. 1997). However, more courts have concluded that the statutes are applicable to deception in the actual practice of medicine. *See* Bridge v. Corning Life Sciences, Inc., 997 F. Supp. 551 (D. Vt. 1998) (concluding that medical provider's misrepresentation regarding whether it had examined pap smear slide was actionable under statute); Karlin v. IVF America, Inc., 712 N.E.2d 662 (N.Y. 1999) (concluding that misrepresentations as to the success rate of medical procedure were covered under statute). In one such instance, the state legislature, apparently in response to the decision, later amended the statute to exclude health care providers from coverage. Williamson v. Amrani, 152 P.3d 60 (Kan. 2007), *superseded by statute*.

3. An example of the lawyer-judge bias? One author has proposed the thesis that, when confronted with a legal question that affects the legal profession, a court will select the legal rule it believes benefits the legal profession, provided the result is plausible. Benjamin J. Barton, The Lawyer-Judge Bias in the American Legal System (2011). Are the different outcomes in the cases involving lawyers and other professionals evidence of this type of bias, or are the outcomes not only plausible but desirable and correct?

* * *

3. Enforcement and Remedies

The consumer protection acts in virtually every jurisdiction provide individual consumers with a private right of action. When initially enacted, some statutes only provided for enforcement by the state's attorney general. However, the broad coverage of the statutes rendered this enforcement scheme ineffective. Karlin v. IVF America, Inc., 712 N.E.2d 662, 665 (N.Y. 1999). Thus, by extending a private right of action to individual consumers, states empower private litigants to serve as private attorneys general. Ivey, Barnum & O'Mara v. Indian Harbor Properties, Inc., 461 A.2d 1369 (Conn. 1983).

In order to recover, a plaintiff must, of course, have suffered actual damages. Thus, for example, even if a statute only requires that an act or practice be "likely to deceive" to be covered as a deceptive practice, the practice must actually induce reliance before a consumer may recover. Recall that a plaintiff need not prove an actual intent to deceive in order for an act to be prohibited by most statutes. However, in many states, the plaintiff who establishes that the defendant knowingly or willfully violated the statute may recover treble damages. *See, e.g.*, Ga. Code § 10-1-399(c). Punitive damages are also often available, either provided for explicitly by statute or through decisional law.

Some deceptive practices result in little or no actual injury. In such cases, attorneys would have little incentive to bring suit on behalf of a client absent some other inducement. Indeed, consumers might be dissuaded from bringing suit in such cases. For this reason, the statutes include a variety of remedial devices to encourage enforcement. A significant number of states allow a prevailing plaintiff to recover a statutory minimum amount of damages. In others, a prevailing plaintiff may be entitled to recover attorney's fees, thus providing an incentive to take what otherwise might be an unprofitable case.

Finally, state administrative agencies can enforce the statutes. States' attorneys general are often empowered to issue injunctions or obtain restitution on behalf of affected consumers. In some states, civil and criminal penalties are also available. *See* Fla. Stat. Ann. § 501.2075 (providing for civil penalty not to exceed $10,000 in the case of an action brought by the enforcing authority in a case involving willful violation of the statute).

* * *

B. Fair Debt Collection Practices Act

Exercise 13.4

Andalusia Collections Services (ACS) is a debt collection company. Creditors hire ACS to collect payment from debtors on outstanding accounts. One practice ACS employs is to print form letters on the letterhead of an attorney, Janson, demanding payment of a debt and instructing the debtor to contact ACS. The letters, signed by Janson, typically provide that "I have received instructions from my client to pursue this matter to the fullest extent permissible by law." ACS delivers around 100 of these letters a week to Janson for him to sign. The extent of Janson's review consists of making sure that there is no conflict of interest with any existing client. Janson signs the letters and ACS mails them. Janson receives $2 for each letter he signs. The recipient of one of these letters, Sarah, has brought suit under the Fair Debt Collection Practices Act against ACS and Janson based on the mailing of the letter. Sarah concedes that the debt referenced in the letter is owed. What result?

For years, unfair debt collection practices posed a vexing problem. Debtors who were subjected to misleading, harassing, and invasive attempts to collect a debt sometimes resorted to common law tort theories of recovery such as misrepresentation, intentional infliction of emotional distress, and invasion of privacy. For example, in *Carney v. Rotkin, Schmerin & McIntyre*, 206 Cal. App. 3d 1513, 1527 (Ct. App. 1988), a California court held a plaintiff had stated a claim for IIED when a law firm, in an attempt to collect a debt on behalf of client, falsely told a seventy-four-year-old woman that there was a bench warrant out for her arrest and that the firm would not recall the warrant until the debt was paid in full. The *Restatement (Second) of Torts* recognized high-pressure debt collection practices as a specific situation in which the tort of intentional infliction of emotional distress might apply. Restatement (Second) of Torts § 46 cmt. e (1965). Even prior to the *Restatement*, several courts had allowed for recovery for purely emotional harms stemming from abusive collection tactics. Russell Fraker, Note, *Reformulating Outrage: A Critical Analysis of the Problematic Tort of IIED*, 61 VAND. L. REV. 983, 991 (2008).

Given the limitations posed by these torts, however, some individuals were left without a remedy. In 1977, Congress enacted the Fair Debt Collection Practices Act (FDCPA) to regulate "abusive, deceptive, and unfair debt collection practices" by third-party debt collectors. 15 U.S.C. § 1692 (2006). The FTC has enforcement authority with respect to the Act, but private actions are far more common. Many states have enacted their own debt collection statutes that provide a private right of action.

The FDCPA prohibits the "use of any false, deceptive, or misleading representation" in connection with the collection of a debt. 15 U.S.C. § 1692e. The Act lists, without limitation, sixteen specific examples of such practices. These include making false representations as to a debt's character, amount, or legal status; falsely representing or implying that an individual is an attorney or that the communication is from an attorney; threatening to take any action that cannot legally be taken or that is not intended to be taken; and communicating or threatening to communicate credit information which is known to be false, including the failure to communicate that the debt is disputed. *Id.* § 1692e(2). Importantly, the FDCPA is a strict liability statute. Russell v. Equifax A.R.S., 74 F.3d 30, 33 (2d Cir. 1996).

The FDCPA covers the actions of "debt collectors." Thus, there may sometimes be an issue as to who qualifies as a debt collector. In addition, the Act provides several defenses. Thus, in addition to the question of whether a debt collector's actions are false, deceptive, misleading, or otherwise prohibited by the FDCPA, there is sometimes the question of whether the debt collector can take advantage of a statutory defense. The following cases explore these issues in more detail within the context of attorneys acting as debt collectors.

Focus Questions: *Heintz v. Jenkins*

1. *What is the basis for the Court's holding?*
2. *Do attorneys have reason to be concerned about the Court's holding?*

Heintz v. Jenkins

514 U.S. 291

(1995)

Justice BREYER delivered the opinion of the Court.

The issue before us is whether the term "debt collector" in the Fair Debt Collection Practices Act, 91 Stat. 874, 15 U.S.C. §§1692–1692 (1988 ed. and Supp. V), applies to a lawyer who "regularly," through litigation, tries to collect consumer debts. The Court of Appeals for the Seventh Circuit held that it does. We agree with the Seventh Circuit and we affirm its judgment.

... Among other things, the Act sets out rules that a debt collector must follow for "acquiring location information" about the debtor, §1692b; communicating about the debtor (and the debt) with third parties, §1692c(b); and bringing "[l]egal actions," §1692i. The Act imposes upon "debt collector[s]" who violate its provisions (specifically described) "[c]ivil liability" to those whom they, e.g., harass, mislead, or treat unfairly. §1692k. The Act also authorizes the Federal Trade Commission (FTC) to enforce its provisions. §1692 l(a). The Act's definition of the term "debt collector" includes a person "who regularly collects or attempts to collect, directly or indirectly, debts owed [to] ... another." §1692a(6). And, it limits "debt" to consumer debt, i.e., debts "arising out of ... transaction[s]" that "are primarily for personal, family, or household purposes." §1692a(5).

The plaintiff in this case, Darlene Jenkins, borrowed money from the Gainer Bank in order to buy a car. She defaulted on her loan. The bank's law firm then sued Jenkins in state court to recover the balance due. As part of an effort to settle the suit, a lawyer with that law firm, George Heintz, wrote to Jenkins's lawyer. His letter, in listing the amount she owed under the loan agreement, included $4,173 owed for insurance, bought by the bank because she had not kept the car insured as she had promised to do.

Jenkins then brought this Fair Debt Collection Practices Act suit against Heintz and his firm. She claimed that Heintz's letter violated the Act's prohibitions against trying to collect an amount not "authorized by the agreement creating the debt," §1692f(1), and against making a "false representation of ... the ... amount ... of any debt," §1692e(2)(A). The loan agreement, she conceded, required her to keep the car insured " 'against loss or damage' " and permitted the bank to buy such insurance to protect the car should she fail to do so. But, she said, the $4,173 substitute policy was not the kind of policy the loan agreement had in mind, for it insured the bank not only against "loss or damage" but also against her failure to repay the bank's car loan. Hence, Heintz's "representation" about the "amount" of her "debt" was "false"; amounted to an effort to collect an "amount" not "authorized" by the loan agreement; and thus violated the Act.

Pursuant to Rule 12(b)(6) of the Federal Rules of Civil Procedure, the District Court dismissed Jenkins' Fair Debt Collection lawsuit for failure to state a claim. The court held that the Act does not apply to lawyers engaging in litigation. However, the Court of Appeals for the Seventh Circuit reversed the District Court's judgment, interpreting the Act to apply to litigating lawyers. 25 F.3d 536 (1994). The Seventh Circuit's view in this respect conflicts with that of the Sixth Circuit. *See* Green v. Hocking, 9 F.3d 18 (1993) (per curiam). We granted certiorari to resolve this conflict. And, as we have said, we conclude that the Seventh Circuit is correct. The Act does apply to lawyers engaged in litigation.

There are two rather strong reasons for believing that the Act applies to the litigating activities of lawyers. First, the Act defines the "debt collector[s]" to whom it applies as including those who "regularly collec[t] or attemp[t] to collect, directly or indirectly, [consumer] debts owed or due or asserted to be owed or due another." § 1692a(6). In ordinary English, a lawyer who regularly tries to obtain payment of consumer debts through legal proceedings is a lawyer who regularly "attempts" to "collect" those consumer debts. *See, e.g.*, Black's Law Dictionary 263 (6th ed. 1990) ("To collect a debt or claim is to obtain payment or liquidation of it, either by personal solicitation or legal proceedings").

Second, in 1977, Congress enacted an earlier version of this statute, which contained an express exemption for lawyers. That exemption said that the term "debt collector" did not include "any attorney-at-law collecting a debt as an attorney on behalf of and in the name of a client." Pub.L. 95-109, § 803(6)(F), 91 Stat. 874, 875. In 1986, however, Congress repealed this exemption in its entirety, Pub.L. 99-361, 100 Stat. 768, without creating a narrower, litigation-related, exemption to fill the void. Without more, then, one would think that Congress intended that lawyers be subject to the Act whenever they meet the general "debt collector" definition.

Heintz argues that we should nonetheless read the statute as containing an implied exemption for those debt-collecting activities of lawyers that consist of litigating (including, he assumes, settlement efforts). He relies primarily on three arguments.

First, Heintz argues that many of the Act's requirements, if applied directly to litigating activities, will create harmfully anomalous results that Congress simply could not have intended. We address this argument in light of the fact that, when Congress first wrote the Act's substantive provisions, it had for the most part exempted litigating attorneys from the Act's coverage; that, when Congress later repealed the attorney exemption, it did not revisit the wording of these substantive provisions; and that, for these reasons, some awkwardness is understandable. Particularly when read in this light, we find Heintz's argument unconvincing.

Many of Heintz's "anomalies" are not particularly anomalous. For example, the Sixth Circuit pointed to § 1692e(5), which forbids a "debt collector" to make any "threat to take action that cannot legally be taken." The court reasoned that, were the Act to apply to litigating activities, this provision automatically would make liable any litigating lawyer who brought, and then lost, a claim against a debtor. But, the Act says explicitly that a "debt collector" may not be held liable if he "shows by a preponderance of evidence that the violation was not intentional and resulted from a bona fide error notwithstanding the maintenance of procedures reasonably adapted to avoid any such error." § 1692k(c). Thus, even if we were to assume that the suggested reading of § 1692e(5) is correct, we would not find the result so absurd as to warrant implying an exemption for litigating lawyers. In any event, the assumption would seem unnecessary, for we do not see how the fact that a lawsuit turns out ultimately to be unsuccessful could, by itself, make the bringing of it an "action that cannot legally be taken."

The remaining significant "anomalies" similarly depend for their persuasive force upon readings that courts seem unlikely to endorse. For example, Heintz's strongest "anomaly" argument focuses upon the Act's provisions governing "[c]ommunication in connection with debt collection." § 1692c. One of those provisions requires a "debt collector" not to "communicate further" with a consumer who "notifies" the "debt collector" that he or she "refuses to pay" or wishes the debt collector to "cease further communication." § 1692c(c). In light of this provision, asks Heintz, how can an attorney file a lawsuit against (and thereby communicate with) a nonconsenting consumer or file a motion for summary judgment against that consumer?

We agree with Heintz that it would be odd if the Act empowered a debt-owing consumer to stop the "communications" inherent in an ordinary lawsuit and thereby cause an ordinary debt-collecting lawsuit to grind to a halt. But, it is not necessary to read § 1692c(c) in that way—if only because that provision has exceptions that permit communications "to notify the consumer that the debt collector or creditor may invoke" or "intends to invoke" a "specified remedy" (of a kind "ordinarily invoked by [the] debt collector or creditor"). §§ 1692c(c)(2), (3). Courts can read these exceptions, plausibly, to imply that they authorize the actual invocation of the remedy that the collector "intends to invoke." The language permits such a reading, for an ordinary court-related document does, in fact, "notify" its recipient that the creditor may "invoke" a judicial remedy. Moreover, the interpretation is consistent with the statute's apparent objective of preserving creditors' judicial remedies. We need not authoritatively interpret the Act's conduct-regulating provisions now, however. Rather, we rest our conclusions upon the fact that it is easier to read § 1692c(c) as containing some such additional, implicit, exception than to believe that Congress intended, silently and implicitly, to create a far broader exception, for all litigating attorneys, from the Act itself.

Second, Heintz points to a statement of Congressman Frank Annunzio, one of the sponsors of the 1986 amendment that removed from the Act the language creating a blanket exemption for lawyers. Representative Annunzio stated that, despite the exemption's removal, the Act still would not apply to lawyers' litigating activities. Representative Annunzio said that the Act

> regulates debt collection, not the practice of law. Congress repealed the attorney exemption to the act, not because of attorney[s'] conduct in the courtroom, but because of their conduct in the backroom. Only collection activities, not legal activities, are covered by the act.... The act applies to attorneys when they are collecting debts, not when they are performing tasks of a legal nature.... The act only regulates the conduct of debt collectors, it does not prevent creditors, through their attorneys, from pursuing any legal remedies available to them.

132 Cong.Rec. 30842 (1986).

This statement, however, does not persuade us.

For one thing, the plain language of the Act itself says nothing about retaining the exemption in respect to litigation. The line the statement seeks to draw between "legal" activities and "debt collection" activities was not necessarily apparent to those who debated the legislation, for litigating, at first blush, seems simply one way of collecting a debt. For another thing, when Congress considered the Act, other Congressmen expressed fear that repeal would limit lawyers' "ability to contact third parties in order to facilitate settlements" and "could very easily interfere with a client's right to pursue judicial remedies." H.R.Rep. No. 99-405, p. 11 1985) (dissenting views of Rep. Hiler). They proposed alternative language designed to keep litigation activities outside the Act's scope, but that language was not enacted. *Ibid.* Further, Congressman Annunzio made his statement not during the legislative process, but after the statute became law. It therefore is not a statement upon which other legislators might have relied in voting for or against the Act, but it simply represents the views of one informed person on an issue about which others may (or may not) have thought differently.

Finally, Heintz points to a "Commentary" on the Act by the FTC's staff. It says:

> Attorneys or law firms that engage in traditional debt collection activities (sending dunning letters, making collection calls to consumers) are covered by the [Act], *but those whose practice is limited to legal activities are not covered.*

Federal Trade Commission-Statements of General Policy or Interpretation Staff Commentary on the Fair Debt Collection Practices Act, 53 Fed.Reg. 50097, 50100 (1988) (emphasis added; footnote omitted).

We cannot give conclusive weight to this statement. The Commentary of which this statement is a part says that it "is not binding on the Commission or the public." More importantly, we find nothing either in the Act or elsewhere indicating that Congress intended to authorize the FTC to create this exception from the Act's coverage—an exception that, for the reasons we have set forth above, falls outside the range of reasonable interpretations of the Act's express language.

For these reasons, we agree with the Seventh Circuit that the Act applies to attorneys who "regularly" engage in consumer-debt-collection activity, even when that activity consists of litigation. Its judgment is therefore

Affirmed.

Focus Questions: *Jerman v. Carlisle, McNellie, Rini, Kramer & Ulrich LPA*

1. *What does it mean to say that a violation "was not intentional" under the bona fide error defense?*
2. *What is the basis for the Court's decision?*
3. *Do attorneys have reason to be concerned about the Court's holding?*

Jerman v. Carlisle, McNellie, Rini, Kramer & Ulrich LPA

559 U.S. 573
(2010)

The [FDCPA] contains two exceptions to provisions imposing liability on debt collectors. Section 1692k(c), at issue here, provides that

> [a] debt collector may not be held liable in any action brought under [the FDCPA] if the debt collector shows by a preponderance of evidence that the violation was not intentional and resulted from a bona fide error notwithstanding the maintenance of procedures reasonably adapted to avoid any such error.

The Act also states that none of its provisions imposing liability shall apply to "any act done or omitted in good faith in conformity with any advisory opinion of the [Federal Trade] Commission." § 1692k(e).

B

Respondents in this case are a law firm, Carlisle, McNellie, Rini, Kramer & Ulrich, L.P.A., and one of its attorneys, Adrienne S. Foster (collectively Carlisle). In April 2006, Carlisle filed a complaint in Ohio state court on behalf of a client, Countrywide Home Loans, Inc. Carlisle sought foreclosure of a mortgage held by Countrywide in real property owned by petitioner Karen L. Jerman. The complaint included a "Notice," later served on Jerman, stating that the mortgage debt would be assumed to be valid unless Jerman disputed it in writing. Jerman's lawyer sent a letter disputing the debt, and Carlisle sought verification from Countrywide. When Countrywide acknowledged that Jerman had, in fact, already paid the debt in full, Carlisle withdrew the foreclosure lawsuit.

Jerman then filed her own lawsuit seeking class certification and damages under the FDCPA, contending that Carlisle violated § 1692g by stating that her debt would be assumed valid unless she disputed it in writing.[1] While acknowledging a division of authority on the question, the District Court held that Carlisle had violated § 1692g by requiring Jerman to dispute the debt in writing.[2] The court ultimately granted summary judgment to Carlisle, however, concluding that § 1692k(c) shielded it from liability because the violation was not intentional, resulted from a bona fide error, and occurred despite the maintenance of procedures reasonably adapted to avoid any such error. The Court of Appeals for the Sixth Circuit affirmed. Acknowledging that the Courts of Appeals are divided regarding the scope of the bona fide error defense, and that the "majority view is that the defense is available for clerical and factual errors only," the Sixth Circuit nonetheless held that § 1692k(c) extends to "mistakes of law." Noting that a parallel bona fide error defense in the Truth in Lending Act (TILA), 15 U.S.C. § 1640(c), expressly excludes legal errors, the court observed that Congress has amended the FDCPA several times since 1977 without excluding mistakes of law from § 1692k(c).

We granted certiorari to resolve the conflict of authority as to the scope of the FDCPA's bona fide error defense ...

II

A

The parties disagree about whether a "violation" resulting from a debt collector's misinterpretation of the legal requirements of the FDCPA can ever be "not intentional" under § 1692k(c). Jerman contends that when a debt collector intentionally commits the act giving rise to the violation (here, sending a notice that included the "in writing" language), a misunderstanding about what the Act requires cannot render the violation "not intentional," given the general rule that mistake or ignorance of law is no defense. Carlisle and the dissent, in contrast, argue that nothing in the statutory text excludes legal errors from the category of "bona fide error[s]" covered by § 1692k(c) and note that the Act refers not to an unintentional "act" but rather an unintentional "violation." The latter term, they contend, evinces Congress' intent to impose liability only when a party knows its conduct is unlawful. Carlisle urges us, therefore, to read § 1692k(c) to encompass "all types of error," including mistakes of law.

We decline to adopt the expansive reading of § 1692k(c) that Carlisle proposes. We have long recognized the "common maxim, familiar to all minds, that ignorance of the law will not excuse any person, either civilly or criminally." Our law is therefore no stranger to the possibility that an act may be "intentional" for purposes of civil liability, even if the actor lacked actual knowledge that her conduct violated the law. In *Kolstad v. American Dental Assn.*, 527 U.S. 526, 119 S.Ct. 2118, 144 L.Ed.2d 494 (1999), for instance, we addressed a provision of the Civil Rights Act of 1991 authorizing compensatory and punitive damages for "intentional discrimination," 42 U.S.C. § 1981a, but limiting punitive damages to conduct undertaken "with malice or with reckless indifference to the federally protected rights of an aggrieved individual," § 1981a(b)(1). We observed that in some circumstances "intentional discrimination" could occur without giving rise to punitive damages liability, such as where an employer is "unaware of the relevant federal prohibition" or acts with the "distinct belief that its discrimination is lawful." *See also* W. Keeton, D. Dobbs, R. Keeton, & D. Owen, Prosser and Keeton on Law of Torts 110 (5th ed.

---

1. Section 1692g(a)(3) requires a debt collector, within five days of an "initial communication" about the collection of a debt, to send the consumer a written notice containing, *inter alia*, "a statement that unless the consumer, within thirty days after receipt of the notice, disputes the validity of the debt, or any portion thereof, the debt will be assumed to be valid by the debt collector."

2. The District Court ... held that the plain language of § 1692g does not impose an "in writing" requirement on consumers.

1984) ("[I]f one intentionally interferes with the interests of others, he is often subject to liability notwithstanding the invasion was made under an erroneous belief as to some ... legal matter that would have justified the conduct"); Restatement (Second) of Torts § 164, and Comment e (1963–1964) (intentional tort of trespass can be committed despite the actor's mistaken belief that she has a legal right to enter the property).

Likely for this reason, when Congress has intended to provide a mistake-of-law defense to civil liability, it has often done so more explicitly than here....

Congress also did not confine liability under the FDCPA to "willful" violations, a term more often understood in the civil context to excuse mistakes of law.

...

We draw additional support for the conclusion that bona fide errors in § 1692k(c) do not include mistaken interpretations of the FDCPA, from the requirement that a debt collector maintain "procedures reasonably adapted to avoid any such error." The dictionary defines "procedure" as "a series of steps followed in a regular orderly definite way." WEBSTER'S THIRD NEW INTERNATIONAL DICTIONARY 1807 (1976). In that light, the statutory phrase is more naturally read to apply to processes that have mechanical or other such "regular orderly" steps to avoid mistakes—for instance, the kind of internal controls a debt collector might adopt to ensure its employees do not communicate with consumers at the wrong time of day, § 1692c(a)(1), or make false representations as to the amount of a debt, § 1692e(2). The dissent, like the Court of Appeals, finds nothing unusual in attorney debt collectors maintaining procedures to avoid legal error. We do not dispute that some entities may maintain procedures to avoid legal errors. But legal reasoning is not a mechanical or strictly linear process. For this reason, we find force in the suggestion by the Government (as amicus curiae supporting Jerman) that the broad statutory requirement of procedures reasonably designed to avoid "any" bona fide error indicates that the relevant procedures are ones that help to avoid errors like clerical or factual mistakes. Such procedures are more likely to avoid error than those applicable to legal reasoning, particularly in the context of a comprehensive and complex federal statute such as the FDCPA that imposes open-ended prohibitions on, inter alia, "false, deceptive," § 1692e, or "unfair" practices, § 1692f.

B

Carlisle, its amici, and the dissent raise the additional concern that our reading will have unworkable practical consequences for debt collecting lawyers. Carlisle claims the FDCPA's private enforcement provisions have fostered a "cottage industry" of professional plaintiffs who sue debt collectors for trivial violations of the Act. If debt collecting attorneys can be held personally liable for their reasonable misinterpretations of the requirements of the Act, Carlisle and its amici foresee a flood of lawsuits against creditors' lawyers by plaintiffs (and their attorneys) seeking damages and attorney's fees. The threat of such liability, in the dissent's view, creates an irreconcilable conflict between an attorney's personal financial interest and her ethical obligation of zealous advocacy on behalf of a client: An attorney uncertain about what the FDCPA requires must choose between, on the one hand, exposing herself to liability and, on the other, resolving the legal ambiguity against her client's interest or advising the client to settle—even where there is substantial legal authority for a position favoring the client.

We do not believe our holding today portends such grave consequences. For one, the FDCPA contains several provisions that expressly guard against abusive lawsuits, thereby mitigating the financial risk to creditors' attorneys. When an alleged violation is trivial, the "actual damage[s]" sustained, § 1692k(a)(1), will likely be de minimis or even zero. The Act sets a cap on "additional" damages, § 1692k(a)(2), and vests courts with discretion to adjust such damages where a violation is based on a good-faith error, § 1692k(b). One amicus suggests that attorney's fees may shape financial incentives even where actual and statutory damages are modest. The statute does contemplate an award of costs and "a reasonable attorney's fee as determined by the court" in the case of "any successful action to enforce the foregoing liability." § 1692k(a)(3). But courts have discretion in calculating reasonable attorney's fees under this statute, and § 1692k(a)(3) authorizes courts to award attorney's fees to the defendant if a plaintiff's suit "was brought in bad faith and for the purpose of harassment."

Lower courts have taken different views about when, and whether, § 1692k requires an award of attorney's fees. *Compare* Tolentino v. Friedman, 46 F.3d 645 (C.A.7 1995) (award of fees to a successful plaintiff "mandatory"), and *Emanuel, supra*, at 808–09 (same, even where the plaintiff suffered no actual damages), *with Graziano*, 950 F.2d, at 114, and n. 13 (attorney's fees may be denied for plaintiff's "bad faith conduct"), and Johnson v. Eaton, 80 F.3d 148, 150–152 (C.A.5 1996) ("attorney's fees ... are only available [under § 1692k] where the plaintiff has succeeded in establishing that the defendant is liable for actual and/or additional damages"; this reading "will deter suits brought only as a means of generating attorney's fees"). We need not resolve these issues today to express doubt that our reading of § 1692k(c) will impose unmanageable burdens on debt collecting lawyers.

...

To the extent the FDCPA imposes some constraints on a lawyer's advocacy on behalf of a client, it is hardly unique in our law. "[A]n attorney's ethical duty to advance the interests of his client is limited by an equally solemn duty to comply with the law and standards of professional conduct." Nix v. Whiteside, 475 U.S. 157, 168, 106 S.Ct. 988, 89 L.Ed.2d 123 (1986). Lawyers face sanctions, among other things, for suits presented "for any improper purpose, such as to harass, cause unnecessary delay, or needlessly increase the cost of litigation." Fed. Rules Civ. Proc. 11(b), (c). Model rules of professional conduct adopted by many States impose outer bounds on an attorney's pursuit of a client's interests. *See, e.g.*, ABA Model Rules of Professional Conduct 3.1 (2009) (requiring nonfrivolous basis in law and fact for claims asserted); 4.1 (truthfulness to third parties). In some circumstances, lawyers may face personal liability for conduct undertaken during representation of a client. *See, e.g.*, Central Bank of Denver, N.A. v. First Interstate Bank of Denver, N. A., 511 U.S. 164, 191, 114 S.Ct. 1439, 128 L.Ed.2d 119 (1994) ("Any person or entity, including a lawyer, ... who employs a manipulative device or makes a material misstatement (or omission) on which a purchaser or seller of securities relies may be liable as a primary violator under [Securities and Exchange Commission Rule] 10b-5").

Moreover, a lawyer's interest in avoiding FDCPA liability may not always be adverse to her client. Some courts have held clients vicariously liable for their lawyers' violations of the FDCPA. *See, e.g.*, Fox v. Citicorp Credit Servs., Inc., 15 F.3d 1507, 1516 (C.A.9 1994); *see also* First Interstate Bank of Fort Collins, N.A. v. Soucie, 924 P.2d 1200, 1202 (Colo.App.1996).

The suggestion that our reading of § 1692k(c) will create unworkable consequences is also undermined by the existence of numerous state consumer protection and debt collection statutes that contain bona fide error defenses that are either silent as to, or expressly exclude, legal errors. Several States have enacted debt collection statutes that contain neither an exemption for attorney debt collectors nor any bona fide error defense at all. *See, e.g.*, Mass. Gen. Laws, ch. 93, § 49 (West 2008); Md. Com. Law Code Ann.

§ 14-203 (Lexis 2005); Ore.Rev.Stat. § 646.641 (2007); Wis. Stat. § 427.105 (2007–2008). More generally, a group of 21 States as amici supporting Jerman inform us they are aware of "no [judicial] decisions interpreting a parallel state bona fide error provision [in a civil regulatory statute] to immunize a defendant's mistake of law," except in a minority of statutes that expressly provide to the contrary. *See* Brief for State of New York et al. as Amici Curiae 11, and n. 6. Neither Carlisle and its amici nor the dissent demonstrate that lawyers have suffered drastic consequences under these state regimes.

...

In sum, we do not foresee that our decision today will place unmanageable burdens on lawyers practicing in the debt collection industry. To the extent debt collecting lawyers face liability for mistaken interpretations of the requirements of the FDCPA, Carlisle, its amici, and the dissent have not shown that "the result [will be] so absurd as to warrant" disregarding the weight of textual authority discussed above. *Heintz*, 514 U.S., at 295, 115 S.Ct. 1489. Absent such a showing, arguments that the Act strikes an undesirable balance in assigning the risks of legal misinterpretation are properly addressed to Congress. To the extent Congress is persuaded that the policy concerns identified by the dissent require a recalibration of the FDCPA's liability scheme, it is, of course, free to amend the statute accordingly. Congress has wide latitude, for instance, to revise § 1692k to excuse some or all mistakes of law or grant broader discretion to district courts to adjust a plaintiff's recovery. This Court may not, however, read more into § 1692k(c) than the statutory language naturally supports. We therefore hold that the bona fide error defense in § 1692k(c) does not apply to a violation of the FDCPA resulting from a debt collector's incorrect interpretation of the requirements of that statute

For the reasons discussed above, the judgment of the United States Court of Appeals for the Sixth Circuit is reversed, and the case is remanded for further proceedings consistent with this opinion.

Justice KENNEDY, with whom Justice ALITO joins, dissenting.

The statute under consideration is the Fair Debt Collection Practices Act (FDCPA), 15 U.S.C. § 1692 et seq. The statute excepts from liability a debt collector's "bona fide error[s]," provided that they were "not intentional" and reasonable procedures have been maintained to avoid them. § 1692k(c). The Court today interprets this exception to exclude legal errors. In doing so, it adopts a questionable interpretation and rejects a straightforward, quite reasonable interpretation of the statute's plain terms. Its decision aligns the judicial system with those who would use litigation to enrich themselves at the expense of attorneys who strictly follow and adhere to professional and ethical standards.

* * *

1. Subsequent amendment. Congress amended the FDCPA after *Heintz* to provide that the section of the Act making actionable a debt collector's failure to include in a communication the fact that the debt collector is attempting to collect a debt does not apply to a formal pleading made in connection with a legal action. 15 U.S.C. § 1692e(11).

2. Other prohibited conduct. Like the FDCPA, state statutes prohibit a variety of unfair practices. These include communicating directly with a consumer who is represented by an attorney, *see, e.g.*, Col. Rev. Stat. § 12-14-105(1)(b), and communicating regarding the debt with third parties without the debtor's consent. *Id.* § 12-14-105(2). Section 1692c(b) of the FDCPA prohibits a debt collector from communicating "with any person other than the consumer, his attorney," and other designated individuals without the consumer's consent. In *Evon v. Law Offices of Sidney Mickell*, 2012 WL 3104620 (Aug. 1, 2012 9th Cir.), the Ninth Circuit Court of Appeals held that a law firm violated this portion of the Act when it sent a debt collection letter to the plaintiff's workplace marked "in care of" the plaintiff's employer. Is the decision correct as a matter of statutory construction? What is the problem with the law firm's actions?

3. Professional identity and threats of criminal prosecution. Initially, the ABA's Model Code of Professional Responsibility prohibited a lawyer from threatening to present criminal charges solely to obtain an advantage in a civil matter. DR 7-105 (1980). This would include attempts to collect a debt on behalf of a client. The Model Rules of Professional Conduct deleted this prohibition. Despite this, a near majority of jurisdictions have retained the prohibition. *See* Alex B. Long, *Lawyers Intentionally Inflicting Emotional Distress*, 42 SETON HALL L. REV. 55, 101 (2012). Should lawyers be permitted to threaten criminal charges solely to obtain an advantage in a civil matter? Would you do it?

* * *

C. Attorney Deceit Statutes

Focus Questions: *Amalfitano v. Rosenberg*

1. *Why could the plaintiff in* Amalfitano *not recover under a common law fraudulent misrepresentation theory?*
2 *What are the most important features of the statute at issue in* Amalfitano?

Amalfitano v. Rosenberg

903 N.E.2d 265
(N.Y. 2009)

READ, J.

The United States Court of Appeals for the Second Circuit has certified two questions to us regarding the application of section 487 of the Judiciary Law insofar as it provides that

> [a]n attorney or counselor who: ...
>
> [i]s guilty of any deceit or collusion, or consents to any deceit or collusion, with intent to deceive the court or any party ...
>
> [i]s guilty of a misdemeanor, and in addition to the punishment prescribed therefor by the penal law, he forfeits to the party injured treble damages, to be recovered in a civil action."

The questions arise out of defendant Armand Rosenberg's appeal from a judgment of the United States District Court for the Southern District of New York, finding that Rosenberg violated section 487 and awarding plaintiffs Vivia and Gerard Amalfitano three times their costs to defeat a lawsuit brought by Rosenberg on behalf of Peter Costalas (*Amalfitano v. Rosenberg*, 428 F.Supp.2d 196 [S.D.N.Y. 2006]). [The lawyer, Rosenberg, on behalf of his clients, had filed a complaint containing false allegations against the Amalfitanos. Rosenberg also knowingly made false representations in a motion for summary judgment and submitted an affidavit containing false statements to the state trial court. The trial court granted the Amalfitanos' motion to dismiss the fraud claim. In appealing the dismissal, Rosenberg again submitted the false affidavit and several erroneous documents to the appellate court. The appellate court was deceived by Rosenberg's actions and reversed the trial court's order. The trial court—not deceived by Rosenberg's actions—once again granted the Amalfitanos' motion to dismiss following pretrial discovery. The Amalfitanos then brought this section 487 claim against Rosenberg in federal court, seeking to recover the costs incurred in having to defend against Rosenberg's deceptive acts.] On appeal, the Second Circuit concluded that it could affirm the District Court's judgment "in its entirety" only if, in addition to Rosenberg's actual deceit of the Appellate Division, his "attempted deceit" of the trial court—"the false allegations in the complaint in the Costalas litigation" representing that Peter Costalas was a partner in 27 Whitehall Street Group—would "support[ ] a cause of action under section 487 and was the proximate cause of the Amalfitanos' damages in defending the litigation from its inception" (Amalfitano v. Rosenberg, 533 F.3d 117, 125 [2d Cir. 2008]).

I.
Certified Question No. 1

"Can a successful lawsuit for treble damages brought under N.Y. Jud. Law § 487 be based on an attempted but unsuccessful deceit?"

Rosenberg equates forfeiture under Judiciary Law § 487 with a tort claim for fraud. And under New York common law, "[t]o maintain an action based on fraudulent representations ... in tort for damages, it is sufficient to show that the defendant knowingly uttered a falsehood intending to deprive the plaintiff of a benefit and that the plaintiff was thereby deceived and damaged" (Channel Master Corp. v. Aluminium Ltd. Sales, 4 N.Y.2d 403, 406–07, 176 N.Y.S.2d 259, 151 N.E.2d 833 [1958] [emphasis added]). Thus, Rosenberg argues, section 487 does not permit recovery for an attempted but unsuccessful deceit practiced on a court. And here, the trial judge was concededly never fooled by misrepresentations regarding Peter Costalas's partnership status.

As the District Court correctly observed, however, Judiciary Law § 487 does not derive from common-law fraud. Instead, as the Amalfitanos point out, section 487 descends from the first Statute of Westminster, which was adopted by the Parliament summoned by King Edward I of England in 1275. The relevant provision of that statute specified that

> if any Serjeant, Pleader, or other, do any manner of Deceit or Collusion in the King's Court, or consent [unto it,] in deceit of the Court [or] to beguile the Court, or the Party, and thereof be attainted, he shall be imprisoned for a Year and a Day, and from thenceforth shall not be heard to plead in [that] Court for any Man; and if he be no Pleader, he shall be imprisoned in like manner by the Space of a Year and a Day at least; and if the Trespass require greater Punishment, it shall be at the King's Pleasure (3 Edw, ch. 29; *see generally* THOMAS PITT TASWELL-LANGMEAD, ENGLISH CONSTITUTIONAL HISTORY, at 153–154 [Theodore F.T. Plucknett ed., Sweet & Maxwell, 10th ed. 1946]).

Five centuries later, in 1787, the Legislature adopted a law with strikingly similar language, and added an award of treble damages, as follows:

> And be it further enacted ... [t]hat if any counsellor, attorney, solicitor, pleader, advocate, proctor, or other, do any manner of deceit or collusion, in any court of justice, or consent unto it in deceit of the court, or to beguile the court or the party, and thereof be convicted, he shall be punished by fine and imprisonment and shall moreover pay to the party grieved, treble damages, and costs of suit (L. 1787, ch. 35, § 5).

In 1830, the Legislature carried forward virtually identical language in the Revised Statutes of New York, prescribing that

> [a]ny counsellor, attorney or solicitor, who shall be guilty of any deceit or collusion, or shall consent to any deceit or collusion, with intent to deceive the court or any party, shall be deemed guilty of a misdemeanor, and on conviction shall be punished by fine or imprisonment, or both, at the discretion of the court. He shall also forfeit to the party injured by his deceit or collusion, treble damages, to be recovered in a civil action (2 Rev. Stat of NY, part III, ch. III, tit II, art 3, §69, at 215–16 [2d ed. 1836]).

The Legislature later codified this misdemeanor crime and the additional civil forfeiture remedy as section 148 of the Penal Code of 1881, providing that

> [a]n attorney or counselor who ...
>
> [i]s guilty of any deceit or collusion, or consents to any deceit or collusion, with intent to deceive the court or any party as prohibited by section 70 of the Code of Civil Procedure; ...
>
> [i]s guilty of a misdemeanor, and in addition to the punishment prescribed therefor by this Code, he forfeits to the party injured treble damages, to be recovered in a civil action" (L. 1881, ch. 676, §148[1]).

Section 70 of the Code of Civil Procedure, cross-referenced in section 148, similarly stated that "[a]n attorney or counsellor, who is guilty of any deceit or collusion, or consents to any deceit or collusion, with intent to deceive the court or a party, forfeits, to the party injured by his deceit or collusion, treble damages. He is also guilty of a misdemeanor." The derivation note accompanying section 70 includes the following comment: "As to the meaning of the word, 'deceit', as used in this section, *see* Looff v. Lawton, 14 Hun, 588" (Code of Civil Procedure of the State of New York with Notes by Montgomery H. Throop [Weed, Parsons and Company 1881]).

In *Looff*, the plaintiffs accused their attorney of gulling them into bringing an unnecessary lawsuit, motivated solely by his desire to collect a large fee to represent them. In discussing the meaning of the word "deceit" in section 70 (and, by extension, section 148), the General Term of the Supreme Court opined that the Legislature intended an expansive reading rather than "confining the term to common law or statutory cheats" (Looff v. Lawton, 14 Hun 588, 589 [2d Dept.1878]). To support this interpretation, the court reasoned that because there was already a civil action at common law for fraud and damage that an injured party might pursue,

> [t]here was no occasion ... for another statute to punish, or to give an action for the 'deceit' of lawyers, unless the Legislature intended that that class of persons should be liable for acts which would be insufficient to establish a crime or a cause of action against citizens generally. The statute is limited to a peculiar class of citizens, from whom the law exacts a reasonable degree of skill, and the utmost good faith in the conduct and management of the business intrusted to them ... To mislead the court or a party is to deceive it; and, if knowingly done, constitutes criminal deceit under the statute cited (*id.* at 590).

Section 148 was subsequently recodified as section 273 of the Penal Law of 1909. In conjunction with the Legislature's adoption of the revised Penal Law of 1965, section 148 was transferred from the Penal Law to the Judiciary Law as section 487 (see L. 1965, ch. 1031, §123). There it remains today—the modern-day counterpart of a statute dating from the first decades after Magna Carta; its language virtually (and remarkably) unchanged from that of a law adopted by New York's Legislature two years before the United States Constitution was ratified.

As this history shows, section 487 is not a codification of a common-law cause of action for fraud. Rather, section 487 is a unique statute of ancient origin in the criminal law of England. The operative language at issue—"guilty of any deceit"—focuses on the attorney's intent to deceive, not the deceit's success. And as the District Court pointed out, section 487 was for many years placed in the state's penal law, which "supports the argument that the more appropriate context for analysis is not the law applicable to comparable civil torts but rather criminal law, where an attempt to commit an underlying offense is punishable as well [as] the underlying offense itself" (*Amalfitano*, 428 F.Supp.2d at 210). Further, to limit forfeiture under section 487 to successful deceits would run counter to the statute's evident intent to enforce an attorney's special obligation to protect the integrity of the courts and foster their truth-seeking function.

II.
Certified Question No. 2

"In the course of such a lawsuit, may the costs of defending litigation instituted by a complaint containing a material misrepresentation of fact be treated as the proximate result of the misrepresentation if the court upon which the deceit was attempted at no time acted on the belief that the misrepresentation was true?" (533 F.3d at 126).

In light of our answer to the first question, recovery of treble damages under Judiciary Law § 487 does not depend upon the court's belief in a material misrepresentation of fact in a complaint. When a party commences an action grounded in a material misrepresentation of fact, the opposing party is obligated to defend or default and necessarily incurs legal expenses. Because, in such a case, the lawsuit could not have gone forward in the absence of the material misrepresentation, that party's legal expenses in defending the lawsuit may be treated as the proximate result of the misrepresentation.

Accordingly, the certified questions should be answered in accordance with this opinion.

* * *

1. Attorney deceit statutes. At least twelve jurisdictions—including New York and California—currently have statutes that single out lawyers who engage in deceit or collusion. Most of them use language similar to that of New York's statute. Alex B. Long, *Attorney Deceit Statutes: Promoting Professionalism Through Criminal Prosecutions and Treble Damages*, 44 U.C. Davis L. Rev. 413 (2010).

2. Interpretation of the statutes. Unlike the New York Court of Appeals, most courts have interpreted attorney deceit statutes in a limited fashion, concluding that they merely codify common law fraudulent misrepresentation claims. Are you convinced by *Amalfitano*'s use of history in support of its interpretation? Do you have any concerns about interpreting such statutes as broadly as the New York Court of Appeals did?

3. Other applications. In what other circumstances might an attorney deceit statute, as interpreted in *Amalfitano*, be of use to a plaintiff in the case of dishonest conduct on the part of a lawyer?

Exercise 13.5

Alice, a lawyer, represented Bob as part of a real estate transaction with Carol. Carol alleges that, during the course of negotiations, Alice withheld material factual information concerning the property and affirmatively misrepresented several material facts, all to the detriment of Carol. Carol now sues Alice under the jurisdiction's attorney deceit statute, which reads as follows:

> An attorney or counselor who is guilty of deceit or collusion, or consents thereto, with intent to deceive a court or judge, or a party to an action or proceeding, or brings suit or commences proceedings without authority therefor, is liable to be disbarred, and shall forfeit to the injured party treble damages, to be recovered in a civil action.

You represent Alice. Can you make an argument, based on the statutory language, that the statute does not provide a remedy to Carol?

Chapter 14

Interference with Contractual Relations

Exercise 14.1: Chapter Problem

Memo to: Associate
From: Partner

AJL Jewelers obtained financing from Treeline Capital Corp. as part of a major stock purchase. AJL Jewelers was interested in making another stock purchase with respect to another company, but Treeline was unwilling to offer better terms. Therefore, AJL Jewelers began shopping around. Eventually, AJL entered into a financing deal with Lookout Business Credit Corp. to finance the new purchase. However, Lookout later learned some disturbing information about several AJL officials and their prior criminal convictions and decided to void the deal. Not only did Lookout void the financing deal, a Lookout representative (who formerly worked for Treeline) contacted Treeline and informed Treeline that Lookout had been in negotiations with AJL. The representative also informed Treeline about the information regarding the prior convictions and volunteered his opinion to Treeline that AJL was "a bad risk" based on this information. As a result, Treeline terminated its agreement with AJL, as it had a legal right to do. AJL has now sued Lookout in state court in Oregon for interfering with its contractual relationship with Treeline.

AJL has an expert who is willing to testify that although there are no formal regulations or industry standards on the subject, Lookout's actions in revealing the financing deal and its cancellation amounted to a violation of established customs in the banking industry. In addition, you know that Lookout's actions amounted to a violation of its own code of ethics distributed to all employees. We represent Lookout. I am considering filing a motion for summary judgment. What are our best arguments?

If there is one theme that permeates the discussion of tortious interference claims, it is uncertainty. For example, Professor Dan Dobbs has stated the problem with the interference torts "lies in the complete absence of any principle that will explain to us what judgments to make and why it is that liability sometimes is and sometimes is not imposed." Dan B. Dobbs, *Tortious Interference with Contractual Relationships*, 34 Ark. L. Rev. 335, 346 (1980). That is quite a significant problem. If there is a second theme that permeates the discussion, it is the expansive nature of such claims. Although often thought of as a business tort, interference claims are increasingly asserted in a variety of contexts. Indeed, the flexible nature of the interference torts make them a useful cause of action in a host of situations. However, this also presents a somewhat disturbing problem. As one author has said, "tortious interference law is troubling because it is expanding despite its lack of clear principles or doctrinal foundations." Gary Myers, *The Differing Treatment of Efficiency and Competition in Antitrust and Tortious Interference Law*, 77 MINN. L. REV. 1097, 1110 (1993). Critics have leveled a host of other criticisms concerning the interference torts, most notably their anticompetitive tendencies.

Courts and commentators sometimes speak generically about "tortious interference" claims. In reality, there are two separate interference torts: interference with contractual relations and interference with prospective contractual relations. The fact that there are actually two variants of the interference torts helps contribute to the uncertainty surrounding interference claims.

The following chapter attempts to sort through the doctrinal confusion. The chapter examines the evolution of the torts and the emerging trend among courts to develop clearer rules based upon coherent principles. The chapter also attempts to provide a sample of the various ways in which interference claims may arise, with a particular focus on how such claims might arise in a lawyer's professional life.

* * *

A. Original Development of the Torts

The modern versions of the interference torts can be traced back to the British case of *Lumley v. Gye*, 2 El. & Bl. 216 (1853). *Lumley* involved a suit by the manager and lessee of the Queen's Theatre, who had contracted with Johanna Wagner, a singer. The contract provided that Wagner would sing for the theatre "for a certain time" and could not sing or use her talents elsewhere. The defendant lured Wagner away, and the plaintiff sued. The Court of the Queen's Bench held that the defendant was liable for enticing Wagner away. Importantly, there was no suggestion that the defendant employed any kind of independently wrongful means, such as defaming the plaintiff, in order to accomplish his purpose. Instead, the defendant's act of intentionally causing Wagner to breach her contract was itself the wrong.

U.S. law gradually developed along similar lines throughout much of the 20th century. Later cases extended *Lumley*'s reasoning to interferences with other relationships that were not reduced to contract form. Like *Lumley*, some cases involved attempts to lure employees away from their employers. Others involved other forms of competition. For example, *Imperial Ice Co. v. Rossier*, 112 P.2d 631 (Cal. 1941) involved a defendant who induced an individual to breach the individual's non-compete agreement with the plaintiff, a business rival. There, the California Supreme Court held that "an action will lie for inducing a breach of contract by the use of moral, social, or economic pressures, in themselves lawful, unless there is sufficient justification for such inducement." *Id.* at 632.

* * *

1.The Prima Facie Tort Approach

Focus Questions: *Chaves v. Johnson*

1. *What is the basis for Johnson's liability?*
2. *Johnson and Chaves were competitors. Why weren't Johnson's actions a form of privileged competition?*

Chaves v. Johnson

335 S.E.2d 97
(Va. 1985)

RUSSELL, Justice.

[The plaintiff, Chaves, sued Johnson upon a theory of, *inter alia*, tortious interference with contract rights. The jury awarded damages to Chaves.] The trial court set the verdict aside and entered judgment for the defendant. We granted the plaintiff an appeal.

Juan O. Chaves is a licensed architect practicing in the Fredericksburg area. In September 1978, after soliciting bids from architects, the City of Fredericksburg awarded him a contract for architectural services. The contract provided that Chaves would make a study of the City's governmental space needs, would review the availability of existing properties to meet those needs, and would render complete architectural services with respect to additional construction work desired by the City. His fee was to be $3500 for the space study and 10% of construction costs for new construction. The contract was not specific as to the new construction desired, but at the time of its execution the City contemplated the renovation and conversion of an existing Post Office Building on Princess Anne Street into a new City Hall. Chaves was directed to develop a schematic design and a cost estimate for the project.

Chaves' cost estimate, submitted in April 1979, was for $723,720, plus his fee of $72,372, plus an allowance of $100,000 for furniture. The City Council members had contemplated spending less than $275,000 on the project. Chaves informed the City Council, "This is what you tell me you need. It's going to cost way in excess of what you want. Please tell me what to do." The Public Works Committee decided the cost of renovating the Post Office was too high and asked Chaves to investigate alternatives. He did a study of a potential new City Hall to be built on Caroline Street. Chaves submitted a plan for that project in June 1979.

H.C. Johnson, Jr., was another licensed architect practicing in the Fredericksburg area. He had submitted a competing bid for the City's Architectural Services Contract, quoting a lower fee, and was annoyed when the award was made to Chaves. Johnson testified:

> It was important to me to let City Council know that I felt it was a reflection on me, and a reflection on my professional ability, and a reflection on my professional standing in the community, that it became public knowledge that they had by-passed me, they have not considered my proposal, they have hired somebody who does not have the experience that I have had; and at the same time, pay him fifty percent more. Now, that's got to tell somebody something.

On July 23, 1979, while the City Council was at an impasse concerning the cost of a new City Hall, Johnson wrote the following letter to the City Council:

> July 23, 1979
>
> Fredericksburg City Council
> Fredericksburg, Virginia
>
> Re: Proposed City Hall
> Architectural Project
>
> Members of Council:
>
> Concerning the proposed City Hall Architectural Project. Over a prolonged period of time since Council selected an Architect for the above project it has come to my attention that members of Council did not review, or did not have, all relevant information when making the decision.
>
> If having been aware of the facts it seems unreasonable to me that Council would retain an Architect who has had no prior experience in this type of project and agree to pay an Architectural fee that is over 50% more than what could be considered a reasonable fee.
>
> I have been told by members of Council that they have never seen the proposal that I submitted, in response to Mr. Funk's request, and were not aware that I was really interested in the project.
>
> I have also been told that a member of Council told other members of Council that I was too busy to work on the project. This is absolutely not true. Had I been too busy I would not have submitted a proposal or told Mr. Funk, or stated in my proposal, that I was extremely interested in the project.
>
> In view of the fact that I am a registered Architect, a permanent resident of the area, have maintained an office in the City for thirteen years and have paid many thousands of dollars to the City Treasurer in the form of Business License Tax, and have had as much experience as any Architect in the State with respect to this type of project, have submitted a reasonable fee schedule and have expressed a sincere desire to be considered for the project, it seems a considerable reflection on my professional reputation, as well as questionable judgement on Council's part, to retain an Architect of no past experience and agree to pay him an unjustifiably high fee.
>
> Because of my failure to request a proper interview, which I had assumed would be an appropriate formality, at the time of the original architectural selection concerning the Post Office I do not necessarily feel that I am entitled to further consideration concerning that particular project, even though I feel that Council did not give my proposal fair and impartial consideration.
>
> However, if it is Council's intention to consider a new City Hall at any location other than the Post Office I would at this time request that my original proposal be reviewed and reconsidered and a new architectural contract be awarded based on the requirements of the new project and the merits of those submitting proposals.
>
> Further, if it is Council's intention to accept and review unsolicited architectural concepts for a new City Hall I would also appreciate some consideration with respect to such a presentation.
>
> If you have not seen my original proposal I have enclosed a copy for your review. Of considerable importance, I feel, is the fact that I stated I was extremely

> interested in the project, that my fee in the $700,000.00 to $800,000.00 range would have 6.5% of the construction cost, and that a study and determination of space needs was a part of my basic fee. If you also review the other proposals submitted and the contract that was eventually entered into by the City it is clear that all facts were not considered when a decision was reached. It seems to me that on a project of this type the public interest is being poorly served if members of Council do not review all information that is readily available to them when making a decision involving hundreds of thousand (possibly millions) of dollars, and as a result select the person or firm who is readily available, is best qualified, and proposes to do the work for the most reasonable fee.
>
> I ask only that all relevant facts and information receive fair and impartial consideration.
>
> Sincerely,
>
> H. C. Johnson, Jr.
> Architect

Johnson hand delivered a copy of this letter to each council member, accompanied by a copy of his fee schedule and a list of his professional qualifications.

A week following the receipt of Johnson's letter, the Public Works Committee, consisting of five councilmen, held a closed executive session and thereafter, in a public meeting, voted to recommend that City Council terminate Chaves' contract. The seconder of the motion stated that he was voting to terminate the contract because "it had been pointed out to him" that Chaves' fees were "excessive" and his experience "not sufficient." Two weeks later, at a formal meeting, the City Council voted to accept the committee's recommendation and terminate Chaves' contract. No reason was stated for the Council's action.

After Chaves' termination, the City Council solicited new bids for architectural services. Johnson's bid was accepted, although lower bids were received.

Chaves filed a motion for judgment against Johnson [on a theory of tortious interference with contract rights, seeking $107,145 in actual and consequential damages.]

At trial, eight of the eleven City Council members testified. Each denied that he had been influenced by Johnson's letter in deciding to vote to terminate Chaves' contract. Several councilmen cited specific areas of dissatisfaction with Chaves' schematic design. One councilman testified that he had decided as early as April 1979 that Chaves should be replaced and had discussed the matter with other councilmen. He also admitted that he had gone to Johnson's office a few days before Johnson wrote the letter of July 23, and had discussed the matter with Johnson, who had a copy of Chaves' design on his desk.

[The jury] returned a verdict awarding Chaves $70,000 actual damages....

The trial court sustained Johnson's motion to set aside the verdict on the tortious interference count on the primary ground that there was no evidence to support the jury's finding that Johnson's letter was the proximate cause of Chaves' discharge. The court relied on the testimony of the eight councilmen that they had been motivated by other factors.

We have not previously had occasion to consider [the tort of tortious interference with contract], although in *Worrie v. Boze*, 198 Va. 533, 95 S.E.2d 192 (1956), we affirmed a judgment granting relief for a tortious conspiracy to procure a breach of contract. There, we said: "It is well settled that the right to performance of a contract and the right to reap profits therefrom are property rights which are entitled to protection in the courts. Consequently, suits for procuring breach of contract proceed on this basis." Code § 18.2-499 provides criminal penalties and Code § 18.2-500 provides civil penalties for such conspiracies.

A right of action for tortious interference with contract rights was recognized by a majority of the judges of the Queen's Bench in Lumley v. Gye, 2 El. & Bl. 216, 118 Eng.Rep. 749 (1853). It has also been recognized by the Supreme Court of the United States, *Angle v. Chicago, etc., R.R. Co.*, 151 U.S. 1, (1894), and by many of our sister states, *see, e.g., Imperial Ice Co. v. Rossier*, 18 Cal.2d 33, 112 P.2d 631 (1941). The tort is succinctly described in *Restatement (Second) Torts* § 766 (1977):

Intentional Interference with
Performance of Contract
by Third Party

> One who intentionally and improperly interferes with the performance of a contract (except a contract to marry) between another and a third person by inducing or otherwise causing the third person not to perform the contract, is subject to liability to the other for the pecuniary loss resulting to the other from the failure of the third person to perform the contract.

The elements required for a prima facie showing of the tort are: (1) the existence of a valid contractual relationship or business expectancy; (2) knowledge of the relationship or expectancy on the part of the interferor; (3) intentional interference inducing or causing a breach or termination of the relationship or expectancy; and (4) resultant damage to the party whose relationship or expectancy has been disrupted. Thus, the interferor's knowledge of the business relationship and his intent to disturb it are requisite elements; malice is not. *Restatement, supra*, § 766 comment s.

An affirmative defense, for which the burden rests upon the defendant, is justification or privilege. It is similar, but not identical, to the defense of qualified privilege in the law of defamation. It is based upon the relationships between the parties and the balance to be struck between the social desirability of protecting the business relationship, on one hand, and the interferor's freedom of action on the other. Specific grounds for the defense, discussed seriatim in *Restatement, supra*, §§ 768–772 are: legitimate business competition, financial interest, responsibility for the welfare of another, directing business policy, and the giving of requested advice.

At trial, Johnson moved to strike Chaves' evidence on the ground of privilege or justification, and assigned cross-error to the court's refusal to grant his motion. On appeal, he argues that his letter to the City Council members was justified on the basis of financial self-interest; freedom of speech; and the right of a taxpayer to complain of public expenditures.

The trial court correctly overruled Johnson's motion to strike. Some jurisdictions have held that a competitor is justified by economic self-interest in causing a third person not to enter into a prospective business relationship with another competitor, or not to continue an existing contract terminable at will, provided no "intentional, improper interference" is used. His conduct is tortious, however, if he induces the third party to breach an existing contract which is not terminable at will. Cumberland Glass Mfg. Co. v. DeWitt, 120 Md. 381, 87 A. 927 (1913), *aff'd*, 237 U.S. 447, 35 S.Ct. 636, 59 L.Ed. 1042 (1915). *Restatement, supra*, § 768. Chaves' contract with the City was terminable only for cause, not at will.

We are unpersuaded by Johnson's freedom-of-speech argument. By logical extension, it would apply to any verbal conduct, however tortious, and would completely destroy the right of action universally recognized. Our constitutional guarantees of free speech, as we have seen, protect expressions of opinion from actions for defamation. Those constitutional guarantees have never been construed, however, to protect either criminal or tortious conduct. Thus, obscenity, "fighting words," *Chaplinsky v. New Hampshire*, 315 U.S. 568, 572 (1942) and defamatory words, *Time, Inc. v. Firestone*, 424 U.S. 448 (1976), remain outside the scope of constitutionally protected free speech. The tort complained of here is an intentional wrong to the property rights of another, accomplished by words, not defamatory in themselves, but employed in pursuance of a scheme designed wrongfully to enrich the speaker at the expense of the victim. The law provides a remedy in such cases, and the constitutional guarantees of free speech afford no more protection to the speaker than they do to any other tortfeasor who employs words to commit a criminal or a civil wrong.

The trial court set aside the verdict for tortious interference on three grounds: (1) that no proximate cause was established, (2) that no intent to interfere on Johnson's part was established, and (3) that the evidence negated malice on Johnson's part. As stated above, malice is not required. Regarding proximate cause, the court relied on the unanimous statements of the eight councilmen who testified that they were not motivated by Johnson's letter in deciding to discharge Chaves. The jury, however, was not required to accept the councilmen's testimony. It was entitled to rely on the circumstantial evidence surrounding Johnson's relationships with certain councilmen, the timing of his letter, and particularly Chaves' testimony that the seconder of the motion to terminate his contract, after receiving Johnson's letter, explained his vote in a public meeting as based on Chaves' "excessive" fees and "not sufficient" experience which "had been pointed out to him." This evidence was received without objection and was unrefuted. It furnished sufficient support for the jury's finding of proximate cause.

Regarding Johnson's intent, the court relied on the statement in Johnson's letter that he realized that he was too late to compete for the Post Office renovation, but wished to be considered for any other City Hall plan the council might undertake. The court considered this a clear indication that Johnson lacked any intent to interfere with Chaves' existing contract, but was asking only to be considered for any future contract the City might award. This view was based on the erroneous assumption that Chaves' contract was limited to the Post Office renovation. As noted above, the contract was for architectural services for any project the City might decide upon, at any location.

We hold that the court erred in setting aside the verdict for actual damages based upon the count for tortious interference with contract rights. Accordingly, we will reverse the judgment in part, reinstate the verdict as to actual damages, and enter final judgment here for $70,000.00.

* * *

1. Justification/Privilege. *Chaves* lists several recognized privileges to interfere (or justifications for interfering) with another's business relations. This chapter will eventually address each of them.

2. Criticisms and uncertainty. *Chaves* is noteworthy for drawing a distinction between interferences with existing contracts and interferences with a prospective contractual relationship, at least in the case of competition. However, courts have sometimes been unclear where to draw the line between permissible vs. impermissible interferences, depending upon which type of business relationship was at issue. The first *Restatement* *of Torts*, for example, generally failed to distinguish between the two situations and instead provided that one who purposely caused a third person not to perform a contract with another or not to "*enter into* or continue a business relation with" another was subject to liability, unless a privilege attached. Restatement of Torts § 766 (emphasis added). This state of affairs led to two main criticisms:

(1) The torts were anti-competitive in nature. One member of the American Law Institute is said to have commented, "foreign lawyers reading the *Restatement* as an original matter would find it astounding that the whole competitive order of American industry is prima facie illegal." Harvey S. Perlman, *Interference with Contract and Other Economic Expectancies*, 49 U. CHI. L. REV. 61, 79 (1982) (quoting Carl Auerbach).

(2) The torts were unclear as to their bases of liability. There is often little question that a defendant intended to interfere with the plaintiff's relationship with another. Thus, the real question in most cases is whether there is a good reason to make the defendant pay for any damages caused by the intentional interference. Here, the decisional law has not been particularly clear. Courts frequently said that a "malicious" interference was actionable, but "malice" frequently seemed to mean simply that the defendant acted intentionally. The result, according to Dean Prosser, was "a rather broad and undefined tort in which no specific conduct is proscribed and in which liability turns on the purpose for which the defendant acts, with the indistinct notion that the purposes must be considered improper in some undefined way." W. PAGE KEETON ET AL., PROSSER AND KEETON ON THE LAW OF TORTS, § 129, at 979 (5th ed. 1984).

* * *

2. The *Restatement (Second) of Torts* Balancing-of-Factors Approach

The authors of the *Restatement (Second) of Torts* eventually attempted to provide greater clarity to the interference torts. They largely failed. The authors separated the torts of interference with contract (§ 766) and interference with prospective contractual relations (§ 766B). However, the black-letter rules for the two sections are essentially the same. The authors also largely did away with the concept of privilege. Instead, they provided that one who "intentionally and *improperly*" interferes with another's relation is subject to liability. Another section, § 767, provided a list of seven factors to consider in determining whether the interference was improper:

(a) the nature of the actor's conduct,

(b) the actor's motive,

(c) the interests of the other with which the actor's conduct interferes,

(d) the interests sought to be advanced by the actor,

(e) the social interests in protecting the freedom of action of the actor and the contractual interests of the other,

(f) the proximity or remoteness of the actor's conduct to the interference and

(g) the relations between the parties.

Although there is only liability where the defendant "intentionally and improperly interferes," the authors declined to definitively resolve whether the plaintiff bears the burden of establishing impropriety or whether the burden of showing propriety is on the defendant. *Id.* § 767 cmt. b. Reaction to the *Restatement*'s approach and multi-factor test has been mixed at best. Although courts frequently rely upon the *Restatement*, few have adopted the balancing-of-factors approached detailed in § 767.

* * *

3. The Improper Purpose or Improper Means Test

Focus Questions: *Top Service Body Shop, Inc. v. Allstate Ins. Co.*

1. *How does the test articulated in* Top Service *differ from the test contained in § 767 of the Restatement (Second) of Torts? From* Chaves?
2. *What would it take to establish that a defendant acted with an "improper purpose"?*

Top Service Body Shop, Inc. v. Allstate Ins. Co.

582 P.2d 1365
(Or. 1978)

LINDE, Justice.

Plaintiff, the operator of an automobile body repair shop in Coos Bay, Oregon, sued defendant insurance company for general and punitive damages for injuries alleged to result from defendant's wrongful practices in directing insurance claimants to have repairs made at body shops other than plaintiff's. The complaint pleaded causes of action grounded in two theories: First, tortious interference with plaintiff's business, and second, inducement of other body shops to accord defendant discriminatory price advantages prohibited by statute.... Defendant answered by general denials and an affirmative defense to the tort claim asserting a privilege of acting in its own legitimate financial interests. Plaintiff replied that defendant's methods and intent took its actions beyond any such privilege.

The trial resulted in jury verdicts for plaintiff in amounts of $20,000 compensatory and $250,000 punitive damages on the tort claim and $45,000 in treble damages on the price discrimination claim. On defendant's motion, the trial court entered judgments notwithstanding the verdicts on both causes of action, primarily for failure of proof. The court also allowed defendant's alternative motion for a new trial pursuant to ORS 18.140(3). On appeal, plaintiff assigns as error the rulings on these motions and also two rulings excluding evidence offered by it during the trial.

I. The claim of tortious interference.

Although other jurisdictions have decided numerous claims of tortious interference with business relations, this court has had few occasions to consider the elements of this tort.

Either the pursuit of an improper objective of harming plaintiff or the use of wrongful means that in fact cause injury to plaintiff's contractual or business relationships may give rise to a tort claim for those injuries. PROSSER, HANDBOOK OF THE LAW OF TORTS

§ 130 at 952 (4th ed. 1971). However, efforts to consolidate both recognized and unsettled lines of development into a general theory of "tortious interference" have brought to the surface the difficulties of defining the elements of so general a tort without sweeping within its terms a wide variety of socially very different conduct.[3] These difficulties are shown by the changing treatment of the subject in the American Law Institute's *Restatement of the Law of Torts*. The main problem is what weight to give to the defendant's objective in interfering with plaintiff's contract or with plaintiff's prospective business relations. If the focus in defining the tort is on defendant's wrongful motive or use of wrongful means, this element will likely be a necessary part of plaintiff's case. If the tort is defined primarily as an invasion of plaintiff's protected interests, defendant's reasons are likely to be treated as questions of justification or privilege. Section 766 of the first *Restatement of Torts* read:

> Except as stated in Section 698, one who, without a privilege to do so, induces or otherwise purposely causes a third person not to
>
> (a) perform a contract with another, or
>
> (b) enter into or continue a business relation with another is liable to the other for the harm caused thereby.

...

In preparing the *Restatement (Second) of Torts* in 1969, the change to liability based simply on unprivileged intent was not accepted even with respect to inducing or causing breaches of existing contracts. The result was a revision by the succeeding Reporter, Dean John W. Wade, of the *Restatement* chapter dealing with the tort of interference with existing or prospective contracts or, as the Reporter described it, "interference with advantageous economic relations," which proposed significant changes in the analysis. *See* Restatement (Second) of Torts § 766 (Tent. Draft No. 23, 1977). As the *Restatement* now stands, such interference would give rise to liability if it is both intentional and affirmatively improper (replacing reliance on lack of "privilege" in the definition of the tort), and a purpose to harm the injured party would be one factor making the interference improper. Restatement (Second) of Torts §§ 766–767 (Tent. Draft No. 23, 1977).

The evolution of this "restatement" of the tort is significant here because it corresponds to a similar division in the recent decisions in this state....

[T]he decision in *Nees v. Hocks*, 272 Or. 210, 536 P.2d 512 (1975), rejected the concept that every intentional infliction of harm is prima facie a tort unless justified. Finding that this concept was no longer needed to escape the rigidity of the common-law forms of pleading, the court concluded that it created as many difficulties as it solved. However, the court found that the plaintiff had effectively pleaded and proved that her discharge by defendant was tortious by reason of an improper motive.

We conclude that the approach of *Nees v. Hocks* is equally appropriate to claims of tort liability for intentional interference with contractual or other economic relations. In summary, such a claim is made out when interference resulting in injury to another is wrongful by some measure beyond the fact of the interference itself. Defendant's liability may arise from improper motives or from the use of improper means. They may be

---

3. During one period of history, the tort of interference with contracts was a main legal weapon against labor organization. *See, e. g.*, Hitchman Coal & Coke Co. v. Mitchell, 245 U.S. 229, 38 S.Ct. 65, 62 L.Ed. 260 (1917) (injunction); Vegelahn v. Guntner, 167 Mass. 92, 44 N.E. 1077 (1896); Prosser, Handbook of the Law of Torts s 129 at 946–947 (4th ed. 1971).

wrongful by reason of a statute or other regulation, or a recognized rule of common law, or perhaps an established standard of a trade or profession. No question of privilege arises unless the interference would be wrongful but for the privilege; it becomes an issue only if the acts charged would be tortious on the part of an unprivileged defendant. Even a recognized privilege may be overcome when the means used by defendant are not justified by the reason for recognizing the privilege. To this extent we agree with the analysis of the second *Restatement*.[12]

In the present case, Top Service pleaded both improper motives and improper means of interference. It alleged that Allstate sought to and did induce Top Service's patrons not to have Top Service repair their automobiles, making false statements about the quality of plaintiff's workmanship and threats about withdrawing insurance coverage or subjecting the settlement of claims to possible arbitration. It also alleged that this was done "with the sole design of injuring Plaintiff and destroying his business," and in an endeavor to "compel Plaintiff to abandon the same." If proved, along with damages and causation, these allegations satisfy the elements of the tort we have reviewed above.

Defendant contended successfully in the trial court that the evidence, taken most favorably to plaintiff, was insufficient to support a verdict for plaintiff. Judge Warden's order recited two grounds for allowing the motion for judgment n.o.v. on the first cause of action. The first was that "there was no evidence that defendant's conduct was the result of a specific intent directed at the plaintiff or that its purpose was to interfere with the plaintiff, as such." Any impact on plaintiff of defendant's dealings with its insurance claimants was described as "incidental and collateral." The second ground was that defendant acted only within its legal privilege of dealing with its insurance claimants in pursuit of its own lawful business interests.

As to the first issue, Top Service does not really argue that there was direct evidence to show that Allstate had acted with the destructive design quoted above. It claims that even without direct evidence of a specific purpose of defendant to destroy Top Service's business, the jury could have inferred such a purpose from evidence of defendant's conduct in directing customers to other body repair shops. But the record will not support an inference that Allstate had any design or purpose to inflict injury on Top Service as such, even short of the "sole design" to put Top Service out of business that the complaint alleged.

Taken most favorably to plaintiff, as is proper after a verdict for plaintiff, the evidence showed that Allstate has a practice of designating certain repair shops in the locality as "competitive shops" to which it prefers to send insurance claimants for whose repairs Allstate is obligated; that Top Service at one time was a "drive-in" shop for Allstate, where claimants would be directed for an estimate by an Allstate insurance adjuster; that after a dispute Top Service's owner decided that it would not continue as a drive-in shop for Allstate; and that thereafter Allstate adjusters would actively discourage claimants under its insurance policies from taking work to be paid for by Allstate to Top Service, sending them instead to other shops on its preferred list. As specific bases for an inference of destructive purpose, Top Service lists two occasions when Allstate adjusters disparaged

---

12. We need not in this case discuss the "factors" approach of section 767, cited by plaintiff, which poses unresolved difficulties with respect to pleading, proof, and the function of court and jury. *See* Restatement (Second) of Torts s 767, Comments J, k, l (Tent. Draft No. 23, 1977). For other difficulties inherent in "balancing" as an approach to individual cases rather than to characteristic types of relationship, see the thorough opinion in Continental Research, Inc. v. Cruttenden, Podesta & Miller, 222 F. Supp. 190, 216–217 (D. Minn.1963).

the quality of Top Service's work (apart from its relative cost), although Allstate personnel had generally considered Top Service a high quality shop; Allstate's willingness to disappoint its own insured who preferred Top Service; one occasion when Allstate took its option to "total" a car, i.e. to pay off its value, when the insured wanted it repaired at Top Service; and finally Allstate's resort to "improper and unlawful means" to direct business away from Top Service to other shops. Without setting forth here the excerpts of the record cited by plaintiff, we agree with the trial court that these acts were wholly consistent with Allstate's pursuit of its own business purposes as it saw them and did not suffice to support an inference of the alleged improper purpose to injure Top Service. The court's ruling on this point was not error.

Plaintiff contends that its case did not depend solely on proof of Allstate's wrongful motive. It argues that, contrary to the trial court's conclusion, Allstate would not be privileged to interfere with plaintiff's business relations by unlawful or otherwise improper means even in pursuit of its own business objectives. As unlawful or improper practices, plaintiff points to defendant's disparagement of its services, the price discriminations [mentioned earlier in the opinion], and violation of other statutory policies [including a statute prohibiting the disparagement of goods or services by making false representations]. Plaintiff's contention may well be a correct view of the law, as we have reviewed it above, but it does not help plaintiff on this appeal. The difficulty is that the case was submitted to the jury solely on the theory of liability for purposely seeking to harm plaintiff's business. Even if defendant might also have been liable on an alternative theory of tortious interference by improper means, we cannot reinstate the verdict on that theory, which was not presented to the jury. Since the trial court did not err in its ruling under the theory on which the case was submitted, the judgment on the first cause of action must be affirmed.

[With regard to Top Services's second claim, Top Service made out a prima facie case of price discrimination in regard to charges that Allstate received a 5% discount from a competing body shop and that some shops accepted Allstate's estimates of repair costs based on a schedule of painting costs developed by Allstate itself, which was substantially lower than the manuals otherwise used by body shops to estimate these painting costs. However, the evidence did not warrant finding that there were actual or potential anti-competitive effects of the discounts and paint schedules so as to permit recovery on theory that Allstate obtained discriminatory price concessions.]

* * *

The role of malice. Section 767 of the *Restatement (Second) of Torts* directs the factfinder to consider the defendant's motive in interfering and "the interests sought to be advanced by the actor." A comment explains that the factfinder should consider whether the defendant "was motivated, in whole or in part, by a desire to interfere with the other's contractual relations. If this was the sole motive the interference is almost certain to be held improper." *Id.* §767 cmt. d. In an influential law review article, Professor Harvey S. Perlman was highly critical of the reliance on a defendant's purpose or motive in interfering as a basis for imposing liability in interference cases. "Proof of motivation," Perlman argued, "is error-prone and carries social costs. In addition, pure malice is not a perfect predictor of anticompetitive effect, because an actor motivated by pure malice may choose competitive means to accomplish his purpose: if TP hates B for personal reasons and spitefully searches for a more advantageous opportunity for A so as to interfere with B's contract with A, he nonetheless may produce a social benefit." Harvey S. Perlman, *Interference with Contract and Other Economic Expectancies*, 49 U. Chi. L. Rev. 61, 95 (1982). What role, if any, should malice play in the analysis of whether a defendant's interference was improper?

B. Modern Developments: Interference with Contract vs. Interference with Prospective Contract vs. Interference with Contracts Terminable At-Will

There remains a considerable amount of disagreement regarding the proper treatment of interference claims. However, a few trends have started to develop within the past two decades. The following section examines two of those trends as interference law continues to stumble toward something (hopefully) like coherence.

1. Interference with Contract vs. Interference with Prospective Contract

---

Focus Questions: *Della Penna v. Toyota Motor Sales, U.S.A., Inc.*

1. *How does the test articulated in* Della Penna *differ from the other tests described above?*
2. *Why does the court adopt the test it does?*

Della Penna v. Toyota Motor Sales, U.S.A., Inc.

902 P.2d 740
(Cal. 1995)

ARABIAN, Justice.

We granted review to reexamine, in light of divergent rulings from the Court of Appeal and a doctrinal evolution among other state high courts, the elements of the tort variously known as interference with "prospective economic advantage," "prospective contractual relations," or "prospective economic relations," and the allocation of the burdens of proof between the parties to such an action.

I

John Della Penna, an automobile wholesaler doing business as Pacific Motors, brought this action for damages against Toyota Motor Sales, U.S.A., Inc., and its Lexus division, alleging that certain business conduct of defendants both violated provisions of the Cartwright Act, California's state antitrust statute (Bus. & Prof.Code, § 16700 et seq.), and constituted an intentional interference with his economic relations. The impetus for Della Penna's suit arose out of the 1989 introduction into the American luxury car market of Toyota's Lexus automobile. Prior to introducing the Lexus, the evidence at trial showed, both the manufacturer, Toyota Motor Corporation, and defendant, the American distributor, had been concerned at the possibility that a resale market might develop for the Lexus in Japan. Even though the car was manufactured in Japan, Toyota's marketing strategy was to bar the vehicle's sale on the Japanese domestic market until after the American roll-out; even then, sales in Japan would only be under a different brand name, the "Celsior." Fearing that auto wholesalers in the United States might re-export Lexus models back to Japan for resale, and concerned that, with production and the availability of Lexus models in the American market limited, re-exports would jeopardize its fledgling network of American Lexus dealers, Toyota inserted in its dealership agreements a "no export" clause, providing that the dealer was "authorized to sell [Lexus automobiles] only to customers located in the United States. [Dealer] agrees that it will not sell [Lexus automobiles] for resale or use outside the United States. [Dealer] agrees to abide by any export policy established by [distributor]."

Following the introduction into the American market, it soon became apparent that some domestic Lexus units were being diverted for foreign sales, principally to Japan. To counter this effect, Toyota managers wrote to their retail dealers, reminding them of the "no-export" policy and explaining that exports for foreign resale could jeopardize the supply of Lexus automobiles available for the United States market. In addition, Toyota compiled a list of "offenders"—dealers and others believed by Toyota to be involved heavily in the developing Lexus foreign resale market—which it distributed to Lexus dealers in the United States. American Lexus dealers were also warned that doing business with those whose names appeared on the "offenders" list might lead to a series of graduated sanctions, from reducing a dealer's allocation to possible reevaluation of the dealer's franchise agreement.

During the years 1989 and 1990, plaintiff Della Penna did a profitable business as an auto wholesaler purchasing Lexus automobiles, chiefly from the Lexus of Stevens Creek retail outlet, at near retail price and exporting them to Japan for resale. By late 1990, however, plaintiff's sources began to dry up, primarily as a result of the "offenders list." Stevens Creek ceased selling models to plaintiff; gradually other sources declined to sell to him as well.

In February 1991, plaintiff filed this lawsuit against Toyota Motors, U.S.A., Inc., alleging both state antitrust claims under the Cartwright Act and interference with his economic relationship with Lexus retail dealers. At the close of plaintiff's case-in-chief, the trial court granted Toyota's motion for nonsuit with respect to the remaining Cartwright Act claim (plaintiff had previously abandoned a related claim—unfair competition—prior to trial). The tort cause of action went to the jury, however, under the standard BAJI instructions applicable to such claims with one significant exception. At the request of defendant and over plaintiff's objection, the trial judge modified BAJI No. 7.82—the basic instruction identifying the elements of the tort and indicating the burden of proof—to require plaintiff to prove that defendant's alleged interfering conduct was "wrongful."[1]

The jury returned a divided verdict, nine to three, in favor of Toyota. After Della Penna's motion for a new trial was denied, he appealed. In an unpublished disposition, the Court of Appeal unanimously reversed the trial court's judgment, ruling that a plaintiff

---

1. The standard instruction governing "intentional interference with prospective economic advantage," BAJI No. 7.82, describes the essential elements of the claim as (1) an economic relationship between the plaintiff and another, "containing a probable future economic benefit or advantage to plaintiff," (2) defendant's knowledge of the existence of the relationship, (3) that defendant "intentionally engaged in acts or conduct designed to interfere with or disrupt" the relationship, (4) actual disruption, and (5) damage to the plaintiff as a result of defendant's acts. The modification sought by defendant and adopted by the trial court consisted in adding the word "wrongful" in element (3) between the words "in" and "acts." The trial court also read to the jury plaintiff's special jury instruction defining the "wrongful acts" required to support liability as conduct "outside the realm of legitimate business transactions.... Wrongfulness may lie in the method used or by virtue of an improper motive."

alleging intentional interference with economic relations is not required to establish "wrongfulness" as an element of its prima facie case, and that it was prejudicial error for the trial court to have read the jury an amended instruction to that effect. The Court of Appeal remanded the case to the trial court for a new trial; we then granted Toyota's petition for review and now reverse.

II

B

[By the time of the *Restatement (Second) of Torts* reformulation in § 766B] an increasing number of state high courts had traveled well beyond the *Second Restatement*'s reforms by redefining and otherwise recasting the elements of the economic relations tort and the burdens surrounding its proof and defenses. In *Top Service Body Shop, Inc. v. Allstate Ins. Co.,* (1978) 283 Or. 201, 582 P.2d 1365 (*Top Service*), the Oregon Supreme Court, assessing this "most fluid and rapidly growing tort," noted that "efforts to consolidate both recognized and unsettled lines of development into a general theory of 'tortious interference' have brought to the surface the difficulties of defining the elements of so general a tort without sweeping within its terms a wide variety of socially very different conduct."

Recognizing the force of these criticisms, the court went on to hold in *Top Service, supra,* that a claim of interference with economic relations "is made out when interference resulting in injury to another is wrongful by some measure beyond the fact of the interference itself. Defendant's liability may arise from improper motives or from the use of improper means. They may be wrongful by reason of a statute or other regulation, or a recognized rule of common law, or perhaps an established standard of a trade or profession. No question of privilege arises unless the interference would be wrongful but for the privilege; it becomes an issue only if the acts charged would be tortious on the part of an unprivileged defendant."

Over the past decade or so, close to a majority of the high courts of American jurisdictions have imported into the economic relations tort variations on the *Top Service* line of reasoning, explicitly approving a rule that requires the plaintiff in such a suit to plead and prove the alleged interference was either "wrongful," "improper," "illegal," "independently tortious" or some variant on these formulations.

III

In California, the development of the economic relations tort has paralleled its evolution in other jurisdictions. For many years this court declined to adopt the holding of *Lumley v. Gye,* on the ground that, as we reasoned in *Boyson v. Thorn* (1893) 98 Cal. 578, 33 P. 492, "[i]t is a truism of the law that an act which does not amount to a legal injury cannot be actionable because it is done with a bad intent.... If it is right, and the *means* used to procure the breach are right, the motive cannot make it a wrong...." (*Id.* at pp. 583–584, 33 P. 492, italics in original.) In *Imperial Ice Co. v. Rossier* (1941) 18 Cal.2d 33, 112 P.2d 631, however, a unanimous court, speaking through Justice Traynor, pronounced these statements in *Boyson* "not necessary to the decision" and directed that they be "disregarded." (*Id.* at p. 38, 112 P.2d 631.) California thus joined the majority of jurisdictions in adopting the view of the first *Restatement of Torts* by stating that "an action will lie for unjustifiably inducing a breach of contract."

In the aftermath of *Imperial Ice Co. v. Rossier,* our early economic relations cases were principally of two types, either the classic master and servant pattern of the pre-*Lumley v. Gye* cases (*see, e.g.,* Buxbom v. Smith (1944) 23 Cal.2d 535, 548, 145 P.2d 305 [hiring away of plaintiff's employees by defendant, after plaintiff had built up his business to distribute defendant's publication and defendant had breached distribution contract, held actionable as "an unfair method of interference with advantageous relations"]) or those involving circumscribed kinds of business relations in which the plaintiff, typically a real estate broker or attorney working on a contingency, sued to recover fees after defendant had refused to share property sales proceeds or a personal injury.

[W]e are thus presented with the opportunity to consider whether to expressly reconstruct the formal elements of the interference with economic relations tort to achieve a closer alignment with the practice of the trial courts, emerging views within the Court of Appeal, the rulings of many other state high courts, and the critiques of leading commentators. We believe that we should.

IV

In searching for a means to recast the elements of the economic relations tort and allocate the associated burdens of proof, we are guided by an overmastering concern articulated by high courts of other jurisdictions and legal commentators: The need to draw and enforce a sharpened distinction between claims for the tortious disruption of an existing contract and claims that a prospective contractual or economic relationship has been interfered with by the defendant. Many of the cases do in fact acknowledge a greater array of justificatory defenses against claims of interference with prospective relations. Still, in our view and that of several other courts and commentators, the notion that the two torts are analytically unitary and derive from a common principle sacrifices practical wisdom to theoretical insight, promoting the idea that the interests invaded are of nearly equal dignity. They are not.

The courts provide a damage remedy against third party conduct intended to disrupt an existing contract precisely because the exchange of promises resulting in such a formally cemented economic relationship is deemed worthy of protection from interference by a stranger to the agreement. Economic relationships short of contractual, however, should stand on a different legal footing as far as the potential for tort liability is reckoned. Because ours is a culture firmly wedded to the social rewards of commercial contests, the law usually takes care to draw lines of legal liability in a way that maximizes areas of competition free of legal penalties.

A doctrine that blurs the analytical line between interference with an existing business contract and interference with commercial relations less than contractual is one that invites both uncertainty in conduct and unpredictability of its legal effect. The notion that inducing the breach of an existing contract is simply a subevent of the "more inclusive" class of acts that interfere with economic relations, while perhaps theoretically unobjectionable, has been mischievous as a practical matter. Our courts should, in short, firmly distinguish the two kinds of business contexts, bringing a greater solicitude to those relationships that have ripened into agreements, while recognizing that relationships short of that subsist in a zone where the rewards and risks of competition are dominant.

Beyond that, we need not tread today. It is sufficient to dispose of the issue before us in this case by holding that a plaintiff seeking to recover for alleged interference with prospective economic relations has the burden of pleading and proving that the defendant's interference was wrongful "by some measure beyond the fact of the interference itself." (*Top Service*, *supra*, 582 P.2d at p. 1371.) It follows that the trial court did not commit error when it modified BAJI No. 7.82 to require the jury to find that defendant's interference was "wrongful." And because the instruction defining "wrongful conduct" given the jury by the trial court was offered by plaintiff himself, we have no occasion to review its sufficiency in this case. The question of whether additional refinements to the plaintiff's pleading and proof burdens merit adoption by California courts—questions embracing the precise scope of "wrongfulness," or whether a "disinterested malevolence," in Justice Holmes's words (American Bank & Trust Co. v. Federal Reserve Bank (1921) 256 U.S. 350, 358, 41 S.Ct. 499, 500, 65 L.Ed. 983) is an actionable interference in itself, or whether the underlying policy justification for the tort, the efficient allocation of social resources, justifies including as actionable conduct that is recognized as anticompetitive under established state and federal positive law (*see, e.g.*, Perlman, *Interference with Contract and Other Economic Expectancies; A Clash of Tort and Contract Doctrine, supra*, 49 U.Chi.L.Rev. 61)—are matters that can await another day and a more appropriate case.

CONCLUSION

We hold that a plaintiff seeking to recover for an alleged interference with prospective contractual or economic relations must plead and prove as part of its case-in-chief that the defendant not only knowingly interfered with the plaintiff's expectancy, but engaged in conduct that was wrongful by some legal measure other than the fact of interference itself. The judgment of the Court of Appeal is reversed and the cause is remanded with directions to affirm the judgment of the trial court.

MOSK, Justice, concurring.

One reason for the common law's near-incoherence on the tort of intentional interference with prospective economic advantage may be discovered in its doctrinal basis.

The prima facie tort doctrine exhibits a general deficiency. Perhaps it has resulted in a kind of "internal systematic development of the subject matter." (Brown, *The Rise and Threatened Demise of the Prima Facie Tort Principle, supra*, 54 Nw.U.L.Rev. at p. 563.) But if it has, it has done so by sacrificing an external connection to society. "The idea is that 'intentional infliction of harm' is, prima facie, a tort. The problem is that almost any legitimate act can cause 'intentional' harm...." (Dobbs, *Tortious Interference With Contractual Relationships, supra*, 34 Ark.L.Rev. at pp. 337–338, fn. 18.) Therefore, "[i]t must be understood that intentional infliction of harm ... covers a multitude of desirable acts as well as a multitude of sins." (*Id.* at p. 345; *see* Top Service Body Shop v. Allstate Ins. Co. (1978) 283 Or. 201, 205 [582 P.2d 1365, 1368]; Leigh Furniture and Carpet Co. v. Isom (Utah 1982) 657 P.2d 293, 303 [following *Top Service Body Shop*].) "The prima facie tort rule, then, is not a rule about wrongdoing at all. It seems to be a philosophical effort to state all"—or at least much—of "tort law in a single sentence rather than an effort to state a meaningful principle." (Dobbs, *Tortious Interference With Contractual Relationships, supra*, 34 Ark.L.Rev. at p. 345.)

The prima facie tort doctrine exhibits a specific deficiency with regard to the tort of intentional interference with prospective economic advantage. "Since not all interference [is] actionable, or even morally wrong, it cannot be said that there [is] some principle against interference. Since there is no hint in such abstract statements of liability as to what might constitute a defense it is difficult to believe that there is actually any principle involved at all. It has rather the faded ambience of a 'universal truth' once thought to be discoverable in law. In any event, this [leaves] the defendant in an interference case knowing he [is] entitled to some defense, but not knowing what defenses would be accounted sufficient." (Dobbs, *Tortious Interference With Contractual Relationships, supra*, 34 Ark.L.Rev. at p. 345.)

Further, liability under the tort may threaten values of greater breadth and higher dignity than those of the tort itself.

One is the common law's policy of freedom of competition. "'The policy of the common law has always been in favor of free competition, which proverbially is the life of trade. So long as the plaintiff's contractual relations are merely contemplated or potential, it is considered to be in the interest of the public that any competitor should be free to divert them to himself by all fair and reasonable means.... In short, it is no tort to beat a business rival to prospective customers. Thus, in the absence of prohibition by statute, illegitimate means, or some other unlawful element, a defendant seeking to increase his own business may cut rates or prices, allow discounts or rebates, enter into secret negotiations behind the plaintiff's back, refuse to deal with him or threaten to discharge employees who do, or even refuse to deal with third parties unless they cease dealing with the plaintiff, all without incurring liability.'" (A-Mark Coin Co. v. General Mills, Inc. (1983) 148 Cal.App.3d 312, 323–324, 195 Cal.Rptr. 859).

...

With all this said, we are put to the question: What are we to do about the tort of intentional interference with prospective economic advantage?

In view of the foregoing, the only reasonable choice is reformulation. Indeed, an undertaking of this sort is compelled by the almost unanimous agreement, referred to above, that the interfering party should be not be allowed to interfere with impunity at all times and under all circumstances.

To this end, we should clearly define the tort, basing it on stable and circumscribed ground, and eschewing the prima facie tort doctrine, the "protectionist" premise, and the interfering party's motive. Our focus should be on objective conduct and consequences. Further, our concern should be with such conduct and consequences as are unlawful.

It follows that the tort may be satisfied by intentional interference with prospective economic advantage by independently tortious means.

* * *

1. Subsequent developments in California. *Della Penna* left for another day the question of what the phrase "by some measure beyond the fact of the interference itself" actually means. In *Korea Supply Co. v. Lockheed Martin Corp.*, 63 P.3d 937 (Cal. 2003), the California Supreme Court condensed this idea somewhat, and explained that a plaintiff bears the burden of establishing, in addition to the other elements of the tort, "an independently wrongful act." An act is independently wrongful "if it is unlawful, that is, if it is proscribed by some constitutional, statutory, regulatory, common law, or other determinable legal standard." *Id.* at 954.

2. Decoupling the interference torts. A number of other courts have similarly decoupled the torts of interference with contract and interference with prospective contractual relations. For example, after adopting the prima facie tort approach in the case of interference with contractual relations in *Chaves v. Johnson, supra*, the Virginia Supreme Court later distinguished cases of interference with mere prospective contractual relations. In these cases, the court held, that in addition to establishing that the defendant knowingly and intentionally interfered with a prospective contractual relation, thereby causing loss, a plaintiff must also establish that the defendant "used improper means or methods to interfere with the expectancy." Maximus, Inc. v. Lockheed Information Management Systems Co., Inc., 493 S.E.2d 375, 378 (Va. 1997).

3. Independently wrongful acts. *Korea Supply* attempted to clarify *Della Penna*'s holding. But what exactly does it mean to say that a defendant accomplished an interference through "independently wrongful acts" or "improper means or methods"? *Korea Supply* says the defendant's conduct must be "proscribed by some constitutional, statutory, regulatory, common law, or other determinable legal standard"—does this mean the defendant's actions have to amount to a separate, freestanding tort? If so, what purpose does the tort of interference with prospective contractual relations serve?

In *Wal-Mart Stores, Inc. v. Sturges*, 52 S.W.3d 711 (Tex. 2001), the Texas Supreme Court decoupled the interference torts in much the same manner that *Della Penna* and *Maximus, Inc.* did. The Court held that "to recover for tortious interference with a prospective business relation a plaintiff must prove that the defendant's conduct was independently tortious or wrongful." Importantly, the court clarified that by the phrase "independently tortious,"

> we do not mean that the plaintiff must be able to prove an independent tort. Rather, we mean only that the plaintiff must prove that the defendant's conduct would be actionable under a recognized tort. Thus, for example, a plaintiff may recover for tortious interference from a defendant who makes fraudulent statements about the plaintiff to a third person without proving that the third person was actually defrauded. If, on the other hand, the defendant's statements are not intended to deceive, ... then they are not actionable.

Id. at 726. Elsewhere, the court explained that "independently tortious" conduct is conduct "that would violate some other recognized tort *duty*." *Id.* at 713 (emphasis added). Thus, "a defendant who threatened a customer with bodily harm if he did business with the plaintiff would be liable for interference because his conduct toward the customer—assault—was independently tortious," even if the plaintiff could not recover from the defendant for assault. *Id.* "Conduct that is merely 'sharp' or unfair is not actionable and cannot be the basis for an action for tortious interference with prospective relations, and we disapprove of cases that suggest the contrary." *Id.* at 726.

4. Violation of professional standards as improper interference. According to the *Restatement (Second) of Torts*, violation of a professional code of conduct or established custom or practice may be evidence of improper interference. Restatement (Second) of Torts § 767 cmt. c. Would such a violation qualify as an independently wrongful act under the *Della Penna* approach?

Exercise 14.2

You represent Company A, which is being sued by Company B, in a jurisdiction that follows the *Della Penna* approach, for tortiously interfering with Company B's prospective contractual relationship with Company C. Company B alleges that Company A acted with an improper purpose in interfering with its prospective relation with Company C. Company A and Company B are business competitors who both sell the same type of product. Company A's president, Steve, decided not to renew a service contract Company A had with Company C, and instead chose to do business with Company D. Company C had expected Company A to renew its contract and had been planning to use the profits from the deal to purchase goods from Company B. But since the contract was not renewed, Company C did not have enough money to purchase the goods from Company B and, therefore, decided not to enter into a contract with Company B. You speak with several officials at Company A, who tell you that Company D offered a better deal than Company C offered and that this led to the decision to choose Company D over Company C. Accordingly, you file an answer on behalf of Company A, denying any improper purpose on Company A's part. As part of your answer, you also cite the following rule (derived from § 768 of the *Restatement (Second) of Torts*) as to when legitimate business competition is privileged (or is not improper):

> (1) One who intentionally causes a third person not to enter into a prospective contractual relation with another who is his competitor or not to continue an existing contract terminable at will does not interfere improperly with the other's relation if
>
> > (a) the relation concerns a matter involved in the competition between the actor and the other and
> >
> > (b) the actor does not employ wrongful means and
> >
> > (c) his action does not create or continue an unlawful restraint of trade and
> >
> > (d) his purpose is at least in part to advance his interest in competing with the other.

Company A's president, Steve, is now set to be deposed by Company C's lawyer. While preparing Steve for his deposition, you ask him why Company A chose not to renew with Company C. Steve tells you that he makes all of the decisions for the company. He says he knew all about the negotiations between Company B and Company C and figured that by not renewing the contract with Company C, "we could really hurt Company B's bottom line since Company C wouldn't be able to buy from Company B. Plus, I can't stand Company B's president, Dwight. I hate that SOB. The fact that I was able to squeeze a better deal out of Company D was just the icing on the cake."

Rule 3.4(b) of the ABA *Model Rules of Professional Conduct* prohibits a lawyer from counseling a witness to testify falsely. What is your advice to Steve regarding how he should phrase his answers to any questions regarding his decision not to renew with Company C?

---

2. Interference with Contracts Terminable At-Will

Focus Questions: *Reeves v. Hanlon*

1. *Most of the defendants' actions in this case might be relevant to a claim that they interfered with the plaintiffs' contractual relations with their clients. But why are they relevant for purposes of the claims in this case?*
2. *Does it make sense to treat contracts that are terminable at will in a manner different than other kinds of contracts?*

Reeves v. Hanlon

95 P.3d 513

(Cal. 2004)

The primary issue presented is whether a defendant may be held liable under an intentional interference theory for having induced an at-will employee to quit working for the plaintiff.

Factual and Procedural Background

Plaintiffs Robert L. Reeves and Robert L. Reeves & Associates, A Professional Law Corporation, brought the instant lawsuit against defendants Daniel P. Hanlon, Colin T. Greene, and Hanlon & Greene, A Professional Corporation (H & G). The operative complaint included the following allegations: In 1995, Reeves's law firm, which emphasized immigration law and litigation, employed Hanlon as an attorney. In 1997, the firm employed Greene as an associate attorney. In 1998, Reeves entered into an agreement with Hanlon whereby Hanlon could earn an equity position in a law firm to be formed; thereafter, the firm's name was changed to "Reeves and Hanlon, Professional Law Corporation." On or about June 30, 1999, both Hanlon and Greene resigned from Reeves's firm without notice or warning. They improperly persuaded plaintiffs' employees to join H & G, personally solicited plaintiffs' clients to discharge plaintiffs and to instead obtain services from H & G, misappropriated plaintiffs' trade secrets, destroyed computer files and data, and withheld plaintiffs' property, including a corporate car. The complaint asserted 14 causes of action, including intentional interference with contractual relationships, interference with prospective business opportunity, conspiracy to interfere with prospective economic advantage, misappropriation of confidential information in violation of the UTSA, unauthorized use of a corporate car, and destruction of corporate property.

... The evening of their resignations, defendants personally solicited plaintiffs' key employees. As a result, plaintiffs lost nine employees over the next 60 days, six of them joining defendants' new firm....

The Court of Appeal reversed the trial court's order denying in part the motion to tax costs and remanded for entry of a new order regarding costs. It affirmed the judgment in all other respects. As relevant here, the appellate court concluded that plaintiffs' interference claims were legally sound and substantially supported by the record, and also that their misappropriation of trade secrets claim was substantially supported.

Discussion

A. Intentional Interference with At-Will Employment Relations

Preliminarily, we state what is not at issue here. We have not been asked to review the propriety of the determinations by the trial court and the Court of Appeal that defendants are liable to plaintiffs for their tortious interference with plaintiffs' client relations and prospective client opportunities. Accordingly, we accept in full the Court of Appeal's conclusion that "[t]here is direct evidence that [Hanlon's and Greene's] departure was calculated to cripple the Reeves firm's ability to provide legal services: they left abruptly, damaged computer files, removed firm property, and failed to provide adequate guidance concerning their open cases. There is also evidence indicating that Hanlon and Greene phoned far more clients than the 40 or so clients they admitted to contacting, and [that] they exploited these clients' lack of facility with English and ignored their rights concerning the selection of counsel [citation]."

While the issue here does concern defendants' interference with plaintiffs' employee relations, we emphasize the following matters also are not in dispute. First, it is not disputed that the nine employees who left Reeves's firm, including the six who joined H & G, had employment relationships with plaintiffs that they could terminate at will. Second, we accept as undisputed the Court of Appeal's conclusion that the record contains substantial evidence that defendants "mounted a campaign against the Reeves firm involving destruction of computer records, misuse of confidential information, and unethical conduct, of which the cultivation of employee discontent was only a component. This campaign unfairly impaired the Reeves firm's ability to retain its employees." Third, we accept the Court of Appeal's additional determination that the record contains substantial evidence that plaintiffs incurred expenses, above the historical baseline, of $20,009.19 for employee recruitment to mitigate damages.

What is disputed is the Court of Appeal's legal conclusion that "an employer may recover for interference with the employment contracts of its at-will employees by a third party when the third party does not show that its conduct in hiring the employees was justifiable or legitimate." Relying primarily on *GAB Business Services, Inc. v. Lindsey & Newsom Claim Services, Inc.* (2000) 83 Cal.App.4th 409, 99 Cal.Rptr.2d 665 (*GAB*), defendants argue California law does not and should not recognize a cause of action in favor of an employer against another employer for interference with contractual relations by virtue of an offer of employment to an at-will employee.

May the tort of interference with contractual relations be predicated upon interference with an at-will contract? Historically, the answer is yes. A third party's "interference with an at-will contract is actionable interference with the contractual relationship" because the contractual relationship is at the will of the parties, not at the will of outsiders.

More specifically, may such tort be based on interference with an at-will employment relationship? Again, historically, the answer is yes. (*E.g.*, Savage v. Pacific Gas & Electric Co. (1993) 21 Cal.App.4th 434, 448, 26 Cal.Rptr.2d 305 tort of interference with contractual relations may be based on an at-will employment contract).

As reflected in our decisional and statutory law, however, it has long been the public policy of our state that "[a] former employee has the right to engage in a competitive business for himself and to enter into competition with his former employer, even for the business of ... his former employer, provided such competition is fairly and legally conducted." (Continental Car-Na-Var Corp. v. Moseley (1944) 24 Cal.2d 104, 110, 148 P.2d 9; Bus. & Prof.Code, § 16600 [generally recognizing as void any agreement "by which anyone is restrained from engaging in a lawful profession, trade, or business of any kind"].) Consistent with this policy favoring competition, decisions involving parties in competition readily indicate that certain competitive conduct is nonactionable when it interferes with the at-will contract relations of another. Buxbom v. Smith (1944) 23 Cal.2d 535, 145 P.2d 305 (*Buxbom*), for example, explained that "where the means of interference involve no more than recognized trade practices such as advertising or price-cutting, the plaintiff's loss as a result of the competitive strife is deemed *damnum absque injuria*."

More to the point here, *Buxbom* observed that "it is not ordinarily a tort to hire the employees of another for use in the hirer's business." As *Buxbom* explained, however, this general rule is subject to one significant limitation: "This immunity against liability is not retained ... if unfair methods are used in interfering in such advantageous relations." In *Buxbom*, the record established that the defendant gained an unfair advantage over the plaintiff through "deceptive dealings" and "false promises" made in connection with a distribution contract between the parties that the defendant had no intention of performing. He "deliberately induced the plaintiff to buildup his distributing organization" to perform the contract and in a matter of weeks became the plaintiff's sole customer. Once the defendant acquired this strategic position, he breached the distribution contract "to cut off the work required to sustain plaintiff's organization" and "to prevent plaintiff from competing effectively for the retention of [his] employees."

Buxbom first indicated that the defendant's breach of the distribution contract was "a wrong and in itself actionable," but then proceeded to find the breach also constituted "an unfair method of interference with advantageous relations." Its reasoning was this: "Although defendant's conduct may not have been tortious if he had merely broken the contract and subsequently decided to hire plaintiff's employees," he was "guilty of a tortious interference in the relationship between the plaintiff and his employees" because he "intentionally utilized" the breach of the distribution contract "as the means of depriving plaintiff of his employees."

Subsequent to *Buxbom*, the court in *Diodes, Inc. v. Franzen* (1968) 260 Cal.App.2d 244, 67 Cal.Rptr. 19 (*Diodes*) reiterated the so-called privilege of competition, as applied in the context of employment relations, as follows: "Even though the relationship between an employer and his employee is an advantageous one, no actionable wrong is committed by a competitor who solicits his competitor's employees or who hires away one or more of his competitor's employees who are not under contract, so long as the inducement to leave is not accompanied by unlawful action." "However, if either the defecting employee or the competitor uses unfair or deceptive means to effectuate new employment, or either of them is guilty of some concomitant, unconscionable conduct, the injured former employer has a cause of action to recover for the detriment he has thereby suffered."

... Where no unlawful methods are used, public policy generally supports a competitor's right to offer more pay or better terms to another's employee, so long as the employee is free to leave. As Judge Learned Hand observed long ago, if the law were to the contrary, the result "would be intolerable, both to such employers as could use the employe[e] more effectively and to such employe[e]s as might receive added pay. It would put an end to any kind of competition." (*Triangle Film Corp. v. Artcraft Pictures Corp.* (2d Cir. 1918) 250 F. 981, 982.) Or as *Diodes* put it: "The interests of the employee in his own mobility and betterment are deemed paramount to the competitive business interests of the employers, where neither the employee nor his new employer has committed any illegal act accompanying the employment change."

Moreover, the economic relationship between parties to contracts that are terminable at will is distinguishable from the relationship between parties to other legally binding contracts. We have explained the policy generally protecting contracts this way: "The courts provide a damage remedy against third party conduct intended to disrupt an existing contract precisely because the exchange of promises resulting in such a formally cemented economic relationship is deemed worthy of protection from interference by a stranger to the agreement. Economic relationships short of contractual, however, should stand on a different legal footing as far as the potential for tort liability is reckoned." (Della Penna v. Toyota Motor Sales, U.S.A., Inc. (1995) 11 Cal.4th 376, 392, 45 Cal.Rptr.2d 436, 902 P.2d 740.)

But as the *Restatement Second of Torts* explains, if a party to a contract with the plaintiff is free to terminate the contractual relation when he chooses, "there is still a subsisting contract relation; but any interference with it that induces its termination is primarily an interference with the future relation between the parties, and the plaintiff has no legal assurance of them. As for the future hopes he has no legal right but only an expectancy;

and when the contract is terminated by the choice of [a contracting party] there is no breach of it. The competitor is therefore free, for his own competitive advantage, to obtain the future benefits for himself by causing the termination. Thus, he may offer better contract terms, as by offering an employee of the plaintiff more money to work for him or by offering a seller higher prices for goods, and he may make use of persuasion or other suitable means, all without liability." (Rest.2d Torts, § 768, com. i.) Under this analysis, an interference with an at-will contract properly is viewed as an interference with a prospective economic advantage, a tort that similarly compensates for the loss of an advantageous economic relationship but does not require the existence of a legally binding contract.

Consistent with the decisions recognizing that an intentional interference with an at-will contract may be actionable, but mindful that an interference as such is primarily an interference with the future relation between the contracting parties, we hold that a plaintiff may recover damages for intentional interference with an at-will employment relation under the same California standard applicable to claims for intentional interference with prospective economic advantage. That is, to recover for a defendant's interference with an at-will employment relation, a plaintiff must plead and prove that the defendant engaged in an independently wrongful act—i.e., an act "proscribed by some constitutional, statutory, regulatory, common law, or other determinable legal standard" (*Korea Supply, supra*, 29 Cal.4th at p. 1159, 131 Cal.Rptr.2d 29, 63 P.3d 937)—that induced an at-will employee to leave the plaintiff.[7] Under this standard, a defendant is not subject to liability for intentional interference if the interference consists merely of extending a job offer that induces an employee to terminate his or her at-will employment.

We now address whether application of the principles we announce today calls for affirmance of the $20,009.19 award against defendants. We conclude it does. Here, it is undisputed that Hanlon and Greene engaged in unlawful and unethical conduct in mounting a campaign to deliberately disrupt plaintiffs' business. Greene had been chair of plaintiffs' litigation department, and Hanlon had been responsible for over 500 client matters, and both had assumed fiduciary duties to plaintiffs. When the two abruptly resigned without notice, they left no status reports or list of pending matters or deadlines on which they were working. Not only did they leave without providing such information, they acted unlawfully to delete and destroy plaintiffs' computer files containing client documents and forms. Additionally, Hanlon and Greene misappropriated confidential information, improperly solicited plaintiffs' clients, and cultivated employee discontent. While the computer files and the confidential information all appear to have pertained to plaintiffs' clients, not their employees, and while Hanlon and Greene waited until after their resignations to offer jobs to plaintiffs' employees, we cannot conclude the trial court abused its discretion in finding that defendants' unlawful and unethical actions were designed in part to interfere with and disrupt plaintiffs' relationships with their key at-will employees.

In short, defendants did not simply extend job offers to plaintiffs' at-will employees. Rather, defendants purposely engaged in unlawful acts that crippled plaintiffs' business operations and caused plaintiffs' personnel to terminate their at-will employment contracts.

---

7. Because the wrongful conduct in this case pertains only to the termination of at-will contracts, we need not and do not express an opinion whether an independent wrongfulness requirement would be appropriate for cases in which a defendant allegedly induces the breach of an otherwise enforceable term of an at-will contract.

Accordingly, the Court of Appeal properly upheld the award of $20,009.19 for damages attributable to that wrongful conduct.

* * *

1. **What's really going on here?** Are you persuaded by the court's arguments with respect to why defendants' actions (destroying files, appropriating confidential information, etc.) are relevant to the claim that they improperly interfered with the plaintiff's relationships with its employees?

2. **Application beyond employment relationships.** Some courts have declined to extend *Reeves*' holding beyond employment relationships. Bill A. Duffy, Inc. v. Scott, 2009 WL 1125959, *5 (N.D. Cal. Apr 27, 2009). Other courts have adopted *Reeves*'s logic and treat interference claims involving interferences with any type of terminable at-will contract in the same manner as interferences with prospective contractual relationships. Genesis Telecommunications, LLC v. Moore, 2010 WL 6407918, *9 (D.S.C. Oct 18, 2010) (customer relationships); Duggins v. Adams, 360 S.E.2d 832 (Va. 1987) (terminable at-will sales contract). Some courts, either through inattention or explicit choice, have not drawn a distinction between interferences with contracts terminable at will and more traditional contracts. Hall v. Integon Life Ins. Co., 454 So. 2d 1338, 1344 (Ala. 1984).

3. **Interference claims as an alternative to wrongful discharge claims.** The employment at-will rule referenced in *Reeves* makes it difficult for employees to recover from their employers for what they perceive to be wrongful firings. While there are sometimes statutory (e.g., Title VII) or common-law (e.g., claims of wrongful discharge in violation of public policy) remedies available, these theories may provide only limited protection. As a result, some employees have turned to tortious interference claims as a way around these limitations. One common complaint is that a manager or supervisor acted out of malice in bringing about the discharge of an employee. *See* Halvorsen v. Aramark Uniform Services, Inc., 65 Cal. App. 4th 1383 (Cal. Ct. App. 1998). What problem might an employee face in attempting to bring an interference claim against a manager or supervisor who caused the employer to fire the plaintiff?

4. **Interference claims as an alternative to defamation claims.** Based largely on fear of defamation claims, most employers have adopted a policy of providing only limited information about a current or former employee in response to a request for an employment reference. Markita D. Cooper, *Job Reference Immunity Statutes: Prevalent but Irrelevant*, 11 Cornell J.L. & Pub. Pol'y 1, 3 (2001). Since truth is a defense to a defamation claim, an employer who provides truthful information as part of a reference should escape liability. But should an employer who provides truthful, yet damaging information in an employment reference escape liability under an interference theory? What if the employer is motivated solely by malice and includes information irrelevant to the issue of whether an individual would make a good employee? Most courts have held that providing truthful information is never improper, regardless of the defendant's motive or the relevance of the information provided. *See, e.g.*, Tiernan v. Charleston Area Med. Ctr., 506 S.E.2d 578 (W.Va. 1998). However, a few courts have held that truth is not an absolute defense in the context of an interference claim and that a defendant's motive may render an intentional interference actionable. *See* C.N.C. Chem. Corp. v. Pennwalt Corp., 690 F. Supp. 139, 143 (D.R.I. 1988); Collincini v. Honeywell, Inc., 601 A.2d 292, 295 (Pa. Super. Ct. 1991); Pratt v. Prodata Inc., 885 P.2d 786, 790 (Utah 1994).

* * *

C. Recognized Privileges or Instances in Which a Defendant Does Not Improperly Interfere

Several of the cases so far in this chapter have alluded to recognized privileges or instances in which a defendant's interference is not improper. For example, *Chaves* and *Reeves* both referenced the widely-recognized competition "privilege" and Exercise 14.2 explored it in greater detail. Some of the material in the rest of the chapter explores the other common situations in which bright-line rules have emerged that excuse a defendant's interference. Below is a brief description of these rules.

1. Defendant with a financial interest in the business of another. One who has a financial interest in the business of another and who intentionally causes that party not to enter into a contractual relationship with the plaintiff does not interfere improperly with that relationship if she does not employ wrongful means and acts to protect her interest from being prejudiced by the relationship. Restatement (Second) of Torts § 769. Thus, the creditor who, in order to protect his financial interest, persuades the debtor not to do business with the plaintiff should not be held liable, provided he does not employ improper means. Although the *Restatement* limits the rule to interferences with prospective contractual relations, some courts have extended the rule to interferences with contracts terminable at will. *See* Geib v. Alan Wood Steel Co., 419 F. Supp. 1205 (E.D. Pa. 1976).

2. Defendant responsible for the welfare of another. One who is charged with responsibility for the welfare of another and who intentionally causes that person not to perform a contract or not to enter into a prospective contractual relationship with the plaintiff does not interfere improperly if he does not employ wrongful means and acts to protect the welfare of the person. Restatement (Second) of Torts § 770. The rule would apply to a parent-child relationship, as well as relationships like those of attorney and client. Brown Mackie College v. Graham, 981 F.2d 1149, 1153 (10th Cir. 1992).

3. Defendant providing truthful information or honest advice within the scope of a request for the advice. Section 772 of the Restatement (Second) of Torts lists two types of action that do not amount to improper interference. First, as discussed *supra*, a defendant who provides truthful information to another that causes the other not to perform a contract or not to enter into a prospective contractual relationship does not interfere improperly. Restatement (Second) of Torts § 772(a). This is true even if the defendant is motivated solely by spite or ill will. At the same time, the so-called "advisor's privilege" shields from liability the defendant who provides honest advice within the scope of a request for the advice. *Id.* § 772(b).

4. Defendant asserting a bona fide claim. Employer believes that Former Employee is about to violate the non-compete agreement the parties signed by entering into a new employment relationship with Prospective Employer. Employer honestly and in good faith believes the non-compete agreement to be valid. Therefore, Employer notifies Prospective Employer that it plans to take whatever legal action is necessary to enforce the non-compete agreement if Prospective Employer hires Former Employee. As a result, Prospective Employer decides not to hire Former Employee. Employer has not interfered improperly. Emery v. Merrimack Valley Wood Products, Inc., 701 F.2d 985 (1st Cir. 1983); Restatement (Second) of Torts § 773.

* * *

D. Damages

Regardless of which test a jurisdiction employs, the existence of economic damages is an element of the tort. Therefore, unless the defendant's interference resulted in pecuniary harm, the plaintiff's claim should fail. One issue perhaps still lurking in this chapter relates to damages: why would a plaintiff ever sue a defendant for causing another to breach a contract when the plaintiff already has a remedy against the breaching party? The answer, of course, is the availability of punitive damages. Generally, a plaintiff cannot recover punitive damages in a breach of contract claim. However, punitive damages may be recoverable against the party who induced the breach under the tort theory of interference with contract.

Another situation in which an interference claim may be an attractive alternative to a breach of contract claim is where the plaintiff has not yet entered into a contract with another party. In this situation, a breach of contract action would not be available. Thus, the tort of interference with prospective contractual relations might provide a remedy where contract law fails to do so.

The interference torts are largely economic in nature. Therefore, benefit of the bargain damages are available as are consequential damages proximately caused by the interference, provided they can be established with reasonable certainty. However, emotional distress damages and damages for actual harm to reputation may also be compensable, provided they could reasonably be expected to result from the interference. Restatement (Second) of Torts § 774a.

One problem that may arise in interference cases is the potential for a plaintiff to double dip when it comes to damages.

Exercise 14.3

Greg improperly induces Bob to breach his contract with Grant. This breach results in $12,000 lost profits. As a result of the breach, Grant also winds up losing another $7,000 as part of a related deal that fell through. The $7,000 loss was not foreseeable by Bob, although Greg's purpose in inducing the breach was, in part, to cause this loss to Grant.

(a) Assuming Grant is able to collect $12,000 damages from Bob, how much can he recover from Greg in an interference action?

(b) Assume now that, for whatever reason, Grant is not able to collect the $12,000 from Bob. How much can he recover from Greg in an interference action?

E. Special Issues: Interference Claims in the Legal Profession

Interference claims have arisen in a host of situations in the legal setting. In some cases, the interference relates to the actual practice of law. For example, in *Mantia v. Hanson*, 79 P.3d 404 (Or. Ct. App. 2003), the plaintiff sued one of its former employees for interfering with the plaintiff's business by filing frivolous lawsuits against the plaintiff. In addition to suing the former employee, the plaintiff also sued the defendant-law firm for asserting the supposedly baseless claims on behalf of the law firm's client. While recognizing the possibility that the filing of frivolous claims could amount to improper interference, the court granted summary judgment to the law firm.

More common, however, are instances in which the interference involves what might be called the business of law. These are cases in which the defendant—acting much like any business person—takes action that results in the loss of the plaintiff-attorney's expected fee. Consistent with the courts' inconsistent treatment of interference claims more generally, the outcome of these cases is somewhat difficult to predict.

Interference claims in the legal setting present many of the same problems discussed previously. However, the unique nature of the attorney-client relationship and the special rules that have developed to govern that relationship may present courts with challenging issues. For one, attorney-client relationships are terminable at the will of the client. This presents courts that have decoupled the interference torts with the challenge of how to classify an interference with an attorney-client relationship. In addition, if, as some courts have stated, an interference is wrongful because it involves the use of means that violate established ethics rules of a profession, interference claims in the legal setting may require resort to the ethical rules governing lawyers.

1. Advising Clients

Focus Questions: *Los Angeles Airways, Inc. v. Davis*

1. *Which of the relevant privileges/rules regarding improper interference discussed in Part C above does the* Davis *case raise?*
2. *Is the court's holding with respect to the mixed motives of the defendant too permissive? Or, is it just realistic? What other standard might a court adopt instead?*
3. Davis, *which applies California law, was decided prior to* Della Penna *and* Reeves. *Would the result be any different under that approach?*

Los Angeles Airways, Inc. v. Davis

687 F.2d 321
(9th Cir. 1982)

REINHARDT, Circuit Judge.

Plaintiff-Appellant in this diversity action appeals from an order granting summary judgment for the defendant based on the defendant's claim of privilege....

I.

Appellant Los Angeles Airways (hereinafter "LAA") brought this action against Appellee Chester C. Davis for tortious interference with its contractual relationship with Summa Corporation (formerly Hughes Tool Company) and Hughes Air Corporation. LAA specifically alleged that Davis wrongfully, intentionally, and maliciously induced Howard Hughes to cause Summa Corporation and Hughes Air Corporation to breach an oral agreement with LAA to purchase all of LAA's assets and liabilities. Davis' answer denied the existence of an oral agreement to purchase LAA and claimed, by way of affirmative defense, that if his conduct did induce a breach of the alleged agreement, he was privileged to act in such manner. During the period of negotiations between LAA, Summa, and Hughes Air Corporation, Davis served as general counsel for Summa, as attorney for Howard Hughes and Hughes Air Corporation, and as an officer and director of Hughes Air Corporation. Davis subsequently became a director of the Summa Corporation.

Seven years after the initiation of this action and shortly before the matter was scheduled for trial, Davis filed a motion for summary judgment based solely on the affirmative defense of privilege to induce breach of contract. Davis based his claim of privilege on his status as attorney for Summa, Hughes Air Corporation, and Howard Hughes, as an officer, director, or agent of Summa and Hughes Air Corporation, and as an agent of Howard Hughes. Davis' motion was supported by his affidavit in which he stated that all communications with Howard Hughes regarding the acquisition of LAA were undertaken at the request of one of his three principals. Davis denied advising anyone to breach any agreement regarding the proposed acquisition and denied communicating incorrect information to Hughes regarding the acquisition. However, for the purposes of the motion for summary judgment only, Davis assumed that an oral agreement existed between LAA and the Hughes' interests and that any breach of the agreement was caused by Davis' advising and informing his principals.

In its opposition to Davis' motion for summary judgment, LAA asserted that the privilege of a fiduciary to interfere in his principal's contractual relations does not apply when the means used are unlawful. LAA asserted that in response to a request by Howard Hughes to determine whether any commitments had been made in the LAA acquisition negotiations, Davis falsely reported to Hughes that he was unable to obtain meaningful information on the commitments made to LAA from Robert Maheu, Chief Executive Officer of Hughes Nevada Operations, Francis T. Fox, Director of Aviation for Hughes Tool Company, or Edward P. Morgan, a Washington D. C. attorney representing the Hughes' interests in the negotiations. LAA also asserted that Davis sent a financial report to Hughes at his request on the financial condition of LAA without explaining that much of LAA's financial difficulty arose from the delay in the proposed acquisition. LAA then asserted that Davis' purpose in doing this was to convince Hughes to refuse to permit the Purchase Contract to be signed and the acquisition thereby consummated, in order to cause LAA to collapse into bankruptcy and commence litigation against the Hughes' interests. This was in turn intended by Davis to undermine Robert Maheu's position while at the same time enhancing Davis' own position. It was also intended to permit Hughes to later acquire LAA's assets through a purchase at liquidation prices.

On appeal, LAA argues that the privilege does not apply when a fiduciary acts to promote his own self-interest rather than the interests of his principal.[2] LAA contends that intent and motive are questions of fact that cannot be resolved on a motion for summary judgment.

II

In reviewing the motion for summary judgment, we must view the evidence and the factual inferences drawn from the evidence in the light most favorable to the party opposing the motion for summary judgment. On appeal, LAA asserts that because the privilege claimed by Davis is qualified and not absolute, there is a triable issue of fact as to Davis' intent in responding as he did to Howard Hughes' requests regarding the LAA negotiations. Our review of the motion for summary judgment is guided by the law of privilege in California. We must determine if, under the facts presented and the law of privilege in California, Davis' intent in advising Howard Hughes presents a triable issue of material fact.

A. The Law of Privilege in California

The determination of whether the privilege applies in a particular instance requires a two step analysis. The first step is to determine if the relationship between the parties involves the type of interests that the privilege is designed to protect. The second step is to determine whether, in light of the nature and importance of the above relationship, the advisor's intent in inducing the breach was proper. This second step in the analysis is necessary because, as LAA correctly contends, the privilege is qualified and not absolute. Where the intent is not proper, the privilege is lost.

1. The existence and scope of the privilege

The existence and scope of the privilege to induce a breach of contract must be determined by reference to the societal interests which it is designed to protect. The privilege exists whenever a person induces a breach of contract through lawful means in order to protect an interest that has a greater social value than the mere stability of the particular contract in question. Imperial Ice Co. v. Rossier, 18 Cal.2d at 35, 112 P.2d at 632. The privilege is designed in part to protect the important interests served by the confidential relationship between a fiduciary and his principal.

LAA does not dispute the fact that the requests from Hughes were directed to Davis in his capacity as a fiduciary, either as attorney for the Hughes interests or as an agent, officer or director of those interests. Neither LAA nor Davis has clearly identified in what capacity Davis responded to Hughes' requests. Nor has either party suggested how the existence or scope of the privilege is affected by a determination as to which capacity Davis was acting in when he responded to Hughes' inquiries-attorney or business advisor. Davis argues that he is protected in either capacity, while LAA responds that if the scope

2. In the court below, LAA opposed the motion for summary judgment on the ground that the means used by Davis in advising Hughes were unlawful. "(P) laintiff contends Chester C. Davis misled and deceived Howard Hughes with respect to details of a commitment to purchase the assets of Los Angeles Airways...." Plaintiff's Opposition to Motion for Summary Judgment, at 3. Although LAA explained in the court below that Davis' reason for allegedly deceiving Hughes was to undermine Maheu's position in the Hughes empire, LAA did not contend in the trial court that such intent would defeat Davis' claim of privilege. On appeal, however, LAA has abandoned its earlier position that Davis cannot claim the privilege because the means used were unlawful, and now claims that Davis was not protected by the privilege because he acted with the intent to elevate his standing in the Hughes empire by undermining Robert Maheu's position.

of the privilege varies with the capacity in which Davis acted, this court should assume that Davis acted in the capacity with the narrowest privilege.

If Davis were acting in his fiduciary capacity as an agent, officer or director of the Hughes' interests, he could clearly claim the protection of the privilege in California, subject to its qualifications, based on his relationship with the Hughes' interests. The privilege is sometimes described in California law as the "manager's privilege." The manager's privilege has most frequently arisen in the context of employer-employee relations. Thus, a manager is said to be privileged to induce the breach of an employment contract between his employer and another employee. The privilege also extends to non-employees who serve as business advisors or agents and is applicable to advice relating to contracts generally, not just employment agreements. *See, e.g.*, Olivet v. Frischling, 104 Cal.App.3d at 841, 164 Cal.Rptr. at 91–92 (privilege claimed by members of board of directors and attorneys for corporation, contract involved purchase and leaseback of equipment). A business advisor may counsel his principal to breach a contract that he reasonably believes to be harmful to his principal's best interests.

Davis would have occupied at least as significant a fiduciary role if he provided his advice as an attorney rather than as a business advisor. Attorneys are frequently called upon by their clients to provide advice regarding the validity of contracts and the consequences of their breach. An attorney can claim the protection of the privilege to induce breach of contract, subject to its qualifications, when he provides his advice in the course of his representation of a client. Davis could thus also base his claim of privilege on his status as attorney for Hughes and the Hughes' interests.

As noted above, LAA argues that if the availability of the privilege depends on which role Davis was acting in when he advised Hughes, i.e., attorney or business advisor, we should resolve any ambiguity as to Davis' role against him. It is clear in this case, however, that Davis had a qualified privilege to advise breach of contract in his capacity as either attorney or business advisor for Hughes. Because Davis would have been protected in either capacity, we need not consider whether there is a difference in the scope of the privilege or which privilege is applicable to an advisor who acts in two different capacities for one principal.

2. Intent: qualification on the exercise of the privilege

The protection of the privilege may be lost if the advisor acts with improper intent. In determining whether an advisor's intent will result in the loss of the privilege, it is necessary to evaluate his intent in light of the societal interests which the privilege is designed to promote. LAA argues that because intent is a highly subjective question, it is inappropriate to decide the issue of intent on a motion for summary judgment. We agree with LAA's general statement of the law. Where there is a dispute as to the advisor's intent, summary judgment cannot be used to resolve questions of material fact. However, in this case LAA claims that Davis' intent was to cause LAA to collapse into bankruptcy and commence litigation against the Hughes' interests. This was in turn intended by Davis to undermine Robert Maheu's position while at the same time enhancing Davis' position. It was also intended to permit Hughes to later acquire LAA's assets at liquidation prices.

Even fully accepting LAA's statement of Davis' intent, we conclude that Davis' conduct was protected by the privilege. Thus no triable issue of material fact exists.

... In this case, ... LAA contends that Davis' advice was intended, *inter alia*, to secure a benefit for Hughes: the acquisition of LAA at a "distress price." The fact that Davis also hoped that the advice would promote his standing in the eyes of Hughes does not negate Davis' intent to benefit his principal. [No] reported California decision has explicitly addressed the situation in which an advisor is alleged to have acted with a "mixed motive," i.e., with the intent to benefit his employer's interest as well as his own. We must therefore resolve this question as we believe the California Supreme Court would if faced with the same facts.

We conclude that where, as here, an advisor is motivated in part by a desire to benefit his principal, his conduct in inducing a breach of contract should be privileged. The privilege is designed to further certain societal interests by fostering uninhibited advice by agents to their principals. The goal of the privilege is promoted by protecting advice that is motivated, even in part, by a good faith intent to benefit the principal's interest.

We believe that advice by an agent to a principal is rarely, if ever, motivated purely by a desire to benefit only the principal. An agent naturally hopes that by providing beneficial advice to his principal, the agent will benefit indirectly by gaining the further trust and confidence of his principal. If the protection of the privilege were denied every time that an advisor acted with such mixed motive, the privilege would be greatly diminished and the societal interests it was designed to promote would be frustrated. We do not believe that the California Supreme Court would so eviscerate the privilege, and we decline to do so.

Although we need not reach the question, we also seriously doubt that a desire to advance one's own career with an employer (even at the expense of a fellow employee's) would in any event constitute the type of motivation that causes loss of the privilege.

The order of the district court granting summary judgment is AFFIRMED.

* * *

1. Model Rule comparison. Model Rule 2.1 of the ABA's *Model Rules of Professional Conduct* requires a lawyer to "render candid advice," which may include not just legal matters but "moral, economic, social and political factors, that may be relevant to the client's situation." The lawyer's duty to provide advice requires that the lawyer exercise "independent professional judgment." *Id.* If the lawyer's ability to exercise independent professional judgment is materially limited by the lawyer's own personal interests, the lawyer has a disqualifying conflict of interest. *Id.* R. 1.7. What relevance, if any, should these rules have on the application of the rule regarding advice discussed in *Davis*?

2. Volunteering advice. If a defendant-lawyer argues that no liability should attach because the defendant provided honest advice to a contracting party, should it matter that the defendant-lawyer volunteered advice to a client without awaiting a request?

* * *

2. Interference with an Attorney's Ability to Collect a Fee

a. "Stealing" Clients

Focus Questions: *Nostrame v. Santiago*

1. *For purposes of permitting competition, should attorney-client relationships be treated like other kinds of terminable at-will contracts? Is there a reason to allow greater latitude to interfere? Lesser latitude?*
2. *What would be an example of "wrongful means" an attorney might employ to lure away a client?*

Nostrame v. Santiago

22 A.3d 20

(N.J. Super. A.D. 2011)

SKILLMAN, J.A.D. (retired and temporarily assigned on recall).

The primary issue presented by this appeal is whether an attorney who is discharged by his client and replaced by a successor attorney may maintain an action for tortious interference with contract against the successor attorney.

I.

Plaintiff Frank Nostrame, a New Jersey attorney, was retained by defendant Natividad Santiago on January 18, 2007, to represent her in connection with a proposed medical malpractice action, apparently under a contingent fee agreement. Plaintiff performed certain preliminary work, and on May 23, 2007, he filed a complaint on her behalf.

On May 31, 2007, Santiago entered into a contingent fee retainer agreement with defendant Mazie, Slater, Katz and Freeman, LLC (Mazie Slater), a New Jersey law firm, to represent her in the medical malpractice action. On that day, Santiago sent a letter to plaintiff discharging him as her attorney and directing him to turn over his file to Mazie Slater.

After retaining experts to support Santiago's malpractice claim and engaging in substantial discovery, Mazie Slater settled the claim on her behalf for a total of $1,200,000. Under Mazie Slater's contingent fee agreement with Santiago, this settlement resulted in an attorney's fee of $358,396.31.

Plaintiff asserted a lien of $11,623.75 on that fee for the legal work he performed in connection with Santiago's malpractice action. The trial court eventually determined that plaintiff was entitled to the full amount of his lien. Mazie Slater has now paid plaintiff that amount, which is not at issue in this appeal.

In addition to asserting a lien against the Mazie Slater contingent fee for the services he performed before his discharge, plaintiff brought this tortious interference with contract action against Mazie Slater. Plaintiff's complaint alleged in pertinent part that "Natividad Santiago was induced to discharge plaintiff and dissolve the contingent fee contract between them by [Mazie Slater]." The complaint named not only Mazie Slater but also Santiago, her daughter Betsy Santiago, and fictitious John Does as defendants. The complaint did not include any specific allegation with respect to Betsy Santiago. However, the complaint alleged that unnamed "John Does without legal justification interfered with the contractual relation between Natividad Santiago and plaintiff [by] contact[ing] the office of [Mazie Slater] for the purpose of creating a contractual relation between [Mazie Slater] and Natividad Santiago and to terminate the contractual relation between Natividad Santiago and plaintiff."

Shortly after the filing of this complaint, Mazie Slater filed a motion to dismiss on its own behalf and on behalf of Natividad and Betsy Santiago.

The trial court denied defendants' motion to dismiss. We granted defendants' motion for leave to appeal from this denial.

II.

Before considering the maintainability of a claim for tortious interference with contract by a discharged attorney against a successor attorney, we first consider the nature of a contract between an attorney and client. In *Jacob v. Norris, McLaughlin & Marcus*, 128 N.J. 10, 607 A.2d 142 (1992), the Court concluded that a provision in a law firm partnership agreement that barred withdrawing partners from collecting termination compensation if they continued to represent firm clients was invalid. In reaching this conclusion, the Court stated that "[a] client is always entitled to be represented by counsel of his own choosing," and that an attorney "may do nothing which restricts the right of the client to repose confidence in any counsel of his choice." *Id.* at 20, 607 A.2d 142 (quoting Dwyer v. Jung, 133 N.J.Super. 343, 346–47, 336 A.2d 498 (Ch.Div.), *aff'd*, 137 N.J.Super. 135, 348 A.2d 208 (App.Div.1975)). Thus, although a client is liable for the payment of services rendered during the course of an attorney-client relationship, the client is free to discharge the attorney at any time without being subject to suit for breach of contract. *See* Glick v. Barclays De Zoete Wedd, Inc., 300 N.J.Super. 299, 309, 692 A.2d 1004 (App.Div.1997); Restatement (Third) of the Law Governing Lawyers § 32(1) (2000). A client's freedom to terminate the attorney-client relationship unilaterally means that a contract between an attorney and client is a contract that is "terminable at will." Glick, *supra*, 300 N.J.Super. at 309, 692 A.2d 1004; *see* Alex B. Long, *The Business of Law & Tortious Interference*, 36 St. Mary's L.J. 925, 939–44 (2005).

With this understanding of the nature of a contract between an attorney and client, we turn to the question whether a discharged attorney may maintain an action against a successor attorney for tortious interference with contract. In considering claims for tortious interference with existing or prospective contractual relations, our courts generally follow the principles set forth in the *Restatement (Second) of Torts* (1979).

The elements of a cause of action for tortious interference with contract are set forth in section 766 of the Restatement, which states:

> One who intentionally and improperly interferes with the performance of a contract (except a contract to marry) between another and a third person by inducing or otherwise causing the third person not to perform the contract, is subject to liability to the other for the pecuniary loss resulting to the other from the failure of the third person to perform the contract.

A claim for tortious interference with a contract that is terminable at will, such as a contract between attorney and client, falls within section 766. *Id.* § 766 cmt. g. However, the comments to the *Restatement* recognize that a determination of the viability of such a claim may require a different analysis than other tortious interference with contract claims, particularly if the defendant is a competitor of the claimant:

> One's interest in a contract terminable at will is primarily an interest in future relations between the parties, and he has no legal assurance of them. For this reason, an interference with this interest is closely analogous to interference with prospective contractual relations.... If the defendant was a competitor regarding the business involved in the contract, his interference with the contract may be not improper.

Section 767 of the *Restatement* sets forth a series of general factors that a court should consider in determining whether an alleged interference with a contract was improper ... However, those general factors do not need to be addressed if a case falls within one of the "special situations" addressed in sections 768 through 773 of the *Restatement. Id.* § 767 cmt. a.

One of those special situations—an alleged tortious interference with contract by a competitor seeking to pursue its own economic interests by encouraging a prospective customer to discontinue a terminable at will contract with another party—is addressed by section 768(1) of the *Restatement*, which states:

> One who intentionally causes a third person not to enter into a prospective contractual relation with another who is his competitor or not to continue an existing contract terminable at will does not interfere improperly with the other's relation if
>
> (a) the relation concerns a matter involved in the competition between the actor and the other and
>
> (b) the actor does not employ wrongful means and
>
> (c) his action does not create or continue an unlawful restraint of trade and
>
> (d) his purpose is at least in part to advance his interest in competing with the other.

...

Under the plain terms of section 768(1) of the *Restatement*, Mazie Slater's alleged inducement of Santiago to discharge plaintiff as her attorney in the medical malpractice action did not constitute a tortious interference with contract. The contract between plaintiff and Santiago "concern[ed] a matter involved in the competition between [Mazie Slater] and [plaintiff]," *id.* §768(1)(a), because both Mazie Slater and plaintiff are attorneys who represent clients in medical malpractice actions. Plaintiff's complaint does not allege that Mazie Slater employed any "wrongful means," such as fraud or defamation, *see id.* §768 cmt. e, to induce Santiago to discharge him, id. §768(1)(b), or that Santiago's discharge of him and retention of Mazie Slater would "create or continue an unlawful restraint of trade," *id.* §768(1)(c). Moreover, it is undisputed that Mazie Slater's "purpose" in allegedly inducing Santiago to discharge plaintiff was "at least in part to advance [its] interest in competing with [plaintiff.]" *Id.* §768(1)(d). Therefore, we conclude that under section 768 of the *Restatement*, plaintiff's complaint does not state a cause of action against Mazie Slater for tortious interference with contract.

This conclusion is reinforced by the fact that the contractual relationship at issue in this case is a contract between an attorney and client. Whatever interest plaintiff may have had in maintaining his contract with Santiago was outweighed by her interest in exercising her right to select counsel of her own choosing, including her right to discharge plaintiff, and to retain new counsel who she believed could better represent her in the medical malpractice action. *See Jacob*, *supra*, 128 N.J. at 18–24, 607 A.2d 142. Our Supreme Court has described a "client's freedom of choice" as a "paramount interest." *Id.* at 22, 607 A.2d 142. Hence, the courts should not recognize a cause of action for tortious interference with a contract between an attorney and client that could impede that freedom of choice unless the alleged interference involves wrongful means, such as fraud or defamation.

Plaintiff suggests that even though his complaint does not allege that Mazie Slater used any "wrongful means" to induce Santiago to discharge him and retain Mazie Slater, he should be allowed to conduct discovery to determine whether such wrongful means may have been used. Our courts ordinarily take a liberal view in determining whether a complaint states a cause of action. However, New Jersey is a "fact" rather than a "notice" pleading jurisdiction, which means that a plaintiff must allege facts to support his or her claim rather than merely reciting the elements of a cause of action. A plaintiff cannot simply assert that "any essential facts that the court may find lacking can be dredged up in discovery."

We also note that permitting discovery to proceed based on the kind of conclusionary allegations contained in plaintiff's complaint could have a chilling effect upon a client's exercise of the right to select counsel of his or her choosing. Plaintiff's complaint joined not only Mazie Slater but also Santiago and her daughter Betsy as defendants. Plaintiff now recognizes that he has no basis for a claim against Natividad Santiago because a party cannot tortiously interfere with his or her own contract. *See Printing Mart*, *supra*, 116 N.J. at 752–53, 563 A.2d 31. Nevertheless, plaintiff contends that he needed to join

Santiago as a defendant to obtain discovery from her. This contention is obviously incorrect; discovery may be obtained from a person without joining that person as a party. However, the threat of joinder as a defendant or being required to submit to a deposition in this kind of action could deter a client in the position of Santiago from exercising her right to change counsel. Furthermore, the prospect of being sued for tortious interference with contract could cause a potential successor attorney such as Mazie Slater to decline representation of a client previously represented by another attorney, especially in a smaller case, thus interfering with a client's right to seek counsel of his or her choosing. Therefore, the facts alleged in plaintiff's complaint do not provide an adequate legal foundation for him to be allowed to proceed with discovery.

III.

Finally, we consider plaintiff's tortious interference claim against Betsy Santiago. This claim requires only brief discussion. Section 770 of the *Restatement* states:

> One who, charged with responsibility for the welfare of a third person, intentionally causes that person not to perform a contract or enter into a prospective contractual relation with another, does not interfere improperly with the other's relation if the actor
>
> (a) does not employ wrongful means and
>
> (b) acts to protect the welfare of the third person.

This rule "deals with cases in which, by ordinary standards of decent conduct, one is charged with some responsibility for the protection of the welfare of another." *Id.* § 770 cmt. b. We have no hesitancy concluding that "by ordinary standards of decent conduct" a daughter may encourage her mother to terminate a contract that is terminable at will without being subjected to possible liability for tortious interference with contract, at least in the absence of any allegation that she used wrongful means.

Accordingly, the order denying defendants' motion to dismiss is reversed.

* * *

1. Unethical solicitation as interference? The *Nostrame* opinion is unclear as to how Santiago came to be represented by Mazie Slater. Should it make any difference to the outcome of the case if it turned out that Mazie Slater, knowing that Santiago was already represented by the plaintiff, nonetheless solicited Santiago's business? Would the manner in which Mazie Slater solicited Santiago make any difference to the interference claim?

ABA Model Rule 7.3 places limits on the ability of a lawyer to solicit a prospective client. A lawyer may not solicit, in real-time, a prospective client unless, *inter alia*, the lawyer has a prior professional, personal, or family relationship with the prospective client. A lawyer generally has greater latitude to solicit by written means, but the written solicitation of a person known to be in need of legal services must include a disclaimer indicating that the writing amounts to an advertisement. Why do the rules draw these distinctions? The Model Rules do not specifically prohibit a lawyer from soliciting the client of another lawyer. Should there be such a rule?

2. Legal advice leading to representation. What if, instead, Santiago approached Mazie Slater because he was unhappy with the representation he was receiving from the plaintiff and wanted advice about his options? If Mazie Slater honestly advised Santiago that the plaintiff was doing a poor job and should be fired and then solicited Santiago's business, would that be improper interference?

3. Departing attorney interference. One common scenario involves an attorney who leaves his or her law firm and brings along some client for whom the attorney has done work. Breach of fiduciary duty might be one possible claim. Interference is another. As is frequently the situation with interference claims, the scenario involves conflicting policy concerns. On one side, ABA Formal Ethics Opinion 99-414 advised that, given the importance of a client's right to choose a lawyer, an attorney who is responsible for the client's representation or who plays a principal role in the law firm's delivery of legal services in an active matter has a *duty* to notify the client of the attorney's impending departure. The departing attorney should not urge the client to sever the client's relationship with the firm or disparage the firm, but the attorney may indicate a willingness to continue the representation of the client. In addition, it is well settled that although a fiduciary cannot actually compete with a principal prior to departure, a fiduciary is permitted to make preparations to compete with the principal prior to departure. Meehan v. Shaughnessy, 535 N.E.2d 1255, 1264–65 (Mass. 1989). On the other side are concerns about the departing attorney's duty of loyalty to the firm, undue pressure on clients, and the use of any improper means on the part of the departing attorney. One judge, outraged by the solicitation of firm clients by departing associates, remarked, "[t]aking the heart and soul of the benefactor is immoral, illegal and repulsive. If they want their own firm, let them get their own clients." Adler, Barish, Daniels, Levin & Creskoff v. Epstein, 382 A.2d 1226, 1233 (Pa. Super. Ct. 1977), *rev'd*, 393 A.2d 1175 (Pa. 1978).

The *Restatement (Third) of the Law Governing Lawyers* attempts to strike a compromise. The *Restatement* proceeds from the assumption that the clients are clients of the firm. Prior to the departure of a lawyer from the firm, the lawyer may solicit clients "on whose matters the lawyer is actively and substantially working," but only after the lawyer has informed the firm of the lawyer's intent to contact firm clients for that purpose. (Of course, pre-departure solicitation involving the use of otherwise improper means, such as fraud, would be improper.) *After* the lawyer has left the firm, the lawyer is free to solicit firm clients to the same extent as any non-firm lawyer. Restatement (Third) of the Law Governing Lawyers § 9. At this point, the departed lawyer is now a competitor.

4. Professional identity and solicitation. Imagine you are a young associate a law firm and have long dreamed of hanging out your own shingle and starting your own practice. You decide to go ahead and take the leap of faith. Do you see anything wrong with contacting firm clients for whom you have done work in the past in the hopes that they might be interested in coming with you? In contacting firm clients for whom you are currently doing work? Suppose you call a firm client for whom you are currently doing substantial work. You tell the client that you are planning on leaving the firm and setting up your own shop. The client then begins to ask you some specific questions about why you are leaving, what your hourly rate will be, what sort of services you will provide, etc. What can you say in response?

b. Improper Settlement

Focus Questions: *Liston v. Home Insurance Co.* and *Ingalsbe v. Stewart Agency Co.*

1. *The courts in both cases appear to be applying the prima facie tort approach outlined at the beginning of the chapter. Would the result in either case have been any different under the approach from* Reeves *outlined earlier?*
2. *Do the defendants' actions justify liability?*

Liston v. Home Insurance Co.

659 F. Supp. 276
(S.D. Miss. 1986)

[Kathy Stewart was injured in an automobile accident on April 19, 1981. After the accident, she entered into an agreement with the plaintiff, William Liston, whereby Liston would represent her on a contingency fee basis in her personal injury claim against the other driver, Barclay. Under the agreement, Liston would be paid 33 1/3% of any amount recovered if the case were settled without suit, or 40% of any amount recovered after suit was filed. Barclay's insurer was Home Insurance Co. Jo Reynolds was the Home representative who was handling the claim. Reynolds was aware that Stewart was represented by Liston. For roughly 16 months following the accident, Reynolds attempted to obtain an itemization of Stewart's medical bills from Liston, but Liston never complied and stopped responding to Reynolds' inquiries. Eventually, Stewart began to receive past-due statements and letters threatening to garnish her wages from the hospital that had provided medical treatment and received letters threatening to garnish her wages to pay such overdue bills. On August 20, 1982, she wrote Home requesting that a settlement be made on her claim in the amount of $2577.15. Home did not respond to this letter.]

On September 17, 1982, she reiterated the settlement request in a letter denominated "Second Request!" Reynolds responded by phoning Stewart on October 1, 1982.... The substance of Stewart's communication to Reynolds was as follows: that the Stewarts were still receiving a number of bills owing as a result of the accident; that Liston had made no attempt to settle the case; that Stewart did not know what was going on in the case and that therefore she was going to handle it herself. In response to Reynolds' question regarding whether Liston was still representing her in the claim, Stewart stated that she could not get in touch with him so she had decided to handle it on her own. Reynolds then instructed Stewart to get all her medical bills together, plus documentation of other losses including lost wages, and to send them to the Home office. After receiving all necessary documentation, Reynolds again contacted Stewart on January 6, 1983. The parties negotiated a settlement of the claim for $3575, representing payment of Stewart's medical bills and her claimed lost wages, plus $1000 in cash. A general release was signed by the Stewarts on January 10, 1983, and a check was remitted to the Stewarts upon receipt of the release.

It was undisputed at trial that Reynolds made no attempt to verify Stewart's vague references to Liston's continuing involvement in the case. She neither called Liston's office nor sent Liston copies of the two settlement request letters from Kathy Stewart. The court specifically finds that Stewart did not represent to Reynolds in the October 1, 1982 phone conversation that Liston was presently relieved or had withdrawn from the case. Even if the court were to fully credit Reynolds' testimony—that Stewart told her that she and her husband were going to terminate Liston—regarding that conversation, the information she possessed was insufficient to relieve her of a responsibility to at least verify with Liston the extent of his involvement at that point. The court concludes that Reynolds had no reasonable basis for undertaking direct negotiations with Stewart without going first through Liston.

Liston did not learn of the settlement until the fall of 1984, when he instructed his partner, Alan Lancaster, to update some old files. [Upon learning of the settlement, Liston brought an action for interference with contractual relations.]

Intentional Interference with Contractual Relations

The Mississippi Supreme Court, the decisions of which this court is Erie-bound to apply, recognizes the tort of intentional interference with a contractual relation. One who intentionally and improperly interferes with the performance of a contract between another and a third person by inducing or otherwise causing the third person not to perform the contract, is subject to liability to the other for pecuniary loss resulting to the other from the failure of the third person to perform the contract. The elements of a cause of action for wrongful interference with a contract are well established.

(1) that the acts were intentional and willful;

(2) that they were calculated to cause damage to the plaintiffs in their lawful business;

(3) that they were done with the unlawful purpose of causing damage and loss, without right or justifiable cause on the part of defendant (which constitutes malice); and

(4) that actual damage and loss resulted.

... Once plaintiff has established a prima facie case of interference, the defendant may rebut with proof that his actions were either without knowledge of the existence of the contract, or were justified. Mid-Continent Telephone Corp. v. Home Telephone Co., 319 F.Supp. 1176, 1200 (N.D.Miss.1970).

Plaintiffs have clearly established a prima facie case of interference. Reynolds was obviously aware of the existence of the Liston-Stewart contract when she responded to Kathy Stewart's settlement pleas. She was also aware that settling Stewart's claim for $3575 would result in actual damage and loss to Liston under his contract with Stewart; indeed, Reynolds was aware that settling the case with the financially-distressed Stewarts would result in substantial savings for Home. She was also aware of the well-established policy of Home specifically, and the insurance industry generally, of never dealing directly with a client who is represented by an attorney. It would have been a simple and prudent matter to merely send Liston copies of Stewart's settlement request letters, or to resist direct communication with her until Liston's continued representation or lack thereof was verified.

Home argues, however, that Reynolds' actions were justified by the actions of Liston and statements of Stewart indicating that the contract had been abandoned. A contract will be treated as abandoned when acts or conduct on the part of one party inconsistent with the existence of the contract are acquiesced in by the other party. *See generally* 17 Am.Jur.2d Contracts § 484. Such acts or conduct must be positive and unequivocal to support a finding of abandonment. *Id.* No such acts or conduct exist here. Mere passage of time and inaction under the contract, especially in light of the peculiar nature of Stewart's injuries and the fact that she had six years from date of her injury to bring a cause of action against Home, cannot constitute abandonment. The insurance company had no right to assume that Liston had abandoned Kathy Stewart because he would not volunteer information to a claims representative, or had exercised his professional judgment to withhold immediate action on the claim pending a determination on permanent injury. Good business practices and simple prudence would have required more investigation into the extent of Liston's continuing involvement in the case. Thus, the court concludes that Reynolds' actions in settling the claim were not justified, were unlawful and were reasonably calculated to cause damage and loss to both Liston and his client.

The question of damages is difficult of precise calculation. [T]he limits of Home's liability to Stewart, as set out in the policy issued to Barclay, were $10,000. On initial assessment of Stewart's claim, Home itself set a reserve of $8000 to cover its exposure. Both Liston and his expert, Charles Merkel, testified that the reasonable value of Stewart's case if it were tried to a jury would be between $10,000 and $25,000. Both testified that they would have settled the claim for $10,000, that figure representing both the low side of their estimate of the value of the case if tried and the limits of the subject policy. Therefore, the court is of the opinion that a reasonable settlement value on Stewart's claim had Liston been involved in settlement negotiations would have been $10,000. Liston is entitled to recover $3333.33 from Home pursuant to his employment contract with the Stewarts.

Ingalsbe v. Stewart Agency, Inc.

869 So. 2d 30
(Fla. App. 4 Dist. 2004)

FARMER, C.J.

Basically the facts are these. Appellants [Lawyer] were retained by their Client to sue appellees [Dealer] under the Lemon Law. Lawyer and Client agreed in writing to a fee with 3 different alternatives for calculating the actual amount due. Under the contract the amount due would be either:

(A) 40% of the amount recovered plus an additional 5% (or $10,000 if greater than 5%) for any appeal, or

(B) the amount set by the Court under the attorney's fee statutes in Lemon Law cases if greater than 40% of Client's recovery; or

(C) if Client settled the case against the advice of the Lawyer, Client would pay $300 per hour for all time reasonably spent on the matter.

Suit was filed, and the case was tried to a jury, which awarded some $21,000 in damages. On an appeal of that judgment, we reversed upon a holding that the court improperly excluded defensive evidence and remanded for a new trial.

At some point after remand, Dealer approached Client personally and urged they settle the claim without any lawyers. Dealer and Client reached an agreement whereby Dealer agreed to pay Client $35,000 in damages, as well as attorneys fees in the amount of 33 1/3% of the recovery and costs. When Dealer learned the actual terms of the fee agreement, Dealer increased the fee percentage to 40% of the recovery, plus $10,000 for the appeal that had been previously taken. Dealer tendered the 40% plus $10,000 to Lawyer, asserting he had tendered payment in full. Lawyer rejected Dealer's tender and instead sued Dealer for interfering with his fee agreement.

[W]e begin with an acknowledgment that Dealer was privileged to propose and conclude a settlement because of the importance the law places on settlements of civil disputes.[2] But there is nothing inherent in the right to settle lawsuits that would compel a corollary right to interfere with a fee contract between one of the settling parties and his lawyer. Without such a legally recognized right, Dealer was not privileged to use the

2. Robbie v. City of Miami, 469 So.2d 1384, 1385 (Fla.1985) ("[S]ettlements are highly favored and will be enforced whenever possible."); Feldman v. Kritch, 824 So.2d 274, 277 (Fla. 4th DCA 2002) ("Settlements are highly favored as a means to conserve judicial resources, and will be enforced when it is possible to do so.").

right to settle in such a way as to interfere with the obligation of Client arising from the clear language of the fee contract. Dealer could not thereby set up a settlement imperative directing which contractual alternative for calculating the fee would be controlling after the settlement. Nor could Dealer bind Lawyer to an involuntary rescission of one or more of the contract's reasonable alternatives simply by committing to paying only the one most favorable to Dealer. No legitimate interest of Dealer and Client in settling their dispute gives them a privilege to interfere with Lawyer's fee contract in such a way as to restrict the fee due to only the lowest among the contract's reasonable alternatives.

By structuring the settlement in this case to limit the attorney's fees to only the first alternative of a percentage of the recovery, Dealer was interfering with Lawyer's entitlement to a fee under the alternative fee provisions regarding a fee set by the court and a fee based on an hourly rate. These alternative fee provisions were of obvious importance for the underlying claim that was the subject of the fee agreement. In consumer cases, such as those under the Lemon Law, the actual amount of damages may often be quite modest as against the probable amount of legal work required to achieve them. It is the recognition of that imbalance that is behind the Legislative decision to create an entitlement to fees by statute. Without the possibility that a reasonable fee will be set by the court, consumers may find it impossible to interest lawyers into litigating such claims. In short, if the defendants in such cases were privileged to interfere with the very provision that allows consumers to vindicate such statutory rights, the statutes would become mere ornaments in the statutory code.

REVERSED

GROSS, J., dissenting.

Allowing a tortious interference cause of action in this case will severely impinge on a client's right to settle a lawsuit, a right which takes paramount importance in our system.

It is inconceivable that a tort could arise out of these facts. As one federal court construing Florida law has written:

> [I]t is clear that an attorney never has the right to prohibit his client from settling an action in good faith. A client by virtue of a contract with his attorney is not made an indentured servant, a puppet on counsel's string, nor a chair in the courtroom. Counsel should advise, analyze, argue, and recommend, but his role is not that of an imperator whose edicts must prevail over the client's desire. He has no authoritarian settlement thwarting rights by virtue of his employment.

Singleton v. Foreman, 435 F.2d 962, 970 (5th Cir.1970) (citations omitted).

From the Client's perspective, the settlement was in good faith. The settlement far exceeded the amount of damages set at the first trial. At a second trial, the risk for the Client was enhanced, because the evidence omitted at the first trial would be heard by the jury. The Client was not "required to hazard the outcome of litigation, rather than settle the suit, simply because his attorneys [were] employed on a contingent fee basis." Sentco, Inc. v. McCulloh, 84 So.2d 498, 499 (Fla.1955); *see also* Statement of Client's Rights for Contingency Fees 10, R. Regulating Fla. Bar 4-1.5 ("You, the client, have the right to make the final decision regarding settlement of a case.... [Y]ou must make the final decision to accept or reject a settlement.").

The primacy of the Client's right to settle a lawsuit compels the conclusion that the Attorneys have failed to state a cause of action for tortious interference.

* * *

1. Model Rule comparison. Rule 4.2 of the ABA Model Rules of Professional Conduct prohibits a lawyer from communicating "about the subject of the representation with a person the lawyer knows to be represented by another lawyer in the matter," unless the lawyer has the consent of the other lawyer.

2. Lessons for lawyers? Imagine that you represent a defendant in a civil matter. The plaintiff contacts you and, like in *Liston*, tells you that she doesn't know what is going on with her case, that she hasn't been able to get in touch with her own lawyer, and wishes to settle directly without the assistance of her lawyer. This is the same lawyer who has stopped returning your phone calls when you have tried to initiate settlement discussions. What do you do?

3. The Litigation Privilege

Exercise 14.4

You are the trial judge in a tortious interference action brought by the Jackson Law Firm (Jackson) against the Martin Law Firm (Martin). The claim stems from the actions of Martin in a personal injury case in which Jackson represented the defendant. In answering interrogatories in the personal injury litigation, the defendant listed Dwight Fidrych, an attorney with the Jackson firm, as one of several people who had knowledge of facts relevant to the personal injury action. After receiving the answers to the interrogatories, the plaintiff, represented by Martin, moved to disqualify Fidrych and the Jackson firm as the defendant's attorneys. In moving to disqualify Fidrych and the Jackson firm, Martin certified to the trial court that it would be calling Fidrych as a witness at trial. Under the applicable disciplinary rules, Fidrych's participation as a witness would merit disqualification of his firm as well. As a result of Martin's certification, the trial judge disqualified Fidrych and the Jackson firm as counsel for the defendant. Martin, however, never subpoenaed Fidrych for trial, never called him as a witness at trial, and never notified the court that it would not be calling him as a witness. At trial, a final judgment was entered in favor of the plaintiff against the defendant in the amount of $638,237.

In this action, the Jackson firm sued the Martin firm in for tortious interference with a contractual relationship, alleging that Martin intentionally and in bad faith disqualified Fidrych to prevent the Jackson firm from representing the defendant. Martin has moved to dismiss this action on the grounds that its actions were protected by the absolute immunity afforded to statements or actions taken during a judicial proceeding that often applies in defamation claims. You are the trial judge. Will you grant the motion? Why or why not?

Chapter 15

Invasion of Privacy

Exercise 15.1: Chapter Problem

A couple of years ago, Nicollet, Inc. became concerned that one of its employees was selling company secrets to a competitor, so it hired a computer forensics expert to search the employee's company-provided computers. After confirming its suspicions about the theft, the company sent out a company-wide email, informing its employees that the employee in question had been fired and why the firing had occurred. Now the company is thinking about doing something similar with another problem employee. The employee in question has been making noises about possibly suing Nicollet for disability discrimination. The employee's supervisor believes the employee is exaggerating the extent of her physical limitations in an attempt to avoid being fired for poor work performance. Therefore, the company is interested in finding out whether the employee has been speaking to a lawyer and what she has been saying. The supervisor has heard rumors that the employee has been keeping a journal of what the employee believes to be harassing and discriminatory behavior on the part of her supervisor. Therefore, the supervisor has suggested conducting a search of the employee's office and workspace. A human resources person at Nicollet has called you, asking for your advice about how to proceed.

The creation of a tort action based upon an invasion of privacy is typically credited to a late 19th-century law review article by Samuel D. Warren and Louis V. Brandeis. Warren and Brandeis, *The Right to Privacy*, 4 HARV.L.REV. 193 (1890). There are four recognized types of invasion of privacy tort claims: (1) intrusion upon the seclusion; (2) publicity given to private life (or public disclosure of private facts); (3) misappropriation of one's right of publicity; and (4) false light. Some jurisdictions recognize some forms of the tort but not others. Although they are all lumped under the heading of "invasion of privacy," each theory is designed to address a particular type of harm.

* * *

A. Intrusion upon the Seclusion

Focus Questions: *McLain v. Boise Cascade Corp., Mark v. Seattle Times,* and *Tagouma v. Investigative Consultant Services, Inc.*

1. *Which part (or parts) of the Restatement test, as adopted by the courts, did the plaintiff fail to satisfy in* McLain? *In* Mark? *In* Tagouma?
2. *What qualifies as "seclusion"?*
3. *What makes an intrusion "highly offensive to a reasonable person"?*

McLain v. Boise Cascade Corp.

533 P.2d 343
(Or. 1975)

McALLISTER, Justice.

Plaintiff was employed by Boise Cascade Corporation as a glue mixer. On May 19, 1972 he strained his back when he fell while carrying a 100 pound sack of flour to a glue machine. Plaintiff was taken to the office of Dr. D. H. Searing in Salem. Dr. Searing sent plaintiff to the hospital where he was placed in traction. On June 6, 1972, Dr. Searing wrote to Richard Cyphert, then in charge of the Boise Cascade Workmen's Compensation program, advising that plaintiff might be disabled for as much as 12 months. Dr. John D. White was called in as a consultant. He performed a myelogram on plaintiff and reported to Mr. Cyphert that he found no evidence of nerve root or lumbar disc disease and that it was possible that plaintiff was 'consciously malingering.' Cyphert received this letter on June 22, 1972.

On the basis of Dr. White's report Mr. Cyphert notified plaintiff his compensation payments would be terminated. At about that time Mr. Cyphert also was informed that plaintiff was performing part-time work for a mortuary while he was ostensibly disabled. On June 27, 1972 plaintiff received a written release from Dr. White permitting him to return to work with the restriction that he was not to lift more than 50 pounds. Plaintiff returned to work and was assigned an easier job, but was unable to work due to continued pain in his hip.

Plaintiff then consulted an attorney, who filed a request for a hearing with the Workmen's Compensation Board asking that plaintiff's temporary disability payments be reinstated. Mr. Cyphert received a copy of this request on July 5, 1972. On July 12, 1972 Mr. Cyphert hired the defendant United Diversified Services, Inc., to conduct a surveillance of the plaintiff to check the validity of plaintiff's claim of injury. United assigned two of its employees, Rick Oulette and Steve Collette, to conduct a surveillance. The two investigators took 18 rolls of movie film of plaintiff while he was engaged in various activities on his property outside his home. Some of the film showed plaintiff mowing his lawn, rototilling his garden and fishing from a bridge near his home.

Plaintiff lived at Independence on a large square lot containing slightly more than two acres. The property is bounded on the north by the Hopville Road, on the east by a pond, on the west by property owned by Lindsey Ward, a neighbor. To the south is a field which apparently also belongs to Mr. Ward.

Some of the film of plaintiff was taken from a barn behind plaintiff's house, which apparently belonged to Ward, although the record is not clear on that point. Other film was taken by Collette while plaintiff was fishing from a bridge on the Hopville Road near the northeast corner of plaintiff's property. The record is not clear as to where Mr. Collette was standing while taking that film. The remaining rolls of film were taken by Mr. Collette from a point near some walnut trees at the southeast corner of plaintiff's property.

There was a barbed wire fence a short distance west of the east boundary of plaintiff's tract and west of the row of walnut trees from which some of the film was taken. Collette testified that he stayed east of the fence and did not know that he was on plaintiff's land. He testified, however, that he crossed over a fence under the bridge near the northeast corner of plaintiff's property in order to get to his vantage point near the walnut trees. He probably trespassed on plaintiff's property when he crossed the fence, but that does not appear clearly from the record.

On one occasion while Collette was near the walnut trees he was seen by plaintiff. When Collette realized he had been seen he left the area. He had parked his pickup truck on Ward's property near the southwest corner of plaintiff's tract, but abandoned the pickup when he was spotted by McLain and retrieved his truck later.

McLain did not learn about the film and picture taking until the film was shown at the Workmen's Compensation Hearing.

United's investigators did not question any of plaintiff's neighbors or friends and limited their activities to taking pictures while plaintiff was engaged in various activities outside his home. Plaintiff testified that these activities could have been viewed either by neighbors or passersby on the highway. Plaintiff further testified that he was not embarrassed or upset by anything that appeared in the films. He said:

> Q You did all of the things that were shown in the film? There was no deception in the film?
>
> A No.
>
> Q You agree that what you saw there was what you did?
>
> A Right.
>
> Q And you weren't embarrassed by it or mad or upset?
>
> A No, the only thing I was mad about was the fact they snuck around behind my back.
>
> Q The thing that really bothered you was that somebody filmed you without telling you, isn't that right?
>
> A Right.
>
> Q Other than that, it just made you mad that somebody did that without telling you? Other than that, that is all there was to it?
>
> A Right. And I didn't think anybody had any right on my property without permission.

It is now well established in Oregon that damages may be recovered for violation of privacy.

The general rule permitting recovery for such intrusion is stated in *Restatement of the Law of Torts 2d*, ... as follows:

> One who intentionally intrudes, physically or otherwise, upon the solitude or seclusion of another or his private affairs or concerns, is subject to liability to

> the other for invasion of his privacy, if the intrusion would be highly offensive to a reasonable person.

Restatement (Second) of Torts §652B (1977).* *See, also*, PROSSER, TORTS (4th ed. 1971), 807; *Prosser, Privacy*, 48 CAL.L.REV. 383, 389 (1960).

It is also well established that one who seeks to recover damages for alleged injuries must expect that his claim will be investigated and he waives his right of privacy to the extent of a reasonable investigation. Tucker v. American Employers' Ins. Co., 171 So.2d 437, 13 A.L.R.3d 1020 (Fla.App.1965); Souder v. Pendleton Detectives, Inc., 88 So.2d 716 (La.App.1956); Forster v. Manchester, 410 Pa. 192, 189 A.2d 147, 150 (1963); Ellenberg v. Pinkerton's, Inc., 125 Ga.App. 648, 188 S.E.2d 911 (1972). We quote from the Annotation, *Right of Privacy-Surveillance*, 13 A.L.R.3d 1025, 1027:

> Where the surveillance, shadowing, and trailing is conducted in a reasonable manner, it has been held that owing to the social utility of exposing fraudulent claims and because of the fact that some sort of investigation is necessary to uncover fictitious injuries, an unobtrusive investigation, even though inadvertently made apparent to the person being investigated, does not constitute an actionable invasion of his privacy.

In *Forster v. Manchester, supra*, 189 A.2d at 150, the court stated:

> It is not uncommon for defendants in accident cases to employ investigators to check on the validity of claims against them. Thus, by making a claim for personal injuries appellant must expect reasonable inquiry and investigation to be made of her claim and to this extent her interest in privacy is circumscribed....

If the surveillance is conducted in a reasonable and unobtrusive manner the defendant will incur no liability for invasion of privacy. On the other hand, if the surveillance is conducted in an unreasonable and obtrusive manner the defendant will be liable for invasion of privacy.

In this case we think the court below properly granted a nonsuit for the cause of action for invasion of privacy. In the first place, the surveillance and picture taking were done in such an unobtrusive manner that plaintiff was not aware that he was being watched and filmed. In the second place, plaintiff conceded that his activities which were filmed could have been observed by his neighbors or passersby on the road running in front of his property. Undoubtedly the investigators trespassed on plaintiff's land while watching and taking pictures of him, but it is also clear that the trespass was on the periphery of plaintiff's property and did not constitute an unreasonable surveillance 'highly offensive to a reasonable [person].'

Plaintiff does not contend that the surveillance in this case was per se actionable. Plaintiff contends only that the surveillance became actionable when the investigators trespassed on plaintiff's property. Plaintiff's brief states the issue as follows:

> The issue before this Court is whether trespass upon another's homestead for the purpose of conducting an unauthorized surveillance gives rise to an action for violation of the right of privacy,....

We think trespass is only one factor to be considered in determining whether the surveillance was unreasonable. Trespass to peer in windows and to annoy or harass the

* Editor's note: The original version of the opinion included the language from a draft of the *Restatement*. This version includes the language from the final version of the *Restatement*, which is nearly identical to the draft version.

occupant may be unreasonable. Trespass alone cannot automatically change an otherwise reasonable surveillance into an unreasonable one. The one trespass which was observed by plaintiff did not alert him to the fact that he was being watched or that his activities were being filmed. The record is clear that the trespass was confined to a narrow strip along the east boundary of plaintiff's property. All the surveillance in this case was done during daylight hours and when plaintiff was exposed to public view by his neighbors and passersby.

By the same reasoning we think the court did not err in striking the claim for punitive damages in the cause of action for trespass. Assuming that the trespass in this case was intentional there was no evidence of intent to harm, harass or annoy the plaintiff. The surveillance took place near the boundaries of plaintiff's property. The trespass was unlawful, but did not injure plaintiff, nor was it intended to injure him. We think the court property withdrew from consideration by the jury the claim for punitive damages on account of the trespass.

* * *

Elements or a sliding scale? In a subsequent decision, the Oregon Supreme Court broke the intrusion upon the seclusion down into three separate elements: (1) an intentional intrusion, physical or otherwise, (2) upon the plaintiff's solitude or seclusion or private affairs or concerns, (3) which would be highly offensive to a reasonable person. Mauri v. Smith, 929 P.2d 307, 310 (Or. 1996). As you read the next case, consider whether this tort is best viewed as consisting of separate elements or as more of a sliding scale.

* * *

Mark v. Seattle Times

635 P.2d 1081
(Wash. 1981)

[Plaintiff brought defamation and invasion of privacy claims against several media outlets involving news coverage of Medicaid fraud charges filed against Albert M. Mark, a pharmacist.]

During its January 7, 1977 news broadcast, KING-TV also showed a film clip of Mark talking on the telephone inside one of his pharmacies. This film was taken by a KING-TV camera operator who had arrived at the pharmacy after it was closed and had walked up a drive leased to tenants. He apparently placed the camera against the window and used spotlights to illuminate the interior of the pharmacy. The telecast of the interior scene took approximately 13 seconds, the remainder of the 53-second film clip consisting of exterior shots.

Tort liability for intrusion, the only interest which Mark on appeal claims was violated, has been described as follows:

> One who intentionally intrudes, physically or otherwise, upon the solitude or seclusion of another or his private affairs or concerns, is subject to liability to the other for invasion of his privacy, if the intrusion would be highly offensive to a reasonable person.

Restatement (Second) of Torts s 652B at 378 (1977). The interference with a plaintiff's seclusion must be a substantial one resulting from conduct of a kind that would be offensive and objectionable to the ordinary person. Restatement (Second) of Torts s 652B, comment d at 380 (1977); W. Prosser, Torts 808 (4th ed. 1971).

> It is clear also that the thing into which there is intrusion or prying must be, and be entitled to be, private.... On the public street, or in any other public place, the plaintiff has no legal right to be alone; and it is no invasion of his privacy to do no more than follow him about and watch him there. Neither is it such an invasion to take his photograph in such a place, since this amounts to nothing more than making a record, not differing essentially from a full written description, of a public sight which anyone would be free to see (footnotes omitted).

W. Prosser, Torts 808–09 (4th ed. 1971).

A court has found an actionable intrusion where the press gained entrance by subterfuge to the home of an accused and photographed him there, publishing the photographs without his consent. Dietemann v. TIME, Inc., 449 F.2d 245 (9th Cir. 1971). A similar result occurred where a news photographer published a picture taken surreptitiously of a patient in her hospital bed. Barber v. TIME, Inc., 348 Mo. 1199, 159 S.W.2d 291 (1942).

In *McLain v. Boise Cascade Corp.*, 271 Or. 549, 533 P.2d 343 (1975), a plaintiff brought an intrusion action against his employer and a private investigator, whom the employer had hired to investigate plaintiff's suspected fraudulent workers' compensation claims. The investigator crossed plaintiff's property line on a number of occasions to photograph plaintiff in various activities around his residence. In affirming the trial court's granting of an involuntary nonsuit, the Oregon Supreme Court said:

> (P)laintiff conceded that his activities which were filmed could have been observed by his neighbors or passersby on the road running in front of his property. Undoubtedly the investigators trespassed on plaintiff's land while watching and taking pictures of him, but it is also clear that the trespass was on the periphery of plaintiff's property and did not constitute an unreasonable surveillance "highly offensive to a reasonable [person]."

McLain, at 556, 533 P.2d 343.

Here, the affidavits and other material submitted with KING Broadcasting Company's motion for summary judgment, construed most favorably to Mark, establish that Mark, his wife, and a friend were inside one of Mark's pharmacies in the early evening. The store was closed and the door was locked. The KING-TV cameraman walked up a driveway leased to tenants of the building, placed his camera against the window of the store, and photographed the interior, including Mark, who was on the telephone. The film clip, as shown on the air, was 53 seconds long, with Mark visible for 13 seconds.

There was a factual dispute over whether the cameraman was on public or private property at the time he shot the film. Even if Mark's version were true (that the property was private), however, the place from which the film was shot was open to the public and thus any passerby could have viewed the scene recorded by the camera. *McLain*, at 556, 533 P.2d 343.[7] Moreover, a person accused of a crime loses some of his or her claims to privacy. Hodgeman v. Olsen, 86 Wash. 615, 150 P. 1122 (1915); Frith v. Associated Press, 176 F.Supp. 671 (E.D.S.C.1959). *See generally Annot., Waiver or Loss of Right of*

---

7. The present case differs factually from *McLain v. Boise Cascade Co.*, 271 Or. 549, 533 P.2d 343 (1975), where defendant's employees went uninvited onto private property in order to photograph plaintiff. We express no opinion as to the publication of photographs taken by a trespasser, but note that in the present case it is undisputed that the public had an implied invitation to come upon that portion of Mark's property from which the KING-TV cameraman shot his film.

Privacy, 57 A.L.R.3d 16 (1974). Since the intrusion in the present case was a minimal one, publication lasted only 13 seconds, Mark was not shown in any embarrassing positions, and his facial features were not recognizable, we hold there could be no actionable claim in these circumstances.

* * *

Tagouma v. Investigative Consultant Services, Inc.

4 A.3d 170

(Pa. Super. 2010)

[Appellant, Ahmed Tagouma, was videotaped by a private investigator for 45 minutes on a Sony 8 mm video camera with a zoom feature while praying inside an Islamic Center. The investigator had been hired by Tagouma's employer, which was contesting Tagouma's claim for workers compensation.]

Before we examine the merits of Appellant's claim, we note that a workers' compensation claimant has a diminished expectation of privacy. Our Supreme Court's 1963 pronouncement in *Forster v. Manchester*, 410 Pa. 192, 189 A.2d 147 (1963) provided that there was no cause of action for invasion of privacy when a private investigator, Manchester, followed and took photos of Forster on public streets subsequent to her claim for personal injuries sustained in a car accident. Ultimately, our Supreme Court determined:

> It is not uncommon for defendants in accident cases to employ investigators to check on the validity of claims against them. Thus, by making a claim for personal injuries appellant must expect reasonable inquiry and investigation to be made of her claim and to this extent her interest in privacy is circumscribed. It should be noted that all of the surveillances took place in the open on public thoroughfares where appellant's activities could be observed by passers-by. To this extent appellant has exposed herself to public observation and therefore is not entitled to the same degree of privacy that she would enjoy within the confines of her own home.
>
> Moving to the question of whether [the investigator's] conduct is reasonable, we feel that there is much social utility to be gained from these investigations. It is in the best interests of society that valid claims be ascertained and fabricated claims be exposed.

Forster, 189 A.2d at 150. Here, Appellant had a claim for workers' compensation benefits. Appellees were hired by Appellant's employer to perform surveillance of him. Appellant "must expect reasonable [...] investigation" and, thus, his "interest in privacy [was] circumscribed."

[A]lthough very little case law in the civil context exists, we have examined the expectation of privacy in the criminal context for additional direction. The Fourth Amendment of the United States Constitution and Article I, Section 8 of the Pennsylvania Constitution afford citizens the right to be free from unreasonable search and seizure:

> The Fourth Amendment protects "[t]he right of the people to be secure in their persons, houses, papers, and effects against unreasonable searches and seizures." U.S. Const. amend. IV; Pa. Const. art. 1, § 8. A search within the meaning of the Fourth Amendment "occurs when 'an expectation of privacy that society is prepared to consider reasonable is infringed.'" Maryland v. Macon, 472 U.S. 463, 469, 105 S.Ct. 2778, 2782, 86 L.Ed.2d 370 (1985) (quoting United

> States v. Jacobsen, 466 U.S. 109, 113, 104 S.Ct. 1652, 1656, 80 L.Ed.2d 85 (1984)). Whether or not a person who invokes the protection of the Fourth Amendment may claim a "reasonable expectation of privacy" is determined by two inquiries: (1) whether, by his conduct, the person has "exhibited an actual (subjective) expectation of privacy;" and (2) whether that expectation of privacy is "one that society is prepared to recognize as reasonable." Smith v. Maryland, 442 U.S. 735, 740, 99 S.Ct. 2577, 2580, 61 L.Ed.2d 220 (1979) (citing Katz v. United States, 389 U.S. 347, 88 S.Ct. 507, 19 L.Ed.2d 576 (1967) (Harlan, J., concurring)).
>
> It is now well established that a person cannot have a reasonable or justifiable expectation of privacy in things or activities which are generally visible from some public vantage point. California v. Ciraolo, 476 U.S. 207, 211, 106 S.Ct. 1809, 1812, 90 L.Ed.2d 210 (1986).

Commonwealth v. Lemanski, 365 Pa.Super. 332, 529 A.2d 1085, 1091 (1987). Pennsylvania appellate courts have found, in the criminal arena, no expectation of privacy in the following places: an airport, a vehicle parked on a public street, a front porch, a rooftop, a courthouse, or a storefront.

Based on all of the foregoing, in the case sub judice, Appellant has failed to show that he had an expectation of privacy while praying in public. First, Appellant had a diminished expectation of privacy because of his workers' compensation claim. Second, it is undisputed that the Islamic Center was open to the public and Appellant was praying directly in front of a plate glass window. Appellant contends that the act of worship is entitled to a reasonable expectation of privacy because "even though he participated in the worship service with others, he sought to keep the service free from interference of the world[,] and in particular to keep his prayers to his god private to himself...." Such an argument is a red herring. In essence, Appellant asks this Court to create a privacy expectation based on religion, but ignores the fact that he was in public at the time of surveillance. However, merely assigning a purpose to the activity cannot save Appellant's claim for intrusion upon seclusion. For purposes of the tort, Appellant's physical activities and not his thoughts, prayers, or even expressions of prayer were viewed. Witnessing Appellant kneeling in the Al-Hikmeh Institute would be no different than viewing someone kneeling in another public forum. Based upon our standard of review and applicable law, we discern no abuse of discretion by the trial court in granting Appellee's motion for summary judgment and dismissing Appellant's complaint. As such, Appellant's first issue fails.

In his second issue presented, Appellant argues that Zeigler's use of vision enhanced photographic equipment was impermissible. He contends that the Islamic Center was secluded because: (1) it was set back from Carlisle Pike behind two buildings that partially obstructed it on either side; (2) was located at a much lower elevation than the main road; (3) there was no parking or a sidewalk on Carlisle Pike, thereby limiting pedestrian observers; (4) the speed limit was 40 miles per hour on Carlisle Pike, making it virtually impossible for drivers to get more than a quick glimpse of the Center; (5) all of the surrounding businesses were closed; and (6) the parking lot across the street where Zeigler took photos was 82 yards away. Appellant maintains that "the permissible distance for videotaping [should] be the same distance that the human eye can see" otherwise the privacy standards of the Commonwealth "would be the horrors of George Orwell's novel 1984."

Under both the Fourth Amendment and the Pennsylvania Constitution, there is no expectation of privacy if police have lawful access to objects seen in plain view. Commonwealth v. Dean, 940 A.2d 514, 519 (Pa.Super.2008). Pennsylvania appellate courts have consistently concluded that law enforcement is permitted to use various types of vision-enhancing equipment from a lawful vantage point, without violating an expectation of privacy. *See* Commonwealth v. Jenkins, 401 Pa.Super. 580, 585 A.2d 1078 (1991) (police observation of two narcotic street transactions through binoculars was proper); Commonwealth v. Lawson, 454 Pa. 23, 309 A.2d 391 (1973) (same); Commonwealth v. Hernley, 216 Pa.Super. 177, 263 A.2d 904 (1970) (FBI agent's observation of illegal activities while standing on a ladder using binoculars was not unreasonable); Commonwealth v. Jones, 978 A.2d 1000 (Pa.Super.2009) (use of police vehicle's spotlight to illuminate the porch of a suspected drug house at night did not infringe on reasonable expectations of privacy); Commonwealth v. Beals, 313 Pa.Super. 346, 459 A.2d 1263 (1983) (no reasonable expectation of privacy in an open field where police took aerial photographs by helicopter); *compare* Commonwealth v. Lemanski, 365 Pa.Super. 332, 529 A.2d 1085 (1987) (violation of expectation of privacy when police observed, through a zoom lens, illegal activity in a residential greenhouse from an unlawful vantage point); Commonwealth v. Gindlesperger, 560 Pa. 222, 743 A.2d 898 (1999) (police use of thermal imaging device to scan private residence for heat from suspected marijuana growing operation was impermissible).

In this case, it is undisputed that Zeigler was standing at a lawful vantage point in the parking lot across the street from the Islamic Center. His use of a zoom lens, similar to using binoculars, was not unreasonable. Moreover, the Islamic Center was not completely obstructed from the view from the street. Zeigler could have just as easily walked down the public driveway and taken photos from directly outside the window.

Based on the foregoing, we conclude that Appellant failed to establish his right to privacy, even with Zeigler's use of vision-enhanced photographic equipment, and Appellant's second issue fails.

* * *

1. The concept of "seclusion." *McLain* and *Mark* involve intrusions into physical spaces. However, an intrusion upon the seclusion claim may also arise from intrusions into other areas. In *Vernars v. Young*, 539 F.2d 966 (3d Cir. 1976), the defendant, an officer of a corporation, read mail belonging to the plaintiff (also an officer) that had been marked "personal," but delivered to the corporation. The Third Circuit concluded that the plaintiff had a privacy interest in the contents of the mail, the intrusion upon which could serve as a basis for a tort claim. The court stated that, as a general matter, private individuals "have a reasonable expectation that their personal mail will not be opened and read by unauthorized persons." *Id.* at 969. Courts have also held that an individual's conversations with others may be "secluded" for purposes of a privacy claim. Shulman v. Grp. W Prods., Inc., 955 P.2d 469, 491 (Cal. 1998).

2. The concept of a "highly offensive" intrusion. To be actionable, the intrusion must be of a substantial nature, stemming from "conduct to which the reasonable man would strongly object." Restatement (Second) of Torts § 652B cmt. d.

3. Privacy statutes. There are a host of state and federal statutes dealing with privacy rights, including eavesdropping, wiretapping, and electronic surveillance statutes, that limit information-gathering. Electronic Communication Privacy Act, 18 U.S.C § 2510 et seq.; Stored Communications Act (SCA), 18 U.S.C § 2701 et seq. Other statutes address an individual's right to privacy with respect to information concerning an individual's health or medical history. Health Insurance Portability and Accountability Act (HIPAA), 42 U.S.C. § 1320d-2(a); Americans with Disabilities Act (ADA), 42 U.S.C. § 12112(d).

4. Using investigators and other agents to obtain information. Note that a lawyer is prohibited from using a non-lawyer to accomplish what a lawyer is ethically prohibited from doing and may be subject to discipline for the conduct of a non-lawyer retained by the lawyer that would violate the lawyer's own ethical obligations if the lawyer fails to properly supervise the non-lawyer. ABA Model Rules of Professional Conduct R. 8.4(a); *id.* R. 5.3(c).

Focus Questions: *Shulman v. Group W Productions, Inc.*

1. *How could the plaintiffs have had a reasonable expectation of privacy?*
2. *How could a jury find that any intrusion was highly offensive to a reasonable person?*

Shulman v. Group W Productions, Inc.

955 P.2d 469
(Cal. 1998)

In the present case, we address the balance between privacy and press freedom in the commonplace context of an automobile accident....

FACTS AND PROCEDURAL HISTORY

On June 24, 1990, plaintiffs Ruth and Wayne Shulman, mother and son, were injured when the car in which they and two other family members were riding on interstate 10 in Riverside County flew off the highway and tumbled down an embankment into a drainage ditch on state-owned property, coming to rest upside down. Ruth, the most seriously injured of the two, was pinned under the car. Ruth and Wayne both had to be cut free from the vehicle by the device known as "the jaws of life."

A rescue helicopter operated by Mercy Air was dispatched to the scene. The flight nurse, who would perform the medical care at the scene and on the way to the hospital, was Laura Carnahan. Also on board were the pilot, a medic and Joel Cooke, a video camera operator employed by defendants Group W Productions, Inc., and 4MN Productions. Cooke was recording the rescue operation for later broadcast.

Cooke roamed the accident scene, videotaping the rescue. Nurse Carnahan wore a wireless microphone that picked up her conversations with both Ruth and the other rescue personnel. Cooke's tape was edited into a piece approximately nine minutes long, which, with the addition of narrative voice-over, was broadcast on September 29, 1990, as a segment of *On Scene: Emergency Response.*

The segment begins with the Mercy Air helicopter shown on its way to the accident site. The narrator's voice is heard in the background, setting the scene and describing in general terms what has happened. The pilot can be heard speaking with rescue workers on the ground in order to prepare for his landing. As the helicopter touches down, the narrator says "[F]our of the patients are leaving by ground ambulance. Two are still trapped inside." (The first part of this statement was wrong, since only four persons were in the car to start.) After Carnahan steps from the helicopter, she can be seen and heard speaking about the situation with various rescue workers. A firefighter assures her they will hose down the area to prevent any fire from the wrecked car.

The videotape shows only a glimpse of Wayne, and his voice is never heard. Ruth is shown several times, either by brief shots of a limb or her torso, or with her features blocked by others or obscured by an oxygen mask. She is also heard speaking several times. Carnahan calls her "Ruth" and her last name is not mentioned on the broadcast.

While Ruth is still trapped under the car, Carnahan asks Ruth's age. Ruth responds, "I'm old." On further questioning, Ruth reveals she is 47, and Carnahan observes that "it's all relative. You're not that old." During her extrication from the car, Ruth asks at least twice if she is dreaming. At one point she asks Carnahan, who has told her she will be taken to the hospital in a helicopter: "Are you teasing?" At another point she says: "This is terrible. Am I dreaming?" She also asks what happened and where the rest of her family is, repeating the questions even after being told she was in an accident and the other family members are being cared for. While being loaded into the helicopter on a stretcher, Ruth says: "I just want to die." Carnahan reassures her that she is "going to do real well," but Ruth repeats: "I just want to die. I don't want to go through this."

Ruth and Wayne are placed in the helicopter, and its door is closed. The narrator states: "Once airborne, Laura and [the flight medic] will update their patients' vital signs and establish communications with the waiting trauma teams at Loma Linda." Carnahan, speaking into what appears to be a radio microphone, transmits some of Ruth's vital signs and states that Ruth cannot move her feet and has no sensation. The video footage during the helicopter ride includes a few seconds of Ruth's face, covered by an oxygen mask. Wayne is neither shown nor heard.

The helicopter lands on the hospital roof. With the door open, Ruth states while being taken out: "My upper back hurts." Carnahan replies: "Your upper back hurts." That's what you were saying up there." Ruth states: "I don't feel that great." Carnahan responds: "You probably don't."

Finally, Ruth is shown being moved from the helicopter into the hospital. The narrator concludes by stating: "Once inside both patients will be further evaluated and moved into emergency surgery if need be. Thanks to the efforts of the crew of Mercy Air, the firefighters, medics and police who responded, patients' lives were saved." As the segment ends, a brief, written epilogue appears on the screen, stating: "Laura's patient spent months in the hospital. She suffered severe back injuries. The others were all released much sooner."

The accident left Ruth a paraplegic. When the segment was broadcast, Wayne phoned Ruth in her hospital room and told her to turn on the television because "Channel 4 is showing our accident now." Shortly afterward, several hospital workers came into the room to mention that a videotaped segment of her accident was being shown. Ruth was "shocked, so to speak, that this would be run and I would be exploited, have my privacy invaded, which is what I felt had happened." She did not know her rescue had been recorded in this manner and had never consented to the recording or broadcast. Ruth had the impression from the broadcast "that I was kind of talking non-stop, and I remember hearing some of the things I said, which were not very pleasant." Asked at deposition what part of the broadcast material she considered private, Ruth explained: "I think the whole scene was pretty private. It was pretty gruesome, the parts that I saw, my knee sticking out of the car. I certainly did not look my best, and I don't feel it's for the public to see. I was not at my best in what I was thinking and what I was saying and what was being shown, and it's not for the public to see this trauma that I was going through."

Ruth and Wayne sued the producers of *On Scene: Emergency Response*, as well as others.

[The trial court granted the media defendants' summary judgment motion. The Court of Appeal reversed and remanded for further proceedings, but on limited grounds.] First, the Court of Appeal held plaintiffs had no reasonable expectation of privacy in the events at the accident scene itself.... Once inside the helicopter, however, the court next reasoned, plaintiffs did have a reasonable expectation of privacy ...

Of the four privacy torts identified by Prosser, the tort of intrusion into private places, conversations or matter is perhaps the one that best captures the common understanding of an "invasion of privacy." It encompasses unconsented-to physical intrusion into the home, hospital room or other place the privacy of which is legally recognized, as well as unwarranted sensory intrusions such as eavesdropping, wiretapping, and visual or photographic spying. (*See Rest.2d Torts*, § 652B, com. b., pp. 378–379, and illustrations.) It is in the intrusion cases that invasion of privacy is most clearly seen as an affront to individual dignity.

Despite its conceptual centrality, the intrusion tort has received less judicial attention than the private facts tort, and its parameters are less clearly defined. The leading California decision is *Miller v. National Broadcasting Co., supra*, 187 Cal.App.3d 1463, 232 Cal.Rptr. 668. *Miller*, which like the present case involved a news organization's videotaping the work of emergency medical personnel, adopted the *Restatement*'s formulation of the cause of action: "One who intentionally intrudes, physically or otherwise, upon the solitude or seclusion of another or his private affairs or concerns, is subject to liability to the other for invasion of his privacy, if the intrusion would be highly offensive to a reasonable person." (*Rest.2d Torts*, § 652B; Miller, *supra*, 187 Cal.App.3d at p. 1482, 232 Cal.Rptr. 668.)

As stated in *Miller* and the *Restatement*, therefore, the action for intrusion has two elements: (1) intrusion into a private place, conversation or matter, (2) in a manner highly offensive to a reasonable person. We consider the elements in that order.

We ask first whether defendants "intentionally intrude[d], physically or otherwise, upon the solitude or seclusion of another," that is, into a place or conversation private to Wayne or Ruth. "[T]here is no liability for the examination of a public record concerning the plaintiff.... [Or] for observing him or even taking his photograph while he is walking on the public highway...." (*Rest.2d Torts*, § 652B) To prove actionable intrusion, the plaintiff must show the defendant penetrated some zone of physical or sensory privacy surrounding, or obtained unwanted access to data about, the plaintiff. The tort is proven only if the plaintiff had an objectively reasonable expectation of seclusion or solitude in the place, conversation or data source.

Cameraman Cooke's mere presence at the accident scene and filming of the events occurring there cannot be deemed either a physical or sensory intrusion on plaintiffs' seclusion. Plaintiffs had no right of ownership or possession of the property where the rescue took place, nor any actual control of the premises. Nor could they have had a reasonable expectation that members of the media would be excluded or prevented from photographing the scene; for journalists to attend and record the scenes of accidents and rescues is in no way unusual or unexpected.

Two aspects of defendants' conduct, however, raise triable issues of intrusion on seclusion. First, a triable issue exists as to whether both plaintiffs had an objectively reasonable expectation of privacy in the interior of the rescue helicopter, which served as an ambulance. Although the attendance of reporters and photographers at the scene of an accident is to be expected, we are aware of no law or custom permitting the press to ride in ambulances or enter hospital rooms during treatment without the patient's consent. Other than the two patients and Cooke, only three people were present in the helicopter, all Mercy Air staff. As the Court of Appeal observed, "[i]t is neither the custom nor the habit of our society that any member of the public at large or its media representatives may hitch a ride in an ambulance and ogle as paramedics care for an injured stranger." (*See also* Green v. Chicago Tribune Co., supra, 221 Ill.Dec. 342, 675 N.E.2d at p. 252 [hospital room not public place]; Barber v. Time, Inc., *supra*, 159 S.W.2d at p. 295 ["Certainly, if there is any right of privacy at all, it should include the right to obtain medical treatment at home or in a hospital ... without personal publicity."].)

Second, Ruth was entitled to a degree of privacy in her conversations with Carnahan and other medical rescuers at the accident scene, and in Carnahan's conversations conveying medical information regarding Ruth to the hospital base. Cooke, perhaps, did not intrude into that zone of privacy merely by being present at a place where he could hear such conversations with unaided ears. But by placing a microphone on Carnahan's person, amplifying and recording what she said and heard, defendants may have listened in on conversations the parties could reasonably have expected to be private.

The Court of Appeal held plaintiffs had no reasonable expectation of privacy at the accident scene itself because the scene was within the sight and hearing of members of the public. The summary judgment record, however, does not support the Court of Appeal's conclusion; instead, it reflects, at the least, the existence of triable issues as to the privacy of certain conversations at the accident scene, as in the helicopter. The videotapes (broadcast and raw footage) show the rescue did not take place "on a heavily traveled highway," as the Court of Appeal stated, but in a ditch many yards from and below the rural superhighway, which is raised somewhat at that point to bridge a nearby crossroad. From the tapes it appears unlikely the plaintiffs' extrication from their car and medical treatment at the scene could have been observed by any persons who, in the lower court's words, "passed by" on the roadway. Even more unlikely is that any passersby on the road could have heard Ruth's conversation with Nurse Carnahan or the other rescuers.

Whether Ruth expected her conversations with Nurse Carnahan or the other rescuers to remain private and whether any such expectation was reasonable are, on the state of the record before us, questions for the jury. We note, however, that several existing legal protections for communications could support the conclusion that Ruth possessed a reasonable expectation of privacy in her conversations with Nurse Carnahan and the other rescuers. A patient's conversation with a provider of medical care in the course of treatment including emergency treatment, carries a traditional and legally well-established expectation of privacy. (See Evid. Code, §§ 990–1007 [physician-patient privilege]; Civ.Code, §§ 56–56.37 [Confidentiality of Medical Information Act].).

Ruth's claim, of course, does not require her to prove a statutory violation, only to prove that she had an objectively reasonable expectation of privacy in her conversations. Whether the circumstances of Ruth's extrication and helicopter rescue would reasonably have indicated to defendants, or to their agent, Cooke, that Ruth would desire and expect her communications to Carnahan and the other rescuers to be confined to them alone, and therefore not to be electronically transmitted and recorded, is a triable issue of fact in this case. As observed earlier, whether anyone present (other than Cooke) was a mere observer, uninvolved in the rescue effort, is unclear from the summary judgment record. Also unclear is who, if anyone, could overhear conversations between Ruth and Carnahan, which were transmitted by a microphone on Carnahan's person, amplified and recorded by defendants. We cannot say, as a matter of law, that Cooke should not have perceived he might be intruding on a confidential communication when he recorded a seriously injured patient's conversations with medical personnel.

We turn to the second element of the intrusion tort, offensiveness of the intrusion. In a widely followed passage, the *Miller* court explained that determining offensiveness requires consideration of all the circumstances of the intrusion, including its degree and setting and the intruder's "motives and objectives." The *Miller* court concluded that reasonable people could regard the camera crew's conduct in filming a man's emergency medical treatment in his home, without seeking or obtaining his or his wife's consent, as showing "a cavalier disregard for ordinary citizens' rights of privacy" and, hence, as highly offensive.

We agree with the *Miller* court that all the circumstances of an intrusion, including the motives or justification of the intruder, are pertinent to the offensiveness element.[17] Motivation or justification becomes particularly important when the intrusion is by a member of the print or broadcast press in the pursuit of news material. Although, as will be discussed more fully later, the First Amendment does not immunize the press from liability for torts or crimes committed in an effort to gather news the constitutional protection of the press does reflect the strong societal interest in effective and complete reporting of events, an interest that may—as a matter of tort law—justify an intrusion that would otherwise be considered offensive. While refusing to recognize a broad privilege in newsgathering against application of generally applicable laws, the United States Supreme Court has also observed that "without some protection for seeking out the news, freedom of the press could be eviscerated." (*Branzburg v. Hayes* 408 U.S. 665, 681 (1972).

In deciding, therefore, whether a reporter's alleged intrusion into private matters (i.e., physical space, conversation or data) is "offensive" and hence actionable as an invasion of privacy, courts must consider the extent to which the intrusion was, under the circumstances, justified by the legitimate motive of gathering the news. Information collecting techniques that may be highly offensive when done for socially unprotected reasons—for purposes of harassment, blackmail or prurient curiosity, for example—may not be offensive to a reasonable person when employed by journalists in pursuit of a socially or politically important story.

The mere fact the intruder was in pursuit of a "story" does not, however, generally justify an otherwise offensive intrusion; offensiveness depends as well on the particular method of investigation used. At one extreme, " 'routine ... reporting techniques,' " such as asking questions of people with information ("including those with confidential or restricted information") could rarely, if ever, be deemed an actionable intrusion. At the other extreme, violation of well-established legal areas of physical or sensory privacy—trespass into a home or tapping a personal telephone line, for example—could rarely, if ever, be justified by a reporter's need to get the story. Such acts would be deemed highly offensive even if the information sought was of weighty public concern; they would also be outside any protection the Constitution provides to newsgathering.

Between these extremes lie difficult cases, many involving the use of photographic and electronic recording equipment. Equipment such as hidden cameras and miniature cordless and directional microphones are powerful investigative tools for newsgathering, but may also be used in ways that severely threaten personal privacy. California tort law provides no bright line on this question; each case must be taken on its facts.

On this summary judgment record, we believe a jury could find defendants' recording of Ruth's communications to Carnahan and other rescuers, and filming in the air ambulance, to be " 'highly offensive to a reasonable person.' " With regard to the depth of the intrusion, a reasonable jury could find highly offensive the placement of a microphone on a medical rescuer in order to intercept what would otherwise be private conversations

---

17. Among other factors, an intrusion may be deemed more offensive to the extent the intruder's behavior created a risk that the target's efforts to evade or resist the intrusion would lead to physical harm to the intruder, the target or others.

with an injured patient. In that setting, as defendants could and should have foreseen, the patient would not know her words were being recorded and would not have occasion to ask about, and object or consent to, recording. Defendants, it could reasonably be said, took calculated advantage of the patient's "vulnerability and confusion." Arguably, the last thing an injured accident victim should have to worry about while being pried from her wrecked car is that a television producer may be recording everything she says to medical personnel for the possible edification and entertainment of casual television viewers.

For much the same reason, a jury could reasonably regard entering and riding in an ambulance—whether on the ground or in the air—with two seriously injured patients to be an egregious intrusion on a place of expected seclusion. Again, the patients, at least in this case, were hardly in a position to keep careful watch on who was riding with them, or to inquire as to everyone's business and consent or object to their presence. A jury could reasonably believe that fundamental respect for human dignity requires the patients' anxious journey be taken only with those whose care is solely for them and out of sight of the prying eyes (or cameras) of others.

Nor can we say as a matter of law that defendants' motive—to gather usable material for a potentially newsworthy story—necessarily privileged their intrusive conduct as a matter of common law tort liability. A reasonable jury could conclude the producers' desire to get footage that would convey the "feel" of the event—the real sights and sounds of a difficult rescue—did not justify either placing a microphone on Nurse Carnahan or filming inside the rescue helicopter. Although defendants' purposes could scarcely be regarded as evil or malicious (in the colloquial sense), their behavior could, even in light of their motives, be thought to show a highly offensive lack of sensitivity and respect for plaintiffs' privacy. A reasonable jury could find that defendants, in placing a microphone on an emergency treatment nurse and recording her conversation with a distressed, disoriented and severely injured patient, without the patient's knowledge or consent, acted with highly offensive disrespect for the patient's personal privacy comparable to, if not quite as extreme as, the disrespect and insensitivity demonstrated in Miller.

Turning to the question of constitutional protection for newsgathering, one finds the decisional law reflects a general rule of nonprotection: the press in its newsgathering activities enjoys no immunity or exemption from generally applicable laws.

Courts have impliedly recognized that a generally applicable law might, under some circumstances, impose an "impermissible burden" on newsgathering such a burden might be found in a law that, as applied to the press, would result in "a significant constriction of the flow of news to the public" and thus "eviscerate[ ]" the freedom of the press. (Branzburg v. Hayes, *supra*, 408 U.S. at pp. 693, 681, 92 S.Ct. at pp. 2662, 2656.) No basis exists, however, for concluding that ... the intrusion tort places such a burden on the press, either in general or under the circumstances of this case. The conduct of journalism does not depend, as a general matter, on the use of secret devices to record private conversations. More specifically, nothing in the record or briefing here suggests that reporting on automobile accidents and medical rescue activities depends on secretly recording accident victims' conversations with rescue personnel or on filming inside an occupied ambulance. Thus, if any exception exists to the general rule that "the First Amendment does not guarantee the press a constitutional right of special access to information not available to the public generally." such exception is inapplicable here.

Defendants urge a rule more protective of press investigative activity. Specifically, they seek a holding that "when intrusion claims are brought in the context of newsgathering conduct, that conduct be deemed protected so long as (1) the information being gathered is about a matter of legitimate concern to the public and (2) the underlying conduct is lawful (i.e., was undertaken without fraud, trespass, etc.)." Neither tort law nor constitutional precedent and policy supports such a broad privilege.

As to constitutional policy, we repeat that the threat of infringement on the liberties of the press from intrusion liability is minor compared with the threat from liability for publication of private facts. Indeed, the distinction led one influential commentator to assert flatly that "[i]ntrusion does not raise first amendment difficulties since its perpetration does not involve speech or other expression." Such a broad statement is probably not warranted; a liability rule, for example, that punished as intrusive a reporter's merely asking questions about matters an organization or person did not choose to publicize would likely be deemed an impermissible restriction on press freedom. But no constitutional precedent or principle of which we are aware gives a reporter general license to intrude in an objectively offensive manner into private places, conversations or matters merely because the reporter thinks he or she may thereby find something that will warrant publication or broadcast.

* * *

California has an anti-paparazzi statute on the books. Cal. Civil Code § 1708.8. The statute makes clear that it does not preempt any common law privacy claims an individual may have. But the statute does add to the common law, both in terms of defining impermissible intrusions and remedies.

Cal. Civil Code § 1708.8

(a) A person is liable for physical invasion of privacy when the defendant knowingly enters onto the land of another person without permission or otherwise committed a trespass in order to physically invade the privacy of the plaintiff with the intent to capture any type of visual image, sound recording, or other physical impression of the plaintiff engaging in a personal or familial activity and the physical invasion occurs in a manner that is offensive to a reasonable person.

(b) A person is liable for constructive invasion of privacy when the defendant attempts to capture, in a manner that is offensive to a reasonable person, any type of visual image, sound recording, or other physical impression of the plaintiff engaging in a personal or familial activity under circumstances in which the plaintiff had a reasonable expectation of privacy, through the use of a visual or auditory enhancing device, regardless of whether there is a physical trespass, if this image, sound recording, or other physical impression could not have been achieved without a trespass unless the visual or auditory enhancing device was used.

(c) An assault or false imprisonment committed with the intent to capture any type of visual image, sound recording, or other physical impression of the plaintiff is subject to subdivisions (d), (e), and (h).

(d) A person who commits any act described in subdivision (a), (b), or (c) is liable for up to three times the amount of any general and special damages that are proximately caused by the violation of this section. This person may also be liable for punitive damages, subject to proof according to Section 3294. If the plaintiff proves that the invasion of privacy was committed for a commercial purpose, the defendant shall also be subject to disgorgement to the plaintiff of any proceeds or other consideration obtained as a result of the violation of this section. A person who comes within the description of this subdivision is also subject to a civil fine of not less than five thousand dollars ($5,000) and not more than fifty thousand dollars ($50,000).

(e) A person who directs, solicits, actually induces, or actually causes another person, regardless of whether there is an employer-employee relationship, to violate any provision of subdivision (a), (b), or (c) is liable for any general, special, and consequential damages resulting from each said violation. In addition, the person that directs, solicits, actually induces, or actually causes another person, regardless of whether there is an employer-employee relationship, to violate this section shall be liable for punitive damages to the extent that an employer would be subject to punitive damages pursuant to subdivision (b) of Section 3294. A person who comes within the description of this subdivision is also subject to a civil fine of not less than five thousand dollars ($5,000) and not more than fifty thousand dollars ($50,000).

(f)(1) The transmission, publication, broadcast, sale, offer for sale, or other use of any visual image, sound recording, or other physical impression that was taken or captured in violation of subdivision (a), (b), or (c) shall not constitute a violation of this section unless the person, in the first transaction following the taking or capture of the visual image, sound recording, or other physical impression, publicly transmitted, published, broadcast, sold or offered for sale, the visual image, sound recording, or other physical impression with actual knowledge that it was taken or captured in violation of subdivision (a), (b), or (c), and provide compensation, consideration, or remuneration, monetary or otherwise, for the rights to the unlawfully obtained visual image, sound recording, or other physical impression.

* * *

1. **The scope of the statute.** Look at paragraph (b) of the statute. Does it provide any meaningful clarification of the concept of "seclusion" or "reasonable expectation of privacy"? Does the statute go far enough in terms of dealing with paparazzi? Too far?

2. **Application.** Would the outcomes in *McLain*, *Mark*, and/or *Tagouma* have changed if this statute had been in place?

Exercise 15.2

Husband, unbeknownst to Wife, installs a video camera in the ceiling of the couple's bedroom and records wife while the couple is still living together. After the couple divorces, Wife sues Husband on an invasion of privacy theory. Should the claim be dismissed?

Exercise 15.3

Reread the facts in Exercise 15.1 at the beginning of the chapter. Imagine that you are the lawyer representing the employee in question in this matter. The employee recently sent you an email on her personal Gmail account, telling her about a recent incident with her supervisor. However, she accessed the account from her employer-provided work computer. If the employer searches her computer and finds this email, (a) would she have an invasion of privacy claim and (b) will the contents still be protected by the attorney-client privilege? Do you have any ethical obligations here concerning your client?

Exercise 15.4

Reread the facts in Exercise 15.1 at the beginning of the chapter. Imagine that you are a lawyer who represents an employer who would like to be able to search an employee's computer if, in the employer's opinion, such a search is necessary. What is your advice?

Exercise 15.5

Bobby, a seventh-grader with a Facebook account, is the plaintiff in a personal injury action against Alice, an adult. Alice's lawyer, Carol, poses as a school friend of Bobby's in the hopes that Bobby will "friend" Carol. Bobby does so, thus giving Carol access to Bobby's Facebook page. Carol routinely goes to this page and gathers information that she hopes to use in the personal injury matter. Bobby's lawyer eventually learns what Carol has done. Is Carol subject to liability? Should she be?

B. Publicity Given to Private Life

Focus Questions: *Ozer v. Borquez*

1. *What should happen on remand?*
2. *What purpose is served by this tort that isn't already served by the tort of defamation?*

Ozer v. Borquez

940 P.2d 371
(Colo. 1997)

Chief Justice VOLLACK delivered the Opinion of the Court.

In June of 1990, Borquez began working as an associate attorney for Ozer & Mullen, P.C. (the Ozer law firm). During his employment with the Ozer law firm, Borquez received three merit raises, the last of which was awarded on February 15, 1992, eleven days prior to his termination.

On February 19, 1992, Borquez, who is homosexual, learned that his partner was diagnosed with Acquired Immune Deficiency Syndrome (AIDS). Borquez' physician advised him that he should be tested for the human immunodeficiency virus (HIV) immediately. Borquez was anxious about his health and determined that he could not effectively represent a client in a deposition that afternoon and an arbitration hearing the following day. Borquez subsequently telephoned his secretary and attempted to arrange for a colleague to fill in for him at the deposition and hearing. Borquez' secretary and another staff member told the president and shareholder of the law firm, Robert Ozer (Ozer), about Borquez' telephone call. Ozer then directed Borquez' secretary to transfer to him any further telephone calls from Borquez.

Borquez and Ozer subsequently spoke twice on the telephone. During the second conversation, Borquez decided that he would disclose his situation to Ozer. Borquez asked Ozer to keep the information he was about to disclose confidential, but Ozer made no reply. Borquez then told Ozer that he was homosexual, that his partner had been diagnosed with AIDS, and that he needed to be tested for HIV. Ozer responded by stating that he would handle the deposition and arbitration hearing and that Borquez should "do what [he needed] to do."

After speaking with Borquez, Ozer telephoned his wife, Renee Ozer, and told her of Borquez' disclosure.[1] Additionally, Ozer informed the law firm's office manager about Borquez' situation and discussed Borquez' disclosure with two of the law firm's secretaries. On February 21, 1992, Borquez returned to the office and became upset when he learned that everyone in the law firm knew about his situation. Later that afternoon, Ozer met with Borquez and told him that Ozer had not agreed to keep Borquez' disclosure confidential.

On February 26, 1992, one week after Borquez made his disclosure to Ozer, Borquez was fired. The Ozer law firm asserted that Borquez was terminated due to the law firm's poor financial circumstances. Borquez filed suit against the Ozer law firm and against Ozer as an individual, claiming wrongful discharge and invasion of privacy.

... The jury found in favor of Borquez and awarded him damages totaling $90,841. The jury set compensatory damages at $30,841 for the wrongful discharge claim and $20,000 for the invasion of privacy claim, and awarded exemplary damages in the sum of $40,000.

II.

[The court reversed the lower court on the wrongful discharge claim.]

III.

It is generally recognized by a majority of jurisdictions that the right of privacy may be invaded in four different ways: (1) unreasonable intrusion upon the seclusion of another; (2) appropriation of another's name or likeness; (3) unreasonable publicity given to another's private life; and (4) publicity that unreasonably places another in a false light before the public. More specifically, a majority of jurisdictions have recognized that the right of privacy encompasses a tort claim based on unreasonable publicity given to one's private life.

In accordance with these jurisdictions, we now recognize in Colorado a tort claim for invasion of privacy in the nature of unreasonable publicity given to one's private life. In order to prevail on such a claim, we hold that the following requirements must be met:

1. Renee Ozer, a shareholder of the Ozer law firm and the supervisor of the Colorado Springs and Pueblo offices of the law firm, in turn disclosed Borquez' situation to a staff attorney at the Colorado Springs office.

(1) the fact or facts disclosed must be private in nature; (2) the disclosure must be made to the public; (3) the disclosure must be one which would be highly offensive to a reasonable person; (4) the fact or facts disclosed cannot be of legitimate concern to the public; and (5) the defendant acted with reckless disregard of the private nature of the fact or facts disclosed.

The first requirement of a tort claim for invasion of privacy in the nature of unreasonable publicity given to one's private life is that the facts disclosed be private in nature. The disclosure of facts that are already public will not support a claim for invasion of privacy. *See* Aquino v. Bulletin Co., 190 Pa.Super. 528, 154 A.2d 422, 426–27 (1959) (holding that issuance of marriage license or divorce decree was matter of public record and could be disclosed without invading right of privacy); Alarcon v. Murphy, 201 Cal.App.3d 1, 248 Cal.Rptr. 26, 29–30 (1988) (holding that arrest warrant which was part of court file is public record and could be disclosed without violating right of privacy). In contrast, facts related to an individual's sexual relations, or "unpleasant or disgraceful" illnesses, are considered private in nature and the disclosure of such facts constitutes an invasion of the individual's right of privacy. Restatement (Second) of Torts §652D cmt. b (1976).

The second requirement of a tort claim for invasion of privacy based on unreasonable publicity given to one's private life is that the disclosure be made to the public. The requirement of public disclosure connotes publicity, which requires communication to the public in general or to a large number of persons, as distinguished from one individual or a few.[7] *See* Brown v. Mullarkey, 632 S.W.2d 507, 509–10 (Mo.Ct.App.1982) (holding that no public disclosure occurred when plaintiff's personnel file was released to attorneys representing defendant in personal injury suit); Porten v. University of San Francisco, 64 Cal.App.3d 825, 134 Cal.Rptr. 839, 841 (1976) (holding that no public disclosure occurred when plaintiff's school grades were disclosed to scholarship and loan commission because grades were not released to public in general or large number of persons).

Although the disclosure must be made to the general public or to a large number of persons, there is no threshold number which constitutes "a large number" of persons. Rather, the facts and circumstances of a particular case must be taken into consideration in determining whether the disclosure was sufficiently public so as to support a claim for invasion of privacy. *See, e.g.*, Kinsey v. Macur, 107 Cal.App.3d 265, 165 Cal.Rptr. 608, 611 (1980) (holding that defendant's dissemination of copies of a letter to only twenty people constituted public disclosure).

The third requirement of a tort claim for invasion of privacy in the nature of unreasonable publicity given to one's private life is that the disclosure be one which would be highly offensive to a reasonable person. The term "highly offensive" has been construed to mean that the disclosure would cause emotional distress or embarrassment to a reasonable person. The determination of whether a disclosure is highly offensive to the reasonable person is a question of fact and depends on the circumstances of a particular case. *Compare* Urbaniak v. Newton, 226 Cal.App.3d 1128, 277 Cal.Rptr. 354, 360 (1991) (holding that disclosure of HIV positive status was highly offensive to reasonable person) *with* Virgil v. Sports

7. We note that public disclosure may occur where the defendant merely initiates the process whereby the information is eventually disclosed to a large number of persons. *See* Beaumont v. Brown, 401 Mich. 80, 257 N.W.2d 522, 530 (1977).

Illustrated, 424 F.Supp. 1286, 1289 (S.D.Cal.1976) (holding that disclosure of person's unflattering habits and idiosyncrasies was not highly offensive to reasonable person).

The fourth requirement of a tort claim for invasion of privacy in the nature of unreasonable publicity given to one's private life is that the facts disclosed are not of legitimate concern to the public. The right of privacy may potentially clash with the rights of free speech and free press guaranteed by the United States and Colorado Constitutions. The rights of free speech and free press protect the public's access to information on matters of legitimate public concern. *See* Cox Broadcasting Corp. v. Cohn, 420 U.S. 469, 491–92, 95 S.Ct. 1029, 1044–45, 43 L.Ed.2d 328 (1975).[8] As such, the right of the individual to keep information private must be balanced against the right to disseminate newsworthy information to the public. *See* Gilbert v. Medical Econs. Co., 665 F.2d 305, 307 (10th Cir.1981). As the Tenth Circuit Court of Appeals stated in *Gilbert*, "to properly balance freedom of the press against the right of privacy, every private fact disclosed in an otherwise truthful, newsworthy publication must have some substantial relevance to a matter of legitimate public interest." *Id.* at 308; *see also* Virgil v. Time, Inc., 527 F.2d 1122, 1129 (9th Cir.1975) (holding that liability may be imposed for invasion of privacy only if matter publicized is of a kind which is not of legitimate concern to public).

The term newsworthy is defined as "[a]ny information disseminated 'for purposes of education, amusement or enlightenment, when the public may reasonably be expected to have a legitimate interest in what is published.'" *Gilbert*, 665 F.2d at 308 (quoting Restatement (Second) of Torts §652D cmt. j (1976)). In determining whether a subject is of legitimate public interest, "[t]he line is to be drawn when the publicity ceases to be the giving of information to which the public is entitled, and becomes a morbid and sensational prying into private lives for its own sake." Restatement (Second) of Torts §652D cmt. h (1976). The newsworthiness test "properly restricts liability for public disclosure of private facts to the extreme case, thereby providing the breathing space needed by the press." *Gilbert*, 665 F.2d at 308. As such, the requirement that the facts disclosed must not be of legitimate concern to the public protects the rights of free speech and free press guaranteed by the United States and Colorado Constitutions.

The final requirement of a tort claim for invasion of privacy in the nature of unreasonable publicity given to one's private life is that the defendant acted with reckless disregard of the private nature of the fact or facts disclosed. A person acts with reckless disregard if, at the time of the publicity, the person knew or should have known that the fact or facts disclosed were private in nature.

Accordingly, we recognize in Colorado a tort claim for invasion of privacy in the nature of unreasonable publicity given to one's private life. We therefore affirm the court of appeals' recognition of this tort claim.

IV.

The final issue before us is whether the court of appeals correctly held that the jury was properly instructed on Borquez' invasion of privacy tort claim based on unreasonable

---

8. In *Cox*, 420 U.S. at 491, 95 S.Ct. at 1044, the United States Supreme Court held that under the First Amendment, a plaintiff could not recover for publicity of facts that were a matter of public record. However, the Court explicitly declined to address the broader question of whether a plaintiff could constitutionally recover for publicity of private facts that are not a matter of public record. *See id.*

publicity given to one's private life. As discussed in section III above, this tort claim requires public disclosure of private facts. Public disclosure connotes publicity, and the term "publicity" is distinct from the term "publication." *See* Restatement (Second) of Torts § 652D cmt. a (1976). The term "publicity" requires communication to the public in general or to a large number of persons rather than to just one individual or a few. In contrast, the term "publication," as it is applied in defamation claims, "is a word of art, which includes any communication by the defendant to a third person." Restatement (Second) of Torts § 652D cmt. a (1976).

In the current case, the trial court instructed the jury regarding the public disclosure requirement of Borquez' claim for invasion of privacy as follows:

> A statement is "published" when it is communicated orally to and is understood by some person other than the plaintiff.

Instruction No. 7. The trial court thus instructed the jury that the public disclosure requirement was met if Ozer's disclosure was simply made to "some other person" rather than to a large number of persons or the general public. The effect of this instruction was to permit the jury to render a verdict in favor of Borquez if it found that Ozer disclosed to any single individual the fact of Borquez' homosexuality and exposure to AIDS. However, the public disclosure requirement renders Ozer liable for Borquez' invasion of privacy claim only if Ozer disclosed Borquez' situation to a large number of persons or the general public. Because the trial court instructed the jury regarding the term "publication" rather than "publicity," and because the terms "publication" and "publicity" are not interchangeable, we hold that the trial court's instruction was erroneous. We therefore reverse the court of appeals' holding on this issue.

* * *

1. **Special relationship with "the public."** Some courts have held that the publication element "may be satisfied by proof of disclosure to a very limited number of people when a special relationship exists between the plaintiff and 'the public' to whom the information has been disclosed." McSurely v. McClellan, 753 F.2d 88, 112 (D.C. Cir. 1985); Miller v. Motorola, Inc., 560 N.E.2d 900 (Ill. Ct. App. 1990).

2. **Privacy statutes.** Some privacy statutes not only limit the ability of one to intrude into designated areas but also limit the ability to distribute the information acquired as a result of that intrusion. HIPAA, 42 U.S.C. § 1320d-2(b)(ii); ADA, 42 U.S.C. § 12112(d)(3)(B).

Exercise 15.6

Neil was attempting a hostile takeover of Stills, Inc. In an attempt to resist the takeover, the members of the Stills Board of Directors placed Neil under surveillance in an attempt to uncover embarrassing information. Their efforts were rewarded when they learned that Neil was engaged in an extramarital affair. They disclosed this information to Neil's wife, who promptly hired a lawyer and divorced Neil. Eventually, Neil's affair became fodder for the tabloids. At the same time, the board informed some of Stills, Inc.'s larger shareholders of the fact that Neil had been convicted of a felony 20 years earlier and sent along the indictment, some docket information, and Neil's mug shot. Could Neil recover for either disclosure under Colorado law? What if the person attempting the takeover was Donald Trump instead of Neil?

Exercise 15.7

Robert posts a highly embarrassing story about Tobin on Robert's Facebook page. The page is accessible only to Robert's 25 Facebook friends. Given the highly embarrassing and humorous details of the story, the facts concerning Tobin go viral after Robert's Facebook friends tell their friends, who tell their friends, who tell their friends, etc. Can Tobin satisfy the publicity element if he sues under the theory advanced in *Ozer*?

Exercise 15.8

Bruce was a citizen of the state of Arklahoma who had been deprived of certain state benefits. He submitted a request under the state Freedom of Information Act (FOIA), requesting the names and home addresses of employees in the state agency that had denied his benefits. Under state law, employees whose information is subject to a FOIA request may contest the disclosure of the information. In this instance, ten employees contested the disclosure. Five of these employees established that they had gone to considerable lengths to keep their personal information (including their home addresses) private. These measures included using a post office box as an address, keeping their names off mailing lists, and keeping their names and addresses out of phone book listings.

Section 1 of Arklahoma's FOIA provides, "[e]xcept as otherwise provided by any federal law or state statute [including the exceptions to the act], all records maintained or kept on file by any public agency ... shall be public records and every person shall have the right to inspect such records promptly during regular office or business hours or to receive a copy of such records in accordance with the provisions of this Act." Section 2 contains the relevant exceptions, one of which provides in relevant part that "[n]othing in the Freedom of Information Act shall be construed to require disclosure of ... (2) Personnel or medical files and similar files the disclosure of which would constitute an invasion of personal privacy...." The Arklahoma Supreme Court has held that the appropriate test for invasion of personal privacy under Section 2 is essentially the same as that delineated in *Ozer v. Borquez* above.

Is disclosure of the employees' addresses required? Is it required for all of the addresses?

Focus Questions: *Winegard v. Lawson*

1. *Why does the plaintiff's claim fail?*
2. *Regardless of whether you agree with the court's interpretation of the statute at issue, is the court's decision sound from a policy standpoint? How might it impact the advice a lawyer gives to a client in a future case?*

Winegard v. Lawson

260 N.W.2d 816
(Iowa 1977)

McCORMICK, Justice.

Plaintiff John R. Winegard filed a petition in two divisions seeking damages for invasion of privacy and defamation against defendants Richard A. Larsen, Stephen L. Schalk, and Robert Bradfield, members of a Davenport law firm. The trial court sustained defendants' motion for summary judgment on the invasion of privacy claim, and plaintiff appeals from that ruling. We affirm.

The questions here are (1) whether an invasion of privacy action can be based on oral statements, (2) whether the confidentiality provisions of § 598.26, The Code, apply to filings in this court, and (3) whether the record shows a genuine issue of material fact upon which plaintiff is entitled to trial.

Plaintiff's action is predicated on statements allegedly made by one or more of the defendants to a reporter for the Des Moines Register and Tribune Company concerning a Des Moines County dissolution of marriage action in which plaintiff was respondent....

In this action plaintiff contends his privacy was invaded by the alleged statements to the reporter. He singles out the following parts of resulting newspaper articles as showing actionable statements:

1. (from the *Des Moines Tribune* of January 8, 1975)

> Mrs. Winegard's attorney, Stephen Schalk, of Davenport, said the two exchanged wedding rings during a return flight from Las Vegas in 1971 and have held themselves out to the community as husband and wife since that time.
>
> A daughter from one of Sally Ann Winegard's previous marriages had her name changed to Winegard by the two adults, according to the attorney.

2. (from the *Des Moines Register* of January 9, 1975)

> Sally Ann Winegard's attorney, Stephen Schalk of Davenport said the two exchanged wedding rings during a return flight from Las Vegas in 1971 and have held themselves out to the community as husband and wife since that time.
>
> A daughter from one of Sally Ann Winegard's previous marriages had her last name changed to Winegard by the two adults, according to the attorney.

3. (from *The Hawkeye*, of Burlington, on January 9, 1975)

> The pair has allegedly lived together since 1971. Her attorney, Stephen Schalk of Davenport has said they exchanged wedding rings that year and have since shown themselves to the community as husband and wife.

Defendants alleged in their motion for summary judgment that no genuine issue of material fact existed to preclude judgment for them as a matter of law. In support of their motion they introduced trial court findings of fact and conclusions of law from the dissolution action, a copy of a complaint filed by plaintiff in federal court in an effort to halt discovery of his financial affairs in the dissolution case, and the Polk County district court ruling denying plaintiff's motion to compel discovery of the newspaper reporter. In resisting the motion, plaintiff introduced an affidavit in which he denied the truth of the statements attributed to Schalk in the newspaper articles, copies of motions filed by him in the Polk County action, copies of the petition for certiorari and writ of certiorari issued to the Polk County district court, orders of this court sequestering documents relating to the dissolution action in the certiorari case in this court, and an affidavit that the dissolution trial was closed to the public.

The specific legal issues on which the motion for summary judgment was heard were raised in a brief which defendants filed with their motion. After hearing the motion, the trial court overruled it as to the defamation division of the petition but sustained it as to the invasion of privacy division. The court held defendants were entitled to summary judgment on the invasion of privacy claim § 598.26 cannot be the basis of a civil suit, the facts alleged to invade plaintiff's privacy were made public by him when he filed his complaint in the federal court and his application for interlocutory appeal with this court in the dissolution case, and statements which accurately report a judicial proceeding do not constitute an invasion of privacy. This appeal by plaintiff ensued.

I. Are oral statements actionable? [The court concluded that they are.]

II. Do the confidentiality provisions of Code § 598.26 apply in this court? The trial court held plaintiff's invasion of privacy claim could not be based on § 598.26, The Code. This statute provides for confidentiality, in defined circumstances, of the record and evidence in dissolution of marriage cases and includes a misdemeanor penalty for violation. The court's holding rested on two bases. The first was that a violation of the statute will not support a civil action for invasion of privacy. The other was that its protection is not available here in any event.

The statute provides:

> The record and evidence in all cases where a marriage dissolution is sought shall be closed to all but the court and its officers, and access thereto shall be refused until a decree of dissolution has been entered. If the action is dismissed judgment for costs shall be entered in the judgment docket and lien index. The clerk shall maintain a separate docket for dissolution of marriage actions. No officer or other person shall permit a copy of any of the testimony, or pleading, or the substance thereof, to be made available to any person other than a party or attorney to the action. Nothing in this section shall be construed to prohibit publication of the original notice as provided by the rules of civil procedure. Violation of the provisions of this section shall be a public offense, punishable by a fine of not more than one hundred dollars, or imprisonment in the county jail not more than thirty days, or by both such fine and imprisonment.

The first basis relied on by the trial court is untenable. We have recognized that those within the protection of criminal statutes in Iowa have a statutory right to civil remedies for harm caused by their violation in all cases. As a party to the dissolution action involved here, plaintiff is in the class protected by § 598.26. Therefore he is not barred from seeking to recover for alleged harm caused by violation of the statute.

The second basis relied on by the trial court presents a more complex problem. [T]he dissolution action was bifurcated by agreement of counsel, and the question of the existence of the marriage was litigated first. The dissolution trial court, Judge D. B. Hendrickson, subsequently filed an eleven page document denominated "Findings of Fact and Conclusions of Law." This ruling is not limited to reciting findings of fact. Much of it consists of a summary of the testimony of the two parties. The court concluded the ruling by holding "John and Sally are husband and wife by virtue of a common law marriage."

On October 21, 1974, plaintiff filed with this court an application for permission to appeal Judge Hendrickson's ruling attaching a copy of the ruling as an exhibit. The application was denied on November 26, 1974. We entered an ordered sequestering this file on February 15, 1975.

We must decide the issue in the present appeal. If § 598.26 applies to records of this court, plaintiff did not lose its protection by filing the Hendrickson ruling with our clerk when he sought permission to appeal. We need not decide what the effect would be of our maintaining the appeal papers as a public record prior to the February 1975 sequestration order because we hold § 598.26 does not apply to proceedings in this court.

Principles governing statutory interpretation are summarized in *Iowa National Industrial Loan Company v. Iowa Department of Revenue*, 224 N.W.2d 437, 439–440 (Iowa 1974). We search for legislative intent. Statutes which restrict access to court records are in derogation of the common law and are to be strictly construed. Mulford v. Davey, 64 Nev. 506, 186 P.2d 360 (1947). If the legislature desires secrecy in the judicial process, it must say so plainly.

Code chapter 598 concerns district court actions for dissolution of marriage in Iowa. Those actions ordinarily proceed to conclusion in district court. In order to foster conciliation and discourage the parties from a public freezing of position, the legislature provided in § 598.26 for confidentiality of the record and evidence in the case "until a decree of dissolution has been entered." The statute limits access to "the court and its officers." The duty to maintain a separate docket is imposed on "(t)he clerk."

Numerous references to "the court" and "the clerk" occur in chapter 598 outside of § 598.26. It is manifest that these terms refer to the district court, which has original jurisdiction of dissolution actions, and the clerk who serves that court. *See, e.g.*, s 598.11 ("The court may order either party to pay the clerk...."); § 598.15 ("The petition may be presented to the court...."); § 598.17 ("A decree dissolving the marriage may be entered when the court is satisfied...."). We hold the terms "court" and "clerk" have the same meaning in § 598.26 as they do in the other sections of chapter 598. They refer to the district court and its clerk; they do not include the supreme court and its clerk.

Assuming appeal of a ruling before final decree, it would be impossible for this court to make even its opinion public if § 598.26 reached the records of this court. The statute purports to require secrecy until final decree of dissolution is entered. Yet our opinions are a matter of public record. See § 684.12, The Code.

We believe the legislature intended § 598.26 to apply only to the record and evidence in district court. This enables the statutory purpose to be accomplished in most cases. An appeal prior to final decree in a dissolution action is exceptional and is beyond the scope of § 598.26.

Perhaps the purpose of § 598.26 would be unduly attenuated in any event if it did extend to the appellate level. A dissolution litigant who seeks review of an interlocutory order is usually frozen into an adversary position from which he is unlikely to retreat. It is anomalous in the present case that this plaintiff, who aggressively contends no marriage exists, seeks a civil remedy under the aegis of a statute designed to encourage reconciliation.

We hold plaintiff's application for interlocutory appeal, with Judge Hendrickson's findings and conclusions attached, became a matter of public record when it was filed in this court. Therefore, for purposes of the present case, the information in it was public and not private. The portion of the record and evidence which remained in the district court retained its confidentiality.

On this basis, we agree with the trial court that § 598.26 provided no protection to plaintiff from disclosure of the information in the Hendrickson ruling.

III. Is there a genuine issue of material fact for trial? The trial court held the public nature of the Hendrickson findings and conclusions was sufficient to establish the public nature of the information in the statements attributed to defendant Schalk in the news stories, eliminating them as a basis for invasion of privacy.

We think the Hendrickson ruling is important here for several reasons. It shows the testimony of the parties in the dissolution action. Because it was a public record at the time the alleged Schalk statements were made, it provides a basis for determining whether plaintiff had a right of privacy regarding the information contained in those statements.

[According to] §652D [of the *Restatement (Second) of Torts*]:

> One who gives publicity to a matter concerning the private life of another is subject to liability to the other for invasion of his privacy, if the matter publicized is of a kind that
>
> (a) would be highly offensive to a reasonable person, and
>
> (b) is not of legitimate concern to the public.

As noted in Comment b under §652D, this rule applies only to publicity given to matters concerning the private, as distinguished from the public, life of an individual and "(t)here is no liability when the defendant merely gives further publicity to information about the plaintiff that is already public." This theory is available only when the defendant has publicly disclosed private facts. Under this rule defendants could not be held liable for publicizing matters contained in Judge Hendrickson's ruling. Plaintiff had no right as of October 21, 1974, to keep that information secret.

...

Under the record, we find defendants established that no genuine issue of fact existed from which a trier of fact could find the alleged statements invaded plaintiff's privacy on any cognizable theory. The trial court was correct in entering summary judgment on that division of the petition. The court's ruling on the defamation division is not before us, and we intimate no view on it.

* * *

1. Oral statements and publicity. Warren and Brandeis originally surmised that invasion of privacy claims should be limited to written publications unless an oral statement resulted in special injury. Warren and Brandeis, *The Right to Privacy*, 4 Harv.L.Rev. 193, 217 (1890). Today, however, most courts recognize a claim of public disclosure of private facts based upon oral statements resulting in publicity. Winegard v. Larsen, 260 N.W.2d 816, 819 (Iowa 1977).

2. Constitutional concerns. In *Florida Star v. B.J.F.*, 491 U.S. 524 (1989), a newspaper reporter-trainee published the name of a rape victim in a news story. The reporter obtained the name from a police report involving the rape. A Florida statute made it unlawful to "print, publish, or broadcast ... in any instrument of mass communication" the name of the victim of a sexual offense." The victim sued the paper, alleging that the paper had negligently violated the statute. The Supreme Court held that imposing damages in this instance would violate the First Amendment. While stopping short of holding that the publication of truthful information may never be actionable, the Court did say that "where a newspaper publishes truthful information which it has lawfully obtained, punishment may lawfully be imposed, if at all, only when narrowly tailored to a state interest of the highest order." *Id.* at 541. An earlier Supreme Court decision reached a similar conclusion where a broadcasting company identified a rape victim in violation of a state statute during coverage of an open trial. Cox Broadcasting Corporation v. Cohn, 420 U.S. 469 (1975). The Iowa Supreme Court was able to distinguish *Winegard* on the grounds that the dissolution trial had not been open to the public in the first place.

* * *

C. False Light

Focus Question: *Magenis v. Fisher Broadcasting, Inc.*

1. *How does a false light claim differ from a defamation claim?*
2. *Should false light claims and defamation claims have different statutes of limitation?*

Magenis v. Fisher Broadcasting, Inc.

798 P.2d 1106
(Or. App. 1990)

BUTTLER, Presiding Judge.

Plaintiffs, Timothy and Kathy Magenis and their four minor children, filed their complaint on November 18, 1987, alleging that defendants "trespassed upon ... plaintiffs' seclusion" when they accompanied police officers, who were executing a warrant to search plaintiffs' residence, and filmed the raid with video cameras and that defendants placed them in a false light by broadcasting the film on television.

In the "false light" claim, plaintiffs allege, in part:

> Defendants unreasonably placed plaintiffs in a false light before the public by broadcasting over defendant Fisher Broadcasting, Inc.'s television station, KATU, on May 9, 1986, that plaintiffs were involved with stolen vehicles and narcotics.

It is apparent on the face of the complaint that the action was filed more than one year after the alleged publicity. The trial court reasoned that the essence of the claim was that plaintiffs had been libeled or slandered; accordingly, it struck the false light claim as to Timothy and Kathy, on the ground that it is barred by the one-year limitation applicable to libel and slander. ORS 12.120(2). Plaintiffs argue that, because "false light" is a theory of recovery for invasion of privacy and because it is not a necessary element of a false light claim that the plaintiff be defamed, the defamation Statute of Limitations does not apply. Rather, they contend that ORS 12.110(1), the "catch-all" tort limitation [which has a two-year limit], is applicable.

In *Dean v. Guard Publishing Co.*, 73 Or.App. 656, 699 P.2d 1158 (1985), we held that the "false light" aspect of the tort of invasion of privacy is actionable in Oregon. We adopted the elements as stated in *Restatement (Second) Torts* § 652:

> One who gives publicity to a matter concerning another that places the other before the public in a false light is subject to liability to the other for invasion of his privacy, if

(a) the false light in which the other was placed would be highly offensive to a reasonable person, and

(b) the actor has knowledge of or acted in reckless disregard as to the falsity of the publicized matter and the false light in which the other would be placed.

As we stated in *Dean*, the torts of false light and defamation are similar. Both require proof that the published material was not true. They are theoretically distinct, however, in that a defamation action is primarily concerned with damage to reputation, while a claim of false light addresses the plaintiff's interest in being left alone and compensates for mental and emotional suffering resulting from the invasion. Prosser and Keeton, Torts 864, § 117 (5th ed 1984). A person need not be defamed to bring a false light claim:

> "It is enough that he is given unreasonable and highly objectionable publicity that attributes to him characteristics, conduct or beliefs that are false, and so is placed before the public in a false position. When this is the case and the matter attributed to the plaintiff is not defamatory, the rule here stated affords a different remedy, not available in an action for defamation." Restatement (Second) Torts § 652E, comment b.

Thus, although not all false light cases are actionable as defamation, all defamation cases involving publicity are potentially actionable as false light claims. When the published statement complained of is both false and defamatory, the plaintiff may proceed on either theory, or both.

Some courts, focusing on the fact that the tort of false light is distinct from defamation, have held that it should be treated separately for purposes of the Statute of Limitations. They generally conclude, as plaintiffs here contend, that the "catch-all" tort limitation should apply. *See* Rinsley v. Brandt, 446 F.Supp. 850 (D.Kan.1977).

The similarities of the two torts have led other courts to conclude that the Statute of Limitations for defamation should apply to the tort of false light. Smith v. Esquire, Inc., 494 F.Supp. 967 (D.Md.1980); Wiener v. Superior Court of Los Angeles County, 58 Cal.App.3rd, 130 Cal.Rptr. 61 (1976); Eastwood v. Cascade Broadcasting Co., 106 Wash.2d 466, 722 P.2d 1295 (1986). In *Smith*, the court reasoned that to hold otherwise would allow the plaintiff in any defamation action where there has been a general publication to avoid the one year statute merely by characterizing the claim as invasion of privacy. *Smith v. Esquire, Inc., supra*, 494 F.Supp. at 970.

No Oregon case has addressed the question. However, the Supreme Court's decision in *Coe v. Statesman-Journal Co.*, 277 Or. 117, 560 P.2d 254 (1977), leads us to conclude that the defamation limitation applies. There, the plaintiff was a public official who was also a candidate for public office. Before the election, the defendant published in its newspaper an article about a third party who was a convicted embezzler with a criminal record and published a picture of the plaintiff with a caption bearing the third party's name and a picture of the third party bearing the plaintiff's name. The plaintiff filed a claim for negligent injury to his reputation.

In deciding that ORS 12.120(2), the libel and slander statute, applied, the court reasoned that an action seeking damages for injury to reputation is defamation, whether the defendant's alleged acts were negligent, inadvertent or intentional. Similarly, here, although plaintiffs characterized their claim as "false light," the alleged false light-that "plaintiffs were involved with stolen vehicles and narcotics"—is plainly defamatory. Plaintiffs could have filed a claim for defamation. That being the case, we conclude that the specific defamation Statute of Limitations controls. To hold otherwise would permit a plaintiff to elect the longer limitation period of ORS 12.110(1) simply by characterizing a defamation claim as one for false light. We conclude that, when a claim characterized as false light alleges facts that also constitute a claim for defamation, the claim must be filed within the period for bringing a defamation claim. We affirm the trial court's ruling that the false light claims of Timothy and Kathy are barred by ORS 12.120(2).

* * *

Judicial reluctance to recognize false light claims. Although a majority of courts to consider the issue have recognized false light claims, Meyerkord v. Zipatoni Co., 276 S.W.3d 319, 326 (Mo. Ct. App. 2008), a significant number have refused to do so. Many of the courts that have refused to recognize the tort have done because of concerns over the overlap with defamation, "but without the attendant protections of the First Amendment." Jews for Jesus, Inc. v. Rapp, 997 So. 2d 1098, 1100 (Fla. 2008); *see also* Patricia Avidan, Comment, *Protecting the Media's First Amendment Rights in Florida: Making False Light Plaintiffs Play by Defamation Rules*, 35 Stetson L. Rev. 227, 226 (2005).

Exercise 15.9

For each of the following, decide whether the plaintiff can make out a prima facie case of defamation, false light, or both:

(a) Newspaper runs a story about teenage drug use and promiscuity in the local community. The photograph appearing above the headline of the story is of Plaintiff and other teenagers.

(b) Plaintiff sued the organization Jews for Jesus, an organization which has views regarding Jesus Christ that are in conflict with traditional tenets of Judaism. The organization's newsletter ran a story, written by Plaintiff's stepson, which said that Plaintiff, who is Jewish, had become a believer in the organization's beliefs.

(c) Plaintiff posed for photographs that were to be used in advertisement. Without her permission, the photographer sold one of the photos to a book publisher, which placed the photo on the cover of a book. The cover of the book described the book as an autobiographical account of a woman who married a man who wound up going mad and describes the book as a story of "marriage and madness." The photo of Plaintiff appears in a shattered picture frame on the cover of the book.

D. Misappropriation of the Right of Publicity

Of the four types of invasion of privacy, the first three covered in this chapter are primarily concerned with compensating a victim for the loss of dignity and emotional distress suffered as a result of the invasion. The final type of privacy claim—known generically as misappropriation of the right of publicity—is concerned with a different type of harm. Although misappropriation claims fit uneasily under the heading of invasion of privacy, the privacy torts initially got their start with what was essentially a misappropriation claim. Roberson v. Rochester Folding Box Co., 64 N.E. 442 (N.Y. 1902) involved a plaintiff's claim that the defendant, a flour company, used her picture without her permission in order to sell its product. Over a decade earlier, Samuel Warren and future Supreme Court Justice Louis Brandeis had argued in a law review article in favor of a tort that would recognize one's right of privacy. *The Right to Privacy*, 4 Harv. L. Rev. 193 (1890). The New York Court of Appeals rejected the plaintiff's argument in *Roberson* that the defendant had invaded her privacy. However, the New York legislature responded by enacting a statutory right of privacy that prohibits a defendant from using an individual's "name, portrait, picture or voice ... for advertising purposes or for the purposes of trade without ... written consent" and provides a private right of action for a violation. N.Y. Civil Rights Law §§ 50, 51. As described by one court, "[t]he sort of commercial exploitation prohibited and compensable if violated is solicitation for patronage." Costanza v. Seinfeld, 693 N.Y.S.2d 897, 900 (N.Y. Sup. Ct. 1999). Thus, "works of fiction and satire do not fall within the narrow scope of the statutory phrases 'advertising' and 'trade.'" Hampton v. Guare, 195 A.D.2d 366, 366 (N.Y. A.D. 1993). New York's approach proved to be influential.

Focus Questions: *Doe v. TCI Cablevision*

1. *Would the plaintiff have had a triable claim if the plaintiff and the character in the comic had completely different names, but the traits of the character would nonetheless lead the audience to understand that the traits were referring to the plaintiff?*
2. *How does the standard articulated by the court differ from the other standards the court identifies with respect to the First Amendment issues implicated by the tort?*

Doe v. TCI Cablevision

110 S.W.3d 363
(Mo. 2003)

STEPHEN N. LIMBAUGH, JR., Judge.

Appellant Anthony Twist, also known as Tony Twist, is a former professional hockey player in the National Hockey League. After learning of the existence of a comic book, titled *Spawn*, that contained a villainous character sharing his name, Twist brought misappropriation of name and defamation claims against respondents, the creators, publishers and marketers of Spawn and related promotional products. Respondents defended on First Amendment grounds. The circuit court dismissed the defamation count, but allowed the misappropriation of name count to go to trial, which resulted in a jury verdict in favor of Twist in the amount of $24,500,000. The circuit court, however, granted respondents' motion for judgment notwithstanding the verdict and, in the alternative, ordered a new trial in the event that its judgment notwithstanding the verdict was overturned on appeal. A request for injunctive relief was also denied. After appeal to the Court of Appeals, Eastern District, this Court granted transfer. Mo. Const. art. V, sec. 10.

I.

Tony Twist began his NHL career in 1988 playing for the St. Louis Blues, later to be transferred to the Quebec Nordiques, only to return to St. Louis where he finished his career in 1999, due to injuries suffered in a motorcycle accident. During his hockey career, Twist became the League's preeminent "enforcer," a player whose chief responsibility was to protect goal scorers from physical assaults by opponents. In that role, Twist was notorious for his violent tactics on the ice. Describing Twist, a Sports Illustrated writer said: "It takes a special talent to stand on skates and beat someone senseless, and no one does it better than the St. Louis Blues left winger." Austin Murphy, Fighting For A Living: St. Louis Blues Enforcer Tony Twist, Whose Pugilistic Talents Appear To Run In The Family, Doesn't Pull Any Punches On The Job, Sports Illustrated, Mar. 16, 1998, at 42. The article goes on to quote Twist as saying, "I want to hurt them. I want to end the fight as soon as possible and I want the guy to remember it." *Id.*

Despite his well-deserved reputation as a tough-guy "enforcer," or perhaps because of that reputation, Twist was immensely popular with the hometown fans. He endorsed products, appeared on radio and television, hosted the "Tony Twist" television talk show for two years, and became actively involved with several children's charities. It is undisputed that Twist engaged in these activities to foster a positive image of himself in the community and to prepare for a career after hockey as a sports commentator and product endorser.

Respondent Todd McFarlane, an avowed hockey fan and president of Todd McFarlane Productions, Inc. (TMP), created Spawn in 1992. TMP employs the writers, artists and creative staff responsible for production of the comic book. *Spawn* is marketed and distributed monthly by Image Comics, Inc., which was formed by McFarlane and others.

Spawn is "a dark and surreal fantasy" centered on a character named Al Simmons, a CIA assassin who was killed by the Mafia and descended to hell upon death. Simmons, having made a deal with the devil, was transformed into the creature *Spawn* and returned to earth to commit various violent and sexual acts on the devil's behalf. In 1993, a fictional character named "Anthony 'Tony Twist' Twistelli" was added to the *Spawn* storyline. The fictional "Tony Twist" is a Mafia don whose list of evil deeds includes multiple murders, abduction of children and sex with prostitutes. The fictional and real Tony Twist bear no physical resemblance to each other and, aside from the common nickname, are similar only in that each can be characterized as having an "enforcer" or tough-guy persona.

Each issue of the *Spawn* comic book contains a section entitled "Spawning Ground" in which fan letters are published and McFarlane responds to fan questions. In the September 1994 issue, McFarlane admitted that some of the *Spawn* characters were named after professional hockey players, including the "Tony Twist" character: "Antonio Twistelli, a/k/a Tony Twist, is actually the name of a hockey player of the Quebec Nordiques."

In 1997, Twist became aware of the existence of *Spawn* and of the comic book's use of his name for that of the villainous character. On one occasion, several young hockey fans approached Twist's mother with *Spawn* trading cards depicting the Mafia character "Tony Twist." ...

In October 1997, Twist filed suit against McFarlane and various companies associated with the *Spawn* comic book (collectively "respondents"), seeking an injunction and damages for, inter alia, misappropriation of name and defamation, the latter claim being later dismissed. McFarlane and the other defendants filed motions for summary judgment asserting First Amendment protection from a prosecution of the misappropriation of name claim, but the motions were overruled.

At trial, McFarlane denied that the comic book character was "about" the real-life Tony Twist despite the fact that the names were the same. McFarlane also denied that he or the other defendants had attained any benefit by using Twist's name. Twist, however, presented evidence that McFarlane and the other defendants had indeed benefited by using his name. For example, Twist introduced evidence suggesting that in marketing *Spawn* products, McFarlane directly targeted hockey fans—Twist's primary fan base—by producing and licensing *Spawn* logo hockey pucks, hockey jerseys and toy zambonis. On cross-examination, McFarlane admitted that on one occasion defendants sponsored "*Spawn* Night" at a minor league hockey game, where McFarlane personally appeared and distributed *Spawn* products, including products containing the "Tony Twist" character. Another "*Spawn* Night" was planned to take place at a subsequent NHL game, but the event never occurred. On the issue of damages, Twist, through purported expert testimony, offered a formula for determining the fair market value that McFarlane and the other defendants should have paid Twist to use his name. In addition, Twist introduced evidence that his association with the *Spawn* character resulted in a diminution in the commercial value of his name as an endorser of products. To that end, Sean Philips, a former executive of a sports nutrition company, testified that his company withdrew a $100,000 offer to Twist to serve as the company's product endorser after Philips learned that Twist's name was associated with the evil Mafia don in the *Spawn* comic book.

II.

The tort of misappropriation of name is one of four recognized torts falling under the general heading of invasion of privacy. The interest protected by the misappropriation of name tort "is the interest of the individual in the exclusive use of his own identity, in so far as it is represented by his name or likeness, and in so far as the use may be of benefit to him or others." Restatement (Second) of Torts sec. 652C cmt. a (1977). Recently, development of the misappropriation of name tort has given rise to a separate yet similar tort termed the "right of publicity," which is said to "protect a person from losing the benefit of their [sic] work in creating a publicly recognizable persona." Bear Foot, Inc. v. Chandler, 965 S.W.2d 386, 389 (Mo.App.1998). Though facially similar, the protections afforded by each tort are slightly different: "the [misappropriation of name tort] protects against intrusion upon an individual's private self-esteem and dignity, while the right of publicity protects against commercial loss caused by appropriation of an individual's [identity] for commercial exploitation." 4 J. Thomas McCarthy, McCarthy on Trademarks and Unfair Competition sec. 28.6 (4th ed.2003).

Because the two torts differ in the type of protection that each seeks to provide, there are corresponding differences between the types of damages that may be recovered. In a misappropriation of name action, a plaintiff may recover damages not only for pecuniary loss, but also for mental or emotional distress and suffering. By contrast, in a right of publicity action, "the measure of damages properly focuses on the pecuniary loss to the plaintiff or the unjust pecuniary gain to the defendant." Restatement (Third) of Unfair Competition sec. 49 cmt. b.

In this case, Twist seeks to recover the amount of the fair market value that respondents should have paid to use his name in connection with *Spawn* products and for damage done to the commercial value—in effect the endorsement value—of his name. Therefore, Twist's case, though brought as a misappropriation of name action, is more precisely labeled a right of publicity action—a point that both parties appear to concede in their briefs.

Despite the differences in the types of damages that may be recovered, the elements of the two torts are essentially the same. To establish the misappropriation tort, the plaintiff must prove that the defendant used the plaintiff's name without consent to obtain some advantage. Nemani v. St. Louis Univ., 33 S.W.3d 184, 185 (Mo. banc 2000). In a right of publicity action, the plaintiff must prove the same elements as in a misappropriation suit, with the minor exception that the plaintiff must prove that the defendant used the name to obtain a commercial advantage. Restatement (Third) of Unfair Competition sec. 46; *see also* Restatement (Second) of Torts sec. 652C cmt. b (explaining that, in contrast, the misappropriation of name tort applies when plaintiff's name is used for commercial or non-commercial advantage). Given the similarity of elements of the two actions, Missouri cases analyzing the tort of misappropriation of name are pertinent to our recognition of a right of publicity claim.

In *Nemani*, the plaintiff, a research professor, brought suit against St. Louis University after the university used plaintiff's name in support of a federal grant application. This Court, reviewing the claim as a misappropriation of name tort, held that a defendant is liable under the tort when it uses a plaintiff's name without consent to obtain an advantage. However, this Court was careful to point out that "[n]ot all uses of another's name are tortious":

> It is the plaintiff's name as a *symbol of [his] identity* that is involved here, and not [his name] as a mere name. Name appropriation occurs where a defendant makes use of the name to pirate the plaintiff's identity for some advantage.

Id. (citations omitted) (emphasis added).

To summarize, in view of *Nemani* and ... consistent with the *Restatement (Third) of Unfair Competition*, the elements of a right of publicity action include: (1) That defendant used plaintiff's name as a symbol of his identity (2) without consent (3) and with the intent to obtain a commercial advantage.

In this case, the circuit court's entry of JNOV was based on a finding that Twist failed to make a submissible case on the commercial advantage element. In addition, and though the court implicitly held otherwise, respondents claim that the grant of JNOV also was justified because Twist failed to prove that his name was used as "symbol of his identity."

A.

Respondents' initial contention that Twist did not prove that his name was used as a "symbol of his identity" is spurious. To establish that a defendant used a plaintiff's name as a symbol of his identity, "the name used by the defendant must be understood by the audience as referring to the plaintiff." Restatement (Third) of Unfair Competition sec. 46 cmt. d. In resolving this issue, the fact-finder may consider evidence including "the nature and extent of the identifying characteristics used by the defendant, the defendant's intent, the fame of the plaintiff, evidence of actual identification made by third persons, and surveys or other evidence indicating the perceptions of the audience." Restatement (Third) of Unfair Competition sec. 46 cmt. d.

Here, all parties agree that the "Tony Twist" character is not "about" him, in that the character does not physically resemble Twist nor does the Spawn story line attempt to track Twist's real life. Instead, Twist maintains that the sharing of the same (and most unusual) name and the common persona of a tough-guy "enforcer" create an unmistakable correlation between Twist the hockey player and Twist the Mafia don that, when coupled with Twist's fame as a NHL star, conclusively establishes that respondents used his name and identity. This Court agrees. Indeed, respondent McFarlane appears to have conceded the point by informing his readers in separate issues of *Spawn* ... that the hockey player Tony Twist was the basis for the comic book character's name.

Arguably, without these concessions, some Spawn readers may not have made the connection between Twist and his fictional counterpart. However, other evidence at trial clearly demonstrated that, at some point, *Spawn*'s readers did in fact make the connection, for both Twist and his mother were approached by young hockey fans under the belief that appellant was somehow affiliated with the *Spawn* character. On this record, respondents cannot seriously maintain that a good many purchasers of *Spawn* did not readily understand that respondents' use of the name referred to appellant. Accordingly, this Court holds that Twist presented sufficient evidence to prove that his name was used as a symbol of his identity.

B.

Twist contends, and this Court again agrees, that the evidence admitted at trial was sufficient to establish respondents' intent to gain a commercial advantage by using Twist's name to attract consumer attention to *Spawn* comic books and related products. As the Ninth Circuit noted in *Abdul-Jabbar v. General Motors Corp.*, 85 F.3d 407, 416 (9th Cir.1996), "The first step toward selling a product or service is to attract the consumers' attention" (citation omitted). *See also id.* at 415 (holding that to the extent that defendant's use of plaintiff's name attracted consumers' attention to its product, defendant gained a commercial advantage); *Henley*, 46 F.Supp.2d at 597 (holding that the commercial advantage or benefit element is shown if by using plaintiff's name or likeness in the product defendant sought "to catch the eye of the consumer and make the [product] more interesting"); Restatement (Third) of Unfair Competition sec. 47 cmt. c. At a minimum, respondents' statements and actions reveal their intent to create the impression that Twist was somehow associated with the *Spawn* comic book, and this alone is sufficient to establish the commercial advantage element in a right of publicity action. *See* Abdul-Jabbar, 85 F.3d at 414–16; Carson v. Here's Johnny Portable Toilets, Inc., 698 F.2d 831, 835–36 (6th Cir.1983) (holding that defendants violated plaintiff Johnny Carson's right of publicity when it used the phrase, "Here's Johnny," in its advertisement); *Henley*, 46 F.Supp.2d at 592–93 (holding in right of publicity case that defendant's use of the words, "Don's Henley," in advertisement was intended to elicit an association with plaintiff Don Henley).

But this is not all. At trial, Twist introduced evidence that respondents marketed their products directly to hockey fans. For example, respondents produced and distributed *Spawn* hockey jerseys and pucks and sponsored a "*Spawn* Night" at a minor league hockey game where other *Spawn* products were distributed, including products featuring the character "Tony Twist." Additionally, Twist points to McFarlane's statement in the November 1994 issue of *Spawn*, in which he promised readers that "they will continue to see current and past hockey players' names in [his] books." This statement, Twist correctly contends, amounts to an inducement to *Spawn* readers, especially those who are also hockey fans, to continue to purchase the comic book in order to see the name Tony Twist and other hockey players. This is evidence from which the jury could infer that respondents used his name to obtain a commercial advantage.

III.

Having determined that Twist made a submissible case at trial, we next address whether the right of publicity claim is nevertheless prohibited by the First Amendment. Courts throughout the country have struggled with this issue. Of course, not all speech is protected under the First Amendment, and in cases like this, courts often will weigh the state's interest in protecting a plaintiff's property right to the commercial value of his or her name and identity against the defendant's right to free speech.

Zacchini v. Scripps-Howard Broadcasting Co., 433 U.S. 562, 97 S.Ct. 2849, 53 L.Ed.2d 965 (1977), is the first and only right of publicity case decided by the Supreme Court. The case involved the unauthorized broadcast of a videotape of the plaintiff's 15-second "human cannonball" act during a nightly news program. The plaintiff brought suit under the state-recognized tort of right of publicity, alleging that the unauthorized broadcast amounted to an "unlawful appropriation" of his "professional property," and the defendant broadcasting company defended on First Amendment grounds. In balancing the respective parties' interests, the Court held, "Wherever the line in particular situations is to be drawn between media reports that are protected and those that are not, we are quite sure that the First and Fourteenth Amendments do not immunize the media when they broadcast a performer's entire act without his consent." *Zacchini*, 433 U.S. at 574–75, 97 S.Ct. 2849. Because the *Zacchini* Court limited its holding to the particular facts of the case—the appropriation of plaintiff's "entire act"—it does not control the case at hand. Nonetheless, there are larger lessons that are certainly applicable.

First, the Court acknowledged, as had many lower courts previously, that the right of publicity is not always trumped by the right of free speech. Explaining the competing right of publicity interests, the Court observed that "[t]he rationale for protecting the right of publicity is the straightforward one of preventing unjust enrichment by the theft of goodwill. No social purpose is served by having the defendant get free some aspect of the plaintiff that would have market value and for which he would normally pay." *Id.* at 576, 97 S.Ct. 2849.

Second, the Court distinguished claims for right of publicity or name appropriateness from claims for defamation like those adjudicated in *New York Times v. Sullivan*, 376 U.S. 254, 84 S.Ct. 710, 11 L.Ed.2d 686 (1964), and *Hustler Magazine v. Falwell*, 485 U.S. 46, 108 S.Ct. 876, 99 L.Ed.2d 41 (1988), and claims for "publicity that places plaintiff in a 'false light'" like that adjudicated in *Time, Inc. v. Hill*, 385 U.S. 374, 87 S.Ct. 534, 17 L.Ed.2d 456 (1967). Because property interests are involved in the former categories but not the latter, the Court refused to apply the *New York Times v. Sullivan* "actual malice" standard that speech is privileged unless it was "knowingly false or was published with reckless disregard for the truth." As the Court later made clear in *Hustler*, *Zacchini* stands for the proposition that "the 'actual malice' standard does not apply to the tort of appropriation of a right of publicity...." 485 U.S. at 52, 108 S.Ct. 876.

Right to publicity cases, both before and after *Zacchini*, focus instead on the threshold legal question of whether the use of a person's name and identity is "expressive," in which case it is fully protected, or "commercial," in which case it is generally not protected. For instance, the use of a person's identity in news, entertainment, and creative works for the purpose of communicating information or expressive ideas about that person is protected "expressive" speech. On the other hand, the use of a person's identity for purely commercial purposes, like advertising goods or services or the use of a person's name or likeness on merchandise, is rarely protected.

Several approaches have been offered to distinguish between expressive speech and commercial speech. The *Restatement*, for example, employs a "relatedness" test that protects the use of another person's name or identity in a work that is "related to" that person. The catalogue of "related" uses includes "the use of a person's name or likeness in news reporting, whether in newspapers, magazines, or broadcast news ... use in entertainment and other creative works, including both fiction and nonfiction ... use as part of an article published in a fan magazine or in a feature story broadcast on an entertainment program ... dissemination of an unauthorized print or broadcast biography, [and use] of another's identity in a novel, play, or motion picture...." Restatement (Third) of Unfair Competition sec. 47 cmt. c at 549. The proviso to that list, however, is that "if the name or likeness is used solely to attract attention to a work that is not related to the identified person, the user may be subject to liability for a use of the other's identity in advertising...." *Id.* (emphasis added).

California courts use a different approach, called the "transformative test," that was most recently invoked in *Winter v. D.C. Comics*, 30 Cal.4th 881, 134 Cal.Rptr.2d 634, 69 P.3d 473 (2003), a case with a remarkably similar fact situation. In that case, Johnny and Edgar Winters, well-known musicians with albino complexions and long white hair, brought a right of publicity action against defendant D.C. Comics for its publication of a comic book featuring the characters "Johnny and Edgar Autumn," half-worm, half-human creatures with pale faces and long white hair. On appeal, the California Supreme Court considered whether the action was barred by the First Amendment and employed "'what is essentially a balancing test between the First Amendment and the right of publicity based on whether the work in question adds significant creative elements so as to be transformed into something more than a mere celebrity likeness or imitation.'" *Id.* at 475. Concluding that the comic book characters "Johnny and Edgar Autumn" "are not just conventional depictions of plaintiffs but contain significant expressive content other than plaintiffs' mere likenesses," id. at 479, the Court held that the characters were sufficiently transformed so as to entitle the comic book to full First Amendment protection.

The weakness of the *Restatement*'s "relatedness" test and California's "transformative" test is that they give too little consideration to the fact that many uses of a person's name and identity have both expressive and commercial components. These tests operate to preclude a cause of action whenever the use of the name and identity is in any way expressive, regardless of its commercial exploitation. Under the relatedness test, use of a person's name and identity is actionable only when the use is solely commercial and is otherwise unrelated to that person. Under the transformative test, the transformation or fictionalized characterization of a person's celebrity status is not actionable even if its sole purpose is the commercial use of that person's name and identity. Though these tests purport to balance the prospective interests involved, there is no balancing at all—once the use is determined to be expressive, it is protected. At least one commentator, however, has advocated the use of a more balanced balancing test—a sort of predominant use test—that better addresses the cases where speech is both expressive and commercial:

> If a product is being sold that predominantly exploits the commercial value of an individual's identity, that product should be held to violate the right of publicity and not be protected by the First Amendment, even if there is some "expressive" content in it that might qualify as "speech" in other circumstances. If, on the other hand, the predominant purpose of the product is to make an expressive comment on or about a celebrity, the expressive values could be given greater weight.

[Mark S. Lee, *Agents of Chaos: Judicial Confusion in Defining the Right of Publicity-Free Speech Interface*, 23 Loy. L.A. Ent. L.Rev. 471, 500 (2003).]

The relative merit of these several tests can be seen when applied to the unusual circumstances of the case at hand. As discussed, Twist made a submissible case that respondents' use of his name and identity was for a commercial advantage. Nonetheless, there is still an expressive component in the use of his name and identity as a metaphorical reference to tough-guy "enforcers." And yet, respondents agree (perhaps to avoid a defamation claim) that the use was not a parody or other expressive comment or a fictionalized account of the real Twist. As such, the metaphorical reference to Twist, though a literary device, has very little literary value compared to its commercial value. On the record here, the use and identity of Twist's name has become predominantly a ploy to sell comic books and related products rather than an artistic or literary expression, and under these circumstances, free speech must give way to the right of publicity.

V.

In addition to the misappropriation of name claim, Twist sought equitable relief from the circuit court in the form of a permanent injunction prohibiting respondents from using his "name, commercial image, persona, autograph and/or likeness for any purpose without his consent" (emphasis added). The court denied equitable relief concluding, inter alia, that the injunction sought was overbroad because it could "interfere with legitimate and proper action by the defendants in the future." This Court holds that the circuit court was correct in doing so, because, as respondents state in their brief, the requested injunction attempted to prohibit respondents "from engaging in a variety of expressive activities unrelated to the subject matter of this lawsuit and undoubtedly protected by the First Amendment—e.g., a parody of plaintiff, a commentary on his fighting style, a factual report on this lawsuit."

VI.

For the foregoing reasons, the circuit court's judgment notwithstanding the verdict is reversed, the judgment granting a new trial is affirmed, the judgment denying injunctive relief is affirmed, and the case is remanded.

* * *

1. The Lanham Act. In addition to a common-law or, perhaps, statutory right of publicity claim, a celebrity in Twist's general situation might also have a claim under the federal Lanham Act. 15 U.S.C. § 1125. The Lanham Act recognizes that a celebrity may have a property interest in her name or identity that is "akin to that of a person holding a trademark." Parks v. LaFace Records, 329 F.3d 437, 447 (6th Cir. 2003). In order to prevail under a false advertising claim under the Lanham Act, a plaintiff must establish that the use of the plaintiff's name or identity "is likely to cause confusion among consumers as to the 'affiliation, connection, or association' between the celebrity and the defendant's goods or services or as to the celebrity's participation in the 'origin, sponsorship, or approval' of the defendant's goods or services." *Id.* at 446. Thus, for example, civil rights icon Rosa Parks was able to raise a triable Lanham Act issue regarding whether the song *Rosa Parks* by the musical group OutKast "misleads consumers into believing that the song is about her or that she is affiliated with the Defendants, or has sponsored or approved the *Rosa Parks* song." *Id.* First Amendment concerns play a role in resolution of Lanham Act claims just as they do in common-law or statutory right of publicity cases.

2. Privileges. The *Restatement (Second) of Torts* takes the position that the absolute and conditional privileges that apply to defamation claims also apply to invasion of privacy claims. Restatement (Second) of Torts §§ 652F, 652G. Thus, for example, a defendant charged with false light version of invasion of privacy may successfully argue that he was acting in order to protect his own legitimate interest or that he shared a common interest with the recipient. *See* Washburn v. Lavoie, 437 F.3d 84, 92 (D.C. Cir. 2006).

Chapter 16

Misuse of the Legal Process

Exercise 16.1: Chapter Problem

Memo to Associate
Re: TV Connect Defense

We represent TV Connect, a provider of television programming. The company was originally represented by another law firm, which filed separate complaints on behalf of TV Connect against a number of individuals, including an individual named Denise Wayne. The complaints were all similar in that they alleged various statutory theories of recovery under federal law for similar acts. Most of these complaints (including the one filed against Wayne) have been dismissed. We recently received the following complaint filed against TV Connect. Please read it over so that we can discuss.

United States District Court for the Eastern District of Michigan,
Kalamazoo Division

Denise WAYNE, Plaintiff

v.

TV CONNECT, James Osterberg, Osterberg,
Asheton & Alexander, LLC., Defendants.

C. A. No. 2: 14–____.

July 14, 2014.

Denise Wayne ("Plaintiff"), hereafter states as her Complaint against the defendant TV Connect the following:

[Various facts about the parties and a jurisdictional statement are omitted.]

9. Over the past several years TV Connect has attempted to stop the sale and the distribution of electronic equipment that it claims can be used along with other system devices to intercept its satellite signal. Specifically, TV Connect has raided certain companies that sold electronic devices over the Internet and acquired their electronic databases which included information relating to sales, invoices, and communications with customers.

10. After obtaining this electronic information, TV Connect and its investigators, attorneys, agents, and/or employees engaged in the practice of manufacturing documents by transforming the electronic information into purported sales invoices in order to demonstrate admissible "proof" of purchase of certain electronic equipment.

11. Using the manufactured evidence (i.e. purported sales invoices) TV Connect has sent out over 100,000 letters as a part of its anti-piracy campaign to customers

indicating that they were in possession of a "Pirate Access Device" subjecting them to fines of up to $10,000.00 and other civil and criminal sanctions.

12. TV Connect concedes and admits that

(1) the devices in and of themselves cannot be utilized to intercept and view its television signal, but rather requires a variety of additional hardware and software to be synchronized before the devices can be used for the alleged purpose

(2) without all the necessary equipment it is physically impossible to gain access and accomplish the alleged actions stated in its Complaint;

(3) said devices have other legitimate applications and that there have been instances where individuals have been wrongly sued.

13. TV Connect's so called anti-piracy campaign of sending out letters and filing lawsuits based on unsupported allegations is a part of a calculated strategy to extort financial settlements sums from thousands of individuals nationwide who have committed no offense at all.

14. The Plaintiff has never attempted to use or assist any other person in the use of equipment which may illegally intercept or decode TV Connect's satellite programming and Plaintiff has never viewed any unauthorized programming from TV Connect.

15. In 2012, Plaintiff received a letter from TV Connect End User Group as a part of its anti-piracy campaign accusing him and his wife of possessing "illegal signal theft devices" and using said devices for unauthorized viewing of TV Connect's programming.

16. TV Connect and/or its agents, representatives, or investigators demanded that the Plaintiff 1.) Surrender his personal property, 2.) Execute a written statement that he would not purchase or use an illegal signal device to view unauthorized reception of TV Connect's programming, and 3.) Pay a monetary sum in the amount of Three Thousand Five Hundred Dollars ($3,500.00).

17. Throughout all contacts and conversations with TV Connect and its agents, Plaintiff has maintained that he did not possess any illegal equipment and has never viewed any unauthorized programming of TV Connect.

COUNT ONE—WRONGFUL INITIATION OF CIVIL PROCEEDINGS

18. Plaintiff incorporates by reference the allegations contained in paragraphs 1–17.

19. In response, TV Connect, through its attorneys, filed a frivolous lawsuit without any proof or knowledge that the Plaintiff purchased or used said equipment for the purposes alleged. Indeed, Plaintiff was granted summary judgment in TV Connect's action against her.

20. Upon reasonable investigation TV Connect and its attorneys, James Osterberg, Osterberg, Asheton & Alexander, either knew or should have known that Plaintiff did not engage in any illegal actions alleged in the complaint.

21. TV Connect itself and through its agents, under the guise of a anti-piracy campaign, have actually engaged in a mass mailing scam based on unsupported allegations and threats without offering any evidence of signal theft that has already generated millions of dollars in revenue for TV Connect.

22. The lawsuits, including the suit against the Plaintiff, were not filed for the stated purpose of obtaining a financial sum from the targeted defendant but had the ulterior motivation of providing additional persuasive and threatening force to their letter campaign, in that recipients receiving such letters were threatened into paying the extortion sum knowing they would eventually be sued if they failed to comply.

23. TV Connect improperly failed to dismiss its frivolous claims against the Plaintiff for fear that dismissal would adversely affect its litigation efforts and national letter campaign, which is being followed by numerous national media sources, by decreasing its ability to extort further settlements from other parties faced with meritless claims.

24. After filing suit against the Plaintiff, TV Connect has continued to send out thousands of identical letters and lawsuits without any reasonable investigation or verification of its "signal theft" claims.

24. In their demand letters, press releases, and news publications TV Connect emphasizes their efforts to sue those individuals that do not comply with their settlement demands. That the reference to the lawsuits including the Plaintiff is a part of their strategy to threaten others into paying additional settlement amounts.

25. TV Connect and/or its attorneys in filing thousands of suits including the suit against the Plaintiff was for the purpose of threatening and intimidating other individuals into complying with their settlement demands.

26. TV Connect and/or its attorneys improperly utilized the process of this court in an attempt to extort financial settlement sums from thousands of individuals nationwide, constituting an illegitimate purpose collateral to the purported reasons for this action.

COUNT TWO—ABUSE OF PROCESS

27. [The complaint essentially repeats the allegations contained in Count One.]

One of the most common complaints about the legal system is that parties misuse it. Parties and their lawyers file frivolous charges and motions, causing emotional strain and expense on others. Parties and their lawyers misuse the discovery process, sometimes going so far as to destroy relevant evidence. This chapter examines five different liability theories designed to address these kinds of misuses of the legal system.

First, there are the three common law torts that are designed specifically to address misuse of the legal process: malicious prosecution, wrongful initiation of civil proceedings, and abuse of process. The first two torts are often grouped together as "malicious prosecution" claims, but, as will be seen, they are actually distinct torts. The third, abuse of process, is a tort of somewhat uncertain contours that is frequently mistaken for malicious prosecution or wrongful initiation.

The fourth legal remedy discussed in this chapter, anti-SLAPP statutes, developed in response to concerns that some parties were using the filing of frivolous lawsuits to silence free speech. The fifth and final theory discussed in this chapter, spoliation of evidence, deals with a different form of misconduct: destruction of evidence relevant to a legal proceeding.

* * *

A. Malicious Prosecution

1. In General

A person who causes the commencement or continuation of a criminal proceeding without probable cause and for an improper purpose is subject to liability for malicious prosecution if the proceeding terminates in favor of the accused. *See* Restatement (Second) of Torts § 655. "It is frequently said that actions for malicious prosecution are not favored in the law." Browning-Ferris Indus., Inc. v. Lieck, 881 S.W.2d 288, 291 (Tex. 1994). This is perhaps something of an overstatement, but it is true that the tort of malicious prosecution is defined more precisely and painstakingly than some other torts. The reason is that the tort seeks to find "the delicate balance between protecting against wrongful prosecution and encouraging reporting of criminal conduct." *Id.* Therefore, each element of the tort serves an important gatekeeping function.

a. Causing the Commencement or Continuation of a Criminal Proceeding

In order to establish liability, a plaintiff must first show that the defendant caused the commencement or continuation of a criminal proceeding. The term "criminal proceeding" includes "any proceeding in which the state or other government seeks to bring an offender to justice by prosecuting him." Restatement (Second) of Torts § 654 cmt. a. Criminal proceedings are initiated upon the issuance of a warrant for the plaintiff's arrest or upon a grand jury indictment. Criminal proceedings are also initiated upon the arrest of a plaintiff, even in the absence of a warrant. *Id.* § 654.

The defendant must be a proximate cause of the commencement or continuation of the proceeding. Leisinger v. Jacobson, 651 N.W.2d 693, 698 (S.D. 2002). Obviously, a prosecutor may commence a criminal proceeding, but a private citizen also may cause the commencement of a proceeding. For example, if the defendant knows that the information provided or the accusation made is false, and the decision maker, in the exercise of his or her discretion, initiates charges as a result of the information, the defendant's conduct may be actionable. *Id.* § 653 cmt. g; *see also* Tranum v. Broadway, 283 S.W.3d 403, 417 (Tex. Ct. App. 2008). Similarly, a defendant may face liability when someone else causes the commencement of a proceeding, but the defendant plays an active role in procuring the continuation of the proceeding. On the other hand, the fact that the defendant cooperates with law enforcement in the prosecution of the plaintiff is insufficient to establish causation. Similarly, it is not ordinarily sufficient that the defendant calls the police and provides information about criminal behavior that results in the plaintiff's arrest, provided the responding officer has the discretion to decide whether to institute criminal proceedings. Ziemba v. Fo'cs'le, Inc., 475 N.E.2d 1223, 1225 (Mass. Ct. App. 1985); Restatement (Second) of Torts § 653 cmts. d & g.

Exercise 16.2

For each example that follows, decide whether the defendant initiated a criminal proceeding or procured the initiation or continuation of a criminal proceeding:

(a) Defendant's actions cause a proceeding to be commenced to determine whether Plaintiff should be involuntarily committed due to his insanity.

(b) Several weeks after charging Plaintiff with a crime, Prosecutor comes to realize that Plaintiff is innocent of the charges. Despite this, Prosecutor does not drop the charges and continues the prosecution. *See* Restatement (Second) of Torts § 655.

(c) District Attorney initiates criminal proceedings against Plaintiff. The primary reason why she does so is because she receives pressure from a wealthy political backer. Plaintiff sues the political backer for malicious prosecution.

(d) Defendant, a neighbor of Plaintiff, notifies the police that Plaintiff is engaged in illegal activity. Police officers conduct their own investigation into the suspected illegal activity and decide to arrest Plaintiff.

(e) Defendant, a neighbor of Alice, convinces Alice to come forward with accusations of criminal conduct against Plaintiff. Prior to her conversation with Defendant, Alice had no intention of contacting the authorities about Plaintiff. Plaintiff is arrested as a result of Alice's complaint. *See* Restatement (Second) of Torts § 653 cmt. f.

(f) Defendant knowingly provides false testimony at Plaintiff's criminal trial and withholds other exculpatory evidence while testifying. After being exonerated, Plaintiff sues Defendant for continuing the original proceeding against her.

b. Without Probable Cause

A malicious prosecution plaintiff must also establish that the defendant initiated the criminal proceeding without probable cause. The existence of probable cause is ordinarily a question of law for the court. Matthews v. Blue Cross & Blue Shield of Michigan, 572 N.W.2d 603, 611 (Mich. 1998). In order to have probable cause, a defendant who causes the initiation of a criminal proceeding must reasonably believe, based on the facts known to the defendant at the time, that the accused committed the acts in question and that those acts amount to a crime. Restatement (Second) of Torts § 653.

Exercise 16.3

For each example that follows, decide whether the defendant had probable cause when the proceeding was initiated or procured:

(a) Defendant misplaced his MP3 player. Defendant honestly believes that Plaintiff, the only recent visitor to Defendant's house, stole it. Defendant, without searching his house for the MP3 player, demands that Prosecutor initiate criminal proceedings against Plaintiff. The next day, Defendant discovers that the MP3 player had fallen behind the dresser.

(b) Defendant reasonably believed that Plaintiff had stolen his car and therefore put pressure on Prosecutor to bring criminal charges against Plaintiff. While the proceedings were pending, Defendant learned information that established Plaintiff's innocence. However, Defendant failed to inform Prosecutor of this evidence and the prosecution continued. *See* Restatement (Second) of Torts § 655 cmt. c.; Clarke v. Montgomery Ward & Co., 298 F.2d 346, 348 (4th Cir. 1962).

(c) As a result of political pressure brought to bear by a private citizen, a grand jury was convened to consider charges against Plaintiff. After deliberation, the grand jury refuses to indict Plaintiff. *See* Restatement (Second) of Torts § 664.

---

c. For an Improper Purpose

As the name of the tort would suggest, malice is often said to be an element of a malicious prosecution claim. However, malice in the senses of ill will or personal animosity is not necessarily a requirement. What is required is that the defendant's primary purpose in commencing the proceedings was something other than to bring an offender to justice. MacRea v. Brant, 230 A.2d 753, 756 (N.H. 1967). The only proper purpose for commencing criminal proceedings is to see justice done; any other purpose that predominates—whether it be ill will or a desire to benefit personally from the plaintiff's incarceration—is improper.

d. Termination of the Proceeding in Favor of the Accused

To prevail, a plaintiff must also establish that the underlying criminal proceeding terminated in favor of the plaintiff (the accused). In order for the proceeding to have terminated in the accused's favor, the final disposition must be such "as to indicate the innocence of the accused." Restatement (Second) of Torts § 660 cmt. a. Thus, for example, the fact that an individual accused of first-degree murder was convicted of manslaughter, rather than murder, due to a plea deal does not indicate the individual's innocence with respect to the murder charge.

Exercise 16.4

For each example that follows, decide whether the underlying criminal proceeding terminated in the accused's favor:

(a) After deliberation, a grand jury refuses to indict Plaintiff.

(b) In light of the fact that Plaintiff was elderly and was unlikely to live for more than a few more months, Prosecutor abandons the prosecution of Plaintiff.

(c) Plaintiff is convicted of a crime. She exhausts all her appeals and is in prison for 10 years before new DNA evidence is discovered, conclusively establishing Plaintiff's innocence of the crime. As a result, Plaintiff is pardoned and her arrest and court record are expunged from the record. She then sues the party who commenced the proceeding against her.

---

e. Damages

A malicious prosecution plaintiff is entitled to recover for the expenses incurred in defending against the wrongful prosecution (such as attorney's fees). A plaintiff is also entitled to recover for any other pecuniary losses caused by the defendant's actions, including such things as damage to reputation, loss of business, or loss of present or prospective employment. If the plaintiff is arrested or imprisoned as part of the proceedings, the plaintiff is entitled to collect for any harm caused by the arrest or imprisonment, including any resulting emotional distress. Restatement (Second) of Torts § 671.

f. Defenses

Exercise 16.5

Embarrassed by a recent high-profile murder of a member of organized crime, Local Official pressures D.A. to prosecute someone for the crime. When the D.A. replies that she has no leads, Local Official looks at the wall in D.A.'s office, which contains photographs of various organized crime members, and randomly throws a dart at the wall. The dart hits the photograph of an individual in a rival organized crime family. Local Official says, "Convict that guy. I don't care if he did it or not. We need to let the public know that we are tough on crime." D.A. does as she is ordered and obtains a first-degree murder indictment against Junior "Two Stomachs" Carbone. The trial lasts less than a day as the government's witnesses against Carbone are exposed as liars and no admissible evidence is introduced linking Carbone to the murder. Under withering criticism from the judge (who opined, "I know a D.A. can indict a ham sandwich but there clearly was no way D.A. could reasonably have believed she had probable cause to bring these charges"), D.A. voluntarily dismisses the charges against Carbone.

Carbone professes his outrage and brings malicious prosecution claims against D.A. and Local Official. However, several witnesses now come forward and are prepared to testify that they were actually present at the time of the murder and saw Carbone pull the trigger.

Assuming all of the evidence mentioned above in Junior Carbone's case is introduced and believed by the jury in the malicious prosecution trial, should Carbone prevail?

(1) Plaintiff's Guilt

The fact that the malicious prosecution is, in fact, guilty of the underlying criminal charge is an affirmative defense that may be pled by the malicious prosecution defendant. The plaintiff's guilt is a bar to recovery even when the plaintiff has been acquitted of the underlying charge. Since the plaintiff's guilt is an affirmative defense, the defendant bears the burden of establishing it. The standard of proof is the more lenient preponderance of evidence standard used in civil trials rather than criminal law's proof beyond a reasonable doubt standard. Sessoms v. Union Savings & Trust Co., 338 F.2d 752 (6th Cir. 1964).

* * *

(2) Prosecutorial Immunity

The well-established rule is that a public prosecutor is not liable for malicious prosecution. Matthews v. Blue Cross & Blue Shield of Michigan, 572 N.W.2d 603, 609 (Mich. 1998). Given the vital role that criminal prosecutions play, the privilege enjoyed by public prosecutors acting within the scope of their duties is absolute in nature. The privilege does not extend to police officers or other law enforcement officials. Belt v. Ritter, 189 N.W.2d 221 (Mich. 1971).

* * *

B. Wrongful Initiation of Civil Proceedings

Like malicious prosecution, the tort of wrongful initiation of civil proceedings is based upon the misuse of the legal process. But instead of wrongfully commencing criminal proceedings, the wrongful initiation defendant commences civil proceedings. Some jurisdictions use the term "malicious prosecution" in a generic sense to cover both torts. However, the elements of the tort are not necessarily interchangeable.

Focus Questions: *Friedman v. Dozorc*

1. *What is the "English rule" and why does the court retain it?*
2. *One court has said that "[a]n attorney has probable cause to represent a client in litigation when, after a reasonable investigation and industrious search of legal authority, he has an honest belief that his client's claim is tenable in the forum in which it is to be tried."* Tool Research & Engineering Corp. v. Henigson, *46 Cal.App.3d 675, 683 (1975). Is that the standard the Friedman court adopts for the probable cause element?*

Friedman v. Dozorc

312 N.W.2d 585
(Mich. 1981)

* * *

LEVIN, Justice.

The plaintiff is a physician who, after successfully defending in a medical malpractice action, brought this action against the attorneys who had represented the plaintiffs in the former action. Dr. Friedman sought under a number of theories to recover damages for being compelled to defend against an allegedly groundless medical malpractice action....

Leona Serafin entered Outer Drive Hospital in May, 1970, for treatment of gynecological problems.... While in the hospital, Mrs. Serafin was referred to the present plaintiff, Dr. Friedman, for urological consultation. Dr. Friedman recommended surgical removal of a kidney stone..., and the operation was performed on May 20, 1970.... [S]he died five days after the surgery. An autopsy was performed the next day; the report identified the cause of death as thrombotic thrombocytopenic purpura, a rare and uniformly fatal blood disease, the cause and cure of which are unknown.

On January 11, 1972, attorneys Dozorc and Golden, the defendants in this action, filed a malpractice action ... against [Outer Drive Hospital, Dr. Friedman, and others]. In December, 1974, the case went to trial in Wayne Circuit Court. No expert testimony tending to show that any of the defendants had breached accepted professional standards in making the decision to perform the elective surgery or in the manner of its performance was presented as part of the plaintiff's case. The judge entered a directed verdict of no cause of action in favor of Dr. Friedman and the other defendants at the close of the plaintiff's proofs....

Dr. Friedman commenced the present action on March 17, 1976....

II

[The court rejected the plaintiff's argument that a lawyer who initiates a civil action owes a duty to his client's adversary and other foreseeable third parties who may be affected to conduct a reasonable investigation and re-examination of the facts and law so that the attorney will have an adequate basis for a good-faith belief that the client has a tenable claim. The court concluded that recognizing such a duty would create a irreconcilable conflict of interest for the lawyer.]

IV

A

The recognition of an action for malicious prosecution developed as an adjunct to the English practice of awarding costs to the prevailing party in certain aggravated cases where the costs remedy was thought to be inadequate and the defendant had suffered damages beyond the expense and travail normally incident to defending a lawsuit. In 1698 three categories of damage which would support an action for malicious prosecution were identified: injury to one's fame (as by a scandalous allegation), injury to one's person or liberty, and injury to one's property. To this day the English courts do not recognize actions for malicious prosecution of either criminal or civil proceedings unless one of these types of injury, as narrowly defined by the cases, is present.

A substantial number of American jurisdictions today follow some form of "English rule" to the effect that "in the absence of an arrest, seizure, or special damage, the successful civil defendant has no remedy, despite the fact that his antagonist proceeded against him maliciously and without probable cause." A larger number of jurisdictions, some say a majority, follow an "American rule" permitting actions for malicious prosecution of civil proceedings without requiring the plaintiff to show special injury.

B

The plaintiff's complaint does not allege special injury. We are satisfied that Michigan has not significantly departed from the English rule and we decline to do so today....

C

... In seeking a remedy for the excessive litigiousness of our society, we would do well to cast off the limitations of a perspective which ascribes curative power only to lawsuits.

We turn to a consideration of Dean Prosser's criticisms of the three reasons commonly advanced by courts for adhering to the English rule. First, to the assertion that the costs awarded to the prevailing party are intended as the exclusive remedy for the damages incurred by virtue of the wrongful litigation, Prosser responds that "in the United States, where the costs are set by statute at trivial amounts, and no attorney's fees are allowed, there can be no pretense at compensation even for the expenses of the litigation itself." This argument is compelling, but it does not necessarily justify an award of compensation absent the hardship of special injury or dictate that an award of compensation be assessed in a separate lawsuit. Second, to the arguments that an unrestricted tort of wrongful civil proceedings will deter honest litigants and that an innocent party must bear the costs of litigation as the price of a system which permits free access to the courts, Prosser answers that "there is no policy in favor of vexatious suits known to be groundless, which are a real and often a serious injury." But a tort action is not the only means of deterring groundless litigation, and other devices may be less intimidating to good-faith litigants. Finally, in response to the claim that recognition of the tort action will produce interminable litigation, Prosser argues that the heavy burden of proof which the plaintiff bears in such actions will safeguard bona fide litigants and prevent an endless chain of countersuits. But if few plaintiffs will recover in the subsequent action, one may wonder whether there is any point in recognizing the expanded cause of action. If the subsequent action does not succeed, both parties are left to bear the expenses of two futile lawsuits, and court time has been wasted as well.

Although this case arises upon the plaintiff doctor's assertions that the defendant attorneys wrongfully prosecuted a medical malpractice action against him, if we were to eliminate the special injury requirement that expansion of the tort of malicious prosecution would not be limited to countersuits against attorneys by aggrieved physicians. An action for malicious prosecution of civil proceedings could be brought by any former defendant-person, firm or corporation, private or public—in whose favor a prior civil suit terminated, against the former plaintiff or the plaintiff's attorney or both. In expanding the availability of such an action the Court would not merely provide a remedy for those required to defend groundless medical malpractice actions, but would arm all prevailing defendants with an instrument of retaliation, whether the prior action sounded in tort, contract or an altogether different area of law.

This is strong medicine—too strong for the affliction it is intended to cure. To be sure, successful defense of the former action is no assurance of recovery in a subsequent tort action, but the unrestricted availability of such an action introduces a new strategic weapon into the arsenal of defense litigators, particularly those whose clients can afford to devote extensive resources to prophylactic intimidation.

At present, a plaintiff and his attorney who know that they have less than an airtight case must, in deciding whether to continue the case or in evaluating a settlement offer, consider whether if they proceed to trial they will invest more and recover less or nothing. If the instant plaintiff's approach is adopted, all plaintiffs and their attorneys henceforth must also weigh the likelihood that if they persevere in the action and receive an unfavorable decision, they will not only take nothing but also be forced to defend an action for malicious prosecution of civil proceedings. Even if the plaintiff and his attorney had abundant cause for bringing and continuing the action and acted without malice, the expense and annoyance foreseeably involved in even a successful defense of the countersuit may induce them to abandon a problematic claim or to settle the case for less than they would otherwise accept. Some will say amen, but this would push the pendulum too far in favor of the defense, more than is necessary to rectify the evil to which this effort is directed....

Permitting a tort action for wrongful civil proceedings to be maintained absent special injury to the plaintiff could easily generate a surprising number of such actions. Not only doctors, but most defendants, react to a lawsuit with hurt feelings and outrage. They may impute malicious motives to the plaintiff and the opposing attorney and be eager to exact retribution if they prevail. There is no shortage of lawyers who are eager to develop new specialties and would be willing to accept such actions on a contingent fee basis. Some product manufacturers and insurance companies may routinely file countersuits with a view to inhibiting plaintiffs or their attorneys from commencing actions against them or their insureds. The indiscriminate filing of countersuits may lead to actions for wrongfully proceeding with a wrongful civil proceedings action. Embittered litigants whose differences are more emotional than legal will have added opportunities to continue their strife.

The cure for an excess of litigation is not more litigation. Meritorious as well as frivolous claims are likely to be deterred. There are sure to be those who would use the courts and such an expanded tort remedy as a retaliatory or punitive device without regard to the likelihood of recovery or who would seek a means of recovering the actual costs of defending the first action without regard to whether it was truly vexatious.

V

Apart from special injury, elements of a tort action for malicious prosecution of civil proceedings are (1) prior proceedings terminated in favor of the present plaintiff, (2) absence of probable cause for those proceedings, and (3) "malice" more informatively described by the *Restatement* as "a purpose other than that of securing the proper adjudication of the claim in which the proceedings are based."

The following discussion addresses the chief concern of this case: the conditions under which the attorney for an unsuccessful plaintiff may be held liable.

The absence of probable cause in bringing a civil action may not be established merely by showing that the action was successfully defended. To require an attorney to advance only those claims that will ultimately be successful would place an intolerable burden on the right of access to the courts.

DR 7-102(A) and the other professional standards to which plaintiff refers consistently incorporate a requirement of scienter as to groundlessness or vexatiousness, not a requirement that the lawyer take affirmative measures to verify the factual basis of his client's position. A lawyer is entitled to accept his client's version of the facts and to proceed on the assumption that they are true absent compelling evidence to the contrary....

The *Restatement*'s definition of probable cause provides ample guidance whether damages are sought from a lawyer, his client or both:

> One who takes an active part in the initiation, continuation or procurement of civil proceedings against another has probable cause for doing so if he reasonably believes in the existence of the facts upon which the claim is based, and either
>
> (a) correctly or reasonably believes that under those facts the claim may be valid under the applicable law, or
>
> (b) believes to this effect in reliance upon the advice of counsel, sought in good faith and given after full disclosure of all relevant facts within his knowledge and information.

As applied to a plaintiff's lawyer, this standard would allow lack of probable cause to be found where the lawyer proceeded with knowledge that the claim had no factual or legal basis, but would impose no obligation to investigate if the lawyer could reasonably believe the facts to be as the client alleged.

B

This Court has said, in opinions addressed to the tort of malicious prosecution, that malice may be inferred from the facts that establish want of probable cause, although the jury is not required to draw that inference. This rule, developed in cases where damages were sought from a lay person who initiated proceedings, fails to make sufficient allowance for the lawyer's role as advocate and should not be applied in determining whether a lawyer acted for an improper purpose.

A client's total lack of belief that the action he initiates or continues can succeed is persuasive evidence of intent to harass or injure the defendant by bringing the action. But a lawyer who is unaware of such a client's improper purpose may, despite a personal lack of belief in any possible success of the action, see the client and the claim through to an appropriate conclusion without risking liability. Restatement 2d, Torts, § 674, comment d, states:

> An attorney who initiates a civil proceeding on behalf of his client or one who takes any steps in the proceeding is not liable if he has probable cause for his action (see § 675); and even if he has no probable cause and is convinced that his client's claim is unfounded, he is still not liable if he acts primarily for the purpose of aiding his client in obtaining a proper adjudication of his claim. (*See* § 676). An attorney is not required or expected to prejudge his client's claim, and although he is fully aware that its chances of success are comparatively slight, it is his responsibility to present it to the court for adjudication if his client so insists after he has explained to the client the nature of the chances.

The *Restatement* defines the mental element of the tort of wrongful civil proceedings as "a purpose other than that of securing the proper adjudication of the claim in which the proceedings are based." A finding of an improper purpose on the part of the unsuccessful attorney must be supported by evidence independent of the evidence establishing that the action was brought without probable cause.

LEVIN, Justice (concurring).

[T]his Court can appropriately devise an approach to wrongful litigation which is capable of providing both an appropriate measure of deterrence and reasonable compensation for wronged litigants without imperiling the right of free access to the courts. The remedy, quite simply, is to recognize the inadequacy of existing provisions for the taxation of costs and to adopt a new and distinct court rule authorizing the judge to whom a civil action is assigned to order payment of the prevailing party's actual expenses, including reasonable attorneys' fees and limited consequential damages, where the action was wrongfully initiated, defended or continued. Depending upon the circumstances, payment might be required of the attorney, the client or both. The factual questions implicit in such an evaluation of the losing side's conduct would be resolved by the judge after a prompt post-termination hearing at which the parties could call witnesses and they and their attorneys could testify.

Exercise 16.6

In what respect, if any, does the complaint from the Chapter Problem involving TV Connect fail to state a claim of wrongful initiation of civil proceedings against

TV Connect? Against TV Connect's attorneys, James Osterberg, Osterberg, Asheton & Alexander?

---

1. Model Rule comparison. Comment 2 to ABA Model Rule 3.1 requires that lawyers "inform themselves about the facts of their clients' cases and the applicable law and determine that they can make a good faith argument in support of their clients' positions." A lawyer's duty of competence requires adequate preparation, including "inquiry into and analysis of" the facts and law concerning the client's matter. *Id.* Rule 1.1 cmt. 5.

2. Malicious defense. In *Aranson v. Schroeder*, 671 A.2d 1023, 1028–29 (N.H. 1995), the New Hampshire Supreme Court recognized the tort of malicious defense. As defined by the court, the tort mirrors the tort of wrongful initiation or malicious prosecution, but from the defense perspective. Thus, one who initiates or continues a defense in a civil proceeding without probable cause primarily for an improper purpose (such as to delay) and who causes damages may be held liable. Virtually every other court to consider the matter has refused to recognize the tort, however. Young v. Allstate Ins. Co., 198 P.3d 666, 681–82 (Haw. 2008).

* * *

C. Abuse of Process

The final common law theory dealing with misuse of the legal process is the tort of abuse of process. The theory is conceptually similar to the malicious prosecution and wrongful initiation torts. However, abuse of process differs in important respects.

Focus Questions: *Bd. of Educ. v. Farmingdale*, *Young v. Allstate Ins. Co.*, and *Bonner v. Chicago Title Ins. Co.*

1. *What is the difference between abuse of process and wrongful initiation of civil proceedings? Under what circumstances could a plaintiff prevail under an abuse of process theory but not under a wrongful initiation theory?*
2. *What is the primary difference between the elements of an abuse of process claims as stated by the* Farmingdale *and* Young *courts?*
3. *How does the* Bonner *court's "corroborating act" requirement relate to the* Young *court's "willful act" requirement?*

Board of Education of Farmingdale Union Free School Dist. v. Farmingdale

343 N.E.2d 278
(N.Y. 1975)

WACHTLER, Judge.

This appeal, arising in the context of an apparently bitter dispute between a school district and a teachers' association, concerns the seldom considered tort of abuse of process. The school district contends that the association and its attorney are liable for abusing legal process by subpoenaing, with the intent to harass and to injure, 87 teachers and refusing to stagger their appearances. As a result the school district was compelled to hire substitutes in order to avert a total shutdown. The issue on appeal is whether the complaint states a cause of action.

The controversy began in March, 1972 when a number of teachers employed by the district were absent from their classes on two successive days. The school district considered this illegal and the teachers' association was charged with violating the so-called Taylor law (Civil Service Law, s 210, subd. 1) by the Public Employees Relations Board (PERB). The association vehemently denied having engaged in or condoned a strike and the matter was scheduled for a hearing to be held on October 5, 6, 10 and 11.

The complaint contains the following version of the ensuing events. Sometime between September 5, 1972 and October 5, 1972, the attorney for the association prepared and issued judicial subpoenas duces tecum to 87 teachers in order to compel their attendance as witnesses on October 5. The school district learned of these subpoenas on or about October 3, 1972 when the individual teachers requested approved absences from teaching duties in accordance with the collective bargaining agreement. The complaint further alleges that the district's prompt oral request that the majority of teachers be excused from attendance at the initial hearing date was refused by the defendant. Indeed, the defendant refused even to grant the request to stagger the appearances. Consequently all 87 teachers attended the hearing and 77 substitute teachers were hired to replace them. Based on these allegations, the school district asserts three causes of action.

The first alleges an abuse of process in that the defendants wrongfully and maliciously and with intent to injure and harass the plaintiff issued 87 subpoenas with knowledge that all the teachers could not have possibly testified on the initial hearing date. As damages for this cause of action plaintiff seeks the amount expended to engage substitute teachers and an amount representing the aggregate salary of the subpoenaed teachers. The second cause of action reiterates the allegations of the first and prays for punitive damages; while the third alleges defendants' conduct constituted a prima facie tort. Defendants moved to dismiss primarily for failure to state a cause of action Special Term denied this motion and the Appellate Division affirmed with one Justice dissenting.

In its broadest sense, abuse of process may be defined as the misuse or perversion of regularly issued legal process for a purpose not justified by the nature of the process....

Abuse of process, i.e., causing process to issue lawfully but to accomplish some unjustified purpose, is frequently confused with malicious prosecution, i.e., maliciously causing process to issue without justification. Although much of the confusion is dispelled on careful analysis, it must be noted that both torts possess the common element of improper purpose in the use of legal process and both were spawned from the action for trespass on the case in the nature of conspiracy.

Despite the paucity of New York authority, three essential elements of the tort of abuse of process can be distilled from the preceding history and case law. First, there must be regularly issued process, civil or criminal, compelling the performance or forbearance of some prescribed act. Next, the person activating the process must be moved by a purpose to do harm without that which has been traditionally described as economic or social excuse or justification Lastly, defendant must be seeking some collateral advantage or corresponding detriment to the plaintiff which is outside the legitimate ends of the process.

Assuming the truth of the facts pleaded along with every favorable inference and applying the above principles, we find that the complaint before us is sufficient to state a cause of action for abuse of process. The subpoenas here were regularly issued process, defendants were motivated by an intent to harass and to injure, and the refusal to comply with a reasonable request to stagger the appearances was sufficient to support an inference that the process was being perverted to inflict economic harm on the school district.

While it is true that public policy mandates free access to the courts for redress of wrongs and our adversarial system cannot function without zealous advocacy, it is also true that legal procedure must be utilized in a manner consonant with the purpose for which that procedure was designed. Where process is manipulated to achieve some collateral advantage, whether it be denominated extortion, blackmail or retribution, the tort of abuse of process will be available to the injured party.

The appellants raise several arguments against the sufficiency of this complaint. The most troublesome contention raised is that it is standard, appropriate and proper practice to subpoena all witnesses for the first day of any judicial proceeding. While we acknowledge this as appropriate procedure and in no way intend this decision to proscribe it, we are obligated to determine appeals in the context in which they are presented. Here we consider solely whether the complaint states a valid cause of action. If the proof at trial establishes that defendants attempted to reach a reasonable accommodation at a time when the accommodation would have been effectual, the cause of action will be defeated. However, on its face an allegation that defendants subpoenaed 87 persons with full knowledge that they all could not and would not testify and that this was done maliciously with the intent to injure and to harass plaintiff spells out an abuse of process. Another factor to be weighed at trial is whether the testimony of so many witnesses was material and necessary. As this complaint is framed, it may be inferred that defendants were effecting a not too subtle threat which should be actionable.

The dissent in the Appellate Division responds to this point by noting that the school district was not a party to the PERB proceeding, therefore defendants did not stand to gain collateral advantage, a requisite element of the alleged tort. While it is true that plaintiff was not a party to that proceeding, it is equally true that they were not disinterested bystanders. More important the deliberate premeditated infliction of economic injury without economic or social excuse or justification is an improper objective which will give rise to a cause of action for abuse of process.

In the same vein, defendants contend that the school district cannot bring this action because the alleged abusive process was not issued against them. Although there is support for this proposition (*see, generally, Restatement, Torts,* s 682) we reject it. To hold that the party whom the defendants seek to injure and who has suffered economic injury lacks standing would be to defy reality. Accordingly, the tort of abuse of process will be available to nonrecipients of process provided they are the target and victim of the perversion of that process.

Turning to the question of damages, we note that to sustain the first cause of action plaintiff must allege and prove actual or special damages in order to recover Plaintiff has satisfied this requirement by asserting damages in the amount expended to hire substitutes. However, we reject the claim for damages representing the salaries paid to the subpoenaed teachers. There is no justification for that element of damages, particularly in view of the fact that these were approved absences within the meaning of the collective bargaining agreement. Accordingly, that element of damages should be stricken from the complaint.

As to the second cause of action for punitive damages we see no obstacle to its maintenance, contingent on the establishment of malice.

* * *

Young v. Allstate Ins. Co.

198 P.3d 666
(Hawaii 2008)

[According to the allegations in the complaint, Plaintiff, age 87, was injured when his car was rear-ended by Fujimoto, who was insured by Allstate. Fujimoto admitted to Allstate that he had fallen asleep at the wheel. Allstate wrote to Plaintiff, promised to treat Plaintiff fairly, and informed Plaintiff that he did not need an attorney. Allstate eventually offered to settle with Plaintiff for $5,300 after Plaintiff had already incurred $6,000 in medical expenses and was still receiving treatment for a variety of injuries. Plaintiff eventually rejected the offer and filed suit. Allstate raised a number of defenses, including comparative fault. The case was sent to arbitration, at which point the arbitrator awarded Plaintiff over $45,000 in damages. Allstate appealed, refused to raise its offer of $5,300, and made an offer of judgment pursuant to Hawaii Rule of Civil Procedure 68 in the amount of $5,300. Eventually, Plaintiff prevailed at trial and the jury awarded $198,971.71. Following trial, Plaintiff brought claims of abuse of process, malicious defense, intentional infliction of emotional distress, and breach of the implied covenant of good faith and fair dealing for making false accusations about Plaintiff during the process, refusing to settle, and appealing the arbitration award in bad faith.]

This court has declared that there are two essential elements in a claim for abuse of process: "(1) an ulterior purpose and (2) a wilful act in the use of the process which is not proper in the regular conduct of the proceeding." Chung v. McCabe Hamilton & Renny Co., Ltd., 109 Hawai'i 520, 529, 128 P.3d 833, 842 (2006); *see also* Restatement (Second) of Torts ("Restatement of Torts") § 682 (1977) ("One who uses a legal process, whether criminal or civil, against another primarily to accomplish a purpose for which it is not designed, is subject to liability to the other for harm caused by the abuse of process.").

Preliminarily, the Defendants argue that the circuit court correctly dismissed Young's claim of abuse of process because "none of the alleged acts involved the use of judicial process." As the Supreme Court of California stated, however, "'[p]rocess,' as used in the tort of 'abuse of process,'... has been interpreted broadly to encompass the *entire range of 'procedures' incident to litigation.*" Barquis v. Merchants Collection Ass'n, 7 Cal.3d 94, 104 n. 4, 496 P.2d 817, 824 n. 4, (1972) (emphasis added). Here, Young's first amended complaint alleged that Defendants used process when they (1) appealed the arbitration award and forced the dispute to trial, (2) raised affirmative defenses in Fujimoto's answer, (3) made an HRCP Rule 68 offer of judgment, and (4) opposed Young's motions for attorneys' fees, costs, and prejudgment interest. These allegations sufficiently support that Defendants resorted to "process," inasmuch as these actions utilized procedures that were incident to the litigation. Accordingly, we next address whether Young's allegations sufficiently state that (1) the Defendants had an "ulterior purpose" and (2) performed "a wilful act in the use of the process which is not proper in the regular conduct of the proceeding."

1. "ulterior purpose"

In this case, the first amended complaint alleges that the Defendants used process in order to prevail in the underlying case through trial or settlement. While that general aim was clearly legitimate in the regular conduct of the underlying case, it also alleged that the Defendants used process to implement the CCPR plan, employing "scorched earth litigation tactics" to punish Young and to "send a message" to claimants and the plaintiffs' bar nationwide. In our view, that objective is patently illegitimate.[10] Whether that improper purpose was, in fact, the Defendants' primary motivation constitutes a question of fact that cannot be resolved by way of an HRCP Rule 12(b)(6) motion to dismiss. *See Givens*, 75 S.W.3d at 403 (concluding that, although the defendants may have used interrogatories and subpoenas solely for their lawful and intended purpose of gathering information relating to the merits of the case, their intention involved a question of fact not properly decided on a motion to dismiss). Accordingly, we conclude that the allegations sufficiently state that the Defendants employed process primarily for an ulterior purpose.

2. "a wilful act in the use of process which is not proper in the regular conduct of the proceeding"

We next reach the second element of the abuse of process claim: whether the defendant committed " 'a wilful act in the use of the process which is not proper in the regular conduct of the proceeding.' " Young fails to identify such an act by Allstate.

Young appears to allege that, by advancing unreasonably low settlement offers, Allstate engaged in improper willful acts. Offers to settle the claims at issue in a case are "proper," if not encouraged, in the regular conduct of proceedings. A contrary rule would have a "devastating effect on the settlement process," because parties would be wary of making settlement offers if such offers could provide the "essential ingredient" to subject them to a second lawsuit for abuse of process.

Aside from the settlement offers, the only other willful act alleged in the first amended complaint was the Defendants' use of process itself. The most recent edition of Professor Prosser's treatise on torts teaches that "*[s]ome definite act or threat* not authorized by the process, or aimed at an objective not legitimate in the use of the process, *is required*; and *there is no liability where the defendant has done nothing more than carry out the process to its authorized conclusion, even though with bad intentions*." PROSSER AND KEETON ON TORTS § 121, at 898 (5th ed., W. Page Keeton et al. eds., 1984) (emphases added) (footnotes omitted). Thus, more is required than the issuance of the process itself.

In the present matter, Young's first amended complaint alleged that the Defendants sought to further an improper purpose when they employed the legal processes of filing an answer, appealing the arbitration award and taking the dispute to trial, making a HRCP Rule 68 offer of judgment, and opposing Young's requests for attorneys' fees, costs, and prejudgment interest. In our view, the Defendants' use of such processes, without more, did not constitute "willful" acts that were, in themselves, antithetical to the legitimate conduct of the underlying case. *See* Tellefsen v. Key Sys. Transit Lines, 198 Cal.App.2d

10. *See* Crackel v. Allstate Ins. Co., 208 Ariz. 252, 92 P.3d 882, 890 (Ct.App.2004) (concluding that, in using court procedures pursuant to the CCPR plan, Allstate improperly used "the prospect of sustained and expensive litigation as a 'club' in an attempt to coerce [the claimants], and similarly situated claimants, to surrender those causes of action that sought only modest damages"); *Nienstedt*, 651 P.2d at 882 (recognizing that discovery procedures were used for an ulterior purpose where they were employed "to expose the injured party to excessive attorney's fees and legal expenses"); Givens v. Mullikin, 75 S.W.3d 383, 402 (Tenn. 2002) (concluding that it was improper to employ discovery procedures in order "to wear the mettle of the opposing party to reach a favorable termination of the cause unrelated to its merits").

611, 615, 17 Cal.Rptr. 919, 922 (1961) ("[M]erely taking a frivolous appeal is not enough to constitute an abuse of process.... There is no allegation of any act of defendant using such appeal for other than its proper purpose."); ... Hawkins v. Webster, 78 N.C.App. 589, 337 S.E.2d 682, 685 (1985) (holding that the defendant's filing of "answers, which contained falsehoods," was "not the type of improper act upon which a proper claim of abuse of process may be founded").

To summarize, although the first amended complaint sufficiently alleged that the Defendants employed processes and that their primary purpose in utilizing those processes was improper, it did not show that the Defendants committed a willful act not proper in the regular conduct of the underlying case. Accordingly, we hold that the circuit court correctly dismissed Young's abuse of process claim.

* * *

Bonner v. Chicago Title Ins. Co.

487 N.W.2d 807
(Mich. App. 1992)

To recover pursuant to a theory of abuse of process, a plaintiff must plead and prove (1) an ulterior purpose, and (2) an act in the use of process that is improper in the regular prosecution of the proceeding. In *Vallance v. Brewbaker*, 161 Mich.App. 642, 646, 411 N.W.2d 808 (1987), this Court described a meritorious claim of abuse of process as a situation where the defendant has used a proper legal procedure for a purpose collateral to the intended use of that procedure. The Court further stated that there must be some corroborating act that demonstrates the ulterior purpose. *Id.* A bad motive alone will not establish an abuse of process. *Id.*

In this case, plaintiffs alleged in their original complaint that Chicago Title abused the legal process by vigorously presenting groundless defenses in defending the Pomnichowskis in their earlier lawsuit. However, plaintiffs did not allege an act by Chicago Title that demonstrates that the defenses raised were raised with the alleged improper ulterior motive. Thus, the dismissal of plaintiffs' claim of abuse of process was proper.

* * *

1. Damages. A small minority of jurisdictions require a plaintiff to "establish that an arrest of the person or a seizure of property of the plaintiff resulted from the abuse of process." One Thousand Fleet Ltd. Partnership v. Guerriero, 694 A.2d 952, 960 (Md. 1997).

2. The litigation privilege. Courts tend to recognize the existence of the litigation privilege in abuse of process cases more than they do in malicious prosecution or wrongful initiation cases. *See* Silberg v. Anderson, 786 P.2d 365, 371 (1990) (extending absolute litigation privilege for all torts, including abuse of process, except malicious prosecution).

3. Model Rule comparison. The ABA's older *Model Code of Professional Responsibility* specifically prohibited a lawyer from threatening to present criminal charges solely to obtain an advantage in a civil matter. DR 7-105 (1980). The new Model Rules did not retain the prohibition, and a subsequent ethics opinion noted that the omission was intentional. ABA Ethics Opinion 92-363. Despite this, the rules of professional conduct in roughly half of the states still prohibit a lawyer from threatening criminal prosecution in order to gain an advantage in a separate civil proceeding.

Exercise 16.7

In what respect, if any, does the complaint from the Chapter Problem involving TV Connect fail to state a claim of abuse of process against TV Connect? Against TV Connect's attorneys, James Osterberg, Osterberg, Asheton & Alexander?

D. Anti-SLAPP Statutes

Statutes may also regulate the misuse of the legal process. Strategic Lawsuits Against Public Participation (SLAPPs) "are generally meritless suits brought by large private interests to deter common citizens from exercising their political or legal rights or to punish them for doing so." Wilcox v. Superior Court, 33 Cal. Rptr. 2d 446, 450 (Ct. App. 1994). Over half of all jurisdictions now have anti-SLAPP statutes in place to address this problem. Carson Hilary Barylak, Note, *Reducing Uncertainty in Anti-SLAPP Protection*, 71 Ohio St. L.J. 845, 847 (2010).

Focus Questions: *Wilcox v. Superior Court*

1. *Why, according to* Wilcox, *are abuse of process and wrongful initiation claims inadequate to deal with the problem of SLAPPs?*
2. *How do anti-SLAPP statutes address those inadequacies?*

Wilcox v. Superior Court

33 Cal.Rptr.2d 446
(Cal. Ct. App. 1994)

JOHNSON, Associate Justice.

In her petition for writ of mandate Sondra Wilcox, a cross-defendant below, challenges the ruling of the trial court denying her motion to strike the cross-complaint against her for damages and injunctive relief based on restraint of trade and defamation. The motion to strike was based on California's anti-SLAPP (strategic lawsuits against public participation) suit statute (Code Civ.Proc., §425.16). We issued an alternative writ of mandate and stayed proceedings in the trial court pending our decision on the merits. For the reasons set forth below we have determined the cross-complaint is subject to a motion to strike under the anti-SLAPP-suit statute and cross-complainants have failed to establish a probability they will prevail on their claims against petitioner.

FACTS AND PROCEEDINGS BELOW

This cause and its companion, *Saunders v. Superior Court* (1994), 27 Cal.App.4th 832, 33 Cal.Rptr.2d 438, arise out of the practice of "direct contracting" under which a certified shorthand reporter or association of reporters contracts with a major consumer of reporter services, such as an insurance company, for the exclusive right to report depositions taken by attorneys representing that consumer.

Plaintiffs in *Saunders* are certified shorthand reporters who brought suit against defendants, also certified shorthand reporters, alleging "direct contracting" as practiced by defendants constitutes an unfair business practice, intentional interference with plaintiffs' prospective economic advantages and interference with existing contracts. The reporter defendants in *Saunders* are members of an association known as the California Reporting Alliance, referred to by the parties as CRA or the Alliance. Also named as defendants are two insurance companies which entered into "direct contracting" agreements with the reporter defendants through CRA. Petitioner Wilcox is not a plaintiff in the *Saunders* suit but she did make a financial contribution to support the litigation.

The reporter defendants in *Saunders* filed a cross-complaint against the plaintiffs in that action as well as other individuals including Wilcox and her reporting agency for defamation and conspiracy to unlawfully restrain trade through a boycott of defendants' reporting services. (We will refer to Wilcox and her agency together as "Wilcox" or "petitioner.")

The first amended cross-complaint alleges Wilcox distributed a memorandum to various other shorthand reporters which stated, among other things: many shorthand reporting agencies were banding together "to 'permanently put the Alliance to rest once and for all' "; reporters were suing CRA and its members for extortion and racketeering; and reporters should tell attorneys representing insurance companies and their policyholders about this litigation so that the "threat" might be enough to make the insurers "back off" from entering into direct contracting agreements with CRA. The memorandum asked each reporter to contribute $100 to the lawsuit against CRA. The cross-complaint also alleges Wilcox told CRA members she would no longer refer them any work or network with them because they were affiliated with CRA.

Characterizing the cross-complaint as a SLAPP suit, Wilcox filed a motion to strike as to her and her reporting agency pursuant to Code of Civil Procedure section 425.16. The trial court denied the motion on the ground "the responding parties have proffered sufficient evidence in opposition to the motion to establish the probability they will prevail on their claims."

Wilcox filed a petition for writ of mandate in this court seeking to overturn the trial court's denial of her motion to strike. As previously noted, we issued an alternative writ and stayed the proceedings below.

DISCUSSION

I. OVERVIEW OF STRATEGIC LAWSUITS AGAINST PUBLIC PARTICIPATION ("SLAPP" SUITS).

Litigation which has come to be known as SLAPP, is defined by the sociologists who coined the term as "civil lawsuits ... that are aimed at preventing citizens from exercising their political rights or punishing those who have done so." (Canan & Pring, *Strategic Lawsuits Against Public Participation* (1988) 35 Soc.Probs. 506.) The paradigm SLAPP is a suit filed by a large land developer against environmental activists or a neighborhood association intended to chill the defendants' continued political or legal opposition to the developers' plans. SLAPPs, however, are by no means limited to environmental issues (*see, e.g.*, Brownsville Golden Age Nursing Home, Inc. v. Wells (3d Cir.1988) 839 F.2d 155, 157 [suit by nursing home against private citizens who had complained to government officials about conditions in plaintiff's facility]), nor are the defendants necessarily local organizations with limited resources. (*See, e.g.*, Sierra Club v. Butz (N.D.Cal.1972) 349 F.Supp. 934.)

The favored causes of action in SLAPP suits are defamation, various business torts such as interference with prospective economic advantage, nuisance and intentional infliction of emotional distress. Plaintiffs in these actions typically ask for damages which would be ruinous to the defendants.

SLAPP suits are brought to obtain an economic advantage over the defendant, not to vindicate a legally cognizable right of the plaintiff. Indeed, one of the common characteristics of a SLAPP suit is its lack of merit. But lack of merit is not of concern to the plaintiff because the plaintiff does not expect to succeed in the lawsuit, only to tie up the defendant's resources for a sufficient length of time to accomplish plaintiff's underlying objective. As long as the defendant is forced to devote its time, energy and financial resources to combating the lawsuit its ability to combat the plaintiff in the political arena is substantially diminished. The SLAPP strategy also works even if the matter is already in litigation because the defendant/cross-complainant hopes to drive up the cost of litigation to the point where the plaintiff/cross-defendant will abandon its case or have less resources available to prosecute its action against the defendant/cross-complainant and to deter future litigation.

Thus, while SLAPP suits "masquerade as ordinary lawsuits" the conceptual features which reveal them as SLAPPs are that they are generally meritless suits brought by large private interests to deter common citizens from exercising their political or legal rights or to punish them for doing so. Because winning is not a SLAPP plaintiff's primary motivation, defendants' traditional safeguards against meritless actions, (suits for malicious prosecution and abuse of process, requests for sanctions) are inadequate to counter SLAPPs. Instead, the SLAPPer considers any damage or sanction award which the SLAPPee might eventually recover as merely a cost of doing business. By the time a SLAPP victim can win a "SLAPP-back" suit years later the SLAPP plaintiff will probably already have accomplished its underlying objective. Furthermore, retaliation against the SLAPPer may be counter-productive because it ties up the SLAPPee's resources even longer than defending the SLAPP suit itself.

For these reasons, courts and legislatures have looked for procedural remedies which would allow prompt exposure and dismissal of SLAPP suits.

California's response to SLAPP suits was to enact Code of Civil Procedure section 425.16, discussed below.

II. CALIFORNIA'S LEGISLATIVE RESPONSE TO SLAPP SUITS.

Senate Bill 1264, 1991–1994 Regular Session, added a new section 425.16 to the Code of Civil Procedure effective January 1, 1993. (Stats.1992, ch. 726, § 2.)

This legislation provides in relevant part:

> (a) The Legislature finds and declares that there has been a disturbing increase in lawsuits brought primarily to chill the valid exercise of the constitutional rights of freedom of speech and petition for the redress of grievances. The Legislature finds and declares that it is in the public interest to encourage continued participation in matters of public significance, and that this participation should not be chilled through abuse of the judicial process. To this end, this section shall be construed broadly.
>
> (b)(1) A cause of action against a person arising from any act of that person in furtherance of the person's right of petition or free speech under the United

States Constitution or the California Constitution in connection with a public issue shall be subject to a special motion to strike, unless the court determines that the plaintiff has established that there is a probability that the plaintiff will prevail on the claim.

(2) In making its determination, the court shall consider the pleadings, and supporting and opposing affidavits stating the facts upon which the liability or defense is based.

(3) If the court determines that the plaintiff has established a probability that he or she will prevail on the claim, neither that determination nor the fact of that determination shall be admissible in evidence at any later stage of the case, or in any subsequent action, and no burden of proof or degree of proof otherwise applicable shall be affected by that determination in any later stage of the case or in any subsequent proceeding.

...

(e) As used in this section, "act in furtherance of a person's right of petition or free speech under the United States or California Constitution in connection with a public issue" includes: (1) any written or oral statement or writing made before a legislative, executive, or judicial proceeding, or any other official proceeding authorized by law, (2) any written or oral statement or writing made in connection with an issue under consideration or review by a legislative, executive, or judicial body, or any other official proceeding authorized by law, (3) any written or oral statement or writing made in a place open to the public or a public forum in connection with an issue of public interest, or (4) any other conduct in furtherance of the exercise of the constitutional right of petition or the constitutional right of free speech in connection with a public issue or an issue of public interest.

(f) The special motion may be filed within 60 days of the service of the complaint or, in the court's discretion, at any later time upon terms it deems proper. The motion shall be scheduled by the clerk of the court for a hearing not more than 30 days after the service of the motion unless the docket conditions of the court require a later hearing.

(g) All discovery proceedings in the action shall be stayed upon the filing of a notice of motion made pursuant to this section. The stay of discovery shall remain in effect until notice of entry of the order ruling on the motion. The court, on noticed motion and for good cause shown, may order that specified discovery be conducted notwithstanding this subdivision.*

The parties raise four issues under the anti-SLAPP statute. (1) Do any of the causes of action against petitioner arise from an act of petitioner in furtherance of her First Amendment rights so as to trigger a special motion to strike under the statute? (2) Who has the burden of proof on this issue? (3) Assuming a special motion to strike is triggered by the cross-complaint, what showing must the cross-complainants make in order to establish a "probability" they will prevail on their claims? (4) Did the trial court err in finding cross-complainants established such a probability? We address these issues below.

---

* Editor's note: The statutory language included here is the current statutory language, which replaces the older version of the statute included in the decision.

III. PETITIONER MADE A SUFFICIENT SHOWING THE CAUSES OF ACTION AGAINST HER AROSE FROM ACTS IN FURTHERANCE OF HER RIGHTS OF PETITION AND FREE SPEECH IN CONNECTION WITH A PUBLIC ISSUE.

A. The Defendant in an Alleged SLAPP Suit Bears the Initial Burden of Showing the Suit Falls Within the Class of Suits Subject to the Special Motion to Strike.

As noted above, section 425.16 does not apply in every case where the defendant may be able to raise a First Amendment defense to a cause of action. Rather, it is limited to exposing and dismissing SLAPP suits—lawsuits "brought primarily to chill the valid exercise of the constitutional rights of freedom of speech and petition for the redress of grievances" "in connection with a public issue." (§425.16, subds. (a), (b).)

Although the statute clearly places the burden on the plaintiff or cross-complainant to establish a probability of prevailing on the claim (§425.16, subd. (b)), this burden does not arise unless the claim is one falling within the ambit of the statute. The statute is silent as to whether the defendant, as the moving party, has the burden of establishing the action arises out of acts in furtherance of defendant's First Amendment rights in connection with a public issue or whether the plaintiff bears the burden of showing its claim does not arise out of such acts by the defendant....

Traditionally, a party seeking to benefit from a statute bears the burden of making a prima facie showing the statute applies to her. We see no reason why that rule should not apply to a party seeking a special motion to strike under section 425.16. It is not only logical to put this burden on the party seeking the benefit of section 425.16, it is fundamentally fair that before putting the plaintiff to the burden of establishing probability of success on the merits the defendant be required to show imposing that burden is justified by the nature of the plaintiff's complaint.

We conclude, therefore, the statute requires the defendant to make a prima facie showing the plaintiff's suit arises "from any act of [defendant] in furtherance of [defendant's] right of petition or free speech under the United States or California Constitution in connection with a public issue." (§425.16, subd. (b).) The defendant may meet this burden by showing the act which forms the basis for the plaintiff's cause of action was a written or oral statement made before a legislative, executive, or judicial proceeding; or such a statement in connection with an issue under consideration or review by a legislative, executive, or judicial body; or such a statement was made in a place open to the public or a public forum in connection with an issue of public interest; [or any other conduct in furtherance of the exercise of the constitutional right of petition or the constitutional right of free speech in connection with a public issue or an issue of public interest.] (§425.16, subd. (e).) Thus, if the defendant's act was a lawsuit against a developer the defendant would have a prima facie First Amendment defense. (Pacific Gas & Electric Co. v. Bear Stearns & Co. (1990) 50 Cal.3d 1118, 1136–1137, 270 Cal.Rptr. 1, 791 P.2d 587.) But, if the defendant's act was burning down the developer's office as a political protest the defendant's motion to strike could be summarily denied without putting the developer to the burden of establishing the probability of success on the merits in a tort suit against defendant.

It should be noted the definition of an "act in furtherance of" a person's First Amendment rights is not limited to oral and written statements. §425.16, subd. (e).) Thus if the plaintiff's suit arises out of the defendant's constitutionally protected conduct, such as a peaceful economic boycott the plaintiff should be required to satisfy the statute's requirements.

B. Petitioner Made a Sufficient Showing the Causes of Action Against Her Arose From Acts in Furtherance of Her Rights of Petition and Free Speech in Connection With a Public Issue.

Cross-complainants concede the issue of "direct contracting" is a public issue within the meaning of section 425.16, subdivisions (b) and (e). They contend, however, petitioner failed to show the acts alleged in the cross-complaint were done "in connection with" the consideration of direct contracting by any legislative, executive or judicial body as required by those same subdivisions. They argue there is no rational connection between legislative, administrative and judicial challenges to direct contracting and petitioner's alleged defamatory statements and conspiracy with others to injure cross-complainants in their businesses.

This argument points up why traditional pleading-based motions such as demurrers and motions to strike are ineffective in combating SLAPP's and why the Legislature believed there was a need for a "special motion to strike" as authorized by section 425.16. In a SLAPP complaint the defendant's act of petitioning the government is made to appear as defamation, interference with business relations, restraint of trade and the like. For this reason the Legislature provided, in determining a motion under the anti-SLAPP statute, "the court shall consider the pleadings and supporting and opposing affidavits stating the facts upon which the liability or defense is based." (§ 425.16, subd. (b).)

Here petitioner's alleged defamatory statements were clearly made in connection with the underlying judicial challenge to direct contracting. As shown by the cross-complaint itself those statements were made in the context of exhorting shorthand reporters to contribute to the cost of pursing that litigation. Thus, there is a strong showing those statements are rationally connected to the litigation itself.

As to the claims involving restraint of trade, "the constitutional right to petition for redress of grievances [establishes] that there is no antitrust liability for petitioning any branch of government, even if the motive is anticompetitive." There is case law supporting the proposition petitioning includes acts designed to influence public opinion concerning an issue before a legislative or administrative body. Eastern R.R. Presidents' Conference v. Noerr Motor Freight, Inc. (1961) 365 U.S. 127, 142–144, 81 S.Ct. 523, 532–533, 5 L.Ed.2d 464 (hereafter *Noerr*); Webb v. Fury, *supra*, 282 S.E.2d at p. 42. Moreover, the fact a defendant's petitioning activity includes an economic boycott does not necessarily deprive that activity of constitutional protection. (NAACP v. Claiborne Hardware, *supra*, 458 U.S. at pp. 913–914, 102 S.Ct. at pp. 3425–3426; State of Mo. v. Nat. Organization for Women, *supra*, 620 F.2d at p. 1315.) Assuming petitioner engaged in a conspiracy to boycott the cross-complaining shorthand reporters, an allegation she denies, such activity is at least arguably protected by the petition clause of the First Amendment and the trial court properly shifted the burden to the cross-complainants on this issue.

IV. THE CROSS-COMPLAINANTS FAILED TO SATISFY THE REQUIREMENT OF SHOWING A PROBABILITY THEY WILL PREVAIL ON THEIR CLAIMS AGAINST PETITIONER.

A. To Establish "A Probability That the Plaintiff Will Prevail on the Claim" the Plaintiff Must Make a Prima Facie Showing of Facts Which Would, If Proved at Trial, Support a Judgment in Plaintiff's Favor.

Section 425.16, subdivision (b) requires the plaintiff to establish "a probability that the plaintiff will prevail on the claim." We must first determine what the Legislature meant by a "probability" the plaintiff will prevail....

Cases involving similar statutes have held the requirement of establishing a substantial or reasonable probability of success means only that the plaintiff must demonstrate the complaint is legally sufficient and supported by a sufficient prima facie showing of facts to sustain a favorable judgment if the evidence submitted by the plaintiff is credited. If either of these requirements is not met, the motion to strike must be granted; if both are satisfied, it must be denied. This standard is much like that used in determining a motion for nonsuit or directed verdict.

We believe section 425.16, subdivision (b) should be given a similar construction. As discussed above, SLAPP suits are distinguishable from ordinary tort suits by their lack of merit. One of the purposes of section 425.16 … is to eliminate such meritless litigation at an early stage. This statutory purpose is met by requiring the plaintiff to demonstrate sufficient facts to establish a prima facie case.

B. Cross-complainants Failed to Establish a Probability of Prevailing on the Defamation Claim Against Petitioner.

[The court concluded that assuming Wilcox's statements were defamatory, "the fundamental right to petition the government for redress of grievances provides Wilcox with at least a qualified privilege which the cross-complainants have not demonstrated they can overcome."]

C. Cross-complainants Failed to Establish a Probability of Prevailing on the Conspiracy Claims Against Petitioner.

In addition to the claim for defamation based on petitioner's own statements, the cross-complaint seeks to impose liability on petitioner for conspiring with the other cross-defendants to defame cross-complainants, injure them through unlawful and unfair business practices and intentional interference with their prospective business relationships. [The court concluded that "[t]he cross-complainants in this action have failed to produce legally sufficient evidence Wilcox concurred with at least one other person in a tortious scheme to injure cross-complainants."]

DISPOSITION

Let a peremptory writ issue directing the respondent court to vacate its order denying petitioner's motion to strike and to enter a new and different order striking the cross-complaint in its entirety as to cross-defendants Sondra Wilcox and Sondra K. Wilcox & Associates, Inc.

Focus Questions: *Mendoza v. Hamzeh*

1. *Why didn't Mendoza bring an abuse of process claim instead of the other claims asserted?*
2. *Is a demand letter that threatens litigation unless the recipient pays a disputed sum covered by the anti-SLAPP statute?*

Mendoza v. Hamzeh

155 Cal.Rptr.3d 832
(Cal. Ct. App. 2013)

CHANEY, J.

BACKGROUND

In May 2011, plaintiff Miguel Mendoza filed this action against attorney Reed Hamzeh, asserting causes of action for civil extortion, intentional infliction of emotional distress and unfair business practices. The lawsuit arises from a May 6, 2009 letter (the demand letter) Hamzeh sent to Mendoza while Hamzeh was representing a client named Guy Chow regarding a dispute between Chow and Mendoza. The dispute concerned Mendoza's employment as the manager of Chow's print and copy business.

The demand letter from Hamzeh to Mendoza begins: "As you are aware, I have been retained to represent Media Print & Copy ('Media'). We are in the process of uncovering the substantial fraud, conversion and breaches of contract that your client has committed on my client.... To date we have uncovered damages exceeding $75,000, not including interest applied thereto, punitive damages and attorneys' fees. If your client does not agree to cooperate with our investigation and provide us with a repayment of such damages caused, we will be forced to proceed with filing a legal action against him, as well as reporting him to the California Attorney General, the Los Angeles District Attorney, the Internal Revenue Service regarding tax fraud, the Better Business Bureau, as well as to customers and vendors with whom he may be perpetrating the same fraud upon [sic]." The letter goes on to list Mendoza's alleged transgressions, including failure to pay Media's employees, sales taxes and bills.

In his complaint in this action, Mendoza asserts "Hamzeh's threat to report Mendoza to the California Attorney General, the Los Angeles District Attorney, and the Internal Revenue Service constitute[s] the crime of extortion under California law." As set forth above, based on the demand letter, Mendoza brought causes of action against Hamzeh for civil extortion, intentional infliction of emotional distress and unfair business practices.

In September 2011, Hamzeh filed his anti-SLAPP motion, asking the trial court to strike Mendoza's complaint on grounds the demand letter constitutes a protected litigation communication under the anti-SLAPP statute and Mendoza cannot establish a probability of prevailing on his claims because they are barred by the litigation and common interest privileges (Civ.Code, § 47, subds.(b) & (c)). Hamzeh argued he was entitled to attorney fees and costs under section 425.16, subdivision (c)(1).

On October 20, 2011, before filing an opposition to the anti-SLAPP motion, Mendoza's counsel sent a letter to Hamzeh's counsel stating his intention to seek an award of attorney fees under section 425.16, subdivision (c), on grounds the anti-SLAPP motion was frivolous or solely intended to cause unnecessary delay. Mendoza's counsel argued Hamzeh failed to cite in his anti-SLAPP motion the "controlling" California Supreme Court case, *Flatley v. Mauro* (2006) 39 Cal.4th 299, 305, 46 Cal.Rptr.3d 606, 139 P.3d 2 (*Flatley*), holding settlement communications which constitute criminal extortion as a matter of law are not covered by the anti-SLAPP statute. Mendoza's counsel asserted "There is little doubt that Mr. Hamzeh committed extortion when he threatened to report my client to the California Attorney General, the Los Angeles District Attorney, the Internal Revenue Service, the Better Business Bureau, etc. unless my client agreed to pay all damages allegedly caused (which at the time of the letter was represented to be in excess of $75,000) and to cooperate with their investigation."

Hamzeh did not withdraw his anti-SLAPP motion so, on December 1, 2011, Mendoza filed his opposition to the motion and sought attorney fees. Hamzeh filed a reply brief arguing "*Flatley* is inapposite because Hamzeh did not commit a crime" (capitalized and bold font omitted).

After hearing oral argument, the trial court denied the anti-SLAPP motion, concluding the communication at issue was not covered by the anti-SLAPP statute based on the holding in *Flatley, supra.* The court awarded Mendoza $3,150 in attorney fees.

DISCUSSION

I. Anti-SLAPP Motion

...

B. Section 425.16

In evaluating an anti-SLAPP motion, we conduct a two-step analysis. First, we must decide whether the defendant "has made a threshold showing that the challenged cause of action arises from protected activity." For these purposes, protected activity "includes: (1) any written or oral statement or writing made before a legislative, executive, or judicial proceeding, or any other official proceeding authorized by law, (2) any written or oral statement or writing made in connection with an issue under consideration or review by a legislative, executive, or judicial body, or any other official proceeding authorized by law, (3) any written or oral statement or writing made in a place open to the public or a public forum in connection with an issue of public interest, or (4) any other conduct in furtherance of the exercise of the constitutional right of petition or the constitutional right of free speech in connection with a public issue or an issue of public interest." (§425.16, subd. (e).)

Second, if the defendant makes this threshold showing, we decide whether the plaintiff "has demonstrated a probability of prevailing on the claim."

C. *Flatley, supra,* 39 Cal.4th 299, 46 Cal.Rptr.3d 606, 139 P.3d 2

In *Flatley, supra,* the California Supreme Court concluded the anti-SLAPP statute does not apply to communications which constitute criminal extortion as a matter of law because such communications are "unprotected by constitutional guarantees of free speech or petition." As the *Flatley* Court set forth:

> "Extortion is the obtaining of property from another, with his consent... induced by a wrongful use of force or fear...." (Pen.Code, §518.) Fear, for purposes of extortion "may be induced by a threat, either: [¶] ... [¶] 2. To accuse the individual threatened... of any crime; or, [¶] 3. To expose, or impute to him... any deformity, disgrace or crime[.]" (Pen.Code, §519.) "Every person who, with intent to extort any money or other property from another, sends or delivers to any person any letter or other writing, whether subscribed or not, expressing or implying, or adapted to imply, any threat such as is specified in Section 519, is punishable in the same manner as if such money or property were actually obtained by means of such threat." (Pen.Code, §523.)"

(*Flatley, supra,* 39 Cal.4th at p. 326, 46 Cal.Rptr.3d 606, 139 P.3d 2.)

The threat to report a crime may constitute extortion even if the victim did in fact commit a crime. The threat to report a crime may in and of itself be legal. But when the threat to report a crime is coupled with a demand for money, the threat becomes illegal, regardless of whether the victim in fact owed the money demanded. "The law does not contemplate the use of criminal process as a means of collecting a debt." [*Flatley*] "Attorneys are not exempt from these principles in their professional conduct. Indeed, the Rules of Professional Conduct specifically prohibit attorneys from 'threaten[ing] to present criminal, administration, or disciplinary charges to obtain an advantage in a civil dispute.' (Cal. Rules of Prof. Conduct, rule 5-100(A).)" (*Id.* at p. 327, 46 Cal.Rptr.3d 606, 139 P.3d 2.)

Of the anti-SLAPP cases the parties cite, *Flatley* has the most similar fact pattern to the case before us. As stated in the Supreme Court's opinion: "Plaintiff Michael Flatley, a well-known entertainer, sued defendant D. Dean Mauro, an attorney, for civil extortion, intentional infliction of emotional distress and wrongful interference with economic advantage. Flatley's action was based on a demand letter Mauro sent to Flatley on behalf of Tyna Marie Robertson, a woman who claimed that Flatley had raped her, and on subsequent telephone calls Mauro made to Flatley's attorneys, demanding a seven-figure payment to settle Robertson's claims. Mauro filed a motion to strike Flatley's complaint under the anti-SLAPP statute."

In concluding the communications constituted extortion as a matter of law, and therefore the anti-SLAPP statute did not apply, the Supreme Court explained: "At the core of Mauro's letter are threats to publicly accuse Flatley of rape and to report and publicly accuse him of other unspecified violations of various laws unless he 'settled' by paying a sum of money to Robertson of which Mauro would receive 40 percent. In his follow-up phone calls, Mauro named the price of his and Robertson's silence as 'seven figures' or, at minimum, $1 million." Mauro also insinuated in the demand letter that Flatley had committed "various criminal offenses involving immigration and tax law as well as violations of the Social Security Act."

Mauro argued the litigation privilege set forth in Civil Code section 47, subdivision (b), applied to the demand letter. The Supreme Court concluded, regardless of whether the litigation privilege applied to the threats in the demand letter, such threats "are nonetheless not protected under the anti-SLAPP statute because the litigation privilege and the anti-SLAPP statute are substantively different statutes that serve quite different purposes, and it is not consistent with the language or the purpose of the anti-SLAPP statute to protect such threats."

D. Analysis

The anti-SLAPP statute does not apply to the threats at issue in Hamzeh's demand letter. Hamzeh threatened to report Mendoza "to the California Attorney General, the Los Angeles District Attorney, the Internal Revenue Service regarding tax fraud, [and] the Better Business Bureau," and to disclose the alleged wrongdoing to Mendoza's customers and vendors if Mendoza did not pay "damages exceeding $75,000." Regardless of whether Mendoza committed any crime or wrongdoing or owed Chow money, Hamzeh's threat to report criminal conduct to enforcement agencies and to Mendoza's customers and vendors, coupled with a demand for money, constitutes "criminal extortion as a matter of law," as articulated in *Flatley*.

The fact Hamzeh did not list specific crimes in the demand letter does not mean the threat is not extortionate. "'[T]he accusations need only be such as to put the intended victim of the extortion in fear of being accused of some crime. The more vague and general the terms of the accusation the better it would subserve the purpose of the accuser in magnifying the fears of his victim....'" (*Flatley, supra*, 39 Cal.4th at p. 327, 46 Cal.Rptr.3d 606, 139 P.3d 2.)

Hamzeh asserts, in applying *Flatley* to the present case, "the trial court read *Flatley* too broadly." We acknowledge the attorney's conduct in *Flatley* was more egregious than Hamzeh's conduct, in terms of nature and number of threats. Moreover, as Hamzeh points out, the Supreme Court "emphasize[d] that [its] conclusion that Mauro's communications constituted criminal extortion as a matter of law are based on the specific and extreme circumstances of this case."

Regardless of whether the threat in Hamzeh's demand letter may be characterized as particularly extreme or egregious, it still constitutes criminal extortion as a matter of law....

We do not read *Flatley* to mean the anti-SLAPP statute applies to some litigation communications which satisfy the criteria for criminal extortion if such communications are not particularly extreme or egregious. The rule must be a bright line rule. The anti-SLAPP statute does not apply to litigation communications which constitute criminal extortion as a matter of law.

The trial court did not err in denying Hamzeh's anti-SLAPP motion because the anti-SLAPP statute does not apply to the threat in Hamzeh's demand letter on which Mendoza's complaint is based. Because Hamzeh did not make a threshold showing any cause of action in Mendoza's complaint arises from protected activity, we need not decide whether Mendoza has demonstrated a probability of prevailing on his causes of action (the second step in the two-step anti-SLAPP analysis).

DISPOSITION

The order denying Hamzeh's anti-SLAPP motion and awarding attorney fees to Mendoza is affirmed. Mendoza is entitled to recover attorney fees and costs on appeal in amounts to be determined by the trial court.

* * *

1. **Prevailing parties.** The defendant (the party asserting it has been SLAPPed) who prevails on the motion to strike is entitled to collect attorney's fees and costs under California's anti-SLAPP statute. If the motion to strike is determined to be frivolous, the plaintiff (the alleged SLAPPer) is entitled to collect fees. § 425.16(c)(1).

2. **Intent to chill?** In *Equilon Enterprises v. Consumer Cause, Inc.*, 52 P.3d 685 (Cal. 2002), the California Supreme Court clarified that the party moving to strike need not establish that the alleged SLAPPer acted with the intent to chill the defendant's exercise of constitutionally protected speech or petition rights.

3. **Litigation and prelitigation conduct.** A lawyer's litigation or prelitigation conduct taken in anticipation of litigation may be the subject of an anti-SLAPP motion. Shekhter v. Financial Indemnity Co., 89 Cal.App.4th 141 (2001). However, *Mendoza* holds that conduct amounting to civil extortion does not qualify as protected activity. What other kinds of litigation-related conduct is not covered by an anti-SLAPP statute? Assume that a lawyer's former client sues the lawyer, alleging the lawyer is now representing a new client against the former client in violation of the jurisdiction's conflict of interest rules. Assume further that the former client claims the lawyer has also used confidential information against the former client in the course of the new representation in violation of the rules of professional conduct. The lawyer then brings a motion to strike under California's anti-SLAPP statute, arguing that he engaged in protected litigation conduct. Has the lawyer engaged in protected conduct for purposes of the first prong of the analysis?

Exercise 16.8

Ronald Trujillo was an employee of AmericanBank, the largest bank in the U.S. Trujillo managed client accounts. AmericanBank's largest customer was Mason Dixon, Inc., a multinational corporation. Mason Dixon experienced financial difficulties and had trouble repaying some of its loans from AmericanBank. As a result, Trujillo instructed another AmericanBank employee to refuse to make another loan to Mason Dixon. Angered, Mason Dixon withdrew all of its accounts from AmericanBank. Officials from AmericanBank requested and were granted an emergency meeting with Mason Dixon officials to discuss the situation. During the meeting, Mason Dixon officials allegedly made false and defamatory statements about Trujillo's intelligence, business acumen, and professional ethics. Eventually, AmericanBank was successful in convincing Mason Dixon to resume its business with AmericanBank. However, Trujillo was fired the day after the meeting due to his handling of the Mason Dixon matter.

Trujillo sued Mason Dixon on theories of defamation and tortious interference with his employment relationship with AmericanBank. In response, Mason Dixon filed an anti-SLAPP motion pursuant to California's statute. Based on the information presented, what should be the result?

E. Spoliation of Evidence

Focus Questions: *Cedars-Sinai Medical Center v. Superior Court*

1. *Why is the court unwilling to recognize the tort of spoliation of evidence?*
2. *Do you find those reasons persuasive?*

Cedars-Sinai Medical Center v. Superior Court

954 P.2d 511
(Cal. 1998)

KENNARD, Justice.

Plaintiff, a child injured during birth, alleges that defendant hospital intentionally destroyed evidence relevant to his malpractice action against the hospital. He seeks to bring a separate tort cause of action against defendant hospital for its alleged intentional spoliation—that is, intentional destruction or suppression—of evidence.

I

Plaintiff Kristopher Schon Bowyer, through his guardian ad litem, brought a medical malpractice action against defendant Cedars-Sinai Medical Center (hereafter sometimes hospital) and others for injuries he allegedly sustained because of oxygen deprivation during birth. In the course of pretrial discovery, plaintiff's attorney sought from defendant hospital copies of plaintiff's medical records; defendant hospital was unable to locate certain records, including fetal monitoring strips recording plaintiff's heartbeat during labor.

Plaintiff's attorney thereafter filed a second amended complaint, adding a cause of action for intentional spoliation of evidence and alleging that the hospital had intentionally destroyed the missing records to prevent plaintiff from prevailing in his malpractice action. The complaint sought punitive damages on plaintiff's cause of action for intentional spoliation. Defendant hospital moved to strike plaintiff's punitive damages claim on the ground that plaintiff had not complied with Code of Civil Procedure section 425.13, and the trial court granted the motion. Under section 425.13, a plaintiff may not file a complaint seeking punitive damages in an action arising out of the professional negligence of a health care provider unless the court grants an order permitting the complaint to be filed; the court may grant the order only if the plaintiff establishes through affidavits a substantial probability of prevailing on the punitive damages claim.

Plaintiff then moved under Code of Civil Procedure section 425.13 for leave to file a third amended complaint seeking punitive damages. The trial court granted plaintiff's motion. Defendant hospital petitioned the Court of Appeal for a writ of mandate. After issuing the alternative writ, the Court of Appeal denied defendant's petition in a written opinion holding that section 425.13 did not apply to plaintiff's claim of intentional spoliation because the alleged spoliation did not occur while defendant hospital was rendering professional medical services to plaintiff. We granted review to decide whether this court should recognize a tort remedy for the intentional destruction or suppression of evidence by a party to the underlying litigation and, if so, whether section 425.13 applies to claims for punitive damages for acts of intentional spoliation by a health care provider.

II

At the threshold of this case stands the question of whether this court should recognize a tort remedy for the intentional spoliation of evidence by a party to the underlying cause of action to which the evidence is relevant (what we shall term a "first party" spoliator) when, as here, the spoliation is or reasonably should have been discovered before the trial or other decision on the merits of the underlying cause of action. This court has not previously addressed the question of whether tort remedies should exist for acts of spoliation.

In considering whether to create a tort remedy for intentional first party spoliation that is or reasonably should have been discovered before trial of the underlying action, we begin with certain general principles of tort law. "A tort, whether intentional or negligent, involves a violation of a legal duty, imposed by statute, contract or otherwise, owed by the defendant to the person injured." (5 Witkin, Summary of Cal. Law (9th ed. 1988) Torts, §6, p. 61.) At issue here is whether to impose on parties to a lawsuit a duty to avoid the intentional destruction of evidence relevant to the lawsuit. As we have stated, the concept of duty "'is a shorthand statement of a conclusion, rather than an aid to analysis in itself.'" (Dillon v. Legg (1968) 68 Cal.2d 728, 734, 69 Cal.Rptr. 72, 441 P.2d 912.) It is "only an expression of the sum total of those considerations of policy which lead the law to say that the particular plaintiff is entitled to protection." (*Ibid.*) Thus, we must examine and weigh the relevant "considerations of policy" that favor or oppose a tort remedy for intentional first party spoliation.

No one doubts that the intentional destruction of evidence should be condemned. Destroying evidence can destroy fairness and justice, for it increases the risk of an erroneous decision on the merits of the underlying cause of action. Destroying evidence can also increase the costs of litigation as parties attempt to reconstruct the destroyed evidence or to develop other evidence, which may be less accessible, less persuasive, or both.

That alone, however, is not enough to justify creating tort liability for such conduct. We must also determine whether a tort remedy for the intentional first party spoliation of evidence would ultimately create social benefits exceeding those created by existing remedies for such conduct, and outweighing any costs and burdens it would impose. Three concerns in particular stand out here: the conflict between a tort remedy for intentional first party spoliation and the policy against creating derivative tort remedies for litigation-related misconduct; the strength of existing nontort remedies for spoliation; and the uncertainty of the fact of harm in spoliation cases.

Our inquiry into whether to create a tort remedy for the intentional spoliation of evidence must begin with a recognition that using tort law to correct misconduct arising during litigation raises policy considerations not present in deciding whether to create tort remedies for harms arising in other contexts. In the past, we have favored remedying litigation-related misconduct by sanctions imposed within the underlying lawsuit rather than by creating new derivative torts. In *Sheldon Appel Co. v. Albert & Oliker* (1989) 47 Cal.3d 863, 873, 254 Cal.Rptr. 336, 765 P.2d 498, we rejected a proposed expansion of the tort of malicious prosecution with the following observation: "While the filing of frivolous lawsuits is certainly improper and cannot in any way be condoned, in our view the better means of addressing the problem of unjustified litigation is through the adoption of measures facilitating the speedy resolution of the initial lawsuit and authorizing the imposition of sanctions for frivolous or delaying conduct within that first action itself, rather than through an expansion of the opportunities for initiating one or more additional rounds of malicious prosecution litigation after the first action has been concluded."

On other occasions as well, we have warned of the dangers of creating new torts to remedy litigation-related misconduct.... [I]n *Silberg v. Anderson* (1990) 50 Cal.3d 205, 266 Cal.Rptr. 638, 786 P.2d 365, in the course of discussing the litigation communications privilege (Civ. Code, §47, subd. 2), we observed: "[T]he law places upon litigants the burden of exposing during trial the bias of witnesses and the falsity of evidence, thereby enhancing the finality of judgments and avoiding an unending roundelay of litigation.... [¶] For our justice system to function, it is necessary that litigants assume responsibility for the complete litigation of their cause during the proceedings. To allow a litigant to attack the integrity of evidence after the proceedings have concluded, except in the most narrowly circumscribed situations, such as extrinsic fraud, would impermissibly burden, if not inundate, our justice system."

Perjury, like spoliation, undermines the search for truth and fairness by creating a false picture of the evidence before the trier of fact. Perjury does so by creating false evidence; spoliation does so by destroying authentic evidence. Yet we have held that there is no civil remedy in damages against a witness who commits perjury when testifying. (Taylor v. Bidwell (1884) 65 Cal. 489, 490, 4 P. 491.) In reaching that conclusion, we relied on a New York case that concluded "it would be productive of endless litigation" to permit the victim of a judgment allegedly based on false testimony to bring an action for damages. (Smith v. Lewis (N.Y. 1808) 3 Johns. 157, 168 (Kent, C.J.).

[O]ne Court of Appeal later held that there can be no tort action for the concealment or withholding of evidence. (Agnew v. Parks (1959) 172 Cal.App.2d 756, 765–766, 343 P.2d 118.) Other Court of Appeal decisions have rejected other attempts, put forward under a variety of legal theories, to seek damages for the presentation of false evidence.

These cases denying a tort remedy for the presentation of false evidence or the suppression of evidence rest on a concern for the finality of adjudication. This same concern underlies another line of cases that forbid direct or collateral attack on a judgment on the ground that evidence was falsified, concealed, or suppressed. After the time for seeking a new trial has expired and any appeals have been exhausted, a final judgment may not be directly attacked and set aside on the ground that evidence has been suppressed, concealed, or falsified; in the language of the cases, such fraud is "intrinsic" rather than "extrinsic." Similarly, under the doctrines of res judicata and collateral estoppel a judgment may not be collaterally attacked on the ground that evidence was falsified or destroyed.

As we explained more than a century ago, the rule against vacating judgments on the ground of false evidence or other intrinsic fraud serves the important interest of finality in adjudication: "[W]e think it is settled beyond controversy that a decree will not be vacated merely because it was obtained by forged documents or perjured testimony. The reason of this rule is, that there must be an end of litigation; and when parties have once submitted a matter ... for investigation and determination, and when they have exhausted every means for reviewing such determination in the same proceeding, it must be regarded as final and conclusive.... [¶] ... [W]hen [the aggrieved party] has a trial, he must be prepared to meet and expose perjury then and there.... The trial is his opportunity for making the truth appear. If, unfortunately, he fails, being overborne by perjured testimony, and if he likewise fails to show the injustice that has been done him on motion for a new trial, and the judgment is affirmed on appeal, he is without remedy. The wrong, in such case, is of course a most grievous one, and no doubt the legislature and the courts would be glad to redress it if a rule could be devised that would remedy the evil without producing mischiefs far worse than the evil to be remedied. Endless litigation, in which nothing was ever finally determined, would be worse than occasional miscarriages of justice...." (Pico v. Cohn, ... 91 Cal. 129, 133–134, 27 P. 537)

Weighing against our recognition of a tort cause of action for spoliation in this case are both the strong policy favoring use of nontort remedies rather than derivative tort causes of action to punish and correct litigation misconduct and the prohibition against attacking adjudications on the ground that evidence was falsified or destroyed. In particular, there are a number of nontort remedies that seek to punish and deter the intentional spoliation of evidence.

Chief among these is the evidentiary inference that evidence which one party has destroyed or rendered unavailable was unfavorable to that party. This evidentiary inference, currently set forth in Evidence Code section 413 and in the standard civil jury instructions, has a long common law history. For example, in the case of *Armory v. Delamirie* (1722 K.B.) 93 Eng. Rep. 664, a chimney sweep sought to recover a jewel he had given to a jeweler for appraisal. When the jeweler failed to produce the jewel at trial, the court instructed the jury "that unless the [jeweler] did produce the jewel, and shew it not to be of the finest water, they should presume the strongest against him, and make the value of the best jewels the measure of their damages...." (*Ibid.*) This court, too, has long recognized the appropriateness of this inference. (Fox v. Hale & Norcross S.M. Co. (1895) 108 Cal. 369, 415–417, 41 P. 308.)

As presently set forth in Evidence Code section 413, this inference is as follows: "In determining what inferences to draw from the evidence or facts in the case against a party, the trier of fact may consider, among other things, the party's ... willful suppression of evidence relating thereto...." The standard California jury instructions include an instruction on this inference as well: "If you find that a party willfully suppressed evidence in order to prevent its being presented in this trial, you may consider that fact in determining what inferences to draw from the evidence." (BAJI No. 2.03 (8th ed.1994)). Trial courts, of course, are not bound by the suggested language of the standard BAJI instruction and are free to adapt it to fit the circumstances of the case, including the egregiousness of the spoliation and the strength and nature of the inference arising from the spoliation.

In addition to the evidentiary inference, our discovery laws provide a broad range of sanctions for conduct that amounts to a "[misuse] of the discovery process." (Code Civ. Proc., § 2023.) Section 2023 of the Code of Civil Procedure gives examples of misuses of discovery, including "[f]ailing to respond or to submit to an authorized method of discovery" (*id.*, subd. (a)(4)) or "[m]aking an evasive response to discovery." (*Id.*, subd. (a)(6).) Destroying evidence in response to a discovery request after litigation has commenced would surely be a misuse of discovery within the meaning of section 2023, as would such destruction in anticipation of a discovery request.

The sanctions under Code of Civil Procedure section 2023 are potent. They include monetary sanctions, contempt sanctions, issue sanctions ordering that designated facts be taken as established or precluding the offending party from supporting or opposing designated claims or defenses, evidence sanctions prohibiting the offending party from introducing designated matters into evidence, and terminating sanctions that include striking part or all of the pleadings, dismissing part or all of the action, or granting a default judgment against the offending party. Plaintiff remains free to seek these remedies in this case.

Another important deterrent to spoliation is the customary involvement of lawyers in the preservation of their clients' evidence and the State Bar of California disciplinary sanctions that can be imposed on attorneys who participate in the spoliation of evidence. As a practical matter, modern civil discovery statutes encourage a lawyer to marshal and take charge of the client's evidence, most often at an early stage of the litigation. In doing so, a lawyer customarily instructs the client to preserve and maintain any potentially relevant evidence, not only because it is right for the client to do so but also because the lawyer recognizes that, even if the evidence is unfavorable, the negative inferences that would flow from its intentional destruction are likely to harm the client as much as or more than the evidence itself.

In addition, the risk that a client's act of spoliation may suggest that the lawyer was also somehow involved encourages lawyers to take steps to protect against the spoliation of evidence. Lawyers are subject to discipline, including suspension and disbarment, for participating in the suppression or destruction of evidence. (Bus. & Prof.Code, § 6106 ["The commission of any act involving moral turpitude, dishonesty or corruption ... constitutes a cause for disbarment or suspension."]; *id.*, § 6077 [attorneys subject to discipline for breach of Rules of Professional Conduct]; Rules Prof. Conduct, rule 5-220 ["A member shall not suppress any evidence that the member or the member's client has a legal obligation to reveal or to produce."]). The purposeful destruction of evidence by a client while represented by a lawyer may raise suspicions that the lawyer participated as well. Even if these suspicions are incorrect, a prudent lawyer will wish to avoid them and the burden of disciplinary proceedings to which they may give rise and will take affirmative steps to preserve and safeguard relevant evidence.

Finally, Penal Code section 135 creates criminal penalties for spoliation. "Every person who, knowing that any book, paper, record, instrument in writing, or other matter or thing, is about to be produced in evidence upon any trial, inquiry, or investigation whatever, authorized by law, willfully destroys or conceals the same, with intent thereby to prevent it from being produced, is guilty of a misdemeanor." (*Ibid.*)

These nontort remedies for spoliation are both extensive and apparently effective for, although real, the problem of spoliation does not appear to be widespread. The committee of distinguished judges and attorneys in charge of preparing the standard California jury instructions describes as "relatively rare [the] case in which evidence has been willfully suppressed." The reported California cases describing instances of intentional spoliation are not numerous. The infrequency of spoliation suggests that existing remedies are generally effective at deterring spoliation.

III

Another consideration weighing against recognition of a tort remedy for intentional first party spoliation is the uncertainty of the fact of harm in spoliation cases. It seems likely that in a substantial proportion of spoliation cases the fact of harm will be irreducibly uncertain. In such cases, even if the jury infers from the act of spoliation that the spoliated evidence was somehow unfavorable to the spoliator, there will typically be no way of telling what precisely the evidence would have shown and how much it would have weighed in the spoliation victim's favor. Without knowing the content and weight of the spoliated evidence, it would be impossible for the jury to meaningfully assess what role the missing evidence would have played in the determination of the underlying action. The jury could only speculate as to what the nature of the spoliated evidence was and what effect it might have had on the outcome of the underlying litigation.

One court considering the question has observed the following: "[I]t is impossible to know what the destroyed evidence would have shown.... It would seem to be sheer guesswork, even presuming that the destroyed evidence went against the spoliator, to calculate what it would have contributed to the plaintiff's success on the merits of the underlying lawsuit.... The lost evidence may have concerned a relevant, but relatively trivial matter. If evidence would not have helped to establish plaintiff's case an award of damages for its destruction would work a windfall for the plaintiff." (Petrik v. Monarch Printing Corp. (1986) 150 Ill.App.3d 248, 260–261, 103 Ill.Dec. 774, 501 N.E.2d 1312, 1320.)

In the many spoliation cases in which the fact of harm is uncertain, a tort remedy for first party spoliation would not accurately compensate for losses caused by spoliation or correct errors in the determination of the issues in the underlying litigation. In the past, we have considered the uncertainty of determining hypothetically whether a particular plaintiff would have prevailed on a legal claim as sufficient reason for refusing to recognize a tort remedy for other forms of wrongful conduct. (Taylor v. Hopper (1929) 207 Cal. 102, 103–105, 276 P. 990 [refusing to recognize a cause of action for fraudulent inducement of a settlement of a legal claim because, given the uncertainty of whether the plaintiff would have prevailed on the legal claim, "there is no practicable measure of damages for the action sought to be maintained"]; *see also* Agnew v. Parks, supra, 172 Cal.App.2d 756, 768–769, 343 P.2d 118 [rejecting action for fraud that allegedly caused plaintiff to lose a prior lawsuit because of uncertainty as to whether plaintiff would have prevailed in the absence of the alleged fraud].)

IV

The costs that a tort remedy would impose also weigh against creation of a spoliation tort remedy. The uncertainty of the fact of harm, in addition to making a tort remedy a poor instrument for compensating spoliation victims, would create the risk of erroneous determinations of spoliation liability (that is, findings of liability in cases in which availability of the spoliated evidence would not have changed the outcome of the underlying litigation). An erroneous determination of spoliation liability would enable the spoliation victim to recover damages, or avoid liability, for the underlying cause of action when the spoliation victim would not have done so had the evidence been in existence. The availability of punitive damages would only magnify the cost of erroneous liability determinations. The risk of erroneous spoliation liability could also impose indirect costs by causing persons or entities to take extraordinary measures to preserve for an indefinite period documents and things of no apparent value solely to avoid the possibility of spoliation liability if years later those items turn out to have some potential relevance to future litigation.

There is also the cost to defendants and courts of litigating meritless spoliation actions. A separate tort remedy would be subject to abuse, for in many cases potentially relevant evidence will no longer exist at the time of trial, not because it was intentionally destroyed but simply because it has been discarded or misplaced in the ordinary course of events. Many corporations and other entities, for example, have document retention policies under which they destroy at stated intervals documents for which they anticipate having no further need. The mere fact of destruction, however, would permit a disappointed litigant to sue the prevailing party for spoliation, and in many cases the issue of the defendant's purpose in destroying the evidence, like many other issues turning on intent and state of mind, could only be resolved at trial. In this case, for example, plaintiff contends that "a trier of fact could easily find intentional spoliation of evidence" from the mere fact that defendant hospital no longer possesses the records in question.

Moreover, if, as plaintiff seeks to do here, a spoliation tort cause of action were tried jointly with the claims in the underlying action, a significant potential for jury confusion and inconsistency would arise. The jury in such a case logically would first consider the underlying claims; for if it awards the spoliation victim complete relief on the underlying claims, then the spoliation has caused no harm to the spoliation victim's position in the underlying litigation. In doing so, the jury would consider any acts of spoliation by applying the evidentiary inference of Evidence Code section 413. If the jury rejects the spoliation victim's position on the underlying claims, it has either rejected application of the evidentiary inference to the case before it (e.g., because the spoliation victim has not demonstrated that the spoliation was intentional), or has determined that, even applying the inference in favor of the spoliation victim, the other evidence in the case compels a different result. The jury would then consider and decide the spoliation tort claim; in doing so, however, it would necessarily be reconsidering its adjudication that either no intentional spoliation occurred or that the spoliated evidence would not have led to a different result. At the least, this would be confusing to the jury; at most, it would lead to inconsistent results.

On the other hand, pursuing a spoliation tort remedy in a proceeding separate from the underlying action would result in duplicative proceedings without avoiding the potential for inconsistent results. The spoliation action would require a "retrial within a trial," for all of the evidence in the underlying action would have to be presented again so that the spoliation jury could determine what effect the spoliated evidence would have had in light of all the other evidence. This duplication of effort would be burdensome both to the parties and to the judicial system, and it would also produce an even greater risk of inconsistent results than would deciding a spoliation tort cause of action as part of the underlying litigation.

Nor would an intentional first party spoliation tort cause of action offset these costs by significantly increasing deterrence of the destruction of evidence beyond that afforded by existing remedies. It seems dubious that a tort remedy would increase the frequency with which destruction comes to light and thereby increase deterrence. As discussed above, the motive and opportunity to discover instances of spoliation are at their greatest during discovery in the underlying action. There is no reason to conclude that instances of spoliation that remain hidden during discovery in the underlying action would come to light afterward solely by reason of the existence of a tort remedy. Nor, given the uncertainty of harm from acts of evidence destruction, would a tort remedy increase deterrence by more accurately compensating the spoliation victim and thus reducing the benefit to the spoliator.

CONCLUSION

As we noted at the outset, the intentional spoliation of evidence by a party to the litigation to which it is relevant is an unqualified wrong. We conclude, however, that it is the rare case in which a tort remedy for an intentionally caused harm is not appropriate....

Accordingly, we hold that there is no tort remedy for the intentional spoliation of evidence by a party to the cause of action to which the spoliated evidence is relevant, in cases in which, as here, the spoliation victim knows or should have known of the alleged spoliation before the trial or other decision on the merits of the underlying action.[4] We reverse the decision of the Court of Appeal denying the petition for a writ of mandate and remand the cause with directions to that court to issue a writ instructing the trial court to vacate its order granting plaintiff leave to file his third amended complaint.

Focus Questions: *Rosenblit v. Zimmerman*

1. *How does the holding in* Rosenblit *differ from* Cedars-Sinai*?*
2. *What effect, if any, should the court's holding have on the plaintiff's recovery on the fraudulent concealment claim?*

Rosenblit v. Zimmerman

766 A.2d 749
(N.J. 2001)

LONG, J.

This case involves a physician who deliberately destroyed and altered medical records in anticipation of a patient's malpractice lawsuit against him. By happenstance, the patient obtained the original records prior to trial. The jury returned a verdict in favor of the physician in the malpractice action. The patient later recovered a judgment for fraudulent concealment of evidence. Both parties appealed. We are called upon here to determine what remedies are available to a plaintiff in these circumstances.

...

Several jurisdictions have recognized a new tort of intentional spoliation of evidence. Hazen v. Municipality of Anchorage, 718 P.2d 456, 463–64 (Alaska 1986) (recognizing "intentional interference with prospective civil action by spoilation of evidence" as an independent cause of action in Alaska); Coleman v. Eddy Potash, Inc., 120 N.M. 645, 905

4. We do not decide here whether a tort cause of action for spoliation should be recognized in cases of "third party" spoliation (spoliation by a nonparty to any cause of action to which the evidence is relevant) or in cases of first party spoliation in which the spoliation victim neither knows nor should have known of the spoliation until after a decision on the merits of the underlying action.

P.2d 185, 189 (1995) (holding that New Mexico recognizes a cause of action for intentional spoliation of evidence); Smith v. Howard Johnson Co., 67 Ohio St.3d 28, 615 N.E.2d 1037, 1038 (1993) (certifying that Ohio would recognize intentional spoliation claims).

Those jurisdictions have set forth the elements of the tort as follows: (1) the existence of pending or probable litigation involving the plaintiff; (2) defendant's knowledge of the pendency or fact of the litigation; (3) intentional destruction of evidence by the defendant designed to disrupt the plaintiff's case; (4) disruption of the plaintiff's case; and (5) damages proximately caused by the defendant's acts. Kristin Adamski, Comment, *A Funny Thing Happened on the Way to the Courtroom: Spoliation of Evidence in Illinois*, 32 J. Marshall L. Rev. 325, 333 (1999).

Some courts have refused to recognize any tort action to remedy spoliation, holding instead that the evidentiary rules, along with adverse inferences will suffice. That, of course, is true only if the spoliation is discovered in time for the underlying litigation, or so soon afterward that the litigant has an opportunity under the rules to seek relief from judgment and retry his or her case.

Other courts have refused to recognize a new tort because they conceive of spoliation as remediable under existing tort principles. New Jersey falls into that category.

In *Viviano v. CBS, Inc.*, 251 N.J. Super. 113, 119–20, 597 A.2d 543 (App. Div. 1991), *certif. denied*, 127 N.J. 565, 606 A.2d 375 (1992), the plaintiff brought suit against her employer for fraudulently concealing the only available information relevant to her product liability case against the manufacturer of the press machine that injured her at work. A jury awarded her compensatory and punitive damages for the intentional fraudulent concealment. On appeal, the defendant argued, among other things, that there was no tort remedy for its conduct. The Appellate Division disagreed, invoking State of N.J., Dep't of Environ. Protect. v. Ventron Corp., 94 N.J. 473, 503–04, 468 A.2d 150 (1983), where we described the elements of the tort of fraudulent concealment of evidence in another context:

> The deliberate concealment or nondisclosure by the seller of a material fact or defect not readily observable to the purchaser, with the buyer relying upon the seller to his detriment.

Viviano properly denominated the conduct of destruction of litigation evidence as spoliation and, in so doing, cited cases and commentaries that recognized an independent tort remedy for that conduct. Adhering to the well established principle that the recognition of a new cause of action is reserved to the Legislature and the Supreme Court, *Viviano* did not recognize a novel cause of action for spoliation, but identified a pre-existing tort remedy for that conduct: fraudulent concealment. The court held that the plaintiff had proven the elements set forth in *Ventron*. Those elements have been summarized as follows:

> (1) That defendants had a legal obligation to disclose the evidence to plaintiff; (2) that the evidence was material to the plaintiff's case; (3) that the plaintiff could not have readily learned of the concealed information without defendant disclosing it; (4) that the defendant intentionally failed to disclose the evidence to the plaintiff; and (5) that the plaintiff was harmed by relying on the nondisclosure.

We fully approve of that approach. Our only difference with *Viviano* is in its articulation of the elements of the tort of fraudulent concealment. In our view, a slight modification more aptly describes what must be proved when fraudulent concealment occurs in a litigation context. The elements that must be established by a plaintiff in such a fraudulent concealment action are:

(1) That defendant in the fraudulent concealment action had a legal obligation to disclose evidence in connection with an existing or pending litigation;

(2) That the evidence was material to the litigation;

(3) That plaintiff could not reasonably have obtained access to the evidence from another source;

(4) That defendant intentionally withheld, altered or destroyed the evidence with purpose to disrupt the litigation;

(5) That plaintiff was damaged in the underlying action by having to rely on an evidential record that did not contain the evidence defendant concealed.

We are satisfied that those elements properly reflect the application of fraudulent concealment principles in a litigation setting. We hold that the tort of fraudulent concealment, as adopted, may be invoked as a remedy for spoliation where those elements exist. Such conduct cannot go undeterred and unpunished and those aggrieved by it should be made whole with compensatory damages and, if the elements of the Punitive Damages Act, N.J.S.A. 2A:15-5.12, are met, punitive damages for intentional wrongdoing.

...

A party's access to the remedies we have catalogued will depend upon the point in the litigation process that the concealment or destruction is uncovered. If it is revealed in time for the underlying litigation, the spoliation inference may be invoked. In addition, the injured party may amend his or her complaint to add a count for fraudulent concealment. As the trial court realized here, those counts will require bifurcation because the fraudulent concealment remedy depends on the jury's assessment of the underlying cause of action. In that instance, after the jury has returned a verdict in the bifurcated underlying action, it will be required to determine whether the elements of the tort of fraudulent concealment have been established, and, if so, whether damages are warranted. Further, the plaintiff may be awarded discovery sanctions if the court determines that they are justified in light of the outcome in the fraudulent concealment trial.

If, however, the spoliation is not discovered until after the underlying action has been lost or otherwise seriously inhibited, the plaintiff may file a separate tort action. In such an action, plaintiff will be required to establish the elements of the tort of fraudulent concealment. To do so, the fundamentals of the underlying litigation will also require exposition. Unless such an action is allowed, a belatedly discovered spoliation claim would be without a meaningful remedy. Obviously the plaintiff in such an action also could recover discovery sanctions if the court determines that they are warranted in light of the jury verdict.

* * *

1. Model Rule comparison. Rule 3.4(a) of the ABA *Model Rules of Professional Conduct* prohibits a lawyer from unlawfully obstructing another party's access to evidence or unlawfully altering, destroying, or concealing a document or other material having potential evidentiary value. The rule also prohibits a lawyer from counseling or assisting another to do the same.

2. Negligent spoliation. Some states recognize claims for negligent spoliation of evidence. *See, e.g.*, Oliver v. Stimson Lumber Co., 993 P.2d 11 (Mont. 1999); Holmes v. Amerex Rent-A-Car, 710 A.2d 846 (D.C. 1998). To recover, a plaintiff typically must establish:

(1) a potential civil action; (2) a legal duty to preserve evidence relevant to the potential civil action; (3) destruction of that evidence; (4) significant impairment

in the ability to prove the lawsuit; (5) a causal relationship between the evidence destruction and the inability to prove the lawsuit; and (6) resulting damages.

Bart. S. Wilhoit, *Spoliation of Evidence: The Viability of Four Emerging Torts*, 46 UCLA L. Rev. 631, 645 (1998).

3. Third-party spoliation claims. *Cedars-Sinai* and *Rosenblit* were first-party spoliation cases—cases in which a party to litigation destroyed or concealed evidence. In contrast, third-party spoliation claims involve spoliation of evidence by a non-party. Courts are split as to whether to recognize such claims. *See* Oliver v. Stimson Lumber Co., 993 P.2d 11 (Mont. 1999) (recognizing claim against employer's workers' compensation insurance carrier); Downen v. Redd, 242 S.W.3d 273 (Ark. 2006) (refusing to recognize a claim based upon the employer's disposal of a product that was the subject of a product liability action against the manufacturer); Temple Community Hospital v. Superior Court, 976 P.2d 223 (Cal. 1999) (refusing to recognize third-party spoliation claims).

Exercise 16.9

You are an in-house lawyer for a large corporation in a jurisdiction that recognizes the torts of intentional and negligent spoliation. One day, your client receives a demand letter from another attorney accusing the client of breaching a contract and various acts of unfair competition. The letter threatens litigation unless tens of thousands of dollars are paid immediately. The letter identifies six employees as having been the primary players in what the letter alleges was a conspiracy involving another company. The employees supposedly engaged in this conspiracy over the course of three years. The letter alleges that, among other things, the employee in question sent confidential and defamatory material to the other company in a number of emails.

Is your client under any duty at this point to preserve evidence related to this possible lawsuit? Are you, as a lawyer, under any duty? What, if anything, should you tell your client regarding this matter? At what point would the client be subject to tort liability if he or she destroyed relevant evidence?

Part 5

Other Tort Theories

Chapter 17

Aiding and Abetting and Civil Conspiracy

Exercise 17.1: Chapter Problem

Linda and Michael lived together as a couple for five years. During that time, Michael did not have a regular job. Instead, he told Linda that he made his money by buying and selling gold coins and then investing the proceeds from the sales. Despite not having a job, Michael would leave the house most every evening for a few hours, and return home with gold coins.

With Linda's knowledge, Michael installed a smelting furnace in the garage and used it to melt gold into bars. He then sold the bars to refiners in other states. Linda typed transmittal letters for these sales, and in general did the secretarial work for Michael's business. The buyers of Michael's goods made their checks payable to Linda, and she deposited them in her own bank accounts. She kept all of the records on these transactions. Interestingly, the records she kept recorded all of the payments coming in from buyers, but recorded no money going out to the sellers from whom Michael had bought the gold. At the end of five years, the couple had accumulated over $1 million from Michael's business.

Eventually, Michael was arrested for shooting and killing the owner of a home in the course of an attempted burglary. As it turned out, Michael had been burglarizing homes for the entire course of his relationship with Linda. All of his "gold coins" were, in fact, gold coins and other gold objects stolen during the course of the burglaries. The victim's family sued Michael under a wrongful death theory and also seeks to hold Linda liable for aiding and abetting Michael in the homicide. The jury found Linda liable. Should the verdict be overturned?

As the cases in this chapter illustrate, one may be held civilly liable based, in part, on the tortious conduct of another, who is the primary wrongdoer. Although courts sometimes describe this liability as being vicarious in nature, this portrayal is not strictly accurate if one views the act of assisting another in a wrong as a separate wrong. One may be held vicariously liable for the torts of another despite having done absolutely nothing to encourage or assist the other. With the legal theories discussed in this chapter, the defendants have actually done something to merit liability, even if they are not the primary wrongdoers.

The *Restatement (Second) of Torts* groups the kinds of cases covered in this chapter under the heading of "Persons Acting in Concert." *Id.* § 876. This description covers two primary theories of liability: liability for aiding and abetting another's tortious conduct and civil conspiracy. You probably covered the criminal law equivalents in your required

Criminal Law course. There is some dispute as to whether these are free-standing torts, or, as some decisions seem to suggest, aiding and abetting another's commission of a tort is simply a basis for imposing joint liability under the other tort theory. *See* Central Bank of Denver, N.A. v. First Interstate Bank of Denver, N., 511 U.S. 164, 171 (1994); *see also* Eastern Trading Co. v. Refco, Inc., 229 F.3d 617, 623 (7th Cir. 2000) ("[T]here is no tort of aiding and abetting.").

Regardless of whether these are separate torts or simply another way of saying that a defendant is liable for the primary wrongdoer's wrongdoing, the questions of whether one aided and abetted another's wrong or was part of a conspiracy is analytically distinct from the question of whether the elements of the underlying tort are satisfied. Moreover, when a lawyer is accused of assisting a client in the commission of some type of wrongful act, the phrase "aiding and abetting" is often thrown around. Therefore, between the two concepts discussed in this chapter, aiding and abetting is probably the more relevant for lawyers in terms of their professional lives. Thus, the chapter focuses primarily on aiding and abetting liability, including aiding and abetting client fraud (including securities fraud) and aiding and abetting a breach of fiduciary duty. The chapter ends with a brief look at civil conspiracy.

* * *

A. Aiding and Abetting Wrongful Conduct in General

Rael v. Cadena

604 P.2d 822
(N.M. Ct. App. 1979)

LOPEZ, Judge.

The issue on appeal is whether a person present at a battery who verbally encourages the assailant, but does not physically assist him, is civilly liable for the battery.

On a visit in Emilio Cadena's home, Eddie Rael was severely beaten on the head and torso by Emilio's nephew, Manuel Cadena. As a result of the beating, he suffered a fractured rib and was hospitalized. Eddie Rael testified that once the attack had started, Emilio yelled to Manuel in Spanish, "Kill him!" and "Hit him more!" The trial court sitting without a jury found that Emilio encouraged Manuel while Manuel was beating Eddie. Based on this finding, the court held the Cadenas jointly and severally liable for the battery.

Emilio urges that in order for the trial court to have held him jointly liable for the battery, it had to find either that he and Manuel acted in concert, or that Manuel beat the injured Eddie as a result of Emilio's encouragement. This is a misstatement of the law.

This is an issue of first impression in New Mexico. It is clear, however, that in the United States, civil liability for assault and battery is not limited to the direct perpetrator, but extends to any person who by any means aids or encourages the act. According to the *Restatement*:

> (f)or harm resulting to a third person from the tortious conduct of another, one is subject to liability if he
>
> . . .

> (b) knows that the other's conduct constitutes a breach of duty and gives substantial assistance or encouragement to the other so to conduct himself....

Restatement (Second) of Torts s 876 (1979).

Although liability cannot be predicated upon mere presence at a battery, verbal encouragement at the scene gives rise to liability.... Because he yelled encouragement to his nephew while the latter was beating Eddie Rael, Emilio Cadena is jointly liable with his nephew for the battery.

The judgment of the trial court is affirmed.

* * *

1. The prima facie case. Although defined in various ways, the tort of aiding and abetting requires a plaintiff to establish that (1) the party whom the defendant aids performed a wrongful act that caused an injury; (2) the defendant was aware of his role as part of an overall illegal or tortious activity at the time that he provides the assistance; (3) the defendant knowingly and substantially assisted or encouraged the principal violation. Halberstam v. Welch, 705 F.2d 472, 477 (D.C. Cir. 1983). One may be liable for aiding and abetting negligent activity, although liability stemming from intentional misconduct is more common.

2. Encouragement. Note that substantial encouragement (as opposed to actual action) is sufficient to establish liability. According to the *Restatement*, "Advice or encouragement to act operates as a moral support to a tortfeasor and if the act encouraged is known to be tortious it has the same effect upon the liability of the adviser as participation or physical assistance." Restatement (Second) of Torts § 876 cmt. d.

3. Substantial assistance or encouragement. The primary issue in many cases is whether the defendant's assistance or encouragement was substantial enough to warrant liability. The *Restatement* lists five factors to consider in making this determination: "[1] the nature of the act encouraged, [2] the amount of assistance given by the defendant, [3] his presence or absence at the time of the tort, [4] his relation to the other [tortfeasor] and [5] his state of mind." *Id.* There is also an aspect of causation to the analysis. A defendant is not liable for wrongful acts committed by the other person that were not foreseeable.

Exercise 17.2

In which of the following situations have the defendants aided and abetted another in an unlawful act?

(a) Prior to the start of class, a group of students begins throwing erasers at each other as part of fun and games. One of the erasers went off course and struck an innocent bystander, Plaintiff, in the eye, causing her to suffer an injury and lose an eye. Defendant did not throw any of the erasers during the eraser fight, but did retrieve erasers from the ground and hand them to the combatants, including the one that struck Plaintiff.

(b) Defendant, a photographer, sells a photograph of Plaintiff to Publisher, knowing in advance that Publisher plans to alter the photograph in such a way as to defame Plaintiff.

(c) Angered over Plaintiff's failure to return a down payment, Husband physically assaults Plaintiff. Defendant, his wife, had previously instructed Husband to retrieve the down payment, drove Husband over to Plaintiff's house, watched and did nothing as Husband beat Plaintiff, and then drove Husband home after the incident. Defendant did not know in advance that Husband planned to assault Plaintiff.

B. Aiding and Abetting a Client's Wrongful Acts

Focus Questions: *Tensfeldt v. Haberman*

1. *What is the basis for imposing liability upon LaBudde in this case?*
2. *What would the result have been if LaBudde had advised his client to rewrite the will himself in the manner the client wanted? What if LaBudde had simply provided his client with a list of possible options instead of actually drafting the will in the way the client wanted?*

Tensfeldt v. Haberman

768 N.W.2d 641
(Wis. 2009)

ANN WALSH BRADLEY, J.

This case is before this court on certification from the court of appeals pursuant to Wis. Stat. (Rule) § 809.61. It involves a dispute between the children of the deceased, Robert Tensfeldt, and the two attorneys who provided his estate planning services, Attorneys LaBudde and Haberman. Both the children and Attorney LaBudde appealed a circuit court order on their cross motions for summary judgment.

I

Robert Tensfeldt and his first wife, Ruth, had three children—Christine, Robert William, and John. When Robert and Ruth divorced in 1974, they entered into an agreement stipulating to various terms of the divorce. The divorce court determined that the stipulation was "fair and reasonable" and incorporated the stipulation into the divorce judgment.

One of the terms of the stipulation provides that Robert would make and maintain a will leaving two-thirds of his net estate to the children:

> Will in Favor of Children: Simultaneously with the execution of this Stipulation, [Robert] shall execute and shall hereafter keep in effect, a Will leaving not less than two-thirds (2/3) of his net estate outright to the three adult children of the parties, or to their heirs by right of representation. Except as herein provided, [Robert] shall have the right to make such disposition of his estate as he may desire, except as limited herein, and further, except as limited by the requirements set forth in [the provision dealing with unpaid alimony.] As used herein, the term "net estate" shall mean [Robert's] gross estate passing under his Will (or otherwise, upon the occasion of his death), less funeral and burial expenses, ad-

ministration fees and expenses, debts and claims against the estate, and Federal and State taxes.

Robert married his second wife, Constance, in 1975. They remained married until Robert's death in 2000. Robert and Constance had no children together, although Constance had three children from a previous marriage. In 1978, Robert executed a will that was compliant with the stipulation and order—one-third of the net estate went to Constance, and two-thirds of the net estate went to his children or their issue.

In 1980, Robert retained Attorney LaBudde (LaBudde) of Michael Best & Friedrich, LLP to provide estate planning services. It is undisputed that Robert made LaBudde aware of his obligation to his children from the outset. When Robert initially met with LaBudde, he gave the attorney a copy of the divorce judgment and stipulation. LaBudde told Robert that he had three choices: comply with the stipulation; negotiate with the children to alter his obligation; or ignore the stipulation, knowing that the children might contest Robert's will upon his death. Robert chose the third option, and in 1981, LaBudde drafted an estate plan that did not leave two-thirds of the net estate outright to the Tensfeldt children.

After Robert executed the non-compliant estate plan, LaBudde received a letter from Robert's divorce attorney, J.M. Slechta. Attorney Slechta wrote:

> Since you have drafted a will for Mr. Robert Tensfeldt of Oconomowoc, I recalled that in his divorce in 1974 in which proceedings I represented him, it was agreed in the Stipulation made part of the judgment, some restrictions on the disposition of his estate.... Realizing this might have some effect upon the disposition which you have proposed I am enclosing a copy of such stipulation for your examination. There does not seem to be any sanction against disposition of assets during his lifetime.

LaBudde wrote back:

> Your letter ... asks whether Mr. Tensfeldt's most recent Will ... violates his obligations under that decree....
>
> In my opinion, Mr. Tensfeldt's present Will needs some revision in light of the obligations under the divorce decree, of which I was unaware until receipt of your letter. On the other hand, the so-called "Economic Recovery Tax Act of 1981" does, as you know, offer significant new estate and gift tax advantages which may be available to Mr. Tensfeldt to some extent despite the decree.

Robert and LaBudde never changed the estate plan to bring it into compliance with the divorce stipulation and judgment. Even though Robert and Constance moved to Florida in 1985, they continued to retain the attorneys at Michael Best & Friedrich to handle their estate planning. Over the course of 12 years, LaBudde drafted and executed a series of revisions to the plan for Robert, including the 1992 plan that was in effect when Robert died. None of the revised plans left at least two-thirds of his net estate outright to the three adult children of his first marriage.

Attorney LaBudde later scaled back his practice, and Robert first consulted with Attorney Haberman (Haberman) in 1994. In 1999, Robert met with Haberman to discuss his estate plan in depth. According to a memo from his file, Haberman "carefully outlined the assets passing to his children and his wife's children, and [Robert] decided to leave things as they are and make no changes" to the 1992 estate plan.

According to the 1992 plan, after Robert's death the Tensfeldt children would receive some money and property up front. However, the majority of Robert's estate would pour into an inter vivos trust. Constance would receive an income from the trust during her life, and after Constance's death her children would receive a cash payment from the trust. The Tensfeldt children would receive the remainder of the balance.

Robert died in 2000. Robert's son and Constance were appointed personal representatives of the estate, and Haberman was retained as counsel. At that point, Haberman learned about the divorce stipulation, and he told Constance and the Tensfeldt children about its existence.

The estate was probated in Florida, with Haberman as the attorney representing the estate. This probate action turned into a lengthy dispute, encompassing two independent actions in the Florida circuit court. Initially, the Tensfeldt children sued to enforce the stipulation and order promising them two-thirds of Robert's net estate outright. Constance objected to the claim, elected against the will, and expressed her intention to continue to receive income under the inter vivos trust. The children objected to Constance's election and argued that it was untimely....

The court determined that Constance's election was timely, that she was entitled to partial distribution of her elective share, and that ... she was also entitled to receive income from the trust. Further, the court held that the children's claim for two-thirds of the estate was barred by the 20-year statute of limitations for judgments.

The children appealed both determinations.... Ultimately, the parties settled the dispute.

After settling, the children filed suit in Wisconsin against Attorneys LaBudde and Haberman. They alleged various intentional torts, including aiding and abetting and civil conspiracy, as well as negligence against LaBudde for helping Robert violate the divorce judgment. Further, they alleged negligence against Haberman, arguing that they have been injured because of his failure to [properly] advise Robert.... In addition, they asserted that LaBudde and Haberman's law firm, Michael Best & Friedrich LLP, was liable for claims against the two attorneys. Following discovery, all parties moved for summary judgment.

The circuit court determined that as a matter of law LaBudde aided and abetted Robert's violation of the divorce judgment and set trial for the issues of causation and damages. Further, the court determined that the civil conspiracy and negligence claims against LaBudde presented questions of fact for the jury to decide. However, the court dismissed all claims against Haberman, concluding that he was negligent as a matter of law but that the evidence that his negligence had actually caused harm to the children was speculative.

The children appealed and LaBudde cross-appealed. The court of appeals certified the cross-appeal to this court.... We accepted jurisdiction of the entire case pursuant to Wis. Stat. § 809.61 and address the questions as argued and briefed by the parties.

III. Intentional Tort Claims Against Attorney LaBudde

The Tensfeldt children allege that between 1980 and 1992, Attorney LaBudde assisted Robert in unlawfully violating a court order mandating that Robert make and maintain a specific will. During that time, LaBudde drafted five wills for Robert, each of them non-compliant with a divorce judgment. The circuit court determined that these actions constituted aiding and abetting as a matter of law:

> The parties stipulate that Robert desired to violate the judgment requiring him to leave two-thirds of his net estate to the Children, an indisputably unlawful act. See Wis. Stat. § 785.01(1)(b). However, to do so, he needed help in drafting his will, and LaBudde provided this assistance. There is also no question that

> LaBudde intended that the will would violate the judgment. He was aware of the court's judgment and knew that the will he drafted violated it. Since there are no disputed material facts and the only inferences that can be drawn from them lead to the conclusion that LaBudde aided and abetted Robert in his violation of a court judgment and consciously intended to do so, summary judgment is appropriate.

The court then scheduled trial on the issue of damages.

LaBudde disagrees with the court's determination.... He argues that either qualified immunity or the good faith advice privilege bars the claim of aiding and abetting....

C. Is LaBudde Protected by Either Immunity or Privilege?

... LaBudde raises the defenses of qualified immunity and good faith advice. He argues that an attorney is not liable to third parties for acts committed on behalf of his client in the exercise of his professional responsibilities as an attorney. He cites *Yorgan v. Durkin* for the proposition that "[t]he well established rule of law in Wisconsin is that absent fraud or certain public policy considerations, an attorney is not liable to third parties for acts committed in the exercise of his duties as an attorney." 2006 WI 60, ¶ 27, 290 Wis.2d 671, 715 N.W.2d 160.

We agree that in most cases, an attorney is immune from liability to third parties based on the attorney's failure to perform a duty owed to a client. However, failure to perform an obligation to a client is entirely distinct from conduct that assists the client committing an unlawful act to the detriment of a third party.

In *Yorgan v. Durkin*, we refused to hold an attorney personally liable for the fees his client owed to a chiropractor. The client had directed Attorney Durkin to pay the chiropractor's fees out of the proceeds she received from a personal injury lawsuit, but Durkin failed to follow his client's instructions. The chiropractor brought suit against Durkin, alleging that Durkin was liable to third party creditors for failing to properly settle his client's obligations. We concluded that the public policy factors "implicated by the nature of the situation at hand" did not weigh in favor of imposing liability to third party creditors.

The public policy implicated by the nature of this case weighs differently. Under these facts, the public policy balance favors liability. Unlike in *Yorgan v. Durkin*, the theory of liability advanced by the Tensfeldt children is not vicarious. It is not based on LaBudde's failure to fulfill a professional obligation to Robert to the detriment of the Tensfeldt children. Indeed, the parties agree that Robert asked LaBudde to draft the will in violation of the court judgment, and LaBudde was not negligent in performing this service. In contrast to *Yorgan v. Durkin*, the basis for liability here is that LaBudde knowingly assisted the commission of the unlawful act.[25]

We are mindful that a violation of the rules does not impose civil liability on an attorney per se. Yorgan v. Durkin, 715 N.W.2d 160.

---

25. The Supreme Court Rules of professional conduct for attorneys provide guidance regarding the scope of representation. An attorney "shall not counsel a client to engage, or assist a client, in conduct that the lawyer knows is criminal or fraudulent[.]" SCR 20:1.2(d) (2008). We have stated that "[t]here is a critical distinction between presenting an analysis of legal aspects of questionable conduct and recommending the means by which a crime or fraud might be committed with impunity." *Id.* cmt. 9. If a client insists upon pursuing an unlawful course of conduct, the attorney has one option-withdraw from the representation of the client. SCR 20:1.16(a)(1).

A thorough discussion of an attorney's liability to third parties is found in *Strid v. Converse*, 111 Wis.2d 418, 331 N.W.2d 350 (1983). In that case, we stated that immunity is not available when the attorney engages in fraudulent or unlawful acts:

> [An attorney] is duty bound ... to exercise good faith. He must not be guilty of any fraudulent acts, and he must be free from any unlawful conspiracy with either his client, the judge, or any other person, which might have a tendency to either frustrate the administration of justice or to obtain for his client something to which he is not justly and fairly entitled.

Further, the court concluded:

> [T]he immunity of an attorney who is acting in a professional capacity is qualified rather than absolute. The immunity from liability to third parties extends to an attorney who pursues in good faith his or her client's interest on a matter fairly debatable in the law. However, the immunity does not apply when the attorney acts in a malicious, fraudulent or tortious manner which frustrates the administration of justice or to obtain something for the client to which the client is not justly entitled.

Here, LaBudde drafted documents that obtained for Robert something he was not legally entitled to—an estate plan that violated a court judgment requiring Robert to leave two-thirds of his net estate to his children outright. Under these circumstances, LaBudde is not entitled to qualified immunity.

LaBudde also argues that he is entitled to the good faith advice privilege. This privilege is based on the *Restatement (Second) of Torts* § 772 (1979), which this court has neither adopted nor rejected as applied to attorneys. Notably, this section of the *Restatement* focuses on advice leading to a breach of contract:

> One who intentionally causes a third person not to perform a contract or not to enter into a prospective contractual relation with another does not interfere improperly with the other's contractual relation, by giving the third person
>
> (a) truthful information, or
>
> (b) honest advice within the scope of a request for the advice.

We acknowledge that in some circumstances, an attorney may in good faith advise a client to breach a contract. That is not the situation before us today.

The action here is not for breach of contract. Rather, it is an action in tort for assisting a client to unlawfully violate a court judgment. Further, LaBudde did not merely give advice. He drafted an estate plan that violated the judgment. We conclude that, under these facts, LaBudde is not entitled to this privilege.

In sum, we determine that the circuit court properly concluded that LaBudde is liable as a matter of law for aiding and abetting his client's unlawful act. The divorce judgment was enforceable at the time it was entered and at the time Robert asked LaBudde to draft an estate plan that violated the judgment. Under these facts, LaBudde is not entitled to either qualified immunity or the good faith advice privilege.

* * *

1. Model Rule comparison. Footnote 25 in *Tensfeldt* contains Wisconsin's prohibition on an attorney's counseling or assisting a client in conduct the attorney knows is criminal or fraudulent. Rule 1.2(d) of the ABA *Model Rules of Professional Conduct* contains the same language and also includes the same comment concerning the distinction between presenting analysis of questionable conduct and advising a client as to the means to accomplish a crime or fraud. How are the tort rule from *Tensfeldt* and the disciplinary rule contained in Rule 1.2(d) related?

2. **Application of the advice privilege.** In the context of claims of tortious interference with contractual relations, courts have generally held that a lawyer is privileged to advise a client to breach a contract. *See* Los Angeles Airways, Inc. v. Davis, 687 F.2d 321 (9th Cir. 1982); McDonald v. Stewart, 182 N.W.2d 437 (Minn. 1970). Should aiding and abetting be available in such cases as an alternative theory?

Exercise 17.3

Lawyer prepares a contract for Client for the sale of Client's land to Buyer, thus concluding Lawyer's representation of Client. Client signs the contract and forwards to it to Buyer for her signature. Lawyer subsequently learns of information that establishes that Client's sale will amount to fraud upon Buyer. The relevant jurisdiction's rules of professional conduct for lawyers permit a lawyer to reveal information relating to the representation of a client to the extent reasonably necessary "to prevent the client from committing a crime or fraud that is reasonably certain to result in substantial injury to the financial interests or property of another and in furtherance of which the client has used or is using the lawyer's services." However, Lawyer remains silent and Client goes ahead and commits the fraud upon Buyer. Has Lawyer aided and abetted Client's fraud?

Focus Questions: *Stoneridge Inv. Partners, LLC v. Scientific-Atlanta*

1. *What happens to Scientific–Atlanta, Inc. and Motorola, Inc. after this decision?*
2. *What does this decision mean for corporate lawyers?*

Stoneridge Inv. Partners, LLC v. Scientific-Atlanta

552 U.S. 148
(2008)

Justice KENNEDY delivered the opinion of the Court.

We consider the reach of the private right of action the Court has found implied in § 10(b) of the Securities Exchange Act of 1934, 48 Stat. 891, as amended, 15 U.S.C. § 78j(b), and SEC Rule 10b-5, 17 CFR § 240.10b-5 (2007). In this suit investors alleged losses after purchasing common stock. They sought to impose liability on entities who, acting both as customers and suppliers, agreed to arrangements that allowed the investors' company to mislead its auditor and issue a misleading financial statement affecting the stock price.

I

This class-action suit by investors was filed against Charter Communications, Inc., in the United States District Court for the Eastern District of Missouri. Stoneridge Investment Partners, LLC, a limited liability company organized under the laws of Delaware, was the lead plaintiff and is petitioner here.

Charter issued the financial statements and the securities in question. It was a named defendant along with some of its executives and Arthur Andersen LLP, Charter's independent auditor during the period in question. We are concerned, though, with two other defendants, respondents here. Respondents are Scientific-Atlanta, Inc., and Motorola, Inc. They were suppliers, and later customers, of Charter.

For purposes of this proceeding, we take these facts, alleged by petitioner, to be true. Charter, a cable operator, engaged in a variety of fraudulent practices so its quarterly reports would meet Wall Street expectations for cable subscriber growth and operating cash flow. The fraud included misclassification of its customer base; delayed reporting of terminated customers; improper capitalization of costs that should have been shown as expenses; and manipulation of the company's billing cutoff dates to inflate reported revenues. In late 2000, Charter executives realized that, despite these efforts, the company would miss projected operating cash flow numbers by $15 to $20 million. To help meet the shortfall, Charter decided to alter its existing arrangements with respondents, Scientific-Atlanta and Motorola. Petitioner's theory as to whether Arthur Andersen was altogether misled or, on the other hand, knew the structure of the contract arrangements and was complicit to some degree, is not clear at this stage of the case. The point, however, is neither controlling nor significant for our present disposition, and in our decision we assume it was misled.

Respondents supplied Charter with the digital cable converter (set top) boxes that Charter furnished to its customers. Charter arranged to overpay respondents $20 for each set top box it purchased until the end of the year, with the understanding that respondents would return the overpayment by purchasing advertising from Charter. The transactions, it is alleged, had no economic substance; but, because Charter would then record the advertising purchases as revenue and capitalize its purchase of the set top boxes, in violation of generally accepted accounting principles, the transactions would enable Charter to fool its auditor into approving a financial statement showing it met projected revenue and operating cash flow numbers. Respondents agreed to the arrangement.

So that Arthur Andersen would not discover the link between Charter's increased payments for the boxes and the advertising purchases, the companies drafted documents to make it appear the transactions were unrelated and conducted in the ordinary course of business. Following a request from Charter, Scientific-Atlanta sent documents to Charter stating—falsely—that it had increased production costs. It raised the price for set top boxes for the rest of 2000 by $20 per box. As for Motorola, in a written contract Charter agreed to purchase from Motorola a specific number of set top boxes and pay liquidated damages of $20 for each unit it did not take. The contract was made with the expectation Charter would fail to purchase all the units and pay Motorola the liquidated damages.

To return the additional money from the set top box sales, Scientific-Atlanta and Motorola signed contracts with Charter to purchase advertising time for a price higher than fair value. The new set top box agreements were backdated to make it appear that they were negotiated a month before the advertising agreements. The backdating was important to convey the impression that the negotiations were unconnected, a point Arthur Andersen considered necessary for separate treatment of the transactions. Charter recorded the advertising payments to inflate revenue and operating cash flow by approximately $17 million. The inflated number was shown on financial statements filed with the Securities and Exchange Commission (SEC) and reported to the public.

Respondents had no role in preparing or disseminating Charter's financial statements. And their own financial statements booked the transactions as a wash, under generally accepted accounting principles. It is alleged respondents knew or were in reckless disregard of Charter's intention to use the transactions to inflate its revenues and knew the resulting financial statements issued by Charter would be relied upon by research analysts and investors.

Petitioner filed a securities fraud class action on behalf of purchasers of Charter stock alleging that, by participating in the transactions, respondents violated § 10(b) of the Securities Exchange Act of 1934 and SEC Rule 10b-5.

The District Court granted respondents' motion to dismiss for failure to state a claim on which relief can be granted. The United States Court of Appeals for the Eighth Circuit affirmed. In its view the allegations did not show that respondents made misstatements relied upon by the public or that they violated a duty to disclose; and on this premise it found no violation of § 10(b) by respondents. At most, the court observed, respondents had aided and abetted Charter's misstatement of its financial results; but, it noted, there is no private right of action for aiding and abetting a § 10(b) violation. *See* Central Bank of Denver, N.A. v. First Interstate Bank of Denver, N. A., 511 U.S. 164, 191 (1994).

Decisions of the Courts of Appeals are in conflict respecting when, if ever, an injured investor may rely upon § 10(b) to recover from a party that neither makes a public misstatement nor violates a duty to disclose but does participate in a scheme to violate § 10(b). *Compare* Simpson v. AOL Time Warner Inc., 452 F.3d 1040 (C.A.9 2006), *with* Regents of Univ. of Cal. v. Credit Suisse First Boston (USA), Inc., 482 F.3d 372 (C.A.5 2007). We granted certiorari.

II

Section 10(b) of the Securities Exchange Act makes it

> unlawful for any person, directly or indirectly, by the use of any means or instrumentality of interstate commerce or of the mails, or of any facility of any national securities exchange ... [t]o use or employ, in connection with the purchase or sale of any security ... any manipulative or deceptive device or contrivance in contravention of such rules and regulations as the Commission may prescribe as necessary or appropriate in the public interest or for the protection of investors. 15 U.S.C. § 78j.

The SEC, pursuant to this section, promulgated Rule 10b-5, which makes it unlawful

> (a) To employ any device, scheme, or artifice to defraud,
>
> (b) To make any untrue statement of a material fact or to omit to state a material fact necessary in order to make the statements made, in the light of the circumstances under which they were made, not misleading, or
>
> (c) To engage in any act, practice, or course of business which operates or would operate as a fraud or deceit upon any person, in connection with the purchase or sale of any security." 17 CFR § 240.10b-5.

Rule 10b-5 encompasses only conduct already prohibited by § 10(b). United States v. O'Hagan, 521 U.S. 642, 651 (1997). Though the text of the Securities Exchange Act does not provide for a private cause of action for § 10(b) violations, the Court has found a right of action implied in the words of the statute and its implementing regulation. Superintendent of Ins. of N.Y. v. Bankers Life & Casualty Co., 404 U.S. 6, 13, n. 9 (1971). In a typical § 10(b) private action a plaintiff must prove (1) a material misrepresentation or omission by the defendant; (2) scienter; (3) a connection between the misrepresentation or omission and the purchase or sale of a security; (4) reliance upon the misrepresentation or omission; (5) economic loss; and (6) loss causation. *See* Dura Pharmaceuticals, Inc. v. Broudo, 544 U.S. 336, 341–342 (2005).

In *Central Bank*, the Court determined that § 10(b) liability did not extend to aiders and abettors. The Court found the scope of § 10(b) to be delimited by the text, which makes no mention of aiding and abetting liability. The Court doubted the implied § 10(b) action should extend to aiders and abettors when none of the express causes of action in the securities Acts included that liability. It added the following:

> Were we to allow the aiding and abetting action proposed in this case, the defendant could be liable without any showing that the plaintiff relied upon the aider and abettor's statements or actions.... Allowing plaintiffs to circumvent the reliance requirement would disregard the careful limits on 10b-5 recovery mandated by our earlier cases.

The decision in *Central Bank* led to calls for Congress to create an express cause of action for aiding and abetting within the Securities Exchange Act. Then-SEC Chairman Arthur Levitt, testifying before the Senate Securities Subcommittee, cited *Central Bank* and recommended that aiding and abetting liability in private claims be established. S. Hearing No. 103-759, pp. 13–14 (1994). Congress did not follow this course. Instead, in § 104 of the Private Securities Litigation Reform Act of 1995 (PSLRA), 109 Stat. 757, it directed prosecution of aiders and abettors by the SEC. 15 U.S.C. § 78t(e).

The § 10(b) implied private right of action does not extend to aiders and abettors. The conduct of a secondary actor must satisfy each of the elements or preconditions for liability; and we consider whether the allegations here are sufficient to do so.

III

The Court of Appeals concluded petitioner had not alleged that respondents engaged in a deceptive act within the reach of the § 10(b) private right of action, noting that only misstatements, omissions by one who has a duty to disclose, and manipulative trading practices (where "manipulative" is a term of art, *see, e.g.*, Santa Fe Industries, Inc. v. Green, 430 U.S. 462, 476–477, 97 S.Ct. 1292, 51 L.Ed.2d 480 (1977)) are deceptive within the meaning of the rule. 443 F.3d, at 992. If this conclusion were read to suggest there must be a specific oral or written statement before there could be liability under § 10(b) or Rule 10b-5, it would be erroneous. Conduct itself can be deceptive, as respondents concede. In this case, moreover, respondents' course of conduct included both oral and written statements, such as the backdated contracts agreed to by Charter and respondents.

A different interpretation of the holding from the Court of Appeals opinion is that the court was stating only that any deceptive statement or act respondents made was not actionable because it did not have the requisite proximate relation to the investors' harm. That conclusion is consistent with our own determination that respondents' acts or statements were not relied upon by the investors and that, as a result, liability cannot be imposed upon respondents.

A

Reliance by the plaintiff upon the defendant's deceptive acts is an essential element of the § 10(b) private cause of action. It ensures that, for liability to arise, the "requisite causal connection between a defendant's misrepresentation and a plaintiff's injury" exists as a predicate for liability. Basic Inc. v. Levinson, 485 U.S. 224, 243, 108 S.Ct. 978, (1988).

We have found a rebuttable presumption of reliance in two different circumstances. First, if there is an omission of a material fact by one with a duty to disclose, the investor to whom the duty was owed need not provide specific proof of reliance. Second, under the fraud-on-the-market doctrine, reliance is presumed when the statements at issue become public. The public information is reflected in the market price of the security. Then it can be assumed that an investor who buys or sells stock at the market price relies upon the statement.

Neither presumption applies here. Respondents had no duty to disclose; and their deceptive acts were not communicated to the public. No member of the investing public had knowledge, either actual or presumed, of respondents' deceptive acts during the relevant times. Petitioner, as a result, cannot show reliance upon any of respondents' actions except in an indirect chain that we find too remote for liability.

* * *

1. Secondary actor liability. Recall from Chapter 11 that the general rule is that unless a false statement is attributed to a secondary actor in a securities fraud case, there is no liability for securities fraud. "[P]articipation in the creation of those statements amounts, at most, to aiding and abetting securities fraud." Pacific Investment Management Co. v. Mayer Brown, LLP, 603 F.3d 144, 148 (2d Cir. 2010).

2. The *Central Bank* decision. In *Central Bank*, the Court concluded that the statutory text did not provide for an aiding and abetting claim. But in addition, the Court pointed out that aiding and abetting has not been adopted as a separate tort in all jurisdictions and, therefore, there was no "deeply rooted background of aiding and abetting tort liability" that might justify the conclusion that Congress intended to allow for such a civil remedy in the case of a violation of the statute. Central Bank of Denver, N.A. v. First Interstate Bank of Denver, N. A., 511 U.S. 164, 184 (1994).

3. Fraud on the market. The Supreme Court has explained the basis of the fraud-on-the-market theory mentioned in *Stoneridge*: "An investor who buys or sells stock at the price set by the market does so in reliance on the integrity of that price. Because most publicly available information is reflected in market price, an investor's reliance on any public material misrepresentations, therefore, may be presumed for purposes of a Rule 10b-5 action." Basic Inc. v. Levinson, 485 U.S. 224, 247 (1988).

4. Aiding and abetting liability under other federal statutes. There is no generally applicable federal aiding and abetting civil statute. But as the Court pointed out in *Central Bank*, a number of federal statutes do include a provision allowing for recovery where one has aided and abetted another in the violation of a statute. 511 U.S. at 182. These include the Internal Revenue Code, 26 U.S.C. §6701, the Commodity Exchange Act, 7 U.S.C. §25(a)(1), as well as other securities laws.

Exercise 17.4

Imagine a case involving the same facts as in *Stoneridge* but with two big differences: (1) Charter was not a publicly-traded entity and (2) Charter engaged in inflating its revenues in an attempt to make itself appear more attractive to Stoneridge so that Stoneridge would purchase Charter's assets for a higher price. Could Stoneridge recover from Scientific-Atlanta, Inc. and Motorola on aiding and abetting theory?

C. Aiding and Abetting Breach of Fiduciary Duty

As mentioned in *Tensfeldt*, another possible theory is aiding and abetting a client's breach of fiduciary duty. Some plaintiffs have succeeded on such claims. *See* S & K Sales Co. v. Nike, Inc., 816 F.2d 843 (2d Cir. 1987) (affirming jury verdict against company for aiding and abetting an employee's breach of fiduciary duty). However, courts are currently divided on the question of whether to recognize such claims when brought against lawyers. *See generally* Paula Schaefer, *The Future of Inadvertent Disclosure: The Lingering Need to Revise Professional Conduct Rules*, 69 Md. L. Rev. 195 (2010); Katerina P. Lewinbuk, *Let's Sue All the Lawyers: The Rise of Claims Against Lawyers for Aiding and Abetting a Client's Breach of Fiduciary Duty*, 40 Ariz. St. L.J. 135, 166 (2008).

Focus Questions: *Thornwood, Inc. v. Jenner & Block* and *Reynolds v. Schrock*

1. *Under what circumstances may an attorney be held liable for aiding and abetting a client's breach of fiduciary duty under the* Thornwood *approach? The* Reynolds *approach?*
2. *What is the rationale for extending a privilege to lawyers where they provide substantial assistance or encouragement to a client's breach of fiduciary duty?*
3. *Does the* Reynolds *court provide sufficient guidance to help future courts decide whether a lawyer's actions are privileged?*

Thornwood, Inc. v. Jenner & Block

799 N.E.2d 756
(Ill. App. 1 Dist. 2003)

In February 1991, Thomas A. Thornton and James Follensbee (Follensbee), through James Follensbee & Associates and JF+A Properties, Ltd., formed the Thornwood Venture Limited Partnership (Partnership) for the purpose of developing Thornton's Kane County farm as a residential community and golf course (Thornwood Golf Course). Thornton contributed 550 acres of land and an option to buy an additional 180 acres of land. Thornton further agreed to fund the Partnership's endeavors until it was able to secure equity investors. Follensbee contributed his expertise and experience as an architect, engineer, and real estate developer to the Partnership. In exchange, Thornton received a 75% ownership interest in the Partnership. Follensbee received a 25% ownership interest and the right to be compensated for his services as the Partnership's managing general partner.

The Partnership consumed significant funds in its efforts to develop the Property. By October 1994, Thornton had expended cash and incurred debt of more than $8 million for the Partnership. Follensbee made numerous efforts to recruit investors for the Partnership. In 1994, for instance, Follensbee approached PGA Tour Golf Course Properties, Inc. (PGA), and Potomac Sports Properties, Inc. (Potomac), regarding the possibility of developing Thornwood Golf Course as a PGA Tournament Players Course (TPC). The benefits of such a partnership could have been substantial....

Thus, the Partnership was likely to experience tremendous revenue growth if Thornwood Golf Course was a TPC. Unfortunately, in a letter dated June 8, 1994, the PGA indicated that it would not be willing to work with the Partnership "unless the developer [was] willing to start over." Follensbee delivered a copy of the letter to Thornton and told him that "the PGA and [Potomac's] involvement in the development project was not feasible."

Nevertheless, Follensbee continued to pursue partnership negotiations with the PGA and Potomac. Without disclosing his continued negotiations, Follensbee began making plans with the PGA and Potomac regarding the layout of the golf course, the division of profits, and the duties of the Partnership, the PGA, and Potomac. None of these plans involved Thornton; nor were they disclosed to Thornton.

In the midst of Follensbee's undisclosed efforts to recruit the PGA and Potomac as partners, Thornton confronted Follensbee regarding the significant expenditures he had made to fund Follensbee's development activities. Thornton's assets were quickly dissipating into the Partnership without any indication that the Partnership was likely to have any success in the near future; thus, Thornton indicated to Follensbee that he desired to liquidate the Partnership or sell his interest. Follensbee responded that he would sue Thornton before he would allow liquidation of the Partnership. Alternatively, he indicated that he would be interested in purchasing Thornton's interest in the Partnership. At that time, Follensbee did not inform Thornton that his interest was likely to gain significant value in the near future because of the agreement Follensbee was negotiating with the PGA and Potomac. Instead, Follensbee enlisted the services of Jenner & Block to assist him in acquiring Thornton's interest in the Partnership. Jenner & Block also participated in Follensbee's negotiations with the PGA and Potomac. On January 11, 1995, Follensbee and Thornton executed a settlement agreement (settlement agreement), which provided the requirements and terms for Follensbee to acquire Thornton's interest in the Partnership. Alternatively, the settlement agreement provided for the liquidation of the Partnership. Significantly, the settlement agreement contained mutual releases between the parties....

Additionally, Thornton contemporaneously executed a release (Jenner & Block Release) purporting to relieve Jenner & Block, Follensbee's attorneys:

> from any liability from any and all claims, counterclaims, controversies, actions, causes of actions, demands, debts, damages, costs, attorneys fees, or liabilities of any nature whatsoever in law of [sic] in equity, whether known or hereinafter discovered, that arose out of events that have occurred from the beginning of time until the date hereof.

At the time Thornton signed the releases, he was not aware that Follensbee had continued negotiations with the PGA and Potomac and reached a conditional agreement for their involvement in Thornwood Golf Course. Thornton did not become aware of Follensbee's actions until November 1998, almost four years after he signed the releases. Nevertheless, Jenner & Block contends that these releases bar Thornton's claims. The trial court agreed and dismissed the complaint....

Partners have a fiduciary relationship. Consequently, they "owe one another a duty of full disclosure of material facts when making a settlement and obtaining a release." [The court concluded that the releases did not necessarily bar the plaintiff's claims.]

Jenner & Block urges that even if we find the releases do not bar Thornton's claims, we should affirm the dismissal of the complaint because it fails to state any claims upon which relief can be granted. We disagree....

Although Illinois courts have never found an attorney liable for aiding and abetting his client in the commission of a tort, the courts have not prohibited such actions. In *Reuben H. Donnelley Corp. v. Brauer*, 275 Ill.App.3d 300, 211 Ill.Dec. 779, 655 N.E.2d 1162 (1995), for instance, the court considered a claim of aiding and abetting made against one defendant and his attorneys. While not specifically considering whether the claim could be maintained against the attorneys as a matter of law, the court implicitly accepted that such a claim could be maintained when it held that there could be no liability because the underlying conduct involved a breach of contract, not a tort.

Similarly, Illinois courts recognize that claims for conspiracy may be maintained against attorneys where there is evidence that the attorneys participated in a conspiracy with their clients. Accordingly, we see no reason to impose a per se bar that prevents imposing liability upon attorneys who knowingly and substantially assist their clients in causing another party's injury. As we have recognized, "'[o]ne may not use his license to practice law as a shield to protect himself from the consequences of his participation in an unlawful or illegal conspiracy.'" Celano v. Frederick, 54 Ill.App.2d 393, 400, 203 N.E.2d 774 (1964), quoting Wahlgren v. Bausch & Lomb Optical Co., 68 F.2d 660, 664 (7th Cir.1934). The same policy should prevent an attorney from escaping liability for knowingly and substantially assisting a client in the commission of a tort.

Certainly, as Jenner & Block points out, mere receipt of copies of letters authored by Follensbee, which expose his breach of fiduciary duty, probably does not constitute aiding and abetting under Illinois law. Here, however, Thornton alleges more. He alleges that Jenner & Block aided and abetted by knowingly and substantially assisting Follensbee in breaching his fiduciary duty by (1) communicating the competitive advantages available to the Partnership from the PGA/TPC plan to other parties, but specifically not to Thornton; (2) expressing Follensbee's interest in purchasing Thornton's interest in the Partnership and negotiating the purchase of that interest without disclosing to Thornton the continued negotiations with the PGA and Potomac; (3) reviewing and counseling Follensbee with regard to the production of investment offering memoranda, financial projections, and marketing literature, which purposely failed to identify Thornton as a partner; and (4) drafting, negotiating, reviewing, and executing documents, including the Jenner & Block and Follensbee Releases, relating to the purchase of Thornton's interest and the PGA/TPC Plan with knowledge that Thornton was not aware of the PGA/TPC plan. All of these acts are alleged to have been perpetrated by Jenner & Block while it had knowledge that Thornton and Follensbee were partners, that Follensbee had a duty to disclose the PGA/TPC plan to Thornton, and that Follensbee did not disclose the PGA/TPC plan to Thornton despite having the opportunity and duty to do so. Importantly, Thornton is not required to prove his allegations at this time. Thus, even though Thornton may face an uphill battle in proving his claims, we cannot at this time affirm the dismissal of his complaint.

Reynolds v. Schrock

142 P.3d 1062
(Or. 2006)

BALMER, J.

This case requires us to determine whether a lawyer may be liable to a third party for aiding and abetting a client's breach of fiduciary duty, and, if the lawyer may be so liable, what circumstances must exist to impose liability. Plaintiff sued defendant for breach of fiduciary duty, and he also sued defendant's lawyer for his role in that alleged breach. The trial court entered summary judgment in the lawyer's favor, and the Court of Appeals reversed.

I. FACTS

We take the facts from the Court of Appeals opinion and the record. Because this case comes to us on summary judgment, we review the facts in the manner most favorable to plaintiff, the nonmoving party. Plaintiff was a naturopathic physician, and defendant Donna Schrock was one of plaintiff's patients. Plaintiff and Schrock bought two parcels of land together. In 1999, Schrock filed two separate actions against plaintiff. The first action concerned the jointly owned land, and the second alleged that, in the course of the doctor-patient relationship, plaintiff had engaged in improper sexual conduct with Schrock. The two actions were consolidated, and the parties later settled them in an agreement negotiated and drafted by their respective lawyers, including Schrock's lawyer, defendant Charles Markley. The settlement agreement provided, in part, that plaintiff would transfer his share of one of the two jointly owned properties (the "lodge property") to Schrock and that Schrock and plaintiff together would sell the second property (the "timber property") and transfer the proceeds to plaintiff. If the proceeds of the timber property sale were less than $500,000, then Schrock would pay plaintiff the difference and Schrock would grant plaintiff a security interest for that amount in the lodge property to secure the payment. If the proceeds of the timber property sale equaled or exceeded $500,000, then Schrock would owe plaintiff nothing and plaintiff would have no security interest in the lodge property.

After the parties signed the settlement agreement, plaintiff transferred his interest in the lodge property to Schrock. Markley then advised Schrock that, in his opinion, nothing in the settlement agreement expressly required her to retain the lodge property in anticipation of the possible creation of a security interest in plaintiff's favor. Schrock, with Markley's assistance and without plaintiff's knowledge, sold the lodge property to a third party before the parties sold the timber property. Markley asked the escrow officer handling the sale to keep the sale confidential. Markley also advised Schrock that she could revoke the consent that she had given earlier to plaintiff's plan to sell the jointly owned timber property. In Markley's view, plaintiff had failed to provide Schrock with information about the value of the timber property prior to arranging to sell it, contrary to a requirement in the settlement agreement, and that breach freed Schrock from any obligation to consent to the sale of the timber property. Based on Markley's advice, and with Markley's assistance, Schrock revoked her consent to the sale of the timber property.

II. PROCEEDINGS BELOW

Plaintiff sued Schrock and Markley over their actions in connection with the implementation of the settlement agreement. As to Schrock, plaintiff alleged, among other things, that the settlement agreement had created fiduciary duties between Schrock and plaintiff as joint venturers. Plaintiff asserted that Schrock, by selling the lodge property and revoking her consent to the sale of the timber property, had breached her fiduciary duty to plaintiff and the implied covenant of good faith and fair dealing that was part of the settlement agreement.[3] He further alleged that Schrock had converted his interest in the lodge property by selling that property and retaining the proceeds.

3. Both the claim for breach of fiduciary duty and the claim for breach of the covenant of good faith and fair dealing arose from the duties that plaintiff and Schrock allegedly owed one another as a result of the settlement agreement. The parties and the courts below treated the claims as a single claim for breach of fiduciary duty, and we do as well.

Plaintiff's complaint alleged that Markley was jointly liable with Schrock because he had aided and abetted Schrock's torts by giving her "substantial assistance and encouragement" in the commission of the torts and acting "in concert with [her] pursuant to a common design...." ... Plaintiff and Schrock later settled, leaving Markley as the only remaining defendant.

Markley moved for summary judgment, and the trial court granted his motion, stating, in part:

> "[T]he only evidence is that Mr. Markley advised his client of what she could do given the language of the agreements.... [T]here is no evidence that he was doing anything other than acting as Ms. Schrock's lawyer. Mr. Markley had no duty to the plaintiff.... [His] duty runs only to his client."

On appeal, plaintiff assigned error to the trial court's judgment in Markley's favor on the "joint-liability tort claims"—that is, the claims that Markley was jointly liable with Schrock for breach of fiduciary duty and conversion. The Court of Appeals affirmed the trial court's judgment in Markley's favor on the conversion claim. Reynolds, The court, however, reversed the judgment on the breach of fiduciary duty claim. The Court of Appeals held that this court's precedents did not exempt a lawyer from liability for assisting in a client's breach of fiduciary duty and that the Court of Appeals' case law suggested that a lawyer for a fiduciary could be liable for knowingly aiding or assisting a fiduciary in a breach of duty. As noted, Markley sought review, which we allowed.

III. ANALYSIS

A. Liability for Assisting a Breach of Fiduciary Duty

We begin our analysis, as do the parties, with this court's decision in *Granewich v. Harding*, 329 Or. 47, 985 P.2d 788 (1999). That case provides a reasonable starting point because it involved claims for breach of fiduciary duty, including a claim against a lawyer for assisting others in breaching fiduciary duties that they owed to the plaintiff. Plaintiff argues that *Granewich* describes the elements required to state a claim and holds that a lawyer in Markley's position may be liable for assisting in a client's breach of fiduciary duty. In our view, however, *Granewich* does not provide a complete answer to the questions that this case raises.

The plaintiff in *Granewich*, a minority shareholder in a corporation, alleged that the corporation's two majority shareholders had breached their fiduciary duty to him by effectuating a corporate "squeeze-out." The plaintiff also asserted a separate claim against the corporation's lawyer, alleging that the lawyer had assisted the other defendants in that squeeze-out. This court held that the lawyer could be liable for aiding and abetting the other defendants' breach of fiduciary duty, even though the lawyer had no independent fiduciary duty to the plaintiff. However, the *Granewich* opinion specifically noted that the defendant lawyer in that case had represented the corporation, not the other defendants (the majority shareholders), and that the plaintiff had alleged that the lawyer's actions had fallen "outside the scope of any legitimate employment on behalf of the corporation." Therefore, in *Granewich*, this court did not consider or answer the question that is at the core of this case: whether, and under what circumstances, a third party may assert a claim against a lawyer, acting in a professional capacity, for assisting a client in breaching the client's fiduciary duty.

Under *Granewich* and the *Restatement*, a person who acts "in concert with" or "gives substantial assistance or encouragement" to a fiduciary who breaches a duty to a third party may be liable for the resulting harm. Markley argues, however, that that general rule does not apply when a lawyer, in the context of a lawyer-client relationship, advises a client who breaches a fiduciary duty to a third party. The *Restatement* labels any such exemption from liability that the law otherwise would impose as a "privilege." *See Restatement* § 890 ("One who otherwise would be liable for a tort is not liable if he acts in pursuance of and within the limits of a privilege...."). We therefore consider whether the fact that Markley was acting as Schrock's lawyer when he engaged in the challenged conduct created a privilege that protects Markley from liability. If that status does create such a privilege, then we must consider the circumstances in which the privilege applies.

B. Privilege Against Joint Liability for a Lawyer Assisting a Client's Breach of Fiduciary Duty

This court has not considered previously what privileges, if any, protect a person from liability for substantially assisting another in a breach of fiduciary duty. However, several cases have considered privileges as they relate to claims for interference with contractual relations brought against advisors or agents who acted on behalf of another person or entity. Those cases are instructive, because, like the present case, they involve claims against a person for actions on behalf of a client or principal that allegedly harmed a third party.

In *Wampler v. Palmerton*, 250 Or. 65, 439 P.2d 601 (1968), the plaintiff sued a corporation's financial advisors for intentional interference with contractual relations for advising the corporation to breach its contract with the plaintiff. This court noted that the advisors owed a "duty of advice and action" to the corporation and that imposing liability on those advisors would paralyze the corporation's ability to act and to secure advice on how to act. The court therefore recognized a privilege against liability for corporate advisors who act in good faith and for the benefit of the corporation. Indeed, the court noted, the privilege protects the advisor from liability "even though plaintiff argues that the defendants intended to cause the corporation to take an unfair advantage of the plaintiff by means of the breach of contract."

In *Welch v. Bancorp Management Advisors*, 296 Or. 208, 214, 675 P.2d 172 (1983), this court again considered the issue of when an agent can be liable in tort for actions that the agent takes on behalf of its principal and that cause harm to a third party. In that case, a real estate developer alleged that a lender had agreed to provide financing for a project but had breached that agreement based on "misrepresentations" and "false advice" given to the lender by its investment committee. The developer sought to recover from the investment committee members for tortious interference with the financing agreement. Relying on its earlier decision[] in *Wampler*..., this court held that the investment committee had been acting as the agent of the lender and therefore was immunized from tort liability if its actions had been within the scope of its authority:

> An agent acting as a financial advisor is thus privileged to interfere with or induce breach of the principal's contracts or business relations with third parties, as long as the agent's actions are within the scope of his employment and taken with an intent to further the best interests of the principal.

Welch, 296 Or. at 218, 675 P.2d 172; *see also id.* at 216–17, 675 P.2d 172 ("[T]he proper test is whether the agent acts within the scope of his authority and with the intent to benefit the principal.").

This court, in the cases described above, protected from liability defendants who owed duties to an entity or person and who, in the course of performing those duties, harmed a third party. This court recognized a qualified privilege in those cases because it was necessary to protect important relationships between the defendant and the entity or person—the financial advisor and the corporation in *Wampler*, ... and the investment committee and the lender in *Welch*. That is, this court, in exercising its common-law authority to define tortious conduct, implicitly concluded that the effective performance of the duties arising from those relationships required that the person performing those duties have a qualified privilege from tort liability.

The principle underlying the cases just discussed—that, for individuals and corporations to obtain the advice and assistance that they must receive from their agents, the agents must have some protection from tort liability to third parties—assists us in determining the rule that should be applied in this case. Not every relationship between a person who breaches a contract or a fiduciary duty and one who substantially assists in such a breach necessarily justifies recognition of a privilege against liability. However, we think that the lawyer-client relationship is one that does. That is true, in our view, because safeguarding the lawyer-client relationship protects more than just an individual or entity in any particular case or transaction; it is integral to the protection of the legal system itself. Myriad business transactions, as well as civil, criminal, and administrative proceedings, require that the client have the assistance of a lawyer. And a variety of doctrines, from the rules against conflicts of interest to the confidential nature of lawyer-client communications, demonstrate the ways in which the legal system protects the lawyer-client relationship.

Moreover, ... a third party's claim against the lawyer that puts the lawyer at odds with the client will compromise the lawyer-client relationship. A lawyer who is sued for substantially assisting a client's breach of fiduciary duty becomes subject to divided loyalties. As this court has recognized, lawyers cannot serve their clients adequately when their own self-interest—in these examples, the need to protect themselves from potential tort claims by third parties—pulls in the opposite direction. *See, e.g.,* In re Jeffery, 321 Or. 360, 898 P.2d 752 (1995) (conflict of interest for lawyer to represent client in criminal case in which lawyer also was implicated); *see also Restatement of Lawyers* § 121 comment b (conflict compromises client's expectation of effective representation). Moreover, allowing a claim against the lawyer may raise issues of lawyer-client privilege, if the preparation of an adequate defense for the lawyer would require the disclosure of privileged communications.

To summarize the discussion above, this court's earlier decisions hold that a person may be jointly liable with another for substantially assisting in the other's breach of a fiduciary duty owed to a third party, if the person knows that the other's conduct constitutes a breach of that fiduciary duty. *Granewich*, 329 Or. at 57, 985 P.2d 788. Our tort case law also makes clear, however, that, if a person's conduct as an agent or on behalf of another comes within the scope of a privilege, then the person is not liable to the third party. In this case, we extend those well-recognized principles to a context that we have not previously considered and hold that a lawyer acting on behalf of a client and within the scope of the lawyer-client relationship is protected by such a privilege and is not liable for assisting the client in conduct that breaches the client's fiduciary duty to a third party. Accordingly, for a third party to hold a lawyer liable for substantially assisting in a client's breach of fiduciary duty, the third party must prove that the lawyer acted outside the scope of the lawyer-client relationship.

Several features of the rule regarding the circumstances in which a lawyer's conduct may be privileged are particularly important. First, the rule places the burden on the plaintiff to show that the lawyer was acting outside the scope of the lawyer-client relationship.

Second, the rule protects lawyers only for actions of the kind that permissibly may be taken by lawyers in the course of representing their clients. It does not protect lawyer conduct that is unrelated to the representation of a client, even if the conduct involves a person who is a client. Because such unrelated conduct is, by definition, outside the scope of the lawyer-client relationship, no important public interest would be served by extending the qualified privilege to cover it. For the same reason, the rule does not protect lawyers who are representing clients but who act only in their own self-interest and contrary to their clients' interest. Similarly, this court would consider actions by a lawyer that fall within the "crime or fraud" exception to the lawyer-client privilege, OEC 503(4)(a), and Rule of Professional Conduct 1.6(b)(1), to be outside the lawyer-client relationship when evaluating whether a lawyer's conduct is protected.

The Court of Appeals, in this case, like other courts that have considered similar claims by nonclients against lawyers, struggled to reconcile the client's need for a lawyer's confidentiality, advice, and assistance with the desire to hold lawyers accountable for "affirmative conduct that actually furthers the client's breach of fiduciary duty, done by the attorney with knowledge that he or she is furthering the breach." For that reason, the court held that, although a lawyer could be jointly liable under the principles of *Restatement*, section 876(a) and (b), for assisting a client that breached its fiduciary duty, "a strict and narrow construction best protects the attorney-client relationship without conferring on attorneys a license to help fiduciaries breach their duties." *Id.*

In our view, the test that we hold applicable here—whether the lawyer's conduct fell outside the permissible scope of the lawyer-client relationship—often will lead to the same result as the tests adopted in the cases described above. It does so, however, in a more predictable and useful way, because it focuses on the scope of the lawyer-client relationship—and the legal rules, such as OEC 503(4)(a), that help define that scope—rather than on the fine line between "advice" and "assistance" or between "substantial assistance" and other assistance. We acknowledge that the test does not identify a bright line between liability and immunity, but it nevertheless uses concepts tied directly to the lawyer's role in representing the client and existing sources of law regarding the scope of that role.

C. Application of the Privilege

We now return to the facts of this case. Like the parties and the courts below, we assume for these purposes that Schrock breached a fiduciary duty to plaintiff and that Markley knowingly provided substantial assistance to her or acted in concert with her in so doing. We focus on whether Markley, as Schrock's lawyer, has a qualified privilege from liability to plaintiff for assisting in that breach of duty. Here, plaintiff had "the burden of negating [the] qualified privilege ... as part of his affirmative case." *Straube*, 287 Or. at 371, 600 P.2d 371. On summary judgment, therefore, plaintiff had the burden of producing evidence that would show that Markley's conduct was not privileged because it fell outside the permissible scope of his role as Schrock's lawyer.

Taken in the light most favorable to plaintiff, the summary judgment record shows that Markley took four actions that plaintiff asserts are relevant to his claims. First, Markley advised Schrock that the settlement agreement did not require her to retain the lodge property in anticipation of the possibility that plaintiff's security interest would attach to it and assisted her in selling it. Second, he called the escrow officer and asked her not to tell anyone about the pending sale of the property. Third, he assisted Schrock in revoking her consent to sell the timber property. Finally, he accepted substantial fees for performing legal work for Schrock, including the foregoing three actions.

Nowhere has plaintiff suggested, and nothing in the record indicates, that any aspect of Markley's advice and assistance to Schrock fell outside the scope of the lawyer-client relationship or the assistance that a lawyer properly provides for a client. There is no credible claim that Markley's conduct violated any applicable statute. No evidence in the summary judgment record suggests that Markley's or Schrock's conduct was criminal or fraudulent. Whether or not Markley's interpretation of the agreement was correct—a determination that we need not make here—the purpose of the privilege requires that lawyers be able to assess the legal problems that their clients bring to them and discuss the full range of available solutions. Moreover, lawyers must be able to assist their clients in implementing those solutions, to the extent that that assistance falls within the legitimate scope of the lawyer-client relationship. Although courts may not always agree with the legal advice that a lawyer provides, protecting a lawyer from liability to a third party for advising a client is essential to the administration of justice.

Plaintiff argues that we should interpret Markley's acceptance of fees as a self-interested act that fell outside the scope of the qualified privilege. We disagree. Whether Markley took no fee or an hourly fee or a contingent fee is irrelevant to the central question whether his actions fell within the scope of the lawyer-client relationship. If anything, Markley's acceptance of a fee supports his claim that he was acting as Schrock's lawyer, although there is no evidence here that he was not acting as her lawyer.

The summary judgment record reveals no evidence from which a reasonable jury could find that Markley acted outside the scope of the lawyer-client relationship in his representation of Schrock. Markley's conduct therefore falls within the scope of the privilege that we have described above. The trial court was correct in granting Markley's motion for summary judgment.

Exercise 17.5

You are a trial judge in a jurisdiction with no precedent on the issues in *Thornwood* and *Reynolds*. A case comes to you involving the same issues. Which approach will you adopt? What policy considerations are most important to you in reaching your decision?

Professional identity. Imagine that in *Thornwood, Inc. v. Jenner & Block*, Follensbee comes to you in your professional capacity as a lawyer at the point in the story where Thornton had confronted Follensbee regarding the significant expenditures he had made to fund Follensbee's development activities. Follensbee tells you that he has been negotiating in secret with the PGA and Potomac and is interested in acquiring Thornton's interest in the partnership, but does not wish to tell Thornton about the likely increase in value as a result of the negotiation with the PGA and Potomac. What do you say to him?

* * *

D. Civil Conspiracy

As mentioned in the introduction to this chapter, the other basis of liability that might arise when persons act in concert is civil conspiracy. As defined by one court, the elements of a civil conspiracy claim are

> (1) an agreement between two or more persons; (2) to participate in an unlawful act, or a lawful act in an unlawful manner; (3) an injury caused by an unlawful

overt act performed by one of the parties to the agreement; (4) which overt act was done pursuant to and in furtherance of the common scheme.

Halberstam v. Welch, 705 F.2d 472, 477 (D.C. Cir. 1983).

There is obviously some similarity between conspiracy and aiding and abetting. But, as the D.C. Circuit observed, "[t]here is a qualitative difference between proving an agreement to participate in a tortious line of conduct, and proving knowing action that substantially aids tortious conduct. In some situations, the trier of fact cannot reasonably infer an agreement from substantial assistance or encouragement. A court must then ensure that all the elements of the separate basis of aiding-abetting have been satisfied." An example would be *Rael v. Cadena*, the decision from the beginning of this chapter.

Focus Questions: *McLaughlin v. Copeland*

1. *Did Veazey's co-conspirator engage in an unlawful act?*
2. *What concerns do you see in permitting civil conspiracy claims against defense lawyers based on their attempts to contest or settle a claim on behalf of their clients?*
3. *Why would a plaintiff ever bring a conspiracy clam against a party when the other co-conspirator was the one who committed the underlying wrongful act?*

McLaughlin v. Copeland

455 F. Supp. 749
(D. Del. 1978)

BLAIR, District Judge, Sitting by Designation.

The plaintiff, Francis X. McLaughlin, alleges that defendants Lammot du Pont Copeland Junior and Senior conspired with Thomas A. Shaheen (and others) to defraud the creditors of the Winthrop Lawrence Corporation. Winthrop Lawrence is allegedly co-owned by Copeland Jr. and a corporation controlled by Shaheen.

In 1970, Winthrop Lawrence and Copeland Jr. filed Chapter XI bankruptcy petitions in Baltimore and Wilmington, respectively. Defendant Veasey and his law firm were retained to represent Copeland Jr. in the Wilmington bankruptcy proceeding. McLaughlin appeared in that proceeding on behalf of Pappas, one of Copeland Jr.'s alleged creditors, and made several references to the allegedly fraudulent and potentially criminal activities of the Copelands. Shortly thereafter, McLaughlin advised the defendants that his client, who was also a claimant against Winthrop, had instructed him to file a class action against Copeland Sr., Copeland Jr., and others on behalf of all creditors of the Winthrop Lawrence Corporation.

The basic thrust of McLaughlin's complaint is that after learning of his investigation of their misconduct, the defendants became fearful that the plaintiff would publicly expose the Copelands' allegedly fraudulent activities and entered into an agreement to "discredit, defame and damage" him in an effort to forestall exposure and force the abandonment of the threatened class action. This scheme to discredit McLaughlin is alleged to have included an attempt to entice the plaintiff into committing the crime of extortion and violating DR 7-105 of the *Code of Professional Responsibility* in connection with his representation of Pappas. It is this alleged conspiracy which forms the basis of plaintiff's suit.

McLaughlin contends that Veasey, acting for himself, his client Copeland Jr., and Copeland Sr., "undertook a concerted effort to discover something 'actionable against'" either McLaughlin or his client, and that this effort increased when Veasey was informed of McLaughlin's intention to submit the results of his investigation to a congressional committee for referral to the Justice Department or the F.B.I.

In February of 1975 McLaughlin and Veasey met in Baltimore to discuss settlement of Pappas' claim against Copeland Jr. It is alleged by McLaughlin that Veasey's true purpose in attending the meeting was to "induce, entice or otherwise entrap" the plaintiff into violating the *Code of Professional Responsibility*'s rule against "threatening a criminal prosecution to obtain advantage in a civil matter." Plaintiff further alleges that when this plan failed, Veasey maliciously and falsely prepared a memorandum suggesting that McLaughlin had committed the crime of extortion and violated the *Code of Professional Responsibility*. The gravamen of his complaint is that Veasey's subsequent transmission of the memorandum, supporting documents from his file, and an explanatory letter dated March 5th to the judge presiding at the Wilmington bankruptcy proceeding together with the publication of copies of the March 5th letter to the attorneys of record in that proceeding, constituted libel and malicious interference in his business as a practicing attorney.

Upon receipt of the March 5th letter and enclosures, Judge Schwartz referred the matter to the Disciplinary Board of the District of Columbia Bar which concluded, after a hearing, that the evidence was insufficient to support a finding that McLaughlin had violated the Code of Professional Responsibility. McLaughlin contends that Veasey's publication of the letter and supporting documents to Judge Schwartz "caused" a false and malicious complaint to be instituted against him with the disciplinary board, and that both the initial publication to the judge and attorneys, and the initiation of the disciplinary proceeding were acts in furtherance of a pre-existing conspiracy between Veasey and the Copelands. These allegations are divided into three counts: libel (Count II), civil conspiracy to libel, discredit and otherwise damage (Count I), and malicious interference with business (Count III). Defendants have moved to dismiss the complaint pursuant to F.R.Civ.P. 12(b)(6).

[The court concluded that the March 5th letter was absolutely privileged for purposes of the libel and malicious interference claims and, therefore, dismissed the claims.]

Civil Conspiracy

The gravamen of an action in civil conspiracy is not the conspiracy itself but the underlying wrong which would be actionable absent the conspiracy. "In order for a civil action for conspiracy to be maintained, there must be, in addition to a confederation of two or more persons, (1) some unlawful act done in furtherance of the conspiracy, and (2) actual legal damage resulting to the victim-plaintiff." Van Royen v. Lacey, 262 Md. 94, 97, 277 A.2d 13, 14 (1971). McLaughlin's complaint does not allege facts sufficient to meet this test.

The letter of March 5th is absolutely privileged and therefore cannot give rise to an action in defamation or interference with business. If the letter cannot give rise to a tort action, it cannot support an action in conspiracy to commit a tort, for it is well settled that "(n)o action in tort lies for conspiracy to do something unless the acts actually done, if done by one person, would constitute a tort." Domchick v. Greenbelt Consumer Services, 200 Md. 36, 42, 87 A.2d 831, 834 (1952).

In his memorandum in opposition to defendants' motion to dismiss, McLaughlin contends that even if Veasey's letter is absolutely privileged, "there are other tortious overt acts" in furtherance of the alleged conspiracy, "the most important one being the February 21, 1975 meeting in which Veasey's only purpose was to try and 'obtain something actionable against McLaughlin.'" This issue was conclusively resolved in the jurisdictional opinion which concluded that:

> Analytically, the question of jurisdiction for Counts I and III is the same as for Count II: was there a tortious act or omission in Maryland causing injury to McLaughlin? The act which is alleged to have occurred in Maryland is the February 21, 1975 meeting. The meeting was not the proximate cause of the alleged injury to the plaintiff. While it certainly was one of a preliminary number of acts leading to the mailings, if Veasey had returned to Wilmington and done nothing, there would be nothing upon which plaintiff could base a cause of action.

Since the only ostensibly tortious act, the mailing of the March 5th letter, is privileged and cannot give rise to a cause of action, McLaughlin is left with literally nothing upon which to base his suit. He does not allege that he was damaged by any act other than the publication of Veasey's letter, and it is axiomatic that "there is no such thing as a civil action for conspiracy but rather an action for damages caused by acts committed pursuant to a former conspiracy." Benoit v. Amalgamated Local 299 United E. R. & M. W., 150 Conn. 266, 276, 188 A.2d 499, 503 (1963).

* * *

Protection for attorneys. Cal. Civ. Code § 1714.10 provides: "No cause of action against an attorney for a civil conspiracy with his or her client arising from any attempt to contest or compromise a claim or dispute, and which is based upon the attorney's representation of the client, shall be included in a complaint or other pleading unless the court enters an order allowing the pleading that includes the claim for civil conspiracy to be filed after the court determines that the party seeking to file the pleading has established that there is a reasonable probability that the party will prevail in the action." Why would the California legislature adopt such a rule?

Chapter 18

Bad Faith

Every contract includes an implied duty of good faith and fair dealing. This includes insurance agreements. An insurer has an "implied-in-law duty to act in good faith and deal fairly with the insured to ensure that the policy benefits are received." Christian v. American Home Assurance Co., 577 P.2d 899, 901 (Okla.1977). The breach of this contractual duty may result in a tort claim of bad faith. Although the tort is rooted in a breach of an implied contractual duty, one of the obvious benefits of being able to bring a claim sounding in tort rather than contract is the availability of punitive damages. There are two distinct species of bad faith claims: (1) first-party claims, involving a claim by the insured based on the insurer's failure to cover the insured's losses and (2) third-party claims, involving a claim by the insured based on the insurer's failure to settle a claim brought by a third party against the insured within the insured's policy limits.

A. First-Party Claims

Focus Questions: *Gonzalez v. Blue Cross/Blue Shield of Alabama*

1. *When does an insurer's refusal to pay a claim amount to bad faith?*
2. *What would it have taken in this case for the Gonzalezes to create a genuine issue of material fact on the bad faith claim?*

Gonzalez v. Blue Cross/Blue Shield of Alabama

689 So.2d 812
(Ala. 1997)

SHORES, Justice.

Marco A. Gonzalez and his wife Theresa Gonzalez sued Blue Cross/Blue Shield of Alabama ("Blue Cross") and Alfa Mutual Insurance Company ("Alfa Mutual"), after Blue Cross had refused to pay insurance claims relating to the birth of the Gonzalezes' son.

Against both defendants the Gonzalezes stated claims of breach of contract and bad faith failure to pay an insurance claim, and they also stated a claim of fraud against Alfa Mutual. The trial court entered a summary judgment for Blue Cross on the bad faith claim and a summary judgment for Alfa Mutual on all claims and made those summary judgments final pursuant to Rule 54(b), Ala. R. Civ. P. The Gonzalezes appeal. We affirm.

The Gonzalezes sought family health insurance coverage. On January 28, 1993, they completed and signed a "Blue Cross and Blue Shield Application for Health Coverage" and then submitted this application to the Alfa Service Center in Pelham, Alabama. Under a contract with Alfa Services, Blue Cross acts as the claims administrator for the Alfa Health Plan, the policy for which the Gonzalezes applied. Blue Cross approved the application and mailed a "Certificate of Alfa Group Health Benefits" ("the certificate") to the Gonzalezes. The final page of the application is entitled "Conditions of Enrollment"; the conditions stated there include an acknowledgment that the insured understands that maternity care benefits would be covered under the insurance policy but would be subject to a 365-day waiting period:

> I, the undersigned, represent that:
>
> ....
>
> 7. I understand that the program I am applying for will not cover myself or my enrolled dependents until 365 days after my effective date of coverage for ... maternity benefits....

The certificate issued to the Gonzalezes contained a similar explanation of the 365-day waiting period for maternity benefits:

> Each female Subscriber or wife of a male Subscriber covered by Family Coverage Including Maternity Benefits must serve a waiting period of 365 consecutive days before benefits for maternity care are available to her under this Contract. The 365-day waiting period begins the date on which she is covered by Family coverage Including Maternity Benefits. The entire 365-day waiting period must be served before she receives services or supplies or is admitted to the Hospital for Maternity Care except when the pregnancy terminates before her expected delivery date which, if carried to full term, would have occurred after the expiration of the 365-day waiting period.

Under these provisions, the Gonzalezes' waiting period for maternity benefits began on March 1, 1993, the effective date of their coverage, and would expire on February 28, 1994.

Marco Gonzalez, who is an attorney at law, alleges that he was not told, before he submitted the application and a $650 check to cover the first premium, that there was a 365-day waiting period for maternity benefits.... Marco Gonzalez also alleges that he did not read the application before signing it and did not read the certificate until after Blue Cross had rejected the claim relating to the birth of his son.

On June 30, 1993, during an examination by her family doctor, Dr. Bryan McClelland, Mrs. Gonzalez discovered that she was pregnant. The following day, she visited her obstetrician-gynecologist, Dr. Robert May, who confirmed Dr. McClelland's findings. Because Dr. May was nearing retirement, the Gonzalezes chose Dr. William Somerall to care for Mrs. Gonzalez during her pregnancy and to deliver the baby. On September 8, 1993, Mrs. Gonzalez visited Dr. Robert Ryan, who performed an ultrasound examination. After the claim for this service was submitted for payment, Blue Cross requested the results of the ultrasound examination to determine the applicability of the waiting period to Mrs. Gonzalez's pregnancy. On November 12, 1993, Blue Cross received the ultrasound computer printout, which listed the first day of Mrs. Gonzalez's last menstrual period as May 23, 1993, showed that the fetus had a gestational age of about 15.6 weeks, and designated the expected delivery date as February 26, 1994. The accompanying report from Dr. Ryan said that the clinical expected delivery date was February 27, 1994. Both of these due dates were before the expiration of the waiting period on February 28, 1994.

On February 22, 1994, Mrs. Gonzalez was admitted to Brookwood Medical Center and there gave birth on February 24, 1994, to a nine-pound, five-ounce, baby boy. It is undisputed that the actual delivery date came before the expiration of the waiting period. The claims associated with the delivery, which included the hospital admission, the delivery itself, and an epidural, were submitted to Blue Cross for payment. Blue Cross paid claims on March 14 and March 28, 1994, for the delivery and the epidural, respectively. But on March 31, 1994, Blue Cross rejected the $8,031.90 claim for Mrs. Gonzalez's hospital stay from February 22 to February 26, 1994. On April 13, 1994, Blue Cross paid the claim for the ultrasound examination, which had been performed by Dr. Ryan on September 8, 1993. However, Blue Cross later determined that this ultrasound claim, as well as the claims for the delivery and the epidural, had all been paid in error, and it requested refunds of amounts it had initially paid for these services.

After being notified that Blue Cross had rejected the hospital admission claim, Mr. Gonzalez wrote two letters, dated May 2 and May 18, 1994, to Brookwood Medical Center, requesting information and documentation regarding why that claim had been rejected. Copies of these letters were also sent to Blue Cross. On June 6, 1994, Martha Melton, a Blue Cross customer service representative, wrote to Mr. Gonzalez, acknowledging receipt of his letters and stating that Mrs. Gonzalez's medical records had been forwarded to the Blue Cross medical review staff. On June 20, 1994, the Gonzalezes received a letter, by certified mail, from Brookwood Medical Center with an enclosed copy of a Blue Cross remittance notice dated March 31, 1994, stating that benefits were unavailable for Mrs. Gonzalez's hospital admission because the waiting period specified in the contract had not been served. Also on June 20, Blue Cross sent Mr. Gonzalez a letter offering the same explanation—that the hospital admission claim had been rejected because of the 365-day waiting period. In reply, Mr. Gonzalez wrote another letter to Blue Cross, dated July 13, 1994, enclosing copies of a letter from Dr. McClelland and a record from Dr. May stating that Mrs. Gonzalez's positive pregnancy test was given on June 30, 1993, and that the first day of her last menstrual period was documented as June 21, 1993. Mr. Gonzalez claimed that this information he submitted indicated an expected delivery date that was after February 28, 1994, and thus was outside the waiting period. Lynn Farley, medical director with Blue Cross, wrote back, explaining that this new information provided by Drs. McClelland and May conflicted with the previously submitted ultrasound records from Dr. Ryan that Blue Cross had reviewed. Farley's letter further stated that, in light of the conflicting information, Blue Cross had requested additional records from Drs. Somerall and May and that Blue Cross would reconsider whether the hospital admission claim would be paid. The Gonzalezes did not wait for a response from Blue Cross, but filed this action on August 17, 1994.

I. The Bad Faith Claim Against Blue Cross

The Gonzalezes argue that on their bad faith claim against Blue Cross they presented evidence creating genuine issues of material fact for a jury to decide and, therefore, that the trial judge erred by granting Blue Cross's motion for summary judgment.

This Court first recognized an actionable tort for an insurer's bad faith refusal to pay an insurance claim in *Chavers v. National Security Fire & Cas. Ins. Co.*, 405 So.2d 1 (Ala. 1981). "Bad faith is the intentional failure by an insurer to perform the duty of good faith and fair dealing implied by law." Koch v. State Farm Fire & Cas. Co., 565 So.2d 226, 229 (Ala. 1990). In *Chavers* the Court held:

> [A]n actionable tort arises [from] an insurer's intentional refusal to settle a direct claim where there is either '(1) no lawful basis for the refusal coupled with actual knowledge of that fact or (2) intentional failure to determine whether or not there was any lawful basis for such refusal.'

405 So.2d at 7. The Gonzalezes' bad faith claim rests on the second tier of the *Chavers* test, which was clarified in *Gulf Atlantic Life Ins. Co. v. Barnes*, 405 So.2d 916, 924 (Ala. 1981):

> "The second tier of the test is an elaboration on the first. The trier of fact, by finding, on the part of the insurer, an 'intentional failure to determine whether or not there was any lawful basis for refusal,' may use that fact as an element of proof that no lawful basis for refusal ever existed. The relevant question before the trier of fact would be whether a claim was properly investigated and whether the results of the investigation were subjected to a cognitive evaluation and review. Implicit in that test is the conclusion that the knowledge or reckless disregard of the lack of a legitimate or reasonable basis may be inferred and imputed to an insurance company when there is a reckless indifference to facts or to proof submitted by the insured."

The elements of a bad faith claim were summarized in *National Security Fire & Cas. Co. v. Bowen*, 417 So.2d 179 (Ala. 1982), as follows:

> An insurer is liable for its refusal to pay a direct claim when there is no lawful basis for the refusal coupled with actual knowledge of that fact. Chavers v. National Security Fire [& Cas.] Co., [405 So.2d 1 (Ala. 1981)]. No lawful basis 'means that the insurer lacks a legitimate or arguable reason for failing to pay the claim.' Gulf Atlantic Life Ins. Co. v. Barnes, [405 So.2d 916 (Ala. 1981)]. When a claim is 'fairly debatable,' the insurer is entitled to debate it, whether the debate concerns a matter of fact or law. *Ibid.*
>
> 
>
> Under those authorities the plaintiff in a 'bad faith refusal' case has the burden of proving:
>
> (a) an insurance contract between the parties and a breach thereof by the defendant;
>
> (b) an intentional refusal to pay the insured's claim;
>
> (c) the absence of any reasonably legitimate or arguable reason for that refusal (the absence of a debatable reason);
>
> (d) the insurer's actual knowledge of the absence of any legitimate or arguable reason;
>
> (e) if intentional failure to determine the existence of a lawful basis is relied upon, the plaintiff must prove the insurer's intentional failure to determine whether there is a legitimate or arguable reason to refuse to pay the claim.
>
> In short, plaintiff must go beyond a mere showing of nonpayment and prove a bad faith nonpayment, a nonpayment without any reasonable ground for dispute. Or, stated differently, the plaintiff must show that the insurance company had no legal or factual defense to the insurance claim.
>
> The 'debatable reason' under (c) above means an arguable reason, one that is open to debate or question.

417 So.2d at 183.

In *Blackburn v. Fidelity & Deposit Co.*, 667 So.2d 661, 668 (Ala.1995), we stated:

> In bad faith cases involving an insurer's refusal to pay an insurance claim, this Court has established the 'directed verdict on the contract claim' standard. In *National Savings Life Ins. Co. v. Dutton*, 419 So.2d 1357, 1362 (Ala. 1982), we stated:

> 'In the normal case in order for a plaintiff to make out a prima facie case of bad faith refusal to pay an insurance claim, the proof offered must show that the plaintiff is entitled to a directed verdict on the contract claim, and, thus, entitled to recover on the contract claim as a matter of law. Ordinarily, if the evidence produced by either side creates a fact issue with regard to the validity of the claim and, thus, the legitimacy of the denial thereof, the tort claim must fail and should not be submitted to the jury.'
>
> However, in *Thomas v. Principal Financial Group*, 566 So.2d 735 (Ala.1990), we noted that the 'directed verdict on the contract claim' test was not applicable to decide every bad faith claim. Citing *Continental Assurance Co. v. Kountz*, 461 So.2d 802 (Ala.1984), and *Gulf Atlantic Life Ins. Co. v. Barnes*, 405 So.2d 916 (Ala.1981), we held that even if an insured was not entitled to a directed verdict on the contract claim, the bad faith claim could be submitted to the jury if 'the insurer either intentionally or recklessly failed to properly investigate the claim or subject the results to a cognitive evaluation and review.' *Thomas, supra*, at 744.

Thus, the issue before this Court is whether the Gonzalezes presented substantial evidence that Blue Cross failed to properly investigate the Gonzalezes' claims or to subject the results of its investigation to a "cognitive evaluation and review."

The policy issued to the Gonzalezes specifically requires that coverage be in effect for 365 days before maternity benefits will be provided. As previously noted, the effective date of the policy in this case was March 1, 1993, so the waiting period for maternity benefits expired on February 28, 1994. Mrs. Gonzalez gave birth on February 24, 1994, before the expiration of the waiting period. However, the policy also specifies that maternity benefits would be provided "when the pregnancy terminates before [the] expected delivery date which, if carried to full term, would have occurred after the expiration of the 365-day waiting period." Thus, because the actual birth of the Gonzalezes' baby came before the expiration of the waiting period, the maternity care services rendered to Mrs. Gonzalez would be covered under the policy only if the expected delivery date was after the expiration of the waiting period on February 28, 1994.

The record shows that on November 1, 1993, Blue Cross requested the records of Mrs. Gonzalez's ultrasound examination that had been performed on September 8, 1993, by Dr. Ryan, in order to determine the applicability of the waiting period. It is undisputed that Blue Cross received both the computer printout indicating the results of that examination and showing an expected delivery date of February 26, 1994, and the accompanying report from Dr. Ryan stating that the clinical expected delivery date was February 27, 1994. In addition, Mrs. Gonzalez's Hospital "Admission Summary, Delivery and Newborn Record" from Brookwood Medical Center also lists the expected delivery date as February 27, 1994, and it states the gestational age as approximately 39.2 weeks and states that the baby was nine-pounds, five-ounces and that the pregnancy was considered full-term. (C.R. 110) Each of these documents, all of which show the dates of actual delivery and expected delivery to be before the expiration of the waiting period, was sufficient to establish an arguable or debatable reason for denying the claim.

The Gonzalezes counter by arguing that there is no evidence that the information in Mrs. Gonzalez's file was actually considered by Blue Cross medical review personnel until after the claim was initially rejected on March 31, 1994. The Gonzalezes correctly argue that Blue Cross cannot defeat a bad faith claim by advancing reasons for the denial, no matter how valid, that were discovered only after it had rejected an investigation of the claim. "Whether an insurance company is justified in denying a claim under a policy must be judged by what was before it at the time the decision was made." *Dutton*, 419 So.2d at 1362. However, Blue Cross records show that Mrs. Gonzalez's file, which included the ultrasound results and Dr. Ryan's report, both of which indicated due dates that would come before the expiration of the waiting period, had been forwarded for medical review as of November 29, 1993. (C.R. 452) In addition, the record also shows that at least by January 25, 1994, Blue Cross was aware that Mrs. Gonzalez's expected delivery date was February 26, 1994, and it also shows that by January 25 Blue Cross had already determined that the exclusion (for the case of a baby born during the waiting period whose full-term delivery would have come after the waiting period had ended) could be applicable. (C.R. 449.)

The Gonzalezes next argue that Blue Cross failed to properly evaluate their claim, arguing that when Blue Cross rejected their claim it had not yet discovered or considered the information from Drs. May and McClelland that indicated an expected delivery date outside the waiting period. Blue Cross did not receive this information until Mr. Gonzalez submitted it with his letter dated June 13, 1994, several months after Blue Cross had initially denied the claim. However, the record indicates no reason for Blue Cross to believe that the information already in its possession was incorrect or incomplete. Even assuming that Blue Cross had considered the records submitted by Drs. May and McClelland and had then denied the claim, the ultrasound results and the hospital delivery records in Blue Cross's possession showing that both the actual and the expected delivery dates were before the expiration of the waiting period still would provide at least an arguable or debatable basis for Blue Cross to deny the claim; and once Mr. Gonzalez submitted the conflicting information regarding the expected date of delivery, Blue Cross agreed to reopen the file and to review its determination that it had a valid reason to deny the claim. Thus, the Gonzalezes cannot complain that Blue Cross did not properly investigate the claim once it received evidence indicating that the denial of benefits might have been incorrect. We conclude that the trial court properly entered the summary judgment in favor of Blue Cross on the claim of bad faith.

...

III. The Summary Judgment for Alfa Mutual

[The Gonzalezes also appealed the summary judgment on their claims for breach of contract and bad faith against Alfa Mutual. The court concluded that no insurance contract existed between Gonzalez and Alfa Mutual.]

We have noted above, in our discussion of the elements of an action for bad faith failure to pay an insurance claim, that the plaintiff in such an action has the burden of proving the existence of an insurance contract between the parties and a breach thereof by the defendant. See *Bowen*, 417 So.2d at 183. Because we have already determined that the trial court correctly held that evidence showed there was no contract of insurance between the Gonzalezes and Alfa Mutual, we must also conclude that the Gonzalezes failed to present the evidence necessary to defeat the summary judgment motion as to their bad faith claim against Alfa Mutual. The Gonzalezes offered no evidence that there was an insurance contract between the parties and that the insurer had breached that contract.

...

V. Conclusion

The trial court correctly entered the summary judgment for Blue Cross on the claim of bad faith and correctly entered the summary judgment for Alfa Mutual on all claims.

Those judgments are affirmed.

* * *

Other forms of bad faith. Other forms of recognized first-party bad faith include conducting an "outcome-oriented" investigation of the facts that ignored facts favorable to the insured, State Farm Fire & Cas. v. Simmons, 857 S.W.2d 126 (Tex. App. 1993); requiring the insured to provide unnecessarily detailed information during an investigation into fire damage (including how many corn flakes were in the cereal box prior to a house fire), Hatch v. State Farm Fire & Cas., 842 P.2d 1089 (Wyo. 1992); and destroying evidence favorable to the insured. Upthegrove Hardware, Inc. v. Penn. Lumbermans Mutual Ins. Co., 431 N.W.2d 689 (Wis. Ct. App. 1988).

Exercise 18.1

A fire caused extensive damage to Candace's house in Alabama. She filed a claim with her insurer, Flynn Insurance. As part of its investigation, Flynn hired Jerry Ferriday, a private fire investigator, to investigate the origins of the fire. Ferriday concluded that the fire had probably been set intentionally. This conclusion was at odds with the conclusion of the fire marshal, who concluded that the fire was an accident. Ferriday's conclusion caused Flynn to look into Candace's financial situation to see if she had some motive to set the fire herself. The investigation found that Candace had lost her job just prior to the fire and had substantial credit card debt, but that she found a new job several weeks after the fire damaged her home. Based on this investigation, Flynn decided to deny Candace's claim. Candace then brought a bad faith claim against Flynn in state court in Alabama. What is the likely result?

Exercise 18.2

Jeremy held a homeowner's policy with AEI Insurance Co. Jeremy's house was damaged during a storm, so Jeremy filed a claim with AEI. The storm resulted in numerous claims being filed in the locality, some of them fraudulent in nature. AEI retained O.J. Norberg, a local attorney, to assist in the settlement of the various claims brought by people insured by AEI. Upon Norberg's advice, AEI engaged in extensive investigation of Jeremy (including near constant surveillance over a period of several weeks, photographing and videotaping him, and speaking to friends and neighbors about his personal habits), which lasted for nearly 8 months. During this time, AEI refused to pay Jeremy's claims, stating it was not through investigating his claims. Eventually, Jeremy brought a bad faith claim against AEI and Norberg. What is the likely result of both claims?

B. Third-Party Claims

Focus Questions: *O'Neill v. Gallant Ins. Co.*

1. *As you will see when you read the decision, there is sufficient evidence from which a jury could conclude that Moss, the decision maker for the insurer, made a colossally bad decision with respect to settlement of the victim's claim. Would this be enough to support a jury verdict for bad faith? What does bad faith mean in this context?*
2. *Why was the punitive damages award appropriate in this case?*

O'Neill v. Gallant Ins. Co.

769 N.E.2d 100
(Ill. App. 2002)

Justice KUEHN delivered the opinion of the court:

In this case, an insurance company took its small stake in the outcome of a personal-injury claim, $20,000 worth of liability coverage purchased by one of its customers, and transformed it into a multimillion-dollar judgment against the carrier. For reasons that are not entirely clear, John Moss, executive vice president of Warrior Insurance Group,[1] the person primarily responsible for this action, bypassed a chance to settle an insured's obvious liability for catastrophic personal injuries, and to do so within the insurance policy limits. His decision turned $20,000 worth of contractual duty into a $3,010,063 judgment for a bad-faith refusal to settle within the policy limits.

This remarkable wizardry had its origins on October 31, 1996. On that Halloween day, a Gallant Insurance Company customer named Christine Narvaez drove her insured automobile onto the parking lot of a busy Granite City supermarket. Christine had her two-year-old grandchild with her. The youngster was riding, unconstrained, in a booster seat. Christine saw a friend and decided to stop for a brief chat. She parked and exited the car, leaving the keys in the ignition and the motor running. Thus, circumstances awaited the mischief that her unattended two-year-old grandchild could glean from being left alone in a car with its engine running.

Gallant Insurance Company's insured played quite a Halloween trick on shoppers in the vicinity of her car. The trick treated Marguerite O'Neill to lifelong confinement in a nursing home. It only took a moment for Christine's little nipper to crawl behind the wheel, slip the car into gear, and set it into motion. As the car rolled out of control, it collided with two other cars and two pedestrians. Mrs. O'Neill was the most severely damaged victim of Christine's negligence.

Mrs. O'Neill was in her eighties and could not physically evade the slow-moving car as it approached her. The insured's vehicle pinned her between it and another car and slowly crushed her trapped body. Mrs. O'Neill was pried loose and airlifted to St. Louis

1. The defendant in this suit, Gallant Insurance Company, is a part of the Warrior Insurance Group. In the companies' hierarchies, John Moss oversees certain Gallant Insurance Company departments. Further details about the relationship of the two companies are included later in the body of this opinion.

University Hospital Trauma Center, where she spent the next month in the intensive care unit. Her body suffered a crushed hip, a broken arm, four cracked ribs, and two fractured fingers. She lost more than 40% of her blood supply as a result of internal bleeding. The blood loss triggered respiratory shock. Mrs. O'Neill was given a tracheotomy and was placed on a respirator for 24 days.

The accident had lasting consequences. It deprived Mrs. O'Neill of the ability to live life independently of others. It placed her into a nursing home, where she remains to this day.

Gallant Insurance Company (Gallant) insured Christine with the statutory minimum amount of coverage against liability arising out of the operation of her car. Consequently, there was only $20,000 worth of coverage to address the catastrophic damages that Christine's negligence wrought. Not including her other damages, Mrs. O'Neill's medical bills amounted to $105,000.

Mrs. O'Neill's attorney demanded the policy limits in settlement of her claim. He offered a complete release from liability for Christine, provided that Gallant would promptly tender its check for Christine's $20,000 liability coverage. Gallant was given 30 days to decide. Confronted with a case of obvious liability with potential damages far in excess of the policy limits, Gallant did not dignify the demand with a response. The 30 days passed and Gallant remained silent. It did not try to negotiate. It did not attempt a counteroffer. It did not even tell Christine that the elderly lady that she hurt was willing to forego a personal judgment for more than the amount with which Christine was insured. Gallant simply ignored the offer to settle, and a window of opportunity to protect its customer from an excess judgment closed.

Moss bypassed the chance to authorize the payment of the coverage that Christine had purchased from Gallant. As a result of his decision, Christine suffered a large excess judgment. Gallant's refusal to even respond to an invitation for settlement occurred under baffling circumstances.

Gallant's initial adjuster noted in the claims diary that Christine was clearly negligent and that Gallant was responsible for the damages that she caused. His opinion was reviewed by an immediate supervisor and a claims director, and both concurred in his liability evaluation. Based upon that opinion, Gallant paid the two property-damage claims that stemmed from the accident. When Mrs. O'Neill registered her claim through a lawyer, the claim was forwarded to a more seasoned adjuster. She examined her younger counterpart's work, conducted her own independent investigation of the claim, and before a demand was even made, recommended the payment of the $20,000 policy limits. A claims manager reviewed this recommendation. She wrote to Moss and conveyed her opinion that the policy limits should be tendered.

Gallant did not have a claims department. It was one of two subsidiaries of Warrior Insurance Group, the company that handled all claims. Moss was the executive vice president of Warrior Insurance Group (Warrior). None of Warrior's 12 claims adjusters had the authority to settle a claim for $20,000. Warrior's two claims directors lacked such authority. Even Warrior's claims manager could not authorize a $20,000 settlement. Only Moss and Warrior's chief executive officer could authorize any Gallant settlement payment in excess of $15,000.

Warrior's claims manager, someone with a decidedly conservative approach to the settlement of automobile liability claims, wrote and advised Moss that the tender of the policy limits was a necessary step "in order to make sure that the policyholder's interests were treated with equal weight as the company's interests."

Moss also heard from the lawyers Gallant hired to defend against Mrs. O'Neill's lawsuit. At the time, Gallant so valued their work that it had the firm handling 500 active files, all on a flat-fee billing basis. Two weeks prior to the settlement demand's expiration, those lawyers wrote to Moss with an evaluation and a recommendation. Christine's lawyers told him that liability was clear. They also told him that the verdict potential on that obvious liability rested within a dollar range 15 to 30 times the amount of coverage. Two weeks before the chance to settle within the policy limits was forever lost, Christine's lawyers urged Moss to tender those limits. In their professional judgment, it was clearly the prudent thing to do.

Moss decided to reject everyone's advice. His decision to disregard the adjusters' opinions, the director's opinion, his claims manager's opinion, and Christine's lawyers' opinions occurred without explanation or notation in the claims diary. Much later, at the trial of this case, Moss's testimony, the linchpin of the defense against the bad-faith claim, revealed the reason behind the decision. Moss actually testified, under oath, that he believed in good faith that Christine was not liable for anyone's injuries.

Almost a year after the demand to settle for the policy limits had expired, and only a few days before the trial on the underlying personal-injury action was to begin, Moss decided to authorize an offer of $20,000 in order to settle the case. By that time, Mrs. O'Neill had no interest in accepting such an offer. She had incurred more than $3,000 in costs readying the case for a trial, and there was no offer to defray them. Mrs. O'Neill's economic losses as a result of the accident had nearly doubled since the demand expired, and her contingency-fee structure had also increased. On the eve of trial, Mrs. O'Neill was intent on seeing what kind of an award a jury would return. Hopefully, Christine would personally satisfy the amount by which the jury's award might exceed Christine's insurance coverage.

Moss preferred a last-minute offer of the policy limits to a jury test of his good-faith belief that liability was lacking. Unfortunately, he made the decision to forego his belief too late. The chance to obtain a release in return for $20,000 had come and gone.

A few days after Mrs. O'Neill's refusal of Gallant's offer, a jury found for her and against Christine and awarded $731,063 in damages. The verdict came as no surprise to anyone in Gallant who was ever entrusted with the task of evaluating the claim. We are not even sure that it surprised Moss. Gallant's lawyers asked him to send a $20,000 company check, and he complied, before the verdict was even returned. Christine owed Mrs. O'Neill $711,063. The only reason that she owed it was her carrier's decision not to meet the demand for the policy limits. Moss's good-faith belief that there was no liability on Christine's part proved to be misplaced. The mistake resulted in Christine's financial ruin.

A supplementary action was commenced in order to enforce the judgment against Christine. Her potential claim against Gallant for its failure to settle Mrs. O'Neill's claim within the policy limits was assigned to Mrs. O'Neill, who then brought this lawsuit against Gallant. The case was tried to a jury. The jury found in Mrs. O'Neill's favor and awarded actual damages in the sum of $710,063[2] and punitive damages in the sum of $2.3 million. Interest was also awarded.

---

2. The amount of damages awarded by the jury in the original negligence case against Gallant's insured was $711,063. That verdict was the foundation for this subsequent bad-faith case against Gallant. In this case, the jury returned a verdict for actual damages in the amount of $710,063. The record does not reflect, and counsel for the parties do not offer, any explanation for the $1,000 discrepancy.

A significant part of the evidence presented against Gallant consisted of the pattern of conduct engaged in by Gallant over the five years leading up to this bad-faith action. Mrs. O'Neill presented 44 known cases where Gallant's Illinois customers suffered excess judgments after Gallant passed up the opportunity to settle within the policy limits. Most of the excess judgments occurred on John Moss's watch. The dollar amount by which the excess judgments exceeded policy limits totaled $10,849,313. This staggering total was accumulated through jury awards on automobile accident cases, a class of personal injury generally known for miserly jury verdicts. All but $449,313 of this amount was awarded after Moss took over control of the settlement process in June of 1997.

Gallant argues that the jury's verdict, based upon the finding that Gallant acted in bad faith in its handling of Mrs. O'Neill's claim, is contrary to the manifest weight of the evidence. This is a question that we review with deference to the jury. Its findings will not be overturned unless they are "manifestly erroneous." Fritzsche v. Union Pacific R.R. Co., 303 Ill.App.3d 276, 287, 236 Ill.Dec. 594, 707 N.E.2d 721, 729 (1999).

Where an insurer is pursued for its refusal to settle a claim, "bad faith" lies in an insurer's failure to give at least equal consideration to the insured's interests when the insurer arrives at a decision on whether to settle the claim. *See* Mid-America Bank & Trust Co. v. Commercial Union Insurance Co., 587 N.E.2d 81, 84 (Ill.1992). This is precisely the standard set forth by Donna Hedl, Warrior's claims manager, when she wrote Moss and gave her opinion of how Mrs. O'Neill's claim should be handled. She wrote that the policy limits should be tendered "in order to make sure that the policyholder's interests were treated with equal weight as the company's interests." Her admission, standing alone, provides ample evidence of bad faith. However, there was other evidence of bad faith to support the jury's verdict.

We have identified seven factors pertinent to the assessment of bad faith, and every one of them supports this jury's verdict.

I.

The advice of the insurance company's own adjusters is a factor to be considered. *See* Phelan v. State Farm Mutual Automobile Insurance Co., 448 N.E.2d 579, 585 (Ill. 1983).

Moss, Gallant's decision-maker and the only one authorized to advance a settlement offer in this case, was urged by every level of claims department employee to tender the policy limits. The claim's initial adjuster, his supervisor, and a claims director all concurred in their evaluation of the insured's liability. As a consequence, Gallant paid the property-damage claims in full within 30 days of the occurrence.

The next adjuster who reviewed the file concurred in the conclusions already reached by three other claims department employees. She recommended the payment of the policy limits before Mrs. O'Neill even made a demand. Her supervisor, the claims manager, also recommended the payment of the policy limits. Her recommendation was particularly damaging to Gallant.

Donna Hedl had adjusted claims for Gallant and other nonstandard insurance companies for more than 25 years. Historically, she conceded the payment of claims grudgingly. She subscribed to the conservative philosophy that no claim should be paid absent clear negligence on the part of the insured. Moss had to admit at the trial that he appreciated how she employed this philosophy and that she served the company well. He found her to be a most able and competent adjuster. This left little to offer in support of why he would not follow her advice and tender the policy limits.

II.

A refusal to negotiate is a factor to be considered. Cernocky v. Indemnity Insurance Co. of North America, 216 N.E.2d 198, 205 (Ill. 1966).

Mrs. O'Neill's attorney wrote to Gallant with a firm offer to settle for $20,000. Gallant did not respond. It did not make a counteroffer, request more time to evaluate the demand, or even dignify the attempt to settle with the courtesy of an answer. Donna Hedl admitted that a timely response to a policy-limits demand, even if it is a rejection of the demand, is of critical importance. It keeps open the lines of communication toward compromise and settlement.

III.

The advice of defense counsel is a factor to be considered. Olympia Fields Country Club v. Bankers Indemnity Insurance Co., 60 N.E.2d 896, 906–07 (Ill. 1945).

At a time when Mrs. O'Neill's policy-limits demand remained open, Christine's lawyers advised Moss of their professional opinion that Christine would be held civilly liable for Mrs. O'Neill's damages. The lawyers whom Gallant hired to champion Christine's defense gave Moss this evaluation, together with their estimate that the verdict range would likely fall between $300,000 and $600,000. Christine's lawyers urged a settlement for the policy limits two weeks before Mrs. O'Neill's offer expired. The attorneys would later increase the verdict potential to an amount in excess of $1 million. The notice of a verdict potential of more than 50 times the policy limits did not prompt Gallant to initiate negotiations or to tender the policy limits.

IV.

Communication with the insured, keeping her fully aware of the claimant's willingness to settle for the amount of coverage, is a factor to be considered. Bailey v. Prudence Mutual Casualty Co., 429 F.2d 1388, 1390 (7th Cir.1970).

Here, Gallant and the attorneys Gallant hired never bothered telling Christine that Mrs. O'Neill was willing to settle for her policy limits, until months after the offer expired. When defense counsel belatedly advised Christine of the settlement offer, the substance of the offer was not conveyed, and Christine was misled by being told that the company was still evaluating the demand. The demand had expired. There was nothing to evaluate. Moss decided not to respond to the demand, despite everyone's advice to meet it.

Gallant did not give its policyholder an opportunity to protect herself. Its failure to timely communicate with its customer and its false statements when it did communicate signal bad faith. *Bailey*, 429 F.2d at 1390.

V.

Inadequate investigation and defense is a factor to be considered. Ballard v. Citizens Casualty Co. of New York, 196 F.2d 96, 102 (7th Cir.1952).

Here, the complaint in Mrs. O'Neill's lawsuit against Christine alleged that the insured failed to use an adequate child restraint system. If Christine had any defense to the lawsuit, it was predicated upon the reasonableness of her belief that the booster seat that her grandchild was sitting in was sufficient to restrain the child while she left him unattended in a car with the engine running. The booster seat was a critical piece of evidence.

It should have been clear to Gallant, if it believed in such a defense, that the failure to produce the booster seat at the trial invited a strong inference that the insured either knew or should have known that the booster seat was entirely inadequate to restrain the child. Notwithstanding, Gallant never inspected the booster seat, never photographed the seat, and never warned Christine to preserve the booster seat for use as evidence at the trial. Gallant's neglect had two consequences: Christine disposed of the booster seat and, because she was unable to produce the seat, the jury received the missing-evidence instruction in the underlying case.

After their assessment of clear liability and massive verdict potential and after Moss's refusal to follow their recommendation based upon that assessment, Christine's lawyers formulated a discovery plan. They proposed taking the deposition of 13 potential witnesses. One of the reasons was their stated desire to minimize the predicted excess verdict. Apparently, Gallant did not consider that goal very important. Only two depositions were authorized.

VI.

A substantial prospect of an adverse verdict is a factor to be considered. *Phelan*, 448 N.E.2d at 585.

The odds of a jury rejecting Mrs. O'Neill's claim were astronomical. Everyone knew the score. From Gallant's most novice adjuster up the chain of command to a seasoned veteran of 25 years, everyone predicted that Christine would lose and that the verdict would top the coverage. Defense counsel knew what was going to happen. They predicted it. Everyone, save Moss, got it right. It took the jury only 40 minutes to deliberate to a verdict and award Mrs. O'Neill $731,063.

VII.

The potential for damages to exceed the policy limits is a factor to be considered. *Mid-America Bank & Trust Co.*, 587 N.E.2d at 84.

Gallant knew from the lawyers it hired to protect Christine's interests that the verdict potential was, at a minimum, 15 times the amount of insurance protection. The medical bills alone were more than five times that protection. The decision to reject the chance to settle a claim of this magnitude signals bad faith.

Gallant tries to shield its decision to forego the settlement offer with its decision to file and pursue a motion for summary judgment. It points out that after the motion was denied, it offered the policy limits. This facade of good faith is belied by the lawyers Gallant hired to protect Christine's interests. Christine's lawyers, the same ones who urged Moss to protect her by tendering the policy limits, had absolutely no faith in the prospects of prevailing on the summary judgment motion. From the moment that it was filed, they believed that it would fail, as indeed it did.

The filing of a motion that lacked merit did not insulate Moss from the unreasonable decision to ignore everyone's opinion and allow a settlement offer to expire without a response. If it did, insurance companies would acquire free license to play roulette with their customers' money, even in cases where circumstances compel the immediate payment of insurance proceeds in order to protect those customers. The filing of a summary judgment motion in lieu of meeting a demand that everyone in the company deemed valid is precisely the sort of gambling with an insured's money that the doctrine of bad faith was designed to prevent.

In the final analysis, Gallant's argument rests upon Moss's self-serving testimony that he acted in good faith when he rejected the chance to settle, because he believed that

Christine was not liable. The jury obviously found him less than credible. It had good reason. Moss's professed belief flew in the face of everyone who ever evaluated this case, and there were many. Three Gallant adjusters believed that Christine was liable. A Gallant claims director believed that Christine was liable. Gallant's sole claims manager, who had been evaluating liability in automobile accident claims for 25 years and who denied all claims in the absence of clear negligence, believed that Christine was liable. Everyone in the law firm that Gallant hired, a firm entrusted to handle more than 500 active claims for Gallant, believed that Christine was liable. And the 12 people Gallant selected to determine liability at the trial believed that Christine was liable. Without a great deal of experience in such matters, they decided that issue and fixed the amount of damages in less than an hour of deliberation.

Despite Moss's professed belief, Gallant had promptly paid the lesser claims of people hurt because of Christine's negligence. Despite Moss's professed belief, he tried to pay all of the coverage on the eve of the trial. And last but not least, despite Moss's professed belief, after the verdict was returned, Gallant paid its $20,000, closed its file, and walked away. Moss would not authorize an appeal of the liability question. Christine was left to fend for herself and somehow mount an appeal of the $710,063 excess judgment on her own.

holding The jury's finding of bad faith was not against the manifest weight of the evidence.

We turn to the question of whether punitive damages can be awarded for an insurance company's bad-faith refusal to settle. We hold that they can.

Gallant notes that no Illinois case has ever authorized common law punitive damages against an insurance carrier based upon a bad-faith refusal to settle a third party's liability claim. There are other jurisdictions that have allowed punitive damages in certain cases where the insurance company's bad faith was particularly egregious. Cain v. State Farm Mutual Automobile Insurance Co., 47 Cal.App.3d 783, 121 Cal.Rptr. 200 (1975); Campbell v. Government Employees Insurance Co., 306 So.2d 525 (Fla.1974); Newport v. USAA, 2000 OK 59, 11 P.3d 190 (2000); Shamblin v. Nationwide Mutual Insurance Co., 183 W.Va. 585, 396 S.E.2d 766 (1990). We think that where the insurer's conduct exceeds mere negligence and, like here, demonstrates to a jury's satisfaction that the refusal to settle within policy limits was engaged in with utter indifference and reckless disregard for its policyholder's financial welfare, punitive damages can be awarded.

Rule

Although punitive damages are not the law's favorite, Illinois has traditionally authorized the recovery of punitive damages in tort cases involving intentional misconduct or a breach of fiduciary duty. Cirrincione v. Johnson, 703 N.E.2d 67, 70 (Ill. 1998). "Illinois courts are not hesitant to award punitive damages in cases where there has been a flagrant breach of fiduciary responsibility." Central Bank-Granite City v. Ziaee, 544 N.E.2d 1121, 1128 (Ill. 1989).

Gallant cites to numerous cases where, in varying contexts, courts have held that no fiduciary relationship exists between an insurer and an insured. However, when a liability insurance company employs policy terms that obtain the irrevocable power to determine whether an offer to compromise a personal-injury claim will be accepted or rejected, it creates a fiduciary relationship between it and the insured with resulting duties that grow out of that relationship.

Gallant's policy terms vested it with exclusive control over Mrs. O'Neill's claim and the defense against her lawsuit. Gallant reserved the right to hire the policyholder's lawyer. It also retained the absolute discretion to determine whether a settlement offer should be accepted or rejected. The policy terms rendered the policyholder helpless in the absence of Gallant's good faith. As was demonstrated by the staggering excess judgment total under Moss's command, in the absence of good faith, Gallant's policyholders confronted significant risks of personal exposure.

"'Under policies like those here involved, the insurer and the insured owe to each other the duty to exercise the utmost good faith. While the insurance company, in determining whether to accept or reject an offer of compromise, may properly give consideration to its own interests, it must, in good faith, give at least equal consideration to the interests of the insured [,] and if it fails to do so[,] it acts in bad faith.'" *Cernocky*, 216 N.E.2d at 204–05.

Courts must offer vigilant protection to those who find themselves in a position of vulnerability in a fiduciary relationship.

Gallant insures mostly high-risk drivers. Illinois requires those high-risk drivers to obtain liability coverage in order to drive. Consequently, they pay dearly to acquire liability coverage and, almost universally, purchase only the statutory minimum. For the most part, Gallant's customer base represents a class of driver extremely vulnerable to insurance practices performed in bad faith and contrary to an insured's interests. This was certainly the case here. Christine had certain known mental health problems and was hardly well-to-do. She could not afford to hire her own attorney to protect her from her fiduciary. Based upon Gallant's treatment, she could have used private counsel. Such assistance might have set Gallant right when *it wrote to inform Christine that it would defend her under a reservation of rights*—when Gallant falsely claimed that it did not have to provide coverage.* Such assistance might have set Gallant right when *it failed to respond to the settlement demand and, thereafter, falsely claimed that it was still evaluating the demand.* Finally, independent counsel might have suggested to Moss that his faith in a lack of liability, and his refusal to pay because of it, carried a duty to defend the liability question on appeal. Counsel might have made Moss understand that under the circumstances of his claimed decision-making, he could not simply walk away from the adverse verdict by tendering the amount of coverage. His oversight of Christine's interests was still in play. Gallant insures mostly high-risk drivers. Illinois requires those high-risk drivers to obtain liability coverage in order to drive. Consequently, they pay dearly to acquire liability coverage and, almost universally, purchase only the statutory minimum. For the most part, Gallant's customer base represents a class of driver extremely vulnerable to insurance practices performed in bad faith and contrary to an insured's interests. This was certainly the case here. Christine had certain known mental health problems and was hardly well-to-do. She could not afford to hire her own attorney to protect her from her fiduciary. Based upon Gallant's treatment, she could have used private counsel. Such assistance might have set Gallant right when it wrote to inform Christine that it would defend her under a reservation of rights—when Gallant falsely claimed that it did not have to provide coverage. Such assistance might have set Gallant right when it failed to respond to the settlement demand and, thereafter, falsely claimed that it was still evaluating the demand. Finally, independent counsel might have suggested to Moss that his faith in a lack of liability, and his refusal to pay because of it, carried a duty to defend the

* [Editor's note: A "reservation of rights" letter is the device insurance companies use to undertake the defense of an insured while reserving the right to later assert that the claim falls outside coverage, thus protecting itself from the claim that the insurer waived any defenses it might have with respect to paying the claim.]

liability question on appeal. Counsel might have made Moss understand that under the circumstances of his claimed decision-making, he could not simply walk away from the adverse verdict by tendering the amount of coverage. His oversight of Christine's interests was still in play.

In a case like this one, we think that punitive damages for a bad-faith refusal to settle are appropriate and warranted. After all, punitive damages are designed to deter misconduct. Hopefully, the availability of punitive damages can provide some degree of deterrent against unscrupulous insurers who would otherwise take advantage of customers and abuse their fiduciary relationship in order to promote their own economic self-interest. Gallant needed to be told through the award of punitive damages that it had to stop its common practice of ignoring policy-limit demands in serious cases where liability was clear-cut. It had to be punished for a pattern of misconduct that exposed its policyholders to more than $10 million in excess judgments.

Gallant challenges the evidence of wrongdoing and contends that it did not establish the kind of misconduct that calls for a punitive-damages award. A jury enjoys wide latitude in deciding whether a defendant's misconduct is sufficiently egregious to warrant the imposition of punitive damages. We will not disturb a finding of liability for punitive damages unless it is against the manifest weight of the evidence.

We need not belabor the evidence of bad faith that supports punitive damages. Suffice it to say, there was ample evidence from which a jury could reasonably infer that Gallant deliberately chose to gamble with Christine's financial security, in the hope of merely delaying the payment of minimal policy limits. It would have been quite reasonable for jurors to conclude that Gallant threw Christine's financial future to the wind for the small amount of revenue it could derive from its $20,000 before a judgment could be rendered. Of course, jurors could have also reasonably inferred from the evidence that the nontender of money until the eve of the trial was a calculated design, widespread in its application and utilized on numerous claims where it was obvious that the coverage would ultimately have to be paid. By exposing a lot of its customers to excess judgments in order to delay the payment of valid third-party claims, Gallant could amass considerable revenue. Hence, jurors possessed evidence from which they could reasonably conclude that corporate greed motivated Gallant's breach of fiduciary duty and that its greed was pervasive—that Gallant routinely betrayed its customers' interests by deliberate design.

At a minimum, based upon the evidence presented, the jury was entitled to believe that Gallant's conduct showed an utter indifference and a reckless disregard for its policyholder's financial welfare and that Gallant breached a fiduciary duty to factor that welfare into its decision-making. Such a finding surpasses the threshold for the imposition of punitive damages.

Finally, Gallant argues that the punitive-damages award is grossly excessive, unreasonable, unwarranted by the evidence, and a violation of due process.

We review the determination on a challenge to the size of a punitive-damages award de novo. The constitutionality of such an award depends upon its size. Fundamental fairness embodied in due process prohibits "grossly excessive" punitive damages. BMW of North America, Inc. v. Gore, 517 U.S. 559, 574 (1996). The United States Supreme Court has established three criteria to consider when determining whether an award of punitive damages is "grossly excessive": "the degree of reprehensibility of the [conduct]; the disparity between the harm or potential harm suffered by [the plaintiff] and his punitive damages award; and the difference between this remedy and the civil penalties authorized or imposed in comparable cases." *BMW of North America, Inc.*, 517 U.S. at 575.

We must side with Mrs. O'Neill and against Gallant on the extent to which the evidence established the existence of reprehensible conduct on the part of Christine's insurance provider. If the term "reprehensible" means shameful, i.e., conduct deserving of severe reproach, Gallant's treatment of Christine, and others who bought insurance from it, was truly reprehensible.

We can start with Gallant's treatment of Christine, who suffered from a mental illness and who totally lacked financial resources. Christine was completely dependent upon Gallant for help in handling her exposure to financial ruin. It hired the lawyers to champion her defense. It employed a team of professional adjusters and an experienced claims manager. It had the money to pay for a complete release from liability. It possessed the means to protect Christine's financial future.

Gallant also possessed the experience to know that if Christine was found liable, the injuries that she caused meant certain bankruptcy for her, given her meager policy limits. It also possessed the experience to understand that, in terms of Christine's predicament, a policy-limits demand was "God-sent."

In assessing the degree of reprehensibility, we think it fair to conclude that Gallant blatantly ignored its policyholder's financial security and did virtually nothing to protect her, despite a golden opportunity to do so. Its decision to bypass a settlement of Mrs. O'Neill's claim for the payment of $20,000 is inexplicable. Its conduct toward Christine was shameful. Its explanation for the misconduct only compounded it.

However, the conduct that the jury punished was conduct that extended beyond the handling of Christine's case. The jury learned that Gallant's treatment of Christine was but the tip of the iceberg. Below the surface lay a host of excess judgments occurring under similar circumstances. Moss routinely withheld Gallant's money in cases where legitimate claims could have been settled for customers' policy limits. Gallant's misconduct went far beyond the mismanagement of its fiduciary duty in one isolated case where it should have settled a claim.

Gallant's view of its fiduciary responsibility to Christine was a view that it shared with its other customers. Gallant policyholders suffered more than $10 million in excess judgments, the result of numerous lawsuits where policy-limit demands were cavalierly ignored. There is a pattern to Gallant's misconduct that pervades its handling of third-party claims.

The second consideration in the determination of an award's excessiveness is the disparity between the harm actually suffered and the sum of punitive damages. Here, that disparity is not excessive. Gallant's misconduct caused Christine to suffer a $710,063 excess judgment. The punitive damages were only slightly higher than triple the actual damages. This proportion of actual damages to punitive damages is not out of line with cases that have found punitive-damages awards constitutional.

Finally, the jury's award is in line with punishment meted out in comparable cases. Gallant had fair warning that an abuse of fiduciary duty had potentially grave consequences.

We find that the punitive-damages award was not grossly excessive. The jury's award of $2.3 million to punish Gallant for its misconduct did not deprive Gallant of due process under the fourteenth amendment.

* * *

1. Bad faith failure to settle. *O'Neill* is typical of third-party bad faith claims. With these claims, the insurer fails to settle a third party's claim within the insured's policy limits, thus leaving the insured liable for any excess judgment.

Exercise 18.3

Insured was involved in an auto accident for which he was almost totally at fault. The accident left the victim, a minor, with brain damage and other injuries. Insurer investigated the accident and concluded the day after it occurred that Insured was almost totally at fault, that the victim's injuries were severe, and that the limit of Insured's policy was $25,000. Six weeks after the accident, the lawyer for the victim offered to settle the matter for the policy limit. Insurer did not respond to this offer, nor did it inform Insured of the offer. By this point, the victim's family was in dire financial straits. Six weeks later, the lawyer for the victim made a formal demand to settle the matter for the policy limit and gave Insured 10 days to respond. Insured did not respond within 10 days, but did offer the policy limit six weeks later. The victim refused this offer and proceeded to trial, where he won a jury verdict far in excess of $25,000. Facing payment for the excess, Insured filed a bad faith action against Insurer. What result? Should it matter if the victim imposes the short time limit with the hopes that the insurer will not meet it, thus allowing the insured to assign his or her right to bring a bad faith action for any excess judgment to the victim?

---

2. The tripartite relationship. As part of the insurance agreement, the insurer typically retains the right to settle a claim within the limits of the policy and agrees to pay for the defense of the insured. This includes the costs associated with hiring a lawyer. This results in the formation of a tripartite relationship: the relationship between insurer, insured, and lawyer. Who is the lawyer's client in this relationship—insurer, insured, or both? Some courts (perhaps a majority) have concluded that the lawyer has two clients. Others (as is perhaps the trend) have concluded that the lawyer's only client is the insured, despite the fact that the lawyer is being paid by the insurer and is likely to have more contact with the insurer than the insured. Why does the issue matter?

Exercise 18.4

Doctor Fletcher was sued for malpractice. His insurance carrier, Flynn Insurance Co., hired Isabella Robson, a lawyer, to represent Fletcher. After reviewing the case and speaking with plaintiff's counsel, Flynn instructed Robson to settle the case for a modest sum as agreed upon with plaintiff's counsel. However, no one informed Fletcher about the settlement. Fletcher adamantly opposed any settlement, insisting she had done nothing wrong. After she learned the case had settled, Fletcher sued Flynn for breach of contract and bad faith. She also sued Robson for breach of fiduciary duty and malpractice for failing to inform her about the proposed settlement. What result?

Exercise 18.5

Imagine that you are one of the lawyers in the firm that Gallant hired in *O'Neill*. As the court said, your firm currently has 500 active files with Gallant. You are familiar with all of the facts associated with the O'Neill accident and

Moss's reluctance to settle, even after you have advised him that the verdict potential rested within a dollar range 15 to 30 times the amount of coverage and that he should settle for the policy limits. The time to accept the plaintiff's settlement offer is about to run out. What should you do?

---

3. Punitive damages. Successful bad faith actions often lead to punitive damages awards. In *State Farm Mut. Auto. Ins. Co. v. Campbell*, 538 U.S. 408 (2003), the United States Supreme Court held that a punitive damages award of $145 million in a bad faith action offended the Due Process Clause of the Fourteenth Amendment. Part of the Court's justification was that the jury punished State Farm for conduct involving other parties "that bore no relation to the [plaintiffs'] harm." A few years later, the Court concluded that although a jury may consider the fact that a defendant's conduct caused harm to others when assessing the reprehensibility of the defendant's conduct, it cannot directly punish the defendant for harm caused to others. Phillip Morris USA v. Williams, 549 U.S. 346 (2007). Could the punitive damages award in *O'Neill* be sustained under that standard?

Chapter 19

Wrongful Discharge in Violation of Public Policy

Exercise 19.1: Chapter Problem

Kevin Garner was a driver and security guard for Landon Armored Trucks, Inc. One day, Garner made a scheduled stop at a local bank. Garner's partner went inside the bank and Garner stayed in the truck. A few minutes later, Garner saw a bank manager come running out of the bank screaming for help. She was being chased by a man with a knife. Garner exited the truck and locked it. By the time Garner got out of the truck, the bank manager had escaped, but the man with the knife was in the process of abducting a pedestrian at knife point and dragging her into the bank. Garner followed the man into the bank, where he saw his partner pointing his gun at the suspect. Garner's partner shouted at the suspect and distracted him while Garner tackled the suspect and subdued him until police arrived.

That afternoon, Garner was fired for violating Landon Armored Trucks' policy prohibiting guards from leaving a company truck unattended. Garner has now sued the company, alleging wrongful discharge in violation of public policy. You represent Garner. What potential arguments can you make on his behalf? What legal research do you need to do in order to make those arguments?

The most basic rule governing the workplace is the at-will employment rule. Under this rule, absent an agreement to the contrary, a court will assume that the employment is at-will, meaning an employer is free to discharge an employee for a good reason, a bad reason, or no reason at all. At-will employees also enjoy the same freedom to resign. The at-will rule is the default rule in nearly every jurisdiction.

Obviously, application of the rule can sometimes be quite harsh. *See, e.g.*, Green v. Bryant, 887 F. Supp. 798 (E.D. Pa. 1995) (dismissing complaint of employee who was fired after being beaten and raped by her husband because employer feared that husband might come to the workplace and commit future violence). There are, however, some limitations to the rule's reach. Various state and federal statutes prohibit discrimination on the basis of race, sex, age, and other characteristics. *See, e.g.*, Title VII, 42 U.S.C. §2000e-2(a)(1) (2006). However, employees are sometimes fired for reasons that would strike most as being unfair but that are not prohibited by these statutes. Moreover, while the at-will rule is frequently defended on the grounds that it provides both parties with the freedom to act in what they believe to be in their best interests, many have questioned this justification, citing the inequality of bargaining power between employer and employee in the typical case.

As a result of some of these concerns, many courts in the 1980s began to carve out common-law exceptions to the common-law employment at-will rule. Some of the exceptions were contract-based. *See, e.g.*, Thompson v. St. Regis Paper Co., 685 P.2d 1081 (Wash. 1984) (concluding that statements contained in an employee handbook can amount to a contractual limitation on an employer's ability to discharge an employee). The most common tort-based exception was the tort of wrongful discharge in violation of public policy. Wrongful discharge claims typically take one of four forms, each of which is discussed below. While not every jurisdiction recognizes each kind of claim, most recognize at least one or two. *But see* Arrow Air, Inc. v. Walsh, 645 So. 2d 422, 424 (Fla. 1994) (noting that Florida has never recognized the tort).

A. Exercising a Right

Focus Questions: *Feliciano v. 7-Eleven, Inc.*

1. *How does the* Feliciano *court attempt to balance the potentially competing interests of employer, employee, and the public at large?*
2. *How is a court to determine when the discharge of an employee threatens public policy?*

Feliciano v. 7-Eleven, Inc.

559 S.E.2d 713
(W.Va. 2001)

FACTUAL AND PROCEDURAL HISTORY

The plaintiff, Antonio Feliciano [hereinafter referred to as "Feliciano"], was employed as a retail sales clerk by the defendant, 7-Eleven, Inc. [hereinafter referred to as "7-Eleven"], at its Baker Heights store, located in Berkeley County, West Virginia. At approximately 4:00 a.m. on July 14, 2000, a woman, wearing a mask and pointing a firearm, demanded that store employees, including Feliciano, give her the store's money. During this incident, certain employees emptied the cash register and, while the woman was focused upon another employee, Feliciano grabbed and disarmed her. Feliciano continued to restrain the would-be robber until local law enforcement authorities arrived on the scene and apprehended her.

Following this incident, 7-Eleven terminated Feliciano, who was an at will employee, for failure to comply with its company policy which prohibits employees from subduing or otherwise interfering with a store robbery. Feliciano then filed a civil action against 7-Eleven in the Circuit Court of Berkeley County alleging that he had been wrongfully discharged, in contravention of West Virginia public policy, for exercising his right to self-defense. The defendant removed the suit to the United States District Court for the Northern District of West Virginia, Martinsburg Division, based upon diversity of citizenship and moved to dismiss Feliciano's claim, contending that he had failed to state a claim upon which relief could be granted. In considering this motion, the district court encountered a legal conundrum which it has certified to this Court. Applying West Virginia substantive law, the court ruled, by order entered February 28, 2001, that, "unless the West Virginia Supreme Court of Appeals holds otherwise, the Court concludes that self-defense is not a substantial public policy in West Virginia," which ruling, if upheld, would result in the dismissal of Feliciano's complaint for failure to state a meritorious claim for wrongful discharge. Pursuant to this decision, the district court certifies its question of law to this Court.

DISCUSSION

Before definitively deciding the question certified for our determination, it is helpful to briefly review basic concepts of employment law applicable to the case *sub judice*. In the State of West Virginia, employers and employees alike are generally governed by the at will employment doctrine. Pursuant to this body of law, "[w]hen a contract of employment is of indefinite duration it may be terminated at any time by either party to the contract." Syl. pt. 2, Wright v. Standard Ultramarine & Color Co., 141 W.Va. 368, 90 S.E.2d 459 (1955). The practical effect of this doctrine, then, is that "an at-will employee serves at the will and pleasure of his or her employer and can be discharged at any time, with or without cause." Kanagy v. Fiesta Salons, Inc., 208 W.Va. 526, 529, 541 S.E.2d 616, 619 (2000) (citation omitted). Nevertheless, " 'the employer is not so absolute a sovereign of the job that there are not limits to his prerogative.' " *Id.*

Accordingly, a cause of action for wrongful discharge exists when an aggrieved employee can demonstrate that his/her employer acted contrary to substantial public policy in effectuating the termination. "[P]ublic policy" is that principle of law which holds that no person can lawfully do that which has a tendency to be injurious to the public or against public good even though no actual injury may have resulted therefrom in a particular case to the public." Cordle v. General Hugh Mercer Corp., 174 W.Va. at 325, 325 S.E.2d at 114. Whether a particular factor motivating a discharge from employment is a matter of public policy is dictated by reference to various authorities: "[t]o identify the sources of public policy for purposes of determining whether a retaliatory discharge has occurred, we look to established precepts in our constitution, legislative enactments, legislatively approved regulations, and judicial opinions." Syl. pt. 2, Birthisel v. Tri-Cities Health Servs. Corp., 188 W.Va. 371, 424 S.E.2d 606 (1992). However, in order to sustain a cause of action for wrongful discharge, the public policy relied upon must not just exist; it must be substantial. "Inherent in the term 'substantial public policy' is the concept that the policy will provide specific guidance to a reasonable person." Syl. pt. 3, Birthisel, 188 W.Va. 371, 424 S.E.2d 606. Moreover,

> [t]he term "substantial public policy" implies that the policy principle will be clearly recognized simply because it is substantial. An employer should not be exposed to liability where a public policy standard is too general to provide any specific guidance or is so vague that it is subject to different interpretations.

Id. Thus, to be substantial, a public policy must not just be recognizable as such but must be so widely regarded as to be evident to employers and employees alike.

Turning now to the issue presently before us, we must decide whether self-defense is a substantial public policy exception so as to support a cause of action for wrongful discharge. In our prior decision of *Birthisel*, we observed that the sources of public policy include constitutional authority, statutory and regulatory provisions, and principles of common law. An examination of the West Virginia Constitution and the legislation of this State, however, suggest that while both bodies of law briefly mention an individual's right to defend him/herself, neither clearly expresses this view as a definite statement of public policy. *See, e.g.*, W. Va. Const. art. III, § 22 (securing an individual's "right to keep and bear arms for the defense of self"); W. Va.Code § 61-7-1 (1989) (Repl.Vol.2000) (acknowledging the right to bear arms for self-defense). *See also* W. Va.Code § 61-6-21(e) (1987) (Repl.Vol.2000) (permitting the teaching of self-defense techniques in civil rights context).

The jurisprudential history of this State, however, clearly demonstrates the existence of a public policy favoring an individual's right to defend him/herself. From the earliest reported cases to present day decisions, this Court has repeatedly recognized and safeguarded an individual's right to defend him/herself against an unprovoked assailant. In the course of these opinions, we have defined the nature of the right to self-defense.... In the course of rendering these rulings, we have also clarified the essential elements of this offense.

Similarly, we have refined the circumstances under which a defendant may avail him/herself of a self-defense argument and crafted various procedural rules to govern the assertion of this affirmative defense. In fact, the right to self-defense is so entrenched in the common law of this State that, some eighty years ago, this Court, while considering a defendant's plea of self-defense, obviated the need for meaningful discussion thereof by remarking that "[t]he law of self-defense is so well understood and has been so many times laid down by prior decisions as to need no additional affirmation in this case." State v. Miller, 85 W.Va. 326, 329, 102 S.E. 303, 304 (1919). Furthermore, we previously have recognized that the right to self-defense extends to one's place of employment:

> [i]n defending himself, his family or his property from the assault of an intruder, one is not limited to his immediate home or castle; his right to stand his ground in defense thereof without retreating extends to his place of business also and where it is necessary he may take the life of his assailant or intruder.

Syl. pt. 7, State v. Laura, 93 W.Va. 250, 116 S.E. 251 (1923). Hence, it goes without saying that an individual's right to self-defense in West Virginia has been sufficiently established in and clarified by our State's common law so as to render it a substantial public policy.

While we recognize this substantial public policy of an employee's right to defend him/herself against bodily injury, we nevertheless must also be mindful of an employer's corresponding duty to safeguard its employees and patrons. Thus, while a particular employee may assert his/her right to self-defense, an employer also has an interest in protecting its staff and customers from harm that may befall them as a result of the employee's actions in defending him/herself. For example, in the case *sub judice*, it is quite possible that someone, be it Feliciano, his coworker, or an innocent bystander, could have been injured in the course of Feliciano's attempts to defend himself. While it is indeed quite fortunate that no such injuries resulted, we must still account for this very real possibility. Accordingly, we find that while an employee has a right to self-defense, such right must necessarily be limited in its scope and available in only the most dangerous of circumstances. Therefore, we hold that when an at will employee has been discharged from his/her employment based upon his/ her exercise of self-defense in response to lethal imminent danger, such right of self-defense constitutes a substantial public policy exception to the at will employment doctrine and will sustain a cause of action for wrongful discharge. Consistent with our prior precedent, we hold further that an employer may rebut an employee's prima facie case of wrongful discharge resulting from the employee's use of self-defense in response to lethal imminent danger by demonstrating that it had a plausible and legitimate business reason to justify the discharge.

As this case is presently before the Court upon certification of a question of law, we are not at liberty to decide whether the facts support Feliciano's cause of action for wrongful discharge. However, as guidance for future cases, we find the following elements of the tort of wrongful discharge, as enumerated by the United States Court of Appeals for the Sixth Circuit in *Godfredson v. Hess & Clark, Inc.*, 173 F.3d 365 (6th Cir.1999), to be particularly instructive to a determination of whether an employee has successfully presented a claim of relief for wrongful discharge in contravention of substantial public policy:

> 1. [Whether a] clear public policy existed and was manifested in a state or federal constitution, statute or administrative regulation, or in the common law (the clarity element).
>
> 2. [Whether] dismissing employees under circumstances like those involved in the plaintiff's dismissal would jeopardize the public policy (the jeopardy element).
>
> 3. [Whether t]he plaintiff's dismissal was motivated by conduct related to the public policy (the causation element).
>
> 4. [Whether t]he employer lacked overriding legitimate business justification for the dismissal (the overriding justification element).

173 F.3d at 375. This succinct summation merely reiterates the procedures we previously have delineated in the foregoing discussion and decision of this case.

CONCLUSION

In conclusion, we answer the question certified by the United States District Court for the Northern District of West Virginia in the affirmative, but with limitation. Thus, the right of self-defense in response to lethal imminent danger is a substantial public policy exception to the at will employment doctrine and will support a cause of action for wrongful discharge. An aggrieved employer may then rebut the presumption of a wrongful discharge by demonstrating that it had a plausible and legitimate business reason for terminating its employee.

* * *

1. Sources of public policy. *Feliciano* is somewhat unusual in that the court is willing to look to the common law to help divine public policy. Some courts have expressly held that public policy must be evidenced by a constitutional or statutory provision. Brockmeyer v. Dun & Bradstreet, 335 N.W.2d 834, 840 (Wis. 1983). Others have recognized administrative regulations as a source of public policy, at least where the regulations are rooted in existing legislation. Green v. Ralee Engineering Co., 960 P.2d 1046, 1054 (Cal. 1998). However, "[w]ith few exceptions, courts recognizing a cause of action for wrongful discharge have to some extent relied on statutory expressions of public policy as a basis for the employee's claim." Adler v. Am. Standard Corp., 432 A.2d 464, 469 (Md. 1981).

2. Codes of professional conduct. Some courts have held that codes of professional conduct are capable of articulating public policy. *See* Rocky Mountain Hosp. & Med. Serv. v. Mariani, 916 P.2d 519, 525 (Colo. 1996) (concluding that rules of professional conduct governing accountants may articulate public policy for purposes of a wrongful discharge claim). When, if ever, should a professional code of conduct be deemed capable of articulating public policy?

3. Exercising a statutory right. Because many courts limit the sources of public policy to statutes, the exception to the at-will rule at issue in *Feliciano* is often referred to as "exercising a statutory right." The most obvious example would be discharging an employee for filing a claim for workers' compensation benefits. Frampton v. Central Ind. Gas Co., 297 N.E.2d 425 (Ind. 1973). Indeed, some decisions speak exclusively of exercising a statutory right and seem limited to the case of filing a claim for workers' compensation. *See* Campbell v. Eli Lilly & Co., 413 N.E.2d 1054, 1060 (Ind. Ct. App. 1980).

* * *

B. Fulfilling a Public Obligation

Firing an employee for fulfilling some type of public obligation may also violate public policy. The classic example is firing an employee for serving jury duty. Nees v. Hocks, 536 P.2d 512 (Or. 1975). Other examples include firing an employee for enforcing building codes related to public safety when it was the employee's job to do so, *Parada v. City of Colton*, 29 Cal.Rptr.2d 309 (Cal. App. 4 Dist. 1994), and for giving truthful testimony under oath. Trexler v. Norfolk Southern Ry. Co. 957 F. Supp. 772 (M.D.N.C. 1997). Importantly, an employee must actually be under an obligation to take a particular action before the employee will have a wrongful discharge claim if fired for having taken that action. *See* Babick v. Oregon Arena Corp., 40 P.3d 1059 (Or. 2002) (affirming dismissal of security guards wrongful discharge claim based on guards' lawful arrests of individuals because no statute required guards to make the arrests).

* * *

C. Whistleblowing

Focus Questions: *Balla v. Gambro, Inc.*

1. *What are the sources of public policy in this matter?*
2. *Why does the fact that the plaintiff is an attorney make a difference in this case?*

Balla v. Gambro, Inc.

584 N.E.2d 104
(Ill. 1991)

Justice CLARK delivered the opinion of the court:

The issue in this case is whether in-house counsel should be allowed the remedy of an action for retaliatory discharge.

Appellee, Roger Balla, formerly in-house counsel for Gambro, Inc. (Gambro), filed a retaliatory discharge action against Gambro, its affiliate Gambro Dialysatoren, KG (Gambro Germany), its parent company Gambro Lundia, AB (Gambro Sweden), and the president of Gambro in the circuit court of Cook County (Gambro, Gambro Germany and Gambro Sweden collectively referred to as appellants). Appellee alleged that he was fired in contravention of Illinois public policy and sought damages for the discharge. The trial court dismissed the action on appellants' motion for summary judgment. The appellate court reversed. We granted appellant's petition for leave to appeal and allowed amicus curiae briefs from the American Corporate Counsel Association and Illinois State Bar Association.

Gambro is a distributor of kidney dialysis equipment manufactured by Gambro Germany. Among the products distributed by Gambro are dialyzers which filter excess fluid and toxic substances from the blood of patients with no or impaired kidney function. The manufacture and sale of dialyzers is regulated by the United States Food and Drug Administration (FDA); the Federal Food, Drug, and Cosmetic Act (Federal Act) (21 U.S.C. § 331 et seq. (1988)); FDA regulations (21 C.F.R. §§ 820.150 through 820.198 (1987)); and the Illinois Food, Drug and Cosmetic Act (Ill.Rev.Stat.1985, ch. 56 1/2, par. 501 et seq.).

Appellee, Roger J. Balla, is and was at all times throughout this controversy an attorney licensed to practice law in the State of Illinois. On March 17, 1980, appellee executed an employment agreement with Gambro which contained the terms of appellee's employment. Generally, the employment agreement provided that appellee would "be responsible for all legal matters within the company and for personnel within the company's sales office." Appellee held the title of director of administration at Gambro. As director of administration, appellee's specific responsibilities included, *inter alia*: advising, counseling and representing management on legal matters; establishing and administering personnel policies; coordinating and overseeing corporate activities to assure compliance with applicable laws and regulations, and preventing or minimizing legal or administrative proceedings; and coordinating the activities of the manager of regulatory affairs. Regarding this last responsibility, under Gambro's corporate hierarchy, appellee supervised the manager of regulatory affairs, and the manager reported directly to appellee.

In August 1983, the manager of regulatory affairs for Gambro left the company and appellee assumed the manager's specific duties. Although appellee's original employment agreement was not modified to reflect his new position, his annual compensation was increased and Gambro's corporate organizational chart referred to appellee's positions as "Dir. of Admin./Personnel; General Counsel; Mgr. of Regulatory Affairs." The job description for the position described the manager as an individual "responsible for ensuring awareness of and compliance with federal, state and local laws and regulations affecting the company's operations and products." Requirements for the position were a bachelor of science degree and three to five years in the medical device field plus two years experience in the area of government regulations. The individual in the position prior to appellee was not an attorney.

In July 1985 Gambro Germany informed Gambro in a letter that certain dialyzers it had manufactured, the clearances of which varied from the package insert, were about to be shipped to Gambro. Referring to these dialyzers, Gambro Germany advised Gambro:

> For acute patients risk is that the acute uremic situation will not be improved in spite of the treatment, giving continuous high levels of potassium, phosphate and urea/creatine. The chronic patient may note the effect as a slow progression of the uremic situation and depending on the interval between medical check-ups the medical risk may not be overlooked.

Appellee told the president of Gambro to reject the shipment because the dialyzers did not comply with FDA regulations. The president notified Gambro Germany of its decision to reject the shipment on July 12, 1985.

However, one week later the president informed Gambro Germany that Gambro would accept the dialyzers and "sell [them] to a unit that is not currently our customer but who buys only on price." Appellee contends that he was not informed by the president of the decision to accept the dialyzers but became aware of it through other Gambro employees. Appellee maintains that he spoke with the president in August regarding the company's decision to accept the dialyzers and told the president that he would do whatever necessary to stop the sale of the dialyzers.

On September 4, 1985, appellee was discharged from Gambro's employment by its president. The following day, appellee reported the shipment of the dialyzers to the FDA. The FDA seized the shipment and determined the product to be "adulterated within the meaning of section 501(h) of the [Federal Act]."

On March 19, 1986, appellee filed a four-count complaint in tort for retaliatory discharge seeking $22 million in damages. Counts III and IV for emotional distress were dismissed from the action, as was the president in an order entered by the trial court on November 5, 1986.

On July 28, 1987, Gambro filed a motion for summary judgment. Gambro argued that appellee, as an attorney, was precluded from filing a retaliatory discharge action in light of the appellate court opinion in *Herbster v. North American Co. for Life & Health Insurance*, 501 N.E.2d 343 (Ill. 1986).... Appellee argued that the plaintiff in *Herbster* was in-house counsel for a corporation whose duties were restricted to legal, whereas he served as the director of administration and personnel and manager of regulatory affairs as well as general counsel for Gambro. Appellee argued that a question of fact existed as to whether he was discharged for the performance of a purely legal function.

On November 30, 1988, the trial court granted appellants' motion for summary judgment.... On appeal, the court below held that an attorney is not barred as a matter of law from bringing an action for retaliatory discharge. Rather, determination of whether an attorney has standing to bring the action was based on the following three-part test:

> (1) whether [the attorney's] discharge resulted from information he learned as a 'layman' in a nonlegal position; (2) whether [the attorney] learned the information as a result of the attorney/client relationship, if so, whether the information was privileged, and if it was privileged, whether the privilege was waived; and (3) whether there were any countervailing public policies favoring disclosure of privileged information learned from the attorney/client relationship."

The court remanded for a determination of these questions of fact.

We agree with the trial court that appellee does not have a cause of action against Gambro for retaliatory discharge under the facts of the case at bar. Generally, this court adheres to the proposition that "an employer may discharge an employee-at-will for any reason or for no reason [at all]." However, in *Kelsay v. Motorola, Inc.*, 384 N.E.2d 353 (Ill. 1978) this court first recognized the limited and narrow tort of retaliatory discharge. In *Kelsay*, an at-will employee was fired for filing a worker's compensation claim against her employer. After examining the history and purpose behind the Workers' Compensation Act to determine the public policy behind its enactment, this court held that the employee should have a cause of action for retaliatory discharge. This court stressed that if employers could fire employees for filing workers' compensation claims, the public policy behind the enactment of the Workers' Compensation Act would be frustrated.

Subsequently, in *Palmateer v. International Harvester Co.*, 421 N.E.2d 876 (Ill. 1981) this court again examined the tort of retaliatory discharge. In *Palmateer*, an employee was discharged for informing the police of suspected criminal activities of a co-employee, and because he agreed to provide assistance in any investigation and trial of the matter.

Based on the public policy favoring the investigation and prosecution of crime, this court held that the employee had a cause of action for retaliatory discharge. Further, we stated:

> All that is required [to bring a cause of action for retaliatory discharge] is that the employer discharge the employee in retaliation for the employee's activities, and that the discharge be in contravention of a clearly mandated public policy.

Palmateer, 421 N.E.2d 876.

In this case it appears that Gambro discharged appellee, an employee of Gambro, in retaliation for his activities, and this discharge was in contravention of a clearly mandated public policy. Appellee allegedly told the president of Gambro that he would do whatever was necessary to stop the sale of the "misbranded and/or adulterated" dialyzers. In appellee's eyes, the use of these dialyzers could cause death or serious bodily harm to patients. As we have stated before, "[t]here is no public policy more important or more fundamental than the one favoring the effective protection of the lives and property of citizens." However, in this case, appellee was not just an employee of Gambro, but also general counsel for Gambro.

As noted earlier, in *Herbster v. North American Co. for Life & Health Insurance*, 501 N.E.2d 343 (Ill. 1986) our appellate court held that the plaintiff, an employee and chief legal counsel for the defendant company, did not have a claim for retaliatory discharge against the company due to the presence of the attorney-client relationship. Under the facts of that case, the defendant company allegedly requested the plaintiff to destroy or remove discovery information which had been requested in lawsuits pending against the company. The plaintiff refused arguing that such conduct would constitute fraud and violate several provisions of the Illinois Code of Professional Responsibility. Subsequently, the defendant company discharged the plaintiff.

The appellate court refused to extend the tort of retaliatory discharge to the plaintiff in *Herbster* primarily because of the special relationship between an attorney and client. The court stated:

> The mutual trust, exchanges of confidence, reliance on judgment, and personal nature of the attorney-client relationship demonstrate the unique position attorneys occupy in our society.

The appellate court recited a list of factors which make the attorney-client relationship special such as: the attorney-client privilege regarding confidential communications, the fiduciary duty an attorney owes to a client, the right of the client to terminate the relationship with or without cause, and the fact that a client has exclusive control over the subject matter of the litigation and a client may dismiss or settle a cause of action regardless of the attorney's advice. Thus, in *Herbster*, since the plaintiff's duties pertained strictly to legal matters, the appellate court determined that the plaintiff did not have a claim for retaliatory discharge.

We agree with the conclusion reached in *Herbster* that, generally, in-house counsel do not have a claim under the tort of retaliatory discharge. However, we base our decision as much on the nature and purpose of the tort of retaliatory discharge, as on the effect on the attorney-client relationship that extending the tort would have. In addition, at this time, we caution that our holding is confined by the fact that appellee is and was at all times throughout this controversy an attorney licensed to practice law in the State of Illinois. Appellee is and was subject to the Illinois Code of Professional Responsibility adopted by this court. The tort of retaliatory discharge is a limited and narrow exception to the general rule of at-will employment. The tort seeks to achieve "a proper balance ...

among the employer's interest in operating a business efficiently and profitably, the employee's interest in earning a livelihood, and society's interest in seeing its public policies carried out." Further, as stated in *Palmateer*, *"[t]he foundation of the tort of retaliatory discharge lies in the protection of public policy. . . ."* (emphasis added).

In this case, the public policy to be protected, that of protecting the lives and property of citizens, is adequately safeguarded without extending the tort of retaliatory discharge to in-house counsel. Appellee was required under the Rules of Professional Conduct to report Gambro's intention to sell the "misbranded and/or adulterated" dialyzers. Rule 1.6(b) of the Rules of Professional Conduct reads:

> A lawyer *shall* reveal information about a client to the extent it appears necessary to prevent the client from committing an act that would result in death or serious bodily injury (emphasis added).

Appellee alleges, and the FDA's seizure of the dialyzers indicates, that the use of the dialyzers would cause death or serious bodily injury. Thus, under the above-cited rule, appellee was under the mandate of this court to report the sale of these dialyzers.

In his brief to this court, appellee argues that not extending the tort of retaliatory discharge to in-house counsel would present attorneys with a "Hobson's choice." According to appellee, in-house counsel would face two alternatives: either comply with the client/employer's wishes and risk both the loss of a professional license and exposure to criminal sanctions, or decline to comply with client/employer's wishes and risk the loss of a full-time job and the attendant benefits. We disagree. Unlike the employees in *Kelsay* which this court recognized would be left with the difficult decision of choosing between whether to file a workers' compensation claim and risk being fired, or retaining their jobs and losing their right to a remedy, in-house counsel plainly are not confronted with such a dilemma. In-house counsel do not have a choice of whether to follow their ethical obligations as attorneys licensed to practice law, or follow the illegal and unethical demands of their clients. In-house counsel must abide by the Rules of Professional Conduct. Appellee had no choice but to report to the FDA Gambro's intention to sell or distribute these dialyzers, and consequently protect the aforementioned public policy.

In addition, we believe that extending the tort of retaliatory discharge to in-house counsel would have an undesirable effect on the attorney-client relationship that exists between these employers and their in-house counsel. Generally, a client may discharge his attorney at any time, with or without cause. This rule applies equally to in-house counsel as it does to outside counsel. Further, this rule "recognizes that the relationship between an attorney and client is based on trust and that the client must have confidence in his attorney in order to ensure that the relationship will function properly." As stated in *Herbster*, "the attorney is placed in the unique position of maintaining a close relationship with a client where the attorney receives secrets, disclosures, and information that otherwise would not be divulged to intimate friends." We believe that if in-house counsel are granted the right to sue their employers for retaliatory discharge, employers might be less willing to be forthright and candid with their in-house counsel. Employers might be hesitant to turn to their in-house counsel for advice regarding potentially questionable corporate conduct knowing that their in-house counsel could use this information in a retaliatory discharge suit.

We recognize that under the Illinois Rules of Professional Conduct, attorneys shall reveal client confidences or secrets in certain situations and thus one might expect employers/clients to be naturally hesitant to rely on in-house counsel for advice regarding this potentially questionable conduct. However, . . . [i]f extending the tort of retaliatory discharge might have a chilling effect on the communications between the employer/client and the in-house counsel, we believe that it is more wise to refrain from doing so.

In light of our decision that in-house counsel generally are not entitled to bring a cause of action for retaliatory discharge against their employer/client, we must consider appellee's argument that he learned of the dialyzers' defect and Gambro's noncompliance with FDA regulations in his role as manager of regulatory affairs at Gambro, and not as corporate counsel. Appellee argues that, if he did learn of Gambro's alleged violation of FDA regulations as manager of regulatory affairs, and acted pursuant to his duties as manager of regulatory affairs, he is merely an "employee" at Gambro and therefore should be entitled to bring a cause of action for retaliatory discharge. The appellate court in this matter agreed with appellee and held that a question of fact exists as to whether "[appellee's] discharge resulted from information he learned as a 'layman' in a nonlegal position."

We disagree.... In this case, there is no issue of fact as to whether appellee learned of Gambro's violations of FDA regulations as a "layman," as opposed to general counsel for Gambro. After examining the pleadings, exhibits and appellee's deposition testimony, we find that appellee was acting as Gambro's general counsel throughout this ordeal. As noted earlier, at the time of this controversy, appellee not only was acting as general counsel for Gambro, but also was its manager of regulatory affairs. Under the corporate hierarchy at Gambro, the corporate counsel supervised the manager of regulatory affairs. Thus, appellee "supervised" himself in his role as manager of regulatory affairs. More importantly, based on the official job descriptions supplied by Gambro, it is clear that the general counsel and the manager of regulatory affairs performed essentially the same roles with regards to FDA compliance.... Thus, both roles had equivalent duties for assuring compliance with FDA regulations.

For the foregoing reasons, the decision of the appellate court is reversed, and the decision of the trial court is affirmed.

Justice FREEMAN, dissenting:

I respectfully dissent from the decision of my colleagues. In concluding that the plaintiff attorney, serving as corporate in-house counsel, should not be allowed a claim for retaliatory discharge, the majority first reasons that the public policy implicated in this case, i.e., protecting the lives and property of Illinois citizens, is adequately safeguarded by the lawyer's ethical obligation to reveal information about a client as necessary to prevent acts that would result in death or serious bodily harm. I find this reasoning fatally flawed.

The majority so reasons because, as a matter of law, an attorney cannot even contemplate ignoring his ethical obligations in favor of continuing in his employment. I agree with this conclusion "as a matter of law." However, to say that the categorical nature of ethical obligations is sufficient to ensure that the ethical obligations will be satisfied simply ignores reality. Specifically, it ignores that, as unfortunate for society as it may be, attorneys are no less human than nonattorneys and, thus, no less given to the temptation to either ignore or rationalize away their ethical obligations when complying therewith may render them unable to feed and support their families.

I would like to believe, as my colleagues apparently conclude, that attorneys will always "do the right thing" because the law says that they must. However, my knowledge of human nature, which is not much greater than the average layman's, and, sadly, the recent scandals involving the bench and bar of Illinois are more than sufficient to dispel such a belief. Just as the ethical obligations of the lawyers and judges involved in those scandals were inadequate to ensure that they would not break the law, I am afraid that the lawyer's ethical obligation to "blow the whistle" is likewise an inadequate safeguard for the public policy of protecting lives and property of Illinois citizens.

... An attorney should not be punished simply because he has ethical obligations imposed upon him over and above the general obligation to obey the law which all men have. Nor should a corporate employer be protected simply because the employee it has discharged for "blowing the whistle" happens to be an attorney.

Ultimately, the court's decision in the instant case does nothing to encourage respect for the law by corporate employers nor to encourage respect by attorneys for their ethical obligations. Therefore, I must respectfully dissent.

* * *

1. Model Rule comparison. Under Illinois' Rules of Professional Conduct, a lawyer was required to disclose information relating to the representation of a client to the extent necessary to prevent death or substantial bodily harm. While some jurisdictions impose a similar mandatory obligation on the part of attorneys, Rule 1.6(b)(1) of the ABA's *Model Rules of Professional Conduct* provide that a lawyer may (but is not required) to disclose information under these circumstances.

2. Other decisions. Most courts have rejected *Balla*'s reasoning and held that there is no per se bar to an in-house lawyer's wrongful discharge claim. *See* Heckman v. Zurich Holding Co. of America, 242 F.R.D. 606, 608 (D. Kan. 2007) (citing cases and holding that former in-house attorney could pursue a wrongful discharge claim). One reason why courts have rejected *Balla* is that Model Rule 1.6(b)(5) expressly provides that a lawyer may disclose client information to the extent reasonably necessary "to establish a claim ... on behalf of the lawyer in a controversy between the lawyer and the client."

Focus Questions: *Weiss v. Lonnquist*

1. *Why does the plaintiff's claim fail?*
2. *What does it mean to say that a law provides an "adequate alternative means of promoting the public policy" at issue?*
3. *What would the result have been if the plaintiff had filed a disciplinary complaint against the defendant?*

Weiss v. Lonnquist

293 P.3d 1264

(Wash. App. Div. 1 2013)

[Reba Weiss was an employee at the Law Offices of Judith A. Lonnquist, PS, a labor and employment law firm. Weiss was assigned the task of drafting a summary judgment response on behalf of a discharged employee. While reviewing the case file, Weiss became convinced that the client had committed perjury during her deposition and that Lonnquist had persuaded her to do so.]

On August 6, 2007, Weiss told Lonnquist she was unwilling to work on Jane Doe's case because of the ethical issue. Lonnquist, according to Weiss, said she was "not happy about this." Lonnquist relieved Weiss of the assignment and wrote the summary judgment response herself. Lonnquist's view was that Jane Doe did not commit perjury ... [Lonnquist fired Weiss shortly thereafter.]

Weiss considered filing a bar complaint against Lonnquist. She decided against it because, as she explained in her deposition, "I wanted to pursue a civil action and I knew that they would put the bar complaint on hold if there was a civil action pending." She believed the bar process was inadequate because it would not address the wrongful termination. In May 2008, Weiss sued Lonnquist and her law firm, alleging wrongful termination in violation of public policy, willful withholding of wages, defamation, outrage, and negligent infliction of emotional distress.

The jury found for Weiss on her claim of wrongful discharge and her wage claims.

THE PUBLIC POLICY TORT CLAIM

Wrongful discharge in violation of public policy is an intentional tort. In 1996, the Supreme Court set forth the four elements of the tort:

> (1) The plaintiffs must prove the existence of a clear public policy (the clarity element)....
>
> (2) The plaintiffs must prove that discouraging the conduct in which they engaged would jeopardize the public policy (the jeopardy element)....
>
> (3) The plaintiffs must prove that the public-policy-linked conduct caused the dismissal (the causation element)....
>
> (4) The defendant must not be able to offer an overriding justification for the dismissal (the absence of justification element).

Gardner v. Loomis Armored, Inc., 128 Wash.2d 931, 941, 913 P.2d 377 (1996) (emphasis omitted).

THE JEOPARDY ELEMENT

... The jeopardy element sets up a relatively high bar. A plaintiff must show that she engaged in particular conduct and the conduct directly relates to the public policy, or was necessary for the effective enforcement of the public policy. The plaintiff must prove that discouraging the conduct that she engaged in would jeopardize the public policy. Of particular importance here, this means the plaintiff also must show that other means of promoting the public policy are inadequate. If there are other adequate means available, the public policy is not in jeopardy and a private cause of action need not be recognized. *Korslund*, 156 Wash.2d at 184, 125 P.3d 119. "The jeopardy element guarantees an employer's personnel management decisions will not be challenged unless a public policy is genuinely threatened." *Gardner*, 128 Wash.2d at 941–42, 913 P.2d 377. "The question of whether adequate alternative means for promoting a public policy exist presents a question of law as long as 'the inquiry is limited to examining existing laws to determine whether they provide adequate alternative means of promoting the public policy.'" *Cudney*, 172 Wash.2d at 528–29, 259 P.3d 244, *quoting Korslund*, 156 Wash.2d at 182, 125 P.3d 119.

Washington State has an established system for investigating and adjudicating alleged violations of the Rules of Professional Conduct. As attorneys, both Lonnquist and Weiss are subject to these rules. The public policy Weiss invokes as the primary basis for her tort claim against Lonnquist is embodied in RPC 3.3, entitled "Candor Toward the Tribunal," although she also cites RPC 3.1, 4.1, 5.1, and 8.4. The rule provides in relevant part:

> (a) A lawyer shall not knowingly:
>
> (1) make a false statement of fact or law to a tribunal or fail to correct a false statement of material fact or law previously made to the tribunal by the lawyer;

> (2) fail to disclose a material fact to a tribunal when disclosure is necessary to avoid assisting a criminal or fraudulent act by the client unless such disclosure is prohibited by Rule 1.6;
>
> ....
>
> (4) offer evidence that the lawyer knows to be false.

RPC 3.3.

1. The bar disciplinary process was available to Weiss.

A rule entitled "Reporting Professional Misconduct" provides, "A lawyer who knows that another lawyer has committed a violation of the Rules of Professional Conduct that raises a substantial question as to that lawyer's honesty, trustworthiness or fitness as a lawyer in other respects, should inform the appropriate professional authority." RPC 8.3(a). However, the rule goes on to say that a lawyer is not permitted to report the professional misconduct of another lawyer "if doing so would require the lawyer to disclose information otherwise protected by Rule 1.6." RPC 8.3(c).

Weiss contends the Rules of Professional Conduct made the bar disciplinary process unavailable to her under the circumstances. Relying on RPC 1.6 and *In re Disciplinary Proceeding Against Schafer,* 149 Wash.2d 148, 66 P.3d 1036 (2003), Weiss contends it was not possible for her to file a bar complaint because to do so would have meant unethically disclosing information about Jane Doe.

The rule provides in relevant part as follows:

> (a) A lawyer shall not reveal information relating to the representation of a client unless the client gives informed consent, the disclosure is impliedly authorized in order to carry out the representation or the disclosure is permitted by paragraph (b).
>
> (b) A lawyer to the extent the lawyer reasonably believes necessary:
>
> ....
>
> (2) may reveal information relating to the representation of a client to prevent the client from committing a crime;
>
> (3) may reveal information relating to the representation of a client to prevent, mitigate or rectify substantial injury to the financial interests or property of another that is reasonably certain to result or has resulted from the client's commission of a crime or fraud in furtherance of which the client has used the lawyer's services;
>
> ....
>
> (6) may reveal information relating to the representation of a client to comply with a court order.

RPC 1.6.

Because of the exceptions in RPC 1.6(b), the protection accorded to client information in RPC 1.6(a) is not the insuperable obstacle that Weiss portrays it to be. Weiss believed Jane Doe had committed perjury and was planning to continue her perjury, with Lonnquist's complicity and to the detriment of Jane Doe's former employer, as the case went forward. Under RPC 1.6(b)(2) and (b)(3), Weiss was permitted to reveal the information she had relating to her representation of Jane Doe, to the extent she reasonably believed necessary.

Because the information was not protected by RPC 1.6, Weiss could have—and per RPC 8.3(a) "should" have—informed the state bar association about Lonnquist's alleged role in suborning perjury by Jane Doe. Lonnquist would then have the right to reveal to the bar association additional information relating to her representation of Jane Doe to the extent she reasonably believed necessary to establish her defense. RPC 1.6(b)(5) & cmt. 10. Under the bar association's own Rules for Enforcement of Legal Conduct, the bar association would then have the obligation to keep the information about Jane Doe strictly confidential, unless Jane Doe consented to the release. ELC 3.2(b).

Instead of reporting Lonnquist to the state bar, Weiss chose to begin a civil lawsuit against Lonnquist. In the course of that lawsuit, she herself demanded that Lonnquist disclose confidential information about Jane Doe. The court ordered disclosure, conditioned upon redaction of Jane Doe's true name. It is hard to see how Jane Doe's confidential information was better protected in a public trial than it would have been in the relative privacy of an investigation and hearing by the bar association.

2. The bar disciplinary process is an adequate means of promoting the public policy rooted in the rules of professional conduct.

When Weiss refused to engage in the conduct she perceived as unethical, the public policy she was promoting was the policy demanding candor to the tribunal as set forth in the Rules of Professional Conduct. And she concedes that the disciplinary rules of the bar "may offer an adequate alternative means of protecting that public policy because the Washington State Bar Association has the authority and the ability to sanction an attorney who is found to be in violation of the rule." This concession is appropriate and significant because it is ultimately dispositive.

Weiss contends, however, that there is another public policy at stake for which the disciplinary rules provide no remedy. Weiss claims there is a general public policy that employees should be protected from retaliation when they refuse to comply with the employer's directive to engage in unethical conduct. The bar association had the power to discipline Lonnquist, but it did not have the power to reinstate Weiss in her job or compensate her for losing it. Weiss argues that her case is to be distinguished from Cudney on the basis that the bar disciplinary process provides no remedy for retaliation.

It is true that the bar association provides no comparable remedy offering personal relief and protection from retaliation for an attorney who refuses her supervisor's directive to engage in conduct she perceives as unethical. But we do not [believe] that alternative remedies, to be adequate, must provide relief personal to the employee. The Supreme Court has repeatedly emphasized that it does not matter whether or not the alternative means of enforcing the public policy grants a particular aggrieved employee any private remedy. In *Hubbard v. Spokane County*, 146 Wash.2d 699, 50 P.3d 602 (2002), the Supreme Court was utterly clear on this point. "The other means of promoting the public policy need not be available to a particular individual so long as the other means are adequate to safeguard the public policy." *Hubbard*, 146 Wash.2d at 717, 50 P.3d 602. The plaintiff must show that the actions she took were the "'only available adequate means'" to promote the public policy. *Cudney*, 172 Wash.2d at 530, 259 P.3d 244, quoting Danny v. Laidlaw Transit Servs., Inc., 165 Wash.2d 200, 222, 193 P.3d 128 (2008).

The public policy tort may be available where an employee is discharged in retaliation for refusing to commit an illegal act. But Weiss cites no case supporting her theory that the public policy tort is available to an employee who is discharged in retaliation for refusing to commit an illegal act where that employee has refused to engage with a professional disciplinary system specifically designed to receive and address complaints about the employer.

... A civil suit cannot be the only available adequate means to vindicate the Rules of Professional Conduct when the bar association itself is specifically entrusted with the enforcement of those rules, has expertise in interpreting them, and stands ready to investigate complaints.

... We might have a different case if Weiss had reported Lonnquist to the bar association and had been discharged for taking that action. Weiss would then have been in a better position to argue that her civil suit was necessary for the effective enforcement of public policy. But Weiss decided against filing a bar complaint, preferring to pursue a civil action. Her theory that she was enforcing a public policy against retaliation simply circles back to the argument that a remedy is inadequate unless it provides compensation and other individualized relief to the aggrieved employee. As discussed above, the Supreme Court has rejected that argument.

Because Weiss failed as a matter of law to satisfy the jeopardy element of the tort of wrongful discharge, her suit should have been dismissed on summary judgment.

* * *

1. Preventing the Hobson's Choice. One of the common justifications offered for recognizing wrongful discharge claims is that an employee should not be forced to choose between keeping his job and complying with some other recognized duty, whether the duty involves fulfilling a public obligation, complying with an ethical obligation, or refusing to commit an unlawful act. Martin Marietta v. Lorenz, 823 P.2d 100, 109 (Colo.1992). Are the decisions in *Balla* and *Weiss* consistent with that idea?

2. Lawyers and job duties. A lawyer pursuing a wrongful discharge claim may face another obstacle. In *Kidwell v. Sybaritic, Inc.*, 784 N.W.2d 220 (Minn. 2010), an in-house lawyer was fired after sending an email to management about the "pervasive culture of dishonesty" within the company, including possible violations of law. The Minnesota Supreme Court held that the lawyer's subsequent whistleblower claim failed as a matter of law, in part, because it was his job as in-house counsel to notify management of such problems. "An employee cannot be said to have 'blown the whistle' when the employee's report is made because it is the employee's job to investigate and report wrongdoing." *Id.* at 228.

* * *

D. Refusing to Commit an Unlawful Act

Focus Questions: *Sabine Pilot Service, Inc. v. Hauck* and *Johnston v. Del Mar Distributing Co., Inc.*

1. *What is the basis for the exception recognized in* Sabine Pilot*?*
2. *What is the basis for the* Johnston *court's extension of* Sabine Pilot's *holding?*

Sabine Pilot Service, Inc. v. Hauck

687 S.W.2d 733
(Tex. 1985)

WALLACE, Justice.

Hauck was a deckhand for Sabine. He testified in deposition that he was instructed that one of his duties each day was to pump the bilges of the boat on which he worked.

He observed a placard posted on the boat which stated that it was illegal to pump the bilges into the water. He called the United States Coast Guard and an officer confirmed that pumping bilges into the water was illegal; therefore, he refused to do so. He further testified that he was fired for refusing to illegally pump the bilges into the water.

Sabine testified through one of its officers that Hauck was discharged because he refused to swab the deck, man a radio watch and other derelictions of duty.

The sole issue for our determination is whether an allegation by an employee that he was discharged for refusing to perform an illegal act states a cause of action. This court in *East Line & R.R.R. Co. v. Scott*, 72 Tex. 70, 75, 10 S.W. 99, 102 (1888), held that employment for an indefinite term may be terminated at will and without cause. The courts of Texas have steadfastly refused to vary from that holding. However, in the last 30 years the courts of 22 states have made exceptions to the employment-at-will doctrine and numerous commentators have advocated exceptions to the doctrine. The exceptions advocated by the commentators and adopted by various courts range from very liberal and broad exceptions to very narrow and closely defined ones.

Sabine contends that any exception to the employment-at-will doctrine should be statutorily created. The Legislature has created exceptions to this doctrine. TEX.REV.CIV.STAT.ANN. art. 8307c (discharge for filing a worker's compensation claim); TEX.REV.CIV.STAT.ANN. art. 5207a (discharge based on union membership or non-membership); TEX.REV.CIV.STAT.ANN. art. 5765 § 7A (discharge because of active duty in the State Military Forces); TEX.REV.CIV.STAT.ANN. art. 5207b (discharge because of jury service); TEX.REV.CIV.STAT.ANN. art. 5221k § 1.02, Texas Commission on Human Rights Act (discharge based on race, color, handicap, religion, national origin, age or sex). Although the Legislature has created those exceptions to the doctrine, this court is free to judicially amend a judicially created doctrine.

Upon careful consideration of the changes in American society and in the employer/employee relationship during the intervening 97 years since the *East Line & R.R.R. Co. v. Scott decision*, we hold that the situation which led to that decision has changed in certain respects. We now hold that public policy, as expressed in the laws of this state and the United States which carry criminal penalties, requires a very narrow exception to the employment-at-will doctrine announced in *East Line & R.R.R. Co. v. Scott.* That narrow exception covers only the discharge of an employee for the sole reason that the employee refused to perform an illegal act. We further hold that in the trial of such a case it is the plaintiff's burden to prove by a preponderance of the evidence that his discharge was for no reason other than his refusal to perform an illegal act.

KILGARLIN, Justice, concurring.

I concur with this judgment which gives Michael Hauck an opportunity to prove to a trier of fact that he was discharged for refusing to violate a law. Moreover, I heartily applaud the court's acknowledgement of the vital need for a public policy exception to the employment at will doctrine. Absolute employment at will is a relic of early industrial times, conjuring up visions of the sweat shops described by Charles Dickens and his contemporaries. The doctrine belongs in a museum, not in our law. As it was a judicially promulgated doctrine, this court has the burden and the duty of amending it to reflect social and economic changes. Our duty to update this doctrine is particularly urgent when the doctrine is used as leverage to incite violations of our state and federal laws. Allowing an employer to require an employee to break a law or face termination cannot help but promote a thorough disrespect for the laws and legal institutions of our society.

* * *

Johnston v. Del Mar Distributing Co., Inc.

776 S.W.2d 768
(Tex.App.—Corpus Christi 1989)

BENAVIDES, Justice.

Nancy Johnston, appellant, brought suit against her employer, Del Mar Distributing Co., Inc., alleging that her employment had been wrongfully terminated. Del Mar filed a motion for summary judgment in the trial court alleging that appellant's pleadings failed to state a cause of action. After a hearing on the motion, the trial court agreed with Del Mar and granted its motion for summary judgment.

The record reveals that the only documents before the trial court in the instant case were the pleadings of the parties, Del Mar's motion for summary judgment, and appellant's response to the motion. As a general rule, pleadings, even if verified, do not constitute summary judgment evidence. In the instant case, however, Del Mar's summary judgment was based solely on the ground that appellant's petition failed to state a cause of action; therefore, it is proper to consider the pleadings in our review of the summary judgment.

In her petition, appellant alleged that she was employed by Del Mar during the summer of 1987. As a part of her duties, she was required to prepare shipping documents for goods being sent from Del Mar's warehouse located in Corpus Christi, Texas to other cities in Texas. One day, Del Mar instructed appellant to package a semi-automatic weapon (for delivery to a grocery store in Brownsville, Texas) and to label the contents of the package as "fishing gear." Ultimately, the package was to be given to United Parcel Service for shipping. Appellant was required to sign her name to the shipping documents; therefore, she was concerned that her actions might be in violation of some firearm regulation or a regulation of the United Postal Service. Accordingly, she sought the advice of the United States Treasury Department Bureau of Alcohol, Tobacco & Firearms (hereinafter referred to as "the Bureau"). A few days after she contacted the Bureau, appellant was fired. Appellant brought suit for wrongful termination alleging that her employment was terminated solely in retaliation for contacting the Bureau.[3]

Del Mar asserted in its motion that, notwithstanding the above described facts, appellant's cause of action was barred by the employment-at-will doctrine. Specifically, Del Mar asserted that since appellant's employment was for an indefinite amount of time, she was an employee-at-will and it had the absolute right to terminate her employment for any reason or no reason at all.

It is well-settled that Texas adheres to the traditional employment-at-will doctrine....

Today, the absolute employment-at-will doctrine is increasingly seen as a "relic of early industrial times" and a "harsh anachronism." Sabine Pilot Service, Inc. v. Hauck, 687 S.W.2d 733, 735 (Tex.1985) (Kilgarlin, J., concurring). Accordingly, our Legislature has enacted some exceptions to this doctrine, i.e., an employer may not fire an employee for (1) membership or non-membership in a labor union, (2) serving on a jury, (3) filing a workmen's compensation claim, (4) being on active military duty, (5) being of a particular race, color, handicap, religion, national origin, age, or sex.

Recently, the Texas Supreme Court, recognizing the need to amend the employment-at-will doctrine, invoked its judicial authority to create a very narrow common law

3. Appellant's petition can be construed as alleging that she was fired because (1) she inquired into whether her acts were illegal; and (2) she reported suspected violations to a regulatory agency (commonly referred to as "whistleblowing").

exception to the doctrine. *Sabine Pilot*, 687 S.W.2d at 735. In *Sabine Pilot*, the Texas Supreme Court was faced with a narrow issue for consideration, i.e., whether an allegation by an employee that he or she was discharged for refusing to perform an illegal act stated a cause of action. *Id.* The Court held that

> public policy, *as expressed in the laws* of this state and the United States which *carry criminal penalties*, requires a very *narrow* exception to the employment-at-will doctrine ... [t]hat *narrow* exception covers only the discharge of an employee for the *sole* reason that the employee refused to perform an *illegal act.*

Id. (emphasis ours).

Since the Court was faced only with this narrow issue, it did not carve out any other "public policy" exceptions to the doctrine. However, as Justice Kilgarlin noted in his concurring opinion, the decision does not preclude the Court from expanding the exception when warranted in a proper case. *Id.*

Del Mar, in its motion for summary judgment, argued that the narrow exception created in *Sabine Pilot* did not apply to the instant case because mislabeling the contents of a package is not a criminal offense under state or federal laws....

While we acknowledge that the facts of this case are distinguishable from the facts in *Sabine Pilot*, we nonetheless find that the public policy exception created in *Sabine Pilot* applies to the instant case.

On appeal, appellant alleges that her petition did state a cause of action pursuant to the public policy exception announced in *Sabine Pilot.* In her brief, appellant contends that since Texas law currently provides that an employee has a cause of action when she is fired for refusing to perform an illegal act, it necessarily follows that an employee states a cause of action where she alleges that she is fired for simply inquiring into whether or not she is committing illegal acts. To hold otherwise, she argues, would have a chilling effect on the public policy exception announced in *Sabine Pilot.* We agree.

It is implicit that in order to refuse to do an illegal act, an employee must either know or suspect that the requested act is illegal. In some cases it will be patently obvious that the act is illegal (murder, robbery, theft, etc.); however, in other cases it may not be so apparent. Since ignorance of the law is no defense to a criminal prosecution, it is reasonable to expect that if an employee has a good faith belief that a required act might be illegal, she will try to find out whether the act is in fact illegal prior to deciding what course of action to take. If an employer is allowed to terminate the employee at this point, the public policy exception announced in Sabine Pilot would have little or no effect. To hold otherwise would force an employee, who suspects that a requested act might be illegal, to: (1) subject herself to possible discharge if she attempts to find out if the act is in fact illegal; or (2) remain ignorant, perform the act and, if it turns out to be illegal, face possible criminal sanctions.

We hold that since the law recognizes that it is against public policy to allow an employer to coerce its employee to commit a criminal act in furtherance of its own interest, then it is necessarily inferred that the same public policy prohibits the discharge of an employee who in good faith attempts to find out if the act is illegal. It is important to note that we are not creating a new exception to the employment-at-will doctrine. Rather, we are merely enforcing the narrow public policy exception which was created in *Sabine Pilot.*

Therefore, we find that the *Sabine Pilot* exception necessarily covers a situation where an employee has a good faith belief that her employer has requested her to perform an act which may subject her to criminal penalties. Public policy demands that she be allowed to investigate into whether such actions are legal so that she can determine what course of action to take (i.e., whether or not to perform the act).

Furthermore, it is the opinion of this Court that the question of whether or not the requested act was in fact illegal is irrelevant to the determination of this case. We hold that where a plaintiff's employment is terminated for attempting to find out from a regulatory agency if a requested act is illegal, it is not necessary to prove that the requested act was in fact illegal. A plaintiff must, however, establish that she had a good faith belief that the requested act might be illegal, and that such belief was reasonable. Accordingly, we sustain appellant's third and fourth points of error.

Del Mar also contends, for the first time on appeal, that this case involves a "whistleblower" fact situation because appellant was fired for reporting suspected illegal activity to a police agency. Del Mar asks this Court not to create a "whistleblower" exception to the employment-at-will doctrine since neither the Legislature nor the Supreme Court has created such an exception. Del Mar cites Tex.R.Civ.Stat.Ann. art. 6252-16a, § 2 (Vernon Supp.1989) in support of its position.

Article 6252-16a, § 2 provides that a governmental employee cannot be fired because she reports suspected illegal activity to a police agency. Del Mar argues that we must exercise judicial restraint since the Legislature had the opportunity to include employees of the private sector, but declined to do so.

It is well-settled in Texas that a motion for summary judgment shall state with specificity the grounds upon which the movant is relying. Tex.R.Civ.P. 166a(c). Any issues that are not specifically before the trial court at the hearing on the motion may not be considered for the first time on appeal.

Since, in the instant case, Del Mar did not specifically assert this issue in its motion for summary judgment, we will not consider it for the first time on appeal.[5]

The judgment of the trial court is reversed and remanded for trial.

* * *

1. Collapsing categories. Note that *Sabine Pilot* recognized only one narrow category of cases as an exception to the at-will rule. Texas continues to recognize only this category of cases as an exception to the at-will rule. *See* Ed Rachal Foundation v. D'Unger, 207 S.W.3d 330, 332 (Tex. 2006) (refusing to recognize a whistleblower exception). But in *Johnston*, the distinction between refusing to commit an illegal act and whistleblowing is blurry at best. Does it make sense to try to fit cases into these types of cubbyholes or should the analysis be more general in nature?

2. Correct conclusions vs. reasonable beliefs. Should an employee be required to be correct about whether an act is illegal before she is protected? *See* Callantine v. Staff Builders, Inc., 271 F.3d 1124 (8th Cir. 2001) (applying Missouri law and rejecting employee's claim where there was no evidence that the act in question was illegal); Clark v. Modern Group Ltd., 9 F.3d 321, 332 (3d Cir. 1993) (applying Pennsylvania law and stating that an employee's good faith but mistaken belief about the legality of conduct is an insufficient basis for recognizing wrongful discharge claim).

---

5. Nonetheless, we add that our holdings in the determination of appellant's points of error three and four are not to be construed as creating a whistleblower exception to the employment-at-will doctrine.

Exercise 19.2: Summary Problem

You are an associate at the Biggs Law Firm. One of the paralegals at the firm, Biff, is a former lawyer who was disbarred a few years ago. You recently learned that Biff, under instructions from Willie, a partner in the firm, sometimes drafts legal documents and engages in other activities that amount to the unauthorized practice of law in the relevant jurisdiction. There is a rule of professional conduct in your jurisdiction that requires a lawyer who knows that another lawyer has engaged in a violation of the rules of professional conduct that raises a substantial question as to the other lawyer's honesty, trustworthiness, or fitness to practice law in other respects to report the other lawyer to the jurisdiction's lawyer disciplinary board. You express your concerns about the conduct of Biff and Willie to the firm's managing partner. Specifically, you mention that you think that Willie's conduct raises a substantial question about his fitness to practice law and that you or someone at the firm is required by the jurisdiction's rules of professional conduct to notify the jurisdiction's disciplinary authorities. The partner tells you that he will look into the matter and get back to you. A week goes by; Willie is not fired, but you are. You are contemplating filing a wrongful discharge suit against the firm. What are your best arguments for recovery and what legal research do you need to do in order to better analyze your case?

Index